Edwin Sturtevant

STURTEVANT'S

EDIBLE PLANTS OF THE WORLD

EDITED

BY

U. P. HEDRICK

DOVER PUBLICATIONS, INC.

NEW YORK

Published in Canada by General Publishing
Company, Ltd., 30 Lesmill Road, Don Mills,
Toronto, Ontario.
Published in the United Kingdom by Constable
and Company, Ltd., 10 Orange Street, London WC 2.

This Dover edition, first published in 1972, is an
unabridged and unaltered republication of the work
originally published by J. B. Lyon Company, Albany,
in 1919 for the State of New York as the Department
of Agriculture's Twenty-seventh *Annual Report,*
Volume 2, Part II [Report of the New York
Agricultural Experiment Station for the Year 1919].
The original title was *Sturtevant's Notes on Edible
Plants.*

International Standard Book Number: 0-486-20459-6
Library of Congress Catalog Card Number: 76-184690

Manufactured in the United States of America
Dover Publications, Inc.
180 Varick Street
New York, N. Y. 10014

To the Board of Control of the New York Agricultural Experiment Station:

GENTLEMEN.— It.gives me peculiar pleasure to transmit to you for publication a manuscript prepared from notes by Dr. E. Lewis Sturtevant, the distinguished first Director of this Station, the publication to be known as "Sturtevant's Notes on Edible Plants."

Dr. Sturtevant was one of that group of men who early espoused the cause of agricultural science in the United States, a field in which he became distinguished, his studies in economic botany being one of his notable achievements. When he retired in 1887 as Director of this Station, he left behind him a voluminous manuscript consisting of a compilation of existing knowledge on the edible food plants of the world, a piece of work involving a laborious and extended research in botanical literature. For twenty years this manuscript remained untouched, when Dr. U. P. Hedrick undertook its editing, a difficult and arduous task, well performed, in order that so valuable a collection of knowledge might become available to botanists and to students of food economics.

It is especially appropriate that such a volume should be issued at this time. Food problems are becoming more and more acute as the demand for food increasingly overshadows the supply. Primitive peoples depended upon food resources which are now neglected. Other sources of possible human nutrition have doubtless remained untouched, and the time may come when a comprehensive utilization of food plants will be essential to human sustenance. It is believed, therefore, that the information so ably brought together by Dr. Sturtevant cannot fail to become increasingly useful.

Very respectfully,

W. H. JORDAN

Director

NEW YORK AGRICULTURAL
EXPERIMENT STATION
GENEVA, N. Y.
June 1, 1919.

PREFACE

All who have attempted to study the origin and history of cultivated plants must have been struck with the paucity and inaccuracy of information on the subject. For nearly nineteen hundred years, to be written in Pliny was proof sufficient; yet much of Pliny's history is inaccurate though still repeated in periodicals and popular works. Linnaeus, the great systematizer, gave the origin of most of the plants he described; but of these, De Candolle, by long odds the best plant historian, says, " three out of four of Linnaeus' indications of the original home of cultivated plants are incomplete or incorrect." De Candolle, in his turn, usually accurate, is exceedingly scant, giving the origin of but 249 cultivated plants, not all edible, while Sturtevant, in the text in hand, puts down 2897 which may be used for food, most of which are cultivated.

The query at once comes to mind as to the respects in which Sturtevant adds new knowledge on an old subject. New knowledge may be found on the following subjects: (1) The original home of many esculents is given for the first time. (2) New landmarks in the histories of edible plants are pointed out. (3) An effort is made to mention all cultivated esculents. (4) Though the book contains much new information as to the history of the food plants of the Old World, it is especially full and accurate in the discussion of the esculents of the New World. (5) Sturtevant presents much new information on the variations that have been produced in plants by cultivation. (6) His book adds much to geographical botany. (7) He contributes much data for the study of acclimatization.

It is pertinent to inquire as to the qualifications and opportunities Sturtevant may have had to illuminate so vast a subject as that of edible plants. To answer this query, and for the added reason that a book can be used with greatest profit only when its author is known, a brief biography of Sturtevant follows this *Preface.*

Sturtevant's Notes on Edible Plants is a compilation from four sources, namely: the first seven reports of the New York State Agricultural Experiment Station; a manuscript of 1600 closely written imperial octavo sheets

entitled, *Notes on Edible Plants*, left at this Station by the author; a series
of articles in the *American Naturalist* on the history of garden vegetables,
running for four years beginning with 1887; and between forty and fifty
thousand card index notes which belong in part to this Station and in part
to the Missouri Botanical Garden.   The material used was written previous
to 1892, the author having spent at least a quarter-century in its preparation.
The editor must now state what his task has been.

With so great a wealth of material much has had to be discarded.
A great mass of cultural notes has not been used.   Descriptions of many
varieties of many species were discarded.   Vernacular names in many
languages and dialects were omitted.   Botanical synonyms have had to
be left out.   Sturtevant's discussions of edible fungi, while full for the time
in which they were written, are, in the light of recent research, so scant and
fragmentary that the editor, unable to revise or add to them, has with
many regrets excluded them.   The unused material amounts to several
times that used.

After sorting the material, the next task was to arrange it for publication.
This work fell into four well-defined divisions of labor:

First, some standard of botanical nomenclature had to be adopted that
the many botanical names from the several hundred authors quoted by
Sturtevant could be made to conform as far as possible to one standard.
Index Kewensis was taken as the authority best suited for the work in hand;
this standard has seldom been departed from even though departure seemed
most necessary in the light of later botanical studies; to have begun making
departures would have entailed too great a task.

Second, Sturtevant's citations to literature, except in the series of
articles in the *American Naturalist*, usually consist only of the name of
the book and the author.   Since a book such as this is almost worthless
without full citations, these, as far as possible, have been completed and
verified, a task requiring borrowed books from a dozen or more libraries
and the labor of several persons for months.   Even after great effort to
insure fullness and correctness, no doubt many mistakes have crept into
the citations.

Third, biblIographical information is given in detail, since to cite
unknown authors is a worthless procedure.   It seems a simple task to
catalog a collection of books.   But the difficulties, especially in the case
of early books, were found to be many.   Anonymous writers, *noms de plume*,
cross-references, borrowed material, numerous editions, works of com-

mentators and editors bearing the names of original authors, all confuse and make the task of the bibliographer complex and difficult.

Fourth, the material had to be arranged. Sturtevant in his discussions of vegetables in the reports of this Station, in his card index of edible plants and in his *History of Garden Vegetables* in the *American Naturalist*, arranges the plants in accordance with the English vernacular names; but in his partly completed manuscript, undoubtedly written with the expectation of publishing, the plants are arranged alphabetically according to genera. The last plan seemed to suit the present work best and was adopted. The natural order of the genera is given; species are alphabetically arranged under each genera; while, to make them as prominent as possible, English vernacular names are printed in capitals after the species. The vernacular names are those used by the authorities quoted or are taken from standard botanical text-books.

While the changes and omissions made by the editor leave that which remains substantially as written by Dr. Sturtevant, yet there has been so much cutting and fitting that it would be unjust to hold Sturtevant responsible for infelicities that may appear. Despite the editor's efforts to retain the diction, style and individuality of Dr. Sturtevant, the quality of the work is no doubt marred by passing through hands other than those of the author.

The following acknowledgments must be recorded: The editor is grateful to Dr. Sturtevant's children for permission to publish their father's work; and to his associates in the Horticultural Department of this Station for assistance in reading the manuscript and proof of the book, especially to J. W. Wellington who has had charge of standardizing botanical names, verifying references and preparing the bibliography.

U. P. HEDRICK,

Horticulturist, New York Agricultural Experiment Station.

EDWARD LEWIS STURTEVANT

Edward Lewis Sturtevant, farmer, botanist, physician and author, was one of the giants of his time in the science of agriculture. Through natural endowment, industry and rare mental attainments, he accomplished more than most men in scientific research by his own efforts. But, possibly, he achieved even more through his influence on his fellow-workmen than by his own endeavors. Rare, indeed, are the men in any field of attainment who have furnished so freely as he from an inexhaustible store of information unfailing aid and inspiration to those who worked with him. The happy combination of these two qualities, work and ability to help others work, led Sturtevant to success significant enough to make him one of the honor men of agriculture in the United States. From this brief and incommensurate tribute, we pass to a sketch of Sturtevant's active life.

As to genealogy, the line of descent runs from Samuel, the first Sturtevant in America, who landed in Plymouth in 1642, through generations living in Plympton and Wareham, Massachusetts, to Consider Sturtevant who purchased a farm at Winthrop, Maine, in 1810. Here Dr. Sturtevant's father was born but later moved to Boston, the birthplace of Dr. Sturtevant. His mother was Mary Haight Leggett from a family of fighting Quakers who settled at West Farm, New York, about 1700.

Born in Boston, January 23, 1842, Sturtevant, as a child, was taken by his parents to Philadelphia and here, with little time intervening, his father and mother died. Young Sturtevant's aunt, a Mrs. Benson, became his guardian, and with her the lad moved to Winthrop, Maine, the birthplace of his father. His early school days were spent in New Jersey, though later he prepared for college at Blue Hill, Maine. His preliminary education finished, Sturtevant, in 1859, entered Bowdoin College, to remain until 1861, when, at the urgent call of the country for college men to serve in the civil strife then raging, he enlisted in the Union army.

To classical Bowdoin, Sturtevant owed much for his ability to write. Few scientists who have written so much and so rapidly, have written as well. His English is not ornate but is vivid, terse, logical, happy in phrasing and seldom at loss for the proper word. To classical Bowdoin, too, Sturtevant owes his remarkable ability to use languages. Greek, Latin, French and German in the written form were familiar to him, and he was able to read, more or less well, scientific treatises in several other of the European languages. Though he was not graduated with his class at Bowdoin, the college later gave him her degree of Bachelor of Arts and still later further honored him with her Master of Arts.

Sturtevant entered the Union army in September, 1861, as First Lieutenant of Company G, 74th Regiment of Maine Volunteers. It speaks well for the youth of barely twenty-one that the following January he became Captain of his company. Company G was a part of the 19th Army Corps which, during Captain Sturtevant's service in it, was stationed on the lower Mississippi where, possibly, its most important work was the siege of Port Hudson. A part of Sturtevant's time in the army was spent on the staff of General Nickerson, 3d Brigade, 2d Division, serving with the rank of Captain. Possibilities of further service, higher promotion, or, on the other hand, death or wounds on the battle field, were cut short by an attack of typhoid malaria which so incapacitated him that he returned home in 1863, his career in the army ended.

The next landmark in Sturtevant's life is a course in the Harvard Medical School from which he received a degree in 1866. But, possessed of a degree from one of the leading medical colleges in the country, he did not begin the practice of medicine, and, in fact, never followed the profession. We may assume, however, that the training in a medical school turned his attention to science, for, possibly, the best science in American institutions at this time was to be found in a few leading schools of medicine. The year following the completion of the medical course was spent with his brother Thomas in Boston.

In 1867, E. Lewis, Joseph N. and Thomas L. Sturtevant purchased land at South Framingham, Massachusetts. The farm soon became famous, under the name " Waushakum Farm," for a series of brilliant experiments in agriculture which are still models in experimental acumen and conscientious execution. Here, almost at once, E. Lewis Sturtevant began the foundation of a great agricultural and botanical library, one possibly not surpassed in these fields of science by any other private collection, while, as it was eventually developed, for Prelinnean works it is still unsurpassed by any other American library. Here, too, almost at once, Sturtevant started the studies of cultivated plants recorded in this volume.

The immediate concern of the Sturtevant brothers, however, was the development of a model dairy farm of Ayrshire cattle. Waushakum Farm soon became the home of this breed. Several scientific aspects of this work with Ayrshires are worth noting. Milk records of the herd and of individual animals, covering many milking periods, were kept and still constitute, according to dairymen of our day, a most valuable contribution to dairying. As an outcome of their researches with this breed, a monograph of 252 pages was published on Ayrshire cattle by the brothers in 1875. Out of their work with Ayrshires came the North American Ayrshire Register published by E. Lewis and Joseph N. Sturtevant in several annual volumes. These books are still in use by breeders of Ayrshires and are of permanent value as records of the breed. E. Lewis Sturtevant in particular gave attention to the physiology of milk and milk secretion. His studies of fat globules in milk of different breeds of cows attracted much attention in the agricultural press, and he was soon in great demand as a speaker before agricultural and dairy associations.

But even in these first days on Waushakum Farm, the Ayrshires did not occupy all of his time. One is amazed in looking through the agricultural papers of the late sixties and early seventies at the number of articles signed by E. L. Sturtevant — still in his twenties. These early articles show originality, intense curiosity in regard to everything new, scientific imagination, a mind fertile in fruitful ideas and tremendous industry. These first articles in the press, too, show that he early possessed initiative, a trait which he retained throughout his scientific life. In all of his work it was seldom that he had to seek ideas or suggestions from others, though he was possessed of a mind which appreciated new trains of thought, and many there were of his day who could speak of his kindly interest in the work of others.

Indian corn attracted Sturtevant from the first. No sooner had he settled on Waushakum Farm than he began a botanical and cultural study of maize which he continued to the time of his death. The first fruits of his work with corn was the introduction of an improved variety of Yellow Flint, the new sort being called "Waushakum." This variety was wonderfully productive, yields of 125 bushels of shelled corn to the acre being common. Breeding this new variety was a piece of practical work that brought the head of Waushakum Farm more prominence in agriculture than any of his scientific work, "scientific farming" at that time not being in high repute with tillers of the soil.

Sturtevant wrote much on Indian corn, contributing many short articles on its culture on the farm and several long treatises on its botany and the classification of its many varieties. Perhaps the most notable of the scientific articles are in the *Bulletin of the Torrey Botanical Society* for August, 1894, and Bulletin 57 on *Varieties of Corn* from the United States Department of Agriculture. The last-named work is a monograph on maize which is still the best authority on this valuable plant and a permanent tide mark, as it were, to show Sturtevant's ability in working up the history of cultivated plants. Besides setting forth the botany of corn, this bulletin describes 800 varieties, gives their synonyms and establishes a scientific nomenclature for Indian corn. The varieties are placed in groups in accordance with their relationship, thus giving to scientist and farmer a classification of this immensely variable plant.

To Sturtevant is given the credit of having built the first lysimeter in America. This instrument, to measure the percolation of water through a certain depth of soil, was put in on the Waushakum Farm in 1875. It covered five-thousandths of an acre and measured water percolations to the depth of twenty-five inches. Records from the apparatus were kept from late in 1875 to the beginning of 1880 — a little more than four full years. The results, presented in papers at several scientific meetings, and freely discussed in the agricultural press, gave him high standing among agricultural experimenters in America.

In spite of duties that must have claimed much of his time on Waushakum Farm, Sturtevant found time to undertake investigations in many diverse fields of agriculture. As the years advanced, he put more and more energy in the rapidly growing field of agricultural research until finally experimentation came to claim most of his attention. His eminence in research on Waushakum Farm brought him many opportunities to speak and write on agricultural affairs, in which work his facile pen and ready speech greatly enhanced his reputation as an experimenter. A natural outcome of his growth in the work he had chosen was that his services should be sought in scientific institutions having to do with agriculture. In 1882, the Board of Control of the New York State Agricultural Experiment Station, located at Geneva, New York, selected him Director of the Station, an institution just created by the State Legislature, and asked him to organize the work.

Perhaps Sturtevant was the more ready to give up Waushakum Farm and devote his whole time to scientific research for the reason that in 1879, the trio that had for twelve years made the farm famous was broken by the death of one of the three brothers, Joseph N. Sturtevant. The association of these two brothers had been so close that the obituary of Joseph, written by E. L. Sturtevant for the *Scientific Farmer*, becomes of interest in this biography. We publish it in full:

"Joseph N. Sturtevant, born April 1, 1844; died Jan. 19, 1879. Member of the Massachusetts State Board of Agriculture 1873–5. A brief record of a short but useful life. And yet this life, which struggled with the difficulties brought about by ill health from birth, made the most of the few well moments, and has made an impress upon agricultural thought which shall continue even if the originator be unrecognized and forgotten. Honest in thought as in action, caring nothing for applause, a true philanthropist in all that constitutes the word, a careful thinker, considerate towards the opinions of others, and yet possessing a positiveness of character which came through conviction, his advice was often sought and seldom unheeded. Without personal vanity, as delicate as a woman towards the rights of others, a mind trained to goodness for its own sake, one who believed in good because of the good, and hated evil because of the evil, the future life was lost sight of in the present, and there was nothing additional that religion could bring, because he was true religion itself in every fibre of body and movement of mind. His creed,—

"'What is excellent,
As God lives in permanent.'

And his life and creed were as one; and he was one who held familiar converse with self, and was trustful of man's power to do the right as well as to think it, and looked upon wrong as the mar which came through the self rather than others, and in purity of thought sought that purity of life which distinguished him.

"He has appeared before the public as one of the authors of *The Dairy Cow, Ayrshire*, as one of the editors of the *North American Ayrshire Register*, and as contributor to our various agricultural papers. In the *Scientific Farmer* he has contributed many articles without signature, some signed J. N. S., others signed Zelco, and a few under his own name. He commenced writing for the *Country Gentleman* in 1868, using the *nom de plume* of Zelco, and although this was his favorite paper before the close connection with the *Scientific Farmer* arose, yet he wrote occasionally for the *Massachusetts Ploughman*, *New England Farmer*, *National Live Stock Journal*, and other papers, but usually upon request. The series of

'In and Out Papers,' written under the *nom de plume* of Alex. B., in the *Scientific Farmer*, commencing with the May number for 1876, and continuing till the farewell in the April number for 1878, when his health broke down, has received marked attention, and showed the possibilities of a literary career, had only the health which admitted of close and continuous application been granted.

"The trio at Waushakum Farm is now broken. Three brothers purchased the farm and formed one life in 1866, and for twelve years there have been harmonious thought and action,— and now — and now — a wearying sense of desolation."

The invitation to take up work in New York was accepted and Dr. Sturtevant moved at once to Geneva to become, in his new work in agricultural research, an explorer in an almost virgin field. The splendid institutions we now have, created by the Hatch Act of Congress, did not come into existence until 1888. But six other States had planned to begin experimental work in agriculture, four of which had made modest starts, but as yet not much had been accomplished. There were but few models in the Old World, and these were established in very different environment. The financial support was meager, and encouragement from those the Station sought to serve was correspondingly small. The new Director had to deal with the fundamentals of agricultural research at a time when few men could see the need of such research, and almost no one could be found to help carry the work forward.

Under many difficulties and discouragements, Dr. Sturtevant began to develop the Station. His plan was more comprehensive than any other yet conceived in America. All phases of agriculture as carried on in New York were to be recognized. Horticulture, live-stock and crop departments were organized with chemical and botanical departments as handmaids. A notable group of men was brought to form the new staff and within a few years, gauged by the time and opportunity, the Station was doing epoch-making work. One needs only to name the staff, everyone destined to make a high name for himself in his field of endeavor, to measure the high standard Sturtevant set. Thus, in the Third Annual Report of the Station, the Director has as his staff: C. S. Plumb, Assistant to the Director; Emmett S. Goff, Horticulturist; J. C. Arthur, Botanist; S. Moulton Babcock, Chemist; and E. F. Ladd, Assistant Chemist. These men helped to lay broad and deep the foundation of the Station.

Dr. Sturtevant was Director of the New York Station from July,

1882, to March, 1887 — not quite five years. Much of his time must have been taken up with executive work incidental to a new institution. Yet the six reports of the Station show much real research material, and much extension work, more needed then than now, that speak well for the initiative and industry of the Director and his small staff. Be it remembered that in these early days there were no laboratories and but scant equipment, with only the small sum of $20,000 annually available for maintenance, salaries and improvements. The Board of Control confessedly did not have clear ideas of the function of the Station, and there were many opponents in the press, and even on the farms, who lost no opportunities to criticise.

One of the best measures of the man can be found in the initial policy of the Station as determined by Dr. Sturtevant. Widely divergent opinions prevailed as to the work of such institutions. Dr. Sturtevant asserted that the function of a Station was to " discover, verify and disseminate." He saw clearly from the very first the need of well-established fundamental principles in agriculture and set his staff at the work of discovering principles. His scientific work on Waushakum Farm had taught him that there were many possible errors in prevailing experimental work, and he at once set about determining their source and the best means of minimizing them. During his stay at the New York Station, in several reports he urged the importance of learning how to experiment, how to interpret results and pointed out errors in certain kinds of experimentation. He believed that the management and responsibility for a station should rest with the Director alone as the only way in which unity and continuity of direction could be secured. Those conversant with experiment stations must see how generally these views of Dr. Sturtevant now prevail and must give him credit for very materially helping to found the splendid system of present-day experiment stations.

These five years at Geneva added greatly to Dr. Sturtevant's store of knowledge of cultivated plants. During the time he was Director, all the varieties of cultivated esculents that could be obtained were grown on the grounds of the Station. The early volumes of the reports of this Station are filled with descriptions of varieties of cultivated plants grown on the grounds. Now, it is certain that if additions are to be made to the knowledge of the origin of cultivated plants, such additions must come largely from experimental observations of the plants themselves to ascertain the stages through which they have come from the wild to the cultivated form. The remarkable collection of plants grown under Dr. Sturtevant's direction gave, as this text shows on many pages, an unsurpassed opportunity to study plants in the steps they have taken from first cultivation to their present forms.

Dr. Sturtevant's opportunities for research in books during this directorship was hardly less remarkable. The Sturtevant Prelinnean Library, now in the Missouri Botanical Garden, numbers over 500 titles in several languages. These, with most of the more modern texts on plants, gave him sources of information then possessed by few other students of plants, for many of the rarer books were inaccessible to Americans of Sturtevant's time. In this great library, the patience and erudition of Dr. Sturtevant became priceless. Here, he sought historical mention of edible plants; travelers' descriptions of them; the names of the many esculents used by various peoples; their geographical distributions; their various uses; cultural treatments; the connections of food plants with great migrations of mankind both in ancient and modern times. He studied selection as affected by the likes and dislikes of various peoples, and gave particular attention to the studies of archaeologists on the material remains of plants.

In 1887, Dr. Sturtevant gave up his charge of the Station at Geneva and returned to the old home at South Framingham. But the opportunity for experimental work on Waushakum Farm had passed. The city had encroached upon the country, and where had been pastures and farm fields were now town lots and dwellings. The inclination for research which throughout his life had animated Sturtevant, now took the turn, more than ever, of research in books. Near the old home, into which he moved with his family, he housed his library in a small building and set to work. Always diligent with the pen, and his favorite subject the history of plants, there is no question but that he now determined to put in permanent form the many articles he had printed here and there on the origin, history and variations in cultivated plants. His manuscripts, notes and the articles in *American Naturalist* indicate such a determination. Had not ill health and untimely death intervened, it is probable that Sturtevant would have put forth the volume which now, a quarter-century later, comes from the hands of an editor.

The idea of writing a history of food plants came to Dr. Sturtevant long before his retirement from active professional work — in fact must have been in his mind from college days. His books were well under way and much had been accomplished as early as 1880, for in April of that year he wrote to the *Country Gentleman* asking its readers to give him information on the introduction of food plants, for seeds of new or curious esculents, for reports on the foods of agricultural Indians, stating the purpose of these questions as follows: " I am collecting the material for writing a *Flora Dietica*, or a history of food plants, with especial reference to the distribution and variation of cultivated plants. My inquiries thus far embrace 1,185 genera, and (including probably some synonyms) 3,087 species of food plants." Then follow numerous questions, after which he further states: " Geographical botany, acclimatization through variations, the increase of varieties with the increase of knowledge and the spread of civilization, what man has done and what man can hope to do in modifying vegetable growth to his use and support — is a subject of great interest as well as importance; and it seems desirable that information which can be obtained now, while our country is not yet wholly occupied, should be put upon record against the time when the ascertaining of these facts will be more difficult."

The manuscripts at the disposal of the editor show Dr. Sturtevant to have been an omnivorous reader. A glance at the foot-note citations to literature in this text shows the remarkable range of his readings in agriculture, botany, science, history, travel and general literature. Besides the mass of material from which this text has been taken, there is in the possession of the Geneva Station the manuscript of an *Encyclopedia of Agriculture and Allied Subjects*, work at which, as the title page says, began March 3, 1879. This encyclopedia, unfortunately for all engaged in agriculture, was completed only to the letter M. Its 1200, closely written, large-size pages form, as far as they go, a full dictionary on agriculture. In addition to the manuscripts left at this Station, are card notes on agricultural, botanical and historical matters, while another set, with but few duplicates of cards, are in the possession of the Missouri Botanical Garden. This set, much the better of the two, was put in shape and presented to the Missouri Botanical Garden only a few weeks before Dr. Sturtevant's death.

In addition to his experimental and executive work, his *Notes on Edible Plants* and the *Encyclopedia of Agriculture*, Sturtevant found time to contribute hundreds of articles, long and short, to the agricultural and scientific press. Those of most note are recorded in the bibliography which follows, but the total output of his thirty years of literary work is better gaged as to quantity by a series of scrapbooks in which he systematically preserved his pen contributions. There are twelve volumes of these scrapbooks filled with newspaper and magazine articles, the earliest written being dated November 2, 1867, and the last October 6, 1896. Besides these, there are two volumes containing sixty-four pamphlets most of which are named in the accompanying bibliography. Thus roughly to state the quantity of a man's work may seem to indicate only the prodigality of his pen. So to judge Dr. Sturtevant does him a great injustice, for everything to which he set his pen is thoughtful, lucid and logical even if not always adorned by grace of expression. There is often in his writings a happy turn of phrase, and the inevitable word usually turns up at the right place

The newspapers of the two States in which he lived furnished the medium through which Dr. Sturtevant reached the general reader, and for the farmer he had at his command the agricultural press of the whole country. Contributions of scientific character were published in *American Naturalist*, *Botanical Gazette*, *Garden and Forest*, *Torrey Botanical Club Bulletin* and *Science*. The indexes of the magazines, during the time of Sturtevant's active work, furnish sufficient clues to his contributions.

For a little more than two years, Dr. Sturtevant was associated with E. H. Libby, as editor of the *Scientific Farmer*, after which, for nearly a year and a half, he was sole editor. The joint editorship began in March, 1876, and ended in May, 1878, the magazine being discontinued in October, 1879. The *Scientific Farmer* was in all matters pertaining to agriculture abreast of the times — in most matters in advance of the times — notwithstanding which it was not a financial success, and, becoming too heavy a drain on its owner's pocket, was discontinued. The magazine was published before the days of experiment station bulletins and contains the gist of the agricultural investigations then being carried on, most of it being reported by the investigators themselves. As editor, Dr. Sturtevant assumed the role of analyst of the scientific work in the agriculture of the times, using, as all must agree, singularly good judgment and discrimination in his discussions of the work of others.

One of the great pleasures of Dr. Sturtevant's life seems to have been active participation in the several scientific societies to which he belonged. He was long a Fellow in the American Association for the Advancement of Science; he was one of the founders of the Society for the Promotion of Agricultural Science, serving as its first secretary and fourth president; while in Massachusetts, he was active in the Massachusetts Horticultural Society; and during his directorship of the New York Station was one of the leaders in the Western New York Horticultural Society. He was, too, at various times, a member of several general agricultural and dairymen's organizations. He was never a passive member in any of the societies in which he was interested and to those named, in particular, presented many papers, while the minutes of the meetings record that his voice was heard in all important discussions.

Dr. Sturtevant's wedded life began in 1864 when he married Mary Elizabeth Mann. To this happy union were born four children, two sons and two daughters, the wife and mother dying in 1875. In 1883, he again married, taking as his wife Hattie Mann, sister to the first wife. By this marriage there was one son. Dr. Sturtevant's colleagues at Geneva, to several of whom the writer is indebted for much information, speak of the devotion of the husband and father to his family and say that he rarely sought companionship outside the home circle and that, on their part, mother and children were devoted to the head of the household and constantly gave him substantial help in his work. The eldest daughter, Grace Sturtevant, talented with pencil and brush, made the drawings and colored sketches to illustrate her father's writings on peppers and sweet potatoes, while those of maize, published in the Report of the New York Station for 1884, were done by Mrs. Sturtevant.

In 1893, Dr. Sturtevant was a victim of one of the epidemics of grippe which each returning winter ravaged the country. He never fully recovered from this attack and his health began to fail until shortly it was found that tuberculosis had secured firm hold. With the hope that the disease might be thrown off, three winters were passed in California with temporary but not permanent relief. July 30, 1898, he passed away. It was a fitting death; he passed quietly to sleep in the old home on Waushakum Farm to which his work had given distinguished name.

A BIBLIOGRAPHY OF STURTEVANT'S WRITINGS

The bibliography of Dr. Sturtevant's principal writings discloses a lasting basis for his high place among agricultural experimenters. For this bibliography the reader is indebted to Professor C. S. Plumb of the Ohio State University, assistant to Dr. Sturtevant while Director of the New York Experiment Station, an intimate friend, and one who best knew his work. The bibliography was prepared for the Missouri Botanical Garden and was printed in the *Tenth Annual Report* of that institution.

Why the Ayrshire Cow should be the Dairyman's Choice. *Trans. Vermont Dairymen's Association*, 1872, pp. 150–159.

Cost of a Crop of Corn to the Massachusetts Farmer. *Agriculture of Massachusetts*, 1872–73, part II, pp. 80–89.

Ayrshire Points. *Ohio Agricultural Report*, 1872, pp. 261–270. Reprinted in *Mark Lane Express*, London, Eng., Feb. 3, 1873; in *Farmers' Magazine*, London, May, 1873, p. 230; and in the *North British Agriculturist*, Edinburgh, Scotland, July 16, 1873.

The Claims of the Ayrshire Cow upon the Dairy Farmer. *Trans. N. Y. State Agr. Society*, 1872–76, pp. 266–279. Copied in *Gardeners' Chronicle* and *Agricultural Gazette*, England, May 3, 1873, p. 624.

Food, Physiology and Force. *N. H. Agriculture*, 1874, p. 157. Also in *Scientific Farmer*, July, 1879, p. 89, and *Scientific American* Supplement, No. 186.

Milk: Physiological and Miscellaneous. A Prize Essay. *Transactions New York State Agricultural Society*, 1872–76, pp. 91–124, plates III.

Milk: Some Considerations concerning its Morphology. *Report Massachusetts State Board of Agriculture*, 1873–74, pp. 374–388.

Milk: Its typal Relations, etc. A lecture before the Vermont Dairymen's Association, Jan. 21, 1874. Printed for the author, 1874, pp. 20, figs. 3. Also in *9th Report American Dairymen's Association*.

Physiological Considerations concerning Feeding for Butter and Cheese. *Report Connecticut Board of Agriculture*, 1874, pp. 67, figs. 4.

Cream. *American Dairymen's Association Report*, 1874, p. 39. Also in *New England Farmer*, Jan. 23, 1875.

Associate Dairying. The appendix to Flints' *Milch Cows and Dairy Farming*. No name signed.

The Wild Cattle of Scotland, or White Forest Breed. *American Naturalist*, vol. VIII, March, 1874, pp. 135–145.

The Law of Inheritance; or the Philosophy of Breeding. *Twenty-second Annual Report Massachusetts State Board of Agriculture*, 1875, pp. 48.

Chemical Corn Growing. *Trans. Middlesex South Agricultural Society*, 1875, pp. 11–32.

The Dairy Cow. A Monograph of the Ayrshire Breed of Cattle. By E. Lewis Sturtevant, M. D., and Joseph N. Sturtevant, of Waushakum Farm, South Framingham, Mass. With an appendix on Ayrshire.

Jersey and Dutch Milks; their Formation and Peculiarities. Boston, Mass. A. Williams & Co., 1875. Cloth, 12 mo., pp. 252. Illustrated.

The Dairy Cow — What she is and whence she came. *Report Maine State Board of Agriculture*, 1875–76, pp. 112–125.

Plant Food and Agriculture. *Report Connecticut Board of Agriculture*, 1876, pp. 14.

American Agricultural Literature. *Proc. Fifth Annual Session National Agr. Congress*, Philadelphia, Sept. 12–14, 1876, pp. 30–37.

Agriculture. *Report Massachusetts State Commissioners to the Centennial Exhibition at Philadelphia*, 1876, pp. 49–53.

Philosophy of Dairying. *Trans. American Dairymen's Association*, 1876, pp. 90.

Inter Cultural Tillage. *Report Connecticut State Board of Agriculture*, 1877–78, pp. 42.

Dairying *vs.* Thoroughbred Bulls. *Trans. Vermont Dairymen's Association*, 1876, pp. 60.

Fertilizer Laws. *Agriculture of Pennsylvania*, 1877, pp. 108.

Corn Culture. *Ibid.*, 1878, pp. 252–256.

Seed Breeding. *Report Connecticut Board of Agriculture*, 1878, pp. 149–187. Reprinted in *Monthly Journal of Science*, Aug., 1879.

Seed Corn. *Report Maine State Board of Agriculture*, 1878–79, pp. 30–47.

Fertility. *Journal American Agricultural Association*, vol. 1.

Corn Culture at Waushakum Farm. *Trans. New York State Agricultural Society*, vol. 32, 1872–76, pp. 170–176.

Indian Corn. *Trans. New York State Agricultural Society*, 1872–76, pp. 37–74.

Some Thoughts and Facts concerning the Food of Man. *Report Connecticut Board of Agriculture*, 1880, pp. 114–155.

Seedless Fruits. *Trans. Mass. Horticultural Society*, part I, 1880, pp. 29.

Deerfoot Farm Centrifugal Dairy. *Report United States Commissioner of Agriculture*, pp. 629–651, plates III. Reprinted in *Journal of Royal Agricultural Society of England*, Second Series, vol. XVIII, 1882, pp. 475–495.

Thoughts on Agricultural Education. *Report Connecticut State Board of Agriculture*, 1881, pp. 19.

The Growing of Corn. *Twenty-eighth Annual Report of the Massachusetts State Board of Agriculture*, 1881, pp. 77–130.

Lysimeter Records. *Proc. American Assoc. for Advancement of Science*, 1881, pp. 37–39.

Experimental Observations on the Potato. *Trans. N. Y. State Agricultural Society*, 1877–82, pp. 261–265.

The Need of a Better Seed Supply. *Ibid.*, pp. 286–289.

Conditions Necessary to Success in Dairying. *Report New York State Dairymen's Association*, 1883, pp. 56–60.

Relations between Seeding and Quality in certain Vegetables and Fruits. *Proc. Society for the Promotion of Agr. Science*, vol. I, 1883, pp. 109–118.

Different Modes of Cutting Potatoes for Planting. *Ibid.*, pp. 77–78.

Agricultural Botany. *Proc. Society for the Promotion of Agri. Science*, 1883, p. 7. Also *Trans. American Association for the Advancement of Science*, 1883, pp. 293–295, Abstract.

History of Cereal Plants. *Sibley's Grain and Farm Seeds Annual*, 1883, pp. 5–14.

Maize: An Attempt at Classification. Rochester, N. Y., 1884, pp. 9. Illustrated. Printed for private distribution only.

Agricultural Botany. *American Naturalist*, June, 1884, pp. 573–577, fig. 3.

Hungarian Grass. *Trans. N. Y. State Agricultural Society*, vol. 33, 1877–82, pp. 208–220.

Experiment Stations. *Ibid.*, pp. 235–243.

The Feeding of Spoiled Brewer's Grains. *Report New York State Dairymen's Association*, 1884, pp. 46–64.

Influence of Isolation upon Vegetation. *Proc. American Association for the Advancement of Science*, 1884.

Dairy Interests in General. *Report New York State Dairymen's Association*, 1884, pp. 102–108.

The Work of the Station. *Ninth Annual Report New York State Dairymen's Association*, 1885, pp. 25–29.

A List of Edible Fungi. *Trans. Mass. Horticultural Society*, 1881, pp. 322–348.

Germination Studies. *Proc. Amer. Assn. for the Advancement of Science*, 1885, pp. 287–291.

An Observation on the Hybridization and Cross Breeding of Plants. *Proc. Amer. Assn. for Adv. of Science*, vol. 34, 1885, pp. 283–287.

Germination Studies. *Ibid.*, pp. 287–291.

Lowest Germination of Maize. *Botanical Gazette*, April, 1885, pp. 259–261.

Cultivated Food Plants. *Proc. Society for the Promotion of Agricultural Science*, 1885, pp. 59–72.

Indian Corn and the Indian. *American Naturalist*, March, 1885, pp. 225–234.

Kitchen Garden Esculents of American Origin. *American Naturalist*, I, May, 1885, pp. 444–457. II, June, 1885, pp. 542–552. III, July, 1885, pp. 658–669.

Horticultural Botany. *Proc. Western New York Hort. Society* for 1886, pp. 25–32.

A Study of the Dandelion. *American Naturalist*, Jan. 1886, pp. 5–9. Illustrated.

A Study of Garden Lettuce. *American Naturalist*, March, 1886, pp. 230–233.

History of Celery. *American Naturalist*, July, 1886, pp. 599–606, figs. 3.

History of Garden Vegetables. *American Naturalist*, 1887, vol. 21, pp. 49–59; 125–133; 321–333; 433–444; 701–712; 826–833; 903–912; 975–985. 1888, vol. 22, pp. 420–433; 802–808; 979–987. 1890, vol. 24, pp. 30–48; 143–157; 629–646; 719–744.

The Dandelion and the Lettuce. *Proc. Society for Promotion of Agricultural Science*, 1886, vol. 3, pp. 40–44.

A Study in Agricultural Botany. *Ibid.*, 1886, vol. 4, pp. 68–73.

Atavism the Result of Cross Breeding in Lettuce. *Ibid.*, 1886, vol. 4, pp. 73–74.

History of the Currant. *Proc. Western New York Hort. Society*, 1887.

Seed Germination — A Study. *Agricultural Science*, Feb., 1887.

Capsicum umbilicatum. *Bull. Torrey Botanical Club*, April, 1888.

Capsicum fasiculatum. *Ibid.*, May, 1888.

Notes on the History of the Strawberry. *Trans. Mass. Horticultural Society*, 1888, pp. 191–204.

Seedless Fruits. *Memoirs Torrey Botanical Club*, vol. 1, part 4, 1890.

Ensilage Experiments in 1884–1885 at the New York State Agricultural Experiment Station. *Trans. New York State Agr. Society*, 1889, pp. 116–120.

Forage Crops: Maize and Sorghum. *Ibid.*, pp. 135–143.

Agricultural Botany. *Ibid.*, pp. 335–338.

Edible Plants of the World. *Agricultural Science*, vol. 3, no. 7, 1889, pp. 174–178.

The Tomato. *Report Maryland Experiment Station*, 1889, p. 18.

Huckleberries and Blueberries. *Trans. Mass. Hort. Society*, 1890, pp. 17–38.

Concerning some names for Cucurbitae. *Bull. Torrey Botanical Club*, October, 1891.

Notes on Maize. *Bull. Torrey Botanical Club*, vol. 21, 1894, pp. 319–343; 503–523.

Paramount Fertilizers. *Report Mass. State Board of Agriculture*, 1888, pp. 37–55.

Report of the New York State Agricultural Experiment Station, 1882–1887, first six volumes. The following are the special topics reported on by Dr. Sturtevant:

1882. Organization of Station work. Experiments with wheat, barley and oats. Studies on Maize. Experiments with potatoes. Forage crops.

1883. Botanical notes. Studies on Maize. Station-grown seeds. Weight of seeds. Relation of feed to milk. Experiments with potatoes. Experiments with corn. Experiments with grasses.

1884. Feeding experiments and milk analysis. Study of milk. Experiments with potatoes. Wheat improvement. Experiments with corn. Germination of seeds. Study of maize, including sweet, pop and dent corn.

1885. Starch waste as cattle food. Ensilage and forage crops. Studies on corn. Fertilizers on potatoes. Tests on germination of maize and other seeds. The sweet corns.

1886. Cattle feeding experiments. Temperature and crops. Vitality of seeds as influenced by age. Experiments with cabbage. Studies of Indian corn.

1887. Feeding for beef. Experiments with potatoes. Seed germinations.

NOTES ON EDIBLE PLANTS

Aberia caffra Harv. & Sond. *Bixineae.*   KAI APPLE.   KAU APPLE.   KEI APPLE.

South Africa.   The fruits are of a golden-yellow color, about the size of a small apple. They are used by the natives for making a preserve and are so exceedingly acid when fresh that the Dutch settlers prepare them for their tables, as a pickle, without vinegar.[1]

Abronia arenaria Menzies.   *Nyctagineae.*

Seashore of Oregon and California.   The root is stout and fusiform, often several feet long.[2]   The Chinook Indians eat it.[3]

Abrus precatorius Linn. *Leguminosae.*   CORAL-BEAD PLANT.   LOVE PEA.   RED-BEAD VINE.   ROSARY-PEA TREE.   WILD LICORICE.

A plant common within the tropics in the Old World, principally upon the shores. The beauty of the seeds, their use as beads and for necklaces, and their nourishing qualities, have combined to scatter the plant.[4]   The seeds are used in Egypt as a pulse, but Don[5] says they are the hardest and most indigestible of all the pea tribe.   Brandis[6] says the root is a poor substitute for licorice.

Abutilon esculentum A. St. Hil.   *Malvaceae.*

Brazil.   The Brazilians eat the corolla of this native plant cooked as a vegetable.[7]

A. indicum Sweet

Old World tropics.   The raw flowers are eaten in Arabia.[8]   The leaves contain a large quantity of mucilage.

Acacia *Leguminosae.*

From various acacias comes gum arabic which is stated by some to be a highly nutritious article of food.   During the whole time of the gum harvest in Barbary, the Moors of the desert live almost entirely upon it.   It is claimed that six ounces are sufficient for the support of a man during twenty-four hours.   Gum arabic is also used as food by the

---

[1] Jackson, J. R.   *Treas. Bot.* 2:1255.   1876.

[2] Brewer and Watson *Bot. Cal.* 2:4.   1880.   (*A. latifolia*)

[3] Brown, R.   *Bot. Soc. Edinb.* 9:381.   1868.

[4] De Candolle, A.   *Geog. Bot.* 2:769.   1855.

[5] Don, G.   *Hist. Dichl. Pls.* 2:342.   1832.

[6] Brandis, D.   *Forest Fl.* 139.   1876.

[7] Saint Hilaire, A.   *Fl. Bras. Merid.* 1:160.   1825.

[8] Forskal *Fl. Aeg. Arab.* XCIII.   1775.   (*Hibiscus esculentus*)

Hottentots of southern Africa, and Sparmann states that, in the absence of other provisions, the Bushmen live on it for days together.[1] At Swan River, Australia, an acacia, called manna by the natives, produces a large quantity of gum resembling gum arabic, and this, says Drummond,[2] forms an important article of native food. The experiment of Magendie,[3] however, showed that dogs could not support life on gum, and Dr. Hammond [4] believes that, so far from having any value as an alimentary substance, it is positively injurious.

A. abyssinica Hochst.

Abyssinia. Hildebrant mentions that gum is collected from this species.[5]

A. arabica Willd. BABOOL-BARK. GUM ARABIC TREE. SUNTWOOD.

North and central Africa and southwest Asia. It furnishes a gum arabic of superior quality.[6] The bark, in times of scarcity, is ground and mixed with flour in India,[7] and the gum, mixed with the seeds of sesame, is an article of food with the natives.[8] The gum serves for nourishment, says Humboldt,[9] to several African tribes in their passages through the dessert. In Barbary, the tree is called *atteleh*.

A. bidwilli Benth.

Australia. The roots of young trees are roasted for food after peeling.[10]

A. catechu Willd. CATECHU. KHAIR. WADALEE-GUM TREE.

East Indies. Furnishes catechu, which is chiefly used for chewing in India as an ingredient of the packet of betel leaf.[11]

A. concinna DC. SOAP-POD.

Tropical Asia. The leaves are acid and are used in cookery by the natives of India as a substitute for tamarinds. It is the *fei-tsau-tau* of the Chinese. The beans are about one-half to three-fourths inch in diameter and are edible after roasting.[12]

A. decora Reichb.

Australia. The gum is gathered and eaten by Queensland natives.[13]

A. decurrens Willd. ˙ BLACK WATTLE. GREEN WATTLE. SILVER WATTLE.

Australia. It yields a gum not dissimilar to gum arabic.[14]

---

[1] Rhind, W. *Hist. Veg. King.* 557. 1855.

[2] Hooker, W. J. *Journ. Bot.* 2:359. 1840.

[3] Stille, A. *Therap. Mat. Med.* 1:113. 1874.

[4] Ibid.

[5] Flückiger and Hanbury *Pharm.* 234. 1879.

[6] *U. S. Disp.* 6. 1865.

[7] Brandis, D. *Forest Fl.* 182. 1874.

[8] Drury, H. *Useful Pls. Ind.* 5. 1858.

[9] Humboldt, A. *Polit. Essay New Spain* 2:423. 1811.

[10] Palmer, E. *Journ. Roy. Soc. New So. Wales* 17:93. 1884.

[11] Dutt, U. C. *Mat. Med. Hindus* 158. 1877.

[12] Smith, F. P. *Contrib. Mat. Med. China* 1. 1871.

[13] Palmer, E. *Journ. Roy. Soc. New So. Wales* 17:94. 1884.

[14] Mueller, F. *Sel. Pls.* 4. 1891.

A. ehrenbergiana Hayne

Desert regions of Libya, Nubia, Dongola. It yields a gum arabic.[1]

A. farnesiana Willd. CASSIE-OIL PLANT. HUISACHE. OPOPANAX. POPINAC. SPONGE
TREE. WEST INDIAN BLACKTHORN.

Tropics. This species is cultivated all over India and is indigenous in America from New Orleans, Texas and Mexico, to Buenos Aires and Chile, and is sometimes cultivated. It exudes a gum which is collected in Sind.[2] The flowers distil a delicious perfume.

A. ferruginea DC.

India. The bark steeped in " jaggery water "— fresh, sweet sap from any of several palms — is distilled as an intoxicating liquor. It is very astringent.[3]

A. flexicaulis Benth.

Texas. The thick, woody pods contain round seeds the size of peas which, when boiled, are palatable and nutritious.[4]

A. glaucophylla Steud.

Tropical Africa. This species furnishes gum arabic.[5]

A. gummifera Willd. BARBARY-GUM. MOROCCO-GUM.

North Africa. It yields gum arabic in northern Africa.[6]

A. homalophylla A. Cunn. MYALL-WOOD. VIOLET-WOOD.

This species yields gum in Australia.[7]

A. horrida Willd. CAPE-GUM TREE. DORNBOOM.

South Africa. This is the dornboom plant which exudes a good kind of gum.[8]

A. leucophloea Willd. KUTEERA-GUM.

Southern India. The bark is largely used in the preparation of spirit from sugar and palm-juice, and it is also used in times of scarcity, ground and mixed with flour. The pods are used as a vegetable, and the seeds are ground and mixed with flour.[9]

A. longifolia Willd. SYDNEY GOLDEN WATTLE.

Australia. The Tasmanians roast the pods and eat the starchy seeds.[10]

A. pallida F. Muell.

Australia. The roots of the young trees are roasted and eaten.[11]

---

[1] *U. S. Disp.* 6. 1865.
[2] Brandis, D. *Forest Fl.* 180. 1876.
[3] Drury, H. *Useful Pls. Ind.* 8. 1858
[4] Havard, V. *Proc. U. S. Nat. Mus.* 499 1885.
[5] Flückiger and Hanbury *Pharm.* 234. 1879.
[6] Mueller, F. *Sel. Pls.* 3. 1876.
[7] Baillon, H. *Hist. Pls.* 2:51. 1872.
[8] Mueller, F. *Sel. Pls.* 7. 1891.
[9] Brandis, D. *Forest Fl.* 184. 1874.
[10] Baillon, H. *Hist. Pls.* 2:52. 1872. (*A. sophorae*)
[11] Palmer, E. *Journ. Roy. Soc. New So. Wales* 17:94. 1884.

A. penninervis Sieber. BLACKWOOD. MOUNTAIN HICKORY.

Australia. This species yields gum gonate, or gonatic, in Senegal.[1]

A. senegal Willd. GUM ARABIC TREE.

Old World tropics. The tree forms vast forests in Senegambia. It is called *nebul* by the natives [2] and furnishes gum arabic.

A. seyal Delile GUM ARABIC TREE. THIRSTY THORN. WHISTLING-TREE

North Africa, Upper Egypt and Senegambia. It furnishes the best gum arabic.[3] It is called *glute* by the Arabs of the upper Nile and whistling tree by the natives of Sudan. The holes left by the departure of a gall insect are rendered musical by the wind.[4]

A. stenocarpa Hochst. GUM ARABIC TREE.

Southern Nubia and Abyssinia. The gum of this tree is extensively collected in the region between the Blue Nile and the upper Atbara. It is called *taleh, talha* or *kakul*.[5]

A. suaveolens Willd.

Australia. The aromatic leaves are used in infusions as teas.[6]

A. tortilis Hayne

Arabia, Nubia and the desert of Libya and Dongola. It furnishes the best of gum arabic.[7]

Acaena sanguisorbae Vahl. *Rosaceae.* NEW ZEALAND BUR.

Australia. The leaves are used as a tea by the natives of the Middle Island in New Zealand, according to Lyall. It is the *piri-piri* of the natives.[8]

Acanthorhiza aculeata H. Wendl. *Palmae.*

Mexico. The pulp of the fruit is of a peculiar, delicate, spongy consistence and is pure white and shining on the outside. The juice has a peculiar, penetrating, sweet flavor, is abundant, and is obviously well suited for making palm-wine. The fruit is oblong, about one inch in longest diameter. It is grown in Trinidad.[9]

Acanthosicyos horrida Welw. *Cucurbitaceae.* NARAS.

Tropics of Africa. The fruit grows on a bush from four to five feet high, without leaves and with opposite thorns. It has a coriaceous rind, rough with prickles, is about 15–18 inches around and inside resembles a melon as to seed and pulp. When ripe it has a luscious sub-acid taste.[10] The bushes grow on little knolls of sand. It is described,

---

[1] Baillon, H. *Hist. Pls.* 2:50. 1872. (*A. adstringens*)

[2] Brandis, D. *Forest Fl.* 186. 1874. (*A. verek*)

[3] Mueller, F. *Sel. Pls.* 12. 1891.

[4] Schweinfurth, G. *Heart Afr.* 1:97, 98. 1874. (*A. fistula*)

[5] Flückiger and Hanbury *Pharm.* 206. 1879.

[6] Baillon, H. *Hist. Pls.* 2:56. 1872.

[7] Mueller, F. *Sel. Pls.* 1. 1880.

[8] Black, A. A. *Treas. Bot.* 1:5. 1870.

[9] Prestoe, H. *Trinidad Bot. Gard. Rpt.* 39. 1880. (*Chamaerops stauracantha*)

[10] Alexander, J. E. *Exped. Disc. Afr.* 2:68. 1837.

however, by Anderson [1] as a creeper which produces a kind of prickly gourd about the size of a Swede turnip and of delicious flavor. It constitutes for several months of the year the chief food of the natives, and the seeds are dried and preserved for winter consumption.

Acer dasycarpum Ehrh. *Sapindaceae.* SILVER MAPLE. SOFT MAPLE. WHITE MAPLE.

North America. The sap will make sugar of good quality but less in quantity than the sugar maple.[2] Sugar is made from this species, says Loudon,[3] in districts where the tree abounds, but the produce is not above half that obtained from the sap of the sugar maple.

A. platanoides Linn. NORWAY MAPLE.

Europe and the Orient. From the sap, sugar has been made in Norway, Sweden and in Lithuania.[4]

A. pseudo-platanus Linn. MOCK PLANE. SYCAMORE MAPLE.

Europe and the Orient. In England, children suck the wings of the growing keys for the sake of obtaining the sweet exudation that is upon them.[5] In the western Highlands and some parts of the Continent, the sap is fermented into wine, the trees being first tapped when just coming into leaf.[6] From the sap, sugar may be made but not in remunerative quantities.[7]

A. rubrum Linn. RED MAPLE. SWAMP MAPLE.

North America. The French Canadians make sugar from the sap which they call *plaine*, but the product is not more than half that obtained from the sugar maple.[8] In Maine, sugar is often made from the sap.

A. saccharinum Wangenh. ROCK MAPLE. SUGAR MAPLE.

North America. This large, handsome tree must be included among cultivated food plants, as in some sections of New England groves are protected and transplanted for the use of the tree to furnish sugar. The tree is found from 48° north in Canada, to the mountains in Georgia and from Nova Scotia to Arkansas and the Rocky Mountains. The sap from the trees growing in maple orchards may give as an average one pound of sugar to four gallons of sap, and a single tree may furnish four or five pounds, although extreme yields have been put as high as thirty-three pounds from a single tree. The manufacture of sugar from the sap of the maple was known to the Indians, for Jefferys,[9] 1760, says that in Canada " this tree affords great quantities of a cooling and wholesome liquor from which they make a sort of sugar," and Jonathan Carver,[10] in 1784, says the

[1] Anderson *Lake Ngami* 16. 1856.
[2] Hough, F. B. *Elem. For.* 237, 238. 1882.
[3] Loudon, J. C. *Arb. Frut. Brit.* 1:424. 1854
[4] Loudon, J. C. *Arb. Frut. Brit.* 1:410. 1854.
[5] Loudon, J. C. *Arb. Frut. Brit.* 1:418. 1854.
[6] Johnson, C. P. *Useful Pls. Gt. Brit.* 63. 1862.
[7] Johns, C. A. *Treas. Bot.* 1:8. 1870.
[8] Loudon, J. C. *Arb. Frut. Brit.* 1:427. 1854.
[9] Jefferys, T. *Nat. Hist. Amer.* 41. 1760.
[10] Carver, J. *Travs. No. Amer.* 496. 1778.

Nandowessies Indians of the West "consume the sugar which they have extracted from the maple tree." In 1870, the Winnebagoes and Chippewas are said often to sell to the Northwest Fur Company fifteen thousand pounds of sugar a year. The sugar season among the Indians is a sort of carnival, and boiling candy and pouring it out on the snow to cool is the pastime of the children.

A. tataricum Linn. TARTARIAN MAPLE.

Orient. The Calmucks, after depriving the seeds of their wings, boil them in water and afterwards use them for food, mixed with milk and butter.[1]

Achillea millefolium Linn. *Compositae.* HUNDRED-LEAVED   GRASS.   MILFOIL.   NOSE-
        BLEED.   SANGUINARY.   THOUSAND-SEAL.   YARROW.

Europe, Asia and America. In some parts of Sweden, yarrow is said to be employed as a substitute for hops in the preparation of beer, to which it is supposed to add an intoxicating effect.[2]

Achras sapota Linn. *Sapotaceae.* NASEBERRY.   SAPODILLA.   SAPOTA.

South America. This is a tree found wild in the forests of Venezuela and the Antilles. It has for a long time been introduced into the gardens of the West Indies and South America but has been recently carried to Mauritius, to Java, to the Philippines, and to the continent of India.[3] The sapodilla bears a round berry covered with a rough, brown coat, hard at first, but becoming soft when kept a few days to mellow. The berry is about the size of a small apple and has from 6 to 12 cells with several seeds in each, surrounded by a pulp which in color, consistence, and taste somewhat resembles the pear but is sweeter.[4] The fruit, when tree-ripe, is so full of milk that little rills or veins appear quite through the pulp, which is so acerb that the fruit cannot be eaten until it is as rotten as medlars.[5] In India, Firminger [6] says of its fruit: "a more luscious, cool and agreeable fruit is not to be met with in any country in the world;" and Brandis [7] says: "one of the most pleasant fruits known when completely ripe." It is grown in gardens in Bengal.

Achyranthes bidentata Blume. *Amarantaceae.*

Tropical Asia. The seeds were used as food during a famine in Rajputana, India. Bread made from the seeds was very good. This was considered the best of all substitutes for the usual cereals.[8]

Aciphylla glacialis F. Muell. *Umbelliferae.*

Australia. This species is utilized as an alimentary root.[9]

---

[1] Browne, D. J. *Trees Amer.* 73. 1846.
[2] *U. S. Disp.* 17. 1865.
[3] Unger, F. *U. S. Pat. Off. Rpt.* 349. 1859.
[4] Lunan, J. *Hort. Jam.* 2:2. 1814.
[5] Ibid.
[6] Firminger, T. A. C. *Gard. Ind.* 255. 1874.
[7] Brandis, D. *Forest Fl.* 288. 1874.
[8] King *Bot. Soc. Edinb.* 10:198, 244. 1870. (*A. aspera*)
[9] Baillon, H. *Hist. Pls.* 7:194. 1881.

Aconitum lycoctonum Linn. *Ranunculaceae.* WOLFSBANE.

Middle and northern Europe. The root is collected in Lapland and boiled for food. This species, says Masters in the *Treasury of Botany*, does not possess such virulent properties as others.

A. napellus Linn. ACONITE. BEAR'S-FOOT. FRIAR'S-CAP. HELMET-FLOWER. LUCKIE'S MUTCH. MONKSHOOD. SOLDIER'S-CAP. TURK'S-CAP.

Northern temperate regions. Cultivated in gardens for its flowers. A narcotic poison, aconite, is the product of this species and the plant is given by the Shakers of America as a medicinal herb. In Kunawar, however, the tubers are eaten as a tonic.[1]

Acorus calamus Linn. *Aroideae.* MYRTLE FLAG. SWEET FLAG.

Northern temperate regions. The rhizomes are used by confectioners as a candy, by perfumers in the preparation of aromatic vinegar, by rectifiers to improve the flavor of gin and to give a peculiar taste to certain varieties of beer. In Europe and America, the rhizomes are sometimes cut into slices and candied or otherwise made into a sweetmeat. These rhizomes are to be seen for sale on the street corners of Boston and are frequently chewed to sweeten the breath. In France it is in cultivation as an ornamental water plant.

A. gramineus Soland. GRASS-LEAVED SWEET FLAG.

Japan. The root of this species is said to possess a stronger and more pleasant taste and smell than that of *A. calamus.* It is sometimes cultivated in gardens.

Acrocomia lasiospatha Mart. *Palmae.* MACAW. MUCUJA PALM.

West Indies and Brazil. Its fruit is the size of an apricot, globular and of a greenish-olive color, with a thin layer of firm, edible pulp of an orange color covering the nut, and, though oily and bitter, is much esteemed and eagerly sought after by the natives.[2] This is probably the macaw tree of Wafer.

A. mexicana Karw. COQUITO HABRASO. COYOLI PALM.

Mexico. The fruit, in Mexico, is eaten by the inhabitants but is not much esteemed.

A. sclerocarpa Mart. MUCUJA PALM.

Tropics of America. The young leaves of this palm are eaten as a vegetable. It is cultivated in British hot-houses.[3] The fruit is the size of a crab and contains a sweet, edible kernel. The husks are full of oil.

Acronychia laurifolia Blume. *Rutaceae.* JAMBOL.

Tropics of Asia. The black, juicy, sweetish-acid fruit is an esculent.[4] In Cochin China the young leaves are put in salads. They have the smell of cumin and are not unpleasant.[5] In Ceylon the berries are called jambol.

---

[1] Flückiger and Hanbury *Pharm.* 15. 1879.
[2] Seemann, B. *Pop. Hist. Palms* 48. 1856.
[3] Masters, M. T. *Treas. Bot.* 1:14. 187c.
[4] Don, G. *Hist. Dichl. Pls.* 1:781. 1831. (*Cyminosma pedunculata*)
[5] Ibid.

Actinidia callosa Lindl. *Ternstroemiaceae.* KOKUWA.

Japan and Manchuria. This vine is common in all the valleys of Yesso and extends to central Nippon. It is vigorous in growth and fruits abundantly. The fruit is an oblong, greenish berry about one inch in length; the pulp is of uniform texture, seeds minute and skin thin. When fully ripe it possesses a very delicate flavor.[1]

A. polygama Franch. & Sav.

Northern Japan. This is somewhat less desirable than *A. callosa*, as it fruits less abundantly and the vine is not so rich in foliage.[2]

Adansonia digitata Linn. *Malvaceae.* BAOBAB. CORK TREE. MONKEYBREAD. SOUR
GOURD.

East Indies. This tree has been found in Senegal and Abyssinia, as well as on the west coast of Africa, extending to Angola and thence across the country to Lake Ngami. It is cultivated in many of the warm parts of the world. Mollien,[3] in his *Travels*, states that to the negroes, the Baobab is perhaps the most valuable of vegetables. Its leaves are used for leaven and its bark for cordage and thread. In Senegal, the negroes use the pounded bark and the leaves as we do pepper and salt. Hooker[4] says the leaves are eaten with other food and are considered cooling and useful in restraining excessive perspiration. The fruit is much used by the natives of Sierra Leone. It contains a farinaceous pulp full of seeds, which tastes like gingerbread and has a pleasant acid flavor.[5] Brandis[6] says it is used for preparing an acid beverage. Monteiro[7] says the leaves are good to eat boiled as a vegetable and the seeds are, in Angola, pounded and made into meal for food in times of scarcity; the substance in which they are imbedded is also edible but strongly and agreeably acid.

The earliest description of the Baobab is by Cadamosto, 1454, who found at the mouth of the Senegal, trunks whose circumference he estimated at 112 feet. Perrottet says he has seen these trees 32 feet in diameter and only 70 to 85 feet high.

A. gregorii F. Muell. CREAM OF TARTAR TREE. SOUR GOURD.

Northern Australia. The pulp of its fruit has an agreeable, acid taste like cream of tartar and is peculiarly refreshing in the sultry climates where the tree is found.[8]

Adenanthera abrosperma F. Muell. *Leguminosae.*

Australia. The seeds are roasted in the coals and the kernels are eaten.[9]

A. pavonia Linn. BARBADOES PRIDE. CORAL PEA. RED SANDALWOOD.

One of the largest trees of tropical eastern Asia. The seeds are eaten by the common

---

[1] Penhallow, D. P. *Amer. Nat.* **16**:120. 1882. (*A. arguta*)

[2] Ibid.

[3] Drury, H. *Useful Pls. Ind.* 15. 1858.

[4] Ibid.

[5] Sabine, J. *Trans. Hort. Soc. Lond.* **5**:444. 1824.

[6] Brandis, D. *Forest Fl.* 30. 1874.

[7] Monteiro, J. J. *Angola, River Congo* **1**:128. 1875.

[8] Black, A. A. *Treas. Bot.* **1**:18. 1870.

[9] Palmer, E. *Journ. Roy. Soc. New So. Wales* **17**:94. 1884.

people.[1] It has been introduced into the West Indies and various parts of South America.[2]

Adenophora communis Fisch. *Campanulaceae.*

Eastern Europe. The root is thick and esculent.[3]

Adiantum capillus-veneris Linn. *Polypodiaceae.* CAPILLAIRE. DUDDER GRASS. MAIDEN-HAIR FERN. VENUS' HAIR.

Northern temperate climates. In the Isles of Arran, off the Galway coast of Britain, the inhabitants collect the fronds of this fern, dry them and use them as a substitute for tea.[4]

Aeginetia indica Linn. *Orobanchaceae.*

Tropics of Asia. An annual, leafless, parasitic herb, growing on the roots of various grasses in India and the Indian Archipelago. Prepared with sugar and nutmeg, it is there eaten as an antiscorbutic.[5]

Aegle marmelos Correa. *Rutaceae.* BALL TREE. BELA TREE. BENGAL QUINCE. GOLDEN APPLE.

East Indies. The Bengal quince is held in great veneration by the Hindus. It is sacred to Siva whose worship cannot be accomplished without its leaves. It is incumbent on all Hindus to cultivate and cherish this tree and it is sacrilegious to up-root or cut it down. The Hindoo who expires under a bela tree expects to obtain immediate salvation.[6] The tenacious pulp of the fruit is used in India for sherbet and to form a conserve.[7] Roxburgh observes that the fruit when ripe is delicious to the taste and exquisitely fragrant. Horsfield [8] says it is considered by the Javanese to be very astringent in quality. The Bengal quince is grown in some of the gardens of Cairo. The perfumed pulp within the ligneous husk makes excellent marmalade. The orange-like fruit is very palatable and possesses aperient qualities.[9]

Aegopodium podagraria Linn. *Umbelliferae.* ASHWEED. BISHOP'S-WEED. GOUTWEED. GROUND ASH. HERB GERARD.

Europe and adjoining Asia. Lightfoot [10] says the young leaves are eaten in the spring in Sweden and Switzerland as greens. It is mentioned by Gerarde.[11] In France it is an inmate of the flower garden, especially a variety with variegated leaves.

---

[1] Lunan, J. *Hort. Jam.* 1:7. 1814.

[2] Hooker, W. J. *Journ. Bot.* 4:343. 1842.

[3] Johns, C. A. *Treas. Bot.* 1:19. 1870. (*A. liliifolia*)

[4] Johnson, C. P. *Useful Pls. Gt. Brit.* 295. 1862.

[5] Black, A. A. *Treas. Bot.* 1:23. 1870.

[6] Dutt, U. C. *Mat. Med. Hindus* 129. 1877.

[7] Brandis, D. *Forest Fl.* 57. 1874.

[8] Ainslie, W. *Mat. Ind.* 2:188. 1826.

[9] *Gard. Chron.* 746. 1875.

[10] Lightfoot, J. *Fl. Scot.* 1:170. 1789.

[11] Johns, C. A. *Treas. Bot.* 1:23. 1870.

Aerva lanata Juss. *Amarantaceae.*

Tropical Africa and Arabia. According to Grant,[1] this plant is used on the Upper Nile as a pot-herb.

Aesculus californica Nutt. *Sapindaceae.* CALIFORNIA HORSE-CHESTNUT.

A low-spreading tree of the Pacific Coast of the United States. The chestnuts are made into a gruel or soup by the western Indians.[2] The Indians of California pulverize the nut, extract the bitterness by washing with water and form the residue into a cake to be used as food.[3]

A. hippocastanum Linn. HORSE-CHESTNUT.

Turkey. The common horse-chestnut is cultivated for ornament but never for the purpose of a food supply. It is now known to be a native of Greece or the Balkan Mountains.[4] Pickering[5] says it was made known in 1557; Brandis,[6] that it was cultivated in Vienna in 1576; and Emerson,[7] that it was introduced into the gardens of France in 1615 from Constantinople. John Robinson[8] says that it was known in England about 1580. It was introduced to northeast America, says Pickering,[9] by European colonists. The seeds are bitter and in their ordinary condition inedible but have been used, says Balfour,[10] as a substitute for coffee.

A. indica Coleb.

Himalayas. A lofty tree of the Himalaya Mountains called *kunour* or *pangla.*[11] In times of scarcity, the seeds are used as food, ground and mixed with flour after steeping in water.[12]

A. parviflora Walt. BUCKEYE.

Southern states of America. The fruit, according to Browne,[13] may be eaten boiled or roasted as a chestnut.

Afzelia africana Sm. *Leguminosae.*

African tropics. A portion of the seed is edible.[14]

A. quanzensis Welw. MAKOLA.

Upper Nile. The young purple-tinted leaves are eaten as a spinach.[15]

---

[1] Pickering, C. *Chron. Hist. Pls.* 465. 1879.

[2] Pickering, C. *Chron. Hist. Pls.* 582. 1879.

[3] *U. S. D. A. Rpt.* 405. 1870.

[4] Robinson, J. *Agr. Mass.* 34. 1850.

[5] Pickering, C. *Chron. Hist. Pls.* 892. 1879.

[6] Brandis, D. *Forest Fl.* 104. 1876.

[7] Emerson, G. B. *Trees, Shrubs Mass.* 2:546. 1875.

[8] Robinson, J. *Letter to Dr. Sturtevant* Oct. 13, 1881.

[9] Pickering, C. *Chron. Hist. Pls.* 892. 1879.

[10] Balfour, J. H. *Man. Bot.* 459. 1875.

[11] Pickering, C. *Chron. Hist. Pls.* 735. 1879. (*Pavia indica*)

[12] Brandis, D. *Forest Fl.* 113. 1876.

[13] Browne, D. J. *Trees Amer.* 121. 1846. (*A. macrostachya*)

[14] Baillon, H. *Hist. Pls.* 2:161. 1872.

[15] Speke, J. H. *Journ. Disc. Source Nile* 568. 1864.

Agapetes saligna Benth. & Hook. *Vacciniaceae*.

East Indies. The leaves are used as a substitute for tea by the natives of Sikkim.[1]

Agave americana Linn. *Amaryllideae*. AMERICAN ALOE. CENTURY PLANT. MAGUEY.

Tropical America. The first mention of the agave is by Peter Martyr,[2] contemporary with Columbus, who, speaking of what is probably now Yucatan, says: " They say the fyrst inhabitants lyved contented with the roots of Dates and magueans, which is an herbe much lyke unto that which is commonly called sengrem or orpin." The species of agave, called by the natives *maguey*, grows luxuriantly over the table-lands of Mexico and the neighboring borders and are so useful to the people that Prescott[3] calls the plant the " miracle of nature." From the leaves, a paper resembling the ancient papyrus was manufactured by the Aztecs; the tough fibres of the leaf afforded thread of which coarse stuffs and strong cords were made; the leaf, when washed and dried, is employed by the Indians for smoking like tobacco but being sweet and gummy chokes the pipe; an extract of the leaves is made into balls which lather with water like soap; the thorns on the leaf serve for pins and needles; the dried flower-stems constitute a thatch impervious to water; about Quito, the flower-stem is sweet, subacid, readily ferments and forms a wine called *pulque* of which immense quantities are consumed now as in more ancient times; from this *pulque* is distilled an ardent, not disagreeable but singularly deleterious spirit known as *vino mescal*. The crown of the flower-stem, charred to blackness and mingled with water, forms a black paint which is used by the Apaches to paint their faces; a fine spirit is prepared from the roasted heart by the Papajos and Apaches; the bulbs, or central portion, partly in and partly above the ground are rich in saccharine matter and are the size of a cabbage or sometimes a bushel basket and when roasted are sweet and are used by the Indians as food. Hodge,[4] writing of Arizona, pronounces the bulbs delicious. Bartlett[5] mentions their use by the Apaches, the Pimas, the Coco Maricopas and the Dieguenos Tubis.

The agave was in cultivation in the gardens of Italy in 1586 and Clusius saw it in Spain a little after this time.[6] It is now to be found generally in tropical countries. The variety which furnishes sisal hemp was introduced into Florida in 1838 and in 1855 there was a plantation of 50 acres at Key West.

A. palmeri Engelm.

Arizona. The central bud at certain seasons is roasted and eaten by the Indians and a spirit is also distilled from it.[7]

A. parryi Engelm. MESCAL.

New Mexico and northern Arizona. This plant constitutes one of the staple foods

[1] Hooker, J. D. *Illustr. Himal. Pls.* Pl. XV. A. 1855.

[2] Eden *Hist. Trav.* 142. 1577.

[3] Prescott, W. H. *Conq. Mex.* 1:137. 1843.

[4] Hodge, H. C. *Arizona* 245. 1877.

[5] Bartlett, J. R. *Explor. Texas* 1:292. 1854.

[6] De Candolle, A. *Geog. Bot.* 2:739. 1855.

[7] Newberry *Pop. Sci. Month.* 32:40. 1888.

of the Apaches. When properly prepared, it is saccharine, palatable and wholesome, mildly acid, laxative and antiscorbutic.[1]

A. utahensis Engelm. UTAH ALOE.

Utah and Arizona. The bulb of the root is considered a great delicacy by the Indians, who roast and prepare it for food which is said to be sweet and delicious.[2]

A. wislizeni Engelm.

Mexico. The young stems when they shoot out in the spring are tender and sweet and are eaten with great relish by the Mexicans and Indians.[3]

Aglaia edulis A. Gray. *Meliaceae.*

Fiji Islands and the East Indies. The natives eat the aril which surrounds the seed and call it *gumi.*[4] The fruit is edible, having a watery, cooling, pleasant pulp.[5] The aril is large, succulent and edible.[6]

A. odorata Lour.

China. Firminger[7] says this plant never fruits in Bengal. The flowers are bright yellow, of the size and form of a pin head and are delightfully fragrant. Fortune[8] says it is the *lan-hwa u yu-chu-lan* of China and that the flowers are used for scenting tea. Smith[9] says it is the *san-yeh-lan* of China, that the flowers are used for scenting tea and that the tender leaves are eaten as a vegetable.

Agrimonia eupatoria Linn. *Rosaceae.* AGRIMONY. COCKLEBUR. LIVERWORT. STICKLEWORT.

North temperate regions. The dried leaves are used by country people as a sort of tea but probably only for medicinal qualities.[10]

Agriophyllum gobicum Bunge. *Chenopodiaceae.*

Siberia. The seeds are used as food.[11]

Agropyron repens Beauv. *Gramineae.* QUACK GRASS.

Temperate regions. This is a troublesome weed in many situations yet Withering[12] states that bread has been made from its roots in times of want.

Ailanthus glandulosa Desf. *Simarubeae.* TREE OF HEAVEN. VARNISH TREE.

China. Smith[13] says that the leaves are used to feed silkworms and, in times of scarcity, are used as a vegetable.

---

[1] Havard, V. *Torr. Bot. Club Bul.* 123. 1895.

[2] Case *Bot. Index* 19. 1880.

[3] Havard, V. *Proc. U. S. Nat. Mus.* 519. 1885.

[4] Don, G. *Hist. Dichl. Pls.* 1:683. 1831.

[5] Wight, R. *Illustr. Ind. Bot.* 1:146. 1840. (*Milnea edulis*)

[6] Royle, J. F. *Illustr. Bot. Himal.* 1:140. 1839.

[7] Firminger, T. A. C. *Gard. Ind.* 429. 1874.

[8] Fortune, R. *Resid. Chinese* 201. 1857.

[9] Smith, F. P. *Contrib. Mat. Med. China.* 6. 1871.

[10] Johnson, C. P. *Useful Pls. Gt. Brit.* 95. 1862.

[11] Rigil *Gard. Chron.* 19:472. 1883.

[12] Johnson, C. P. *Useful Pls. Gt. Brit.* 290. 1862.

[13] Smith, F. P. *Contrib. Mat. Med. China* 6. 1871.

Akebia lobata Decne. *Berberideae.*

Japan. The fruits of the wild vines are regularly gathered and marketed in season.[1]

A. quinata Decne.

China. The fruit is of variable size but is usually three or four inches long and two inches in diameter. The pulp is a homogeneous, yellowish-green mass containing 40 to 50 black, oblong seeds. It has a pleasant sweetish, though somewhat insipid taste.[2]

Alangium lamarckii Thw. *Cornaceae.*

A small tree of the tropics of the Old World. On the coast of Malabar, the fruit is an article of food. It affords an edible fruit.[3] The fruit in India is mucilaginous, sweet, somewhat astringent but is eaten.[4]

Albizzia julibbrissin Durazz. *Leguminosae.*

Asia and tropical Africa. The aromatic leaves are used by the Chinese as food.[5] The leaves are said to be edible.[6] The tree is called *nemu* in Japan.[7]

A. lucida Benth.

East Indies. The edible, oily seeds taste like a hazelnut.[8]

A. monilifera F. Muell.

Australia. The pods are roasted when young and are eaten by the natives.[9]

A. montana Benth.

Java. Sometimes used as a condiment in Java.[10]

A. myriophylla Benth.

East Indies. With bark of this tree, the mountaineers make an intoxicating liquor.[11]

A. procera Benth.

Tropical Asia and Australia. In times of scarcity, the bark is mixed with flour.[12]

Albuca major Linn. *Liliaceae.*

South Africa. In Kaffraria, Thunberg [13] says the succulent stalk, which is rather mucilaginous, is chewed by the Hottentots and other travellers by way of quenching thirst.

---

[1] *Amer. Gard.* **12**:140. 1891.

[2] Ibid.

[3] Royle, J. F. *Illustr. Bot. Himal.* **1**:215. 1839.

[4] Brandis, D. *Forest Fl.* 250. 1874.

[5] Bretschneider *Bot. Sin.* 52. 1882. (*Acacia julibrissin*)

[6] Smith, F. P. *Contrib. Mat. Med. China* 2. 1871.

[7] Don, G. *Hist. Dichl. Pls.* **2**:420. 1820. (*Acacia nemu*)

[8] Baillon, H. *Hist. Pls.* **2**:56. 1872. (*Acacia lucida*)

[9] Drury, H. *Useful Pls. Ind.* 9. 1858.

[10] Palmer, E. *Journ. Roy. Soc. New So. Wales* **17**:94. 1884.

[11] Baillon, H. *Hist. Pls.* **2**:58. 1872.

[12] Brandis, D. *Forest Fl.* 176. 1874.

[13] Thunberg, C. P. *Travs.* **1**:146. 1795.

Aletris farinosa Linn. *Haemodoraceae.* AGUE-ROOT. COLIC-ROOT. CROW-CORN. STAR
          GRASS. UNICORN-ROOT.

North America. This plant, says Masters,[1] is one of the most intense bitters known,
but, according to Rafinesque,[2] the Indians eat its bulbs.

Aleurites triloba Forst. *Euphorbiaceae.* CANDLENUT TREE. COUNTRY WALNUT. OTAHEITE
          WALNUT.

Tropical Asia and Pacific Islands. This is a large tree cultivated in tropical countries
for the sake of its nuts. It is native to the eastern islands of the Malayan Archipelago
and of the Samoan group. In the Hawaiian Islands, it occurs in extensive forests. The
kernels of the nut when dried and stuck on a reed are used by the Polynesians as a substitute for candles and as an article of food in New Georgia. When pressed they yield
a large proportion of pure, palatable oil, also used as a drying oil for paint and known as
walnut-oil and artist's-oil.[3]

Alhagi camelorum Fisch. *Leguminosae.* CAMELSTHORN. MANNA-PLANT.

The Orient and central Asia. This indigenous shrub furnishes a manna by
exudation.[4]

A. maurorum Medic. PERSIAN MANNA-PLANT.

North Africa to Hindustan. Near Kandahar and Herat, manna is found and collected on the bushes of this desert plant at flowering time after the spring rains.[5] This
manna is supposed by some to have been the manna of Scripture but others refer the manna
of Scripture to one of the lichens.

Alisma plantago Linn. *Alismaceae.* MAD-DOG WEED. WATER-PLANTAIN.

North temperate zone and Australia. The solid part of the root contains farinaceous
matter and, when deprived of its acrid properties by drying, is eaten by the Calmucks.[6]

Allium akaka Gmel. *Liliaceae.*

Persia. This plant appears in the bazar in Teheren as a vegetable [7] under the name
of *wolag.* It also grows in the Alps. The whole of the young plant is considered a delicacy
and is used as an addition to rice in a pilau.[8]

A. ampeloprasum Linn. GREAT-HEADED GARLIC. LEVANT GARLIC. WILD LEEK.

Europe and the Orient. This is a hardy perennial, remarkable for the size of the
bulbs. The leaves and stems somewhat resemble those of the leek.[9] The peasants in
certain parts of Southern Europe eat it raw and this is its only known use.[10]

---

[1] Masters, M. T. *Treas. Bot.* 1:35. 1870.
[2] Rafinesque, C. S. *Fl. La.* 18. 1817.
[3] Black, A. A. *Treas. Bot.* 1:36. 1870.
[4] Don, G. *Hist. Dichl. Pls.* 2:310. 1832.
[5] Brandis, D. *Forest Fl.* 145. 1876.
[6] Johns, C. A. *Treas. Bot.* 1:38. 1870.
[7] Unger, F. *U. S. Pat. Off. Rpt.* 356. 1859. (*A. latifolium*)
[8] Ibid.
[9] Burr, F. *Field, Gard. Veg.* 124. 1863.
[10] *Bon Jard.* 414. 1882.

A. angulosum Linn. MOUSE GARLIC.

Siberia. Called on the upper Yenisei *mischei-tschesnok*, mouse garlic, and from early times collected and salted for winter use.[1]

A. ascalonicum Linn. SHALLOT.

Cultivated everywhere. The *Askolonion krommoon* of Theophrastus and the *Cepa ascolonia* of Pliny, are supposed to be our shallot but this identity can scarcely be claimed as assured. It is not established that the shallot occurs in a wild state, and De Candolle is inclined to believe it is a form of *A. cepa*, the onion.[2] It is mentioned and figured in nearly all the early botanies, and many repeat the statement of Pliny that it came from Ascalon, a town in Syria, whence the name. Michaud, in his *History of the Crusades*, says that our gardens owe to the holy wars shallots, which take their name from Ascalon.[3] Amatus Lusitanus,[4] 1554, gives Spanish, Italian, French and German names, which go to show its early culture in these countries. In England, shallots are said to have been cultivated in 1633,[5] but McIntosh[6] says they were introduced in 1548; they do not seem to have been known to Gerarde in 1597. In 1633, Worlidge[7] says " eschalots art now from France become an English condiment." Shallots are enumerated for American gardens in 1806.[8] Vilmorin[9] mentions one variety with seven sub-varieties.

The bulbs are compound, separating into what are called cloves, like those of garlic, and are of milder flavor than other cultivated alliums. They are used in cookery as a seasoner in stews and soups, as also in a raw state; the cloves, cut into small sections, form an ingredient in French salads and are also sprinkled over steaks and chops. They make an excellent pickle. In China, the shallot is grown but is not valued as highly as is *A. uliginosum*.[10]

A. canadense Linn. TREE ONION. WILD GARLIC.

North America. There is some hesitation in referring the tree onion of the garden to this wild onion. Loudon[11] refers to it as " the tree, or bulb-bearing, onion, *syn.* Egyptian onion, *A. cepa*, var. *viviparium;* the stem produces bulbs instead of flowers and when these bulbs are planted they produce underground onions of considerable size and, being much stronger flavored than those of any other variety, they go farther in cookery." Booth[12] says, " the bulb-bearing tree onion was introduced into England from Canada in 1820 and is considered to be a vivaparous variety of the common onion, which it resembles in appearance. It differs in its flower-stems being surmounted by a cluster of small green

---

[1] Pickering, C. *Chron. Hist. Pls.* 813. 1879.

[2] De Candolle, A. *Orig. Pls. Cult.* 70. 1885.

[3] Michaud *Hist. Crusades* 3:329. 1853.

[4] Dioscorides, Amatus Lusitanus Ed. 287. 1554.

[5] Miller *Gard. Dict.* 1807.

[6] McIntosh, C. *Book Gard.* 2:27. 1855.

[7] Worlidge, J. *Syst. Hort.* 193. 1683.

[8] McMahon, B. *Amer. Gard. Cal.* 190. 1806.

[9] Vilmorin *Les Pls. Potag.* 200. 1883.

[10] Smith, F. P. *Contrib. Mat. Med. China* 7. 1871.

[11] Loudon, J. C. *Hort.* 661. 1860.

[12] Booth, W. B. *Treas. Bot.* 1:40. 1870.

bulbs instead of bearing flowers and seed." It is a peculiarity of *A. canadense* that it often bears a head of bulbs in the place of flowers; its flavor is very strong; it is found throughout northern United States and Canada. Mueller [1] says its top bulbs are much sought for pickles of superior flavor. Brown [2] says its roots are eaten by some Indians. In 1674, when Marquette [3] and his party journeyed from Green Bay to the present site of Chicago, these onions formed almost the entire source of food. The lumbermen of Maine often used the plant in their broths for flavoring. On the East Branch of the Penobscot, these onions occur in abundance and are bulb-producing on their stalks. They grow in the clefts of ledges and even with the scant soil attain a foot in height. In the lack of definite information, it may be allowable to suggest that the tree onion may be a hybrid variety from this wild species, or possibly the wild species improved by cultivation. The name, Egyptian onion, is against this surmise, while, on the other hand, its apparent origination in Canada is in its favor, as is also the appearance of the growing plants.

A. cepa Linn. ONION.

Persia and Beluchistan. The onion has been known and cultivated as an article of food from the earliest period of history. Its native country is unknown. At the present time it is no longer found growing wild, but all authors ascribe to it an eastern origin. Perhaps it is indigenous from Palestine to India, whence it has extended to China, Cochin China, Japan, Europe, North and South Africa and America. It is mentioned in the Bible as one of the things for which the Israelites longed in the wilderness and complained about to Moses. Herodotus says, in his time there was an inscription on the Great Pyramid stating the sum expended for onions, radishes and garlic, which had been consumed by the laborers during the progress of its erection, as 1600 talents. A variety was cultivated, so excellent that it received worship as a divinity, to the great amusement of the Romans, if Juvenal [4] is to be trusted. Onions were prohibited to the Egyptian priests, who abstained from most kinds of pulse, but they were not excluded from the altars of the gods. Wilkinson [5] says paintings frequently show a priest holding them in his hand, or covering an altar with a bundle of their leaves and roots. They were introduced at private as well as public festivals and brought to table. The onions of Egypt were mild and of an excellent flavor and were eaten raw as well as cooked by persons of all classes.

Hippocrates [6] says that onions were commonly eaten 430 B. C. Theophrastus,[7] 322 B. C., names a number of varieties, the Sardian, Cnidian, Samothracian and Setanison, all named from the places where grown. Dioscorides,[8] 60 A. D., speaks of the onion as long or round, yellow or white. Columella,[9] 42 A. D., speaks of the Marsicam, which

---

[1] Mueller, F. *Sel. Pls.* 28 B. 1891.

[2] Brown, R. *Gard. Chron.* 1320. 1868.

[3] Case *Bot. Index* 34. 1880.

[4] De Candolle, A. *Geog. Bot.* 828. 1855.

[5] Wilkinson, J. G. *Anc. Egypt.* 1:168. 1854.

[6] Hippocrates *Opera* Cornarius Ed. 113. 1546.

[7] Theophrastus *Hist. Pl.* Bodaeus Ed. 761, 785. 1644.

[8] Dioscorides Ruellius Ed. 135. 1529.

[9] Columella lib. 12, c. 10.

the country people call *unionem*, and this word seems to be the origin of our word, onion, the French *ognon*. Pliny,[1] 79 A. D., devotes considerable space to *cepa*, and says the round onion is the best, and that red onions are more highly flavored than the white. Palladius,[2] 210 A. D., gives minute directions for culture. Apicius,[3] 230 A. D., gives a number of recipes for the use of the onion in cookery but its uses by this epicurean writer are rather as a seasoner than as an edible. In the thirteenth century, Albertus Magnus[4] describes the onion but does not include it in his list of garden plants where he speaks of the leek and garlic, by which we would infer, what indeed seems to have been the case with the ancients, that it was in less esteem than these, now minor, vegetables. In the sixteenth century, Amatus Lusitanus[5] says the onion is one of the commonest of vegetables and occurs in red and white varieties, and of various qualities, some sweet, others strong, and yet others intermediate in savor. In 1570, Matthiolus[6] refers to varieties as large and small, long, round and flat, red, bluish, green and white. Laurembergius,[7] 1632, says onions differ in form, some being round, others, oblong; in color, some white, others dark red; in size, some large, others small; in their origin, as German, Danish, Spanish. He says the Roman colonies during the time of Agrippa grew in the gardens of the monasteries a Russian sort which attained sometimes the weight of eight pounds. He calls the Spanish onion oblong, white and large, excelling all other sorts in sweetness and size and says it is grown in large abundance in Holland. At Rome, the sort which brings the highest price in the markets is the Caieta; at Amsterdam, the St. Omer.

There is a tradition in the East, as Glasspoole[8] writes, that when Satan stepped out of the Garden of Eden after the fall of man, onions sprang up from the spot where he placed his right foot and garlic from that where his left foot touched.

Targioni-Tozzetti[9] thinks the onion will probably prove identical with *A. fistulosum* Linn., a species having a rather extended range in the mountains of South Russia and whose southwestern limits are as yet unascertained.

The onion has been an inmate of British gardens, says McIntosh,[10] as long as they deserve the appellation. Chaucer,[11] about 1340, mentions them: "Wel loved he garleek, onyons and ek leekes."

Humboldt[12] says that the primitive Americans were acquainted with the onion and that it was called in Mexican *xonacatl*. Cortez,[13] in speaking of the edibles which they

---

[1] Pliny lib. 19, c. 32.

[2] Palladius lib. 3, c. 24.

[3] Apicius *Opson.* 1709.

[4] Albertus Magnus *Veg.* Jessen Ed. 487. 1867.

[5] Dioscorides Amatus Lusitanus Ed. 273. 1554.

[6] Matthiolus *Comment* 389. 1570.

[7] Laurembergius *Apparat. Plant.* 27. 1632.

[8] Glasspoole, H. G. *Ohio State Bd. Agr. Rpt.* **29**:422. 1874.

[9] Targioni-Tozzetti *Journ. Hort. Soc. Lond.* **9**:147. 1855.

[10] McIntosh, C. *Book Gard.* **2**:31. 1855.

[11] Chaucer *Prologue* V 634. 1340.

[12] De Candolle, A. *Geog. Bot.* **2**:829. 1855.

[13] Ibid.

found on the march to Tenochtitlan, cites onions, leeks and garlic. De Candolle [1] does not think that these names apply to the species cultivated in Europe. Sloane,[2] in the seventeenth century, had seen the onion only in Jamaica in gardens. The word *xonacatl* is not in Hernandez,[3] and Acosta [4] says expressly that the onions and garlics of Peru came originally from Europe. It is probable that onions were among the garden herbs sown by Columbus at Isabela Island in 1494, although they are not specifically mentioned. Peter Martyr [5] speaks of " onyons " in Mexico and this must refer to a period before 1526, the year of his death, seven years after the discovery of Mexico. It is possible that onions, first introduced by the Spaniards to the West Indies, had already found admittance to Mexico, a rapidity of adaptation scarcely impossible to that civilized Aztec race, yet apparently improbable at first thought.

Onions are mentioned by Wm. Wood,[6] 1629–33, as cultivated in Massachusetts; in 1648, they were cultivated in Virginia;[7] and were grown at Mobile, Ala., in 1775.[8] In 1779, onions were among the Indian crops destroyed by Gen. Sullivan [9] near Geneva, N. Y. In 1806, McMahon [10] mentions six varieties in his list of American esculents. In 1828, the potato onion, *A. cepa*, var. *aggregatum* G. Don, is mentioned by Thorburn [11] as a " vegetable of late introduction into our country." Burr [12] describes fourteen varieties.

Vilmorin [13] describes sixty varieties, and there are a number of varieties grown in France which are not noted by him. In form, these may be described as flat, flattened, disc-form, spherical, spherical-flattened, pear-shaped, long. This last form seems to attain an exaggerated length in Japan, where they often equal a foot in length. In 1886, Kizo Tamari,[14] a Japanese commissioner to this country, says, " Our onions do not have large, globular bulbs. They are grown just like celery and have long, white, slender stalks." In addition to the forms mentioned above, are the top onion and the potato onion. The onion is described in many colors, such as white, dull white, silvery white, pearly white, yellowish-green, coppery-yellow, salmon-yellow, greenish-yellow, bright yellow, pale salmon, salmon-pink, coppery-pink, chamois, red, bright red, blood-red, dark red, purplish.

But few of our modern forms are noticed in the early botanies. The following synonymy includes all that are noted, but in establishing it, it must be noted that many of the figures upon which it is founded are quite distinct:

[1] De Candolle, A. *Geog. Bot.* 2:829. 1855.
[2] Ibid.
[3] Ibid.
[4] Ibid.
[5] Eden *Hist. Trav.* 1577.
[6] Wood, W. *New Eng. Prosp.* 2:7. 1634.
[7] *Perf. Desc. Va.* 4. 1649. Force Coll. Tracts 2:1838.
[8] Romans *Nat. Hist. Fla.* 1:115. 1775.
[9] Conover, G. S. *Early Hist. Geneva* 47. 1879.
[10] McMahon, B. *Amer. Gard. Cal.* 582. 1806.
[11] Thorburn *Cat.* 1828.
[12] Burr, F. *Field, Gard. Veg.* 129. 1863.
[13] Vilmorin *Les Pls. Potag.* 51. 1883.
[14] *Amer. Hort.* Sept. 10, 1886.

I.

Bulb flat at bottom, tapering towards stem.

Cepa. Fuchsius, 430. 1542.
Cepa rotunda. Bodaeus, 787. 1644.
Caepe sive Cepa rubra et alba. Bauhin, J. **2**:549. 1651.
Geant de Rocca. Vilm. 387. 1883.
Mammoth Pompeii. American Seedsmen.
Golden Queen. American Seedsmen.
Paris Silverskin. American Seedsmen.
Silver White Etna. American Seedsmen.

The difference at first sight between the crude figure of Fuchsius and the modern varieties is great, but ordinary experience indicates that the changes are no greater than can be observed under selection.

II.

Bulb round at bottom, tapering towards stem.

Zwiblen. Roeszl. 121. 1550.
Cepa. Trag. 737. 1552.
Caepa. Cam. *Epit.* 324. 1586.
Blanc hâtif de Valence. Vilm. 378. 1883.
Neapolitan Marzajola. American Seedsmen.
Round White Silverskin. American Seedsmen.
White Portugal. American Seedsmen.

III.

Bulb roundish, flattened above and below.

Cepa. Matth. 276, 1558; Pin. 215. 1561.
Caepa capitata. Matth. 388. 1570.
Cepe. Lob. *Obs.* 73. 1576; *Icon.* **1**:150. 1591.
Cepa rubra. Ger. 134. 1597.
Cepa rotunda. Dod. 687. 1616.
Rouge gros-plat d'Italie. Vilm. 387. 1883.
Bermuda. American Seedsmen.
Large Flat Madeira. American Seedsmen.
Wethersfield Large Red. American Seedsmen.

IV.

Bulb rounded below, flattened above.

Cepa. Pictorius 82. 1581.
Philadelphia Yellow Dutch, or Strasburg. American Seedsmen.

V.

Bulb spherical, or nearly so.

Cepa. Trag. 737. 1552. Lauremb. 26. 1632.
Cepe. Lob. *Obs.* 73. 1576; *Icon.* **1**:150. 1591.
Cepe alba. Ger. 134. 1597.
Caepa capitata. Matth. 419. 1598.
Juane de Danvers. Vilm. 380. 1883.
Danvers. American Seedsmen.

VI
Bulb concave on the bottom.

Cepa rotunda. Bodaeus 786. 1644.
Extra Early Red. American Seedsmen.

VII.
Bulb oblong.

Caepa. Cam. *Epit.* 324. 1586.
Cepae Hispanica oblonga. Lob. *Icon.* 1:150. 1591.
Cepa oblonga. Dod. 687. 1616; Bodaeus 787. 1644.
Piriform. Vilm. 388. 1883.

VIII.
The top onion.

In 1587, Dalechamp[1] records with great surprise an onion plant which bore small bulbs in the place of seed.

A. cernuum Roth. WILD ONION.

Western New York to Wisconsin and southward. This and *A. canadense* formed almost the entire source of food for Marquette[2] and his party on their journey from Green Bay to the present site of Chicago in the fall of 1674.

A. fistulosum Linn. CIBOUL. TWO-BLADED ONION. WELSH ONION.

Siberia, introduced into England in 1629.[3] The Welsh onion acquired its name from the German walsch (foreign).[4] It never forms a bulb like the common onion but has long, tapering roots and strong fibers.[5] It is grown for its leaves which are used in salads. McIntosh[6] says it has a small, flat, brownish-green bulb which ripens early and keeps well and is useful for pickling. It is very hardy and, as Targioni-Tozzetti[7] thinks, is probably the parent species of the onion. It is mentioned by McMahon[8] in 1806 as one of the American garden esculents; by Randolph in Virginia before 1818; and was cataloged for sale by Thorburn in 1828, as at the present time.

A. neapolitanum Cyr. DAFFODIL GARLIC.

Europe and the Orient. According to Heldreich,[9] it yields roots which are edible.

A. obliquum Linn.

Siberia. From early times the plant has been cultivated on the Tobol as a substitute for garlic.[10]

---

[1] Dalechamp, J. *Hist. Gen. Pl.* (Lugd.) 532. 1587.
[2] Case *Bot. Index* 34. 1880.
[3] Booth, W. B. *Treas. Bot.* 1:40. 1870.
[4] Pickering, C. *Chron. Hist. Pls.* 582. 1879.
[5] Booth, W. B. *Treas. Bot.* 1:40. 1870.
[6] McIntosh, C. *Book Gard.* 2:41. 1855.
[7] Targioni-Tozzetti *Journ. Hort. Soc. Lond.* 9:147. 1855.
[8] McMahon, B. *Amer. Gard. Cal.* 582. 1806.
[9] Mueller, F. *Sel. Pls.* 19. 1880.
[10] Pickering, C *Chron. Hist. Pls.* 813. 1879.

A. odorum Linn. FRAGRANT-FLOWERED GARLIC.

Siberia. This onion is eaten as a vegetable in Japan.[1]

A. oleraceum Linn. FIELD GARLIC.

Europe. The young leaves are used in Sweden to flavor stews and soups or fried with other herbs and are sometimes so employed in Britain but are inferior to those of the cultivated garlic.[2]

A. porrum Linn. LEEK.

Found growing wild in Algiers but the *Bon Jardinier*[3] says it is a native of Switzerland. It has been cultivated from the earliest times. This vegetable was the *prason* of the ancient Greeks, the *porrum* of the Romans, who distinguished two kinds, the *capitatum*, or leek, and the *sectile*, or chives, although Columella,[4] Pliny,[5] and Palladius,[6] indicate these as forms of the same plant brought about through difference of culture, the chive-like form being produced by thick planting. In Europe, the leek was generally known throughout the Middle Ages, and in the earlier botanies some of the figures of the leek represent the two kinds of planting alluded to by the Roman writers. In England, 1726, Townsend[7] says that " leeks are mightily used in the kitchen for broths and sauces." The Israelites complained to Moses of the deprivation from the leeks of Egypt during their wanderings in the wilderness. Pliny[8] states, that in his time the best leeks were brought from Egypt, and names Aricia in Italy as celebrated for them. Leeks were brought into great notice by the fondness for them of the Emperor Nero who used to eat them for several days in every month to clear his voice, which practice led the people to nickname him Porrophagus. The date of its introduction into England is given as 1562, but it certainly was cultivated there earlier, for it has been considered from time immemorial as the badge of Welshmen, who won a victory in the sixth century over the Saxons which they attributed to the leeks they wore by the order of St. David to distinguish them in the battle. It is referred to by Tusser and Gerarde[9] as if in common use in their day.

The leek may vary considerably by culture and often attain a large size; one with the blanched portion a foot long and nine inches in circumference and the leaf fifteen inches in breadth and three feet in length has been recorded.[10] Vilmorin[11] described eight varieties in 1883 but some of these are scarcely distinct. In 1806, McMahon[12] named three varieties among American garden esculents. Leeks are mentioned by Romans[13] as grow-

---

[1] *Gard. Chron.* **25**:458. 1886.

[2] Johnson, C. P. *Useful Pls. of Gt. Brit.* 270. 1862.

[3] *Bon. Jard.* 550. 1882.

[4] Columella lib. 2, c. 8.

[5] Pliny lib. 19, c. 34.

[6] Palladius lib. 3, c. 24.

[7] Townsend *Seedsman* 37. 1726.

[8] McIntosh, C. *Book Gard.* **2**:44. 1855.

[9] Gerarde, J. *Herb.* 139. 1597.

[10] *Gard. Chron.* **26**:599. 1886.

[11] Vilmorin *Les Pls. Potag.* 416. 1883.

[12] McMahon, B. *Amer. Gard. Cal.* 581. 1806.

[13] Romans *Nat. Hist. Fla.* **1**:115. 1775.

ing at Mobile, Ala., in 1775 and as cultivated by the Choctaw Indians.   The reference
to leeks by Cortez is noticed under *A. cepa*, the onion.   The lower, or blanched, portion
is the part generally eaten, and this is used in soups or boiled and served as asparagus.[1]
Buist [2] names six varieties.   The blanched stems are much used in French cookery.

A. reticulatum Fras.

North America.   This is a wild onion whose root is eaten by the Indians.[3]

A. roseum Linn.   ROSY-FLOWERED GARLIC.

Mediterranean countries.   According to Heldreich,[4] this plant yields edible roots.

A. rotundum Linn.

Europe and Asia Minor.   The leaves are eaten by the Greeks of Crimea.[5]

A. rubellum Bieb.

Europe, Siberia and the Orient.   The bulbs are eaten by the hill people of India
and the leaves are dried and preserved as a condiment.[6]

A. sativum Linn.   CLOWN'S TREACLE.   GARLIC.

Europe.   This plant, well known to the ancients, appears to be native to the plains
of western Tartary [7] and at a very early period was transported thence over the whole
of Asia (excepting Japan), north Africa and Europe.   It is believed to be the *skorodon
hemeron* of Dioscorides and the *allium* of Pliny.   It was ranked by the Egyptians among
gods in taking an oath, according to Pliny.   The want of garlics was lamented to Moses
by the Israelites in the wilderness.   Homer [8] makes garlic a part of the entertainment
which Nestor served to his guest, Machaon.   The Romans are said to have disliked it on
account of the strong scent but fed it to their laborers to strengthen them and to their
soldiers to excite courage.   It was in use in England prior to 1548 and both Turner [9] and
Tusser [10] notice it.   Garlic is said to have been introduced in China 140–86 B. C.[11] and to
be found noticed in various Chinese treatises of the fifteenth, sixteenth, seventeenth and
eighteenth centuries.[12]   Loureiro [13] found it under cultivation in Cochin China.

The first mention of garlic in America is by Peter Martyr,[14] who states that Cortez
fed on it in Mexico.   In Peru, Acosta [15] says " the Indians esteem garlike above all
the roots of Europe."   It was cultivated by the Choctaw Indians in gardens before

[1] Burr, F.   *Field, Gard. Veg.* 126.   1863.

[2] Buist, R.   *Fam. Kitch. Gard.* 84.   1851.

[3] Pickering, C.   *Chron. Hist. Pls.* 605.   1879.

[4] Mueller, F.   *Sel. Pls.* 28 B.   1891.

[5] Pallas, P. S.   *Trav. Russia* 2:449.   1803.   (*A. descendens*)

[6] Royle, J. F.   *Illustr. Bot. Himal.* 1:393.   1839.

[7] Pickering *Chron. Hist. Pls.* 145.   1879.

[8] *Treas. Bot.* 1:41.   1870.

[9] Miller *Gard. Dict.* 1807.

[10] McIntosh, C.   *Book Gard.* 2:29.   1855.

[11] Bretschneider, E.   *On the Study* 15.   1870.

[12] Bretschneider, E.   *Bot. Sin.* 59, 78, 83, 85.   1882.

[13] Loureiro *Fl. Cochin.* 201.   1790.

[14] Eden *Hist. Trav.* 1577.

[15] Acosta *Nat. Mor. Hist. Ind.* 261.   1604.   Hakl. Soc. Ed. 1880.

1775 [1] and is mentioned among garden esculents by American writers on gardening in 1806 and since. The plant has the well-known alliaceous odor which is strongly penetrating, especially at midday. It is not as much used by northern people as by those of the south of Europe. In many parts of Europe, the peasantry eat their brown bread with slices of garlic which imparts a flavor agreeable to them. In seed catalogs, the sets are listed while seed is rarely offered. There are two varieties, the common and the pink.

A. schoenoprasum Linn. CHIVE. CIVE.

North temperate zone. This perennial plant seems to be grown in but few American gardens, although McMahon,[2] 1806, included it in his list of American esculents. Chive plants are included at present among the supplies offered in our best seed catalogs. In European gardens, they are cultivated for the leaves which are used in salads, soups and for flavoring. Chives are much used in Scotch families and are considered next to indispensable in omelettes and hence are much more used on the Continent of Europe, particularly in Catholic countries. In England, chives were described by Gerarde[3] as " a pleasant Sawce and good Pot-herb;" by Worlidge[4] in 1683; the chive was among seedsmen's supplies [5] in 1726; and it is recorded as formerly in great request but now of little regard, by Bryant [6] in 1783.

The only indication of variety is found in Noisette,[7] who enumerates the *civette*, the *cive d'Angleterre* and the *cive de Portugal* but says these are the same, only modified by soil. The plant is an humble one and is propagated by the bulbs; for, although it produces flowers, these are invariably sterile according to Vilmorin.

A. scorodoprasum Linn. ROCAMBOLE. SAND LEEK. SPANISH GARLIC.

Europe, Caucasus region and Syria. This species grows wild in the Grecian Islands and probably elsewhere in the Mediterranean regions.[8] Loudon says it is a native of Denmark, formerly cultivated in England for the same purposes as garlic but now comparatively neglected. It is not of ancient culture as it cannot be recognized in the plants of the ancient Greek and Roman authors and finds no mention of garden cultivation by the early botanists. It is the *Scorodoprasum* of Clusius,[9] 1601, and the *Allii genus, ophioscorodon dictum quibusdam*, of J. Bauhin,[10] 1651, but there is no indication of culture in either case. Ray,[11] 1688, does not refer to its cultivation in England. In 1726, however, Townsend [12] says it is " mightly in request; " in 1783, Bryant [13] classes it with edibles.

[1] Romans *Nat. Hist. Fla.* **1**:84. 1775.

[2] McMahon, B. *Amer. Gard. Cal.* 581. 1806.

[3] Gerarde, J. *Herb.* 139. 1597.

[4] Worlidge, J. *Syst. Hort.* 194. 1683.

[5] Townsend *Seedsman* 25. 1726.

[6] Bryant *Fl. Diet.* 92. 1783.

[7] Noisette *Man. Jard.* 353. 1829.

[8] De Candolle, A. *Geog. Bot.* **2**:831. 1855.

[9] Clusius *Hist.* 190. 1601.

[10] Bauhin, J. *Hist. Pl.* **2**:559. 1651.

[11] Ray, J. *Hist. Pl.* **2**:1120. 1688.

[12] Townsend *Seedsman* 25. 1726.

[13] Bryant *Fl. Diet.* 23. 1783.

In France it was grown by Quintyne, 1690. It is mentioned by Gerarde as a cultivated plant in 1596. Its bulbs are smaller than those of garlic, milder in taste and are produced at the points of the stem as well as at its base. Rocambole is mentioned among American garden esculents by McMahon,[1] 1806, by Gardiner and Hepburn,[2] 1818, and by Bridgeman,[3] 1832.

A. senescens Linn.

Europe and Siberia. This species is eaten as a vegetable in Japan.[4]

A. sphaerocephalum Linn. ROUND-HEADED GARLIC.

Europe and Siberia. From early times this species has been eaten by the people about Lake Baikal.[5]

A. stellatum Fras.

North America. " Bulb oblong-ovate and eatable." [6]

A. ursinum Linn. BEAR'S GARLIC. BUCKRAMS. GIPSY ONION. HOG'S GARLIC. RAMSONS.

Europe and northern Asia. Gerarde,[7] 1597, says the leaves were eaten in Holland. They were also valued formerly as a pot-herb in England, though very strong.[8] The bulbs were also used boiled and in salads.[9] In Kamchatka this plant is much prized. The Russians as well as the natives gather it for winter food.[10]

A. vineale Linn. CROW GARLIC. FIELD GARLIC. STAG'S GARLIC.

Europe and now naturalized in northern America near the coast. In England, the leaves are used as are those of garlic.[11]

Allophyllus cobbe Blume. *Sapindaceae.*

Eastern Asia. The berries, which are red in color and about the size of peas, are eaten by the natives.[12]

A. zeylanicus Linn.

Himalayas. The fruit is eaten.[13]

Alocasia indica Schott. *Aroideae.* PAI.

East Indies and south Asia, South Sea Islands and east Australia. The underground stems constitute a valuable and important vegetable of the native dietary in India. The

---

[1] McMahon, B. *Amer. Gard. Cal.* 190. 1806.
[2] Gardiner and Hepburn *Amer. Gard.* 40. 1818.
[3] Bridgeman *Young Gard. Asst.* 89. 1857.
[4] *Gard. Chron.* 25:458. 1886.
[5] Pickering, C. *Chron. Hist. Pls.* 753. 1879.
[6] Wood, A. *Class Book Bot.* 711. 1855.
[7] Gerarde, J. *Herb.* 142. 1597.
[8] Johnson, C. P. *Useful Pls. Gt. Brit.* 271. 1862.
[9] Gerarde, J. *Herb.* 142. 1597.
[10] Glasspoole, H. G. *Ohio State Bd. Agr. Rpt.* 29:428. 1874.
[11] Johnson, C. P. *Useful Pls. Gt. Brit.* 271. 1862.
[12] Ainslie, W. *Mat. Ind.* 2:413. 1826.
[13] Unger, F. *U. S. Pat. Off. Rpt.* 343. 1859. (*Schmidelia africana*)

stems sometimes grow to an immense size and can be preserved for a considerable time, hence they are of great importance in jail dietary when fresh vegetables become scarce in the bazar or jail-garden.[1] For its esculent stems and small, pendulous tubers of its root, it is cultivated in Bengal and is eaten by people of all ranks in their curries. In the Polynesian islands its large tuberous roots are eaten.[2] Wilkes[3] says the natives of the Kingsmill group of islands cultivate this species with great care. The root is said to grow to a very large size.

A. macrorhiza Schott. APE. TARO.

Tropics of Asia, Australia and the islands of the Pacific. The root is eaten in India, after being cooked, but it is inferior to that of *A. esculentum*.[4] The roots are also eaten in tropical America as well as by the people of New Caledonia, who cultivate it.[5] It furnishes the *roasting eddas*[6] of Jamaica and the *tayoea* of Brazil.[7] It is the taro of New Holland, the roots of which, when roasted, afford a staple aliment to the natives.[8] Wilkes[9] states that this plant is the ape of the Tahitians and is cultivated as a vegetable.

Aloe sp. *Liliaceae*. ALOE.

The Banians of the African coast, according to Grant,[10] cut the leaves of an aloe into small pieces, soak them in lime-juice, put them in the sun, and a pickle is thus formed.

Alpinia galanga Willd. *Scitamineae*. GALANGAL. GALINGALE.

Tropical eastern Asia. The root is used in place of ginger in Russia and in some other countries for flavoring a liquor called *nastoika*. By the Tartars, it is taken with tea.[11] In Cochin China the fresh root is used to season fish and for other economic purposes.[12]

A. globosa Horan.

China. The large, round China cardamons are supposed to be produced by this species.[13] The Mongol conquerors of China set great store on this fruit as a spice.[14]

A. striata Hort. AMOMUM. CARDAMOM.

East Indies. This is probably the *amomon* of Dioscorides. It is found in Sumatra, Java and other East Indian islands as far as Burma and produces the round cardamoms of commerce.

[1] Dutt, U. C. *Mat. Med. Hindus* 253. 1877.

[2] Seemann, B. *Fl. Viti.* 286. 1865–1873.

[3] Wilkes, C. *U. S. Explor. Exped.* 5:81. 1845.

[4] Ainslie, W. *Mat. Ind.* 2:463. 1826.

[5] LaBillardière *Voy. Recherche Pérouse* 2:236. 1799.

[6] Hughes, G. *Nat. Hist. Barb.* 227. 1750.

[7] Schomburgkh *Hist. Barb.* 587. 1848.

[8] Hooker, W. J. *Bot. Misc.* 1:259, 261. 1830. (*Caladium glycyrrhiza*)

[9] Wilkes, C. *U. S. Explor. Exped.* 2:51. 1845.

[10] Speke, J. H. *Journ. Disc. Source Nile* 583. 1864.

[11] Flückiger and Hanbury *Pharm.* 641. 1879.

[12] Pickering, C. *Chron. Hist. Pls.* 570. 1879.

[13] Masters, M. T. *Treas. Bot.* 1:52. 1870. (*Amomum globosum*)

[14] Smith, F. P. *Contrib. Mat. Med. China* 14. 1871.

A. uviformis Horan.

Tropical Asia. The fruit is said to be edible.[1]

Alsodeia physiphora Mart. *Violarieae.*

Brazil. Used as a spinach in Brazil.[2] The green leaves are very mucilaginous, and the negroes about Rio Janeiro eat them with their food.[3]

Alsophila lunulata R. Br. *Cyatheaceae.* TREE FERN.

Viti. The young leaves are eaten in times of scarcity.[4]

A. spinulosa Hook.

This is the *pugjik* of the Lepchas who eat the soft, watery pith. It is abundant in East Bengal and the peninsula of India.

Alstroemeria haemantha Ruiz & Pav. *Amaryllideae.* HERB LILY.

Chile. The plant furnishes a farina from its roots.

A. ligtu Linn.

Chile and the mountains of Peru. A farina is obtained from its roots. It is called in Peru *lintu*, in Chile *utat*.[5] Its roots furnish a palatable starch.[6]

A. revoluta Ruiz & Pav.

Chile. Its roots furnish a farina.[7]

A. versicolor Ruiz & Pav.

Chile. A farina is obtained from its roots.[8] In France it is an inmate of the flower garden.

Althaea officinalis Linn. *Malvaceae.* MARSHMALLOW. WHITE MALLOW.

The plant is found wild in Europe and Asia and is naturalized in places in America. It is cultivated extensively in Europe for medicinal purposes, acting as a demulcent. In 812, Charlemagne[9] enjoined its culture in France. Johnson says[10] its leaves may be eaten when boiled.

A. rosea Cav. HOLLYHOCK.

The Orient. This species grows wild in China and in the south of Europe. Forskal[11] says it is cultivated at Cairo for the sake of its leaves, which are esculent and are used

---

[1] Masters, M. T. *Treas. Bot.* 1:534. 1870. (*Globba uviformis*)

[2] Lindley *Veg. King.* 339. 1846. (*Conohoria loboloba*)

[3] Don, G. *Hist. Dichl. Pls.* 1:340. 1831. (*Gonohoria loboloba*)

[4] Seemann, B. *Fl. Viti.* 334. 1865-73.

[5] Pickering, C. *Chron. Hist. Pls.* 661. 1879.

[6] Mueller, F. *Sel. Pls.* 33. 1891. (*A. pallida*)

[7] Pickering, C. *Chron. Hist. Pls.* 661. 1879.

[8] Ibid.

[9] Flückiger and Hanbury *Pharm.* 85. 1879.

[10] Johnson, C. P. *Useful Pls. Gt. Brit.* 59. 1862.

[11] Pickering, C. *Geog. Dist. Ans. Pls.* 47. 1863-1876.

in Egyptian cookery. It possesses similar properties to the marshmallow and is used for similar purposes in Greece.[1]

Amaranthus blitum Linn. *Amarantaceae*. AMARANTHUS. WILD BLITE.

Temperate and tropical zones. The plant finds use as a pot-herb.[2]

A. campestris Willd.

East Indies. This species is one of the pot-herbs of the Hindus.[3]

A. diacanthus Rafin.

North America. Rafinesque[4] says the leaves are good to eat as spinach.

A. gangeticus Linn. AMARANTHUS.

Tropical zone. This amaranthus is cultivated by the natives in endless varieties and is in general use in Bengal. The plant is pulled up by the root and carried to market in that state.[5] The leaves are used as a spinach.[6] Roxburgh[7] says there are four leading varieties cultivated as pot-herbs: Viridis, the common green sort, is most cultivated; Ruber, a beautiful, bright colored variety; Albus, much cultivated in Bengal; Giganteus, is five to eight feet high with a stem as thick as a man's wrist. The soft, succulent stem is sliced and eaten as a salad, or the tops are served as an asparagus.[8] In China, the plant is eaten as a cheap, cooling, spring vegetable by all classes.[9] It is much esteemed as a pot-herb by all ranks of natives.[10] This species is cultivated about Macao and the neighboring part of China and is the most esteemed of all their summer vegetables.[11]

A. paniculatus Linn. PRINCE'S FEATHER. RED AMARANTH.

North America and naturalized in the Orient. This plant is extensively cultivated in India for its seed which is ground into flour. It is very productive. Roxburgh[12] says it will bear half a pound of floury, nutritious seed on a square yard of ground. Titford[13] says it forms an excellent pot-herb in Jamaica when boiled, exactly resembling spinach.

A. polygamus Linn. GOOSE-FOOT.

Tropical Africa and East Indies. This plant is cultivated in India and is used as a pot-herb.[14] It has mucilaginous leaves without taste.[15] This amaranthus is a common

[1] Masters, M. T. *Treas. Bot.* 1:46. 1870.

[2] Balfour *Man. Bot.* 562. 1875.

[3] Ainslie, W. *Mat. Ind.* 2:392. 1826.

[4] Rafinesque, C. S. *Fl. La.* 32. 1817.

[5] Roxburgh, W. *Hort. Beng.* 67. 1814.

[6] Firminger, T. A. C. *Gard. Ind.* 142. 1874.

[7] Ibid.

[8] Ibid.

[9] Smith, F. P. *Contrib. Mat. Med. China* 12. 1871.

[10] Wight, R. *Icon. Pls.* 2:713. 1843. (*A. tristis*)

[11] Livingstone, J. *Trans. Hort. Soc. Lond.* 5:54. 1824. (*A. tristis*)

[12] Mueller, F. *Sel. Pls.* 34. 1891.

[13] Titford, W. J. *Hort. Bot. Amer.* VII of Addenda. 1812. (*A. sanguineus*)

[14] Royle, J. F. *Illustr. Bot. Himal.* 1:321. 1839.

[15] Ibid.

weed everywhere in India and is much used by the natives as a pot-herb.[1] Drury says it is considered very wholesome.[2] This species is the goose-foot of Jamaica, where it is sometimes gathered and used as a green.[3]

A. polystachyus Willd.

East Indies. The species is cultivated in India as a pot-herb for its mucilaginous leaves but is tasteless.[4]

A. retroflexus Linn. GREEN AMARANTH. PIGWEED.

North America. This weed occurs around dwellings in manured soil in the United States whence it was introduced from tropical America.[5] It is an interesting fact that it is cultivated by the Arizona Indians for its seeds.[6]

A. spinosus Linn. PRICKLY CALALUE. THORNY AMARANTH.

Tropical regions. This is a weed in cultivated land in Asia, Africa and America. It is cultivated sometimes as a spinach.[7] In Jamaica, it is frequently used as a vegetable and is wholesome and agreeable.[8] It seems to be the prickly calalue of Long.[9]

A. viridis Linn.

Tropics. This plant is stated by Titford [10] to be an excellent pot-herb in Jamaica and is said to resemble spinach when boiled

Ambelania acida Aubl. *Apocynaceae.*

Guiana. The fruit is edible.[11]

Amelanchier alnifolia Nutt. *Rosaceae.* WESTERN SERVICE BERRY.

North America. In Oregon and Washington, the berries are largely employed as a food by the Indians.[12, 13] The fruit is much larger than that of the eastern service berry; growing in favorable localities, each berry is full half an inch in diameter and very good to eat.

A. canadensis Medic. GRAPE-PEAR. JUNEBERRY. SERVICE BERRY. SHAD. SWEET PEAR.

North America and eastern Asia. This bush or small tree, according to the variety, is a native of the northern portion of America and eastern Asia. Gray [14] describes five

---

[1] Wight, R. *Icon. Pls.* 2:719. 1843. (*A. polygonoides*)
[2] Drury, H. *Useful Plants Ind.* 31. 1858. (*A. polygonoides*)
[3] Lunan, J. *Hort. Jam.* 1:381. 1814.
[4] Royle, J. F. *Illustr. Bot. Himal.* 1:321. 1839.
[5] Gray, A. *Man. Bot.* 412. 1868.
[6] Brewer and Watson *Bot. Cal.* 2:41. 1880.
[7] De Candolle, A. P. *Geog. Bot.* 2:778. 1855.
[8] Lunan, J. *Hort. Jam.* 1:143. 1814.
[9] Long *Hist. Jam.* 3:771. 1774.
[10] Titford, W. J. *Hort. Bot. Amer.* VII of Addenda. 1812. (*A. sanguineus*)
[11] Unger, F. *U. S. Pat. Off. Rpt.* 351. 1859.
[12] Vasey *U. S. D. A. Rpt.* 162. 1875.
[13] Case *Bot. Index* 38. 1881.
[14] Gray, A. *Man. Bot.* 162. 1868.

forms. For many years a Mr. Smith,[1] Cambridge, Massachusetts, has cultivated var. *oblongifolia* in his garden and in 1881 exhibited a plate of very palatable fruit at the Massachusetts Horticultural Society's show. The berries are eaten in large quantities, fresh or dried, by the Indians of the Northwest. The fruit is called by the French in Canada *poires*, in Maine sweet pear [2] and from early times has been dried and eaten by the natives. It is called grape-pear in places, and its fruit is of a purplish color and an agreeable, sweet taste.[3] The pea-sized fruit is said to be the finest fruit of the Saskatchewan country and to be used by the Cree Indians both fresh and dried.[4]

A. vulgaris Moench. AMELANCHIER.

Mountains of Europe and adjoining portions of Asia.[5] This species has long been cultivated in England, where its fruit, though not highly palatable, is eatable. It is valued more for its flowers than its fruit.[6]

Ammobroma sonorae Torr. *Lennoaceae.*

A leafless plant, native of New Mexico. Col. Grey, the original discoverer of this plant, found it in the country of the Papago Indians, a barren, sandy waste, where rain scarcely ever falls, but " where nature has provided for the sustenance of man one of the most nutritious and palatable of vegetables." The plant is roasted upon hot coals and ground with mesquit beans and resembles in taste the sweet potato " but is far more delicate." It is very abundant in the hills; the whole plant, except the top, is buried in the sand.[7]

Amomum. *Scitamineae.* CARDAMOM.

The aromatic and stimulant seeds of many of the plants of the genus *Amomum* are known as cardamoms, as are those of *Elettaria.* The botanical history of the species producing the various kinds is in much confusion. One species at least is named as under cultivation.

A. angustifolium Sonner. GREAT CARDAMOM.

Madagascar. This plant grows on marshy grounds in Madagascar and affords in its seeds the Madagascar, or great cardamoms of commerce. It is called there *longouze*.[8]

A. aromaticum Roxb.

East Indies. The fruit is used as a spice and medicine by the natives and is sold as cardamoms.

A. granum-paradisi Linn. GRAINS OF· PARADISE.

African tropics. The seeds are made use of illegally in England to give a fictitious

---

[1] Smith, B. G.   Note by Sturtevant.

[2] Pickering, C.   *Chron. Hist. Pls.* 804.   1879.   (*A. botryapium*)

[3] Johns, C. A.   *Treas. Bot.* 1:50.   1870.

[4] Don, G.   *Hist. Dichl. Pls.* 2:604.   1832.   (*A. ovalis*)

[5] Pickering, C.   *Chron. Hist. Pls.* 356.   1879.

[6] Johns, C. A.   *Treas. Bot.* 1:50.   1870.

[7] Masters, M. T.   *Treas. Bot.* 2:1260, 1261.   1876.

[8] Pickering, C.   *Chron. Hist. Pls.* 821.   1879.

strength to spirits and beer, but they are not particularly injurious.[1] The seeds resemble and equal camphor in warmth and pungency.[2]

A. maximum Roxb. JAVA CARDAMOM

Java and other Malay islands. This species is said to be cultivated in the mountains of Nepal.

A. melegueta Rosc. MELEGUETA PEPPER.

African tropics. The seeds are exported from Guiana where the plant, supposed to have been brought from Africa, is cultivated by the negroes. The hot and peppery seeds form a valued spice in many parts of India and Africa.

A. villosum Lour.

East Indies and China. This plant is supposed to yield the hairy, round, China cardamoms.[3]

A. xanthioides Wall. BASTARD CARDAMOM.

Burma. In China, says Smith,[4] the seeds are used as a preserve or condiment and are used in flavoring spirit.

Amorphophallus campanulatus Blume. *Aroideae.* AMORPHOPHALLUS. TELINGA POTATO.

Tropical Asia. This plant is much cultivated, especially in the northern Circars, where it is highly esteemed for the wholesomeness and nourishing quality of its roots. The telinga potato is cooked in the manner of the yam and is also used for pickling.[5] When in flower, the odor exhaled is most overpowering, resembling that of carrion, and flies cover the club of the spadix with their eggs. The root is very acrid in a raw state; it is eaten either roasted or boiled. At the Society Islands the fruit is eaten as bread, when breadfruit is scarce and in the Fiji Islands is highly esteemed for its nutritive properties.[6]

A. lyratus Kunth.

East Indies. The roots are eaten by the natives and are thought to be very nutritious. They require, however, to be carefully boiled several times and to be dressed in a particular manner in order to divest them of a somewhat disagreeable taste.[7]

Amphicarpaea edgeworthii Benth. *Leguminosae.* WILD BEAN.

Himalayas. A wild, bean-like plant, the pods of which are gathered while green and used for food.[8]

A. monoica Ell. HOG PEANUT.

North America. A delicate vine growing in rich woodlands which bears two kinds of flowers, the lower ones subterranean and producing fruit. It is a native of eastern

---

[1] Masters, M. T. *Treas. Bot.* 1:52. 1870.

[2] Pickering, C. *Chron. Hist. Pls.* 842. 1879. (*A. grandiflorum*)

[3] Masters, M. T. *Treas. Bot.* 1:52. 1870.

[4] Smith, F. P. *Contrib. Mat. Med. China* 16. 1871.

[5] Drury, H. *Useful Pls. Ind.* 32. 1858.

[6] Seemann, B. *Fl. Viti.* 284. 1865-73.

[7] Drury, H. *Useful Pls. Ind.* 56. 1858. (*Arum lyratum* Roxb.)

[8] Georgeson *Amer. Gard.* 14:85. 1893.

United States.[1] Porcher[2] says that in the South the subterranean pod is cultivated as a vegetable and is called hog peanut.

Anacardium humile St. Hil. *Anacardiaceae.* MONKEY-NUT.

Brazil. The nuts are eaten and conserves are made of the fruit.[3]

A. nanum St. Hil.

Brazil. The nuts are eaten and conserves are made of the fruit.[4]

A. occidentale Linn. CASHEW.

This tree is indigenous to the West Indies, Central America, Guiana, Peru and Brazil in all of which countries it is cultivated. The Portuguese transplanted it as early as the sixteenth century to the East Indies and Indian archipelago. Its existence on the eastern coast of Africa is of still more recent date, while neither China, Japan, or the islands of the Pacific Ocean possess it.[5] The shell of the fruit has thin layers, the intermediate one possessing an acrid, caustic oil, called cardol, which is destroyed by heat, hence the kernels are roasted before being eaten; the younger state of the kernel, however, is pronounced wholesome and delicious when fresh. Drury[6] says the kernels are edible and wholesome, abounding in sweet, milky juice and are used for imparting a flavor to Madeira wine. Ground and mixed with cocoa, they make a good chocolate. The juice of the fruit is expressed, and, when fermented, yields a pleasant wine; distilled, a spirit is drawn from the wine making a good punch. A variety of the tree is grown in Travancore, probably elsewhere, the pericarp of the nuts of which has no oil but may be chewed raw with impunity. An edible oil equal to olive oil or almond oil is procured from the nuts but it is seldom prepared, the kernels being used as a table fruit. A gum, similar to gum arabic, called *cadju gum*, is secreted from this tree. The thickened receptacle of the nut has an agreeable, acid flavor and is edible.[7]

A. rhinocarpus DC. WILD CASHEW.

South America. This is a noble tree of Columbia and British Guiana, where it is called wild cashew. It has pleasant, edible fruits like the cashew. In Panama, according to Seemann, the tree is called *espave*, in New Granada *caracoli*.[8]

Anagallis arvensis Linn. *Primulaceae.* PIMPERNEL. POOR MAN'S WEATHERGLASS. SHEPHERD'S CLOCK.

Europe and temperate Asia. Pimpernel, according to Fraas,[9] is eaten as greens in the Levant. Johnson[10] says it forms a part of salads in France and Germany. The flowers close at the approach of bad weather, hence the name, poor man's weatherglass.

---

[1] Gray, A. *Man. Bot.* 530. 1908.

[2] Porcher, F. P. *Res. So. Fields, Forests* 227. 1869.

[3] Baillon, H. *Hist. Pls.* 5:304. 1878.

[4] Ibid.

[5] Unger, F. *U. S. Pat. Off. Rpt.* 347. 1859.

[6] Drury, H. *Useful Pls. Ind.* 33. 1858.

[7] Masters, M. T. *Treas. Bot.* 1:58. 1870.

[8] Black, A. A. *Treas. Bot.* 2:973. 1870. (*Rhinocarpus*)

[9] Pickering, C. *Chron. Hist. Pls.* 200. 1879.

[10] Johnson, C. P. *Useful Pls. Gt. Brit.* 212. 1862.

Anamirta paniculata Colebr. *Menispermaceae.*

East Indies.   A strong, climbing shrub found in the eastern part of the Indian Peninsula and Malay Islands.   From this plant is produced a deleterious drug illegally used
in England to impart bitterness to beer.[1]

Ananas sativus Schult. *Bromeliaceae.*   PINEAPPLE.

Tropical America.   In 1493, the companions of Columbus, at Guadeloupe island,
first saw the pineapple, the flavor and fragrance of which astonished and delighted them,
as Peter Martyr records.   The first accurate illustration and description appear to have
been given by Oviedo in 1535.   Las Casas,[2] who reached the New World in 1502, mentions the finding by Columbus at Porto Bello of the delicious pineapple.   Oviedo,[3] who
went to America in 1513, mentions in his book three kinds as being then known.   Benzoni,[4]
whose *History of the New World* was published in 1568 and who resided in Mexico from
1541 to 1555, says that no fruit on God's earth could be more agreeable, and Andre Thevet,[5]
a monk, says that in his time, 1555–6, the *nanas* was often preserved in sugar.   De Soto,[6]
1557, speaks of " great pineapples " " of a very good smell and exceeding good taste " in
the Antilles.   Jean de Lery,[7] 1578, describes it in his *Voyage to Brazil* as being of such
excellence that the gods might luxuriate upon it and that it should only be gathered by
the hand of a Venus.   Acosta,[8] 1578, also describes this fruit as of " an excellent smell,
and is very pleasant and delightful in taste, it is full of juice, and of a sweet and sharp
taste."   He calls the plant *ananas*.   Raleigh,[9] 1595, speaks of the " great abundance of
pinas, the princesse of fruits, that grow under the Sun, especially those of Guiana."

Acosta states that the *ananas* was carried from Santa Cruz in Brazil to the West
Indies, and thence to the East Indies and China, but he does not pretend by this that
pineapples were not to be found out of Brazil, for he describes an idol in Mexico, Vitzili-
putzli, as having " in his left hand a white target with the figures of five pineapples, made
of white feathers, set in a crosse."   Stephens,[10] at Tuloom, on the coast of Yucatan, found
what seemed intended to represent a pineapple among the stucco ornaments of a ruin.
We do not know what to make of Wilkinson's[11] statement of one instance of the pineapple
in glazed pottery being among the remains from ancient Egypt.   It has probably been
cultivated in tropical America from time immemorial, as it now rarely bears seeds.
Humboldt[12] mentions pineapples often containing seeds as growing wild in the forests of

[1] Masters, M. T. *Treas. Bot.* 1:58. 1870. (*A. cocculus*)

[2] Irving, W. *Columbus* 2:334. 1848.

[3] McIntosh, C. *Book Gard.* 2:641. 1855.

[4] Ibid.

[5] Ibid.

[6] De Soto *Disc. Conq. Fla.* 1557. Hakl. Soc. Ed. 18. 1851.

[7] Booth, W. B. *Treas. Bot.* 1:60. 1870.

[8] Acosta *Nat. Mor. Hist. Ind.* 1578. Hakl. Soc. Ed. 1:236. 1880.

[9] Raleigh *Disc. Guiana.* Hakl. Soc. Ed. 73. 1848.

[10] Stephens *Trav. Yucatan* 2:406. 1841.

[11] Wilkinson *Anc. Egypt.* 2:36. 1854.

[12] De Candolle, A. P. *Geog. Bot.* 2:927. 1855.

the Orinoco, at Esmeralda; and Schomburgk [1] found the wild fruit, bearing seeds, in considerable quantity throughout Guiana. Piso [2] also mentions a pineapple having many seeds growing wild in Brazil. Titford [3] says this delicious fruit is well known and very common in Jamaica, where there are several sorts. Unger [4] says, in 1592 it was carried to Bengal and probably from Peru by way of the Pacific Ocean to China. Ainslie [5] says that it was introduced in the reign of the Emperor Akbar by the Portuguese who brought the seed from Malacca; that it was naturalized in Java as early as 1599 and was taken thence to Europe. In 1594, it was cultivated in China, brought thither perhaps from America by way of the Philippines.[6] An anonymous writer states that it was quite common in India in 1549 and this is in accord with Acosta's statement.

The pineapple is now grown in abundance about Calcutta, and Firminger [7] describes ten varieties. It is now a common plant in Celebes and the Philippine Islands. The Jesuit, Boymins,[8] mentions it in his *Flora Sinensis* of 1636. A white kind in the East Indies, says Unger,[9] which has run wild, still contains seed in its fruit. In 1777, Captain Cook planted pineapples in various of the Pacific Isles, as at Tongatabu, Friendly Islands, and Society Islands. Afzelius [10] says pineapples grow wild in Sierra Leone and are cultivated by the natives. Don [11] states that they are so abundant in the woods as to obstruct passage and that they bear fruit abundantly.[12] In Angola, wild pines are mentioned by Montiero,[13] and the pineapple is noticed in East Africa by Krapf. R. Brown [14] speaks of the pineapples as existing upon the west coast of Africa but he admits its American origin. In Italy, the first attempts at growing pineapples were made in 1616 but failed. At Leyden, a Dutch gardener was successful in growing them in 1686. The fruit, as imported, was known in England in the time of Cromwell and is again noticed in 1661 and in 1688 from Barbados. The first plants introduced into England came from Holland in 1690, but the first success at culture dates from 1712.

Anaphalis margaritacea Benth. & Hook. *Compositae.* PEARLY EVERLASTING.

North America. Josselyn,[15] prior to 1670, remarks of this plant that "the fishermen when they want tobacco, take this herb: being cut and dried." In France, it is an inmate of the flower garden.

---

[1] Raleigh *Disc. Guiana.* Hakl. Soc. Ed. 74. 1848.

[2] De Candolle, A. P. *Geog. Bot.* 2:927. 1855.

[3] Titford, W. J. *Hort. Bot. Amer.* 54. 1812.

[4] Unger, F. *U. S. Pat. Off. Rpt.* 331. 1859. (*Bromelia ananas*)

[5] Ainslie, W. *Mat. Ind.* 1:315. 1826.

[6] Ibid.

[7] Firminger, T. A. C. *Gard. Ind.* 174. 1874.

[8] *Boston Daily Advertiser* Aug. 10, 1880.

[9] Unger, F. *U. S. Pat. Off. Rpt.* 331. 1859. (*Bromelia ananas*)

[10] Sabine, J. *Trans. Hort. Soc. Lond.* 5:461. 1824. (*Bromelia ananas*)

[11] Ibid.

[12] Ibid.

[13] Montiero, J. J. *Angola, River Congo* 2:298. 1875.

[14] De Candolle, A. *Geog. Bot.* 2:927. 1855.

[15] Josselyn, J. *Voy.* 78. 1663.

Anchomanes hookeri Schott. *Aroideae.*

Eastern equatorial Africa.   The large bulb is boiled and eaten.[1]

Anchusa officinalis Linn. *Boragineae.*   ANCHU.   BUGLOSS.

Europe.   Johnson [2] says, in the south of France and in some parts of Germany, where it is common, the young leaves are eaten as a green vegetable.

Ancistrophyllum secundiflorum G. Mann & H. Wendl. *Palmae.*

African tropics.   The stems are cut into short lengths and are carried by the natives upon long journeys, the soft central parts being eaten after they have been properly roasted.[3]

Andropogon schoenanthus Linn. *Gramineae.*   CAMEL'S HAY.   GERANIUM GRASS.   LEMON
        GRASS.   OIL-PLANT.

Asia, African tropics and subtropics.   This species is commonly cultivated for the fine fragrance of the leaves which are often used for flavoring custard.[4]   When fresh and young, the leaves are used in many parts of the country as a substitute for tea and the white center of the succulent leaf-culms is used to impart a flavor to curries.[5]   The tea made of this grass is considered a wholesome and refreshing beverage, says Wallich,[6] and her Royal Majesty was supplied with the plant from the Royal Gardens, Kew, England.

Aneilema loureirii Hance. *Commelinaceae.*

China.   The plant is cultivated and its tubers are eaten by the Chinese.[7]   They are also eaten in India.[8]

Angelica sylvestris Linn. *Umbelliferae.*   GROUND ASH.   HOLY GHOST.   WILD ANGELICA.

Europe and the adjoining portions of Asia.   On the lower Volga, the young stems are eaten raw by the natives.   Don [9] says it is used as archangelica, but the flavor is more bitter and less grateful.

Angiopteris evecta Hoffm. *Filices.*

A fern of India, the Asiastic and Polynesian Islands.   The caudex, as also the thick part of the stipes, is of a mealy and mucilaginous nature and is eaten by the natives in times of scarcity.[10]

---

[1] Pickering, C.   *Chron. Hist. Pls.* 733.   1879.

[2] Johnson, C. P.   *Useful Pls. Gt. Brit.* 181.   1862.

[3] Williams, B. S.   *Choice Stove, Greenhouse Pls.* 33.   1876.   (*Calamus secondiflorus*)

[4] Firminger, T. A. C.   *Gard. Ind.* 334.   1874.

[5] Drury, H.   *Useful Pls. of Ind.* 37.   1858.   (*A. citratus* Hort.)

[6] Wallich *Pls. Asiat.* 3:48 Pl. 280.   1832.

[7] Royle, J. F.   *Illustr. Bot. Himal.* 1:403.   1839.

[8] Henfrey, A.   *Bot.* 380.   1870.

[9] Don, G.   *Hist. Dichl. Pls.* 3:323.   1834.

[10] Smith, J.   *Dom. Bot.* 171.   1882.

Angraecum fragrans Thou. *Orchideae.* BOURBON TEA. FAHAM TEA.

The leaves of this orchid are very fragrant and are used in Bourbon as tea. It has been introduced into France.[1]

Anisophyllea laurina R. Br. *Rhizophoreae.* MONKEY APPLE.

African tropics. The fruit is sold in the markets of Sierra Leone in the months of April and May; it is described by Don as being superior to any other which is tasted in Africa. It is of the size and shape of a pigeon's egg, red on the sunned side, yellow on the other, its flavor being something between that of the nectarine and a plum.[2]

Annesorhiza capensis Cham. et Schlecht. *Umbelliferae.* ANYSWORTEL.

Cape of Good Hope. The root is eaten.[3]

A. montana Eckl. & Zeyh.

South Africa. The plant has an edible root.[4]

Anona asiatica Linn. *Anonaceae.*

Ceylon and cultivated in Cochin China. The oblong-conical fruit, red on the outside, is filled with a whitish, .eatable pulp but is inferior in flavor to that of *A. squamosa.*

A. cherimolia Mill. CHERIMALLA. CHERIMOYA. CHERIMOYER. CUSTARD APPLE.

American tropics. Originally from Peru, this species seems to be naturalized only in the mountains of Port Royal in Jamaica. Venezuela, New Granada and Brazil know it only as a plant of cultivation. It has been carried to the Cape Verde Islands and to Guinea.[5] The cherimoya is not mentioned among the fruits of Florida by Atwood in 1867 but is included in the American Pomological Society's list for 1879.[6] In 1870, specimens were growing at the United States Conservatory in Washington. The fruit is esteemed by the Peruvians as not inferior to any fruit of the world. Humboldt speaks of it in terms of praise. Herndon[7] says Huanuco is *par excellence* the country of the celebrated cherimoya, and that he has seen it there quite twice as large as it is generally seen in Lima and of the most delicious flavor. Masters says,[8] however, that Europeans do not confirm the claims of the cherimoya to superiority among fruits, and the verdict is probably justified by the scant mention by travellers and the limited diffusion.

A. cinerea Dunal. ANON. SUGAR APPLE. SWEETSOP.

West Indies. This species is placed by Unger[9] among edible fruit-bearing plants.

A. muricata Linn. COROSSOL. PRICKLY CUSTARD APPLE. SOURSOP.

Tropical America. This tree grows wild in Barbados and Jamaica but in Surinam

[1] Lindley, J. *Treas. Bot.* 1:67. 1876.
[2] Sabine, J. *Trans. Hort. Soc. Lond.* 5:446. 1824.
[3] Carruthers, W. *Treas. Bot.* 1:66. 1870.
[4] Mueller, F. *Sel. Pls.* 225. 1876.
[5] Unger, F. *U. S. Pat. Off. Rpt.* 350. 1859.
[6] *Amer. Pom. Soc. Cat.* XLIV. 1879.
[7] Herndon, W. L., and Gibbon, L. *Explor. Vall. Amaz.* 1:117. 1854.
[8] Masters, M. T. *Treas. Bot.* 1:70. 1870.
[9] Unger, F. *U. S. Pat. Off. Rpt.* 350. 1859.

has only escaped from gardens. It is cultivated in the whole of Brazil, Peru and Mexico. In Jamaica, the fruit is sought after only by negroes. The plant has quite recently been carried to Sierra Leone.[1] It is not mentioned among the fruits of Florida by Atwood[2] in 1867 but is included in the American Pomological Society's list for 1879. The smell and taste of the fruit, flowers and whole plant resemble much those of the black currant. The pulp of the fruit, says Lunan,[3] is soft, white and of a sweetish taste, intermixed with oblong, dark colored seeds, and, according to Sloane, the unripe fruit dressed like turnips tastes like them. Morelet[4] says the rind of the fruit is thin, covering a white, unctuous pulp of a peculiar, but delicious, taste, which leaves on the palate a flavor of perfumed cream. It has a peculiarly agreeable flavor although coupled with a biting wild taste. Church[5] says its leaves form corossol tea.

A. paludosa Aubl.

Guiana, growing upon marshy meadows. The species bears elongated, yellow berries, the size of a hen's egg, which have a juicy flesh.[6]

A. palustris Linn. ALLIGATOR APPLE. CORK-WOOD. MONKEY APPLE. POND APPLE.

American and African tropics. The plant bears fruit the size of the fist. The seeds, as large as a bean, lie in an orange-colored pulp of an unsavory taste but which has something of the smell and relish of an orange.[7] The fruit is considered narcotic and even poisonous in Jamaica but of the latter we have, says Lunan,[8] no certain proof. The wood of the tree is so soft and compressible that the people of Jamaica call it corkwood and employ it for stoppers.

A. punctata Aubl.

Guiana. The plant bears a brown, oval, smooth fruit about three inches in diameter with little reticulations on its surface. The flesh is reddish, gritty and filled with little seeds. It has a good flavor and is eaten with pleasure.[9] It is the *pinaou* of Guiana.

A. reticulata Linn. ANON. BULLOCK'S HEART. CORAZON. COROSSOL. CUSTARD APPLE.

Tropical America. Cultivated in Peru, Brazil, in Malabar and the East Indies. This delicious fruit is produced in Florida in excellent perfection as far north as St. Augustine; it is easily propagated from seed. Masters[10] says its yellowish pulp is not so much relished as that of the soursop or cherimoyer. Lunan[11] says, in Jamaica, the fruit is much esteemed by some people. Unger[12] says it is highly prized but he calls the fruit brown,

---

[1] Unger, F.   U. S. Pat. Off. Rpt. 350.   1859.

[2] U. S. D. A. Rpt. 144.   1867.

[3] Lunan, J.   Hort. Jam. 2:180.   1814.

[4] Morelet Trav. Cent. Amer. 21.   1871.

[5] Church, A. H.   Food 203.   1887.

[6] Unger, F.   U. S. Pat. Off. Rpt. 350.   1859.

[7] Sloane, H.   Nat. Hist. Jam. 2:169.   1725.   (A. aquatica)

[8] Lunan, J.   Hort. Jam. 1:11.   1814.

[9] Lindley, J.   Trans. Hort. Soc. Lond. 5:101.   1824.

[10] Masters, M. T.   Treas. Bot. 1:70.   1870.

[11] Lunan, J.   Hort. Jam. 1:256.   1814.

[12] Unger, F.   U. S. Pat. Off. Rpt. 350.   1859.

the size of the fist, while Lunan says brown, shining, of a yellow or orange color, with a reddishness on one side when ripe.

A. senegalensis Pers.

African tropics and Guiana. The fruit is not much larger than a pigeon's egg but its flavor is said, by Savine, to be superior to most of the other fruits of this genus.[1]

A. squamosa Linn. ANON. SUGAR APPLE. SWEETSOP.

It is uncertain whether the native land of this tree is to be looked for in Mexico, or on the plains along the mouth of the Amazon. Von Martius[2] found it forming forest groves in Para. It is cultivated in tropical America and the West Indies and was early transported to China, Cochin China, the Philippines and India. The fruit is conical or pear-shaped with a greenish, imbricated, scaly shell. The flesh is white, full of long, brown granules, very aromatic and of an agreeable strawberry-like, piquant taste.[3] Rhind[4] says the pulp is delicious, having the odor of rose water and tasting like clotted cream mixed with sugar. Masters[5] says the fruit is highly relished by the Creoles but is little esteemed by Europeans. Lunan[6] says it is much esteemed by those who are fond of fruit in which sweet prevails. Drury[7] says the fruit is delicious to the taste and on occasions of famine in India has literally proved the staff of life to the natives.

Anthemis nobilis Linn. *Compositae.* CAMOMILE.

Europe. Naturalized in Delaware. This plant is largely cultivated for medicinal purposes in France, Germany and Italy. It has long been cultivated in kitchen gardens, an infusion of its flowers serving as a domestic remedy. The flowers are occasionally used in the manufacture of bitter beer and, with wormwood, make to a certain extent a substitute for hops. It has been an inmate of American gardens from an early period. In France it is grown in flower-gardens.[8]

Anthericum hispidum Linn. *Liliaceae.* ST. BERNARD'S LILY.

South Africa. The sprouts are eaten as a substitute for asparagus. They are by no means unpalatable, says Carmichael,[9] though a certain clamminess which they possess, that induces the sensation as of pulling hairs from between one's lips, renders them at first unpleasant.

Anthistiria imberbis Retz. *Gramineae.*

Africa. This grass grows in great luxuriance in the Upper Nile region, 5° 5' south, and in famines furnishes the natives with a grain.[10]

[1] Pickering, C. *Chron. Hist. Pls.* 69. 1879.
[2] Unger, F. *U. S. Pat. Off. Rpt.* 350. 1859.
[3] Ibid.
[4] Rhind, W. *Hist. Veg. King.* 375. 1855.
[5] Masters, M. T. *Treas. Bot.* 1:70. 1870.
[6] Lunan, J. *Hort. Jam.* 2:180. 1814.
[7] Drury, H. *Useful Pls. Ind.* 41. 1858.
[8] Vilmorin *Fl. Pl. Ter.* 103. 1870. 3rd Ed.
[9] Hooker, W. J. *Bot. Misc.* 2:264. 1831.
[10] Speke, J. H. *Journ. Disc. Source Nile* 586. 1864. (*A. ciliata*)

Anthocephalus morindaefolius Korth. *Rubiaceae.*

East Indies and Sumatra. This large tree is cultivated in Bengal, North India and elsewhere. The flowers are offered on Hindu shrines. The yellow fruit, the size of a small orange, is eaten.[1] The plant is a native of the Siamese countries.[2]

Anthriscus cerefolium Hoffm. *Umbelliferae.* CHERVIL.

Europe, Orient and north Asia. This is an old fashioned pot-herb, an annual, which appears in garden catalogs. Chervil is said to be a native of Europe and was cultivated in England by Gerarde[3] in 1597. Parkinson[4] says " it is sown in gardens to serve as salad herb." Pliny[5] mentions its use by the Syrians, who cultivated it as a food, and ate it both boiled and raw. Booth[6] says the French and Dutch have scarcely a soup or a salad in which chervil does not form a part and as a seasoner is by many preferred to parsley. It seems still to find occasional use in England, Chervil was cultivated in Brazil in 1647[7] but there are no references to its early use in America. The earlier writers on American gardening mention it, however, from McMahon[8] in 1806. The leaves, when young, are the parts used to impart a warm, aromatic flavor to soups, stews and salads. Gerarde[9] speaks of the roots as being edible. There are curled-leaved varieties

Antidesma bunius Spreng. *Euphorbiaceae.*

A tree of Nepal, Amboina and Malabar. Its shining, deep red, fruits are subacid and palatable.[10] In Java, the fruits are used, principally by Europeans, for preserving.[11]

A. diandrum Spreng.

East Indies. The berries are eaten by the natives.[12] The leaves are acid and are made into preserve.[13]

A. ghesaembilla Gaertn.

East Indies, Malay, Australia and African tropics. The small drupes, dark purple when ripe, with pulp agreeably acid, are eaten.[14]

Apios tuberosa Moench. *Leguminosae.* GROUNDNUT. WILD BEAN.

Northeast America. The tubers are used as food. Kalm[15] says this is the *hopniss* of the Indians on the Delaware, who ate the roots; that the Swedes ate them for want

---

[1] Brandis, D. *Forest Fl.* 261. 1876.

[2] Pickering, C. *Chron. Hist. Pls.* 554. 1879. (*Nauclea cadamba*)

[3] Gerarde, J. *Herb.* 1040. 1633 or 1636.

[4] McIntosh, C. *Book Gard.* 2:171. 1855. (*Chaerophyllum sativum*)

[5] Ibid.

[6] Booth, W. B. *Treas. Bot.* 1:74. 1870.

[7] Churchill *Coll. Voy.* 2:132. 1732.

[8] McMahon, B. *Amer. Gard. Cal.* 191. 1806.

[9] Gerarde, J. *Herb.* 1040. 1633 or 1636.

[10] Wight, R. *Icon. Pls.* 3:Pl. 819.

[11] Black, A. A. *Treas. Bot.* 1:75. 1870.

[12] Black, A. A. *Treas. Bot.* 1:76. 1870.

[13] Brandis, D. *Forest Fl.* 447. 1874.

[14] Ibid.

[15] Kalm, P. *Trav. No. Amer.* 1:400. 1772.

of bread, and that in 1749 some of the English ate them instead of potatoes. Winslow[1] says that the Pilgrims, during their first winter, " were enforced to live on ground nuts." At Port Royal, in 1613, Biencourt[2] and his followers used to scatter about the woods and shores digging ground nuts. In France, the plant is grown in the flower garden.[3]

Apium graveolens Linn. *Umbelliferae.* ACHE. CELERY. SMALLAGE.

A plant of marshy places whose habitat extends from Sweden southward to Algeria, Egypt, Abyssinia and in Asia even to the Caucasus, Baluchistan and the mountains of British India[4] and has been found in Tierra del Fuego,[5,6] in California[7] and in New Zealand. Celery is supposed to be the *selinon* of the Odyssey, the *selinon heleion* of Hippocrates, the *eleioselinon* of Theophrastus and Dioscorides and the *helioselinon* of Pliny and Palladius. It does not seem to have been cultivated, although by some commentators the plant known as smallage has a wild and a cultivated sort. Nor is there one clear statement that this smallage was used as food, for *sativus* means simply planted as distinguished from growing wild, and we may suppose that this Apium, if smallage was meant, was planted for medicinal use. Targioni-Tozzetti[8] says this Apium was considered by the ancients rather as a funereal or ill-omened plant than as an article of food, and that by early modern writers it is mentioned only as a medicinal plant. This seems true, for Fuchsius, 1542, does not speak of its being cultivated and implies a medicinal use alone, as did Walafridus Strabo in the ninth century; Tragus, 1552; Pinaeus, 1561; Pena and Lobel, 1570, and *Ruellius' Dioscorides*, 1529. Camerarius' *Epitome of Matthiolus*, 1586, says planted also in gardens; and Dodonaeus, in his *Pemptades*, 1616, speaks of the wild plant being transferred to gardens but distinctly says not for food use. According to Targioni-Tozzetti,[9] Alamanni, in the sixteenth century, speaks of it, but at the same time praises Alexanders for its sweet roots as an article of food. Bauhin's names, 1623, *Apium palustre* and *Apium officinarum*, indicate medicinal rather than food use, and J. Bauhin's name, *Apium vulgare ingratus*, does not promise much satisfaction in the eating. According to Bretschneider,[10] celery, probably smallage, can be identified in the Chinese work of Kia Sz'mu, the fifth century A. D., and is described as a cultivated plant in the Nung Cheng Ts'nan Shu, 1640. We have mention of a cultivated variety in France by Olivier de Serres, 1623,[11] and in England the seed was sold in 1726 for planting for the use of the plant in soups and broths;[12] and Miller[13] says, 1722, that smallage is one of the

[1] Young, A. *Chron. Pilgr.* 329. 1841.
[2] Parkman, F. *Pion. France* 301. 1894.
[3] Vilmorin *Fl. Pl. Ter.* 105. 1870. 3rd Ed.
[4] De Candolle, A. *Orig. Cult. Pls.* 71. 1885.
[5] Ross, J. C. *Voy. Antarct. Reg.* 2:298. 1847. (*A. antarticum*)
[6] Cook *Voy.* 3:198. 1773.
[7] Nuttall *Jour. Acad. Phila.* 1:183. New ser.
[8] Targioni-Tozzetti *Journ. Hort. Soc. Lond.* 9:144. 1855.
[9] Ibid.
[10] Bretschneider, E. *Bot. Sin.* 78. 1882.
[11] Heuze *Pls. Aliment.* 1:5. 1873.
[12] Townsend *Seedsman* 37. 1726.
[13] Miller *Bot. Offic.* 1722.

herbs eaten to purify the blood. Cultivated smallage is now grown in France under the name *Celeri à couper*, differing but little from the wild form. The number of names that are given to smallage indicate antiquity.

The prevalence of a name derived from one root indicates a recent dispersion of the cultivated variety. Vilmorin[1] gives the following synonyms: French *Celeri*, English *celery*, German *Selleree*, Flanders *Selderij*, Denmark *Selleri*, Italy *Sedano*, Spain *apio*, Portugal *Aipo*. The first mention of the word celery seems to be in Walafridus Strabo's poem entitled *Hortulus*, where he gives the medicinal uses of Apium and in line 335 uses the word as follows: "*Passio tum celeri cedit devicta medelae.*" " The disease then to celery yields, conquered by the remedy," as it may be literally construed, yet the word *celeri* here may be translated quick-acting and this suggests that our word celery was derived from the medicinal uses. Strabo wrote in the ninth century; he was born A. D. 806 or 807, and died in France in 849.

Targioni-Tozzetti[2] says, it is certain that in the sixteenth century celery was grown for the table in Tuscany. There is no mention of celery in Fuchsius, 1542; Tragus, 1552; Matthiolus' *Commentaries*, 1558; Camerarius' *Epitome*, 1558; Pinaeus, 1561; Pena and Lobel, 1570; Gerarde, 1597; Clusius, 1601; Dodonaeus, 1616; or in Bauhin's *Pinax*, 1623; Parkinson's *Paradisus*, 1629, mentions Sellery as a rarity and names it *Apium dulce*. Ray, in his *Historia Plantarum*, 1686, says, " smallage transferred to culture becomes milder and less ungrateful, whence in Italy and France the leaves and stalks are esteemed as delicacies, eaten with oil and pepper." The Italians call this variety *Sceleri* or *Celeri*. The French also use the vegetable and the name. Ray adds that in English gardens the cultivated form often degenerates into smallage. Quintyne, who wrote[3] prior to 1697, the year in which the third edition of his *Complete Gardener* was published, says, in France " we know but one sort of it." Celeri is mentioned, however, as *Apium dulce*, *Celeri Italorum* by Tournefort, 1665.[4] In 1778, Mawe and Abercrombie note two sorts of celery in England, one with the stalks hollow and the other with the stalks solid. In 1726, Townsend[5] distinguished the celeries as smallage and " selery " and the latter he says should be planted " for Winter Sallads, because it is very hot." Tinburg[6] says celery is common among the richer classes in Sweden and is preserved in cellars for winter use. In 1806, McMahon[7] mentions four sorts in his list of garden esculents for American use. It is curious that no mention of a plant that can suggest celery occurs in Bodaeus and Scaliger's edition of Theophrastus, published at Amsterdam in 1644.

There is no clear evidence, then, that smallage was grown by the ancients as a food plant but that if planted at all it was for medicinal use. The first mention of its cultivation as a food plant is by Olivier de Serres, 1623, who called it *ache*, while Parkinson speaks of celery in 1629, and Ray indicates the cultivation as commencing in Italy and

---

[1] Vilmorin *Les Pls. Potag.* 72. 1883.

[2] Targioni-Tozzetti *Journ. Hort. Soc. Lond.* **9:144.** 1855.

[3] Quintyne *Comp. Gard.* 1704.

[4] Tournefort *Inst.* 305. 1719.

[5] Townsend *Seedsman.* 1726.

[6] Tinburg *Hort. Culin.* 25. 1764.

[7] McMahon, B. *Amer. Gard. Cal.* 581. 1806.

extending to France and England. Targioni-Tozzetti states, however, as a certainty that celery was grown in Tuscany in the sixteenth century. The hollow celery is stated by Mawe [1] to have been the original kind and is claimed by Cobbett,[2] even as late as 1821, as being the best.

The first celeries grown seem to have differed but little from the wild plant, and the words celery and (cultivated) smallage were apparently nearly synonymous at one time, as we find cultivated *ache* spoken of in 1623 in France and at later dates *petit celeri* or *celeri à couper*, a variety with hollow stalks, cultivated even at the present time for use of the foliage in soups and broths. Among the earlier varieties we find mention of hollow-stalked, stalks sometimes hollow, and solid-stalked forms; at the present time the hollow-stalked forms have been discarded. Vilmorin [3] describes twelve sorts as distinct and worthy of culture in addition to the *celeri à couper* but in all there is this to be noted, there is but one type.

In Italy and the Levant, where celery is much grown, but not blanched, the green leaves and stalks are used as an ingredient in soups. In England and America, the stalks are always blanched and used raw as a salad or dressed as a dinner vegetable. The seeds are also used for flavoring. In France, celery is said by Robinson [4] never to be as well grown as in England or America. By cultivation, celery, from a suspicious if not poisonous plant, has become transformed into the sweet, crisp, wholesome and most agreeable cultivated vegetable.

A. graveolens rapaceum DC. CELERIAC. TURNIP-ROOTED CELERY.

Europe, Orient, India and California. This variety of celery forms a stout tuber, irregularly rounded, frequently exceeding the size of one's fist, hence it is often termed turnip-rooted celery. In France, it is commonly grown in two varieties. The tuber, generally eaten cooked, is sometimes sliced and used in salads. In Germany, it is commonly used as a vegetable, cooked in soups or cooked and sliced for salads. In England, celeriac is seldom grown. In this country, it is grown only to a limited extent and is used only by our French and German population. When well grown, these bulbs should be solid, tender and delicate.

In 1536, Ruellius,[5] in treating of the *ache*, or uncultivated smallage as would appear from the context, says the root is eaten, both raw and cooked. Rauwolf,[6] who travelled in the East, 1573-75, speaks of *Eppich*, whose roots are eaten as delicacies, with salt and pepper, at Tripoli and Aleppo; and J. Bauhin,[7] who died in 1613, mentions a *Selinum tuberosum, sive Buselini speciem*, as named in Honorius Bellus, which seems to be the first mention of celeriac, as the earlier references quoted may possibly refer to the root of the ordinary sort, although probably not, for at this date the true celery had scarcely been

---

[1] Mawe and Abercrombie *Univ. Gard. Bot.* 1778.
[2] Cobbett, W. *Amer. Gard.* 129. 1846.
[3] Vilmorin *Les Pl. Potag.* 74. 1883.
[4] Robinson, W. *Parks, Gard. Paris* 496. 1878.
[5] Ruellius *Nat. Stirp.* 708. 1536.
[6] Gronovius *Fl. Orient.* 35. 1755.
[7] Bauhin, J. *Hist. Pl.* 2: pt. 3, 101. 1651.

sufficiently developed.   In 1729, Switzer [1] describes the plant in a book devoted to this
and other novelties but adds that he had never seen it; this indicates that celeriac was
little known in England at this date, for he adds that the gentleman, who had long been
an importer of curious seeds, furnished him with a supply from Alexandria.   Celeriac is
again named in England in 1752,[2] 1765,[3] and by succeeding writers but is little known
even at the present time.   In 1806, McMahon [4] includes this in his list of American garden
esculents, as does Randolph for Virginia before 1818.   Burr describes two varieties, and
two varieties are offered in our seed catalogs.   The history of celeriac is particularly
interesting, as we seem to have a record of its first introduction and of a size at that time
which is not approached in modern culture.

Jo. Baptista Porta, a Neapolitan, writes thus in his *Villae*, published at Frankfurt
in 1592 (lib. 10, chap. 21), the translation being liberal: " There is another kind of
celery called Capitatum, which is grown in the gardens of St. Agatha, Theano and other
places in Apulia, granted from nature and unseen and unnamed by the ancients.   Its
bulb is spherical, nearly of the size of a man's head.   It is very sweet, odorous and grateful.   Except in rich land, it degenerates, until it differs from the common apium in no
respects, except in its root, round like a head."

A. prostratum Labill.   AUSTRALIAN CELERY.

Australian and Antarctic regions.   Mueller [5] says this plant can be utilized as a
culinary vegetable.

Apocynum reticulatum Linn.   *Apocynaceae.*   DOGBANE.

East Indies.   According to Unger,[6] this plant furnishes a food.

Aponogeton distachyum Thunb.   *Naiadaceae.*   CAPE ASPARAGUS.   CAPE POND-WEED.

South Africa.   This plant has become naturalized in a stream near Montpelier,
France.   Its flowering spikes, known as water *untjie*, are in South Africa in high repute
as a pickle [7] and also afford a spinach.[8]   In Kaffraria, the roasted roots are reckoned a
great delicacy.[9]

A. fenestrale Hook.   LATTICE-LEAF.   WATER-YAM.

Madagascar.   Ellis [10] says this plant is not only extremely curious but also very
valuable to the natives who, at certain seasons of the year, gather it as an article
of food, the fleshy root, when cooked, yielding a farinaceous substance resembling the
yam.

---

[1] Switzer, S.   *Raising Veg.* 9.   1729.

[2] Miller *Gard. Dict.* 1752, from *Miller Gard. Dict.*   1807.

[3] Stevenson *Gard. Kal.* 30.   1765.

[4] McMahon, B.   *Amer. Gard. Cal.* 581.   1806.

[5] Mueller, F.   *Sel. Pls.* 44.   1891.

[6] Unger, F.   *U. S. Pat. Off. Rpt.* 359.   1859.

[7] Hooker, W. J.   *Bot. Misc.* 2:265.   1831.

[8] Mueller, F.   *Sel. Pls.* 45.   1891.

[9] Thunberg, C. P.   *Trav.* 1:156.   1795.

[10] Ellis, W.   *Three Visits Madagas.* 59.   1859.   (*Ouvirandra fenestralis*)

A. monostachyon Linn. f.

Tropical eastern Asia. The natives relish the small tubers as an article of diet; they are said to be as good as potatoes, and are esteemed a great delicacy.[1]

Aporosa lindleyana Baill. *Euphorbiaceae.*

East Indies. The small, berry-like fruit is edible.[2]

Aquilegia canadensis Linn. *Ranunculaceae.* WILD COLUMBINE.

North America. The roots are eaten by some Indians, according to R. Brown.[3]

Arachis hypogaea Linn. *Leguminosae.* EARTH NUT. EARTH ALMOND. GOOBER. GRASS NUT. GROUND NUT. PEANUT. PINDAR.

Tropical America. This plant is now under cultivation in warm climates for the seeds which are largely eaten as nuts, and from which an oil is extracted to be used as a substitute for olive oil to which it is equal in quality. Although now only under field cultivation in America, yet, in 1806, McMahon[4] included this plant among kitchen-garden esculents. For a long time, writers on botany were uncertain whether the peanut was a native of Africa or of America, but, since Squier[5] has found this seed in jars taken from the mummy graves of Peru, the question of its American origin seems settled. The first writer who notes it, is Oviedo in his *Cronica de las Indias*, who says " the Indians cultivate very much the fruit *mani.*" Before this, the French colonists, sent in 1555 to the Brazilian coast, became acquainted with it under the name of *mandobi.*[6]

The peanut was figured by Laet, 1625,[7] and by Marcgravius, 1648,[8] as the *anchic* of the Peruvians, the *mani* of the Spaniards. It seems to be mentioned by Garcilasso de la Vega,[9] 1609, as being raised by the Indians under the name, *ynchic.* The Spaniards call it *mani* but all the names, he observes, which the Spaniards give to the fruits and vegetables of Peru belong to the language of the Antilles. The fruit is raised underground, he says, and " is very like marrow and has the taste of almonds." Marcgravius,[10] 1648, and Piso,[11] 1658, describe and figure the plant, under the name of *mandubi,* as common and indigenous in Brazil. They cite Monardes,[12] an author late in the sixteenth century, as having found it in Peru with a different name, *anchic.*[13] Father Merolla,[14]

---

[1] Drury, H. *Useful Pls. Ind.* 43. 1858.

[2] Archer *Bot. Soc. Edinb.* 8:163. 1866.

[3] Brown, R. *Gard. Chron.* 1320. 1868.

[4] McMahon, B. *Amer. Gard. Cal.* 581. 1806.

[5] Squier, E. G. *Peru* 81. 1877.

[6] Flückiger and Hanbury *Pharm.* 186. 1879.

[7] Ibid.

[8] De Candolle, A. *Geog. Bot.* 2:963. 1855.

[9] Vega, G. de la. *Roy. Comment.* Hakl. Soc. Ed. 2:360. 1871.

[10] De Candolle, A. *Geog. Bot.* 2:963. 1855.

[11] Ibid.

[12] De Candolle, A. *Geog. Bot.* 2:962. 1855.

[13] Ibid.

[14] Churchill *Coll. Voy.* 1:563. 1744.

1682, under the name of *mandois*, describes a vegetable of Congo which grows " three or four together like vetches but underground and are about the bigness of an ordinary olive. From these milk is extracted like to that drawn from almonds." This may be the peanut. In China, especially in Kwangtung, peanuts are grown in large quantities and their consumption by the people is very great. The peanut was included among garden plants by McMahon, 1806; Burr, 1863, describes three varieties; and Jefferson speaks of its culture in Virginia in 1781. Its culture was introduced into France in 1802,[1] and the peanut was described among pot-herbs by Noisette,[2] 1829.

Aralia cordata Thunb. *Araliaceae.* UDO.

Japan. The young shoots of this species provide an excellent culinary vegetable.[3] They are used in soups in Japan.[4] According to Siebold,[5] this plant is universally cultivated in Japan, in fields and gardens. It is valued for its root which is eaten like scorzonera, but the young stalks are likewise a delicious vegetable.[6]

A. quinquefolia Decne & Planch. GINSENG.

North America. The root is collected in large quantities in the hilly regions of Ohio, western Virginia, Minnesota and other parts of eastern America for export to China where it is valued as a medicine. Some persons in this country are in the habit of chewing the root, having acquired a relish for its taste, and it is chiefly to supply the wants of these that it is kept in the shops.[7]

Araucaria bidwillii Hook. *Coniferae.* BUNYA-BUNYA.

Australia; the *bunya-bunya* of the natives. The cones furnish an edible seed which is roasted. Each tribe of the natives has its own set of trees and each family its own allotment among them. These are handed down from generation to generation with the greatest exactness and are believed to be the only hereditary personal property possessed by the aborigines.

A. brasiliana A. Rich. BRAZILIAN PINE.

Brazil. The seeds are very large and are eatable.[8] They are sold as an article of food in the streets of Rio de Janeiro.

A. imbricata Pav. CHILIAN PINE. MONKEY PUZZLE.

Southern Chili. The seeds are eaten by the Indians, either fresh, boiled or roasted, and from them is distilled a spirituous liquor.[9] Eighteen good-sized trees will yield enough for a man's sustenance all the year round.[10]

---

[1] *Bon Jard.* 685. 1882.
[2] Noisette *Man. Jard.* 329. 1829.
[3] Mueller, F. *Sel. Pls.* 45. 1891.
[4] Bird *Unbeat. Tracks Jap.* 1:244. 1881.
[5] Pickering, C. *Chron. Hist. Pls.* 418. 1879. (*A. edulis*)
[6] Hanbury, D. *Sci. Papers* 261. 1876.
[7] *U. S. Disp.* 636. 1865. (*Panax quinquefolium*)
[8] Gordon, G. *Pinetum* 37. 1875.
[9] Gordon, G. *Pinetum* 41. 1875.
[10] Pickering, C. *Chron. Hist. Pls.* 812. 1879.

Arbutus andrachne Linn. *Ericaceae.* STRAWBERRY TREE.

East Mediterranean countries.[1] Its fruit was eaten during the Golden Age.[2] Don[3] says the fruit seems to be used in Greece.

A. canariensis Duham.

Canary Islands. The berries are made into a sweetmeat.[4]

A. menziesii Pursh. MADRONA.

Pacific Coast of North America. The berries resemble Morello cherries. When ripe they are quite ornamental and are said sometimes to be eaten.[5]

A. unedo Linn. ARBUTE. CANE APPLES. STRAWBERRY TREE.

Mediterranean countries. Theophrastus[6] says the tree produces an edible fruit; Pliny,[7] that it is not worth eating. Sir J. E. Smith[8] describes the fruit as uneatable in Ireland, but W. Wilson[9] says he can testify from repeated experience that the ripe fruit is really very palatable: In Spain, a sugar and a sherbet are obtained from it.

Archangelica atropurpurea Hoffm. *Umbelliferae.* GREAT ANGELICA. MASTERWORT.

North America. This plant is found from New England to Pennsylvania, Wisconsin, and northward. Stille[10] says the stems are sometimes candied. The root is used in domestic medicines as an aromatic and stimulant.

A. gmelini DC. ANGELICA.

Northwest Asia. This species is used for culinary purposes by the Russians in Kamchatka.[11] The root, dug in the autumn of the first year, is used in medicine as an aromatic tonic and possesses the taste and smell of the seeds.

A. officinalis Hoffm. ANGELICA. ARCHANGEL. WILD PARSNIP.

Europe, Siberia and Himalayan regions. This plant is a native of the north of Europe and is found in the high, mountainous regions in south Europe, as in Switzerland and among the Pyrenees. It is also found in Alaska. Angelica is cultivated in various parts of Europe and is occasionally grown in American gardens. The whole plant has a fragrant odor and aromatic properties. Angelica is held in great estimation in Lapland, where the natives strip the stem of leaves, and the soft, internal part, after the outer skin has been pulled off, is eaten raw like an apple or turnip.[12] In Kamchatka, the roots are distilled and a kind of spirit is made from them, and on the islands of Alaska, where

---

[1] Pickering, C. *Chron. Hist. Pls.* 102. 1879.
[2] Ibid.
[3] Don, G. *Hist. Dichl. Pls.* 3:834. 1834.
[4] Andrews *Bot. Reposit.* 10:Pl. 664. 1797.
[5] Newberry *Pacific R. R. Rpt.* 6:23, fig. 1857.
[6] Daubeny, C. *Trees, Shrubs Anc.* 50. 1865.
[7] Bostock and Riley *Nat. Hist. Pliny* 4:516. 1855.
[8] Hooker, W. J. *Journ. Bot.* 1:315. 1834.
[9] Ibid.
[10] Stille, A. *Therap. Mat. Med.* 1:491, 492. 1874.
[11] Don, G. *Hist. Dichl. Pls.* 3:324. 1834.
[12] *Journ. Agr.* 2:174. 1831.

it is abundant and called wild parsnip, it is stated by Dall[1] to be edible. Angelica has been in cultivation in England since 1568. The leaf-stalks were formerly blanched and eaten like celery. The plant is in request for the use of confectioners, who make an excellent sweetmeat with the tender stems, stalks, and ribs of the leaves candied with sugar. The seeds enter into the composition of many liquors. In the north of Europe, the leaves and stalks are still used as a vegetable.

The medicinal properties of the root were highly prized in the Middle Ages. In Pomet,[2] we read that the seed is much used to make angelica comfits as well as the root for medicine. Bryant[3] deems it the best aromatic that Europe produces. This plant must be a native of northern Europe, for there are no references to it in the ancient authors of Greece and Rome, nor is it mentioned by Albertus Magnus in the thirteenth century. By Fuchsius, 1542, and succeeding authors it receives proper attention. The German name, *Heilige Geist Wurz*, implies the estimation in which it was held and offers a clue to the origin of the word Angelica, or angel plant, which occurs in so many languages, as in English, Spanish, Portugese, and Italian, becoming *Angélique* and *Archangélique* in French, and *Angelickwurz* in German. Other names of like import are the modern *Engelwurz* in Germany, *Engelkruid* in Flanders and *Engelwortel* in Holland.

The various figures given by herbalists show the same type of plant, the principal differences to be noted being in the size of the root. Pena and Lobel,[4] 1570, note a smaller variety as cultivated in England, Belgium, and France, and Gesner is quoted by Camerarius[5] as having seen roots of three pounds weight. Bauhin,[6] 1623, says the roots vary, the Swiss-grown being thick, those of Bohemia smaller and blacker.

Garden angelica is noticed amongst American garden medicinal herbs by McMahon,[7] 1806, and the seed is still sold by our seedsmen.

Arctium majus Bernh. *Compositae.* BEGGAR'S BUTTONS. BURDOCK. CLOTBUR. CUCKOLD. GOBO. HARLOCK.

Europe and Asia and occurring as a weed in the United States. In Japan, burdock is said to be cultivated as a vegetable. Gerarde[8] says " the stalke of the *clot-burre* before the burres come forth, the rinde peelld off, being eaten raw with salt and pepper, or boyled in the broth of fat meate, is pleasant to be eaten." Kalm,[9] in his *Travels in North America*, writing of Ticonderoga, N. Y., says: " and the governor told me that its tender shoots are eaten in spring as radishes, after the exterior part is taken off." In Japan, says Johns, the tender stalks are eaten as an asparagus, and its roots are said to be edible. Penhallow[10]

[1] Dall, W. H. *Alaska* 448. 1897.

[2] Pomet *Hist. Drugs* 42. 1748.

[3] Bryant *Fl. Diet.* 53. 1783.

[4] Pena and Lobel *Advers.* 311. 1570.

[5] Camerarius *Hort. Med.* 16. 1588.

[6] Bauhin, C. *Pinax* 155. 1623.

[7] McMahon, B. *Amer. Gard. Cal.* 583. 1806.

[8] Gerarde, J. *Herb.* 811. 1636. 2nd Ed.

[9] Kalm, P. *Trav. No. Amer.* 2:202. 1772.

[10] Penhallow, D. P. *Amer. Nat.* 16:120. 1882. (*Lappa major*)

says the Japanese cultivate the root, but as an article of food it is tasteless, hard and fibrous.

Arctostaphylos alpina Spreng. *Ericaceae.* ALPINE BEARBERRY.

Arctic regions and mountain summits farther south. The berries are eaten in Lapland but are a mawkish food, according to Linnaeus.[1] Richardson[2] says there are two varieties, that both are eaten in the autumn and, though not equal to some of the other native fruits, are not unpleasant. They are called *amprick* by the Russians at the mouth of the Obi.

A. glauca Lindl. MANZANITA.

California. The fruit grows in clusters, is first white, then red and finally black. This berry is regarded as eatable but is dry and of little flavor.[3]

A. tomentosa Lindl. MANZANITA

Southern California. The red berries are used by the Spanish inhabitants of Texas to make a cooling, subacid drink. The fruit is used when not quite ripe as a tart apple. Dried and made into bread and baked in the sun, the fruit is relished by the Indians.[4]

A. uva-ursi Spreng. BEARBERRY. BEAR'S GRAPE. BRAWLINS. CREASHAK. MOUNTAIN
　　　　BOX.

North America and Arctic regions. The Chinook Indians mix its dried leaves with tobacco. It is used for the same purpose by the Crees who call it *tchakoshe-pukk;* by the Chippewaians, who name it *kleh;* and by the Eskimos north of Churchill, by whom it is termed *at-tung-a-wi-at.* It is the *iss-salth* of the Chinooks.[5] Its dry, farinaceous berry is utterly inedible.[6]

Ardisia coriacea Sw. *Myrsineae.* BEEF-WOOD.

West Indies. According to Sloane,[7] the drupes are eaten in Jamaica and are accounted a pleasant dessert.

A. esculenta Pav.

South America. The berries are esculent.[8]

Areca catechu Linn. *Palmae.* ARECA NUT. BETEL NUT. CATECHU. PINANG.

East Indies. This handsome palm is cultivated throughout the Indian Archipelago, in Ceylon and the west side of India for the sake of its seed which is known under the names areca nut, pinang and betel nut; the nut is about the size of a nutmeg. These nuts are consumed, when dry, in great quantity, a small portion being separated, put into a

[1] Don, G. *Hist. Dichl. Pls.* 3:836. 1834.
[2] Richardson, J. *Arctic Explor.* 2:303. 1851.
[3] Newberry *Pacific R. R. Rpt.* 6:22. 1857.
[4] *U. S. D. A. Rpt.* 413. 1870.
[5] Hooker, W. J. *Fl. Bor. Amer.* 2:37. 1840.
[6] Richardson, J. *Arctic Explor.* 2:30. 1851.
[7] Nuttall, T. *No. Amer. Sylva* 2:134. 1865.
[8] Don, G. *Hist. Dichl. Pls.* 4:19. 1838.

leaf of piper-betle over which a little quick-lime is laid, then rolled up and chewed alto-gether.[1] It tinges the saliva red and stains the teeth. Whole shiploads of this nut, so universally in use among the Eastern natives, are exported annually from Sumatra, Malacca, Siam and Cochin China. The heart of the leaves, according to Seemann, is eaten as a salad and has not a bad flavor as Blanco writes.[2]

A. glandiformis Lam.

Moluccas. In Cochin China the leaves are chewed with the betel nut.[3]

A. laxa Buch.-Ham.

Andaman Islands. The nuts of this plant are used instead of the betel nut by the convicts confined on Andaman Islands.[4]

Arenaria peploides Linn. *Caryophylleae.* SEA CHICKWEED.

North temperate and Arctic regions. In Iceland, the plant is fermented and in that state used as food, like sauerkraut; the plant also forms a wholesome vegetable when boiled [5] and is used for a pickle.[6]

Arenga saccharifera Labill. *Palmae.* ARENG PALM.

Tropical eastern Asia. This palm has been called the most useful of all palms. Griffith [7] says, the young albumen preserved in sugar forms one of the well-known pre-serves of the Straits. Brandis [8] says, the heart of the stem contains large quantities of sago, and the cut flower-stalks yield a sugary sap of which sugar and palm-wine are made. Graham [9] says, at Bombay this palm affords tolerably good sago and the sap, palm-wine and sugar. Seemann[10] says, the bud, or cabbage, is eaten. The sap, of which some three quarts a day are collected, furnishes toddy and from this toddy, jaggery sugar is prepared. The seed, freed from its noxious covering, is made into a sweetmeat by the Chinese. From the pith, a species of sago is prepared which, however, has a peculiar flavor.

Argania sideroxylon Roem. et Schult. *Sapotaceae.* ARGAN TREE. MOROCCO IRON-WOOD.

Morocco. From the seeds, the natives extract an oil that is used for cooking and lighting. When ripe, the fruit, which is an egg-shaped drupe, falls from the trees and the goats then enter into competition with their masters for a share in the harvest. The goats, however, swallow the fruit only for the sake of the subacid rind and, being unable to digest the hard seeds, eject them during the process of rumination, when they are gath-ered and added to the general store for oil making.[11]

---

[1] Ainslie, W. *Mat. Ind.* 2:270. 1826.

[2] Seemann, B. *Pop. Hist. Palms* 56. 1856.

[3] Loureiro *Cochin.* 1:568. 1790.

[4] Griffith, W. *Palms Brit. Ind.* 149. 1850.

[5] Johnson, C. P. *Useful Pls. Gt. Brit.* 54. 1862.

[6] Balfour, J. H. *Man. Bot.* 445. 1875. (*Honkeneja peploides*)

[7] Griffith, W. *Palms Brit. Ind.* 164. 1850.

[8] Brandis, D. *Forest Fl.* 551. 1874.

[9] Pickering, C. *Chron. Hist. Pls.* 335. 1879.

[10] Seemann, B. *Pop. Hist. Palms* 64, 67. 1856.

[11] *Pharm. Journ., Trans.* 1878.

Arisaema atrorubens Blume. *Aroideae.* DRAGON ROOT. JACK-IN-THE-PULPIT. INDIAN TURNIP.

North America. Cutler [1] says, the shredded roots and berries are said to have been boiled by the Indians with their venison. Bigelow [2] says, the starch of the root is delicate and nutritious. It must, however, be obtained from the root by boiling in order that the heat may destroy the acrimonious principle.

A. costatum Mart.

Himalayas. This is said by Ellis [3] to be a large aroid, called *ape* in Tahiti, which is frequently planted in dry ground. It is considered inferior to taro.

A. curvatum Kunth.

Himalayas. The Lepchas of India prepare a food called *tong* from the tuberous root. The roots are buried in masses until acetous fermentation sets in and are then dug, washed and cooked, by which means their poisonous properties are in part dispersed, but not entirely, as violent illness sometimes follows a hearty meal of *tong*. [4]

A. tortuosum Schott.

Himalayas. The root is considered esculent by the mountaineers of Nepal. [5]

Arisarum vulgare Targ. *Aroideae.*

Mediterranean regions. In north Africa, the roots are much used in seasons of scarcity. The root, which is not as large as our ordinary walnut, contains an acid juice, which makes it quite uneatable in the natural state. This is, however, removed by repeated washings and the residue is innoxious and nutritive. [6]

Aristotelia macqui L'Herit. *Tiliaceae.* MOUNTAIN CURRANT.

A large shrub called in Chile, *maqui*. The berries, though small, have the pleasant taste of bilberries and are largely consumed in Chile. [7]

A. racemosa Hook.

New Zealand. The natives eat the berries. [8]

Arracacia xanthorrhiza Bancr. *Umbelliferae.* ARRACACHA. PERUVIAN CARROT.

Northern South America. This plant has been cultivated and used as a food from early times in the cooler mountainous districts of northern South America, where the roots form a staple diet of the inhabitants. The root is not unlike a parsnip in shape but more blunt; it is tender when boiled and nutritious, with a flavor between the parsnip and a roasted chestnut. A fecula, analogous to arrowroot, is obtained from it by rasp-

---

[1] Pickering, C. *Chron. Hist. Pls.* 808. 1879. (*Arum triphyllum*)

[2] Bigelow, J. *Med. Bot.* 1:58. 1817.

[3] Ellis, W. *Polyn. Research.* 1:48. 1833.

[4] Moore, T. *Treas. Bot.* 2:1347. 1876.

[5] Wallich *Pls. Asiat.* 2:10, Tab. 114. 1830–32.

[6] Hooker and Ball *Marocco, Gt. Atlas* 342. 1878.

[7] Mueller, F. *Sel. Pls.* 49. 1891.

[8] Black, A. A. *Treas. Bot.* 1:92. 1870.

ing in water. Arracacha yields, according to Boussingault,[1] about 16 tons per acre. The plant is also found in the mountain regions of Central America. The roots are nutritious and palatable and there are yellow, purple and pale varieties.[2] Attempts to naturalize this plant in field culture in Europe have been unsuccessful. It was introduced into Europe in 1829 and again in 1846, but trials in England, France and Switzerland were unsuccessful [3] in obtaining eatable roots. It was grown near New York in 1825 [4] and at Baltimore in 1828 or 1829 [5] but was found to be worthless. Lately introduced into India, it is now fairly established there and Morris [6] considers it a most valuable plant-food, becoming more palatable and desirable the longer it is used. It is generally cultivated [7] in Venezuela, New Granada and Ecuador, and in the temperate regions of these countries, Arracacha is preferred to the potato. The first account which reached Europe concerning this plant was published in the *Annals of Botany* in 1805. It was, however, mentioned in a few words by Alcedo,[8] 1789.

Artemisia abrotanum Linn. *Compositae.* OLD MAN. SOUTHERNWOOD.

Europe and temperate Asia. This artemisia forms an ingredient, says Lindley, in some continental beers.

A. absinthium Linn. ABSINTHE. WORMWOOD.

Cultivated in Europe and in England in cottage gardens on a large scale. Bridgeman,[9] 1832, is the first writer on American gardening who mentions absinthe but now its seeds are cataloged for sale by all our larger dealers. It is classed among medicinal herbs but is largely used in France to flavor the cordial, absinthe, and in America in compounding bitters. The seed is used by the rectifiers of spirits and the plant is largely cultivated in some districts of England for this purpose. It is said occasionally to form an ingredient of sauces in cookery.

A. dracunculus Linn. TARRAGON.

East Europe, the Orient and Himalayan regions. Tarragon was brought to Italy, probably from the shores of the Black Sea, in recent times. The first mention on record is by Simon Seth, in the middle of the twelfth century, but it appears to have been scarcely known as a condiment until the sixteenth century.[10] It was brought to England in or about 1548.[11] The flowers, as Vilmorin says, are always barren, so that the plant can be propagated only by division. Tarragon culture is mentioned by the botanists of the sixteenth century and in England by Gerarde,[12] 1597, and by succeeding authors on gar-

---

[1] Morton *Cyc. Agr.* 1:108. 1869. (*A. esculenta*)

[2] Mueller *Sel. Pls.* 50. 1891.

[3] Heuze *Pls. Aliment.* 2:509. 1873.

[4] *New Eng. Farm.* July 22, 1825.

[5] Couper *Farm. Libr.* 94. 1847.

[6] *Gard. Chron.* 26:50. 1886. (*A. esculenta*)

[7] De Candolle, A. *Orig. Cult. Pls.* 40. 1885.

[8] Don, G. *Hist. Dichl. Pls.* 3:378. 1834.

[9] Bridgeman *Young Gard. Asst.* 108. 1857.

[10] Targioni-Tozzetti *Journ. Hort. Soc. Lond.* 148. 1854.

[11] McIntosh, C. *Book Gard.* 2:167. 1855.

[12] Gerarde, J. *Herb.* 193. 1597.

dening. Rauwolf,[1] 1573–75, found it in the gardens of Tripoli. In America, it is mentioned by McMahon,[2] 1806. Its roots are now included in our leading seed catalogs. Tarragon has a fragrant smell and an aromatic taste for which it is greatly esteemed by the French. In Persia, it has long been customary to use the leaves to create an appetite. Together with the young tips, the leaves are put in salads, in pickles and in vinegar for a fish sauce. They are also eaten with beefsteaks, served with horseradish. Tarragon vinegar, says McIntosh,[3] is much esteemed.

A. maritima Linn. WORM-SEED.

Caucasian region, Siberia and Europe. It is a bitter tonic and aromatic. It was formerly used to make a conserve with sugar.[4]

A. mutellina Vill. ALPINE WORMWOOD.

Europe. The plant is used on the continent in the preparation of *Eau d'absinthe*, which is in request amongst epicures.[5]

A. spicata Wulf. SPIKED WORMWOOD.

Europe. The plant is used on the continent in the preparation of *Eau d'absinthe*.

A. vulgaris Linn. FELLON-HERB. MUGWORT.

Northern temperate regions. Mugwort was employed, says Johnson,[6] to a great extent for flavoring beer before the introduction of the hop. It is still used in England to flavor the home-made beer of the cottagers. On the continent, it is occasionally employed as an aromatic, culinary herb.

Artocarpus brasiliensis Gomez. *Urticaceae*. JACK.

Brazil. Professor Hartt [7] says the jack is cultivated in the province of Bahia and to the north, at Sao Matheus and occasionally as far south as Rio de Janeiro, Brazil. The fruit is of immense size, being sometimes a foot and a half in the longer diameter. The seeds are largely used as food and the pulp is nutritious. In some parts, a kind of farina is prepared from the seeds, but this use is by no means general.

A. hirsuta Lam.

East Indies. The fruit is the size of a large orange. The pulpy substance is much relished by the natives, being almost as good as the fruit of the jack.[8]

A. incisa Linn. f. BREADFRUIT.

This most useful tree is nowhere found growing wild but is now extensively cultivated in warm regions. It is first described by the writer of *Mendana's Voyage to the Marquesas Islands*, 1595. It has been distributed from the Moluccas, by way of Celebes and New Guinea, throughout all the islands of the Pacific Ocean to Tahiti. Breadfruit is also

[1] Gronovius *Fl. Orient.* 106. 1755.

[2] McMahon, B. *Amer. Gard. Cal.* 511. 1806.

[3] McIntosh, C. *Book Gard.* 2:167. 1855.

[4] Johnson, C. P. *Useful Pls. Gt. Brit.* 152. 1862.

[5] Balfour, J. H. *Man. Bot.* 521. 1875.

[6] Johnson, C. P. *Useful Pls. Gt. Brit.* 154. 1862.

[7] Hartt, C. F. *Geog. Braz.* 245. 1870.

[8] Drury, H. *Useful Pls. Ind.* 51. 1858.

naturalized in the Isle of France, in tropical America [1] and bears fruit in Ceylon and Burma.[2] It is more especially an object of care and cultivation in the Marquesas and the Friendly and Society Islands. The tree was conveyed to the Isle of France from Luzon in the Philippines by Sonnerat. In 1792, from Tahiti and Timor, Capt. Bligh, who was commissioned by the British Government for this purpose, took a store of plants and in 1793 landed 333 breadfruit trees at St. Vincent and 347 at Port Royal, Jamaica.[3] In the cultivated breadfruit, the seeds are almost always abortive, leaving their places empty [4] which shows that its cultivation goes back to a remote antiquity. This seedlessness does not hold true, however, of all varieties, of which there are many. Chamisso [5] describes a variety in the Mariana Islands with small fruit containing seeds which are frequently perfect. Sonnerat found in the Philippines a breadfruit, which he considered as wild, which bears ripe seeds of a considerable size.[6] In Tahiti, there are eight varieties without seeds and one variety with seeds which is inferior to the others.[7] Nine varieties are credited by Wilkes [8] to the Fiji Islands and twenty to the Samoan.[9] Captain Cook,[10] at Tahiti, in 1769, describes the fruit as about the size and shape of a child's head, with the surface reticulated not much unlike a truffle, covered with a thin skin and having a core about as big as the handle of a small knife.

The eatable part of breadfruit lies between the skin and the core and is as white as snow and somewhat of the consistence of new bread. It must be roasted before it is eaten. Its taste is insipid, with a slight sweetness, somewhat resembling that of the crumb of wheaten bread mixed with a Jerusalem artichoke. Wilkes [11] says the best varieties when baked or roasted are not unlike a good custard pudding. If the breadfruit is to be preserved, it is scraped from the rind and buried in a pit where it is allowed to ferment, when it subsides into a mass somewhat of the consistency of new cheese. These pits when opened emit a nauseous, fetid, sour odor, and the color of the contents is a greenish-yellow. In this state it is called *mandraiuta*, or native bread, of which several kinds are distinguished. It is said that it will keep several years and is cooked with cocoanut milk, in which state it forms an agreeable and nutritious food. This tree affords one of the most generous sources of nutriment that the world possesses .According to Foster,[12] twenty-seven breadfruit trees, which would cover an English acre with their shade, are sufficient for the support of from ten to twelve people during the eight months of fruit-bearing. Breadfruit is called in Tahiti *maiore*, in Hawaii *aeiore*.[13]

[1] Unger, F.   *U. S. Pat. Off. Rpt.* 315.   1859.

[2] Brandis, D.   *Forest Fl.* 426.   1874.

[3] *Enc. Brit.* 5:301.   1844.   8th Ed.

[4] De Candolle, A. P.   *Veg. Organ.* 2:174.   1840.

[5] Darwin, C.   *Ans. Pls. Domest.* 2:256.   1893.

[6] Forster, J. R.   *Obs.* 179.   1778.   Note.

[7] Lunan, J.   *Hort. Jam.* 1:113.   1814.

[8] Wilkes, C.   *U. S. Explor. Exped.* 3:332.   1845.

[9] Wilkes, C.   *U. S. Explor. Exped.* 2:121.   1845.

[10] Cook *Voyage* 3:207.   1773.

[11] Wilkes, C.   *U. S. Explor. Exped.* 3:333.   1845.

[12] Peschel, O.   *Races Man* 156.   1876.

[13] Pickering, C.   *Chron. Hist. Pls.* 437.   1879.

A. integrifolia Linn. f. JACK.

East Indies. On account of its excellent fruit, this tree is a special object of cultivation on the two Indian peninsulas, in Cochin China and southern China. It has only recently been introduced into the islands of the Pacific Ocean, as well as upon the island of Mauritius, the Antilles and the west coast of Africa. It is scarcely to be doubted that it occurs here and there growing wild and that perhaps Ceylon and the peninsula of Further India may be looked upon as its original native land.[1] The jack seems to be the Indian fruit described by Pliny, who gives the name of the tree as *pala*, of the fruit, *ariena;* and to be the *chagui* of Friar Jordanus,[2] about 1330, whose " fruit is of such size that one is enough for five persons." Firminger[3] says the fruit of this tree is perhaps about one of the largest in existence and is an ill-shapen, unattractive-looking object. The interior is of a soft, fibrous consistency with the edible portions scattered here and there, of about the size and color of a small orange. It is considered delicious by those who can manage to eat it, but it possesses the rich, spicy scent and flavor of the melon to such a powerful degree as to be quite unbearable to persons of a weak stomach, or to those not accustomed to it. There are two varieties in India. Lunan[4] says the thick, gelatinous covering which envelopes the seeds, eaten either raw or fried, is delicious. The round seeds, about half an inch in diameter, eaten roasted, have a very mealy and agreeable taste. The fruit, says Brandis,[5] is an important article of food in Burma, southern India and Ceylon. The tree has a very strong and disagreeable smell.

A. lakoocha Roxb.

Malay and East Indies. The ill-shapen fruit, the size of an orange and of an austere taste, is sometimes eaten. Firminger[6] says also that he has met with those who said they liked it, a fact which he could otherwise have hardly credited. Brandis[7] says the male flower-heads are pickled.

Arum *Aroideae.*

The several species of arum possess a combination of extremely acrid properties, with the presence of a large quantity of farina, which can be separated from the poisonous ingredient by heat or water and in some instances by merely drying. The arums form the most important plants of the tropics. In a single Polynesian Island, Tahiti, the natives have names for 33 arums. Taro, the general name, is grown in vast quantities in the Fiji group on the margins of streams under a system of irrigation. When the root is ripe, the greater part is cut off from the leaves and the portion which is left attached to them is at once replanted. These roots are prepared for use by boiling and are then pounded into a kind of flour, which is preserved until wanted for use. Large quantities of taro are also stored in pits where it becomes solid and is afterwards used by the

---

[1] Unger, F. *U. S. Pat. Off. Rpt.* 315. 1859.
[2] Jordanus, Fr. *Wonders East* Hakl. Soc. Ed. 13. 1863.
[3] Firminger, T. A. C. *Gard. Ind.* 185. 1874.
[4] Lunan, J. *Hort. Jam.* 1:388. 1814.
[5] Brandis, D. *Forest Fl.* 426. 1874.
[6] Firminger, T. A. C. *Gard. Ind.* 188. 1874.
[7] Brandis, D. *Forest Fl.* 427. 1874.

natives as *mandrai*. In former times, the common spotted arum furnished food to the English during the periods of scarcity. It seems impossible to determine in all cases to which species of arum travelers refer in recording the use of this genera of plants. The information given under the heading of the species will show the generality of their use and their importance.

A. dioscoridis Sibth. & Sm.

East Mediterranean countries. Theophrastus mentions that the roots and leaves of this plant, steeped in vinegar, were eaten in ancient Greece. The roots, as Pickering remarks,[1] are cooked and eaten in the Levant.

A. italicum Mill.   ITALIAN ARUM.

Mediterranean countries. This arum is described by Dioscorides, who says its root is eaten either raw or cooked. Westward, the cooked root is further mentioned by Dioscorides as mixed with honey by the Balearic islanders and made into cakes.[2] This plant was in cultivation for seven years in Guernsey for the purpose of making arrow-root from its corms.[3]

A. maculatum Linn.   ADAM-AND-EVE.   BOBBINS.   CUCKOO PINT.   LORDS-AND-LADIES.   STARCH-ROOT.   WAKE ROBIN.

Europe. The thick and tuberous root, while fresh, is extremely acrid, but by heat its injurious qualities are destroyed, and in the isle of Portland the plant was extensively used in the preparation of an arrow-root. According to Sprengel,[4] its roots are cooked and eaten in Albania, and in Slavonia it is made into a kind of bread. The leaves, even of this acrid plant, are said by Pallas [5] to be eaten by the Greeks of Crimea. " Dioscorides showeth that the leaves also are prescribed to be eaten and that they must be eaten after they be dried and boyled." [6]

Arundinaria japonica Sieb. & Zucc.   *Gramineae.*   CANE.

Northern Japan. When the young shoots appear in early summer, they are carefully gathered and, under the name of *take-no-ko*, are used for food as we would employ young asparagus; though by no means so tender as the latter, they make a very desirable dish.[7]

A. macrosperma Michx.   LARGE CANE.

North America. This is the species of cane which forms cane brakes in Virginia, Kentucky and southward. Flint,[8] in his *Western States*, says: " It produces an abundant crop of seed with heads very like those of broom corn. The seeds are farinaceous and are said to be not much inferior to wheat, for which the Indians and occasionally the first settlers substituted it."

---

[1] Pickering, C.   *Chron. Hist. Pls.* 346.   1879.
[2] Pickering, C.   *Chron. Hist. Pls.* 314.   1879.
[3] Seemann, B.   *Journ. Bot.* 1:25.   1863.
[4] Pickering, C.   *Chron. Hist. Pls.* 314.   1879.
[5] Pallas, P. S.   *Trav. Russia* 2:449.   1803.
[6] Gerarde. J.   *Herb.* 835.   1633 or 1636.
[7] Penhallow, D. P.   *Amer. Nat.* 16:121.   1882.
[8] Flint, T.   *West. States* 1:80, 81.   1828.

Asarum canadense Linn. *Aristolochiaceae.* SNAKEROOT. WILD GINGER.

North America. Barton [1] says the dried, pulverized root is commonly used in many parts of our country as a substitute for ginger, and Balfour [2] says it is used as a spice in Canada.

Asclepias syriaca Linn. *Asclepiadeae.* MILKWEED. SILKWEED.

North America. Kalm [3] says the French in Canada use the tender shoots of milkweed in spring, preparing them like asparagus, and that they also make a sugar of the flowers; a very good, brown, palatable sugar. Fremont [4] found the Sioux Indians of the upper Platte eating the young pods, boiling them with the meat of the buffalo. Jefferys,[5] in his *Natural History of Canada*, says: " What they call here the cotton-tree is a plant which sprouts like asparagus to the height of about three feet and is crowned with several tufts of flowers; these are shaken early in the morning before the dew is off of them when there falls from them with the dew a kind of honey, which is reduced into sugar by boiling; the seed is contained in a pod which encloses also a very fine sort of cotton." In 1835, Gen. Dearborn [6] of Massachusetts recommended the use of the young shoots of milkweed as asparagus, and Dewey [7] says the young plant is thus eaten. In France the plant is grown as an ornament.

A. tuberosa Linn. BUTTERFLY WEED. PLEURISYROOT. TUBER-ROOT.

Northeastern America. The tubers are boiled and used by the Indians. The Sioux of the upper Platte prepare from the flowers a crude sugar and also eat the young seed-pods. Some of the Indians of Canada use the tender shoots as an asparagus.[8]

Asimina triloba Dun. *Anonaceae.* PAPAW.

Middle and southern United States. All parts of the tree have a rank smell, and the fruit is relished by few except negroes.[9] Vasey says the fruit, about four inches long, when ripe has a rich, luscious taste. " The pulp of the fruit," says Flint,[10] " resembles egg-custard in consistence and appearance. It has the same creamy feeling in the mouth and unites the taste of eggs, cream, sugar and spice. It is a natural custard, too lucious for the relish of most people. The fruit is nutritious and a great resource to the savages."

Asparagus acerosus Roxb. *Liliaceae.*

East Indies and Burma. This species was found by Mason [11] to be a passable substitute for our garden asparagus.

---

[1] Barton, W. P. C. *Med. Bot.* 2:89. 1818.
[2] Balfour, J. H. *Man. Bot.* 576. 1875.
[3] Kalm, P. *Trav. No. Amer.* 2:202. 1772.
[4] Fremont *Explor. Exped.* 16. 1845.
[5] Jefferys, T. *Nat. Hist. Amer.* 42. 1760.
[6] Dearborn *Me. Farm.* Apr. 10, 1835.
[7] Dewey, C. *Rpt. Herb. Flow. Pls. Mass.* 145. 1840.
[8] Dodge *U. S. D. A. Rpt.* 405. 1870.
[9] Don, G. *Hist. Dichl. Pls.* 1:91. 1831.
[10] Flint, E. *West. States* 1:72. 1828. (*Annona triloba*)
[11] Pickering, C. *Chron. Hist. Pls.* 476. 1879.

A. acutifolius Linn. ASPARAGUS.

Mediterranean regions. The young shoots are eaten in Italy, Spain, Portugal and by the Greeks in Sicily.[1][2] They are thin, bitter and often stringy.

A. adscendens Roxb.

Himalayas and Afghanistan. From this plant is made, according to Modeen Sheriff, the genuine *sufed mush,* called in the Deccan *shakakul-hindi* and used as a substitute for salep.[3]

A. albus Linn. GARDEN-HEDGE.

Western Mediterranean region. The young heads are cut from wild plants and brought to table in Sicily, but they form but a poor substitute for cultivated asparagus.[4]

A. aphyllus Linn.

Mediterranean region. The young shoots are collected and eaten in Greece.[5]

A. laricinus Burch.

A shrubby species of South Africa. Dr. Pappe[6] says that it produces shoots of excellent tenderness and aromatic taste.

A. officinalis Linn. ASPARAGUS.

Europe, Caucasian regions and Siberia. This plant, so much esteemed in its culti-vated state, is a plant of the seashore and river banks of southern Europe and the Crimea. It is now naturalized in many parts of the world. In the southern parts of Russia and Poland, the waste steppes are covered with this plant. Unger[7] says it is not found either wild or cultivated in Greece, but Daubeny[8] says at the present time it is known under the name of *asparaggia,* and Booth[9] says it is common. Probably the mythological men-tion of the asparagus thickets which concealed Perigyne, beloved of Theseus,— the plant, in consequence, being protected by law among the Ionians inhabiting Caria — referred to another species.

Cultivated asparagus seems to have been unknown to the Greeks of the time of Theophrastus and Disocorides, and the word *asparagos* seems to have been used for the wild plant of another species. The Romans of the time of Cato, about 200 B. C., knew it well, and Cato's directions for culture would answer fairly well for the gardeners of today, except that he recommends starting with the seed of the wild plant, and this seems good evidence that the wild and the cultivated forms were then of the same type as they are today. Columella,[10] in the first century, recommends transplanting the young roots from a seed-bed and devotes some space to their after-treatment. He offers choice of

---

[1] Hooker, W. J. *Journ. Bot.* 1:211. 1834.

[2] Mueller, F.   *Sel Pls.* 54. 1891.

[3] Pickering, C. *Chron. Hist. Pls.* 736. 1879.

[4] Hooker, W. J. *Journ. Bot.* 1:211. 1834.

[5] Pickering, C. *Chron. Hist. Pls.* 165. 1879.

[6] Mueller, F.   *Sel. Pls.* 55. 1891.

[7] Unger, F.   *U. S. Pat. Off. Rpt.* 358. 1859.

[8] Daubeny, C. *Trees, Shrubs, Anc.* 127. 1865.

[9] Booth, W. B. *Treas. Bot.* 1:101. 1870.

[10] Columella lib. 9, c. 3.

cultivated seed or that from the wild plant, without indicating preference. Pliny,[1] who also wrote in the first century, says that asparagus, of all the plants of the garden, receives the most praiseworthy care and also praises the good quality of the kind that grows wild in the island of Nesida near the coast of Campania. In his praise of gardens,[2] he says: " Nature has made the asparagus wild, so that any one may gather as found. Behold, the highly-manured asparagus may be seen at Ravenna weighing three pounds." Palladius,[3] an author of the third century, rather praises the sweetness of the wild form found growing among the rocks and recommends transplanting it to such places otherwise worthless for agriculture, but he also gives full directions for garden culture with as much care as did Cato. Gesner [4] quotes Pomponius, who lived in the second century, as saying that there are two kinds, the garden and the wild asparagus, and that the wild asparagus is the more pleasant to eat. Suetonius,[5] about the beginning of the second century, informs us how partial the Emperor Augustus was to asparagus, and Erasmus [6] also mentions it.

A. racemosus Willd. RACEMOSE ASPARAGUS.

East Indies, African tropics and Australia. In India, the tubers are candied as a sweetmeat. This preparation, however, as Dutt states,[7] has scarcely any other taste or flavor besides that of the sugar. Firminger [8] says the preserve prepared from the blanched shoots is very agreeable.

A. sarmentosus Linn.

East Indies. The long, fleshy, whitish root is used as food by the people of Ceylon and, in the candied state, is often brought to India from China.[9]

A. verticillatus Linn.

South Russia. The young shoots, according to Chaubard,[10] are eaten in the Peloponesus.

Asperula odorata Linn. *Rubiaceae.* WOODROOF.

Europe and the adjoining portions of Asia. The flowers are sweet-scented. The herbage is not fragrant when fresh but, after being gathered for a short time, it gives out the perfume of new hay and retains this property for years. In Germany, woodroof is used for imparting a flavor to some of the Rhine wines. In England, it is cultivated occasionally as a garden herb, being used for flavoring cooling drinks. Its seed is advertised in American garden catalogs. Woodroof will thrive in the shade of most trees and grows in all kinds of garden soil.

---

[1] Bostock and Riley. *Nat. Hist. Pliny* 4:188. 1856.

[2] Pliny c. 19.

[3] Palladius lib. 3, c. 24; lib. 4, c. 9.

[4] *Script. Rei Rust.* 1788, *Lexicon,* art. *Asparagus.*

[5] McIntosh, C. *Book Gard.* 2:177. 1855.

[6] Ibid.

[7] Dutt, U. C. *Mat. Med. Hindus* 260. 1877.

[8] Firminger, T. A. C. *Gard. Ind.* 121. 1874.

[9] Ainslie, W. *Mat. Ind.* 2:409. 1826.

[10] Pickering, C. *Chron. Hist. Pls.* 525. 1879.

Asphodeline lutea Reichb. *Liliaceae.* ASPHODEL. JACOB'S ROD. KING'S SPEAR.

Region of the Mediterranean and the Caucasus. This plant is mentioned as covering large tracts of land in Apulia and as being abundant in Sicily. It was fabled to grow in the Elysian fields, and hence the ancient Greeks were wont to place asphodel on the tombs of their friends. The root is mentioned as an esculent by Pythagoras.[1] Pliny[2] says the roots of asphodel were generally roasted under embers and then eaten with salt and oil and when mashed with figs were thought a most excellent dish. Phillips,[3] exercising some imagination, says: "Asphodel was to the ancient Greeks and Romans what the potato now is to us, a bread plant, the value of which cannot be too highly estimated. It has long since given way to its successors in favor."

Aster tripolium Linn. *Compositae.* ASTER.

Northern Africa, Asia, the Orient and Europe. The somewhat fleshy leaves of this aster are occasionally gathered to make a kind of pickle.[4]

Astragalus aboriginorum Richards. *Leguminosae.* ASTRAGALUS.

Arctic North America. The roots are eaten by the Cree and Stone Indians of the Rocky Mountains.[5]

A. adscendens Boiss. & Haussk.

Persia. The plant affords an abundance of gum and also a manna.[6]

A. boeticus Linn. SWEDISH COFFEE.

Mediterranean region. In certain parts of Germany and Hungary, this plant is cultivated for its seeds, which are roasted, ground and used as a substitute for coffee. Its culture is the same as that of the common pea or tare. The name applied to the seeds, Swedish coffee, would indicate that it is also grown in Scandinavia.

A. caryocarpus Ker-Gawl. GROUND PLUM.

Mississippi region of North America. The unripe fruits are edible and are eaten raw or cooked.

A. christianus Linn.

Asia Minor and Syria. In Taurus, the roots of the great, yellow milk-vetch are sought as an article of food.[7]

A. creticus Lam.

Greece. This plant yields tragacanth[8]

A. florulentus Boiss. & Haussk.

Persia. The plant yields a manna.[9]

---

[1] Pickering, C. *Chron. Hist. Pls.* 106. 1879.
[2] Bostock and Riley *Nat. Hist. Pliny* 4:360. 1856.
[3] Phillips, H. *Comp. Kitch. Gard.* 1:35. 1831.
[4] Masters, M. T. *Treas. Bot.* 2:1173. 1870.
[5] Brown, R. *Bot. Soc. Edinb.* 9:381. 1868. (*Phaca aboriginorum*)
[6] Flückiger and Hanbury *Pharm.* 174. 1879.
[7] Fraser, J. B. *Mesopotamia* 354. 1842.
[8] Baillon, H. *Hist. Pls.* 2:378. 1872.
[9] Flückiger and Hanbury *Pharm.* 415. 1879.

A. gummifer Labill.

Syria. This is another species supplying a source of tragacanth.[1]

A. hamosus Linn.

Mediterranean region to India. The plant is grown particularly on account of the singularity of its fruits which, before maturity, resemble certain worms. They are of a mediocre taste but are employed in salads chiefly to cause an innocent surprise.[2]

A. kurdicus Boiss.

Kurdistan and Syria. The plant affords tragacanth.[3]

A. leioclados Boiss.

Persia. Tragacanth is produced by this plant.[4]

A. mexicanus A. DC.

Open plains and prairies from Illinois westward and southward. The unripe fruits are edible and are eaten raw or cooked by travelers.[5]

Astrocaryum acaule Mart. *Palmae.*

Brazil. This is a palm of the Rio Negro. The fruit is edible.[6]

A. murumura Mart. MURUMURA.

A palm of the Brazilian forest. The fruit, according to Kunth, has an agreeable flavor and at first a scent resembling musk but afterwards that of a melon. Wallace states that the fleshy covering of the fruit is rather juicy and is eatable.[7]

A. tucuma Mart.

Upper Amazon and Rio Negro. The fleshy part of the fruit is esteemed for food by the Indians.[8] The yellowish, fibrous pulp is eaten by the natives.[9]

Astronia papetaria Blume. *Melastomaceae.*

A tree of the Moluccas. Its subacid leaves are cooked as a sauce for fish.[10]

Athamanta cervariaefolia DC. *Umbelliferae.* SPIGNEL.

Teneriffe Islands. The root is said to be eaten.[11]

A. cretensis Linn. CANDY CARROT.

Southern Europe. An agreeable liquor is made from the seeds.

A. matthioli Wulf.

Southeastern Europe. The plant has an edible root.[12]

---

[1] *Treas. Bot.* 106. 1870.

[2] Vilmorin *Veg. Gard.* 510, 511. 1885.

[3] Flückiger and Hanbury *Pharm.* 174. 1879.

[4] Ibid.

[5] Gray, A. *Man. Bot.* 132. 1868.

[6] Seemann, B. *Pop. Hist. Palms* 74. 1856.

[7] Ibid.

[8] Seemann, B. *Pop. Hist. Palms* 74. 1856.

[9] Bates, H. W. *Nat. Amaz.* 647. 1879. Humboldt *Libr. Sci.*

[10] Syme, J. T. *Treas. Bot.* 1:106. 1870.

[11] Baillon, H. *Hist. Pls.* 7:192. 1881.

[12] Ibid.

Atherosperma moschatum Labill. *Monimiaceae.* TASMANIAN SASSAFRAS TREE.

Australia. Its aromatic bark has been used as a substitute for tea.[1]

Atriplex halimus Linn. *Chenopodiaceae.* SEA ORACH.

A plant of the seashores of Europe and the Mediterranean countries and salines as far as Siberia. Sea orach is one of the few indigenous plants of Egypt that affords sustenance to man. It is mentioned by Antipharues [2] as esculent; by Dioscorides as cooked and eaten; by Tournefort as eaten in Greece. The men of the Euphrates expedition often used this species as a culinary vegetable.

A. hortensis Linn. BUTTER LEAVES. MOUNTAIN SPINACH. ORACH.

Cosmopolitan. Orach has long been used as a kitchen vegetable in Europe. It was known to the ancient Greeks under the name of *atraphaxis* and Dioscorides writes that it was eaten boiled. It was known to the Romans under the name of *atriplex*. Orach was introduced into English gardens in 1548 and was long used, as it still is, in many countries to correct the acidity and the green color of sorrel. It is grown in three varieties.[3]

Orach was known to Turner [4] in England in 1538, who calls it areche, or red oreche. In 1686, Ray [5] mentions the white and red, as mentioned by Gerarde [6] in 1597. In 1623, Bauhin [7] mentions the red, the white and the dark green. In 1806, three kinds are named by McMahon [8] as in American gardens.

Attalea cohune Mart. *Palmae.* COHUNE PALM.

Honduras. The tree bears a fruit, about the size of a large egg, growing in clusters resembling a bunch of grapes. The kernel tastes somewhat like that of the cocoanut but is far more oleaginous and the oil is superior.[9]

A. compta Mart.

Brazil. The seed-vessels are eaten as a delicacy.[10]

A. excelsa Mart. URUCURI PALM.

Amazon region. Bates [11] says the fruit is similar in size and shape to the date and has a pleasantly flavored, juicy pulp. The Indians did not eat it but he did, although its wholesomeness was questionable.

Avena brevis Roth. *Gramineae.* FLY'S LEG. SHORT OAT.

Europe. The Germans call this species a native plant and say that it grows wild

[1] Smith, J. *Dom. Bot.* 248. 1871.

[2] Pickering, C. *Chron. Hist. Pls.* 12. 1879.

[3] Fraser, J. B. *Mesopotamia* 359. 1842. (*A. orache*)

[4] Turner *Libellus.* 1538.

[5] Ray *Hist. Pl.* 191. 1686.

[6] Gerarde, J. *Herb.* 256. 1597.

[7] Bauhin, C. *Pinax* 119. 1623.

[8] McMahon, B. *Amer. Gard. Cal.* 321. 1806.

[9] Temple, R. *Journ. Soc. Arts* 2:500. No. 81.

[10] Masters, M. T. *Treas. Bot.* 1:110. 1870.

[11] Bates, H. W. *Nat. Amaz.* 719. 1879. Humboldt *Libr. Sci.*

among grain. It is cultivated in mountainous districts of Europe, as in those of Auvergne and Forez, because it ripens quickly, where the country people call it *piedo de mouche*, or fly's leg, because of the appearance of the dark awns.[1] In some parts of France, on account of its excellence for fodder, it is called *avoine a fourrage*.

A. fatua Linn. DRAKE. FLAVER. POTATO OAT. TARTAREAN OAT. WILD OAT.

Europe, the Orient and Asia. This is the common wild oat of California. It may have been introduced by the Spaniards but it is now spread over the whole country many miles from the coast. The grain is gathered by the Indians of California and is used as a bread corn. In 1852, Professor Buckman[2] sowed a plat of ground with seeds collected in 1851 and in 1856 had for the produce poor, but true, samples of what are known as the potato and Tartarean oat. In 1860, the produce was good white Tartarean and potato oats.

A. nuda Linn. NAKED OAT. PEELCORN. PILLCORN.

Southern Europe. This is probably an oat produced by cultivation. The Chinese are said to cultivate a variety of it with a broad, flat rachis. It was growing in England, according to Turner, in 1538. It is now, and has been for some time, among the seeds of our seedsmen.

A. orientalis Schreb. SIBERIAN OAT. TARTAREAN OAT.

Southern Europe and the Orient. Although the name leads to the supposition that this oat had its origin in the dry table-lands of Asia, yet we are not aware, says Lindley,[3] that any evidence exists to show that it is so. We only know it as a cultivated plant. Phillips[4] says the Siberian oat reached England in 1777, and Unger[5] says it was brought from the East to Europe at the end of the preceding century.

A. sativa Linn. HAVER. OAT.

The native land of the common oat is given as Abyssinia by Pickering.[6] Unger[7] says the native land is unknown, although the region along the Danube may pass as such. The oat is probably a domesticated variety of some wild species and may be *A. strigosa* Schreb., found wild in grain fields throughout Europe. Professor Buckman believed *A. fatua* Linn., to be the original species, as in eight years of cultivation he changed this plant into good cultivated varieties. Unger[8] says the Celts and the Germans, as far as can be ascertained, cultivated this oat 2000 years ago, and it seems to have been distributed from Europe into the temperate and cold regions of the whole world. It was known to the Egyptians, Hebrews, Greeks and Romans. De Candolle,[9] however, writes

---

[1] *Bon Jard.* 655. 1882.

[2] Buckman, J. *Treas. Bot.* 1:11. 1870.

[3] Morton *Cyc..Agr.* 1:171. 1869.

[4] Phillips, H. *Comp. Kitch. Gard.* 2:13. 1831.

[5] Unger, F. *U. S. Pat. Off. Rpt.* 302. 1859.

[6] Pickering, C. *Chron. Hist. Pls.* 341. 1879.

[7] Unger, F. *U. S. Pat. Off. Rpt.* 302. 1859.

[8] Ibid.

[9] De Candolle, A. *Geog. Bot.* 2:939. 1855.

that the oat was not cultivated by the Hebrews, the Egyptians, the ancient Greeks or the Romans and is now cultivated in Greece only as an object of curiosity.[1] The oat is not cultivated for human food in India.[2]

This grain is not mentioned in Scripture and hence would seem to be unknown to Egypt or Syria.[3] The plant is noticed by Virgil[4] in his *Georgics* with the implication that its culture was known. Pliny[5] mentions the plant. It is, hence, quite probable that the Romans knew the oat principally as a forage crop. Pliny[6] says that the Germans used oatmeal porridge as food. Dioscorides[7] and Galen[8] make similar statements, but the latter adds that although it is fitter food for beasts than men yet in times of famine it is used by the latter. From an investigation of the lacustrine remains of Switzerland, Heer[9] finds that during the Bronze age oats were known, the oat-grain being somewhat smaller than that produced by our existing varieties. Turner[10] observes, in 1568, that the naked oat grew in Sussex, England. The bearded oat was brought from Barbary and was cultivated in Britain about 1640; the brittle oat came from the south of Europe in 1796; the Spanish oat was introduced in 1770; the Siberian, in 1777; the Pennsylvanian, in 1785; the fan-leaved, from Switzerland in 1791.[11] In Scotland, the oat has long been a bread grain and, about 1850, Peter Lawson[12] gives 40 varieties as cultivated. This cereal was sown by Gosnold[13] on the Elizabeth Islands, Massachusetts, in 1602; is recorded as cultivated in Newfoundland[14] in 1622; was growing at Lynn, Mass.,[15] in 1629–33. It was introduced into New Netherland[16] prior to 1626 and was cultivated in Virginia[17] previous to 1648. The Egyptian, or winter oat, was known in the South in 1800. In 1880, 36 named kinds were grown in the state of Kansas.[18] The oat grows in Norway and Sweden as far north as 64° to 65° but is scarcely known in the south of France, Spain or Italy, and in tropical countries its culture is not attempted.

A. strigosa Schreb. BRISTLE-POINTED OAT. MEAGRE OAT.

Europe. Pickering[19] says this plant is of the Tauro-Caspian countries; it was first

---

[1] De Candolle, A. *Geog. Bot.* 2:939. 1855.

[2] Ibid.

[3] Ibid.

[4] Ibid.

[5] Phillips, H. *Comp. Kitch. Gard.* 2:9. 1831.

[6] Stille, A. *Therap. Mat. Med.* 1:125. 1874.

[7] Ibid.

[8] Ibid.

[9] *Gard. Chron.* 1068. 1866.

[10] Phillips, H. *Comp. Kitch. Gard.* 2:13. 1831.

[11] Ibid.

[12] Lawson, P. *Prize Essays Highland Soc.* 4:312. 1851.

[13] *U. S. Pat. Off. Rpt.* 159. 1853.

[14] Ibid.

[15] Wood, W. *New Eng. Prosp.* 81. 1634.

[16] *U. S. Pat. Off. Rpt.* 159. 1853.

[17] Ibid.

[18] *Kansas Bd. Agr. Rpt.* 19. 1880.

[19] Pickering, C. *Chron. Hist. Pls.* 1031. 1879.

observed in Germany in 1771;[1] by Retz [2] in Sweden in 1779; and the same year by Withering [3] in Britain. Lindley [4] says it is found wild in abundance in grain fields all over Europe. The smallness of the grain renders this oat unfit for cultivation except on poor, mountainous places, where nothing better may be had. The Germans, however, have much improved it

Averrhoa bilimbi Linn. *Geraniaceae.* BILIMBI. BLIMBING. CUCUMBER TREE.

East Indies and China. The fruit is of the form and size of a gherkin, with a smooth, thin, pale green, translucent rind like that of a ripe grape. When ripe, the flesh is as soft as butter and has somewhat the flavor of an unripe gooseberry, too acid to be eaten except when cooked.[5] Brandis [6] speaks of it as pickled or preserved in sugar, and Smith [7] writes that the flowers are made into conserves.

A. carambola Linn. BLIMBING. CARAMBA. CARAMBOLA. COUNTRY GOOSEBERRY.

East Indies and China. This plant has been cultivated for its fruit for ages in tropical and subtropical India. The form of the fruit is oblong, with five prominent angles; its skin is thin, green at first and yellowish afterwards; the flesh is soft and exceedingly juicy like a plum, with a grateful, acid flavor. In Hindustan and Ceylon, the fruit is sometimes as big as the two fists. In Sumatra, there are two sorts which are used chiefly in cookery.[8] In Bengal, there are two varieties, one with acid, the other with sweet fruit,[9] as also in Burma.[10] The fruit is used as a pickle by Europeans and the flowers are said to be made into a conserve.

Avicennia officinalis Linn. *Verbenaceae.* NEW ZEALAND MANGROVE.

Region of the Caspian. This plant transudes a gum which the natives of New Zealand esteem as a food.[11] The kernels are bitter but edible.[12]

Aydendron firmulum Nees. *Laurineae.* PICHURIM BEAN. TODA SPECIE.

Brazil. The Portugese of the Rio Negro, a branch of the Amazon, gather the aromatic seeds, known in trade by the names of the pichurim bean and toda specie. The seed is grated like nutmeg.

Babiana plicata Ker-Gawl. *Irideae.* BABOON-ROOT.

South Africa. The root is sometimes boiled and eaten by the colonists at the Cape.[13]

---

[1] Pickering, C. *Chron. Hist. Pls.* 1031. 1879.
[2] Ibid.
[3] Ibid.
[4] Morton *Cyc. Agr.* 172. 1869.
[5] Firminger, T. A. C. *Gard. Ind.* 236. 1874.
[6] Brandis, D. *Forest Fl.* 46. 1874.
[7] Smith, J. *Dict. Econ. Pls.* 54. 1882.
[8] Lindley, J. *Trans. Hort. Soc. Lond.* 5:115. 1824.
[9] Brandis, D. *Forest Fl.* 46. 1874.
[10] Pickering, C. *Chron. Hist. Pls.* 690. 1879.
[11] Nuttall, T. *No. Amer. Sylva* 2:144. 1865. (*A. resinifera*)
[12] Drury, H. *Useful Pls. Ind.* 57. 1858. (*A. tomentosa*)
[13] Thunberg, C. P. *Trav.* 1:285. 1795. (*Gladiolus plicatus*)

Baccaurea dulcis Muell. *Euphorbiaceae.*

Malayan Archipelago; cultivated in China.[1] The fruits of this species are rather larger than a cherry, nearly round and of a yellowish color. The pulp is luscious and sweet and is greatly eaten in Sumatra, where the tree is called *choopah* and in Malacca, where it goes by the name of *rambeh*.[2]

B. sapida Muell.

East Indies and Malay. This plant is cultivated for its agreeable fruits. The Hindus call it *lutqua*.[3]

B. sp.?

India. Royle[4] says the plant yields the *tampui*, a fruit ranking in point of taste and flavor along with the *lausch*.

Bactris gasipaës H. B. & K. *Palmae.* PEACH PALM.

Venezuela. On the Amazon, says Bates,[5] this plant does not grow wild but has been cultivated from time immemorial by the Indians. The fruit is dry and mealy and may be compared in taste to a mixture of chestnuts and cheese. Bunches of sterile or seedless fruit sometimes occur at Ega and at Para. It is one of the principal articles of food at Ega when in season and is boiled and eaten with treacle and salt. Spencer[6] compares the taste of the mealy pericarp, when cooked, to a mixture of potato and chestnut but says it is superior to either. Seemann[7] says in most instances the seed is abortive, the whole fruit being a farinaceous mass. Humboldt says every cluster contains from 50 to 80 fruits, yellow like apples but purpling as they ripen, two or three inches in diameter, and generally without a kernel; the farinaceous portion is as yellow as the yolk of an egg, slightly saccharine and exceedingly nutritious. He found it cultivated in abundance along the upper Orinoco. In Trinidad, the peach palm is said to be very prolific, bearing two crops a year, at one season the fruit all seedless and another season bearing seeds. The seedless fruits are highly appreciated by natives of all classes.[8]

B. major Jacq. PRICKLY PALM.

West Indies. The fruit is the size of an egg with a succulent, purple coat from which wine may be made. The nut is large, with an oblong kernel and is sold in the markets under the name of *cocorotes*.[9]

B. maraja Mart. MARAJA PALM.

Brazil. This palm has a fruit of a pleasant, acid flavor from which a vinous beverage is prepared.[10]

---

[1] Royle, J. F. *Illustr. Bot. Himal.* 1:136. 1839.
[2] Smith, A. *Treas. Bot.* 2:887. 1870.
[3] Royle, J. F. *Illustr. Bot. Himal.* 1:136. 1839.
[4] Royle, J. F. *Illustr. Bot. Himal.* 1:138. 1839.
[5] Bates, H. W. *Nat. Amaz.* 728. 1879. Humboldt *Libr. Sci.*
[6] Mueller, F. *Sel. Pls.* 63. 1891.
[7] Seemann, B. *Pop. Hist. Palms* 209. 1856.
[8] Prestoe *Trinidad Bot. Gard. Rpt.* 39. 1880. (*Guilielma speciosa*)
[9] Titford, W. J. *Hort. Bot. Amer.* 109. 1812.
[10] Seemann, B. *Pop. Hist. Palms* 98. 1855.

B. minor Jacq. PRICKLY POLE. TOBAGO CANE.

Jamaica. The fruit is dark purple, the size of a cherry and contains an acid juice which Jacquin says is made into a sort of wine. The fruit is edible but not pleasant.[1, 2]

Bagassa guianensis Aubl. *Urticaceae.*

Guiana. The tree bears an orange-shaped edible fruit.[3]

Balanites aegyptica Delile. *Simarubeae.* ZACHUN-OIL TREE.

Northern Africa, Arabia and Palestine. A shrubby, thorny bush of the southern border of the Sahara from the Atlantic to Hindustan.[4] It is called in equatorial Africa *m'choonchoo;* the edible drupe tastes like an intensely bitter date.[5]

Balsamorhiza hookeri Nutt. *Compositae.* BALSAM-ROOT.

Northwestern America. The thick roots of this species are eaten raw by the Nez Percé Indians and have, when cooked, a sweet and rather agreeable taste.[6]

B. sagittata Nutt. OREGON SUNFLOWER.

Northwestern America. The roots are eaten by the Nez Percé Indians in Oregon, after being cooked on hot stones. They have a sweet and rather agreeable taste.[7] Wilkes[8] mentions the Orgeon sunflower of which the seeds, pounded into a meal called *mielito*, are eaten by the Indians of Puget Sound.

Bambusa. *Gramineae.*

In India, the Bambusa flowers so frequently that in Mysore and Orissa the seeds are mixed with honey and eaten like rice.[9] The farina of the seeds is eaten in China.[10] In Amboina, in the East Indies, the young bamboo shoots, cut in slices and pickled, are used as a provision for long voyages and are sold in the markets as a culinary vegetable.[11] In the Himalayas, the young shoots are eaten as a vegetable, and the seeds of a variety called *praong* in Sikkim are boiled and made into cakes or into beer.[12] Williams[13] says: " In China the tender shoots are cultivated for food and are, when four or five inches high, boiled, pickled, and comfited." Fortune[14] says: " In China the young shoots are cultivated for food and are taken to market in large quantities."

---

[1] Titford, W. J. *Hort. Bot. Amer.* 112. 1814. (*Cocos guineensis*)

[2] Lunan, J. *Hort. Jam.* 2:94. 1814.

[3] Masters, M. T. *Treas. Bot.* 1:117. 1870.

[4] Smith, J. *Dom. Bot.* 455. 1871.

[5] Speke, J. H. *Journ. Disc. Source Nile* 564. 1864.

[6] *U. S. D. A. Rpt.* 406. 1870. (*B. incana*)

[7] Black, A. A. *Treas. Bot.* 1:120. 1870. (*B. helianthoides*)

[8] Wilkes, C. *U. S. Explor. Exped.* 4:434. 1845.

[9] Humboldt, A. *Views Nature* 335. 1850.

[10] Williams, S. W. *U. S. Pat. Off. Rpt.* 475. 1860.

[11] La Billardière *Voy. Recherche Pérouse* 1:395. 1799.

[12] Hooker, J. D. *Himal. Journ.* 1:313. 1854.

[13] Williams, S. W. *U. S. Pat. Off. Rpt.* 475. 1860.

[14] Fortune, R. *Resid. Chinese* 190. 1857.

B. arundinacea Willd.   BAMBOO.

East Indies.   The seeds of this and other species of Bambusa have often saved the lives of thousands in times of scarcity in India, as in Orissa in 1812, in Kanara in 1864 and in 1866 [1] in Malda.   The plant bears whitish seed, like rice, and Drury [2] says these seeds are eaten by the poorer classes.

B. tulda Roxb.   BAMBOO.

East Indies and Burma.   In Bengal, the tender young shoots are eaten as pickles by the natives.[3]

Banisteria crotonifolia A. Juss.   *Malpighiaceae.*

Brazil.   The fruit is eaten in Brazil.[4]

Baptisia tinctoria R. Br.   *Leguminosae.*   HORSE-FLY WEED.   WILD INDIGO.

Northeastern America.   Barton [5] says the young shoots of this plant, which resemble asparagus in appearance, have been used in New England as a substitute for asparagus.

Barbarea arcuata Reichb.   *Cruciferae.*   BITTER CRESS.

Europe and Asia.   The plant serves as a bitter cress.

B. praecox R. Br.   AMERICAN CRESS.   BELLE ISLE CRESS.   EARLY WINTER CRESS.   LAND CRESS.   SCURVY GRASS.

Europe.   This cress is occasionally cultivated for salad in the Middle States under the name scurvy grass and is becoming spontaneous farther south.   It is grown in gardens in England as a cress and is used in winter and spring salads.   In Germany, it is generally liked.   In the Mauritius, it is n regular cultivation and is known as early winter cress. In the United States, its seeds are offered in seed catalogs.

B. vulgaris R. Br.   ROCKET.   WINTER CRESS.   YELLOW ROCKET.

Europe and temperate Asia.   This herb of northern climates has been cultivated in gardens in England for a long time as an early salad and also in Scotland, where the bitter leaves are eaten by some.[6]   In early times, rocket was held in some repute [7] but is now banished from cultivation yet appears in gardens as a weed.   The whole herb, says Don,[8] has a nauseous, bitter taste and is in some degree mucilaginous.   In Sweden, the leaves are boiled as a kale.   In New Zealand, the plant is used by the natives as a food under the name, *toi.*   Rocket is included in the list of American garden esculents by McMahon,[9] in 1806.   In 1832, Bridgeman says winter cress is used as a salad in spring and autumn and by some boiled as a spinage.

---

[1] Brandis, D.   *Forest Pl.* 566.   1874.

[2] Drury, H.   *Useful Pls. Ind.* 61.   1858.

[3] Roxburgh, W.   *Hort. Beng.* 2:193.   1814.

[4] Don, G.   *Hist. Dichl. Pls.* 1:635.   1831.

[5] Barton, W. P. C.   *Med. Bot.* 2:61.   1818.

[6] Johnson, C. P.   *Useful Pls. Gt. Brit.* 31.   1862.

[7] Gerarde, J.   *Herb.* 243.   1633 or 1636.   2nd Ed.

[8] Don, G.   *Hist. Dichl. Pls.* 1:159.   1831.

[9] McMahon, B.   *Amer. Gard. Cal.* 581.   1806.   (*Erysimum barbarea*)

Barringtonia alba Blume. *Myrtaceae.* BOTTLE-BRUSH TREE.

Moluccas. The young leaves are eaten raw.[1]

B. butonica Forst.

Islands of the Pacific. This plant has oleaginous seeds and fruits which are eaten green as vegetables.[2]

B. careya F. Muell.

Australia. The fruit is large, with an adherent calyx and is edible.[3]

B. edulis Seem.

Fiji Islands. The rather insipid fruit is eaten either raw or cooked by the natives.[4]

B. excelsa Blume.

India, Cochin China and the Moluccas. The fruit is edible and the young leaves are eaten cooked and in salad.[5]

Basella rubra Linn. *Chenopodiaceae.* MALABAR NIGHTSHADE.

Tropical regions. This twining, herbaceous plant is cultivated in all parts of India, and the succulent stems and leaves are used by the natives as a pot-herb in the way of spinach.[6] In Burma, the species is cultivated and in the Philippines is seemingly wild and eaten by the natives.[7] It is also cultivated in the Mauritius[8] and in every part of India,[9] where it occurs wild.[10] Malabar nightshade was introduced to Europe in 1688[11] and was grown in England in 1691,[12] but these references can hardly apply to the vege-table garden. It is, however, recorded in French gardens in 1824 and 1829.[13] It is grown in France as a vegetable,[14] a superior variety having been introduced from China in 1839.[15] According to Livingstone, it is cultivated as a pot-herb in India.[16] It is a spinach plant which has somewhat the odor of *Ocimum basilicum*.[17] The species is cultivated in almost every part of India as a spinach, and an infusion of the leaves in used as tea.[18] It is called Malabar nightshade by Europeans of India.[19]

[1] Baillon, H. *Hist. Pls.* **6**:350. 1880.

[2] Baillon, H. *Hist. Pls.* **6**:350. 1880. (*B. speciosa*)

[3] Palmer, E. *Journ. Roy. Soc. New So. Wales* **17**:94. 1884.

[4] Seemann, B. *Fl. Viti.* 82. 1865–73.

[5] Baillon, H. *Hist. Pls.* **6**:350. 1880. (*B. coccinea*)

[6] Firminger, T. A. C. *Gard. Ind.* 145. 1874. (*B. alba*)

[7] Pickering, C. *Chron. Hist. Pls.* 696. 1879. (*B. alba*)

[8] Bojer *Hort. Maurit.* 270. 1837.

[9] Drury, H. *Useful Pls. Ind.* 66. 1858. (*B. alba*)

[10] Wight, R. *Icon. Pls.* 896. 1843.

[11] Noisette *Man. Jard.* 559. 1860.

[12] Martyn *Miller's Gard. Dict.* 1807.

[13] Pirolle *L'Hort Franc.* 1824.

[14] Robinson, W. *Parks, Gard. Paris* 503. 1878.

[15] *Bon Jard.* 432. 1882.

[16] Drury, H. *Useful Pls. Ind.* 66. 1858. (*B. alba*)

[17] Mueller, F. *Sel. Pls.* 66. 1891.

[18] Drury, H. *Useful Pls. Ind.* 66. 1858. (*B. alba*)

[19] Ibid.

Bassia butyracea Roxb. *Sapotaceae.* INDIAN-BUTTER. PHOOLWA-OIL PLANT.

East Indies. The pulp of the fruit is eatable. The juice is extracted from the flowers and made into sugar by the natives. It is sold in the Calcutta bazaar and has all the appearance of date sugar, to which it is equal if not superior in quality.[1] An oil is extracted from the seeds, and the oil cake is eaten[2] as also is the pure vegetable butter which is called *chooris* and is sold at a cheap rate.[3]

B. latifolia Roxb. EPIE. MAHOUA. YALLAH-OIL PLANT.

East Indies. The succulent flowers fall by night in large quantities from the tree, are gathered early in the morning, dried in the sun and sold in the bazaars as an important article of food. They have a sickish, sweet taste and smell and are eaten raw or cooked. The ripe and unripe fruit is also eaten, and from the fruit is expressed an edible oil.[4]

B. longifolia Linn. ILLUPIE-OIL PLANT. ILPA.

East Indies. The flowers are eaten by the natives of Mysore, either dried, roasted, or boiled to a jelly.[5] The oil pressed from the fruits is to the common people of India a substitute for ghee and cocoanut oil in their curries.[6]

Batis maritima Linn. *Batideae.* JAMAICA SAMPHIRE. SALTWORT.

Jamaica. This low, erect, succulent plant is used as a pickle.[7]

Bauhinia esculenta Burch. *Leguminosae.*

South Africa. The root is sweet and nutritious.[8]

B. lingua DC.

Moluccas. This species is used as a vegetable.[9]

B. malabarica Roxb.

East Indies and Burma. The acid leaves are eaten.[10]

B. purpurea Linn.

East Indies, Burma and China. The flower-buds are pickled and eaten as a vegetable.[11]

B. tomentosa Linn. ST. THOMAS' TREE.

Asia and tropical Africa. The seeds are eaten in the Punjab,[12] and the leaves are eaten by natives of the Philippines as a substitute for vinegar.

---

[1] Drury, H. *Useful Pls. Ind.* 67. 1858.
[2] Brandis, D. *Forest Fl.* 290. 1874.
[3] Pickering, C. *Chron. Hist. Pls.* 603. 1879.
[4] Brandis, D. *Forest Fl.* 290. 1874.
[5] Brandis, D. *Forest Fl.* 291. 1874.
[6] Don, G. *Hist. Dichl. Pls.* 4:35. 1831.
[7] Smith, J. *Dom. Bot.* 237. 1871.
[8] Unger, F. *U. S. Pat. Off. Rpt.* 328. 1859.
[9] Unger, F. *U. S. Pat. Off. Rpt.* 359. 1859.
[10] Brandis, D. *Forest Fl.* 159. 1874.
[11] Brandis, D. *Forest Fl.* 160. 1874.
[12] Drury, H. *Useful Pls. Ind.* 74. 1873.

B. vahlii Wight & Arn. MALOO CREEPER.

East Indies. The pods are roasted and the seeds are eaten. Its seeds taste, when ripe, like the cashew-nut.

B. variegata Linn. MOUNTAIN EBONY.

East Indies, Burma and China. There are two varieties, one with purplish, the other with whitish flowers. The leaves and flower-buds are eaten as a vegetable and the flower-buds are often pickled in India.[1]

Beckmannia erucaeformis Host. *Gramineae.*

Europe, temperate Asia and North America. According to Engelmann,[2] the seeds are collected for food by the Utah Indians.

Begonia barbata Wall. *Begoniaceae.* BEGONIA.

East Indies and Burma. The leaves, called *tengoor*, are eaten by the natives as a pot-herb.[3] Hooker[4] says the stems of many species are eaten in the Himalayas, when cooked, being pleasantly acid. The stems are made into a sauce in Sikkim.

B. cucullata Willd. BEGONIA.

Brazil. The leaves are used as cooling salads.

B. malabarica Lam. BEGONIA.

East Indies. Henfrey[5] says the plants are eaten as pot-herbs.

B. picta Sm. BEGONIA.

Himalayas. The leaves have an acid taste and are used as food.

Bellis perennis Linn. *Compositae.* ENGLISH DAISY.

Europe and the adjoining portions of Asia. Lightfoot[6] says the taste of the leaves is somewhat acid, and, in scarcity of garden-stuff, they have been used in some countries as a pot-herb

Bellucia aubletii Naud. *Melastomaceae.*

Guiana. A tree of Guiana which has an edible, yellow fruit.[7]

B. brasiliensis Naud.

Brazil. The fruit is edible.[8]

Benincasa cerifera Savi. *Cucurbitaceae.* WAX GOURD. WHITE GOURD. WHITE PUMPKIN.

Asia and African tropics. This annual plant is cultivated in India for its very large, handsome, egg-shaped gourd. The gourd is covered with a pale greenish-white, waxen

---

[1] Brandis, D. *Forest Fl.* 161. 1874.

[2] Brewer and Watson *Bot. Cal.* 2:264. 1880.

[3] Royle, J. F. *Illustr. Bot. Himal.* 1:313. 1839.

[4] Hooker, J. D. *Illustr. Himal. Pls.* Pl. XIII. 1855.

[5] Henfrey, A. *Bot.* 282. 1870.

[6] Lightfoot, J. *Fl. Scot.* 1:487. 1789.

[7] Syme, J. T. *Treas. Bot.* 147. 1870. (*Blakea quinquenervia*)

[8] Baillon, H. *Hist. Pls.* 7:34. 1881.

bloom. It is consumed by the natives [1] in an unripe state in their curries.[2] This gourd is cultivated throughout Asia and its islands and in France as a vegetable.[3] It is described as delicate, quite like the cucumber and preferred by many.[4] The bloom of the fruit forms peetha wax and occurs in sufficient quantity to be collected and made into candles. This cucurbit has been lately introduced into European gardens. According to Bretschneider,[5] it can be identified in a Chinese book of the fifth century and is mentioned as cultivated in Chinese writings of the seventeenth and eighteenth centuries. In 1503–08, Ludovico di Varthema [6] describes this gourd in India under the name *comolanga*. In 1859, Naudin [7] says it is much esteemed in southern Asia, particularly in China, and that the size of its fruit, its excellent keeping qualities, the excellence of its flesh and the ease of its culture should long since have brought it into garden culture. He had seen two varieties: one, the cylindrical, ten to sixteen inches long and one specimen twenty-four inches long by eight to ten inches in diameter, from Algiers; the other, an ovoid fruit, shorter, yet large, from China. The long variety was grown at the New York Agricultural Experiment Station in 1884 from seed from France. The fruit is oblong-cylindrical, resembling very closely a watermelon when unripe but when ripe covered with a heavy glaucous bloom.

This plant is recorded in herbariums as from the Philippine Islands, New Guinea, New Caledonia, Fiji Islands, Tahiti, New Holland and southern China and as cultivated in Japan and in China.[8]

This species is the *Cumbulam* of Rheede *Hort. Mal.*, 8, p. 5, t. 3; the *Camolenga* of Rumphius *Amb.* 5, 395, t. 143; the *Cucurbita Pepo* of Loureiro *Cochinch.* 593.

Berberis angulosa Wall. *Berberideae.* BARBERRY.

India. This is a rare Himalayan species with the largest flowers and fruit of any of the thirteen species found on that range. In Sikkim, it is a shrub four or more feet in height, growing at an elevation of from 11,000 to 13,000 feet, where it forms a striking object in autumn from the rich golden and red coloring of its foliage. The fruit is edible and less acid than that of the common species.[9]

B. aquifolium Pursh. MAHONIA. MOUNTAIN GRAPE. OREGON GRAPE.

Western North America. This shrub is not rare in cultivation as an ornamental. It has deep blue berries in clusters somewhat resembling the frost grape and the flavor is strongly acid. The berries are used as food, and the juice when fermented makes, on the addition of sugar, a palatable and wholesome wine. It is said not to have much value as a fruit. It is common in Utah and its fruit is eaten, being highly prized for its medicinal

---

[1] Firminger, T. A. C. *Gard. Ind.* 126. 1874.

[2] Mueller, F. *Sel. Pl.* 67. 1891.

[3] Robinson, W. *Parks, Gard. Paris* 503. 1878.

[4] *Bon Jard.* 432. 1882.

[5] Bretschneider, E. *Bot. Sin.* 59, 78, 83, 85. 1882.

[6] Jones, J. W. *Trav. Varthema* 1503–08. Hakl. Soc. Ed. 161. 1863.

[7] Naudin *Revue Cucurbit Ann. Sci. Nat.* 4th Ser., t. 12, p. 10.

[8] De Candolle, A. & C. *Monog.* 3:513. 1881.

[9] *Gard. and For.* 443. 1889.

properties.[1] The acid berry is made into confections and eaten as an antiscorbutic, under the name mountain grape.

B. aristata DC. NEPAL BARBERRY.

East Indies. The Nepal barberry produces purple fruits covered with a fine bloom, which in India are dried in the sun like raisins and used like them at the dessert.[2] It is native to the mountains of Hindustan and is called in Arabic *aarghees*.[3] The plants are quite hardy and fruit abundantly in English gardens. Downing cultivated it in America but it gave him no fruit.[4] In Nepal, the berries are dried by the Hill People and are sent down as raisins to the plains.[5]

B. asiatica Roxb. ASIATIC BARBERRY.

Region of Himalayas. According to Lindley, the fruit is round, covered with a thick bloom and has the appearance of the finest raisins. The berries are eaten in India.[6] The plants are quite hardy and fruit abundantly in English gardens.

B. buxifolia Lam. MAGELLAN BARBERRY.

This evergreen shrub is found native from Chile to the Strait of Magellan. According to Dr. Philippi, it is the best of the South American species; the berries are quite large, black, hardly acid and but slightly astringent. The fruit, says Sweet,[7] is used in England both green and ripe as are gooseberries, for making pies and tarts. In Valdivia and Chiloé, provinces of Chile, they are frequently consumed. It has ripened fruit at Edinburgh, and Mr. Cunningham [8] enthusiastically says it is as large as the Hamburg grape and equally good to eat. It is also grown in the gardens of the Horticultural Society, London, from which cions appear to have been distributed. Under the name Black Sweet Magellan, it is noticed as a variety in Downing. It was introduced into England about 1828.

B. canadensis Pursh. AMERICAN BARBERRY.

North America; a species found in the Alleghenies of Virginia and southward but not in Canada.[9] The berries are red and of an agreeable acidity.[10]

B. darwinii Hook. DARWIN'S BARBERRY.

Chile and Patagonia. In Devonshire, England, the cottagers preserve the berries when ripe, and a party of school children admitted to where there are plants in fruit will clear the bushes of every berry as eagerly as if they were black currants.[11]

---

[1] Case *Bot. Index* 10. 1881.

[2] Downing, A. J. *Fr. Fr. Trees Amer.* 244. 1857.

[3] Pickering, C. *Chron. Hist.: Pls.* 708. 1879.

[4] Downing, A. J. *Fr. Fr. Trees Amer.* 244. 1857.

[5] Wight, R. *Illustr. Ind. Bot.* 1:23. 1840. (*B. cristata*)

[6] Brandis, D. *Forest Fl.* 12. 1874.

[7] Sweet, R. *Brit. Flow. Gard.* 1:100. 1831.

[8] Loudon, J. C. *Hort.* 580. 1860. (*B. dulcis*)

[9] Gray, A. *Man. Bot.* 53. 1868.

[10] Pursh, F. *Fl. Amer. Septent.* 1:219. 1814.

[11] *Gard. Chron.* 28:21. 1882.

B. empetrifolia Lam. FUEGIAN BARBERRY.

Region of Magellan Strait. The berry is edible.[1]

B. glauca DC.

New Granada. The berry is edible.[2]

B. lycium Royle. INDIAN BARBERRY.

Himalayan region. In China, the fruit is preserved as in Europe, and the young shoots and leaves are made use of as a vegetable or for infusion as a tea.[3]

B. nepalensis Spreng. MAHONIA.

An evergreen of the Himalayas. The fruits are dried as raisins in the sun and sent down to the plains of India for sale.[4]

B. nervosa Pursh. OREGON GRAPE.

Northwestern America; pine forests of Oregon. The fruit resembles in size and taste that of *B. aquifolium*.[5]

B. pinnata Lag. BLUE BARBERRY.

Mexico; a beautiful, blue-berried barberry very common in New Mexico. It is called by the Mexicans *lena amorilla*. The berries are very pleasant to the taste, being saccharine with a slight acidity.[6]

B. sibirica Pall. SIBERIAN BARBERRY.

Siberia. The berry is edible.[7]

B. sinensis Desf.

China. The berry is edible.[8]

B. tomentosa Ruiz & Pav. HAIRY BARBERRY.

Chile. The berry is edible.[9]

B. trifoliolata Moric.

Western Texas. The bright red, acid berries are used for tarts and are less acid than those of *B. vulgaris*.[10]

B. vulgaris Linn. BARBERRY. JAUNDICE BERRY. PIPRAGE.

Europe and temperate Asia. This barberry is sometimes planted in gardens in England for its fruit. It was early introduced into the gardens of New England and increased so rapidly that in 1754 the Province of Massachusetts passed an act to prevent

---

[1] Baillon, H. *Hist. Pls.* **3**:68. 1874. Note.

[2] Ibid.

[3] Smith, F. P. *Contrib. Mat. Med. China* 37. 1871.

[4] Royle, J. F. *Illustr. Bot. Himal.* **1**:64. 1839.

[5] Case *Bot. Index* 37. 1881.

[6] Bigelow, J. M. *Pacific R. R. Rpt.* **4**:7. 1856.

[7] Baillon, H. *Hist. Pls.* **3**:68. 1874.

[8] Ibid.

[9] Ibid.

[10] Torrey, J. *Bot. U. S. Mex. Bound. Surv.* 31. 1858.

its spreading.[1] The berries are preserved in sugar, in syrup, or candied and are esteemed by some. They are also occasionally pickled in vinegar, or used for flavoring. There are varieties with yellow, white, purple, and black fruits. A celebrated preserve is made from a stoneless variety at Rouen, France. The leaves were formerly used to season meat in England.[2] The berries are imported from Afghanistan into India under the name of currant. A black variety was found by Tournefort[3] on the bank of the Euphrates, the fruit of which is said to be of delicious flavor.

Bertholletia excelsa Humb. & Bonpl. *Myrtaceae.* AMAZON NUT. ALMONDS OF THE AMAZON. BRAZIL NUT. BUTTERNUT. CREAMNUT. PARA NUT. NIGGERTOE.

Brazil. This is one of the most majestic trees of Guiana, Venezuela and Brazil. It furnishes the triangular nuts of commerce everywhere used as a food. It was first described in 1808.[4] An oil is expressed from the kernels and the bark is used in caulking ships.

Besleria violacea Aubl. *Gesneraceae.*

Guiana. The purple berry is edible.[5]

Beta vulgaris Linn. *Chenopodiaceae.* BEET. CHARD. CHILIAN BEET. LEAF-BEET. MANGEL. MANGEL WURZEL. MANGOLD. ROMAN KALE. SEA BEET. SEA-KALE BEET. SICILIAN BEET. SPINACH BEET. SUGAR BEET. SWISS CHARD.

Europe and north Africa. The beet of the garden is essentially a modern vegetable. It is not noted by either Aristotle[6] or Theophrastus,[7] and, although the root of the chard is referred to by Dioscorides and Galen,[8] yet the context indicates medicinal use. Neither Columella, Pliny nor Palladius mentions its culture, but Apicius,[9] in the third century, gives recipes for cooking the root of *Beta*, and Athenaeus,[10] in the second or third century, quotes Diphilus of Siphnos as saying that the beet-root was grateful to the taste and a better food than the cabbage. It is not mentioned by Albertus Magnus[11] in the thirteenth century, but the word *bete* occurs in English recipes for cooking in 1390.

Barbarus,[12] who died in 1493, speaks of the beet as having a single, long, straight, fleshy, sweet root, grateful when eaten, and Ruellius,[13] in France, appropriates the same description in 1536, as does also Fuchsius[14] in 1542; the latter figures the root as described

[1] *Hist. Mass. Hort. Soc.* 30. 1880.
[2] Gerarde, J. *Herb.* 1326. 1633 or 1636.
[3] Tournefort *Voy. Levant* 2:168. 1718.
[4] Humboldt, A. *Views Nat.* 179. 1850.
[5] Don, G. *Hist. Dichl. Pls.* 4:652. 1838.
[6] *Scaliger* Aristotle 29. 1566.
[7] Theophrastus *Hist. Pl.* Bodaeus Ed. 778. 1644.
[8] Fuchsius *Hist. Stirp.* 807. 1542.
[9] Apicius *Opson.* lib. 3, c. 2, p. 2.
[10] Turre, *Dryadum* 443. 1685.
[11] Albertus Magnus *Veg.* Jessen Ed. 1867.
[12] Dioscorides Ruellius Ed. 124. 1529.
[13] Ruellius *Nat. Stirp.* 481. 1536.
[14] Fuchsius *Hist. Stirp.* 807. 1542.

by Barbarus, having several branches and small fibres. In 1558, Matthiolus[1] says the white and black chards are common in Italian gardens but that in Germany they have a red beet with a swollen, turnip-like root which is eaten. In 1570, Pena and Lobel[2] speak of the same plant but apparently as then rare, and, in 1576, Lobel[3] figures this beet, and this figure shows the first indication of an improved form, the root portion being swollen in excess over the portion by the collar. This beet may be considered the prototype of the long, red varieties. In 1586, Camerarius[4] figures a shorter and thicker form, the prototype of our half-long blood beets. This same type is figured by Daleschamp,[5] 1587, and also a new type, the *Beta Romana*, which is said in Lyte's *Dodoens*, 1586,[6] to be a recent acquisition. It may be considered as the prototype of our turnip or globular beets.

Another form is the flat-bottomed red, of which the Egyptian and the Bassano of Vilmorin, as figured, may be taken as the type. The Bassano was to be found in all the markets of Italy in 1841,[7] and the Egyptian was a new sort about Boston in 1869.[8] Nothing is known concerning the history of this type.

The first appearance of the improved beet is recorded in Germany about 1558 and in England about 1576, but the name used, Roman beet, implies introduction from Italy, where the half-long type was known ·in 1584. We may believe Ruellius's reference in 1536 to be for France. In 1631, this beet was in French gardens under the name, *Beta rubra pastinaca*,[9] and the culture of " betteraves " was described in *Le Jardinier Solitaire*, 1612. Gerarde[10] mentions the " Romaine beete " but gives no figure. In 1665, in England, only the Red Roman was listed by Lovell,[11] and the Red beet was the only kind noticed by Townsend,[12] a seedsman, in 1726, and a second sort, the common Long Red, is mentioned in addition by Mawe,[13] 1778, and by Bryant,[14] 1783. In the United States, one kind only was in McMahon's[15] catalog of 1806 — the Red beet, but in 1828 four kinds are offered for sale by Thorburn.[16] At present, Vilmorin[17] describes seventeen varieties and names and partly describes many others.

---

[1] Matthiolus *Comment.* 249. 1558.

[2] Pena and Lobel *Advers.* 93. 1570.

[3] Lobel *Obs.* 124. 1576.

[4] Camerarius *Epit.* 255. 1586.

[5] Dalechamp *Hist. Gen. Pl.* (Lugd.) 532. 1587.

[6] Dodoens *Herb.* 54. 1586. Lyte Ed.

[7] *Gard. Chron.* 183. 1841.

[8] *Trans. Mass. Hort. Soc.* 70. 1869.

[9] Laurembergius *Hort.* 191. 1632.

[10] Gerarde, J. *Herb.* 251. 1597.

[11] Lovell *Herb.* 40. 1665.

[12] Townsend *Seedsman* 22. 1726.

[13] Mawe and Abercrombie *Univ. Gard. Bot.* 1778.

[14] Bryant *Fl. Diet.* 26. 1783.

[15] McMahon, B. *Amer. Gard. Cal.* 580. 1806.

[16] Thorburn *Cat.* 1828.

[17] Vilmorin *Les Pls. Potag.* 35. 1883.

CHARD.

Chard was the *beta* of the ancients and of the Middle Ages. Red chard was noticed by Aristotle [1] about 350 B. C. Theophrastus [2] knew two kinds — the white, called *Sicula*, and the black (or dark green), the most esteemed. Dioscorides [3] also records two kinds. Eudemus, quoted by Athenaeus,[4] in the second century, names four; the sessile, the white, the common and the dark, or swarthy. Among the Romans, chard finds frequent mention, as by Columella,[5] Pliny,[6] Palladius [7] and Apicius.[8] In China is was noticed in writings of the seventh, eighth, fourteenth, sixteenth and seventeenth centuries;[9] in Europe, by all the ancient herbalists.

Chard has no Sanscrit name. The ancient Greeks called the species *teutlion;* the Romans, *beta;* the Arabs, *selg;* the Nabateans, *silq*.[10] Albertus Magnus,[11] in the thirteenth century, uses the word *acelga*, the present name in Portugal and Spain.

The wild form is found in the Canary Isles, the whole of the Mediterranean region as far as the Caspian, Persia and Babylon, perhaps even in western India, as also about the sea-coasts of Britain.[12] It has been sparingly introduced into kitchen-gardens for use as a chard.[13] The red, white, and yellow forms are named from quite early times; the red by Aristotle, the white and dark green by Theophrastus and Disocorides. In 1596, Bauhin [14] describes dark, red, white, yellow, chards with a broad stalk and the sea-beet. These forms, while the types can be recognized, yet have changed their appearance in our cultivated plants, a greater compactness and development being noted as arising from the selection and cultivation which has been so generally accorded in recent times. Among the varieties Vilmorin describes are the White, Swiss, Silver, Curled Swiss, and Chilian.

SEA BEET.

The leaves of the sea beet form an excellent chard and in Ireland are collected from the wild plant and used for food;[15] in England the plant is sometimes cultivated in gardens.[16] This form has been ennobled by careful culture, continued until a mangold was obtained.[17]

---

[1] Scaliger *Aristotle* 69. 1566.

[2] Theophrastus *Hist. Pl.* Bodaeus Ed. 778. 1644.

[3] Matthiolus *Comment.* 248. 1558.

[4] Turre *Dryadum* 442. 1685.

[5] Columella lib. 10, c. 251; lib. 11, c. 3, etc.

[6] Pliny lib. 19, c. 40.

[7] Palladius lib. 3, c. 24.

[8] Apicius *Opson.* lib. 3, c. 2, p. 2.

[9] Bretschneider, E. *Bot. Sin.* 53, 59, 79, 83. 1882.

[10] De Candolle, A. *Orig. Pls. Cult.* 58. 1885.

[11] Albertus Magnus *Veg.* Jessen Ed. 78. 1867.

[12] Morton *Cyc. Agr.* 1:234. 1869.

[13] Targioni-Tozzetti *Trans. Hort. Soc. Lond.* 147. 1854.

[14] Bauhin, C. *Phytopinax* 190. 1596.

[15] Johnson, C. P. *Useful Pls. Gt. Brit.* 215. 1862.

[16] Morton *Cyc. Agr.* 1:234. 1869.

[17] *Agr. Gazette* 218. 1879.

SWISS CHARD.

Swiss chard is deemed by Ray to have been known to Gerarde, 1597, for Gerarde, in his *Herball*, indicates the sportive character of the seed as to color and mentions a height which is attained only by this plant. He says of it, " another sort hereof that was brought unto me from beyond the seas," and particularly notices the great breadth of the stalk; but the color particularly noticed is the red sort. Ray gives as a synonym *Beta italica* Parkinson. Swiss chard is quite variable in the stalks, according to the culture received.

SILVER-LEAF BEET.

The silver-leaf beet (*Poirée blonde à carde blanche* Vilm. 1883) is a lighter green form of swiss chard, as described by Vilmorin, but with shorter and much broader stalk. It seems to be a variety within the changes which can be effected by selection and culture and perhaps can be referred to the Chilean type.

CHILEAN BEET.

The chilean beet is a form usually grown for ornamental purposes. The stalks are often very broad and twisted and the colors very clear and distinct, the leaf puckered and blistered as in the Curled Swiss. In the *Gardeners' Chronicle*,[1] 1844, it is said that " these ornamental plants were introduced to Belgium some ten or twelve years previously." It is yellow or red and varies in all the shades of these two colors. In 1651, J. Bauhin[2] speaks of two kinds of chard as novelties: the one, white, with broad ribs; the other, red. He also speaks of a yellow form, differing from the kind with a boxwood-yellow root. In 1655, Lobel[3] describes a chard with yellowish stems, varied with red. The forms now found are described by their names: Crimson-veined Brazilian, Golden-veined Brazilian, Scarlet-ribbed Chilean, Scarlet-veined Brazilian, Yellow-ribbed Chilean and Red-stalked Chilean.

The modern chards are the broad-leaved ones and all must be considered as variables within a type. This type may be considered as the one referred to by Gerarde in 1597, whose " seedes taken from that plant which was altogether of one colour and sowen, doth bring foorth plants of many and variable colours." Our present varieties now come true to color in most instances but some seeds furnish an experience such as that which Gerarde records.

MANGOLD.

Mangolt was the old German name for chard, or rather for the beet species, but in recent times the mangold is a large-growing root of the beet kind used for forage purposes. In the selections, size and the perfection of the root above ground have been important elements, as well as the desire for novelty, and hence we have a large number of very distinct-appearing sorts: the long red, about two-thirds above ground; the olive-shaped, or oval; the globe; and the flat-bottomed Yellow d'Obendorf. The colors to be noted are red, yellow and white. The size often obtained in single specimens is enormous,

---

[1] *Gard. Chron.* 591. 1844. (*B. brasiliensis*)

[2] Bauhin, J. *Hist. Pl.* 2:961. 1651.

[3] Lobel *Stirp. Illustr.* 84. 1655.

a weight of 135 pounds [1] has been claimed in California, and Gasparin in France vouches for a root weighing 132 pounds.

Very little can be ascertained concerning the history of mangolds. They certainly are of modern introduction. Olivier de Serres,[2] in France, 1629, describes a red beet which was cultivated for cattle-feeding and speaks of it as a recent acquisition from Italy. In England, it is said to have arrived from Metz [3] in 1786; but there is a book advertised of which the following is the title: *Culture and Use of the Mangel Wurzel, a Root of Scarcity*, translated from the French of the Abbé de Commerell, by J. C. Lettson, with colored plates, third edition, 1787,[4] by which it would appear that it was known earlier. McMahon [5] records the mangold as in American culture in 1806. Vilmorin describes sixteen kinds and mentions many others.

SUGAR BEET.

The sugar beet is a selected form from the common beet and scarcely deserves a separate classification. Varieties figured by Vilmorin are all of the type of the half-long red, and agree in being mostly underground and in being very or quite scaly about the collar. The sugar beet has been developed through selection of the roots of high sugar content for the seedbearers. The sugar beet industry was born in France in 1811, and in 1826 the product of the crop was 1,500 tons of sugar. The use of the sugar beet could not, then, have preceded 1811; yet in 1824 five varieties, the *grosse rouge, petite rouge, rouge ronde, jaune* and *blanche* are noted [6] and the French Sugar, or Amber, reached American gardens before 1828.[7] A richness of from 16 to 18 per cent of sugar is now claimed for Vilmorin's new Improved White Sugar.[8]

The discovery of sugar in the beet is credited to Margraff in 1747, having been announced in a memoir read before the Berlin Academy of Sciences.

A partial synonymy of *Beta vulgaris* is as follows:

RED BEETS.

I.

Beta rubra.   Lob. 124.   1576; *Icon.* **1**:248.   1591; Matth. 371.   1598.
B. rubra Romana.   Dod. 620.   1616.
Common Long Red.   Mawe.   1778.
Betterave rouge grosse.   Vilm. 38.   1883.
Long Blood.   Thorb.   1828, 1886.

II.

Beta rubra.   Cam. *Epit.* 256.   1586; Lugd. 535.   1587; Pancov. n. 607.   1673.
Betiola rossa.   Durc. 71.   1617.
Betterave rouge naine.   Vilm. 37.   1883.
Pineapple beet.

---

[1] *U. S. D. A. Rpt.* 597.   1866.

[2] De Candolle, A.   *Geog. Bot.* **2**:831.   1885.

[3] Sinclair, G.   *Hort. Gram. Woburn.* 410.   1824.

[4] Wesley *Nat. Hist. Book Cir.* No. 71.   1886.

[5] McMahon, B.   *Amer. Gard. Cal.* 187.   1806.

[6] Pirolle *L'Hort. Franc.*   1824.

[7] Fessenden *New Amer. Gard.* 40.   1828

[8] Vilmorin *Les Pls. Potag.* 51.   1883.

III.

Beta erythorrhizos Dodo. Lugd. 533. 1587.
Beta rubra radice crassa, alia species. Bauh. J. 2:961. 1651.
B. rubra . . . russa; Beta-rapa. Chabr. 303. 1677.
Turnip-pointed red. Mawe. 1778.
Turnip-rooted red. Bryant 26. 1783.
Early Blood Turnip. Thorb. 1828, 1886.

YELLOW BEETS.
IV.

Beta quarta radice buxea. Caesalp. 1603 from *Mill. Dict.* 1807.
Yellow-rooted. *Mill. Dict.* 1807.
Betterave jaune grosse. Vilm. 41. 1883.

V.

Beta rubra, lutea; Beta-rapa. Chabr. 305. 1677.
Turnip-pointed yellow. Mawe. 1778.
Yellow Turnip. Thorb. 1828.
Betterave jaune ronde sucre. Vilm. 41. 1883.

SEA BEET.
VI.

Beta sylvestris spontanea marina. Lob. *Obs.* 125. 1576.
B. sylvestris maritima. Bauh. *Phytopin.* 191. 1596.
Sea Beet. Ray *Hist.* 1:204. 1686.

WHITE BEET.
VII.

Beta alba lactucae and rumicis folio, etc. *Advers.* 93. 1570.
B. alba vel pallescens, quam Cicla officin. Bauh. *Pin.* 118. 1623.
White Beet. Ray 204. 1686.
Beta cicla. Linn. *Sp.* 322. 1774.
Common White-Leaved. Mawe. 1778.
White-leaved. McMahon 187. 1806.
Spinach-Beet. Loudon. 1860.
Poirée blonde ou commune. Vilm. 421. 1883.

SWISS CHARD.
VIII.

Beta alba? 3. Gerarde 251. 1597.
The Sicilian Broad-Leaved Beet. Ray 205. 1686.
White Beet. Townsend. 1726.
Chard, or Great White Swiss Beet. Mawe. 1778.
Swiss, or Chard Beet. *Mill. Dict.* 1807.
Swiss Chard, or Silver Beet. Buist. 1851.
Silver-Leaf Beet. Burr 292. 1863.
Poirée à carde blanche. Vilm. 421. 1883.

SILVER-LEAF BEET.

IX.

Poirée blonde à carde blanche. Vilm. 1883.

CURLED SWISS CHARD.

X.

Curled-Leaf Beet. Burr 291. 1863.
Beck's Seakale Beet. Gard. Chron. 1865.
Poireé à blanche frisee. Vilm. 1883.

Betula alba Linn. *Cupuliferae.* CANOE BIRCH. LADY BIRCH. PAPER BIRCH. WHITE
BIRCH.

Europe, northern Asia and North America. The bark, reduced to powder, is eaten
by the inhabitants of Kamchatka, beaten up with the ova of the sturgeon,[1] and the inner
bark is ground into a meal and eaten in Lapland in times of dearth.[2] Church[3] says sawdust of birchwood is boiled, baked and then mixed with flour to form bread in Sweden
and Norway. In Alaska, says Dall,[4] the soft, new wood is cut fine and mingled with
tobacco by the economical Indian. From the sap, a wine is made in Derbyshire, England,
and, in 1814, the Russian soldiers near Hamburg intoxicated themselves with this fermented sap. The leaves are used in northern Europe as a substitute for tea,[5] and the
Indians of Maine make from the leaves of the American variety a tea which is relished.
At certain seasons, the sap contains sugar. In Maine, the sap is sometimes collected in
the spring and made into vinegar.

B. lenta Linn. BLACK BIRCH. CHERRY BIRCH. MAHOGANY BIRCH. SWEET BIRCH.

North America. The sap, in Maine, is occasionally converted into vinegar.

B. nigra Linn. RED BIRCH. RIVER BIRCH.

From Massachusetts to Virginia. The sap contains sugar in the spring, according
to Henfrey.[6]

Billardiera mutabilis Salisb. *Pittosporeae.* APPLE-BERRY.

Australia. This species is said by Backhouse[7] to have pleasant, subacid fruit.

Bixa orellana Linn. *Bixineae.* ANNATTO.

South America. This shrub furnishes in the reddish pulp surrounding the seeds
the annatto of commerce, imported from South America and used extensively for coloring
cheese and butter. The culture of this plant is chiefly carried on in Guadeloupe and
Cayenne, where the product is known as *roucou*. It is grown also in the Deccan and

---

[1] Royle, J. F. *Illustr. Bot. Himal.* 1:345. 1839.
[2] Johnson, C. P. *Useful Pls. Gt. Brit.* 241. 1862.
[3] Church, A. H. *Food* 71. 1887.
[4] Dall, W. H. *U. S. D. A. Rpt.* 176. 1868.
[5] Johnson, C. P. *Useful Pls. Gt. Brit.* 241. 1862.
[6] Henfrey, A. *Bot.* 356. 1870.
[7] Syme, J. T. *Treas. Bot.* 1:144. 1870.

other parts of India and the Eastern Archipelago, in the Pacific Islands, Brazil, Peru, and Zanzibar, as Simmonds [1] writes.

Blepharis edulis Pers. *Acanthaceae.*

Persia, Northwestern India, Nubia and tropical Arabia. The leaves are eaten crude.[2]

Blighia sapida Kon. *Sapindaceae.* AKEE FRUIT.

Guinea. This small tree is a native of Guinea and was carried to Jamaica by Captain Bligh [3] in 1793. It is much esteemed in the West Indies as a fruit. The fruit is fleshy, of a red color tinged with yellow, about three inches long by two in width and of a three-sided form. When ripe, it splits down the middle of each side, disclosing three shining, jet-black seeds, seated upon and partly immersed in a white, spongy substance called the aril. This aril is the eatable part. Fruits ripened in the hothouses of England have not been pronounced very desirable. Unger [4] says, however, the seeds have a fine flavor when cooked and roasted with the fleshy aril.

Boerhaavia repens Linn. *Nyctagineae.* HOG-WEED.

Cosmopolitan tropics. According to Ainslie,[5] the leaves are eaten in India, and Graham says in the Deccan it is sometimes eaten by the natives as greens. It is a common and troublesome weed of India. The young leaves are eaten by the natives as greens and made into curries.[6]

Bomarea edulis Herb. *Amaryllideae.* WHITE JERUSALEM ARTICHOKE.

Tropical America. The roots are round and succulent and when boiled are said to be a light and delicate food. A farinaceous or mealy substance is also made of them, from which cream is made, wholesome and very agreeable to the taste. The roots are sold under the name of white Jerusalem artichoke.[7]

B. glaucescens Baker.

Ecuador. The fruit is sought after by children on account of a sweet, gelatinous pulp, resembling that of the pomegranate, in which the seeds are imbedded.[8]

B. salsilla Mirb.

Chile. The tubers are available for human food.[9]

Bombax ceiba Linn. *Malvaceae.* GOD-TREE. SILK-COTTON TREE.

South America. The leaves and buds, when young and tender, are very mucilaginous, like okra, and are boiled as greens by the negroes of Jamaica.[10] The fleshy petals of the

[1] Simmonds, P. L. *Trop. Agr.* 387, 388. 1889.
[2] Pickering, C. *Chron. Hist. Pls.* 425. 1879.
[3] Rhind, W. *Hist. Veg. King.* 367. 1855.
[4] Unger, F. *U. S. Pat. Off. Rpt.* 315. 1859.
[5] Ainslie, W. *Mat. Ind.* 2:205. 1826.
[6] Wight, R. *Icon. Pls.* 874. 1840–1853.
[7] Andrews, C. *Bot. Reposit.* 10:649. 1797. (*Alstroemeria edulis*)
[8] Hooker, W. J. *Bot. Misc.* 2:198, 238. 1831. (*Alstroemeria dulcis*)
[9] *Gard. Chron.* **17**:76. 1882.
[10] Lunan, J. *Hort. Jam.* **1**:243. 1814.

flowers are sometimes prepared as food by the Chinese.[1] The tree is called god-tree in the West Indies, where it is native.

B. malabaricum DC. COTTON TREE.

East Indies, Malay and China. The calyx of the flower-bud is eaten as a vegetable.[2]

B. septenatum Jacq.

Tropical America. The plant furnishes a green vegetable.[3]

Bongardia rauwolfii C. A. Mey. *Berberideae.*

Greece and the Orient. This plant was noticed as early as 1573 by Rauwolf, who spoke of it as the true *chrysogomum* of Dioscorides. The Persians roast or boil the tubers and use them as food, while the leaves are eaten as are those of sorrel.[4]

Boottia cordata Wall. *Hydrocharideae.*

A water plant of Burma. All the green parts are eaten by the Burmese as pot-herbs, for which purpose they are collected in great quantity and carried to the market at Ava.[5]

Boquila trifoliata Decne. *Berberideae.*

Chile. The berries, about the size of a pea, are eaten in Chile.[6] It is commonly called in Chile, *baquil-blianca.*

Borago officinalis Linn. *Boragineae.* BORAGE. COOL-TANKARD. TALEWORT.

Europe, North Africa and Asia Minor. This plant has been distributed throughout the whole of southern and middle Europe even in the humblest gardens and is now cultivated likewise in India, North America and Chile. Its leaves and flowers were used by the ancient Greeks and Romans for cool tankards. The Greeks called it *euphrosynon*, for, when put in a cup of wine, it made those who drank it merry. It has been used in England since the days of Parkinson. In Queen Elizabeth's time, both the leaves and flowers were eaten in salads. It is at present cultivated for use in cooling drinks and is used by some as a substitute for spinach. The leaves contain so much nitre that when dry they burn like match paper.[7] The leaves also serve as a garnish and are likewise pickled. In India, it is cultivated by Europeans for use in country beer to give it a pleasant flavor.[8] Borage is enumerated by Peter Martyr [9] as among the plants cultivated at Isabela Island by the companions of Columbus. It appears in the catalogs of our American seedsmen and is mentioned by almost all of the earlier writers of gardening. The flowering parts of borage are noted or figured by nearly all of the ancient herbalists.

---

[1] Williams, S. W. *Mid. King.* 1:284. 1848.

[2] Brandis, D. *Forest Fl.* 31. 1874.

[3] Unger, F. *U. S. Pat. Off. Rpt.* 359. 1859.

[4] Black, A. A. *Treas. Bot.* 1:156. 1870.

[5] Wallich, N. *Pl. Asiat.* 1:52. Tab. 65. 1830.

[6] Black, A. A. *Treas. Bot.* 1:157. 1870.

[7] McIntosh, C. *Book Gard.* 2:234. 1855.

[8] Ainslie, W. *Mat. Ind.* 2:145. 1826.

[9] Eden *Hist. Trav.* 18. 1577.

Borassus flabellifer Linn. *Palmae.* DOUB PALM. PALMYRA PALM. TALA PALM. WINE
PALM.

A common tree in a large part of Africa south of the Sahara and of tropical eastern
Asia. The fruits, but still more the young seedlings, which are raised on a large scale
for that purpose, are important as an article of food.[1] Livingstone[2] says the fibrous pulp
around the large nuts is of a sweet, fruity taste and is eaten. The natives bury the
nuts until the kernels begin to sprout; when dug up and broken, the inside resembles
coarse potatoes and is prized in times of scarcity as nutritious food. During several
months of the year, palm wine, or *sura*, is obtained in large quantities and when fresh
is a pleasant drink, somewhat like champagne, and not at all intoxicating, though, after
standing a few hours, it becomes highly so. Grant[3] says on the Upper Nile the doub palm
is called by the negroes *m'voomo*, and the boiled roots are eaten in famines by the
Wanyamwezi.

The Palmyra palm is cultivated in India. The pulp of the fruit is eaten raw or roasted,
and a preserve is made of it in Ceylon. The unripe seeds and particularly the young
plant two or three months old are an important article of food. But the most valuable
product of the tree is the sweet sap which runs from the peduncles, cut before flowering, and
is collected in bamboo tubes or in earthern pots tied to the cut peduncle. Nearly all of
the sugar made in Burma and a large proportion of that made in south India is the produce
of this palm. The sap is also fermented into toddy and distilled.[4] Drury[5] says the fruit
and fusiform roots are used as food by the poorer classes in the Northern Circars.
Firminger[6] says the insipid, gelatinous, pellucid pulp of the fruit is eaten by the natives
but is not relished by Europeans. A good preserve may, however, be made from it and is
often used for pickling.

Borbonia cordata Linn. *Leguminosae.*

South Africa. At the Cape of Good Hope, in 1772, Thunberg[7] found the country
people making tea of the leaves.

Boscia senegalensis Lam. *Capparideae.*

African tropics. The seeds are eaten by the negroes of the Senegal.[8]

Boswellia frereana Birdw. *Burseraceae.*

Tropics of Africa. Though growing wild, the trees are carefully watched and even
sometimes propagated. The resin is used in the East for chewing as is that of the mastic
tree.[9]

---

[1] Brandis, D. *Forest Fl.* 545. 1874.

[2] Livingstone, D. and C. *Exped. Zambesi* 112. 1866. (*B. aethiopium*)

[3] Pickering, C. *Chron. Hist. Pls.* 125. 1879. (*B. aethiopium*)

[4] Brandis, D. *Forest Fl.* 544. 1874.

[5] Drury, H. *Useful Pls. Ind.* 84. 1858.

[6] Firminger, T. A. C. *Gard. Ind.* 172. 1874.

[7] Thunberg, C. P. *Trav.* 1:128. 1795.

[8] Baillon, H. *Hist. Pls.* 3:169. 1874.

[9] Flückiger and Hanbury *Pharm.* 153. 1879.

B. serrata Roxb. FRANKINCENSE TREE.

India. In times of famine, the Khnoods and Woodias live on a soup made from the fruit of this tree.[1]

Botrychium virginianum Swartz. *Ophioglassaceae.* RATTLESNAKE FERN.

This large, succulent fern is boiled and eaten in the Himalayas as well as in New Zealand.

Boucerosia incarnata N. E. Br. *Asclepiadeae.*

South Africa. The Hottentots eat it, says Thunberg,[2] after peeling off the edges and prickles.

Bouea burmanica Griff. *Anacardiaceae.*

Burma. The fruit is eaten, that of one variety being intensely sour, of another insipidly sweet.[3]

Bourreria succulenta Jacq. *Boragineae.* CURRANT TREE.

West Indies. The berries are the size of a pea, shining, saffron or orange-colored, pulpy, sweet, succulent and eatable.[4]

Brabejum stellatifolium Linn. *Proteaceae.* WILD CHESTNUT.

South Africa. Thunberg[5] says the Hottentots eat the fruit of this shrub and that it is sometimes used by the country people instead of coffee, the outside rind being taken off and the fruit steeped in water to deprive it of its bitterness; it is then boiled, roasted and ground like coffee.

Brachistus solanaceus Benth. & Hook. f. *Solanaceae.*

Nicaragua. This perennial merits trial culture on account of its large, edible tubers.[6]

Brachystegia appendiculata Benth. *Leguminosae.*

Tropical Africa. The seeds are eaten.[7]

Brachystelma sp.? *Asclepiadeae.*

South Africa. This genus furnishes edible roots in South Africa and those of some species are esteemed as a preserve by the Dutch inhabitants.[8]

Brahea dulcis Mart. *Palmae.*

Peru. This Mexican palm, called *palma dulce* and *soyale*, has a fruit which is a succulent drupe of a yellow color and cherry-size, sweet and edible.[9]

---

[1] Drury, H. *Useful Pls. Ind.* 95. 1873.

[2] Thunberg, C. P. *Trav.* 2:140. 1796. (*Stapelia incarnata*)

[3] Pickering, C. *Chron. Hist. Pls.* 112. 1879. (*B. oppositifolia*)

[4] Lunan, J. *Hort. Jam.* 1:255. 1814.

[5] Thunberg, C. P. *Trav.* 1:129. 1795.

[6] Mueller, F. *Sel. Pls.* 521. 1891. (*Witheringia solanacea*)

[7] Britten, J. *Treas. Bot.* 2:1271. 1876.

[8] Carruthers, W. *Treas. Bot.* 1:164. 1870.

[9] Seemann, B. *Pop. Hist. Palms* 126. 1856.

B. serrulata H. Wendl. SAW PALMETTO.

Southern United States.   A fecula was formerly prepared from the pith by the Florida Indians.

Brasenia schreberi J. F. Gmel. *Nymphaeaceae.* WATER SHIELD.

India, Japan, Australia, Tropical Africa and North America.   The tuberous root-stocks are collected by the California Indians for food.[1]

Brassica. *Cruciferae.* BORECOLE. BROCCOLI. BRUSSELS SPROUTS. CABBAGE. CAULI-
FLOWER.   CHARLOCK.   CHINESE CABBAGE.   COLLARDS.   KALE.   KOHL-RABI.
MUSTARD.   PORTUGAL CABBAGE.   RAPE.   RED CABBAGE.   RUTABAGA.   SAVOY
CABBAGE.   TURNIPS.

This genus, in its cultivated species and varieties, assumes protean forms.   In the cabbage section we have the borecoles and kales, which come nearest to the wild form; green and red cabbage with great, single heads; the savoys with their blistered and wrinkled leaves; brussels sprouts with numerous little heads; broccolis and the cauliflowers with their flowers in an aborted condition and borne in a dense corymb; the stalked cabbage of Jersey, which sometimes attains a height of 16 feet; the Portuguese *couve tronchuda* with the ribs of its leaves greatly thickened; and kohl-rabi.   All of these vegetables are referred by Darwin[2] to *B. oleracea* Linn.   The other cultivated forms of the genus are descended, according to the view adopted by some, from two species, *B. napus* Linn. and *B. rapa* Linn.; but, according to other botanists, from three species; while others again strongly suspect that all these forms, both wild and cultivated, ought to be ranked as a single species.   The genus, as established by Bentham, also includes the mustards.

B. alba Boiss. WHITE MUSTARD.

Europe and the adjoining portions of Asia.   The cultivated plant appears to have been brought from central Asia to China, where the herbage is pickled in winter or used in spring as a pot-herb.[3]   In 1542, Fuchsius,[4] a German writer, says it is planted everywhere in gardens.   In 1597, in England, Gerarde[5] says it is not common but that he has distributed the seed so that he thinks it is reasonably well known.   It is mentioned in American gardens in 1806.[6]   The young leaves, cut close to the ground before the formation of the second series or rough leaves appear, form an esteemed salad.

B. campestris Linn. TURNIP. RAPE. RUTABAGA.

TURNIP.

The turnip, says Unger,[7] is derived from a species growing wild at the present day in Russia and Siberia as well as on the Scandinavian peninsula.   From this, in course

---

[1] Brewer and Watson *Bot. Cal.* 1:16. 1880. (*B. peltata*)

[2] Darwin, C. *Ans. Pls. Domest.* 1:341, 342. 1893.

[3] Smith, F. P. *Contrib. Mat. Med. China* 197. 1871.

[4] Fuchsius *Hist. Stirp.* 537. 1542. (*Sinapsis alba*)

[5] Gerarde, J. *Herb.* 190. 1597.

[6] McMahon, B. *Amer. Gard. Cal.* 582. 1806.

[7] Unger, F. *U. S. Pat. Off. Rpt.* 327. 1859.

of cultivation, a race has been produced as *B. campestris* Linn., and a second as *B. rapa* Linn., our white turnip, with many varieties. The cultivation of this plant, indigenous in the region between the Baltic Sea and the Caucasus, was probably first attempted by the Celts and Germans when they were driven to make use of nutritious roots. Buckman was inclined to the belief that *B. campestris* and *B. napus* are but agrarian forms derived from *B. oleracea*. Nowhere, he asserted, are the first two varieties truly wild but both track cultivation throughout Europe, Asia and America. Lindley says this plant, *B. campestris*, has been found apparently wild in Lapland, Spain, the Crimea and Great Britain but it is difficult to say whether or not it is truly wild. When little changed by cultivation, it is the *colsa*, *colza*, or *colsat*, the *chou oléifère* of the French, an oil-reed plant of great value. This is the *colsa* of Belgium, the east of France, Germany and Switzerland but not of other districts, in which the name is applied to rape. Unger[1] states that this plant, growing wild from the Baltic Sea to the Caucasus, is the *B. campestris oleifera* DC. or *B. colza* Lam. and that its culture, first starting in Belgium, is now extensively carried on in Holstein. De Candolle[2] supposes the Swedish turnip is a variety, analogous to the kohl-rabi among cabbages, but with the root swollen instead of the stem. In its original wild condition, it is a flattish, globular root, with a very fine tail, a narrow neck and a hard, deep yellow flesh. Buckman,[3] by seeding rape and common turnips in mixed rows, secured, through hybridization, a small percentage of malformed swedes, which were greatly improved by careful cultivation. If Bentham was correct in classing *B. napus* with *B. campestris*, the result of Buckman's experiment does not carry the rutabaga outside of *B. campestris* for its origin. Don[4] classifies the rutabaga as *B. campestris* Linn. var. *oleifera*, sub. var. *rutabaga*.

The turnip is of ancient culture. Columella,[5] A. D. 42, says the *napus* and the *rapa* are both grown for the use of man and beast, especially in France; the former does not have a swollen but a slender root, and the latter is the larger and greener. He also speaks of the *Mursian gongylis*, which may be the round turnip, as being especially fine. The distinction between the *napus* and the *rapa* was not always held, as Pliny[6] uses the word *napus* generically and says that there are five kinds, the Corinthian, Cleonaeum, Liothasium, Boeoticum and the Green. The Corinthian, the largest, with an almost bare root, grows on the surface and not, as do the rest, under the soil. The Liothasium, also called Thracium, is the hardest. The Boeoticum is sweet, of a notable roundness and not very long as is the Cleonaeum. At Rome, the Amiternian is in most esteem, next the Nursian, and third our own kind (the green?). In another place, under *rapa*, he mentions the broad-bottom (flat?), the globular, and as the most esteemed, those of Nursia. The *napus* of Amiternum, of a nature quite similar to the *rapa*, succeeds best in a cool place. He mentions that the *rapa* sometimes attains a weight of forty pounds. This weight has, however,

---

[1] Unger, F. *U. S. Pat. Off. Rpt.* 327. 1859.
[2] De Candolle, A. P. *Trans. Hort. Soc. Lond.* 5:25. 1824.
[3] Buckman, J. *Treas. Bot.* 1:165. 1870.
[4] Don, G. *Hist. Dichl. Pls.* 1:241. 1831.
[5] Columella lib. 2, c. 10, etc.; 10, c. 421.
[6] Pliny lib. 19, c. 25; lib. 18, c. 34, 35.

been exceeded in modern times. Matthiolus,[1] 1558, had heard of turnips that weighed a hundred pounds and speaks of having seen long and purple sorts that weighed thirty pounds. Amatus Lusitanus,[2] 1524, speaks of turnips weighing fifty and sixty pounds. In England, in 1792, Martyn [3] says the greatest weight that he is acquainted with is thirty-six pounds. In California, about 1850, a turnip is recorded of one hundred pounds weight.[4]

In the fifteenth century, Booth [5] says the turnip had become known to the Flemings and formed one of their principal crops. The first turnips that were introduced into England, he says, are believed to have come from Holland in 1550. In the time of Henry VIII (1509-1547) according to McIntosh,[6] turnips were used baked or roasted in the ashes and the young shoots were used as a salad and as a spinach. Gerarde [7] describes them in a number of varieties, but the first notice of their field culture is by Weston in 1645. Worlidge, 1668, mentions the turnip fly as an enemy of turnips and Houghton speaks of turnips as food for sheep in 1684. In 1686, Ray says they are sown everywhere in fields and gardens. In 1681, Worlidge says they are chiefly grown in gardens but are also grown to some extent in fields. The turnip was brought to America at a very early period. In 1540, Cartier [8] sowed turnip seed in Canada, during his third voyage. They were also cultivated in Virginia in 1609; [9] are mentioned again in 1648; [10] and by Jefferson in 1781. They are said by Francis Higginson [11] to be in cultivation in Massachusetts in 1629 and are again mentioned by William Wood, 1629-33.[12] They were plentiful about Philadelphia in 1707. Jared Sparks [13] planted them in Connecticut in 1747. In 1775, Romans in his *Natural History of Florida* mentions them. They are also mentioned in South Carolina in 1779. In 1779, General Sullivan destroyed the turnips in the Indian fields at the present Geneva, New York, in the course of his invasion of the Indian country. The common flat turnip was raised as a field crop in Massachusetts and New York as early as 1817.

NAVET, OR FRENCH TURNIP.

(*B. napus esculenta* DC.)

This turnip differs from the *Brassica rapa oblonga* DC. by its smooth and glaucous leaves. It surpasses other turnips by the sweetness of its flavor and furnishes white, yellow and black varieties. It is known as the Navet, or French turnip.[14] This was apparently

---

[1] Matthiolus *Comment.* 240. 1558.

[2] Dioscorides. Amatus Lusitanus Ed. 247. 1554.

[3] Martyn *Fl. Rust.* 1792.

[4] Williams, A. *U. S. Pat. Off. Rpt.* 4. 1851.

[5] Booth, W. B. *Treas. Bot.* 1:167. 1870. (*B. rapa*)

[6] McIntosh, C. *Book Gard.* 2:183. 1855.

[7] Gerarde, J. *Herb.* 177, 178. 1597.

[8] Pinkerton *Coll. Voy.* 12:667. 1812.

[9] *True Decl. Va.* 13. 1610. Force Coll. Tracts 3:1844.

[10] *Perf. Desc. of Va.* 4. Force Coll. Tracts 2:1838.

[11] Higginson, Rev. Francis. *New Eng. Plant.* Mass. Hist. Soc. Coll. 1:118. 1806.

[12] Wood, W. *New Eng. Prosp.* 11. 1634. 1st Ed.

[13] Sparks, J. *Essays Husb.* (1747) 13. 1811.

[14] De Candolle, A. P. *Trans. Hort. Soc. Lond.* 5:26, 30. 1824.

the *napa* of Columella.[1] This turnip was certainly known to the early botanists, yet its synonymy is difficult to be traced from the figures. However, the following are correct:

Napus. Trag. 730. 1552; Matth. 240. 1664; Pin. 144. 1561; Cam. *Epit.* 222. 1586; Dod. 674. 1616; Fischer 1646.

Bunias sive napus. Lob. *Icon.* 1:200. 1591.

Bunias silvestris lobelii. Ger. 181. 1597.

Napi. Dur. C. 304. 1617.

Bunias. Bodaeus 733. 1644.

Napus dulcis. Blackw. t. 410. 1765.

Navet petit de Berlin. Vilm. 360. 1883.

Teltow turnip. Vilm. 580. 1885.

The navets are mentioned as under cultivation in England by Worlidge,[2] 1683; as the French turnip by Wheeler,[3] 1763, and in *Miller's Dictionary,* 1807. Gasparin[4] says the *navet de Berlin,* which often acquires a great size, is much grown in Alsace and in Germany. It is grown in China, according to Bretschneider.[5] This turnip was known in the fifth century.

The Common Flat Turnip.
(*B. rapa depressa* DC.)

This turnip has a large root expanding under the origin of the stem into a think, round, fleshy tuber, flattened at the top and bottom. It has white, yellow, black, red or purple and green varieties. It seems to have been known from ancient times and is described and figured by the earlier botanists. The synonymy is as follows:

A. Flattened both above and below.

Rapum. Matth. 240. 1554; Cam. *Epit.* 218. 1586.

Rapum sive rapa. Pin. 143. 1561.

Rapa. Dur. C. 386. 1617.

Navet turnip. Vilm. 583. 1883.

B. Flattened, but pointed below.

Orbiculatum seu turbinatum rapum. Lob. *Icon.* 1:197. 1791.

Rapum. Porta, *Phytognom.* 120. 1591.

Rapum vulgare. Dod. 673. 1616.

Rave d'Auvergne tardive. Vilm.

C. Globular.

Rapum. Trag. 728. 1552.

Rapa, La Rave. Tourn. 113. 1719.

Navet jaune d'Hollande. Vilm. 370. 1883.

Yellow Dutch. Vilm. 588. 1885.

The Long Turnip.
(*B. rapa oblonga* DC.)

This race of turnip differs from the preceding in having a long or oblong tuber tapering to the radicle. It seems an ancient form, perhaps the Cleonaeum of Pliny.

---

[1] Columella lib. 2, c. 10, etc.; 10, c. 421.

[2] Ibid.

[3] Worlidge, J. *Syst. Hort.* 181. 1683.

[4] Gasparin *Cours Agr.* 4:116.

[5] Bretschneider, E. *Bot. Sin.* 78. 1882.

Vulgare rapum alterum. Trag. 729. 1532.
Rapum longum. Cam. *Epit.* 219. 1586.
Rapum tereti, rotunda, oblongaque radici. Lob. *Icon.* **1**:197. 1591.
Rapum oblongius. Dod. 673. 1616.
Rapum sativum rotundum et oblongum. Bauh. J. **2**:838. 1651.
Rapa, La Rave. Tourn. 113. 1719.
Navet de Briollay. Vilm. 372. 1883.

This account by no means embraces all the turnips now known, as it deals with form only and not with color and habits. In 1828, 13 kinds were in Thorburn's *American Seed Catalog* and in 1887, 33 kinds. In France, 12 kinds were named by Pirolle in 1824 and by Petit in 1826. In 1887, Vilmorin's *Wholesale Seed-list* enumerates 31 kinds.

RAPE.

Bentham [1] classes rape with *B. campestris* Linn. and others are disposed to include it as an agrarian form of *B. oleracea* Linn. Darwin [2] says *B. napus* Linn., in which he places rape, " has given rise to two large groups, namely Swedish turnips (by some believed to be of hybrid origin) and colzas, the seeds of which yield oil." It can be believed quite rationally that the Swedish turnip may have originated in its varieties from *B. campestris* and from hybridization with *B. napus*. To this species, Lindley refers some of the rapes, or coles, the *navette, navette d'hiver,* or *rabette* of the French, and the *repo, ruben* or *winter reps* of the Germans, while the summer rapes he refers to *B. praecox*. Rape is used as an oil plant but is inferior to colza. It is also used in a young state as a salad plant. Of this species there is also a fleshy-rooted variety, the Tetlow turnip, or *navet de Berlin petit* of the French, the root long and spindle-shaped, somewhat resembling a carrot. Its culture in England dates from 1790 but it was well known in 1671 and is noticed by Caspar Bauhin in his *Pinax*. It is much more delicate in flavor than our common turnip. In France and Germany, this Tetlow turnip is extensively cultivated. To what extent our common turnips are indebted to the rapes, seems impossible to say, for Metzger, by culture, converted the biennial, or winter rape, into the annual, or summer rape, varieties which Lindley believes to be specifically distinct. The *Bon Jardinier* [3] says, in general, the early turnips of round form and growing above ground belong to *B. napus* and names the Yellow Malta, Yellow Finland and Montmaquy of our catalogs.

Summer rape is referred by Lindley to *B. praecox* Waldst. & Kit. In the east of France, it is called *navette d'été,* or *navette de mai* and by the Germans *sommer reps*. Some botanists refer summer rape to *B. campestris* Linn. and winter rape to *B. napus* Linn. Rape is also referred to *B. rapa* Linn. The evidence is unusually clear, says Darwin,[4] that rape and the turnip belong to the same species, for the turnip has been observed by Koch and Godron to lose its thick roots in uncultivated soil and when rape and turnips are sown together they cross to such a degree that scarcely a single plant comes true. Summer rape seems to be grown to a far less extent than winter rape.

---

[1] Loudon, J. C. *Hort.* 627. 1860.
[2] Darwin, C. *Ans. Pls. Domest.* **1**:344. 1893.
[3] *Bon Jard.* 534, 535. 1882.
[4] Darwin, C. *Ans. Pls. Domest.* **1**:344. 1893.

RUTABAGA.

The rutabaga of the Swedes, the *navet de Suède*, or *chou de Suède*, or *chou rutabaga*, or *chou navet jaune*, of the French was introduced into England somewhere about the end of the eighteenth century. In the *Maine Farmer* of May 15, 1835,[1] a correspondent, John Burston, states that the rutabaga, swedish turnip, or Lapland turnip — for by all these names was it known — was introduced to this country since the commencement of the present century. Six or more varieties are named in all seed catalogs and Burr[2] describes 11 kinds.

The rutabagas of our gardens include two forms, one with white flesh, the other with yellow. The French call these two classes *chou-navets* and rutabagas respectively. The *chou-navet*, or *Brassica napo-brassica communis* DC., has either purple or white roots; the rutabaga, or *B. napo-brassica Ruta-baga* A. P. DC., has a more regular root, round or oval, yellow both without and within.[3] In English nomenclature, while now the two forms are called by a common name, yet formerly the first constituted the turnip-rooted cabbage. In 1806, the distinction was retained in the United States, McMahon[4] describing the turnip-rooted cabbage and the Swedish turnip, or Rutabaga. As a matter of convenience we shall describe these two classes separately.

The first description of the white-rooted form is by Bauhin[5] in his *Prodromus*, 1620, and it is named again in his *Pinax*,[6] 1623, and is called *napo-brassica*. In 1686, Ray[7] apparently did not know it in England, as he quotes Bauhin's name and description, which states that it is cultivated in Bohemia and is eaten, but Morison,[8] in 1669, catalogs it among the plants in the royal gardens. In France, it is named by Tournefort,[9] in 1700, *Brassica radice napiformi*, or *chou-navet*. In 1778, this was called in England turnip-cabbage with the turnip underground and in the United States, in 1806, turnip-rooted cabbage, as noted above. There are three varieties described by Vilmorin[10] under the names *chou-navet*, *chou turnip*, and *chou de Lapland*, one of which is purple at the collar; apparently these same varieties are named by Noisette[11] in 1829. The white and the red-collared were named by Pirolle,[12] in 1824. This class, as Don[13] says in 1831, is little known in English gardens, though not uncommon in French horticulture.

The rutabaga is said by Sinclair, in the account of the system of husbandry in Scotland, to have been introduced into Scotland about 1781–2, and a quotation in the *Gar-*

[1] *Me. Farm.* May 15, 1835.

[2] Burr, F. *Field, Gard. Veg.* 86. 1863.

[3] De Candolle, A. P. *Trans. Hort. Soc. Lond.* **5**:25. 1824.

[4] McMahon *Amer. Gard. Cal.* 309. 1806.

[5] Bauhin, C. *Prodromus* 54. 1671.

[6] Bauhin, C. *Pin.* **3**:1623.

[7] Ray *Hist. Pl.* 797. 1686.

[8] Morison *Hort. Reg. Bles.* 31. 1669.

[9] Tournefort *Inst.* 219. 1719.

[10] Vilmorin *Les Pls. Potag.* 142. 1883.

[11] Noisette *Man. Jard.* 349. 1829.

[12] Pirolle *L'Hort. Franc.* 1824.

[13] Don, G. *Hist. Dichl. Pls.* **1**:241. 1831.

deners' Chronicle [1] says it was introduced into England in 1790. It is mentioned in 1806 by McMahon as in American gardens, and in 1817 there is a record of an acre of this crop in Illinois.[2] The vernacular names all indicate an origin in Sweden or northern Europe. It is called Swedish turnip or Roota-baga by McMahon, 1806, by *Miller's Dictionary*, 1807, by Cobbett, 1821, and by other authors to the present time. De Candolle, 1821, calls it *navet jaune, navet de Suède, chou de Laponie,* and *chou de Suède;* Pirolle, in 1824, Ruta-baga or *chou navet de Suède,* as does Noisette in 1829. In 1821 Thorburn calls it Ruta-baga, or Russian turnip, and a newspaper writer in 1835 [3] calls it Ruta-baga, Swedish turnip and Lapland turnip. The foreign names given by Don in 1831 include many of the above named and the Italian *navone di Laponia.* Vilmorin [4] in his *Les Plantes Potagères,* 1883, describes three varieties: one with a green collar, one with a purple collar and a third which is early.

B. carinata A. Braun.

This plant is said by Unger [5] to be found wild and cultivated in Abyssinia although it furnishes a very poor cabbage, not to be compared with ours.

B. chinensis Linn.   CHINESE CABBAGE.

The *pe-tsai* of the Chinese is an annual, apparently intermediate between cabbage and the turnip but with much thinner leaves than the former. It is of much more rapid growth than any of the varieties of the European cabbage, so much so, that when sown at midsummer it will ripen seed the same season. Introduced from China in 1837,[6] it has been cultivated and used as greens by a few persons about Paris but it does not appear likely to become a general favorite.[7] It is allied to the kales. Its seeds are ground into a mustard.

But little appears to be recorded concerning the varieties of this cabbage of which the Pak-choi and the Pe-tsai only have reached European culture. It has, however, been long under cultivation in China, as it can be identified in Chinese works on agriculture of the fifth, sixteenth, seventeenth and eighteenth centuries.[8] Loureiro, 1790,[9] says it is also cultivated in Cochin China and varieties are named with white and yellow flowers. The Pak-choi has more resemblance to a chard than to a cabbage, having oblong or oval, dark shining-green leaves upon long, very white and swollen stalks. The Pe-tsai, however, rather resembles a cos lettuce, forming an elongated head, rather full and compact and the leaves are a little wrinkled and undulate at the borders.[10] Both varieties have, however, a common aspect and are annuals.

---

[1] *Gard. Chron.* 346. 1853.

[2] *U. S. Pat. Off. Rpt.* 198. 1854.

[3] *Me. Farm.* May 15, 1835.

[4] Vilmorin *Les Pls. Potag.* 142. 1883.

[5] Unger, F.   *U. S. Pat. Off. Rpt.* 353. 1859.

[6] *Bon Jard.* 533. 1882.

[7] Loudon, J. C.   *Hort.* 627. 1860.

[8] Bretschneider, E.   *Bot. Sin.* 59, 78, 83, 85. 1882.

[9] Loureiro *Fl. Cochin.* 397. 1790.

[10] Vilmorin *Les Pls. Potag.* 407. 1883.

Considering that the round-headed cabbage is the only sort figured by the herbalists, that the pointed-headed early cabbages appeared only at a comparatively recent date, and certain resemblances between Pe-tsai and the long-headed cabbages, it is not an impossible suggestion that these cabbage-forms appeared as the effect of cross-fertilization with the Chinese cabbage. But, until the cabbage family has received more study in its varieties, and the results of hybridization are better understood, no certain conclusion can be reached. It is, however, certain that occasional rare sports, or variables, from the seed of our early, long-headed cabbages show the heavy veining and the limb of the leaf extending down the stalk, suggesting strongly the Chinese type. At present, however, views as to the origin of various types of cabbage must be considered as largely speculative.

B. cretica Lam.

Mediterranean regions. The young shoots were formerly used in Greece.[1]

B. juncea Coss. CHINESE MUSTARD. INDIAN MUSTARD.

The plant is extensively cultivated throughout India, central Africa and generally in warm countries. It is largely grown in south Russia and in the steppes northeast of the Caspian Sea. In 1871–72, British India exported 1418 tons of seed. The oil is used in Russia in the place of olive oil. The powdered seeds furnish a medicinal and culinary mustard.[2]

B. nigra Koch. BLACK MUSTARD.

This is the mustard of the ancients and is cultivated in Alsace, Bohemia, Italy, Holland and England. The plant is found wild in most parts of Europe and has become naturalized in the United States. According to the belief of the ancients, it was first introduced from Egypt and was made known to mankind by Aesculapius, the god of medicine, and Ceres the goddess of seeds. Mustard is mentioned by Pythagoras and was employed in medicine by Hippocrates, 480 B. C. Pliny says the plant grew in Italy without sowing. The ancients ate the young plants as a spinach and used the seeds for supplying mustard.

Black mustard is described as a garden plant by Albertus Magnus[3] in the thirteenth century and is mentioned by the botanists of the sixteenth century. It is, however, more grown as a field crop for its seed, from which the mustard of commerce is derived, yet finds place also as a salad plant. Two varieties are described, the Black Mustard of Sicily and the Large-seeded Black.[4] This mustard was in American gardens in 1806 or earlier. The young plants are now eaten as a salad, the same as are those of *B. alba* and the seeds now furnish the greater portion of our mustard.

B. oleracea acephala DC. BORECOLE. COLE. COLEWORT. KALE.

The chief characteristics of this species of Brassica are that the plants are open, not heading like the cabbages, nor producing eatable flowers like the cauliflowers and broccoli.

---

[1] Unger, F.   *U. S. Pat. Off. Rpt.* 353.   1859.

[2] Flückiger and Hanbury *Pharm.* 64.   1879.

[3] Albertus Magnus *Veg.* 568.   1867.   Jessen Ed.

[4] Vilmorin *Les Pls. Potag.* 356.   1883.

The species has every appearance of being one of the early removes from the original species and is cultivated in many varieties known as kale, greens, sprouts, curlico, with also some distinguishing prefixes as Buda kale, German greens. Some are grown as ornamental plants, being variously curled, laciniated and of beautiful colors. In 1661, Ray journeyed into Scotland and says of the people that " they use much pottage made of coal-wort which they call keal." It is probable that this was the form of cabbage known to the ancients.

The kales represent an extremely variable class of vegetable and have been under cultivation from a most remote period. What the varieties of cabbage were that were known to the ancient Greeks it seems impossible to determine in all cases, but we can hardly question but that some of them belonged to the kales. Many varieties were known to the Romans. Cato,[1] who lived about 201 B. C., describes the Brassica as: the *levis*, large broad-leaves, large-stalked; the *crispa* or *apiacan;* the *lenis*, small-stalked, tender, but rather sharp-tasting. Pliny,[2] in the first century, describes the *Cumana*, with sessile leaf and open head; the *Aricinum*, not excelled in height, the leaves numerous and thick; the *Pompeianum*, tall, the stalk thin at the base, thickening along the leaves; the *brutiana*, with very large leaves, thin stalk, sharp savored; the *sabellica*, admired for its curled leaves, whose thickness exceeds that of the stalk, of very sweet savor; the *Lacuturres*, very large headed, innumerable leaves, the head round, the leaves fleshy; the *Tritianom*, often a foot in diameter and late in going to seed. The first American mention of coleworts is by Sprigley, 1669, for Virginia but this class of the cabbage tribe is probably the one mentioned by Benzoni[3] as growing in Hayti in 1565. In 1806, McMahon[4] recommends for American gardens the green and the brown Aypres and mentions the Red and Thick-leaved Curled, the Siberian, the Scotch and especially recommends Jerusalem kale.

The form of kale known in France as the *chevalier* seems to have been the longest[5] known and we may surmise that its names of *chou caulier* and *caulet* have reference to the period when the word *caulis*, a stalk, had a generic meaning applying to the cabbage race in general. We may hence surmise that this was the common form in ancient times, in like manner as coles or coleworts in more modern times imply the cultivation of kales. This word *coles* or *caulis* is used in the generic sense, for illustration, by Cato, 200 years B. C.; by Columella the first century A. D.; by Palladius in the third; by Vegetius in the fourth century A. D.; and Albertus Magnus in the thirteenth. This race of *chevaliers* may be quite reasonably supposed to be the *levis* of Cato, sometimes called *caulodes*.

According to De Candolle, this race of *chevaliers* has five principal sub-races, of which the following is an incomplete synonymy:

I.

Brassica laevis. Cam. *Epit.* 248. 1586; Matth. *Op.* 366. 1598.
Br. vulgaris sativa. Ger. 244. 1597.
Cavalier branchu. DeCand. *Mem.* 9. 1821.

---

[1] *Script. Rei Rust.* 1:75. 1787.
[2] Pliny lib. 19, c. 41; lib. 20, c. 33.
[3] Benzoni *Hist. New World* Hakl. Soc. Ed. 91. 1857.
[4] McMahon, B. *Amer. Gard. Cal.* 308, 309. 1806.
[5] De Candolle, A. P. *Trans. Hort. Soc. Lond.* 5:7. 1824.

Thousand-headed. Burr 236. 1863.
Chou branchu du Poitou. Vilm. 135. 1883.
Chou mille têtes. Vilm. l. c.

II. a. viridis.

Kol. Roeszl. 87. 1550.
Brassica. Trag. 720. 1552.
Brassica alba vulgaris. Bauh. J. **2**:829. 1651.
Chou vert commun. Decand. *Mem.* 9. 1821.
Cow Cabbage. Burr 232. 1863.
Chou cavalier. Vilm. 134. 1883.
Brassica vulgaris alba. Chabr. 290. 1677.

II. b. rubra.

Brassica primum genus. Fuch. 413. 1542.
Br. rubra prima species. Dalechamp 523. 1587.
Br. rubra. Ger. 244. 1597.
Br. rubra vulgaris. Bauh. J. **2**:831. 1651; Chabr. 270. 1877.
Red cavalier. De Cand. *Mem.* 9. 1821.
Flanders kale. Burr 233. 1863.
Caulet de Flander. Vilm. 134. 1883.

III.

Brassica vulgaris sativa. Lob. *Obs.* 122. 1576; *Icon.* **1**:243. 1591; Dod. 621. 1616.
Br. alba vulgaris. Dalechamp 520. 1587.
Brassica. Dur. C. 76. 1817.
Chou à feuilles de Chêne. De Cand. *Mem.* 10. 1821.
Buda kale. Vilm. 141. 1885.

IV. a.

Brassica secundum genus. Fuch. 414. 1542.
Br. fimbriata. Lob. *Obs.* 124. 1576; *Icon.* 247. 1591.
Br. sativa crispa. Ger. 244. 1597.
Br. crispa. Dod. 622. 1616.
Br. crispa lacinosa. Bauh. J. **2**:832. 1651.
Chou vert frise. De Cand. *Mem.* 10. 1821.
Tall Green Curled. Burr 236. 1863.
Chou frise vert grand. Vilm. 131. 1883.

IV. b.

Brassica crispa, seu apiana. Trag. 721. 1552.
Br. crispa Tragi. Dalechamp 524. 1587.
Br. tenuifolia laciniata. Lob. *Icon.* **1**:246. 1591.
Br. selenoides. Dod. 622. 1616.
Br. tenuissima laciniata. Bauh. J. **2**:832. 1651.
Br. selenoides. Ger. 248. 1597.
Chou plume ou Chou aigrette. De Cand. *Mem.* 11. 1821.
Ornamental kales of our gardens.

V.

Brassica tophosa. Ger. 246. 1547; Bauh. J. **2**:830. 1651.
Br. tophosa Tabernemontano. Chabr. 270. 1677.
Chou palmier. De Cand. *Mem.* 11. 1821; Vilm. 133. 1883.

These forms occur in many varieties, differing in degree only, and of various colors, even variegated. In addition to the above we may mention the proliferous kales, which also occur in several varieties. The following synonyms refer to proliferation only, as the plants in other respects are not similar:—

Brassica asparagoides Dalechampii. Dalechamp 522. 1587.
Brassica prolifera. Ger. 245. 1597.
Brassica prolifera crispa. Ger. 245. 1597.
Cockscomb kale. Burr 232. 1863.
Chou frise prolifère. Vilm. 133. 1883.

THE DWARF KALES.

De Candolle does not bring these into his classification as offering true types, and in this perhaps he is right. Yet, olericulturally considered, they are quite distinct. There are but few varieties. The best marked is the Dwarf Curled, the leaves falling over in a graceful curve and reaching to the ground. This kale can be traced through variations and varieties to our first class, and hence it has probably been derived in recent times through a process of selection, or through the preservation of a natural variation. There is an intermediate type between the Dwarf Curled and the Tall Curled forms in the intermediate Moss Curled.

THE PORTUGAL KALES.

Two kales have the extensive rib system and the general aspect of the Portugal cabbage. These are the *chou brocoli* and the *chou frise de mosbach* of Vilmorin. These bear the same relation to Portugal cabbage that common kale bears to the heading cabbages.

B. oleracea botrytis cymosa DC. BROCCOLI.

The differences between the most highly improved varieties of the broccoli and the cauliflower are very slight; in the less changed forms they become great. Hence two races can be defined, the sprouting broccolis and the cauliflower broccolis. The growth of the broccoli is far more prolonged than that of the cauliflower, and in the European countries it bears its heads the year following that in which it is sown. It is this circumstance that leads us to suspect that the Romans knew the plant and described it under the name *cyma* — "*Cyma a prima sectione praestat proximo vere.*" "*Ex omnibus brassicae generibus suavissima est cyma,*" says Pliny.[1] He also uses the word *cyma* for the seed stalk which rises from the heading cabbage. These excerpts indicate the sprouting broccoli, and the addition of the word *cyma* then, as exists in Italy now, with the word broccoli is used for a secondary meaning, for the tender shoots which at the close of winter are emitted by various kinds of cabbages and turnips preparing to flower.[2]

It is certainly very curious that the early botanists did not describe or figure broccoli. The omission is only explainable under the supposition that it was confounded with the cauliflower, just as Linnaeus brought the cauliflower and the broccoli into one botanical variety. The first notice of broccoli is quoted from *Miller's Dictionary*, edition of 1724,

---

[1] Pliny lib. 19, c. 41; lib. 20, c. 35.
[2] Vilmorin *Les Pls. Potag.* 151. 1883.

in which he says it was a stranger in England until within these five years and was called " sprout colli-flower," or Italian asparagus.[1] In 1729, Switzer[2] says there are several kinds that he has had growing in his garden near London these two years: " that with small, whitish-yellow flowers like the cauliflower; others like the common sprouts and flowers of a colewort; a third with purple flowers; all of which come mixed together, none of them being as yet (at least that I know of) ever sav'd separate." In 1778, Mawe,[3] names the Early Purple, Late Purple, White or Cauliflower-broccoli and the Black. In 1806, McMahon[4] mentions the Roman or Purple, the Neapolitan or White, the Green and the Black. In 1821, Thorburn[5] names the Cape, the White and the Purple, and, in 1828, in his seed list, mentions the Early White, Early Purple, the Large Purple Cape and the White Cape or Cauliflower-broccoli.

The first and third kind of Switzer, 1729, are doubtless the heading broccoli, while the second is probably the sprouting form. These came from Italy and as the seed came mixed, we may assume that varietal distinctions had not as yet become recognized, and that hence all the types of the broccoli now grown have originated from Italy. It is interesting to note, however, that at the Cirencester Agricultural College, about 1860, sorts of broccoli were produced, with other variables, from the seed of wild cabbage.[6]

Vilmorin says:[7] " The sprouting or asparagus broccoli, represents the first form exhibited by the new vegetable when it ceased to be the earliest cabbage and was grown with an especial view to its shoots; after this, by continued selection and successive improvements, varieties were obtained which produced a compact, white head, and some of these varieties were still further improved into kinds which are sufficiently early to commence and complete their entire growth in the course of the same year; these last named kinds are now known as cauliflowers."

B. oleracea bullata gemmifera DC. BRUSSELS SPROUTS.

This vegetable, in this country, grown only in the gardens of amateurs, yet deserving more esteem, has for a type-form a cabbage with an elongated stalk, bearing groups of leaf-buds in the axils of the leaves. Sometimes occurring as a monstrosity, branches instead of heads are developed. Quite frequently an early cabbage, after the true head is removed, will develop small cabbages in the leaf-axils, and thus is formed the *Brassica capitata polycephalos* of Dalechamp,[8] 1587, which he himself describes as a certain unused and rare kind.

Authors[9] have stated that brussels sprouts have been grown from time immemorial about Brussels, in Belgium; but, if this be so, it is strange that they escaped the notice of the

---

[1] Martyn *Miller Gard. Dict.* 1807. Preface.

[2] Switzer *Raising Veg.* 2. 1729.

[3] Mawe and Abercrombie *Univ. Gard. Bot.* 1778.

[4] McMahon, B. *Amer. Gard. Cal.* 310. 1806.

[5] Thorburn *Cat.* 1821.

[6] *Agr. Gaz.* 217. 1879.

[7] Vilmorin *Les Pls. Potag.* 151. 1883.

[8] Dalechamp *Hist. Gen. Pl.* (*Lugd.*) 521. 1587.

[9] Booth, W. B. *Treas. Bot.* 1:167. 1874.

early botanists, who would have certainly noticed a common plant of such striking appearance and have given a figure. Bauhin,[1] indeed, 1623, gives the name *Brassica ex capitibus pluribus conglobata,* and adds that some plants bear 50 heads the size of an egg, but his reference to Dalechamp would lead us to infer that the plant known to him was of the same character as that figured by Dalechamp above noted. Lobel,[2] 1655, refers to a cabbage like a *Brassica polycephalos,* but, as he had not seen it, he says he will affirm nothing. Ray,[3] 1686, refers to a like cabbage.

A. P. De Candolle,[4] 1821, describes brussels sprouts as commonly cultivated in Belgium and implies its general use in French gardens, but Booth [5] says it is only since about 1854 that it has been generally known in England. A correspondent [6] of the *Gardeners' Chronicle,* 1850, however, refers to the tall sorts as generally preferred to the dwarf by the market gardeners about London. In American gardens, it is mentioned in 1806 [7] and this implies its general use in Europe.

But two classes are known, the tall and the dwarf, and but a few minor variations in these classes. The tall is quite distinct in habit and leaf from the dwarf, the former having less crowded sprouts and a more open character of plant, with leaves scarcely blistered or puckered. As, however, there is considerable variation to be noted in seedlings, furnishing connecting links, the two forms may legitimately be considered as one, the difference being no greater than would be explained by the observed power of selection and of the influence for modification which might arise from the influence of cabbage pollen. This fact of their being of but one type, even if with several variables, would seem to indicate a probability that the origin is to be sought for in a sport, and that our present forms have been derived from a suddenly observed variable of the Savoy cabbage type and, as the lack of early mention and the recent nature of modern mention presupposes, at some time scarcely preceding the last century.

Allied to this class is the Tree cabbage, or Jersey cabbage, which attains an extreme height of 16 feet, bearing a comparatively small, open cabbage on the summit, the Thousand-headed cabbage, the Poiton cabbage, and the Marrow cabbage, the stems of which last are succulent enough to be boiled for food. In 1806, McMahon [8] describes brussels sprouts, but he does not include them in his list of American garden esculents so they were not at that time in very general use. Fessenden,[9] 1828, mentions the Thousand-headed cabbage but it does not seem to have been known to him personally. Thorburn,[10] in his catalog for 1828, offers its seed for sale, but one variety only, and in 1881, two varieties.

---

[1] Bauhin, C. *Pinax* 3. 1623.

[2] Lobel *Stirp. Illustr.* 82. 1655.

[3] Ray *Hist. Pl.* 794. 1686.

[4] De Candolle, A. P. *Trans. Hort. Soc. Lond.* 5:15. 1824.

[5] Booth, W. B. *Treas. Bot.* 1:167. 1874.

[6] *Gard. Chron.* 117. 1850.

[7] McMahon, B. *Amer. Gard. Cal.* 580. 1806.

[8] McMahon, B. *Amer. Gard. Cal.* 309. 1806.

[9] Fessenden *New Amer. Gard.* 59. 1828.

[10] Thorburn *Cat.* 1828.

B. oleracea bullata major DC. SAVOY CABBAGE.

This race of cabbage is distinguished by the blistered surface of its leaves and by the formation of a loose or little compacted head. Probably the heading cabbages of the ancient Romans belong to this class, as, in their descriptions, there are no indications of a firm head, and at a later period this form is named as if distinctly Roman. Thus, Ruellius,[1] 1536, describes under the name *romanos* a loose-heading sort of cabbage but does not describe it particularly as a Savoy. This sort probably is the *Brassica italica tenerrima glomerosa flore albo* figured by J. Bauhin,[2] 1651, its origin, judging from the name, being ascribed to Italy; it is also figured by Chabraeus,[3] 1677, under the same name and with the additional names of *Chou d'Italie* and *Chou de Savoys*. In the *Adversaria*[4] and elsewhere, this kind is described as tender and as not extending to northern climates. This form, so carefully pictured as existing under culture, has doubtless been superseded by better varieties. It has been cultivated in English gardens for three centuries.[5] In 1806, McMahon[6] mentions three savoys for American gardens. In 1828, Thorburn offers in his catalog seeds of five varieties and in 1881 offers seed of but three.

B. oleracea capita DC. CABBAGE.

Few plants exhibit so many forms in its variations from the original type as cabbage. No kitchen garden in Europe or America is without it and it is distributed over the greater part of Asia and, in fact, over most of the world. The original plant occurs wild at the present day on the steep, chalk rocks of the sea province of England, on the coast of Denmark and northwestern France and, Lindley says, from Greece to Great Britain in numerous localities. At Dover, England, wild cabbage varies considerably in its foliage and general appearance and in its wild state is used as a culinary vegetable and is of excellent flavor.[7] This wild cabbage is undoubtedly the original of our cultivated varieties, as experiments at the garden of the Royal Agricultural College and at Cirencester resulted in the production of sorts of broccoli, cabbages and greens from wild plants gathered from rocks overhanging the sea in Wales.[8] Lindley groups the leading variations as follows: If the race is vigorous, long jointed and has little tendency to turn its leaves inwards, it forms what are called open cabbages (the kales); if the growth is stunted, the joints short and the leaves inclined to turn inwards, it becomes the heart cabbages; if both these tendencies give way to a preternatural formation of flowers, the cauliflowers are the result. If the stems swell out into a globular form, we have the turnip-rooted cabbages. Other species of *Brassica*, very nearly allied to *B. oleracea* Linn., such as *B. balearica* Richl., *B. insularis* Moris, and *B. cretica* Lam., belong to the Mediterranean flora and some botanists suggest that some of these species, likewise introduced

---

[1] Ruellius *Nat. Pl. Stirp.* 477. 1536.

[2] Bauhin, J. *Hist. Pl.* 2:827. 1651.

[3] Chabraeus *Icon. Sciag.* 269. 1677.

[4] Pena and Lobel *Advers.* 91. 1570.

[5] Booth, W. B. *Treas. Bot.* 1:166. 1870.

[6] McMahon, B. *Amer. Gard. Cal.* 580. 1806.

[7] *Gard. Mag.* 8:54.

[8] *Agr. Gaz.* 217. 1879.

into the gardens and established as cultivated plants, may have mixed with each other
and thus have assisted in giving rise to some of the many races cultivated at the present
day.

The ancient Greeks held cabbage in high esteem and their fables deduce its origin
from the father of their gods; for, they inform us that Jupiter, laboring to explain two
oracles which contradicted each other, perspired and from this divine perspiration the
colewort sprung.[1] Dioscorides[2] mentions two kinds of coleworts, the cultivated and
the wild. Theophrastus[3] names the curled cole, the swath cole and the wild cole. The
Egyptians are said to have worshipped cabbage, and the Greeks and Romans ascribed
to it the happy quality of preserving from drunkenness.[4] Pliny[5] mentions it. Cato[6]
describes one kind as smooth, great, broadleaved, with a big stalk, the second ruffed,
the third with little stalks, tender and very much biting. Regnier[7] says cabbages were
cultivated by the ancient Celts.

Cabbage is one of the most generally cultivated of the vegetables of temperate climates. It grows in Sweden as far north as 67° to 68°. The introduction of cabbage
into European gardens is usually ascribed to the Romans, but Olivier de Serres[8] says the
art of making them head was unknown in France in the ninth century. Disraeli[9] says
that Sir Anthony Ashley of Dorsetshire first planted cabbages in England, and a cabbage
at his feet appears on his monument; before his time they were brought from Holland.
Cabbage is said to have been scarcely known in Scotland until the time of the Common-
wealth, 1649, when it was carried there by some of Cromwell's soldiers.[10] Cabbage was
introduced into America at an early period. In 1540, Cartier[11] in his third voyage to
Canada, sowed cabbages. Cabbages are mentioned by Benzoni[12] as growing in Hayti
in 1556; by Shrigley,[13] in Virginia in 1669; but are not mentioned especially by Jefferson
in 1781. Romans found them in Florida in 1775 and even cultivated by the Choctaw
Indians. They were seen by Nieuhoff in Brazil in 1647. In 1779, cabbages are mentioned among the Indian crops about Geneva, New York, destroyed by Gen. Sullivan in
his expedition of reprisal.[14] In 1806, McMahon[15] mentions for American gardens seven
early and six late sorts. In 1828, Thorburn[16] offered 18 varieties in his seed catalog and

---

[1] Phillips, H. *Comp. Kitch. Gard.* 1:92. 1831.

[2] Gerarde, J. *Herb.* 311. 1833 or 1836. 2nd Ed.

[3] Ibid.

[4] Soyer, A. *Pantroph.* 60. 1853.

[5] Bostock and Riley *Nat. Hist. Pliny*

[6] Cato c. 157, 75.

[7] Regnier *Econ. Pub. Celt.* 438. 1818.

[8] Soyer, A. *Pantroph.* 61. 1853.

[9] Disraeli *Curios. Lit.* 2:329. 1859.

[10] Booth, W. B. *Treas. Bot.* 1:166. 1870.

[11] Pinkerton *Coll. Voy.* 12:667. 1812.

[12] Benzoni *Hist. New World.* Hak. Soc. Ed. 91. 1857.

[13] Shrigley *True Rel. Va. Md.* Force Coll. Tracts 3:5. 1844.

[14] Conover, G. S. *Early Hist. Geneva* 47. 1879.

[15] McMahon, B. *Amer. Gard. Cal.* 580. 1806.

[16] Thorburn *Cat.* 1821.

in 1881, 19. In 1869, Gregory tested 60 named varieties in his experimental garden and in 1875 Landreth tested 51.

The headed cabbage in its perfection of growth and its multitude of varieties, bears every evidence of being of ancient origin. It does not appear, however, to have been known to Dioscorides, or to Theophrastus or Cato, but a few centuries later the presence of cabbage is indicated by Columella [1] and Pliny,[2] who, of his variety, speaks of the head being sometimes a foot in diameter and going to seed the latest of all the sorts known to him. The descriptions are, however, obscure, and we may well believe that if the hard-headed varieties now known had been seen in Rome at this time they would have received mention. Olivier de Serres [3] says: "White cabbages came from the north, and the art of making them head was unknown in the time of Charlemagne." Albertus Magnus,[4] who lived in the twelfth century, seems to refer to a headed cabbage in his *Caputium*, but there is no description. The first unmistakable reference to cabbage [5] is by Ruellius, 1536, who calls them *capucos coles*, or *cabutos* and describes the head as globular and often very large, even a foot and a half in diameter. Yet the word cabaches and caboches, used in England in the fourteenth century, indicates cabbage was then known and was distinguished from coles.[6] Ruellius, also, describes a loose-headed form called *romanos*, and this name and description, when we consider the difficulty of heading cabbages in a warm climate, would lead us to believe that the Roman varieties were not our present solid-heading type but loose-headed and perhaps of the savoy class.

Our present cabbages are divided by De Candolle [7] into five types or races: the flat-headed, the round-headed, the egg-shaped, the elliptic and the conical. Within each class are many sub-varieties. In Vilmorin's *Les Plantes Potagères*, 1883, 57 kinds are described, and others are mentioned by name. In the *Report of the New York Agricultural Experiment Station for 1886*, 70 varieties are described, excluding synonyms. In both cases the savoys are treated as a separate class and are not included. The histories of De Candolle's forms are as follows:

FLAT-HEADED CABBAGE.

Type, Quintal. The first appearance of this form is in Pancovius Herbarium, 1673, No. 612. A Common Flatwinter, probably this form, is mentioned by Wheeler,[8] 1763; the Flat-topped is described by Mawe,[9] 1778. The varieties that are now esteemed are remarkably flat and solid.

ROUND CABBAGE.

Type, Early Dutch Drumhead. This appears to be the earliest form, as it is the only kind figured in early botanies and was hence presumably the only, or, perhaps, the

---

[1] Columella lib. 10, c. 1, p. 138.

[2] Pliny lib. 19, c. 41, p. 187.

[3] Soyer, A. *Pantroph.* 61. 1853.

[4] Albertus Magnus *Veg.* lib. 7, c. 90. 1867. Jessen Ed.

[5] Ruellius *Nat. Stirp.* 477. 1536.

[6] *The Forme of Cury* 1390 in Warner *Antiq. Culin.* 1791.

[7] De Candolle, A. P. *Trans. Hort. Soc. Lond.* 5:7. 1824.

[8] Wheeler *Bot., Gard. Dict.* 79. 1763.

[9] Mawe and Abercrombie *Univ. Gard. Bot.* 1778.

principal sort known during several centuries. The following synonymy is taken from drawings only and hence there can be no mistake in regard to the type:

Brassicae quartum genus. Fuch. 416. 1542.
Kappiskraut. Roeszl. 87. 1550.
Caulis capitulatis. Trag. 717. 1552.
Brassica capitata. Matth. 247. 1558; Pin. 163. 1561; Cam. *Epit.* 250. 1586.
Kol oder Kabiskraut. Pict. 90. 1581.
Brassica alba sessilis glomerata, aut capitata Lactucae habitu. Lobel *Icon.* **1**:243. 1591.
Brassica capitata albida. Dalechamp **1**:521. 1587; Dod. *Pempt.* 623. 1616.
Brassica capuccia. Dur. C. 78. 1617.
Brassica capitata alba. Bod. 777. 1644; Bauh. J. **1**:826. 1651; Chabr. 269. 1677.

The descriptive synonymy includes the *losed* cabbage, a great round cabbage of Lyte's *Dodoens*, 1586; the White Cabbage Cole of Gerarde, 1597; the White Cabbage of Ray, 1686; the *chou pomme blanc* of Tournefort, 1719; the English of Townsend, 1726; the Common White of Wheeler, 1763; the English or Late, of Stevenson, 1765; the Common Round White of Mawe, 1778.

EGG-SHAPED CABBAGE.

Type, the Sugar-loaf. Vilmorin[1] remarks of this variety, the Sugar-loaf, that, although a very old variety and well known in every country in Europe, it does not appear to be extensively grown anywhere. It is called *chou chicon* in France[2] and *bundee kobee* in India.[3] It is mentioned by name by Townsend,[4] 1726; by Wheeler,[5] 1763; by Stevenson,[6] 1765; and by Mawe,[7] 1778. Perhaps the Large-sided cabbage of Worlidge[8] and the Long-sided cabbage of Quintyne[9] belong to this division.

ELLIPTIC CABBAGE.

Type, Early York. This is first mentioned by Stevenson,[10] 1765, and he refers to it as a well-known sort. According to Burr, it came originally from Flanders. There are now many varieties of this class.

CONICAL CABBAGE.

Type, Filderkraut. This race is described by Lamarck,[11] 1783, and, if there is any constancy between the name and the variety during long periods, is found in the Battersea, named by Townsend in 1726 and by a whole line of succeeding writers.

It is certainly very singular that but one of these races of cabbage received the notice of the older botanists (excepting the one flat-topped given by Chabraeus, 1677),

---

[1] Vilmorin *Veg. Gard.* 110. 1885.
[2] Vilmorin *Veg. Gard.* 109. 1885.
[3] Speede *Ind. Handb. Gard.* 112. 1842.
[4] Townsend *Seedsman* 26. 1726.
[5] Wheeler *Bot. Gard. Dict.* 79. 1765.
[6] Stevenson *Gard. Kal.* 26, 119. 1765.
[7] Mawe and Abercrombie *Univ. Gard. Bot.* 1778.
[8] Worlidge, J. *Syst. Hort.* 202. 1683.
[9] Quintyne *Comp. Gard.* 189. 1693. Evelyn Ed.
[10] Stevenson *Gard. Kal.* 26. 119, 1765.
[11] Don, G. *Hist. Dichl. Pls.* **1**:228. 1831.

as their characteristics are extremely well marked and form extreme contrasts between the conical, or pointed, and the spherical-headed. We must, hence, believe that they either originated or came into use in a recent period. How they came and whence they came, must be decided from a special study, in which the effect of hybridization may become a feature. From the study of sports that occasionally appear in the garden, the suggestion may be offered that at least some of these races have been derived from crossings with some form of the Chinese cabbage, whereby form has become transferred while the other characteristics of the Chinese species have disappeared. On the other hand, the savoy class, believed to have origin from the same source as the cabbage, has oval or oblong heads, which have been noted by the herbalists.

It is very remarkable, says Unger, that the European and Asiatic names used for different species of cabbage may all be referred to four roots. The names *kopf kohl* (German), *cabus* (French), *cabbage* (English), *kappes, kraut, kapost, kaposta, kapsta* (Tartar), *kopee* (Beng.), *kopi* (Hindu), have a manifest relation to the Celto-Slavic root *cap* or *kap*, which in Celtic means head. *Brassica* of Pliny is derived from the Celtic, *bresic* cabbage. The Celto-Germanico-Greek root *caul* may be detected in the word *kaol*, the Grecian *kaulion* of Theophrastus, the Latin *caulis;* also in the words *caulx, cavolo, coan, kohl, kale, kaal* (Norwegian), *kohl* (Swedish), *col* (Spanish), *kelum* (Persian); finally, the Greco-Germanic root *cramb, krambe,* passes into *krumb, karumb* of the Arabians. The want of a Sanscrit name shows that the cabbage tribe first found its way at a later period to India and China. This tribe is not mentioned as in Japan by Thunberg, 1775.

B. oleracea capitata rubra DC. RED CABBAGE.

This is a very distinct and probably a very ancient kind of a peculiar purple color and solid heading. It is cultivated in a number of varieties and in 1854 the seed of Red Savoy was distributed from the United States Patent Office. One variety is mentioned for American gardens by McMahon,[1] 1806, and one variety only by Thorburn,[2] 1828 and 1881, but several distinct sorts can now be obtained from seedsmen. Burr,[3] 1863, describes three reds and one so deeply colored as to be called black.

The first certain mention of this cabbage is in 1570, in Pena and Lobel's *Adversaria,*[4] and figures are given by Gerarde, 1597,[5] Matthiolus, 1598,[6] Dodonaeus, 1616,[7] and J. Bauhin, 1651.[8] These figures are all of the spherical-headed type. In 1638,[9] Ray notices the variability in the colors upon which a number of our seedsmen's varieties are founded. The oblong or the pointed-headed types which now occur cannot be traced. The solidity of the head and the perfectness of the form in this class of cabbage indicate long culture

---

[1] McMahon, B. *Amer. Gard. Cal.* 580. 1806.
[2] Thorburn *Cat.* 1828.
[3] Burr, F. *Field, Gard. Veg.* 266, 267. 1863.
[4] Pena and Lobel *Advers.* 91. 1570.
[5] Gerarde, J. *Herb.* 246. 1597.
[6] Matthiolus *Opera* 367. 1598.
[7] Dodonaeus *Pempt.* 621. 1616.
[8] Bauhin, J. *Hist. Pl.* 2:832. 1651.
[9] Ray *Hist. Pl.* 795. 1686.

and a remote origin. In England, they have never attained much standing for general use,[1] and, as in this country, are principally grown for pickling.

COLLARDS OR COLEWORT.

As grown in the United States, collards, or colewort, are sowings of an early variety of cabbage in rows about one foot apart to be cut for use as a spinach when about six or eight inches high. Other directions for culture are to sow seeds as for cabbage in June, July and August for succession, transplant when one month old in rows a foot apart each way, and hoe frequently. The collard plants are kept for sale by seedsmen, rather than the cabbage seed under this name. In the Southern States, collards are extensively grown and used for greens and after frost the flavor is esteemed delicious.

B. oleracea caulo-rapa communis DC. KOHL-RABI.

This is a dwarf-growing plant with the stem swelled out so as to resemble a turnip above ground. There is no certain identification of this race in ancient writings. The *bunidia* of Pliny [2] seems rather to be the rutabaga, as he says it is between a radish and a rape. The *gorgylis* of Theophrastus [3] and Galen [4] seems also to be the rutabaga, for Galen says the root contained within the earth is hard unless cooked. In 1554, Matthiolus [5] speaks of the kohl-rabi as having lately come into Italy. Between 1573 and 1575, Rauwolf [6] saw it in the gardens of Tripoli and Aleppo. Lobel,[7] 1570, Camerarius,[8] 1586, Dalechamp,[9] 1587, and other of the older botanists figure or describe it as under European culture.

Kohl-rabi, in the view of some writers, is a cross between cabbage and rape, and many of the names applied to it convey this idea. This view is probably a mistaken one, as the plant in its sportings under culture tends to the form of the Marrow cabbage, from which it is probably a derivation. In 1884, two kohl-rabi plants were growing in pots in the greenhouse at the New York Agricultural Experiment Station; one of these extended itself until it became a Marrow cabbage and when planted out in the spring attained its growth as a Marrow cabbage. This idea of its origin finds countenance in the figures of the older botanists; thus, Camerarius, 1586, figures a plant as a kohl-rabi which in all essential points resembles a Marrow cabbage, tapering from a small stem into a long kohl-rabi, with a flat top like the Marrow cabbage. The figures given by Lobel,[10] 1591, Dodonaeus,[11] 1616, and Bodaeus,[12] 1644, when compared with Camerarius' figure, suggest

---

[1] Worlidge, J. *Syst. Hort.* 203. 1683.

[2] Pliny lib. 20, c. 2.

[3] Theophrastus lib. 7, c. 4.

[4] Galen *Aliment.* 1547.

[5] Matthiolus *Comment* 248. 1554.

[6] Gronovius *Fl. Orient* 81. 1755.

[7] Pena and Lobel *Advers.* 92. 1570.

[8] Camerarius *Epit.* 251. 1586.

[9] Dalechamp *Hist. Gen. Pl.* (Lugd.) 522. 1587.

[10] Lobel *Icon.* 246. 1591.

[11] Dodonaeus *Pempt.* 625. 1616.

[12] Theophrastus *Hist. Pl.* Bodaeus Ed. 777. 1644.

the Marrow cabbage. A long, highly improved form, not now under culture, is figured by Gerarde,[1] 1597, J. Bauhin,[2] 1651, and Chabraeus,[3] 1677, and the modern form is given by Gerarde and by Matthiolus,[4] 1598. A very unimproved form, out of harmony with the other figures, is given by Dalechamp,[5] 1587, and Castor Durante,[6] 1617. The synonymy can be tabulated as below:

I.

Caulorapum. Cap. *Epit.* 251. 1586.

II.

Rapa Br. peregrine, caule rapum gerens. Lob. *Icon.* 246. 1591.
Br. caule rapum gerens. Dod. *Pempt.* 625. 1616.
Rapa brassica. Bodaus 777. 1644.

III.

Caulo rapum longum. Ger. 250. 1597.
Br. caulorapa. Bauh. J. 2:830. 1651.
Br. caulorapa sivè Rapo caulis. Chabr. 270. 1677.

IV.

Caulorapum rotundum. Ger. 250. 1597.
Brassica gongylodes. Matth. *Opera* 367. 1598.

V.

Brassica raposa. Dalechamp 522. 1587.
Bradica raposa. Dur. C. 1617. app.

Matthiolus, as we have stated, says the plant came into Germany from Italy; Pena and Lobel say it came from Greece; Gerarde, that it grows in Italy, Spain and Germany, whence he received seeds. This plant was an inmate of the Old Physic Garden in Edinburgh before 1683. In 1734, it was first brought into field culture in Ireland; in Scotland in 1805; and in England in 1837. In the United States, it was mentioned by McMahon,[7] 1806. Fessenden,[8] 1828, names two varieties, one the above-ground and the other the below-ground turnip-rooted. Darwin [9] speaks of the recently formed new race, already including nine subvarieties, in which the enlarged part lies beneath the ground like a turnip. Two varieties are used in France in ornamental gardening, the leaves being cut and frizzled, and the artichoke-leaved variety is greatly prized for decoration by confectioners. These excerpts indicate a southern origin, for this vegetable and the Marrow cabbage are very sensitive to cold. The more highly improved forms, as figured in our synonymy, are in authors of northern or central Europe, while the unimproved forms are given by more southern writers. This indicates that the present kohl-

---

[1] Gerarde, J. *Herb.* 250. 1597.

[2] Bauhin, J. *Hist. Pl.* 2:830. 1651.

[3] Chabraeus *Icon. Sciag.* 270. 1677.

[4] Matthiolus *Opera* 367. 1598.

[5] Dalechamp *Hist. Gen. Pl.* (Lugd.) 1587.

[6] Durante, C. *Herb.* app. 1617.

[7] McMahon, B. *Amer. Gard. Cal.* 309. 1806.

[8] Fessenden *New Amer. Gard.* 59. 1828.

[9] Darwin, C. *Ans. and Pls. Domest.* 1:342. 1893.

rabi received its development in northern countries. The varieties now grown are the White and Purple, in early and late forms, the Curled-leaf, or Neapolitan, and the Artichoke-leaved.

B. olearacea costata oblonga DC. PORTUGAL CABBAGE.

This cabbage is easily recognizable through the great expansion of the midribs and veins of the leaf, in some cases forming quite half of the leaf, the midrib losing its identity in the multitude of radiating, branching veins. In some plants the petioles are winged clear to the base. Nearly all the names applied to this form indicate its distribution, at least in late years, from Portugal, whence it reached English gardens about 1821 [1] and American gardens, under the name of Portugal Cabbage, about 1850.[2] It should be remarked, however, that a *chou à la grosse côte* was in French gardens in 1612 [3] and in three varieties in 1824.

This cabbage varies in a direction parallel to that of the common cabbage, or has forms which can be classed with the kales and the heading cabbages of at least two types.

The peculiarity of the ribs or veins occasionally appears among the variables from the seed of the common cabbage, hence atavism as the result of a cross can be reasonably inferred. As to the origin of this form, opinion, at the present stage of studies, must be largely speculative but we may reasonably believe that it originated from a different form or a different set of hybridizations than did the common cabbage. The synonymy appears to be:

> *Choux à la grosse côte.* Jard. Solit. 1612.
> *Chou blond aux grosses côtes.* Bosc. *Dict.* 4, 43. 1789.
> *Brassica oleracea aceppala costata.* DC. *Syst.* 2:584. 1821.
> *B. oleracea costata.* DC. *Trans. Hort. Soc. Lond. M.* 5:12. 1824.
> *Chou aux grosses côtes.* Vilm. 1883.

B. sinapistrum Boiss. CHARLOCK. FIELD MUSTARD.

This is an European plant now occurring as a weed in cultivated fields in America. In seasons of scarcity, in the Hebrides, the soft stems and leaves are boiled in milk and eaten. It is so employed in Sweden and Ireland. Its seeds form a good substitute for mustard.

Bridelia retusa Spreng. *Euphorbiaceae.*

A tree of eastern Asia. The fruit is sweetish and eatable.[4]

Brodiaea grandiflora Sm. *Liliaceae.* CALIFORNIAN HYACINTH.

Northwestern America. Its fruit is eaten by the Indians.[5] In France, it is grown in the flower garden.[6]

---

[1] De Candolle, A. P. *Trans. Hort. Soc. Lond.* 5:12. 1821.
[2] Buist, R. *Fam. Kitch. Gard.* 1851. Preface.
[3] *Jard. Solit.* 158. 1612.
[4] Brandis, D. *Forest Fl.* 449. 1876.
[5] Pickering, C. *Chron. Hist. Pls.* 605. 1879.
[6] Vilmorin *Fl. Pl. Ter.* 174. 1870. 3rd Ed.

Bromelia Sp. *Bromeliaceae.*

In the Malay Archipelago, Wallace[1] left two men for a month, by accident, on an island near Ceram, who " subsisted on the roots and tender flower-stalks of a species of Bromelia, on shell fish and on a few turtle's eggs."

Brosium alicastrum Sw. *Urticaceae.* ALICASTRUM SNAKEWOOD. BREADNUT.

American tropics. The fruit, boiled with salt-fish, pork, beef or pickle, has frequently been the support of the negro and poorer sorts of white people in times of scarcity and has proved a wholesome and not unpleasant food.[2]

B. galactodendron D. Don. COW-TREE. MILK-TREE.

Guiana; the *palo de vaca, arbol de leche,* or cow-tree of Venezuela. Humboldt[3] says: " On the barren flank of a rock grows a tree with coriaceous and dry leaves. Its large, woody roots can scarcely penetrate into the stone. For several months of the year not a single shower moistens its foliage. Its branches appear dead and dried; but when the trunk is pierced there flows from it a sweet and nourishing milk. It is at the rising of the sun that this vegetable fountain is most abundant. The negroes and natives are then seen hastening from all quarters, furnished with large bowls to receive the milk which grows yellow and thickens at its surface. Some empty their bowls under the tree itself, others carry the juice home to their children." This tree seems to have been noticed first by Laet[4] in 1633, in the province of Camana. The plant, according to Desvaux, is one of the *palo de vaca* or cow-trees of South America. From incisions in the bark, milky sap is procured, which is drunk by the inhabitants as a milk. Its use is accompanied by a sensation of astringency in the lips and palate. This cow-tree is grown in Ceylon and India, for Brandis[5] says it yields large quantities of thick, gluey milk without any acridity, that it is drunk extensively, and that it is very wholesome and nourishing.

Broussonetia papyrifera Vent. *Urticaceae.* PAPER MULBERRY. TAPA-CLOTH TREE.

A tree of the islands of the Pacific, China and Japan. It is cultivated for the inner bark which is used for making a paper as well as textile fabrics.[6] The fleshy part of the compound fruit is saccharine and edible.[7]

Bruguiera gymnorrhiza Lam. *Rhizophoreae.*

Muddy tropical shores from Hindustan to the Samoan Islands. Its fruit, leaves and bark are eaten by the natives in the Malayan Archipelago.[8]

Bryonia alba Linn. *Cucurbitaceae.* WHITE BRYONY.

West Mediterranean countries. Loudon says the young shoots are edible.

[1] Wallace, A. R. *Malay Arch.* 526. 1869.
[2] Browne *U. S. D. A. Rpt.* 198. 1870.
[3] Humboldt, A. *Trav.* 2:48, 49. 1889.
[4] Humboldt, A. *Trav.* 2:48. 1889.
[5] Brandis, D. *Forest Fl.* 427. 1876.
[6] Mueller, F. *Sel. Pls.* 78. 1891.
[7] Hanbury, D. *Sci. Papers* 231. 1876.
[8] Pickering, C. *Chron. Hist. Pls.* 300. 1879.

B. dioica Jacq. RED BRYONY. WILD HOP.

Europe and adjoining Asia. Loudon says the young shoots of red bryony are edible.
Masters [1] says that the plant has a fetid odor and possesses acrid, emetic and pungent
properties.

Buchanania lancifolia Roxb. *Anacardiaceae.* CHEEROJEE-OIL PLANT.

East Indies and Burma. The tender, unripe fruit is eaten by the natives in their
curries.[2]

B. latifolia Roxb.

Tropical India and Burma. The fruit, says Brandis,[3] has a pleasant, sweetish, subacid flavor and is an important article of food of the hill tribes of central India. The
kernel of the seed tastes somewhat like the pistachio nut and is used largely in native sweetmeats. Drury [4] says these kernels are a general substitute for almonds among the natives
and are much esteemed in confectionery or are roasted and eaten with milk.

Bumelia lanuginosa Pers. *Sapotaceae.* FALSE BUCKTHORN.

North America. This is a low bush of southern United States which, according to
Nuttall,[5] bears an edible fruit as large as a small date.

B. reclinata Vent. WESTERN BUCKTHORN.

Southwestern United States. In California, Torrey [6] says the fruit is sweet and
edible and nearly three-quarters of an inch long.

Bunias erucago Linn. *Cruciferae.*

Mediterranean countries. In Italy, Unger [7] says this species serves as a salad for
the poor.

B. orientalis Linn. HILL MUSTARD. TURKISH ROCKET.

Eastern Europe and Asia Minor. This plant is called *dikaia retka* on the Lower
Volga. Its stems are eaten raw. This rocket was cultivated in 1739 by Philip Miller
in the Botanic Garden of Chelsea and was first introduced into field culture in England,
as a forage plant, by Arthur Young. The young leaves are recommended by Vilmorin [8]
either as a salad or boiled.

Bupleurum falcatum Linn. *Umbelliferae.* HARE'S EAR.

Europe, Orient, Northern Asia and Himalayan region. The leaves are used for food
in China [9] and Japan.[10]

---

[1] Masters, M. T. *Treas. Bot.* 1:176. 1870.

[2] Drury, H. *Useful Pls. Ind.* 89. 1858.

[3] Brandis, D. *Forest Fl.* 127. 1874.

[4] Drury, H. *Useful Pls. Ind.* 89. 1858.

[5] Nuttall, T. *No. Amer. Sylva* 2:106. 1865. (*B. macrocarpa*)

[6] Torrey, J. *Bot. U. S., Mex. Bound. Surv.* 2:109. 1859.

[7] Unger, F. *U. S. Pat. Off. Rpt.* 354. 1859.

[8] Vilmorin *Les Pls. Potag.* 54. 1883.

[9] Bretschneider, E. *Bot. Sin.* 51. 1882.

[10] Georgeson *Amer. Gard.* 13:7. 1892. Fig. p. 9.

B. octoradiatum Bunge.

Northern China. In China, the tender shoots of this apparently foreign plant are edible.[1]

B. rotundifolium Linn. THOROUGH WAX.

Europe, Caucasus region and Persia. "Hippocrates hath commended it in meats for salads and potherbs."[2]

Burasaia madagascariensis DC. *Menispermaceae.*

Madagascar. This plant has edible fruit.[3]

Bursera gummifera Linn. *Burseraceae.* AMERICAN GUM TREE. INDIAN BIRCH.

American tropics. An infusion of the leaves is occasionally used as a domestic substitute for tea.[4]

B. icicariba Baill.

Brazil. The tree is said to have edible, aromatic fruit. It yields the *elemi* of Brazil.[5]

B. javanica Baill.

Java. This plant is the *tingulong* of the Javanese, who eat the leaves and fruit.[6]

Butomus umbellatus Linn. *Alismaceae.* FLOWERING RUSH. GRASSY RUSH. WATER GLADIOLUS.

Europe and adjoining Asia. Unger[7] says, in Norway, the rhizomes serve as material for a bread. Johns[8] says, in the north of Asia, the root is roasted and eaten. Lindley[9] says the rhizomes are acrid and bitter, as well as the seeds but are eaten among the savages. In France, it is grown in flower gardens as an aquatic.[10]

Butyrospermum parkii Kotschy. *Sapotaceae.* BUTTER TREE. SHEA TREE.

Tropical west Africa. Shea, or galam, butter is obtained from the kernel of the fruit and serves the natives as a substitute for butter. This butter is highly commended by Park.[11] The tree is called *meepampa* in equatorial Africa.[12]

Buxus sempervirens Linn. *Euphorbiaceae.* BOX.

Europe, Orient and temperate Asia. In France and some other parts of the

[1] Smith, F. P. *Contrib. Mat. Med. China* 45. 1871.
[2] Gerarde, J. *Herb.* 608. 1633 or 1636. 2nd Ed.
[3] Baillon, H. *Hist. Pls.* 3:70. 1874.
[4] Sargent *U. S. Census* 9:32. 1884.
[5] Baillon, H. *Hist. Pls.* 5:297. 1878.
[6] Ibid.
[7] Unger, F. *U. S. Pat. Off. Rpt.* 308. 1859.
[8] Johns, C. A. *Treas. Bot.* 1:183. 1870.
[9] Lindley, J. *Veg. King.* 208. 1846.
[10] Vilmorin *Fl. Pl. Ter.* 185. 1870. 3rd Ed.
[11] Don, G. *Hist. Dich. Pls.* 4:36. 1838.
[12] Pickering, C. *Chron. Hist. Pls.* 426. 1879. (*Bassia parkii*)

continent, the leaves of the box have been used as a substitute for hops in beer, but Johnson[1] says they cannot be wholesome and would probably prove very injurious.

Byrsonima crassifolia H. B. & K. *Malpighiaceae.*

A small tree of New Granada and Panama. The small, acid berries are eaten.[2]

B. spicata Rich. SHOEMAKER'S TREE.

Tropical America. The yellow, acid berries are good eating but astringent.[3]

Cadaba farinosa Forsk. *Capparideae.*

A shrub of tropical Africa and Arabia. Spinach is made from the leaves.[4]

Caesalpinia pulcherrima Sw. *Leguminosae.* PEACOCK FLOWER. PRIDE OF BARBADOS.

Cosmopolitan tropics. The green seeds are eaten raw and have the taste of peas.[5]

Cajanus indicus Spreng. *Leguminosae.* ANGOLA PEA. CATJANG. CONGO PEA. DAHL.
GRANDUE. NO-EYE PEA. PIGEON PEA. TOOR. URHUR.

East Indies. The pigeon pea is a perennial shrub, though treated generally as an annual when in cultivation. It is now naturalized in the West Indies, in tropical America and in Africa. The variety Bicolor grows from three to six feet high and is called the Congo pea in Jamaica. The variety Flavus grows from five to ten feet high and is called in Jamaica no-eye pea, pigeon pea and Angola pea.[6] Dr. MacFayden[7] says there are few tropical plants so valuable. Lunan[8] says the pea when young and properly cooked is very little inferior as a green vegetable to English peas and when old is an excellent ingredient in soups. Berlanger[9] says at Martinique there are several varieties greatly used, and that the seeds both fresh and dried are delicious. In Egypt, on the richest soil, says Mueller,[10] 4000 pounds of peas have been produced to the acre, and the plant lasts for three years, growing 15 feet tall. This variety is said by Pickering[11] to be native of equatorial Africa. In India, the seeds of the two varieties are much esteemed, ranking, with the natives, third amongst their leguminous seeds.[12] Elliott[13] says the pulse when split is in great and general esteem and forms the most generally used article of diet among all classes in India. At Zanzibar, the seeds are a principal article of diet. It is both cultivated and wild all over India as well as in all parts of tropical Africa. It certainly is one of the oldest cultivated

---

[1] Johnson, C. P. *Useful Pls. Gt. Brit.* 228. 1862.
[2] Smith, A. *Treas. Bot.* 1:185. 1870. (*B. cumingiana*)
[3] Ibid.
[4] Speke, J. H. *Journ. Disc. Source Nile* 561. 1864.
[5] *Proc. Amer. Acad. Art. Sci.* 425. 1886.
[6] Smith, A. *Treas. Bot.* 1:189. 1870.
[7] Macfayden *Jam.* 1:296. 1837.
[8] Lunan, J. *Hort. Jam.* 2:64. 1814.
[9] Berlanger *Trans. N. Y. Agr. Soc.* 568. 1858.
[10] Mueller, F. *Sel. Pls.* 82. 1891.
[11] Pickering, C. *Chron. Hist. Pls.* 443. 1879. (*C. flavus*)
[12] Drury, H. *Useful Pls. Ind.* 95, 1858.
[13] Elliott, W. *Bot. Soc. Edinb.* 7:294. 1863.

plants in the world, a fact attested by its presence in ancient tombs. Schweinfurth states that it is found in Egyptian tombs of the twelfth dynasty (2200–2400 B. C.) [1]

Cakile maritima Scop. *Cruciferae.* SEA ROCKET.

Europe, northern Africa and North America. Kalm [2] says the sea rocket furnishes a root in Canada which is pounded, mixed with flour and eaten, when there is a scarcity of bread.

Caladium bicolor Vent. *Aroideae.*

South America. The corms are eaten roasted or boiled. [3] The leaves are eaten, boiled as a vegetable, in the West Indies. [4]

Calamus rotang Linn. *Palmae.* RATTAN CANE.

East Indies. Thunberg [5] saw the fruit of the rattan exposed for sale in Batavia. When ripe this fruit is roundish, as large as a hazelnut and is covered with small, shining scales, laid like shingles, one upon the other. The natives generally suck out the subacid pulp which surrounds the kernel by way of quenching their thirst. Sometimes the fruit is pickled with salt and eaten at tea-time. This palm furnishes rattan canes.

Calathea allouia Lindl. *Scitamineae.*

Guiana. This species is cultivated in the West Indies and, according to Lindley, [6] furnishes one of the arrowroots of commerce.

Calendula officinalis Linn. *Compositae.* GOLDINS GOLDS. POT MARIGOLD.

Southern Europe. This marigold was cultivated in England prior to 1573. The petals of the flowers are occasionally used in broths and soups in Britain and Holland and are also used for coloring butter. [7] In 1806, it was included in McMahon's [8] list of aromatic, pot and sweet herbs of American gardens. There are a number of ornamental varieties, and the species is to be found in many of our country gardens. The plant is described in nearly all of the early herbals and is mentioned by Albertus Magnus in the thirteenth century.

Calla palustris Linn. *Aroideae.* WATER ARUM. WATER DRAGON.

Europe, Northern Asia and North America. The rootstocks of this plant yield eatable starch, prepared by drying and grinding them and then heating the powder until the acrid properties are dissipated. [9]

---

[1] *Nature* 19:315. 1884.

[2] Kalm, P. *Trav. No. Amer.* 2:345. 1772. (*Bunias cakile*)

[3] Henfrey, A. *Bot.* 371. 1870.

[4] Masters, M. T. *Treas. Bot.* 1:190. 1870. (*C. sagittaefolium*)

[5] Thunberg, C. P. *Trav.* 2:277. 1796.

[6] Lindley, J. *Veg. King.* 169. 1846. (*Maranta allouia*)

[7] Loudon, J. C. *Enc. Pls.* 741. 1855.

[8] McMahon, B. *Amer. Gard. Cal.* 583. 1806.

[9] Masters, M. T. *Treas. Bot.* 1:194. 1870.

Callicarpa lanata Linn. *Verbenaceae.*

East Indies. The bark has a peculiar, subaromatic and slightly bitter taste and is chewed by the Cinghalese when they cannot obtain betel leaves.[1]

Calligonum pallasia L'Herit. *Polygonaceae.*

Caspian region, Russia and Siberia. The roots when pounded are said to furnish a mucilaginous, edible substance resembling gum tragacanth.[2]

C. polygonoides Linn.

Armenia, Persia and northwestern India. The abortive flowers, which fall in great numbers, are, in the south Punjab and sometimes in Sind, swept up, made into bread, or cooked with ghee and eaten.[3]

Callirhoe involucrata A. Gray. *Malvaceae.* POPPY MALLOW.

Northwestern America. The large, tapering root of this plant is said to be edible.[4] It is an inmate of the flower garden in France.[5]

C. pedata A. Gray. PIMPLE MALLOW.

Northwestern America. The roots of this species resemble those of a parsnip and are used as food by the Indians of Nebraska and Idaho.[6] In France it is grown in flower gardens.[7]

Calluna vulgaris Salisb. *Ericaceae.* HEATH.

Europe and North America. The Celtic tribes had a method of preparing an intoxicating drink from a decoction of heath. This beverage, mixed with wild honey, was their common drink at feasts.[8] In the Hebrides, says Johnson,[9] a kind of beer is formed by fermenting a mixture of two parts of heath tops and one of malt. The Picts had a mode of preparing beer or wine from the flowers of the heath.

Calochortus elegans Pursh. *Liliaceae.* STAR TULIP.

Pacific northwest of America. The root of this plant is eaten by the Indians.[10]

C. luteus Dougl. BUTTERFLY TULIP. SEGO LILY.

Western United States. This plant has a small, bulbous root about the size of a walnut, very palatable and nutritious and much used by the Indian tribes of Utah as an article of food.[11] The Mormons during their first years in Utah consumed the root in large quantities.

[1] Ainslie, W. *Mat. Ind.* 2:180. 1826.

[2] Syme, J. T. *Treas. Bot.* 2:937. 1870. (*Pterococcus aphyllus*)

[3] Brandis, D. *Forest. Fl.* 372. 1874.

[4] Stansbury, H. *Rpt. Gt. Salt Lake* 384. 1853.

[5] Vilmorin *Fl. Pl. Ter.* 199. 1870. 3rd Ed.

[6] *U. S. D. A. Rpt.* 406. 1870.

[7] Vilmorin *Fl. Pl. Ter.* 199. 1870. 3rd Ed.

[8] Hogg, W. *Journ. Agr.* 6:43. 1836.

[9] Johnson, C. P. *Useful Pls. Gt. Brit.* 167. 1862. (*Erica vulgaris*)

[10] Pickering, C. *Chron. Hist. Pls.* 582. 1879.

[11] Stansbury, H. *Rpt. Salt Lake* 160, 208, 397. 1853.

Calophyllum inophyllum Linn. *Guttiferae.* ALEXANDRIAN LAUREL. POONAY-OIL PLANT.

Old world tropics. The fruit when ripe is red and sweet and is eaten by the natives. An oil is expressed from it and is used in lamps.[1]

Calotropis gigantea Ait. *Asclepiadeae.* BOW-STRING HEMP.

East India. According to Twemlow,[2] an intoxicating liquor called *bar* is obtained from the plant by the Hill People about Mahableshwur. According to Royle,[3] it yields a kind of manna.

Caltha palustris Linn. *Ranunculaceae.* COWSLIP. MARSH MARIGOLD. MEADOW BRIGHT.

Of northern climates. This well-known plant, says Gray,[4] is used as a potherb in spring when coming into flower, under the name of cowslip. In the Southern States, the flower-buds are pickled for use as a substitute for capers.[5]

Calycanthus floridus Linn. *Calycanthaceae.* CAROLINA ALLSPICE.

North America. The aromatic bark is said to be used as a substitute for cinnamon.[6]

Calyptranthes aromatica St. Hil. *Myrtaceae.*

South Brazil. Mueller[7] says the flower-buds can be used as cloves; the berries, as allspice.

C. obscura DC.

Brazil. The fruit is sold in Rio Janeiro as an aromatic and astringent.

C. paniculata Ruiz & Pav.

Peru. The fruit is used as a substitute for cloves.

C. schiediana Berg.

Mexico. In Mexico, the fruit is used as cloves.

Calystegia sepium R. Br. *Convolvulaceae.* BINDWEED.

Temperate climates. It has edible stalks[8] which are eaten by the Hindus.[9] The roots are said to be boiled and eaten by the Chinese, who manage, says Smith,[10] to cook and digest almost every root or tuber in spite of the warnings of botanists and chemists.

C. soldanella R. Br. SEA BINDWEED.

Temperate climates. The tender stalks of the sea bindweed are pickled.[11] The

---

[1] Drury, H. *Useful Pls. Ind.* 1858. (*C. spurium*)

[2] Pickering, C. *Chron. Hist. Pls.* 596. 1879. (*Asclepias gigantea*)

[3] Ibid.

[4] Gray, A. *Man. Bot.* 404. 1908.

[5] Porcher, F. P. *Res. So. Fields, Forests* 17. 1869.

[6] Black, A. A. *Treas. Bot.* 1:203. 1870.

[7] Mueller, F. *Sel. Pls.* 85. 1891.

[8] Royle, J. F. *Illustr. Bot. Himal.* 1:308. 1839.

[9] Ainslie, W. *Mat. Ind.* 2:220. 1826.

[10] Smith, F. P. *Contrib. Mat. Med. China* 47. 1871.

[11] Don, G. *Hist. Dichl. Pls.* 4:297. 1838.

young shoots, says Johnson,[1] were gathered formerly by the people on the southern coasts
of England and pickled as a substitute for samphire.

Camassia esculenta Lindl. *Liliaceae.* COMMON CAMASS. KAMOSH. QUAMASH.

Northwestern America. The root forms the greater part of the vegetable food of the
Indians on the northwest coast of America and Vancouver Island and is called kamosh
or quamash. This bulbous root is said to be of delicious flavor and highly nutritious,
but Lewis[2] says it causes bowel complaints if eaten in quantity. This plant covers many
plains and is dug by the women and stored for eating, roasted or boiled. The bulbs, when
boiled in water, yield a very good molasses, which is much prized and is used on festival
occasions by various tribes of Indians. In France, it is an inmate of the flower garden.[3]

Camelina sativa Crantz. *Cruciferae.* FALSE FLAX. GOLD-OF-PLEASURE. OIL-SEED PLANT.
SIBERIAN OIL-SEED.

Europe and temperate Asia. This plant occurs in northeastern America as a noxious
weed in flax fields, having been introduced from Europe. It was regularly cultivated in
the mediaeval ages in Germany and Russia[4] and is now cultivated in Flanders. The
stem yields a fiber, but the stalks seem to be used only in broom making. The seeds
yield an oil which is used for culinary and other purposes.[5] In 1854, the seeds of this plant
were distributed from the United States Patent Office. It was called in Britain gold-of-
pleasure even in the time of Gerarde. The seeds are sometimes imported into England
under the name dodder seed, but they have no relation to the true dodder which is a far
different plant.

Camellia sasanqua Thunb. *Ternstroemiaceae.* TEA-OIL PLANT.

Japan and China. This plant was introduced from China to England in 1811. It
yields a nut from which an oil is expressed in China, equal, it is said, to olive oil. In Japan
the dried leaves are mixed with tea to give it a grateful odor.[6]

C. thea Link. TEA.

China. This is the species to which the cultivated varieties of tea are all referred.
In its various forms it is now found in China and Japan, in the mountains that separate
China from the Burmese territories, especially in upper Assam, in Nepal, in the islands
of Bourbon, Java, St. Helena and Madeira, in Brazil and experimentally in the United
States. The first mention of tea seems to have been by Giovanni Pietro Maffei in his
Historiae Indicae, 1589, from which it appears that it was then called by the Chinese *chia.*
Giovanni Botero in his *Della Cause della grandezza....della citta,* 1589, says the Chinese
have an herb from which they extract a delicate juice, which they use instead of wine.
In 1615, an Englishman in Japan, in the employment of the East India Company,

[1] Johnson, C. P.   *Useful Pls. Gt. Brit.* 181.   1862.   (*Convolvulus soldanella*)
[2] Pursh, F.   *Fl. Amer. Septent.* 1:226, 227.   1814.   (*Phalangium bulbosum*)
[3] Vilmorin *Fl. Pl. Ter.* 204.   1870.   3rd Ed.
[4] Pickering, C.   *Chron. Hist. Pls.* 353.   1879.
[5] Don, G.   *Hist. Dichl. Pls.* 1:214.   1831.
[6] Don, G.   *Hist. Dichl. Pls.* 1:579.   1831.

sent to a brother official at Macao for a " pot of the best *chaw*," and this is supposed to be the earliest known mention by an Englishman. Adam Olearius [1] describes the use of tea in Persia in 1633, and says — his book being published in 1647 — " this herb is now so well known in most parts of Europe, where many persons of quality use it with good success." In 1638, Mandelslo [2] visited Japan and about this time wrote of the *tsia* or tea of Japan.

Prior to 1657, tea was occasionally sold in England at prices ranging from $30 to $50 a pound. In 1661, Mr. Pepys, secretary of the British Admiralty, speaks of " tea (a China drink) of which I had never drank before," and in 1664, the Dutch India Company presented two pounds and two ounces to the King of England as a rare and valuable offering and in 1667 this company imported 100 pounds. In 1725, there were imported into England 370,323 pounds; in 1775, the quantity had increased to 5,648,188 pounds. In 1863, upwards of 136,000,000 pounds were imported of which 85,206,779 pounds were entered for home consumption. In 1863, the United States received 29,761,037 pounds and 72,077,951 pounds in 1880.

In 1810, the first tea plants were carried to Rio Janeiro, together with several hundred Chinese experienced in its culture. The government trials do not seem to have resulted favorably but later, the business being taken up by individuals, its culture seems to be meeting with success and the tea of Brazil, called by its Chinese name of *cha*, enters quite largely into domestic consumption. In 1848, Junius Smith,[3] of South Carolina, imported a number of shrubs and planted them at Greenville. At about the same time some 32,000 plants were imported from China and distributed through the agency of the Patent Office. In 1878, the Department of Agriculture distributed 69,000 plants. In Louisiana, in 1870, a plantation of tea shrubs, three to four hundred in number, is said to have existed.

Campanula edulis Forsk. *Campanulaceae.* BELLFLOWER.
Arabia. The root is thick, sapid and is eaten by children.[4]

C. persicifolia Linn. PEACH BELLS.
Europe and north Asia. This plant has been used as food in England but has long since fallen into disuse.[5] In France it is called *cloche* and is grown as a flowering plant.[6]

C. rapunculoides Linn. CREEPING BELLFLOWER.
Europe and temperate Asia. This plant may be substituted in cultivation for rampion.[7] It has long since fallen into disuse.[8]

C. rapunculus Linn. RAMPION.
Europe, Orient, north Africa and northern Asia. This biennial plant was formerly much cultivated in gardens for its roots as well as its leaves. Loudon says the latter are excellent, eaten raw as a salad or boiled as a spinach, and the root, which has the flavor

[1] *Enc. Brit.* 1:88. 1860. 8th Ed.
[2] *Enc. Brit.* 21:89. 1860. 8th Ed.
[3] *U. S. Pat. Off. Rpt.* 7. 1859.
[4] Don, G. *Hist. Dichl. Pls.* 3:753. 1834.
[5] Johnson, C. P. *Useful Pls. Gt. Brit.* 162. 1862.
[6] Vilmorin *Fl. Pl. Ter.* 217. 1870. 3rd Ed.
[7] Johns, C. A. *Treas. Bot.* 1:208. 1874.
[8] Johnson, C. P. *Useful Pls. Gt. Brit.* 162. 1862.

of walnuts, is also eaten raw like a radish or mixed with salads, either raw or boiled and cold. It is much cultivated in France and Italy, says Johns.[1]

Rampion is recorded in gardens by Pena and Lobel,[2] 1570, and is figured by Tragus,[3] 1552, Lobel,[4] 1576, as well as by other writers of this period, as an improved root. In 1726, Townsend[5] says it is to be found in only few English gardens; and Bryant,[6] 1783, says it is much cultivated in France but in England is now little regarded. It is recorded in American gardens in 1806, 1819 and 1821. As late as 1877, an English writer says rampion is a desirable addition to winter salads.[7]

Campomanesia aromatica Griseb. *Myrtaceae.* GUAVA STRAWBERRY.

Guiana and Cayenne. At Martinique, where this shrub is cultivated, it is called guava strawberry, because the flavor of its delicate pulp reminds one of the Pine strawberry.[8] The fruit is edible.[9]

C. lineatifolia Ruiz & Pav.

Peru. This species furnishes edible fruit.[10]

Canarina campanulata Linn. *Campanulaceae.*

Canary Islands. The fleshy capsule, roots and young shoots are said to be edible.[11]

Canarium album Raeusch. *Burseraceae.* CANARIUM

A tree native of China and Cochin China, Anam and the Philippines. The fruit is pickled and used as olives.[12]

C. commune Linn. CHINESE OLIVE. JAVA ALMOND. WILD ALMOND.

Moluccas. This fine-looking tree is cultivated for the sake of its fruit which, in taste, is something like an almond. An oil is expressed from the seed which in Java is used in lamps and when fresh is mixed with food. Bread is also made from its nuts in the island of Celebes. In Ceylon, the nut is called wild almond by Europeans and is eaten.

C. edule Hook. f.

Tropical Africa. This is the *safu* of the island of St. Thomas in the Gulf of Guinea, where its fruit is much esteemed. In taste, the fruit is bitter and astringent; it is usually roasted.

C. pimela Kon.

Cochin China, China and Java. The black fruit is sometimes pickled.[13]

[1] Johns, C. A. *Treas. Bot.* 1:208. 1874.
[2] Pena and Lobel *Advers.* 91. 1570.
[3] Tragus *Stirp.* 725. 1552.
[4] Lobel *Obs.* 178. 1576.
[5] Townsend *Seedsman* 23. 1726.
[6] Bryant *Fl. Diet.* 27. 1783.
[7] Hobday, E. *Cottage Gard.* 113. 1877.
[8] Berlanger *Trans. N. Y. Agr. Soc.* 677. 1864. (*Psidium aromaticum*)
[9] Unger, F. *U. S. Pat. Off. Rpt.* 349. 1859. (*Psidium aromaticum*)
[10] Ibid.
[11] Syme, J. T. *Treas. Bot.* 1:212. 1870.
[12] Don, G. *Hist. Dichl. Pls.* 2:85. 1832.
[13] Ibid.

C. sylvestre Gaertn.

Amboina. The plant bears nuts with edible kernels.[1]

Canavalia ensiformis DC. *Leguminosae.* HORSE BEAN. OVERLOOK. SWORD BEAN.

Tropical Africa. This climbing plant is commonly cultivated about Bombay. The half-grown pods are eaten.[2] It is cultivated in the Peninsula for its esculent pods;[3] in Burma to a small extent, where its young pods are eaten;[4] and also in the Philippines.[5] The plant is common in woods in the East Indies, tropical Africa, Mexico, Brazil and the West Indies. It is called *overlook* by the negroes of Jamaica.[6] Elliott[7] says it is found only in a cultivated state and is probably the domesticated form of *C. virosa.* Firminger[8] says it is a native vegetable of India, the pod large, flat, sword-shaped, fully nine inches long, and more than an inch and a quarter wide. Though rather coarse-looking, yet when sliced and boiled, is exceedingly tender and little, if any, inferior to the French bean. Roxburgh[9] describes three varieties: flowers and seeds red; flowers white and seeds red; flowers and large seed white. This last variety is considered the best and is used on the tables of Europeans as well as by the natives of Sylhet where it is indigenous. Drury[10] says it is a common plant in hedges and thickets and in cultivation. It is called in India *mukhun seen.*[11]

Canella alba Murr. *Canellaceae.* WILD CINNAMON.

West Indies. The bark is employed by the negroes as a condiment and has some reputation as an antiscorbutic.[12]

Canna achiras Gill. *Scitamineae.* CANNA.

South Africa. This plant is said to furnish tubers used as food in Peru and Chile.[13] It is one of the species cultivated in the West Indies for the manufacture of the arrowroot known as *tous les mois* according to Balfour.[14]

C. coccinea Mill. INDIAN SHOT.

East Indies. This plant is said by Mueller[15] and Balfour to yield the *tous les mois* of the West Indies.

---

[1] Don, G. *Hist. Dichl. Pls.* 2:85. 1832.

[2] Pickering, C. *Chron. Hist. Pls.* 686. 1879.

[3] Ibid.

[4] Ibid.

[5] Ibid.

[6] Smith, A. *Treas. Bot.* 1:212. 1870. (*C. gladiata*)

[7] Elliott, W. *Bot. Soc. Edinb.* 7:296. 1863. (*C. gladiata*)

[8] Firminger, T. A. C. *Gard. Ind.* 148. 1874.

[9] Ibid.

[10] Drury, H. *Useful Pls. Ind.* 105. 1858.

[11] Firminger, T. A. C. *Gard. Ind.* 148. 1874.

[12] *U. S. Disp.* 198. 1865.

[13] Lindley, J. *Med. Econ. Bot.* 50. 1849.

[14] Balfour, J. H. *Bot. Man.* 607. 1875.

[15] Mueller, F. *Sel. Pls.* 88. 1891.

C. edulis Ker-Gawl.

American tropics. This plant is cultivated in the islands of St. Christopher, Trinidad and probably elsewhere. The tubers are said to be quite large and when rasped to a pulp furnish, by washing and straining, one of the classes of arrowroot known as *tous les mois*.[1, 2] It is one of the hardiest of arrowroot plants. It is the *adeira*[3] or *achiras*[4] of Peru.

C. glauca Linn.

Mexico and West Indies. This is one of the West Indian arrowroot cannas.[5]

Cannabis sativa Linn.   *Urticaceae.*   FIMBLE.   GALLOW GRASS.   HEMP.

Caspian, central Asia and northwestern Himalayas. Hemp is spontaneous in the north of India and in Siberia. It has also been found wild in the Caucasus and in the north of China. Its native country is probably the region of the Caspian. Hemp was cultivated by the Celts.[6] The Scythians, according to Herodotus,[7] cultivated it. The Hebrews and the ancient Egyptians did not know it, for no mention is made of it in the sacred books and it does not appear in the envelopes of the mummies. Its culture is ancient throughout the southern provinces of India as a textile plant and for the stimulating properties of the leaves, flowers and seeds.[8] Dioscorides[9] alludes to the strength of the ropes made from its fibre and the use of the seeds in medicine. Galen refers to it medicinally. It was known in China as early as A. D. 220.[10] It was introduced into the United States before 1639, as Wm. Wood[11] mentions it.

Hempseed was served fried for dessert by the ancients.[12] In Russia, Poland and neighboring countries, the peasants are extremely fond of parched hempseed and it is eaten even by the nobility. The oil expressed from the seed is much used as food during the time of the fasts in the Volga region.[13] The plant is cultivated by the Hottentots for the purpose of smoking and it is used in like manner by the negroes of Brazil.[14] In the East, hemp is grown largely for the sake of the *churras*, or resin, which possesses intoxicating properties. The Arabs smoke the sun-dried leaf mixed with tobacco in huge pipes,[15] while the Africans smoke the hemp alone. For fibre purposes and for seed, the plant is largely grown in Russia and North America.

---

[1] Mueller, F.   *Sel. Pls.* 88.   1891.

[2] Balfour, J. H.   *Bot. Man.* 607.   1875.

[3] Mueller, F.   *Sel. Pls.* 88.   1891.

[4] Pickering, C.   *Chron. Hist. Pls.* 717.   1879.

[5] Mueller, F.   *Sel. Pls.* 88.   1891.

[6] De Candolle, A.   *Geog. Bot.* 2:835.   1855.

[7] Ibid.

[8] Ibid.

[9] Targioni-Tozzetti *Journ. Hort. Soc. Lond.* 9:149.   1855.

[10] Stille, A.   *Therap. Mat. Med.* 1:955.   1874.

[11] Pickering, C.   *Chron. Hist. Pls.* 77.   1879.

[12] Soyer, A.   *Pantroph.* 48.   1853.

[13] Loudon, J. C.   *Enc. Agr.* 107.   1866.

[14] Stille, A.   *Therap. Mat. Med.* 1:957.   1874.

[15] Masters, M. T.   *Treas. Bot.* 1:214.   1870.

Capparis aphylla Roth. *Capparideae.* CAPER. KUREEL.

Northern Africa, Arabia and East Indies. In India, the bud of this plant is eaten as a potherb, and the fruit is largely consumed by the natives, both green and ripe [1] and is formed into a pickle.[2] In Sind, the flower-buds are used as a pickle, and the unripe fruit is cooked and eaten. Both the ripe and unripe fruit, prepared into a bitter-tasting pickle, is exported into Hindustan.[3] Its fruit, before ripening, is cooked and eaten by the Banians of Arabia.[4] The African species is described by Barth [5] as forming one of the characteristic features in the vegetation of Africa from the desert to the Niger, the dried berries constituting an important article of food, while the roots when burned yield no small quantity of salt.

C. horrida Linn. f. CAPER.

Tropical Asia and Malays. In the southern Punjab and Sind, the fruit is pickled.

C. spinosa Linn. CAPER.

Mediterranean regions, East Indies and Orient. This species furnishes buds which are substituted for the capers of commerce.[6] It is used as a caper.[7] The preserved buds have received wide distribution as a vegetable. The caper was known to the ancient Greeks, and the renowned Phryne, at the first period of her residence in Athens, was a dealer in capers.[8] The Greeks of the Crimea, according to Pallas,[9] eat the sprouts, which resemble those of asparagus, as well as the bud, shoot, and, in short, every eatable part of the shrub. Wilkinson [10] states that the fruit of the Egyptian caper, or *lussef,* is very large, like a small cucumber, about two and a half inches long and is eaten by the Arabs. According to Ruellius,[11] Aristotle and Theophrastus describe the plant as not cultivated in gardens, but in his time, 1536, it was in the gardens of France. In Sind and the Punjab, the fruit is pickled and eaten. It is now cultivated in the south of Europe for the flower-buds, which furnish the capers of commerce. About 1755, capers were imported into South Carolina by Henry Laurens.[12] They were raised successfully for two years in Louisiana, before 1854, but the plants afterwards perished by frost.[13]

C. tomentosa Lam. KOWANGEE.

This is the *kowangee* of tropical Africa. In famines at Madi, spinach is made from its leaves.[14]

---

[1] Drury, H. *Useful Pls. Ind.* 3. 1873.
[2] Royle, J. F. *Illustr. Bot. Himal.* 1:73. 1839.
[3] Brandis, D. *Forest Fl.* 14. 1874.
[4] Forskal *Fl. Aeg. Arab.* 82. 1775.
[5] Masters, M. T. *Treas. Bot.* 1:217. 1870. (*C. sodada*)
[6] Pickering, C. *Chron. Hist. Pls.* 140. 1879.
[7] Unger, F. *U. S. Pat. Off. Rpt.* 359. 1859.
[8] Ibid.
[9] Pallas, P. S. *Trav. Russia* 2:449. 1803.
[10] Wilkinson, J. G. *Anc. Egypt.* 2:29. 1854.
[11] Ruellius *Nat. Stirp.* 561. 1536
[12] *Hist. Mass. Hort. Soc.* 29. 1880.
[13] Bry, H. M. *U. S. Pat. Off. Rpt.* 225. 1854.
[14] Speke, J. H. *Journ. Disc. Source Nile* 562. 1864.

Capraria biflora Linn. *Scrophularineae.* GOAT-WEED. JAMAICA TEA. SMART WEED. WEST INDIA TEA.

Tropical America. Lunan[1] says the leaves not only resemble those of tea but make an equally agreeable decoction. Titford[2] says an infusion of them is a very good beverage.

Capsella bursa-pastoris Medic. *Cruciferae.* MOTHER'S HEART. SHEPHERD'S PURSE.

Temperate regions. One of the commonest of weeds, this plant has accompanied Europeans in all their navigations and established itself wherever they have settled to till the soil. Johns[3] says it was formerly used as a potherb. Johnson[4] says, as improved by cultivation, "it is used in America as a green vegetable, being largely raised about Philadelphia for sale in the markets." Darlington,[5] the botanist, who lived near Philadelphia, calls it "a worthless little intruder from Europe," and we are disposed to believe that the statement of its culture is one of the errors which are copied from book to book. In China, it is collected by the poor and largely eaten as food.[6]

Capsicum. *Solanaceae.*

Tropical America. Ancient Sanscrit or Chinese names for the genus are not known. The first mention that is on record is by Peter Martyr[7] in his epistle dated Sept. 1493, when he says Columbus brought home with him "pepper more pungent than that from Caucasus." In his *Decades of the Ocean* he says: "There are innumerable Kyndes of Ages, the varietie whereof, is known by theyr leaves and flowers. One kind of these, is called *guanaguax*, this is white both within and without. Another named *guaraguei* is of violet colour without and white within. *Squi* are whyte within and without. *Tunna* is altogether of violet colours. *Hobos* is yelowe both of skynne and inner substance. There is an other named *atibunicix*, the skynne of this is of violet coloure and the substance white. *Aniguamar* hath his skynne also of violet coloure and is white within. *Guaccaracca* hath a white skynne and the substance of violet colour. There are many other, which are not yet brought to us." This variability indicates an antiquity of cultivation.

Veytia[8] says the Olmecs raised chilis before the time of the Toltecs. Sahagun[9] mentions capsium more frequently than any other herb among the edible dishes of the Aztecs. Acosta[10] says it is the principal sauce and the only spice of the Indians. Bancroft[11] says it was eaten by the Nahuathan natives both green and dry, whole and

[1] Lunan, J. *Hort. Jam.* 2:217. 1814.

[2] Titford, W. J. *Hort. Bot. Amer.* 79. 1811.

[3] Johns, C. A. *Treas. Bot.* 1:218. 1870.

[4] Johnson, C. P. *Useful Pls. Gt. Brit.* 49. 1862.

[5] Darlington, W. *Weeds, Useful Pls.* 50. 1860.

[6] Smith, F. P. *Contrib. Mat. Med. China* 196. 1871.

[7] Irving, W. *Columbus* 3:425. 1849.

[8] Bancroft, H. H. *Native Races* 2:343. 1882. Note.

[9] Bancroft, H. H. *Native Races* 2:175. 1882.

[10] Bancroft, H. H. *Native Races* 2:355. 1882.

[11] Ibid.

ground. Garcilasso de la Vega [1] speaks of it as an ancient vegetable in Peru, and one variety was especially valued by royalty. The earliest reference to this genus seems to be by Chanca,[2] physician to the fleet of Columbus, in his second voyage, and occurs in a letter written in 1494 to the Chapter of Seville. Capsicum and its uses are more particularly described by Oviedo,[3] who reached tropical America from Spain in 1514.

Hans Stade,[4] about 1550, mentions the capsicum of the continent of America as being of two kinds: " The one yellow, the other red, both, however, grow in like manner. When green it is as large as the haws that grow on hawthorns. It is a small shrub, about half a fathom high and has small leaves; it is full of peppers which burn the mouth." Lignon in his *History of the Barbadoes*, 1647 to 1653, describes two sorts in Barbados: " The one so like a child's corall, as not to be discerned at the distance of two paces, a crimson and scarlet mixt; the fruit about three inches long and shines more than the best pollisht corall. The other, of the same colour and glistening as much but shaped like a large button of a cloak; both of one and the same quality; both violently strong and growing on a little shrub no bigger than a gooseberry bush." Long [5] says there are about 15 varieties of capsicum in Jamaica, which are found in most parts of the island. Those which are most commonly noticed are the Bell, Goat, Bonnett, Bird, Olive, Hen, Barbary, Finger and Cherry. Of these the Bell is esteemed most proper for pickling. Wafer,[6] 1699, speaking of the Isthmus, says: " They have two sorts of pepper, the one called Bell-pepper, the other Bird-pepper, each sort growing on a weed or shrubby bush about a yard high. The Bird-pepper has the smaller leaf and is most esteemed by the Indians."

Garcilasso de la Vega [7] in his *Royal Commentaries*, 1609, says the most common pepper in Peru is thick, somewhat long, and without a point. This is called *rocot uchu*, or thick pepper, to distinguish it from the next kind. They eat it green and before it assumes its ripe color, which is red. There are others yellow and others brown, though in Spain only the red kind has been seen. There is another kind the length of a geme, a little more or less, and the thickness of the little finger. These were considered a nobler kind and were reserved for the use of the royal family. Another kind of pepper is small and round, exactly like a cherry with its stalk. They call it *chinchi uchu* and it bears far more than the others. It is grown in small quantities and for that reason is the more highly esteemed. Molina [8] says many species of the pimento, called by the Indians *thapi*, " are cultivated in Chili, among others the annual pimento which is there perennial, the berry pimento, and the pimento with a subligenous stalk." Capsicums were eaten in large quantities by the ancient inhabitants of tropical America, and the natives of Guiana now eat the fruit in such abundance as would not be credited by an European unless he were to see it. In Sonora and New Mexico, at the present time, they are universally grown, and

---

[1] Vega *Roy. Comment.* Hak. Soc. Ed. 2:365. 1871.
[2] Flückiger and Hanbury *Pharm.* 406. 1879.
[3] Ibid.
[4] *Captiv. Hans Stade.* Hakl. Soc. Ed. 166. 1874.
[5] Long *Hist. Jam.* 3:721. 1774.
[6] Wafer *Voy. Isthmus Amer.* 100. 1699.
[7] Vega *Roy. Comment.* Hakl. Soc. Ed. 2:365. 1871.
[8] Molina *Hist. Chili* 1:95. 1808.

the pods while green are eaten with various substances, under the name of *chille verde*, while the dishes prepared with the red pods are called *chille colorom*.[1]

Capsicum was brought to Spain by Columbus[2] in 1493. It is mentioned in England in 1548 and was seen by Clusius[3] in Moravia in 1585. Clusius asserts that the plant was brought to India by the Portuguese. Gerarde[4] says these plants are brought from foreign countries, as Guinea, India and those parts, into Spain and Italy, whence we have received seed for our English gardens. There are many peppers, some of which it is more convenient to describe as species

C. annuum Linn. CAYENNE PEPPER. CHILLIES. GUINEA PEPPER. PIMENTO. RED PEPPER.

Tropical regions. Booth[5] says this species was introduced into Europe by the Spaniards and that it was cultivated in England in 1548. The fruits are variable, some being yellow, others red and others black. The pods, according to Loudon,[6] are long or short, round or cherry-shaped. In lower Hungary, the variety now very largely cultivated for commercial purposes, has a spherical, scarlet fruit. It is cultivated in India,[7] in America, and, indeed, almost everywhere in warm countries.

C. baccatum Linn. BIRD PEPPER. BIRDS-EYE PEPPER.

Tropical regions. Booth[8] says this species is indigenous to both the East and West Indies and has been grown in England since 1731. The pods are erect, roundish, egg-shaped, very pungent. It was probably early introduced into India as shown by the belief that it is native. It is used like other red peppers by the Mexicans who call it *chipatane*.[9]

C. cerasiforme Mill. CHERRY PEPPER.

Tropics. Its stem is 12 to 15 inches high; fruit erect, of a deep, rich, glossy scarlet when ripe; of intense piquancy. A variety occurs with larger, more conical and pendent pods, and there is also a variety with yellow fruit.[10]

C. frutescens Linn. AGE. CHILI PEPPER. GOAT PEPPER. SPUR PEPPER.

Tropical America. This plant is considered by some botanists as a native of India, as it has constantly been found in a wild state in the Eastern Islands, but Rumphius[11] argues its American origin from its being so constantly called Chile. It is the *aji* or *uchu* seen by Cieza de Leon[12] in 1532–50, during his travels in Peru and even now is a favorite condiment with the Peruvian Indians. This pepper is cultivated in every part of India,

[1] *U. S. D. A. Rpt.* 425. 1870.
[2] Irving, W. *Colum.* 1:238. 1848.
[3] Flückiger and Hanbury *Pharm.* 406. 1879.
[4] Gerarde, J. *Herb.* 365. 1633 or 1636. 2nd Ed.
[5] Booth, W. B. *Treas. Bot.* 1:219. 1870.
[6] Loudon, J. C. *Hort.* 607. 1860.
[7] Firminger, T. A. C. *Gard. Ind.* 153. 1874.
[8] Booth, W. B. *Treas. Bot.* 1:219. 1870.
[9] Torrey, J. *Bot. U. S. Mex. Bound. Surv.* 152. 1859. (*C. microphyllum*)
[10] Burr, F. *Field, Gard. Veg.* 621. 1863.
[11] Ainslie, W. *Mat. Ind.* 1:306. 1826.
[12] Markham, C. R. *Trav. Cieza de Leon* 1532–50. Hakl. Soc. Ed. 232. 1864. Note.

in two varieties, the red and the yellow,[1] and in Cochin China.[2] In Ceylon there are three varieties, a red, a yellow and a black.[3] It has been in English gardens since 1656. Its long, obtuse pods are very pungent and in their green and ripe state are used for pickling, for making Chile vinegar; the ripe berries are used for making cayenne pepper. Burr[4] describes the fruit as quite small, cone-shaped, coral-red when ripe, and intensely acrid but says it will not succeed in open culture in the north.

C. minimum Roxb. CAYENNE PEPPER.

Philippine Islands. This is said to be the cayenne pepper of India.[5,6] Wight[7] says this pepper is eaten by the natives of India but is not preferred. It grows also on the coast of Guinea and is recognized as a source of capsicum by the British Pharmacopoeia.[8] It is intensely pungent.

C. tetragonum Mill. BONNET PEPPER. LUNAN PEPPER. PAPRIKA. TURKISH PEPPER.

Tropical regions. This species is said by Booth[9] to be the bonnet pepper of Jamaica. The fruits are very fleshy and have a depressed form like a Scotch bonnet. In lower Hungary, under the name *paprika*, the cultivation gives employment to some 2500 families. The fruit is red, some three and a half to five inches long, and three-quarters of an inch to an inch in diameter.

McMahon, 1806,[10] says capsicums are in much estimation for culinary purposes and mentions the Large Heart-shaped as the best. He names also the Cherry, Bell and Long Podded. In 1826, Thorburn[11] offers in his catalog five varieties, the Long or Cayenne, the Tomato-shaped or Squash, the Bell or Ox-heart, the Cherry and the Bird or West Indian. In 1881 he offers ten varieties.

GROUPS OF CAPSICUM.

In the varieties under present cultivation, we have distinct characters in the calyx of several of the groups and in the fruit being pendulous or erect. It is worthy of note that the pendulous varieties have a pendulous bloom as well as fruit, and the erect varieties have erect bloom. Some heavy fruits are erect, while some light fruits are pendulous. Another distinct character is the flavor of the fruit, as for instance all the sweet peppers have a like calyx, and a like color. While again there may seem at first to be considerable variability in the fruits even on the same plant, yet a more careful examination shows that this variability is more apparent than real and comes from a suppression or distortion of growth, all really being of a similar type.

---

[1] Ainslie, W. *Mat. Ind.* 1:306. 1826.
[2] Ibid.
[3] Moon *Indig. Exot. Pls. Ceylon* 1824.
[4] Burr, F. *Field, Gard. Veg.* 619. 1863.
[5] Drury, H. *Useful Pls. Ind.* 111. 1873.
[6] Flückiger and Hanbury *Pharm.* 406. 1879.
[7] Firminger, T. A. C. *Gard. Ind.* 153. 1874. (*C. fastigiatum*)
[8] *U. S. Disp.* 207. 1865. (*C. fastigatum*)
[9] Booth, W. B. *Treas. Bot.* 1:219. 1870.
[10] McMahon, B. *Amer. Gard. Cal.* 319. 1806.
[11] Thorburn *Cat.* 1828.

This history of the botany of the groups can best be seen by the synonymy, which is founded upon figures given with the descriptions.

I.

THE CALYX EMBRACING THE FRUIT.

(a) *Fruits pendulous.*

This form seems to have been the first introduced and presents fruits of extreme pungency and is undoubtedly that described as brought to Europe by Columbus. It presents varieties with straight and recurved fruit and the fruit when ripe is often much contorted and wrinkled.

Capsicum longum. DC. from Fingerhuth.
Siliquastrum tertium. Langer Indianischer pfeffer. Fuch. 733. 1542.
Siliquastrum minus. Fuch. l. c. 732.
Indianischer pfeffer. Saliquastrum. Roeszl. 214. 1550.
Indianischer pfeffer. Trag. 928. 1552.
Piper indicum. Cam. *Epit.* 347. 1586.
Capsicum oblongius Dodonaei. Dalechamp 632. 1587.
Piper indicum minus recurvis siliquis. Hort. Eyst. 1613, 1713.
Piper indicum maximum longum. Hort. Eyst. 1613, 1713.
Capsicum recurvis siliquis. Dod. 716. 1616.
Piper Calecuticum, sive Capsicum oblongius. Bauh. J. 2:943. 1650.
Siliquastrum, Ind. pfeffer. Pancov. n. 296. 1673.
Piper Capsicum. Chabr. 297. 1677.
Piment de Cayenne. Vilm. 151. 1885.
Long Red Cayenne. Ferry.
Mexican Indian, four varieties, one of the exact variety of Fuch. 1542.
Siliquastrum majus. Fuch. 732. 1542.
Long Yellow Cayenne. Hend.
Capsicum longum luteum. Fingerhuth.

(b) *Fruits erect.*

Capsicum annuum acuminatum. Fingerhuth.
Piper ind. minimum erectum. Hort. Eyst. 1613, 1713.
Piper ind. medium longum erectum. Hort. Eyst. 1613, 1713.
Piper longum minus siliquis recurvis. Jonston *Dendrog.* 56. 1662.
Pigment du Chili. Vilm. 410. 1883.
Chili pepper. Vilm. 151. 1885.
Red Cluster. Vilm.
Yellow Chili. Hend.

II.

CALYX PATERIFORM, NOT COVERING THE FLATTENED BASE OF THE FRUIT.

(a) *Fruits long, tapering, pendent.*

Piper indicum sive siliquastrum. Pin. 12. 1561.
Capsicum actuarii. Lob. *Obs.* 172, 1576; *Icon.* **1**:316. 1591.
Capsicum majus. Dalechamp 632. 1587.
Capsicum longioribus siliquis. Ger. 292. 1597.
Piper indicum. Matth. *Op.* 434. 1598.
Capsicum oblongioribus siliquis. Dod. 716. 1616.
Pepe d'India. Dur. C. 344. 1617.

Figures 13 and 14. Piso *De Ind.* 226. 1658.
Guinea pepper or garden coral. Pomet 125. 1748.
Piper indicum bicolor. Blackw. *Herb.* n. 129, f. 2. 1754.
Piment rouge long. Vilm. 409. 1883.
Long Red capsicum or Guinea. Vilm. 150. 1885.

(b) *Fruits short, rounding, pendent.*
Siliquastrum quartum. Fuch. 734. 1542.
Siliquastrum cordatum. Cam. *Epit.* 348. 1586.

Fig. 2 and 6. Piso 225. 1658.
Piper cordatum. Jonston *Dendrog.* 56. 1662.
Capsicum cordiforme, Mill. Fingerhuth.
Oxheart. Thorb.
New Oxheart. Thorb.

III.
Calyx Funnel-form, not Embracing Base of Fruit.

(a) *Fruit pendent, long.*
Piper indicum medium. Hort. Eyst. 1613, 1713.
Piper siliquis flavis. Hort. Eyst. 1613, 1713.
Piper indicum aureum latum. Hort. Eyst. 1613, 1713.

Fig. in Hernandez. *Nova Hisp.* 137. 1651.
Piper indicum longioribus siliquis rubi. Sweert. t. 35, f. 3. 1654.
Piper vulgatissime. Jonston t. 56. 1662.
Piper oblongum recurvis siliquis. Jonston t. 56. 1662.
Capsicum fructu conico albicante, per maturitaken minato. Dill. t. 60. 1774.
Piment jaune long. Vilm. 409. 1883.
Long Yellow Capsicum. Vilm. 151. 1885.

(b) *Fruits pendent, round.*
Siliquastrum rotundum. Cam. *Epit.* 348. 1586.
Piper rotundum majus surrectum. Jonston t. 56. 1662.

Figure 5. Piso 225. 1658.
Cherry Red, of some seedsmen.

(c) *Fruits erect, round.*
Piper minimum siliquis rotundis. Hort. Eyst. 1613, 1713.
Capsicum cersasiforme. Fingerhuth.
Piment cerise. Vilm. 411. 1883.
Cherry Pepper. Burr 621. 1863; Vilm. 152. 1885.

IV.
Calyx Funnel-form, as Large as Base; Fruit More or Less Irregularly Swollen, not Pointed, Pendent.

Capsicum luteum. Lam. Fingerhuth. t. 8.
Prince of Wales, of some seedsmen (yellow).
(Perhaps) *Capsicum latum Dodanaei.* Dalechamp 632. 1587.
Capsicum latis siliquis. Dod. 717. 1616.
Capsicum siliquis latiore and rotundiore. Bauh. J. **2**:943. 1651.
Piper capsicum siliqui latiori et rotundiore. Chabr. 297. 1677.

V.

CALYX SET IN CONCAVITY OF FRUIT.

This character perhaps results only from the swollen condition of the fruit as produced by selection and culture. As, however, it appears constant in our seedsmen's varieties, it may answer our purpose here.

(a) *Fruit very much flattened.*
Piper indicum rotundum maximum. Hort. Eyst. 1613, 1713.
Solanum mordeus, etc., Bonnet Pepper. Pluk. *Phyt.* t. 227, p. 1. 1691.
Capsicum tetragonum. Fingerhuth t. 10.
Piment tomato. Vilm. 413. 1886.
Red Tomato capsicum or American bonnet. Vilm. 154. 1885.

(b) *Fruit squarish, angular, very much swollen, large.*

This group includes the Bell, Sweet Mountain, Monstrous, and Spanish Mammoth of Vilmorin; the Giant Emperor, Golden Dawn, etc. of American seedsmen. The varieties of this class seem referable to *Capsicum annuum rugulosum* Fing., *C. grossum pomiforme* Fing. and *C. angulosum* Fing. but these have not yet been sufficiently studied.

Group V embraces the sweet peppers and none other. A sweet kind is noted by Acosta,[1] 1604, and it is perhaps the *rocot uchu* of Peru, as mentioned by Garcilasso de la Vega.[2] Sweet peppers are also referred to by Piso,[3] 1648.

Occasionally *Capsicum baccatum* Linn. is grown, but the species is too southern for general use in the North. Its synonymy follows:

Capsicum, Piper indicum brevioribus siliquis. Lob. *Obs.* 172. 1576; *Icon.* **1**:317. 1591.
Capsicum brasilianum. Dalechamp 633. 1587; Pancov. n. 297. 1673.
Capsicum minimis siliquis. Ger. 292. 1597; Dod. 717. 1616.
Fig. 8. Piso *De Ind.* 225. 1658.
Peperis capsici varietas, siliqua parva, etc. Chabr. 297. 1677.
Capsicum baccatum Linn. Fingerhuth t. 4.
Small Red Cayenne. Briggs *Seed Cat.* 1874.

Caragana ambigua Stocks. *Leguminosae.*

Baluchistan. The flowers are eaten by the Brahmans in Baluchistan, where it is called *shinalak.*[4]

C. arborescens Lam. SIBERIAN PEA TREE.

Siberia. The seeds are of culinary value but are used particularly for feeding poultry.[5]

Cardamine amara Linn. *Cruciferae.* BITTER CRESS.

Europe and northern Asia. Lightfoot [6] says the young leaves are acrid and bitter

---

[1] Acosta *Nat. Mor. Hist. Ind.* 266. 1604. Grimestone Ed.
[2] Vega *Roy. Comment.* Hakl. Soc. Ed. **2**:365. 1871.
[3] Piso *Hist. Rerum Nat. Bras.* 108. 1648.
[4] Brandis, D. *Forest Fl.* 134. 1876.
[5] Mueller, F. *Sel. Pls.* 90. 1891.
[6] Lightfoot, J. *Fl. Scot.* **1**:350. 1789.

but do not taste amiss in salads. Johnson [1] says the leaves are often employed by country people in salads, their taste, although pungent and bitter, is not unpleasant.

C. diphylla Wood. PEPPER-ROOT.

North America. The long, crisp rootstocks taste like water cress.[2] Pursh says they are of a pungent, mustard-like taste and are used by the natives as mustard.

C. glacialis DC. SCURVY GRASS.

Capt. Cook found this scurvy plant in plenty about the Strait of Magellan in damp places and used it as an antiscorbutic.

C. hirsuta Linn. HAIRY CRESS. LAMB'S CRESS. SCURVY GRASS.

Temperate and subtropical regions. Ross [3] calls this the scurvy grass of Tierra del Fuego; it is edible. Lightfoot [4] says the young leaves, in Scotland, make a good salad, and Johns [5] says the leaves and flowers form an agreeable salad. In the United States, Elliott [6] and Dewey [7] both say the common bitter cress is used as a salad.

C. nasturtioides Bert.

Chile. The plant is eaten as a cress.[8]

C. pratensis Linn. CUCKOO FLOWER. LADY'S SMOCK. MAYFLOWER. MEADOW CRESS.

Temperate zone. This is an insignificant and nearly worthless salad plant, native to the whole of Europe, northern Asia and Arctic America, extending to Vermont and Wisconsin. It has a piquant savor and is used as water cress. It is recorded as cultivated in the vegetable garden in France by Noisette,[9] 1829, and by Vilmorin,[10] 1883, yet, as Decaisne and Naudin [11] remark, but rarely. There is no record of its cultivation in England, but in America it is described by Burr [12] in four varieties, differing in the flowers, and as having become naturalized to a limited extent, a fact which implies a certain cultivation. Its seed is not offered in our catalogs.

C. rotundifolia Michx. ROUND-LEAVED CUCKOO FLOWERS. WATER-CRESS.

Northern America. The leaves, says Gray,[13] " have just the taste of the English water-cress."

C. sarmentosa Forst. f.

Islands of the Pacific. This plant is eaten as a cress in New Caledonia.[14]

[1] Johnson, C. P. *Useful Pls. Gt. Brit.* 29. 1862.

[2] Gray, A. *Man. Bot.* 65. 1868. (*Dentaria diphylla*)

[3] Ross *Voy. Antarct. Reg.* 2:300. 1847.

[4] Lightfoot, J. *Fl. Scot.* 1:349. 1789.

[5] Johns, C. A. *Treas. Bot.* 1:221. 1870.

[6] Elliott, S. *Bot. So. Car., Ga.* 2:144. 1824. (*C. pennsylvanicum*)

[7] Dewey, C. *Rpt. Herb. Flow. Pls. Mass.* 36. 1840. (*C. pensylvanica*)

[8] Unger, F. *U. S. Pat. Off. Rpt.* 356. 1859.

[9] Noisette *Man. Jard.* 356. 1829.

[10] Vilmorin *Les Pls. Potag.* 198. 1883.

[11] Decaisne and Naudin *Man. Jard.* 4:227. 1866.

[12] Burr, F. *Field, Gard. Veg.* 344. 1863.

[13] Gray, A. *Man. Bot.* 66. 1868.

[14] Seemann, B. *Fl. Viti.* 5. 1865–73.

Cardiopteris lobata Wall. *Olacineae.*

East Indies. It has oleraceous leaves, edible but almost insipid.[1]

Cardiospermum halicacabum Linn. *Sapindaceae.* BALLOON VINE. HEART PEA. WINTER CHERRY.

Tropics. This climbing vine, ornamental on account of its inflated pods, is said by Pickering[2] to be native of subtropical North America and by Black[3] to occur in all tropical countries. In Burma, according to Mason,[4] it is grown in great quantities as a vegetable. In the Moluccas, as Drury[5] states, the leaves are cooked. In equatorial Africa, it is common and the leaves are made into spinach by the natives as Grant[6] observed.

Careya arborea Roxb. *Myrtaceae.* SLOW-MATCH TREE.

East India. The fruit is eaten.[7]

Carica citriformis Jacq. f. *Passifloreae.*

African Tropics. This plant bears a fruit the size of an orange, eatable but insipid.[8]

C. microcarpa Jacq.

South America. The plant bears fruit the size of a cherry.[9]

C. papaya Linn. MELON TREE. PAPAYA. PAPAW.

American tropics. The papaw tree is indigenous in Brazil, Surinam and the West Indies and from these places has been taken to the Congo. Its transfer to the East Indies may have occurred soon after the discovery of America, for, as early as 1626, seeds were brought from the East Indies to Nepal. Its further distribution to China, Japan and the islands of the Pacific Ocean took place only in the last century.[10] Linschoten[11] says, it came from the East Indies to the Philippines and was taken thence to Goa. In east Florida, it grows well. Of the fruit, Wm. S. Allen of Florida, writes that it is often as large as a melon, yet the best varieties for eating — those having the best flavor — are no larger than a very large pear. The fruit is used extensively in south Florida and Cuba for making tough meat tender. The toughest meat is made tender by putting a few of the leaves or the green fruit of the pawpaw tree into the pot with the meat and boiling. In a few minutes, the meat will cleave from the bones and be as tender as one could wish.

Dr. Morris read before the Maryland Academy of Science a paper by Mr. Lugger in

---

[1] Baillon, H. *Hist. Pls.* 5:307. 1878. (*C. rumphii*)
[2] Pickering, C. *Chron. Hist. Pls.* 567. 1879.
[3] Black, A. A. *Treas. Bot.* 1:222. 1870.
[4] Pickering, C. *Chron. Hist. Pls.* 567. 1879.
[5] Drury, H. *Useful Pls. Ind.* 112. 1873.
[6] Pickering, C. *Chron. Hist. Pls.* 567. 1879.
[7] Lindley, J. *Veg. King.* 755. 1846.
[8] Don, G. *Hist. Dichl. Pls.* 3:44. 1834.
[9] Don, G. *Hist. Dichl. Pls.* 3:45. 1834.
[10] Unger, F. *U. S. Pat. Off. Rpt.* 331. 1859.
[11] Nuttall, T. *No. Amer. Sylva* 2:115, 116. 1865.

which the fruit is said to attain a weight of 15 pounds, is melon-shaped, and marked as melons are with longitudinally-colored stripes. The fruit may be sliced and pickled. The ripe fruit is eaten with sugar or salt and pepper. The seeds are egg-shaped, strong-flavored and used as a spice. The leaves have the property of making meat wrapped up in them tender. Brandis[1] also says, meat becomes tender by washing it with water impregnated with the milky juice, or by suspending the joint under the tree. Williams[2] says, the Chinese are acquainted with this property and make use of it sometimes to soften the flesh of ancient hens and cocks by hanging the newly-killed birds in the tree, or by feeding them upon the fruit beforehand. The Chinese also eat the leaves. Herndon[3] says, on the mountains of Peru, the fruit is of the size of a common muskmelon, with a green skin and yellow pulp, which is eaten and is very sweet and of a delicate flavor. Hartt[4] says the *mamao*, a species of Carica in Brazil, furnishes a large and savory fruit full of seeds. Brandis[5] calls the ripe fruit in India sweet and pleasant, and says the unripe fruit is eaten as a vegetable and preserved. Wilkes[6] says, it is prized by the natives of Fiji, and Gray[7] says the fruit is a favorite esculent of the Sandwich Islanders. The tree bears in a year or 18 months from seed and is cultivated in tropical climates.

C. posopora Linn.

Peru and Chile. This species bears yellow, pear-shaped, edible fruit.[8]

Carissa grandiflora, A. DC. *Apocynaceae.* AMATUNGULA. CARAUNDA. NATAL PLUM.

South Africa. The flavor is subacid and agreeable and the fruit is much prized in Natal for preserving.[9]

Carlina acanthifolia All. *Compositae.* ACANTHUS-LEAVED THISTLE.

Mediterranean region. The receptacle of the flowers may be used like that of an artichoke.

C. vulgaris Linn. CARLINE THISTLE.

Europe and northern Asia. The receptacles of the flowers are used like an artichoke.

Carlotea formosissimum Arruda. Family unknown.

Pernambuco. The tuberous root, abounding with soft and nutritive fecula, has afforded assistance to the people in parts of Brazil, in times of drought.[10]

C. speciosa Arruda.

Pernambuco. The tuberous roots have found use in Brazil.

---

[1] Brandis, D. *Forest Fl.* 245. 1874.

[2] Williams, S. W. *Mid. King.* 1:284. 1848.

[3] Herndon, W. L., and Gibbon, L. *Explor. Vall. Amaz.* 1:87. 1854.

[4] Hartt *Geog. Braz.* 217. 1870.

[5] Brandis, D. *Forest Fl.* 245. 1876.

[6] Wilkes, C. *U. S. Explor. Exped.* 3:334. 1845.

[7] Gray, A. *Bot. U. S. Explor. Exped.* 640. 1854.

[8] Don, G. *Hist. Dichl. Pls.* 3:44. 1834.

[9] Jackson, J. R. *Treas. Bot.* 2:1263. 1876. (*Arduina grandiflora*)

[10] Koster *Trav. Braz.* 2:368. 1817.

Carpodinus acida Sabine. *Apocynaceae.*

A climbing shrub of Sierra Leone. The fruit has a sharp, acid taste, with some little bitterness, which prevents its being agreeable; it is, however, much liked by the natives.[1]

C. dulcis Sabine. SWEET PISHAMIN.

Sierra Leone. The fruit is yellow externally, in size and appearance resembling a lime. When broken or cut it yields a quantity of sweet, milky juice. The pulp, in which many large seeds are found, is also agreeable and sweet.[2]

Carthamus tinctorius Linn. *Compositae.* FALSE SAFFRON. SAFFLOWER.

Old World; extensively cultivated in India, China and other parts of Asia; also in Egypt, southern Europe and in South America. Under the name of safflower, the flowers are used largely for dyeing. Phillips[3] says the flowers are used in Spain and in the Levant to color foods. The oil from the seeds in India is used for lamps and for culinary purposes, says Drury.[4] In South America, as well as in Jamaica, as Ainslie[5] writes, the flowers are much used for coloring broths and ragouts. They were so used in England in the time of Parkinson.[6] In American seed catalogs, the seed is offered under the name of saffron but the true saffron is the product of a crocus.

Carum bulbocastanum Koch. *Umbelliferae.* PIGNUT.

Europe and Asia. The tuberous roots serve as a culinary vegetable and the fruit as a condiment.[7] Lightfoot[8] says the roots are bulbous and taste like a chestnut; in some parts of England they are boiled in broth and served at the table.[9] Pallas says the roots are eaten by the Tartars.

C. capense Sond.

South Africa. The. edible, aromatic root is called *feukel-wortel.*

C. carvi Linn. CARAWAY. KUMMEL.

Europe, Orient and northern Asia. This biennial plant is described by Dioscorides and mentioned by Galen. Pliny states that it derives its name from its native country, Caria, and that it is used chiefly in the culinary art. Caraway is now cultivated largely for its seed in England, particularly in Essex, in Iceland where it is apparently wild,[10] in Morocco and elsewhere. The seeds are exported from Finland, Russia, Germany, Prussia, North Holland and Morocco.[11] The seeds are used in confectionery and distillation. In England, the seed is used by cottagers to mix with their bread, and caraway-

[1] Sabine, J.   *Trans. Hort. Soc. Lond.* 5:456.   1824.

[2] Sabine, J.   *Trans. Hort. Soc. Lond.* 5:455.   1824.

[3] Phillips, H.   *Comp. Kitch. Gard.* 2:202.   1831.

[4] Drury, H.   *Useful Pls. Ind.* 116.   1873.

[5] Ainslie, W.   *Mat. Ind.* 2:364.   1826.

[6] Parkinson *Par. Terr.* 329.   1904.   (Reprint of 1629.)

[7] Mueller, F.   *Sel. Pls.* 93.   1891.

[8] Lightfoot, J.   *Fl. Scot.* 1:156.   1789.   (*Bunium bulbocastanum*)

[9] Pallas, P. S.   *Trav. Russia* 2:189.   1803.   (*Bunium bulbocastanum*)

[10] Babington *Journ. Linn. Soc. Bot.* 11:310.   1871.

[11] Flückiger and Hanbury *Pharm.* 273.   1879.

seed bread may often be found in restaurants in the United States.   In Schleswig-
Holstein and Holland, they are added to a skim-milk cheese called Kummel cheese.   The
roots are edible and were considered by Parkinson[1] to be superior to parsnips and are
still eaten in northern Europe.   The young leaves form a good salad and the larger ones
may be boiled and eaten as a spinach.[2]   Lightfoot[3] says the young leaves are good in
soups and the roots are by some esteemed a delicate food.   It was cultivated in American
gardens in 1806 and is still to be found.

The seeds of caraway were found by O. Heer[4] in the debris of the lake habitations
of Switzerland, which establishes the antiquity of the plant in Europe.   This fact renders
it more probable that the *Careum* of Pliny[5] is this plant, as also its use by Apicius[6] would
indicate.   It is mentioned as cultivated in Morocco by Edrisi in the twelfth century.
In the Arab writings, quoted by Ibn Baytar, a Mauro-Spaniard of the thirteenth century,
it is likewise named; and Fleuckiger and Hanbury think the use of this spice commenced
at about this period.   Caraway is not noticed by St. Isidore, Archbishop of Seville in
the seventh century, although he notices dill, coriander, anise, and parsley; nor is it named
by St. Hildegard in Germany in the twelfth century.   But, on the other hand, two German
medicine books of the twelfth and thirteenth centuries use the word *cumich*, which is still
the popular name in southern Germany.   In the same period the seeds appear to have
been used by the Welsh physicians of Myddvai, and caraway was certainly in use in England at the close of the fourteenth century and is named in Turner's *Libellus*, 1538, as
also in *The Forme of Cury*, 1390.

C. copticum Benth. & Hook. f.

Europe, north Africa and northern Asia.   This small plant is very much cultivated
during the cold season in Bengal, where it is called *ajowan, ajonan* or *javanee*.   The seeds
have an aromatic smell and warm pungent taste and are used in India for culinary purposes as spices with betel nuts and paw leaves and as a carminative medicine.[7]   The
seeds are said to have the flavor of thyme.

C. ferulaefolium Boiss.

Mediterranean region.   This plant is a perennial herb with small, edible tubers.[8]
Its whitish and bitterish roots are said by Dioscorides to be eaten both raw and cooked.
In Cyprus, these roots are still cooked and eaten.

C. gairdneri A. Gray.   EDIBLE-ROOTED CARAWAY.

Western North America   The root is a prominent article of food among the California Indians.[9]   The Nez Percé Indians collect the tuberous roots and boil them like

---

[1] Parkinson *Par. Terr.* 515. 1904. (Reprint of 1629.)

[2] Johnson, C. P.   *Useful Pls. Gt. Brit.* 113.   1862.

[3] Lightfoot, J.   *Fl. Scot.* 1:169.   1789.

[4] *Gard. Chron.* 1068.   1866.

[5] Pliny lib. 19, c. 49.

[6] Apicius lib. 1, c. 30; 2, c. 4; 8, c. 2.

[7] Dutt, U. C.   *Mat. Med. Hindus* 173.   1877.

[8] Mueller, F.   *Sel. Pls.* 93.   1891.

[9] Brewer and Watson *Bot. Cal.* 1:259.   1880.

potatoes.   They are the size of a man's finger, of a very agreeable taste, with a cream-like flavor.[1]

C. kelloggii A. Gray.

California.   The root is used by the Indians of California as a food.[2]

C. petroselinum Benth. & Hook. f.   PARSLEY.

Old World.   Parsley is cultivated everywhere in gardens, for use as a seasoning and as a garnish.   Eaten with any dish strongly seasoned with onions, it takes off the smell of onion and prevents the after taste.   It excels other herbs for communicating flavor to soups and stews.   Among the Greeks and Romans, parsley formed part of the festive garlands, and Pliny states that in his time there was not a salad or a sauce presented at table without it.   The ancients supposed that its grateful smell absorbed the inebriating fumes of wine and by that means prevented intoxication.   Parsley seems to be the *apium* of the ancient Romans, the *selinon* of Theophrastus,[3] who, 322 B. C., describes two varie-ties; one with crowded, dense leaves, the other with more open and broader leafage. Columella,[4] 42 A. D., speaks of the broad-leaved and curled sorts and gives directions for the culture of each; and Pliny,[5] 79 A. D., mentions the cultivated form as having varieties with a thick leaf and a crisp leaf, evidently copying from Theophrastus.   He adds, how-ever, apparently from his own observation, that *apium* is in general esteem, for the sprays find use in large quantities in broths and give a peculiar palatability to condimental foods. In Achaea, it is used, so he says, for the victor's crown in the Nemean games.

A little later, Galen,[6] 164 A. D., praises parsley as among the commonest of foods, sweet and grateful to the stomach, and says that some eat it with *smyrnium* mixed with the leaves of lettuce.   Palladius,[7] about 210 A. D., mentions the method of procuring the curled form from the common and says that old seed germinates more freely than fresh seed.   (This is a peculiarity of parsley seed at present and is directly the opposite to that of celery seed.)   Apicius,[8] 230 A. D., a writer on cookery, makes use of the *apium viride* and of the seed.   In the thirteenth century, Albertus Magnus [9] speaks of *apium* and *petroselinum* as being kitchen-garden plants; he speaks of each as being an herb the first year, a vegetable the second year of growth.   He says *apium* has broader and larger leaves than *petroselinum* and that *petroselinum* has leaves like the *cicuta;* and that the *petrose-linum* is more of a medicine than a food.

Booth [10] states that parsley was introduced into England in 1548 from Sardinia.   In addition to its general use, in Cornwall where it is much esteemed, it is largely used in

---

[1] *U. S. D. A. Rpt.* 407.   1870.   (*Endosmia gairdneri*)

[2] Brewer and Watson *Bot. Cal.* 1:259.   1880.

[3] Theophrastus lib. 7, c. 4.

[4] Columella lib. 11, c. 3.

[5] Pliny lib. 19, c. 37, c. 46; lib. 20, c. 44.

[6] Galen *Aliment.* lib. 2, 154.   1547.

[7] Palladius lib. 5, c. 3.

[8] Apicius *Opson.*   1709.

[9] Albertus Magnus *Veg.*   Jessen Ed. 1867.

[10] Booth, W. B.   *Treas. Bot.* 1:79.   1870.

parsley pies. The plant is now naturalized in some parts of England and Scotland. Parsley is mentioned as seen on the coast of Massachusetts by Verazzano,[1] about 1524, but this is undoubtedly an error. Two kinds, the common and curled, are mentioned for our gardens by McMahon,[2] 1806. Fessenden,[3] 1828, names three sorts, and Thorburn,[4] 1881, four sorts.

At the present time we have five forms; the common or plain-leaved, the celery-leaved or Neapolitan, the curled, the fern-leaved and the Hamburg, or turnip-rooted.

I.
PLAIN-LEAVED PARSLEY.

The plain-leaved form is not now much grown, having been superseded by the more ornamental, curled forms. In 1552, Tragus[5] says there is no kitchen-garden in Germany without it and it is used by the rich as well as the poor. Matthiolus,[6] 1558 and 1570, says it is one of the most common plants of the garden. In 1778, Mawe[7] says it is the sort most commonly grown in English gardens but many prefer the curled kinds; in 1834, Don[8] says it is seldom cultivated. It was in American gardens in 1806.

Apium hortense. Matth. 362. 1558; 512. 1570; 562. 1598; Pin. 333. 1561; Dalechamp 700. 1587; Lob. *Icon.* 706. 1591; Ger. 861. 1597; Dod. 694. 1616.
Garden parsley. Lyte *Dod.* 696. 1586.
Common parsley. Ray 448. 1686; McMahon 127. 1806.
Plane parsley. Mawe 1778.
Common plain-leaved. Don **3**:279. 1834.
Plain parsley. Burr. 433. 1863.
Persil commun. Vilm. 403. 1883.

II.
THE CELERY-LEAVED OR NEAPOLITAN.

The Celery-leaved, or Neapolitan, is scarcely known outside of Naples. It differs from common parsley in the large size of its leaves and leaf-stalks and it may be blanched as a celery.[9] It was introduced into France by Vilmorin in 1823.[10] Pliny mentions parsleys with thick stalks and says the stalks of some are white. This may be the *Apium hortense maximum* of Bauhin,[11] 1596, as the description applies well. He says it is now grown in gardens and was first called English Apium. He does not mention it in his *Pinax*, 1623, under the same name, but under that of *latifolium*. Linnaeus[12] considers this to be *Ligusticum peregrinum*.

---

[1] Tytler *Prog. Disc. No. Coast Amer.* 36. 1833.
[2] McMahon, B. *Amer. Gard. Cal.* 127. 1806.
[3] Fessenden *New Amer. Gard.* 222. 1828.
[4] Thorburn *Cat.* 1881.
[5] Tragus *Stirp.* 459. 1552.
[6] Matthiolus *Comment.* 362. 1558; 512. 1570.
[7] Mawe and Abercrombie *Univ. Gard. Bot.* 1778. (*Apium petroselinum*)
[8] Don, G. *Hist. Dich. Pls.* **3**:279. 1834.
[9] Vilmorin *Les Pls. Potag.* 404. 1883.
[10] Pirolle *L'Hort. Franc.* 1823; *Bon Jard.* 254. 1824–25.
[11] Bauhin, C. *Phytopinax* 268. 1596.
[12] Linnaeus *Sp. Pl.* 1680. 2nd Ed.

Persil celeri ou de Naples.   *L'Hort. Franc.* 1824.
Naples or Celery-leaved.   Burr 434.   1863.
Persil grand de Naples.   Vilm. 404.   1883.

III.
CURLED PARSLEY.

Of these, there are many varieties, differing but in degree, such as the Curled, Extra Curled, Moss Curled and Triple Curled.   Pena and Lobel,[1] 1570, mention this form and say it is very elegant and rare, brought from the mountains the past year and grown in gardens, the leaves curled on the borders, very graceful and tremulous, with minute incisions.   In the synonymy, many of the figures do not exhibit the curled aspect which the name and description indicate; hence, we make two divisions, the curled and the very curled.   The curled was in American gardens preceding 1806.

(a) *The curled.*
   Apium crispum sive multifidum.   Ger. 861.   1597. cum ic.
   Apium crispum.   Matth. *Op.* 562.   1598. cum ic.
(b) *Very curled.*
   Apium crispatum.   Advers. 315.   1570; Dalechamp 700.   1587.
   Apium.   Cam. *Epit.* 526.   1586.
   Petroselinum vulgo, crispum.   Bauh. J. **3**:pt. 2, 97.   1651.
   Curled.   Townsend 33.   1726; Mawe 1778; McMahon 127.   1806. Thorb. *Kal.*   1821.
   Apium crispum.   Mill. *Dict.* 1731, from *Mill. Dict.* 1807.
   Apium petroselinum.   Bryant 24.   1783.
   Curled or Double.   Fessenden 222.   1828; Bridgeman 1832.
   Persil frisé.   *L'Hort. Franc.* 1824; Vilm. 404.   1883.
   Dwarf curled.   Fessenden 222.   1828; Burr 432.   1863.
   Curled leaved.   Don **3**:279.   1834.

IV.
FERN-LEAVED PARSLEY.

The Fern-leaved has leaves which are not curled but are divided into a very great number of small, thread-like segments and is of a very dark green color.   It is included in American seed catalogs of 1878.   This form seems, however, to be described by Bauhin in his edition of Matthiolus, 1598, as a kind with leaves of the coriander, but with very many extending from one branch, lacinate and the stem-leaves unlike the coriander because long and narrow.

V.
HAMBURG OR TURNIP-ROOTED.

Hamburg parsley is grown for its roots, which are used as are parsnips.   It seems to have been used in Germany in 1542,[2] or earlier, but its use was indicated as of Holland origin even then in the name used, Dutch parsley.   It did not reach England until long after.   In 1726, Townsend,[3] a seedsman, had heard that " the people in Holland boil the roots of it and eat it as a good dish."   Miller[4] is said to have introduced it in 1727

---

[1] Pena and Lobel *Advers.* 315.   1570.

[2] Fuchsius *Hist. Stirp.* 573.   1542.

[3] Townsend *Seedsman* 33.   1726.

[4] Martyn *Miller Gard. Dict.*   1807.

and to have grown it himself for some years before it became appreciated. In 1778,[1] it is said to be called Hamburg parsley and to be in esteem. In 1783, Bryant mentions its frequent occurrence in the London markets. It was in American gardens in 1806.

> *Oreoselinum.* Fuch. 573. 1542.
> *Petroselinum.* Trag. 459. 1552.
> *Apium.* Cam. *Epit.* 526. 1586.
> *Apium hortense Fuchsii.* Bauh. J. **3**:pt. 2, 97. 1651.
> *Apium latifolium.* Mill. *Dict.* 1737.
> *Dutch parsley.* Gard. *Kal.* 127. 1765.
> *Hamburg parsley.* Mawe 1778.
> *Broad-leaved.* Mawe 1778.
> *Hamburg or large rooted.* McMahon 1806; Burr 433. 1863.
> *Large rooted.* Thorb. *Kal.* 1821.
> *Persil tubéreux.* L'Hort. Franc. 1824.
> *Persil à grosse racine.* Vilm. 405. 1883.

A *persil panaché* (plumed parsley) is mentioned by Pirolle, in *L'Hort. Français,* 1824.

C. segentum Benth. & Hook. f.

Europe. This is an aromatic, annual herb available for culinary purposes.[2]

C. sylvestre Baill.

East Indies. This plant is used as a carminative by the natives.[3]

Carya alba Nutt. *Juglandeae.* SHAGBARK HICKORY. SHELLBARK HICKORY.

North America. In 1773, at an Indian village in the South, Bartram[4] noticed a cultivated plantation of the shellbark hickory, the trees thriving and bearing better than those left to nature. Emerson[5] says this tree ought to be cultivated for its nuts which differ exceedingly in different soils and situations and often on individual trees growing in immediate proximity. In 1775, Romans[6] speaks of the Florida Indians using hickory nuts in plenty and making a milky liquor of them, which they called milk of nuts. He says: " This milk they are very fond of and eat it with sweet potatoes in it." The hickory nut now not only furnishes food to a large number of the Indians of the far West but is an important article in our markets and is even exported to Britain.

C. microcarpa Nutt. SMALL-FRUITED HICKORY.

Eastern North America. The nuts are edible but not prized.

C. olivaeformis Nutt. PECAN.

A slender tree of eastern North America from Illinois southward. The delicious pecan is well known in our markets and is exported to Europe. It was eaten by the Indians and called by them *pecaunes,* and an oil expressed from it was used by the natives of

---

[1] Mawe and Abercrombie *Univ. Gard. Bot.* 1778.
[2] Mueller, F. *Sel. Pls.* 94. 1891.
[3] Royle, J. F. *Illustr. Bot. Himal.* 1:229. 1839.
[4] *Hist. Mass. Hort. Soc.* 28. 1880.
[5] Emerson, G. B. *Trees, Shrubs Mass.* 1:217. 1875.
[6] Romans *Nat. Hist. Fla.* 1:68. 1775.

Louisiana to season their food.[1] Its use at or near Madrid on the Mississippi by the Indians is mentioned in the *Portuguese Relation*[2] of De Soto's expedition. The pecan is now extensively cultivated in the Southern States for its fruit.

C. porcina Nutt. BROOM HICKORY. PIGNUT.

North America. The pignut is a large tree of Eastern United States. The nuts are variable in form, hard and tough, the kernel sweetish or bitterish but occasionally eaten by children.

C. sulcata Nutt. BIG SHELLBARK. KING NUT.

Pennsylvania to Illinois and Kentucky. The nuts of this tree are eaten by the Indians and are considered of fine quality. This is one of the species recommended for culture by the American Pomological Society.

C. tomentosa Nutt. MOCKER NUT. SQUARE NUT. WHITE-HEART HICKORY.

Eastern North America. This hickory bears a nut with a very thick and hard shell. The kernel is sweet and in some varieties is as large as in the shellbark, but the difficulty of extracting it makes it far less valuable. A variety is found with prominent angles, called square nut.[3]

Caryocar amygdaliferum Cav. *Ternstroemiaceae*. CARYOCAR.

A high tree in Ecuador. The kernel of the nut is edible and has the taste of almonds.[4] This is the *almendron* of Mariquita. " The nuts are fine." [5]

C. amygdaliforme Ruiz & Pav.

Peru. The tree bears nuts that taste like almonds.[6]

C. brasiliense St. Hil. PIQUIA-OIL PLANT.

Brazil. This species bears an oily, mucilaginous fruit, containing a sort of chestnut eaten in times of famine.[7] This is perhaps the *Acantacaryx pinguis* Arruda, a large tree that produces most abundantly a fruit the size of an orange, of which the pulp is oily, feculous and nourishing. It is the delight of the inhabitants of Ceara and Piauhy and is called *piqui*.[8]

C. butyrosum Willd.

Guiana. This plant is cultivated for its nuts in Cayenne. These are esculent and taste somewhat like a Brazil nut.[9] It is called *pekea* by the natives of Guiana. It furnishes a timber valuable for shipbuilding.[10]

---

[1] Pickering, C. *Chron. Hist. Pls.* 749. 1879.

[2] De Soto *Disc., Conq. Fla.* Hakl. Soc. Ed. 9:94. 1841.

[3] Emerson, G. B. *Trees, Shrubs Mass.* 1:222. 1875.

[4] Don, G. *Hist. Dichl. Pls.* 1:654. 1831.

[5] Humboldt, A. *Trav.* 2:368. 1889.

[6] Don, G. *Hist. Dichl. Pls.* 1:654. 1831.

[7] Burton, R. F. *Explor. Braz.* 1:76. 1869.

[8] Koster, H. *Trav. Braz.* 2:364. 1817.

[9] Don, G. *Hist. Dichl. Pls.* 1:654. 1831.

[10] Smith, A. *Treas. Bot.* 1:229. 1870.

C. glabrum Pers.

Guiana. It furnishes edible nuts.[1] It is sometimes cultivated, and the trees are much used in shipbuilding and for other purposes. The natives make much use of the nuts.

C. nuciferum Linn. BUTTERNUT.

A lofty tree of British Guiana which produces the *souari* or butternut of the English markets. These nuts are shaped something like a kidney flattened upon two sides and have an exceedingly hard, woody shell of a rich, reddish-brown color, covered all over with round wart-like protuberances, which encloses a large, white kernel of a pleasant, nutty taste yielding a bland oil by pressure.[2]

C. tomentosum Willd. BUTTERNUT.

Guiana. The plant bears a sweet and edible nut.[3]

Caryota obtusa Griff. *Palmae.*

A very large palm of the Mishmi Mountains in India. The central part of the trunk is used by the natives as food.[4]

C. urens Linn. JAGGERY PALM. TODDY PALM. WINE PALM.

Malabar, Bengal, Assam and various other parts of India. The center of the stem is generally soft, the cells being filled with sago-like farina, which is made into bread and eaten as gruel. But the main value of this palm consists in the abundance of sweet sap which is obtained from the cut spadix and which is either fermented or boiled down into syrup and sugar.[5]

Casearia esculenta Roxb. *Samydaceae.*

Tropical Asia. The leaves are eaten by the natives.[6]

Casimiroa edulis La Llave. *Rutaceae.* MEXICAN APPLE. WHITE SAPOTA.

Mexico. This tree grows wild and is cultivated in the states of Sinaloa, Durango and elsewhere in Mexico and is known by the name of *zapote blanco*. The fruit is about an inch in diameter, pale yellow in color and is most palatable when near decay. It has a very rich, subacid taste, and the native Californians are very fond of it.[7] Masters[8] says its fruit has an agreeable taste but induces sleep and is unwholesome and that the seeds are poisonous.

---

[1] Don, G. *Hist. Dichl. Pls.* 1:654. 1831.
[2] Smith, A. *Treas. Bot.* 1:229. 1870.
[3] Don, G. *Hist. Dichl. Pls.* 1:654. 1831.
[4] Griffith, W. *Palms Brit. Ind.* 170. 1850.
[5] Brandis, D. *Forest Fl.* 550. 1876.
[6] Black, A. A. *Treas. Bot.* 1:231. 1870.
[7] *Cal. State Bd. Hort. Rpt.* 80. 1880.
[8] Masters, M. T. *Treas. Bot.* 1:232. 1870.

Cassia auriculata Linn. *Leguminosae.* CASSIA.

East Indies. In some parts of the country, a spirituous liquor is prepared by adding the bruised bark to a solution of molasses and allowing the mixture to ferment.[1]

C. fistula Linn.

Tropical Asia. This handsome tree has been introduced into the West Indies and northern Africa, whence its pods are imported for use in medicine. In Mysore, stalks of it are put in the ground and worshipped. It is classed by Unger[2] as among the little-used vegetable foods, the pulp apparently being eaten. This pulp about the seeds is, however, a strong purgative.

C. occidentalis Linn. STINKING WEED.

Cosmopolitan tropics. Rafinesque[3] says the pods of this plant are long, with many seeds, which the countrymen use instead of coffee. It is found in tropical and subtropical America[4] and in both Indies.[5] It has been carried to the Philippines, and its seeds, while tender, are eaten by boys.[6] Naturalized in the Mauritius, the natives use the roasted seeds as a substitute for coffee. Livingstone found the seeds used as coffee in interior Africa.

C. sophera Linn. CACAY.

Old World tropics. This plant is said by Unger[7] to be used as a vegetable in Amboina.

Cassytha cuscutiformis (?) *Laurineae.* DODDER-LAUREL.

The white drupes of this north Australian species are edible. The plants are semi-parasitical and are often called dodder-laurel.[8]

C. filiformis Linn.

Cosmopolitan tropics. The plant is put as a seasoning into buttermilk and is much used for this purpose by the Brahmans in southern India.[9] In Yemen, its berries are eaten by boys.[10]

Castanea dentata Borkh. *Cupuliferae.* AMERICAN CHESTNUT.

Southward from Maine as far as Florida and westward as far as Michigan but not in the prairie regions. Chestnuts were mixed with pottage by the Indians of New England and they now appear in season in all our markets and are sold roasted on the streets of our cities. The American variety bears smaller and sweeter nuts than the European.

[1] Drury, H.   *Useful Pls. Ind.* 120.   1873.

[2] Unger, F.   *U. S. Pat. Off. Rpt.* 333.   1859.

[3] Rafinesque, C. S.   *Fl. La.* 100.   1817.   (*C. ciliata*)

[4] Pickering, C.   *Chron. Hist. Pls.* 752.   1879.

[5] Masters, M. T.   *Treas. Bot.* 1:232.   1870.

[6] Pickering, C.   *Chron. Hist. Pls.* 752.   1879.

[7] Unger, F.   *U. S. Pat. Off. Rpt.* 359.   1859.

[8] Black, A. A.   *Treas. Bot.* 1:234.   1870.

[9] Drury, H.   *Useful Pls. Ind.* 123.   1873.

[10] Pickering, C.   *Chron. Hist. Pls.* 729.   1879.

C. pumila Mill. CHINQUAPIN.

Southern United States. Pursh [1] says the nuts are sweet and delicious; Vasey,[2] that they are not comparable to those of *C. dentata* but are eaten by children.

C. sativa Mill. EUROPEAN CHESTNUT.

Europe, Japan and North America. The native country of the chestnut is given by Targioni-Tozzetti [3] as the south of Europe from Spain to Caucasus; Pickering [4] says, eastern Asia. Other writers say it was first introduced into Europe from Sardis in Asia Minor; it is called *Sardinian balanos* by Dioscorides and *Dios balanos* by Theophrastus. It is evident from the writings of Virgil that chestnuts were abundant in Italy in his time. There are now many varieties cultivated. Chestnuts which bear nuts of a very large size are grown in Madeira. In places, chestnuts form the usual food of the common people, as in the Apennine mountains of Italy, in Savoy and the south of France. They are used not only boiled and roasted but also in puddings, cakes and bread. Chestnuts afford a great part of the food of the peasants in the mountains of Madeira.[5] In Sicily, chestnuts afford the poorer class of people their principal food in some parts of the isle; bread and puddings are made of the flour.[6] In Tuscany, they are ground into flour and chiefly used in the form of porridge or pudding. In the coffee-houses of Lucca, Pescia and Pistoja, patés, muffins, tarts and other articles are made of chestnuts and are considered delicious.[7] In Morea, chestnuts now form the principal food of the people for the whole year.[8] Xenophon states that the children of the Persian nobility were fattened on chestnuts. In the valleys inhabited by the Waldenses, in the Cevennes and in a great part of Spain, the chestnut furnishes nutriment for the common people. Charlemagne commended the propagation of chestnuts to his people.[9] In modern Europe, only the fruits of cultivated varieties are considered suitable for food.[10] This species is enumerated by Thunberg [11] as among the edible plants of Japan.

Castanospermum australe A. Cunn. & Fraser. *Leguminosae.* MORETON BAY CHESTNUT.

Australia. Fraser [12] says the fruit is eaten by the natives on all occasions and when roasted has the flavor of a Spanish chestnut. Europeans, from necessity, have subsisted on the fruit for two days, the raw fruit griping but the roasted being innoxious.

Catesbaea spinosa Linn. *Rubiaceae.*

A shrub of the West Indies. The fruit is yellow, pulpy and of an agreeable taste.[13]

---

[1] Pursh, F. *Fl. Amer. Septent.* 2:625. 1814.
[2] Vasey *U. S. D. A. Rpt.* 175. 1875.
[3] Thompson, R. *Treas. Bot.* 1:235. 1870.
[4] Pickering, C. *Chron. Hist. Pls.* 77. 1879. (*C. vesca*)
[5] Phillips, H. *Comp. Orch.* 86. 1831.
[6] Hooker, W. J. *Lond. Journ. Bot.* 1:144. 1834.
[7] Loudon, J. C. *Enc. Agr.* 53. 1866.
[8] Loudon, J. C. *Enc. Agr.* 122. 1866.
[9] Unger, F. *U. S. Pat. Off. Rpt.* 313. 1859. (*C. vesca*)
[10] Emerson, G. B. *Trees, Shrubs Mass.* 1:189. 1875. (*C. vesca*)
[11] Thunberg, C. P. *Fl. Jap.* 195. 1784. (*Fagus castanea*)
[12] Hooker, W. J. *Bot. Misc.* 1:243. 1830.
[13] Masters, M. T. *Treas. Bot.* 1:239. 1870.

Catha edulis Forsk. *Celastrineae.* ARABIAN TEA. KAT.

A shrub of tropical Africa. The leaves are used by the Arabs in the preparation of a beverage possessing properties analogous to those of tea and coffee. Large quantities of twigs with the leaves attached are annually brought to Aden from the interior. The shrub is called by the natives *cafta.*[1] Prior to the introduction of coffee, says Pickering,[2] the use of kat was established in Yemen by Ali Schadheli ben Omar. Various virtues are attributed to the leaves which are eaten with avidity by the Arabs.

Caucalis anthriscus Huds. *Umbelliferae.* HEDGE PARSLEY.

Europe. Wilkinson[3] says this is the *anthriscum* of Pliny, now called in Arabic *gezzer e'shaytan,* and that it is esculent.

C. daucoides Linn. BASTARD PARSLEY. BUD PARSLEY. HEN'S FOOT.

Europe and temperate Asia. Gerarde[4] calls this plant bastard parsley and hen's foot. It is the *sesslis* of the Egyptians. It was called a potherb by Dioscorides and Pliny, and Galen says it is pickled for salads in winter.

Caulanthus crassicaulis S. Wats. *Cruciferae.* WILD CABBAGE.

Western regions of America. It is sometimes used as a food, says Rothrock,[5] when a better substitute cannot be found.

Cavendishia sp.? *Vacciniaceae.*

Frigid regions of the Andes of Peru. This is a tall, evergreen shrub with pink, edible berries the size of a cherry.[6]

Ceanothus americanus Linn. *Rhamneae.* MOUNTAIN SWEET. NEW JERSEY TEA. WILD SNOWBALL.

North America. The leaves were used as a substitute for tea during the American Revolution.[7]

Cecropia peltata Linn. *Urticaceae.* INDIAN SNAKEWOOD. TRUMPET TREE.

American tropics. The young buds are eaten as a potherb.[8]

Cedrela odorata Linn. *Meliaceae.* BARBADOES CEDAR. CIGAR-BOX WOOD.

South America. Smith[9] says, in China the leaves of this tree are eaten in the spring when quite tender.

---

[1] Smith, A. *Treas. Bot.* 1:239. 1870.

[2] Pickering, C. *Chron. Hist. Pls.* 811. 1879. (*Celastrus edulis*)

[3] Wilkinson, J. G. *Anc. Egypt.* 2:33. 1854.

[4] Gerarde, J. *Herb.* 1023. 1633 or 1636. 2nd Ed.

[5] Rothrock, J. T. *U. S. Geog. Surv. Bot.* 6:41. 1878.

[6] Mueller, F. *Sel. Pls.* 498. 1891. (*Vaccinium alatum*)

[7] Gray, A. *Man. Bot.* 115. 5th Ed.

[8] Smith, A. *Treas. Bot.* 1:242. 1870.

[9] Smith, F. P. *Contrib. Mat. Med. China* 56. 1871.

Cedronella cana Hook. *Labiatae.* HOARY BALM OF GILEAD.

Mexico. This pretty and very fragrant plant is useful for putting in a claret cup.[1]

Cedrus libani Barrel. *Coniferae.* CEDAR OF LEBANON.

Asia Minor, Syria, Afghanistan, Himalayan region and Algeria. A kind of manna was anciently collected from this tree.[2]

Celastrus macrocarpus Ruiz & Pav. *Celastrineae.* STAFF TREE.

Peru. It has savory, alimentary buds. The seeds yield an edible oil.[3]

C. scandens Linn. BITTER SWEET. STAFF VINE. WAXWORK.

Northern North America. The Chippewa Indians use the tender branches. The plant has a thick bark which is sweetish and palatable when boiled.[4]

Celosia argentea Linn. *Amarantaceae.*

Cosmopolitan tropics. In China, this plant is a troublesome weed in flax fields but is gathered and consumed as a vegetable.[5] In France, it is grown in flower gardens.[6]

C. trigyna Linn.

Tropical Africa. According to Grant,[7] this plant is eaten as a potherb.

Celtis australis Linn. *Urticaceae.* CELTIS. EUROPEAN NETTLE. HONEYBERRY. LOTE TREE.

Europe, temperate Asia and East Indies. The European nettle is a native of Barbary and is grown as a shade tree in the south of France and Italy. Dr. Hogg[8] considers it to be the lote tree of the ancients, " *lotos to dendron* " of Dioscorides and Theophrastus; Sibthorp and Stackhouse are of the same opinion. The fruit is about the size of a small cherry, yellow, dark brown or black. The modern Greeks are very fond of the fruits; they are also eaten in Spain. They are called in Greece honeyberries and are insipidly sweet. In India, Brandis[9] says a large, blackish or purple kind is called *roku* on the Sutlej; a smaller yellow or orange kind *choku.*

C. occidentalis Linn. HACKBERRY. NETTLE TREE. SUGARBERRY.

Southern and Western United States. This celtis is a fine forest tree. The fruits are sweet and edible.[10]

C. tala Gill.

Mexico. This is the *cranjero* or *cranxero* of the Mexicans. The berries of this shrub are of the size of small peas, oval, orange-yellow and somewhat edible though astringent.[11]

---

[1] *Gard. Chron.* 17:559. 1882.

[2] Geoffrey *Mat. Med.* 2:584. 1741.

[3] Baillon, H. *Hist. Pls.* 6:26. 1880.

[4] *U. S. D. A. Rpt.* 422. 1870.

[5] Smith, F. P. *Contrib. Mat. Med. China* 57. 1871.

[6] Vilmorin *Fl. Pl. Ter.* 237. 3rd Ed.

[7] Pickering, C. *Chron. Hist. Pls.* 465. 1879.

[8] Hooker, W. J. *Lond. Journ. Bot.* 1:203. 1834.

[9] Brandis, D. *Forest Fl.* 428. 1874.

[10] Gray, A. *Man. Bot.* 443. 1868.

[11] Torrey, J. *U. S. Pat. Off. Rpt.* 253. 1857.

Centaurea calcitrapa Linn. *Compositae.* CALTROPS. STAR THISTLE.

Europe, north Africa and temperate Asia. The young stems and leaves, according to Forskal,[1] are eaten raw in Egypt.

C. chamaerhaponticum Ball.

Mediterranean coasts. In Algeria, according to Desfontaenes,[2] the root is edible and not unpleasant to the taste.

C. pygmaea Benth. & Hook. f.

Mediterranean countries. The roots have an agreeable flavor and are eaten by the Arabs in some parts of Africa.[3]

Centranthus macrosiphon Boiss. *Valerianeae.* LONG-SPURRED VALERIAN.

Spain. Valerian is an annual cultivated in gardens for its handsome, rose-colored flowers and is used as a salad in some countries, notably in France. It appears to combine all that belongs to corn salad, with a peculiar slight bitterness which imparts to it a more distinct and agreeable flavor.

C. ruber DC. FOX'S BRUSH. RED VALERIAN.

Red Valerian is said to be eaten as a salad in southern Italy.[4]

Centrosema macrocarpum Benth. *Leguminosae.*

British Guiana. The beans are eaten by the Indians, according to Schomburgk.[5] The leaves, according to A. A. Black, are also eaten.

Cephalotaxus drupacea Sieb. & Zucc. *Coniferae.* PLUM-FRUITED YEW.

Japan. The female plant bears a stone-fruit closely resembling a plum in structure. The flesh is thick, juicy and remarkably sweet, with a faint suggestion of the pine in its flavor.[6]

Ceratonia siliqua Linn. *Leguminosae.* ALGAROBA BEAN. CAROB TREE. LOCUST BEAN.
ST. JOHN'S BREAD.

This tree is indigenous in Spain and Algeria, the eastern part of the Mediterranean region, in Syria;[7] and is found in Malta, the Balearic Islands, in southern Italy, in Turkey, Greece and Grecian Islands, in Asia Minor, Palestine and the north of Africa.[8] It was found by Denham[9] and Clapperton[10] in the Kingdom of Bornu, in the center of Africa. The pods being filled with a saccharine pulp, are eaten both green and dry and were a

---

[1] Pickering, C. *Chron. Hist. Pls.* 140. 1879.
[2] Black, A. A. *Treas. Bot.* 2:970. 1870. (*Rhaponticum acaule*)
[3] Hooker and Ball *Marocco, Gt. Atlas* 292. 1878. (*Cynara acaulis*)
[4] Thompson, W. *Treas. Bot.* 1:247. 1870.
[5] Hooker, W. J. *Journ. Bot.* 2:59. 1840.
[6] Brooks, W. P. *Trans. Mass. Hort. Soc.* 52. 1890.
[7] Brandis, D. *Forest Fl.* 166. 1874.
[8] Hooker, W. J. *Journ. Bot.* 1:114. 1834.
[9] Ibid.
[10] Ibid.

favorite food with the ancients; there are specimens preserved in the museum at Naples which were exhumed from a house in Pompeii. The Egyptians extracted from the husk of the pod a sort of honey, with which they preserved fruits; in Sicily, a spirit and a sirup are prepared from them;[1] in the island of Diu or Standia, the luscious pulp contained in the pod is eaten by the poor and children and is also made into a sherbet. These pods are imported into the Punjab as food for man, horses, pigs and cattle[2] and are imported into England occasionally as a cattle food.[3] In 1854, seeds of this tree were distributed from the United States Patent Office.[4]

Ceratostema grandiflorum Ruiz & Pav. *Vacciniaceae.*

Peruvian Andes. This tall, evergreen shrub produces berries of a pleasant, acidulous taste.[5]

Cercis canadensis Linn. *Leguminosae.* JUDAS TREE. REDBUD.

North America. The French Canadians use the flowers in salads and pickles.[6]

C. siliquastrum Linn. JUDAS TREE. LOVE TREE.

Mediterranean countries. The pods are gathered and used with other raw vegetables by the Greeks and Turks in salads, to which they give an agreeable odor and taste.[7] The flowers are also made into fritters with batter and the flower-buds are pickled in vinegar.[8]

Cereus caespitosus Engelm. & A. Gray. *Cacteae.*

Texas. The fruit, rarely an inch long, is edible, and the fleshy part of the stem is also eaten by the inhabitants of New Mexico.[9] The fruit is of a purplish color and very good, resembling a gooseberry. The Mexicans eat the fleshy part of the stem as a vegetable, first carefully freeing it of spines.[10]

C. dasyacanthus Engelm.

Southwestern North America. The fruit is one to one and one-half inches in diameter, green or greenish-purple, and when fully ripe is delicious to eat, much like a gooseberry.[11]

C. dubius Engelm.

Southwestern North America. The ripe fruit, one to one and one-half inches long, green or rarely purplish, is insipid or pleasantly acid.[12]

C. engelmanni Parry.

Southwestern North America. This plant bears a deliciously palatable fruit.[13]

---

[1] Hooker, W. J. *Journ. Bot.* 1:113. 1834.

[2] Brandis, D. *Forest Fl.* 166. 1874.

[3] Church, A. H. *Foods* 124. 1887.

[4] *U. S. Pat. Off. Rpt.* 27. 1854.

[5] Mueller, F. *Sel. Pls.* 499. 1891. (*Vaccinium grandiflorum*)

[6] Browne, D. J. *Trees Amer.* 222. 1846.

[7] Walsh, R. *Trans. Hort. Soc. Lond.* 6:34. 1826.

[8] Johns, C. A. *Treas. Bot.* 1:256. 1870.

[9] Fendler, A., and Gray, A. *Pl. Fendl.* 50. 1849.

[10] Smith, A. *Treas. Bot.* 1:439. 1870. (*Echinocereus pectinatus*)

[11] Fendler, A., and Gray, A. *Pl. Fendl.* 50. 1849.

[12] Ibid.

[13] Parry *Bot. U. S. Mex. Bound.* 21. 1854.

C. enneacanthus Engelm.

Southwestern North America. The berry is pleasant to eat.[1]

C. fendleri Engelm.

New Mexico. The purplish-green fruit is edible.[2]

C. giganteus Engelm.

Texas. This cactus yields a fruit sweet and delicious. The Indians collect it in large quantities and make a sirup or conserve from the juice, which serves them as a luxury as well as for sustenance. The Mexicans call the tree *suwarrow;* the Indians, *harsee.* The sirup manufactured from the juice is called *sistor.*[3] Engelmann says the crimson-colored pulp is sweet, rather insipid and of the consistency of a fresh fig. Hodge,[4] in Arizona, calls the fruit delicious, having the combined flavor of the peach, strawberry and fig.

C. greggii Engelm.

Texas. The plant has a bright scarlet, fleshy, edible berry.[5]

C. polyacanthus Engelm.

Texas. It bears a berry of a pleasant taste.[6]

C. quisco C. Gay

Chile. The sweetish, mucilaginous fruits are available for desserts.[7]

C. thurberi Engelm.

New Mexico. This plant grows in the Papago Indian country on the borders of Arizona and Sonora and attains a height of 18 to 20 feet and a diameter of four to six inches and bears two crops of fruit a year. The fruit is, according to Engelmann, three inches through, like a large orange, of delicious taste, the crimson pulp being dotted with numerous, black seeds. The seeds, after passing through the digestive canal, are collected, according to Baegert and Clavigero,[8] and pounded into a meal used in forming a food. Venegas,[9] in his *History of California*, describes the fruit as growing to the boughs, the pulp resembling that of a fig only more soft and luscious. In some, it is white; in some red; and in others yellow but always of an exquisite taste; some again are wholly sweet, others of a grateful acid. This cactus is called *pithaya* by the Mexicans and affords a staple sustenance for the Papago Indians.

Ceropegia bulbosa Roxb. *Asclepiadeae.*

East Indies. Roxburgh [10] says, " men eat every part."

---

[1] Fendler, A., and Gray, A. *Pl. Fendl.* 50. 1849.

[2] Ibid.

[3] Bigelow *Pacific R. R. Rpt.* 4:13. 1856.

[4] Hodge, H. C. *Ariz.* 243. 1877.

[5] Fendler, A., and Gray, A. *Pl. Fendl.* 50. 1849.

[6] Ibid.

[7] Mueller, F. *Sel. Pls.* 106. 1891.

[8] *Smithsonian Inst. Rpt.* 365. 1863.

[9] Venegas *Hist. Cal.* 1:42. 1759.

[10] Roxburgh, W. *Pls. Corom. Coast* 1:11, t. 7. 1795.

C. tuberosa Roxb.

East Indies. Every part is esculent; the roots are eaten raw.[1]

Cervantesia tomentosa Ruiz & Pav. *Santalaceae.*

Peru. Its seeds are edible.[2]

Cetraria islandica Linn. *Lichenes.* ICELAND MOSS.

Iceland moss is found in the northern regions of both continents and on elevated mountains farther south. It serves as food to the people of Iceland and Lapland; the bitterness is first extracted with water, after which the plant is pounded up into meal for bread or boiled with milk.[3]

Chaerophyllum bulbosum Linn. *Umbelliferae.* PARSNIP CHERVIL. TURNIP-ROOTED
   CHERVIL.

Europe and Asia Minor. In Bavaria, this vegetable is found growing wild but is said to have been first introduced from Siberia. Burnett[4] alludes to it as deleterious, but Haller[5] affirms that the Kalmucks eat the roots with their fish and commend them as a nutritive and agreeable food. Booth[6] says it is a native of France and, although known to British gardeners since its introduction in 1726, it is only within the last few years that attention has been directed to its culture as an esculent vegetable. In size and shape, the root attains the dimensions of a small Dutch carrot. It is outwardly of a grey color, but when cut the flesh is white, mealy and by no means unpleasant to the taste. F. Webster,[7] consul at Munich, Bavaria, in 1864, sent some seed to this country and says: " The great value of this vegetable, as an acquisition to an American gardener, is not only its deliciousness to the epicure but the earliness of its maturity, fully supplying the place of potatoes." The seed is now offered in our seed catalogs. The wild plant is described by Camerarius,[8] 1588 and by Clusius,[9] 1601, and is also named by Bauhin,[10] 1623. As a cultivated plant, it seems to have been first noted about 1855, when the root is described as seldom so large as a hazelnut, while in 1861 it had attained the size and shape of the French round carrot.[11] This chervil appeared in American seed catalogs in 1884, or earlier, and was described by Burr[12] for American gardens in 1863. It was known in England in 1726 but was not under culture.[13]

---

[1] Roxburgh, W. *Pls. Corom. Coast* **1**:12, t. 9. 1795.

[2] Mueller, F. *Sel. Pls.* 107. 1891.

[3] *U. S. Disp.* 244. 1865.

[4] Burnett *U. S. D. A. Rpt.* 500. 1864.

[5] Haller *U. S. D. A. Rpt.* 500. 1864.

[6] Booth, W. B. *Treas. Bot.* **1**:74. 1870.

[7] *U. S. D. A. Rpt.* 500. 1864.

[8] Camerarius *Hort. Med.* 1588.

[9] Clusius *Hist.* **2**:200. 1601.

[10] Bauhin, C. *Pinax* 161. 1623.

[11] *Gard. Chron.* 887, 906. 1861.

[12] Burr, F. *Field, Gard. Veg.* 31. 1863.

[13] Booth, W. B. *Treas. Bot.* **1**:74. 1870.

C. tuberosum Royle.

In the Himalayas, the tuberous roots are eaten and are called *sham*.[1]

Chamaedorea elegans Mart.   *Palmae.*

South America.   The young, unexpanded flower-spikes are used as a vegetable.

C. tepejilote Liebm.

Mexico.   The flowers, when still enclosed in the spathes, are highly esteemed as a culinary vegetable.[2]

Chamaerops humilis Linn.   *Palmae.*   DWARF FAN-PALM.   PALMETTO.

West Mediterranean countries.   The young shoots or suckers from the bottom of the plant, called *cafaglioni*, are eaten by the Italians.   In Barbary, the lower part of the young stems and the roots are eaten by the Moors.[3]

Chelidonium sinense DC.   *Papaveraceae.*

China.   The leaves were eaten as a food in China in the fourteenth century.[4]

Chenopodium album Linn.   *Chenopodiaceae.*   LAMB'S QUARTER.   PIGWEED.   WHITE GOOSE-
   FOOT.

Temperate and tropical regions.   Remnants of this plant have been found in the early lake villages of Switzerland.   In the Hebrides, it was observed by Lightfoot[5] to be boiled and eaten as greens.   In the United States, it is used as a spinach.   The young, tender plants are collected by the Navajoes, the Pueblo Indians of New Mexico, all the tribes of Arizona, the Diggers of California and the Utahs, and boiled as a spinach or are eaten raw.   The seeds are gathered by many tribes, ground into a flour and made into a bread or mush.[6]

C. ambrosioides Linn.   MEXICAN TEA.

Temperate and tropical regions.   This herb is called in Mexican *epazolt*.   The plant is cooked and eaten by the natives.   It was called at Verona, in 1745, the *allemand* because drunk in infusion by the Germans.   It seems to be indigenous to tropical America.

C. auricomum Lindl.   AUSTRALIAN SPINACH.

Australia.   This plant is a native of the interior of Australia and has lately come into use in England as a substitute for spinach, according to J. Smith.[7]   Mueller[8] calls this spinach palatable and nutritious.

C. bonus-henricus Linn.   ALL GOOD.   FAT HEN.   GOOD-KING-HENRY.   GOOSEFOOT.   MERCURY.
   WILD SPINACH.

Europe, now sparingly naturalized around dwellings in the United States.   Under

[1] Royle, J. F.   *Illustr. Bot. Himal.* 1:231.   1839.

[2] Seemann, B.   *Pop. Hist. Palms* 139.   1856.

[3] Andrews *Bot. Reposit.* 9: Pl. 599.   1797.

[4] Bretschneider, E.   *Bot. Sin.* 51.   1882.

[5] Lightfoot, J.   *Fl. Scot.* 1:149.   1789.

[6] *U. S. D. A. Rpt.* 419.   1870.

[7] Smith, J.   *Dom. Bot.* 235.   1871.

[8] Mueller, F.   *Sel. Pls.* 109.   1891.

the curious names of fat-hen and good-king-Henry, this plant was formerly largely cultivated in the gardens in England as a potherb, and even in the beginning of the present
century was still esteemed in Lincolnshire and some of the Midland counties but is now
little used. Lightfoot [1] says, in Scotland, the young leaves in the spring are often eaten
as greens and are very good. Glasspoole [2] says, in Lincolnshire, it was preferred to garden
spinach, and the young shoots used to be peeled and eaten as asparagus. The plant is
now but rarely cultivated. Gerarde speaks of it in 1597 as a wild plant only, while Ray,
1686, refers to it as frequently among vegetables. Bryant, 1783, says: " formerly cultivated in English gardens but of late neglected, although certainly of sufficient merit."
In 1807, *Miller's Gardener's Dictionary* says it is generally in gardens about Boston in
Lincolnshire and is there preferred to spinach. It cannot ever have received very general
culture as it is only indicated as a wayside plant by Tragus, 1552; Lobel, 1570 and 1576;
Camerarius, 1586; Dalechamp, 1587; Matthiolus, 1598; and Chabraeus, 1677. Its value
as an antiscorbutic finds recognition in its names, *bonus Henricus* and *tota bona*.

C. capitatum Aschers. BLITE. STRAWBERRY BLITE.

Northern and southern regions. Gerarde [3] says: " it is one of the potherbes that
be unsavory or without taste, whose substance is waterish." The fruit, though insipid,
is said formerly to have been employed in cookery. The leaves have a spinach-like flavor
and may be used as a substitute for it. [4] Unger [5] says even the blite or strawberry spinach
finds consumers for its insipid, strawberry-like fruit. The plant is found indigenous and
common from Western New York to Lake Superior and northward. [6] *Blitum capitatum*,
if Linnaeus's synonymy can be trusted, was known to Bauhin, [7] 1623, and by Ray, [8] 1686.
Miller's *Gardener's Dictionary* refers it to J. Bauhin [9] who received the plant in 1651.
The species was, during this time, little known outside of botanical gardens.

C. quinoa Willd. PETTY RICE. QUINOA.

South America. This plant, indigenous to the Pacific slopes of the Andes, constituted
the most important article of food of the inhabitants of New Granada, Peru and Chile
at the time of the discovery of America, and at the present day is still extensively cultivated on account of its seeds, which are used extensively by the poorer inhabitants. There
are several varieties, of which the white is cultivated in Europe as a spinach plant, rather
than for its seeds. However prepared, the seed, says Thompson, is unpalatable to strangers.
Gibbon,[10] who saw the plant in Bolivia, says that when boiled like rice and eaten with
milk, the seeds are very savory. Seeds from France but originally from Peru, were dis-

[1] Lightfoot, J. *Fl. Scot.* 1:147. 1789.
[2] Glasspoole, H. G. *Rpt. Ohio State Bd. Agr.* 528. 1875.
[3] Gerarde, J. *Herb.* 321. 1633 or 1636. 2nd Ed.
[4] Thompson, W. *Treas. Bot.* 1:150. 1870. (*Blitum capitatum*)
[5] Unger, F. *U. S. Pat. Off. Rpt.* 357. 1859. (*Blitum capitatum*)
[6] Gray, A. *Man. Bot.* 408. 1868. (*Blitum capitatum*)
[7] Bauhin, C. *Pinax* n. 7. 119. 1623.
[8] Ray *Hist. Pl.* 1: n. 5, 7. 197. 1686.
[9] Bauhin, J. *Hist. Pl.* 2:973. 1651.
[10] Herndon, W. L., and Gibbon, L. *Explor. Valley Amaz.* 2:139. 1854.

tributed from the United States Patent Office in 1854. Garcilasso de la Vega[1] says it was called *quinua* by the natives of Peru and *mujo* by the Spaniards. He says: " Both the Indians and the Spanish eat the tender leaf in their dishes, because they are savory and very wholesome. They also eat the grain in the soups, prepared in various ways." A black-seeded variety, cultivated in gardens, is mentioned by Feuille,[2] in Peru, preceding 1725. It was introduced into France in 1785[3] but has not had very extended use. Molina[4] says in Chile there is a variety called *dahue* by the Indians which has greyish leaves and produces a white grain. The grain of the *quinua* serves for making a very pleasant stomachic beverage; that of the *dahue*, on being boiled, lengthens out in the form of worms and is excellent in soup. The leaves are also eaten and are tender and of an agreeable taste.

Chiogenes serpyllifolia Salisb. *Vacciniaceae.* CREEPING SNOWBERRY.

North America and Japan. The berry is white, edible, juicy and of an agreeable, subacid taste with a pleasant checkerberry flavor.[5] The Indians of Maine use the leaves of the creeping snowberry for tea.[6]

Chloranthus inconspicuus Sw. *Chloranthaceae.*

China and Japan. This plant furnishes the flowers which serve to scent some sorts of tea,[7] particularly an expensive sort called *chu-lan-cha.*[8]

Chlorogalum pomeridianum Kunth. *Liliaceae.* AMOLE. SOAPPLANT. WILD POTATO.

California. The egg-shaped bulb is one to three inches in diameter. Cooking eliminates all the acrid properties, rendering the bulb good, wholesome food.[9]

Chondodendron tomentosum Ruiz & Pav. *Menispermaceae.* WILD GRAPE.

Peru. This plant is called by the Peruvians wild grape on account of the form of the fruit and its acid and not unpleasant flavor.[10]

Chondrilla juncea Linn. *Compositae.*

Southern Europe and adjoining Asia. This plant is mentioned by Dorotheus as good for cooking and for the stomach; it is enumerated by Pliny as among the esculent plants of Egypt.[11]

C. prenanthoides Vill.

East Mediterranean countries and mountains of Yemen. This plant is enumerated by Pliny as among the esculents of Egypt. Forskal says it is eaten raw in Yemen.[12]

---

[1] Vega *Roy. Comment.* Hakl. Soc. Ed. 2:358.
[2] Feuillee *Peru* 3:Ap. 16, t. x. 1725.
[3] Heuze, G. *Pls. Aliment.* 2:259. 1873.
[4] Molina *Hist. Chili* 1:91. 1808.
[5] Emerson, G. B. *Trees, Shrubs Mass.* 2:460. 1875. (*C. hispidula*)
[6] Thoreau *Me. Woods* 270. 1877. (*C. hispidula*)
[7] Williams, S. W. *Mid. King.* 1:282. 1848.
[8] Smith, F. P. *Contrib. Mat. Med. China* 61. 1871.
[9] Harvard, V. *Torr. Bot. Club Bul.* 22:114. 1895.
[10] Masters, M. T. *Treas. Bot.* 1:274. 1870. (*C. convolvulaceum*)
[11] Pickering, C. *Chron. Hist. Pls.* 281. 1879.
[12] Pickering, C. *Chron. Hist. Pls.* 361. 1879. (*Prenanthes chondrilloides*)

Chondris crispus Lyngb. *Rhodophyceae.* CARRAGEEN. IRISH MOSS. PEARL MOSS.

This alga is found on the western coast of Ireland, England and Europe and also on the eastern coast of the United States. It has been used as a food and medicine by the Irish peasants from time immemorial. It is collected for the market and is largely used as a food for invalids under the names carrageen, Irish moss and pearl moss.

Choretrum candollei F. Muell. *Santalaceae.* WILD CURRANTS.

A shrub bearing greenish-red berries which are called wild currants in New South Wales. They have a pleasant, acid taste combined with a certain degree of astringency. Mixed with other fruit, they are used for preserves and in the preparation of cooling, acid beverages.[1]

Chorispora tenella DC. *Cruciferae.*

Central Asia. The leaves of this plant are described as a good, early salad by Pallas in his *Travels in Russia.*

Chrysanthemum balsamita Linn. *Compositae.* ALECOST. COSTMARY.

West Mediterranean countries. This plant is common in every cottage garden in England, where it was introduced in 1568. The leaves possess a strong, balsamic odor and are sometimes put in salads but it has ceased to be grown for culinary purposes and even in France is only occasionally used. The leaves were formerly used in England to flavor ale and negus, hence the name alecost. In the United States, it is mentioned by Burr,[2] 1863, who names one variety. It is grown in Constantinople.[3]

C. leucanthemum Linn. MARGUERITE. OX-EYE DAISY. WHITE DAISY. WHITEWEED.

Europe. Johnson[4] says the leaves may be eaten as salad. The plant is the well-known flower of our fields, where it has become naturalized from Europe.

C. segetum Linn. CORN CHRYSANTHEMUM. CORN MARIGOLD.

Europe, north Africa and western Asia. The stalks and leaves, " as Dioscorides saith, are eaten as other pot herbes are."[5] In northern Japan and China, Miss Bird[6] describes a cultivated form of chrysanthemum as occurring frequently in patches and says the petals are partially boiled and are eaten with vinegar as a dainty.

Chrysobalanus ellipticus Soland. *Rosaceae.* COCO PLUM.

African tropics. This plant bears a damson-sized fruit with a black, thin skin and is eaten.[7]

C. icaco Linn. COCO PLUM.

African and American tropics. This tree-like shrub, with its fruit similar to the damson, grows wild as well as cultivated in the forests along the shores of South America and in

---

[1] Smith, A. *Treas. Bot.* 2:674. 1870. (*Leptomeria billardieri*)

[2] Burr, F. *Field, Gard. Veg.* 416. 1863. (*Balsamita vulgaris*)

[3] Forskal *Fl. Aeg. Arab.* 32. 1775.

[4] Johnson, C. P. *Useful Pls. Gt. Brit.* 161. 1862.

[5] Gerarde, J. *Herb.* 745. 1633 or 1636. 2nd Ed.

[6] Bird *Unbeat. Tracks Jap.* 1:175. 1881.

[7] Don, G. *Hist. Dichl. Pls.* 2:477. 1832.

Florida.[1] Browne[2] says in Jamaica the fruit is perfectly insipid but contains a large nut inclosing a kernel of very delicious flavor. The fruits in the West Indies, prepared with sugar, form a favorite conserve with the Spanish colonists, and large quantities are annually exported from Cuba. On the African coast it occurs from the Senegal to the Congo. The fruit is eaten by the natives of Angola and, according to Montiero,[3] is like a round, black-purple plum, tasteless and astringent. Sabine[4] says: " the fruit is about the size of an Orleans plum but is rounder, of a yellow color, with a flesh soft and juicy, the flavor having much resemblance to that of noyau."

Chrysophyllum africanum A. DC. *Sapotaceae.*

African tropics. This is a tall tree of Sierra Leone, whose fruit is in request.[5]

C. argenteum Jacq.

Martinique. The fruit, the size of a plum, contains a soft, bluish, edible pulp.[6]

C. cainito Linn. STAR APPLE.

West Indies. This tree has been cultivated from time immemorial in the West Indies but nowhere is found wild.[7] It seems to have been observed by Cieza de Leon[8] in his travels in Peru, 1532–50, and is called *caymitos.* Lunan[9] says some trees bear fruit with a purple and some with a white skin and pulp, which when soft is like jelly, with milky veins and has a sweet and pleasant taste.

C. glabrum Jacq.

Martinique. The fruit is blue, of the form and size of a small olive and is seldom eaten except by children.[10]

C. michino H. B. & K.

New Granada. The fruit is yellow outside, whitish and clammy inside and is very grateful.[11]

C. microcarpum Sw.

Haiti. The fruit is the size of a gooseberry, of a very sweet, delicious taste.[12]

C. monopyrenum Sw. DAMSON PLUM OF JAMAICA.

West Indies. The fruit is oval and about the size of a Bergamot pear. It contains a white, clammy juice when fresh, which, after being kept a few days, becomes sweet,

---

[1] Unger, F.   *U. S. Pat. Off. Rpt.* 349. 1859.

[2] Lunan, J. *Hort. Jam.* 1:211. 1814.

[3] Montiero, J. J. *Angola, River Congo* 2:298. 1875.

[4] Sabine, J. *Trans. Hort. Soc. Lond.* 5:453. 1824. (*C. luteus*)

[5] Sabine, J. *Trans. Hort. Soc. Lond.* 5:458. 1824.

[6] Don, G. *Hist. Dichl. Pls.* 4: 32. 1838.

[7] De Candolle, A. *Orig. Pls. Cult.* 285. 1885.

[8] Markham, C. R. *Trav. Cieza de Leon.* Hakl. Soc. Ed. 33:234. 1864.

[9] Lunan, J. *Hort. Jam.* 2:202. 1814.

[10] Don, G. *Hist. Dichl. Pls.* 4:32. 1838.

[11] Ibid.

[12] Ibid.

and delicious. It frequently contains four or five black seeds about the size of pumpkin seeds.[1]

C. obovatum Sabine.

African tropics. The fruit is the size of an apple, with a short apex and is much inferior to the star apple of the West Indies.

C. pruniferum F. Muell.

Australia. The fruit is of a plum-like appearance and is edible.[2]

C. roxburghii G. Don. PITAKARA. STAR APPLE.

Asiatic tropics. The fruit is greedily eaten by the natives.[3] It is the size of a small crab, yellow when ripe, smooth and is greedily eaten although insipid. The pulp is tolerably firm but is exceedingly clammy, adhering to the lips or knife with great tenacity.[4]

Chrysosplenium alternifolium Linn. *Saxifrageae.* GOLDEN SAXIFRAGE.

Europe, northern Asia and North America. The leaves are eaten as a salad in the Vosges Mountains.[5]

C. oppositifolium Linn.

Europe, northern Asia and East Indies. In some countries, this plant is eaten as a salad.[6] The leaves are eaten in salad and soup.[7]

Cicer arietinum Linn. *Leguminosae.* CHICK-PEA. EGYPTIAN PEA.

Europe, Orient and the East Indies. This plant is represented as growing wild in the Caucasus, in Greece and elsewhere; it is also found escaped from cultivation in the fields of middle Europe. The Jews, Greeks and Egyptians cultivated it in ancient times. It is extensively cultivated at the present time in the south of Europe, in the Levant, in Egypt as far as Abyssinia and in India. The seeds vary in size and color in the different varieties. In Paris, they are much used for soups. In India, they are ground into a meal and either eaten in puddings or made into cakes. They are also toasted or parched and made into a sort of comfit. In India, says Wight:[8] " The leaves of the plant secrete an acid which the natives collect by spreading a cloth over night on the plant and wringing out the dew in the morning. They then use it as vinegar or for forming a cooling drink." In 1854, the seed was distributed from the United States Patent Office.[9]

The shape of the unripe seed, which singularly resembles a ram's head, may account for its being regarded as unclean by the Egyptians of the time of Herodotus.[10] It was

---

[1] Lunan, J. *Hort. Jam.* 1:259. 1814.

[2] Mueller, F. *Sel. Pls.* 298. 1891. (*Niemeyera prunifera*)

[3] Royle, J. F. *Illustr. Bot. Himal.* 1:263. 1839.

[4] Don, G. *Hist. Dichl. Pls.* 4:33. 1838.

[5] Johns, C. A. *Treas. Bot.* 1:280. 1870.

[6] Johnson, C. P. *Useful Pls. Gt. Brit.* 110. 1862.

[7] Baillon, H. *Hist. Pls.* 3:418. 1874. Note.

[8] Wight, R. *Illustr. Ind. Bot.* 1: 192. 1840.

[9] *U. S. Pat. Off. Rpt.* XVI. 1854. Preface.

[10] Pickering, C. *Geog. Dist. Ans. Pls.* 380. 1863–1876.

in common use in ancient Rome and varieties are mentioned by Columella [1] and Pliny,[2] the latter naming the white and black, the Dove of Venus pea, and many kinds differing from each other in size. Albertus Magnus,[3] in the thirteenth century, mentions the red, the white and the black sorts, and this mention of colors is continued by the herbalists of the sixteenth, seventeenth, and eighteenth centuries. The white chick-pea is the sort now generally grown in France, where the dried seeds find large use in soups. The red variety is now extensively grown in eastern countries, and the black sort is described as more curious than useful.

Cichorium endivia Linn. *Compositae.* ENDIVE.

Europe and the Orient. This is a widely distributed plant, probably of East Indian origin, where certainly, says Unger,[4] " The same plant is met with wild about Patna and Kamaon, as well as in Nepal." Others deem it a native plant of Sicily. It was used as an esculent from a very early period by the Egyptians and was known to the Greeks Ovid mentions it in his tale of *Philemon and Baucis*, Columella also refers to it as common in his day, and Pliny states it was eaten in his time as a salad and as a potherb. It was in cultivation in England as early as 1548.[5] It is not known when the endive was first used in the United States, but McMahon,[6] 1806, mentions the Green Curled, White Curled and the Broad-leaved in cultivation. In 1828 and 1881, Thorburn offers the seed of these varieties only.

There are two distinct forms of endive, the curled and the broad-leaved. The first does not seem to have been known to the ancients, although Dioscorides [7] and Pliny [8] name two kinds. In the thirteenth century, Albertus Magnus [9] names also two kinds, the one with narrower leaves than the other; and in 1542 Fuchsius [10] figures two kinds of like description, and like forms are noted in nearly all the earlier botanies. A curled, broad-leaved form is figured by Camerarius,[11] 1586; Dalechamp,[12] 1587; and Gerarde,[13] 1597. Endive is described in the *Adversaria*,[14] 1570. The authors named furnish what may reasonably be considered as the types of the four kinds of broad-leaved endives described by Vilmorin.[15] The origin of the curled endives, of which Vilmorin describes twelve, is difficult to trace. The peculiar truncate appearance of the seed-stalks is very

---

[1] Columella lib. 9, c. 1.

[2] Bostock and Riley *Nat. Hist. Pliny* 4:46.   1856.

[3] Albertus Magnus *Veg.*   Jessen Ed. 490.   1867.

[4] Unger, F.   *U. S. Pat. Off. Rpt.* 353.   1859.

[5] McIntosh, C.   *Book Gard.* 2:159.   1855.

[6] McMahon, B.   *Amer. Gard. Cal.* 581.   1806.

[7] Dioscorides lib. 2, c. 147.

[8] Pliny lib. 20, c. 29, 32.

[9] Albertus Magnus *Veg.* Jessen Ed. 508.   1867.

[10] Fuchsius *Hist. Stirp.* 677, 678.

[11] Camerarius *Epit.* 283.   1586.

[12] Dalechamp *Hist. Gen. Pl.* (Lugd.) 557.   1587.

[13] Gerarde, J.   *Herb.* 221.   1597.

[14] Pena and Lobel *Advers.* 86.   1570.

[15] Vilmorin *Les Pls. Potag.* 95.   1883.

conspicuous, and this feature would lead one to suspect that the type is to be seen in the *Seris sativa* of Lobel,[1] but the resemblances are quite remote. This is the *Cichorium latioris folii* of Dodonaeus,[2] 1616. The endives were in English gardens as well-known plants in 1778[3] and were named among seedsmen's supplies in 1726.[4] They were in the United States prior to 1806.[5]

C. intybus Linn. BARBE DE CAPUCHIN. CHICORY. SUCCORY. WITLOOF.

Europe and the Orient. Wild chicory has been used from time immemorial as a salad-plant and, forced in darkness, affords the highly-esteemed vegetable in France known as barbe de capuchin. It has also large-rooted varieties and these, when treated in like manner, form the vegetable known in Belgium as witloof.

Whether chicory was cultivated by the ancients there is reason to doubt, although they knew the wild plant and its uses as a vegetable. It is not mentioned in the descriptive list of garden vegetables in use in the thirteenth century, as given by Albertus Magnus.[6] Ruellis,[7] 1535, mentions two kinds but does not imply cultivation; nor does Fuschius,[8] 1542, who likewise names two kinds, one of which is our dandelion. It is treated of by Tragus,[9] 1552; Matthiolus,[10] 1558; the *Adversaria*,[11] 1570; Lobel,[12] 1576; Camerarius,[13] 1586; Dalechamp,[14] 1587; Gerarde,[15] 1597; but with no mention of cultivation. Although not mentioned in Lyte's translation of *Dodonaeus*, 1586, as cultivated, yet, in Dodonaeus' *Pemptades*, 1616, it is said not only to occur wild throughout all Germany but to be cultivated in gardens. This is the first mention of culture noted. In 1686, Ray[16] says " it is sown in gardens and occurs wild in England." The seed occurs among seedsmen's supplies in 1726.[17]

At the present time, chicory is grown for the use of its leaves in salads and for its root to be used as an adulterant for coffee. The smooth, tapering root, which seems such an improved form in our modern varieties, is beautifully figured by Camerarius in 1586. The common chicory grown for salads is but the wild plant little changed and with the divided leaves as figured by the herbalists. The entire-leaved form with a tendency to a red midrib also occurs in nature and may be considered as the near prototype of the Magde-

---

[1] Lobel *Obs.* 114. 1576.
[2] Dodonaeus *Pempt.* 634. 1616.
[3] Mawe and Abercrombie *Univ. Gard. Bot.* 1778.
[4] Townsend *Seedsman* 20. 1726.
[5] McMahon, B. *Amer. Gard. Cal.* 581. 1806.
[6] Albertus Magnus lib. 7, tract 2, c. 2.
[7] Ruellius *Nat. Stirp.* 495. 1536.
[8] Fuchsius *Hist. Stirp.* 679. 1542.
[9] Tragus *Stirp.* 272. 1552.
[10] Matthiolus *Comment.* 258. 1558.
[11] Pena and Lobel *Advers.* 82. 1570.
[12] Lobel *Pl. Stirp. Hist.* 114. 1576.
[13] Camerarius *Epit.* 285. 1586.
[14] Dalechamp *Hist. Gen. Pl.* (Lugd.) 557. 1587.
[15] Gerarde, J. *Herb.* 235. 1597.
[16] Ray *Hist. Pl.* 1:255. 1686.
[17] Townsend *Seedsman* 33. 1726.

burg large-rooted and of the red Italian sorts. The variegated chicory, the curled-leaved and the broad-leaved may have their prototypes in nature if sought for but at present must remain unexplained. The common, the spotted-leaved and the large-rooted were in French culture in 1826.[1]

Cinnamomum cassia Blume. *Laurineae.* CASSIA. CINNAMON.

China, Sumatra, Ceylon and other parts of eastern Asia. This plant yields a cinnamon of commerce. Cinnamon seems to have been known to the ancient natives inhabitating the countries bordering on the Levant. It is the *kinnamomon* of Herodotus, a name which he states the Greeks learned from the Phoenicians. It is spoken of in *Exodus*, is referred to by Hippocrates, Dioscorides, Pliny and others of the ancient writers. The inner bark of the shoots is the portion used. Nearly every species of the genus yields its bark to commerce, including not less than six species on the Malabar coast and in Ceylon, and nearly twice as many more in the eastern part of Asia and in the islands of the Eastern Archipelago. Cassia bark resembles the true cinnamon but is thicker, coarser and not as delicately flavored. Both are used for flavoring confectionery and in cooking.

C. culilawan Blume.

Malays, China, Moluccas and Cochin China. The bark of this species is said to have the flavor of cloves and is used as a condiment.

C. iners Reinw.

Burma, Malays, tropical Hindustan and Siam. In India, the natives use the bark as a condiment in their curries. In southern India, the more mature fruits are collected for use but are very inferior to the Chinese cassia buds.[2] Among the Ghauts, the bark is put in curries as a spice.[3]

C. loureirii Nees.

Cochin China and Japan. From the bark of this plant is made a cinnamon of which the finest kind is superior to that of Ceylon.

C. nitidum Blume.

Java, Ceylon and India. This plant furnishes a spice.

C. sintok Blume.

Malays and Java. The plant possesses an aromatic bark.

C. tamala T. Nees & Eberm.

Himalayan region. This plant furnishes leaves that are essential ingredients in Indian cookery.[4]

C. zeylanicum Nees. CINNAMON.

East Indies and Malays. This plant is largely cultivated in Ceylon for its bark. Its cultivation is said to have commenced about 1770, but the plant was known in a wild

---

[1] Petit *Dict. Jard.* 1826.
[2] Flückiger and Hanbury *Pharm.* 480. 1879.
[3] Pickering, C. *Chron. Hist. Pls.* 394. 1879.
[4] Dutt, U. C. *Mat. Med. Hindus* 224. 1877.

state long before. Herodotus says: " the bark was the lining taken from birds' nests built with clay against the face of precipitous mountains in those countries where Bacchus was nurtured." It has been cultivated for some time in Mauritius, the West Indies, Brazil and other tropical countries.

Cistus ladaniferus Linn. *Cistineae.* LAUDANUM.

Western Mediterranean regions. This species, which furnishes the laudanum of Spain and Portugal, is often to be met with in gardens. Loudon [1] says the gum which exudes from it is eaten by the common people.

C. villosus Linn. SHAGGY ROCK-ROSE.

Spain. This plant is used in Greece in preparing infusions similar to tea. It is the *cistus mas* of the ancients.[2]

Citriobatus sp.? *Pittosporeae.* NATIVE ORANGE. ORANGE THORN.

Australia. A species of this genera is the native orange and orange thorn of the Australian colonists. The fruit is an orange berry with a leathery skin, subglobular, about one and one-half inches through and is eaten by the natives.[3]

Citrullus colocynthis Schrad. *Cucurbitaceae.* BITTER GOURD. COLOCYNTH.

Tropical Africa. This creeping plant grows abundantly in the Sahara, in Arabia, on the Coromandel coast and in some of the islands of the Aegean. The fruit, which is about as large as an orange, contains an extremely bitter and drastic pulp, from which the drug colocynth is obtained.[4] Thunberg [5] says this gourd is rendered so perfectly mild at the Cape of Good Hope, by being properly pickled, that it is eaten by the natives and by the colonists. The gourds are also made into preserves with sugar, having been previously pierced all over with knives and then boiled in six or seven waters until all the bitterness disappears. Gypsies eat the kernel of the seed freed from the seed-skin by a slight roasting. Flückiger [6] says the seed kernels are used as a food in the African desert, after being carefully deprived of their coatings. Stille [7] says they are reported to be mild, oleaginous and nutritious. Captain Lyon [8] speaks also of their use in northern Africa. In India, according to Vaupell,[9] there is a sweet variety which is edible and cultivated.

C. vulgaris Schrad. WATERMELON.

Tropical Africa. The watermelon has succeeded especially well under American culture, the varieties being many in number and continuously increasing, either through importation or through the process of selection. The size has also become enormous

---

[1] Loudon, J. C. *Enc. Agr.* 117. 1866.

[2] Baillon, H. *Hist. Pls.* 4:337. 1875. Note.

[3] Syme, J. T. *Treas. Bot.* 1:290. 1870.

[4] Flückiger, F. A. *Sci. Record* 63. 1874.

[5] Thunberg, C. P. *Trav.* 2:171. 1796.

[6] Flückiger, F. A. *Sci. Record* 63. 1874.

[7] Stille, A. *Therap. Mat. Med.* 2:428. 1874.

[8] *U. S. Disp.* 315. 1865.

[9] Pickering, C. *Chron. Hist. Pls.* 253. 1879.

selected specimens sometimes weighing 96 pounds or even more. The varieties vary in shape from round to oblong and in color from a light green to almost a black, self-colored or striped with paler green or marbled. The flesh may be white, cream-color, honey-color, pale red, red or scarlet. The seeds are white, white with two black spots, cream-colored tipped with brown and a brown stripe around the edge, yellow with a black stripe round the margin and with black spots, dark brown, reddish-brown, russet-brown, black, sculptured or as if engraved with ornamental characters, and pink or red.

The watermelon is mentioned by the early botanists and described as of large size, but it must be considered that this fruit even now is not as successfully grown in Europe as in more southern countries. That none or few types have originated under modern culture is indicated by an examination into the early records.

Size.— Cardanus,[1] 1556, writes that the size is sometimes so great that a man can scarcely embrace the fruit with his expanded arms. Marcgravius,[2] 1648, describes those of Brazil as being as large as a man's head, sometimes larger, sometimes smaller. In 1686, Ray [3] says the size is such as to be scarcely grasped with the two hands; this is what J. Bauhin [4] wrote many years earlier for he died in 1613. The figures in the earlier botanies, of which there are many, all indicate a smalll-sized fruit, although the description is usually of a "large" or "very large" fruit.

Shape.— Round fruits are mentioned by Fuchsius,[5] 1542; by Cardanus,[6] 1556; Garcia ab Horto,[7] 1567; Marcgravius,[8] 1648; Piso,[9] 1658; and Ray,[10] 1686. Subround or roundish, by Camerarius,[11] 1586; and Gerarde,[12] 1597. Oblong by Garcia ab Horto,[13] 1567; Lourerio,[14] 1790. Oval, by Garcia ab Horto,[15] 1567. Elliptical, by Marcgravius,[16] 1648; and Ray,[17] 1686.

Color.— Grass-green, by Fuchsius,[18] 1542. Green, by Albertus Magnus, thirteenth century; Bauhin,[19] 1596; Gerarde,[20] 1597. Grass-green and spotted, by Matthiolus,[21] 1570;

---

[1] Cardanus *Rerum var.* 185. 1581.

[2] Marcgravius *Hist. Rerum Nat. Bras.* 22. 1648.

[3] Ray *Hist. Pl.* 643. 1686.

[4] Bauhin, J. *Hist. Pl.* 1650.

[5] Fuchsius *Hist. Stirp.* 702. 1542.

[6] Cardanus *Rerum var.* 184. 1556.

[7] Horto, G. ab. *Aromatum* 237. 1567.

[8] Marcgravius *Hist. Rerum Nat. Bras.* 22. 1648.

[9] Pisc *De Ind.* 263. 1658.

[10] Ray *Hist. Pl.* 643. 1686.

[11] Camerarius *Epit.* 22. 1648.

[12] Gerarde, J. *Herb.* 767. 1597.

[13] Horto, G. ab. *Aromatum* 237. 1567.

[14] Loureiro *Fl. Cochin.* 594. 1790.

[15] Horto, G. ab. *Aromatum* 237. 1567.

[16] Marcgravius *Hist. Rerum Nat. Bras.* 22. 1648. (Piso)

[17] Ray *Hist. Pl.* 643. 1686.

[18] Fuchsius *Hist. Stirp.* 702. 1542.

[19] Bauhin, C. *Phytopinax* 622. 1596.

[20] Gerarde, J. *Herb.* 767. 1597.

[21] Matthiolus *Comment.* 369. 1570.

Camerarius,[1] 1596; Dalechamp,[2] 1587. Green and spotted, by Bauhin,[3] 1596. Blackish, by Gerarde,[4] 1597.

Flesh.— Red, by Bauhin,[5] 1596; 1623,[6] Marcgravius,[7] 1648. White, by Bauhin,[8] 1596, 1623;[9] Chabraeus,[10] 1677. Scarlet, by Marcgravius,[11] 1648. Pale red, by Piso,[12] 1658; Loureiro,[13] 1790. Yellow, by Bryant,[14] 1783. Flesh-color, by Josselyn, 1663.

Seed.— Chestnut-brown, by Fuchsius,[15] 1542. Purple-red, by Tragus,[16] 1552. Black, by Matthiolus,[17] 1570; Camerarius,[18] 1596; Dalechamp,[19] 1587; Bauhin,[20] 1596; J. Bauhin,[21] 1651. Red, by Matthiolus,[22] 1570; Bauhin,[23] 1596; Sloane,[24] 1696; Bryant,[25] 1783. Reddish, by Camerarius,[26] 1586. Brown, by Bauhin,[27] 1596; Marcgravius,[28] 1648. Raven-black, by Marcgravius,[29] 1648. White, by J. Bauhin,[30] 1651. Sculptured, by Forskal,[31] 1775.

It is interesting to note that the older writers described some varieties as sweet, others as insipid and acid. Livingstone[32] describes the wild watermelons of South Africa as some sweet and wholesome, others bitter and deleterious. The bitter or acid forms do not now appear in our culture.

The most surprising plant of the South African desert, writes Livingstone, is the *kengwe* or *keme*, the watermelon. In years when more than the usual quantity of rain

---

[1] Camerarius *Epit.* 297. 1586.

[2] Dalechamp *Hist. Gen. Pl.* (Lugd.) 625. 1597.

[3] Bauhin, C. *Phytopinax* 622. 1596.

[4] Gerarde, J. *Herb.* 767. 1597.

[5] Bauhin, C. *Phytopinax* 622. 1596.

[6] Bauhin, C. *Pinax* 312. 1623.

[7] Marcgravius *Hist. Rerum Nat. Bras.* 22. 1648. (Piso)

[8] Bauhin, C. *Phytopinax* 622. 1596.

[9] Bauhin, C. *Pinax* 312. 1623.

[10] Chabraeus *Icon. Sciag.* 133. 1677.

[11] Marcgravius *Hist. Rerum Nat. Bras.* 22. 1648. (Piso)

[12] Piso *De Ind.* 263. 1658.

[13] Lourerio *Fl. Cochin.* 594. 1790.

[14] Bryant *Fl. Diet.* 269. 1783.

[15] Fuchsius *Hist. Stirp.* 702. 1542.

[16] Tragus *Stirp.* 832. 1552.

[17] Matthiolus *Comment.* 369. 1570.

[18] Camerarius *Epit.* 297. 1586.

[19] Dalechamp *Hist. Gen. Pl.* (Lugd.) 625. 1587.

[20] Bauhin, C. *Phytopinax* 622. 1596.

[21] Bauhin, J. *Hist. Pl.* 2:236. 1651.

[22] Matthiolus *Comment.* 369. 1570.

[23] Bauhin, C. *Phytopinax* 622. 1596.

[24] Sloane, H. *Cat.* 103. 1696.

[25] Bryant *Fl. Diet.* 269. 1783.

[26] Camerarius *Epit.* 297. 1586.

[27] Bauhin *Phytopinax* 622. 1596.

[28] Marcgravius *Hist. Rerum Nat. Bras.* 22. 1648. (Piso)

[29] Ibid.

[30] Bauhin, J. *Hist. Pl.* 2:236. 1651.

[31] Forskal, P. *Fl. Aeg. Arab.* 1:122, 167. 1775.

[32] Livingstone, D. *Trav. Research. So. Afr.* 54. 1858.

falls, vast tracts of the country are literally covered with these melons. Some are sweet, and others so bitter that they are named by the Boers the " bitter watermelon." The bitter ones are deleterious, but the sweet are quite wholesome. As this missionary observer was not a botanist, it is possible that this species may have been the colocynth, *Citrullus colocynthis*, or a hybrid of the colocynth and the watermelon.

Rauwolf,[1] 1574, found the watermelon growing in abundance in the gardens of Tripoli, Rama and Aleppo under the name *bathieca*, the root of which word, says R. Thompson,[2] is from the Hebrew *abattichim*, one of the fruits of Egypt which the Jews regretted in the wilderness. The watermelon still forms the chief food and drink of the inhabitants of Egypt for several months in the year. In Bagdad, also, it is a staple summer food. Pallas says in southern Russia the people make a beer from their abundant crops of watermelons, with the addition of hops. They also make a conserve or marmalade from the fruit, which is an excellent substitute for syrup or molasses. In 1662, Nieuhoff[3] found the watermelon called *batiek* by the Indians of Batavia, some being white, others red and the seeds black. This melon is said to have been introduced into Britain in 1597. By European colonists, says Pickering,[4] it was carried to Brazil and the West Indies, to eastern North America, to the islands of the Pacific, to New Zealand and Australia.

Watermelons are mentioned by Master Graves[5] as abounding in Massachusetts in 1629, and shortly after Josselyn[6] speaks of it as a fruit " proper to the countrie. The flesh of it is of a flesh-colour . . . and excellent against the stone." " A large fruit, but nothing near so big as a pompion; colour smoother, and of a sad grass-green, rounder, or, more rightly, sap-green; with some yellowness admixt when ripe. The seeds are black; the flesh, or pulpe, exceeding juicy." Before 1664, according to Hilton,[7] watermelons were cultivated by the Florida Indians. In 1673, Father Marquette,[8] who descended the Wisconsin and Mississippi Rivers, speaks of melons, " which are excellent, especially those with a red seed." In 1822, Woods[9] says of the Illinois region: " Watermelons are also in great plenty, of vast size; some I suppose weigh 20 pounds. They are more like pumpkins in outward appearance than melons. They are round or oblong, generally green, or a green and whitish color on the outside, and white or pale on the inside, with many black seeds in them, very juicy, in flavor like rich water, and sweet and mawkish, but cool and pleasant." In 1747, Jared Eliot mentions watermelons in Connecticut, the seed of which came originally from Archangel in Russia. In 1799, watermelons were raised by the tribes on the Colorado River. In 1806, McMahon[10] describes four kinds. They are now cultivated throughout the warm regions of the globe.

[1] Ray, J.   *Trav. through Low Countries* 2:16.   1738.

[2] Thompson, R.   *Treas. Bot.* 1:357.   1870.

[3] Churchill *Coll. Voy.* 2:289.   1732.

[4] Pickering, C.   *Chron. Hist. Pls.* 72.   1879.

[5] Graves *Mass. Hist. Soc. Coll.* 1:124.   1806.

[6] Josselyn, J.   *Voy.* 101.   1865.

[7] Hilton *Rel. Fla.* 8.   1664.   Force Coll. Tracts 4: No. 2.   1846.

[8] *Ill. Hort. Soc. Trans.* 125.   1876.

[9] Woods, J.   *Ill. Country* 226, 227.   1822.

[10] McMahon, B.   *Amer. Gard. Cal.* 582.   1806.   (*Cucurbita citrullus*)

Citrus. *Rutaceae*. BERGAMOT. CITRON. GRAPE FRUIT. LEMON. LIME. ORANGE. POMELO SHADDOCK.

The determination of the species of this genus seems to be in confusion, as might be expected from the great variability of this favorite fruit so long under cultivation. Linnaeus[1] established two species, *Citrus aurantium*, comprising the sweet and bitter orange and the shaddock; and *Citrus medica*, comprising the lime, lemon and citron. Risso and Poiteau[2] recognized eight species, *C. bergamia*, the bergamot, *C. limetta*, the sweet lime with white flowers, *C. decumana*, the shaddock, *C. lumia*, the sweet lemon, *C. limonum*, the lemon, and *C. medica*, the citron. In 1818, Risso[3] describes 169 varieties and figures 105. The mass of evidence collected by Professor Targioni-Tozzetti[4] seems to show that oranges were first brought from India into Arabia in the ninth century, that they were unknown in Europe, or at any rate in Italy, in the eleventh, but were shortly afterwards carried westward by the Moors. They were in cultivation at Seville towards the end of the twelfth century, and at Palermo in the thirteenth and probably also in Italy, for it is said that St. Domine planted an orange for the convent of S. Sabina in Rome in the year 1200. In the course of the same century, the crusaders found citrons, oranges and lemons very abundant in Palestine, and in the fourteenth century both oranges and lemons became common in several parts of Italy.

They must have been early introduced to America, for Humboldt[5] says "it would seem as if the whole island of Cuba had been originally a forest of palm, lemon and wild orange trees," and he thinks the oranges, which bear a small fruit, are probably anterior to the arrival of Europeans, who transported thither the *agrumi* of the gardens. Caldlouch[6] says the Brazilians affirm that the small, bitter orange, which bears the name of *loranjo do terra* and is found wild far from the habitations of man, is of American origin, De Soto,[7] 1557, mentions oranges in the Antilles as bearing fruit all the year, and, in 1587, Cavendish[8] found an orchard with lemons and oranges at Puna, South America, and off San Blas lemons and oranges were brought to the ships. In 1693–94, Phillips speaks of the wild orange as apparently indigenous in Mexico, Porto Rico, Barbados and the Bermudas, as well as in Brazil and the Cape Verde Islands.[9]

The citron appears to have been the only one of this genus known in ancient Rome and is probably the *melea persike* of Theophrastus and the *persika mala* of Dioscorides. Lindley says those who have bestowed the most pains in the investigation of Indian botany, and in whose judgment we should place the most confidence, have come to the conclusion that the citron, orange, lemon, lime and their numerous varieties now in circulation, are all derived from one botanical species.

[1] Brandis, D. *Forest Fl.* 51. 1876.

[2] Ibid.

[3] Wood, A. *Class Book Bot.* 275. 1864.

[4] Targioni-Tozzetti *Journ. Hort. Soc. Lond.* 9:173. 1855.

[5] Humboldt, A. *Trav.* 3:171. 1889.

[6] Ibid.

[7] De Soto *Disc. Conq. Fla.* Hakl. Soc. Ed. 19. 1851.

[8] *Lives Voy. Drake, Cavendish* 136. 1854.

[9] Nuttall, T. *No. Amer. Sylva* 2:54. 1865.

C. aurantium Linn. BERGAMONT. BITTER ORANGE. SEVILLE ORANGE. SWEET ORANGE.

Tropical eastern Asia. The sweet orange began to be cultivated in Europe about the middle of the fifteenth century. Phillips[1] says it was introduced at Lisbon in 1548 by Juan de Castro, a celebrated Portuguese warrior, and from this one tree all the European orange trees of this sort were propagated. This tree was said to have been alive at Lisbon in 1823. One of the first importations of oranges into England occurred A. D. 1290, in which year a Spanish ship laden with this fruit arrived at Portsmouth; of this cargo the Queen of Edward I bought seven.[2] Gallesio[3] says the sweet orange reached Europe through Persia to Syria, and thence to the shores of Italy and the south of France, being carried by the Arabs. It was seen by Friar Jordanus[4] in India about 1330. In the year 1500, says Loudon,[5] there was only one orange-tree in France, which had been planted in 1421 at Pempeluna in Navarre, and this tree is still living. In 1791, Bartram[6] refers to the orange as growing abundantly in Florida, as is apparent from the context, and in 1871 Dr. Baldwin writes, " you may eat oranges from morning to night at every plantation along the shore (of the St. Johns), while the wild trees, bending with their golden fruit over the water, present an enchanting appearance." Oranges are also found in Louisiana and in California (they were seen by Father Baegert[7] in 1751) and are now quite extensively grown for market in the extreme southern states. They are imported to our Atlantic ports from the Mediterranean, the Azores and also from the West Indies. At San Francisco, large quantities are received from Tahiti and Mexico and a few from Hawaii. There are numerous varieties grown, some of which are so distinct as to be described as botanical species.

BERGAMOT.

The bergamot first appeared in the latter part of the seventeenth century. It is not mentioned in the grand work on orange trees by Ferrari,[8] 1676, nor by Lanzani,[9] 1690, nor Quintinye,[10] 1692. It seems to be first mentioned in a little book called *La Parfumeur François*,[11] published at Lyons in 1693.[12] There are several varieties.

BIGARADE ORANGE. SOUR ORANGE. BITTER ORANGE. SEVILLE ORANGE.

The sour orange is extensively cultivated in the warmer parts of the Mediterranean region, especially in Spain, and exists under many varieties. It was probably the first orange cultivated in Europe.[13] The sour orange was not mentioned by Nearchus among

---

[1] Phillips, H. *Comp. Orch.* 266. 1831.

[2] Flückiger and Hanbury *Pharm.* 112. 1879.

[3] Gallesio *Treas. Bot.* 1:292. 1870.

[4] Jordanus, Fr. *Wonders East.* 1330. Hakl. Soc. Ed. 15. 1863.

[5] Loudon, J. C. *Hort.* 608. 1860.

[6] Bartram, W. *Trav. No., So. Car.* 144. 1791.

[7] *Smithsonian Inst. Rpt.* 356. 1863.

[8] Flückiger and Hanbury *Pharm.* 109. 1879.

[9] Ibid.

[10] Ibid.

[11] Ibid.

[12] Ibid.

[13] Flückiger and Hanbury *Pharm.* 111. 1879.

the productions of the country which is watered by the Indus, but the Arabs, pushing farther into the interior than Alexander the Great, found the orange, and brought it into Arabia in the ninth century. It reached Italy in the eleventh century and was in cultivation about Seville at the close of the twelfth and at Palermo in the thirteenth century. Gallesio [1] states that it was introduced from Arabia and the north of Africa into Spain. Pickering,[2] states that the bitter orange was cultivated in Sicily in A. D. 1002. The sour orange had become naturalized in the forests of Essequibo, about Vera Cruz and near Mexico City, in 1568; in Brazil in 1587;[3] in Porto Rico, Barbados and the Bermudas,[4] Cape Verde islands and in Florida at early dates. There are many varieties and the fruit of a curious one consists of an orange within an orange.

TANGERINE. MANDARIN.

This fruit is rare in China but abundant in Cochin China. The fruit is round, a little compressed, red inside as well as out. It is the most agreeable of all oranges.[5] Loudon [6] says the thin rind is loose, so much so that when ripe the pulp may be shaken about as a kernel in some nuts. The flesh, of a deep orange color, possesses a superior flavor. Williams [7] says it is the most delicious of the oranges of China.

C. decumana Murr. GRAPE FRUIT. POMELO. PUMMELO. SHADDOCK.

Tropical Asia. The shaddock was first carried from China to the West Indies early in the eighteenth century. It occurs in several varieties and both the red and white kinds are considered by Wilkes [8] indigenous to the Fiji Islands. In 1777, they were somewhat distributed by Capt. Cook in his voyage of discovery.

C. japonica Thunb. KUMQUAT.

Japan and China. The fruit is about the size of a cherry or gooseberry. It is cultivated in China and Japan and is found near Canton in China. The small, oblong, reddish-yellow fruit contains but five sections under a very thin skin; the pulp is sweet and agreeable.[9]

C. javanica Blume. JAVA LEMON.

Java. This cultivated species bears small, roundish, slightly acid fruits.[10]

C. limonia Osbeck. LEMON.

Tropical Asia. De Candolle[11] says the lemon was unknown to the ancient Romans

[1] Gallesio *Treas. Bot.* 1:292. 1870.

[2] Pickering, C. *Chron. Hist. Pls.* 656. 1879.

[3] *Lives Voy. Drake, Cavendish* 136. 1854.

[4] Nuttall, T. *No. Amer. Sylva* 2:54. 1865.

[5] Gallesio, G. *Traité Citrus* 32. 1811.

[6] Loudon, J. C. *Hort.* 608. 1860.

[7] Williams, S. W. *U. S. Pat. Off. Rpt.* 475. 1860.

[8] Wilkes, C. *U. S. Explor. Exped.* 3:335. 1845.

[9] De Candolle, A. *Geog. Bot.* 2:870. 1855.

[10] Ibid.

[11] De Candolle, A. *Geog. Bot.* 2:865. 1855.

and Greeks, and that its culture extended into the West only with the conquests of the Arabs. It is mentioned in the *Book of Nabathae* on Agriculture which is supposed to date from the third or fourth century of our era. The Arabs brought the lemon in the tenth century from the gardens of Omar into Palestine and Egypt. Jacques de Vitry, writing in the thirteenth century, very well describes the lemon, which he had seen in Palestine. About 1330, Friar Jordanus,[1] saw in India "other lemons sour like ours" which would indicate its existence in India before that date. It was cultivated in Genoa, about the middle of the fifteenth century and as early as 1494 in the Azores.[2] From the north of India, the lemon appears to have passed eastward into Cochin China and China and westward into Europe; it has become naturalized in the West Indies and various parts of America. There are numerous varieties. Some are cultivated in Florida to a limited extent. They are mentioned in California in 1751–68 by Father Baegert.[3]

LIME.

In Jamaica, the lime is quite naturalized. The fruit is nearly globose, small, yellow when ripe, with a thin skin and an abundance of pure, acid juice.[4] This fruit is largely imported into the United States, in its natural form, pickled and in the form of lime juice. About 1755, Henry Laurens[5] imported limes into South Carolina.

SWEET LEMON.

The fruit has the rind and the flesh of a lemon but the pulp is sweet. There are many varieties in Italy.

C. medica Linn. CITRON.

Tropical Asia; indigenous to and still found wild in the mountains of east India. The citron is the only member of the orange tribe, the fruit of which was known in ancient Rome. The tree appears to have been cultivated in Palestine in the time of Josephus and was introduced into Italy about the third century. In 1003, it was much grown near Naples.[6] Hogg[7] thinks this is the *melea medike* of Theophrastus, 322 B. C., and *mela medika e kedromela* of Dioscorides.[8] Rhind says it was first cultivated in Italy by Palladius in the second century. Royle[9] found it growing wild in the forests of northern India. In Media and Persia, the citron is found only in the cultivated state. It is now distributed throughout the whole of southern Europe, also in Brazil and in the Congo.[10] Fruits are used chiefly in a candied form.

---

[1] Jordanus, Fr. *Wonders, East.* Hakl. Soc. Ed. 15. 1863.
[2] Flückiger and Hanbury *Pharm.* 103. 1879.
[3] *Smithsonian Inst. Rpt.* 356. 1863.
[4] Brandis, D. *Forest Fl.* 54. 1876.
[5] Loudon, J. C. *Hort.* 609. 1860.
[6] Flückiger and Hanbury *Pharm.* 115. 1879.
[7] Hooker, W. J. *Journ. Bot.* 1:105. 1831.
[8] Rhind, W. *Hist. Veg. King.* 353. 1855.
[9] Unger, F. *U. S. Pat. Off. Rpt.* 337. 1859.
[10] Ibid.

Cladothrix lanuginosa Nutt.   *Amarantaceae.*

California and Mexico.   According to Schott,[1] the Mexicans use a decoction of the plant as a tea.

Clausena excavata Burm. f.   *Rutaceae.*   WHAMPLE.

East India and Malay Archipelago.   This shrub of China and the Moluccas is cultivated in the West Indies.   The fruit has a good deal the taste of the grape, accompanied with a peculiar flavor, being very grateful to the palate.[2]   The fruit is borne in clusters, resembling, when ripe, a diminutive lemon, about the size of an acorn.   It contains three large seeds which nearly fill the interior.   The scanty pulp has an anise-seed flavor.[3] Williams[4] says in China it is pleasantly acid and held in esteem, as it also is in the Indian archipelago.   About two bushels are produced on a tree.

Clavija sp.   *Myrsineae.*

A genus of South American shrubs or small trees.   The fruits are fleshy and contain numerous seeds embedded in a pulp which is said to be eatable.   They vary in size, but are seldom larger than a pigeon's egg.[5]

Claydonia rangiferina (Linn.) Web.   *Lichenes.*   REINDEER MOSS.

Northern regions.   Reindeer moss is sometimes eaten by the people of Norway and is crisp and agreeable.   Reindeer moss, says Kalm,[6] grows plentifully in the woods around Quebec.   M. Gaulthier and several other gentlemen told him that the French, on their long voyages through the woods, in pursuit of their fur trade with the Indians, sometimes boil this moss and drink the decoction for want of better food when their provisions are exhausted.

Claytonia caroliniana Michx.   *Portulaceae.*

Eastern United States.   This plant has edible bulbs much prized by Indians.[7]

C. exigua Torr. & Gray.

California.   The succulent leaves are in popular use as a potherb in California.[8]

C. megarrhiza Parry.

Western North America.   This plant has a long, fleshy taproot but it is confined to the summits of the Rocky Mountains and is seldom available.[9]

C. perfoliata Donn.   CUBAN SPINACH.

North America.   This species, according to Robinson,[10] is cultivated in France as a

---

[1] Torrey, J.   *U. S. Mex. Bound. Surv.* 181.   1859.   (*Alternanthera lanuginosa*)

[2] Hooker, W. J.   *Journ. Bot.* **7**:135.   1855. (*Cookia punctata*)

[3] Firminger, T. A. C.   *Gard. Ind.* 217.   1874.   (*Cookia punctata*)

[4] Williams, S. W.   *U. S. Pat. Off. Rpt.* 475.   1860.

[5] Black, A. A.   *Treas. Bot.* **1**:296.   1870.

[6] Kalm, P.   *Trav. No. Amer.*   **2**:287, 288.   1772.   (*Lichen rangiferinus*)

[7] Havard, V.   *Torr. Bot. Club Bul.* **22**:107.   1895.

[8] Brewer and Watson *Bot. Cal.* **1**:76.   1880.

[9] Havard, V.   *Torr. Bot. Club Bul.* **22**:107.   1895.

[10] Robinson, W.   *Parks, Gard. Paris* 503.   1878.

salad plant.   The foliage is used in England, according to Loudon,[1] as a spinach.   De
Candolle [2] says it is occasionally cultivated there.   *C. perfoliata* of Cuba is an annual
employed as a spinach in France in place of purslane.[3]   It was first described in 1794
but in 1829 was not named by Noisette [4] for French gardens; in 1855 it was said by De
Candolle [5] to be occasionally cultivated as a vegetable in England.   It is now included
by Vilmorin among French vegetables.

C. sibirica Linn.   SIBERIAN PURSLANE.

Northern Asia and northwestern North America.   This species is eaten both raw
and cooked by the Indians of Alaska.[6]

C. tuberosa Pall.

Kamchatka and eastern Siberia.   The tubers are edible.[7]

C. virginica Linn.   SPRING BEAUTY.

Eastern United States.   This species has edible bulbs, much prized by the Indians.[8]

Clematis flammula Linn.   *Ranunculaceae.*   VIRGIN'S BOWER.

Mediterranean countries.   The young shoots, when boiled, may be eaten.

Cleome chelidonii Linn.   *Capparideae.*   SPIDER-FLOWER.

East Indies.   The seeds are used by the natives as a mustard in their curries, on
account of their pungency.[9]

C. felina Linn. f.

East Indies.   In India, the flowers are used to flavor salads.[10]

C. heptaphylla Linn.

American tropics.   The leaves are eaten.

C. viscosa Linn.

Old World tropics.   This plant has an acrid taste, something like mustard, and is
eaten by the natives among other herbs as a salad.[11]   The seeds, being pungent, are used
in curries as a mustard.[12]   Its seeds are eaten as a condiment like mustard.[13]   The seeds
are used in curries.[14]

---

[1] Dewey, C.   *Rpt. Herb. Flow. Pls. Mass.* 92.   1840.
[2] De Candolle, A.   *Geog. Bot.* 2:662.   1855.
[3] *Bon Jard.* 476.   1882.
[4] Noisette *Man. Jard.* 1829.
[5] De Candolle, A.   *Geog. Bot.* 2:662.   1855.
[6] *U. S. Nat. Herb.* 3:330.   1896.
[7] Don, G.   *Hist. Dichl. Pls.* 3:82.   1834.
[8] Havard, V.   *Torr. Bot. Club Bul.* 22:107.   1895.
[9] Royle, J. F.   *Illustr. Bot. Himal.* 1:73.   1839.
[10] Baillon, H.   *Hist. Pls.* 3:169.   1874.
[11] Pickering, C.   *Chron. Hist. Pls.* 736.   1879.   (*Polanisia icosandra*)
[12] Royle, J. F.   *Illustr. Bot. Himal.* 1:73.   1839.
[13] Baillon, H.   *Hist. Pls.* 3:169.   1874.
[14] Speede *Ind. Handb. Gard.* 50.   1842.   Supplement.

Clerodendron serratum Spreng. *Verbenaceae.*

Tropical India and Burma. Its flowers and leaves are eaten.[1]

Clethra tinifolia Sw. *Ericaceae.* SOAP-WOOD. SWEET PEPPER. WILD PEAR.

Tropical America, Jamaica and southern Brazil. In Jamaica the trees bear a green, roundish berry of which the pulp is sweet, white, mealy and includes a hard, brownish-black stone. These berries are gathered and eaten as a pleasant dessert.[2]

Cleyera theoides Choisy. *Ternstroemiaceae.*

West Indies. Henfrey[3] says the leaves of this plant furnish a tea in Panama.

Clidemia sp.? *Melastomaceae.* INDIAN CURRANT.

Tropical America. A genus of shrubs the berry of which is fleshy and edible.[4]

C. dependens D. Don.

Peru. This shrub furnishes a gooseberry-like fruit of little value.[5]

Cliffortia ilicifolia Linn. *Rosaceae.* EVERGREEN OAK.

South Africa. The leaves have been used in Africa as a tea substitute.[6]

Clinogyne dichotoma Salisb. *Scitamineae.* MARANTA

East Indies and Malays. The maranta is cultivated in the East Indies for arrowroot.[7]

Clitoria ternatea Linn. *Leguminosae.* BUTTERFLY PEA.

Mountains of Madagascar and Mauritius. In the Philippines, the pods are sometimes eaten.[8] In Amboina, the flowers are used to tinge boiled rice a cerulean color.[9]

Cnicus eriophorus Roth. *Compositae.*

Europe and Asia Minor. This thistle is said to have been cultivated by M. Lecoq[10] in France and is pronounced by him a savory vegetable. The receptacles of this plant, says Lightfoot,[11] are pulpy and esculent, like those of the artichoke.

C. oleraceus Linn.

Northern Europe and Asia. The leaves of this thistle are cooked and eaten by the Russians.[12] In France, it is in flower gardens.[13] The plant is included among vegetables

---

[1] Pickering, C. *Chron. Hist. Pls.* 739. 1879.

[2] Lunan, J. *Hort. Jam.* 1:65. 1814.

[3] Henfrey, A. *Bot.* 230. 1870. (*Freziera theoides*)

[4] Syme, J. T. *Treas. Bot.* 1:298. 1870.

[5] Unger, F. *U. S. Pat. Off. Rpt.* 351. 1859. (*Melastoma spicatum*)

[6] *Gard. Chron.* 20:766. 1883.

[7] Masters, M. T. *Treas. Bot.* 2:720. 1870. (*Maranta ramosissima*)

[8] Pickering, C. *Chron. Hist. Pls.* 606. 1879.

[9] Ibid.

[10] Ambank *U. S. Pat. Off. Rpt.* 655. 1851. (*Cirsium eriophorum*)

[11] Lightfoot, J. *Fl. Scot.* 1:455. 1789.

[12] Pickering, C. *Chron. Hist. Pls.* 784. 1879.

[13] Vilmorin *Fl. Pl. Ter.* 275. 1870. 3rd Ed. (*Cirsium eriophorum*)

by Vilmorin,[1] although he says it does not appear to be cultivated. The swollen rootstock, gathered before the plant flowers, was formerly used as a table-vegetable. It does not appear to have ever reached American gardens.

C. palustris Willd.

Europe and Asia Minor. In Evelyn's time, the stalks were employed, as were those of the milk-thistle, for food.[2] Lightfoot[3] says the stalks are esculent, after being peeled and boiled.

C. serratuloides Roth.

Siberia. The roots are eaten.[4]

C. virginianus Pursh.

North America. The roots are about the size of carrots, are sweet and well flavored but require a long preparation. They are eaten by the western Indians.[5]

Coccinia indica Wight & Arn. *Cucurbitaceae.* SCARLET-FRUITED GOURD.

Tropical Asia. The fruit of this plant, so common in every hedge, is eaten by the natives in their curries and when fully ripe is eaten by birds.[6]

C. moimoi M. Roem.

Tropical Arabia and Africa. The fruit is eaten.[7]

Coccoloba uvifera Linn. *Polygonaceae.* KINO. SEASIDE GRAPE.

Shores of the West Indies and neighboring portions of tropical America. Its fruit is eatable and commonly sold in markets but is not much esteemed.[8] As grown in India, the fruit is reddish-purple, pear-shaped, sweetish-acid and is borne in drooping racemes. The fruit consists of the fleshy perianth which encloses a solitary seed.[9]

Cocculus cebatha DC. *Menispermaceae.*

A woody vine of tropical Arabia. The ripe berries are acrid but edible, and a spirituous liquor is obtained from them.[10]

C. limacia DC.

Eastern Asia. The berries are acid and edible.[11]

Cochlearia armoracia Linn. *Cruciferae.* HORSERADISH. RED COLE.

Europe. This well-known condimental plant is indigenous to eastern Europe from

[1] Vilmorin *Les Pls. Potag.* 157. 1883.

[2] Johnson, C. P. *Useful Pls. Gt. Brit.* 150. 1862.

[3] Lightfoot, J. *Fl. Scot.* 1:454. 1789.

[4] Pickering, C. *Chron. Hist. Pls.* 793. 1879. (*Cirsium serratuloides*)

[5] Fremont *Explor. Exped.* 146, 159. 1845. (*Cirsium virginianum*)

[6] Wight, R. *Illustr. Bot.* 2:27. 1850.

[7] Pickering, C. *Chron. Hist. Pls.* 390. 1879. (*Turia moghadd*)

[8] Lindley, J. *Med. Econ. Bot.* 126. 1849.

[9] Brandis, D. *Forest Fl.* 373. 1874.

[10] Pickering, C. *Chron. Hist. Pls.* 712. 1879.

[11] Royle, J. F. *Illustr. Bot. Himal.* 1:62. 1839.

the Caspian through Russia and Poland to Finland and is now spontaneous in the United States. Both the leaves and roots were eaten in Germany during the Middle Ages but their use was not common in England until a much later period. This plant cannot be identified with certainty with the *armoracia* of the Romans.[1] If it be the *armoracia* of Palladius,[2] which is a wild plant transferred to the garden, it is very curious that its use is not mentioned by Apicius[3] in his work on cookery, of the same century. Zanonius[4] deems horseradish to be the *draba* of Dioscorides. It seems to be the *raphanus* of Albertus Magnus,[5] who lived in the thirteenth century; he speaks of the plant as wild and domesticated, but its culture then was probably for medicinal purposes alone, as indicated by him. Its culture in Italy, in 1563, is implied by Ruellius[6] under the name *armoracia* but Castor Durante,[7] 1617, does not describe it. In Germany, its culture as a condimental plant is mentioned by Fuchsius,[8] 1542, and by later writers. In 1587, Dalechamp[9] speaks of its culture in Germany but does not mention it in France. Lyte,[10] 1586, mentions the wild plant and its uses as a condiment in England but does not imply culture. Horseradish, though known in England as red cole in 1568, is not mentioned by Turner[11] as used in food, nor is it noticed by Boorde,[12] 1542, in his chapter on edible roots in the *Dyetary of Helth*. Gerarde[13] speaks of it as used by the Germans, and Coles, in *Adam in Eden*, states that the root sliced thin and mixed with vinegar is eaten as a sauce with meat as among the Germans.[14] In the United States, horseradish is in general cultivation for market purposes. It was included by McMahon,[15] 1806, in his list of garden esculents.

C. danica Linn.

Northern and Arctic regions. This species is employed as a salad plant.[16]

C. macrocarpa Waldst. & Kit.

Hungary and Transylvania. The root may be used as a horseradish but it is less acrid.[17]

C. officinalis Linn. SCURVY GRASS. SPOONWORT.

Arctic regions. This species is used occasionally as a cress and is cultivated in gardens

[1] De Candolle, A. *Orig. Pls. Cult.* 34. 1885.
[2] Palladius lib. 4, c. 9; lib. 11, c. 2; lib. 12, c. 6.
[3] Apicius *Opson.* 1709.
[4] Zanonius *Stirp. Hist.* t. 15, p. 23. 1742.
[5] Albertus Magnus *Veg.* lib. 6, tract 2, c. 16. 1867. Jessen Ed.
[6] Ruellius *Nat. Stirp.* 466. 1536.
[7] Durante, C. *Herb.* 1617.
[8] Fuchsius *Hist. Stirp.* 660. 1542.
[9] Dalechamp *Hist. Gen. Pl.* (Lugd.) 636. 1587.
[10] Dodoens *Herb.* 688. 1586. Lyte Ed.
[11] Flückiger and Hanbury *Pharm.* 66. 1879.
[12] Ibid.
[13] Gerarde, J. *Herb.* 242. 1633 or 1636. 2nd Ed.
[14] Flückiger and Hanbury *Pharm.* 66. 1879.
[15] McMahon, B. *Amer. Gard. Cal.* 582. 1806.
[16] Unger, F. *U. S. Pat. Off. Rpt.* 356. 1859.
[17] Don, G. *Hist. Dichl. Pls.* 1:188. 1831.

for that purpose. It is a common plant in some parts of Scotland, and Lightfoot [1] says
" it is eaten in sallads as an antiscorbutic." It serves as a scurvy grass in Alaska. [2]

Cocos australis Mart. *Palmae.*

Paraguay. This palm bears a fruit somewhat the shape and size of an acorn, with
a pointed tip and is of a beautiful golden-yellow color somewhat tinged or spotted with
red when ripe. At maturity, it is soft and pulpy, the flesh yellow, succulent and somewhat
fibrous. The flavor is delicious, resembling that of a pineapple. [3]

C. butyracea Linn. f. OIL PALM. WINE PALM.

South America. This is the *palma de vino* of the Magdalena. This tree is cut down
and a cavity excavated in its trunk near the top. In three days, this cavity is found filled
with a yellowish-white juice, very limpid, with a sweet and vinous flavor. During 18
or 20 days, the palm-tree wine is daily collected; the last is less sweet but more alcoholic
and more highly esteemed. One tree yields as much as 18 bottles of sap, each bottle
containing 42 cubic inches, or about three and a quarter gallons. [4]

C. coronata Mart.

Brazil. This species yields a pith, which the Indians make into bread, and a nut from
which an oil is extracted. [5]

C. nucifera Linn. COCOANUT.

Tropics. The centers of the geographical range of this palm are the islands and
countries bordering the Indian and Pacific oceans [6] but it is now extensively cultivated
throughout the tropics. About 1330, it was described in India, and quite correctly too,
under the name of *nargil*, by Friar Jordanus. [7] In 1524, the cocoanut was seen by Pizarro [8]
in an Indian coast village of Peru. In the vicinity of Key West and as far north as Jupiter
Inlet, the cocoanut is found, having been first introduced about 1840 by the wrecking
of a vessel that threw a quantity of these nuts upon the beach. Thirty species of cocoanut
are said by Simmonds [9] to be described [7] and named in the East. Firminger [10] mentions
ten varieties in India. Captain Cook found several sorts at Batavia. Ellis [11] says there
are many varieties in Tahiti. The nuts are much used as a food. When the embryo is
unformed, the fruit furnishes sweet palm-milk, a further development supplies a white,
sweet and aromatic kernel; it finally becomes still firmer and then possesses a pleasant,
sweet oil. In the Fiji Islands, the kernel of the old nut is scraped, pressed through a
grater, and the pulp thus formed is mixed with grasses and scented woods and suffered

[1] Lightfoot, J. *Fl. Scot.* 1:343. 1789.

[2] Dall, W. H. *U. S. D. A. Rpt.* 187. 1868. (*C. fenestrata*)

[3] *Garden* 11. 1876.

[4] Humboldt, A. *Trav.* 3:210. 1889.

[5] Seemann, B. *Pop. Hist. Palms* 173. 1856.

[6] Seemann, B. *Pop. Hist. Palms* 157. 1856.

[7] Jordanus, Fr. *Wonders, East* 1330. Hakl. Soc. Ed. 15. 1863.

[8] Prescott, W. H. *Conq. Peru* 1:218. 1860.

[9] Simmonds, P. L. *Trop. Agr.* 229, 230. 1889.

[10] Firminger, T. A. C. *Gard. Ind.* 269. 1874.

[11] Ellis, W. *Polyn. Research.* 1:57. 1833.

to stand in the sun, which causes the oil to rise to the top, when it is skimmed off. The residuum, called *kora*, is pounded or mashed, wrapped in banana leaves and then buried under salt water covered with piles of stones. This preparation is a common food of the natives.[1] Toddy or palm-wine, is also made from the sap of the flower-spathes.

C. oleracea Mart. IRAIBA PALM.

Brazil. The leaf-buds, or cabbages, are edible.[2]

C. ventricosa Arruda.

Brazil. The oily pulp of the fruit and the almond of the inner stone is eaten and is sold in the markets. The pith contains a fecula which is extracted in times of want and is eaten.[3]

Codiaeum variegatum Blume. *Euphorbiaceae.*

India. This species is used as a vegetable.[4]

Coffea arabica Linn. *Rubiaceae.* COFFEE.

Arabia and African tropics. This shrub is found wild in Abyssinia[5] and in the Sudan where it forms forests.[6] It is mentioned as seen from the mid-Niger to Sierra Leone and from the west coast to Monrovia. In the territory west of Braganza, says Livingstone,[7] wild coffee is abundant, and the people even make their huts of coffee trees. On or about the equator, says Grant,[8] the *m'wanee*, or coffee, is cultivated in considerable quantities but the berry is eaten raw as a stimulant, never drunk in an infusion by the Wanyambo. The Ugundi, says Long,[9] never make a decoction of coffee but chew the grain raw; this is a general custom. The Unyoro, says Burton,[10] have a plantation of coffee about almost every hut door. According to the Arabian tradition, says Krapf,[11] the civet-cat brought the coffee-bean to the mountains of the Arusi and Ilta-Gallas, where it grew and was long cultivated, until an enterprising merchant carried the coffee plant, five hundred years ago, to Arabia where it soon became acclimated.

About the fifteenth century, writes Phillips,[12] the use of coffee appears to have been introduced from Persia to Aden on the Red Sea. It was progressively used at Mecca, Medina, and Cairo; hence it continued its progress to Damascus and Aleppo. From these two places, it was introduced into Constantinople in the year 1554. Rauwolf,[13] who was in the Levant in 1573, was the first European author who made any men-

---

[1] Wilkes, C. *U. S. Explor. Exped.* 3:334. 1845.

[2] Seemann, B. *Pop. Hist. Palms* 180. 1856.

[3] Koster, H. *Trav. Braz.* 2:366. 1817.

[4] Unger, F. *U. S. Pat. Off. Rpt.* 359. 1859. (*C. chrysosticton*)

[5] De Candolle, A. P. *Geog. Bot.* 2:969. 1855.

[6] Ibid.

[7] Livingstone, D. *Trav. Research. So. Afr.* 466. 1858.

[8] Speke, J. H. *Journ. Disc. Source Nile* 571. 1864.

[9] Long, C. C. *Cent. Afr.* 142. 1877.

[10] Burton, R. F. *Lake Reg. Cent. Afr.* 399. 1860.

[11] Krapf *Trav. East Afr.* 47.

[12] Phillips, H. *Comp. Orch.* 104. 1831.

[13] Phillips, H. *Comp. Orch.* 105. 1831.

tion of coffee, but the first who has particularly described it, is Prosper Alpinus,[1] 1591, and 1592. The Venetians seem to be the next who used coffee. This beverage was noticed by two English travellers at the beginning of the seventeenth century, Biddulph[2] about 1603 and William Finch[3] in 1607. Lord Bacon[4] mentions it in 1624. M. Thevenot[5] taught the French to drink coffee on his return from the East in 1657. It was fashionable and more widely known in Paris in 1669. Coffee is said to have been first brought to England in 1641, but Evelyn[6] says in his diary, 1637. It was first publicly known in London in 1652. According to other accounts, the custom of drinking coffee originated with the Abyssinians, by whom the plant had been cultivated from time immemorial, and was introduced to Aden in the early part of the fifteenth century, whence its use gradually extended over Arabia.

Towards the end of the seventeenth century, the Dutch transported the plant to Batavia, and thence a plant was sent to the botanic gardens at Amsterdam, where it was propagated, and in 1714 a tree was presented to Louis XIV. A tree was imported into the Isle of Bourbon in 1720. One account asserts that the French introduced it to Martinique in 1717 and another states that the Dutch had previously taken it to Surinam. It reached Jamaica in 1728. It seems certain that we are indebted to the progeny of a single plant for all the coffee now imported from Brazil and the West Indies. It was introduced to Celebes in 1822.[7] In Java and Sumatra, the leaves of the coffee plant are used as a substitute for coffee.[8] In 1879, four trees were known to have been grown and successfully fruited in Florida.

C. liberica Hiern. LIBERIAN COFFEE.

Tropical Africa. This seems to be a distinct species, which furnishes the Liberian coffee. It was received in Trinidad from Kew Gardens, England, in 1875.[9]

Coix lacryma-jobi Linn. *Gramineae.* JOB'S TEARS.

Tropical Asia. The seeds may be ground to flour and made into a coarse but nourishing bread which is utilized in times of scarcity.[10]

Cola acuminata Schott & Endl. *Sterculiaceae.* COLANUT. GOORANUT. KOLANUT.

Tropical Africa. This tree, a native of tropical Africa, is cultivated in Brazil and the West Indies. Under the name of cola or kolla or goora-nuts, the seeds are extensively used as a sort of condiment by the natives of western and central tropical Africa and likewise by the negroes in the West Indies and Brazil.[11] There are several

---

[1] Phillips, H. *Comp. Orch.* 105. 1831.

[2] Ibid.

[3] Ibid.

[4] Ibid.

[5] Phillips, H. *Comp. Orch.* 106. 1831.

[6] Ibid.

[7] Wallace, A. R. *Malay Arch.* 251. 1869.

[8] Hanbury, D. *Sci. Papers* 84. 1876.

[9] Prestoe *Rpt. Bot. Gard. Trinidad* 21. 1880.

[10] Long *Hist. Jam.* 3:831. 1774.

[11] Smith, A. *Treas. Bot.* 1:311. 1870.

varieties. Father Carli [1] noticed them in Congo in 1667 under the name of *colla*. Barth [2] says the chief article of African produce in the Kano markets is the guro or kolanut, which forms an important article of trade and which has become to the natives as necessary as coffee or tea is to us. The nuts contain the alkaloid thein. A small piece of one of their seeds is chewed before each meal as a promoter of digestion; it is also supposed to improve the flavor of anything eaten after it or, as Father Carli [3] says, " they have a little bitterness but the water drank after makes them very sweet." This plant was introduced into Martinique about 1836. Its amylaceous seeds, of a not very agreeable taste, are much sought after by the negroes. [4]

Colea telfairii Boj. *Bignoniaceae.*
Madagascar. The fruit is eaten.

Coleus aromaticus Benth. *Labiatae.* COLEUS. COUNTRY BORAGE.
East Indies. This is the country borage of India. Every part of the plant is delightfully fragrant, and the leaves are frequently eaten and mixed with various articles of food in India. [5] In Burma, it is in common use as a potherb. A purple coleus was observed in cultivation in northern Japan by Miss Bird, [6] the leaves of which are eaten as spinach.

C. barbatus Benth.
East Indies and tropical Africa. About Bombay, this species is commonly cultivated in the gardens of the natives for the roots, which are pickled. [7]

C. spicatus Benth.
East Indies. Wilkinson [8] quotes Pliny as saying that the Egyptians grew this plant for making chaplets and for food.

Colocasia antiquorum Schott. *Aroideae.* DASHEEN. TARO.
Tropical Asia. This is very probably an Indian plant, as it is cultivated in the whole of central Asia in very numerous varieties and has a Sanscrit name. It was carried westward in the earliest times and is cultivated in the delta of Egypt under the name of *Quolkas*. [9] Clusius, writing in 1601, had seen it in Portugal. The Spaniards are said to call it *alcoleaz* and to have received it from Africa. [10] Boissier [11] cites it as common in middle Spain. Lunan [12] says there are several varieties cultivated in Jamaica which are preferred by the negroes

---

[1] Churchill *Coll. Voy.* 1:501. 1744.
[2] Barth, H. *Trav. Disc. No., Cent. Afr.* 1:514. 1857.
[3] Churchill *Coll. Voy.* 1:501. 1744.
[4] Berlanger *Trans. N. Y. Agr. Soc.* 568. 1858. (*Sterculia acuminata*)
[5] Drury, H. *Useful Pls. Ind.* 154. 1873.
[6] Bird *Unbeat. Tracks Jap.* 1:175. 1881.
[7] Pickering, C. *Chron. Hist. Pls.* 732. 1879.
[8] Wilkinson, J. G. *Anc. Egypt.* 2:34. 1854. (*Ocymum zatarhendi*)
[9] De Candolle, A. *Geog. Bot.* 2:817. 1855. (*Arum colocasia*)
[10] Ibid.
[11] Ibid.
[12] Lunan *Hort. Jam.* 1:212. 1814.

to yams. In 1844, this species was cultivated by Needham Davis[1] of South Carolina, who says one acre of rich, damp soil will produce one thousand bushels by the second year. In India, colocasias are universally cultivated and the roots are without acrimony.[2] The tubers, says Firminger,[3] resemble in outward appearance those of the Jerusalem artichoke. They are not in great request with Europeans in Bengal where potatoes may be had all the year through but in the Northwest Provinces, where potatoes are unobtainable during the summer months, they are much consumed in the way of a substitute. Their flavor is not unlike salsify. The plant is cultivated extensively by the Polynesians, who call it taro; the tubers are largely consumed and the young leaves are eaten as a spinach.[4]

C. antiquorum esculenta Schott. ELEPHANT'S EAR. KALO. TARO.

This plant is largely grown in Tahiti, and Ellis[5] says the natives have distinct names for 33 of the varieties. Nordoff[6] says more than 30 varieties of kalo are cultivated in the Hawaiian Islands and adds that all the kinds are acrid except one which is so mild that it may be eaten raw. Simpson[7] says, " Kalo forms the principal food of the lower class of the Sandwich Islanders and is cultivated with great care in small enclosures kept wet." From the root a sort of paste called *poi* is made. Masters[8] says it is called taro, and the rootstocks furnish a staple diet. It is also grown in the Philippines[9] and is enumerated by Thunberg[10] among the edible plants of Japan. In Jamaica, Sloane[11] says the roots are eaten as potatoes, but the chief use of the vegetable, says Lunan,[12] is as a green, and it is as delicate, wholesome, and agreeable a one as any in the world. In soup it is excellent, for such is the tenderness of the leaves that they, in a manner, dissolve and afford a rich, pleasing and mucilaginous ingredient. It is very generally cultivated in Jamaica. Adams[13] found the boiled leaves very palatable in the Philippines but the uncooked leaves were so acrid as to be poisonous. At Hongkong, the tubers are eaten under the name of *cocoas*. In Europe and America it is grown as an ornamental plant.

C. indica Hassk.

Southern Asia. This plant is cultivated in Bengal for its esculent stems and the small, pendulous tubers of its root, which are eaten by people of all ranks in their curries.[14]

---

[1] Davis, N.   *Trans. N. Y. Agr. Soc.* 517.   1845.

[2] Royle, J. F.   *Illustr. Bot. Himal.* 1:406.   1839.

[3] Firminger, T. A. C.   *Gard. Ind.* III.   1874.

[4] Seemann, B.   *Fl. Viti.* 285.   1865-73.

[5] Ellis, W.   *Polyn. Research.* 1:48.   1833.

[6] Nordhoff, C.   *No. Cal., Sandwich Is.* 253.   1874.   Notes.

[7] Simpson, G.   *Journ. Around World* 2:33.   1847.

[8] Masters, M. T.   *Treas. Bot.* 1:315.   1870.

[9] Adams, A.   *Voy. Samarang* 2:339.   1848.

[10] Thunberg, C. P.   *Fl. Jap.* 234.   1784.   (*Arum esculentum*)

[11] Sloane, H.   *Nat. Hist. Jam.* 1:167.   1707.   (*Arum minus*)

[12] Lunan, J.   *Hort. Jam.* 1:415.   1814.

[13] Adams, A.   *Voy. Samarang* 2:339.   1848.

[14] Wight, R.   *Icon. Pls.* 3:794.   Bears no date.   (*Arum indica*)

Royle [1] says it is much cultivated about the huts of the natives. It is also cultivated in Brazil [2] and is found in East Australia. The acridity is expelled from this plant by cooking. [3]

Combretum butyrosum Tul. *Combretaceae.* BUTTER TREE.

Tropical Africa. The Kaffirs call the fatty substance obtained from the fruit *chiquito.* It is largely used by them as an admixture to their food and is also exported. [4]

Commelina angustifolia? *Commelinaceae.*

The rhizomes contain a good deal of starch mixed with mucilage and are therefore fit for food when cooked. [5]

C. coelestis Willd. BLUE SPIDERWORT.

Mexico. The rhizomes are used as food in India. [6]

C. communis Linn.

China. In China, this plant is much cultivated as a potherb, which is eaten in spring. [7]

C. latifolia Hochst.

Abyssinia. It is used as a potherb. [8]

C. striata?

The rhizomes are suitable for food. [9]

Comocladia integrifolia Jacq. *Anacardiaceae.* BURN-WOOD. MAIDEN PLUM. PAPAW-WOOD.

Tropical America. Lunan [10] says the fruit is eatable but not inviting. The maiden plum of the West Indies, says Morris, [11] is grown as a fruit in the Public Gardens of Jamaica.

Conanthera bifolia Ruiz & Pav. *Haemodoraceae.*

Chile. The natives of the country make use of the root of this plant in their soups and it is very pleasant to the taste. Molina [12] says the bulbs, when boiled or roasted, are an excellent food. It is called *illmu.*

Condalia mexicana Schlecht. *Rhamneae.*

Northern Mexico. The berries are similar to those of *C. obovata.* [13]

---

[1] Royle, J. F. *Illustr. Bot. Himal.* 1:407. 1839.

[2] Masters, M. T. *Treas. Bot.* 1:315. 1870.

[3] Mueller, F. *Sel. Pls.* 125. 1891.

[4] Mueller, F. *Sel. Pls.* 126. 1891.

[5] Lindley, J. *Veg. King.* 188. 1853.

[6] Henfrey, A. *Bot.* 380. 1870.

[7] Smith, F. P. *Contrib. Mat. Med. China* 69. 1871. (*Commelyna polygama*)

[8] Pickering, C. *Chron. Hist. Pls.* 466. 1879.

[9] Lindley, J. *Veg. King.* 188. 1853.

[10] Lunan, J. *Hort. Jam.* 1:475. 1814.

[11] Morris *Rpt. Pub. Gard. Jam.* 35. 1880.

[12] Molina *Hist. Chili* 1:96. 1808. (*Bermudiana bulbosa*)

[13] Havard, V. *Proc. U. S. Nat. Mus.* 509. 1885.

C. obovata Hook. BLUE-WOOD. TEXAN LOGWOOD.

Texas. This plant is a shrub of San Antonio, Texas and westward. The small, deep red berry is acidulous, edible and is used in jellies.[1]

C. spathulata A. Gray.

Western Texas. The berries are similar to those of *C. obovata*.[2]

Conferva sp. *Confervae.*

Green cakes are made of the slimy river confervae in Japan, which, pressed and dried, are used as food.

Conium maculatum Linn. *Umbelliferae.* HERB BENNET. POISON HEMLOCK.

Europe and the Orient. Poison hemlock has become naturalized in northeastern America from Europe. Although poisonous, says Carpenter,[3] in the south of England, it is comparatively harmless in London and is eaten as a potherb by the peasants of Russia.

Conopodium denudatum Koch. *Umbelliferae.* ARNUT. EARTH CHESTNUT. JURNUT.
          KIPPERNUT. PIGNUT.

Western Europe. The small, tuberous roots of this herb, when boiled or roasted, are available for food and are known as earth chestnuts.[4] In England, says Don,[5] the tubers are frequently dug and eaten by children. When boiled, they are very pleasant. The roots, says Johnson,[6] are edible but are little eaten in England except by children.

Convolvulus arvensis Linn. *Convolvulaceae.* FIELD BINDWEED.

Old World tropics, middle Asia and naturalized in America from Europe. This plant gives its flavor to the liquor called *noyeau*, imported from Martinique, according to Lindley.[7] It reached Philadelphia in 1876 in the packing of exhibits at the Centennial.

Copaifera coleosperma Benth. *Leguminosae.*

Tropical Africa. The aril is used in preparing a nourishing drink.[8]

C. hymenaeifolia Moric.

Cuba. This species is said to be the *mosibe* of eastern tropical Africa, a tree which yields a red-skinned, fattening, bean-like seed.[9]

Corchorus acutangulus Lam. *Tiliaceae.*

Cosmopolitan tropics. This plant is the *papau ockroe* of the Barbados and is eaten by the negroes as a salad and potherb.[10]

---

[1] Havard, V. *Proc. U. S. Nat. Mus.* 509. 1885.

[2] Ibid.

[3] Carpenter, W. B. *Veg. Phys. Bot.* 203. 1850.

[4] Mueller, F. *Sel. Pls.* 126. 1891.

[5] Don, G. *Hist. Dichl. Pls.* 3:291. 1834.

[6] Johnson, C. P. *Useful Pls. Gt. Brit.* 114. 1862. (*Bunium flexuosum*)

[7] Lindley, J. *Med. Econ. Bot.* 209. 1849. (*C. dissectus*)

[8] Masters, M. T. *Treas. Bot.* 2:1282. 1876.

[9] *Treas. Bot.* 2:1319. 1876.

[10] De Candolle, A. *Geog. Bot.* 2:1026. 1855.

C. antichorus Raeusch.

Old World tropics. The whole plant is boiled as a potherb.[1]

C. capsularis Linn. JUTE.

Cosmopolitan tropics. This plant is extensively cultivated in Bengal for its fiber, which forms one of the jutes of commerce so extensively exported from Calcutta.[2] It was introduced into the United States shortly before 1870 and placed under experimental culture,[3] and, in 1873, favorable reports of its success came from many of the southern states. The young shoots are much used as a potherb in Egypt and in India.[4]

C. olitorius Linn. CORCHORUS. JEW'S MALLOW.

Cosmopolitan tropics. This plant yields some of the jute of commerce but is better known as a plant of the kitchen in tropical countries. It is cultivated in Egypt, India and in France. In Aleppo, it is grown by the Jews, hence the name, Jew's mallow. The leaves are used as a potherb.[5]

It is mentioned by Pliny [6] among Egyptian potherbs, and Alpinus,[7] 1592, says that no herb is more commonly used among the Egyptian foods. Forskal [8] also mentions its cultivation in Egypt and notes it among the cultivated esculents of Arabia. In India, it occurs wild and the leaves are gathered and eaten as spinach.[9] In tropical Africa, it is both spontaneous and cultivated as a vegetable [10] and it is in the vegetable gardens of Mauritius.[11] In Jamaica, the plant is frequently met with in gardens but has, in a great measure, ceased to be cultivated, although the leaves are used as a spinach.[12] It is now cultivated in French gardens for its young leaves, which are eaten in salads.[13] It is recorded by Burr [14] as in American gardens in 1863 but the plant seems not to have been mentioned by other writers as growing in this country.

C. procumbens Boj.

Tropical Africa. This plant was carried to the Mauritius where it is cultivated in kitchen gardens.[15]

C. siliquosus Linn. BROOM-WEED.

Tropical America. This plant is called *té* by the inhabitants of Panama who use its leaves as a tea substitute.[16]

[1] Don, G. *Hist. Dichl. Pls.* 1:542. 1831. (*Antichorus depressus*)

[2] Brandis, D. *Forest Fl.* 57. 1876.

[3] *U. S. D. A. Rpt.* 15. 1870.

[4] Smith, A. *Treas. Bot.* 1:329. 1870.

[5] Ibid.

[6] Bostock and Riley *Nat. Hist. Pliny* 4:349. 1856.

[7] Alpinius *Pl. Aegypt.* 39. 1592.

[8] Forskal *Fl. Aeg. Arab.* xciii, 101. 1775.

[9] Speede *Ind. Handb. Gard.* 155. 1842. (*C. obtorius*)

[10] Oliver, D. *Fl. Trop. Afr.* 1:262. 1868.

[11] Bojer, W. *Hort. Maurit.* 42. 1837.

[12] Macfadyen *Jam.* 1:108. 1837.

[13] Vilmorin *Les Pls. Potag.* 168. 1883.

[14] Burr, F. *Field, Gard. Veg.* 338. 1863.

[15] Pickering, C. *Chron. Hist.* 380. 1879.

[16] Smith, A. *Treas. Bot.* 1:329. 1870.

C. tridens Linn.

Cosmopolitan tropics.   It is used as a potherb in Egypt.[1]

C. trilocularis Linn.

Old World tropics.   In Arabia this plant is used as a potherb.[2]   It is used as a potherb in Sennaar and Cordova, where it is native.[3]

Cordia collococca Linn.   *Boragineae.*   CLAMMY CHERRY.

Jamaica.   The fruit is red, with a sweetish pulp and is edible.

C. loureiri Roem. et Schult.

China.   The drupe is red, small, acid and edible.[4]

C. myxa Linn.   ASSYRIAN PLUM.   SELU.

Tropical Asia and Australia.   The tender, young fruit is eaten as a vegetable and
is pickled in India.   The ripe fruit is also eaten.   The kernel tastes somewhat like a filbert
and that of the cultivated tree is better.[5]

C. obliqua Willd.

Tropical India.   The young fruit is pickled and is also eaten as a vegetable.[6]

C. rothii Roem. et Schult.

Western India.   The fruit is eaten.[7]

C. sebestena Linn.

Tropical America.   The plant bears a mucilaginous, edible fruit.   Nuttall [8] says it
has been observed growing at Key West, Florida.

C. vestita Hook. f. & Thoms.

Himalayan region.   The fruit is filled with a gelatinous pulp, which is eaten and is
preferred to that of *C. myxa.*[9]

Cordyline indivisa Steud.   *Liliaceae.*   DRACAENA.   TI.

New Zealand.   The berries are eaten by the New Zealanders.[10]

C. terminalis Kunth.   DRACAENA.   TI.

Tropical Asia and Australia.   This plant, common in the islands of the Papuan
Archipelago, is there cultivated.   In the Samoan Islands, some 20 varieties, mostly edible,
are distinguished by name.[11]   The thick, fleshy roots contain large quantities of saccharine

[1] Unger, F.   *U. S. Pat. Off. Rpt.* 355.   1859.

[2] Don, G.   *Hist. Dichl. Pls.* 1:543.   1831.

[3] Unger, F.   *U. S. Pat. Off. Rpt.* 356.   1859.

[4] Don, G.   *Hist. Dichl. Pls.* 4:376.   1838.

[5] Brandis, D.   *Forest Fl.* 336.   1874.

[6] Drury, H.   *Useful Pls. Ind.* 158.   1873.

[7] Pickering, C.   *Chron. Hist. Pls.* 594.   1879.   *(C. angustifolia)*

[8] Nuttall, T.   *No. Amer. Sylva* 2:147.   1865.

[9] Brandis, D.   *Forest Fl.* 338.   1874.

[10] Unger, F.   *U. S. Pat. Off. Rpt.* 347.   1859.   *(Dracaena indivisa)*

[11] Pickering, C.   *Chron. Hist. Pls.* 438.   1879.   *(Dracaena terminalis)*

matter and, when baked, become very agreeable to the taste.[1] The baked ti root, says Ellis,[2] macerated in water, is fermented and then a very intoxicating liquor is obtained from it by distillation. The large, tuberous roots are eaten by the natives of Viti.[3] The tuberous root often weighs from 10 to 14 pounds and, after being baked on hot stoves, much resembles in taste and degree of sweetness stock licorice. The Fijians chew it, or use it to sweeten puddings.[4] The root is roasted and eaten.[5]

Coriandrum sativum Linn. *Umbelliferae.* CORIANDER.

Southern Europe and the Orient. The seeds of this plant were used as a spice by the Jews and the Romans. The plant was well known in Britain prior to the Norman conquest and was employed in ancient English medicine and cookery.[6] Coriander was cultivated in American gardens prior to 1670.[7] The seeds are carminative and aromatic and are used for flavoring, in confectionery and also by distillers. The young leaves are put into soups and salads. In the environs of Bombay, the seeds are much used by the Musselmans in their curries.[8] They are largely used by the natives of India as a condiment and with betelnuts and pau leaves.[9] In Burma, the seeds are used as a condiment in curries.[10] The ripe fruits of coriander have served as a spice and a seasoning from very remote times, its seeds having been found in Egyptian tombs of the twenty-first dynasty;[11] a thousand or so years later, Pliny [12] says the best coriander came to Italy from Egypt. Cato,[13] in the third century before Christ, recommends coriander as a seasoning; Columella,[14] in the first century of our era and Palladius,[15] in the third, direct its planting. The plant was well known in Britain prior to the Norman conquest [16] and was carried to Massachusetts before 1670.[17] In China, it can be identified in an agricultural treatise of the fifth century and is classed as cultivated by later writers of the sixteenth and eighteenth centuries.[18] In Cochin China, it is recorded as less grown than in China.[19] In India, it is largely used by the natives as a condiment.[20] Coriander has reached Paraguay and is

---

[1] Wilkes, C. *U. S. Explor. Exped.* **3**:337. 1845.

[2] Ellis, W. *Polyn. Research.* **2**:102. 1833. (*Dracaena terminalis*)

[3] Seemann, B. *Fl. Viti.* 311. 1865-73.

[4] Ibid.

[5] Mueller, F. *Sel. Pls.* 129. 1891.

[6] Flückiger and Hanbury *Pharm.* 293. 1879.

[7] Pickering, C. *Chron. Hist. Pls.* 142. 1879.

[8] Ibid.

[9] Dutt, U. C. *Mat. Med. Hindus* 175. 1877.

[10] Pickering, C. *Chron. Hist. Pls.* 142. 1889.

[11] *Nature* 113. 1883.

[12] Pliny lib. 20, c. 82.

[13] Cato c. 157.

[14] Columella lib. 6, c. 33; lib. 10, c. 244; lib. 11, c. 3.

[15] Palladius lib. 3, c. 24; lib. 4, c. 9, etc.

[16] Flückiger and Hanbury *Pharm.* 329. 1879.

[17] Josselyn, J. *New Eng. Rar.* 146. 1865.

[18] Bretschneider, E. *Bot. Sin.* 78, 59, 85. 1882.

[19] Loureiro *Fl. Cochin.* 180. 1790.

[20] Dutt, U. C. *Mat. Med. Hindus* 175. 1877.

in especial esteem for condimental purposes in some parts of Peru.[1] Notwithstanding this extended period of cultivation, no indication of varieties under cultivation is found.

Coriaria nepalensis Wall. *Coriarieae.* TANNER'S TREE.

Himalayan region and China. Brandis[2] says the fruit is eaten but is said to cause thirst or colic. J. Smith[3] says the fruit is eaten and is not unwholesome.

C. ruscifolia Linn. DEU.

Peru and Chili. The baccate, fructiferous perianth yields a palatable, purple juice, which is much liked by the natives and from which a kind of wine may be made, but the seeds are poisonous.[4]

C. sarmentosa Forst. f. WINEBERRY.

New Zealand. The fruit affords a refreshing wine to the natives but the seeds are poisonous. It is called *tutu.*[5]

Cornus amomum Mill. *Cornaceae.* KINNIKINNIK.

North America. In Louisiana, this plant is said by Rafinesque[6] to have black fruit very good to eat.

C. canadensis Linn. BUNCHBERRY. DWARF CARNEL.

North America. This species occurs from Pennsylvania to Labrador on the east and to Sitka on the northwest. The scarlet berries are well known to children, being pleasant but without much taste. They are sometimes made into puddings.[7]

C. capitata Wall.

Himalayan region. This plant was introduced into English gardens about 1833 as an ornamental. The fruit is sweetish, mingled with a little bitter taste, and is eaten and made into preserves in India.[8]

C. macrophylla Wall. LARGE-LEAVED DOGWOOD.

Himalayan region, China and Japan. The round, smooth, small berries are eaten in India.[9]

C. mas Linn. CORNELIAN CHERRY. CORNUS. SORBET.

Europe and Asia Minor. The cornelian cherry was formerly cultivated for its fruits which were used in tarts. There are a number of varieties. De Candolle[10] mentions one with a yellow fruit. Duhamel[11] says there are three varieties in France and Germany;

---

[1] Johnson, C. P. *Useful Pls. Gt. Brit.* 125. 1862.
[2] Brandis, D. *Forest Fl.* 128. 1876.
[3] Smith, J. *Dom. Bot.* 132. 1882.
[4] Gray, A. *Bot. U. S. Explor. Exped.* 306. 1854.
[5] Smith, J. *Dom. Bot.* 132. 1882.
[6] Rafinesque, C. S. *Fl. La.* 78. 1817. (*C. polygamus*)
[7] Emerson, G. B. *Trees, Shrubs Mass.* 2:470. 1875.
[8] Brandis, D. *Forest Fl.* 254. 1874.
[9] Brandis, D. *Forest Fl.* 252. 1874.
[10] De Candolle, A. *Geog. Bot.* 2:1083. 1855.
[11] Loudon, J. C. *Hort.* 581. 1860.

one with wax-colored fruit, another with white fruit and a third with fleshy, round fruit. Don [1] says the fruit is gratefully acid and is called *sorbet* by the Turks. A. Smith [2] says the harsh, acid fruits are scarcely eatable but are sold in the markets in some parts of Germany to be eaten by children or made into sweetmeats and tarts. J. Smith [3] says the fruit is of a cornelian color, of the size of a small plum, not very palatable, but is eaten in some parts as a substitute for olives; it is also preserved, is used in confectionery and, in Turkey, serves as a flavoring for sherbets. In Norway, the flowers are used for flavoring distilled spirits.

C. sanguinea Linn. CORNEL DOGWOOD. DOGBERRY. DOGWOOD. PEGWOOD.

Europe and northern Asia. The fruit is said to contain a large quantity of oil used for the table and in brewing.

C. stolonifera Michx. RED-OSIER.

North America. Thoreau [4] found the bark in use by the Indians of Maine for smoking, under the name *magnoxigill*, Indian tobacco. Nuttall [5] says the fruit, though bitter and unpalatable, is eaten by the Indians of the Missouri River.

C. suecica Linn. KINNIKINNIK.

North America. The berries are gathered in the autumn by the western Eskimo and preserved by being frozen in wooden boxes out of which they are cut with an axe.[6] In central New York, this plant is called *kinnikinnik* by the Indians.[7]

Correa alba Andr. *Rutaceae.*

Australia. Henfrey [8] says the leaves are used by the Australian settlers for a tea.

Corydalis bulbosa DC. *Papaveraceae.* FUMEWORT.

Northern Europe. This species has a tuberous root, which, when boiled, furnishes the Kalmuck Tartars with a starchy substance much eaten by them.[9]

Corylus americana Walt. *Cupuliferae.* HAZELNUT.

North America. This species bears well-flavored nuts but they are smaller and thicker shelled than the European hazel. The nuts are extensively gathered as a food by the Indians in some places.[10]

C. avellana Linn. COBNUT. FILBERT. HAZELNUT.

Europe and Asia Minor. This species includes not only the hazelnut but all of the European varieties of filbert. It was cultivated by the Romans, and Pliny says the name

[1] Don, G. *Hist. Dichl. Pls.* 3:400. 1834.
[2] Smith, A. *Treas. Bot.* 1:333. 1870.
[3] Smith, J. *Dom. Bot.* 134. 1882.
[4] Thoreau *Me. Woods* 223. 1877.
[5] Nuttall, T. *Gen. No. Amer. Pls.* 1:98. 1818. (*C. canadensis*)
[6] Seemann, B. *Anthrop. Journ.* 3:ccciii. 1865.
[7] Pickering, C. *Chron. Hist. Pls.* 807. 1879. (*C. sericea*)
[8] Henfrey, A. *Bot.* 246. 1870.
[9] Johnson, C. P. *Useful Pls. Gt. Brit.* 21. 1862. (*C. solida*)
[10] Brown, R. *Bot. Soc. Edinb.* 9:383. 1868.

is derived from Abellina in Asia, supposed to be the valley of Damascus. Pliny [1] adds that it had been brought into Greece from Pontus, hence it was also called *nux pontica*. The nut was called by Theophrastus, *heraclotic nuts*, from Heraclea — now Ponderachi — on the Asiatic shore of the Black Sea. These names probably refer to particular varieties as the species is common in Europe and adjoining Asia. In Peacham's [2] *Emblems*, we find it stated that the name filbert is derived from Philibert, a king of France, who " caused by arte sundry kinds to be brought forth." There are a number of varieties. The best nuts come from Spain and are known as Barcelona nuts. Cobnuts and filberts are largely grown in Kent, England. In Kazan, Russia, the nuts are so plentiful that an oil used as food is expressed from them. Filberts were among the seeds mentioned in the Memorandum [3] of Mar. 16, 1629, to be sent to the Massachusetts Company and are now to be occasionally found in gardens in Virginia and elsewhere.

C. colurna Linn. COBNUT.

Eastern Europe, Asia Minor and Himalayan region. This plant furnishes the imported cobnuts of Britain. The kernels form an important article of food in some parts of the hills of India.[4] The nuts are known in England as cobnuts or Turkish nuts. This tree was carried from Pontus to Macedonia and Thrace and has been distributed throughout Italy. It was brought to Germany in the sixteenth century.[5]

C. ferox Wall.

Himalayan region. This species bears a small, thick-shelled nut, in taste like the common hazel.

C. rostrata Ait. BEAKED HAZELNUT.

Northeastern America. The plant bears a well-flavored nut.

C. tubulosa Willd. LAMBERT'S NUT. LOMBARDY-NUT.

Asia Minor and Southern Europe. This species furnishes the Lombardy, or Lambert's nut.

Corynocarpus laevigata Forst. *Anacardiaceae.* NEW ZEALAND LAUREL.

New Zealand. The pulp of the drupe of this tree is edible, but the embryo is considered poisonous until steeped in salt water. Bennett [6] says it is valued for its fruit and seeds, the former of the size of a plum, pulpy in the interior and sweet. The seeds are used in times of scarcity and contain a tasteless, farinaceous substance. The new seeds are, however, poisonous until steamed for a day and soaked.

Corypha gebanga Blume. *Palmae.* GEBANG PALM.

Malay. The pithy substance of the trunk yields a sort of sago.[7]

---

[1] Thompson, R. *Treas. Bot.* 1:336. 1870.

[2] Disraeli *Curios. Lit.* 2:332. 1858. Note.

[3] *Mass. Records* 1:24.

[4] Brandis, D. *Forest Fl.* 494. 1876.

[5] Unger, F. *U. S. Pat. Off. Rpt.* 321. 1859.

[6] Bennett, G. *Gath. Nat. Austral.* 346. 1860.

[7] Seemann, B. *Pop. Hist. Palms* 187. 1856.

Costus speciosus Sm. *Scitamineae.* WILD GINGER.

East Indies and Malay. Ainslie [1] says the natives of India preserve the root and deem it very wholesome. Lunan [2] says the roots of wild ginger are sometimes used as ginger but are not as good. Browne [3] says this species is found everywhere in the woods of Jamaica.

Cotyledon edulis Brewer. *Crassulaceae.*

California. The young leaves are eaten by the Indians. [4]

C. spinosa Linn.

North America. The leaves are agreeably acid and are eaten. [5]

C. umbilicus Linn. NAVELWORT.

Europe and the adjoining portions of Asia. This plant is classed by Loudon as a spinach.

Couepia chrysocalyx Benth. *Rosaceae.*

Brazil. This beautiful tree is said by Mr. Spruce [6] to grow plentifully along the Amazon River from the Barra upward. The Indians plant it near their houses for the sake of its edible fruits.

C. guianensis Aubl.

Guiana. The seed is edible. The fruit contains a sweet oil like that of the almond. [7]

Couma utilis Muell. *Apocynaceae.*

Brazil. This species bears a fruit known as *couma* which is said by Bates to be delicious. The fruit is a berry containing several seeds embedded in a pulp.

Couroupita guianensis Aubl. *Myrtaceae.* CANNON-BALL TREE.

Guiana and Cayenne. The pulp of the fruit is vinous, white, acid and not disagreeable. [8]

Crambe cordifolia Stev. *Cruciferae.* COLEWORT.

Persia and the Caucasus to Thibet and the Himalayas. The root and foliage afford an esculent. [9]

C. maritima Linn. SEA KALE. SCURVY GRASS.

This plant is found growing upon the sandy shores of the North Sea, the Atlantic Ocean and of the Mediterranean Sea. It appears to have been known to the Romans,

[1] Ainslie, W. *Mat. Ind.* 2:165. 1826.
[2] Lunan, J. *Hort. Jam.* 2:281. 1814.
[3] Ainslie, W. *Mat. Ind.* 2:167. 1826.
[4] Brewer and Watson *Bot. Cal.* 1:211. 1880.
[5] Pickering, C. *Chron. Hist. Pls.* 812. 1879. (*Sedum spinosum*)
[6] Black, A. A. *Treas. Bot.* 1:341. 1870.
[7] Don, G. *Hist. Dichl. Pls.* 2:478. 1832. (*Acioa guianensis*)
[8] Don, G. *Hist. Dichl. Pls.* 2:875. 1832.
[9] Mueller, F. *Sel. Pls.* 131. 1891.

who gathered it in a wild state and preserved it in barrels for use during long voyages.[1]
Although Crambe is recorded by Pena and Lobel,[2] Dalechamp,[3] Gerarde,[4] and Ray [5] as
wild on the coast of Britain and as fit for food, yet it was brought into English culture
from Italy,[6] a few years preceding 1765, and the seed sold at a high price as a rarity.   In
1778,[7] it is said to " be now cultivated in many gardens as a choice esculent;" in 1795,[8]
it was advertised in the London market.   According to Heuze,[9] it was first cultivated
in France by Quintyne, gardener to Louis XIV, but it is not mentioned in Quintyne
of 1693; it, however, is mentioned by the French works on gardening of 1824 [10] and
onward.   Parkinson notices it in England in 1629 and Bryant [11] does also, about 1783,
but Philip Miller [12] first wrote upon it as an esculent in 1731, saying the people of Sussex
gather the wild plants in the spring.   It is recorded that bundles of it were exposed for
sale in the Chichester markets in 1753 but it was not known about London until 1767.
In 1789, Lightfoot [13] speaks of " the young leaves covered up with sand and blanched
while growing," constituting when boiled a great delicacy.   Sea kale is now very popular
in English markets and is largely used in France, the blanched stems and leaf-stalks being
the parts used.   It is mentioned by McMahon,[14] 1609, in his list of American esculents.
In 1809, John Lowell, Roxbury, Massachusetts, cultivated it and in 1814 introduced it
to the notice of the public.   In 1828, Thorburn,[15] in his seed catalog of that year, says
it " is very little known in the United States, though a most excellent garden vegetable
and highly deserving of cultivation."   The same might be said now, although its seeds
are advertised for sale in all leading seed lists.

C. orientalis Linn.

Asia Minor and Persia.   Pallas [16] says the Russians use it.   Its roots resemble those
of horseradish, but they are often thicker than the human arm.   The root is dug for the
use of the table as a substitute for horseradish, and the younger stalks may be dressed
in the same manner as broccoli.

C. tatarica Jacq.   TARTAR BREAD-PLANT.

Eastern Europe and northern Asia.   This is a plant of the steppes region along the

---

[1] McIntosh Book Gard. 103.   1855.
[2] Pena and Lobel Advers. 92.   1570.
[3] Dalechamp Hist. Gen. Pl. (Lugd.) 526.   1587.
[4] Gerarde, J.   Herb. 248.   1597.
[5] Ray Hist. Pl. 838.   1686.
[6] Stevenson Gard. Kal. 22.   1765.
[7] Mawe and Abercrombie Univ. Gard. Bot.   1778.
[8] Gard. Chron. 25:626.   1886.   New Series.
[9] Heuze, G.   Pls. Alim. 2:667.   1873.
[10] Pirolle L'Hort. Franc.   1824.
[11] Bryant Fl. Diet. 124.   1783.
[12] Miller Gard. Dict.   1731.   1st Ed.
[13] Lightfoot, J.   Fl. Scot. 1:364.   1789.
[14] McMahon, B.   Amer. Gard. Cal. 583.   1806.
[15] Thorburn Cat. 86.   1828.
[16] Pallas, P. S.   Trav. Russia 1:373.   1802.

Lower Danube, Dneiper and the Don. The root is fleshy, sweet and the thickness of a man's arm. It is eaten raw as a salad in Hungary, as well as cooked, as is the case with the young shoots of the stem. In times of famine, it has been used as bread in Hungary and, says Unger,[1] it is probable that it was the *chara caesaris* which the soldiers of Julius Caesar used as bread.

Craniolaria annua Linn. *Pedalineae.*

Tropical America. The fleshy and sweet root is preserved in sugar by the Creoles as a delicacy.[2]

Crataegus aestivalis Torr & Gray. *Rosaceae.* CRATAEGUS.

North America. The tree bears a juicy, pleasant-flavored fruit which is much used.[3] The fruit is said by Elliott [4] to be large, red, acid and used for tarts and preserves.

C. azarolus Linn. AZAROLE.

Asia Minor and Persia. Azarole is much cultivated for its fruits, which are the size of a cherry, red, with sometimes a tinge of yellow, and are said to have a very agreeable flavor.[5] The fruit is eaten in Sicily, in Italy and the Levant, being sometimes served as dessert, and is much used for preserves. It is common about Jerusalem, where its fruit is collected for preserves.[6] It is, according to Stackhouse, the *mespile anthedon* of Theophrastus.

C. coccinea Linn.

Eastern United States. Gray [7] says the fruit is scarcely eatable. Elliott [8] says the fruit is red, large and eatable. The fruit is eaten fresh or mingled with choke cherries and service berries and is pressed into cakes and dried for winter use by the western Indians.[9] The small, purplish fruits are edible.[10]

C. douglasii Lindl.

Michigan and the Northwest. This species bears a small, sweet, black fruit ripening in August. It is largely collected by the Indians.

C. flava. SUMMER HAW. YELLOW-FRUITED THORN.

North America. The fruit is said by Elliott to be oval, red and well flavored.

C. orientalis Bieb. EASTERN THORN.

Greece and Asia Minor. In the Crimea, this species bears little apples, sometimes

---

[1] Unger, F. *U. S. Pat. Off. Rpt.* 354. 1859.

[2] Dickie, G. D. *Treas. Bot.* 1:344. 1870.

[3] Wood, A. *Class Book Bot.* 331. 1864.

[4] Elliott, S. *Bot. So. Car., Ga.* 1:547–553. 1821.

[5] Andrews *Bot. Reposit* 9:Pl. 579. 1797.

[6] Smith, J. *Dom. Bot.* 407. 1871.

[7] Gray, A. *Man. Bot.* 160. 1868.

[8] Elliott, S. *Bot. So. Car., Ga.* 1:553. 1821.

[9] *U. S. D. A. Rpt.* 413. 1870.

[10] Wood, A. *Class Book Bot.* 332. 1865.

of a bright yellow and at other times of a lively red color, an agreeable fruit, much improved by grafting.[1]

C. oxyacantha Linn. HAWTHORN. QUICK. QUICK-SET THORN. WHITE THORN.

Europe and temperate Asia. The fruit is said by Don[2] to be mealy, insipid, dark red and occasionally yellow. Johnson[3] says it is seldom eaten in England except by children. Lightfoot[4] says that when thoroughly ripe it is eaten by the Highlanders. In Kamchatka, the natives eat the fruits and make a kind of wine by fermenting them with water. In India, says Brandis,[5] the tree is cultivated for its fruit.

C. parvifolia Ait. DWARF THORN.

North America. The greenish-yellow fruit is eatable.[6]

C. pentagyna Waldst. & Kit.

Europe and Asia. The plant grows wild in the hills west of Pekin. The red fruit is much larger than the ordinary crataegus; it is collected and an excellent sweetmeat is prepared therefrom.[7]

C. pubescens Steud.

Mexico. A jelly is made from the fruit, resembling that of the quince.[8]

C. sanguinea Pall.

Russia and Siberia. In Germany, this species yields edible fruits.

C. subvillosa Schrad.

Eastern Asia and North America. The large, red fruit, often downy, is edible and of an agreeable flavor.[9]

C. tanacetifolia Pers.

Armenia. The fruit resembles a small apple, about an inch in diameter, and is eaten in Armenia.[10] The Armenians relish the fruits, which resemble small apples, with five roundings like the ribs of a melon, a little hairy, pale green inclining to yellow, with a raised navel of five leaves.[11]

C. tomentosa Linn. BLACK THORN. PEAR THORN.

Eastern United States. This species is said, in the Michigan Pomological Society's catalog of 1879, to bear an edible fruit, often of pleasant flavor but which varies much in quality. Probably, this is the " hawes of white thorn neere as good as our cherries in

---

[1] Pallas, P. S. *Trav. Russia* **2**:174. 1803.

[2] Don, G. *Hist. Dichl. Pls.* **2**:600. 1832.

[3] Johnson, C. P. *Useful Pls. Gt. Brit.* 98. 1862.

[4] Lightfoot, J. *Fl. Scot.* **1**:256. 1789.

[5] Brandis, D. *Forest Fl.* 207. 1874.

[6] Elliott, S. *Bot. So. Car., Ga.* **1**:547. 1821.

[7] Bretschneider, E. *On Study* 11. 1870. (*C. pinnatifida*)

[8] Watson *Proc. Amer. Acad. Sci.* 411. 1887.

[9] Sargent *U. S. Census* **9**:78. 1884.

[10] Loudon, J. C. *Arb. Frut. Brit.* **2**: 828. 1844.

[11] Tournefort *Voy. Levant* **2**:172. 1718.

England," noted by Rev. Francis Higginson.[1] Wood says:[2] " The white thorn affords hawes as big as an English cherrie which is esteemed above a cherrie for his goodneese and pleasantnesse to the taste." Josselyn[3] says of it: " Hawthorn: the berries being as big as services and very good to eat and not so stringent as the hawes in England." The fruit is somewhat hard and tough but is eatable and rather agreeable to the taste.[4]

Crataeva magna DC. *Capparideae.*
Cochin China. The roundish, ash-colored fruits are eatable.[5]

C. obovata Vahl.
Madagascar. The fruit is eatable.[6]

C. religiosa Forst. f.
Old World tropics. In equatorial Africa, the fresh shoots are made into spinach and the young branches into tooth-scrubbers.[7] In India, this plant furnishes food for man.[8]

C. tapia Linn. GARLIC PEAR.
South America. The fruit is edible but not very good.[9] It is the size of a small orange, eatable but not pleasant.[10] In Jamaica, the fruit is spherical, orange-sized, with a hard, brown shell, a mealy pulp like that of a pear, sweetish, smelling like garlic, and near the center there are many kidney-shaped seeds. It is edible but not very pleasant.[11]

Crescentia cujete Linn. *Bignoniaceae.* CALABASH TREE.
Tropical America. The fruit of this tree resembles a gourd. The plant is found wild or cultivated in various parts of tropical America and in the West Indies. The hard, woody shell of the fruit is made to serve many useful domestic purposes in the household economy of the people of these countries, such as basins, cups, spoons, water-bottles and pails. Wafer,[12] apparently, speaks of this tree and of *C. cucurbitina* during his visit to the Isthmus, 1679–86: " There are two sorts of these trees but the difference is chiefly in the fruit; that of the one being sweet, the other bitter. The substance of both is spongy and juicy. That of the sweeter sort does not incline to a tart, sourish taste. The Indians, however, eat them frequently on a march, tho they are not very delightful. They only suck out the juice and spit out the rest. The bitter sort is not eatable." Henfrey[13] says the subacid pulp of the fruit is eaten; Seemann,[14] that it affords food to the negroes.

---

[1] *Mass. Hist. Soc. Coll.* 1st Ser. 1:118. 1806. Reprint of 1792.

[2] Wood, W. *New Eng. Prosp.* 1st Ed. 16. 1634.

[3] Josselyn, W. *Rar.* 93. 1865.

[4] Emerson, G. B. *Trees, Shrubs Mass.* 1:495. 1875.

[5] Don, G. *Hist. Dichl. Pls.* 1:276. 1831.

[6] Ibid.

[7] Speke, J. H. *Journ. Disc. Source Nile* 561. 1864. (*C. adansonii*)

[8] Unger, F. *U. S. Pat. Off. Rpt.* 337. 1859.

[9] Ainslie, W. *Mat. Ind.* 2:197. 1826.

[10] Grisebach, A. H. R. *Fl. Brit. W. Ind.* 17. 1864.

[11] Lunan, J. *Hort. Jam.* 1:317. 1814.

[12] Wafer *Voy. Isth. Amer.* 93. 1699.

[13] Henfrey, A. *Bot.* 331. 1870.

[14] Hooker, W. J. *Journ. Bot.* 9:143. 1857.

Nuttall[1] says the plant is found at Key West, Florida, and that the fruit is eaten by the Indians in time of scarcity while the unripe fruit is candied with sugar.

Crithmum maritimum Linn.   *Umbelliferae.*   SAMPHIRE.   SEA FENNEL.

Europe.   This is a seaside plant, found on rocky shores from the Crimea to Land's End, England, and extends even to the Caucasus.   The whole plant is " of a spicie taste with a certaine saltnesse " on which account it has been long held in great repute as an ingredient in salads.   It was declared by Gerarde[2] to be " the pleasantest sauce." Samphire is cultivated in English gardens for its seed pods, which make a warm, aromatic pickle, and for its leaves, which are used in salads,[3] but it is oftener collected from the shores.   In Jamaica, as Titford[4] declares, it forms an agreeable and wholesome pickle. In France, it is cultivated for its leaves which, pickled with vinegar, enter into salads and seasonings.[5]   The first mention of its culture is by Quintyne,[6] in France, 1690; it is again mentioned by Stevenson,[7] in England, 1765; and its use as a potherb by the poor, as well as a pickle, is noticed by Bryant,[8] 1783.   It is noticed in American gardens in 1821.[9]

Crocus cancellatus Herb.   *Irideae.*

Asia Minor.   This plant is said by Unger[10] to be brought to market in Damascus, when the bulb is about sprouting, and is much prized as a vegetable.

C. sativus Linn.   SAFFRON.

Greece and Asia Minor.   This plant was formerly cultivated in England and is now spontaneous.   It is cultivated in Austria, France and Spain for the deep, orange-colored stigmas of the flowers, which are used for coloring.   It was not cultivated in France before the Crusades, the bulbs from Avignon being introduced about the end of the fourteenth century.[11]   Loudon[12] says saffron is used in sauces and for coloring by the Spaniards and Poles.   In England and France, it enters into creams, biscuits, preserves and liquors and is used for coloring butter and cheese.   The Mongols use it in cooking.[13]   Under the Hebrew name, *carcom*, the plant is alluded to by Solomon; and as *krokos*, by Homer, Hippocrates, Theophrastus and Theocritus.   Virgil and Columella mention it and Cilicia and Sicily are both alluded to by Dioscorides and Pliny as localities celebrated for this drug. Throughout the middle ages, frequent notices are found of its occurrence in commerce and in cultivation.

---

[1] Nuttall, T.   *No. Amer. Sylva* 2:136.   1865.
[2] Johns, C. A.   *Treas. Bot.* 1:348.   1870.
[3] Loudon, J. C.   *Enc. Pls.* 213.   1855.
[4] Titford, W. J.   *Hort. Bot. Amer.* 51.   1812.
[5] *Bon. Jard.* 549.   1882.
[6] Quintyne *Comp. Gard.* 105.   1693.
[7] Stevenson *Gard. Kal.* 102.   1765.
[8] Bryant *Fl. Diet.* 136.   1783.
[9] Cobbett, W.   *Amer. Gard.* 159.   1846.
[10] Unger, F.   *U. S. Pat. Off. Rpt.* 311.   1859.   (*C. edulis*)
[11] *Gard. Chron.* 671.   1848.
[12] Loudon, J. C.   *Enc. Agr.* 943.   1866.
[13] Smith, F. P.   *Contrib. Mat. Med. China* 189.   1871.

Crotalaria glauca Willd. *Leguminosae.*

African tropics. The people of Madi eat its flowers, pods and leaves as spinach.[1]

C. laburnifolia Linn.

Asiatic tropics. This is an upright, perennial plant, bearing short, black and light brown beans the size of soy beans. It is sometimes cultivated.[2]

Croton corymbulosus Rothr. *Euphorbiaceae.* CHAPARRAL TEA. ENCENILLA.

North America. An infusion of the flowering tops makes a very palatable drink, one much used by the Mexicans and Indians as well as by colored (U. S.) soldiers who prefer it to coffee.[3]

Cryptocarya moschata Nees & Mart. *Laurineae.* BRAZILIAN NUTMEG.

Brazil. This tree produces the spice known as Brazilian nutmegs.[4]

C. peumus Nees.

Chile. The fruit is edible.[5]

Cryptotaenia canadensis DC. *Umbelliferae.* HONEWORT.

North America. This species is very generally cultivated in Japan. The tips are used as greens and to flavor soups; the blanched stems are used as a salad and a potherb; the root also is utilized.[6]

Cucumeropsis edulis Cogn. *Cucurbitaceae.*

Tropical Africa. This is a cucumber-like plant which bears edible fruits of one foot in length and three inches in diameter.[7]

Cucumis anguria Linn. *Cucurbitaceae.* BUR CUCUMBER. GHERKIN. GOAREBERRY GOURD. WEST INDIAN GHERKIN. WILD CUCUMBER.

West Indies. This is the wild cucumber of Hughes. It is a native of the West Indies, and the green fruit is eaten there but it is far inferior to the common cucumber. Sloane [8] says the fruit is of a pale green color, oval, as big as a walnut, having many short, blunt, thick tubercles, sharper than those of other cucumbers, and that within the pulp are a great many small seeds like those of other cucumbers. It is cultivated in Jamaica, but oftener the fruits are collected from the wild plants. In France, it is called *Concombre arada* and is sometimes grown in gardens, the fruit being called sweet and excellent when grown under good circumstances of soil. This vegetable is described by Marcgravius [9] in Brazil 1648, the name *Cucumis sylvestris Brazileae* indicating an uncultivated plant. Ten years later,

---

[1] Speke, J. H. *Journ. Disc. Source Nile* 565. 1864.

[2] Georgeson *Amer. Gard.* 14:85. 1893.

[3] Havard, V. *Torr. Bot. Club Bul.* 23:46. 1896.

[4] Masters, M. T. *Treas. Bot.* 1:354. 1870.

[5] Molina *Hist. Chili* 1:129. 1808. (*Peumus mammosa*)

[6] Georgeson *Amer. Gard.* 12:714. 1891.

[7] Mueller, F. *Sel. Pls.* 131. 1891. (*Corynosicyos edulis*)

[8] Sloane, H. *Nat. Hist. Jam.* 1:227. 1774.

[9] Marcgravius *Hist. Rerum Nat. Bras.* 44. 1648.

Piso[1] also described it as a wild plant of Brazil under the name *guarervaoba* or *cucumer asinius* and gives a figure. It has also been found in the Antilles and in continental tropical and subtropical America, New Granada and South Florida.[2] It is not mentioned as cultivated in Jamaica by Sloane,[3] 1696. Its fruit is mentioned as being used in soups and pickles, apparently gathered from the wild plant, by Long,[4] 1774, Titford,[5] 1812, and Lunan,[6] 1814. It is, however, cultivated in French Guiana and Antiqua.[7] Although described by Ray,[8] 1686 and 1704, and grown by Miller in his botanic garden in 1755, it yet does not appear to be in the vegetable gardens of England in 1807,[9] although it was known in the gardens of the United States[10] in 1806. In France, it was under cultivation in 1824 and 1829[11] but apparently was abandoned and was reintroduced by Vilmorin in 1858.[12]

C. longipes Hook. f.

The fruit tastes like a cucumber.[13]

C. melo Linn. CANTALOUPE. MELON. MUSKMELON.

Old World tropics. Naudin[14] divides the varieties of melon into ten sections, which differ not only in their fruits but also in their leaves and their entire habit or mode of growth. Some melons are no larger than small plums, others weigh as much as 66 pounds; one variety has a scarlet fruit; another is only one inch in diameter but three feet long and is coiled in a serpentine manner in all directions. The fruit of one variety can scarcely be distinguished from cucumbers; one Algerian variety suddenly splits up into sections when ripe. The melons of our gardens may be divided into two sections: those with green flesh, as the citron and nutmeg; those with yellow flesh, as the Christiana, cantaloupe and Persian melons, with very thin skins and melting honey-like flesh of delicious flavor. In England, melons with red, green, and white flesh are cultivated.

By the earlier and unscientific travellers, the term melon has been used to signify watermelons, the Macock gourd of Virginia, and it has even been applied to pumpkins by our early horticulturists. The names used by the ancient writers and translated by some to mean melon, seem also in doubt. Thus, according to Fraas,[15] the *sikua* of Theophrastus[16]

---

[1] Piso *Hist. Rerum Nat. Bras.* 264. 1648.

[2] Naudin *Ann. Sci. Nat.* 8, 12. No year.

[3] Sloane, H. *Cat.* 103. 1696.

[4] Long *Hist. Jam.* 801. 1774.

[5] Titford, W. J. *Hort. Bot. Amer.* 100. 1812.

[6] Lunan, J. *Hort. Jam.* 1:254. 1814.

[7] De Candolle, A. & C. *Monog.* 3:501. 1881.

[8] Ray *Hist. Pl.* 1686; *Suppl.* 333. 1704.

[9] Miller *Gard. Dict.* 1807.

[10] McMahon, B. *Amer. Gard. Cal.* 581.. 1806.

[11] Pirolle *L'Hort. Franc.* 1824.

[12] Naudin *Ann. Sci. Nat.* 8, 12.

[13] Oliver *Fl. Trop. Afr.* 2:547. 1871.

[14] Sachs *Bot.* 925. 1882.

[15] De Candolle, A. *Geog. Bot.* 2:905. 1855.

[16] Ibid.

was the melon. In Liddell and Scott's *Lexicon*, the definition is given " a fruit like the melon or gourd but eaten ripe." Fraas [1] says the melon is the *pepon* of Dioscorides.[2] The *Lexicon* says " *sikuos pepon*, or more frequently *o pepon*, a kind of gourd or melon not eaten till quite ripe." Fraas [3] says " the melon is the *melopepon* of Galen and the *melo* of Pliny." [4] Andrews' *Latin Lexicon* gives under *melopepo* " an apple-shaped melon, cucumber melon, not eaten till fully ripe." Pliny, on the other hand, says in Greece in his day it was named *peponia*. In Italy, in 1539, the names of *pepone, melone* and *mellone* were applied to it. In Sardinia, where it is remarked by De Candolle [5] that Roman traditions are well preserved, it is called *meloni*. As a summary, we may believe that although " a kind of gourd not eaten until fully ripe " may have been cultivated in ancient Greece and Rome, or even by the Jews under their Kings, as Unger [6] asserts, yet the admiration of the authors of the sixteenth century for the perfume and exquisite taste of the melon, as contrasted with the silence of the Romans, who were not less epicurean, is assuredly a proof that the melon had not at that time, even if known, attained its present luscious and perfumed properties, and it is an indication, as De Candolle [7] observes, " of the novelty of the fruit in Europe." When we consider, moreover, the rapidity of its diffusion through the savage tribes of America to remote regions, we cannot believe that a fruit so easily transported through its seed could have remained secluded during such a long period of history.

Albertus Magnus,[8] in the thirteenth century, says, melons, which some call *pepones*, have the seed and the flower very nearly like those of the cucumber and also says, in speaking of the cucumber, that the seeds are like those of the *pepo*. Under the head of watermelon, *citrullus*, he calls the melon *pepo*, and says it has a smooth, green skin, but the *pepo* is commonly yellow and of an uneven surface and as if round, semi-circular sections were orderly arranged together. In 1536, Ruellius [9] describes our melon as the *pepo;* in 1542, Fuchsius [10] describes the melon, but figures it under the name of *pepo*. In 1550, Roeszlin [11] figures the melon under the name of *pepo*, and in 1558 Matthiolus [12] figures it under the name of melon. The Greek name of *pepon*, and the Italian, German, Spanish and French of melon, variously spelled, are given among synonyms by various authors [13] of the sixteenth century; *melones sive pepones* are used by Pinaeus,[14] 1561;

---

[1] De Candolle, A. *Geog. Bot.* 2:905. 1855.

[2] Ibid.

[3] Ibid.

[4] Ibid.

[5] Ibid.

[6] Unger, F. *U. S. Pat. Off. Rpt.* 333. 1859.

[7] De Candolle, A. *Geog. Bot.* 2:906. 1855.

[8] Albertus Magnus *Veg.* 501. 1867. Jessen Ed.

[9] Ruellius *Nat. Stirp.* 503. 1536.

[10] Fuchsius *Hist. Stirp.* 701, 702. 1542.

[11] Roeszlin *Kreuterb.* 116. 1550.

[12] Matthiolus *Comment.* 262. 1558.

[13] Pinaeus *Hist. Pl.* 194. 1561. Camerarius *Epit.* 296. 1586.

[14] Pinaeus *Hist. Pl.* 194. 1561.

melone and *pepone* by Castor Durante,[1] 1617, and by Gerarde[2] in England, 1597. Melons and *pompions* are used synonymously, and the melon is called *muske-melon* or *million*.

Whether the ancients knew the melon is a matter of doubt. Dioscorides,[3] in the first century, says the flesh or pulp (*cara*) of the *pepo* used in food is diuretic. Pliny,[4] about the same period, says a new form of cucumber has lately appeared in Campania called *melopepo*, which grows on the ground in a round form, and he adds, as a remarkable circumstance, in addition to their color and odor, that when ripe, although not suspended, yet the fruit separates from the stem at maturity. Galen,[5] in the second century, treating of medicinal properties, says the autumn fruits (*i. e.*, ripe) do not excite vomiting as do the unripe, and further says mankind abstains from the inner flesh of the *pepo*, where the seed is borne but eats it in the *melopepo*. A half-century later, Palladius[6] gives directions for planting *melones* and speaks of them as being sweet and odorous. Apicius,[7] a writer on cookery, about 230 A. D., directs that *pepones* and *melones* be served with various spices corresponding in part to present customs, and Nonnius, an author of the sixth century, speaks of cucumbers which are odoriferous.[8] In the seventh century, Paulus Agineta,[9] a medical writer, mentions the medicinal properties of the *melopepo* as being of the same character but less than that of the *pepo*, and separates these from the *cucurbita* and *cucumis*, not differing from Galen, already quoted.

From these remarks concerning odor and sweetness, which particularly apply to our melon, and the mention of the spontaneous falling of the ripe fruit, a characteristic of no other garden vegetable, we are inclined to believe that these references are to the melon, and more especially so as the authors of the sixteenth and following centuries make mention of many varieties, as Amatus Lusitanus,[10] 1554, who says, *quorum varietas ingens est*, and proceeds to mention some as thin skinned, others as thicker skinned, some red fleshed, others white.

In 1259, Tch'ang Te, according to Bretschneider,[11] found melons, grapes and pomegranates of excellent quality in Turkestan. This Chinese traveller may have brought seeds to China, where Loureiro[12] states the melons are of poor quality and whence they did not spread, for Rumphius[13] asserts that melons were carried into the islands of the Asiatic Archipelago by the Portuguese. Smith,[14] however, in his *Materia Medica of*

[1] Durante, C. *Herb.* 345. 1617.

[2] Gerarde, J. *Herb.* 770, 775. 1597.

[3] Dioscorides *Vergelius Ed.* 210. 1532.

[4] Pliny lib. 19, c. 23.

[5] Galen *De Aliment.* lib. 2; Gregorius Ed. 97. 1547.

[6] Palladius lib. 4, c. 9; lib. 5, c. 3; lib. 6, c. 15.

[7] Apicius *Opson.* 82. 1709.

[8] Nonnius Quoted from Lister in Apulius, *l. c.*

[9] Aegineta, P. *Pharm. Simp.* 76. 1531.

[10] Dioscorides Amatus Lusitanus Ed. 265. 1554.

[11] Schuyler *Turkistan* 1:399. 1876.

[12] De Candolle, A. *Geog. Bot.* 2:907. 1855.

[13] Ibid.

[14] Smith, F. P. *Contrib. Mat. Med. China* 80. 1871.

China, says Chang K'ien, the noted legate of the Han dynasty, seems to have brought this " foreign cucumber " from central Asia to China, where it is now largely cultivated and eaten both raw and in a pickle. According to Pasquier, melons were unknown in central or northern Europe until the reign of Charles VIII, 1483–1498, King of France, who brought them from Italy. We find a statement by J. Smith [1] that they were supposed to have been first introduced from Egypt into Rome. They were perhaps known commonly in Spain before 1493, for Columbus on his second voyage found melons " already grown, fit to eat, tho' it was not above two months since the seed was put into the ground." In 1507, Martin Baumgarten,[2] travelling in Palestine, mentions melons as brought to him by the inhabitants. In 1513, Herrera,[3] a Spanish writer, says, " if the melon is good, it is the best fruit that exists, and none other is preferable to it. If it is bad, it is a bad thing, we are wont to say that the good are like good women, and the bad like bad women." In the time of Matthiolus,[4] 1570, many excellent varieties were cultivated. The melon has been cultivated in England, says Don,[5] since 1570, but the precise date of its introduction is unknown, though originally brought from Jamaica.

The culture of the melon is not very ancient, says De Candolle,[6] and the plant has never been found wild in the Mediterranean region, in Africa, in India or the Indian Archipelago. It is now extensively cultivated in Armenia, Ispahan, Bokhara and elsewhere in Asia; in Greece, South Russia, Italy and the shores of the Mediterranean. About 1519, the Emperor Baber is said to have shed tears over a melon of Turkestan which he cut up in India after his conquest, its flavor bringing his native country to his recollection. In China, it is cultivated but, as Loureiro [7] says, is of poor quality. In Japan, Thunberg,[8] 1776, says the melon is much cultivated, but the more recent writers on Japan are very sparing of epithets conveying ideas of qualities. Capt. Cook apparently distributed the melon in suitable climates along his course around the world, as he has left record of so doing at many places; as, the Lefooga Islands, May 1777, at Hiraheime, October, 1777.

Columbus is recorded as finding melons at Isabela Island in 1494 on his return from his second voyage, and the first grown in the New World are to be dated March 29, 1494. The rapidity and extent of their diffusion may be gathered from the following mentions. In 1516, " melons different from those here " were seen by Pascual de Andagoya [9] in Central America. In Sept. 1535, Jacques Cartier mentions the Indians at Hochelega, now Montreal, as having " musk mellons." [10] In 1881, muskmelons from Montreal appeared

[1] Smith, J. *Dom. Bot.* 386. 1871.
[2] Churchill *Coll. Voy.* 1:343. 1744.
[3] De Candolle, A. *Geog. Bot.* 2:906. 1855.
[4] Ibid.
[5] Don, G. *Hist. Dichl. Pls.* 3:5. 1834.
[6] De Candolle, A. *Geog. Bot.* 2:907. 1855.
[7] Ibid.
[8] Ibid.
[9] Andagoya, P. de. *Narrative* Hakl. Soc. Ed. 29. 1865.
[10] Pinkerton *Coll. Voy.* 12:656. 1812.

in the Boston market.　In 1749, Kalm [1] found at Quebec melons abounding and always eaten with sugar.　In 1540, Lopez de Gomara,[2] in the expedition to New Mexico, makes several mentions of melons.　In 1542, the army of the Viceroy of Mexico sent to Cibolo found the melon already there.　In 1583, Antonis de Espejo found melons cultivated by the Choctaw Indians.　In 1744, the melon is mentioned as cultivated by the Coco Maricopas Indians by Father Sedelmayer, and melons are mentioned on the Colorado River by Vinegas, 1758.　In 1565, melons are reported by Benzoni [3] as abounding in Hayti, but melon seeds appear not to have been planted in the Bermudas until 1609.[4]

Muskmelons are said to have been grown in Virginia in 1609 [5] and are again mentioned in 1848.[6]　In 1609, melons are mentioned by Hudson [7] as found on the Hudson River. Muskmelons are mentioned by Master Graves [8] in his letter of 1629 as abounding in New England and again by Wm. Woods,[9] 1629–33.　According to *Hilton's Relation*,[10] muskmelons were cultivated by the Florida Indians prior to 1664.　In 1673 the melon is said to have been cultivated by the Indians of Illinois, and Father Marquette [11] pronounced them excellent, especially those with a red seed.　In 1822, Woods [12] says: " There are many sorts of sweet melons, and much difference in size in the various kinds.　I have only noticed musk, of a large size, and nutmeg, a smaller one; and a small, pale colored melon of a rich taste, but there are other sorts with which I am unacquainted."　In 1683, some melon seeds were sown by the Spaniards on the Island of California.　The Indians about Philadelphia grew melons preceding 1748, according to Kalm.[13]　In Brazil, melons are mentioned by Nieuhoff,[14] 1647, and by Father Angelo,[15] 1666.

In various parts of Africa, as in Senegal and Abeokuta, and in China, the seeds are collected and an oil expressed which is used for food and other purposes and is also exported.　In 1860, the production in Senegal was 62,266 kilos., and a considerable amount was shipped from Chefoo, China, in 1875.　During the Civil War many farmers in the southern states made molasses and sugar from muskmelons and cantaloupes.　In Kentucky, an occasional experiment has been made in converting a surplusage of melons into syrups with considerable success.

[1] Kalm, P.　*Trav. No. Amer.* 2:324.　1772.

[2] *Pacific R. R. Rpt.* 3:111.　1856.

[3] Benzoni *Hist. New World* Hakl. Soc. Ed. 91.　1857.

[4] *Newes from Barmudas* 20.　1613.　Force Coll. Tracts 3: No. 3.　1844.

[5] *True Decl. Va.* London 13.　1610.　Force Coll. Tracts 3: No. 3.　1844.

[6] *New Desc. Va.* Mass. Hist. Coll. 19:122.　1832.

[7] *N. Y. Agr. Soc. Trans.* 359.　1850.

[8] *Mass. Hist. Soc. Coll.* 1st Ser. 1:124.　1806.　Reprint of 1792.

[9] Woods, W.　*New Eng. Prosp.* Prince Soc. Ed. 15.　1865.

[10] Hilton *Rel. Fla.* 8.　1664–68.　Force Coll. Tracts 4: No. 2.　1846.

[11] Marquette, Fr.　*Trans. Ill. Hort. Soc.* 125.　1876.

[12] Woods, J.　*Ill. Country* 226.　1822.

[13] Watson *Annals Phil.* 442.　1856.

[14] Churchill *Coll. Voy.* 2:132.　1732.

[15] Churchill *Coll. Voy.* 1:489.　1744.

NOTES ON CLASSIFICATION.

1. Early and late melons, as also winter melons, are described by Amatus,[1] 1554; summer and winter, by Bauhin,[2] 1623.

2. White- and red-fleshed are described by Amatus, 1554; yellow-fleshed by Dodonaeus, 1616; green-fleshed by Marcgravius[3] 1648; green, golden, pale yellow and ashen by Bauhin,[4] 1623.

3. Sugar melons are named *sucrinos* by Ruellius,[5] 1536; *succrades rouges* and *succrades blanches* by Chabraeus,[6] 1677; and *succris* and *succredes* by Dalechamp,[7] 1587.

4. Netted melons are named by Camerarius,[8] 1586, as also the ribbed. The warted are mentioned in the *Adversaria*,[9] 1570; rough, warted and smooth, by Bauhin,[10] 1623.

5. The round, long, oval and pear-form are mentioned by Gerarde,[11] 1597; the quince form, by Dalechamp,[12] 1587; the oblong, by Dodonaeus, 1616; the round, oblong, depressed, or flat, by Bauhin,[13] 1623.

C. melo dudaim Naud. DUDAIM MELON. POMEGRANATE MELON. QUEEN ANNE'S-POCKET MELON.

Equatorial Africa. The fruit is globose-ovate, as large as a lemon, and not edible but is cultivated for its strong and pleasant odor. It has a very fragrant, musky smell and a whitish, flaccid, insipid pulp.[14]

C. melo flexuosus Naud. SNAKE CUCUMBER. SNAKE MELON.

East Indies. This melon is cultivated in Japan and is called by the Dutch *banket melon*.[15]

C. prophetarum Linn. GLOBE CUCUMBER.

Arabia and tropical Africa. The flesh of this cucumber is scanty and too bitter to be edible, says Vilmorin,[16] who includes it among the plants of the kitchen garden. Burr [17] says the fruit is sometimes eaten boiled, but is generally pickled in its green state like the common cucumber and adds that it is not worthy of cultivation.

---

[1] Dioscorides Amatus Lusitanus Ed. 265. 1554.

[2] Bauhin *Pinax* 310, 311. 1623.

[3] Marcgravius *Hist. Rerum Nat. Bras.* 22. 1648. (Piso)

[4] Bauhin, C. *Pinax* 310, 311. 1623.

[5] Ruellius *Nat. Stirp.* 503. 1536.

[6] Chabraeus *Icon. Sciag.* 134. 1677.

[7] Dalechamp *Hist. Gen. Pl.* (Lugd.) 623. 1587.

[8] Camerarius *Epit.* 296. 1586.

[9] Pena and Lobel *Advers.* 285. 1570.

[10] Bauhin, C. *Pinax* 310, 311. 1623.

[11] Gerarde, J. *Herb.* 770, 775. 1597.

[12] Dalechamp *Hist. Gen. Pl.* (Lugd.) 623 1587.

[13] Bauhin, C. *Pinax* 310, 311. 1623.

[14] Don, G. *Hist. Dichl. Pls.* 3:27. 1834.

[15] Ibid.

[16] Vilmorin *Veg. Gard.* 227. 1885.

[17] Burr *Field, Gard. Veg.* 179. 1863.

C. sativus Linn. CUCUMBER.

East Indies. The origin of the cucumber is usually ascribed to Asia and Egypt. Dr. Hooker[1] believes the wild plants inhabit the Himalayas from Kumaun to Sikkim. It has been a plant of cultivation from the most remote times, but De Candolle[2] finds no support for the common belief of its presence in ancient Egypt at the time of the Israelite migration into the wilderness, although its culture in western Asia is indicated from philological data as more than 3000 years old. The cucumber is said to have been brought into China from the west, 140–86 B. C.;[3] it can be identified in a Chinese work on agriculture of the fifth century and is described by Chinese authors of 1590 and 1640.[4] Cucumbers were known to the ancient Greeks[5] and to the Romans, and Pliny[6] even mentions their forced culture. They find mention in the Middle Ages and in the botanies from Ruellius, 1536, onward. The cucumber is believed to be the *sikus hemeros* of Dioscorides, and the *sikuos* of Theophrastus. Pliny[7] says cucumbers were much grown in Africa as well as in Italy in his time, and that the Emperor Tiberius had cucumbers at his table every day in the year. We find reference to them in France in the ninth century, for Charlemagne ordered cucumbers to be planted on his estate. In Gough's[8] *British Topography*, cucumbers are stated to have been common in England in the time of Edward III, 1327, but during the wars of the houses of York and Lancaster, their cultivation was neglected, the plant was lost, and they were reintroduced only in 1573. In 1629, Parkinson[9] says " in many countries they use to eate coccumbers as wee doe apples or Peares," and they are thus eaten and relished at the present day in southern Russia and in Japan.

Cucumbers were grown by Columbus[10] at Hayti in 1494. In 1535, Cartier[11] mentions " very great cucumbers" cultivated by the Indians about Hochelaga, now Montreal. In 1539, De Soto[12] found in Florida at Apalache " cucumbers better than those of Spain " and also at other villages, and, in 1562, Ribault[13] mentions them as cultivated by the Florida Indians. According to Capt. John Smith,[14] Captains Amidos and Barlow mention cucumbers in Virginia in 1584 and they are mentioned as being cultivated there in 1609.[15] Cucumbers were among the Indian vegetables destroyed by General Sullivan in 1779[16]

[1] Burbidge, F. W. *Cult. Pls.* 277. 1877.

[2] De Candolle, A. *Orig. Pls. Cult.* 266. 1885.

[3] Bretschneider, E. *On Study* 15. 1870.

[4] Bretschneider, E. *Bot. Sin.* 78, 59, 83. 1882.

[5] Theophratus *Hist. Pl.* Bodaeus Ed. 1644.

[6] Pliny lib. 19, c. 23.

[7] McIntosh, C. *Book Gard.* 2:663. 1855.

[8] Ibid.

[9] Parkinson *Par. Terr.* 524. 1904. (Reprint of 1629)

[10] Irving, W. *Columbus* 1:380. 1859.

[11] Pinkerton *Coll. Voy.* 12:652. 1812.

[12] De Soto *Disc. Conq. Fla.* Hakl. Soc. Ed. 9:44. 1851.

[13] Hakluyt, R. *Coll. Divers Voy. Amer.* Hakl. Soc. Ed. 7:102. 1840.

[14] Pinkerton *Coll. Voy.* 13:6. 1812.

[15] *True Decl. Va.* 13. 1610. Force Coll. Tracts. 3: No. 3. 1844.

[16] Conover, G. S. *Early Hist. Geneva* 45. 1879.

in the Indian fields about Kashong, near the present Geneva, N. Y. At the Bermudas, "cowcumbers" were planted in 1609.[1] In Massachusetts, they are mentioned in 1629 by Rev. Francis Higginson;[2] William Wood[3] mentions them in his *New England's Prospects*, 1629–33. In Brazil, cucumbers were seen by Nieuhoff[4] in 1647 and by Father Angelo[5] in 1666.

There are a great number of varieties varying from the small gherkin to the mammoth English varieties which attain a length of twenty inches or more. The cultivated gherkin is a variety used exclusively for pickling and was in American gardens in 1806. At Unyanyembe, Central Africa, and other places where the cucumber grows almost wild, says Burton,[6] the Arabs derive from its seed an admirable salad oil, which in flavor equals and perhaps surpasses the finest produce of the olive. Vilmorin in *Les Plantes Potagères*, 1883, describes 30 varieties. Most, if not all, of these as well as others including 59 different names have been grown on the grounds of the New York Agricultural Experiment Station. While some of the varieties grown differ but little, yet there are many kinds which are extraordinarily distinct.

TYPES OF CUCUMBERS.

The types of our common cucumbers are fairly well figured in the ancient botanies, but the fruit is far inferior in appearance to those we grow today, being apparently more rugged and less symmetrical. The following synonymy is established from figures and descriptions:

I.

Cucumis sativus vulgaris. Fuch. 697. 1542.
Cucumis sativus. Roeszl. 116. 1550; Cam. *Epit.* 294. 1586.
Cucumis. Trag. 831. 1552; Fischer 1646.
Cucumis vulgaris. Ger. 762, 1597; Chabr. 134. 1677.
Concombre. Tourn. t. 32. 1719.
? *Short Green*. Park. *Par.* 1629.
? *Short Green Prickly*. Mawe 1778; *Mill. Dict.* 1807.
Early Green Cluster. *Mill. Dict.* 1807.
Green Cluster. Thorb. 1828.
Early Cluster of American seedsmen.

II.

A second form, very near to the above, but longer, less rounding and more prickly has a synonymy as below:

Cucumeres. Matth. 282. 1558.
Cucumis sativus. Dalechamp 1:620. 1587.
Cucumeres sativi and *esculenti* Lob. *Icon.* 1:638. 1591.
Cucumis vulgaris Dod. 662. 1616.
Cedruolo. Dur. C. 103. 1617.

---

[1] *Newes from Barmudas* 20. 1613. Force Coll. Tracts. **3**: No. 3. 1844.

[2] *Mass. Hist. Soc. Coll.* 1st Ser. **1**:118. 1806. (Reprint of 1792)

[3] Wood, W. *New Eng. Prosp.* 15. 1865.

[4] Churchill *Coll. Voy.* **1**:132. 1732.

[5] Churchill *Coll. Voy.* **1**:489. 1744.

[6] Burton, R. F. *Lake Reg. Cent. Afr.* 465. 1860.

Cucumis vulgaris, viridis, and *albis.* Bauh. J. **2**:246. 1651.
Long Green Prickly. Mill. Dict. 1807.
Early Frame. Thorb. Cat. 1828 and 1886.

III.

The third form is the smooth and medium-long cucumbers, which, while they have a diversity of size, yet have a common shape and smoothness. Such are:

? Cucumer sativus. Pin. 192. 1561.
Concombre. Tourn. t. 32. 1719.
? Large Smooth Green Roman. Mawe, 1778; Mill. Dict. 1807.
Long Smooth Green Turkey. Mawe 1778; Mill. Dict. 1807.
Long Green Turkey. Thorb. Cat. 1828.
Turkey Long Green or *Long Green.* Landreth. 1885.
Greek, or *Athenian.* Vilm. 1885.

IV.

The fourth form includes those known as English, which are distinct in their excessive length, smoothness and freedom from seeds, although in a botanical classification they would be united with the preceding, from which, doubtless, they have originated. The synonymy for these would scarcely be justified had it not been observed that the tendency of the fruit is to curve under conditions of ordinary culture:

Cucumis longus. Cam. Epit. 295. 1586.
Cucumis longus eidem. Baugh. J. **2**:248. 1651.
Green Turkey Cucumber. Bryant 267. 1783.
Long Green English varieties. Vilm. 163. 1883.

V.

The Bonneuil Large White Cucumber, grown largely about Paris for the use of perfumes, is quite distinct from all other varieties, the fruit being ovoid, perceptibly flattened from end to end in three or four places, thus producing an angular appearance. We may suspect that Gerarde figured this type in his cucumber, which came from Spain into Germany, as his figure bears a striking resemblance in the form of the fruit and in the leaf:

Cucumis ex Hispanico semine natus. Ger. 764. 1597.
Cucumis sativus major. Bauh. Pin. 310. 1623. (excl. Fuch.)
Bonneuil Large White. Vilm. 222. 1885.
White Dutch. A. Blanc. No. 6133.

VI.

Another type of cucumbers is made up of those which have lately appeared under the name of Russian. Nothing is known of their history. They are very distinct and resemble a melon more than a cucumber, at least in external appearance:

1. *The Early Russian,* small, oval and smooth.
2. *The Russian Gherkin,* obovate and ribbed like a melon.
3. *The Russian Netted,* oval and densely covered with a fine net-work.

The appearance of new types indicates that we have by no means exhausted the possibilities of this species. The Turkie cucumber of Gerarde is not now to be recognized under culture; nor are the *Cucumer minor pyriformis* of Gerarde and of J. Bauhin and the *Cucumis pyriformis* of C. Bauhin, *Phytopinax,* 1596.

If the synonymy be closely examined, it will be noted that some of the figures represent cucumbers as highly improved as at the present day. The *Cucumis longus* of J. Bauhin is figured as if equalling our longest and best English forms; the *concombre* of Tournefort is also a highly improved form, as is also the *cucumeres* of Matthiolus, 1558.

Cucurbita maxima Duchesne. *Cucurbitaceae.* TURBAN SQUASH.

Nativity undetermined. The Turban squash is easily recognized by its form, to which it is indebted for its name. This is possibly the Chilean mamillary Indian gourd of Molina,[1] described as with spheroidal fruit with a large nipple at the end, the pulp sweet and tasting like the sweet potato. In 1856, Naudin [2] describes *le turban rouge* and *le turban nouveau du Brésil,* the latter of recent introduction from South America. Its description accords with the *Cucurbita clypeiformis tuberoso* and *verrucoso*, seen by J. Bauhin [3] in 1607. The Zapilliot, from Brazil, advertised by Gregory in 1880, and said by Vilmorin to have reached France from South America about 1860, resembles the Turban squash in shape. This evidence, such as it is, points to South America as the starting point of this form.

The squashes of our markets, par excellence, are the marrows and the Hubbard, with other varieties of the succulent-stemmed. These found representation in our seed catalog in 1828,[4] in the variety called Com. Porter's Valparaiso, which was brought from Chile shortly after the war of 1812. In the *New England Farmer*, September 11, 1824, notice is made of a kind of melon-squash or pumpkin from Chile, which is possibly the Valparaiso. The Hubbard squash is said by Gregory, its introducer in 1857, to be of unknown origin but to resemble a kind which was brought by a sea captain from the West Indies. The Marblehead, also introduced by Gregory and distributed in 1867, is said to have come directly from the West Indies. The Autumnal Marrow or Ohio, was introduced in 1832 and was exhibited at the rooms of the Massachusetts Horticultural Society.

The Turban squash does not appear in any of the figures or descriptions of the herbalists, except as hereinafter noted for Lobel.

C. moschata Duchesne. CANADA CROOKNECK. CUSHAW. WINTER CROOKNECK.

Nativity undetermined. The Winter Crookneck squash seems to have been first recorded by Ray,[5] who received the seeds from Sir Hans Sloane and planted them in his garden. This is the variety now known as the Striped. It has apparently been grown in New England from the earliest times and often attains a large size. Josselyn [6] refers to a cucurbit that may be this, the fruit " longish like a gourd," the very comparison made by Ray. Kalm [7] mentions a winter squash in New Jersey called " crooked neck," and Carver, 1776, speaks of " crane-necks " being preserved in the West for winter supply.

---

[1] Molina *Hist. Chili* 1:93. 1808.

[2] Naudin *Ann. Sci. Nat.* 4th ser.

[3] Bauhin, J. *Hist. Pl.* 2:227. 1651.

[4] Thorburn *Cat.* 1828.

[5] Ray *Hist. Pl.* 1:642. 1686.

[6] Josselyn, J. *New Eng. Rar.* 89. 1672.

[7] Kalm, P. *Trav. No. Amer.* 1:271. 1772.

A subvariety, the Puritan,[1] answers to Beverley's[2] description of a form which he calls *Cushaw*, an Indian name recognizable in the *Ecushaw* of Hariot, 1586. This form was grown at the New York Agricultural Experiment Station in 1884 from seed obtained from the Seminoles of Florida and appears synonymous with the Neapolitan, to which Vilmorin applies the French synonym, *courge de la Florida*.

C. pepo Linn.   GOURD.   PUMPKIN.   SQUASH.

THE SQUASH.

Nativity undetermined. The word "squash" seems to have been derived from the American aborigines and in particular from those tribes occupying the northeastern Atlantic coast. It seems to have been originally applied to the summer squash. Roger Williams[3] writes the word "askutasquash,"—"their vine apples,— which the English from them call squashes; about the bigness of apples, of several colors." Josselyn[4] gives another form to the word, writing, "squashes," "but more truly 'squoutersquashes,' a kind of mellon or rather gourd, for they sometimes degenerate into gourds. Some of these are green, some yellow, some longish, like a gourd; others round, like an apple; all of them pleasant food boyled and buttered, and seasoned with spice. But the yellow squash — called an apple squash (because like an apple), and about the bigness of a pome water — is the best kind." This apple squash, by name at least, as also by the description so far as applicable, is even now known to culture but is rarely grown on account of its small size.[5]

Van der Donck, after speaking of the pumpkins of New Netherlands, 1642–53, adds: "The natives have another species of this vegetable peculiar to themselves, called by our people *quaasiens*, a name derived from the aborignes, as the plant was not known to us before our intercourse with them. It is a delightful fruit, as well to the eye on account of its fine variety of colors, as to the mouth for its agreeable taste. . . . It is gathered in summer, and when it is planted in the middle of April, the fruit is fit for eating by the first of June. They do not wait for it to ripen before making use of the fruit, but only until it has attained a certain size. They gather the squashes, and immediately place them on the fire without any further trouble."[6] In 1683, Worlidge uses the word squash, saying: "There are lesser sorts of them (pompeons) that are lately brought into request that are called 'squashes,' the edible fruit whereof, boyled and serv'd up with powdered beef is esteemed a good sawce." Kalm,[7] in his *Travels*, says distinctly: "The squashes of the Indians, which now are cultivated by Europeans, belong to those kind of gourds which ripen before any other." These squashes of New England were apparently called "sitroules" by Champlain,[8] 1605, who describes them "as big as the fist." Lahon-

[1] Burr, F.   *Field, Gard. Veg.* 221.   1863.

[2] Beverley *Hist. Va.* 124.   1705.

[3] Williams, R.   *Key.* 1643.   Narragansett Ed. 1:125.   1866.

[4] Josselyn, J.   *New Eng. Rar.* 109.   1865.   Orig. 1672.

[5] Burr, F.   *Field, Gard. Veg.* 207.   1863.

[6] Gray, A.   *Amer. Journ. Sci.* 377.   1883.

[7] Kalm, P.   *Trav. No. Amer.* 1:110.   1772.

[8] Champlain *Voy.*   Prince Soc. Ed. 2:64, 75.   1878.

tan,[1] 1703, calls the squashes of southern Canada " citrouilles " and compares them with the melon, which indicates a round form.

These " squashes," now nearly abandoned in culture, would seem to be synonymous, in some of their varieties at least, with the Maycock of Virginia and the Virginian watermelon described in Gerarde's *Herball* [2] as early as 1621.

The Perfect Gem squash, introduced in 1881, seems to belong to this class and is very correctly figured by Tragus,[3] 1552, who says they are called *Mala indica*, or, in German, *Indianisch apffel*, and occur in four colors; saffron-yellow, creamy-white, orange, and black. He also gives the name *Sommer apffel*, which indicates an early squash, and the names *zucco de Syria* and *zucco de Peru*, which indicate a foreign origin. To identify this squash, with its claim of recent introduction, as synonymous with Tragus' *Cucumis, seu zucco marinus*, may seem unjustifiable. The Perfect Gem and Tragus plants have the following points in common: fruit of like form and size; so also the leaf, if the proportions between leaf and fruit as figured may be trusted; seed sweet in both; color alike, "*Quae candida foris* and *quae ex pallido lutea sunt poma*." The plants are runners in both. Compared also with the description of the Maycock, it appears to be the same in all but color. A curious instance of survival seems to be here noted, or else the regaining of a lost form through atavism. A careful comparison with the figures and the description given would seem to bring together as synonyms:

Cucumis marinus. Fuch. 699. 1542. Roeszl. 116. 1550.
Cucumis vel zucco marinus. Trag. 835. 1552,
Cucurbita indica rotunda. Dalechamp 1:116. 1587.
Pepo rotundis minor. Dod. 666. 1616.
Pepo minor rotundis. Bodaeus 783. 1644.
Cucurbitae folio aspero, sive zucchae. Icon. IV., Chabr. 130. 1673.
The Maycock. Ger. 919. 1633.
The Perfect Gem. 1881.

The distinctions between the various forms of cucurbits seem to have been kept in mind by the vernacular writers, who did not use the words pompion and gourd, as synonyms. Thus, in 1535, Cartier [4] mentions as found among the Indians of Hochelega, now Montreal, " pompions, gourds." In 1586, Hariot [5] mentions in Virginia " pompions, melons, and gourds;" Captain John Smith [6] " pumpions and macocks;" Strachey,[7] who was in Virginia in 1610, mentions " macocks and pumpions " as differing. " Pumpions and gourds " are named by Smith [8] for New England in 1614. In 1648, at the mouth of the Susquehanna, mention is made of " symnels and maycocks." [9]

---

[1] Lahontan, L.   *New Voy. Amer.* 2:61.   1735.
[2] Gerarde, J.   *Herb.* 919, 921.   1633.
[3] Tragus *Stirp.* 835.   1552.
[4] Pinkerton *Coll. Voy.* 12:656.   1812.
[5] Pinkerton *Coll. Voy.* 12:596.   1812.
[6] Pinkerton *Coll. Voy.* 13:33.   1812.
[7] Strachey *Trav. Va.*   Hakl. Soc. Ed. 72.   1849.
[8] Smith *Desc. New Eng.* 16.   1616.   Force Coll. Tracts 2:No. 1.   1838.
[9] *Desc. New Albion* 28.   1648.   Force Coll. Tracts 2:No. 7.   1838.

The word "squash," in its early use, we may conclude, applied to those varieties of cucurbits which furnish a summer vegetable and was carefully distinguished from the pumpkin. Kalm,[1] in the eighteenth century, distinguishes between pumpkins, gourds and squashes. The latter are the early sorts; the gourd includes the late sorts useful for winter supplies; and under the term pompion, or melon, the latter name and contemporary use gives the impression of roundness and size, are included sorts grown for stock. Jonathan Carver,[2] soon after Kalm, gives indication of the confusion now existing in the definition of what constitutes a pumpkin and a squash when he says " the melon or pumpkin, which by some are called squashes," and he names among other forms the same variety, the crookneck or craneneck, as he calls it, which Kalm classed among gourds.

At the present time, the word squash is used only in America, gourds, pumpkins, and marrows being the equivalent English names, and the American use of the word is so confusing that it can only be defined as applying to those varieties of cucurbits which are grown in gardens for table use; the word pumpkin applies to those varieties grown in fields for stock purposes; and the word gourd to those ornamental forms with a woody rind and bitter flesh, or to the Lagenaria.

The form of cucurbit now so generally known as Bush or Summer Squash is correctly figured in 1673 by Pancovius,[3] under the name of *Melopepo clypeatus* Tab. What may be the fruit, was figured by Lobel,[4] 1591; by Dodonaeus,[5] 1616; and similar fruit with the vine and leaf, by Dalechamp,[6] 1587; Gerarde,[7] 1597; Dodonaeus, 1616; and by J. Bauhin,[8] 1651. By Ray,[9] 1686, it is called in the vernacular " the Buckler," or " Simnel-Gourd." This word cymling or cymbling, used at the present day in the southern states for the Scalloped Bush Squash in particular, was used in 1648 in *A Description of New Albion* but spelled " Symnels." Jefferson [10] wrote the word " cymling." In 1675, Thomson, in a poem entitled *New England's Crisis*, uses the word " cimnel," and distinguishes it from the pumpkin. There is no clue as to the origin of the word, but it was very possibly of aboriginal origin, as its use has not been transferred to Europe. In England this squash is called Crown Gourd and Custard Marrow; in the United States generally, it is the Scalloped Squash, from its shape, though locally, Cymling or Patty-pan, the latter name derived from the resemblance to a crimped pan used in the kitchen for baking cakes. It was first noticed in Europe in the sixteenth century and has the following synonymy:

Cucurbita laciniata. Dalechamp 1:618. 1587.
Melopepo latior clypeiformis. Lob. *Icon.* 1:642. 1591.

---

[1] Kalm, P. *Trav. No. Amer.* 1:271, 272. 1772.
[2] Carver, J. *Trav. No. Amer.* 525. 1778.
[3] Pancovius *Herbarium* No. 920. 1673.
[4] Lobel *Icon.* 1:642. 1591.
[5] Dodonaeus *Pempt.* 667. 1616.
[6] Dalechamp *Hist. Gen. Pl.* (Lugd.) 1:618. 1587.
[7] Gerarde, J. *Herb.* 774. 1597.
[8] Bauhin, J. *Hist. Pl.* 2:224. 1651.
[9] Ray *Hist. Pl.* 1:648. 1686.
[10] Jefferson *Notes Va.* 1803.

Pepo maximum clypeatus. Ger. 774. 1597.

Pepo latus. Dod. 666. 1616.

Pepo latiorus fructus. Dod. 667. 1616.

Cucurbita clypeiformis sive Siciliana melopepon latus a nonnulis vocata. Bauh. J. 2:224. 1651. (First known to him in 1561.)

Melopepo clypeatus. Pancov. n. 920. 1653.

The Bucklet, or Simnel-Gourd. Ray *Hist.* **1**:648. 1686.

Summer Scolloped.

The Bush Crookneck is also called a squash. Notwithstanding its peculiar shape and usually warted condition, it does not seem to have received much mention by the early colonists and seems to have escaped the attention of the pre-Linnean botanists, who were so apt to figure new forms. The most we know is that the varietal name Summer Crookneck appeared in our garden catalogs in 1828,[1] and it is perhaps referred to by Champlain in 1605. It is now recommended in France rather as an ornamental plant than for kitchen use.[2]

The Pineapple squash, in its perfect form, is of a remarkably distinctive character on account of its acorn shape and regular projection. As grown, however, the fruit is quite variable and can be closely identified with the *Pepo indicus angulosus* of Gerarde[3] and is very well described by Ray,[4] 1686. This variety was introduced in 1884 by Landreth from seed which came originally from Chile. It is a winter squash, creamy white when harvested, of a deep yellow at a later period.

The Pumpkin.

The word " pumpkin " is derived from the Greek *pepon*, Latin *pepo*. In the ancient Greek, it was used by Galen as a compound to indicate ripe fruit as *sikuopepona*, ripe cucumber; as, also, by Theophrastus *peponeas* and Hippocrates *sikuon peponia*.[5] The word *pepo* was transferred in Latin to large fruit, for Pliny[6] says distinctly that *cucumeres*, when of excessive size, are called *pepones*. By the commentators, the word *pepo* is often applied to the melon. Fuchsius,[7] 1542, figures the melon under the Latin name *pepo*, German, *pfeben;* and Scaliger,[8] 1566, Dalechamp,[9] 1587, and Castor Durante,[10] 1617, apply this term *pepo* or *pepon* likewise to the melon. The derivatives from the word *pepo* appear in the various European languages as follows:

Belgian: *pepoenem*, Lob. *Obs.* 1576; *pompeon*, Marcg. 1648, Vilm. 1883.

English: *pepon*, Lyte 1586; *pompon*, Lyte 1586; *pompion*, Ger. 1597; *pumpion*, J. Smith 1606; *pumpkin*, Townsend 1726.

---

[1] Thorburn *Cat.* 1828.

[2] Vilmorin *Les Pls. Potag.* 184. 1883.

[3] Gerarde, J. *Herb.* 774. 1597.

[4] Ray *Hist. Pl.* **1**:641. 1686.

[5] Theophrastus *Hist. Pl.* Bodaeus Ed. 781. 1644.

[6] Grandsagne *Hist. Nat. Pline* 19, c. 23. 1829-33.

[7] Fuchsius *Hist. Stirp.* 701. 1542.

[8] Scaliger *Aristotle* 79, 110. 1566.

[9] Dalechamp *Hist. Gen. Pl.* (Lugd.) **1**:623. 1587.

[10] Durante, C. *Herb.* 1617.

French: *pompons*, Ruel. 1536; *pepon*, Dod. Gal. 1559.

Italian: *popone*, Don. 1834.

Swedish: *pumpa*, Tengborg 1764; *pompa*, Webst. *Dict.*

In English, the words " melon " and " million " were early applied to the pumpkin, as by Lyte 1586, Gerarde 1597 and 1633, and by a number of the early narrators of voy ages of discovery.   Pumpkins were called gourds by Lobel, 1586, and by Gerarde, 1597, and the word gourd is at present in use in England to embrace the whole class and is equivalent to the French *courge*.   In France, the word *courge* is given by Matthiolus, 1558, and Pinaeus, 1561, and seems to have been used as applicable to the pumpkin by early navigators, as by Cartier, 1535.   The word *courge* was also applicable to the lagenarias 1536, 1561, 1586, 1587, 1597, 1598, 1617, 1651, 1673 and 1772, and was shared with the pumpkin and squash in 1883.

Our earliest travelers and historians often recognized in the pumpkin a different fruit from the *courge*, the gourd, or the melon.   Cartier, on the St. Lawrence, 1584, dis criminates by using the words " *gros melons, concombres* and *courges* " [1] or in a translation " pompions, gourds, cucumbers." [2]   In 1586, a French name for what appears to be the summer squash is given by Lyte as *concombre marin*.   With this class, we may interpret Cartier's names into *gros melons*, pumpkins, *concombres*, summer squashes, and *courge*, winter crooknecks, as the shape and hard shell of this variety would suggest the gourd or lagenaria.   In 1586, Hariot, in Virginia,[3] says: " Macoks were, according to their several forms, called by us pompions, melons and gourds, because they are of the like forms as those kinds in England.   In Virginia, such of several forms are of one taste, and very good, and so also spring from one seed.   They are of two sorts: one is ripe in the space of a month, and the other in two months."   Hariot, apparently, confuses all the forms with the macock, which, as we have shown in our notes on squashes, appears identical with the type of the Perfect Gem squash, or the *Cucumis marinus* of Fuchsius. The larger sorts may be his pompions, the round ones his melons, and the cushaw type his gourds; for, as we shall observe, the use of the word pompion seems to include size, and that of gourd, a hard rind.   Acosta,[4] indeed, speaks of the Indian pompions in treating of the large-sized fruits.   Capt. John Smith,[5] in his *Virginia*, separates his pumpions and macocks, both planted by the Indians amongst their corn and in his description of New England, 1614, speaks of " pumpions and gourds."   This would seem to indicate that he had a distinction in mind, and we may infer that the word pompion was used for the like productions of the two localities and that the word gourd in New England referred to the hard-rind or winter squashes; for, Master Graves [6] refers to Indian pompions, Rev. Francis Higginson [7] to pompions, and Wood [8] to pompions and isquouter-squashes in

---

[1] Cartier *Bref. Recit.*   1545.   Reimpr. Tross.   1863.

[2] Pinkerton *Coll. Voy.* 12:656.   1812.

[3] Pinkerton *Coll. Voy.* 12:596.   1812.

[4] Acosta *Nat. Mor. Hist. Ind.* 264.   1604.

[5] Pinkerton *Coll. Voy.* 12:33.   1812.

[6] *Mass. Hist. Soc. Coll.* 1:118, 124.   1806.   Reprint of 1792.

[7] Ibid.

[8] Wood, W.   *New Eng. Prosp.* 15.   1865.

New England soon after its colonization. Josselyn,[1] about the same period, names also gourds, as quoted in our notes on the squash. Kalm,[2] about the middle of the eighteenth century, traveling in New Jersey, names " squashes of the Indians," which are a summer fruit, " gourds," meaning the winter crookneck, and " melons," which we may conclude are pumpkins; Jonathan Carver,[3] 1776, speaks of the melon or pumpkin, called by some squashes, and says the smaller sorts are for summer use, the crane-neck for winter use and names the Large Oblong. In 1822, Woods[4] speaks of pompons, or pumpions, in Illinois, as often weighing from 40 to 60 pounds.

The common field pumpkin of America is in New England carried back traditionally to the early settlement and occurs under several forms, which have received names that are usually quite local. Such form-varieties may be tabulated alphabetically, as below, from Burr:

Canada. Form oblate. 14 in. diam., 10 in. deep. Deep orange-yellow.
Cheese. Flattened. 16 in. diam., 10 in. deep. Deep reddish-orange.
Common Yellow. Rounded. 12 in. diam., 14 in. deep. Clear orange-yellow.
Long Yellow. Oval. 10 in. diam., 20 in. deep. Bright orange-yellow.
Nantucket. Various. 18 in. diam., 10 in. deep. Deep green.

I.
THE CANADA PUMPKIN.

The Canada pumpkin is of an oblate form inclining to conic, and is deeply and regularly ribbed and, when well grown, of comparatively large size. It is somewhat variable in size and shape, however, as usually seen. The following synonymy is justified:

Cucurbitae indianae and perefrinae. Pin. 191. 1561.
Cucurbita indica, rotunda. Dalechamp **1**:616. 1587.
Pepo rotundus compressus melonis effigie. Lob. *Obs.* 365. 1576; *Icon.* **1**:642. 1591.
(?) *Pepo indicum minor rotundus.* Ger. 774. 1597.
Pepo silvestris. Dod. 668. 1616.
Melopepo. Tourn. t. 34. 1719.
Canada Pumpkin. Vermont Pumpkin.

II.
CHEESE PUMPKIN.

The fruit is much flattened, deeply and rather regularly ribbed, broadly dishing about cavity and basin. It varies somewhat widely in the proportional breadth and diameter.

Melopepo compressus alter. Lob. *Icon.* **1**:643. 1591.
Pepo maximus compressus. Ger. 774. 1597.
Cucurbita genus, sive Melopepo compressus alter, Lobelio. Bauh. J. **2**:266. 1651.
Large Cheese. Fessenden 1828; Bridgeman 1832.
Cheese.

This variety, says Burr, was extensively disseminated in the United States at the time of the American Revolution and was introduced into New England by returning soldiers.

---

[1] Josselyn, J. *New Eng. Rar.* 109. 1865. Orig. 1672.
[2] Kalm, P. *Trav. No. Amer.* 1:271, 272. 1772.
[3] Carver, J. *Trav. No. Amer.* 211. 1776.
[4] Woods, J. *Ill. Country* 122. 1822.

III.
COMMON YELLOW FIELD.

The fruit is rounded, a little deeper than broad, flattened at the ends, and rather regularly and more or less prominently ribbed.

Cucurbita indica. Cam. *Epit.* 293.   1586.
Melopepo teres. Lob. *Icon.* **1**:643.   1591.
Pepo maximus rotundus. Ger. 773.   1597.
Cucurbita aspera Icon. I. Bauh. J. **2**:218.   1651.
Cucurbita folio aspero, zucha. Chabr. 130.   1673.
Common Yellow Field Pumpkin.

IV.
LONG YELLOW.

The fruit is oval, much elongated, the length nearly, or often twice, the diameter, of large size, somewhat ribbed, but with markings less distinct than those of the Common Yellow.

Cucumis Turcicus. Fuch. 698.   1542.
Melopepo. Roeszl. 116.   1550.
Pepo. Trag. 831.   1552.
Cucurbita indica longa. Dalechamp **1**:617.   1587.
Pepo maximus oblongus. Ger. 773.   1597.
Pepo major oblongus. Dod. 635.   1616; Bodaeus 782.   1644.
Cucurbita folio aspero, zucha. Chabr. 130.   1673.
Long Yellow Field Pumpkin.

The *Jurumu Lusitanus Bobora* of Marcgravius [1] and Piso [2] would seem to belong here except for the leaves, but the figure is a poor one.

These forms just mentioned, all have that something in their common appearance that at once expresses a close relationship and to the casual observer does not express differences.

We now pass to some other forms, also known as pumpkins, but to which the term squash is sometimes applied.

The Nantucket pumpkin occurs in various forms under this name, but the form referred to, specimens of which have been examined, belongs to *Cucurbita pepo* Cogn., and is of an oblong form, swollen in the middle and indistinctly ribbed. It is covered more or less completely with warty protuberances and is of a greenish-black color when ripe, becoming mellowed toward orange in spots by keeping. It seems closely allied to the *courge sucrière du Brésil* of Vilmorin. It is not the *Cucurbita verrucosa* of Dalechamp, 1587, nor of J. Bauhin, 1651, as in these figures the leaves are represented as entire and the fruit as melon-formed and ribbed.

In 1884, there appeared in our seedmen's catalogs, under the name of Tennessee Sweet Potato pumpkin, a variety very distinct, of medium size, pear-shape, little ribbed, creamy-white, striped with green, and the stem swollen and fleshy. Of its history nothing has been ascertained, but it bears a strong likeness in shape to a tracing of a piece of " pumpkin pottery " exhumed from the western mounds. In Lobel's history, 1576, and

---

[1] Piso *Hist. Rerum Nat. Bras.* 44.   1648.
[2] Piso *De Ind.* 264.   1658.

in his plates, 1591, appear figures of a plant which in both leaf and fruit represents fairly well our variety. These figures are of interest as being the only ones yet found in the ancient botanies which represent a fruit with a swollen, herbaceous stem. The following is the synonymy:

Pepo oblongus vulgatissimus. Lob. *Obs.* 365. 1576.
Pepo oblongus. Lobel *Icon.* 1:641. 1591.
Tennessee Sweet Potato Pumpkin.

Numerous series of pumpkins are listed in the catalogs of our seedsmen and some of a form quite distinct from those here noticed but not as yet sufficiently studied to be classified. However, much may yet be learned through the examination of complete sets of varieties within each of the three described species of cucurbita which furnish fruits for consumption. Notwithstanding the ready crossings which are so apt to occur within the ascribed species, there yet seems to exist a permanency of types which is simply marvellous, and which would seem to lend countenance to the belief that there is need of revision of the species and a closer study of the various groups or types which appear to have remained constant during centuries of cultivation.

If we consider the stability of types and the record of variations that appear in cultivated plants, and the additional fact that, so far as determined, the originals of cultivated types have their prototype in nature and are not the products of culture, it seems reasonable to suppose that the record of the appearance of types will throw light upon the country of their origin. From this standpoint, we may, hence, conclude that, as the present types have all been recorded in the Old World since the fifteenth century and were not recorded before the fourteenth, there must be a connection between the time of the discovery of America and the time of the appearance of pumpkins and squashes in Europe.

THE GOURD.

The word, gourd, is believed to be derived from the Latin *cucurbita*, but it takes on various forms in the various European languages. It is spelled " gowrde " by Turner, 1538; " gourde " by Lobel, 1576; and " gourd " by Lyte, 1586. In France, it is given as *courgen* and *cohurden* by Ruellius, 1536, but appears in its present form, *courge*, in Pinaeus, 1561. Dalechamp used *coucourde*, 1587, a name which now appears as *cougourde* in Vilmorin. The Belgian name appears as *cauwoord* in Lyte, 1586; and the Spanish name, *calabassa*, with a slight change of spelling, has remained constant from 1561 to 1864, as has the *zucca* of the Italians and the *kurbs* of the Germans.

The gourd belonging to *Lagenaria vulgaris* is but rarely cultivated in the United States except as an ornamental plant and as such shares a place with the small, hard-shelled cucurbita which are known as fancy gourds. In some localities, however, under the name of Sugar Trough gourd, a lagenaria is grown for the use of the shell of the fruit as a pail. What is worthy of note is the fact that this type of fruit does not appear in the drawings of the botanists of the early period, nor in the seed catalogs of Europe at the present time. In the *Tupi Dictionary* of Father Ruiz de Montaga,[1] 1639,

---

[1] Gray & Trumbull *Amer. Journ. Sci.* 372. 1883.

among the gourd names are " iacvi-gourd, like a great dish or bowl," which may mean this form. When we examine descriptions, this gourd may perhaps be recognized in Columella's account, "*Sive globosi corporis, atque utero minumum quae vasta tumescit*," [1] and used for storing pitch or honey; yet a reference to his prose description [2] rather contradicts the conjecture and leads us to believe that he describes only the necked form, and this form seems to have been known only to Palladius.[3] Pliny [4] describes two kinds, the one climbing, the other trailing. Walafridus Strabo,[5] in the ninth century, seems to describe the *plebeia* of Pliny as a cucurbita and the *cameraria* as a pepo. The former, apparently, was a necked form and the latter, one in which the neck has mostly disappeared leaving an oval fruit. Albertus Magnus,[6] in the thirteenth century, describes the cucurbita as bearing its seed "*in vase magno*," which implies the necked form. The following types are illustrated by the various herbalists:

TYPES OF GOURDS.

I.

Cucurbita oblonga.   Fuch. 370.   1542.
Cucurbita plebeia.   Roeszl. 115.   1550.
Cucurbita.   Trag. 824.   1552.
Curcubita longa.   Cardan. 222.   1556.
Cucurbita.   Matth. 261.   1558; Pinaeus 190.   1561; Cam. *Epit.* 292.   1586.
Cucurbita sive zuccha, omnium maxima anguina.   Lob. *Obs.* 366.   1576; *Icon.* **1**:644.
     1591.
Cucurbita cameraria longa.   Dalechamp **1**:615.   1587.
Cucurbita anguina.   Ger. 777.   1597.
Cucurbita oblonga.   Matth. 392.   1598.
Cucurbita longior.   Dod.   1616.
Zucca.   Dur., C.   488.   1617.
Cucurbita anguina longa.   Bodaeus 784.   1644.
Cucurbita longa, folio molli, flore albo.   Bauh., J. **2**:214.   1651; Chabr. 129.   1673.
Courge massue très longue.   Vilm. 190.   1883.
Club Gourd.

II.

————— Ruellius frontispiece 1536.
Cucurbita minor.   Fuch. 369.   1542.
Cucurbita.   Trag. 824.   1552; Matth. 261.   1558; Cam. *Epit.* 292.   1586.
Cucurbita marina.   Cardan. 222.   1556.
Cucurbita cameraria.   Dalechamp **1**:615.   1587.
Cucurbita lagenaria sylvestris.   Ger. 779.   1597.
Cucurbita prior.   Dod. 668.   1616.
Zucca.   Dur., C.   488.   1617.
Courge pélérine.   Vilm. 191.   1883.
Bottle Gourd.

---

[1] Columella lib. 10, c. 383.
[2] Columella lib. 11, c. 3.
[3] Palladius lib. 9, c. 9.
[4] Pliny lib. 19, c. 24.
[5] Macer Floridus *Vir. Herb.*   Sillig Ed. 146, 147.   1832.
[6] Albertus Magnus *Veg.* Jessen Ed. 500.   1867.

III.

Cucurbita calebasse.   Tourn. 7.36.   1719.
Courge siphon.   Vilm. 190.   1883.
Dipper Gourd.

IV.

Cucurbita major.   Fuch. 368.   1542.
Cucurbita cameraria.   Roeszl. 115.   1550.
Cucurbita.   Trag. 824.   1552; Matth. 261.   1558.
Cucurbita cameraria major.   Dalechamp 1:616.   1587.
Cucurbita lagenaria.   Ger. 777.   1597.
Cucurbita major sessilis.   Matth. 393.   1598.
Cucurbita lagenaria rotunda.   Bodaeus 784.   1644.
Cucurbita latior, folio molli, flore albo.   Bauh. J. 1:215.   1651; Chabr. 129.   1673.
Sugar Trough Gourd.

V.

Cucurbita.   Matth. 261.   1558; Dalechamp 1:615.   1587.
Courge plate de corse.   Vilm. 191.   1883.

This classification, it is to be remarked, is not intended for exact synonymy but to represent the like types of fruit-form. Within these classes there is a wide variation in size and proportion.

Whether the lagenaria gourds existed in the New World before the discovery by Columbus, as great an investigator as Gray[1] considers worthy of examination, and quoted Oviedo for the period about 1526 as noting the long and round or banded and all the other shapes they usually have in Spain, as being much used in the West Indies and the mainland for carrying water. He indicates that there are varieties of spontaneous growth as well as those under cultivation. The occurrence, however, of the so-called fancy gourds of *Cucurbita pepo*, of hard rind, of gourd shape, and often of gourd bitterness, render difficult the identification of species through the uses. The *Relation of the Voyage of Amerigo Vespucci*,[2] 1489, mentions the Indians of Trinidad and of the coast of Paris as carrying about their necks small, dried gourds filled with the plant they are accustomed to chew, or with a certain whitish flour; but this record could as well have been made from the *Cucurbita pepo* gourds as from the lagenaria gourds. The further mention that each woman carried a cucurbita containing water might seem to refer to gourds.

Acosta[3] speaks of the Indians of Peru making floats of gourds, for swimming, and says, " there are a thousand kinds of Calebasses; some are so deformed in their bigness that of the rind cut in the midst and cleansed, they make as it were, baskets to put in all their meat, for their dinner; of the lesser, they make vessels to eat and drink in." Bodaeus'[4] quotation in Latin, reads differently in a free translation: " They grow in the province of Chile to a wonderful size, and are called *capallas*. They are of an indefinite number of kinds; some are monstrous in their immense size, and when cut open and cleaned, furnish various vessels. Of the smaller they most ingeniously make cups and saucers." In

---

[1] Gray and Trumbull *Amer. Journ. Sci.* 370.   1883.
[2] Ibid.
[3] Acosta *Nat. Hist. Ind.* 177, 238.   1604.   Grimestone Ed.
[4] Theophrastus *Hist. Pl.* Bodaeus Ed. 784.   1644.

1624, Bodaeus received from the West Indies some seed which bore fruit "*Quae humanum crassitudinem et longitudinem superaret,*" which fully justifies Acosta's idea of size. The *Anonymous Portugal of Brasil*[1] says: " Some pompions so big that they can use them for vessels to carry water, and they hold two pecks or more." Baro,[2] 1647, also speaks of "*Courges et calebasses si grandes et profondes qu'elles servent comme de magazin,*" and Laet[3] mentions "*Pepones tam vastae, ut Indigenae iis utantur pro vasis quibus aquam aggerunt.*" These large-sized gourds were not, however, confined to America. Bodaeus, as we have noted, grew fruits deformed in their bigness, to use Acosta's term, from West Indian seed, and Cardanus[4] says he has seen gourds (he gives a figure which is a gourd) weighing 80 and 122 pounds. Bauhin[5] records the club gourd as sometimes three feet long; Ray,[6] as five or six feet long; and Forskal,[7] the bottle gourd as 18 inches in diameter. These records of size are all, however, of a date following the discovery of America, and the seed of these large varieties might have come from American sources, as is recorded in one case by Bodaeus.

The lagenaria gourd is of Old World origin, for water-flasks of the lagenaria have been found in Egyptian tombs of the twelfth dynasty, or 2200 or 2400 years B. C.,[8] and they are described by the ancient writers. That the gourd reached America at an early period, perhaps preceding the discovery,[9] we cannot doubt for Marcgravius notes a cucurbit with a white flower and of lagenarian form, in Brazil in 1648;[10] but there is not sufficient evidence to establish its appearance in America before brought by the colonists. What the " calabazas " were which served for water-vessels, and were apparently of considerable size, cannot at present be surmised. It is possible that there are varieties of *Cucurbita pepo* not yet introduced to notice that would answer the conditions. It is also less possible that gourd-shaped clay vessels might have been used and were recorded by not over-careful narrators as gourds. In 1595, Mendana, on his voyage to the Solomon Islands, said " Spanish pumpkins "[11] at the islands of Dominica and Santa Cruz, or according to another translation,[12] " pumpkins of Castile." It would seem by this reference that, whether the " calabaza " of the original Spanish referred to gourds or pumpkins, it did not take many years for this noticeable class of fruits to receive a wide distribution, and it might further imply that Mendana, setting forth from the western coast of America, discriminated between the American pumpkin, or pumpkin proper, and the Spanish pumpkin or gourd.

---

[1] Sloane, H. *Cat.* 100. 1696.

[2] Ibid.

[3] Ibid.

[4] Cardanus *De Rerum Var.* 222. 1586.

[5] Bauhin, C. *Pinax* 313. 1623.

[6] Ray *Hist. Pl.* 1:638. 1686.

[7] Forskal *Fl. Aeg.-Arab.* 167. 1775.

[8] Schweinfurth in *Nature* 314. 1883.

[9] Fruits of the lagenaria are at present carried to the coast of Iceland by ocean currents.

[10] Piso *Hist. Rerum Nat. Bras.* 44. 1648.

[11] Dalrymple *Coll. Voy.* 1:88. 1770.

[12] De Morga *Philippine Is.* Hakl. Soc. Ed. 68, 70. 1868.

Cudrania javanensis Tréc. *Urticaceae.*

Tropical Asia, Africa and Australia. The fruit is a compound, irregularly-shaped berry as large as a small custard apple, formed of the enlarged fleshy perianths and receptacle, each perianth enclosing a one-seeded nut.[1] The fruit is edible and of a pleasant taste.[2]

Cuminum cyminum Linn. *Umbelliferae.* CUMIN.

Mediterranean region. This is a small, annual plant indigenous to the upper regions of the Nile but was carried at an early period by cultivation to Arabia, India and China, as well as to the countries bordering on the Mediterranean.[3] It is referred to by the prophet Isaiah[4] and is mentioned in Matthew.[5] Pliny[6] calls it the best appetizer of all the condiments and says the Ethiopian and the African are of superior quality but that some prefer the Egyptian. During the Middle Ages, cumin was one of the species in most common use and is mentioned in Normandy in 716, in England between 1264 and 1400 and is enumerated in 1419 among the merchandise taxed in the city of London. It is mentioned in many of the herbals of the sixteenth and seventeenth centuries and is recorded as under cultivation in England in 1594.[7] In India, the seeds form an ingredient of curry powders and pickles[8] and in France find use in cookery.[9] In Holland, cheeses are sometimes flavored with cumin. The seed is occasionally advertised in American seed catalogs[10] but is probably very rarely grown.

Cupania americana Linn. *Sapindaceae.*

Mexico. The sweet, chestnut-like seeds are used in the West Indies as a food.[11] The seeds have the flavor of chestnut or sweet acorns and are used on the banks of the Orinoco to make a fermented liquor.[12]

Curculigo orchioides Gaertn. *Amaryllideae.*

Tropical Asia. In the Mariana Islands, the roots are eaten.[13]

Curcuma amada Roxb. *Scitamineae.* AMADA. GINGER. MANGO.

East Indies. The fresh root possesses the smell of a green mango and is used in India as a vegetable and condiment.[14]

---

[1] Brandis, D. *Forest Fl.* 425. 1876.

[2] Mueller, F. *Sel. Pls.* 137. 1891.

[3] Flückiger and Hanbury *Pharm.* 331. 1879. [7]

[4] Isaiah c. 28, 25–27.

[5] Matthew c. 23, 23.

[6] Pliny lib. 19, c. 47.

[7] Miller *Gard. Dict.* 1807.

[8] Dutt, U. C. *Mat. Med. Hindus* 173. 1877.

[9] Vilmorin *Les Pls. Potag.* 199. 1883.

[10] Vick *Cat.* 1884.

[11] Unger, F. *U. S. Pat. Off. Rpt.* 315. 1859. (*C. tomentosa*)

[12] Baillon, H. *Hist. Pls.* 5:387. 1878.

[13] Moore, T. *Treas. Bot.* 1:363. 1870. (*C. stans*)

[14] Dutt, U. C. *Mat. Med. Hindus* 257. 1877.

C. angustifolia Roxb. ARROWROOT.

Himalayan region. The root had long been an article of food amongst the natives of India before it was particularly noticed by Europeans.[1] It furnishes an arrowroot of a yellow tinge which does not thicken in boiling water.[2] This East Indian arrowroot is exported from Travancore.[3] It forms a good substitute for the West Indian arrowroot and is sold in the bazaars.[4]

C. leucorhiza Roxb.

East Indies. The tubers yield a starch which forms an excellent arrowroot that is sold in the bazaars.[5]

C. longa Linn. TURMERIC.

Tropical Asia. This plant is extensively cultivated in India for its tubers which are an essential ingredient of native curry powders, according to Dutt.[6] The substance called turmeric is made from the old tubers of this and perhaps other species. The young, colorless tubers furnish a sort of arrowroot.[7]

C. rubescens Roxb.

East Indies. This plant furnishes an excellent arrowroot from its tubers, which is eaten by the natives and sold in the bazaars.[8]

C. zedoaria Rosc. ZEDOARY.

Himalayas. This plant yields a product used as turmeric.

Cyamopsis psoraloides DC. *Leguminosae.*

East Indies. This species is cultivated about Bombay for the sake of the pods which are eaten like French beans,[9] and is grown also by the natives of Burma who esteem it a good vegetable.[10] Wight [11] says " the young beans are with reason much prized by the natives as a culinary pulse and merit more attention from Europeans, as they are a pleasant and delicate vegetable."

Cyanella capensis Linn. *Haemodoraceae.*

South Africa. A kind of onion is obtained from this plant and roasted for the table by the farmers of Kaffraria.[12]

Cyathea dealbata Swartz. *Cyatheaceae.* SILVERY TREE-FERN.

The pith of this tree-fern is said to be eaten in New Zealand.[13]

---

[1] Ainslie, W. *Mat. Ind.* 1:19. 1826.

[2] Firminger, T. A. C. *Gard. Ind.* 114. 1874.

[3] Pickering, C. *Chron. Hist. Pls.* 579. 1879.

[4] Royle, J. F. *Illustr. Bot. Himal.* 1:359. 1839.

[5] Ibid.

[6] Dutt, U. C. *Mat. Med. Hindus* 255. 1877.

[7] Masters, M. T. *Treas. Bot.* 1:363. 1870.

[8] Royle, J. F. *Illustr. Bot. Himal.* 359. 1839.

[9] Pickering, C. *Chron. Hist. Pls.* 332. 1879.

[10] Ibid.

[11] Wight *Illustr. Ind. Bot.* 1:191. 1840.

[12] Thunberg, C. D. *Trav.* 2:14. 1796.

[13] Moore, T. *Treas. Bot.* 1:366. 1870.

C. medullaris Swartz. BLACK-STEMMED TREE-FERN.

The pith of this plant, a coarse sago, is eaten in times of scarcity in New Zealand. In the *Voyage of the Novara* it is said that the whole stalk, often 20 feet high, is edible and is sufficient to maintain a considerable number of persons. The pith, when cooked and dried in the sun, is an excellent substitute for sago. It is also to be found in Queensland and the Pacific isles.[1]

Cycas circinalis Linn. *Cycadaceae.* SAGO PALM.

Tropical eastern Asia and the Malayan Archipelago. Captain Cook speaks of the inhabitants of Prince Island eating the nuts, which poisoned his hogs and made some of the crew sick. He adds, however, that they are sliced and dried and after steeping in fresh water for three minutes and dried a second time they are eaten in times of scarcity as a food, mixed with rice. In Malabar, Drury says a kind of sago prepared from the nuts is much used by the poorer classes. Pickering[2] says on the Comoro Islands it is a common esculent; Blanco[3] says on the Philippines its fruit is sometimes eaten; Rumphius[4] says it is eaten on the Moluccas; J. Smith[5] says a kind of sago is obtained from the stem.

C. revoluta Thunb.

Subtropical Japan. Thunberg[6] says a small morsel of the pith of the stem is sufficient to sustain life a long time and on that account the plant is jealously preserved for the use of the Japanese army. The drupes are also eaten. J. Smith[7] says it occurs also in China and New Guinea.

Cyclopia genistoides Vent. *Leguminosae.* BUSH TEA.
South Africa. An infusion of its leaves is used as a tea.[8]

C. subternata Vog.
South Africa. This is also a tea substitute, according to Church.[9]

Cymbidium canaliculatum R. Br. *Orchideae.*
Australia. The tubers of this plant are used by the blacks of Wide Bay.[10]

Cymopterus fendleri A. Gray. *Umbelliferae.*
Texas and New Mexico. This plant emits, when in decoction, a peculiarly strong and pleasant odor. It is sometimes used as a stuffing for mutton.[11]

---

[1] Smith, J. *Dom. Bot.* 171. 1882.
[2] Pickering, C. *Chron. Hist. Pls.* 304. 1879.
[3] Ibid.
[4] Ibid.
[5] Smith, J. *Dom. Bot.* 146. 1882.
[6] Thunberg, C. P. *Fl. Jap.* 229. 1784.
[7] Smith, J. *Dict. Econ. Pls.* 146. 1882.
[8] Church *Gard. Chron.* **20**:766. 1883.
[9] Ibid. (*C. vogelii*)
[10] Palmer, E. *Journ. Roy. Soc. New So. Wales* **17**:97. 1884.
[11] Rothrock, J. T. *U. S. Geog. Surv. Bot.* **6**:45. 1878.

C. glomeratus DC.

Western states of North America.   The root is edible.[1]

C. montanus Torr. & Gray.   GAMOTE.

Western North America.   This plant is called by the Mexicans gamote or camote.[2] The root is spindle-shaped, parsnip-like but much softer, sweeter and more tender than the parsnip.   This root is collected largely by the Mexicans and also by the Ute and Piute Indians.[3]

Cynara cardunculus Linn.   *Compositae.*   ARTICHOKE.   CARDOON.

CARDOON.

Mediterranean region and common in its wild form in southern Europe and a portion of central Asia.   Cardoon was known, according to Targioni-Tozzetti,[4] to the ancient Romans and was cultivated for the leaf-stalks which were eaten.   Some commentators say that both the Greeks and Romans procured this vegetable from the coast of Africa, about Carthage, and also from Sicily.   Dioscorides mentions it.   Pliny [5] says it was much esteemed in Rome and obtained a higher price than any other garden herb.   In more recent times, Ruellius,[6] 1536, speaks of the use of the herb as a food, after the manner of asparagus.   Matthiolus,[7] 1558, says there are many varieties in the gardens which are commonly called *cardoni* by the Etruscans, and that, diligently cultivated, these are tender, crisp, and white and are eaten with salt and pepper.   The plant is mentioned by Parkinson, 1629, under the name of *Cardus esculentus* but its introduction into England is stated to have been in 1656 or 1658.

Cardoon is now cultivated in but few English gardens.   On the continent of Europe, it is regarded as a wholesome esculent and in France is much used, the stalks of the inner leaves, rendered crisp and tender by blanching, serving as a salad.   Five varieties are esteemed there.   Townsend,[8] in his tour through Spain mentions that in some parts of that country they never use rennet for cheese but substitute the down of this plant from which they make an infusion.   In the present day, the flowers of cardoon are carefully dried and used for the same purpose.   McMahon [9] includes it in his list of American esculents in 1806 and says " it has been a long time used for culinary purposes, such as for salads, soups and stewing."   Thorburn [10] includes it in his seed catalogs of 1828 and 1882.   In the Banda Oriental, says Darwin,[11] very many, probably several hundred, square miles are covered by one mass of these prickly plants and are impenetrable by man or beast.   Over the undulating plains where these great beds occur, nothing else can now live.

---

[1] Mueller, F.   *Sel. Pls.* 91.   1880.

[2] Torrey *Pacific R. R. Rpt.* 4:92.   1856.

[3] Bigelow, J. M.   *Pacific R. R. Rpt.* 4:9.   1856.

[4] Targioni-Tozzetti *Journ. Hort. Soc. Lond.* 142.   1854.

[5] Pliny lib. 19, c. 43.

[6] Ruellius *Nat. Stirp.* 643.   1536.

[7] Matthiolus *Comment.* 322.   1558.

[8] Glasspoole, H. G.   *Ohio State Bd. Agr. Rpt.* 536.   1875.

[9] McMahon, B.   *Amer. Gard. Cal.* 581.   1806.

[10] Thorburn *Cat.* 1828.   1882.

[11] Darwin, C.   *Voy. H. M. S. Beagle* 119.   1845.

Vilmorin [1] describes five varieties: the *Cardon de Tours*, the *Cardon plein inerme*, the *Cardon d'Espagne*, the *Cardon Puvis*, and the *Cardon à côtes rouges*.

The first of these, the *Cardon de Tours*, is very spiny and we may reasonably believe it to be the sort figured by Matthiolus,[2] 1598, under the name of *Carduus aculeatus*. It is named in French works on gardening in 1824, 1826 and 1829.[3] Its English name is Prickly-Solid cardoon; in Spain it is called *Cardo espinoso*. It holds first place in the estimation of the market gardeners of Tours and Paris.

The *Cardon plein inerme* is scarcely spiny, is a little larger than the preceding but otherwise closely resembles it. J. Bauhin [4] had never seen spineless cardoons. It is spoken of in 1824 in French books on gardening. It is called, in England, Smooth-Solid cardoon and has also names in Germany, Italy and Spain.

The *Cardon d'Espagne* is very large and not spiny and is principally grown in the southern portions of Europe. We may resonably speculate that this is the sort named by Pliny as coming from Cordoba. *Cardons d'Espagne* have their cultivation described in *Le Jardinier Solitaire*, 1612. A " Spanish cardoon " is described by Townsend [5] in England, 1726, and the same name is used by McMahon [6] in America, 1806. This is the *Cynara integrifolia* of Vahl.

The *Cardon Puvis*, or Artichoke-leaved, is spineless and is grown largely in the vicinity of Lyons, France. It finds mention in the French books on gardening of 1824 and 1829, as previously enumerated.

The *Cardon à côtes rouges*, or Red-stemmed, is so named from having the ribs tinged with red. It is called a recent sort by Burr in 1863.

From a botanical point of view we have two types in these plants, the armed and the unarmed; but these characters are by no means to be considered as very constant, as in the Smooth-Solid we have an intermediate form. From an olericultural point of view, we have but one type throughout but a greater or less perfection. A better acquaintance with the wild forms would, doubtless, show to us the prototypes of the variety differences as existing in nature.

ARTICHOKE.

The artichoke is a cultivated form of cardoon. To the ancient Romans, it was known only in the shape of cardoon. It seems quite certain that there is no description in Dioscorides and Theophrastus, among the Greeks, nor in Columella, Palladius and Pliny, among the Romans, but that can with better grace be referred to the cardoon than to the artichoke. To the writers of the sixteenth century, the artichoke and its uses were well known. *Le Jardinier Solitaire*, an anonymous work published in 1612, recommends three varieties for the garden. In Italy, the first record of the artichoke cultivated for the receptacle of the flowers was at Naples, in the beginning or middle of the fifteenth

---

[1] Vilmorin, *Les Pls. Potag.* 59, 60. 1883.

[2] Matthiolus *Opera* 496. 1598.

[3] Pirolle *L'Hort. Franc.* 1824.

[4] Bauhin, J. *Hist. Pl.* 50. 1651.

[5] Townsend *Seedsman* 29. 1726.

[6] McMahon, B. *Amer. Gard. Cal.* 581. 1806.

century. It was thence carried to Florence in 1466 and at Venice, Ermolao Barbaro who died as late as 1493, knew of only a single plant grown as a novelty in a private garden, although it soon after became a staple article of food over a great part of the peninsula. In France, three varieties are commonly grown. It seems to have been unknown in England, says Booth,[1] until introduced from Italy in 1548 and is even now but little grown there, yet in France it is highly esteemed. In the United States, in 1806, McMahon[2] mentions two species, *C. scolymus*, or French, and *C. hortensis*, or Globe. Of the second, he mentions two varieties. In 1818, the artichoke is mentioned by Gardiner and Hepburn and also by John Randolph[3] of Virginia; in 1828, by Fessenden;[4] and in 1832 by Bridgeman,[5] who names two kinds. In 1828, Thorburn[6] offers in his catalog the seeds of the Green Globe and in 1882 of the French Green Globe and the Large Paris. The parts used are the lower parts of the leaves or scales of the calyx and the fleshy receptacles of the flowers freed from the bristles and seed down. In France, where it is much esteemed, the tender, central leaf-stalk is blanched and eaten like cardoons.

The most prominent distinction between varieties as grown in the garden, is the presence or absence of spines. Although J. Bauhin,[7] 1651, says that seed from the same plant may produce both sorts, probably this comes from cross-fertilization between the kinds, and the absence or presence of spines is a true distinction. Pragus describes both forms in 1552, as do the majority of succeeding writers.

A second division is made from the form of the heads, the conical-headed and the globe.

I.

Conical-headed.

Of the varieties sufficiently described by Vilmorin, four belong to this class and they are all spiny. This form seems to constitute the French artichoke of English writers. The following synonymy seems justifiable:

Scolymus. Trag. 866. 1552. *cum ic.*
Carduus, vulgo Carciofi. I. Matth. 322. 1558.
Carduus aculeatus. Cam. *Epit.* 438. 1586. *cum ic;* Matth. ed. of 1598. 496. *cum ic.*
Thistle, or Prickly Artichoke. Lyte's *Dod.* 603. 1586.
Cinara sylvestris. Ger. 291. 1597. fig.
Carduus sive Scolymus sativus, spinosos. Bauh. J. 3:48. 1651. *cum ic.*
Artichokes, Violet. Quintyne 187; 1693; 178. 1704.
Conical-headed Green French. Mawe 1778.
French Artichoke. *Mill. Dict.* 1807; Amer. Gard. Books 1806, 1819, 1828, 1832, etc.
Vert de Provence. Vilm. 16. 1883.
De Roscoff. Vilm. 1. c.
De Saint Laud oblong. Vilm. 1. c.
Sucre de Gênes. Vilm. 1. c.

---

[1] Booth, W. B. *Treas. Bot.* 1:372. 1870.
[2] McMahon, B. *Amer. Gard. Cal.* 196. 1806.
[3] Randolph, J. *Treat. Gard.* 1818.
[4] Fessenden *New Amer. Gard.* 18. 1828.
[5] Bridgeman *Young Gard. Asst.* 31. 1857.
[6] Thorburn *Cat.* 1828.
[7] Bauhin, J. *Hist. Pl.* 3:48. 1651.

II.

GLOBULAR-HEADED.

To this form belong two of Vilmorin's varieties and various other varieties as described by other writers. The synonymy which seems to apply is:

Scolymus. Fuch. 792. 1542. *cum ic.*
Cardui alterum genus. Trag. 866. 1552.
Carduus, vulgo Carciofi. II. Matth. 322. 1558.
Carduus non aculeatus. Cam. *Epit.* 437. 1586. *cum ic.*; Matth. 497. 1598. *cum ic.*
Right artichoke. Lyte's *Dod.* 603. 1586.
Cinara maxima ex Anglia delata. Lob. *Icon.* **2**: 3. 1591.
Cinara maxima alba. Ger. 991. 1597. fig.
Cinara maxima anglica. Ger. 1. c.
Green or White. Quintyne 187. 1593; 178. 1704.
Red. Quintyne 1. c.
Globular-headed Red Dutch. Mawe 1778.
Globe Artichoke. Mill. *Dict.* 1807; Amer. Gard. Books 1806, 1819, 1828, etc.
Gros vert de Laon. Vilm. 1883.
Violet de Provence. Vilm. 1. c.

The color of the heads also found mention in the early writers. In the first division, the green is mentioned by Tragus, 1552; by Mawe, 1778; and by *Miller's Dictionary*, 1807; the purple by Quintyne, 1693. In the Globe class, the white is named by Gerarde, 1597; and by Quintyne, 1693; and the red by Gerarde, 1597; by Quintyne, 1693; and by Mawe, 1778; and Parkinson, 1629, named the red and the white.

The so-called wild plants of the herbalists seem to offer like variations to those we have noted in the cultivated forms, but the difficulty of identification renders it inexpedient to state a fixed conclusion. The heads are certainly no larger now than they were 250 years ago, for the *Hortus Eystettensis* figures one 15 inches in diameter. The long period during which the larger part of the present varieties have been known seems to justify the belief that modern origination has not been frequent. *Le Jardinier Solitaire*, 1612, describes early varieties, *le blanc, le rouge* and *le violet.* Worlidge, 1683, says there are several kinds, and he names the tender and the hardy sort. McMahon names the French and two varieties of the Globe in America in 1806. In 1824, in France, there were the *blanc, rouge, violet* and the *gros vert de Laon.* Petit 1826, adds *sucre de gênes* to the list. Noisette, 1829, adds the *camus de Brittany.*

The name given by Ruellius[1] to the artichoke in France, 1536, is *articols*, from the Italian *articoclos.* He says it comes from *arcocum* of the Ligurians, *cocali* signifying the cone of the pine. The Romans call it *carchiophos.* The plant and the name came to France from Italy.

C. integrifolia Vahl. SPANISH CARDOON.

Spain. The plants are of large size, the midribs being very succulent and solid.[2]

Cynoglossum sp.? *Boragineae.* HOUND'S TONGUE.

Himalayas. Hooker[3] says one species is used as a potherb.

---

[1] Ruellius *Nat. Stirp.* 644. 1536.
[2] McIntosh, C. *Book Gard.* **2**:130. 1855.
[3] Hooker, J. D. *Himal. Journ.* **2**:68. 1854.

Cynometra cauliflora Linn. *Leguminosae.* NAM-NAM.

East Indies and Malays. The fruit in shape resembles a kidney. It is about three inches long and the outside is very rough. It is seldom eaten raw but, fried with batter, it makes a good fritter. Wight [1] says the fruit is much esteemed in the Eastern Islands.

Cyperus bulbosus Vahl. *Cyperaceae.*

Africa and East Indies. Drury [2] says the roots are used as flour in times of scarcity in India and are eaten roasted or boiled, tasting like potatoes. Royle [3] says they are palatable.

C. esculentus Linn. CHUFA. EARTH ALMOND. ZULU NUTS.

South Europe and north Africa; introduced in America and now runs wild on the banks of the Delaware and other rivers from Pennsylvania to Carolina. The roots are very sweet and are eaten by children. [4] The chufa was distributed from the United States Patent Office in 1854 and has received a spasmodic culture in gardens. It is much cultivated in southern Europe, Asia and Africa, becoming of importance at Valence, in Galicia, and in the environs of Rosetta and Damietta, Egypt. [5] In Hungary, it is grown for the seeds, to be used as a coffee substitute, [6] but in general for its tubers which are sweet, nutty and palatable. These bulbs, says Bryant, [7] are greatly esteemed in Italy and some parts of Germany and are frequently brought to table by way of dessert. At Constantinople, the tubers appear in the markets and are eaten raw or made into a conserve. [8] Gerarde, 1633, speaks of their extensive use in Italy, and of their being hawked about the streets and, at Verona, eaten as dainties. [9] They now appear in the English markets under the name of Zulu nuts. [10] The chufa must also have been esteemed in ancient times, for tubers have been found in Egyptian tombs of the twelfth dynasty, or from 2200 to 2400 years before Christ. [11] Notwithstanding the long continued culture of this plant, there are no varieties described.

C. papyrus Linn. PAPYRUS.

Sicily, Syria and tropical Africa. This plant is the ancient papyrus. Hogg [12] says it was used as food by the ancients, who chewed it either raw, boiled or roasted, for the sake of its sweet juice.

C. rotundus Linn. NUT GRASS.

Cosmopolitan. The tubers are eaten by the North American Indians. [13]

---

[1] Wight, R. *Illustr. Ind. Bot.* **1**:196. 1840.

[2] Drury, H. *Useful Pls. Ind.* 173. 1873.

[3] Royle, J. F. *Illustr. Bot. Himal.* **1**:414. 1839.

[4] Pursh, F. *Fl. Amer. Septent.* **1**:52. 1814.

[5] Heuze *Pls. Alim.* **2**:551. 1873.

[6] Loudon, J. C. *Enc. Agr.* 98. 1866.

[7] Bryant *Fl. Diet.* 29. 1783.

[8] Walsh, R. *Trans. Hort. Soc. Lond.* **6**:50. 1826.

[9] Gerarde, J. *Herb.* 32. 1633.

[10] *Gard. Chron.* **17**:838. 1882.

[11] Schweinfurth in *Nature* 314. 1883.

[12] Drury, H. *Useful Pls. Ind.* 173. 1873.

[13] Havard, V. *Torr. Bot. Club Bul.* **22**:115. 1895.

Cyphia sp.? *Campanulaceae.*

South Africa. The Hottentots are said to eat the tuberous roots of at least one species of these herbaceous, twining plants.[1]

C. digitata Wild.

South Africa. The roots are bulbous, esculent, and fleshy.[2]

Cyphomandra hartwegi Sendt. *Solanaceae.*

New Granda. The berry is reddish, about the size of a pigeon's egg and is two-celled. It appears to be the fruit sold in the markets of Lima, where it is commonly used for cooking in lieu of the ordinary tomato, the flavor of which it resembles. Tweddie says it is used in Buenos Aires.[3]

Cytisus scoparius Link. *Leguminosae,* BROOM. SCOTCH BROOM.

Middle Europe. Before the introduction of hops, says Johnson,[4] broom tops were often used to communicate a slightly bitter flavor to beer. The young flower-buds are occasionally pickled and used as a substitute for capers. The seeds, when roasted, are used as a coffee substitute in France.

Dacrydium cupressinum Soland. *Coniferae.* IMOU PINE. RED PINE. RIMU.

A lofty tree of New Zealand. The fleshy cup of the nut is eatable, and a beverage like spruce-beer is made from its young shoots.[5]

Dahlia variabilis Desf. *Compositae.* DAHLIA.

Mexico. The dahlia was first introduced into Spain in 1787, and three specimens reached Paris in 1802.[6] Its petals may be used in salads. It was first cultivated for its tubers but these were found to be uneatable.

Daphne oleoides Schreb. *Thymelaeaceae.* DAPHNE.

Europe and Asia Minor. The berries are eaten but are said to cause nausea and vomiting. On the Sutlej a spirit is distilled from them.[7]

Dasylirion texanum Scheele. *Liliaceae.*

Texas. The bases of the leaves and the young stems are full of nutritious pulp which supplies, when cooked, a useful and palatable food.[8]

Datura metel Linn. *Solanaceae.* DOWNY THORNAPPLE.

American tropics. This species grows abundantly along the Colorado River in Arizona. The Mohaves gather the leaves and roots, bruise and mix them with water and then let the mixture stand several hours after which the liquid is drawn off. The

[1] *Treas. Bot.* 1:374. 1870.

[2] Don, G. *Hist. Dichl. Pls.* 3:718. 1834.

[3] Miers, J. *Illustr. So. Amer. Pls.* 1:39. 1840.

[4] Johnson, C. P. *Useful Pls. Gt. Brit.* 70. 1862.

[5] Smith, J. *Dom. Bot.* 353. 1888.

[6] Bushman *Journ. Agr.* 2:30. 1831.

[7] Brandis, D. *Forest Fl.* 384. 1876.

[8] Havard, V. *Proc. U. S. Nat. Mus.* 517. 1885.

product is a highly narcotic drink producing a stupefying effect which it is not easy to remove. The Mohaves will often drink this nauseating liquid, as they are fond of any kind of intoxication.[1]

D. sanguinea Ruiz & Pav.

South America. The Peruvians prepare an intoxicating beverage from the seeds, which induces stupefaction and furious delirium if partaken of in large quantities.[2] The Arabs of central Africa are said by Burton [3] to dry the leaves, the flowers and the rind of the rootlets, the latter being considered the strongest preparation, and smoke them in a common bowl or in a waterpipe. It is esteemed by them a sovereign remedy for asthma and influenza.

Daucus carota Linn. *Umbelliferae.* CARROT.

Europe and the adjoining portions of Asia and introduced in North and South America, China and Cochin China. The root, says Don,[4] is slender, aromatic and sweetish. The roots are employed in the Hebrides as an article of food, being eaten raw, and are collected by the young women for distribution as dainties among their acquaintances on Sundays and at their dances. This wild plant is the original of the cultivated carrot, for, by cultivation and selection, Vilmorin-Andrieux obtained in the space of three years roots as fleshy and as large as those of the garden carrot from the thin, wiry roots of the wild species. Carrots are now cultivated throughout Europe and in Paris are a most popular vegetable. In some regions, sugar has been made from them but its manufacture was not found profitable. In Germany, a substitute for coffee has been made of carrots chopped up into small pieces and browned.[5] In Sweden, carrots grow as high as latitude 66° to 67° north. In Asia, the carrots of the Mahratta and Mysore countries are considered to be of especially fine quality.

The carrot and the parsnip, if known to them, seem to have been confounded in the description by the ancients, and we find little evidence that the cultivated carrot was known to the Greek writers, to whom the wild carrot was certainly known.[6] The ancient writers usually gave prominence to the medical efficacy of herbs; and if our supposition is correct that their carrots were of the wild form, we have evidence of the existence of the yellow and red roots in nature, the prototypes of these colors now found in our cultivated varieties. Pliny [7] says: " They cultivate a plant in Syria like *staphylinos*, the wild carrot, which some call *gingidium*, yet more slender and more bitter, and of the same properties, which is eaten cooked or raw, and is of great service as a stomachic; also a fourth kind, resembling a pastinac asomewhat, called by us *Gallicam*, but by the Greeks *daucon*." This comparison with a parsnip and also the name is suggestive of the cultivated carrot. Galen, a Greek physician of the second century, implies cultivation of the carrot when he

---

[1] *U. S. D. A. Rpt.* 423.   1870.

[2] Masters, M. T.   *Treas. Bot.* 1:386.   1870.

[3] Ibid.

[4] Don, G.   *Hist. Dichl. Pls.* 3:354.   1834.

[5] Johnson, C. P.   *Useful Pls. Gt. Brit.* 120.   1862.

[6] Theophrastus *Hist. Pl.* Bodaeus Ed. 1119, 1122.   1644.

[7] Pliny lib. 20, c. 16; lib. 19, c. 27.

says the root of the wild carrot is less fit to be eaten than that of the domestic.[1] In the thirteenth century, however, Albertus Magnus treats of the plants under field culture, garden culture, orchard culture and vineyard culture, and yet, while naming the parsnip, makes no mention of the carrot — if the word *pastinaca* really means the parsnip. One may believe, however, that the *pastinaca* of Albertus Magnus is the carrot for, in the sixteenth century, Ammonius[2] gives the name for the carrot *pastenei*, as applying to *Pastinaca sativa* and *agrestis*. Barbarus, who died in 1493, and Virgil[3] both describe the carrot under the name pastinaca; and Apicius,[4] a writer on cookery in the third century, gives directions for preparing the *Carota seu pastinaca*, which can apply only to the carrot. Dioscorides[5] uses the word *carota* as applying to *Pastinaca silvestris* in the first century. Columella[6] and Palladius[7] both mention the *pastinaca* as a garden plant but say nothing that cannot better apply to the carrot than to the parsnip. Macer Floridus[8, 9] also treats of what may be the carrot under *pastinaca* and says no roots afford better food.

Hence, we believe that the carrot was cultivated by the ancients but was not a very general food-plant and did not attain the modern appreciation; that the word *pastinaca*, or *cariotam*, or *carota*, in those times was applied to both the cultivated and the wild form; and we suspect that the word *Gallicam*, used by Pliny in the first century, indicates that the cultivated root reached Italy from France, where now it is in such exaggerated esteem.

The *siasron* of Dioscorides and the *siser* of Columella and Pliny may have been a form of the carrot but we can attain no certainty from the descriptions. The fact that the grouping of the roots which occurs in the skirret, into which authors translate *siser*, is not mentioned by the ancients — a distinction almost too important to be overlooked — and that the short carrot was called *siser* by botanists of the sixteenth century, are arguments in favor of *siser* being a carrot. On the other hand, we should scarcely expect a distinction being made between *pastinaca* and *siser*, were both as similar in the plant as are the two forms of carrot at present.

The carrot is now found under cultivation and as an escape throughout a large portion of the world. In China, it is noticed in the Yuan dynasty, as brought from western Asia, 1280–1368,[10] and is classed as a kitchen vegetable in the sixteenth, seventeenth and eighteenth centuries by various Chinese authors.[11, 12] In India, the carrot is said to have come first from Persia and is now cultivated in abundance in the Mahratta and Mysore countries.[13] The carrot is enumerated among the edible plants of Japan by

[1] Matthiolus *Opera* 570. 1598.

[2] Ammonius *Med. Herb.* 186. 1539.

[3] Dioscorides Ruellius Ed. 174. 1529.

[4] Apicius lib. 3, c. 21.

[5] Dioscorides Ruelius Ed. 174. 1529.

[6] Columella lib. 11, c. 3.

[7] Palladius c. 24.

[8] Macer Floridus *Vir. Herb.* L. 1284, Sillig Ed. 1832.

[9] Macer Floridus *Herb. Virt.* Pictorius Ed. 95. 1581.

[10] Bretschneider, E. *On Study* 17. 1870.

[11] Bretschneider, E. *Bot. Sin.* 59, 83, 85. 1882.

[12] Smith, F. P. *Contrib. Mat. Med. China* 51. 1871.

[13] Ainslie, W. *Mat. Ind.* 1:57. 1826.

Thunberg[1] and earlier by Kaempfer.[2]   The kind now described by a Japanese authority [3] is an inch and a half in diameter at the crown, nearly two feet and a half long, and of a high color.   The carrot is now cultivated in the Mauritius, where also it has become spontaneous.   It is recorded in Arabia by Forskal [4] and was seen growing — both the yellow and the red — by Rauwolf at Aleppo in the sixteenth century.[5]   In Europe, its culture was mentioned by nearly all of the herbalists and by writers on gardening subjects, the red or purple kind finding mention by Ruellius,[6] 1536.   In England, the yellow and dark red, both long forms, are noticed by Gerarde,[7] 1597, and the species is supposed to have been introduced by the Dutch in 1558.   In the *Surveyors' Dialogue*, 1604, it is stated that carrot roots are then grown in England and sometimes by farmers.[8]   In the New World, carrots are mentioned at Margarita Island by Hawkins, 1565 [9] (and this implies that they were well known in England at this date); are mentioned in Brazil, 1647;[10] in Virginia, 1609 [11] and 1648; [12] and in Massachusetts, 1629.[13]   In 1779, carrots were among the Indian foods destroyed by General Sullivan near Geneva, New York.[14]   So fond of carrots are the Flathead Indians, of Oregon, that the children cannot forbear stealing them from the fields, although honest as regards other articles.[15]

TYPES OF CARROTS.

The types of modern carrot are the tap-rooted and the premorse-rooted with a number of subtypes, which are very distinct in appearance.   The synonymy, in part, is as below:

I.

THE LONG, TAPER-POINTED FORMS.

Pastinaca sativa prima.   Fuch. 682.   1542.
Moren. Roeszl. 106.   1550.
Staphylinus.   Trag. 442.   1552.
Carota.   Cam. *Epit.* 509.   1586 (very highly improved); Matth. 549.   1598.
Pastinaca sativa Diosc. Daucus Theophrasti.   Lob. *Icon.* **1**:720.   1591.
Pastinaca sativa tenuifolia.   Ger. 872.   1597.
Pastinaca sativa rubens.   Dod. 678.   1616.
Long yellows, red, and whites of modern culture.

---

[1] Thunberg *Fl. Jap.* 117, xxxiii.   1784.

[2] Kaempfer, E.   *Amoen.* 822.   1712.

[3] *Amer. Hort.*   Sept. 9, 1886.

[4] Forskal *Fl. Aeg. Arab.* xciii.   1775.

[5] Gronovious *Fl. Orient.* 32.   1755.

[6] Ruellius *Nat. Stirp.* 699.   1536.

[7] Gerarde, J.   *Herb.* 872.   1597.

[8] *Gard. Chron.* 346.   1853.

[9] Hawkins, Sir John.   *Second Voy.* Hakl. Soc. Ed. **57**:27.   1878.

[10] Churchill *Coll. Voy.* 2:132.   1732.

[11] *True Decl. Va.* 13.   1610.   Force Coll. Tracts 3:   1844.

[12] *Perf. Desc. Va.* 4.   1649.   Force Coll. Tracts 2:   1838.

[13] Higginson *Mass. Hist. Soc. Coll.* 1st ser. **1**:118.   1806.

[14] Conover, G. S.   *Early Hist. Geneva.* 47.   1879.

[15] *Pacific R. R. Rpt.* **1**:295.   1855.

II.

THE HALF-LONG, TAPER-POINTED FORMS.

Pastinaca sativa altera. Fuch. 683. 1542.
Siser. Matth. *Comment.* 242. 1558; Pin. 147. 1561.
Siser alterum. Cam. *Epit.* 227. 1586.
Carota. Dur. C. 95. 1617.
Blanche des Vosges. Vilm. 70. 1883.
Danvers Half-long of American gardens.

III.

PREMORSE-ROOTED FORMS.

The premorse forms offer a number of subtypes which are very distinct, some being nearly spherical, others cylindrical, and yet others tapering, but all ending abruptly at the base, the tap-root starting from a flat, or nearly flat, surface. This appearance seems to be modern.

The spherical.— The earliest mention of this type is in France in 1824, 1826 and 1829, as the *Courte de Pollande*.[1], [2], [3]. It is figured by Decaisne and Naudin,[4] and, in a more improved form, by Vilmorin in 1883.

The cylindrical.— The carrots of this type are remarkably distinct and have foi types the Carentan and the Coreless of Vilmorin. The first was in American seed-catalogs in 1878.

The tapering.— A number of varieties belong to this class, of which the Early Horn is the type. This was mentioned for American gardens by McMahon,[5] 1806, and by succeeding authors.

In view of the confusion in early times in the naming of the carrot, it is desirable to offer a list of the names used by various authors, with the dates. The first, or long carrot, was called in England, *carot*, Lyte, 1586: In France, *carota*, Ruel., 1536; *carottes*, *pastenades*, Pin., 1561; *pastenade jaune, pastenade rouge*, Lyte, 1586; *carotte, racine jaune*, Ger., 1597: In Germany, *Pastenei*, Ammon., 1539; *Pastiney Pastinachen*, Fuch., 1542; *geel Ruben, rohte Ruben, weissen Ruben*, Trag., 1552; *Mohren*, Rosz., 1550; *Moren*, Pin., 1561; *gelbe Ruben, weissen Ruben*, Rauwolf, 1582; *rot Mohren, weisse Mohren*, Cam., 1586: In Dutch, *geel peen, pooten, geel mostilen, caroten*, Lyte, 1586: In Italy, *carota*, Pin., 1561; *carota* and *carotola*, Cam., 1586; *pastinaca*, Ger., 1597; Dod., 1616: In Spain, *canahoria*, Ger., 1597; and *pastenagues, cenoura*, Dod., 1616.

The half-long, taper-pointed carrot was called *siser* by Matthiolus in 1558: In France, *carottes blanche*, Pin. 1561; but his other names applicable to the skirret are the *chervy*, *giroles* or *carottes blanches*, Cam. *Epit.* 1586: In Germany, *Gierlin* or *Girgellin*, Cam. 1586: In Italy, *carota bianca*, Cam. 1586; *carotta, carocola*, Dur. C. 1617: In Spain, *chirivias.* Camerarius, 1586, says they were planted in gardens and even in fields throughout Germany and Bohemia.

---

[1] Pirolle *L'Hort. Franc.* 1824.

[2] Petit *Dict. Jard.* 1826.

[3] Noisette *Man. Jard.* 1829.

[4] Decaisne and Naudin *Man. Jard.* 4:125.

[5] McMahon, B. *Amer. Gard. Cal.* 313. 1806.

The various forms of the carrot have probably their prototypes in nature but as yet the evidence is a little deficient.   We may suspect the general resemblance of the Altringham to the Japanese variety, already mentioned, to be somewhat more than accidental and to signify the original introduction of this variety from Japan.   We have, in the attempts at amelioration, noted the appearance of forms of types similar to those under cultivation. The presumptive evidence is in favor of the view that all cultivated types are removes from nature, not new originations by man; yet the proof is not as decisive as could be wished.[1]

D. gingidium Linn.

Europe and north Africa.   This is the *gingidium* of the ancients, according to Sprengel. " There is, saith Galen, great increase of *gingidium* in Syria, and it is eaten.   .   .   . Diascorides doth also write the same: this pote herbe, (saith he) is eaten raw, sodden, and preserved with great good to the stomacke."[3]

Debregeasia edulis Wedd.   *Urticaceae.*

Japan.   The plant is called *janatsi-itsigo* or *toon itsigo*.   Its berries are edible.[4]

Decaisnea insignis Hook. f. & Thoms.   *Berberideae.*

Himalayas.   The fruit is of a pale yellow color and is full of a white, juicy pulp that is very sweet and pleasant; the fruit is eagerly sought after by the Lepchas.[5]

Dendrobium speciosum Sm.   *Orchideae.*   ROCK-LILY.

Australia.   This orchid, found growing upon rocks, has large pseudo-bulbs, the size of cucumbers, which are said to be eaten by the natives.[6]

Dendrocalamus hamiltonii Nees & Arn.   *Gramineae.*

Himalayas.   This stately bamboo is called *pao* by the Lepchas and *wah* by the Mechis in Sikkim.   The young shoots are boiled and eaten.[7]

Desmoncus prunifer Poepp.   *Palmae.*

Peru.   The acid-sweet fruit is edible.[8]

Detarium senegalense J. F. Gmel.   *Leguminosae.*   DATTOCK.

Tropical Africa.   The fruits are about the size of an apricot.   Underneath the thin outer covering there is a quantity of green, farinaceous, edible pulp intermixed with stringy fibres that proceed from the inner and bony covering which encloses the single seed.   There are two varieties; one bitter, the other sweet.   The latter is sold in the markets and is prized by the negroes.[9]

---

[1] *Proc. Soc. Prom. Agr. Sci.* 68.   1886.

[2] Sprengel *Hist.* 1:164.   1817.

[3] Gerarde, J.   *Herb.* 2nd Ed.   1042.   1633 or 1636.

[4] Mueller, F.   *Sel. Pls.* 150.   1891.

[5] Hooker, J. D.   *Illustr. Himal. Pls.* Plate X.   1855.

[6] Smith, J.   *Dom. Bot.* 184.   1871.

[7] Brandis, D.   *Forest Fl.* 570.   1876.

[8] Seemann, B.   *Pop. Hist. of Palms* 188.   1856.

[9] Black, A. A.   *Treas. Bot.* 1:396.   1870.

Dialium guineese Willd. *Leguminosae.* VELVET TAMARIND.

Tropical Africa. The pod, about the size and form of a filbert, is covered with a black, velvety down, while the farinaceous pulp, which surrounds the seeds, has an agreeably acid taste and is commonly eaten.[1]

D. indum Linn. TAMARIND PLUM.

Java. The plant has a delicious pulp, resembling that of the tamarind but not quite so acid.[2]

D. ovoideum Thw.

Ceylon. The fruits are sold in the bazaars. They have an agreeable, acid flavor.[3]

Dicypellium caryophyllatum Nees. *Laurineae.*

Tropical America. The bark furnishes clove cassia.[4] It is called by French colonists *bois de rose;* in Carib, *licari kanali.*[5]

Dieffenbachia seguine Schott. *Aroideae.* DUMB CANE.

Tropical America. A wholesome starch is prepared from the stem, although the juice of the plant is so excessively acrid as to cause the mouth of any one biting it to swell and thus to prevent articulation for several days.[6]

Digera arvensis Forsk. *Amarantaceae.*

Asia and tropical Africa. A very common, procumbent shrub of India, frequent in cultivated ground. The leaves and tender tops are used by the natives in their curries.[7]

Dillenia indica Linn. *Dilleniaceae.*

Tropical Asia. The subacid, mucilaginous fruit, the size of an orange, is eaten in the Eastern Archipelago. The fleshy leaves of the calyx which surrounds the ripe fruit have an agreeable, acid taste and are eaten raw or cooked, or made into sherbets, or serve for jellies in India. They are commonly used in curries. The large amount of fiber they contain is objectionable. This is the *chulta* of India.[8] In the Philippines, the juice of the fruit serves as vinegar.

D. pentagyna Roxb.

East Indies. The flower-buds and young fruits have a pleasant, acid flavor and are eaten raw or cooked in Oudh and central India. The ripe fruits are also eaten.

D. scabrella Roxb. SANDPAPER TREE.

Himalayan region. The fleshy leaves of the calyx have a pleasantly acid taste and

---

[1] Black, A. A. *Treas. Bot.* 1:397. 1870. (*D. acutifolium*)

[2] Ibid.

[3] Ibid.

[4] Masters, M. T. *Treas. Bot.* 1:405. 1870.

[5] Pickering, C. *Chron. Hist. Pls.* 674. 1879.

[6] Smith, A. *Treas. Bot.* 1:406. 1870.

[7] Wight, R. *Icon. Pls.* 2:732. 1843. (*Desmochaeta muricata*)

[8] Firminger, T. A. C. *Gard. Ind.* 211. 1874. (*D. speciosa*)

are used in curries.[1]   In Burma, the green fruit is brought to the bazaars and is considered
a favorite vegetable.[2]

D. serrata Thunb.

Malay.   The fruit is the size of an orange and has a sweetish, acid taste.[3]   It is eaten
in the Eastern Archipelago.

Dimorphandra mora Benth. & Hook. f.   *Leguminosae.*

A gigantic timber-tree of British Guiana.   The seeds, says Brown,[4] are used by the
natives as food, being boiled, grated, and then mixed with cassava meal, giving it a brown
color but a pleasant and sweetish taste.   The seeds of another species are likewise used.

Dioon edule Lindl.   *Cycadaceae.*

Mexico.   The seeds yield a starch used as arrowroot.[5]

Dioscorea.   *Dioscoreaceae.*   YAMS.

Under the general name of yams the large, fleshy, tuberous roots of several species
of Dioscorea are cultivated in tropical and subtropical countries.   Many varieties
known only in cultivation are described as species by some authors.   In the Fiji Islands
alone, says Milne,[6] there are upwards of 50 varieties, some growing to an enormous
size, occasionally weighing from 50 to 80 pounds but the general average is from two to
eight pounds.   In Australia, according to Drummond,[7] there is a native yam which affords
the principal vegetable food of the natives.

D. aculeata Linn.   BIRCH-RIND YAM.   GOA POTATO.

Tropical Asia.   This yam is said to be a native of tropical, eastern Asia, and is cultivated in the Indian Archipelago, the Pacific islands and the West Indies.   The root
is of a sweetish taste and Dr. Seemann[8] regarded it as one of the finest esculent roots of
the globe.   It is cultivated in India[9] and the tubers are dug, in the cold season, in the
forests and sold in the bazaars.[10]   A variety cultivated at Caracas has a very delicious
taste,[11] though Lunan,[12] at Jamaica, says this yam is slightly bitter.   This yam is said by
Seemann, at Viti, never to flower or fruit.

D. alata Linn.   WHITE YAM.

Tropical Asia.   This plant is cultivated in the tropics of the whole earth.   Unger[13]

[1] Wallich *Pl. Asiat.* 1:21.   Tab. 22.   1830.
[2] Pickering, C.   *Chron. Hist. Pls.* 112.   1879.   (*D. scabia*)
[3] Don, G.   *Hist. Dichl. Pls.* 1:78.   1831.
[4] Brown, C. B.   *Camp Life Brit. Guiana* 383.   1876.   (*Mora excelsa*)
[5] Lindley, J.   *Bot. Reg. Misc.* 59.   1843.
[6] Milne, W.   *Bot. Soc. Edinb.* 6:263.   1860.
[7] Hooker, W. J.   *Journ. Bot.* 2:355.   1840.
[8] Mueller, F.   *Sel. Pls.* 153.   1891.
[9] Roxburgh, W.   *Hort. Beng.* 72.   1814.
[10] Drury, H.   *Useful Pls. Ind.* 183.   1873.
[11] Mueller, Γ.   *Sel. Pls.* 153.   1891.
[12] Lunan, J.   *Hort. Jam.* 2:309, 310.   1814.
[13] Unger, F.   *U. S. Pat. Off. Rpt.* 310.   1859.

says the Indian Archipelago and the southern portions of the Indian continent is the starting point of this yam, thence it was carried first to the eastern coast of Africa, next to the west coast and thence to America, whence the names *yam* and *igname* are derived from the negroes. In the negro daliect of Guinea, the word *yam* means " to eat." This is the species most generally cultivated in the Indian Archipelago, the small islands of the Pacific and the Indian continent.[1] It is universally cultivated in the Carnatic region.[2] There are several varieties in Jamaica, where it is called white yam.[3]

D. atropurpurea Roxb. MALACCA YAM. RANGOON YAM.

Siamese countries. The Malacca yam is cultivated in India and is known in Calcutta as the rangoon yam.[4] It is called in Burma *myouk-nee* and is cultivated.[5]

D. bulbifera Linn. AIR POTATO.

Tropical Asia. Less cultivated than many others, this yam is found wild in the Indian Archipelago, upon the Indian continent as far as Silhet and Nepal to Madagascar.[6] Grant[7] found it in central Africa. The bulbs are like the Brazil-nut in size and shape, cut l'ke a potato when unripe and are very good boiled. Schweinfurth[8] says it is called *nyitti* and the bulbs which protrude from the axils of the leaves, in shape like a great Brazil-nut, resemble a potato in taste and bulk. In the Samoan and Tonga group of islands, the root is not considered edible. In India, the flowers and roots are eaten by the poorer classes, the very bitter root being soaked in lye to extract the bitterness, but a variety occurs which is naturally sweet.[9] In Jamaica, it is cultivated by the negroes for the bulbs of the stem.[10] It was seen in a garden at Mobile, Alabama, by Wm. Bartram,[11] about 1733, under cultivation for its edible roots.

D. cayenensis Lam.

Tropical South America. The root is edible.

D. daemona Roxb.

East Indies. The plant is called *kywae* and its very acrid root is eaten by the Karens in times of scarcity.[12]

D. decaisneana Carr.

China. The root is edible and was introduced into France as a garden plant but is now forgotten, although it is perhaps valuable.[13]

---

[1] De Candolle, A. *Geog. Bot.* 821. 1855.
[2] Wight, R. *Icon. Pls.* 3:Pl. 810. No date.
[3] Lunan, J. *Hort. Jam.* 2:309. 1814.
[4] Firminger, T. A. C. *Gard. Ind.* 122. 1874.
[5] Pickering, C. *Chron. Hist. Pls.* 714. 1879.
[6] De Candolle, A. *Geog. Bot.* 2:821. 1855.
[7] Speke, J. H. *Journ. Disc. Source Nile* 584. 1864.
[8] Schweinfurth, G. *Heart. Afr.* 1:251. 1874. (*Helmia bulbifera*)
[9] Pickering, C. *Chron. Hist. Pls.* 416. 1879.
[10] Lunan, J. *Hort. Jam.* 2:310. 1814.
[11] *Hist. Mass. Hort. Soc.* 27. 1880.
[12] Pickering, C. *Chron. Hist. Pls.* 589. 1879.
[13] *Bon Jard.* 514. 1882.

D. deltoidea Wall.

East Indies. This species occurs both wild and cultivated in the Indian Archipelago;[1] its roots are eaten.

D. divaricata Blanco. CHINESE POTATO. CHINESE YAM. CINNAMON VINE. YAM.

Philippine Islands, China and everywhere cultivated in several varieties. This yam was received in France in 1851 from Shanghai, and was introduced into the United States, in 1855, by the Patent Office Department. It has not fulfilled expectation in the United States and is now grown principally as an ornamental climber. It was observed in Japan by Thunberg.[2]

D. fasciculata Roxb. YAM.

Tropical eastern Asia. This species is cultivated largely about Calcutta, and a starch is made from its tubers.[3] Firminger[4] says this is a very distinct kind of yam, the tubers about the size, form and color of large kidney potatoes; when well cooked, it has a greater resemblance in mealiness and flavor to the potato than any other yam he knows of. It is much cultivated in the Philippines by the natives and is much esteemed.[5]

D. globosa Roxb. YAM.

East Indies. This species is much cultivated in India as yielding the best kind of yam and is much esteemed both by Europeans and natives.[6] Roxburgh[7] says it is the most esteemed yam in Bengal, but Firminger[8] thinks it not equal in quality to other varieties. In Burma, Mason[9] says it is the best of the white-rooted kinds.

D. hastifolia Nees. YAM.

Australia. The tubers are largely consumed by the aborigines for food, and this is the only plant on which they bestow any kind of cultivation.[10]

D. japonica Thunb.

Japan. The roots, cut into slices and boiled, have a very pleasant taste.[11]

D. nummularia Lam. TIVOLO YAM.

Moluccas. This yam has cylindrical roots as thick as an arm and of excellent quality.[12]

D. oppositifolia Linn. YAM.

East Indies. This is one of the edible yams.[13]

---

[1] De Candolle, A. *Geog. Bot.* 2:821. 1855.

[2] Thunberg, C. P. *Fl. Jap.* 150. 1784.

[3] Drury, H. *Useful Pls. Ind.* 183. 1873.

[4] Firminger, T. A. C. *Gard. Ind.* 122. 1874.

[5] Pickering, C. *Chron. Hist. Pls.* 865. 1879. (*D. tugui*)

[6] Drury, H. *Useful Pls. Ind.* 183. 1873.

[7] Mueller, F. *Sel. Pls.* 154. 1891.

[8] Firminger, T. A. C. *Gard. Ind.* 121. 1874.

[9] Pickering, C. *Chron. Hist. Pls.* 862. 1879.

[10] Mueller, F. *Sel. Pls.* 154. 1891.

[11] Thunberg, C. P. *Trav.* 3:84. 1796.

[12] Mueller, F. *Sel. Pls.* 155. 1891.

[13] Ibid.

D. pentaphylla Linn. YAM.

Tropical Asia. In India, this yam is common in jungles and is found in the South Sea Islands. Wight [1] has never seen it cultivated in India, although the natives dig the tubers to eat. It is cultivated in Amboina and sometimes in Viti.[2] In India, the male flowers are sold in the bazaars and eaten as greens.[3] The tubers are eaten in Viti [4] and Hawaii.[5] It is a good yam.[6] Graham [7] says the tubers are dreadfully nauseous and intensely bitter even after being boiled. They are put into toddy to render it more potent, as they have intoxicating properties, and a few slices are sufficient. In China, the " nauseous tubers are sometimes cooked and eaten." [8]

D. piperifolia Humb. & Bonpl.

South America. This species has edible roots.[9]

D. purpurea Roxb. PONDICHERRY SWEET POTATO.

East Indies. The Pondicherry sweet potato is known only in a cultivated state,[10] and was brought to India from the Mauritius, where it is much grown. The tuber is of a dull, crimson-red outside and of a glistening white within.

D. quinqueloba Thunb. YAM.

Japan. This species is an edible yam of Japan.[11]

D. rubella Roxb. YAM.

East Indies. This is a common but very excellent yam of India, as good perhaps as any in cultivation. The tuber is of great size, crimson-red on the outside and of a glistening white within.

D. sativa Linn. YAM.

Tropics. Pickering [12] states that this species is found in tropical America and is cultivated by the Waraus of the delta of the Orinoco. The word *igname* was heard by Vespucius on the coast of Para and was found by Cabral, in 1500, applied in Brazil to a root from which bread was made. This yam was carried by European colonists to the Malayan Archipelago. Its roots, says Seemann,[13] are acrid and require to be soaked before boiling. Browne [14] says it is cultivated in the southern United States for its large, flattened and sometimes palmated roots, which are boiled, roasted and eaten like the potato.

---

[1] Wight, R. *Icon. Pls.* 3:814. No date.
[2] Seemann, B. *Fl. Viti.* 308. 1865-73.
[3] Drury, H. *Useful Pls. Ind.* 183. 1873.
[4] Seemann, B. *Fl. Viti.* 108. 1865-73.
[5] Pickering, C. *Chron. Hist. Pls.* 416. 1879.
[6] Mueller, F. *Sel. Pls.* 155. 1891.
[7] Pickering, C. *Chron. Hist. Pls.* 729. 1879.
[8] Smith, F. P. *Contrib. Mat. Med. China* 86. 1871.
[9] Mueller, F. *Sel. Pls.* 155. 1891.
[10] Drury, H. *Useful Pls. Ind.* 183. 1873.
[11] Mueller, F. *Sel. Pls.* 155. 1891.
[12] Pickering, C. *Chron. Hist. Pls.* 714. 1879.
[13] Seemann, B. *Fl. Viti.* 307. 1865-73.
[14] *U. S. Pat. Off. Rpt.* 389. 1854.

D. spicata Roth.

East Indies.   It has edible roots.[1]

D. tomentosa Koen.   DOYALA YAM.

East Indies.   This is the Doyala yam of India.[2]

D. trifida Linn.   INDIAN YAM.

Guiana and Central America.   This species is cultivated as an edible yam.[3]

D. triloba Lam.   YAM.

Guiana.   This is the smallest and most delicate of the yams grown in Jamaica.   It seldom exceeds eight or nine inches in length and two or three in diameter and is generally smaller.   The roots have a pleasant, sweetish taste, very agreeable to most palates.[4]

Diospyros chloroxylon Roxb.   *Ebenaceae.*

East Indies.   This Indian tree has a cherry-like fruit which is very palatable.[5]   The fruit is sweetish, clammy and subastringent but edible.[6]

D. decandra Lour.

Cochin China.   The berry is large, nearly globular, pulpy, yellowish when ripe; its taste is sweet and austere, combined with a disagreeable smell.   It is, however, sold in the markets and eaten.[7]

D. discolor Willd.   MANGOSTEEN.

Philippine Islands.   This species is commonly cultivated in many islands of the East and has also been introduced into the West Indies.   The fruit is like a large quince and in some places is called mangosteen.   Its flavor is agreeable.[8]   The fruit of this tree is brown, with a pink-colored, fleshy rind, the pulp firm and white and the flavor agreeable. It is cultivated in the Isle of France for its fruit.[9]

D. dodecandra Lour.

Cochin China.   The berry is pale, with a sweetish, astringent, edible and pleasant pulp.[10]

D. ebenum Koen.   EAST INDIAN EBONY.

This plant bears an edible fruit.[11]

D. embryopteris Pers.

East Indies.   The fruit of this tree of India is not unlike a russet apple, pulpy, of

[1] Mueller, F.   *Sel. Pls.* 155.   1891.

[2] Mueller, F.   *Sel. Pls.* 156.   1891.

[3] Ibid

[4] Lunan, J.   *Hort. Jam.* 2:309.   1814.

[5] Roxburgh, W.   *Pls. Corom.* 1:38.   1795.

[6] Royle, J. F.   *Illustr. Bot. Himal.* 1:262.   1839.

[7] Don, G.   *Hist. Dichl. Pls.* 4:39.   1838.

[8] Smith, J.   *Dict. Econ. Pls.* 254.   1882.   (*D. mabola*)

[9] Don, G.   *Hist. Dichl. Pls.* 4:40.   1838.   (*D. mabola*)

[10] Don, G.   *Hist. Dichl. Pls.* 4:41.   1838.

[11] Unger, F.   *U. S. Pat. Off. Rpt.* 339.   1859.   (*D. ebanaster*)

unattractive yellow color and covered with a rust-colored farina. It is occasionally eaten but is not palatable.[1] It is eaten by the natives.[2]

D. kaki Linn. DATE PLUM. JAPANESE PERSIMMON. KAKI. KEG-FIG.

Japan. This plant has been cultivated in Japan for a long period and has produced many varieties, some of which are seedless. The fruit, in general, is as large as an ordinary apple, of a bright color, and contains a semi-transparent pulp. The tree is cultivated in India and in China and was seen in Japan by Thunberg,[3] 1776. It was introduced into the United States from Japan by the Perry expedition and one of these trees is still growing at Washington. About 1864, others were imported; in 1877, 5000 plants in ten varieties were brought to America. This persimmon is now grown in California, Georgia and elsewhere. The fruit is described as delicious by all who have eaten the best varieties.

D. lanceaefolia Roxb.

East India. This is an eastern fruit, said by Kotschy [4] to have a taste similar to chocolate.

D. lotus Linn. FALSE LOTE-TREE.

Temperate Asia. The fruit is the size of a cherry, yellow when ripe, sweet with astringency.[5] The sweetish fruit is much prized by the Afghan tribes, who eat it fresh or dried [6] and use it in sherbets.

D. melanoxylon Roxb. COROMANDEL EBONY.

East Indies and Ceylon. The yellow fruit is about one to one and one-half inches through, with soft, sweet, slightly astringent flesh, which is eaten and is refreshing.[7]

D. obtusifolia Willd.

South America. This is the *sapota negro*, with small, black, edible fruit.[8]

D. pentamera Woods & F. Muell. GRAY PLUM.

Eastern tropical Australia. The fruits, which are produced in great abundance, are eaten by the aborigines.[9]

D. pilosanthera Blanco.

Philippines. The fruit of this tree is eaten.[10]

D. tetrasperma Sw. WATTLE TREE.

Jamaica. The fruit is eaten by negroes.[11]

---

[1] Ainslie, W. *Mat. Ind.* 2:278. 1826.
[2] Drury, H. *Useful Pls. Ind.* 195. 1873.
[3] Thunberg, C. P. *Fl. Jap.* 157. 1784.
[4] Unger, F. *U. S. Pat. Off. Rpt.* 344. 1859.
[5] Don, G. *Hist. Dichl. Pls.* 4:38. 1838.
[6] Brandis, D. *Forest Fl.* 298. 1874.
[7] Brandis, D. *Forest Fl.* 296. 1874.
[8] Don, G. *Hist. Dichl. Pls.* 4:39. 1838.
[9] Black, A. A. *Treas. Bot.* 1:223. 1870.
[10] Pickering, C. *Chron. Hist. of Pls.* 917. 1879.
[11] Lunan, J. *Hort. Jam.* 2:318. 1814.

D. texana Scheele. BLACK PERSIMMON.

Mexico. This is the black persimmon of the Americans and the *sapote-pieto* of the Mexicans of western Texas. The black, cherry-like fruit is melting and very sweet.[1]

D. tomentosa Roxb. EBONY.

East Indies. The sweetish, clammy and subastringent fruit of this plant is eaten.

D. toposia Buch.-Ham.

East Indies. The fruit of this species is sweetish, clammy, and subastringent but edible.[2]

D. virginiana Linn. PERSIMMON.

North America, found wild from the 42nd parallel to Texas, often attaining the size of a large tree. This plant is the persimmon, *piakmine*, or *pessimmon* of America, called by the Louisiana natives *ougoufle*. Loaves made of the substance of prunes " like unto brickes, also plummes of the making and bigness of nuts and have three or four stones in them " were seen by DeSoto on the Mississippi. It is called *mespilorum* by LeMoyne in Florida; " *mespila* unfit to eat until soft and tender " by Hariot on the Roanoke; *pessimmens* by Strachey on the James River; and *medlars* on the Hudson by the remonstrants against the policy of Stuyvesant.[3] The fruit is plum-like, about an inch in diameter, exceedingly astringent when green, yellow when ripe, and sweet and edible after exposure to frost. Porcher [4] says the fruit, when matured, is very sweet and pleasant to the taste and yields on distillation, after fermentation, a quantity of spirits. A beer is made of it. Mixed with flour, a pleasant bread may be prepared. Occasional varieties are found with fruit double the size of the ordinary kind. The best persimmons ripen soft and sweet, having a clear, thin, transparent skin without any roughness. Flint,[5] in his *Western States*, says when the small, blue persimmon is thoroughly ripened, it is even sweeter than the fig and is a delicious fruit. It is sometimes cultivated in America and is also to be found in some gardens in Europe.

Dipladenia tenuifolia A. DC. *Apocynaceae.*

Brazil. This plant is called by the inhabitants of Sertao, Brazil, *cauhy*, and the tuberous root, which is the size and color of a large, black turnip-radish, is eaten by them when cooked and is said to be very palatable; in the raw state it tastes not unlike a turnip.[6]

Diplazium esculentum. *Polypodioceae.*

This fern, according to Royle,[7] is employed as food in the Himalayas.

---

[1] Lindenheimer *U. S. D. A. Rpt.* 166. 1875.
[2] Royle, J. F. *Illustr. Bot. Himal.* 1:262. 1839.
[3] Pickering, C. *Chron. Hist. Pls.* 770. 1879.
[4] Porcher, F. P. *Res. So. Fields, Forests* 424. 1869.
[5] Flint, T. *West. States* 1:73. 1828.
[6] Gardner, G. *Trav. Braz.* 179. 1846.
[7] Royle, J. F. *Illustr. Bot. Himal.* 1:429. 1839.

Diplothemium maritimum Mart. *Palmae.* COAST PALM.

A palm of Brazil. The fruit, an ovate or obovate drupe, is yellow and has a fibrous, acid-sweet flesh, which is eaten by the Indians.[1]

Diposis bulbocastanum DC. *Umbelliferae.*

Chile. The tubers are edible.[2]

Dobera roxburghii Planch. *Salvadoraceae.*

East Indies and South Africa. This is a large tree called in Yemen *dober;*[3] the fruit is eaten.

Dolichandrone stipulata Benth. & Hook. f. *Bignoniaceae.*

Burma. The flowers, according to Mason,[4] are brought to market for food.

Dolichos biflorus Linn. *Leguminosae.* HORSE GRAIN.

Old World tropics. This is the horse grain of the East Indies. The bean occurs in white, brown and black. The seeds are boiled in India for the horses, and the liquor that remains is used by the lower class of servants in their own food.[5] There are varieties with gray and black seeds; the natives use the seeds in their curries.[6]

D. hastatus Lour.

East Africa. This plant is cultivated on the east coast of Africa and the seeds are eaten by the natives.[7]

D. lablab Linn. BONAVISTA BEAN. HYACINTH BEAN. LABLAB.

Tropics of India and China. A number of varieties of this bean are cultivated in Asiatic countries for the pulse and the tender pods. There is a great diversity in the color of the flowers, size and shape of pod and color of seeds. Roxburgh[8] describes var. *rectum*, pods straight, seeds reddish, flowers white, large; called *pauch-seem:* Var. *falcatum minus*, pods falcate, size of the little finger, flowers white, largish; called *baghonuko-seem:* Var. *falcatum majus*, pods falcate, flowers purple; called *dood-pituli-seem:* Var. *gladiatum flore albo*, pods gladiate-clavate, length of the little finger, flowers white; called *sada-jamai-puli-seem:* Var. *gladiatum flore purpureo*, called *pituli-jamai-puli-seem:* Var. *macrocarpum*, the largest of all, pods six to eight inches long, seeds black with a white eye, flowers red; called *gychi-seem.*

A great number of synonyms which have been assigned to this species is indicative of the variable character of the plant. In India, where it is much cultivated, four eatable varieties which are offered for sale in the bazaars during the cold season, are thus described

---

[1] Seemann, B. *Pop. Hist. Palms* 190. 1856.

[2] Mueller, F. *Sel. Pls.* 158. 1891.

[3] Pickering, C. *Chron. Hist. Pls.* 390. 1879. (*D. glabra*)

[4] Pickering, C. *Chron. Hist. Pls.* 112. 1879. (*Bignonia stipulata*)

[5] Elliott, W. *Bot. Soc. Edinb.* 7:293. 1863. (*D. uniflorus*)

[6] Drury, H. *Useful Pls. Ind.* 186. 1873.

[7] Don, G. *Hist. Dichl. Pls.* 2:358. 1832.

[8] Firminger, T. A. C. *Gard. Ind.* 150. 1874.

by Roxburgh:[1]   Var. *albiflorum*, the *shevet-seem*, flowers white, smallish, cultivated in gardens as a pole bean; the tender pods are eaten, the seeds never; the plant has a disagreeable smell: Var. *rubiflorum*, the *jeea-seem*, flowers red, cultivated and much esteemed by the natives: Var. *purpurascens*, the *goordal-seem*, a large variety with large, purple flowers: Var. *purpureum*, the *ruk-to-seem*, stem and large flowers purple, the pods deep purple.   Wight[2] calls the species a very valuable pulse generally esteemed by all classes of natives and very extensively cultivated in Mysore.   In Jamaica, it is called the bonavista-bean and is cultivated in most parts of the country.   The bean is a wholesome, palatable food and is in general use.[3]   On the east coast of Africa, the leaves are dried and made into a spinach.[4]

D. sesquipedalis Linn.   ASPARAGUS BEAN.   YARD-LONG BEAN.

South America.   This bean was first described by Linnaeus,[5] 1763.   It reached England in 1781.[6]   Linnaeus gives its habitat as America and Jacquin received it from the West Indies.   Martens[7] considers it as a synonym of *Dolichos sinensis* Linn.   Loureiro's description of *D. sinensis* certainly applies well to the asparagus bean, and Loureiro[8] thinks the *D. sesquipedalis* of Linnaeus the same.   He refers to Rumphius's *Amboina*, 1.9, c. 22, tab. 134, as representing his plant, and this work, published in 1750, antedates the description of Linnaeus.   Probably this is an East Indian plant, introduced into the West Indies.

The name, asparagus bean, comes from the use of the green pods as a vegetable, and a tender, asparagus-like dish it is.   The name at Naples, *fagiolo e maccarone*, conveys the same idea.   The pods grow very long, oftentimes two feet in length, hence the name, yard-long bean, often used.   The asparagus, or yard-long, bean is mentioned for American gardens in 1828[9] and probably was introduced earlier.   It is mentioned for French gardens under the name of *haricot asperge* in 1829.[10]   There are no varieties known to our seedsmen, but Vilmorin offers one, the *Dolique de Cuba*.[11]

D. sphaerospermus DC.   BLACK-EYED PEA.

Jamaica.   This is the black-eyed pea of the Barbados.[12]   It is a native of Jamaica, and the seeds are sweet and as good for food as any of the kidney beans.

D. umbellatus Thunb.

Japan.   The seeds and pods are used in the preparation of a starch and meal.[13]   There

[1] Firminger, T. A. C.   *Gard. Ind.* 149.   1874.

[2] Wight, R.   *Illustr. Ind. Bot.* 1:192.   1840.   (*Lablab vulgaris*)

[3] Long *Hist. Jam.* 3:785.   1774.

[4] Speke, J. H.   *Journ. Disc. Source Nile* 567.   1864.   (*Lablab vulgaris*)

[5] Linnaeus *Sp. Pl.* 1019.   1763.

[6] Martyn *Miller Gard. Dict.*   1807.

[7] Martens *Gartenbohnen* 100.   1869.

[8] Loureiro *Fl. Cochin.* 436.   1790.

[9] Fessenden *New Amer. Gard.* 36.   1828.

[10] Noisette *Man. Jard.*   1829.

[11] Thorburn *Cat.*   1828.

[12] Don, G.   *Hist. Dichl. Pls.* 2:360.   1832.

[13] *Gard. Chron.* 25:458.   1886.

are several varieties of this plant under culture; some of them are pole beans, others dwarf.[1]

Doryanthes excelsa Correa. *Amaryllideae.* GIANT LILY.

Australia. A liliaceous plant 24 feet high of which the stem is roasted and eaten by the Australians.[2]

Dovyalis zizyphoides E. Mey. *Bixineae.*

South Africa. The red berries are edible.[3]

Dracaena draco Linn. *Liliaceae.* DRAGON-TREE.

Canary Islands. The dragon tree furnished dragons-blood once considerably exported from the Canaries. At Porto Santo, one of the Madeira Islands, Cada Mosto in 1454 found the tree yielding " a kind of fruit, like to our cherries but yellow, which grows ripe in March and is of a most exquisite taste." [4]

Dracontium polyphyllum Linn. *Aroideae.*

South America. The roots serve as food to the natives of the Pacific isles.[5]

Dracontomelon sylvestre Blume. *Anacardiaceae.*

Borneo. This species is planted at Rewa, Fiji Islands. Pickering, in *Races of Man*, mentions the fruit under the name *canarium* and says it is sour and edible.[6]

Dregea volubilis Benth. *Asclepiadeae.*

East Indies. " I have been informed," says Ainslie,[7] " that the leaves are amongst those which are occasionally eaten as greens by the natives of lower India but I am doubtful of this, considering the general character of the genus."

Drimys aromatica F. Muell. *Magnoliaceae.* PEPPER TREE.

Australia. The ripe fruit is black, Hooker [8] says, and the whole plant is highly aromatic and pungent, hence its seeds and berries are sometimes used as pepper.

D. winteri Forst. NEW GRANADA WINTER-BARK.

South America. The bark of the variety *montana* is used in Brazil as a seasoning.[9]

Drosera rotundifolia Linn. *Droseraceae.* LUSTWORT. SUNDEW.

Northern regions. The round-leaved sundew is said by Figuer [10] to be acrid and caustic, and in Italy a liquor called *rossoli* is distilled from its juices. It curdles milk.

---

[1] Georgeson *Amer. Gard.* **14**:84. 1893.

[2] Pickering, C. *Chron. Hist. Pls.* 564. 1879.

[3] Don, G. *Hist. Dichl. Pls.* **1**:292. 1831. (*Flacourtia rhamnoides*)

[4] *Gen. Coll. Voy. Portugese* 50. 1789.

[5] De Candolle, A. *Geog. Bot.* **2**:827. 1855.

[6] Gray, A. *Bot. U. S. Explor. Exped.* 375. 1854.

[7] Ainslie, W. *Mat. Ind.* **2**:155. 1826. (*Asclepias volubilis*)

[8] Hooker, W. J. *Journ. Bot.* **2**:404. 1840. (*Tasmania aromatica*)

[9] Don, G. *Hist. Dichl. Pls.* **1**:80. 1831. (*D. granatensis*)

[10] Figuier *Veg. World* 405. 1867.

Dryas octopetala Linn. *Rosaceae.* MOUNTAIN AVENS.

Northern temperate and arctic regions. In Iceland, the leaves of this plant are used as a substitute for tea.[1]

Duguetia longifolia Baill. *Anonaceae.*

Guiana, Peru and Trinidad. The fruit is nearly round, as big as a Reinette apple, the surface divided by reticulated divisions, the skin thin, and the red, delicate, viscous flesh excellent and very agreeable.[2] It is very much prized by the Caribs.[3]

Durio oxleyanus Griff. *Malvaceae.*

Malay Islands. This is probably the form of the durian from which the cultivated species has originated.[4]

D. zibethinus Murr. DURIAN.

Malayan Archipelago. Accounts of this far-famed fruit had reached Europe as early as 1640, as Parkinson[5] mentions it. The fruit is of the size of a man's head and the seed, with its enveloping pulp, about the size of a hen's egg. The pulp is a pure white, resembling *blanc mange* and as delicious in taste as the finest cream. The odor is, however, intolerable. Wallace[6] says that to eat durians is a sensation worth a voyage to the East to experience. The unripe fruit is used as a vegetable. Bayard Taylor[7] says: " Of all fruits, at first the most intolerable but said by those who have smothered their prejudices, to be of all fruits, at last, the most indispensable. When it is brought to you at first, you clamor till it is removed; if there are durians in the next room to you, you cannot sleep. Chloride of lime and disinfectants seem to be its necessary remedy. To eat it, seems to be the sacrifice of self respect; but endure it for a while, with closed nostrils, taste it once or twice, and you will cry for durians thenceforth, even — I blush to write it — even before the glorious mongosteen."

Durville utilia Bory. *Algae.*

This seaweed is employed in soups in Chile.[8]

Dysoxylum spectabile Hook. f. *Meliaceae.*

A tree of New Zealand, called by the inhabitants *kohe*, or *wahahe*. Its leaves have a bitter taste and are employed as a substitute for hops.[9]

Echinocactus hamatocanthus Muehlenpf. *Cactaceae.*

Mexico. The ripe fruit is red and " as delicious as that of the strawberry cactus."[10]

---

[1] Buysman, M. *Gard. Chron.* **26**:810. 1886.
[2] Lindley, J. *Trans. Hort. Soc. Lond.* **5**:101. 1824. (*Anona longifolia*)
[3] Unger, F. *U. S. Pat. Off. Rpt.* 351. 1859. (*Anona longifolia*)
[4] Masters, M. T. *Treas. Bot.* **2**:1290. 1876.
[5] Pickering, C. *Chron. Hist. Pls.* 816. 1879.
[6] Wallace, A. R. *Malay Arch.* 85, 86. 1869.
[7] Taylor, B. *Siam* 193. 1892.
[8] Berkeley, M. J. *Treas. Bot.* **1**:37. 1870.
[9] Smith, A. *Treas. Bot.* **1**:570. 1870.
[10] Havard, V. *U. S. Nat. Herb.* **3**:365. 1896.

E. horizonthalonius Lem.

Mexico. This species furnishes fruits which are sliced, candied and sold as confections.[1]

E. longihamatus Gal.

Mexico. Fruit red, edible and of good quality.[2]

E. viridescens Nutt.

California. The fruit is of the shape and taste of a gooseberry.[3]

E. wislizeni Engelm.

Western North America. This cactus is called by the Mexicans *visnada*, or *biznacha*. The seeds are small and black and when parched and pulverized, make good gruel and even bread. The pulp of the fruit is rather sour and is not much eaten. Travellers, in passing through the cactus wastes, often resort to this plant to quench their thirst, its interior containing a soft, white, watery substance of slightly acid taste, which is rather pleasant when chewed. Pieces of this, soaked in a sirup or sugar and dried, are as good as candied citron, which they resemble in taste and substance. This plant, in some of its preparations, furnishes a favorite food to the Yabapais and Apache Indians of Arizona.[4]

Echinophora spinosa Linn. *Umbelliferae.* PRICKLY SAMPHIRE. SEA PARSNIP.

Europe. The roots of prickly samphire are eatable, with the flavor of parsnips, and the young leaves make excellent pickles.

Eclipta erecta Linn. *Compositae.*

Cosmopolitan tropics. About Bombay, this plant, a common weed, is sometimes eaten by the natives as a potherb.[5]

Ehretia acuminata R. Br. *Boragineae.*

Asia and Australian tropics. The drupe is red-orange, or nearly black when ripe, as large as a small pea. The unripe fruit is pickled in India. When ripe it is insipidly sweet and is eaten.[6]

E. elliptica DC.

Texas and Mexico. This plant is a small tree with fruit the size of a large pea, yellow, with a thin, edible pulp.[7]

E. laevis Roxb.

Asia and Australian tropics. The inner bark, in times of famine, is mixed with flour and eaten. The fruit is tasteless but is eaten.[8]

---

[1] Havard, V. *U. S. Nat. Herb.* 3:360. 1896.

[2] Havard, V. *Proc. U. S. Nat. Mus.* 520. 1885.

[3] Engelmann *Bot. Works* 191. 1887.

[4] *U. S. D. A. Rpt.* 417. 1870. Fig.

[5] Pickering, C. *Chron. Hist. Pls.* 700. 1879. (*E. prostrata*)

[6] Brandis, D. *Forest Fl.* 340. 1874. (*E. serrata*)

[7] Torrey, J. *Bot. U. S. Mex. Bound. Surv.* 2:136. 1859.

[8] Brandis, D. *Forest Fl.* 340. 1874.

E. tinifolia Linn. BASTARD CHERRY.

West Indies.   The berries are the size of a currant and are frequently eaten.[1]

Elaeagnus angustifolia Linn. *Elaeagnaceae.* OLEASTER. WILD OLIVE.

Europe and northern Asia.   The wild olive is a tree mainly cultivated for its fruit, which, in general, is acid and eatable.   In Greece, it is sweetish-acid and mealy when ripe.[2]   The fruit is commonly sold in the markets of Constantinople.   It abounds in a dry, mealy, saccharine substance which is sweet and pleasant.[3]   The fruit is eaten in Nepal; it is cultivated in Thibet; and in Persia appears as dessert under the name of *zinzeyd.*   A spirit is distilled from the fruit in Yarkand.[4]

E. argentea Pursh. SILVERBERRY.

North America.   About Hudson's Bay this shrub produces a dry, farinaceous, edible drupe about the size of a small cherry.[5]

E. latifolia Linn. OLEASTER. WILD OLIVE.

Tropical Asia.   The fruit is olive-shaped and larger than an olive.   It is eaten in Nepal [6] and the mountains of Hindustan and Siam.   The oleaster, or wild olive, has a fruit the size and form of a damson, has a stone in the center and when ripe is of a pale red or cherry color.   It is very acrid and though not generally considered an edible fruit in India, yet, when cooked and sweetened with sugar, makes a very agreeable compote.[7]   Brandis [8] says the acid, somewhat astringent fruit is eaten.   It is abundant on the Neilgherries, says Wight,[9] and the fruit is edible and also makes a good tart.

E. perrottetii Schlecht. PHILIPPINE OLEASTER.

Philippine Islands.   The fruit of the Philippine oleaster has the taste of the best cherries.[10]

E. umbellata Thunb.

Japan.   The small, succulent fruit is eaten in India.[11]

Elaeis guineensis Jacq. *Palmae.* MACAW-FAT. OIL PALM.

Tropical Africa and introduced to tropical America.   The bright yellow drupe with shiny, purple-black point, though nauseous to the taste, is eaten in Africa.   *Mawezi,* or palm oil, of the consistency of honey, is rudely extracted from this palm and despite its flavor, is universally used in cooking.   This palm is also tapped for toddy.[12]   Palm

[1] Lunan, J. *Hort. Jam.* 1:61.   1814.

[2] Brandis, D. *Forest Fl.* 390.   1874.

[3] Walsh, R. *Trans. Hort. Soc. Lond.* 6:36.   1826.

[4] Brandis, D. *Forest Fl.* 390.   1874.

[5] Nuttall, T. *Gen. No. Amer. Pls.* 1:97.   1818.

[6] Royle, J. F. *Illustr. Bot. Himal.* 1:323.   1839.

[7] Firminger, T. A. C. *Gard. Ind.* 182.   1874.

[8] Brandis, D. *Forest Fl.* 390.   1874.

[9] Wight, R. *Icon. Pls.* 5: Pl.   1856.   1852.

[10] Unger, F. *U. S. Pat. Off. Rpt.* 343.   1859.

[11] Brandis, D. *Forest Fl.* 390.   1876.

[12] Burton, R. F. *Lake Reg. Cent. Afr.* 316.   1860.

chop, a dish prepared at Angola from the fresh nut, is pronounced most excellent by Montiero,[1] who also describes the fresh wine as delicious. Lunan [2] says the roasted nuts taste very much like the outside fat of roasted mutton, and that the negroes are fond of the oil which sometimes makes an ingredient in their foods. Hartt [3] says this palm is the *dendes* of Brazil, the *caiauhe* of the Amazons, and that the oil is much used for culinary purposes.

Elaeocarpus dentatus Vahl. *Tiliaceae.*

New Zealand. The pulp surrounding the stone of the fruit is eatable, and in India the fruits are either used in curries or pickled like olives.[4]

E. floribundus Blume.

Tropical Asia. The fruit is an article of food.[5] In India, the fruit, called in Bengal *julpai*, of the size and shape of an olive, is pickled. [6]

E. munroii Mast.

East Indies. The olive-sized fruit is eaten by the natives.[7]

Elaeodendron glaucum Pers. *Celastrineae.* CEYLON TEA.

Tropical Asia. This plant has been introduced from Ceylon under the name of Ceylon tea.[8]

E. orientale Jacq. OLIVE-WOOD.

Mauritius Islands, Madagascar and Burma, where it is called *let-pet-ben*. Its leaves are used by the natives for tea.[9]

E. sphaerophyllum Presl.

South Africa. The drupaceous fruits are edible.[10]

Eleocharis tuberosa Schult. *Cyperaceae.* WATER-CHESTNUT.

East Indies. This plant is grown in southern China for its roots, for which there is a great demand in all Chinese towns.[11] Royle [12] says it is the *pi-tsi* of the Chinese and that the round, turnip-shaped tubers are eaten. Loudon [13] calls it the water-chestnut and says it is grown in tanks by the Chinese for the tubers. Ainslie [14] says the root is

---

[1] Montiero *Angola, River Congo* 1:96, 97. 1875.

[2] Lunan, J. *Hort. Jam.* 2:26. 1814.

[3] Hartt *Geog. Braz.* 270. 1870.

[4] Smith, A. *Treas. Bot.* 1:444. 1870. (*E. hinau*)

[5] Lindley, J. *Trans. Hort. Soc. Lond.* 5:120. 1824. (*E. serratus*)

[6] Brandis, D. *Forest Fl.* 44. 1874. (*E. serratus*)

[7] Dyer, W. T. *Treas. Bot.* 2:1318. 1876. (*Monocera munroii*)

[8] Don, G. *Hist. Dichl. Pls.* 2:12. 1832.

[9] Pickering, C. *Chron. Hist. Pls.* 590. 1879.

[10] Baillon, H. *Hist. Pls.* 6:27. 1880.

[11] Fortune, R. ·*Wand. China* 307. 1847.

[12] Royle, J. F. *Illustr. Bot. Himal.* 1:413, 414. 1839.

[13] Loudon, J. C. *Enc. Agr.* 158. 1866. (*Scirpus tuberosus*)

[14] Ainslie, W. *Mat. Ind.* 2:342. 1826. (*Scirpus tuberosus*)

in high estimation either for the pot or as a medicine.   This rush can be subjected to regular cultivation in ponds, says Mueller,[1] for the sake of its edible, wholesome tubers.   It is largely cultivated all over China.   The tuber is sweet and juicy with a chestnut flavor and is universally used as food.   A kind of arrowroot is made from it.[2]

Elettaria cardamomum Maton. *Scitamineae*. CEYLON CARDAMOM.

East Indies. From time immemorial, great numbers of the natives have derived a livelihood from the cultivation of this plant.   The fruit is used as an aromatic in medicine throughout the East Indies and is largely consumed as a condiment.   It furnishes the Ceylon cardamom and the large cardamom of Guibourt mentioned in his history of drugs. It is cultivated in Crete.[3]

Eleusine aegyptiaca Desf. *Gramineae*. ELEUSINE.

Cosmopolitan tropics and subtropics. This grass grows most abundantly on waste ground, also on the flat roofs of the Arab houses in Unganyembe.   The natives gather the ears, dry them in the sun, beat out the grain on the rocks, grind and make a stir-about of it.[4]   Its grain is used in southern India.   It has a small seed, covered in part with a bearded husk through which the shining seed is seen.

E. coracana Gaertn. ELEUSINE. NATCHNEE. RAGEE.

South America, East Indies and Egypt. This grass is cultivated on a large scale in many tropical countries.   It is the most productive of all the Indian cereals, says Elliott,[5] and is the staple grain of the Mysore country.   In Sikkim, says Hooker,[6] the seeds are fermented to make a drink called *murwa*.   On the Coromandel coast, writes Ainslie,[7] it is a useful and most valuable grain, which is eaten and prized by the natives.   The grain is of the size of a mustard seed and is dark in color; it is either made into cakes, or is eaten as a porridge; it is pleasant to the taste and in its nature aperient.   It is enumerated by Thunberg[8] among the edible plants of Japan.   Grant[9] found this grass cultivated everywhere along his route through central Africa.   Its flour, if soaked for a night in water, makes a very fair unleavened bread.   A coarse beer, tasting pleasantly bitter, is also made from this grain mixed with that of *durra*.   Schweinfurth[10] says it is called *telaboon* by the Arabians, by the Abyssinians *tocusso* and is grown only in the poorest soils. It has a disagreeable taste and makes only a wretched sort of pop.   It has been grown in small quantities at the Michigan Agricultural College.[11]

[1] Mueller, F.   *Sel. Pls.* 226. 1891.   (*Heleocharis tuberosa*)
[2] Smith, F. P.   *Contrib. Mat. Med. China* 92. 1871.
[3] Masters, M. T.   *Treas. Bot.* 1:446. 1870.
[4] Speke, J. H.   *Journ. Disc. Source Nile* 587. 1864.
[5] Elliott, W.   *Bot. Soc. Edinb.* 7:288. 1863.
[6] Hooker, J. D.   *Journ. Hort. Soc. Lond.* 23. 1852.
[7] Ainslie, W.   *Mat. Ind.* 1:245. 1826. (*Cynosurus coracanus*)
[8] Thunberg, C. P.   *Fl. Jap.* xl. 1784. (*Cynosurus coracanus*)
[9] Speke, J. H.   *Journ. Disc. Source Nile* 587. 1864.
[10] Schweinfurth, G.   *Heart Afr.* 1:248. 1874.
[11] Beal, W. J.   *Rur. N. Y.*   Nov. 2, 1878.

E. tocussa Fresen.

Abyssinia. This plant furnishes a bread corn and is called *dagussa*.[1] Parkyns,[2] who ate of the bread in Abyssinia, says its taste is unpleasant as it leaves a gritty, sandy taste in the mouth and passes through the stomach with but little change. Its native country is given by Unger as the East Indies.

Elymus arenarius Linn. *Gramineae.* LYME GRASS. RANCHERIA GRASS.

Europe and western North America. The seed of this grass is threshed out and eaten by the Digger Indians.[3] It is indigenous to France and is used as an ornamental plant in gardens.[4]

Embelia nagushia D. Don. *Myrsineae.*

Himalayan region. The fruits are eaten in Sikkim as well as the leaves, which are sour to the taste.[5]

E. ribes Burm. f.

Tropical Asia. In Silhet, the berries are collected and used to adulterate black pepper.[6]

Emilia sonchifolia DC. *Compositae.*

Asia and tropical Africa. The leaves are eaten raw in salads in China.[7] Its leaves are eaten raw in salads, according to Murray.[8] In France, it is grown in flower gardens.[9]

Empetrum nigrum Linn. *Empetraceae.* CRAKEBERRY. CROWBERRY. MONOX.

Arctic and subarctic climates. The berries are eaten by the Scotch and Russian peasantry. The fruits are black, about the size of juniper berries, of a firm, fleshy substance and are insipid in taste.[10] They are consumed in a ripe or dry state by the Indians of the Northwest, are eaten by the Tuski of Alaska [11] and are gathered in autumn by the western Eskimo and frozen for winter food.[12]

Encephalartos caffer Miq. *Cycadaceae.* HOTTENTOT BREAD-FRUIT. KAFFIR BREAD.

South Africa. The interior of the trunk and the center of the ripe female cones contain a spongy, farinaceous pith, made use of by the Kaffirs as food.[13] On the female cone,

---

[1] Unger, F.   *U. S. Pat. Off. Rpt.* 306.   1859.

[2] Parkyns, M.   *Life Abyss.* 1:308.   1856.

[3] Newberry *Pacific R. R. Rpt.* 6:92.   1857.

[4] Vilmorin *Fl. Pl. Ter.* 362.   1870.   3rd Ed.

[5] Hooker, J. D.   *Treas. Bot.* 1:276.   1870.   (*Choripetalum undulatum*)

[6] Brandis, D.   *Forest Fl.* 284.   1874.

[7] Drury, H.   *Useful Pls. Ind.* 196.   1873.

[8] Ainslie, W.   *Mat. Ind.* 2:213.   1826.

[9] Vilmorin *Fl. Pl. Ter.* 186.   1870.   3rd Ed.   (*Cacalia sonchifolia*)

[10] Johns, C. A.   *Treas. Bot.* 1:449.   1870.

[11] Dall, W. H.   *Alaska* 379.   1897.

[12] Seemann, B.   *Anthrop. Journ.* 3:ccciii.   1865.

[13] Masters, M. T.   *Treas. Bot.* 1:450.   1870.

seeds as large as unshelled Jordan almonds are contained between the scales, and are surrounded with a reddish pulp, which is good to eat.[1]   Barrow[2] says it is used by the Kaffirs as food.   The stem, when stripped of its leaves, resembles a large pineapple.   The Kaffirs bury it for some months in the ground, then pound it, and extract a quantity of farinaceous matter of the nature of sago.   This sago is a favorite food with the natives and is not unacceptable to the Dutch settlers when better food cannot be had.

Enhalus koenigii Rich.   *Hydrocharideae.*   SEA FRUIT.

Sumatra.   The fruits are called *berak laut*, or sea fruit.   The seeds are slightly farinaceous and taste like chestnuts soaked in salt water.   This fruit is round, hairy and generally much covered with mud.[3]

Enhydra paludosa DC.   *Compositae.*

East Indies, Malay and Australia.   The leaves of this water plant are eaten by the natives as a vegetable.[4]   It is the *kingeka* of Bengal.

Entada scandens Benth.   *Leguminosae.*   SWORD BEAN.

Tropical shores from India to the Polynesian Islands.   The seeds are flat and brown and are eaten cooked[5] like chestnuts in Sumatra and Java,[6] and the pods furnish food in the West Indies.[7]   In Jamaica, Lunan[8] says the beans, after being long soaked in water, are boiled and eaten by some negroes.

E. wahlbergia Harv.

South Africa.   In central Africa, the bitter roots are eaten.[9]

Enteromorpha compressa (Linn.) Grev.   *Algae.*

This is one of the edible seaweeds of Japan.

Ephedra distachya Linn.   *Gnetaceae.*   SEA GRAPE.

China and south Russia.   The fruit is eaten by the Russian peasants and by the wandering hordes of Great Tartary.[10]   The fruit is eaten by the Chinese and is mucilaginous, with a slightly acid or pungent flavor.[11]   The fruit is ovoid, succulent, sweet, pale or bright red when ripe.   It is eaten in some places, as on the Sutlej.[12]

---

[1] Thunberg, C. P.   *Trav.* 2:66.   1796.   (*Zamia caffra*)

[2] Ainslie, W.   *Mat. Ind.* 1:363.   1826.

[3] Hooker, W. J.   *Lond. Journ. Bot.* 7:165.   1855.

[4] Dutt, U. C.   *Mat. Med. Hindus* 185.   1877.

[5] Brandis, D.   *Forest Fl.* 168.   1874.

[6] Pickering, C.   *Chron. Hist. Pls.* 775.   1879.

[7] Ibid.

[8] Lunan, J.   *Hort. Jam.* 1:137.   1814.

[9] Schweinfurth, G.   *Heart Afr.* 1:268.   1874.

[10] Balfour, J. H.   *Treas. Bot.* 1:454.   1870.

[11] Smith, F. P.   *Contrib. Mat. Med. China* 93.   1871.

[12] Brandis, D.   *Forest Fl.* 501.   1874.

Epilobium angustifolium Linn. *Onagrarieae.* FIREWEED. WILLOW-HERB.

Northern climates. In England, says Johnson,[1] the leaves are much used for the adulteration of tea. The leaves form a wholesome vegetable when boiled, and the young shoots make a good substitute for asparagus. The people of Kamchatka, says Lightfoot,[2] eat the young shoots which creep under the ground and they brew a sort of ale from the dried pith. Richardson[3] says the young leaves, under the name of *l'herbe fret*, are used by the Canadian voyagers as a potherb.

E. latifolium Linn.

Northern and arctic regions. This species furnishes a vegetable of poor quality for northern Asia and Iceland.[4]

E. tetragonum Linn. SQUARE-STEMMED WILLOW-HERB.

Europe. This plant is used as a vegetable in Iceland and northern Asia.[5]

Equisetum fluviatile Linn. *Equisetaceae.* HORSETAIL. JOINT GRASS. SCRUB GRASS.

Europe and adjoining Asia. The starch contained in the tubers of the rhizome is nutritious, according to Lindley.[6] This is the plant which was eaten by the Romans under the name *equisetum*. Coles, in his *Adam in Eden*, speaking of horsetails, says, " the young heads are dressed by some like asparagus, or being boyled are often bestrewed with flower and fried to be eaten."

E. hyemale Linn. DUTCH RUSH. HORSETAIL. SCOURING RUSH. SHAVE GRASS.

Northern climates. Lindley[7] says, it serves as food in time of famine.

Eremurus spectabilis Bieb. *Liliaceae.*

Asia Minor and Persia. In May and June the young shoots are sold as a vegetable in the villages of the Caucasus, Kurdistan and Crimea. The flavor is intermediate between spinach and purslane and is by no means a disagreeable vegetable.[8]

Eriobotrya japonica Lindl. *Rosaceae.* JAPANESE PLUM. LOQUAT.

A fruit tree indigenous in Japan and China and much cultivated in India. The loquat was first made known by Kempfer in 1690. It was brought to Europe by the French in 1784 and in 1787 was imported from Canton to Kew. It has not fruited at Paris in the open air but is successfully cultivated in the south of France, and its fruit is common in the markets of Toulon. At Malta, it succeeds admirably. In Florida, it is spoken of as if well known under the name of Japanese plum in 1867, ripening its fruit in February and March. In the Gulf States, it is said to do well, the fruit is the size of a large plum, juicy, subacid, refreshing, and altogether delightful and unique in flavor

---

[1] Johnson, C. P. *Useful Pls. Gt. Brit.* 104. 1862.

[2] Lightfoot, J. *Fl. Scot.* 1:197. 1789.

[3] Hooker, W. J. *Fl. Bor. Amer.* 1:205. 1840.

[4] Unger, F. *U. S. Pat. Off. Rpt.* 359. 1859.

[5] Ibid.

[6] Lindley, J. *Med. Econ. Bot.* 22. 1849.

[7] Ibid.

[8] Calvert, H. *Gard. Chron.* 596. 1855.

and quality.[1] In China the tree grows as far north as Fuhchau but does not produce as good fruit as in Canton. It is a more acid fruit than the apple and serves for cooking rather than as a table fruit. It resembles the medlar but is superior to it in flavor and size.

Eriodendron anfractuosum DC. *Malvaceae.* CABBAGE-WOOD. CEIBA.

Asia and tropical Africa. The fruit is eaten in India sometimes cooked and sometimes raw.[2] At Celebes, the seeds are eaten.[3]

Erioglossum edule Blume. *Sapindaceae.*

A shrub or small tree of Java and the islands of the Indian Archipelago. The fruit is edible.[4] A cider is made in Java from the pericarp of the fruit.[5]

Erisma japura Spruce. *Vochysiaceae.* JAPURA.

Brazil. The kernel of the red fruit is pleasant eating both raw and boiled. By a process of boiling and leaving in running water for several weeks, and then pounding in a mortar, it is made into a sort of butter, which is eaten with fish and game, being mixed in the gravy. People who can get over its vile smell, which is never lost, find it exceedingly savory.[6]

Erodium cicutarium L'Herit. *Geraniaceae.* PIN GRASS. STORKSBILL. WILD MUSK.

Europe and introduced into America. This plant, when young, is gathered and cooked, or eaten raw by the Blackfeet, Shoshone and Digger Indians. Fremont [7] saw it thus used, and R. Brown [8] says it is the pin grass of the Californians of which the stem is edible.

E. jacquinianum Fisch.

In Egypt, the tubercles are eaten.[9]

Eruca sativa Mill. *Cruciferae.* ROCKET.

Mediterranean region and western Asia. Rocket is called "a good salat-herbe" by Gerarde, and Don [10] says the leaves and tender stalks form an agreeable salad. Syme [11] says it is used in southern Europe as a salad. It is cultivated for its leaves and stalks which are used as a salad. Walsh [12] says, it is a fetid, offensive plant but is highly esteemed by the Greeks and Turks, who prefer it to any other salad. It was cultivated by the ancient Romans. Albertus Magnus,[13] in the thirteenth century, speaks of it in gardens;

[1] Redmond, D. *Amer. Pom. Soc. Rpt.* 56. 1875. (*Mespilus japonica*)
[2] Baillon, H. *Hist. Pls.* 4:116. 1875.
[3] Ainslie, W. *Mat. Ind.* 2:96. 1826.
[4] Brandis, D. *Forest Fl.* 108. 1876.
[5] Baillon, H. *Hist. Pls.* 5:387. 1878. (*Pancovia edulis*)
[6] Black, A. A. *Treas. Bot.* 1:464. 1870.
[7] Fremont *Explor. Exped.* 243. 1845.
[8] Brown, R. *Bot. Soc. Edinb.* 9:385. 1868.
[9] Baillon, H. *Hist. Pls.* 5:32. 1878. (*E. hirtum*)
[10] Don, G. *Hist. Dichl. Pls.* 1:53. 1831.
[11] Syme, J. T. *Treas. Bot.* 1:465. 1870.
[12] Walsh, R. *Trans. Hort. Soc. Lond.* 6:53. 1826. (*Brassica eruca*)
[13] Albertus Magnus *Veg.* Jessen Ed. 507. 1867.

so also does Ruellius,[1] 1536, who uses nearly the present French name, *roqueta*. In 1586, Camerarius[2] says it is planted most abundantly in gardens. In 1726, Townsend[3] says it is not now very common in English gardens, and in 1807 *Miller's Dictionary*[4] says it has been long rejected. Rocket was in American gardens in 1854 or earlier[5] and is yet included by Vilmorin[6] among European vegetables.

Eryngium maritimum Linn. *Umbelliferae.* SEA ERYNGO. SEA HOLLY. SEA-HOLM.

Asia Minor and the seashores along the Mediterranean and Atlantic as far as Denmark. The young, tender shoots, when blanched, may be eaten like asparagus. The roots are candied and sold as candied eryngo. When boiled or roasted, the roots resemble chestnuts and are palatable and nutritious.[7]

Erythrina indica Lam. *Leguminosae.* CORAL TREE.

Tropical Asia and Australia. This is a small tree commonly cultivated for supporting the weak stems of the pepper plant. In Ceylon the young, tender leaves are eaten in curries.[8]

Erythronium dens-canis Linn. *Liliaceae.* DOG'S-TOOTH VIOLET.

Europe and northern Asia. The Tartars collect and dry the bulbs and boil them with milk or broth.[9]

E. grandiflorum Pursh. DOG'S-TOOTH VIOLET.

Interior Oregon. The roots of this plant are eaten by some Indians.[10]

Erythroxylum coca Lam. *Lineae.* COCA. SPADIC.

A shrub of the Peruvian Andes cultivated from early times for its leaves which are used as a masticatory.[11] This use of the leaves under the name, coca, is common throughout the greater part of Peru, Quito, New Granada, and also on the banks of the Rio Negro, where it is known as *spadic*. It forms an article of commerce among the Indians and is largely cultivated in Bolivia. These leaves contain an alkaloid analogous to thein and exert, when chewed, a stimulant action.

Eschscholzia sp.? *Papaveraceae.*

China. This plant is grown in gardens and is used as a potherb or condiment.[12]

[1] Ruellius *Nat. Stirp.* 513. 1536.

[2] Camerarius *Epit.* 306. 1586.

[3] Townsend *Seedsman* 18. 1726.

[4] Martyn *Miller Gard. Dict.* 1807.

[5] Brown *U. S. Pat. Off. Rpt.* 377. 1854. (*Brassica eruca*)

[6] Vilmorin *Les Pls. Potag.* 541. 1883.

[7] Smith, J. *Dict. Econ. Pls.* 373. 1882.

[8] Smith, A. *Treas. Bot.* 1:468. 1870.

[9] Gmelin *Fl. Sibir.* 1:39. 1747.

[10] Brown, R. *Bot. Soc. Edinb.* 9:380. 1868.

[11] Pickering, C. *Chron. Hist. Pls.* 799. 1879.

[12] Smith, F. P. *Contrib. Mat. Med. China* 94. 1871.

Escobedia scabrifolia Ruiz & Pav. *Scrophularineae.*

Tropical America. The roots are said to be used for coloring gravies.[1]

Eucalyptus dumosa A. Cunn. *Myrtaceae.* MALLEE.

Australia. A manna called *lerp* is produced upon the leaves, which the natives use for food. It is said to be a secretion from an insect.

E. gunnii Hook. f. CIDER TREE.

Australia. This plant yields a cool, refreshing liquid from wounds made in the bark during spring.[2]

E. oleosa F. Muell. MALLEE.

Australia. The water drained from the roots is clear and good and is used by the natives of Queensland when no other water is obtainable.[3]

E. terminalis F. Muell.

Australia. Manna is procured from the leaves and small branches.[4]

Eucheuna speciosum Berk. *Algae.* JELLY PLANT.

This is the jelly plant of Australia and is one of the best species for making jelly, size and cement.

Euclea pseudebenus E. Mey. *Ebenaceae.*

South Africa. The fleshy, glaucous, brownish fruits, the size of a pea, are sweet and slightly astringent and are eaten by the natives of South Africa under the name *embolo.*[5]

E. undulata Thunb.

South Africa. The small, black berry is edible.[6] This is the *guarri* bush of South Africa. The sweet berries are eaten by the Hottentots or, bruised and fermented, they yield a vinegar.[7]

Eugenia acris Wight & Arn. *Myrtaceae.* WILD CLOVE.

East Indies and West Indies. In Jamaica, the aromatic, astringent leaves are often used in sauce and the berries for culinary purposes.[8] In Hindustan, it is called *lung.*[9]

E. apiculata DC.

Chile. The fruit is eaten.[10]

[1] Spruce *Gard. Chron.* 17:20. 1882.

[2] Smith, A. *Treas. Bot.* 1:472. 1870.

[3] Palmer, E. *Journ. Roy. Soc. New So. Wales* 17:106. 1884.

[4] Palmer, E. *Journ. Roy. Soc. New So. Wales* 17:98. 1884.

[5] *Gard. Chron.* 584. 1875.

[6] Mueller, F. *Sel. Pls.* 192. 1891.

[7] Thunberg, C. P. *Trav.* 1:202. 1795.

[8] Lunan, J. *Hort. Jam.* 1:76. 1814. (*Myrtus acris*)

[9] Pickering, C. *Chron. Hist. Pls.* 609. 1879.

[10] Baillon, H. *Hist. Pls.* 6:347. 1880.

E. aquea Burm. f.

A tree of India, called *lal jumrool*.   The fruit is the size of a small apple, is of a waxy appearance and of somewhat aromatic taste but is hardly eatable.   There are two varieties, a white and a pale rose-colored fruit.[1]

E. arnottiana Wight.

East Indies.   The fruit is eaten by the natives of India, though, owing to its astringency, it is by no means palatable.[2]

E. arrabidae Berg.

Brazil.   The berries are eaten.[3]

E. brasiliensis Lam.   BRAZIL CHERRY.

Brazil.   This species furnishes an edible fruit.[4]   It is grown under the name of Brazil cherry in the Public Gardens of Jamaica.[5]

E. caryophyllata Thunb.   CLOVE.

The clove tree is a handsome evergreen, native of the Moluccas.   It was introduced to the Mauritius in 1770, thence to Cayenne in 1773; to Zanzibar about the end of the century [6] and to Jamaica in 1789.[7]   The cloves of commerce are the unexpanded flower-buds.   Cloves were known to the ancient Greek and Roman writers.   They were brought from the far East to Ceylon in the days of Cosmas Indicopleustes, in the first half of the sixth century, and were known in the Mediterranean countries to Paulus Aegineta, A. D. 634.[8]   Clove stalks were an article of import into Europe during the Middle Ages.   Clove leaves were imported into Palestine in the twelfth century and were sold at Frankfort in Germany about 1450.   The stalks are still an object of trade from Zanzibar, where they are called by the natives *vikunia;* they are tolerably aromatic, and are used for adulterating ground cloves.[9]   For many years, the Dutch exercised a strict monopoly in the growth of this spice, by restricting its cultivation to the island of Amboina and even extirpating all but a limited number of the trees, but they are now grown in the West Indies and elsewhere.

E. catinga Baill.

Guiana.   The fruit is eaten.[10]

E. cauliflora Berg.

Brazil.   The *jacbuticaba* grows wild in the woods of the south of Brazil and is also cultivated in most of the gardens in the diamond and gold districts.   The fruit is

[1] Firminger, T. A. C.   *Gard. Ind.* 266.   1874.   (*Jambosa aquea*)

[2] Wight, R.   *Icon. Pls.* 3: Pl. 999.   No date.

[3] Baillon, H.   *Hist. Pls.* 6:347.   1880.

[4] Unger, F.   *U. S. Pat. Off. Rpt.* 349.   1859.

[5] Morris *Rpt. Pub. Gard. Jam.* 35.   1880.

[6] Flückiger and Hanbury *Pharm.* 249.   1879.

[7] Morris *Rpt. Pub. Gard. Jam.* 35.   1880.

[8] Pickering, C.   *Chron. Hist. Pls.* 574.   1879.   (*Caryophyllus aromaticus*)

[9] Flückiger and Hanbury *Pharm.* 254, 255.   1879.

[10] Baillon, H.   *Hist. Pls.* 6:344.   1880.

black, about the size of a Green Gage plum, of a pulpy consistency and very refreshing.[1] Unger [2] says the fruit is of the size of an Oxheart cherry and under the tender, black epidermis there is a white, soft and even juicy flesh in which are two or three seeds. It is inferior in taste to our cherry. In Brazil, it is much esteemed. It has been planted in the Antilles and even introduced into the East Indies.

E. cordifolia Wight.

Ceylon. The fruit is an inch in diameter.[3]

E. darwinii Hook. f.

Chile. The fruits are eaten.[4]

E. dichotoma DC.

North America and West Indies. The small, edible fruit is of an agreeable, aromatic flavor.[5]

E. disticha DC.   WILD COFFEE.

Jamaica. The fruit is eaten in the Antilles.[6]

E. djouat Perr.

Philippine Islands. It yields an edible fruit.[7]

E. dulcis Berg.

Brazil. The berries are eaten.[8]

E. dysenterica DC.

Brazil. This is an excellent dessert fruit.

E. edulis Benth. & Hook. f.

Brazil. The berries are eaten.

E. floribunda West.

Santa Cruz. The fruit is edible.[9]

E. formosa Cambess.

Brazil. The berries are eaten.[10]

E. fragrans Willd.   ZEBRA-WOOD.

West Indies. The fruit is eaten in the Antilles.[11]

E. guabiju Berg.

Region of Argentina. The berries are eaten in Brazil.[12]

---

[1] Gardner Trav. Braz. 343. 1846.
[2] Unger, F.   U. S. Pat. Off. Rpt. 349.   1859.
[3] Mueller, F.   Sel. Pls. 192. 1891.
[4] Baillon, H.   Hist. Pls. 6:347. 1880.
[5] Sargent U. S. Census 9:88. 1884.
[6] Baillon, H.   Hist. Pls. 6:347. 1880.
[7] Unger, F.   U. S. Pat. Off. Rpt. 336. 1859.
[8] Baillon, H.   Hist. Pls. 6:347. 1880.
[9] Unger, F.   U. S. Pat. Off. Rpt. 349. 1859.
[10] Baillon, H.   Hist. Pls. 6:347. 1880.
[11] Ibid.
[12] Ibid.

E. inocarpa DC.

Brazil. The fruit is about the size of a plum, with a fibrous, acid-sweet flesh.[1]

E. itacolumensis Berg.

Brazil. The berries are eaten.[2]

E. jambolana Lam. BLACK PLUM. JAMBOLAN. JAMBOLAN PLUM. JAMBOOL. JAMBU. JAVA PLUM.

Asia and Australian tropics. This tree yields in India, says Dutt,[3] an abundant crop of subacid, edible fruits. In some places, the fruit attains the size of a pigeon egg and is of superior quality. Brandis[4] says the fruit has a harsh but sweetish flavor, somewhat astringent and acid, and is much eaten by the natives of India. Firminger[5] compares it to a damson in appearance and to a radish in taste.

E. jambos Linn. MALABAR PLUM. ROSE APPLE.

Tropical eastern Asia. The tree is cultivated in many parts of India for its fruit, which is of the size of a small apple, with a delicate, rose-water perfume but dry and hardly worth eating.[6] It can hardly be considered eatable, being of a poor flavor and of a dry, pithy consistency[7] but is made into preserves.[8] The tree was introduced into Jamaica in 1762. The rind, says Lunan,[9] has a sweetish, watery taste, with a flavor like roses but it is not in much esteem as a fruit.[10] It was introduced into Florida by C. Codrington,[11] Jacksonville, before 1877.

E. javanica Lam. JAMBOSA. JUMROOL.

A moderate-sized tree of the islands of the Indian Archipelago. The fruit is the size of a small apple, pure white, shining, wax-like and has a raw, watery, insipid taste. It is hardly fit to be eaten.[12]

E. ligustrina Miq.

Brazil. The berries are eaten in Brazil.

E. lineata DC. GUAVA BERRY.

West Indies. A small tree of Tortola. The fruit is small and excellent for dessert. It is also used for a preserve and forms a favorite cordial.[13]

E. longipes Berg.

Florida. The small, red fruit with the flavor of cranberries is edible.[14]

---

[1] Baillon, H. *Hist. Pls.* **6**:347. 1880.

[2] Ibid.

[3] Dutt, U. C. *Mat. Med. Hindus* 164. 1877.

[4] Brandis, D. *Forest Fl.* 234. 1874.

[5] Firminger, T. A. C. *Gard. Ind.* 264. 1874. (*Syzygium jambolanum*)

[6] Brandis, D. *Forest Fl.* 233. 1874.

[7] Firminger, T. A. C. *Gard. Ind.* 265. 1874. (*Jambosa vulgaris*)

[8] Smith, J. *Dom. Bot.* 371. 1871.

[9] Lunan, J. *Hort. Jam.* **2**:127. 1814.

[10] Ibid.

[11] *Amer. Pom. Soc. Rpt.* 66. 1877. (*Jambosa vulgaris*)

[12] Firminger, T. A. C. *Gard. Ind.* 266. 1874. (*Jambosa alba*)

[13] Smith, J. *Dict. Econ. Pls.* 202. 1882.

[14] Sargent *U. S. Census* **9**:89. 1884.

E. luschnathiana Klotzsch.

Brazil.   The berries are eaten.

E. mabaeoides Wight.

Ceylon.   The fruit is the size of a small cherry.

E. macrocarpa Roxb.

East Indies, where it is called *chalta-jamb*.   The fruit is eaten by the natives.[1]

E. makapa Mer. et Lens (?).   JAMBOSINE.

This tree is cultivated in the Mauritius under several varieties.   The fruit is pear-shaped and edible.[2]   The jambosine was introduced into Florida at Jacksonville before 1877.[3]

E. malaccensis Linn.   JAMBOS.   LARGE-FRUITED   ROSE   APPLE.   MALAY   APPLE.   ROSE
          APPLE.

A tree of the Moluccas, cultivated in the Indian Archipelago, Pacific islands, China and India.   " The fruit," says Capt. Cook, at Batavia, " is of a deep red color and an oval shape; the largest, which are always the best, are not bigger than a small apple; they are pleasant and cooling, though they have not much flavor."   Rheede says the fruit is of the size and shape of a moderate pear, white with a blush of red, of a very agreeable, vinous taste and smell.   Firminger[4] says the fruit is of the size and form of a very small apple, perfectly smooth, of a pure, translucent white, with a beautiful blush of crimson and that some persons eat it but it is not worth eating.   Seemann[5] says that it is quince-shaped, with an apple-like smell and delicate flavor.   In 1839, a specimen of the fruit grown under glass at Cambridge, Massachusetts, was exhibited at the Massachusetts Horticultural Society's exhibition[6] and the fruit was pronounced most delicious, partaking of the fragrance of the rose with the sweetness of the peach.   The flowers are preserved by the Dutch at Amboina and are frequently eaten as a salad.[7]

E. myrobalana DC.

Brazil.   The berries are eaten in Brazil.[8]

E. nhanica Cambess.

Brazil.   The berries are used as a table fruit.[9]

E. oblata Roxb.

East Indies.   It is called *goolam* and is cultivated for its fruit.[10]

---

[1] Wight, R.   *Icon. Pls.* **2**: Pl.   612.   1843.

[2] Unger, F.   *U. S. Pat. Off. Rpt.* 336.   1859.   (*Jambosa makapa*)

[3] *Amer. Pom. Soc. Rpt.* 66.   1877.   (*Jambosa makapa*)

[4] Firminger, T. A. C.   *Gard. Ind.* 265.   1874.   (*Jambosa malaccensis*)

[5] Seemann, B.   *Fl. Viti.* 77.   1865–73.

[6] *Hist. Mass. Hort. Soc.* 249.   1880.

[7] Andrews *Bot. Reposit.* **7**:458.   1797.

[8] Baillon, H.   *Hist. Pls.* **6**:347.   1880.

[9] Mueller, F.   *Sel. Pls.* 193.   1891.

[10] Wight, R.   *Icon. Pls.* **2**: Pl. 622.   1843.

E. operculata Roxb.

Tropical Asia. The fruit is round, of the size and appearance of small, black cherries and is very generally eaten in Chittagong.[1] The fruit is eaten.[2]

E. pisiformis Cambess.

Brazil. The berries are eaten.[3]

E. pitanga Kiaersk. PITANGA.

Brazil. Hartt[4] says its refreshingly acid, red fruit is eaten.

E. procera Poir. IRONWOOD.

Santo Domingo and south Florida, where it is called ironwood. The round berry, the size of a pepper, is edible.[5]

E. pseudopsidium Jacq.

Martinique. The fruit is edible and is held in considerable esteem in the West Indies.[6]

E. pulchella Roxb.

Moluccas. It bears a fruit like the black currant.[7]

E. pumila Gardn.

Brazil. The berries are eaten in Guiana.[8]

E. pyriformis Cambess.

Brazil. The fruit is the size of a pear.[9]

E. rariflora Benth.

Fiji Islands. The fruit resembles a cherry in size and shape and is edible.[10]

E. revoluta Wight.

East Indies. The berries are an inch in diameter.[11]

E. richii A. Gray.

Pacific islands. In Viti, the agreeably-smelling fruit is eaten.[12]

E. suborbicularis Benth.

Australia. The fruit is large, red, with small stone and is eaten when ripe.[13]

---

[1] Wight, R. *Icon. Pls.* 2: Pl. 615. 1843.
[2] Brandis, D. *Forest Fl.* 235. 1874,
[3] Baillon, H. *Hist. Pls.* 6:347. 1880.
[4] Hartt *Geog. Braz.* 59. 1870.
[5] Don, G. *Hist. Dichl. Pls.* 2:855. 1832.
[6] Ibid.
[7] Wight, R. *Icon. Pls.* 2: Pl. 628. 1843.
[8] Baillon, H. *Hist. Pls.* 6:347. 1880.
[9] Mueller, F. *Sel. Pls.* 193. 1891.
[10] Seemann, B. *Fl. Viti.* 79. 1865-73.
[11] Mueller, F. *Sel. Pls.* 193. 1891.
[12] Seemann, B. *Fl. Viti.* 78. 1865-73.
[13] Palmer, E. *Journ. Roy. Soc. New So. Wales* 17:98. 1884.

E. supraaxillaris Spring. TALA.

Southern Brazil. The fruit is large and edible.[1]

E. temu Hook. & Arn.

Chile. The fruit is eaten.[2]

E. uniflora Linn. BRAZIL CHERRY. CAYENNE CHERRY. PITANGA. SURINAM CHERRY.

Tropical America, where it is called *pitanga*. In India, this species appears to be cultivated under the names of Brazil cherry and cherry of Cayenne. The fruit of this large shrub is about the size of a button and is considered agreeable by the natives.[3]

E. zeyheri Harv.

South Africa. The berries are the size of a cherry and are edible.[4]

Eulophia campestris Wall. *Orchideae.* SALEP.

East Indies. This plant furnishes the salep collected in Cashmere.[5]

E. herbacea Lindl. SALEP.

East Indies. This species furnishes the salep of the Indian bazaars known as *saleb misri*.[6]

Euonymus japonicus Linn. f. *Celastrineae.* JAPANESE SPINDLE TREE.

China and Japan. In China, the leaves of this tree are eaten when young.[7]

Eupatorium triplinerve Vahl. *Compositae.*

Tropical America. An infusion of the leaves has an agreeable and somewhat spicy taste and is a good dict drink. Dyer says the plant is now chiefly cultivated at the island of Bourbon, for the purpose of being dried and sent to France, where it is used as a tea substitute.[8]

Euphorbia balsamifera Ait. *Euphorbiaceae.* BALSAM SPURGE.

Canary Islands. Its juice is thickened to a jelly and eaten by the natives.[9]

E. canariensis Linn.

Canary Islands. The natives of Teneriffe are in the habit of removing the bark and then sucking the inner portion of the stem to quench their thirst.

E. edulis Lour.

Cochin China. It is mentioned as a potherb.[10]

[1] Mueller, F. *Sel. Pls.* 193. 1891.
[2] Baillon, H. *Hist. Pls.* 6:347. 1880.
[3] Firminger, T. A. C. *Gard. Ind.* 264. 1874. (*E. michelii*)
[4] Mueller, F. *Sel. Pls.* 194. 1891.
[5] Archer, T. C. *Profit. Pls.* 85. 1865.
[6] Flückiger and Hanbury *Pharm.* 655. 1879.
[7] Smith, F. P. *Contrib. Mat. Med. China* 94. 1871.
[8] Ainslie, W. *Mat. Ind.* 2:35. 1826.
[9] Pickering, C. *Chron. Hist. Pls.* 467. 1879.
[10] Masters, M. T. *Treas. Bot.* 1:477. 1870.

E. lathyris Linn. CAPER SPURGE.

Southern Europe. The seeds are used as a substitute for capers[1] but, says Johnson,[2] they are extremely acrid and require long steeping in salt and water and afterwards in vinegar.

Euphoria informis Poir. *Sapindaceae.*

Cochin China. Its fruit is eaten in China.[3]

Euryale ferox Salisb. *Nymphaeceae.* GORGON. PRICKLY WATER-LILY.

East India and China. This aquatic plant is frequently cultivated in India and China for its floury seeds. In China, it is said to have been in cultivation for upwards of 3000 years.[4] The fruit is round, soft, pulpy and the size of a small orange; it contains from 8 to 15 round, black seeds as large as peas, which are eaten roasted. The pulp is also eaten. Smith[5] says, in China, it is much cultivated for the stems, rhizomes and seeds, all of which contain much starch and are eaten.

Euterpe edulis Mart. *Palmae.* ASSAI PALM.

Tropical America. The long, terminal bud of this Brazilian palm is pronounced by Gardner[6] equal to asparagus in flavor when cooked.

E. montana R. Grah.

Islands of New Spain. The terminal leaf-bud is used as a cabbage.[7]

E. oleracea Mart. ASSAI PALM.

Brazil. Bates[8] says the fruit forms a universal article of diet in all parts of Brazil. It is the size of a cherry, round and contains but a small portion of pulp, which is made, with the addition of water, into a thick, violet-colored beverage. Mrs. Agassiz[9] pronounces this diet drink as very good, eaten with sugar and farina of the mandioc. The terminal leaf-bud is used as a cabbage.[10]

Eutrema wasabi Maxim. *Cruciferae.* JAPANESE HORSERADISH.

Japan. This is Japanese horseradish, which grows wild on the coast and is cultivated in small quantities, rasped and eaten with fish. The best roots are cultivated only in clear spring water running down the mountain valleys.

Evernia prunastri Linn. *Lichenes.* ACH.

Northern Europe, America and Asia. This lichen was observed by Sibthorp and

---

[1] Loudon, J. C. *Hort.* 689. 1860.
[2] Johnson, C. P. *Useful Pls. Gt. Brit.* 226. 1862.
[3] Don, G. *Hist. Dichl. Pls.* 1:670. 1831. (*Nephelium informe*)
[4] Hooker, J. D. *Himal. Journ.* 2:255. 1854.
[5] Smith, F. P. *Contrib. Mat. Med. China* 75. 1871.
[6] Gardner, G. *Trav. Braz.* 396. 1846.
[7] Seemann, B. *Pop. Hist. Palms* 206. 1856.
[8] Bates, H. W. *Nat. Amaz.* 647. Humboldt *Libr. Sci.* 1879.
[9] Agassiz *Journ. Braz.* 140. 1868.
[10] Seemann, B. *Pop. Hist. Palms* 206. 1856.

Bory[1] on the branches of plum and other trees throughout Greece and around Constantinople. According to Forskal, it is imported in shiploads from Greece into Egypt and mixed in bread. According to Lindley, it has a peculiar power of imbibing and retaining odors.

Exocarpus cupressiformis Labill. *Santalaceae.* AUSTRALIAN CURRANTS.

Australia. The fruit is eaten and is made into preserves.[2]

Fagopyrum cymosum Meissn. *Polygonaceae.* PERENNIAL BUCKWHEAT.

Himalayas and China. This is a common Himalayan plant which forms an excellent spinach and is called *pullop-bi*.[3] It occurs also in China.[4] The plant seeds badly and hence is not valued as a cereal.

F. esculentum Moench. BRANK. BUCKWHEAT. NOTCH-SEEDED BUCKWHEAT.

Europe and northern Asia. Buckwheat seems to have been unknown to the Greeks and Romans. It grows wild in Nepal, China and Siberia and is supposed to have been brought to Europe at the beginning of the sixteenth century from northern Asia. According to Buckman,[5] it is mentioned in a German Bible printed in 1522. It is mentioned by Tragus,[6] 1552, as cultivated in the Odenwald under the name of *heydenkorn*. Caesalpinus,[7] 1583, describes it as cultivated, probably in Italy under the name of *formentone aliis saresinum*. Dodoenaeus,[8] 1616, says it was much cultivated in Germany and Brabant. It must have secured early admittance to America, for samples of American growth were sent to Holland by the colony of Manhattan Island as early as 1626. It is at present cultivated in the United States as a field crop, as also in northern Europe, in China, Japan and elsewhere. Fraser[9] found large fields of it at 11,405 feet elevation near the temple of Milun in the Himalayas. In northern India and Ceylon, it is of recent introduction and its cultivation is confined to narrow limits. Notch-seeded buckwheat is a native of the mountainous districts of China and Nepal, where it is cultivated for its seeds.[10]

F. tataricum Gaertn. TARTARIAN BUCKWHEAT.

Europe and northern Asia. Tartarian buckwheat is of the same origin as buckwheat, though it is much less widely distributed and was introduced at a much later period into Europe.[11] It has been cultivated from time immemorial in Nepal and on the confines of China.

Fagus ferruginea Ait. *Cupuliferae.* AMERICAN BEECH.

North America. The nuts are esteemed delicious and are found in season in the

---

[1] Sibthorp, J. *Fl. Graecae* **2**:314. 1813. (*Borrera prunastri*)

[2] Smith, A. *Treas. Bot.* **2**:674. 1870. (*Leptomeria acerba*)

[3] Hooker, J. D. *Himal. Journ.* **2**:31. 1854. (*Polygonum cymosum*)

[4] Mueller, F. *Sel. Pls.* 196. 1891.

[5] Pickering, C. *Geog. Distrib. Ans. Pls.* **1**:137. 1863–1876.

[6] De Candolle, A. *Geog. Bot.* **2**:953. 1855. (*Polygonum fagopyrum*)

[7] Ibid.

[8] Ibid.

[9] Fraser *Enc. Brit.* **17**:630. 1859. 8th Ed.

[10] Mueller, F. *Sel. Pls.* 124. 1880.

[11] Unger, F. *U. S. Pat. Off. Rpt.* 306, 307. 1859. (*Polygonum tataricum*)

Boston markets.   Porcher[1] says the young leaves are used by the common people of the South as a potherb.   In Maine, the buds are eaten by the Indians.

F. sylvatica Linn.   EUROPEAN BEECH.

Europe.   In Hanover, the oil of the nut is used as a salad oil and as a substitute for butter.[2]   In France, the nuts are roasted and serve as a substitute for coffee.[3]   Sawdust of beech wood is boiled in water, baked and then mixed with flour to form the material for bread in Norway and Sweden.[4]

Farsetia clypeata R. Br.   *Cruciferae.*

Southern Europe and the Orient.   This plant has the same properties as the cresses.[5]

Fedia cornucopiae Gaertn.   *Valerianeae.*   HORN-OF-PLENTY.   VALERIAN.

Mediterranean region.   According to Robinson,[6] this species is grown in France as a salad plant.   It is also grown in flower gardens.[7]

Feronia elephantum Correa.   *Rutaceae.*   ELEPHANT APPLE.   WOOD APPLE.[1]

East Indies.   The fruit is of the size of a large apple and is covered with a hard, gray, scabrous, woody rind.   The pulp is universally eaten on the coast of Coromandel.[8]   The interior of the fruit, says Firminger[9] is filled with a brown, soft, mealy substance, rather acid and smelling of rancid butter.   Brandis[10] says a jelly is made of it in India, and Wight[11] says that this very pleasant jelly resembles black-currant jelly.   Dutt[12] says it is cultivated in India for its fruit, the pulp of which is eaten and made into a *chatni*.

Ferula assa-foetida Linn.   *Umbelliferae.*   ASAFETIDA.   FOOD-OF-THE-GODS.

Persia and Afghanistan.   Asafetida is called food-of-the-gods by the Persians, who hold the juice in high esteem as a condiment,[13] eat the leaves as greens and the root when roasted.   Gerarde[14] says it is reported to be eaten in Apulia.   The young shoots and heads are considered by the Khirgls as a great delicacy.   The fetid odor disappears on boiling.[15]

F. longifolia Fisch.

South Russia.   The aromatic, long roots are esteemed as a vegetable.[16]

[1] Porcher, F. P.   *Res. So. Fields, Forests* 275.   1869.   (*F. americana*)

[2] Hooker, W. J.   *Lond. Journ. Bot.* 7:184.   1855.

[3] Loudon, J. C.   *Arb. Frut. Brit.* 3:1963.   1854.

[4] Church, A. H.   *Food* 71.   1887.

[5] Baillon, H.   *Hist. Pls.* 3:225.   1874.

[6] Robinson, W.   *Parks, Gard. Paris* 504.   1878.

[7] Vilmorin *Fl. Pl. Ter.*   1179.   1870.   3rd Ed.   (*Valeriana cornucopiae*)

[8] Lindley, J.   *Trans. Hort. Soc. Lond.* 5:118.   1824.

[9] Firminger, T. A. C.   *Gard. Ind.* 218.   1874.

[10] Brandis, D.   *Forest Fl.* 57.   1874.

[11] Pickering, C.   *Chron. Hist. Pls.* 370.   1879.

[12] Dutt, U. C.   *Mat. Med. Hindus* 131.   1877.

[13] Smith, J.   *Dict. Econ. Pls.* 26.   1882.

[14] Gerarde, J.   *Herb.* 2nd Ed.   1057.   1633 or 36.

[15] Schuyler *Turkistan* 1:228.   1876.

[16] Mueller, F.   *Sel. Pls.* 199.   1891.

F. narthex Boiss. ASAFETIDA.

Baltistan.   Kaempfer says that in Afghanistan and Khorassan there are two varieties, one called *Kama-i-gawi*, which is grazed by cattle and used as a potherb and the other called *Kama-i-anguza*, which affords the asafetida of commerce.   Among the Mohammedan and Hindu population of India, the gum is generally used as a condiment and, in regions where the plant grows, the fresh leaves are cooked as an article of diet.[1]

Ficus aspera Forst. f. Fig.   *Urticaceae.*   TONGUE FIG.

Islands of New Hebrides.   This is a tropical species of fig whose fruit may be eaten.[2]

F. benghalensis Linn.   BANYAN.

East Indies and African tropics.   The sweetish fruit of the banyan is eaten in India in times of scarcity.

F. brassii R. Br.

A shrub of Sierra Leone.   It bears an edible fruit about as large as that of the white Ischia fig.[3]

F. carica Linn.   FIG.

Europe, Orient and Africa.   The fig is indigenous, says Unger,[4] in Syria, Persia, Asia Minor, Greece and north Africa and has been cultivated in these countries from time immemorial and even as far as southern Germany.   The fig had its place as a fruit tree in the garden of Alcinous.   According to one Grecian tradition, Dionysius Sycetes was the discoverer of the fig tree; according to another, Demeter brought the first fig tree to Greece; a third tradition states that the fig tree grew up from the thunderbolt of Jupiter.   The fig is mentioned by Athenaeus, Columella and Macrobius, and six varieties were known in Italy in the time of Cato.   Pliny enumerates 29 sorts in his time.   At the present time, no less than 40 varieties are enumerated for Sicily by Dr. Presl.   The fig tree is enumerated among the fruit trees of Charlemagne.   It was carried to England in 1525 or 1548 by Cardinal Pole.[5]   Cortez carried the fig tree to Mexico in 1560,[6] and figs are mentioned as cultivated in Virginia in 1669 [7] and were observed growing out of the ruins of Frederica, Georgia, by Wm. Bartram,[8] about 1773, and at Pearl Island near New Orleans.   Downing [2] describes 15 varieties as the most desirable sorts for this country and says the fig reached here in 1790.

F. cooperi Hort.

Tropical America.   The purple fruit, at the Department of Agriculture Conservatory, February 16, 1880, was edible but was not very attractive.[10]

---

[1] Flückiger and Hanbury *Pharm.* 283.   1879.

[2] Unger, F.   *U. S. Pat. Off. Rpt.* 332.   1859.

[3] Sabine, J.   *Trans. Hort. Soc. Lond.* **5**:448.   1824.

[4] Unger, F.   *U. S. Pat. Off. Rpt.* 331.   1859.

[5] Thompson, R.   *Treas. Bot.* **1**:493.   1870.

[6] Unger, F.   *U S. Pat. Off. Rpt.* 331.   1859.

[7] Shrigley, N.   *True Rel. Va., Md.* 5.   1669.   Force Coll. Tracts. **3**:   1844.

[8] Bartram, W.   *Hist. Mass. Hort. Soc.* 27.   1880.

[9] Downing, A. J.   *Fr. Fr. Trees Amer.* 291.   1857.

[10] Sturtevant, Dr.   Visit to Wash. Feb. 16, 1880.

F. cunia Buch.-Ham.

Tropical Asia. The fruit is eaten.[1]

F. erecta Thunb.

Himalayas, China and Japan. In Japan, the small figs are sometimes eaten.[2]

F. forskalaei Vahl.

Tropical Arabia. The fruit is not agreeable but is eaten.

F. glomerata Roxb.

A large tree of tropical eastern Asia. The ripe fruit is eaten. In times of scarcity, the unripe fruit is pounded, mixed with flour and made into cakes.[3] In the Konckans, the natives sometimes eat the fruit which outwardly resembles the common fig.[4] The fruit is edible but insipid and is usually found full of insects. In Cebu, in times of drought, the inhabitants have no other resources for water than cutting the root.[5]

F. granatum Forst. f.

New Hebrides. A tropical species with fruit that is eaten.[6]

F. heterophylla Linn. f.

Tropical Asia. The fruit is eaten by the natives of India.[7]

F. hirta Vahl.

Tropical Asia and Malay. The fruit is eaten by the natives of India.[8]

F. infectoria Roxb.

Tropical Asia and Malay. The fruit, in racemes, is nearly round, of a reddish color when ripe, and about the size of a small plum. It is eaten by the common people.[9]

F. palmata Forsk.

Tropical Asia, Arabia and East Indies. In the hills of India, this fig is eaten largely and is succulent, sweet and pleasant.[10]

F. persica Boiss.

A shrub found wild about Shiraz, Persia. The fruit is edible but not very palatable.[11]

F. religiosa Linn. PEEPUL. SACRED FIG.

East Indies. In central India, the young leaf-buds are eaten as a vegetable by the Hill Tribes in times of scarcity.[12]

---

[1] Brandis, D. *Forest Fl.* 421. 1874.

[2] Thunberg, C. P. *Trav.* 3:62. 1796.

[3] Brandis, D. *Forest Fl.* 422. 1874.

[4] Pickering, C. *Chron. Hist. Pls.* 414. 1879.

[5] Ibid.

[6] Unger, F. *U. S. Pat. Off. Rpt.* 332. 1859.

[7] Royle, J. F. *Illustr. Bot. Himal.* 1:337. 1839.

[8] Ibid.

[9] Ainslie, W. *Mat. Ind.* 2:30. 1826.

[10] Brandis, D. *Forest Fl.* 419. 1876.

[11] Unger, F. *U. S. Pat. Off. Rpt.* 332. 1859.

[12] Brandis, D. *Forest Fl.* 415. 1876.

F. roxburghii Wall.

Burma and Himalayan regions. The fruit is eaten by the natives in their curries.[1]

F. rumphii Blume.

Himalayan regions and Malay. This is a large tree cultivated in the Darrang district of Assam for rearing the lakh insect. The fruit is eaten.[2]

F. sur Forsk.

Mountains of Yemen. The fruit is edible.[3]

F. sycomorus Linn. ASSES FIG. SYCOMORE.

North Africa. The fruit is somewhat aromatic and is brought to the markets at Cairo and is eaten throughout the entire East.[4] The figs are sweet and delicate. They were selected by the ancient Egyptians as the fruit given by the goddess Netpe to those who were worthy of admission to the regions of eternal happiness.[5]

Flacourtia cataphracta Roxb. *Bixineae.* PUNEALA PLUM.

East Indies. The puneala plum is a fruit of India, better in flavor than a sloe but inferior to a poor plum. It makes an excellent stew.[6]

F. inermis Roxb. LOOY-LOOY.

Moluccas. This species is cultivated in the Moluccas for its pleasant, edible fruit. It is a little tree bearing a berry of reddish-purple color, the size of a small cherry and has five angles.[7] The reddish-purple berries are of a pleasant, acid taste; they are called *ṭomi-tomi* in India.[8] The fruit, called by the Malays *koorkup*, though rather too acid to be eaten raw, is esteemed for tarts and pies.[9] In Ceylon, it is called by the natives *lowi lowi;* by the English looy-looy. The fruit makes an excellent jelly, resembling and as good as currant jelly, and is also used for tarts.[10]

F. montana J. Grah.

East Indies. It is called *attuck ka jhar.* The fruit, the size of a crab apple, is eaten by the natives.[11]

F. ramontchi L'Herit. BATOKO PLUM. MADAGASCAR PLUM.

East Indies, Malay and Madagascar. The fruit is of the size of a plum, of a sharp but sweetish taste.[12] It is common in the jungles of India. The fruit, when fully ripe, is

---

[1] Wight, R. *Icon. Pls.* 2: Pl. 673. 1843. (*F. macrophylla*)

[2] Brandis, D. *Forest Fl.* 417. 1874. (*F. cordifolia*)

[3] Pickering, C. *Chron. Hist. Pls.* 366. 1879.

[4] Unger, F. *U. S. Pat. Off. Rpt.* 344. 1859.

[5] Figuier *Veg. World* 343. 1867.

[6] Firminger, T. A. C. *Gard. Ind.* 197. 1874.

[7] Roxburgh, W. *Pls. Corom. Coast* 3:16. 1819.

[8] Firminger, T. A. C. *Gard. Ind.* 197. 1874.

[9] Hooker, W. J. *Bot. Misc.* 1:289. 1830.

[10] Hooker, W. J. *Journ. Bot.* 2:226. 1840.

[11] Pickering, C. *Chron. Hist. Pls.* 743. 1879. (*F. crenata*)

[12] Smith, J. *Dict. Econ. Pls.* 331. 1882.

of a pleasant acid taste and very refreshing.[1]   At Bombay, the fruit is eaten but is by no means good.[2]   The fruit is eaten.[3]

F. sepiaria Roxb.

East Indies and Malay.   In Coromandel, the berries are sold in the market.[4]   The fruit has a pleasant, acid taste and is very refreshing.[5]   At Bombay, its berries are eaten.[6]

Flagellaria indica Linn.   *Flagellarieae.*

Tropical shores from Africa to the Samoan Islands.   In Fiji, the ears of this plant are eaten.[7]

Flemingia tuberosa Dalzell.   *Leguminosae.*

East Indies.   The tubers are said to be edible.[8]

F. vestita Benth.   FLEMINGIA.

Himalayan region.   This prostrate plant is cultivated in many parts of northwest India for the sake of its edible, tuberous roots, which are nearly elliptical and about an inch long.[9]

Fluggea leucopyrus Willd.   *Euphorbiaceae.*

East Indies.   The small, round, whitish-colored fruit is a little bitter to the taste but is eaten in India by the poor.[10]

F. microcarpa Blume.

Old World tropics.   The fruit, a white, globose, dehiscent berry, one-sixth inch in diameter, is eaten.[11]   The berries are eaten by the natives of eastern tropical Africa.[12]

Foeniculum vulgare Mill.   *Umbelliferae.*   FENNEL.   FINOCHIO.

Europe.   Fennel was cultivated by the Romans as a garden herb and was so much used in the kitchen that there were few meats seasoned, or vinegar sauces served without it.[13]   It was used as a condiment by our English forefathers.   The plant is a native of temperate Europe and Asia.   It is now largely cultivated in central Europe, Saxony, Franconia and Wurtemburg, in the south of France, in Italy, in India and in China. Fennel was included among American garden herbs by McMahon,[14] 1806.   Darwin [15] found

---

[1] Wight, R.   *Illustr. Ind. Bot.* **1**:37.   1840.
[2] Pickering, C.   *Chron. Hist.* 692.   1879.
[3] Brandis, D.   *Forest Fl.* 18.   1874.
[4] Roxburgh, W.   *Pls. Corom. Coast* **1**:48.   1795
[5] Wight, R.   *Illustr. Ind. Bot.* **1**:37.   1840.
[6] Pickering, C.   *Chron. Hist. Pls.* 725.   1879.
[7] Seemann, B.   *Fl. Viti.* 315.   1865-73.
[8] Mueller, F.   *Sel. Pls.* 207.   1891.
[9] Black, A. A.   *Treas. Bot.* **1**:499.   1870.
[10] Ainslie, W.   *Mat. Ind.* **2**:449.   1826.
[11] Brandis, D.   *Forest Fl.* 415.   1874.
[12] Black, A. A.   *Treas. Bot.* **1**:501.   1870.   (*F. abyssinica*)
[13] McIntosh, C.   *Book Gard.* **2**:5.   1855.
[14] McMahon, B.   *Amer. Gard. Cal.* 583.   1806.   (*Anethum foeniculum*)
[15] Darwin, C.   *Voy. H. M. S. Beagle* 119.   1884.

it growing wild in the neighborhood of Buenos Aires, Montivideo and other towns. The leaves are used in sauces, the stalks eaten in salads, and the seeds are employed in confectionery and for flavoring liquors. Fennel is constantly mentioned in the Anglo-Saxon medical recipes which date as early, at least, as the eleventh century. The diffusion of the plant in central Europe was stimulated by Charlemagne, who enjoined its cultivation on the imperial farms. Fennel shoots, fennel water and fennel seed are all mentioned in an ancient record of Spanish agriculture of 961 A. D.[1] There are three different forms recognized, all believed to belong to the common species.

BITTER FENNEL.

In 1863, Burr[2] describes a common and a dark-leaved form; in 1586, Lyte's *Dodoens' Herball* describes in like manner two varieties. This is the common wild sort, hardy and often spontaneous as an escape from gardens. Bitter fennel is the *Anethum foeniculum* Linn., 1763, and the *Foeniculum* of Camerarius,[3] 1586. Sometimes, but rarely, the leaves are used for seasoning but the plant is grown chiefly for its seeds which are largely used in flavoring liquors. Bitter fennel appears to be the common fennel or *finckle* of Ray, 1686, and the *foennel* and *fyncle* of Turner, 1538.

SWEET FENNEL.

This form is cultivated more frequently as a garden plant than the preceding, and its seeds are also an object of commerce. As the plant grows old, the fruits of each succeeding season gradually change in shape and diminish in size, until, at the end of four or five years, they are hardly to be distinguished from those of the bitter fennel. This curious fact was noted by Tabernaemontanus, 1588, and was systematically proved by Guibort, 1869.[4] This kind has, however, remained distinct from an early date. It is described by Albertus Magnus[5] in the thirteenth century and by Charlemagne in the ninth. It is mentioned throughout Europe, in Asia, and in America as an aromatic, garden herb. The famous *carosella*, so extensively used in Naples, scarcely known in any other place, is referred by authors to *F. piperitum* DC. The plant is used while in the state of running to bloom; the stems, fresh and tender, are broken and served raw, still enclosed in the expanded leaf-stalks.[6] This use is, perhaps, referred to by Amatus Lusitanus,[7] 1554, when, in speaking of finocchio, he says the swollen stalk is collected and said to be eaten.

FINOCCHIO.

This form is very distinct in its broad leaf-stalks, which, overlapping each other at the base of the stem, form a bulbous enlargement, firm, white and sweet inside. This

---

[1] Flückiger and Hanbury *Pharm.* 308. 1879.

[2] Burr, F. *Field, Gard. Veg.* 420. 1863.

[3] Dodoens *Herb.* 305. 1586. Lyte Ed.

[4] Flückiger and Hanbury *Pharm.* 308. 1879.

[5] Albertus Magnus *Beg.* Jessen Ed. 517. 1867.

[5] Vilmorin *Veg. Gard.* 246. 1885.

[7] Dioscorides Amatus Lusitanus Ed. 338. 1554.

seems to be the *finochi*, or Italian fennel, stated by Switzer,[1] 1729, to have but recently been introduced to English culture and yet rare in 1765.[2] The first distinct mention is by Mawe,[3] 1778, under the name of Azorian Dwarf or finocchio. It is again described in a very perfect form by Bryant,[4] 1783, under the name of Sweet Azorian fennel. According to *Miller's Dictionary*, 1807, it is the *F. azoricum* Miller, 1737. Ray,[5] 1686, uses the name *Foeniculum dulce azoricum*, but his description is hardly sufficient. Finocchio is described for American gardens in 1806.[6] It does not seem to have entered general culture except in Italy. The type of this fennel seems to be figured by J. Bauhin, 1651, and by Chabraeus, 1677, under the name *Foeniculum rotundum flore albo*.

Fragaria. *Rosaceae*. STRAWBERRY.

The Latin word for the strawberry, *Fraga*, has given name to the botanical genus *Fragaria*, which includes our edible species. Ruellius, 1536, says the French word *fresas* was applied to the fruit on account of the excellent sweetness of its odor, *odore suavissimum*, and taste; in 1554, this was spelled *frayses* by Amatus Lusitanicus, but the modern word *fraise* appeared in the form *fraises*, in Fuchsius, 1542, and Estienne, 1545. The Italian *fraghe* and *fragole*, as used by Matthiolus, 1571, and *fragola* as used by Zvingerus, 1696, and the modern Italians, appear to have come directly from the Latin; while the Spanish *fresa* and *fresera* must have had the same immediate origin as the French. Some of the ancient commentators and botanists seem to have derived the Latin name from *fragrans*, sweet-smelling, for Turner in his *Libellus*, 1538, says "*fragum non fragrum (ut quidam scioli scribunt)*," and Amatus Lusitanicus, 1554, writes *fragra*. The latter quotes Servius, a grammarian of the fifteenth century, as calling the fruit *terrestria mora*,— earth mulberry,—(or, following Dorstenius who wrote in 1540, "*fructus terrae et mora terrestria*)," whence the Spanish and Portuguese *murangaos*, (the modern Portuguese *moranguoiro*). The manner of the fruit-bearing, near the ground, seems to have been the character of the plant more generally observed, however, than that of the fruit, for we have Virgil's verse, "*humi nascentia fraga*," child of the soil, and Pliny's epithet, "*terrestribus fragis*," ground strawberry, as distinguishing from the *Arbutus unedo* Linn. or strawberry tree, as also the modern vernacular appellations, such as the Belgian *eertbesien*, Danish *jordbeer*, German *erdbeere*, Netherland *aerdbesie*, while even the English strawberry, the Anglo-Saxon *streowberie*, spelled in modern fashion by Turner in 1538, is said to have been derived from the spreading nature of the runners of the plant, and to have come originally from the observed *strewed*, anciently *strawed*, condition of the stems, and reading as if written *strawedberry* plant. It was called *straeberry* by Lidgate in the fifteenth century.

The classical history of the strawberry can be written very shortly. Virgil refers to the "*humi nascentia fraga*" in his third *Eclogue;* Ovid to the "*arbuteos fructus montanaque fraga*" in his *Metamorphoses*, book I, v. 104, as furnishing a food of the golden

---

[1] Switzer *Raising Veg.* 1729.

[2] Stevenson *Gard. Kal.* 46. 1765.

[3] Mawe and Abercrombie *Univ. Gard. Bot.* 1778. (*Anethum azoricum*)

[4] Bryant *Fl. Diet.* 53. 1783.

[5] Ray *Hist. Pl.* 458. 1686.

[6] McMahon, B. *Amer. Gard. Cal.* 199. 1806.

age and again in the 13th book, "*mollia fraga;*" and Pliny mentions the plant by name in his lib. xxi, c. 50, and separates the ground strawberry from the arbutus tree in his lib. xv, c. 28.   The fruit is not mentioned in the cook-book ascribed to Apicius Coelius, an author supposed to have lived about A. D. 230.   The Greeks seem to have had no knowledge of the plant or fruit; at least there is no word in their writings which commentators have agreed in interpreting as applying to the strawberry.   Nicolaus Myripsicus, an author of the tenth century, uses the word *phragouli*, and Forskal, in the eighteenth century, found the word *phraouli* in use for the strawberry by the Greeks about Belgrade.   Fraas gives the latter word for the modern Greek, and Sibthorp the word *kovkoumaria*, which resembles the ancient Greek *komaros* or *komaron*, applied to the arbutus tree, whose fruit has a superficial resemblance to the strawberry.

Neither the strawberry nor its cultivation is mentioned by Ibnal-awam, an author of the tenth century, unusually full and complete in his treatment of garden, orchard, and field products, nor by Albertus Magnus, who died A. D. 1280.   It is not mentioned in *The Forme of Cury*, a roll of ancient English cookery compiled about A. D. 1390 by two master cooks of King Richard II; nor in *Ancient Cookery*, a recipe book of 1381; nor at the Inthronization Feast of George Neville, Archbishop of York, in 1504.   The fruit was, however, known in London in the time of Henry VI, for in a poem by John Lidgate, who died about 1483, we find

> " Then unto London I dyde me hye,
>   Of all the land it bearyeth the pryse;
> ' Gode pescode,' one began to cry —
> ' Strabery rype, and cherrys in the ryse.' "

The strawberry is figured fairly well in the *Ortus Sanitatis*, 1511, c. 188, but there is no mention of culture.   Ruellius, however, 1536, speaks of it as growing wild in shady situations, says gardens furnish a larger fruit, and mentions even a white variety. Fuchsius, 1542, also speaks of the larger garden variety, and Estinne, 1545, (perhaps also in his first edition of the *De Re Hortensi*, 1535), says strawberries are used as delicacies on the table, with sugar and cream, or wine, and that they are of the size of a hazelnut; he says the plants bear most palatable fruit, red, especially when they are fully ripe; that some grow on the mountains and woods, and are wild, but that some cultivated ones are so odorous that nothing can be more so, and that these are larger, and some are white, others red, yet others are both red and white.

Cultivated strawberries are also noted by many authors of the sixteenth century, as by Mizaldus, 1560; Pena and Lobel in 1571; and in 1586 Lyte's *Dodoens* records, " they be also much planted in gardens."   Porta, 1592, regards them as among the delicacies of the garden and the delights of the palate.   Hyll, 1593, says " they be much eaten at all men's tables," and that " they will grow in gardens unto the bigness of a mulberry." *Le Jardinier Solitaire*, 1612, gives directions for planting, and Parkinson, 1629, notes a number of varieties.   As to size, Dorstenius, 1540, speaks of them as of the size of a hazelnut; Bauhin, 1596, as being double the size of the wild; the *Hortus Eystettensis*, 1613, figures berries one and three-eighths inches in diameter; Parkinson, in 1629, as " neere five inches about;" Plat, 1653, as two inches about in bigness; Vaillant, 1727, as an inch and sometimes more in diameter. It remained for Frezier, who discovered *Fragaria chiloensis*, and brought it to Europe in 1712, to describe fruit as of the size of a walnut, sometimes as large as an egg; and Burbridge, a recent writer, says that in the Equatorial Andes, in the province of Ambato, there are strawberries growing wild, equal in size and flavor to some of our best varieties.

The strawberry plant is variable in nature, and it seems probable that the type of all the varieties noted under cultivation may be found in the wild plant, if diligently sought for. In the Maine fields there are plants of *Fragaria vesca* with roundish, as well as elongated fruit; of *Fragaria virginiana* with roundish berries and elongated berries, with berries having a distinct neck and those not necked; of a deep red, scarlet, and palish color; with large fruit and small fruit; with large growth and small growth, according to the fertility of the soil.

As to color of fruit, white strawberries, to be referred to *Fragaria vesca*, are mentioned by Ruellius, 1536, and by a host of following writers. Peck has found white berries of this species about Skaneateles, New York. A white-fruited variety of *F. virginiana* is noted by Dewey as abundant in the eastern portion of Berkshire County, Massachusetts. Molina records that the Chile strawberry, *Fragaria chiloensis*, in Chile has red, white, and yellow-fruited varieties, and Frezier, who introduced the species to Europe in 1712, calls the fruit pale red. Gmelin in his *Flora Sibirica*, 1768, mentions three varieties of *Fragaria vesca;* one with a larger flower and fruit, one with white fruit; a third with winged petioles and berries an inch long. This last variety seems to answer to those forms of strawberry plants occasionally found among the seedlings at the New York Agricultural Experiment Station, which have extra leaflets upon the stem of the petiole. Five-leaved strawberry plants are noted by many of the early writers; an account of such plants may also be found in the *Report of the New York Agricultural Experiment Station* for 1877.

Variegated-leaved forms are named by Tournefort, 1719, and a number of varieties by Mawe in 1778. Such forms were also noted among the seedling Alpines at the New York Station in 1887. Don, in his *History of Dichlamydeous Plants*, 1832, describes *Fragaria vesca* as varying into red, white, and black fruit, as without runners, as double flowered, as with stamens transformed into flowers, as without petals and with foliaceous sepals; *F. majaufea* Duch., as varying into green, red, and purple fruit; *F. breslingea* Duch., as having varieties with usually five-lobed leaves; *F. elatior* as possessing a curled-leaved form; *F. grandiflora* as furnishing a variegated-leaved form; and *F. chiloensis* as having red-fleshed and white-fleshed fruit. Among the variations to be also noted is that of losing all its leaves in winter ascribed to the *F. viridis* Weston, and the twice-bearing habit of the Alpines, *F. vesca* Linn., var. *a*.

The earliest cultivated variety with a distinct nomenclature seems to be the Le Chapiron, of the Gallobelgians, a variety with a large, pale-colored berry, so named by Lobel, in 1576, and called by him Chapiton in the index to his *Icones*, 1591. (The Capiton of Tournefort, 1719, seems to correspond to the modern Hautbois class.) The name, Le Capiton, occurs also in the *Hortus Regius Parisiis*, 1665. It is quite probable that the Caprons mentioned by Quintinye in 1672, are the same or a similar variety, as both kinds are to be referred to *Fragaria elatior* Ehrh.

The first mention of the cultivation of the various classes of the strawberry may best be placed under the titles of the ascribed species, in part neglecting probable synonymy and neglecting all introductions not preceding the nineteenth century.

1536. *Fresas* (red and white). Ruell. *Stirp.* 598. 1536.= *Fragaria vesca* Linn.

1542. *Fragaria major.* Fuch. *Hist.* 854. 1542; 808. 1551; 931. 1555.

1545. *Fraises.* Estienne *De Re Hort.* 88. 1545. *L'Agric.* 75. 1570.

1560. *Fraga* (red and white). Mizald. *Secret.* 104. 1560.

1576. *Fragaria* and *Fragra majora alba. Gallobelgis des Chapirons.* Lob. *Obs.* 396. 1576. (See 1613.)

1583. *Fragaria* and *Fraga alterum genus.* Dod. *Pempt.* 660. 1583; 671. 1616.

1586. *Fraga alba.* Cam. *Epit.* 766. 1586.= *Fragaria vesca* Linn. var.

1586. Strawberries. Lyte's *Dodoens* 93. 1586.= *Fragaria vesca* Linn.

1592. *Fragole* (red and white). Porta. *Villae.* 748. 1592.= *Fragaria vesca* Linn.

1596. *Fructa duplo majore vulgari.* Bauh. *Phytopin.* 653. 1596.

1597. Another sort, . . . fruite greene when it is ripe. Ger. *Herb.* 845. 1597.= *Fragaria vesca* var. *a, Mill. Dict.*

1597. *Fragaria* and *Fraga.* Ger. *Herb.* 845. 1597.= *Fragaria vesca* Linn. *Mill. Dict.*

1597. *Fragaria* and *Fraga subalba.* Ger. *Herb.* 844. 1597.= *Fragaria vesca* Linn., var. *a, Mill. Dict.*

1612. *Fraisiers.* Le *Jard. Solit.* 382. 1612.

1613. *Caperonnier unisexe. Le Caperon. Fraise-abricot. Fraise-framboise. Hautboy. Chapetons,* Lob. Duch. in Lam. *Enc.* 1786. (See 1576.) = *Fragaria elatior* Ehrh. *Fraise capron framboise* Vilm.

1620. *Fragaria virginiana.* Don. *Hist. Dichl. Pls.* **2:** 542. (See 1623, 1629, 1633.) According to Sprengel, fig. 8 in the *Hortus Eystettensis* 1613, is this species.

1623. *Fraga acque magna ac in Anglia in Virginia crescunt.* Bauh. *Pin.* 326. 1623. (See 1620.)

1623. *Fragaria fructu parvi pruni magnitudini.* Bauh. *Pin.* 326. 1623.= *Fragaria elatior.*

1629. From Brussels. Park. *Par.* 528. 1629. *Caperonnier royal?* (See 1770.)

1629. Greene Strawberry. Park. *Par.* 528. 1629. See *Breslinge d'Angleterre.* Probably the Green, of Downing *Fruits* 685. 1866.=(?) *Fragaria elatior.*

1629. White Strawberry. Park. *Par.* 528. 1629.

1629. Bohemia Strawberry. Park. *Par.* 528. 1629.= *Fragaria vesca* Linn., var. *b, Mill. Dict.*

1629. Virginia. Park. *Par.* 528. 1629. (See 1620, 1623.) = *Fragaria Virginiana* Ehrh.

1529. *Quoimio de Virginia. Fraisier ecarlate.* Duch. in Lam. *Enc.* = *Fragaria virginiana* Ehrh. *Fraisier ecarlate de virginie* Vilm.

1629. *Breslinge d'Angleterre. Fraisier vert.* Duch. in Lam. *Enc.* The Greene Strawberry of Park. *Par.* 528. 1629.= *Fragaria elatior ?*

1633. *Canadana pariter insolitae magnitudinis fraga adrepsit.* Ferrarius *Cult.* 379. 1633. (See 1620.) = *Fragaria virginiana* Ehrh.

1640. *Fraisier double et couronne. Fraisier à trochet.* Duch. in Lam. *Enc.* = *Fragaria vesca* Linn., var. *e,* Don. See Blackw. t. 77, f. 3.

1651. *Fragaria ferens fragar rubra et alba.* Bauh. J. *Hist.* **2:** 395. 1651.= *Fragaria vesca.* var. *b.* Willd. *Sp.* **2:** 1091.= *F. fructu albo.* Bauh. *Pin.* 326. 1623.

1653. Strawberries from the woods. Plat. *Gard. Eden.* 38, 93. 1653.= *Fragaria vesca* Linn.

1655. *Fraisier fressant. Fraisier de Montreuil. Le Capiton.* H. R. P. 1665. Tourn. 1719. Duch. in Lam. *Enc.* = *Fragaria vesca* Linn. *Fraise de Montreuil* Vilm.

1680. *Fragaria Anglica duplici petalorum serie.* Mor. *Hist.* 2, 186. 1680. (See 1640.)

1686. *Fragaria hortensis major.* Mor. *Hist.* s. 2, t. 19, f. 1.= *? Fragaria vesca* Linn. var. *b*, Mill. *Dict.*

1693. *Caprons.* Quint. *Comp. Gard.* 146. 1693.

1712. *Frutiller. Fraisier du Chili.* Duch. in Lam. *Enc. Fragaria Chiloense.* Pers. *Syn.* 2, 53. Carried to England in 1727. *Mill. Dict.* 1807.= *Fragaria Chiloensis* Duch. *Fraisier du Chili vrai* Vilm.

1722. Bradley, in his Observations this year, names the White Wood, Scarlet Wood, and Hautbois.

1726. *Fragaria fructu parvi pruni magnitudine. Fraga fructu magno. Eyst.* 1613. Rupp. *Jen.* 86. 1726.= *Fragaria elatior* Willd. *Sp.* **2**:1091.

1739. *Fragaria hortensis fructu maximo.* Weimn. *Icon.* t. 514, f. d. 1738.= *? Fragaria elatior.*

1742. *Fragaria fructu rotundo suavissimo flore duplici.* Zann. *Hist.* 112. 1742. (See 1640, 1680.)

1742. *Fragaria hispidis.* C. B. 327. *Tertium fragariae genus.* Trag. 500. Mapp. *Alsat.* 110. 1742.= *Fragaria collina.* Willd. *Sp.* **2**:1093.

1744. *Fragaria vulgaris.* C. T. 326. Morandi 9, t. 7, ic. 3. 1744.= *Fragaria vesca* Linn. Willd. *Sp.* **2**:1091.

1748. *Fraisier buisson. Fraisier sans coulant.* Duch. in Lam. *Enc.*= *Fraisier des Alpes sans filets.* Vilm. *Les Pls. Potag.* 222. 1883.= *Fragaria alpina* Pers. var.

1757. *Fragaria hortensis fructu majore.* Zinn. *Got.* 138. 1757.

1759. *Fragaria grandiflora.* Don. *Hist. Dichl. Pls.* **2**:542.

1762. *Fragaria vesca, b pratensis.* Linn. *Sp.* 709. 1762.= *Fragaria elatior.* Willd. *Sp.* **2**:1091.

1762. *Quoimios de Harlem. Fraisier Ananas.* Duch. in Lam. *Enc.*= *Fragaria grandiflora* Ehrh. *Fraisier Ananas.* Vilm. (See 1759.)

1764. *Fragaria semperflorens.* Duch. in Lam. *Enc.*= *Fraisier des Alpes, Fragaria alpina* Pers. A red and a white variety among others described by Vilmorin *Les Pls. Potag.* 221. 1883.

1765. Stevenson, in his *Gardeners' Kalendar* of this year, names the American, Coped White, Green, Scarlet, Long Red, Dutch, English Garden, Polonian, and Wood.

1765. *Breslinge de Suède. Fraisier Brugnon.* Duch. in Lam. *Enc.*= *Fragaria elatior* Willd.= *F. vesca* var. *pratensis* Linn. (See 1762.) Cited by Linnaeus in *Fl. Lap.* 1737.

1766. *Majaufe de Provence.* Duch. in Lam. *Enc. Fraisier de Bargemont*, observed in the year 1583 by Caesalpinus = *Fragaria collina* Ehrh. var., according to Vilmorin.

1766. *Breslinge d'Allemagne.* Duch. in Lam. *Enc.*= *Fragaria collina* Ehrh. *Fraisier étoile.* Vilm.

1768. *Breslinge de Bourgogne. Fraisier Marteau.* Duch. in Lam. *Enc.*

1770. *Le Caperonnier Royal.* Duch. in Lam. *Enc.*= Probably the Prolific or Conical. Downing *Fruits* 680. 1866. (See 1629.) = *Fragaria elatior..*

1770. *Quoimio de Clagny.* Duch. in Lam. *Enc.*

1772. *Fragaria Virginiana campestre.* Bryant *Fl. Diet.* 163. 1783.

1778. Mawe and Abercrombie in their *Universal Gardener* of this year, name: *Wood* strawberries, red-fruited, white, greenish, pineapple-tasted, double-blossomed, with gold-striped leaves, with silver-striped leaves. *Virginian:* Common scarlet, roundish-leaved large scarlet, striped-leaved scarlet. *Hautboy* or *Musky:* Oval-fruited, globular-fruited, pine-shaped, green-fruited, red-blossomed, white-striped leaved, yellow-striped leaved. *Chili:* Round pale red, oblong pale red, round scarlet Carolina, white. *Alpine* or *Monthly:* Scarlet-red, white.

1786.   *Quoimio de Bath. Fraisier de Bath.* Duch. in Lam. *Enc.*=*Fragaria grandiflora*
        Ehrh. Don. *Hist. Dichl. Pls.* **2**:545.

1786.   *Quoimio de Carolina. Fraisier de Carolina.* Duch. in Lam. *Enc.*=*Fragaria*
        grandiflora Ehrh. *Frasier Ananas.* Vilm.

1786.   *Quoimio de Cantorberie. Fraiser-Quoimo.* Duch. in Lam. *Enc.*=*Fragaria chiloensis.*
        Don. *Hist. Dichl. Pls.* **2**:545.

1786.   *Fragaria sylvestris.* Duch. in Lam. *Enc.*=*Fragaria vulgaris.* C. B. 1623.=*F.*
        sylvestris vel *montana.* Cam. *Epit.* 765. 1586. (See 1653.) Probably the same
        as *Fresas,* Ruell. 1536.=*Fragaria vesca* Linn.

1786.   *Fragaria minor.* Duch. in Lam. *Enc.*=*Fragaria vesca* Linn. var. *c.* Don.

1790.   *Fragaria vesca* (China). Lour. *Cochinch.* 325. 1790.

1798.   *Fragaria collina* Ehrh. Don. *Hist. Dichl. Pls.* **2**:542. (See 1766.)

We hence find the following as the dates of the mention of the species under cultivation, the synonyms taken from Steudel:—

> *Fragaria vesca* Linn. 1536, 1586, 1592, 1597, 1629, 1640, 1651, 1653, 1655, 1680,
>   1742, 1744, 1786.
> *Fragaria elatior* Ehrh.=*F. vesca* var. *pratensis* Linn. 1576, 1613, 1623, 1629, 1726,
>   1739, 1762, 1765, 1770.
> *Fragaria virginiana* Ehrh. 1620, 1623, 1627, 1633, 1772.
> *Fragaria chiloensis* Ehrh.=*F. vesca* var. *chiloensis* Linn. 1712, 1786.
> *Fragaria collina* Ehrh.=*F. hispida* Duch. 1742, 1766, 1798. (*Fragaria alpina*
>   Pers.) 1748, 1764.
> *Fragaria grandiflora* Ehrh.=*F. ananassa* Duch.=*F. vesca* var. *ananas* Ait. 1759,
>   1762, 1786.

Although this outline, confessedly imperfect, shows that strawberry culture had
received some attention preceding the present century, and that a considerable number
of varieties had been secured, yet it is in modern times that through the growing of seedlings, and the facilities for reaping a reward for alleged improvements, varieties have
become overwhelming in number. In remote times, even towards the close of the last
century, growers were wont to seek their supplies from the woods and fields; now the
nurseryman is applied to. This increase in varieties may best be indicated by giving
in tabular form the number of varieties that have been mentioned by garden writers of
various dates.

		Kinds Named.
1545.	Estienne *De Re Hortensi*	2
1612.	*Le Jardinier Solitaire*	1
1629.	Parkinson *Paradisus*	6
1680.	Morison *Hist.*	8
1692.	Quintinye *Complete Gardener*	3
1719.	Tournefort *Inst.*	10
1765.	Stevenson *Gard. Kal.*	9
1771.	Miller *Dict.*	8
1778.	Mawe *Gard.*	23
1786.	Duch. in Lam. *Enc.*	25
1807.	*Miller's Dict.*	8
1824.	Pirolle *L'Hort. Franc.*	14
1826.	Petit *Du Jard. Petit.*	10

The modern varieties under American culture have usually large berries with more or less sunken seeds, with the trusses lower than the leaves, and seem to belong mostly to the species represented in nature by *Fragaria virginiana*, although they are supposed hybridizations with *Fragaria chiloensis*, and, in the higher-flavored class, with *Fragaria elatior*. Certain it is that, in growing seedlings from our improved varieties, reversions often occur to varieties referable to the Hautbois and Chilean sorts, from which hybridization can be inferred. One notes as of common occurrence that seedlings from high-flavored varieties are very likely to furnish some plants of the Hautbois class, and even scarcely, if at all, distinguishable from named varieties of the Hautbois with which there has been opportunity for close comparison. From large-berried varieties of diminished flavor, and which occasionally throw hollowed berries, the reversion occasionally produces plants unmistakably of the Chilean type. In other cases we have noticed reversions to forms of *Fragaria vesca*.

These circumstances all lead towards establishing the mingled parentage of our varieties under cultivation, and render the classification of cultivated varieties somewhat difficult. Vilmorin seems to have separated varieties into natural groupings under the headings: Wood strawberries, *Fragaria vesca* Linn.; Alpine strawberries, *Fragaria alpina* Pers.; Short-runnered *Fragaria collina* Ehrh.; Hautbois, *Fragaria elatior* Ehrh.; Scarlet, *Fragaria virginiana* Ehrh.; Chile, *Fragaria chiloensis* Duch.; Pineapple, *Fragaria grandiflora* Ehrh., and Hybrid (*Fragaria hybrida*)? Under the latter distribution, to which he does not venture the Latin nomenclature, he does not recognize sufficient identity of character for general description, but one may well believe that an extended acquaintance with varieties will enable a description to be formulated which will make of this group a species by convenience, or, otherwise expressed, a historical species, with a number of subspecies (for convenience) which shall simplify the question of arrangement and which will enable us to secure a quicker identification of varieties.

The changes which have been produced, or have appeared under cultivation, seem comparatively few. 1. Increased size of plant. Yet in nature we find variability in this respect, arising from greater or less fertility or favoring character of the soil and exposure. This increase of size seems also in a measure to have become hereditary. 2. Increased size of berry. In nature we find variability in this respect. All analogical reasoning justifies the belief that this gain may arise through heredity influenced by long series of selections. 3. Firmness of berry. Present knowledge does not admit of assigning a cause for this feature, unless it has been gained through hybridization. 4. Flavor. This seems to be the direct sequence of hybridization, in its more marked aspects; in its lesser aspects it does not seem to exceed that which occurs between natural varieties. 5. Aspect. This seems to have been acquired through the action of hybridization, when the influence of one parent appears to have become predominant. The whole subject of the influences noted and to be ascribed to hybridization must be left for further study.

As an appendix it may be of service to furnish a list of figures of the strawberry plant which antedate the present century.

According to Sprengel the strawberry is not represented upon the monuments of ancient Egypt or Greece. Figures occur as in the following list:

1484. *Fragaria. Herbarius maguntae* c. lxiii.
1499. *Fragaria.* Jacobus de Dondis *Aggregator practicus.* (According to Sprengel.)
1511. *Fragaria. Ortus Sanit.* c. 188.
1536. *Fragaria.* Brunf. 40.
1540. *Fragaria.* Dorst., *Bot.* 131.
1542. *Fragaria major et minor.* Fuch. 853; ib., 1551, 808.
1550. *Fragaria.* Roszl., *Kreut.* 153.
1552. *Fragaria.* Trag. *Stirp.* 500.
1561. *Fragaria.* Pinaeus *Hist.* 480.
1570. *Fragaria.* Matth. *Comment.* 651.
1571. *Fragaria.* Matth. *Compend.* 686.
1576. *Fragaria and fraga.* Lob. *Obs.* 396.
1583. *Fraga altera.* Dod. *Pempt.* 661.
1583. *Fragaria and fraga.* Dod. *Pempt.* 661.
1586. *Fragaria.* Cam. *Epit.* 765.
1587. *Fragaria.* Dalechamp *Hist.* 614.
1588. *Fragaria.* I. Tabern. *Kreut.* 429.
1588. *Fragum album.* II. Tabern. *Kreut.* 429.
1590. *Fragum. Trifolium fragiferum.* Tabern. *Icon.* 118.
1590. *Fragum album.* Tabern. *Icon.* 119.
1591. *Fragaria and fragu.* Lob. *Icon.* 697.
1591. *Fragaria and fragu major subalbida.* Lob. *Icon.* 697.
1597. *Fragaria and fraga.* Ger. *Herb.* 844.
1597. *Fragaria and fraga subalba.* Ger. *Herb.* 844.
1598. *Fragaria fructu albo.* Matth. *Comment.* 721.
1613. *Fragum.* I. Tabern. *Kreut.* 353.
1613. *Fragaria album.* II. Tabern. *Kreut.* 354.
1613. *Fraga fructu magno.* Eyst. Vern. ord. 7, fol. 8, p. 1.
1613. *Fraga fructo albo.* Eyst. Vern. ord. 7, fol. 8, p. 2.
1613. *Fraga fructu rubro.* Eyst. Vern. ord. 7, fol. 8, p. 2.
1616. *Fraga altera.* Dod. *Pempt.* 672.
1616. *Fragaria and fraga.* Dod. *Pempt.* 672.
1617. *Fragaria.* Cast. *Dur.* 192.
1629. *Fraga vulgaris.* Park. *Par.* 527, f. 6.
1629. *Fraga bohemica maxima.* Park. *Par.* 527, f. 7.
1629. *Fraga aculeata.* Park. *Par.* 527, f. 8.
1650. *Fragaria ferens fraga rubra et alba.* Bauh. J. *Hist.* **2**:394.
1654. *Fragaria vel fraga alba.* Sweert. *Flor.* t. 2, f. 7.

1654. *Fragaria vel fraga maxima.* Sweert. *Flor.* t. 2, f. 8.
1654. *Fragaria vel fraga media.* Sweert. *Flor.* t. 2, f. 9.
1677. *Fragaria. Fraga.* Chabr. *Sciag.* 169.
1680. *Fragaria hortensis major.* Mor. *Hist. Ox.* S. 2, t. 19, f. 1.
1680. *Fragaria sylvestris.* Mor. *Hist. Ox.* S. 2, t. 19, f. 2.
1696. *Fragaria.* Zwing. *Theat. Bot.* 864.
1696. *Fraga alba.* Zwing. *Theat. Bot.* 865.
1714. *Fragaria flore pleno fructu rubello.* Barrel. *Icon.* 89.
1714. *Fragaria spinoso fructu.* Barrel. *Icon.* n. 90.
1739. *Fragaria vulgaris.* Weinm. *Iconog.* t. 514, f. c (col.).
1739. *Fragaria hortensis fructo maximo.* Weinm. *Iconog.* t. 514, f. d (col.).
1742. *Fragaria arborea confiore herbaceo.* Zanon. *Hist.* t. 78.
1744. *Fragaria vulgaris.* Morandi t. 7, f. 3.
1749. *Fragaria.* Blackw. *Herb.* t. 77 (col.).
1760. *Fragaria.* Ludw. *Ect.* t. 136 (col.).
1774. *Fragaria chiloensis.* Dillen. *Elth.* t. 120, f. 146.

F. chiloensis Duchesne. GARDEN STRAWBERRY. PINE STRAWBERRY.

Western shores of the New World. This is a dioecious strawberry, bearing very large fruit and called in Chile *quelghen*.[1] The best quality of fruit, according to Molina,[2] came from the Chilean provinces of Puchacay and Huilquilemu. The plant was carried by Frezier in 1712 from Conception to Europe and from Europe was carried to the West Indies.[3] Prince[4] describes the Large Scarlet Chile as imported to this country from Lima, about 1820, and the Montevideo, about 1840, and 14 other varieties originating from this species.

F. collina Ehrh. GREEN STRAWBERRY.

Europe and northern Asia. The fruits are greenish, tinged with red, of a musky, rich, pineapple flavor. Prince enumerates four varieties as cultivated.[5]

F. elatior Ehrh. HAUTBOIS STRAWBERRY.

Europe. The French call this class of strawberries *caprons*. The fruit has a musky flavor which many persons esteem.[6] Prince[7] describes eight varieties in cultivation.

F. vesca Linn. ALPINE STRAWBERRY. PERPETUAL STRAWBERRY. WOOD STRAWBERRY.

Temperate regions. Previous to 1629, the date of the introduction of the Virginian strawberry, this was the species generally gathered in Europe and the fruit referred to by Shakespeare:

" My lord of Ely, when I was last in Holborn,
I saw good strawberries in your garden there."

This species is mentioned by Virgil, Ovid and Pliny as a wild plant. Lyte,[8] in his trans-

---

[1] Pickering, C. *Chron. Hist. Pls.* 892. 1879.
[2] Ibid.
[3] Ibid.
[4] Prince *U. S. Pat. Off. Rpt.* 195. 1861.
[5] Prince *U. S. Pat. Off. Rpt.* 206. 1861.
[6] Thompson, H. *Treas. Bot.* 1:504. 1870.
[7] Prince *U. S. Pat. Off. Rpt.* 205. 1861.
[8] Dodoens *Herb.* 1578. Lyte Ed.

lation of *Dodoens' Herball*, refers to it as growing wild in 1578 and first appearing in an improved variety in cultivation about 1660. A. De Candolle,[1] however, states that it was cultivated in the mediaeval period. Gray[2] says it is indigenous in the United States, particularly northward. In Scandinavia, it ripens beyond 70°.[3] Prince[4] enumerates 10 varieties of the Wood, and 15 varieties of the Alpine, under cultivation. In 1766, Duchesne says, "The King of England was understood to have received the first seed from Turin." It was such a rarity that a pinch of seed sold for a guinea.

F. virginiana Duchesne. SCARLET STRAWBERRY. VIRGINIA STRAWBERRY.

Eastern North America. Called by the New England Indians *wuttahimneash*. The Indians bruised this strawberry with meal in a mortar and made bread. This fruit was mentioned by Edward Winslow[5] in Massachusetts in 1621. The settlers on the ship Arabella, at Salem, June 12, 1630, went ashore and regaled themselves with strawberries.[6] Wood,[7] in his *New England Prospects*, says strawberries were in abundance, "verie large ones, some being two inches about." Roger Williams[8] says "this berry is the wonder of all the fruits growing naturally in these parts. It is of itself excellent; so that one of the chiefest doctors of England was wont to say, that God could have made, but God never did make, a better berry. In some parts where the Indians have planted, I have many times seen as many as would fill a good ship, within few miles compass." This fruit was first mentioned in England, by Parkinson,[9] 1629, but it was a hundred years or more afterwards before attention began to be paid to improved seedlings. Hovey's Seedling was originated in America in 1834. Prince, in 1861, gives a descriptive list of 87 varieties which he refers to this species.

Frankenia portulacaefolia Spreng. *Frankeniaceae.* SEA HEATH.

St. Helena Islands. One of the few plants indigenous in the Island of St. Helena but now, J. Smith[10] says, believed to be extinct. Balfour[11] says the leaves were used in St. Helena as a substitute for tea.

Fraxinus excelsior Linn. *Oleaceae.* ASH.

Temperate regions of the Old World. The keys of the ash were formerly pickled by steeping in salt and vinegar and were eaten as a condiment, a use to which they are still put in Siberia. The leaves are sometimes used to adulterate tea.[12]

---

[1] Pickering, C. *Chron. Hist. Pls.* 378. 1879.
[2] Gray, A. *Man. Bot.* 480. 1908.
[3] DuChaillu *Land Midnight Sun* 1:152. 1882.
[4] Prince *U. S. Pat. Off. Rpt.* 1861.
[5] Young, A. *Chron. Pilgr.* 234. 1841.
[6] Hutchinson *Hist. Mass.* 1:25. Ed. of 1795.
[7] Wood, W. *New Eng. Prosp.* 15. 1865.
[8] Williams, R. *Key* Narragansett Hist. Coll. 1:121. 1643.
[9] Parkinson *Par. Terr.* 528. 1904. (Reprint of 1629).
[10] Smith, J. *Dom. Bot.* 444. 1871.
[11] Balfour, J. H. *Treas. Bot.* 1:506. 1870.
[12] Johnson, C. P. *Useful Pls. Gt. Brit.* 174. 1862.

F. ornus Linn. MANNA ASH.

Mediterranean region and the Orient. The manna ash is indigenous and is cultivated in Sicily and Calabria. When the trees are eight or ten years old, one cut is made every day from the commencement of July to the end of September, from which a whitish, glutinous liquor exudes spontaneously and hardens into manna. Manna is collected during nine years, when the tree is exhausted and is cut down and only a shoot left, which after four or five years becomes in turn productive. Once a week the manna is collected. The yield is about 5 pounds of select and 70 pounds of assorted manna per acre. This tree is the *melia* of Dioscorides, the *meleos* of modern Greece.[1] The seeds are imported into Egypt for culinary and medicinal use and are called bird tongues.[2] *Fraxinus excelsior* Linn. furnishes a little manna in some districts of Sicily.[3]

The manna of Scripture is supposed to be a Lichen, *Parmelia esculenta*, a native of Asia Minor, the Sahara and Persia. Some believe manna to be the exudation found on the stems of *Alhagi maurorum* Medic., a shrubby plant which covers immense plains in Arabia and Palestine and which now furnishes a manna used in India. In Kumaun, as Madden[4] states, the leaves and branches of *Pinus excelsa* Wall., become covered with a liquid exudation which hardens into a kind of manna, sweet, not turpentiny, which is eaten. Tamarisk manna is collected in India from the twigs of *Tamarix articulata* Ehr. and *T. gallica* Ehr., and is used to adulterate sugar as well as for a food by the Bedouin Arabs. *Pyrus glabra* Boiss., affords in Luristan a substance which, according to Hauss-knecht, is collected and is extremely like oak manna. The same traveller states that *Salix fragilis* Linn., and *Scrophularia frigida* Boiss., likewise yield in Persia saccharine exudations. A kind of manna was anciently collected from *Cedrus libani* Linn. Australian manna is found on the leaves of *Eucalyptus viminalis* Labill., *E. mannifera* Mudie and *E. dumosa* A. Cunn.; that from the second species is used as food by the natives. This latter manna is said to be an insect secretion and is called lerp. In Styria, *Larix europaea* DC., exudes a honeyed juice which hardens and is called manna. In Asiatic Turkey, *diarbekir* manna is found on the leaves of dwarf oaks. *Pinus lambertiana* Dougl., of southern Oregon, yields a sort of exudation used by the natives, which resembles manna.

Freycinetia banksii A. Cunn. *Pandaneae.*

New Zealand. The flowers, of a sweetish taste, are eagerly eaten by the natives of New Zealand.[5] This plant is said by Curl to bear the best edible fruit of the country.[6]

F. milnei Seem.

Fiji Islands. According to Milne,[7] the fruit is eaten by the Fijians.

Fritillaria camschatcensis Ker-Gawl. *Liliaceae.* KAMCHATKA LILY.

Eastern Asia. The bitter tubers, says Hooker, are copiously eaten by the Indians

---

[1] Pickering, C. *Chron. Hist. Pls.* 169. 1879. (*Ornus europaea*)
[2] Ibid.
[3] Flückiger and Hanbury *Pharm.* 366. 1874.
[4] Madden, E. *Obs. Himal. Coniferae.* 1850.
[5] Hooker, W. J. *Journ. Bot.* 4:306. 1842.
[6] Curl, W. *Bot. Index* 107. 1880.
[7] Seemann, B. *Fl. Viti.* 283. 1865–73.

of Sitka and are known by the name of *koch*. This plant is enumerated by Dall[1] among the useful indigenous Alaskan plants. In Kamchatka, the women collect the roots, which are used in cookery in various ways; when roasted in embers, they supply the place of bread. Captain Cook[2] said he boiled and ate these roots as potatoes and found them wholesome and pleasant. Royle[3] says the bulbs are eaten in the Himalayan region.

F. lanceolata Pursh. NARROW-LEAVED FRITILLARY.
Western North America. The roots are eaten by some Indians.[4]

Fuchsia corymbiflora Ruiz. & Pav. *Onagrarieae.* FUCHSIA.
Peru. The fruit is said by J. Smith[5] to be wholesome and not unpalatable.

F. denticulata Ruiz. & Pav. FUCHSIA.
Peru. The acid fruits are edible.[6]

F. racemosa Lam. FUCHSIA.
Santo Domingo. It produces edible, acid fruits.[7]

Fusanus acuminatus R. Br. *Santalaceae.* NATIVE PEACHES. QUANDONG NUT.
Australia. Both the succulent outer part and kernel are edible.[8] The seeds are eaten as almonds.[9] Lindley[10] says the fruit is as sweet and useful to the New Hollanders as almonds are to us.

F. persicarius F. Muell.
Australia. The bark of the root of this small variety of the sandal tree is roasted by the Murray tribe of Australian natives in hot ashes and eaten. It has no taste but is very nutritious. The native name is *quantong*.[11]

Galactites tomentosa Moench. *Compositae.*
A plant of the Mediterranean countries, described by Diodorus[12] as an edible thistle and by Dioscorides as eaten, while young, cooked with oil and salt. The tender flower-stem is eaten in the region of the Dardanelles.

Galega officinalis Linn. *Leguminosae.* GOAT'S RUE.
Europe and western Asia. This European herb is recommended by Gerarde[13] as a

---

[1] Dall, W. H. *Alaska* 517. 1897.
[2] Cook *Voyage* 3:118. 1773.
[3] Royle, J. F. *Illustr. Bot. Himal.* 1:388. 1839.
[4] Brown, R. *Bot. Soc. Edinb.* 9:380. 1868.
[5] Smith, J. *Dom. Bot.* 385. 1871.
[6] Unger, F. *U. S. Pat. Off. Rpt.* 351. 1859.
[7] Ibid.
[8] Mueller, F. *Sel. Pls.* 443. 1891.
[9] Henfrey, A. *Bot.* 344. 1870.
[10] Lindley, J. *Veg. King.* 788. 1846.
[11] Hooker, W. J. *Journ. Bot.* 9:267. 1857.
[12] Pickering, C. *Chron. Hist. Pls.* 448. 1879.
[13] Gerarde, J. *Herb.* 2nd ed. 1253. 1633 or 1636.

spinach. It has recently received attention as a possible substitute for clover. In France, it is an inmate of the flower garden.[1]

Galium aparine Linn. *Rubiaceae.* BEDSTRAW. BUR-WEED. CATCH-WEED. CLEAVERS. GOOSE GRASS.

Northern climates. The seeds form one of the best of the substitutes for coffee, according to Johnson,[2] and are so used in Sweden. The dried plant is sometimes used as a tea.

G. verum Linn. CHEESE RENNET. HUNDRED-FOLD. YELLOW BEDSTRAW.

Europe; naturalized in eastern North America. Yellow bedstraw has been used in some parts of England to curdle milk. In Gerarde's time, this plant was used to color the best Cheshire cheese. According to Ray, the flowering tops, distilled with water, yield an acid liquor which forms a pleasant summer drink.[3]

Garcinia cambogia Desr. *Guttiferae.*

East Indies. In the East Indies, the fruit is eaten at meals as an appetizer. It is about two inches in diameter, with a thin, smooth, yellowish rind and a yellow, succulent, sweet pulp.[4] The fruit is of an exceedingly sharp but pleasant acid and the aril, or pulp, is by far the most palatable part.

G. cochinchinensis Choisy.

China. The fruit is about the size of a plum, of a reddish color when ripe and has a juicy, acid pulp. The leaves are used in Amboina as a condiment for fish.[5]

G. cornea Linn.

East Indies. The fruit resembles that of the mangosteen but is sometimes larger.[6]

G. cowa Roxb. COWA. COWA-MANGOSTEEN

East Indies. The fruit is eatable but not palatable. The cowa or cowa-mangosteen, bears a ribbed and russet apricot-colored fruit of the size of an orange and, were it not a trifling degree too acid, would be accounted most delicious. It makes, however, a remarkably fine preserve. In Burma, the fruit is eaten.[7]

G. dulcis Kurz.

Moluccas. The berry is the size of an apple, of a roundish-oval figure and bright yellow hue when ripe. The seeds are enveloped in edible pulp of a darker color than the skin and have a pleasant taste.

G. indica Choisy. COCUM. KOKUM.

East Indies. This is a large tree of the coast region of western India known by the

---

[1] Vilmorin *Fl. Pl. Ter.* 1870. 3rd Ed.

[2] Johnson, C. P. *Useful. Pls. Gt. Brit.* 137. 1862.

[3] Johnson, C. P. *Useful Pls. Gt. Brit.* 136. 1862.

[4] Martyn *Miller Gard. Dict.* 1807. (*Cambogia gutta*)

[5] Don, G. *Hist. Dichl. Pls.* 1:621. 1831. (*Stalagmitis cochinchinensis*)

[6] Don, G. *Hist. Dichl. Pls.* 1:621. 1831. (*Stalagmitis celebica*)

[7] Firminger, T. A. C. *Gard. Ind.* 206. 1874.

natives as the *conca*. The fruit is the size of a small apple and contains an acid, purple pulp. Garcia d'Orta, 1563, says that it has a pleasant, though sour, taste and that the fruit serves to make a vinegar. The oil from the seeds has been used to adulterate butter.[1] About Bombay, it is called kokum, and the fruit is eaten, and oil is obtained from the seeds. It is called *brindas* by the Portuguese at Goa, where cocum oil is used for adulterating ghee or butter.[2]

G. lanceaefolia Roxb.

Himalayas. The plant yields an edible fruit in India.[3]

G. livingstonei T. Anders. AFRICAN MONGOSTEEN.

Tropical Africa. It is grown as a fruit tree in the Public Gardens of Jamaica.[4]

G. mangostana Linn. MONGOSTEEN.

A fruit of the equatorial portion of the Malayan Archipelago and considered by many the most delicious of all fruits. Capt. Cook, in 1770, found it at Batavia and says " it is about the size of a crab apple and of a deep red wine-color; on the top of it are the figures of five or six small triangles found in a circle and at the bottom several hollow, green leaves, which are remains of the blossom. When they are to be eaten, the skin, or rather flesh, must be taken off, under which are found six or seven white kernels placed in a circular order and the pulp with which these are enveloped is the fruit, than which nothing can be more delicious: it is a happy mixture of the tart and the sweet, which is no less wholesome than pleasant." Bayard Taylor [5] says " beautiful to sight, smell and taste, it hangs among its glossy leaves, the prince of fruits. Cut through the shaded green and purple of the rind, and lift the upper half as if it were the cover of a dish, and the pulp of half-transparent, creamy whiteness stands in segments like an orange, but rimmed with darkest crimson where the rind was cut. It looks too beautiful to eat; but how the rarest, sweetest essence of the tropics seems to dwell in it as it melts to your delighted taste." The tree was fruited in English greenhouses in 1855. It is cultivated in the southern and eastern parts of India but does not there attain the same perfection as it does in the Malay Archipelago.[6] Neither does it do well in the West Indies,[7] but Morris [8] says it is cultivated for its fruit in the Public Gardens of Jamaica. In Burma, it is called *men-gu*.[9]

G. morella Desr. GAMBOGE.

East Indies and Malay; a small tree common in Siam and Cambodia. The fruit is a pulpy drupe, about two inches in diameter, of a yellow color and is esteemed as a des-

---

[1] Flückiger and Hanbury *Pharm.* 86. 1879.

[2] Pickering, C. *Chron. Hist. Pls.* 483. 1879.

[3] Royle, J. F. *Illustr. Bot. Himal.* 1:133. 1839.

[4] Morris *Rpt. Pub. Gard. Jam.* 35. 1880.

[5] Taylor, B. *Siam* 268. 1892.

[6] Black, A. A. *Treas. Bot.* 1:519. 1870.

[7] Unger, F. *U. S. Pat. Off. Rpt.* 339. 1859.

[8] Morris *Rpt. Pub. Gard. Jam.* 35. 1880.

[9] Pickering, C. *Chron. Hist. Pls.* 642. 1879.

sert fruit. The plant furnishes the gamboge, the orange-red gum-resin of commerce.[1]
It is called *cochin goraka* and is cultivated in the Public Gardens of Jamaica.[2]

G. ovalifolia Oliver.

African tropics. It yields edible fruit.[3]

G. paniculata Roxb.

Himalayan region. The fruit is edible.[4] The fruit of this species raised in Calcutta
is represented as about the size of a cherry, that of native specimens received from Silhet
about twice as large.[5]

G. pedunculata Roxb.

Himalayan region. The fleshy part of the fruit which covers the seeds and their
juicy envelope, or aril, is in large quantity, of a firm texture and of a very sharp, pleasant,
acid taste. It is used by the natives in their curries and for acidulating water.

G. xanthochymus Hook. f.

East Indies and Malay. The plant bears a round, smooth apple of medium size,
which, when ripe, is of a beautiful, yellow color. The seeds are from one to four, large,
oblong and immersed in pulp. The fruit is very handsome and in taste is little inferior
to many of our apples. Firminger[6] says the fruit is intolerably acid. Drury[7] says that
its orange-like fruit is eaten; Unger,[8] that it is pleasant-tasted.

Gardenia brasiliensis Spreng. *Rubiaceae.*

Brazil. This plant affords, according to J. Smith,[9] an edible fruit about the size of
an orange.

G. gummifera Linn. f.

East Indies. The fruit is eaten.[10] The fruit is eaten in the Circar Mountains of
India.[11]

G. jasminoides Ellis.

China. The flowers are used for scenting tea.[12]

Garuga pinnata Roxb. *Burseraceae.*

Malay and East Indies. The fruit is eaten raw and pickled.[13]

---

[1] Smith, J. *Dict. Econ. Pls.* 189. 1882.
[2] Morris *Rpt. Pub. Gard. Jam.* 35. 1880.
[3] Royle, J. F. *Illustr. Bot. Himal.* 1:133. 1839.
[4] Unger, F. *U. S. Pat. Off. Rpt.* 339. 1859.
[5] Wight, R. *Illustr. Ind. Bot.* 1:125. 1840.
[6] Firminger, T. A. C. *Gard. Ind.* 207. 1874. (*Xanthochymus pictorius*)
[7] Pickering, C. *Chron. Hist. Pls.* 593. 1879. (*Xanthochymus pictorius*)
[8] Unger, F. *U. S. Pat. Off. Rpt.* 336. 1859. (*Xanthochymus pictorius*)
[9] Smith, J. *Dom. Bot.* 334. 1871.
[10] Brandis, D. *Forest Fl.* 270. 1874.
[11] Don, G. *Hist. Dichl. Pls.* 3:497. 1834. (*G. arborea*)
[12] Fortune, R. *Resid. Chinese* 201. 1857. (*G. florida*)
[13] Brandis, D. *Forest Fl.* 62. 1876.

Gastrodia cunninghamii Hook. f. *Orchideae.* PERI-ROOT.

New Zealand. The root of this orchid is eaten by the natives of New Zealand, who call it peri; it is about 18 inches long, as thick as the finger and full of starch.[1]

Gaultheria myrsrinites Hook. *Ericaceae.*

Northern California and Oregon. The fruit is scarlet, aromatic, and is said to be delicious.[2]

G. procumbens Linn. CHECKER BERRY. TEA BERRY. WINTERGREEN.

Northeastern America. The berries are often offered for sale in the markets of Boston; they are pleasantly aromatic and are relished by children. The oil is used for flavoring. The leaves are made into a tea by the Indians of Maine.

G. shallon Pursh. SALAL.

Northwest Pacific Coast. The aromatic, acid berries are rather agreeable to the taste.[3] The fruit is much esteemed by the Indians of the northwest coast [4] and is dried and eaten in winter.[5]

Gaylussacia frondosa Torr. & Gray. *Vacciniaceae.* BLUE TANGLE. DANGLEBERRY. DWARF HUCKLEBERRY.

North America. The fruit is large, bluish, rather acid and is used for puddings. The fruit is sweet and edible according to Gray.[7] In the southern states, the berries are eaten.[8]

G. resinosa Torr. & Gray. BLACK HUCKLEBERRY.

North America. This plant has several varieties and occurs in woodlands and swamps in northeast America. The berries are globular, of a shining black color, and Emerson [9] says are more valued in market than those of other species.

Geitonoplesium cymosum A. Cunn. *Liliaceae.* SHEPHERD'S JOY.

Islands of the Pacific and east Australia. The young shoots offer a fine substitute for asparagus, according to Mueller.[10]

Gelidium corneum Lam. *Algae.* KANTEEN.

This seaweed occurs almost everywhere. In Japan, *kanteen*, or vegetable isinglass, is prepared from it, which is eaten. The cleansed plant is boiled in water, the solution is strained and allowed to set to a jelly in wooden boxes. The jelly is cut into long prisms,

---

[1] Black, A. A. *Treas. Bot.* 1:521. 1870.

[2] Brewer and Watson *Bot. Cal.* 1:455. 1880.

[3] Torrey *Bot. U. S. Mex. Bound. Surv.* 2:108. 1859.

[4] Hooker, W. J. *Fl. Bor. Amer.* 2:36. 1840.

[5] Brown, R. *Bot. Soc. Edinb.* 9:384. 1868.

[6] Emerson, G. B. *Trees, Shrubs Mass.* 2:452. 1875.

[7] Gray, A. *Man. Bot.* 282. 1868.

[8] Elliott, S. *Bot. So. Car., Ga.* 1:496. 1821. (*Vaccinium frondosum*)

[9] Emerson, G. B. *Trees, Shrubs Mass.* 2:451. 1875.

[10] Mueller, F. *Sel. Pls.* 214. 1891.

frozen and then allowed to thaw in the sun. The water runs away as the thawing proceeds, leaving a white skeleton of kanteen. One part will make a firm jelly with 150 parts of water.

Genipa americana Linn. *Rubiaceae.* GENIPAP. MARMALADE BOX.

South America. This plant is cultivated in Brazil, Guiana and other tropical countries for its large, greenish-white, edible fruit.[1] The fruit is as large as an orange and has an agreeable flavor. In Surinam, it is called marmalade box.[2]

Genista tinctoria Linn. *Leguminosae.* DYER'S-BROOM. WOODWAXEN.

Europe in the region of the Caucasus. The buds are pickled and used in sauces as a caper substitute.

Gentiana campestris Linn. *Gentianeae.* GENTIAN.

Europe. Linnaeus[3] says the poorer people of Sweden use this species as a hop to brew with their ale.

G. lutea Linn. YELLOW GENTIAN.

Europe and Asia Minor. The root contains sugar and mucilage, and in Switzerland an esteemed liquor is prepared from it.[4] It is an inmate of the flower garden in France.[5]

Geoffraea superba Humb. & Bonpl. *Leguminosae.* ALMENDOR.

South America. Gardner[6] says this plant produces a fleshy drupe about the size of a walnut which is called *umari* by the Indians. In almost every house, whether Indian or Brazilian, he observed a large pot of this fruit being prepared. The taste of the kernel is not unlike that of boiled beans. It is the *almandora* of the Amazon.[7]

Geranium dissectum Linn. *Geraniaceae.* AUSTRALIAN GERANIUM. NATIVE CARROT.

Europe, northern Asia and Australia. In Tasmania, the roots, called native carrots, are used as food.[8] Drummond[9] saw a species in Swan River Colony, the perennial root shaped like a carrot, which was eaten by the natives.

Geum rivale Linn. *Rosaceae.* INDIAN CHOCOLATE. PURPLE AVENS. WATER AVENS.

Northern temperate regions. Johnson[10] says this plant was often used in olden times to flavor ale and other liquors.

[1] Don, G. *Hist. Dichl. Pls.* 3:495. 1834.

[2] Masters, M. T. *Treas. Bot.* 1:525. 1870.

[3] Lightfoot, J. *Fl. Scot.* 1:153. 1789.

[4] Lindley, J. *Med. Econ. Bot.* 194. 1849.

[5] Vilmorin *Fl. Pl. Ter.* 427. 1870. 3rd Ed.

[6] Gardner, G. *Trav. Braz.* 101. 1846.

[7] Black, A. A. *Treas. Bot.* 1:527. 1870.

[8] Syme, J. T. *Treas. Bot.* 1:528. 1870.

[9] Hooker, W. J. *Journ. Bot.* 2:368. 1840.

[10] Johnson, C. P. *Useful Pls. Gt. Brit.* 88. 1862.

G. urbanum Linn. AVENS. CLOVE-ROOT. HERB BENNETT.

Northern temperate regions, Australia and New Zealand. The root, according to Lindley,[1] is used as an ingredient in some ales.

Gigantochloa apus Kurz. *Gramineae.* BAMBOO.

Java. The young shoots are used as a vegetable.[2]

G. ater Kurz. BAMBOO.

Java. This bamboo in Java attains a height of 70 feet and is extensively cultivated. The young shoots afford a culinary vegetable.[3]

G. robusta Kurz. BAMBOO.

Malay. This bamboo attains the height of a hundred feet. The young shoots are used as a vegetable.[4]

G. verticillata Munro. BAMBOO.

Java. The plant grows to a height of 120 feet, with stems nearly a foot thick. This is one of the most extensively cultivated of all Asiatic bamboos. The young shoots are used as a culinary vegetable.[5]

Gigartina lichnoides Harvey. *Algae.* CEYLON MOSS.

Ceylon moss is a seaweed much used in the East as a nutritive article of food and for giving consistence to other dishes. It is of a very gelatinous nature and when boiled down is almost wholly convertible into jelly.[6]

Ginko biloba Linn. *Coniferae.* GINKO. MAIDEN-HAIR TREE.

China and Japan. The fruit of the ginko is sold in the markets in all Chinese towns and is not unlike dried almonds, only whiter, fuller and more round. The natives seem very fond of it, although it is rarely eaten by Europeans.[7] In Japan, the seeds furnish an oil used for eating and burning.[8] The fruit of the maiden-hair tree is called in China *pa-kwo.* The Chinese consume the nuts of this tree at weddings, the shells being dyed red; they have a fishy taste.[9] This tree is largely cultivated as an ornamental in Europe, Asia and North America.

Gladiolus edulis Burch. *Irideae.* EDIBLE GLADIOLUS.

South Africa. The bulb-like roots are edible and taste like chestnuts when roasted.[10]

---

[1] Pickering, C. *Chron. Hist. Pls.* 506. 1879.

[2] Mueller, F. *Sel. Pls.* 216. 1891.

[3] Ibid.

[4] Ibid.

[5] Ibid.

[6] Harvey, W. H. *Man. Brit. Algae.* 1841.

[7] Fortune, R. *Wand. China* 118. 1847.

[8] Pickering, C. *Chron. Hist. Pls.* 797. 1879.

[9] Smith, F. P. *Contrib. Mat. Med. China* 103. 1871.

[10] Mueller, F. *Sel. Pls.* 217. 1891.

Glaucium flavum Crantz. *Papaveraceae.*

Europe and the Mediterranean regions. This plant furnishes an inodorous and insipid oil of a clear yellow color, sweet, edible and fit for burning.

Gleditschia triacanthos Linn. *Leguminosae.* HONEY LOCUST.

North America. This tree, native of the region about the Mississippi and its tributaries, is cultivated as an ornamental tree both in this country and in Europe. The pods contain numerous seeds enveloped in a sweet, pulpy substance, from which a sugar is said to have been extracted.[1] Porcher[2] says a beer is sometimes made by fermenting the sweet pods while fresh.

Glyceria fluitans R. Br. *Gramineae.* FLOAT GRASS. MANNA GRASS. POLAND MANNA.

Northern temperate regions. The seeds of this grass are collected on the continent and sold as manna seeds for making puddings and gruel.[3] According to Von Heer,[4] it is cultivated in Poland.

Glycine soja Sieb. & Zucc. *Leguminosae.* COFFEE BEAN. SOJA BEAN. SOY BEAN.

Tropical Asia. This bean is much cultivated in tropical Asia for its seeds, which are used as food in India, China and Japan. It is an ingredient of the sauce known as soy. Of late, it has been cultivated as an oil plant. In 1854,[5] two varieties, one white- and the other red-seeded, were obtained from Japan and distributed through the agency of the Patent Office. At the late Vienna Exposition, samples of the seed were shown among the agricultural productions of China, Japan, Mongolia, Transcaucasia and India. Professor Haberland[6] says this plant has been cultivated from early ages and that it grows wild in the Malay Archipelago, Java and the East Indies. In Japan, it is called *miso*.[7] Of late, its seeds have appeared among the novelties in our seed catalogs. According to Bretschneider,[8] a Chinese writing of 163–85 B. C. records that Shen nung, 2800 B. C., sowed the five cereals, and another writing of A. D. 127–200 explains that these five cereals were rice, wheat, *Panicum italicum* Linn., *P. miliaceum* Linn. and the soja bean. The use of this bean as a vegetable is also recorded in authors of the fifth, fourteenth and sixteenth centuries. The first European mention of the soja bean is by Kaempfer,[9] who was in Japan in 1690. In his account of his travels, he gives considerable space to this plant. It also seems to be mentioned by Ray,[10] 1704. This bean is much cultivated in China and Cochin China.[11] There are a large number of varieties.

---

[1] Smith, A. *Treas. Bot.* 1:534. 1870.

[2] Porcher, F. P. *Res. So. Fields, Forest* 229. 1869.

[3] Johnson, C. P. *Useful Pls. Gt. Brit.* 285. 1862.

[4] Heer *Agr. Ohio* 278. 1859.

[5] *U. S. Pat. Off. Rpt.* XV. 1854. Preface. (*Soja hispida*)

[6] *Rutgers Sci. School Rpt.* 55. 1879.

[7] Don, G. *Hist. Dichl. Pls.* 2:357. 1832.

[8] Bretschneider, E. *Bot. Sin.* 75, 78, 52, 59. 1882.

[9] Kaempfer, E. *Amoen.* 1712.

[10] Ray *Hist. Pl.* 438. 1704.

[11] Loureiro *Fl. Cochin.* 441. 1790.

Seeds were brought from Japan to America by the Perry Expedition on its return and were distributed from the United States Patent Office [1] in 1854. In France, seeds were distributed in 1855.[2] In 1869, Martens [3] described 13 varieties.

Glycosmis pentaphylla Correa. *Rutaceae.* JAMAICA MANDARIN ORANGE.

Tropical Asia and Australia. This Asiatic tree is noted for the delicious flavor of its fruit.[4] It is the mandarin orange of Jamaica and is grown as a fruit tree in the Public Gardens of Jamaica.[5] The ripe fruit is eaten.[6]

Glycyrrhiza asperrima Linn. f. *Leguminosae.* WILD LICORICE.

Russia and central Asia. Pallas [7] says the leaves are used by the Kalmucks as a substitute for tea.

G. echinata Linn. WILD LICORICE.

Southern Europe and the Orient. From the root of this herb, a portion of the Italian licorice is prepared. The Russian licorice root is of this species.[8]

G. glabra Linn. LICORICE.

South Europe, northern Africa and Persia. This plant is cultivated in England, Germany and the north of France. Licorice root is used in medicine and in brewing porter.[9] The leaves, called *nakhalsa* are employed by the Mongols as substitutes for tea.[10]

G. lepidota Pursh. WILD LICORICE.

North America. The root is eaten by the Indians of Alaska and the northwestern states.[11]

Gmelina arborea Roxb. *Verbenaceae.*

Tropical India and Burma. The yellow drupe is eaten by the Gonds of the Satpura who protect the tree near villages.[12]

Gnetum gnemon Linn. *Gnetaceae.*

Malay. The seeds are eaten in Amboina, roasted, boiled or fried, and the green leaves are a favorite vegetable, cooked and eaten as spinach.[13]

---

[1] *U. S. Pat. Off. Rpt.* XV. 1854. (*Soja hispida*)

[2] Paillieux *Soja* 5. 1881.

[3] Martens *Gartenbohne* 103, 104, 105. 1869.

[4] Masters, M. T. *Treas. Bot.* 1:537. 1870. (*G. citrifolia*)

[5] Morris *Rpt. Pub. Gard. Jamaica* 35. 1880.

[6] Brandis, D. *Forest Fl.* 50. 1874.

[7] Pickering, C. *Chron. Hist. Pls.* 793. 1879.

[8] Mueller, F. *Sel. Pls.* 217. 1891.

[9] Mueller, F. *Sel. Pls.* 218. 1891.

[10] Pickering, C. *Chron. Hist. Pls.* 753. 1879. (*G. hirsuta*)

[11] *U. S. D. A. Rpt.* 407. 1870.

[12] Brandis, D. *Forest Fl.* 364. 1876.

[13] Figuier *Veg. World* 332. 1867.

Gomortega nitida Ruiz & Pav.

This is a large tree of Chile called *queule* or *keule*. The fruit is the size of a small peach; the eatable part is yellow, not very juicy, but is of a most excellent and grateful taste.[1]

Gomphia jabotapita Sw. *Ochnaceae.* BUTTON TREE.

Tropical America. Piso[2] says the carpels are astringent and are not only eaten raw, but that an oil is expressed from them, which is used in salads.

G. parviflora DC. BUTTON TREE.

Brazil. The oil expressed from the fruit is used for salads.

Goniothalamus walkeri Hook. f. & Thoms. *Anonaceae.*

Ceylon. The roots are very fragrant and are said to contain camphor. They are chewed by the Singhalese.[3]

Gonolobus hispidus Hook. & Arn. *Asclepiadeae.* ANGLE-POD.

South America. The pod is described by Tweedie[4] as being very large, resembling a toad, and is eaten by the natives.

Gossypium herbaceum Linn. *Malvaceae.* COTTON.

Tropical Asia. During the War of the Rebellion, cotton seed came into some use as a substitute for coffee, the seed having been parched and ground.[5] The oil expressed from the seed makes a fine salad oil and is also used for cooking and as a butter substitute.

Gouania domingensis Linn. *Rhamneae.* CHAW-STICK.

West Indies. The stems are used for flavoring cooling beverages.[6]

Gourliea chilensis Clos. *Leguminosae.* CHANAL. CHANAR.

Tropical South America. This plant is called chanar or chanal in Chile and Buenos Aires. According to Tweedie, the pulp of the fruit is used in flavoring sweet wines.[7]

Gracilaria lichenoides L. Harv. *Algae.* AGAR-AGAR.

Coast of Ceylon and the opposing portion of the Malayan Archipelago. This seaweed is highly valued for food in Ceylon and other islands of the East. It abounds in Burma and is of superior quality on the Tenasserim Coast.

---

[1] Lindley, J. *Trans. Hort. Soc. Lond.* 5:104. 1824.

[2] Don, G. *Hist. Dichl. Pls.* 1:816. 1831.

[3] Jackson, J. R. *Treas. Bot.* 2:1299. 1876.

[4] Hooker, W. J. *Journ. Bot.* 1:295. 1834.

[5] Stelle *Amer. Agr. Rev.* 105. 1882.

[6] Smith, A. *Treas. Bot.* 1:545. 1870.

[7] Black, A. A. *Treas. Bot.* 1:545. 1870.

Greigia sphacelata Regel. *Bromeliaceae.*

Chile. The sweet, pulpy fruits, called *chupon*, are greedily eaten by children.

Grevillea sp.? *Proteaceae.* SILK-BARK OAK.

A species at Swan River Colony, Australia, has a large, yellow, spicate inflorescence nearly a foot long. The natives, says Drummond, collect the flowers and suck the honey from them. They call the plant *woadjar*.[1]

Grewia asiatica Linn. *Tiliaceae.*

East Indies. This plant is cultivated in India, says Brandis,[2] for the small, not very succulent, pleasantly acid fruit. The bark of this tree is also employed for making rope. Masters[3] says the small, red fruits, on account of their pleasant, acid taste, are commonly used in India for flavoring sherbets. Firminger[4] says the pea-sized fruits, with a stone in the center, are sour and uneatable. The berries have a pleasant, acid taste and are used for making sherbets.[5]

G. hirsuta Vahl.

Tropical Asia. A shrub or small tree whose pleasant, acid fruit is much used for making sherbets.[6]

G. megalocarpa Beauv.

Tropical Africa. The black fruit is edible.[7]

G. oppositifolia Buch.-Ham.

Hindustan. The berries have a pleasant, acid taste and are used for sherbets.[8] They are also eaten.[9]

G. pilosa Lam.

East Indies and tropical Africa. The fruit of a shrub, probably this, is called *karanto* on the Bassi hills of India and is eaten.[10]

G. populifolia Vahl.

East Indies and tropical Africa. The fruit, with a scanty but pleasant pulp, is eaten in Sind, where it is called *gungo*. In the Punjab, it is called *gangee*.[11]

G. salvifolia Heyne.

East Indies. The small, dry, subacid fruit is eaten in India.[12]

[1] Hooker, W. J. *Journ. Bot.* 2:360. 1840.

[2] Brandis, D. *Forest Fl.* 41. 1874.

[3] Masters, M. T. *Treas. Bot.* 1:552. 1870.

[4] Firminger, T. A. C. *Gard. Ind.* 200. 1874.

[5] Pickering, C. *Chron. Hist. Pls.* 735. 1879. (*G. elastica*)

[6] Royle, J. F. *Illustr. Bot. Himal.* 1:104. 1839.

[7] Don, G. *Hist. Dichl. Pls.* 1:550. 1831.

[8] Drury, H. *Useful Pls. Ind.* 235. 1873.

[9] Brandis, D. *Forest Fl.* 38. 1874.

[10] Brandis, D. *Forest Fl.* 39. 1874.

[11] Brandis, D. *Forest Fl.* 38. 1874.

[12] Brandis, D. *Forest Fl.* 43. 1874.

G. sapida Roxb.

Himalayan region. This plant bears a small but palatable fruit,[1] much used for sherbets.[2]

G. scabrophylla Roxb.

Himalayan region and Burma. The fruit, the size of a gooseberry, is eaten in India [3] and is used for sherbets.[4]

G. tiliaefolia Vahl.

Tropics of Asia and Africa. Its drupe, the size of a pea, is of an agreeable, acid flavor.[5]

G. villosa Wild.

East Indies. The fruit is of the size of a cherry, with a sweet, edible pulp and is eaten in India.[6]

Grias cauliflora Linn. *Myrtaceae.* ANCHOVY PEAR.

West Indies. The anchovy pear is a native of Jamaica, where it forms a high tree. It has for a long time been cultivated in plant houses for the sake of its magnificent foliage. The fruits are pear-shaped, russet-brown drupes and when young are pickled like the mango, which they resemble in taste.[7] This plant is cultivated to a limited extent in extreme southern Florida.[8]

Guazuma tomentosa H. B. & K. *Sterculiaceae.* BASTARD CEDAR.

West Indies; introduced into India. The fruit is filled with mucilage, which is said by Drury [9] to be very agreeable to the taste.

G. ulmifolia Lam. BASTARD CEDAR.

Tropical America. The fruit, says St. Hilaire,[10] is hard and woody but is filled with a mucilage of a sweet and agreeable taste, which can be sucked with pleasure. In Jamaica, says Lunan,[11] the fruit is eaten by the negroes, either raw or boiled as a green.

Guizotia abyssinica Case. *Compositae.* RAMTIL.

Tropical Africa. This plant is a native of Abyssinia, where it is cultivated, as well as in India, for the sake of its seeds, which yield an oil to pressure, bland like that of sesame

[1] Brandis, D.   *Forest Fl.* 42.   1874.

[2] Royle, J. F.   *Illustr. Bot. Himal.* 1:104.   1839.

[3] Brandis, D.   *Forest Fl.* 40.   1874.   (*G. sclerophylla*)

[4] Royle, J. F.   *Illustr. Bot. Himal.* 1:104.   1839.

[5] Brandis, D.   *Forest Fl.* 41.   1874.

[6] Brandis, D.   *Forest Fl.* 39.   1874.

[7] Rhind, W.   *Veg. King.* 374.   1855.

[8] Redmond, D.   *Amer. Pom. Soc. Rpt.* 55.   1875.

[9] Drury, H.   *Useful Pls. Ind.* 236.   1873.

[10] St. Hilaire, A.   *Fl. Bras. Merid.* 1:118.   1825.

[11] Lunan, J.   *Hort. Jam.* 1:60.   1814.

and called ramtil.   This oil is sweet and is used as a condiment and as a burning oil.[1]   It is much used for dressing food in Mysore.[2]

Gundelia tournefortii Linn.   *Compositae.*

Syria, Asia Minor and Persia.   This thistle is grown abundantly in Palestine and is similar to the artichoke.   The young plant, especially the thick stem, with the young and still undeveloped flower-buds, is brought to the market of Jerusalem under the name *cardi* and is sought after as a vegetable.[3]

Gunnera chilensis Lam.   *Halorageae.*

Chile.   The acidulous leaf-stalks serve as a vegetable.[4]   The plant somewhat resembles rhubarb on a gigantic scale.   The inhabitants, says Darwin,[5] eat the stalks, which are subacid.   The leaves are sometimes nearly eight feet in diameter, and the stalk is rather more than a yard high.   It is called *panke.*[6]   In France, it is grown as an ornament.[7]

Gustavia speciosa DC.   *Myrtaceae.*

New Granada.   The small fruits of this tree, according to Humboldt and Bonpland, cause the body of the eater to turn yellow, and, after it remains 24 or 48 hours, nothing can erase the color.[8]

Gymnema lactiferum R. Br.   *Asclepiadeae.*   COW PLANT.

East Indies and Malay.   This is the cow plant of Ceylon, where it is said to yield a mild and copious milk.[9]

Gymnocladus canadensis Lam.   *Leguminosae.*   CHICOT.   KENTUCKY COFFEE-TREE. NICKER-TREE.   STUMP TREE.

North America.   This tree, which occurs in the northern United States and in Canada, is often cultivated for ornamental purposes.   The pods, preserved like those of the tamarind, are said to be wholesome and slightly aperient.   The seeds were employed by the early settlers of Kentucky as a substitute for coffee.[10]

Gynandropsis pentaphylla DC.   *Capparideae.*

Cosmopolitan tropics.   This plant is a well-known esculent in the Upper Nile and throughout equatorial Africa as far as the Congo.[11]   In India, the leaves are eaten by the

---

[1] Black, A. A.   *Treas. Bot.* 1:556.   1870.   (*G. oleifera*)

[2] Ainslie *Mat. Med.* 2:256.   1826.

[3] Unger, F.   *U. S. Pat. Off. Rpt.* 358.   1859.

[4] Mueller, F.   *Sel. Pls.* 224.   1891.

[5] Darwin, C.   *Voy. H. M. S. Beagle* 279.   1884.   (*G. scabra*)

[6] Molina *Hist. Chili* 1:99.   1808.   (*G. tinctoria*)

[7] Vilmorin *Fl. Pl. Ter.* 478.   1870.   3rd Ed.   (*G. scabra*)

[8] Don, G.   *Hist. Dichl. Pls.* 2:870.   1832.

[9] Royle, J. F.   *Illustr. Bot. Himal.* 1:274.   1839.

[10] Browne, D. J.   *Trees Amer.* 219.   1846.

[11] Pickering, C.   *Chron. Hist. Pls.* 648.   1879.   (*Cleome pentaphylla*)

natives,[1] and the seeds are used as a substitute for mustard and yield a good oil.[2] In Jamaica, it is considered a wholesome plant but, from its being a little bitterish, requires repeated boilings to make it palatable.[3]

Gynura sarmentosa DC. *Compositae.*
Malay. In China, the leaves are employed as food.[4]

Gyrophora muhlenbergii Ach. *Lichenes.* ROCK TRIPE.
Arctic climates. Franklin[5] says, when boiled with fish-roe or other animal matter, this lichen is agreeable and nutritious and is eaten by the natives.

G. vellea Linn. Ach. ROCK TRIPE.
Cold regions. This lichen forms a pleasanter food than the other species of this genus.[6]

Haematostaphis barteri Hook. f. *Anacardiaceae.* BLOOD PLUM.
Tropical Africa. The fruit has a pleasant, subacid flavor when ripe. In size and shape it is similar to a grape.[7]

Haemodorum sp.? *Haemodoraceae.*
At Swan River, Australia, Drummond says seven or eight species furnish roots which are eaten by the natives. The roots of all the species are acrid when raw but mild and nutritious when roasted.[8]

Halesia tetraptera Linn. *Styraceae.* SILVER-BELL TREE. WILD OLIVE.
North Carolina to Texas. The ripe fruit is eaten by some people and when green is sometimes made into a pickle.

Hamamelis virginiana Linn. *Hamamelideae.* WITCH-HAZEL.
Northeastern United States. The seeds are used as food, says Balfour.[9] The kernels are oily and eatable, says Lindley.[10] The source of such statements, writes Gray,[11] appears to be the *Medical Flora* of the eccentric Rafinesque, who says the nuts are called pistachio nuts in the Southern States, but Gray[12] has never heard of the seeds being eaten. They are about the size of a grain of barley and have a thick, bony coat.

[1] Ainslie, W. *Mat. Ind.* 2:224. 1826.
[2] Drury, H. *Useful Pls. Ind.* 239. 1873.
[3] Ainslie, W. *Mat. Ind.* 2:224. 1826.
[4] Dickie, G. D. *Treas. Bot.* 1:187. 1870. (*Cacalia procumbens*)
[5] Franklin, J. *Narr. Journ. Polar Seas* 773. 1823.
[6] Ibid.
[7] *Gard. Chron.* 751. 1864.
[8] Hooker, W. J. *Journ. Bot.* 2:355. 1840.
[9] Balfour, J. H. *Man. Bot.* 504. 1875.
[10] Lindley, J. *Veg. King.* 784. 1846.
[11] Gray, A. *Amer. Journ. Sci.* 24:439. 1857.
[12] Ibid.

Hancornia speciosa Gomez. *Apocynaceae.* MANGABA.

Brazil. Gardner[1] says the fruit is about the size of a large plum, streaked a little with red on one side. The flavor is most delicious. Hartt[2] says the fruit is very delicious.

Hedysarum mackenzii Richards. *Leguminosae.* LICORICE-ROOT.

North America. Richardson[3] says at Fort Good Hope, Mackenzie River, this plant furnishes long, flexible roots which taste sweet like licorice and are much eaten in the spring by the natives but become woody and lose their juiciness and crispness as the season advances. This is the licorice-root of the trappers of the Northwest and is also used as a food by the Indians of Alaska.[4]

Heldreichia kotschyi Boiss. *Cruciferae.*

Cilicia. This plant has the same properties as the cresses.[5]

Helianthus annuus Linn. *Compositae.* SUNFLOWER.

North America. This plant is said by Pickering[6] to be a native of western America and is called in Mexico *chimalati*. Gray[7] says it probably belongs to the warmer parts of North America. Other botanists ascribe its origin to Mexico and Peru. Brewer and Watson[8] say in all probability the wild sunflower of the California plains is the original of the cultivated sunflower and that the seeds are now used by the Indians as food. Kalm,[9] 1749, saw the common sunflower cultivated by the Indians at Loretto, Canada, in their maize fields; the seeds were mixed with thin *sagamite* or maize soup. In 1615, the sunflower was seen by Champlain among the Hurons.[10] The seeds are said to be boiled and eaten in Tartary. In Russia, they are ground into a meal, the finer kinds being made into tea-cakes, and in some parts the whole seed is roasted and used as a substitute for coffee.

Gerarde,[11] in England, writes: "We have found by triall, that the buds before they be flowered, boiled and eaten with butter, vinegar and pepper, after the manner of artichokes, an exceeding pleasant meat, surpassing the artichoke far in procuring bodily lust. The same buds with the stalks neere unto the top (the hairness being taken away) broiled upon a gridiron and afterwards eaten with oile, vinegar, and pepper have the like property." In Russia, this plant yields about 50 bushels of seed per acre, from which about 50 gallons of oil are expressed and the oil-cake is said to be superior to that from linseed for the feeding of cattle. This oil is used for culinary purposes in many places in Russia. In Landeshut, Germany, the carefully dried leaf is much used locally for a tobacco. The seed-receptacles

---

[1] Gardner *Trav. Braz.* 65. 1849.

[2] Hartt *Geog. Braz.* 374. 1870.

[3] Richardson, J. *Arctic Explor.* 1:240. 1851. (*H. boreale*)

[4] Dall, W. H. *Alaska* 43. 1897.

[5] Baillon, H. *Hist. Pls.* 3:225. 1874.

[6] Pickering, C. *Chron. Hist. Pls.* 749. 1879.

[7] Gray, A. *Man. Bot.* 255. 1868.

[8] Brewer and Watson *Bot. Cal.* 1:353. 1880.

[9] Kalm, P. *Trav. No. Amer.* 2:309. 1772.

[10] Parkman, F. *Pion. France* 395. 1894.

[11] Gerarde, J. *Herb.* 752. 1633 or 1636.

are made into blotting paper and the inner part of the stalk into a fine writing paper in the manufactories of the province. The stalk, when treated like flax, produces a silky fiber of excellent quality. The green leaves make excellent fodder, and Sir Allen Crockden, in England, is said to grow the plant at Sevenoaks, for the purpose of feeding his stock. The leaves, dried and burned to powder, are valuable, mixed with bran, for milch cows.[1] The seeds are also said to be valuable as a food for sheep. The dried seeds are pounded into a cake and eaten by the Indians of the Northwest.[2]

H. doronicoides Lam

North America. This coarse species with showy heads, of river bottoms from Ohio to Illinois and southward, is most probably, says Gray,[3] the original of the Jerusalem artichoke.

H. giganteus Linn. GIANT SUNFLOWER.

Eastern North America. The Choctaws use the seeds ground to a flour and mixed with maize flour for making a very palatable bread.[4]

H. tuberosus Linn. JERUSALEM ARTICHOKE.

North America. The name, Jerusalem artichoke, is considered to be a corruption of the Italian *Girasoli articocco*, sunflower artichoke. Gray[5] thinks that this esculent originated in the valley of the Mississippi from the species of sunflower, *H. doronicoides*, Lam. It was cultivated by the Huron Indians.[6] In New England, Gookin found the natives mixing Jerusalem artichokes in their pottage. They were growing in Virginia, in 1648[7] and at Mobile, Alabama, in 1775.[8] The sunflower reached Europe in the early part of the seventeenth century, as it is not mentioned in Bauhin's *Phytopinax*, 1596, and is mentioned in his *Pinax*, 1623, where, among other names, he calls it *Crysanthemum e Canada quibusdam, Canada & Artichoki sub terra, aliis*. It is figured by Columna,[9] 1616, and also by Laurembergius,[10] 1632; Ray,[11] 1686, makes the first use found of the name Jerusalem artichoke, though Parkinson used the word in 1640, according to Gray. In 1727, Townsend[12] says "it is a Root fit to be eat about Christmas when it is boiled." Mawe,[13] 1778, says it is by many esteemed. Bryant,[14] 1783, says, "not much cultivated." In 1806, McMahon[15] speaks of it in American gardens and calls it "a wholesome, palatable

---

[1] Simmonds, P. L. *Trop. Agr.* 419. 1889.

[2] Hooker, W. J. *Fl. Bor. Amer.* **1**:313. 1840. (*H. lenticularis*)

[3] Gray, A. *Amer. Journ. Sci.* 348. 1877.

[4] Romans *Nat. Hist. Fla.* 1:84. 1775.

[5] Gray, A. *Amer. Agr.* 142. 1877.

[6] Ibid.

[7] *Perf. Desc. Va.* 4. 1649. Force Coll. Tracts 2: No. 8. 1838.

[8] Romans *Nat. Hist. Fla.* 1:115. 1775.

[9] Columna *Minus cognit. stirp. pars altera.* 13. 1616.

[10] Noisette *Man. Jard.* 1829; Pirolle *L'Hort. France.* 1824.

[11] Laurembergius *Apparat. Plant.* 131. 1632.

[12] Townsend *Seedsman* 23. 1726.

[13] Mawe and Abercrombie *Univ. Gard. Bot.* 1778

[14] Bryant *Fl. Diet.* 33. 1783.

[15] McMahon, B. *Amer. Gard. Cal.* 206. 1806.

food." In 1863, Burr [1] describes varieties with white, purple, red and yellow-skinned tubers.

The history of the Jerusalem artichoke has been well treated by Gray and Trumbull in the *American Journal of Science*, May, 1877, and April, 1883. It was found in culture at the Lew Chew Islands about 1853.[2] We offer a synonymy as below:

> *Flos Solis Farnesianus sive Aster Peruanus tubercosus.* Col. 13. 1616.
> *Helianthemum indicum tuberosum.* Bauh. *Pin.* 277. 1623.
> *De Solis flore tuberoso, seu flore Farnesiano Fabii Columnae.* Aldinus, 91. 1625.
> *Battatas de Canada.* Park. *Par.* 1629.
> *Adenes Canadenses seu flos solis glandulosus.* Lauremb. 132. 1632.
> *Flos Solis pyramidalis, parvo flore, tuberosa radice, Heliotropium indicum.* Ger. 1633.
> *Peruanus solis flos ex Indiis tuberosus.* Col. in Hern. 878, 881. 1651.
> Potatoes of Canada. Coles. 1657.
> *Canada & Artischokki sub terra.* H. R. P. 1665.
> *Chrysanthemum latifolium Brasilianum.* Bauh. *Prod.* 70. 1671.
> *Chrysanthemum Canadense arumosum.* Cat. H. L. B. 1672.
> *Helenium Canadense.* Amman. 1676.
> *Chrysanthemum perenne majus fol, integris, americanum tuberum.* Mor. 1630.
> Jerusalem Artichoke. Ray 335. 1686.
> *Corona solis parvo flore, tuberosa radice.* Tourn. 489. 1719.
> *Helianthus radice tuberosa esculenta,* Hierusalem Artichoke. Clayton. 1739.
> *Helianthus foliis ovato cordatis triplinervus.* Gronov. *Virg.* 129. 1762.
> *Helianthus tuberosus.* Linn. *Sp.* 1277. 1763.

Helichrysum serpyllifolium Less. *Compositae.* HOTTENTOT TEA.

South Africa. This plant is used as a tea substitute under the name of Hottentot tea.[3]

Heliconia bihai Linn. *Scitamineae.* FALSE PLANTAIN.

South America. In the West Indies, the young shoots are eaten by the natives.[4]

H. psittacorum Linn. f. PARROT'S PLANTAIN.

South America. In the West Indies, the shoots are eaten.[5]

Helwingia rusciflora Willd. *Araliaceae.*

Japan. The young leaves, says Balfour,[6] are used in Japan as an esculent.

Hemerocallis sp.? *Liliaceae.* DAY LILY.

Northern Asia. It is somewhat difficult, says Penhallow,[7] to give testimony bearing upon the flavor and desirable qualities of flowers and buds from various species of Hemerocallis. In certain sections of the Island of Yezo, particularly on the pumice for-

---

[1] Burr, F. *Field, Gard. Veg.* 37. 1863.
[2] Birdwood *Veg. Prod. Bomb.* 165. 1865.
[3] *Gard. Chron.* 20:766. 1883.
[4] Masters *Treas. Bot.* 1:575. 1870.
[5] Ibid.
[6] Balfour, J. H. *Treas. Bot.* 1:579. 1870.
[7] Penhallow, D. P. *Amer. Nat.* 16:119. 1882.

mation of the east coast, these plants are very abundant and, at the time of blossoming, the fields for miles along the road on either side are almost uniformly golden-yellow. At such times the Aino women may be seen busily engaged gathering the flowers which they take home to dry or pickle in salt. They are afterwards used in soups.

H. minor Mill.

Northern Asia. In China, the young leaves are eaten and appear to intoxicate or stimulate to some extent. The flowers are eaten as a relish with meat.[1] This species is said by Vilmorin[2] to be a native of Siberia and to be grown in French flower gardens.

Henriettea succosa DC. *Melastomaceae.*

Guinea. The plant furnishes a gooseberry-like fruit of little value.[3]

Henriettella flavescens Triana. *Melastomaceae.*

Guiana. This species furnishes a gooseberry-like fruit of little value.[4]

Heracleum cordatum Presl. *Umbelliferae.* COW PARSNIP.

Sicily. The root is black, sweet scented and is used as angelica by the Sicilians.[5]

H. flavescens Baumg. YELLOW COW PARSNIP.

This plant is used as a food and, in Kamchatka, a spirit called *raka* is prepared from it.[6]

H. lanatum Michx. AMERICAN COW PARSNIP.

Subarctic America. The roots and young stems are eaten by some of the tribes along the Pacific and it is also used by the Crees of the eastern side of the Rocky Mountains as a potherb.[7]

H. pubescens Bieb. DOWNY COW PARSNIP.

The young shoots are filled with a sweet, aromatic juice and are eaten raw by the natives of the Caucasus,[8] where it is native. In France, it is grown in the flower garden.[9]

H. sibiricum Linn.

In Prussia, this plant is sown in April and the next year yields an immense amount of foliage to be used as fodder. It is more especially grown for ewes than for any other kind of stock. In 1854, seed from Germany was distributed from the United States Patent Office.[10] Captain Cook says this plant was formerly a principal ingredient in the cookery of most of the Kamchatka dishes but since the Russians got possession of the country it has been almost entirely appropriated to the purpose of distillation.

---

[1] Smith, F. P. *Contrib. Mat. Med. China* 110. 1871.

[2] Vilmorin *Fl. Pl. Ter.* 507. 1870. 3rd Ed. (*H. graminea*)

[3] Unger, F. *U. S. Pat. Off. Rpt.* 351. 1859. (*Melastoma succosum*)

[4] Unger, F. *U. S. Pat. Off. Rpt.* 351. 1859. (*Melastoma flavescens*)

[5] Don, G. *Hist. Dichl. Pls.* 3:342. 1834.

[6] Don, G. *Hist. Dichl. Pls.* 3:341. 1834.

[7] Brown, R. *Bot. Soc. Edinb.* 9:381. 1868.

[8] Don, G. *Hist. Dichl. Pls.* 3:342. 1868.

[9] Vilmorin *Fl. Pl. Ter.* 163. 1870. 3rd Ed. (*Berce pubescente*)

[10] *U. S. Pat. Off. Rpt.* 1854. Preface.

H. sphondylium Linn.   COW PARSNIP.

Europe, northern Asia and western North America. The people of Ploonia and Lithuania says Gerarde,[1] "use to make drinks with the decoction of this herb and leven or some other thing made of meale, which is used instead of beere and other ordinaire drinks." The young succulent stems, after being stripped of their envelope, are occasionally eaten as a salad in the outer Hebrides. These stalks are much used, says Johnson,[2] in some parts of Asiatic Russia. In Russia and Siberia, the leaf-stalks are dried in the sun and tied up in close bundles, until they acquire a yellow color, when a sweet substance resembling sugar forms upon them, which is eaten as a great delicacy. In Lithuania and Siberia, a spirit is distilled from the stalks, either alone or mixed with bilberries; fermented, they form a kind of beer. The young shoots and leaves may be boiled and eaten as a green vegetable and, when just sprouting from the ground, resemble asparagus in flavor.

H. tuberosum Molina.

Chile. The bulbs are frequently six inches long and three broad; the color is yellow; the taste is pleasant. The plant grows naturally in sandy places near hedges and produces abundantly.[3]

Herpestis monnieria H. B. & K. *Scrophularineae.* WATER HYSSOP.

Cosmopolitan tropics. The Indians eat this herb in their soups.[4]

Hesperocallis undulata A. Gray. *Liliaceae.*

Mexico. The bulb is eaten by the California Indians.[5]

Hibiscus cannabinus Linn. *Malvaceae.* BASTARD JUTE.   DECKANER HEMP.   INDIAN HEMP.

Old World tropics. The stem yields a hemp-like fiber sometimes called Indian hemp, Deckaner hemp, or bastard jute. It is as much cultivated, says Drury,[6] for the sake of its leaves as its fibers. The leaves serve as a sorrel spinach.

H. digitatus Cav.

Brazil and Guiana. The plant is used as a vegetable.[7]

H. esculentus Linn. GOBO.   GOMBO.   GUMBO.   OCRA.   OKRA.

Tropical Africa. Okra has become distributed as a plant of cultivation from Khartum and Sennar throughout Egypt to Palestine and elsewhere. Schweinfurth [8] found its seed pods a favorite vegetable in Nubia and the plant perfectly wild on the White Nile. About Constantinople, okra is largely cultivated and the leaves are used as a demulcent.[9] In

---

[1] Gerarde, J. *Herb.* 1009. 1633 or 1636.

[2] Johnson, C. P. *Useful Pls. Gt. Brit.* 118. 1862.

[3] Molina *Hist. Chili* 1:96. 1808.

[4] Titford, W. J. *Hort. Bot. Amer.* 35. 1811.

[5] Brewer and Watson *Bot. Cal.* 2:158. 1880.

[6] Drury, H. *Useful Pls. Ind.* 243. 1873.

[7] Unger, F. *U. S. Pat. Off. Rpt.* 359. 1859.

[8] Schweinfurth, G. *Heart Afr.* 1:97. 1874.

[9] *Amer. Journ. Pharm.* May 1860.

India, the capsule, familiarly known as the *bendi-kai*, is much esteemed for imparting a mucilaginous thickening to soups, and the young pods are often gathered green and pickled like capers; but Firminger[1] states that, though of an agreeable flavor, the pods, on account of their slimy nature, are not generally in favor with Europeans. Its seeds form one of the best coffee substitutes known.[2] In the south of France, okra is cultivated for its pods. It was carried from Africa to Brazil before 1658,[3] reached Surinam before 1686[4] and is mentioned by Hughes[5] for Barbados in 1750.

In the southern United States, okra has long been a favorite vegetable, the green pods being used when quite young, sliced in soups and similar dishes, to which they impart a thick, viscous or gummy consistency. The ripe seeds, washed and ground, are also said to furnish a palatable substitute for coffee. Okra is mentioned by Kalm,[6] 1748, as growing in gardens in Philadelphia; is mentioned by Jefferson as cultivated in Virginia before 1781; and is included among garden vegetables by McMahon,[7] 1806, and all succeeding writers on American gardening. The green seed pods are used in soups, or stewed and served like asparagus, or when cold made into a salad. The green pods may be preserved for winter use by cutting them in halves, stringing and drying them. The young leaves and pods are also occasionally dried, pulverized and stored in bottles for future use. The stalks of the plant are used for the manufacture of paper. This plant offers a highly esteemed vegetable in southern States and is quite frequently, but neither generally nor extensively, cultivated in northern gardens for use of the pods in soups and stews.

The Spanish Moors appear to have been well acquainted with this plant, which was known to them by the name of *bamiyah*. Abul-Abbas el-Nebati, a native of Seville, learned in plants, who visited Egypt in 1216, describes in unmistakable terms the form of the plant, its seeds and fruit, which last, he remarks, is eaten when young and tender with meal by the Egyptians.[8] The references to this plant in the early botanies are not numerous and the synonymies offered are often incorrect. The following, however, are justified:

Trionum theophrasti. Rauwolf, in Ap. to Dalechamp, 31. 1857. Cum ic.

Alcea aegyptia Clusius *Hist.* 2:27, 1601. Cum ic.

Honorius bellus. In Clus., l. c. 2:311.

Bamia alessandrina. Dur. C. Ap. 1617. Cum ic.

Quingombo. Marcg. *Bras.*, 31, 1648, cum ic.; Piso. *Bras.* 211, 1658. Cum ic.

Malva rosea sive hortensis. Bauh. J. 2:951. 1651.

Ketmia americana annua flore albo, fructu non sulcato longissimo. Commelyn, *Hort. Med.* 150. 1701. Cum ic.

Of these, the last only, that of Commelyn, represents the type of pod of the varieties usually to be found in our gardens, but plants are occasionally to be found bearing pods

---

[1] Firminger, T. A. C. *Gard. Ind.* 141. 1874.

[2] *Bon Jard.* 501. 1882.

[3] Piso *De Ind.* 211. 1658. Marcgravius *Hist. Rerum Nat. Bras.* 31. 1648. (Piso)

[4] Commelin *Hort.* 1:37. 1697.

[5] Hughes, G. *Nat. Hist. Barb.* 210. 1750.

[6] Kalm, P. *Trav. No. Amer.* 1:58. 1772.

[7] McMahon *Amer. Gard. Cal.* 318. 1806.

[8] Flückiger and Hanbury *Pharm.* 94. 1879.

which resemble those figured in the above list. There is little recorded, however, concerning variety, as in the regions where its culture is particularly affected there is a paucity of writers. *Miller's Dictionary*, 1807, mentions that there are different forms of pods in different varieties; in some, not thicker than a man's finger, and five or six inches long; in others, very thick, and not more than two or three inches long; in some, erect; in others, rather inclined. Lunan,[1] in Jamaica, 1814, speaks of the pods being of different size and form in the varieties. In 1831, Don[2] describes a species, the *H. bammia* Link., with very long pods. In 1863, Burr[3] describes four varieties in American gardens; two dwarfs, one pendant-podded and one tall and white-podded. In 1885, at the New York Agricultural Experiment Station, varieties were grown under 11 different names and from these there were three distinct sorts only. Vilmorin,[4] 1885, names but two sorts, the long-fruited and the round-fruited.

H. ficulneus Linn.

Tropics of Asia and Australia. This species is cultivated in Egypt as a vegetable.[5]

H. furcatus Willd.

Old World tropics. This species of hibiscus is used as a vegetable.[6]

H. hirtus Linn.

East Indies and Malay. This species furnishes a vegetable of Bengal and the East Indies.[7]

H. maculatus Lam.

Santo Domingo. This plant is used for food purposes.[8]

H. micranthus Linn. f.

African tropics and East Indies. It is used as a vegetable.[9]

H. rosa-sinensis Linn. CHINESE HIBISCUS.

Old World tropics. This is a well-known ornament of our hot-houses. The people of India[10] and China,[11] prepare a kind of pickle from the petals of the flowers.

H. sabdariffa Linn. INDIAN SORREL. ROSELLE.

Old World tropics. Two varieties, the red and white, are cultivated in most gardens of Jamaica for the flowers which are made, with the help of sugar, into very agreeable tarts and jellies, or fermented into a cooling beverage.[12] Roselle is now cultivated in most

[1] Lunan, J. *Hort. Jam.* 2:12. 1814.

[2] Don, G. *Hist. Dichl. Pls.* 1:480. 1831.

[3] Burr, F. *Field, Gard. Veg.* 614. 1863.

[4] Vilmorin *Veg. Gard.* 357. 1885.

[5] Unger, F. *U. S. Pat. Off. Rpt.* 359. 1859.

[6] Ibid.

[7] Ibid.

[8] Ibid.

[9] Ibid.

[10] Ainslie, W. *Mat. Ind.* 2:359. 1826.

[11] Drury, H. *Useful Pls. Ind.* 244. 1873.

[12] Long *Hist. Jam.* 805. 1774.

gardens of India. The most delicious puddings and tarts, as well as a remarkably fine jelly, are made of the thick, succulent sepals which envelope the fruit. There are two kinds, the red and the white.[1] In Malabar, jellies and tarts are made of the calyces and capsules freed from the seeds [2] as also in Burma.[3] In Unyoro and Ugani, interior Africa, it is cultivated for its bark, seeds and leaves. The bark makes beautiful but short cordage; the leaves make a spinach and the seeds are eaten roasted.[4] Roselle is now rather commonly grown in Florida.

H. syriacus Linn. ROSE OF SHARON.

Old World tropics. In China, the leaves are sometimes made into tea or eaten when young.[5]

H. tiliaceus Linn.

The Tahitians suck the bark when the breadfruit harvest is unproductive, and the New Caledonians eat it.[6]

Hippocratea comosa Sw. *Celastrineae.*

Santo Domingo and West Indies. The seeds are oily and sweet.[7]

H. grahamii Wight.

East Indies. In India, the seed is edible.[8]

Hippophaë rhamnoides Linn. *Elaeagnaceae.* SALLOW THORN. SEA BUCKTHORN.

Europe and temperate Asia. The fruit is acid and, though not very agreeable in flavor, is eaten by children in England. The Siberians and Tartars make a jelly from the berries and eat them with milk and cheese, while the inhabitants of the Gulf of Bothnia prepare from them an agreeable jelly which they use as a condiment with their fish. In some districts of France, a sauce is made of the berries, to be eaten with fish and meat.[9] In Kunawar, the fruit is made into a condiment.[10]

H. salicifolia D. Don. SEA BUCKTHORN.

Nepal. The fruit is eaten in the Himalayas.[11]

Hodgsonia heteroclita Hook. f. & Thomas. *Cucurbitaceae.*

Himalayan regions, Burma and Malay. This plant is a gigantic climber bearing immense, yellowish-white, pendulous blossoms. Its fruit is of rich brown, whose kernels, called *katior-pot* by the Lepchas, are eaten.[12]

---

[1] Firminger, T. A. C. *Gard. Ind.* 200. 1874.

[2] Pickering, C. *Chron. Hist. Pls.* 797. 1879.

[3] Ibid.

[4] Speke, J. H. *Journ. Disc. Source Nile* 563. 1864.

[5] Smith, F. P. *Contrib. Mat. Med. China* 113. 1871.

[6] Seemann, B. *Fl. Viti.* 18. 1865–73.

[7] Baillon, H. *Hist. Pls.* 6:27. 1880.

[8] Wight, R. *Illustr. Ind. Bot.* 1:132. 1840.

[9] Johnson, C. P. *Useful Pls. Gt. Brit.* 238. 1862.

[10] Brandis, D. *Forest Fl.* 389. 1874.

[11] Royle, J. F. *Illustr. Bot. Himal.* 1:323. 1839.

[12] Hooker, J. D. *Himal. Journ.* 2:7, 350. 1854.

Hoffmanseggia stricta Benth. *Leguminosae.*

Mexico. This herb has an esculent, tuberous rootstock.[1]

Holboellia latifolia Wall. *Berberideae.*

Himalayan regions. This is the *kole-pot* of the Lepchas; the fruit is eaten in Sikkim but is mealy and insipid.[2] This plant is called *gophla* and the fruit is eaten.[3]

Hordeum deficiens Steud. *Gramineae.* RED SEA BARLEY.

Abyssinia. This is one of the two-rowed barleys cultivated in Arabia and Abyssinia.[4]

H. distichon Linn. BARLEY.

Parent of cultivated forms. This is the common barley of cultivation and occurs in numerous varieties. Meyer[5] found it growing wild between Lenkoran and Baku; Koch,[6] on the Steppes of Schirwan in the southeast of the Caucasus; Kotschy,[7] in South Persia. Forster[8] reports it as wild in the region near the confluence of the Samara and the Volga. Barley was cultivated, says Pickering,[9] at the time of the invention of writing and standing crops are figured under the fifth, seventh and seventeenth dynasties of Egypt, or about 2440 B. C., 1800 B. C. and 1680 B. C. It is mentioned as among the things that were destroyed by the plagues of Egypt.[10] The flour of barley was the food of the Jewish soldiers.[11] The Egyptians claimed that barley was the first of the cereals made use of by man and trace its introduction to their goddess, Isis. Barley was in all times considered by the Greeks, says Heer,[12] as a sacred grain and was exclusively used in sacrifices and in the great festival held every year at Eleusis in honor of agriculture. Pliny[13] terms it *antiquissimum frumentum*, the most ancient cereal, but, according to Suetonius, it was considered an ignominious food by the Romans. Common barley, says Unger,[14] came to Europe by the way of Egypt; and the Romans were acquainted with the two- and the six-lined barley, and the Greeks with these varieties and the bere barley. Barley was long the grain most extensively cultivated in England. It appears on the coins of the early Britons and was not only the grain from which their progenitors, the Cimbri, made their bread but from which they made their favorite beverage, beer.[15] Herodotus describes beer made from barley as among the drinks of the Egyptians in his

---

[1] Havard, V. *Proc. U. S. Nat. Mus.* 501. 1885.
[2] Hooker, J. D. *Illustr. Himal. Pls.* Pl. X. 1855.
[3] Brandis, D. *Forest Fl.* 571. 1876.
[4] Mueller, F. *Sel. Pls.* 232. 1891.
[5] Unger, F. *U. S. Pat. Off. Rpt.* 302. 1859.
[6] Ibid.
[7] Ibid.
[8] Humboldt, A. *Views Nat.* 129. 1850.
[9] Pickering, C. *Chron. Hist. Pls.* 34. 1879. (*H. vulgare*)
[10] Exodus 9:31.
[11] 2nd Samuel 17:28.
[12] Heer *Agr. Ohio* 14:283. 1859.
[13] Humboldt, A. *Views Nat.* 129. 1850.
[14] Unger, F. *U. S. Pat. Off. Rpt.* 302. 1859.
[15] Johnson, C. W. *Journ. Agr.* 1st Ser. 11:484.

day, 450 B. C., and Pliny, Aristotle, Strabo and Diodorus mention beer. Xenophon, 400 B. C., writes that the people of Armenia used a drink made of fermented barley. Diodorus Siculus says the natives of Galatia prepared a beer from barley, and barley is mentioned in Greece by Sophocles, Dioscorides and others. Tacitus, about A. D. 100, says beer was the common drink of the Germans.

Barley was sown by Gosnold [1] on Martha's Vineyard and the Elizabeth Islands in 1602. Lescarbot [2] sowed barley at Port Royal, Nova Scotia, in 1606, and it was growing in Champlain's garden at Quebec in 1610. Barley was grown by the colonists of the London Company in Virginia in 1611.[3] It appears to have been cultivated in the New Netherlands in 1626.[4] In 1629–33, barley was growing at Lynn, Massachusetts.[5]

Barley can be grown in sheltered valleys as far north as 70° in Lapland and 68° in Siberia.[6] At Fort Yukon, Alaska, it has been grown in small patches, according to Dall.[7]

H. hexastichon Linn. SIX-LINED BARLEY. WINTER BARLEY.

Europe and Asia. This barley is supposed by Lindley [8] to be a domesticated form of *H. distichon*. Unger [9] says the six-lined, or winter barley, was cultivated by the Egyptians, Jews and East Indians in the earliest times and grains of it are found in the mummies of the Egyptian catacombs. Ears are somewhat numerous, says Lubbock,[10] in the ancient lake habitations of Switzerland. In the ears from Wangen, each row has generally ten or eleven grains, which, however, are smaller and shorter than those now grown. There are now in cultivation numerous varieties referred to this form.

H. jubatum Linn. MANED BARLEY. SQUIRREL-TAIL BARLEY.

Seashore and interior salines of the New World. The seeds are especially in request among the Shoshones of southern Oregon.[11] The maned, or squirrel-tail, barley has been known in British gardens since 1782 as an ornamental grass. Its awned spikes are dangerous to cattle.

H. vulgare Linn. BERE. BIG BARLEY. NEPAL BARLEY.

This species furnished the varieties known as bere, or big barley, and appears to be one of the varieties formerly cultivated in Greece. Its native land seems unknown, although Olivier [12] states it grew wild in the region between the Euphrates and the Tigris. Willdenow [13] is inclined to place its native country in the region of the Volga. It is enu-

---

[1] *U. S. Pat. Off. Rpt.* 156. 1853.
[2] Parkman, F. *Pion. France* 266. 1894.
[3] *U. S. Pat. Off. Rpt.* 156. 1853.
[4] Ibid.
[5] Ibid.
[6] *Enc. Brit.* **17**:630. 1859. 8th Edition.
[7] Dall, W. H. *Alaska* 441. 1897.
[8] Morton *Cyc. Agr.* **2**:67. 1869.
[9] Unger, F. *U. S. Pat. Off. Rpt.* 302. 1859.
[10] Lubbock *Amer. Journ. Sci. Art.* **34**:181. 1862. 2nd Series.
[11] Brown, R. *Bot. Soc. Edinb.* **9**:382. 1868.
[12] Unger, F. *U. S. Pat. Off. Rpt.* 302. 1859.
[13] Ibid.

merated by Thunberg[1] among the edible plants of Japan. It is cultivated in Scotland as a spring crop and in Ireland as a winter crop. Nepal barley is cultivated at great elevations on the Himalaya Mountains and in Thibet. The seed has frequently been sent to Europe as a very hardy kind, of quick maturity, but it is chiefly cultivated in botanical gardens. It is a naked-seeded species with much the appearance of wheat. It was introduced into Britain in 1817.[2]

H. zeocriton Linn. BATTLEDORE BARLEY. SPRAT BARLEY.

Parent of cultivated forms. This species is occasionally cultivated in Scotland, and Lindley[3] says it is interesting only from a botanical point of view. He says it is an undoubted result of domestication. Koch[4] collected in the Schirwan part of the Caucasus a kind of grain which he calls *H. spontaneum* and regards as the original wild form of sprat barley.

Hormosippon arcticus Berk. *Algae.*

This alga abounds in the Arctic regions and affords wholesome food, which is far preferable to the *tripe de roche*, as it has none of its bitterness or purgative quality.

Houttuynia cordata Thunb. *Piperaceae.*

Himalayan region, China and Japan. The leaves of this plant are said to be used as a potherb in Nepal.[5] In France, it is an inmate of flower gardens[6] as an aquatic.

Hovenia dulcis Thunb. *Rhamneae.* RAISIN TREE.

Himalayan regions, China and Japan. The tree is cultivated in India for its fruit, which has a pleasant flavor like that of a Bergamot pear.[7] The round fruits, about the size of a pea, are seated at the end of the recurved, fleshy peduncle, which is cylindrical, about an inch long, and is the part eaten.[8]

Humulus lupulus Linn. *Urticaceae.* BINE. HOP.

Northern Europe and not rare in the United States, especially westward on banks of streams. The scaly cones, or catkins, have been used from the remotest period in the brewing of beer. The hop was well known to the Romans and is mentioned by Pliny under the name *lupus salictarius*. Hop gardens are named as existing in France and Germany in the eighth and ninth centuries, and Bohemian and Bavarian hops have been known as esteemed kinds since the eleventh century. The hop was mentioned by Joan di Cuba in his *Ortus Samtatis* as growing in Holland prior to 1485. Hop roots were mentioned in the Memorandum[7] of Mar. 16, 1629, of seeds to be sent to the Massachusetts Company. The plant was also cultivated in New Netherlands as early as 1646, and in

[1] Thunberg *Fl. Jap.* XXXIII. 1784.

[2] Mueller, F. *Sel. Pls.* 232. 1891.

[3] Morton *Cyc. Agr.* 2:68. 1869.

[4] Humboldt, A. *Views Nat.* 130. 1850.

[5] Royle, J. F. *Illustr. Bot. Himal.* 1:331. 1839.

[6] Vilmorin *Fl. Pl. Ter.* 516. 1870. 3rd Ed.

[7] Brandis, D. *Forest Fl.* 94. 1876.

[8] Black, A. A. *Treas. Bot.* 2:599. 1870.

[9] *Mass. Records* 1:24.

Virginia in 1648 it is said, " their Hopps are faire and large, thrive well." [1]   Gerarde [2] says, " The buds or first sprouts which come forth in the Spring are used to be eaten in sallads; yet are they, as Pliny saith, more toothsome than nourishing, for they yield but very small nourishment." Dodoenaeus alludes to this plant as a kitchen herb. He says, " before its tender shoots produce leaves, they are eaten in salads, and are a good and wholesome meat." Hop shoots are now to be found in Covent Garden market and are not infrequently to be seen in other European markets.

The first allusion to the hop as a kitchen herb in America is by Cobbett,[3] 1821. The use of the young shoots is mentioned by Pliny [4] in the first century as collected from the wild plant, rather as a luxury than as a food. Dodonaeus, 1616, refers to the use of the young shoots, as collected apparently from the hop yard, as does also Camerarius,[5] 1586, and others. Emil Pott,[6] in summing up the uses of this plant, says that the tendrils furnish a good vegetable wax and a juice from which a reddish-brown coloring matter can be extracted. Hop ashes are greatly valued in the manufacture of certain Bohemian glasswares. A pulp for paper-making can be satisfactorily bleached, and very serviceable unbleached papers and cardboards are made from this raw material. The fibers can also be used in the manufacture of textile fabrics, and, in Sweden, yarn and linen making from hop fibers has long been an established industry and is constantly increasing in importance and extent. The stalks can also be used for basket and wickerwork. The leaves and the spent hops are excellent food for live stock and especially for sheep.

Hydnora africana Thunb. *Cytinaceae.* JACKAL'S KOST.

South Africa. This plant is found growing on the roots of Euphorbia. It consists of a tubular flower from four to six inches long and may be compared to the socket of a candlestick but three-lobed. The outside is of dull brown and inside of a rosy-red color It possesses an offensive smell like putrid meat. It is, however, said to be eaten by the Hottentots.[7]

Hydrangea thumbergii Siebold. *Saxifrageae.* TEA-OF-HEAVEN.

Japan. The natives use the dried leaves as a substitute for tea.[8] This tea is called *ama-tsja*, tea-of-heaven.

Hydrophyllum appendiculatum Michx. *Hydrophyllaceae.* HAIRY WATERLEAF. WOOLEN
    BREECHES.

Eastern North America. Barton [9] says, in Kentucky, the young shoots are eaten in the spring as a salad and are highly prized by all who eat them.

---

[1] *Perf. Desc. Va.* 3. 1649. Force Coll. Tracts **2**: No. 8. 1838.

[2] Gerarde, J. *Herb.* 885. 2nd Ed. 1633.

[3] Cobbett, W. *Amer. Gard.* 141. 1846.

[4] Pliny lib. 21, 50.

[5] Camerarius *Epit.* 934. 1586.

[6] Pott, Emilin, in *Farm.* 509. 1879.

[7] Smith, J. *Dom. Bot.* 208. 1871.

[8] Don, G. *Hist. Dichl. Pls.* **3**:233. 1834.

[9] Barton, W. P. C. *Med. Bot.* **2**:xiii. 1818.

H. canadense Linn.

North America.   Barton[1] says the roots of this species were eaten by the Indians in times of scarcity.

H. virginicum Linn.   INDIAN SALAD.   SHAWNEE SALAD.

North America.   This plant is called in the western states, according to Serra,[2] Indian salad or Shawnee salad, because eaten as such by the Indians, when tender.   Some of the first settlers ate the plant.

Hygrophila spinosa T. Anders.   *Acanthaceae.*

East India and Malay.   The leaves are used as a potherb.[3]

Hymenaea courbaril Linn.   *Leguminosae.*

A colossal tree of tropical and southern subtropical South America.   The pods contain three or four seeds, inclosed in a whitish substance, as sweet as honey, which the Indians eat with great avidity, though, says Lunan,[4] it is apt to purge when first gathered. Brown,[5] in British Guiana, says this pulp tastes not unlike a dry cake, being sweet and melting in the mouth.   It is called *algarroba* in Panama, *jatal* in Brazil and *simiri* in Guiana.[6]

Hyoseris lucida Linn.   *Compositae.*   SWINE'S SUCCORY.

Egypt.   Wilkinson[7] says this plant is the *hypocheris* of Pliny and is esculent.

Hypelate paniculata Cambess.   *Sapindaceae.*

West Indies.   The fruit is the size of a plum and is edible after roasting.

Hyphaene thebaica Mart.   *Palmae.*   GINGERBREAD TREE.

African tropics.   The fruits which are produced in long clusters, each containing between one and two hundred, are beautifully polished, of a rich, yellowish-brown color and are of irregular form.   In Upper Egypt, they form part of the food of the poorer classes of inhabitants, the part eaten being the fibrous, mealy husk, which tastes almost exactly like gingerbread, but its dry, husky nature renders it unpalatable.[8]

Hypochoeris apargioides Hook. & Arn.   *Compositae.*

Chile.   The root of this perennial herb is used for culinary purposes like that of scorzonera.[9]

[1] Barton, W. P. C.   *Med. Bot.* 2:xiii.   1818.
[2] Serra, C. de.   *Trans. Hort. Soc. Lond.* 4:445.   1822.
[3] Dutt, U. C.   *Mat. Med. Hindus* 216.   1877.
[4] Lunan. J.   *Hort. Jam.* 1:462.   1814.
[5] Brown, C. B.   *Camp Life Brit. Guiana* 180.   1876.
[6] Smith, A.   *Treas. Bot.* 2:608.   1870.
[7] Wilkinson, J. G.   *Anc. Egypt.* 2:33.   1854.
[8] Smith, A.   *Treas. Bot.* 2:613.   1870.
[9] Mueller, F.   *Sel. Pls.* 236.   1891.

H. brasiliensis Griseb.

Southern Brazil. This smooth, perennial herb has the aspect of a sow-thistle. It is sometimes used like endive as a salad.[1]

H. maculata Linn.

Europe and northern Asia. The leaves may be used as a salad.[2]

H. radicata Linn. SPOTTED CAT'S EAR.

Europe and north Africa. This weed of Britain, says Johnson,[3] has been cultivated in gardens but has fallen into disuse. The wild plant may be boiled as a potherb.

H. scorzonerae F. Muell.

Chile. The plant has edible roots.[4]

Hypoxis sp.? *Amaryllideae.*

Labillardière[5] found a species in the forests of New Caledonia, the roots of which are eaten by the natives.

Hyptis spicigara Lam. *Labiatae.*

African tropics. This plant of tropical Africa is called *neeno* and is cultivated by the natives of Gani as a grain. It is eaten roasted by them. They also extract an oil from the seeds, both black and white, of this strongly smelling plant.[6] Schweinfurth[7] says the tiny seeds are brazed to a jelly and are used by the natives of central Africa as an adjunct to their stews and gravies. The Bongo and Niam-Niam, especially, store large quantities.

Hyssopus officinalis Linn. *Labiatae.* HYSSOP.

Europe and temperate Asia. Hyssop was once considerably employed in domestic medicine. From the frequent mention made of it in Scripture, we may infer that it grew wild in Syria and Egypt. In French and Italian cookery, the tops of the young shoots are sometimes used in soups.[8] In 1597, Gerarde[9] figures three varieties; in 1683, Worlidge names it among culinary herbs in England, but says it is more valued for medicine; in 1778, Mawe[10] describes six varieties, and says the plant is generally cultivated in the kitchen garden; in 1806,[11] McMahon includes hyssop in his list of kitchen aromatics for American gardens. Hyssop is mentioned among European garden plants by Albertus Magnus in the thirteenth century and in nearly all the later botanies, Ray enumerating

[1] Black, A. A. *Treas. Bot.* 2:1052. 1870.

[2] Loudon, J. C. *Hort.* 683. 1860.

[3] Johnson, C. P. *Useful Pls. Gt. Brit.* 147. 1862.

[4] Mueller, F. *Sel. Pls.* 236. 1891.

[5] Labillardière *Voy. Recherche La Pérouse* 2:243. 1799.

[6] Speke, J. H. *Journ. Disc. Source Nile* 579. 1864.

[7] Schweinfurth, G. *Heart Afr.* 1:250. 1874.

[8] McIntosh, C. *Book Gard.* 2:241. 1855.

[9] Gerarde, J. *Herb.* 464. 1597.

[10] Mawe and Abercrombie *Univ. Gard. Bot.* 1778.

[11] McMahon, B. *Amer. Gard. Cal.* 583. 1806.

it also as an ornamental plant, in nine varieties. As an ornamental plant, hyssop is deserving of notice but its present use in American gardens must be very limited. It is mentioned by Paulus Aegnita, in the seventh century, as a medicinal plant. It is said by Fessenden,[1] 1828, to be occasionally used as a potherb. At present, it has become naturalized as an escape from gardens in Michigan. In France, hyssop is grown in the flower gardens.[2]

Icacina senegalensis Juss. *Olacineae.*

Tropical Africa. The fruit is about the size of an Orleans plum, of a yellow color, with a flavor much resembling that of noyau.[3]

Idesia polycarpa Maxim. *Bixineae.*

Japan. This large-growing tree is cultivated for its fruits, which are many-seeded berries, the seeds lying in pulp.[4]

Ilex cassine Walt. *Ilicineae.* CASSINA. DAHOON HOLLY. HOLLY. YAUPON.

Eastern North America. Romans says the leaves of the cassina were roasted and made into a decoction by the Creek Indians. The Indians attributed many virtues to the tea and permitted only men to drink it. Along the coast region of Virginia and Carolina, the leaves of yaupon are used as a tea and are an object of sale.

I. fertilis Reiss.

Brazil. This species yields the mild maté, considered equal to the best Paraguay tea.[5]

I. glabra A. Gray. APPALACHIAN TEA. INKBERRY.

Eastern North America. Porcher [6] says the leaves form a tea substitute.

I. paraguensis A. St. Hil. MATÉ. YERBA DE MATÉ.

Paraguay. From this plant comes the well-known maté of South America, which replaces tea in Brazil and Buenos Aires. It is consumed by the thousands of tons.[7]

I. quercifolia Meerb. AMERICAN HOLLY.

Eastern North America. According to Porcher,[8] the leaves afford a tea substitute in the south.

I. verticillata A. Gray. BLACK ALDER. WINTERBERRY.

Porcher [9] says the leaves are substituted for tea.

Iilicium anisatum Linn. *Magnoliaceae.* CHINESE ANISE.

Eastern Asia. The fruit, about an inch in diameter, forms an article of commerce

---

[1] Fessenden *New Amer. Gard.* 164. 1828.

[2] Vilmorin *Fl. Pl. Ter.* 522. 1870. 3rd Ed.

[3] Don, G. *Hist. Dichl. Pls.* 1:582. 1831.

[4] Moore, T. *Treas. Bot.* 2:1307. 1876.

[5] Saunders *U. S. D. A. Rpt.* 217. 1881–82. (*I. gigantea*)

[6] Porcher, F. P. *Res. So. Fields, Forests* 428. 1869.

[7] *U. S. D. A. Rpt.* 193. 1870.

[8] Porcher, F. P. *Res. So. Fields, Forests* 429. 1869.

[9] Porcher, F. P. *Res. So. Fields, Forests* 428. 1869.

amongst Asiatic nations. In 1872, Shanghai received 703,066 pounds. The Chinese mix the fruit with coffee and tea to improve the flavor.[1] The Mohammedans of India season some of their dishes with the capsules,[2] and the capsules are largely imported into Germany, France and Italy for the flavoring of spirits.[3]

Imbricaria malabarica Poir. *Sapotaceae.*
East Indies. The fleshy fruit is edible.[4]

I. maxima Poir.
Island of Bourbon. This species, also, has a fleshy, edible fruit.[5]

Inga buorgoni DC. *Leguminosae.*
Tropical America. The pulp of this·legume is edible.[6]

I. fagifolia Willd.
Tropical America. The seeds are covered with a fleshy, edible pulp.[7]

I. feuillei DC.
Peru. This plant is a native of Peru and is cultivated there in gardens, where it is called *pacay.* The white pulp of its long pods is eaten.[8]

I. insignis Kunth.
Ecuador. The pulp of the legume is edible.[9]

I. marginata Willd.
Tropical America. The legume contains a sweet and sapid edible pulp.[10]

I. spectabilis Willd.
Tropical America. This plant bears a pod with black seeds in sweet, juicy cotton. It was called *guavas* by Cieza de Leon [11] in his travels, 1532–50. It is the *guavo real* of Panama and is commonly cultivated for the white pulp about the seeds.

I. vera Willd. Linn.
Tropical America. The pulp about the seeds is sweet and is eaten by negroes.[12]

Inocarpus edulis Forst. *Leguminosae.* TAHITIAN CHESTNUT.
Islands of the Pacific. The nuts of the *ivi*, or Tahitian chestnut, says Seemann,[13] are eaten in the Fiji Islands, roasted or in a green state, and are soft and pleasant to the

[1] Loudon, J. C. *Arb. Frut. Brit.* 1:258. 1854.

[2] Ainslie, W. *Mat. Ind.* 2:18. 1826.

[3] Flückiger and Hanbury *Pharm.* 20. 1879.

[4] Masters, M. T. *Treas. Bot.* 2:620. 1870.

[5] Ibid.

[6] Unger, F. *U. S. Pat. Off. Rpt.* 333. 1859.

[7] Royle, J. F. *Illustr. Bot. Himal.* 1:183. 1839.

[8] Smith, A. *Treas. Bot.* 2:623. 1870.

[9] Unger, F. *U. S. Pat. Off. Rpt.* 333. 1859.

[10] Don, G. *Hist. Dichl. Pls.* 2:387. 1832. (*I. sapida*)

[11] Markham, C. R. *Trav. Cieza de Leon.* Hakl. Soc. Ed. 16, 99. 1864.

[12] Sloane, H. *Nat. Hist. Jam.* 2:59. 1725.

[13] Seemann, B. *Fl. Viti.* 70, 71. 1865–73.

taste. They are much prized by the natives of the Indian Archipelago and in Machian the inhabitants almost live on them. Labillardière[1] says the fruit is eaten boiled by the natives of the Friendly Islands and the flavor is very much like that of chestnuts. Wilkes[2] says it is the principal food of the mountaineers of Fiji. Voigt[3] says the nuts are edible but are by no means pleasant. The tree is called in Tahiti, *rata*.[4]

Inula crithmoides Linn. *Compositae.*

Mediterranean regions. The leaves are pickled and eaten as a condiment.[5]

Ipomoea aquatica Forsk. *Convolvulaceae.* SWEET POTATO. WATER CONVOLVULUS.

Old World tropics. In the Philippines, the root is cooked and eaten by the natives.[6] This species is often planted by the Chinese around the edges of tanks and pools for the sake of its succulent leaves.[7] It is largely cultivated in central China as a vegetable; it is eaten in the spring and somewhat resembles spinach in flavor.[8]

I. batatas Poir. SWEET POTATO.

Tropics of America. This widely-distributed, cultivated plant, originally of South and Central America, had developed many varieties at the period of its discovery by Columbus. Peter Martyr,[9] 1514, mentions *batatas* as cultivated in Honduras and gives the names of nine varieties. In 1526, Oviedo[10] not only mentions sweet potatoes in the West Indies, but says they often have been carried to Spain, and that he had carried them himself to Avila, in Castile. In Peru, Garcilasso de la Vega[11] says the *apichu* are of four or five different colors, some red, others yellow, others white, and others brown, and this author was contemporary with the conquest. The *camote* of Yucatan, called in the islands *axi* and *batatas*, is mentioned in the fourth voyage of Columbus,[12] and Chanca, physician to the fleet of Columbus, in a letter dated 1494, speaks of *ages* as among the productions of Hispaniola. In Europe, sweet potatoes are mentioned by Cardanus,[13] 1556, and Clusius,[14] 1566, describes the red, or purple, and the pale, or white, sorts as under culture in Spain, and, in 1576, notes that their culture had been attempted in Belgium. Their mention thereafter in the early botanies is frequent.

The culture of sweet potatoes is noted for Virginia before 1650.[15] In 1750, Hughes[16]

---

[1] Labillardière *Voy. Recherche La Pérouse* 2:153. 1799.

[2] Wilkes, C. *U. S. Explor. Exped.* 3:334. 1845.

[3] Pickering, C. *Chron. Hist. Pls.* 437. 1879.

[4] Ibid.

[5] Johnson, C. P. *Useful Pls. Gt. Brit.* 161. 1862. (*Limbarda crithmoides*)

[6] Pickering, C. *Chron. Hist. Pls.* 703. 1879. (*I. reptans*)

[7] Williams, S. W. *Mid. King.* 1:287. 1848. (*Convolvulus reptans*)

[8] Smith, F. A. *Contrib. Mat. Med. China* 71. 1871.

[9] Eden *Hist. Trav.* 88, 143. 1577.

[10] Gray and Trumbull *Am. Jour. Sci.* 248. 1883.

[11] Vega, G. de la. *Roy. Comment.* Hakl. Soc. Ed. 2:359. 1871.

[12] Flückiger and Hanbury *Pharm.* 452. 1879.

[13] Cardanus *Rerum Var.* 189. 1556.

[14] Clusius *Hist.* 297. 1576.

[15] Williams, E. *Virginia* 48. 1650. Force Coll. Tracts 3: No. 11. 1844.

[16] Hughes, G. *Nat. Hist. Barb.* 228. 1750.

says that at least 13 sorts are known at the Barbados. In the Mauritius, Bojer [1] describes the round and long forms, white and purple. At the present time, Vilmorin [2] describes two varieties in France, and in 1863 [3] Burr describes nine varieties in American gardens. Of the varieties now known, not one type can be considered as modern in its appearance. The sweet potato is mentioned in England by Gerarde, [4] 1597, as growing in his garden and he says they grow " in India, Barbarie and Spaine and other hot regions," a state-ment confirmed in part by Clusius, [5] who states in 1601 that he had eaten them in Spain. This plant is noticed by Monardes [6] and by Lobel, [7] 1570–76. Its cultivation has been attempted in different parts of Italy but as yet, so Targioni-Tozzetti [8] writes, without success. The sweet potato reached St. Thomas, off the African coast, before 1563–74. In Ramusio, [9] we find in the Portuguese pilot's relation, " The root which is called by the Indians of Hispaniola *batata* is named *igname* at St. Thomas and is one of the most essen-tial articles of their food."

Rumphius [10] says that the Spaniards carried this root to Manilla and the Moluccas, whence the Portuguese distributed it through the Indian Archipelago. It is figured by Rheede [11] and Rumphius [12] as cultivated in Hindustan and Amboina. In Batavia, it was cultivated in 1665. [13] Firminger [14] speaks of it as one of the native vegetables in common cultivation in all parts of India, the plant producing pink flowers with a purple eye. In China, Mr. Fortune informed Darwin, [15] the plant never yields seeds. In the Hawaiian Islands, Wilkes [16] says there are 33 varieties, 19 of which are of a red color and 14 white. In New Zealand, Tahiti and Fiji, it is called by the same name. In New Zealand, there is a tradition among the natives that it was first brought to the island in canoes composed of pieces of wood sewed together.

Sweet potatoes are mentioned as one of the cultivated products of Virginia in 1648, [17] perhaps in 1610 [18] and are mentioned again by Jefferson, [19] 1781. They are said to have been introduced into New England in 1764 and to have come into general use. John

---

[1] Bojer, W. *Hort. Maurit.* 225. 1837.

[2] Vilmorin *Les Pls. Potag.* 401. 1883. (*Convolvulus batatas*)

[3] Burr, F. *Field, Gard. Veg.* 99. 1863.

[4] Gerarde, J. *Herb.* 2nd Ed. 926. 1633.

[5] De Candolle, A. *Geog. Bot.* 2:822. 1855. (*Batatas edulis*)

[6] Pickering, C. *Chron. Hist. Pls.* 754. 1879. (*Convolvulus edulis*)

[7] Ibid.

[8] Targioni-Tozzetti *Journ. Hort. Soc. Lond.* 141. 1854.

[9] Ramusio *Gen. Coll. Voy. Portugese* 433. 1789.

[10] De Candolle, A. *Geog. Bot.* 2:822. 1855.

[11] Pickering, C. *Chron. Hist. Pls.* 754. 1879. (*Convolvulus edulis*)

[12] Ibid.

[13] Churchill *Coll. Voy.* 2:303. 1732.

[14] Firminger, T. A. C. *Gard. Ind.* 157. 1874.

[15] Darwin, C. *Ans. Pls. Domest.* 2:153. 1893.

[16] Wilkes, C. *U. S. Explor. Exped.* 4:282. 1845.

[17] *Perf. Desc. Va.* 4. 1649. Force Coll. Tracts 2:1838.

[18] *True Decl. Va.* 13. 1610. Force Coll. Tracts 3:1844.

[19] Jefferson *Notes Va.* 54, 55. 1781.

Lowell[1] says that sweet potatoes of excellent quality can be raised about Boston, but they are of no agricultural importance in this region.   In 1773, Bartram saw plantations of sweet potatoes about Indian villages in the South, and Romans refer to their use by the Indians of Florida in 1775.   At the present day, sweet potatoes are quite generally cultivated in tropical and subtropical countries, as in Africa from Zanzibar to Egypt,[2] in India, China, Japan, the Malayan Archipelago, New Zealand, the Pacific islands, tropical America, and southern United States as far north even as New York.   They are grown to a small extent in the south of Europe, Canary Islands and Madeira.

I. batatilla G. Don.

Venezuela.   This species furnishes tubers which are used as sweet potatoes.[3]

I. biloba Forsk.   POHUE.

Borders of the tropics.   Ellis[4] says, in Tahiti, the stalks of the pohue are eaten in times of famine.

I. digitata Linn.

Borders of the tropics.   This species is commonly cultivated for food in western tropical Africa.[5]

I. fastigiata Sweet.   WILD POTATO.

Tropical America.   Humboldt[6] mentions this species as cultivated in America under the name, *batata*.

I. grandiflora Lam.

Tropical America.   Ainslie[7] says, in India, the seeds are eaten when young.

I. hederacea Jacq.

Borders of the tropics.   This species is often cultivated in tropical regions.[8]

I. leptophylla Torr.   MAN-OF-THE-EARTH.   MAN-ROOT.   MOONFLOWER.

Western North America.   The wild potato vine is a showy plant of the deserts of North America and is commonly called man-root or man-of-the-earth, being similar in size and shape to a man's body.   The Cheyennes, Arapahoes and Kioways roast it for food when pressed by hunger but it is by no means palatable or nutritious.   Its enormous size and depth in the ground make its extraction by the ordinary Indian implements a work of much difficulty.[9]

I. macrorrhiza Michx.

Georgia and Florida.   Henfrey[10] says this species has edible, farinaceous roots.

---

[1] Lowell, J.   *Boston Advert.*   1821.   Oct. 27.
[2] Speke, J. H.   *Journ. Disc. Source Nile* 575.   1864.
[3] Mueller, F.   *Sel. Pls.* 240.   1891.
[4] Ellis, W.   *Polyn. Research.* 1:53.   1833.
[5] Smith, A.   *Treas. Bot.* 1:129.   1870.   (*Batatas paniculata*)
[6] De Candolle, A.   *Geog. Bot.* 2:823.   1855.
[7] Ainslie, W.   *Mat. Ind.* 2:219.   1826.
[8] De Candolle, A.   *Geog. Bot.* 2:1043.   1855.   (*Pharbitis hederacea*)
[9] *U. S. D. A. Rpt.* 407.   1870.
[10] Henfrey, A.   *Bot.* 321.   1870.

Dr. Baldwin has been informed that the negroes in the South sometimes eat the roots.[1]

I. mammosa Choisy.

Tropics. According to Forster,[2] this species is cultivated under the name of *umara*, *gumarra*, or *gumalla* in Tahiti and in southern New Zealand.

I. tuberosa Linn. SPANISH WOODBINE.

Tropics. The edible tubers are much like the sweet potato in size, taste and form.[3]

I. turpethum R. Br.

Asia, tropical Australia, Society and Friendly Islands and the New Hebrides. The soft, sweet stem is sucked by the boys of Tahiti.[4]

Iridea edulis Bory. *Algae.*

" It is an unaccountable fact that this plant should have been long confounded with *Rhodymenia palmata* — the true Irish eatable *Dulse*. I have never seen *I. edulis* eaten, but Stackhouse tells us that in Cornwall it is sometimes eaten by fishermen, who crisp it over the fire." [5]

Iris cristata Ait. *Irideae.* CRESTED IRIS.

Mountains of Virginia and southward. Pursh says the root, when chewed, at first occasions a pleasant, sweet taste, which, in a few minutes, turns to a burning sensation by far more pungent than capsicum. The hunters of Virginia use it very frequently to alleviate thirst.

I. ensata Thunb. SWORD-LEAVED IRIS.

Himalayas and northern Asia. This iris is cultivated in Japan for the rootstocks, which furnish starch.[6]

I. japonica Thunb.

Japan. This species is grown in Japan and is used for the same purpose as *I. ensata.*

I. pseudacorus Linn. YELLOW IRIS.

Eastern Asia and Europe. The angular seeds, when ripe, are said to form a good substitute for coffee but must be well roasted before eating.[7]

I. setosa Pall.

Siberia. This species is grown in Japan and is used for the same purpose as *I. ensata.*

I. sibirica Linn. SIBERIAN IRIS.

Europe and northern Asia. This species is grown in Japan and is used for the same purpose as *I. ensata.*

---

[1] Elliott, S. *Bot. So. Car., Ga.* 1:253. 1821.
[2] De Candolle, A. *Geog. Bot.* 2:824. 1855.
[3] De Candolle, A. *Geog. Bot.* 2:823. 1855.
[4] Unger, F. *U. S. Pat. Off. Rpt.* 329. 1859. (*Convolvulus turpethum*)
[5] Harvey, W. H. *Phycol. Brit.* 3: Pl. XCVII. 1846–51.
[6] Georgeson *Amer. Gard.* 13:210. 1892.
[7] Johnson, C. P. *Useful Pls. Gt. Brit.* 267. 1862.

I. sisyrinchium Linn. SPANISH NUT.

Mediterranean, the Orient and Afghanistan. This species has been in cultivation in England since the time of Gerarde, who calls it Spanish nut and says that it is "eaten at the tables of rich and delicious persons in sallads or otherwise." It is a native of the Mediterranean region.[1]

I. tectorum Maxim. WALL IRIS.

Japan. This species is grown in Japan and is used for the same purpose as *I. ensata.*

Irvingia barteri Hook. f. *Simarubeae.* BREAD TREE.

A tree of tropical Africa, called *dika.* Burton[2] says the fruit forms the one sauce of the Fans and is called *ndika.* The kernels are extracted from the stones and roasted like coffee, pounded and poured into a mould. This cheese is scraped and added to boiling meat and vegetables. It forms a pleasant relish for the tasteless plantain. The French export it to adulterate chocolate. The fruit is much used, says Masters,[3] at Sierra Leone.

Isatis indigotica Fortune. *Cruciferae.* WOAD.

China. The leaves are used for food.[4]

Jacquinia caracasena H. B. & K. *Myrsineae.*

Venezuela. The berry is edible. The seeds are imbedded in a sweet, fleshy pulp, according to Don.[5]

Jasminum paniculatum Roxb. *Oleaceae.* JASMINE.

China. This is the *sieu-hing-hwa* of China. The flowers are used for scenting tea.[6]

J. sambac Ait. ARABIAN JASMINE.

Tropical Asia; called *mo-le-hwa* in China. The flowers are used for scenting tea.[7]

Jatropha urens Linn. *Euphorbiaceae.* SPURGE NETTLE. TREAD-SOFTLY.

Southern United States. This plant is called by the negroes tread-softly on account of its stinging hairs. The tuberous roots are said to be eatable like those of the cassava.[8]

Jessenia polycarpa Karst. *Palmae.*

Brazil. A palm of New Granada. The fruit is about the size of a pigeon's egg, violet colored, having a thin, oily, eatable flesh surrounding a fibrous husk which encloses a single, horny seed.[9]

Jubaea spectabilis H. B. & K. *Palmae.* COQUITO PALM. LITTLE COKERNUT.

A palm of Chile cultivated in South America. The sap of this tree is boiled to the

[1] Britten, J. *Treas. Bot.* 2:1352. 1876.

[2] Burton *Anthrop. Rev. Journ.* 1:50. 1863.

[3] Masters, M. T. *Treas. Bot.* 2:717. 1870. (*Mangifera gabonensis*)

[4] Bretschneider, E. *Bot. Sin.* 51. 1882.

[5] Don, G. *Hist. Dichl. Pls.* 4:24. 1838.

[6] Fortune, R. *Resid. Chinese* 201. 1857.

[7] Ibid.

[8] Black, A. A. *Treas. Bot.* 1:303. 1870. (*Cnidoscolus stimulosus*)

[9] Smith, A. *Treas. Bot.* 2:637. 1870.

consistency of treacle and forms the *miel de palma*, palm honey, of Chile, a considerable article of trade, being much esteemed for domestic use as sugar. The trees are felled and the crown of leaves is immediately cut off, when the sap begins to flow and continues for several months, provided a thin slice is shaved off the top each morning, until the tree is exhausted. Each tree yields about 90 gallons. The nuts are used by the Chilean confectioners in the preparation of sweetmeats and have a pleasant, nutty taste. The nuts of the Coquito palm are often called little cokernuts.[1]

Juglans baccata Linn. *Juglandeae*. WALNUT.

West Indies. The nuts are edible and furnish an oil. They are very rich in starch.[2]

J. cinerea Linn. BUTTERNUT.

Eastern North America. The butternut was called by the Narragansett Indians *wussoquat*, and the oil from the nut was used for seasoning their aliments.[3] The nuts were used by the Indians to thicken their pottage. The immature fruit is sometimes used as a pickle and is most excellent. The kernel of the ripe nut is esteemed by those who do not object to its strong and oily taste. The tree is occasionally grown as a shade tree and for its nuts. In 1813, a sample of butternut sugar was sent to the Massachusetts Society for the Promotion of Agriculture.

J. nigra Linn. BLACK WALNUT.

A tree valued for its timber, common in the western states of northeast America. The kernel of the nut is sweet and less oily than the butternut but greatly inferior to the Madeira nut. It is eaten and was a prized food of the Indians.

J. regia Linn. ENGLISH WALNUT. MADEIRA NUT. PERSIAN WALNUT.

This tree extends from Greece and Asia Minor over Lebanon and Persia to the Himalayas. It is abundant in Kashmir, Nepal and neighboring countries and is cultivated in Europe and elsewhere. It is referred to by Theophrastus under the name of *karuon*. According to Pliny, it was introduced into Italy from Persia, but it is mentioned as existing in Italy by Varro, who was born B. C. 116. In many parts of Spain, France, Italy and Germany, the nut forms an important article of food to the people, and in some parts of France considerable quantities of oil are expressed from the kernels to be used in cooking and as a dryiug oil in the arts. In Circassia, sugar is said to be made from the sap. There are many varieties; those of the province of Khosistan in Persia are much esteemed and are sent in great quantities to India. In Georgia, they are of a fine quality.[4] In North China, an almost huskless variety occurs.[5] In France, there is a variety called Titmouse walnut because the shell is so thin that birds, especially the titmouse, can break it and eat the kernel. In the United States, it is called English walnut and two varieties succeed well in Virginia. In western New York, it is occasionally seen in lawns.

---

[1] Smith, A.   *Treas. Bot.* **2**:639.   1870.

[2] Unger, F.   *U. S. Pat. Off. Rpt.* 321.   1859.

[3] Michaux. F. A.   *No. Amer. Sylva* **1**:111.   1865.

[4] Ainslie, W.   *Mat. Ind.* **1**:463.   1826.

[5] Mueller, F.   *Sel. Pls.* 245.   1891.

J. rupestris Engelm.

Western North America.   The small nuts are sweet and edible.[1]

J. sieboldiana Maxim.   JAPANESE WALNUT.

Japan.   The small nuts are of good flavor, borne in large clusters, a dozen or more in one bunch.[2]

Juniperus bermudiana Linn.   *Coniferae.*   BERMUDA CEDAR.

Bermuda Islands.   In 1609, Sir Thomas Gates[3] and Sir George Sommers[4] were wrecked on the Bermudas and in their account say " we have a kinde of Berrie upon the Cedar tree, verie pleasant to eat."   In *Newes from Barmudas,*[5] 1612, it is said, " there are an infinite number of Cedar trees (fairest I think in the world) and those bring forth a verie sweete berrie and wholesome to eat."

J. communis Linn.   JUNIPER.

North temperate and arctic regions.   The berries are used by distillers to flavor gin.   The ripe berries were formerly used in England as a substitute for pepper.   In many parts of Germany, the berries are used as a culinary spice.   In Sweden, they are made into a conserve, also prepared in a beverage and in some places are roasted and used as a coffee substitute.[6]   In France, a kind of beer called *genevrette* is made by fermenting a decoction of equal parts of juniperberries and barley.[7]   In Germany, juniper is used for flavoring sauerkraut.[8]   In Kamaon, India, the berries are added to spirits distilled from barley.[9]   In western North America, the berries are an Indian food.

J. drupacea Labill.   HABBEL.   PLUM JUNIPER.

Greece, Asia Minor and Syria.   The sweet, edible fruit is highly esteemed throughout the Orient, according to Mueller.[10]

J. occidentalis Hook.   CALIFORNIA JUNIPER.

Western North America.   The plant bears a large and tuberculated berry, sweet and nutritious, which has, however, a resinous taste.   The berries are largely consumed by the Indians of Arizona and New Mexico.[11]

J. pachyphlaea Torr.   SWEET-FRUITED JUNIPER.

Mexico.   The berries are purplish, globose, half an inch in diameter and have a sweetish and palatable pulp.[12]

---

[1] Sargent *U. S. Census* **9**:131. 1884.

[2] Georgeson *Amer. Gard.* **12**:266. 1891.

[3] *Newes from Barmudas* 20. 1613. Force Coll. Tracts **3**: 1844.

[4] Ibid.

[5] *Newes from Barmudas* 13. 1613. Force Coll. Tracts **3**: 1844

[6] Phillips H.   *Comp. Orch.* 213, 214. 1831.

[7] Johnson, C. P.   *Useful Fls. Gt. Brit.* 264. 1862.

[8] Barton and Castle *Brit. Fl. Med.* 244. 1877.

[9] Brandis, D.   *Forest Fl.* 536. 1876.

[10] Mueller, F.   *Sel. Pls.* 246. 1891.

[11] *U. S. D. A. Rpt.* 411. 1870.

[12] Havard, V.   *Proc. U. S. Nat. Mus.* 503. 1885.

J. recurva Buch.-Ham. DROOPING JUNIPER.

Himalayan region. In India, the sprigs are used in the distillation of spirits. The shrub is sacred and the resinous twigs are used for incense.[1] This species is used in India in the preparation of an intoxicating liquor and for making yeast.[2]

J. tetragona Schlecht. MEXICAN JUNIPER.

Mexico. The berries are half an inch in diameter, and the Indians are said to use them as food.[3]

Kandelia rheedii Wight & Arn. *Rhizophoreae.*

East Indies and Malay. Its fruit is edible.[4]

Kedrostis rostrata Cogn. *Cucurbitaceae.*

East Indies. The leaves are eaten as greens and are called in Tamil *appakovay.*[6] Royle [7] says the fruit is eaten.

Kigelia pinnata DC. *Bignoniaceae.*

A tree of tropical Africa. The fruit is often two or more feet long and is filled with pulp containing numerous, roundish seeds. Grant [8] says the roasted seeds are eaten in famines.

Kleinhovia hospita Linn. *Sterculiaceae.*

Tropical eastern Asia, the Malayan Archipelago and the Samoan Islands. The leaves are cooked and eaten in the Philippines.[9]

Koelreuteria paniculata Laxm. *Sapindaceae.*

China. The berries, when roasted, are eaten by the Chinese, in spite of their apparent acidity.[10] The leaves are used for food.[11]

Lacis sp.? *Podostemaceae.*

Henfrey says some species are used for food on the Rio Negro and other parts of South America.[12]

Lactuca alpina Benth. & Hook. f. *Compositae.* MOUNTAIN SOW-THISTLE.

Europe. The stem, which is milky, is peeled and eaten raw by the Laplanders; the taste is extremely bitter.[13]

---

[1] Brandis, D. *Forest Fl.* 536. 1876.

[2] *Gard. Chron.* 17:47. 1882. (*J. squamata*)

[3] Torrey, J. *Pacific R. R. Rpt.* 4:141. 1856.

[4] Baillon, H. *Hist. Pls.* 6:301. 1880. Note

[5] Ainslie, W. *Mat. Ind.* 2:21. 1826.

[6] Drury, H. *Useful Pls. Ind.* 88. 1873.

[7] Royle, J. F. *Illustr. Bot. Himal.* 1:219. 1839.

[8] Speke, J. H. *Journ. Disc. Source Nile* 577. 1864.

[9] Pickering, C. *Chron. Hist. Pls.* 743. 1879.

[10] Smith, F. P. *Contrib. Mat. Med. China* 199. 1871.

[11] Bretschneider, E. *Bot. Sin.* 52. 1882.

[12] Henfrey, A. *Bot.* 359. 1870.

[13] Lankester *Veg. Food* 9:191. 1846. *Libr. Entert. Knowl.*

L. scariola Linn. LETTUCE. PRICKLY LETTUCE.

Europe and the Orient. Lettuce, the best of all salad plants, as a cultivated plant has great antiquity. It is evident, by an ancedote related by Herodotus, that lettuce appeared at the royal tables of the Persian kings about 550 B. C.[1] Its medicinal properties as a food-plant were noted by Hippocrates,[2] 430 B. C.; it was praised by Aristotle,[3] 356 B. C.; the species was described by Theophrastus,[4] 322 B. C., and Dioscorides,[5] 60 A. D.; and was mentioned by Galen,[6] 164 A. D., who gives the idea of very general use. Among the Romans, lettuce was very popular. Columella,[7] A. D. 42, describes the Caecilian, Cappadocian, Cyprian and Tartesan. Pliny,[8] A. D. 79, enumerates the Alba, Caecilian, Cappadocian, Crispa, Graeca, Laconicon, Nigra, Purpurea and Rubens. Palladius,[9] 210 A. D., implies varieties and mentions the process of blanching. Martial,[10] A. D. 101, gives to the lettuces of Cappadocia the term *viles*, or cheap, implying abundance. In China, its presence can be identified in the fifth century.[11] In England, Chaucer, about 1340, uses the word in his prologue, " well loved he garlic, onions and lettuce," and lettuce is likewise mentioned by Turner,[12] 1538, who spells the word *lettuse*. It is mentioned by Peter Martyr, 1494, as cultivated on Isabela Island. In 1565, Benzoni[13] speaks of lettuce as abounding in Hayti. In 1647, Nieuhoff[14] saw it cultivated in Brazil. In 1806, McMahon[15] enumerates for American gardens 16 sorts. In 1828, Thorburn's[16] seed catalog offered 13 kinds, and in 1881, 23 kinds.

In the report of the New York Agricultural Experiment Station for 1885, 87 varieties are described with 585 names of synonyms.[17] Vilmorin[18] describes, 1883, one hundred and thirteen kinds as distinct. The numbers of varieties named by various writers at various times are as follows: For France, in 1612, six; in 1690, twenty-one; in 1828, forty; in 1883, one hundred and thirteen. For Holland, in 1720, forty-seven. For England, in 1597, six; in 1629, nine; in 1726, nine; in 1763, fifteen; in 1765, eighteen; in 1807, fourteen. For America, in 1806, sixteen; in 1885, eighty-seven.

The cabbage and cos lettuces are the sorts now principally grown but various other

---

[1] McIntosh, C. *Book Gard.* 2:5. 1855.

[2] Hippocrates *Opera* Cornarius Ed. 113. 1546.

[3] Scaliger *Aristotle* 63. 1566.

[4] Theophratus *Hist. Pl.* Bodaeus Ed. 761. 1644.

[5] Dioscorides Vergelius Ed. 220. 1532. Ruellius Ed. 130. 1529.

[6] Galen *Aliment.* lib. 2. Gregorius Ed. 143. 1547.

[7] Columella lib. 10, c. 181–193, 369.

[8] Pliny lib. 19, c. 38.

[9] Palladius lib. 2, c. 14; lib. 3, c. 24; lib. 4, c. 9, etc.

[10] Martial lib. 5, 79.

[11] Bretschneider, E. *Bot. Sin.* 78. 1882.

[12] Turner *Libellus* 1538.

[13] Benzoni *Hist. New World.* Smythe Ed. 1857.

[14] Churchill *Coll. Voy.*

[15] McMahon, B. *Amer. Gard. Cal.* 581. 1806.

[16] Thorburn *Cat.* 1828.

[17] *N. Y. Agr. Expt. Sta.* (Geneva) *Rpt.* 1885.

[18] Vilmorin *Les Pls. Potag.* 285. 1883.

kinds, such as the curled, are frequently, and the sharp-leaved and oak-leaved are occasionally grown as novelities. In these lettuces there can be offered only the synonymy of a few of the varieties now known — those which indicate the antiquity of our cultivated types.

I.
THE LANCEOLATE-LEAVED TYPE.

Lactuca longifolia. Bauh. *Phytopinat* 200. 1596.
Lattuga franzese. Dur. C. 244. 1617. cum ic.
Lactuca folio oblongo acuto. Bauh. *Pin.* 125. 1623. *Prod.* 60. 1671.
Lactuca longo at valde angusto folio. Bauh. J. **2**:999. 1651; Chabr. 313. 1677.
Deer Tongue. Greg. 1883.

II.
THE COS TYPE.

Pena and Lobel,[1] 1570, say that this form is but rarely grown in France and Germany, although common in the gardens of Italy; and Heuze[2] says it was brought from Rome to France by Rabelais in 1537.

Lactuca intybacea. Lombard Lettuce Ger. 240. 1597.
Lactuca foliis endivae. Matth. *Op.* 399. 1598.
Lactuca Romana longa dulcis. Bauh. J. **2**:998. 1651. Chabr. 313. 1677.
La Romaine Jard. Solit. 1612
Romaines. Vilm. 307. 1883.

We can reasonably believe the lettuce of Camerarius to be very close to the Florence Cos. The Lombard lettuce was grown as a sport in the garden of the New York Agricultural Experiment Station in 1886, and the figures by Bauhin and Chabraeus may well be the Paris Cos. It is not to be understood, however, that these figures represent the improved forms of our present culture but the prototypes from which our plants have appeared, as shown not only by resemblance of leaf-form but through the study of variables in the garden. Ray, 1686, describes the Cos as having light green and dark green varieties, and these, as well as the Spotted Cos, are indicated by Bauhin in 1623.

III.
HEADED LETTUCE.

A.— This is the sort commonly grown, and the figures given in the sixteenth century indicate that the heading habit was even then firmly established. We have the following synonyms to offer, premising that types are referred to:

Luctuca crispa. Matth. 264. 1554; Pin. 195. 1561.
Lattuga. Cast. Dur. 243. 1617.
La royale? Le Jard. Solit. 1612. Quintyne 1690.
Laitue Blonde de Berlin syn. *Laitue royale.* 295. 1884.
Berlin

B.— *Lactuca sativa sessilis sive capitata.* Lob. *Icon.* **1**:242. 1591.
Lactuca capitata. Dod. 645. 1616.
Very Early Dwarf Green.

---

[1] Pena and Lobel *Advers.* 90. 1570.
[2] Heuze. G. *Pls. Aliment* i, v. 1873.

C.— *Lactuca.*   Cam. *Epit.* 298.   1586.
    Lactuca capitata.   Ger. 240.   1597.
    Lactuca crispa.   Matth. 399.   1598.
    Batavians.   Vilm. 1883.
D.— *Lattich.*   Roezl. 167.   1550.
    Green Fringed.

The last identification is from the appearance of the young plant.   The old plant is remarkably different, forming a true rosette.

IV.
CUTTING AND MISCELLANEOUS.

A.— *Lactuca crispa altera* Ger. 240.   1597.
    Lactuca crispa et tenuiter dissecta.   Bauh. J. 2:1000.   1651.
    Chabr. 314.   1677.
    Curled Cutting.
B.— *Lactuca foliis querci.*   Ray 219.   1686.
    Oak-leaved.
C.— *Capitatum cum pluribus capitibus.*   Bauh. J. 2:998.   1651.   Chabr. 313.   1677.
    Egyptian Sprouting.

The minor variations which are now separated into varieties did not receive the same recognition in former times, the same variety name covering what now would be several varieties; thus, Quintyne, 1693, calls *perpignans* both a green and a pale form.   Green, light green, dark green, red and spotted lettuces are named in the old botanies, hence we cannot assert any new types have appeared in modern culture.

Lagenaria vulgaris Ser.   *Cucurbitaceae.*   BOTTLE GOURD.   TRUMPET GOURD.
Tropics.   This plant has been found growing wild with bitter fruit in India,[1] in the moist forests around Deyra Doon.[2]   It is also found wild in Malabar,[3] where it is cultivated in gardens for the gourd which is eaten.   This gourd is one of the commonest of the native vegetables of India, says Firminger,[4] the fruit being of moderate size and having the appearance of two oval gourds united endwise, or, of an inflated bladder compressed by a cord around it.   Cut up in slices, it affords a palatable but rather insipid dish.   About Constantinople, it is called *dolma* and is cultivated, the gourd when young, being cut and boiled with other foods.[5]   In Europe, the variety called *trompette* is eaten.[6]   In China, its soft, downy herbage is sometimes eaten, and the fruit is also eaten but is apt to purge.[7]

Lagerstromia parviflora Roxb.   *Lythrarieae.*   CRAPE MYRTLE.
East Indies.   In India, a sweet gum exudes from wounds in the bark and is eaten.[1]

---

[1] De Candolle, A.   *Geog. Bot.* 2:898.   1855.
[2] Ibid.
[3] Ibid.
[4] Firminger, T. A. C.   *Gard. Ind.* 126.   1874.
[5] Walsh, R.   *Trans. Hort. Soc. Lond.* 6:56.   1826.
[6] De Candolle, A.   *Geog. Bot.* 2:898.   1855.
[7] Smith, F. P.   *Contrib. Mat. Med. China* 128.   1871.
[8] Brandis, D.   *Forest Fl.* 239.   1876.

Lallemantia iberica Fisch. & Mey. *Labiatae.*

Asia Minor and Syria. The seeds are very rich in fat and are used for food, as well as for lighting purposes, in the northwest districts of Persia.

Laminaria digitata Lam. *Algae.* RED-WARE. SEA-GIRDLES. SEA-WAND. SEA-WARE. TANGLE.

The tender stalks of the young fronds of this seaweed are eaten.[1]

L. esculenta Lindbl. BADDERLOCK.

Orkney. The midrib of the stem of this seaweed is eaten.[2]

L. potatorum Labill.

This plant is used as food by the natives of Australia.[3]

L. saccharina Lam.

This seaweed is said to be eaten in Iceland and other northern countries.[4]

Lamium album Linn. *Labiatae.* ARCHANGEL. DEAD-NETTLE. DUMB-NETTLE.

Europe and the Orient. The young leaves are boiled in the spring and eaten as greens by the common people of Sweden.[5]

L. purpureum Linn. ARCHANGEL. RED DEAD-NETTLE.

Europe, northern Asia and naturalized as a weed in some places in the United States. The red dead-nettle, or archangel, is eaten in Sweden as greens in spring.[6]

Landolphia florida Benth. *Apocynaceae.* RUBBER TREE.

Tropical Africa. This species furnishes the *abo* of tropical Africa, eaten by the natives.[7] Montiero[8] describes a species of this genus, probably this, as occurring in Angola and called rubber tree. The fruit, the size of a large orange, is yellow when ripe; the shell is hard and bitter and the inside full of a soft, reddish pulp in which the seeds are contained. This pulp is of an agreeable acid flavor and is much liked by the natives. On the Niger, according to Barter,[9] its fruit, which is very sour, is eaten by the natives under the name of *aboli.*

L. owariensis Beauv.

Tropical Africa. This a climbing plant, the fruit of which is the size of an orange and has a reddish-brown, woody shell and an agreeable, sweetish-acid pulp. It is eaten by the natives and is called *abo.*[10] Schweinfurth says the fruit exceeds in sourness that of the citron and the natives of Djur-land manufacture a beverage from it as refreshing as lemonade.

---

[1] Lindley, J. *Veg. King.* 21. 1846.

[2] Rhind, W. *Veg. King.* 190. 1857.

[3] Lindley, J. *Veg. King.* 21. 1846.

[4] Johnson, C. P. *Useful Pls. Gt. Brit.* 301. 1862.

[5] Lightfoot, J. *Fl. Scot.* 1:308. 1789.

[6] Lightfoot, J. *Fl. Scot.* 1:309. 1789.

[7] Jackson, J. R. *Treas. Bot.* 2:1311. 1876.

[8] Montiero, J. J. *Angola, River Congo* 1:138. 1875.

[9] Barter *Gard. Chron.* 17:472. 1882. New series.

[20] Schweinfurth, G. *Heart Afr.* 1:192. 1874. (*Carpodinus sp.?*)

Lansium domesticum Jack.　*Meliaceae.*

A tree of eastern Asia, cultivated in China. Its fruit is sold in the Canton markets. The fruit is the size of a pigeon's egg, of a yellowish color without and whitish within. It is highly esteemed and is eaten fresh or variously prepared. It is known in the East Indies as *lansa, langsat, lanseh, ayer-ayer* or *bejetlan*.[1] In Borneo, Wallace[2] calls it one of the most delicious of the subacid, tropical fruits.

Lantana trifolia Linn.　*Verbenaceae.*

Tropical America. Sloane says the fruit is more juicy than that of other species and is not unpleasant to eat.[3]

Lapageria rosea Ruiz & Pav.　*Liliaceae.*

Chile. The berries, which are of the size of an egg, are sweet and edible.[4]

Lapsana communis Linn.　*Compositae.*　NIPPLEWORT.

Europe, Orient, northern Asia and naturalized in America. The young leaves in the spring have the taste of radishes and are eaten at Constantinople as a salad. In some parts of England, the common people boil them as greens, but they have a bitter and not agreeable taste.[5]

Lardizabala biternata Ruiz et Pav.　*Berberideae.*

Chile and Peru. The fruit is eatable and is sold in the market. The pulp is sweet and grateful to the taste. It is called in Peru *aquilboguil* or *guilbogin* and in Chile *coguillvochi*.[6]

L. triternata Ruiz & Pav.

Chile. This plant has edible fruit.[7]

Larix europaea DC.　*Coniferae.*　EUROPEAN LARCH.

Europe and northern Asia. The Jakuts of northern Siberia grate the inner bark and use it in a broth of fish, meal, and milk. A kind of sugary matter exudes from the the larch in the summer and is collected under the name of manna, or *briancono*. When the larch forests of Russia take fire, a juice exudes from the scorched trunks which is collected under the name of orenburgh gum.[8]

Larrea mexicana Moric.　*Zygophylleae.*　CREOSOTE PLANT.

Mexico. Travellers chew the twigs to alleviate extreme thirst.[9] The plant is a bright evergreen with foliage resembling that of Buxus.

[1] Seemann, B.　*Treas. Bot.* 2:659.　1870.

[2] Wallace, A. R.　*Malay Arch.* 94.　1869.

[3] Lunan, J.　*Hort. Jam.* 2:294.　1814.

[4] Mueller, F.　*Sel. Pls.* 251.　1891.

[5] Lightfoot, J.　*Fl. Scot.* 1:445.　1789.

[6] Don, G.　*Hist. Dichl. Pls.* 1:103.　1831.

[7] Baillon, H.　*Hist. Pls.* 3:70.　1874.

[8] *U. S. Disp.* 831.　1865.

[9] Greene, E. L.　*Amer. Nat.* 15:25.　1881.

Laserpitium latifolium Linn. *Umbelliferae.* LASEWORT.

Europe. The Romans, says Glasspole,[1] used the root of lasewort, with cumin, in seasoning preserved artichoke.

Latania commersonii J. F. Gmel. *Palmae.*

Bourbon Island. The fruit is eaten by the negroes, says Seemann,[2] but that argues little for their taste, as it has a rather disagreeable flavor.

Lathyrus aphaca Linn. *Leguminosae.* YELLOW-FLOWERED PEA.

Europe and the Orient. The seeds, according to Lindley,[3] are served sometimes at table while young and tender but if eaten abundantly in the ripe state are narcotic, producing severe headache.

L. cicera Linn. LESSER CHICK-PEA. VETCH.

Europe and the Orient. This species is an annual with red flowers, occasionally grown in the south of Europe for its peas, but these are of inferior quality and are said sometimes to be very unwholesome.[4] Vetches were carried to the West Indies by Columbus, says Pickering,[5] but their cultivation at the present day seems unknown in America.

L. magellanicus Lam. CAPE HORN PEA.

Magellan region. The Cape Horn pea was eaten by the sailors of Lord Anson in default of better vegetables but is inferior to the worst sort of cultivated pea.[6]

L. maritimus Bigel. HEATH PEA. SEASIDE PEA.

North America and Europe. The seeds are very bitter. In 1555, the people of a portion of Suffolk County, England, suffering from famine, supported themselves to a great extent by the seeds of this plant.[7]

L. montanus Bernh. BITTER VETCH. HEATH PEA. MOUNTAIN PEA.

Europe and northern Asia. Bitter vetch is a native of Europe and the adjoining portion of Asia and has been cultivated on a small scale in kitchen gardens in Britain. The Highlanders of Scotland have great esteem for the tubercles of the roots; they dry and chew them to give a better relish to their whiskey. In some parts of Scotland a spirit is extracted from them. The tubers are sweet in taste and very nutritious and are sometimes boiled and eaten. In Holland and Flanders, the peas are roasted and served as chestnuts.[8] According to Sprengel,[9] the peas are eaten in Sweden and form an article of commerce. In England, the plant is called heath pea.[10]

---

[1] Glasspole, H. G. *Ohio State Bd. Agr. Rpt.* **30**:533. 1875.
[2] Seemann, B. *Pop. Hist. of Palms* 229. 1856.
[3] Pickering, C. *Chron. Hist. Pls.* 826. 1879.
[4] *Treas. Bot.* **2**:662. 1870.
[5] Pickering, C. *Chron. Hist. Pls.* 220. 1879.
[6] Don, G. *Hist. Dichl. Pls.* **2**:331. 1832. (*Pisum americanum*)
[7] Johnson, C. P. *Useful Pls. Gt. Brit.* 82. 1862. (*Pisum maritimum*)
[8] Don, G. *Hist. Dichl. Pls.* **2**:340. 1832. (*Orobus tuberosus*)
[9] Pickering, C. *Chron. Hist. Pls.* 435. 1879. (*Orobus tuberosus*)
[10] Ibid.

L. ochrus DC.

Mediterranean countries.   This is a species of pea mentioned as cultivated by Phanias of Eresus[1] and   Clemens Alexandrinus.[2]   It is enumerated among the esculent plants of Egypt by Alpinus.[3]   Perhaps this is the pea exhumed by Dr. Schliemann[4] in a carbonized state from the ruins of ancient Greece.

L. sativus Linn.   CHICKLING VETCH.

Europe, north Africa and the Orient.   This vetch is an annual forage herb, the pods of which are available for culinary purposes.   It is superior, according to Langethal, to vetches in quality of fodder and seed but is less productive.[5]   The flour from the peas makes a pleasant bread but is unwholesome; its use in the seventeenth century was forbidden in Wurtemburg by law.   The peasants, however, eat it boiled or mixed with wheat flour in the quantity of one-fourth without any harm.[6]   In many parts of France the seed is used in soups.[7]

This, in many regions, is a forage-plant rather than a vegetable;[8] but in the south and southwest parts of Europe, as in Italy and Spain and also in Turkey[9] and India,[10] it is grown for the use of the seed in soups,[11] as well as in the manner of green peas.[12]   This vetch has been cultivated in southern Europe from a remote period and is mentioned by Columella[13] and Palladius.[14]   According to Heuze,[15] it came from Spain into France in 1640; but this must refer to some variety, for it appears to have been well known to the herbalists of the sixteenth century, as Dodonaeus,[16] 1556, and others.   It was included among American vegetables by Burr, 1863, who mentions two varieties, the one with dun, the other with white, seeds.   This latter form was mentioned by Bauhin, 1623.

L. tuberosus Linn.   DUTCH MICE.   EARTHNUT PEA.

Northern Old World and Uralian plains.   In Holland, Don[17] says, the plant is cultivated for its roots, which are eaten there.   Johnson[18] says in Holland and Germany the roots are roasted as food.   Pallas[19] says they are eaten by the Kalmucks.   These tubers are small but amylaceous and are sometimes called Dutch mice.

---

[1] Pickering, C.   *Chron. Hist. Pls.* 345.   1879.   (*Pisum ochrus*)

[2] Ibid.

[3] Ibid.

[4] Schliemann *Amer. Antiq.* 66.   1880.

[5] Mueller, F.   *Sel. Pls.* 252.   1891.

[6] Don, G.   *Hist. Dichl. Pls.* 2:335.   1832.

[7] *Bon Jard.* 603.   1882.

[8] Decaisne and Naudin *Man. Jard.* 4:316.   1865.

[9] Heuze, G.   *Pls. Aliment* 2:414.   1873.

[10] Birdwood *Veg. Prod. Bomb.* 120.   1865.

[11] *Bon Jard.* 603.   1882.

[12] Noisette *Man. Jard.* 2:377.   1860.

[13] Columella lib. 2, c. 11.

[14] Palladius lib. 4, c. 6.

[15] Heuze, G.   *Pls. Aliment* 2:414.   1873.

[16] Dodonaeus *Frument.* 113.   1556.

[17] Don, G.   *Hist. Dichl. Pls.* 2:332.   1832.

[18] Johnson, C. P.   *Useful Pls. Gt. Brit.* 83.   1862.

[19] Pickering, C.   *Chron. Hist. Pls.* 670.   1879.

The plant is now included among vegetables for the garden by Vilmorin,[1] although he says it is scarcely ever cultivated, but that the tubers are often collected from the wild plant in France. Burr[2] likewise includes this species among American garden plants but we know not upon what authority. In 1783, Bryant[3] says this French weed was cultivated in Holland for its roots, which were carried to market. In Siberia, the tubers are said to be much relished by the Tartars. They are used in Germany. It can scarcely be considered a plant of culture.

Laurelia aromatic Juss. *Monimiaceae.* CHILE LAUREL. PERUVIAN NUTMEG.
A Chilean species whose aromatic seeds are used as a spice in Peru.[4]

Laurencia obtusa Berk. *Algae.* CORSICAN MOSS.
This forms the greater part of what is now sold in the shops of Britain as Corsican moss.

L. pinnatifida Lam. PEPPER DULSE.
This seaweed is called pepper dulse in Scotland, on account of its hot and biting taste,[5] and is used as a condiment when other seaweeds are eaten.[6]

Laurus nobilis Linn. *Laurineae.* BAY. LAUREL. SWEET BAY.
Mediterranean region. The leaves are used by confectioners for flavoring.[7]

Lavandula spica Cav. *Labiatae.* LAVENDER.
Mediterranean regions. This plant appears to be the *nardus stricta* of ancient writers and was by them held in high esteem.[8] There are three varieties, says Burr, in cultivation; it is used as a potherb. It was mentioned for our gardens by McMahon,[9] 1806. Lavender yields oil-of-spike, used by painters on porcelain and by artists in the preparation of varnishes. It is cultivated in Surrey, England, to the extent of 300 acres. It is also grown in Lincolnshire and in Hertfordshire, where, in 1871, about 50 acres were cropped. Mawe, 1778, named four types: the narrow-leaved with blue flowers, the narrow-leaved with white flowers, the broad-leaved and the dwarf.

L. vera DC. LAVENDER.
Mediterranean region. This species was used by the Romans to mix with salads[10] and is occasionally cultivated in our gardens, as the seed appears in our seedsmen's catalogs. There is no satisfactory identification of lavender in the writings of the ancients, although it seems to have been well known to the botanists of the sixteenth century. Its use as

---

[1] Vilmorin *Les Pls. Potag.* 241. 1883.
[2] Burr, F. *Field, Gard. Veg.* 103. 1863.
[3] Bryant *Fl. Diet.* 1783.
[4] Smith, A. *Treas. Bot.* 2:663. 1870. (*L. sempervirens*)
[5] Harvey, W. H. *Phycol. Brit.* 2: Pl. LV. 1846–51.
[6] Lindley, J. *Veg. King.* 24. 1846.
[7] Lindley, J. *Med. Econ. Bot.* 2:664. 1870.
[8] McIntosh, C. *Book Gard.* 2:261. 1855.
[9] McMahon, B. *Amer. Gard. Cal.* 583. 1806.
[10] McIntosh, C. *Book Gard.* 2:7. 1855.

a perfume was indicated as early as the fourteenth century and as a medicine even in the twelfth century.[1] Its seed was in English seedsmen's lists of 1726 [2] for garden culture.

Lecanora affinis Linn. *Lichenes.* CRAB'S EYE.

This lichen is found in Armenia and Algeria, blown about and heaped up by the winds. It is ground with corn in times of scarcity to eke out the scanty supply.

L. esculenta Linn. CUP MOSS.

This lichen was found by Ledebour in the Kirghiz Steppe and in middle Asia, frequently on a barren soil or in clefts of rocks, whence it is often washed down after sudden and violent falls of rain, so as to be collected in considerable quantity and easily gathered for food. The same species was found by Paviot, who procured it in his journey to Ararat, where it is eaten by the natives. In some districts of Persia, in 1828, it covered the ground to a depth of five or six inches in so short a period of time that the people thought it had been rained down from heaven. This lichen is supposed by some to have been the manna of the children of Israel.

Lecythis grandiflora Aubl. *Myrtaceae.*

Guiana. The seeds are palatable.[3]

L. minor Jacq.

New Granada. The fruit is two inches in diameter. The seeds are of an agreeable taste.[4]

L. ollaria Linn. POT TREE.

Tropical America. The fruit is the size of a child's head and is prized for its chestnut-like fruit.[5]

L. zabucajo Aubl.

Guiana. The nuts of this species are rather more than two inches long and one wide, covered with a longitudinally-furrowed, corky shell and grow in large, hard, woody fruits, shaped like urns, measuring about six inches in diameter and having close-fitting lids at the top.[6]

Ledum latifolium Jacq. *Ericaceae.* LABRADOR TEA.

Northern climates. The leaves are said to have been used as a substitute for tea during the Revolutionary War.[7] Lindley [8] says the leaves are used to render beer heady.

---

[1] Flückiger and Hanbury *Pharm.* 476. 1879.

[2] Townsend *Seedsman* 37. 1726.

[3] Don, G. *Hist. Dichl. Pls.* 2:873. 1832.

[4] Ibid.

[5] Unger, F. *U. S. Pat. Off. Rpt.* 315. 1859.

[6] Smith, A. *Treas. Bot.* 2:667. 1870.

[7] Wood *U. S. Disp.* 1546. 1865.

[8] Lindley, J. *Veg. King.* 454. 1846.

L. palustre Linn. MARSH ROSEMARY.

Northern and arctic regions. This plant furnished a tea to Richardson [1] in his arctic journey.

Lens esculenta Moench. *Leguminosae.* LENTIL.

Orient. This was probably one of the first plants brought under cultivation by mankind for food. Lentils were known to the ancient Greeks, Jews and Egyptians. The cultivation of the lentil is very ancient, as it has been found in the Egyptian tombs of the twelfth dynasty, or 2200 to 2400 B. C.[2] It has been found in the lacustrine debris of Switzerland dating from the age of bronze.[3] Lentils are now cultivated extensively throughout most parts of the East, including Egypt, Nubia, Syria and India; likewise in most of the countries of central and southern Europe. Wilkinson [4] states that in ancient Egypt much attention was bestowed on the culture of this useful pulse, and certain varieties became remarkable for their excellence, the lentils of Pelusium being esteemed both in Egypt and in foreign countries. In Egypt and Syria, the seeds are parched and sold in the shops. In France and Spain, there are three varieties cultivated; the small brown or red sort is preferred for haricots and soups, and the yellow lentil is readily convertible into flour and serves as the base of certain adulterated preparations.[5] In England, lentils are but little cultivated, yet two varieties are named: the French, of an ash-gray color; the Egyptian, with a dark skin and of an orange-red color inside. In 1834, seeds of the lentil were distributed from the United States Patent Office.[6]

Leonia glycycarpa Ruiz & Pav. *Violarieae.*

A tree of Peru, the fruit of which is called *achocon.* The fruits are the size of a peach, with a rough, netted skin and sweet pulp, which is eaten by the Peruvians [7] and is much relished.[8]

Leopoldinia major Wallace. *Palmae.* JARA PALM.

Brazil. The Indians of the Rio Negro collect the fruit in large quantities and, by burning and washing, extract a floury substance which they use as a substitute for salt.

Lepidium diffusum DC. *Cruciferae.* DITTANDER.

Louisiana. The plant is eatable as a water cress.[9]

L. draba Linn. HOARY CRESS.

East Mediterranean countries. The plant is cooked and eaten in Cappadocia, and the seeds are substituted for pepper in seasoning.

---

[1] Barrow, J. *Voy. Disc. Arctic Reg.* 379. 1846.
[2] Schweinfurth in *Nature* 314. 1883.
[3] De Candolle, A. *Orig. Pls. Cult.* 322. 1885.
[4] Wilkinson, J. G. *Anc. Egypt.* 1:167. 1854.
[5] *Journ. Agr.* 5:65. 1853. New series.
[6] *U. S. Pat. Off. Rpt.* 16. 1854. (*Ervum lens*)
[7] Smith, J. *Dict. Econ. Pls.* 3. 1882.
[8] Smith, A. *Treas. Bot.* 2:670. 1870.
[9] Don, G. *Hist. Dichl. Pls.* 1:221. 1831. (*Lepidiastrum diffusum*)

L. latifolium Linn. DITTANDER. POOR MAN'S PEPPER.

A cress of Europe, north Africa, middle and north Asia.[1] In Britain, this cress was much used as a pungent condiment before the various substances now employed for such purposes became cheap and hence the common name, poor man's pepper. It was sometimes called dittander, and under that name was cultivated in cottage gardens but is now almost entirely discarded as a culinary vegetable.[2] Loudon[3] says it has roots resembling horseradish, for which it may be used as a substitute, and the leaves are excellent as greens and for salads. Lightfoot[4] mentions the use of the pungent leaves for salads, and Mueller[5] says it is much used for some select sauces.

L. oleraceum Forst. f. NEW ZEALAND CRESS.

New Zealand. This plant is found growing abundantly on the seashores. It is a good antiscorbutic and was eagerly sought after by early voyagers as a remedy for scurvy. The natives call it *eketera*. It is now cultivated in Britain as a potherb.[6]

L. piscidium Forst. f. FISH POISON.

Pacific Islands. This is an extremely pungent cress eaten by seamen as a relish and antiscorbutic.

L. sativum Linn. CRESS. NASTURTIUM.

Orient. De Candolle[7] believes this plant to be a native of Persia, whence it may have spread into the gardens of India, Syria, Greece, Egypt and even as far as Abyssinia. It is said by Xenophon, about 400 B. C., to have been eaten by the Persians before they became acquainted with bread. Pliny, in the first century, speaks of the nasturtium as growing in Arabia, of a remarkable size. Cress finds frequent mention in the Greek and Latin authors. This plant has been cultivated in England since 1548 and is mentioned by Gerarde[8] who says, " Galen saith that the Cresses may be eaten with bread *Velutiobsonium* and so the Ancient Spartans usually did; and the low-countrie men many times doe, who commonly use to feed of Cresses with bread and butter. It is eaten with other sallade herbes, as Tarragon and Rocket; and for this cause it is chiefly sown." In 1806, McMahon[9] mentions three varieties for American gardens. The leaves while young have a warm, pungent taste and are now eaten as a salad, either separately or mixed with lettuce or other salad plants. The curled varieties are used for garnishing. Burr[10] describes five varieties, and four types are now under culture; the common, the curled, the broad-leaved and the golden.[11] The synonomy of these various types is as below, it being premised that the modern varieties vary somewhat in degree only:

[1] Mueller, F. *Sel. Pls.* 255. 1891.

[2] Johnson, C. P. *Useful Pls. Gt. Brit.* 25. 1862.

[3] Loudon, J. C. *Hort.* 687. 1860.

[4] Lightfoot, J. *Fl. Scot.* 1:339. 1789.

[5] Mueller, F. *Sel. Pls.* 255. 1891.

[6] Smith, A. *Treas. Bot.* 2:671. 1870.

[7] De Candolle, A. *Orig. Pls. Cult.* 87. 1885.

[8] Gerarde, J. *Herb.* 250. 1633 or 1636.

[9] McMahon, B. *Amer. Gard. Cal.* 581. 1806.

[10] Burr, F. *Field, Gard. Veg.* 341. 1863.

[11] Vilmorin *Veg. Gard.* 207. 1885.

I.
COMMON CRESS.

Nasturtium hortense. Fuch. 362. 1542; Trag. 82. 1552; Pin. 221. 1561; Ger. 194. 1597; Dod. 711. 1616.

Gartenkress. Roezl. 188. 1550.

Nasturtium. Matth. 280. 1558; Lob. *Obs.* 107. 1576; Cam. *Epit.* 335. 1586; Matth. *Op.* 425. 1598; Chabr. 289. 1677.

Nasturtio. Pictorius Ed. Macer 75. 1581.

Nasturtium hortense commune. Bauh. *Phytopin.* 161. 1596.

Nasturtium hortense vulgatum. Baugh. *Pin.* 102. 1623.

Nasturtium vulgare. Baugh. J. 2:912. 1651.

Common Garden Cress. Ray 825. 1686; Vilm. 207. 1885.

Garden Cress. Townsend 1726.

Lepidium saticum. Linn. *Sp.* 899. 1763.

Common Cress. Stevenson 1785; Bryant 103. 1783; *Miller's Dict.* 1807.

Common Small-Leaved. Mawe 1778.

Cresson alénois commun. Vilm. 194. 1883.

II.
CURLED CRESS.

Nasturtium hortense crispum. Bauh. *Phytopin.* 161. 1596; *Pin.* 104. 1623.

Nasturtium hortense. Linn. Ger. 194. 1597.

Nasturtium crispum augustifolium. Matth. *Op.* 426. 1598.

Nasturtium crispum. Bauhin, Joh. Bauh., J. 2:913. 1651.

Nasturtium hortense crispum latifolium. Bauh. *Prod.* 44. 1671.

Nasturtium hortense crispum angustifolium. Bauh. 43. 1671.

Nasturtium crispum. Chabr. 289. 1677.

Curled Cress. Ray 825. 1686; Townsend 1726; Stevenson 34. 1765; Bryant 103. 1783; McMahon 1806; *Mill. Dict.* 1807.

Lepidium sativum crispum. Linn. *Sp.* 899. 1763.

Cresson frisé. L'*Hort. Franc.* 1824; Petit *Dict.* 1826.

Cresson alénois frisé. Vilm. 195. 1883.

Curled, or *Normandy,* and *Extra-Curled Dwarf.* Vilm. 207. 1885.

III.
BROAD-LEAVED CRESS.

Nasturtium. Cam. *Epit.* 335. 1586.

Nasturtium hortense latifolium. Bauh. *Phytopin* 160. 1596; *Pin.* 103. 1623.

Nasturtium latifolium dioscorideum. Bauh., J. 2:913. 1651.

Nasturtium latifolium. Chabr. 289. 1677.

Broad-Leaved Garden Cress. Ray 825. 1686; Vilm. 207. 1885.

Broad-Leaved. Townsend 1726; Stevenson 34. 1765; Mawe 1778; McMahon 1806; *Mill. Dict.* 1807.

Lepidium latifolium. Linn. *Sp.* 899. 1763.

Cresson à larges feuilles. L'*Hort. Franc.* 1824; Petit 1826.

Cresson alénois à large feuille. Vilm. 195. 1893.

IV.
GOLDEN CRESS.

Cresson doré.   Petit 1826; Noisette 1829.
Golden.   *Hort. Trans.* **6**:583.   1826; Burr 343.   1863;   Vilm. 208.   1885.
Cresson alénois doré.   Vilm. 195.   1883.

It appears as if the types of the modern varieties have not changed through culture, as three are quite ancient, and the fourth is but an ordinary variation of a pale yellowish-green color.   Curled cress seems to have been first observed by J. Bauhin, who furnished his brother, C. Bauhin, with seed preceding 1596.

Leptadenia lancifolia Decne.   *Asclepiadeae.*
Tropical Africa.   The natives of the Upper Nile make spinach of its flowers and tender shoots.[1]

Leptospermum pubescens Lam.   *Myrtaceae.*   TEA TREE.
Tasmania and southeastern Australia.   The leaves were used by the early settlers as a tea substitute.[2]

L. scoparium Forst.   TEA TREE.
Australia.   The leaves were used by Captain Cook in his second voyage as a tea and are reported as furnishing a beverage of a very agreeable, bitter flavor, when the leaves were fresh.[3]

Leucaena esculenta Benth.   *Leguminosae.*
Mexico.   According to Don,[4] this is the *guaxe* of Mexico, the legumes of which are eaten by the Mexicans.

Leucopogon fraseri A. Cunn.   *Epacrideae.*   OTAGO HEATH.
Australia.   A plant whose sweetish, orange-like drupe is edible.

L. richei R. Br.   AUSTRALIAN CURRANTS.
Australia.   The berries are said to have supported the French naturalist Riche, who was lost for three days on the south coast of New Holland.[5]

Levisticum officinale Koch.   *Umbelliferae.*   LOVAGE.
Europe.   Lovage grows wild in the south of Europe and is cultivated in gardens. McMahon, 1806,[6] includes it in his list of kitchen garden, aromatic, pot and sweet herbs, and in 1832 Bridgeman[7] includes it among garden medicinal herbs.   It is now used in eclectic medicine.   At the present day, says Vilmorin,[8] lovage is almost exclusively used

[1] Speke, J. H.   *Journ. Disc. Source Nile* 575.   1864.
[2] Smith, A.   *Treas. Bot.* **2**:674.   1870.   (*L. lanigerum*)
[3] Andrews *Bot. Reposit.* **10**:622.   1797.
[4] Don, G.   *Hist. Dichl. Pls.* **2**:421.   1832.   (*Acacia esculenta*)
[5] Balfour, J. H.   *Treas. Bot.* **1**:453.   1870.
[6] McMahon, B.   *Amer. Gard. Cal.* 583.   1806.
[7] Bridgeman *Young Gard. Asst.* 107.   1857.
[8] Vilmorin *Veg. Gard.* 316.   1885.

in the manufacture of confectionery. Formerly the leafstalks and bottoms of the stems were eaten, blanched like celery. The whole plant has a strong, sweetish, aromatic odor and a warm, pungent taste and is probably grown now in America, as in 1806, rather as a medicinal than as a culinary herb. Lovage appears to have been known to Ruellius,[1] 1536, who calls it *Levisticum officinarum,* and was seen in gardens by Chabraeus,[2] 1677.

Lewisia rediviva Pursh. *Portulaceae.* BUTTER-ROOT. SPATLUM.

Unwooded portions of the interior of Oregon and northern California. The root is boiled and eaten by Indian tribes.[3] The Indians of California call it spatlum. The root is large and fusiform, the outer portion of a dingy color, the inner white and farinaceous. It is considered highly nutritious.[4]

Licania incana Aubl. *Rosaceae.*

Guiana. The fruit is the size of a large olive and is dotted with red; the pulp is white; melting, and of a sweetish taste; the shell, or nut, is bony.[5]

Lichtensteinia pyrethrifolia Cham. & Schlecht. *Umbelliferae.*

South Africa. An intoxicating liquor called *gli* is prepared from this plant by the Hottentots.[6]

Ligusticum scoticum Linn. *Umbelliferae.* SCOTCH LOVAGE.

Subarctic seashores; from Rhode Island, northward, says Gray.[7] This plant is frequent in the outer Hebrides where it is called *shunis* and is sometimes eaten raw as a salad, or boiled as greens,[8] or the root is chewed as a substitute for tobacco when tobacco is scarce.[9] It is sometimes used as a potherb in Britain.[10] In northwest America, the green stem is peeled and eaten by the Indians.[11] The root is acrid but aromatic.

Lilium auratum Lindl. *Liliaceae.* GOLDEN-BANDED LILY.

Japan. In Japan, the bulbs are a common article of diet with the natives and are sold everywhere as a vegetable in the market. When cooked, they are sweet, mucilaginous and without any decided taste to make them objectionable to a newcomer.[12]

L. bulbiferum Linn. BULB-BEARING LILY.

This lily is enumerated by Thunberg[13] among the edible plants of Japan. D. P.

---

[1] Ruellius *Nat. Stirp.* 698. 1536.

[2] Chabraeus *Icon. Sciag.* 401. 1677.

[3] Pickering, C. *Chron. His. Pls.* 604. 1879.

[4] *U. S. D. A. Rpt.* 407. 1870.

[5] Martyn *Miller Gard. Dict.* 1807. (*Hedycrea incana*)

[6] *Treas. Bot.* 1:534. 1870.

[7] Gray, A. *Man. Bot.* 194. 1868.

[8] Lightfoot, J. *Fl. Scot.* 1:160. 1789.

[9] *Journ. Agr.* 2:379. 1831.

[10] Dickie, G. *Treas. Bot.* 2:681. 1870.

[11] Brown, R. *Bot. Soc. Edinb.* 9:385. 1868.

[12] *Amer. Gard.* 74. 1882.

[13] Thunberg *Fl. Jap.* 134. 1784.

Penhallow,[1] who lived several years in Yeso, says that lilies are frequently cultivated there for bulbs, which are sold as a vegetable food in the markets and are very fair eating, being sweet and mealy and resembling a potato. In China, this lily is called *shan-tan;* the bulbs are eaten, and the flowers are served as a relish with meat.[2]

L. canadense Linn. YELLOW LILY.

North America. The roots are eaten by the Indians of the Northwest.[3]

L. concolor Salisb. STAR LILY.

China. This lily is cultivated in Japan as a food plant.[4]

L. japonicum Thunb. JAPANESE LILY.

Japan. Miss Bird[5] found the bulbs of the " white lily," perhaps this species, cultivated and eaten as a vegetable.

L. lancifolium Thunb.

Japan. This species is cultivated in Japan as a food plant.[6]

L. martagon Linn. TURBAN LILY. TURK'S CAP.

Southern Europe. The bulbs are said by Pallas[7] to be eaten by the Cossacks along the Volga.

L. pomponium Linn. TURBAN LILY.

Eastern Asia. This lily is called by the Tartars *askchep,* and the roots are collected for food.[8] These bulbs constitute an important article of food in Kamchatka[9] and are eaten in China.[10]

L. speciosum Thunb. SHOWY LILY.

Japan. This species is cultivated as a food plant in Japan.[11]

L. superbum Linn. TURK'S CAP.

North America. Thoreau[12] says the bulb is eaten by the Indians of Maine in soups and is dug in the autumn for this purpose.

L. tigrinum Ker.-Gawl. TIGER LILY.

China and Japan. Royle[13] says the bulbs are eaten in China. D. P. Penhallow says that this species is cultivated in Yeso for the bulbs, which are sold in the markets

[1] Penhallow, D. P. *Amer. Nat.* **16:**119. 1882.

[2] Smith, F. P. *Contrib. Mat. Med. China* 134. 1871.

[3] Brown, R. *Bot. Soc. Edinb.* **9:**380. 1868.

[4] Georgeson *Amer. Gard.* 212. 1892.

[5] Bird *Unbeat. Tracks Jap.* **1:**238. 1881.

[6] Georgeson *Amer. Gard.* 212. 1892.

[7] Royle, J. F. *Illustr. Bot. Himal.* **1:**388. 1839.

[8] Pickering, C. *Chron. Hist. Pls.* 793. 1879.

[9] Henfrey, A. *Bot.* 377. 1870.

[10] Royle, J. F. *Illustr. Bot. Himal.* **1:**388. 1839.

[11] Georgeson *Amer. Gard.* 212. 1892.

[12] Thoreau *Me. Woods* 248, 249. 1877.

[13] Royle, J. F. *Illustr. Bot. Himal.* **1:**388. 1839.

and are very good eating. Miss Bird[1] also speaks of its cultivation as a vegetable in northern Japan.

Limacia scandens Lour. *Menispermaceae.*

Forests of Cochin China. The drupes are small, smooth, acid and esculent.[2]

Limnanthemum crenatum F. Muell. *Gentianeae.*

Australia. The small, round tubers are roasted for food.[3]

L. nymphoides Hoffmgg. & Link.

Europe and northern Asia. This water plant, with its yellow flowers and round leaves, was formerly eaten in China in spite of its bitterness.[4]

Linaria cymbalaria Mill. *Scrophularineae.* KENILWORTH IVY. PENNYWORT.

Europe. This plant is eaten in southern Europe, says Johnson,[5] as a salad and is a good antiscorbutic. Its taste is not unlike that of cress.

Lindera benzoin Meissn. *Laurineae.* BENJAMIN BUSH. SPICE BUSH.

North America. Barton[6] says the berries partake of the same spicy flavor as the bark and that, during the War of the Revolution, the people of the United States used them dried and powdered as a substitute for allspice. Porcher[7] says the leaves were much used by the Confederate soldiers for making a pleasant, aromatic tea. L. S. Mote[8] says the young twigs and leaves were often used by the early pioneers of Ohio as a substitute for tea and spice.

Linum usitatissimum Linn. *Lineae.* FLAX.

Europe and the Orient. Flax has been in cultivation since the earliest times. It was known to the early Egyptians, as it is mentioned frequently in the Bible as a material for weaving cloth. The cloth used in wrapping mummies has been proved to be made of the fibers of this plant. Flax was also cultivated by the early Romans. Among the Greeks, Alcman, in the seventh century before Christ, the historian Thucydides, and among the Romans, Pliny, mention the seed as employed for human food, and the roasted seed is still eaten by the Abyssinians.[9] In the environs of Bombay, the unripe capsules are used as a food by the natives. In Russia, Belgium, Holland, Prussia and the north of Ireland, flax is extensively grown for its fiber which constitutes the linen of commerce. The seeds, known as linseed, are largely used for expressing an oil, and the press-residue is used for feeding cattle. This plant is largely grown for seed in the United States. We

---

[1] Bird *Unbeat. Tracks Jap.* 1:175. 1881.

[2] Loureiro *Fl. Cochin.* 621. 1790.

[3] Palmer, E. *Journ. Roy. Soc. New So. Wales* 17:100. 1884.

[4] Smith, F. P. *Contrib. Mat. Med. China* 135. 1871.

[5] Johnson, C. P. *Useful Pls. Gt. Brit.* 197. 1862.

[6] Barton, W. P. C. *Med. Bot.* 2:95. 1818.

[7] Porcher, F. P. *Res. So. Fields, Forest* 393. 1869.

[8] Case *Bot. Index* 83. 1880.

[9] Flückiger and Hanbury *Pharm.* 97. 1879.

find mention of the culture of flax in Russia about 969 A. D.   Flax is said to have been introduced into Ireland by the Romans, or even more remotely, by the Phoenicians, but the earliest definite mention of linen in Ireland seems to be about 500 A. D.   In England, the statement is made that it was introduced in 1175 A. D., and Anderson, in his *History of Commerce*, traces some fine linen made in England in 1253.   In New England, the growing of flax commenced with its first settlement, and as early as 1640 it received legislative attention.

Lippia pseudo-thea Schau.   *Verbenaceae.*

Brazil.   In Brazil, an infusion of the leaves is highly esteemed as a tea substitute, under the name of *capitao do matto.*[1]   Lindley[2] says the leaves form an agreeable tea.

Liriodendron tulipifera Linn.   *Magnoliaceae.*   POPLAR.   TULIP TREE.   WHITEWOOD.

Eastern North America.   The root is used to prepare an agreeable liquor.   The Canadians use the root to correct the bitterness of spruce beer and to give it a lemon flavor.[3]

Lissanthe montana R. Br.   *Epacrideae.*

Australia.   The large, white, transparent, fleshy fruits are eaten.[4]

L. sapida R. Br.   AUSTRALIAN CRANBERRY.

Australia.   The berries are red and acid and are made into tarts in New South Wales.[5] A. Smith[6] says the flesh is thin and more like that of the Siberian crab than of the cranberry.

L. strigosa R. Br.

Australia.   The fruit is eaten.[7]

Litobrochia sinuata Brack.   *Filices.*   ROYAL FERN.

Seemann[8] says the leaves of this fern are used as a potherb by the natives of Viti.

Livistona australis Mart.   *Palmae.*   CABBAGE PALM.   GIPPSLAND PALM.

Australia.   The young and tender leaves of this palm are eaten like cabbages.[9]

Lobelia sp.?   *Campanulaceae.*   LOBELIA.

The roots of one species are said by Thunberg[10] to be eaten by the Hottentots.   It is called *karup.*

---

[1] Archer, T. C.   *Profit. Pls.* 126.   1865.   (*Lantana psuedo-thea*)

[2] Lindley, J.   *Veg. King.* 663.   1846.   (*Lantana pseudo-thea*)

[3] Baillon, H.   *Hist. Pls.* 1:177.   1871.

[4] Smith, A.   *Treas. Bot.* 2:688.   1870.

[5] Don, G.   *Hist. Dichl. Pls.* 3:776.   1834.

[6] Smith, A.   *Treas. Bot.* 2:688.   1870.

[7] Don, G.   *Hist. Dichl. Pls.* 3:776.   1834.

[8] Seemann, B.   *Fl. Viti.* 350.   1865-73.

[9] Smith, A.   *Treas. Bot.* 2:690.   1870.

[10] Thunberg *Trav.* 2:150.   1796.

Lodoicea callipyge Comm. *Palmae.* COCO DE MER. DOUBLE COCOANUT.

Seychelles Islands. The heart of the leaves is eaten and is often preserved in vinegar. The fruit is the largest any tree produces, sometimes weighing 40 or 50 pounds, with a length of 18 inches and a circumference of 3 feet. The immature fruit affords a sweet and melting aliment.[1] Brandis[2] says the fruit takes several years to come to maturity.

Lonicera angustifolia Wall. *Caprifoliaceae.* NARROW-LEAVED HONEYSUCKLE.

Himalayan region. The sweet berry, of the size of a pea, is eaten in India.[3]

L. ciliata Muhl. FLY HONEYSUCKLE.

Western North America. In Oregon and California, the fruit is much used by the Indians and is considered good by white hunters.[4]

L. involucrata Banks.

Western North America. The fruit is eaten by the Indians of Oregon and Alaska.[5]

Lophophytum sp.? *Balanophoreae.*

Masters says one species is eaten in Bolivia.[6]

Loranthus exocarpi Behr. *Loranthaceae.*

Australia. The fruit is an oblong drupe about one-half inch in length. It is sweet and is eaten raw.[7]

Loreya arborescens DC. *Melastomaceae.*

Guiana. This species furnishes gooseberry-like fruits of little value, according to Unger.[8]

Lotus edulis Linn. *Leguminosae.* BIRD'S-FOOT TREFOIL.

Mediterranean countries. In Crete, the pods are eaten when young as a string bean by the poorer inhabitants.[9]

L. gebelia Vent.

Orient. The pods are eaten as a string bean about Aleppo.[10]

L. tetragonolobus Linn. WINGED PEA.

Mediterranean region. In France, according to Robinson,[11] this pea is cultivated as a vegetable. The pods were formerly employed, says Johns,[12] as an esculent by the poor

---

[1] Seemann, B. *Pop. Hist. Palms* 244. 1856.

[2] Brandis, D. *Forest Fl.* 545. 1876.

[3] Brandis, D. *Forest Fl.* 255. 1874.

[4] *U. S. D. A. Rpt.* 414. 1870.

[5] Ibid.

[6] Masters, M. T. *Treas. Bot.* 2:695. 1870.

[7] Palmer, E. *Journ. Roy. Soc. New So. Wales* 17:100. 1884.

[8] Unger, F. *U. S. Pat. Off. Rpt.* 351. 1859. (*Melastoma arborescens*)

[9] Don, G. *Hist. Dichl. Pls.* 2:195. 1832.

[10] Don, G. *Hist. Dichl. Pls.* 2:197. 1832.

[11] Robinson *Parks, Gard. Paris* 504. 1878.

[12] Johns, C. A. *Treas. Bot.* 2:1135. 1870.

of Sicily and Spain.   The green pods, says Mueller,[1] serve as a substitute for asparagus. This plant is yet in French gardens for use as a string bean [2] but apparently is not in much request.   In 1726, Townsend [3] an English seedsman, says, " I put them here, because some people eat 'em when they are very young; but in my mind they are not good."   In 1785, Bryant [4] reports this pea as in disuse except in some of the northern counties of England.   Clusius [5] first saw the plant in a druggist's garden, in 1579, called *pisum rubrum*. In 1588, Camerarius [6] speaks of this pea in his *Horticulture* under the name *pisum rubrum*. The winged pea was first seen by J. Bauhin [7] in 1594.   Ray [8] describes it in 1686 but gives no indication of cultivation or use.   Parkinson,[9] 1629, calls it *pisum quadratum* and it is mentioned in the second edition of Gerarde, 1638.   It is recorded in American Gardens by Burr, 1863.

Lucuma bifera Molina.   *Sapotaceae.*   SAPOTA.

Chile.   This tree is cultivated in Chile.   It bears twice a year, early in summer and in autumn, but the autumnal fruit alone produces kernels; these are two and have the appearance of chestnuts.   The fruit is round and a little sloped.   By keeping the fruits some time in straw, they become ameliorated and acquire that pleasant taste which renders them so much esteemed.[10]

L. caimito Roem.

Peru.   The tree is cultivated in Peru.   This fruit is about three inches long with a soft and agreeable pulp.[11]

L. mammosa Gaertn. f.   MAMMEE.   MARMALADE TREE.   SAPOTA.

West Indies and South America.   In the West Indies, this tree is cultivated for its fruit.   The fruit is four or five inches in diameter and is covered with a rough, russet-colored bark; the pulp is dark yellowish, soft, sweet, tasting not unlike a very ripe pear. It makes an excellent marmalade but, eaten raw, has an aperient quality.[12]

L. obovata H. B. & K.   LUCUMA.

Western Peru.   The fruit is solid in consistence and so richly flavored that a small quantity suffices.   It is sold in the markets at Lima.[13]   Garcilasso de la Vega [14] says, " another fruit is called by the Indians of Peru, *rucma;* by the Spaniards, *lucuma*.   It

[1] Mueller, F.   *Sel. Pls.* 121.   1876.

[2] Vilmorin *Les Pls. Potag.* 322.   1883.

[3] Townsend *Seedsman* 7.   1726.

[4] Bryant *Fl. Diet.* 302.   1783.

[5] Clusius *Hist.* 2:244.   1601.

[6] Camerarius *Hort. Med.* 91.   1588.   Fig. 26.

[7] Bauhin, J.   *Hist. Pl.* 2:358.   1651.

[8] Ray *Hist. Pl.* 966.   1686.

[9] Martyn *Miller Gard. Dict.* 1807.

[10] Molina *Hist. Chili* 1:129.   1808.

[11] Don, G.   *Hist. Dichl. Pls.* 4:33.   1838.

[12] Lunan, J.   *Hort. Jam.* 1:480.   1814.

[13] Pickering, C.   *Chron. Hist. Pls.* 662.   1879.

[14] Vega *Roy. Comment.*   Hakl. Soc. Ed. 2:363.   1871.

is a tolerable fruit, not delicate nor pleasant, though sweet rather than sour, and not known to be unwholesome, but it is coarse food. It is about the size and shape of an orange and has a kernel in the center very like a chestnut in color and size but not good to eat, being bitter."

L. serpentaria H. B. & K.

Cuba. This is a doubtful species found in Cuba; the fruit is edible.[1]

L. turbinata Molina.

Chile. This species is cultivated in Chile. The fruit has the form of a whipping-top. By keeping in straw, it ripens into a much-esteemed fruit.[2]

Luffa acutangula Roxb. *Cucurbitaceae.* STRAINER VINE.

Old World tropics. This plant is cultivated in India for food purposes and is said by Drury[3] to be one of the best of the native vegetables and to be much used in curries. Roxburgh says that, when the fruit is boiled and dressed with butter, pepper and salt, it is little inferior to green peas. This club-shaped gourd, about 10 or 12 inches long, is eaten boiled or pickled, but the taste is insipid, says Don.[4] This is the *papengaye* of the negroes of Africa, says Oliver,[5] and presents bitter and poisonous, as well as edible varieties.

L. aegyptiaca Mill. BONNET GOURD. DISH-CLOTH GOURD. LOOF.

Old World tropics. This species is cultivated for its fruit throughout tropical Africa.[6] It is the *sooly-qua* of the Chinese, a club-shaped, wrinkled gourd, said to be eaten. It is cultivated for food purposes in India, where it is called *ghia*.[7] It is considered by the natives of Burma a delicious vegetable.[8] The interior, netted fibers, under the name loof, are used in Turkish baths for fleshrubbers. The plant is grown as a curiosity in American gardens.

Lunaria annua Linn. *Cruciferae.* BOLBONAC. HONESTY. PENNY FLOWER.

Europe. "The seed of the bolbonac is a temperature hot and dry and sharpe of taste and is like in taste and force to the seed of treacle mustard, the roots likewise are somewhat of a biting quality but not much: they are eaten with sallads as certain other roots are."[9]

Lupinus albus Linn. *Leguminosae.* FIELD LUPINE. WOLF-BEAN.

Mediterranean region. This plant has been cultivated since the days of the ancient Egyptians. It was cultivated by the Romans as a legume but does not seem to have

[1] Don, G. *Hist. Dichl. Pls.* 4:34. 1838.

[2] Molina *Hist. Chili* 1:129. 1808.

[3] Pickering, C. *Chron. Hist. Pls.* 413. 1879.

[4] Don, G. *Hist. Dichl. Pls.* 3:29. 1834.

[5] Oliver, D. *Fl. Trop. Afr.* 2:530. 1871.

[6] Ibid.

[7] Royle, J. F. *Illustr. Bot. Himal.* 1:218. 1839.

[8] Pickering, C. *Chron. Hist. Pls.* 818. 1879. (*L. pentandra*)

[9] Gerarde, J. *Herb.* 465. 1633.

entered the Rhine regions until the sixteenth century. Theophrastus speaks of lupine in his *History of Plants* and it is also mentioned by Cato, Columella and Pliny. It is now extensively cultivated in Sicily, Italy and some other countries as a plant for green manuring and for the seeds, which, when boiled to remove their bitterness, are still an article of food in some regions.[1] In 1854, seeds were distributed from the United States Patent Office.[2]

L. hirsutus Linn. BLUE LUPINE.

Mediterranean regions. This plant was cultivated by the Greeks under the name *thermos* and serves now as food for the poorer classes of people, as it did the Cynics. The Mainots, at the present day, bake bread from the seeds. It now grows wild throughout the whole of the Mediterranean region from Portugal and Algiers to the Greek islands and Constantinople.[3]

L. littoralis Dougl.

Northwest America. The tough, branching roots are used by the Columbia River Indians as winter food, being dried. When eaten they are roasted and become farinaceous. Tytler[4] says these are the licorice spoken of by Lewis and Clarke. The native name is *comnuchtan*.

L. luteus Linn. YELLOW LUPINE.

Mediterranean region. The seeds of this plant constitute a nutritious article of food for man. It is cultivated in Italy.[5]

L. perennis Linn. WILD LUPINE.

Eastern North America. Unger[6] says its bitter seeds are eaten from Canada to Florida.

L. termis Forsk.

East Mediterranean countries. This plant is cultivated in Italy and in Egypt for its seeds, which are cooked in salt water and shelled. The peduncles, after being pickled, are eaten without cooking.[7]

Lycium europaeum Linn. *Solanaceae.* BOX THORN.

Mediterranean regions and the Orient. This thorny shrub is used as a hedge plant in Tuscany and Spain, and the young shoots are employed as a vegetable.[8] The globose berry, yellow or red and one-sixth of an inch in diameter, is sweet and without flavor but is eaten in India.[9]

---

[1] *Treas. Bot.* 2:699. 1870.

[2] *U. S. Pat. Off. Rpt.* XV. 1854.

[3] Unger, F.   *U. S. Pat. Off. Rpt.* 316. 1859.

[4] Tytler *Prog. Disc. No. Coast Amer.* 318. 1833.

[5] Burr, F.   *Field, Gard. Veg.* 515. 1863.

[6] Unger, F.   *U. S. Pat. Off. Rpt.* 316. 1859.

[7] Don, G.   *Hist. Dichl. Pls.* 2:365. 1832.

[8] *Treas. Bot.* 2:701. 1870.

[9] Brandis, D.   *Forest Fl.* 345. 1876.

L. ruthenicum Murr. RUSSIAN BOX THORN.

Orient. The small, sweet and flavorless berry is eaten in India.[1]

Lycopersicum esculentum Mill. *Solanaceae.* GOLD APPLE. LOVE APPLE. TOMATO.

Tropical America. Bancroft [2] states the tomato was eaten by the wild tribes of Mexico and by the Nahua nations who called it *tomati*. Humboldt [3] says it was called *tomati* and was sown among maize by the ancient Mexicans. The tomato is mentioned by Acosta,[4] 1590, as among the products of Mexico. The names, *mala Peruviana* and *pomi del Peru*, indicate its transference to Europe from Peru, but Phillips,[5] we know not from what authority, says the tomato appears to have been brought to Europe from Mexico. In the *Treasury of Botany*,[6] it is said to have been introduced to Europe in the early part of the sixteenth century.

The earliest mention of tomatoes is by Matthiolus,[7] 1554, who calls them *pomi d'oro* and says they have but recently appeared in Italy. In 1570, Pena and Lobel [8] give the name gold apple in the German, Belgian, French and English languages, which indicates their presence in those countries at this date. In 1578, Lyte [9] says they are only grown in England in the gardens of " Herboristes." Camerarius, in his *Epitome*, 1586,[10] gives the French name of *pommes d'amours*, which corresponds to Lyte's amorous apples; and, in his *Hortus Medicus*, 1588,[11] he gives the names of *pomum Indium*, and the foreign name of *tumatle ex tumatle americanorum*. Anguillara, 1561, calls them *poma Peruviana.*[12] In Hernandez's *History of Nova Hispania*, 1651, he has a chapter on the *tomatl*, which includes our tomatoes and alkekengis; in 1658, the Portuguese of Java used the word *tomatas*.[13] Acosta,[14] however, preceding 1604, used the word *tomates*, and Sloane,[15] in 1695, tomato. Gerarde says he received seeds of the tomato for his garden from Spain, Italy and other hot countries. The date of its appearance in England is hence put for 1596. Gerarde [16] says (in his second edition) that these love apples are eaten abroad prepared and boiled with pepper, salt and oil and also as a sauce, but " they yield very little nourishment to the bodie, and the same naught and corrupt." C. Bauhin in his *Pinax*, 1596, calls the plant *tumatle Americanorum*. In 1656, Parkinson [17] mentions the tomato as being culti-

---

[1] Brandis, D. *Forest Fl.* 345. 1876.

[2] Bancroft, H. H. *Native Races* 1:624, 653, 1875.

[3] Pickering, C. *Chron. Hist. Pls.* 615. 1879.

[4] Acosta *Nat. Mor. Hist. Ind.* Hakl. Soc. Ed. 1:240. 1880.

[5] Phillips, H. *Comp. Orch.* 225. 1831.

[6] *Treas. Bot.* 2:701. 1870.

[7] Matthiolus *Comment.* 479. 1558; 684. 1570.

[8] Pena and Lobel *Advers.* 108. 1570; 108. 1576.

[9] Dodoens *Herb.* 508. 1578. Lyte Ed.

[10] Camerarius *Epit.* 821. 1586.

[11] Camerarius *Hort. Med.* 130. 1588.

[12] Gray, A. *Amer. Journ. Sci.* 128. 1883.

[13] Bontius De *Ind.* 131. 1658.

[14] Acosta *Nat. Mor. Hist. Ind.* 266. 1604. Hakl. Soc. Ed. 1880.

[15] Sloane, H. *Cat.* 109. 1696.

[16] Gerarde, J. *Herb.* 1st Ed. 275. 1597.

[17] Parkinson *Par. Terr.* 379. 1904. (Reprint of 1629)

vated in England for ornament and curiosity only; while Miller,[1] 1752, says they were much used in soups in his time. In 1812, they were an article of field culture in Italy, especially in Sicily, whence they were sent to Naples and Rome, being extensively used in Italian cookery.

As Thunberg[2] does not mention the tomato in Japan in 1776, we may assume that it had not reached the Japanese at that date. Rumphius,[3] 1755, gives the name as *tomatte* as used by the Malays, which shows it had reached the Eastern Archipelago before this time. In 1840, Wilkes[4] found a distinct variety cultivated in Fiji, of a yellow color and about the size of a small egg. The tomato was even found wild in interior Africa by Grant,[5] about 1860, but the natives had not learned the use of the fruit and were surprised at his eating it. Long,[6] 1774, describes the tomato of Jamaica as very large, compressed at both ends, deeply furrowed all over the sides, filled with a pulpy juice, which has somewhat the taste of gravy, for which reason they are often used in soups and sauces and impart a very grateful flavor; they are likewise fried and served with eggs.

D. J. Brown[7] says that, until about 1834, the tomato was almost wholly unknown in this country as an esculent vegetable, and in the *History of the Massachusetts Horticultural Society*[8] it is said that in 1844 this vegetable was then acquiring that popularity which makes it so indispensable at present. Yet they are mentioned as grown in Virginia by Jefferson[9] in 1781. In 1798, according to a writer in the *Prairie Farmer*, the tomato was brought to Philadelphia by a French refugee from Santo Domingo but was not sold in the markets until 1829. In 1802, it was introduced at Salem, Massachusetts, by an Italian painter, but he found it difficult to persuade people even to taste the fruit. In 1835, tomatoes were sold by the dozen at Quincy Market, Boston. In 1812, they were use in as a food at New Orleans, Louisiana.[10] In 1806, McMahon[11] speaks of tomatoes as being in much estimation for culinary purposes but mentions no varieties. In 1818, Gardiner and Hepburn say that tomatoes make excellent pickles. In 1828, Fessenden[12] quotes the name from Loudon only. In 1832, Bridgeman[13] says tomatoes are much cultivated for soups and sauces.

Thorburn[14] gives directions for their cultivation in his *Gardeners' Kalendar* for 1817, offers but one variety in his seed catalog of 1828, but offers 31 varieties in 1881. T. S. Gold,[15]

[1] Martyn *Miller Gard. Dict.* 1807.

[2] Loudon, J. C. *Enc. Agr.* 57. 1812.

[3] De Candolle, A. *Geog. Bot.* 2:91. 1855.

[4] Wilkes, C. *U. S. Explor. Exped.* 3:335. 1845.

[5] Speke, J. H. *Journ. Disc. Source Nile* 576. 1864.

[6] Long, E. *Hist. Jam.* 3:773. 1774.

[7] Brown, D. J. *U. S. Pat. Off. Rpt.* 384. 1854.

[8] *Hist. Mass. Hort. Soc.* 269. 1880.

[9] Jefferson *Notes Va.* Trenton 55. 1803.

[10] *Hist. Mass. Hort. Soc.* 40. 1880.

[11] McMahon, B. *Amer. Gard. Cal.* 200. 1806.

[12] Fessenden *New Amer. Gard.* 291. 1828. (*Solanum lycopersicum*)

[13] Bridgeman *Young Gard. Asst.* 101. 1857. (*Solanum lycopersicum*)

[14] Thorburn *Gard. Kal.* 1817.

[15] Gold. T. S. *Letter.* Apr. 29, 1880.

Secretary of the Connecticut Board of Agriculture, writes: "we raised our first tomatoes about 1832 as a curiosity, made no use of them though we had heard that the French ate them. They were called love apples." The editor of the *Maine Farmer*,[1] 1835, says tomatoes are cultivated in gardens in Maine, and are "a useful article of diet and should be found on every man's table." The *New York Farmer*[2] of this year has the statement of a correspondent that he had "planted a large quantity of tomatoes," and a Professor Bennett[3] in 1835, in a course of local lectures in the West, refers to the tomato, or Jerusalem apple, as found in abundance in the markets of the West and recommends their dietetic use.

The ribbed tomato, with flattened and more or less ribbed fruit, is the kind first introduced into European culture and is described in the *Adversaria* of 1570, as well as by many succeeding authors, and the earlier figures indicate that it has changed but little under culture and was early known as now in red, golden, yellow, and white varieties. A parti-colored fruit is mentioned by J. Bauhin, 1651, and the type of the bronze-leaved is named by Blackwell, 1770. This ribbed type was probably the kind mentioned by Jefferson[4] as cultivated in Virginia in 1781, as it was the kind whose introduction into general culture is noted from 1806 to about 1830, when their growing was becoming general.

It has the following synonymy, gained from figures:

I.

SYNONYMY OF THE RIBBED TOMATO.

Poma amoris, an Glaucium. Diosc. Lob. *Obs.* 140. 1576.
Poma amoris. Lyte's *Dod.* 440. 1578; Cam. *Epit.* 821. 1586; Ger. 275. 1597;
    Sweert. **2**:20. 1654.
Poma aurea. Dalechamp 628. 1587.
Poma amoris, pomum aureum. Lob. *Icon.* **1**:270. 1591.
Solanum pomiferum, fructu rotundo, molli. Matth. *Op.* 761. 1598.
Poma amoris fructu luteo et rubro. Hort. *Eyst.* 1613; 1713.
Aurea mala. Dod. 458. 1616; 455. 1583.
Pomi d'oro. Dur. C. 372. 1617.
Poma amoris. Park. *Par.* 381. 1629.
Amoris pomum. Blackw. 133. 1750.
Mala aurea. Chabr. 525. 1677; Bauh., J. **3**:620. 1650.
Solanum pomiferum. Mor. *Hist.* s. 13, t. 1, f. 7. 1699.
Lycopersicon galeni. Morandi **8**:53. 1744.
Lycopersicon. Tourn. 62. 1719.
Common Large Red. Mawe 1778.
Morelle pomme d'amour. Descourt **6**:95. 1827.
Tomate rouge grosse. Vilm. 555. 1883.
Large Red. Burr. 646. 1863.

In form, these synonyms are substantially of one variety. The descriptions accompanying and others of the same date mention all the colors now found. In 1719, Tourne-

---

[1] *Me. Farm.* Oct. 16, 1835.
[2] *N. Y. Farm.* Sept. 11, 1835.
[3] Bennett, Dr. *Me. Farm.* Aug. 21, 1835.
[4] Jefferson *Notes Va.* 54. 1803.

fort names a pale red, red, a yellow and a white variety in France, and Mawe, 1778, names but the common large red in England. In 1854, Brown describes but two varieties, the large red and the large yellow, for American gardens.

II.
THE ROUND TOMATO.

Of the round tomato, there are no indications of its being known to the early botanists, the first apparent reference being by Tournefort in 1700,[1] who places among his varieties the *Lycopersicum rubro non striato*, the *non striato*, not fluted or ribbed, implying the round form; and this same variety was catalogued by Tilly[2] at Pisa in 1723. In 1842, some seed of the Fiji Island variety was distributed in Philadelphia, and Wilkes[3] describes the fruit of one variety as round, smooth, yellow, the size of a large peach, and the fruit of two other varieties as the size of a small egg, but gives no other particulars. This is the first certain reference to this group. The large, smooth or round, red and the small, yellow, oval tomato of Browne,[4] 1854, may belong here. Here, also may be classed such varieties as Hathaway's Excelsior, King Humbert and the Plum, and some of the *tomate pomme* varieties of the French.

The round form occasionally appears in the plants from seed of hybrid origin, for when the cross was made between the currant and the tree tomato, some plants thus obtained yielded fruit of the plum type. This, however, may have been atavism. The botanical relations seem nearer to the cherry tomato than to the ordinary forms.

III.
SYNONYMY OF THE CHERRY TOMATO.

The cherry tomato is recorded as growing spontaneously in Peru, in the West Indies,[5] Antilles,[6] southern Texas[7] and New Jersey. There were red and yellow varieties in Europe as early as 1623 and these are mentioned in 1783 by Bryant[8] as if they were the only sorts in general culture in England at this time, but Mawe,[9] 1778, enumerates the large red, as also the red and yellow cherry, as under garden culture. The following is its synonymy, mostly founded on description:

Solanum racemosum cerasorum. Bauh. *Pin.* 167. 1623; *Prod.* 90. 1671.
Solanum amoris minus S. mala aethiopica parva. Park. *Par.* 379. 1629.
Cujus fructus plane similis erat, magnitudine, figura, colore, Strychnodendro. etc. Rechius Notes, Hernand, 296. 1651.
Fructus est cersasi instar (quoad magnitudine). Hort. *Reg. Bles.* 310. 1669.
Solanum pomiferum fructu rotundo, molli parvo rubro plano. Ray **3**:352. 1704.

---

[1] Tournefort *Inst.* 150. 1719.
[2] Tillus *Cat. Hort. Pisa* 106. 1723.
[3] Wilkes, C.   *U. S. Explor. Exped.* **3**:335. 1845.
[4] Browne *U. S. Pat. Off. Rpt.* 385. 1854.
[5] Sloane, H.   *Cat.* 109. 1696.
[6] Descourtilz, M. E.   *Fl. Antill.* **5**:279. 1821–29.
[7] Gray, A.   *Synopt. Fl.* **2**:226. 1878.
[8] Bryant *Fl. Diet.* 1783.
[9] Mawe and Abercrombie *Univ. Gard. Bot.* 1778. (*Solanum lycopersicum*)

Lycopersicum fructu cerasi rubro.   Tourn. 150.   1719.
Lycopersicum fructu cerasi luteo.   Tourn. 150.   1719.
Solanum lycopersicum.   Bryant 212.   1783.
Cherry-fruited.   Mawe 1778.
Cherry.   *Mill. Dict.* 1807;   Burr 649, 652.   1863.
Morelle cerasiforme.   Descourt. **5**:279, 378.   1827.
Lycopersicum cerasifolium.   Noisette 1829.
Cherry-shaped.   Buist 1851.
Tomate cerise.   Vilm. 559.   1883.

This type is probably the normal form of the tomato of the gardens to which the other types given can be referred as varieties.   It is quite variable in some respects, bearing its fruit usually in clusters, occasionally in racemes.   It is now but little grown and only for use in preserves and pickles.

IV.
THE PEAR TOMATO.

The pear tomato, which is to be classed as one of the fancy varieties under cultivation, occurs with both yellow, red, and pale yellow or whitish fruit.   It was described by Dunal in 1813, and in Persoon's *Synopsis* in 1805.[1]   It is mentioned in England in 1819, and both colors were mentioned in the United States by Salisbury,[2] 1848.   The pear tomato is used for garnishing and pickling.   The common names are, pear-shaped and fig.

L. humboldtii Dun.

Brazil.   This tomato is very like the preceding species, but the racemes of the flowers are smaller, the calyx segments never being the length of the corolla, and the berries are one-half smaller, red, and, when cultivated, not less angular than those of *L. esculentum.*[3] This tomato was noticed by Humboldt [4] as under cultivation at La Victoria, Neuva Valencia, and everywhere in the valleys of Arayus, in South America.   It is described by Kunth,[5] 1823, and by Willdenow, about 1806, from plants in the Berlin garden from seeds received from Humboldt.   The fruit, although small, has a fine flavor.   The Turban, Turk's Cap, or Turk's Turban, of our seedsmen, a novelty of 1881, belongs here, although this cultivated variety is probably a monstrous form.

L. pimpinellifolium Mill.   CURRANT TOMATO.

South America.   The currant tomato bears its red fruit, somewhat larger than a common currant, or as large as a very large currant, in two-ranked racemes, which are frequently quite large and abundantly filled.   It grows wild in Peru and Brazil and is figured by Feuillee,[6] 1725, but not as a cultivated plant.   It is described by Linnaeus,[7]

---

[1] Dunal, M. F.   *Synop. Solan.* 110.   1816.

[2] Salisbury *Trans. N. Y. Agr. Soc.* 371.   1848.

[3] Don, G.   *Hist. Dichl. Pls.* **4**:443.   1838.

[4] Humboldt, A.   *Trav.* **2**:20.   1889.

[5] Salisbury *Trans. N. Y. Agr. Soc.* 371.   1848.

[6] Feuillee *Peru* 37, t. 25.   1725.

[7] Linnaeus *Sp. Pl.* 265.   1763.

1763.   The grape, or cluster, tomato is recorded in American gardens by Burr,[1] 1863, and as the red currant tomato by Vilmorin,[2] 1883 and 1885.   It is an exceedingly vigorous and hardy variety with delicate foliage and fruits most abundantly.   The berries make excellent pickles.

According to the test of cross-fertilization, few, if any, of the above groups are true species.   Two only, the cherry and the currant tomato, are recorded in a truly wild condition.   The tomato has, however, been under cultivation from a remote period by the Nahua and other Central American nations and reached Europe and American culture, as all the evidence implies, in an improved condition.   If there is any evidence that any of our so-called types arose spontaneously from the influences of culture, it is not noted. We may well ask, why did not other forms appear during the interval from 1558 to 1623, when but one sort, and that figured as little variable, received the notice of the early botanists?

Maba buxifolia Pers.   *Ebenaceae.*   SATINWOOD.

Asia and African tropics.   The fruit is edible, the taste sweetish and not unpalatable but it is scarcely worth the trouble of eating, the seed being so large in proportion to the pulp.[3]

M. inconstans Griseb.

West Indies.   The fruit, at first yellow, then red, is edible, with an ungrateful smell and an insipid taste.   It is an inch in diameter.[4]

M. major Forst. f.

Fiji Islands and India.   In India, the fruit is eaten.[5]

Macadamia ternifolia F. Muell.   *Proteaceae.*   NUT TREE.

Subtropics of east Australia.   The nuts have the taste of hazels.[6]

Madia sativa Molina.   *Compositae.*   MADIA-OIL PLANT.

Western North and South America.   This plant is cultivated in Chile, France, Germany and Italy for the sake of the limpid and sweet oil which is expressed from its seeds.   This oil is used as a substitute for olive oil.   The seeds yield about 41 per cent to analysis and from 26 to 28 per cent to the oil-press, according to Boussingault, whose experiment in 1840 gave 635 pounds of oil and 1706 pounds of oil cake per acre.   The plant is easily cultivated, requiring management similar to seed clover, but, owing to the glutinous nature of the stems and stalks, the seeds require to be threshed and sown as soon as the crop is cut, otherwise fermentation injures them.[7]

---

[1] Burr, F.   *Field, Gard. Veg.* 646.   1863.

[2] Vilmorin *Veg. Gard.* 573.   1885.   (*Solanum racemiflorum*)

[3] Wight, R.   *Illustr. Ind. Bot.* 2:146.   1850.

[4] Don, G.   *Hist. Dichl. Pls.* 4:39.   1838.   (*Diospyros psidiodes*)

[5] Unger, F.   *U. S. Pat. Off. Rpt.* 337.   1859.

[6] Mueller, F.   *Sel. Pls.* 266.   1891.

[7] Unger, F.   *U. S. D. A. Rpt.* 175.   1870.

Maerua crassifolia Forsk. *Capparideae.*

Arabia. This is an arborescent shrub called in Yemen *maeru*. Its fruit is eaten by boys.[1]

Maesa argentea Wall. *Myrsineae.*

Himalayan region. The round, smooth, white berry, the size of a peppercorn, is eaten.[2]

M. indica Wall.

East Indies and Malay. The very small, globose, white berry is eaten in Nepal. At Bombay it is called *atki*.[3]

Magnolia grandiflora Linn. *Magnoliaceae.* MAGNOLIA.

Eastern North America. The flowers are pickled in some parts of Devonshire, England, and are considered exquisite in flavor.[4]

M. yulan Desf. YULAN.

China. The Chinese pickle the flower-buds, after having removed the calyx, and use them for flavoring rice.[5]

Maieta guianensis Aubl. *Melastomaceae.*

Guiana. The fruit is succulent, edible and of a beautiful red color.[6] This plant furnishes gooseberry-like fruits of little value.[7]

M. heterophylla DC.

Peru. The fruit is eaten.[8]

M. poeppigii Mart.

Peru. The fruit is eaten.[9]

Malpighia angustifolia Linn. *Malpighiaceae*

West Indies. The fruit is edible.[10]

M. aquifolia Linn.

West Indies. The fruit is dark purple when ripe and is edible.[11]

M. berteriana Spreng.

Guadeloupe. The fruit is edible.[12]

---

[1] Pickering, C. *Chron. Hist. Pls.* 390. 1879.
[2] Brandis, D. *Forest Fl.* 283. 1876.
[3] Ibid.
[4] Loudon, J. C. *Hort.* 689. 1860.
[5] Loudon, J. C. *Arb. Frut. Brit.* 1:280. 1854. (*M. conspicua*)
[6] Aublet *Hist. Pls. Guiane* 1:443. 1775.
[7] Unger, F. *U. S. Pat. Off. Rpt.* 351. 1859.
[8] Baillon, H. *Hist. Pls.* 7:35. 1881.
[9] Ibid.
[10] Don, G. *Hist. Dichl. Pls.* 1:634. 1831.
[11] Don, G. *Hist. Dichl. Pls.* 1:635. 1831.
[12] Ibid.

M. cnide Spreng.

Santo Domingo.   The fruit is edible.[1]

M. coccigera Linn.

West Indies.   The fruit is small, purple in color when ripe and is edible.[2]

M. emarginata Moc. & Sesse

Mexico.   The fruit is edible.[3]

M. fucata Ker.-Gawl.

Jamaica.   The berries are edible.[4]

M. glabra Linn.   BARBADOS CHERRY.

Tropical America.   This tree is planted in most gardens in Jamaica and is cultivated for its fruit in tropical America.   The fruit is round, red, of the bigness of a cherry, smooth skinned, and contains, within a reddish, sweetish, copiously juicy pulp, several triangular stones whose sides are so accommodated to one another as to seem to make one round one with several furrows on the outside.[5]   The fruit, says Schomburgk,[6] is much used in Barbados in preserves and tarts and the taste reminds one of the raspberry rather than the cherry.

M. grandiflora Jacq.

Martinique.   The fruit is edible.[7]

M. incana Mill.

Honduras.   The fruit is edible.[8]

M. macrophylla Willd.

Brazil.   The fruit is edible.[9]

M. nitida Crantz.

Venezuela.   The fruit is edible.[10]

M. obovata H. B. & K.

New Granada.   The fruit is edible.[11]

M. punicifolia Linn.

Tropical America.   The fruit is one of the size and shape of a cherry, very succulent, and of a pleasant, acid flavor, says Don.[12]   Lunan[13] says it makes very agreeable tarts and excellent jellies.

---

[1] Don, G.   *Hist. Dichl. Pls.* **1**:634.   1831.

[2] Ibid.

[3] Don, G.   *Hist. Dichl. Pls.* **1**:635.   1831.

[4] Don, G.   *Hist. Dichl. Pls.* **1**:634.   1831.

[5] Sloane, H.   *Nat. Hist. Jam.* **2**:106.   1725.

[6] Lindley, J., and Paxton, J.   *Flow. Gard.* **2**:18.   1852.

[7] Don, G.   *Hist. Dichl. Pls.* **1**:635.   1831.

[8] Ibid.

[9] Ibid.

[10] Ibid.

[11] Don, G.   *Hist. Dichl. Pls.* **1**:636.   1831.

[12] Don, G.   *Hist. Dichl. Pls.* **1**:635.   1831.

[13] Lunan, J.   *Hort. Jam.* **1**:49.   1814.

M. saccharina G. Don. SUGAR PLUM.

Tropical Africa. The fruit is sold in great quantities in the market of Freetown.[1]

M. setosa Spreng.

West Indies. The fruit is edible.[2]

M. urens Linn. COW-ITCH CHERRY.

West Indies. The fruit, says Don,[3] is insipid and is eaten only by children and negroes.

Malva rotundifolia Linn. *Malvaceae.* MALLOW.

Europe and neighboring Asia. In Egypt, especially upon the banks of the Nile, the mallow is extensively cultivated and is used as a potherb by the natives. This plant reached northeast America before 1669 and it is mentioned by Josselyn.[4] It is now naturalized in waste places and in cultivated grounds. The mallow was formerly among the culinary herbs [5] but is used now only in infusion or decoction in medicine on account of its mucilaginous properties. Unger [6] says Pythagoras thought much of this plant as a spinach and among the Greeks, as well as among the Romans, it was at one time much esteemed. Mallow and Asphodell were raised at Delos for the temple of Apollo, as a symbol of the first nourishment of man. It was known to Camerarius,[7] 1588, and was known only to Dodonaeus,[8] 1616, as a cultivated plant. At the present day, the young shoots are used as a salad in southern France and Italy.

M. sylvestris Linn. CHEESES. HIGH MALLOW. MARSH MALLOW.

Europe and temperate Asia. This mallow is sometimes cultivated in our gardens [9] and, on account of its mucilaginous properties, finds use as a demulcent in medicine. It is a native of Europe and has become naturalized in this country. Johnson [10] says the foliage, when boiled, forms a very wholesome vegetable, and the flat seeds are eaten by country people.

M. verticillata Linn. CURLED MALLOW.

Europe, Asia and northern Africa. This plant is used in China as a vegetable.[11]

Mammea americana Linn. *Guttiferae.* MAMMEE APPLE. SOUTH AMERICAN APRICOT.

American tropics. This fine tree of the Antilles is cultivated for its fruit there, as well as in some parts of tropical Africa and Asia. The fruit often attains the size of a child's head and is of a yellow color. The outer rind and the pulp which immediately

---

[1] Don, G. *Hist. Dichl. Pls.* 1:635. 1831.

[2] Don, G. *Hist. Dichl. Pls.* 1:634. 1831.

[3] Ibid.

[4] Pickering, C. *Chron. Hist. Pls.* 348. 1879.

[5] *U. S. Disp.* 1552. 1865.

[6] Unger, F. *U. S. Pat. Off. Rpt.* 359. 1859.

[7] Camerarius *Hort. Med.* 1588.

[8] Dodonaeus *Pempt.* 653. 1616.

[9] *U. S. Disp.* 1552. 1865.

[10] Johnson, C. P. *Useful Pls. Gt. Brit.* 58. 1862.

[11] Unger, F. *U. S. Pat. Off. Rpt.* 359. 1859.

surrounds the seeds are very bitter, but the intermediate flesh is sweet and aromatic and is eaten, cut into slices and steeped in wine or made into preserves of various kinds.[1]

Mammillaria fissurata Engelm. *Cacteae.* DRY WHISKEY.

Mexico. This plant is sometimes called dry whiskey from the fact that when chewed it produces more or less intoxication.

M. meiacantha Engelm.

Texas. The oblong, scarlet berries are very good to eat.[2]

M. simplex Haw.

Tropical America. Unger[3] says its berries are edible. This species yields a milky juice that is sweet and wholesome.

M. vivipara Haw.

Upper Louisiana. The flowers are large and red; the fruit is the size of a grape, green and edible.

Mangifera foetida Lour. *Anacardiaceae.* HORSE MANGO.

A tree of the Malayan Archipelago. The horse mango is cultivated by the Burmese, who esteem the fleshy, strong-scented fruit.[4] Don[5] says it is unwholesome but is eaten by the Malays.

M. indica Linn. MANGO.

Tropical eastern Asia. The mango grows abundantly in India, where many varieties are cultivated, and the fruit of some is esteemed as most delicious. In north and central India, says Brandis,[6] the fruit of ungrafted trees is generally stringy with a strong, turpentine flavor. It, nevertheless, forms an important article of food for large classes of the population. The fruit of good grafts is excellent, soft, juicy and with a delicious, aromatic flavor. In Burma, the mango is not generally grafted, for seeds of a good kind, as a rule[7] produce good fruit of a similar description. This seems to be the fruit seen by Friar Jordanus,[7] about 1300, who calls it *aniba*. The mango was introduced to Jamaica in 1782.[8] In 1880, 21 fruitful and superior varieties were growing at the Botanical Gardens in Trinidad.[9] At Cayenne, it did not exist before the beginning of the present century.[10] Its introduction into Brazil was more ancient as the seeds came thence to Barbados in the middle of the eighteenth century.[11] In Martinique, by grafting, a dozen very distinct

[1] *Treas. Bot.* 2:714. 1870.

[2] Havard, V. *Proc. U. S. Nat. Mus.* 520. 1885.

[3] Unger, F. *U. S. Pat. Off. Rpt.* 333. 1859.

[4] Pickering, C. *Chron. Hist. Pls.* 445. 1879.

[5] Don, G. *Hist. Dichl. Pls.* 2:64. 1832.

[6] Brandis. *Forest Fl.* 126. 1874.

[7] Jordanus Fr. *Wonders East.* Hakl. Soc. Ed. 14. 1863.

[8] Macfadyen *Jam.* 1:221. 1837.

[9] Prestoe *Rpt. Bot. Gard. Trinidad* 32. 1880. Printed in 1881.

[10] De Candolle, A. *Geog. Bot.* 2:876. 1855.

[11] De Candolle, A. *Orig. Cult. Pls.* 202. 1885.

varieties have been established, the quality of which, says Berlanger,[1] in respect to the abundance and flavor of the flesh, places them in the first rank of tropical fruits. In the Mauritius, they cultivate a number of varieties. This tree has been introduced into Florida and is now grown there to a limited extent. In Jamaica, starch is made of the unripe fruit.[2] In India, the unripe fruit is much used in conserves, tarts and pickles, and the kernels of the seeds are boiled and eaten in times of scarcity.[3]

M. sylvatica Roxb.

Himalayan region. The yellow fruit is eaten by the natives, although inferior to the worst kinds of the common mango.[4]

Manihot palmata Muell. *Euphorbiaceae*. SWEET CASSAVA.

Brazil. This is the sweet cassava of eastern equatorial America, where it has been cultivated from early times. The roots of this variety are sweet and may be eaten raw but it is less cultivated than the bitter variety. It is cultivated in Queensland, according to Simmonds,[5] for the production of arrowroot.

M. utilissima Pohl. BITTER CASSAVA. MANIOC. TAPIOCA.

Brazil. The manioc, or bitter cassava, of eastern equatorial South America was cultivated by the Indians of Brazil, Guiana and the warm parts of Mexico before the arrival of Europeans and is now grown in many tropical countries. The root is bitter and a most virulent poison when raw but, when grated to a pulp and the poisonous juice expelled by pressure, it becomes edible after being cooked. The coarse meal forms cassava. The expressed juice, allowed to settle, deposits a large quantity of starch which is known as Brazilian arrowroot, or tapioca. The boiled juice furnishes *cassareep*, a condimental sauce, and from the cakes an intoxicating beverage called *piwarrie* is brewed by the Brazilians. The plant is extremely productive. In Brazil, some 46 different kinds are found. Manioc was naturalized in the Antilles as early as the sixteenth century, says Unger,[6] although its journey around the world by way of the Isle of Bourbon and the East Indies took place at a comparatively late period. It reached the west coast of Africa earlier, and the erroneous opinion has been entertained that it was transplanted from Africa to America. In Africa, at Angola, Livingstone[7] says the Portuguese subsist chiefly on manioc. It is prepared in many ways. The root is roasted or boiled as it comes from the ground; the sweet variety is eaten raw; the root may be fermented in water and then roasted or dried after fermentation; baked, or rasped into meal and cooked as farina; or made into confectionery with butter and sugar; and the green leaves are boiled as a spinach. Grant[8] says it is the staple food of the Zanzibar people, where some kinds can be eaten raw, boiled, fried, roasted or in flour. In India, it is eaten as a

---

[1] Berlanger *Trans. N. Y. Agr. Soc.* **18**:567. 1858.

[2] Brandis, D. *Forest Fl.* 127. 1874.

[3] Masters, M. T. *Treas. Bot.* **2**:716. 1870.

[4] Don, G. *Hist. Dichl. Pls.* **2**:64. 1832.

[5] Simmonds, P. L. *Trop. Agr.* 345. 1889. (*M. janipha*)

[6] Unger, F. *U. S. Pat. Off. Rpt.* 309. 1859.

[7] Livingstone, D. *Trav. Research So. Afr.* 462. 1858.

[8] Speke, J. H. *Journ. Disc. Source Nile* 581. 1864.

staple food. In Burma, the root is boiled and eaten. In the Philippines, manioc is cultivated in many varieties. In 1847, a few dozen plants were introduced to this country and distributed from New York City, and in 1870 some were growing in conservatories in Washington. The first mention of cassava is by Peter Martyr[1] who says "*iucca* is a roote, whereof the best and most delicate bread is made, both in the firme land of these regions and also in Ilandes." In 1497, Americus Vespucius, speaking of the Indians of South America, says, "their most common food is a certain root which they grind into a kind of flour of no unpalatable taste and this root is by some of them called *jucha*, by others *chambi*, and by others *igname*."

Maranta arundinacea Linn. *Scitamineae.* ARROWROOT.

South America. This is the true arrowroot plant of the West Indies, Florida, Mexico and Brazil.[2] It furnishes Cape Colony and Natal arrowroot and Queensland arrowroot in part. It is also cultivated in India, where it was introduced about 1840.[3] In 1849, arrowroot was grown on an experimental scale in Mississippi, and in 1858 it was grown as a staple crop at St. Marys, Georgia. The plant is stated to have been carried from the island of Dominica to Barbados and thence to Jamaica.[4] The starch made from the root is mentioned by Hughes,[5] 1751, and the mode of preparing it is described by Browne,[6] 1789. The Bermuda arrowroot is now most esteemed but it is cultivated in the East Indies, Sierra Leone and South Africa as well. Wilkes[7] found the natives of Fiji making use of arrowroot from the wild plant.

Marathrum foeniculaceum Humb. & Bonpl. *Podostemaceae.*

Mexico and New Granada. This plant resembles seaweed and grows in the rivers of Veraguas. Its young leaf-stalks, when boiled, have a delicate flavor not unlike that of French beans.[8]

Marattia alata Sw. *Marattiaceae.*

The fleshy caudex of this fern is used in the Sandwich Islands as food, when better food is scarce.

M. attenuata Lab.

In the Fiji Islands, the fronds are used as a potherb; they are very tender and taste not unlike spinach. In New Zealand, the soft part of the stem is eaten.

Margyricarpus setosus Ruiz et Pav. *Rosaceae.* PEARL BERRY.

A native of Brazil, says Loudon,[9] on arid hills. It bears pearl-like fruit, resembling that of the mistletoe but differing from it in having a grateful and acid taste.

---

[1] Gray, A. *Amer. Journ. Sci.* 249. 1883.

[2] Mueller, F. *Sel. Pls.* 270. 1891.

[3] Simmonds, P. L. *Trop. Agr.* 345. 1889.

[4] Flückiger and Hanbury *Pharm.* 629. 1879.

[5] Ibid.

[6] Ibid.

[7] Wilkes, C. *U. S. Explor. Exped.* 3:337. 1845.

[8] *Gard. Chron.* 548. 1852.

[9] Loudon, J. C. *Arb. Frut. Brit.* 2:934. 1844.

Mariscus dregeanus Kunth. *Cyperaceae.*

Africa, Asia and Australia. The roots are boiled and eaten by the natives of India, who say they are as good as yams.[1]

Marlea vitiensis Benth. *Cornaceae.*

Australia and islands of the Pacific. This tree in New South Wales and Queensland bears edible fruits.[2]

Marlierea glomerata Berg. *Myrtaceae.* CAMBUCA.

Subtropical Brazil. The fruits attain the size of apricots and are much used for food.[3]

M. tomentosa Cambess. GUAPARANGA.

Brazil. The sweet berries of this tall shrub are of the size of cherries.[4]

Marrubium vulgare Linn. *Labiatae.* HOREHOUND.

Europe, Asia and north Africa. This plant affords a popular domestic remedy and seems in this country to be an inmate of the medicinal herb-garden only. In Europe, the leaves are sometimes employed as a condiment. Although a plant of the Old World, it is now naturalized in the New World from Canada to Buenos Aires and Chile, excepting within the tropics.[5] It is figured by Clusius,[6] 1601, and finds mention by many of the botanists of that period. Pliny [7] refers to *Marrubium* as among medicinal plants in high esteem, and it finds mention by Columella.[8] Albertus Magnus,[9] in the thirteenth century, also refers to its valuable remedial properties in coughs. We may hence believe that, as an herb of domestic medicine, horehound has accompanied emigrants into all the cooler portions of the globe.

Marsilea nardu A. B. *Marsileaceae.* NARDOO. NARDU.

Australia. The spores and spore cases of this plant are used by the aborigines for food, pounded up and baked into bread and also made into a porridge. These preparations furnish a nutritious food, by no means unwholesome, and one free from unpleasant taste but affording sorry fare for civilized man.

Martynia fragrans Lindl. *Pedalineae.*

Mexico. The Apache Indians gather the half-mature seed-pods of this plant and cook them. The pods when ripe are armed with two sharp, horn-like projections and, being softened and split open, are used on braided work to ornament willow baskets.[10]

---

[1] Royle, J. F. *Illustr. Bot. Himal.* 1:414. 1839.

[2] Mueller, F. *Sel. Pls.* 125. 1876.

[3] Mueller, F. *Sel. Pls.* 270. 1891.

[4] Ibid.

[5] De Candolle, A. *Geog. Bot.* 2:751. 1855.

[6] Clusius *Hist.* 2:34. 1601.

[7] Pliny lib. 20, c. 89.

[8] Columella, lib. 10, c. 356.

[9] Albertus Magnus *Veg.* Jessen Ed. 539. 1867.

[10] *U. S. D. A. Rpt.* 422. 1870. (*M. violacea*)

M. lutea Lindl.

Brazil. This species, originally from Brazil, has yellow flowers.[1] It does not appear to be in American gardens nor is its seed advertised by our seedsmen. It reached Europe in 1824.[2] It is described by Vilmorin as under kitchen-garden culture.

M. proboscidea Glox. MARTYNIA. UNICORN PLANT.

Southwestern North America and now naturalized in northeastern America. Martynia is in cultivation in our gardens for its seed-pods, which when young are used for pickling. These seed-pods are green, very downy or hairy, fleshy, oval, an inch and a half in their greatest diameters and taper to a long, slender, incurved horn or beak. It is mentioned under American cultivation in 1841.[3] Martynia was known in England as a plant of ornament in 1738 [4] but has, even yet, scarcely entered the kitchen-garden.

Marumia muscosa Blume. *Melastomaceae.*

Java. Refreshing drinks are prepared from the berries.[5]

M. stellulata Blume

Sumatra and Java. Refreshing drinks are prepared from the berries.[6]

Matisia cordata Humb. & Bonpl. *Malvaceae.* CHUPA-CHUPA. SAPOTA.

A tree of New Granada.[7] The oval fruit, about five inches long and three inches broad, in taste has been compared to an apricot or to a mango. It is sold in the markets of New Granada and Peru.[8]

Matthiola incana R. Br. *Cruciferae.* STOCK.

Mediterranean region. This plant is eaten in time of famine.[9]

M. livida DC.

Egypt and Arabia. This plant is eaten in time of famine.[10]

Mauritia flexuosa Linn. f. *Palmae.* ITA PALM. TREE-OF-LIFE.

Tropical South America. The tree-of-life of the missionaries, says Humboldt,[11] not only affords the Guaraons a safe dwelling during the risings of the Orinoco, but its fruit, its farinaceous pith, its juice, abounding in saccharine matter, and the fibers of its petioles furnish them with food, wine and thread. The fruit has somewhat the taste of an apple and when ripe is yellow within and red without. The sago of the pith is made into a bread.

---

[1] Vilmorin *Les Pls. Potag.* 330. 1883.

[2] Noisette *Man. Jard.* 537. 1829.

[3] Kenrick, W. *New Amer. Orch.* 373. 1841.

[4] *Gard. Chron.* 608. 1843.

[5] Baillon, H. *Hist. Pls.* 7:35. 1881.

[6] Ibid.

[7] Jackson, J. R. *Treas. Bot.* 2:1316. 1876.

[8] Smith, J. *Dict. Econ. Pls.* 116. 1882.

[9] Baillon, H. *Hist. Pls.* 3:222. 1874. Note.

[10] Ibid.

[11] Humboldt, A. *Trav.* 1:331; 2:107; 3:9. 1889.

The flour is called *yuruma* and is very agreeable to the taste, resembling cassava bread rather than the sago of India. From the juice, a slightly acid and extremely refreshing liquor is fermented. The ripe fruit contains first a rich, pulpy nut and last a hard core, Bates [1] says the fruit is a common article of food, although the pulp is sour and unpalatable, at least to European tastes. It is boiled and then eaten with farina. This is the *miriti*. or *ita*, palm of Brazil; the sago-like flour is called *ipuruma*.[2]

M. vinifera Mart. WINE PALM.

Brazil. This palm, says Gardner,[3] produces a great number of nuts about the size of an egg, covered with rhomboidal scales arranged in a spiral. Between these scales and the albuminous substance of the nut, there exists an oily pulp of a reddish color, which the inhabitants of Crato boil with sugar and make into a sweetmeat. In Piauhy, they prepare from this pulp an emulsion, which, when sweetened with sugar, forms a very palatable beverage, but if much used is said to tinge the skin a yellowish color. The juice of the stem also forms a very agreeable drink.

Maximiliana regia Mart. *Palmae.* CUCURITE PALM. INAJA PALM.

Brazil. This is the inaja palm of the Rio Negro [4] and the cucurite palm of Guiana.[5] The terminal leaf-bud furnishes a most delicious cabbage, says Seemann,[6] and the fruit is eaten by the Indians. Brown [7] says the nuts are covered with a yellow, juicy pulp, which is sweet and pleasant to the taste. The outer husk of the fruit, says A. Smith,[8] yields a kind of saline flour used by the natives for seasoning their food.

Medeola virginica Linn. *Liliaceae.* INDIAN CUCUMBER.

Northeast America. The roots are eaten by the Indians, according to Pursh.[9] Cutler [10] says the roots are esculent and of an agreeable taste. Gray [11] says the tuberous, white rootstock has a taste like the cucumber.

Medicago denticulata Willd. *Leguminosae.* BUR CLOVER. SHANGHAI TREFOIL.

North temperate region of the Old World. A fine, broad-leaved variety of this plant was found by Fortune to be much used by the Chinese as a winter vegetable.[12]

M. lupulina Linn. BLACK MEDICK. NONESUCH.

North temperate region of the Old World; naturalized in places in America. In southern California, its seeds are much relished by the Indians.[13]

---

[1] Bates, H. W. *Nat. Amaz.* Humboldt *Libr. Sci.* 647. 1879–80.
[2] Seemann, B. *Pop. Hist. Palms* 252, 253. 1856.
[3] Gardner, G. *Trav. Braz.* 171, 172. 1849.
[4] Agassiz *Journ. Braz.* 338. 1868.
[5] Brown, C. B. *Camp Life Brit. Guiana* 180. 1877.
[6] Seemann, B. *Pop. Hist. Palms* 261, 262. 1856.
[7] Brown, C. B. *Camp Life Brit. Guiana* 180. 1877.
[8] Smith, A. *Treas. Bot.* 2:726. 1870.
[9] Pursh, F. *Fl. Amer. Septent.* 1:244. 1814.
[10] Pickering, C. *Chron. Hist. Pls.* 808. 1879.
[11] Gray, A. *Man. Bot.* 524. 1868.
[12] *Gard. Chron.* 815. 1844.
[13] *U. S. D. A. Rpt.* 419. 1870.

M. platycarpa Trautv.

Siberia.   The plant furnishes a food.[1]

M. sativa Linn.   ALFALFA.   LUCERNE.

Europe and the Orient.   The leaves are eaten by the Chinese as a vegetable.[2]

M. scutellata Mill.   SNAILS.

Mediterranean region.   This plant is not edible but, like the caterpillar-plant, is grown on account of the singular shape of its seed-vessels.   It was in Belgian and German gardens preceding 1616 [3] and in American gardens in 1863 or before.[4]

Melia azadirachta Linn.   *Meliaceae.*   BEAN TREE.   CHINA TREE.   FALSE SYCAMORE.
   PRIDE OF INDIA.

East Indies.   A kind of toddy is obtained by tapping the tree, and from the fruit a medicinal oil, known as bitter oil or *taipoo* oil, is made.

M. azedarach Linn.   SYRIAN BEAD TREE.

A tree of Syria, the north of India and subtropical Japan and China.   It is cultivated for ornament in different parts of the world.   In southern France and Spain, it is planted in avenues.   In our southern states, it adorns the streets of cities and has even become naturalized.   The fruit is a round drupe, about as large as a cherry and yellowish when ripe, is sweetish, and, though said by some to be poisonous, is eaten by children.[5]   In India, from incisions in the trunk near the base made in spring, a sap issues which is used as a cooling drink.[6]   From the fruit, a bitter oil is extracted, called *kohombe* oil, and is used medicinally.   The bitter leaves are used as a potherb in India, being made into soup, or curry, with other vegetables.[7]

Melianthus major Linn.   *Sapindaceae.*   HONEY-FLOWER.

Cape of Good Hope.   The flowers are of a dark brown color, in long, erect racemes a foot or more in length, containing a large quantity of honey, which is collected by the natives.[8]   It is grown in French flower gardens.[9]

Melicocca bijuga Linn.   *Sapindaceae.*   GENIP   HONEY-BERRY.

Tropical America.   The pulp of the fruit, says Mueller,[10] tastes like grapes, and the seeds can be used like sweet chestnuts.   Lunan [11] says the tree was introduced into Jamaica from Surinam.   The seed — rarely more than one — is covered with a deliciously sweet-

---

[1] Unger, F.   *U. S. Pat. Off. Rpt.* 357.   1859.   (*Trigonelia platycarpus*)

[2] Bretschneider, E.   *Bot. Sin.* 53.   1882.

[3] Dodonaeus *Pempt.* 575.   1616.

[4] Burr, F.   *Field, Gard. Veg.* 398.   1863.

[5] *U. S. Disp.* 153.   1865.

[6] Brandis, D.   *Forest Fl.* 67.   1874.

[7] Dutt, U. C.   *Mat. Med. Hindus* 136.   1877.

[8] Smith, J.   *Dom. Bot.* 455.   1871.

[9] Vilmorin *Fl. Pl. Ter.* 690.   1870.   3rd Ed.

[10] Mueller, F.   *Sel. Pls.* 276.   1891.

[11] Lunan, J.   *Hort. Jam.* 1:318.   1814.

acid, gelatinous substance like the yolk of an egg, mixed with very fine fibers adhering tenaciously to the seed; the fleshy part is very agreeable to the taste. Titford [1] calls this pulp pleasant and cooling.

Melicytus ramiflorus Forst. *Violarieae.* MAHOE.

New Zealand. This is the mahoe of New Zealand, not the mahoe of the West Indies, says A. Smith.[2] The fruit of this tree is eaten by the natives.

Melilotus officinalis Lam. *Leguminosae.* MELILOT. MELIST. SWEET CLOVER.

Europe and adjoining Asia. The flowers and seeds are the chief ingredient in flavoring the Gruyère cheese of Switzerland.[3]

Melissa officinalis Linn. *Labiatae.* BALM.

Mediterranean region and the Orient. This aromatic perennial has long been an inmate of gardens for the sake of its herbage, which finds use in seasonings and in the compounding of liquors and perfumes as well as the domestic remedy known as balm tea. The plant in a green state has an agreeable odor of lemons and an austere and slightly aromatic taste, and hence is employed to flavor certain dishes in the absence of lemon thyme.[4] The culture was common with the ancients, as Pliny [5] directs it to be planted, and, as a bee-plant or otherwise, it finds mention by Greek and Latin poets and prose writers.[6] In the Ionian Islands, it is cultivated for bees. In Britain, it is said to have been introduced in 1573. It is mentioned in France by Ruellius,[7] 1536; in England, by Gerarde,[8] 1597, who gives a most excellent figure; and also by Lyte,[9] 1586, and Ray,[10] 1686. Mawe,[11] 1758, says great quantities of balm are cultivated about London for supplying the markets. In the United States, it is included among garden vegetables by McMahon,[12] 1806. As an escape, the plant is found in England [13] and sparingly in the eastern United States.[14] Bertero [15] found it wild on the island of Juan Fernandez.

But one variety is known in our gardens, although the plant is described as being quite variable in nature. This would indicate that cultivation had not produced great changes. The only difference noted in the cultivated plant has been in regard to vigor.

---

[1] Titford, W. J. *Hort. Bot. Amer.* 59. 1812.

[2] Smith, A. *Treas. Bot.* 2:732. 1870.

[3] Don, G. *Hist. Dichl. Pls.* 2:177. 1832.

[4] McIntosh, C. *Book Gard.* 2:236. 1855.

[5] Pliny lib. 21, c. 41.

[6] Theocritus, *Idyll* iv: 25; Dioscorides iii: 118; Varro iii: 116; Columella ix: 9; Virgil, *Georgics* iv; as quoted by Grandsagne, Pliny **8**:485.

[7] Ruellius *Nat. Stirp.* 733. 1536.

[8] Gerarde, J. *Herb.* 558. 1597.

[9] Dodoens *Herb.* 293. 1586. Lyte Ed.

[10] Ray *Hist. Pl.* **1**:570.

[11] Mawe and Abercrombie *Univ. Gard. Bot.* 1778

[12] McMahon, B. *Amer. Gard. Cal.* 512. 1806.

[13] De Candolle, A. *Geog. Bot.* 2:681, 721. 1855.

[14] Gray, A. *Synopt. Fl.* **2**: Pt. i, 361. 1886.

[15] De Candolle, A. *Geog. Bot.* 2:681. 721. 1855.

A variegated variety is recorded by Mawe,[1] 1778, for the ornamental garden. This variation is noted by Vilmorin.[2]

Melocactus communis Link & Otto. *Cacteae.* MELON CACTUS. TURK'S-CAP CACTUS.

South America and the West Indies.[3] According to Unger,[4] this cactus bears an edible fruit.

Melocanna bambusoides Trin. *Gramineae.*

East Indies. The fruit is very large, fleshy like an apple and contains a seed which is said to be very pleasant eating.[5]

Melodinus monogynus Roxb. *Apocynaceae.*

Himalayan region, Malay and China. This plant bears a fruit, says Firminger,[6] as large as a moderate-sized apple, which is said to be eatable and agreeable. Royle[7] says it yields edible fruit. A. Smith[8] says the firm, sweet pulp is eaten by the natives. The berry is red, edible, sweet and somewhat astringent.[9]

Melothria pendula Linn. *Cucurbitaceae.*

North America and West Indies. The fruit, in Jamaica, is the size and shape of a nutmeg, smooth, blackish when ripe, and full of small, white seeds like other cucumbers, lodged within an insipid, cooling pulp. The fruit is eaten pickled when green and is good when fully ripe, according to Sloane.[10]

M. scabra Naud.

Mexico. The fruit is an inch long, resembling little watermelons. It is pickled and eaten raw.[11]

Memecylon edule Roxb. *Melastomaceae.*

Coromandel, tropical India and Burma. The juicy fruit is eaten by the natives when ripe. They have much pulp of a bluish-black color and of an astringent quality.[12] The pulp of the fruit, though rather astringent, is eaten by the natives.[13]

Mentha canadensis Linn. *Labiatae.* MINT.

A plant found on the wet banks of brooks from New England to Kentucky and north-

---

[1] Mawe and Abercrombie *Univ. Gard. Bot.* 1778.
[2] Vilmorin *Fl. Pl. Ter.* 692. 1870. 3rd Ed.
[3] Smith, A. *Treas. Bot.* 2:733. 1870.
[4] Unger, F. *U. S. Pat. Off. Rpt.* 333. 1859.
[5] Masters, M. T. *Treas. Bot.* 2:1317. 1876.
[6] Firminger, T. A. C. *Gard. Ind.* 492. 1874.
[7] Royle, J. F. *Illustr. Bot. Himal.* 1:272. 1839.
[8] Smith, A. *Treas. Bot.* 2:734. 1870.
[9] Don, G. *Hist. Dichl. Pls.* 4:26. 1838. (*Oncinus sp.*)
[10] Lunan, J. *Hort. Jam.* 2:280. 1814.
[11] Watson *Contrib. U. S. Nat. Herb.* 14:414. 1887.
[12] Don, G. *Hist. Dichl. Pls.* 2:654. 1832.
[13] Drury, H. *Useful Pls. Ind.* 290. 1873.

ward, and occasionally cultivated in gardens for the leaves, which are used in flavoring. The Indians of Maine eat mint roasted before the fire and salted and think it nourishing.

M. piperita Linn. PEPPERMINT.

Europe, Asia and northern Africa. Peppermint is grown on a large scale for the sake of its oil, which is obtained by distillation, and which finds extensive use for flavoring candies and cordials and in medicine. There are large centers of its culture in the United States, Europe and Asia. It is grown to a limited extent for the leaves which are used for seasoning. Mint is spoken of as if not a garden plant by Ray,[1] 1724, who describes two varieties, the broad and the narrow leaved. In 1778, it is included by Mawe,[2] among garden herbs; in 1806, it is noticed among American garden plants [3] and is now an escape from cultivation. There is no notice of peppermint preceding 1700, when it is mentioned by Plukenet [4] and Tournefort [5] as a wild plant only.

M. pulegium Linn. PENNYROYAL.

Europe and neighboring Asia. The leaves of pennyroyal are sometimes used as a condiment. Mawe,[6] in England, in 1778, calls it a fine aromatic; it was among American potherbs in 1806.[7] It was in high repute among the ancients and had numerous virtues ascribed to it by both Dioscorides and Pliny. From the frequent references to it in Anglo-Saxon and Welsh works on medicine, we may infer that it was much esteemed in northern Europe.[8] It has now fallen into disuse.

M. viridis Linn. SPEARMINT.

Europe, Asia and north Africa; naturalized in America. This garden herb was well known to the ancients and is mentioned in all early mediaeval lists of plants. Amatus Lusitanus,[9] 1554, says it is always in gardens and later botanists confirm this statement for Europe. It was in American gardens in 1806 [10] and probably far earlier, for it was collected by Clayton in Virginia about 1739 [11] as a naturalized plant.

Mentzelia albicaulis Dougl. *Loaseae.* PRAIRIE LILY.

Western North America. The oily seeds are pounded and used by the Indians in California as an ingredient of their *pinole mantica*, a kind of cake.[12]

Menyanthes trifoliata Linn. *Gentianeae.* BUCKBEAN. MARSH TREFOIL.

Northern Europe, Asia and America. The intense bitter of the leaves of the buck-

[1] Ray, J. *Synop. Method.* 234. 1724.

[2] Mawe and Abercrombie *Univ. Gard. Bot.* 1778.

[3] McMahon *Amer. Gard. Cal.* 583. 1806

[4] Pluc'netius *Almag. Bot.* 129. 1700

[5] Tournefort *Inst.* 1719.

[6] Mawe and Abercrombie *Univ. Gard. Bot.* 1778.

[7] McMahon, B. *Amer. Gard. Cal.* 583. 1806.

[8] Flückiger and Hanbury *Pharm.* 486. 1879.

[9] Dioscorides Amatus Lusitanus Ed. 319. 1554.

[10] McMahon *Amer. Gard. Cal.* 583. 1806.

[11] Gronovius *Fl. Virg.* 89. 1762.

[12] Torrey, J. *Bot. U. S. Mex. Bound. Surv.* 2:67. 1859.

bean has led to its use as a substitute for hops in brewing. Large quantities are said to be collected for the adulteration of beer. It has long been employed in Sweden for this purpose. In Lapland and Finland, the rhizomes are sometimes powdered, washed to get rid of the bitter principle and then made into a kind of bread.[1] In the outer Hebrides, when there is a deficiency of tobacco, the islanders console themselves by chewing the root of the marsh trefoil which has a bitter and acrid taste.[2]

Mercurialis annua Linn. *Euphorbiaceae.* ANNUAL MERCURY.

Europe and north Africa and occasionally found spontaneously growing in the United States. Annual mercury, says Johnson,[3] is eaten in Germany, the poisonous principle which it contains in small quantity being dissipated in boiling.

Meriandra benghalensis Benth. *Labiatae.* BENGAL SAGE.

India. Bengal sage, says Firminger,[4] is in general use in lower Bengal as a substitute for sage but it is rather an indifferent substitute.

Mesembryanthemum acinaciforme Linn. *Ficoideae.* HOTTENTOT FIG.

South Africa. This is one of the Hottentot figs of South Africa. The inner part of the fruit affords, says Mueller,[5] a really palatable and copious food.

M. aequilaterale Haw. PIG'S FACE.

Australia and South America. This is an Australian species whose fruit is eaten by the natives.[6] The inner part of the fruit affords a palatable and copious food, according to Mueller.[7] In California, say Brewer and Watson,[8] the fruit is edible and pleasant. This is perhaps the species referred to by Parry [9] as littoral in southern California and as having an edible, juicy fruit. In Australia, says J. Smith,[10] the watery and insipid fruit is eaten by the natives. Wilhelmi [11] says two varieties of this genus in Australia have fruit of an agreeable flavor and are eaten by the aborigines of the Port Lincoln district.

M. anatomicum Haw. CANNA ROOT. KON.

South Africa. The Hottentots, says Thunberg,[12] come far and near to obtain this shrub with the root, leaves and all, which they beat together and afterwards twist up like pig-tail tobacco; after which they let the mass ferment and keep it by them for chewing, especially when they are thirsty. If it be chewed immediately after the fermentation, it intoxicates.

[1] Johnson, C. P. *Useful Pls. Gt. Brit.* 179. 1862.

[2] *Journ. Agr.* 2:379. 1831.

[3] Johnson, C. P. *Useful Pls. Gt. Brit.* 226. 1862. (*M. perennis*)

[4] Firminger, T. A. C. *Gard. Ind.* 158. 1874.

[5] Mueller, F. *Sel. Pls.* 185. 1880.

[6] Unger, F. *U. S. Pat. Off. Rpt.* 347. 1859.

[7] Mueller, F. *Sel. Pls.* 278. 1891.

[8] Brewer and Watson *Bot. Cal.* 251. 1880.

[9] Parry *Bot. U. S. Mex. Bound. Surv.* 16. 1859.

[10] Smith, J. *Dict. Econ. Pls.* 174. 1882.

[11] Hooker, W. J. *Journ. Bot.* 9:266. 1857.

[12] Thunberg, C. P. *Trav.* 2:89. 1796.

M. crystallinum Linn. ICE PLANT.

Cape of Good Hope. The ice plant was introduced into Europe in 1727.[1] It is advertised in American seed lists[2] of 1881 as a desirable vegetable for boiling like spinach, or for garnishing. Vilmorin[3] says the thickness and slightly acid flavor of the fleshy parts of the leaves have caused it to be used as a fresh table vegetable for summer use in warm, dry countries. It is, however, he adds, not without merit as an ornamental plant. Parry[4] found this species growing in large masses in southern California.

M. edule Linn. HOTTENTOT FIG.

Cape of Good Hope. The mucilaginous capsules, says Captain Carmichael, are the chief material of an agreeable preserve. Figuier[5] says the leaves are pickled as a substitute for the pickled cucumber, and Henfrey says the foliage is eaten at the Cape.

M. forskahlei Hochst.

North Africa. The capsules are soaked and dried by the Bedouins, and the seeds separated for making bread, which, however, is not eaten by other Arabs.

M. pugioniforme Linn.

South Africa. Its leaves form a good substitute for spinach.[6]

M. tortuosum Linn.

South Africa. This species possesses narcotic properties and is chewed by the Hottentots for the purpose of producing intoxication.[7]

Mesua ferrea Linn. *Guttiferae.* IRONWOOD.

Java and East Indies. The fruit is reddish and wrinkled when ripe, with a rind like that of the chestnut. It resembles a chestnut in size, shape, substance and taste.[8]

Metroxylon laeve Mart. *Palmae.* SPINELESS SAGO PALM.

East Indies. This species furnishes a large part of the sago which is exported to Europe.[9, 10]

M. rumphii Mart. PRICKLY SAGO PALM.

East Indies. This palm furnishes, says Seemann,[11] the best sago of the East Indies.

M. sagu Rottb. SAGO PALM.

Sumatra and Malacca. The plant is employed in the preparation of sago for food.

---

[1] Noisette *Man. Jard.* 538. 1829.

[2] Thorburn *Cat.* 1881.

[3] Vilmorin *Veg. Gard.* 275. 1885.

[4] Parry *Bot. U. S. Mex. Bound. Surv.* 2:16. 1859.

[5] Figuier *Veg. World* 438. 1867.

[6] Smith, A. *Treas. Bot.* 2:738. 1870.

[7] Ibid.

[8] Drury, H. *Useful Pls. Ind.* 291. 1873.

[9] Smith, A. *Treas. Bot.* 2:1006. 1870.

[10] Seemann, B. *Pop. Hist. Palms* 263. 1856.

[11] Ibid.

Considerable quantities are made at the Poggy Islands, lying off the west coast of Sumatra, where it forms the principal food of the inhabitants.[1]

M. vitiense Benth. & Hook. f. SAGO PALM.

This is a true sago palm in Viti but its quality, Seemann[2] says, was not known to the natives until he pointed it out to them.

Michelia champaca Linn. *Magnoliaceae.* CHAMPACA. FRAGRANT CHAMPACA.

Malay. The fruit is said to be edible, and in India the tree is cultivated for the exquisite perfume of the flowers.[3]

Micromeria juliana Benth. *Labiatae.* SAVORY.

East Mediterranean region. This savory is mentioned by Gerarde,[4] 1597, as sown in gardens. It is a native of the Mediterranean countries, called in Greece, *ussopo*, in Egypt, *pesalem*.[5] It has disappeared from our seed catalogs.

M. obovata Benth.

West Indies and introduced in Britain in 1783. The species has two varieties. It was recorded by Burr,[6] 1863, as in American gardens but as little used. It is said to be much used for seasoning in its native country. It is now recorded as in cultivation in Europe.

Microseris forsteri Hook. f. *Compositae.*

Australia and New Zealand. This is the native scorzonera of tropical Australia and New Zealand. The root is used as a food by the aborigines.[7] The roots are roasted by the natives and eaten. They have an agreeable taste.[8]

M. sp.?

This plant furnishes a small, succulent, and almost transparent root, full of a bitterish, milky juice. The root is eaten raw by the Nez Percé Indians.[9]

Milium nigricans Ruiz & Pav. *Gramineae.*

Peru. A drink called *ullpu* is obtained from the farina of the seeds.[10]

Millettia atropurpurea Benth. *Leguminosae.*

A tree of Burma and Malay. The tender leaves are said to be eaten.[11]

---

[1] Griffith, W. *Palms Brit. Ind.* 25. 1850. (*Sagus laevis*)

[2] Seemann, B. *Fl. Viti.* 279. 1865–73.

[3] Don, G. *Hist. Dichl. Pls.* 1:81. 1831.

[4] Gerarde, J. *Herb.* 461. 1597.

[5] Pickering, C. *Chron. Hist. Pls.* 343. 1879. (*Satureia juliana*)

[6] Burr, F. *Field, Gard. Veg.* 442. 1863. (*Satureia viminea*)

[7] Mueller, F. *Sel. Pls.* 280. 1891.

[8] Hooker, W. J. *Journ. Bot.* **9**:266. 1857. (*Scorzonera lawrencii*)

[9] *U. S. D. A. Rpt.* 409. 1870. (*Scorzonella ptilophora*)

[10] *Treas. Bot.* **2**:1187. 1876.

[11] Wallich *Pl. Asiat.* **1**:70. Tab. 78. 1830–32.

Mimusops elata Allem. *Sapotaceae.* COW TREE.

Brazil. To this species is referred the *massaranduba*, or cow tree, of the Amazon. Wallace [1] says of it that the fruit is eatable and very good. It is the size of a small apple and full of a rich milk which exudes in abundance when the bark is cut. The milk has about the consistency of thick cream and, but for a very slight, peculiar taste, could scarcely be distinguished from the genuine product of the cow. Bates [2] says the fruit is eaten in Para, where it is sold in the streets. The milk is pleasant with coffee but has a slight rankness when drunk pure; it soon thickens to a glue which is excessively tenacious. He was told that it was not safe to drink much of it. Herndon [3] probably refers to this tree when he says he obtained from the Indians the milk of the cow tree, which they drink fresh, and, when brought to him in a calabash, had a foamy appearance as if just drawn from the cow and looked very rich and tempting. It, however, coagulates very soon and becomes as hard and tenacious as glue.

M. elengi Linn. MEDLAR.

East Indies and Malay. This plant is cultivated on account of its fragrant, star-shaped flowers, which are used in garlands. The small, ovoid, one-seeded berry, yellow when ripe, about an inch long, is eaten, and oil is expressed from the seeds.[4] Dutt [5] says the fruits are sweetish and edible when ripe.

M. hexandra Roxb.

East Indies and south India. This plant is commonly cultivated near villages. In Java, it is cultivated for its fruits which are eaten.[6]

M. kauki Linn.

Burma, Malay and Australia. This tree is found in gardens in Java. The fruit is edible.[7] Dr. Hooker [8] states that this tree is cultivated in China, Manila and Malabar for its esculent, agreeably acid fruit. It is the *khirnee* of India.[9]

M. kummel Bruce.

Abyssinia. This is the *M'nyemvee* of interior Africa, a lofty tree whose one-stoned, dry, orange-yellow or reddish fruit is sweet in taste.[10]

M. manilkara G. Don.

Malabar and the Philippines. This species is cultivated for its fruit, which is of the form and size of an olive and is succulent; the pulp is of a sweetish-acid flavor and contains but one or two seeds.[11]

---

[1] Wallace, A. R. *Trav. Amaz.* 28. 1853.

[2] Bates, H. W. *Nat. Amaz.* Humboldt *Libr. Sci.* 635. 1879-80.

[3] Herndon, W. L., and Gibbon, L. *Explor. Vall. Amaz.* 1:227. 1854.

[4] Brandis, D. *Forest Fl.* 293, 294. 1876.

[5] Dutt, U. C. *Mat. Med. Hindus* 188. 1877.

[6] Brandis, D. *Forest Fl.* 291. 1876. (*M. indica*)

[7] Unger, F. *U. S. Pat. Off. Rpt.* 337. 1859. (*M. balota*)

[8] Firminger, T. A. C. *Gard. Ind.* 255. 1874.

[9] Ibid.

[10] Speke, J. H. *Journ. Disc. Source Nile* 574. 1864.

[11] Don, G. *Hist. Dichl. Pls.* 4:35. 1838.

M. sieberi A. DC.   NASEBERRY.

North America and West Indies.   The fruit is delicious and highly flavored.[1]

Mitchella repens Linn.   *Rubiaceae.*   PARTRIDGE-BERRY.   SQUAW-VINE.

North America and Japan.   The insipid, red fruits are eaten by children.

Mollugo hirta Thunb.   *Ficoideae.*

Tropical and subtropical regions.   This plant is a common potherb in upper India.[2]

Momordica balsamina Linn.   *Cucurbitaceae.*   BALSAM APPLE.

Borders of the tropics.   The balsam apple has purgative qualities but is eaten by the Chinese after careful washing in warm water and subsequent cooking.[3]

M. charantia Linn.

Borders of the tropics.   This vine is very commonly cultivated about Bombay.   In the wet season, the fruit is 12 or 15 inches long, notched and ridged like a crocodile's back and requires to be steeped in salt water before being cooked.[4]   Firminger [5] says the fruit is about the size and form of a hen's egg, pointed at the ends, and covered with little blunt tubercles, of intensely bitter taste, but is much consumed by the natives and is agreeable also to Europeans as an ingredient to flavor their curries by way of variety.   In Patna, there are two varieties: *jethwya*, a plant growing in the heat of spring and dying with the first rains, and *bara masiya*, which lasts throughout the year.   In France, it is grown in the flower garden.[6]

M. dioica Roxb.

East Indies.   This species is under cultivation in India for food purposes; the root is edible.[7]   There are several varieties, says Drury.[8]   The young, green fruits and tuberous roots of the female plant are eaten by the natives, and, in Burma, according to Mason,[9] the small, muricated fruit is occasionally eaten.   At Bombay, this plant is cultivated for the fruit, which is the size of a pigeon's egg and knobbed, says Graham.[10]

Monarda didyma Linn.   *Labiatae.*   BEE BALM.   OSWEGO TEA.

From New England to Wisconsin northward, and southward in the Alleghanies.   It is mentioned by McMahon,[11] 1806, in his list of aromatic pot and sweet herbs.   It is called Oswego tea from the use sometimes made of its leaves.   In France, it is grown in the flower gardens.[12]

---

[1] Vasey   *U. S. D. A. Rpt.* 166.   1875.

[2] Ainslie, W.   *Mat. Ind.* 2:345.   1826.   (*Pharnaceum pentagoneum*)

[3] Smith, F. P.   *Contrib. Mat. Med. China* 91.   1871.

[4] Pickering, C.   *Chron. Hist. Pls.* 462.   1879.

[5] Firminger, T. A. C.   *Gard. Ind.* 125.   1874.

[6] Vilmorin *Fl. Pl. Ter.* 705.   1870.   3rd Ed.

[7] Royle, J. F.   *Illustr. Bot. Himal.* 1:219.   1839.

[8] Drury, H.   *Useful. Pls. Ind.* 296.   1873.

[9] Pickering *Chron. Hist. Pls.* 843.   1879.

[10] Ibid.

[11] McMahon, B.   *Amer. Gard. Cal.* 583.   1806.   (*M. punctata*)

[12] Vilmorin *Fl. Pl. Ter.* 708.   1870.   3rd Ed.

Moneses grandiflora S. F. Gray. *Ericaceae.* MOSSBERRY. ONE-FLOWERED PYROLA.

North and Arctic regions. The fruit is used as food by the Indians of Alaska. The yield of berries is scant, however.[1]

Monochoria vaginalis Presl. *Pontederiaceae.*

Asia and African tropics. This species is esteemed as a medical plant in Japan, Java and on the Coromandel Coast. Its young shoots are edible.[2]

Monodora myristica Dun. *Anonaceae.* JAMAICA NUTMEG.

This tree of Jamaica is supposed to have been introduced from South America, but is with more reason believed to have been taken by the negroes from the west coast of Africa. It is cultivated in Jamaica for its fruits, which furnish Jamaica nutmeg. The seeds contain a quantity of aromatic oil which imparts to them the odor and flavor of nutmegs.[3]

Monstera deliciosa Liebm. *Aroideae.* CERIMAN.

American tropics. This fine plant has been somewhat cultivated in England for its fruit and may now be seen in greenhouses in this country. The leaves are broad, perforated and dark, shining green. The fruit consists of the spadix, the eatable portion of which is of fine texture and very rich, juicy and fragrant, with a flavor somewhat like that of the pineapple and banana combined. The fruit is filled with a sort of spicule, which, unless the fruit be thoroughly ripe, interferes with the pleasure of its eating. In 1874, specimens of the fruit were exhibited before the Massachusetts Horticultural Society and again in 1881. Dobrizhoffer,[4] in his *Account of the Abipones of Paraguay,* 1784, refers to a fruit called *guembe* which is " the more remarkable for its being so little known, even by many who have grown old in Paraguay, for the northern woods of that country only are its native soil. It is about a span long, almost cylindrical in shape, being thicker than a man's fist in the middle but smaller at both extremities, and resembles a pigeon stripped of its feathers, sometimes weighing as much as two pounds. It is entirely covered with a soft, yellowish skin, marked with little knobs and a dark spot in the middle. Its liquid pulp has a very sweet taste but is full of tender thorns, perceivable by the palate only, not by the eye, on which account it must be slowly chewed but quickly swallowed. . . . The stalk which occupies the middle, has something of wood in it and must be thrown away. You cannot imagine how agreeable and wholesome this fruit is. . . . This ponderous fruit grows on a flexible shrub resembling a rope, which entwines itself around high trees." If this description applies to our species, it is certainly remarkable that this ancient missionary did not refer to the open spaces in the leaves.

Moraea edulis Ker-Gawl. *Irideae.*

South Africa. The bulbous root is eaten by the Hottentots. When cooked, it has

---

[1] *U. S. D. A. Rpt.* 414. 1870. (*M. uniflora*)

[2] Case *Bot. Index* 25. 1879.

[3] Smith, A. *Treas. Bot.* 2:752. 1870.

[4] Dobrizhoffer *Acct. Abipones* 1:380. 1784.

the taste of potatoes.[1]   Thunberg [2] says, in Kaffraria, the roots were eaten roasted, boiled, or stewed with milk and appeared to him to be both palatable and nourishing, tasting much like potatoes.

Morinda citrifolia Linn. *Rubiaceae.* AWL TREE. INDIAN MULBERRY.

Tropical shores in Hindustan, throughout the Malayan Archipelago and neighboring Polynesian islands.   Its fruit is a great favorite with the Burmese, served in their curries.[3]   Labillardière [4] says the fruit is in great request among the Friendly Islanders, but its taste is insipid.   Captain Cook states that the fruit is eaten in Tahiti in times of scarcity, and that the taste is very indifferent.

M. tinctoria Roxb. ACH-ROOT. DYERS' MULBERRY.

East Indies and Malay.   According to Brandis,[5] this species is cultivated throughout India.   Don says the green fruits are pickled and eaten with curries.

Moringa aptera Gaertn. *Moringeae.*

Nubia and Arabia.   The seeds are exported to Syria and Palestine for medicinal and alimentary use.[6]

M. concanensis Nimmo.

East Indies and India.   The unripe fruit is eaten.[7]

M. pterygosperma Gaertn. HORSERADISH TREE.

Northwest India.   The horseradish tree is cultivated for its fruit, which is eaten as a vegetable and preserved as a pickle, and for its leaves and flowers which are likewise eaten.[8]   Dutt [9] says it is cultivated for its leaves, flowers and seed-vessels, which are used by the natives in their curries.   The root, says Royle,[10] is universally known to European residents in India as a substitute for horseradish.   Ainslie [11] says the root is generally used and the pods are an excellent vegetable.   According to Firminger,[12] the root serves as a horseradish and the long, unripe seed-pods are used boiled in curries.   It is also cultivated by the Burmese for its pods, but by Europeans it is chiefly valued for its roots.[13]   In the Philippines, the leaves and fruit are cooked and eaten.[14]   In the West Indies, the oil expressed from the seeds is used in salads.[15]

---

[1] Pickering, C. *Chron. Hist. Pls.* 230. 1879. (*Vieusseuxia edulis*)

[2] Thunberg, C. P. *Trav.* 1:144. 1795. (*Iris edulis*)

[3] Pickering, C. *Chron. Hist. Pls.* 423. 1879. (*M. bracteata*)

[4] Labillardière *Voy. Recherche Pérouse* 2:153. 1799.

[5] Brandis, D. *Forest Fl.* 278. 1874.

[6] Baillon, H. *Hist. Pls.* 3:170. 1874.

[7] Brandis, D. *Forest Fl.* 130. 1874.

[8] Ibid.

[9] Dutt, U. C. *Mat. Med. Hindus* 117. 1877.

[10] Royle, J. F. *Illustr. Bot. Himal.* 1:180. 1839.

[11] Ainslie, W. *Mat. Ind.* 1:175. 1826.

[12] Firminger *Gard. Ind.* 130. 1874. (*Hyperanthera moringa*)

[13] Pickering, C. *Chron. Hist. Pls.* 298. 1879.

[14] Ibid.

[15] Ibid.

Moronobea grandiflora Choizy. *Guttiferae.*

A tall tree of Brazil. Arruda [1] says the fruit is nearly of the size of an orange but is oval and contains 23 stones covered with a white pulp of a pleasant taste, being sweet and somewhat acid. It is called *bacuri.*

Morus alba Linn. *Urticaceae.* WHITE MULBERRY.

A tree of China and Japan but naturalized in Europe, Asia and America. It is commonly supposed, says Thompson, [2] that cuttings of the white mulberry were first brought into Tuscany from the Levant in 1434 and in the course of the century this species had almost entirely superceded *M. nigra* for the feeding of silk worms in Italy. The variety *multicaulis* was brought from Manila to Senegal, and some years afterwards to Europe, and was described by Kenrick, [3] 1835, preceding which date it had reached America. In 1773 or 1774, Wm. Bartram [4] noticed large plantations of *M. alba* grafted on *M. rubra* near Charleston, S. C., for the purpose of feeding silk worms, but it is probable that its first introduction was coeval with the interest in silk culture before 1660. The mulberry trees planted in Virginia in 1623 by order of the Colonial Assembly were probably of this species. There are many varieties of *M. alba,* and in India it is cultivated for its fruit, of which some kinds are sweet, some acid, and of all shades of color from white to a deep blackish-purple. In Kashmir and Afghanistan, the fruit furnishes a considerable portion of the food of the inhabitants in autumn and much of it is dried and preserved. [5] In Kabul, there is a white, seedless variety called *shah-toot,* or royal mulberry. The fruits are from two to two and one-half inches long and of the thickness of the small finger, very sweet, and the tree is inexhaustibly prolific. In its season it forms the chief food of the poor. [6]

M. celtidifolia H. B. & K.

Peru to Mexico. The tree bears an edible fruit. [7]

M. indica Linn. AINO MULBERRY.

Tropical Asia. The aino mulberry is cultivated in Bengal for feeding silk worms, [8] and about Bombay its dark red fruit is sold in the bazaars for making tarts.

M. laevigata Wall.

East Indies. This species is found wild and cultivated in the Himalayas and elsewhere in India. The fruit is long, cylindrical, yellowish-white, sweet but insipid. [9] The long, cylindrical, purple fruit is much eaten. [10]

---

[1] Koster, H. *Trav. Braz.* 363. 1817. (*M. esculenta*)
[2] Thompson, R. *Treas. Bot.* 2:758. 1870.
[3] Kenrick, W. *New Amer. Orch.* 225. 1835.
[4] *Hist. Mass. Hort. Soc.* 27. 1880.
[5] Brandis, D. *Forest Fl.* 407. 1876.
[6] Harlan *U. S. Pat. Off. Rpt.* 529. 1861.
[7] Mueller, F. *Sel. Pls.* 285. 1891.
[8] Pickering, C. *Chron. Hist. Pls.* 570. 1879.
[9] Brandis, D. *Forest Fl.* 409. 1874.
[10] Royle, J. F. *Illustr. Bot. Himal.* 1:337. 1839.

M. nigra Linn. BLACK MULBERRY.

Temperate Asia. The black mulberry is a native of north Persia and the Caucasus. It was brought at a very early period to Greece. Theophrastus was acquainted with it and called it *sukamnos*. It is only at a late period that this tree, brought by Lucius Vitellus from Syria to Rome, was successfully reared in Italy, after all earlier experiments, according to Pliny, had been conducted in vain. At the time of Palladius and even in that of Athaneus, the mulberry tree had multiplied but little in that country. The introduction of silk culture under Justinian gave a new importance to this tree, and, from that time to the present, its propagation in western and northern Europe, Denmark and Sweden has taken place very rapidly. It was not till the sixteenth century that this plant was superceded by *M. alba* for the feeding of silk worms.[1] This species, according to Mueller,[2] was planted in France in 1500. In the United States, it is scarcely hardy north of New York, but there and southward it is occasionally cultivated for its fruit. In 1760, Jefferys[3] states it was not found in Louisiana.

M. rubra Linn. RED MULBERRY.

From New England to Illinois and southward.[4] The fruit is preferred, says Emerson,[5] to that of any other species by most people. The tree grows abundantly in northern Missouri and along the rivers of Kansas. In Indian Territory, the large, sweet, black fruit is greatly esteemed by the Indians. This fruit was observed by De Soto[6] on the route to Apalachee, and the tree was seen by Strachey[7] on James River planted around native dwellings.

M. serrata Roxb.

Himalayan region. This species is cultivated in Kunawar. It is common in the Himalayas. The purple fruit is mucilaginous and sweet but not very fleshy.[8]

Mouriria pusa Gardn. *Melastomaceae*. SILVERWOOD.

Brazil. Gardner[9] says the fruit of this Brazilian tree is about the size of a small plum, black in color and resembles much in taste the fruit of *Eugenia cauliflora*. In the province of Ceara, this fruit is much esteemed and is carried through the streets for sale by the Indians. It is called *pusa*.

M. rhizophoraefolia Gardn.

Martinique. The fruit is regularly sold in the markets at St. Vincent, but no high value is set upon it, owing to the very small quantity of sweet pulp which tenaciously

---

[1] Unger, F. *U. S. Pat. Off. Rpt.* 341. 1859.
[2] Mueller, F. *Sel. Pls.* 285. 1891. 8th Ed.
[3] Jefferys, T. *Nat. Hist. Amer.* 1:155. 1760.
[4] Gray, A. *Man. Bot.* 444. 1868.
[5] Emerson, G. B. *Trees, Shrubs Mass.* 1:315. 1875.
[6] Pickering, C. *Chron. Hist Pls.* 770. 1879.
[7] Ibid.
[8] Brandis, D. *Forest Fl.* 409. 1876.
[9] Gardner, G. *Trav. Braz.* 146. 1849.

adheres to the seeds. The outer portion of the fruit is not pleasant to the taste, but the seed has the flavor of filberts.[1]

Mucuna capitata Sweet. *Leguminosae.*

Malay Archipelago and the Himalayas. This species, according to Elliott,[2] is cultivated in native gardens in India and even among some of the Hill Tribes.

M. cochinchinensis Lour.

This species is cultivated in Cochin China for its legumes which are served and eaten as we do string beans.[3]

M. gigantea DC. COWITCH.

East Indies. The beans are eaten by the natives and are esteemed as both palatable and wholesome.[4]

M. monosperma DC. NEGRO BEAN.

East Indies. This is a favorite vegetable with Brahmins.[5]

M. nivea DC.

Bengal and Burma. This species is cultivated by the natives in India. Roxburgh[6] says that, by removing the velvety skin of the large, fleshy, tender pods, they are a most excellent vegetable for the table, and the full-grown beans are scarcely inferior to the large garden beans of Europe. Drury[7] reaffirms this opinion.

M. pruriens DC. COWITCH. COWHAGE.

Tropical Africa. The cowitch, or cowhage, has, says Livingstone,[8] a velvety covering to its pods of minute prickles, which, if touched, enter the pores of the skin and cause a painful tingling. The women, in times of scarcity, collect the pods, kindle a fire of grass over them to destroy the prickles, then soak the beans until they begin to sprout, wash them in pure water and either boil them or pound them into meal. Its name on the Zambezi is *kitedzi*.

M. urens Medic. HORSE-EYE BEAN.

In Jamaica, the legume is said by Plumier to have been eaten by the Caribs but Lunan[9] says it is poisonous.

Muntingia calabura Linn. *Tiliaceae.* CALABUR.

West Indies. This is the *guasem* of Jamaica. An infusion of the leaves is used in the Caracas as a tea.[10]

---

[1] Hooker, W. J. *Bot. Misc.* 1:124. 1830. (*Guildingia psidiodes*)

[2] Elliott, W. *Bot. Soc. Edinb.* 7:297. 1863.

[3] Don, G. *Hist. Dichl. Pls.* 2:342. 1832. (*Macranthus cochinchinensis*)

[4] Hooker, W. J. *Bot. Misc.* 2:352. 1831.

[5] Drury, H. *Useful Pls. Ind.* 299. 1873.

[6] Firminger, T. A. C. *Gard. Ind.* 149. 1874.

[7] Drury, H. *Useful Pls. Ind.* 299. 1873.

[8] Livingstone, D. & C. *Exped. Zambesi* 503. 1866.

[9] Lunan, J. *Hort. Jam.* 1:383. 1814.

[10] *Treas. Bot.* 2:1301. 1876.

Murraya exotica Linn. *Rutaceae.* CHINESE BOX.

Asia and Australian tropics. The fruit is red and edible.[1]

M. koenigii Spreng. CURRY-LEAF TREE.

A tree of tropical Hindustan, cultivated for its leaves, which are used to flavor curries. The leaves are aromatic and fragrant and, with the root and bark, are used medicinally. From the seeds, a medicinal oil called *zimbolee* oil is extracted.[2]

M. longifolia Blume.

Java. The fruit is edible.[3]

Musa chinensis Sweet. *Scitamineae.* CHINESE DWARF BANANA.

China. This very delicious plantain, says Firminger,[4] is of a rich and peculiar flavor. The fruits are borne in enormous bunches, each fruit about 10 inches long, of moderate and uniform shape and thickness, and when ripe are pea-green in color. The bananas are exceedingly difficult to obtain in perfection, as they are uneatable until quite ripe, and on becoming ripe, commence almost immediately to decay. This variety, in 1841, was grown in abundance for the table of the King of France at Versailles and Menton. In 1867, young plants of this dwarf banana were sent to Florida from the United States Department of Agriculture, and now they may be seen quite generally in gardens there. It is quite frequently fruited in greenhouses, being of easy culture and management. Hawkins,[5] 1593, saw small, round, plantains, " green when they are ripe " in Brazil.

M. ensete J. F. Gmel. ABYSSINIAN BANANA.

Tropical Africa. The fruit is dry and inedible, containing a few large, stony seeds, but, says Masters,[6] the base of the flower-stalk is cooked and eaten by the natives. Unger[7] says the fruit is not palatable and is rarely eaten, but the white, marrowy portion of the young stems, freed from the rind and cooked, has the taste of the best wheat bread and, dressed with milk and butter, supplies a very excellent, wholesome diet. The plant occurs even in the Egyptian antiques and seems to have been more widely distributed at an earlier period than at the present. There are large plantations of it at Maitsha and Goutto. The tree grows about 20 feet high and is a striking ornament in our best conservatories.

M. maculata Jacq. BANANA.

Mauritius Islands. The fruit is very spicy and of excellent flavor. This is a tender banana not profitable for cultivation above south Florida.[8]

---

[1] Don, G. *Hist. Dichl. Pls.* 1:585. 1831.

[2] Masters, M. T. *Treas. Bot.* 1:136. 1870. (*Bergera königii*)

[3] Don, G. *Hist. Dichl. Pls.* 1:585. 1831.

[4] Firminger, T. A. C. *Gard. Ind.* 181. 1874.

[5] Hawkins, R. *Voy. So. Seas* 1593. Hakl. Soc. Ed. 50, 93. 1847.

[6] Masters, M. T. *Treas. Bot.* 2:765. 1874.

[7] Unger, F. *U. S. Pat. Off. Rpt.* 352. 1859.

[8] Van Deman *U. S. D. A. Pom. Bul.* No. 1:37. 1887.

M. rosacea Jacq. BANANA.

Tropical Asia. This is the *vai* of Cook, the *fahie* of Wilkes, the *fae* of the natives. It was seen by Wilkes [1] in groves in Tahiti, the fruit borne on an upright spike, of the shape of the banana but twice as large and of a deep golden hue, with pulp of a dark orange color. It is destitute of seeds, of high flavor and greatly esteemed by the natives. On the Fiji Islands, it is found cultivated. The fruit is eaten either roasted or boiled. Ellis [2] says there are nearly 20 kinds of wild bananas, very large and serviceable, in the mountains of Tahiti. In India, says Firminger,[3] this species is called *ram kela* and, when in good condition, is a remarkably fine fruit. The fruit is about seven inches long and rather thin, at first of a very dark red, but ripening to a yellowish-red.

M. sapientum Linn. ADAM'S FIG. BANANA. PLANTAIN.

In general, says Humboldt,[4] the musa, known by every people in the Torrid Zone, though hitherto never found in a wild state, has as great a variety of fruit as the apple or pear. The names " plantain " and " banana " are very discriminately applied, but the term plantain is usually restricted to the larger plants whose fruits are eaten cooked, while the term banana is given to sorts whose fruits are eaten raw. The plantain, says Forster,[5] varies almost *ad infinitum*, like our apple. At Tongatabu, says Captain Cook, they have 15 sorts of plantain. In Tenasserim, says Simmonds,[6] there are 20 varieties, in Ceylon 10 and in Burma 30. The Dacca plantain is 9 inches long. In Madagascar, the plantains are as large as a man's forearm. In the mountains of the Philippines, a single bunch is said to be a load for a man. The banana is cultivated in more varieties in India than is the plantain, says Roxburgh.[7] The plantain is abundant in Africa, according to Burton [8] and other African travelers. In Peru, according to Herndon [9] and others, it abounds. One of the dainties of the Mosquito Indians, says Bancroft,[10] is *bisbire*, the name given to plantains kept in leaves till putrid; it is eaten boiled. The plantain is unquestionably of ancient culture, for one of the Mohammedan traditions is that the leaves used for girdles by Adam and Eve were plantain leaves. Plantains with fruit from 10 to 12 inches long were grown in Louisiana in 1855 and probably earlier. The flesh was eaten roasted, fried or boiled.

It seems probable that the plantain, or banana, was cultivated in South America before the discovery by Columbus. It seems indigenous to the hot regions of the Old World and the New, or at any rate to have been present in the New World before the discovery by Columbus, as banana leaves are found in the *huacas*, or Peruvian tombs,

[1] Wilkes, C. *U. S. Explor. Exped.* 2:28. 1845.

[2] Ellis, W. *Polyn. Research.* 1:59. 1833.

[3] Firminger, T. A. C. *Gard. Ind.* 180. 1874. (*M. rubra*)

[4] Humboldt, A. *Trav.* 1:49. 1889.

[5] Forster *Obs.* 177. 1778.

[6] Simmonds, P. L. *Trop. Agr.* 462. 1889

[7] Roxburgh, W. *Pls. Corom. Coast* 3:74. 1819.

[8] Burton, F. *Lake Reg. Cent. Afr.* 316. 1860.

[9] Herndon, W. L., and Gibbon, L. *Explor. Vall. Amaz.* 1:86. 1854.

[10] Bancroft, H. H. *Native Races* 1:721. 1875.

anterior to the Conquest. Bancroft[1] says the Mexicans offered the "fat banana" at
the shrine of the goddess Centeotl. Roxburgh[2] found bananas growing wild on the coast
of Coromandel. Hooker[3] saw two species wild in the Himalayas. Rumphius and Blanco
saw them in the Philippines. Finlayson found them in the small island of Pulo-ubi near
Siam. Cook[4] and others saw them in Tahiti, and Humboldt mentions the occasional
occurrence of wild bananas in the forests of South America. Although the cultivated
varieties of banana and plantain are usually seedless, yet some wild species produce seeds,
and varieties of the cultivated form occasionally bear seeds. Thus, on the coast of Para,
near the Gulf of Triste, and near Cumaná, according to Humboldt, there are sorts with
seeds; as there are at Manila, according to Meyen;[5] and in Central Africa, according to
Burton.[6] The fruit of these is usually of poor quality. In Calcutta, 1503–08, Varthema[7]
mentions 3 kinds of bananas. Firminger,[8] at the present time names 7 varieties, and
Carey[9] says the cultivated varieties in Bengal are infinite. In Tahiti, according to
Ellis,[10] not fewer than 30 varieties of bananas are cultivated by the natives. In the Fiji
Islands, some 9 varieties are in cultivation according to Wilkes.[11] In Cercado, on the
Amazon, Castelanu[12] says there is an enormous number of varieties of bananas. In
Central Africa, Grant[13] names 6 varieties. Ten varieties are given for Ceylon and 30
for Burma.

The garden of Adam in Seyllan (Ceylon), says Morignolli,[14] about 1350, contains
plantain trees which the natives call figs: " but the plantain has more the character of
a garden plant than of a tree. At first they are not good to eat, but after they have been
kept a while in the house they ripen of themselves and are then of an excellent odor and
still better taste, and they are about the length of the longest of one's fingers." In Calicut,
1503–08, Varthema[15] describes three sorts: " The first sort is called *cianchapalon;* these
are very restorative things to eat. Their color is somewhat yellow, and the bark is very
thin. The second sort is called *cadelapalon,* and they are much superior to the others.
The third sort are bitter." The head of the flowers of the variety known as *kuntela,*
before the sheath in which they are enclosed expands, is often cut off, being esteemed a
most delicate vegetable.

[1] Bancroft, H. H.   *Native Races* 3:351.   1882.

[2] Roxburgh, W.   *Pls. Corom. Coast* 3:74.   1819.

[3] Hooker, J. D.   *Himal. Journ.* 1:143.   1854.

[4] Cook, Capt. *Voy.* 3:207.   1773.

[5] Darwin, C.   *Ans. Pls. Domest.* 2:152.   1893.   Note.

[6] Burton, F.   *Lake Reg. Cent. Afr.* 316.   1860.

[7] Jones, J. W.   *Trav. Varthema.*   Hakl. Soc. Ed. 162.   1863.

[8] Firminger, T. A. C.   *Gard. Ind.* 177–182.   1874.

[9] Roxburgh, W.   *Hort. Beng.* 18.   1814.

[10] Ellis, W.   *Polyn. Research.* 1:59.   1833.

[11] Wilkes, C.   *U. S. Explor. Exped.* 3:333.   1845.

[12] Herndon, W. L., and Gibbon, L.   *Explor. Vall. Amaz.* 1:177.   1854.

[13] Speke, J. H.   *Journ. Disc. Source Nile* 583.   1864.

[14] *Cathay, Way Thither.*   Hakl. Soc. Ed. 360.   1866.

[15] Jones, J. W.   *Trav. Varthema.*   Hakl. Soc. Ed. 162.   1863.

In the Malay Archipelago, says Wallace,[1] many species occur wild in the forests and some produce edible fruits. In 1591, at the Nicobar Islands, near Sumatra, the plantain was seen by May.[2] At Batavia, in 1770, Captain Cook found innumerable sorts but only three were good eating, although others were used for cooking. In New Guinea, in 1770, he found plantains flourishing in a state of the highest perfection. Le Maire,[3] 1616, says this fruit is called *tachouner*. In New Holland Captain Cook found the plantain tree bearing a very small fruit, the pulp well-tasted, but full of seeds, and in another place said to be so full of stones as scarcely to be edible. Both the banana and plantain are now cultivated in Australia in many varieties.

In Polynesia, Mendaña, in 1595, mentions " very fine plantains " at Mendaña Islands and elsewhere. In 1606, de Quiros saw plantains as appears from his memorial to the King of Spain. In 1588, Cavendish[4] had " plantains " brought out in boats to his ships and in 1625 Prince Maurice[5] of Nassau mentions bananas as brought to his ships. Easter Island, when discovered in 1722, had " plantains." In 1778, Captain Cook discovered the Sandwich Islands and found there the banana, and Wilkes,[6] in 1840, says bananas and plantains are abundant. The Fiji Islands were discovered by Tasman in 1643, and they were visited by D'Urville in 1827, although there had been intervening arrivals of Europeans. In 1840 Wilkes[7] found there five or six varieties of banana with insipid fruit and three varieties of plantain cultivated to a great extent, as also the wild species of Tahiti and Samoa. Tahiti was discovered by Wallis in 1767 and visited by Bougain-ville in 1768, and by Cook in 1769. In 1777 Captain Cook speaks of the plantain as being cultivated there and also of wild plantains in the mountains. Ellis[8] says the plantain and banana are indigenous and also cultivated in the native gardens. When Captain Cook discovered Wateroo Island, he found plantains and he mentions them at Atooi, the Annamooka Islands.

The banana is mentioned by Ramusio,[9] 1563–74, as being found in Africa. At the island of St. Thomas, off the coast of Guinea, he says " they have also began to plant that herb, which in one year grows to the height of a tree. It produces fruit like the figs called *muse* in Alexandria, and it is called *abellana* in this island." In 1593, Sir Richard Hawkins[10] says " the plantain is a tree found in most parts of Afrique and America," and describes the fruit as having many varieties: " some great, some lesser, some round, some square, some triangle, most ordinarily of a spanne long " and " no conserve is better, nor of a more pleasing taste." St. John, in his *Adventures in the Libyan Desert*, mentions

---

[1] Wallace, A. R. *Trop. Nat.* 254. 1895.

[2] May, Capt. H. *Voy.* 1591. Hakl. Voy. 10: 196. 1904.

[3] Le Maire and Schoutin *Voy.* 1615. Dalrymple *Coll.* 1770.

[4] *Lives, Voy. Cavendish, Drake* 141. 1854.

[5] *Enc. Brit.* 18:269. 1859.

[6] Wilkes, C. *U. S. Explor. Exped.* 3:333. 1845.

[7] Ibid.

[8] Ellis, W. *Polyn. Research.* 1:59. 1833.

[9] Ramusio *Gen. Coll. Voy. Portugese* 434. 1789.

[10] Hawkins, R. *Voy. So. Seas* 1593. Hakl. Soc. Ed. 49. 1847.

the banana as growing in some of the valleys and in the osais of Siwah. Grant [1] found the plantain the staple ood of the countries one degree on either side of the equator. There are half a dozen varieties, he says, the boiling, baking, drying, fruit and wine-making sorts. The fruit dried, from Ugigi, is like a Normandy pippin; a variety when green and boiled is an excellent vegetable, while another yields a wine resembling hock in flavor. Long [2] says, in Uganda, this fruit grows wild in the greatest luxuriance. The tree is very large and the watery matter contained in the stock serves the natives of Uganda for water, when they cannot procure it elsewhere. The banana is scarcely ever eaten in the ripe state, save by the females, who extract from it an unfermented and delicious liquor. Burton [3] says, in certain parts about Lake Tanganyika, the banana is the staff of life and is apparently an aboriginal of these latitudes. In the hilly countries, there are said to be about a dozen varieties, and a single bunch forms a load for a man. It is found on the islands and on the coast of Zanzibar and rarely in the mountains of Usagara. The best fruit is that grown by the Arabs at Unyamyembe, but this is a poor specimen, coarse and insipid, stringy and full of seeds. Upon the Tanganyika lake, there is a variety larger than the horse-plantain of India, of which the skin is brick-reddish, in places inclined to a rusty brown, the pulp a dull yellow and contains black seeds. The flavor is harsh, strong and drug-like.

In 1526, Thomas Nicols,[4] writing of the " plantano " of the Canary Islands, says it " is like a cucumber and when it is ripe it is blacke and in eating more delicate than any conserve." Oviedo,[5] 1516, says the banana was transplanted hence to the Island of Hispaniola, but the Dominique variety, which is supposed to be the one, does not answer to the description of Nicols. In the Cape Verde Islands, plantains are mentioned as seen by Cavendish at S. Jago in 1586 and also at Fogo Island.

The leaves of the banana, according to Prescott,[6] have been frequently found in the *huacas* of Peru, and plantains and bananas were brought to Pizarro on his visit to Tumbez in 1527. Garcilasso de la Vega [7] says that in the time of the Incas the banana, in the warm and temperate regions, formed the base of the nourishment of the natives. He describes the *musa* of the valley of the Andes; he distinguishes also the small, sweet and aromatic *dominico* and the common banana or *arton*. Oviedo [8] contends that it is not indigenous to the New World but was introduced to Hispaniola in 1516 by Father Thomas de Berlanger and that he transplanted it from the Canary Islands, whither the original slips had been brought from the East Indies. Acosta [9] says " it is the fruits they use most at the Indies and in general in all places, although they say the first beginning comes from Ethiopia." He also says " there is a kinde of small planes, white and very delicate, which in Hispaniola they call *dominiques*. There are others which are stronger and bigger

[1] Speke, J. H.   *Journ. Disc. Source Nile* 533.   1864.

[2] Long, C. C.   *Cent. Afr.* 126.   1877.

[3] Burton, R. F.   *Lake Reg. Cent. Afr.* 316.   1860.

[4] Nicols, Thomas   *Voy.* Hakl. Voy.   **6:**129.   1904.

[5] Robinson, W.   *Hist. Amer.* 476.   1856.

[6] Prescott, W. H.   *Conq. Peru* **1:**139.   1860.   Note.

[7] De Candolle, A.   *Geog. Bot.* **2:**921.   1855.

[8] Robinson, W.   *Hist. Amer.* 476.   1856.   Note.

[9] Acosta *Nat. Mor. Hist. Ind.*   Hakl. Soc. Ed. **1:**243.   1880.

and red of color. There growes none in the Kingdom of Peru but are brought from the Indies, as from Mexico, Guernavaca and other vallies. Upon the firme land and in some islands there are great store of *planes* like unto thick groves." There is a tradition current in Mexico, says Humboldt,[1] that the *platans arton* and the *dominico* varieties were cultivated long before the arrival of the Spaniards. Piso,[2] 1648, says the plant was imported into Brazil and has no Brazilian name, but Lery,[3] 1578, says it is called *paco*. In Columbus' fourth voyage, at Costa Rica, in 1503, Las Casas[4] says " the country produced bananas, plantains, pineapples, cocoanuts, and other fruit." According to Irving,[5] bananas were likewise seen on Guatemala. In 1538, De Soto[6] saw plantains in Cuba. In 1565, Bensoni,[7] in his *History of the New World* says, " the plantain is a fruit much longer than it is broad, and the little ones are much better than the large ones." In 1593, Hawkins[8] writes that the best he has seen in Brazil is on an island called Placentia and these are " small and round and green when they are ripe, whereas the others in ripening become yellow. Those of the West Indies and Guynne are great, and one of them sufficient to satisfie a man." In 1595, Captain Preston and Sommers[9] had plantains brought them from Dominica Island, and the same year Captain Drake found great stores of them at Nombre de Dios. Herrera,[10] who wrote a *General History of the Indies* from 1492 to 1554, says, at Quito, " the plantans have the relish of dry figs but eaten green their taste cannot be ascertained." About 1800, Humboldt[11] ate the fruit of the *dominico* variety on the banks of the Amazon. At the present time, says Herndon,[12] *plantanos*, which is the general name of all kinds of plantains of which last there are several species, are the most common fruit of the Montana. The people eat them raw, roasted, boiled, baked and fried. At Santa Barbara, California, they were growing in the mission gardens in 1793.[13]

M. simiarum Kurz.

From Malacca to the Sunda Islands. About 50 varieties of this species are under cultivation and are called *peesangs*. It surpasses *M. sapientum* in delicacy of flavor.[14]

Muscari racemosum Mill. *Liliaceae.* GRAPE-HYACINTH.

Mediterranean and Caucasian region. The bulbs are eaten in Crete, Zacynthus and Corcyra, as well as in Italy, according to Sprengel.[15]

[1] De Candolle, A. *Geog. Bot.* 2:921. 1855.
[2] De Candolle, A. *Geog. Bot.* 2:924. 1855.
[3] Pickering, C. *Chron. Hist. Pls.* 663. 1879.
[4] Irving, W. *Columbus* 2:349. 1849.
[5] Irving, W. *Columbus* 2:322. 1849.
[6] Pickering, C. *Chron. Hist. Pls.* 663. 1879.
[7] Benzoni *Hist. New World* 1572. Hakl. Soc. Ed. 21:87. 1857.
[8] Hawkins, R. *Voy. So. Seas* 1593. Hakl. Soc. Ed. 50, 93. 1847.
[9] Preston and Sommers 1595. Hakl. Voy. 4:62. 1904.
[10] Herrera *Hist. Amer.* Stevens Trans. 5:61. 1740.
[11] Humboldt, A. *Polit. Essay New Spain* 2:292. 1811.
[12] Herndon, W. L., and Gibbon, L. *Explor. Vall. Amaz.* 86. 1854.
[13] Vancouver, G. *Voy. No. Pacific* 4:401. 1801.
[14] Van Deman *U. S. D. A. Pom. Bul.* 1:37. 1887.
[15] Pickering, C. *Chron. Hist. Pls.* 351. 1879.

Mussaenda frondosa Linn. *Rubiaceae.*

A large shrub of tropical eastern Asia and the neighboring islands. This shrub is common in the Ghauts of India, and its strange-looking, white, calycine leaves are eaten.[1]

Myrica cordifolia Linn. *Myricaceae.* MYRICA.

South Africa. The farmers use the wax from the berries for candles, but the Hottentots eat this wax either with or without meat.[2]

M. faya Ait. CANDLEBERRY MYRTLE.

Madeira, Azores and Canary Islands. This is a small tree whose drupaceous fruits are used for preserves.[3]

M. gale Linn. SWEET GALE.

Of northern climates. The French in Canada call it *laurier* and put the leaves into broth to give it a pleasant taste.[4] In England, the leaves are sometimes used to flavor beer as an agreeable substitute for hops. The berries are employed in France as a spice.[5]

M. nagi Thunb.

Tropical Asia and subtropics. This is the *yang-mae* of China, the *yamomomoki* of Japan and is commonly cultivated in these countries, being held in esteem for its subacid fruits, which are eaten both raw and cooked. They are round, one-seeded drupes of deep red color, with a tuberculated or granulated surface resembling that of the fruit of the strawberry tree.[6] Fortune[7] refers to a species, probably this, called *yang-mae* in China. The wild variety *san*, is a fine Chinese fruit tree usually grafted upon *M. sapida*. It is called *sophee* in Silhet, where the fruit is eaten both raw and cooked.[8] It has an agreeably-flavored fruit, though with too large a stone in proportion to the fleshy part; but this, says Royle,[9] might probably be remedied by cultivation. This fruit tree would probably repay the trouble of culture. The fruit is eaten in India, says Brandis,[10] and is sold in the bazaars of the hills.

Myristica acuminata Lam. *Myristiceae.* NUTMEG.

Madagascar. This species yields nutmegs in Brazil, in the Philippine Islands and in Madagascar.

M. fragrans Houtt. NUTMEG.

Moluccas. The nutmeg tree is found wild in Giolo, Ceram, Amboina, Booro, the western peninsula of New Guinea and in many of the adjacent islands. It has been intro-

---

[1] Pickering, C. *Chron. Hist. Pls.* 300. 1879.
[2] Thunberg, C. P. *Trav.* 1:167. 1795.
[3] Mueller, F. *Sel. Pls.* 289. 1891.
[4] Kalm, P. *Trav. No. Amer.* 2:345. 1772.
[5] Johnson, C. P. *Useful Pls. Gt. Brit.* 239. 1862.
[6] Moore, T. *Treas. Bot.* 2:1319. 1876.
[7] Fortune, R. *Resid. Chinese* 64, 65. 1857.
[8] Moore, T. *Treas. Bot.* 2:1319. 1876.
[9] Royle, J. F. *Illustr. Bot. Himal.* 1:347. 1839.
[10] Brandis, D. *Forest Fl.* 495. 1874.

duced into Benkoelen on the west coast of Sumatra, Malacca, Bengal, Singapore, Penang, Brazil and the West Indies, but it is only in a very few localities that its cultivation has been attended with success.[1]   Nutmegs and mace are now brought into the market almost entirely from the Banda Islands, the entire group occupying no more than 17.6 geographical miles.   The earliest accounts of the nutmeg are in the writings of the Arabian physicians.   They are known to have been at first imported overland into Europe and are mentioned under the name of *karua aromatika* in the addition to Aetius, also by Symeon Sethus.[2]   The fruit is much like a peach, having a longitudinal groove on one side, and bursts into two pieces when the enclosed seed, covered by the false aril or arillode, which constitutes the substance known as mace, is exposed.   The seed itself has a thick, hard, outer shell, which may be removed when dry and which encloses the nucleus of the seed, the nutmeg of commerce.

Myrrhis odorata Scop.   *Umbelliferae.*   ANISE.   MYRRH.   SWEET CHERVIL.   SWEET CICELY.
   South Europe and Asia Minor.   This plant was formerly much cultivated in England as a potherb but is now fallen into disuse.   The leaves were eaten either boiled in soups or stews, or used as a salad in a fresh state.   The leaves and roots are still eaten in Germany and the seed is used occasionally for flavoring.   In Silesia, according to Bryant,[3] the roots are eaten boiled and the green seeds are chopped up and mixed with salads to give them an aromatic flavor.[4]   This aromatic herb can scarcely be considered as an inmate of American gardens, although so recorded by Burr,[5] 1863.   In 1597, Gerarde,[6] says the leaves are " exceeding good, holsom, and pleasant among other sallade herbes, giving the taste of Ainse unto the rest."   In 1778, Mawe [7] records that it is used rarely in England.   Pliny [8] seems to refer to its use in ancient Rome under the name *anthriscus*.   It finds notice in most of the early botanies.

Myrsine capitellata Wall.   *Myrsineae.*
   Tropical Asia.   The small, round drupe is eaten, according to Brandis.[9]

M. semiserrata Wall.
   Himalayan region.   The pea-sized drupe, with a soft, fleshy exocarp, is eaten.[10]

Myrtus arayan H. B. & K.   *Myrtaceae.*
   Peru.   This species is cultivated for ornament and fruit.   The fruit is of a rich, spicy, subacid flavor.[11]

---

[1] Flückiger and Hanbury *Pharm.* 451.   1879.
[2] Pickering, C.   *Chron. Hist. Pls.* 603.   1879.   (*M. moschata*)
[3] Johnson, C. P.   *Useful Pls. Gt. Brit.* 121.   1862.
[4] Ibid.
[5] Burr, F.   *Field, Gard. Veg.* 399.   1863.
[6] Gerarde, J.   *Herb.* 883.   1597.
[7] Mawe and Abercrombie *Univ. Gard. Bot.*   1778.
[8] Pliny lib. 22, c. 38.
[9] Brandis, D.   *Forest Fl.* 286.   1876.
[10] Brandis, D.   *Forest Fl.* 285.   1876.
[11] Watson *Proc. Amer. Acad. Sci.* 412.   1887.

M. communis Linn. MYRTLE.

Southern Europe and the Orient. In Greece, myrtle was sacred to Venus and was a coronary plant. Its fruit is eaten by the modern, as it was by the ancient, Athenians.[1] The dried fruit and flower-buds, says Lindley,[2] were formerly used as a spice and are said still to be so used in Tuscany.

M. molinae Barn.

Chile, where it is called *temo*. Its seeds, Molina[3] says, may be used for coffee.

M. nummularia Poir. CRANBERRY-MYRTLE.

Chile to Fuego and the Falkland Islands. Hooker[4] describes the berries as fleshy, sweet and of agreeable flavor.

M. ugni Molina. CHILEAN GUAVA.

Chile. Don[5] says the fruit is red and musky. The natives express the juice and mix it with water to form a refreshing drink. Mueller[6] says it bears small but pleasantly aromatic berries. The fruit is said to be agreeably flavored and aromatic It fruits abundantly in the greenhouses of England, but its flavor does not recommend it as a table fruit.[7]

Nandina domestica Thunb. *Berberideae.* SACRED BAMBOO.

An evergreen shrub of China and Japan. This species is extensively cultivated for its fruits, which are red berries of the size of a pea.[8]

Nannorrhops ritchieana H. Wendl. *Palmae.*

Baluchistan and Afghanistan. The leaf-bud, or cabbage, and the young inflorescence, as well as the flesh of the fruit, is commonly eaten.[9]

Napoleona imperialis Beauv. *Myrtaceae.*

Western tropical Africa. Henfrey[10] says this plant bears.a large fruit with an edible pulp and a rind containing much tannin.

Narcissus sp.? *Amaryllideae.* NARCISSUS.

On the upper Nile, Grant[11] found a narcissus about eight inches high, with white flowers having a waxy, yellow corona and with leaves tasting of onions. The leaves, cooked with mashed ground-nuts, he says, make a delicious spinach.

Nasturtium amphibium R. Br. *Cruciferae.* WATER CRESS.

North temperate regions. Merat says the " young leaves are eatable in the spring."

---

[1] Hooker, W. J. *Journ. Bot.* 1:118. 1834.

[2] Lindley, J. *Veg. King.* 737. 1853.

[3] Molina *Hist. Chili* 1:123. 1808. (*Temus moschata*)

[4] Mueller, F. *Sel. Pls.* 291. 1891.

[5] Don, G. *Hist. Dichl. Pls.* 2:835. 1832.

[6] Mueller, F. *Sel. Pls.* 291. 1891.

[7] Smith, J. *Dom. Bot.* 371. 1871.

[8] Don, G. *Hist. Dichl. Pls.* 1:118. 1831.

[9] Seemann, B. *Pop. Hist. Palms* 145. 1856. (*Chamaerops ritchiana*)

[10] Henfrey, A. *Bot.* 266. 1870.

[11] Speke, J. H. *Journ. Disc. Source Nile* 583. 1864.

N. indicum DC. INDIAN CRESS.

East Indies, China and Malay. This cress found its way into the gardens of France.[1]

N. officinale R. Br. WATER CRESS.

North temperate regions. The young shoots and leaves of water cress have been used as a salad from time immemorial. Xenophon[2] strongly recommended its use to the Persians, and the Romans recommended it to be eaten with vinegar as a remedy for those whose minds were deranged; hence the Greek proverb, "Eat cress and learn more wit." The first attempt to cultivate water cress by artificial means in Europe is said by Booth[3] to have been at Erfurt, about the middle of the sixteenth century. Gerarde and Lord Bacon[4] wrote strongly in its favor, but, according to Don,[5] it has been cultivated as a salad near London only since 1808. At the present time, it is cultivated in plantations many acres in extent and the demand for this popular salad herb during the season can scarcely be supplied. In America, it is mentioned among garden esculents by McMahon,[6] 1806, and by succeeding writers on gardening. In India, this herb is much prized and is sought after by the Mohammedans.[7]

N. palustre DC. MARSH CRESS.

A wild plant of Europe and northern America, common in wet ditches. It is sometimes used as a cress. According to Dall,[8] this cress is eaten in Alaska.

Nectandra cinnamomoides Nees. *Laurineae.* AMERICAN CINNAMON.

Pickering[9] says the American cinnamon is a tree of the eastern slope of the equatorial Andes and is cultivated in the region about Quito. Its dried calices are brought also from forests to the eastward and are used as a spice.

N. rodioei Hook. GREENHEART.

A tree of Guiana. The timber is much valued in ship building. The fruit, of the size of a small apple, has a single seed about as large as a walnut. Though the fruit is very bitter, its seeds yield a starch which the Indians mix with rotten wood and make into a bitter, disagreeable kind of bread.[10]

Negundo aceroides Moench. *Sapindaceae.* ASH-LEAVED MAPLE. BOX ELDER.

A tree of northern North America. This tree, says Hough,[11] is tapped for sugar in Canada and is now being planted in Illinois for sugar-making. Vasey[12] says experiments

---

[1] Unger, F. *U. S. Pat. Off. Rpt.* 356. 1859.

[2] McIntosh, C. *Book Gard.* 169. 1855.

[3] Booth, W. B. *Treas. Bot.* 2:778. 1870.

[4] McIntosh, C. *Book Gard.* 169. 1855.

[5] Don, G. *Hist. Dichl. Pls.* 1:155. 1831.

[6] McMahon, B. *Amer. Gard. Cal.* 581. 1806. (*Sisymbrium nasturtium*)

[7] Ainslie, W. *Mat. Ind.* 1:95. 1826.

[8] Dall, W. H. *U. S. D. A. Rpt.* 187. 1868.

[9] Pickering, C. *Chron. Hist. Pls.* 845. 1879.

[10] Smith, A. *Treas. Bot.* 2:780. 1870.

[11] Hough, F. B. *Elem. For.* 240. 1882.

[12] Vasey *U. S. D. A. Rpt.* 163. 1872.

in Illinois show the box elder to give more sap and a more saccharine sap than the sugar maple and that this sap makes a whiter sugar.   Douglas[1] says the Crow Indians make sugar from its sap, and Richardson[2] says this is the tree which yields most of the sugar in Rupert's Land.

Nelumbium luteum Willd.   *Nymphaeaceae.*   AMERICAN WATER-LOTUS.   WATER CHIN-
          QUEPIN.   YELLOW NELUMBO.

North America and West Indies.   The seeds are very agreeable to eat and are eagerly sought for by children and Indians.[3]   The long and thick, creeping roots, says Rafinesque,[4] are acrimonious when fresh but are easily deprived of their dangerous juice by washings and are then an agreeable food to the Indians.

N. speciosum Willd.   LOTUS.

Northern Africa and tropical Asia.   The lotus is an eastern flower which seems from time immemorial to have been, in native estimation, the type of the beautiful.   It is held sacred throughout the East, and the deities of the various sects in that quarter of the world are almost invariably represented as either decorated with its flowers, seated or standing on a lotus throne or pedestal, or holding a sceptre framed from its flowers.   It is fabled that the flowers obtained their red color by being dyed w th the blood of Siva when Kamadeva wounded him with the love-shaft arrow.   Lakeshmi is called the lotus-born, from having ascended from the ocean on its flowers.   The lotus is often referred to by the Hindu poets.   The lotus floating in the water is the emblem of the world.   It is also symbolic of the mountain Meru, the residence of the gods and the emblem of female beauty. Both the roots and seeds are esculent, sapid and wholesome and are used as food by the Egyptians.   In China, some parts of India and in Ceylon, the black seeds of this plant, not unlike little acorns in shape, are served at table.   Tennent[5] found them of delicate flavor and not unlike the pine cones of the Apennines.   In the southern provinces of China, large quantities are grown.[6]   The seeds and slices of its hairy root are served at banquets and the roots are pickled for winter use.[7]   In Japan, the stems are eaten.[8]   These stalks are not dissimilar in taste to our broad beet with a somewhat sharp after-taste.   The seeds are also eaten like filberts.   The roots furnish a starch, or arrowroot, in China, called *gaou fun.*[9]

Nemopanthus fascicularis Rafin.   *Ilicineae.*   MOUNTAIN HOLLY.

Northeast North America.   The berries, according to Pickering,[10] are eaten by the Indians.

---

[1] Nuttall, T.   *No. Amer. Sylva* 2:38.   1865.

[2] Richardson, J.   *Arctic Explor.* 2:286.   1851.

[3] Don, G.   *Hist. Dichl. Pls.* 1:124.   1831.

[4] Rafinesque, C. S.   *Fl. La.* 23.   1817.

[5] Tennent, J. E.   *Ceylon* 1:123.   1859.

[6] Fortune, R.   *Wand. China* 307.   1847.

[7] Don, G.   *Hist. Dichl. Pls.* 1:123.   1831.

[8] Pickering, C.   *Chron. Hist. Pls.* 111.   1879.

[9] Hanbury, D.   *Sci. Papers* 240.   1876.

[10] Pickering, C.   *Chron. Hist. Pls.* 804.   1879.   (*N. canadensis*)

Nepenthes distillatoria Linn. *Nepenthaceae.* PITCHER PLANT.

Ceylon. This plant has been introduced into India and is now common in some of the mission gardens and is grown in conservatories in Europe and America. The leaves are broad, oblong, smooth, with a very strong nerve running through the middle, ending in a long tendril, generally twisted, to which hangs a long receptacle or bag, which, on being pressed, yields a sweet, limpid, pleasant, refreshing liquor in such quantity that the contents of six or eight of them are sufficient to quench the thirst of a man.[1]

Nepeta cataria Linn. *Labiatae.* CATNIP.

Europe, Orient and the Himalayas. Catnip holds a place as a condiment.[2] In 1726, Townsend[3] says it is used by some in England to give a high relish in sauces. It is mentioned among the plants of Virginia by Gronovius,[4] as collected by Clayton preceding 1739.

N. glechoma Benth. ALEHOOF. GROUND IVY. NEPETA.

Europe and naturalized in northeastern North America. The leaves are in great repute among the poor in England as a tea[5] and in ancient times were used for flavoring ale.

Nephelium lappaceum Linn. *Sapindaceae.* RAMBUTAN. RAMPOSTAN.

Malay Archipelago, where it is found in the greatest abundance but does not appear to be cultivated. This tree yields the well-known and favorite rambutan fruit which in appearance very much resembles a chestnut with the husk on and, like the chestnut, is covered with small points which are soft and of a deep red color. Under this skin is the fruit, and within the fruit a stone; the eatable part thereof is small in quantity, but it perhaps is more agreeable than any other in the whole vegetable kingdom.

N. litchi Cambess. LICHI.

China, Cambodia and the Philippines. This tree furnishes one of the most common fruits of China. The Chinese recognize some 15 or 20 varieties, but Williams[6] says there are only two or three which are distinctly marked. It has been cultivated for ages in that country and furnishes a large amount of food to the people, a single tree often producing four bushels of fruit. It is now cultivated in Bengal and the West Indies. In Trinidad, says Prestoe,[7] the fruit is of the consistence and flavor of a high class Muscat grape and is invariably relished as delicious by all. The most common variety, says A. Smith,[8] is nearly round, about an inch and a half in diameter, with a thin, brittle shell of red color covered all over with rough, wartlike protuberances; others are larger and heart-shaped. When fresh, they are filled with a white, almost transparent, sweet, jelly-like pulp,

---

[1] Ainslie, W. *Mat. Ind.* 2:93. 1826.

[2] Vilmorin *Les Pls. Potag.* 354. 1883.

[3] Townsend *Seedsman* 36. 1726.

[4] Gronovius *Fl. Virg.* 89. 1762.

[5] Lindley, J. *Med. Econ. Bot.* 221. 1849.

[6] Williams, S. W. *U. S. Pat. Off. Rpt.* 1:450. 1850. (*Dimocarpus litchi*)

[7] Prestoe *Rpt. Bot. Gard. Trinidad* 28. 1880. Printed in 1881.

[8] Smith, A. *Treas. Bot.* 2:784. 1870.

surrounding a rather large, shining, brown seed; after they have been gathered some time, the pulp shrivels and turns black, and the fruit then bears some resemblance to a prune.

N. longana Cambess. LONGAN.

East Indies, Burma and southern China, where it is much cultivated for its fruits, which are sold in the Chinese markets. It is also grown in Bengal. The longan is a smaller fruit than the lichi, varying from half an inch to an inch in diameter and is quite round, with a nearly smooth, brittle skin of a yellowish-brown color. It contains a similar semi-transparent pulp of an agreeable, sweet or subacid flavor.[1]

N. rimosum G. Don.

Malay Archipelago. This species furnishes a fruit which is eaten.[2]

Nephrodium esculentum Don. *Filices.*

In Nepal, says Unger, the rootstocks of this fern are eaten by the natives.[3]

Nephrolepsis cordifolia Presl. *Polypodiaceae.* LADDER FERN.

Mexico, Japan and New Zealand. This fern, says J. Smith, produces underground tubers like small potatoes, which are used for food by the natives of Nepal.

Neptunia oleracea Lour. *Leguminosae.*

Tropics. This plant is used in Cochin China in salads, its spongy, floating stems being crisp and juicy but not easily digested.[4]

Nesodaphne tarairi Hook. f. *Laurineae.* TARAIRE TREE.

New Zealand. The plant bears an ovoid and deep purple fruit used by the aborigines, but, as the seeds contain a poisonous principle, they require to be well boiled in order to make them harmless.[5]

N. tawa Hook. f. TAWA.

New Zealand. The fruit is edible but the seeds are poisonous unless well boiled before eaten.[6]

Nicotiana andicola H. B. & K. *Solanaceae.* TOBACCO.

Peru. This plant grows on the back of the Andes and is similar to cultivated tobacco.[7]

N. chinensis Fisch. TOBACCO.

China. This species is only known in a cultivated state.[8] It is everywhere culti-vated in Cochin China and China.[9] This is the species which Le Conte [10] thinks probably

---

[1] Smith, A. *Treas. Bot.* 2:784. 1870.

[2] Unger, F. *U. S. Pat. Off. Rpt.* 336. 1859.

[3] Unger, F. *U. S. Pat. Off. Rpt.* 329. 1859.

[4] Loureiro *Fl. Cochin.* 654. 1790.

[5] Smith, A. *Treas. Bot.* 2:786. 1870.

[6] Ibid.

[7] Humboldt, A. *Trav.* 2:507. 1889.

[8] De Candolle, A. *Geog. Bot.* 2:850. 1855.

[9] Ibid.

[10] LeConte, J. *Amer. Journ. Pharm.* Sept. 1859.

existed in China before the discovery of America, and he furthermore says that from this the best Cuban tobacco is obtained.

N. clevelandi A. Gray. TOBACCO.

California. Professor Rothrock [1] is of the opinion that the early natives of California smoked the leaves. This tobacco is excessively strong and was found in association with the shell-heaps which occur so abundantly on the coasts of southern and central California.

N. glutinosa Linn. TOBACCO.

South America. According to Humboldt,[2] this species is cultivated in Europe.

N. loxensis H. B. & K. TOBACCO.

The Andes. This species is said by Humboldt [3] to be similar to cultivated tobacco.

N. paniculata Linn. TOBACCO.

South America. This species yields the tobacco of Russia. The young leaves are removed, dried in the shade and buried beneath hay ricks, when they become of a brownish-yellow color.[4]

N. quadrivalvis Pursh. TOBACCO.

Western North America. This tobacco is cultivated by the Arikara and Mandan Indians. The tobacco prepared from it is excellent and the most delicate is formed of the dried flowers.[5] The calyx is very fetid and is preferred to any other part.

N. repanda Willd. TOBACCO.

Mexico. This species is used, according to Masters,[6] in the manufacture of some of the most highly esteemed cigars.

N. rustica Linn. TOBACCO.

Mexico. This species is found in old fields from New York westward and southward, a relic of cultivation by the Indians.[7] It is cultivated in all parts of the globe and has even become wild in Africa. It is supposed to be the kind originally introduced into Europe. It furnishes the East Indian tobacco, also that of the Philippines, and the kinds called Latakia and Turkish, according to Masters.[8] It is the *yetl* cultivated by the ancient Mexicans.[9]

N. tabacum Linn. TOBACCO.

South America. This is the principal species of cultivated tobaccos, a native of America and known to the outer world only after the discovery. It was first seen by Europeans in 1492 when Columbus [10] saw the natives of Cuba having in their mouths a

---

[1] Rothrock, J. T. *Sci. Amer.* 99. 1880.

[2] Humboldt, A. *Trav.* 2:507 note. 1889.

[3] Ibid.

[4] *Enc. Brit.* 18:520. 1859.

[5] Pursh, F. *Fl. Amer. Septent.* 1:141, 142. 1814.

[6] Masters, M. T. *Treas. Bot.* 2:787. 1870.

[7] Gray, A. *Synopt. Fl. No. Amer.* 2:241 pt. 1. 1886.

[8] Masters, M. T. *Treas. Bot.* 2:787. 1870.

[9] Humboldt, A. *Trav.* 1:226. 1889.

[10] *U. S. Pat. Off. Rpt.* 236. 1853.

roll of leaves of which they were inhaling the smoke. Yet it has been maintained by some, as Don Ullva, a Spanish writer, 1787, that the custom of smoking tobacco is of much greater antiquity than the date of the discovery of America, and Le Conte, 1859,[1] deems this probably true. Yet the absence of the mention of a custom so peculiar as smoking by all the earlier writers and travelers seems conclusive evidence against such assertions.

The word tobacco, says Humboldt,[2] belongs to the ancient language of Hayti and Santo Domingo. It did not properly denote the herb but the tube through which the smoke was inhaled. The name of the tobacco pipe in the Delaware language was *haboca*, and tobacco in some form or other was used by almost all the tribes of the American continent from the northwest coast to Patagonia.[3] It was observed in use among the New England tribes;[4, 5] among the Indians of the whole eastern coast by the early colonists;[6] among the Eskimos of the northwest, " who swallow the smoke and revel in a temporary elysium; " among the Konigas for chewing and snuffing; among the Ingaliks of the Yukon, who smoke and snuff; and among the Columbians.[7] The Snake Indians cultivated,[8] it and the California Indians also planted it in gardens as early as 1775.[9] In general, the medicine-pipe is a sacred pledge of friendship among all the northwestern tribes. The Aztecs smoked tobacco in pipes after meals,[10] inhaling the smoke, and also took the dried leaf in the pulverized form of snuff.[11]

Among the Nahua natives, says Bancroft,[12] three kinds of tobacco were used, the *yetl*, signifying tobacco in general, the *picycti* and the *quauyetl*. Columbus found it in use in Yucatan. Humboldt[13] says tobacco has been cultivated from time immemorial by all the native people of the Orinoco, and, at the period of the conquest, the habit of smoking was found to be spread alike over both North and South America. The Indians of Peru, according to De la Vega,[14] did not smoke it but used it in the form of snuff for medicinal purposes.

Cortez[15] seems to be the first European who saw the plant, in 1519, at Tobaco, a province of Yucatan, and it is asserted by some that he sent several plants to Spain this year and from this circumstance the plant derived its name. It seems certain that if the plant was then introduced, it did not became an object of commerce and seems not to have

[1] *Amer. Journ. Pharm.* Sept. 1859.

[2] Humboldt, A. *Trav.* 2:506. 1889.

[3] Prescott, W. H. *Conq. Mex.* 1:154 note. 1843.

[4] Mourt *Relation* 230. Mass. Hist. Soc. Coll. 8: 1802.

[5] Young, A. *Chron. Pilgr.* 363. 1841.

[6] Stille, A. *Therap. Mat. Med.* 2:360. 1874.

[7] Bancroft, H. H. *Native Races* 1:76, 133, 199, 1875.

[8] Irving, W. *Astoria* 381. 1849.

[9] Bancroft, H. H. *Native Races* 1:354 note. 1875.

[10] Prescott, W. H. *Conq. Mex.* 2:126. 1843.

[11] Prescott, W. H. *Conq. Peru* 1:140. 1860.

[12] Bancroft, H. H. *Native Races* 2:287. 1882.

[13] Humboldt, A. *Trav.* 2:507. 1889.

[14] Vega *Roy. Comment.* 1: Hakl. Soc. Ed. 188. 1869.

[15] *Journ. Agr.* 1:756. 1829.

been communicated to any other nation, for it was certainly from Portugal, where it was brought from America, about 1559, that its general diffusion over Europe and the East commenced. In 1560, it was introduced into France by John Nicot, ambassador of France at the Court of Portugal, who, at Lisbon, was presented with a specimen of this plant recently brought from Florida [1] — Humboldt [2] says from Yucatan. So late as the reign of Henry IV, tobacco was raised only in gardens and was used only for medicinal purposes. In the reign of Louis XIII, it began to come into request as a luxury and to be taken in the form of snuff. About this date, it was introduced by St. Croix into Italy and, about the beginning of the seventeenth century, Pope Urban VIII issued a bill prohibiting the using of snuff in churches during divine service. It was about the beginning of the seventeenth century that the tobacco plant was introduced into Russia, either from Portugal or from Italy by the way of Astrakhan, but the notices of it at this date are obscure. About the middle of the sixteenth century, it spread from Italy over Germany and Holland.[3] Tobacco reached India in 1605 [4] and about 1625 or 1626 Amurath IV, Sultan of Turkey, passed a law prohibiting its use on pain of death, and a similar law about this time was passed in Persia. According to some, it reached Hindustan and China between 1560 and 1565. Lobel asserts that tobacco was cultivated in England as early as the year 1570. Phillips [5] says it was brought to England by Drake in 1570, who that year made his first expedition against the Spainards, but Drake did not return until 1573. Its introduction is, however, usually ascribed to Raleigh in 1586, at which time, says Humboldt,[6] whole fields of it were already being cultivated in Portugal.

In 1586, tobacco was in cultivation in Virginia by Raleigh's colonists. In 1611, it was first cultivated by the use of a spade and in 1616 it was cultivated to such an extent that it occupied even the streets of Jamestown. It was cultivated in New Netherlands as early as 1646 and was introduced into Louisiana in 1718.[7] In 1640, tobacco culture in Connecticut was stimulated by legislation which required the colonists to use tobacco of Connecticut growth.

Gesner, who died in 1564, is said to have been the first botanist who mentions tobacco, and he used it for chewing and smoking.[8]

Nigella arvensis Linn. *Ranunculaceae.* WILD FENNEL.

Europe, Mediterranean region and the Orient. The seeds are used as those of *N. sativa* as are also the leaves.

N. damascena Linn. WILD FENNEL.

Mediterranean region. This species is grown in Turkey for its seeds, which are used as a condiment.[9]

---

[1] Stille, A. *Therap. Mat. Med.* 2:360. 1874.

[2] Humboldt, A. *Trav.* 2:507. 1889.

[3] *Journ. Agr.* 1:761. 1829.

[4] Dutt, J. C. *Mat. Med. Hindus* 212. 1877.

[5] Phillips, H. *Comp. Kitch. Gard.* 2:339. 1831.

[6] Humboldt, A. *Trav.* 2:508. note. 1889.

[7] *U. S. Pat. Off. Rpt.* 236, 237. 1853.

[8] Hallam *Lit. Europe* 1:240, 241. 1856.

[9] Archer *Bot. Soc. Edinb.* 8:163. 1866.

N. sativa Linn. BLACK CUMIN. FENNEL FLOWER. NIGELLA. NUTMEG FLOWER. ROMAN CORIANDER.

East Mediterranean and Taurus-Caspian countries and cultivated in various parts of the world. The seeds are employed in some parts of Germany, France and Asia as a condiment. In eastern countries they are commonly used for seasoning curries and other dishes, and the Egyptians spread them on bread and put them on cakes like comfits.[1] The seeds, on account of their aromatic nature, are employed as a spice in cooking, particularly in Italy and southern France.[2] This plant is supposed to be the *gith* of Columella and Pliny, in the first century; of Palladius, in the third and of Charlemagne, in the ninth. The *melanthion* of Columella, in the first century, seems a descriptive name for his *gith*. Black cumin finds mention as cultivated in most of the botanies of the sixteenth and seventeenth centuries; is recorded by Vilmorin[3] among plants of the garden, as also by Burr[4] in 1863; and is now found in the lists of some of our seedsmen.[5]

Nipa fruticans Thunb. *Palmae.* NIPA.

Eastern portion of the Malayan Archipelago. The spathe is convertible into syrup, sugar, vinegar, yeast and strong spirit.[6] The pulpy kernels are used for making sweetmeats.[7]

Nitraria schoberi Linn. *Zygophylleae.* NITRE-BUSH.

Russia, north Asia and Australia. The plant produces a fruit of the size of an olive, of a red color and agreeable flavor, much relished by the natives.[8] The berries, though saltish and insipid, are eaten in the Caspian district.

N. tridentata Desf. LOTUS TREE.

Syria, north Africa and the tropics. This has been supposed, says Masters,[10] to be the true lotus tree of the ancients.

Noronhia emarginata Thou. *Oleaceae.*

A shrub of Madagascar. The plant is now, according to Hooker,[11] cultivated in the Mauritius where the pulp of the fruit is esculent.

Nothoscordum fragrans Kunth. *Liliaceae.*

Africa, Mauritius, North America and Mexico. The Jews of Jamaica use this plant as a garlic to season smoked sausage.[12]

[1] Smith, A. *Treas. Bot.* 2:790. 1870.
[2] Noisette *Man. Jard.* 2:447. 1860.
[3] Vilmorin *Les. Pls. Potag.* 374. 1883.
[4] Burr, F. *Field, Gard. Veg.* 429. 1863.
[5] Vick *Cat.* 1884.
[6] Seemann, B. *Pop. Hist. Palms* 269. 1856.
[7] Ainslie, W. *Mat. Ind.* 453. 1826. (*Cocos nypa*)
[8] Masters, M. T. *Treas. Bot.* 2:791. 1870. (*N. billardieri*)
[9] Gmelin, J. G. *Fl. Sibir.* 2:237. 1747-1769.
[10] Masters, M. T. *Treas. Bot.* 2:791. 1870.
[11] Hooker, W. J. *Bot. Misc.* 2:167. 1831.
[12] Titford, W. J. *Hort. Bot. Amer.* 55. 1812.

Nuphar advena Ait. *Nymphaeaceae.* YELLOW POND LILY. SPATTER-DOCK.

North America. In New England, Josselyn[1] found the roots of the water lily with yellow flowers, after long boiling, eaten by the natives and tasting like sheep-liver. R. Brown[2] says the seeds are a staple article of diet among the Klamaths of southern Oregon. Newberry[3] saw many hundred bushels collected for winter use among the Indians of the western coast and says the seeds taste like those of broom corn and are apparently very nutritious.

N. luteum Sibth. & Sm. YELLOW WATER LILY.

Europe and the adjoining portions of Asia. A refreshing drink is made from its flowers by the Turks,[4] and its roots and leaf-stalks are eaten by the Finns and Russians.[5]

N. polysepalum Engelm.

California. This variety furnishes an important article of food, in its seeds, to the Indians.[6]

Nymphaea alba Linn. *Nymphaeaceae.* FLATTER-DOCK. WHITE WATER LILY.

North temperate region. In France, the rootstocks, according to Masters,[7] are used in the preparation of a kind of beer.

N. ampla DC.

North America and West Indies. The farinaceous rootstocks are eaten.

N. gigantea Hook. AUSTRALIAN WATER LILY.

Australia. The porous seed-stalk is peeled and eaten either raw or roasted. The stalks containing brown or black seed are used while those with light-colored seeds are rejected. The large, rough tubers, growing in the mud with the floating leaves attached, are roasted and are not unlike potatoes, being yellow and dry when cooked.[8]

N. lotus Linn. EGYPTIAN WATER LILY. LOTUS.

Tropical Africa and eastern Asia. The rootstocks contain a sort of starch and are eaten by the poorer classes in India. The small seeds, called *bheta*, are fried in heated sand and make a light, easily digestible food. The roots are also eaten in Ceylon and the seeds are chewed by children.[9] The tubers are much sought after by the natives as an article of food or as a medicine. The capsules and seeds are either pickled or put into curries or ground and mixed with flour to make cakes.

N. stellata Willd.

Asia and tropical Africa. This water lily is distinctly figured, says Pickering,[10] in

---

[1] Josselyn, J. *New Eng. Rar.* 72. 1672.

[2] Brown, R. *Bot. Soc. Edinb.* 9:382. 1868.

[3] Newberry *Pacific R. R. Rpt.* 6:67. 1855.

[4] Pickering *Chron. Hist. Pls.* 135. 1879.

[5] Ibid.

[6] Brewer and Watson *Bot. Cal.* 1:17. 1880.

[7] Masters, M. T. *Treas. Bot.* 2:797. 1870.

[8] Palmer, E. *Journ. Roy. Soc. New So. Wales* 17:101. 1884.

[9] Dutt, U. C. *Mat. Med. Hindus* 109, 110. 1877.

[10] Pickering, C. *Chron. Hist. Pls.* 277. 1879.

the cave temples at Adjunta and in Brahmanical cave temples. In the upper Nile region it is called *macongee-congee*, and the flowers and roots are eaten by the Wahiyon.[1]

Nyssa capitata Walt. *Cornaceae.* OGEECHEE LIME.

On the banks of rivers in the Carolinas. The fruit is large, orange-colored and full of an acid similar to a lime, from which it is known by the name of Ogeechee lime.[2]

N. multiflora Wangenh. BLACK GUM. PEPPERIDGE. SOUR GUM. UPLAND TUPELO.

Eastern North America. The fruit is pleasantly acidulous and is often used for preserves.[3]

N. uniflora Wangenh. LARGE TUPELO. OGEECHEE LIME. WILD OLIVE.

Eastern America. Its fruit, according to Browne,[4] is sold in the Savannah market under the name of Ogeechee lime for the purpose of a preserve.

Ochrocarpos africana Oliver. *Guttiferae.*

Tropical Africa. The fruit is twice the size of a man's fist; the rind is brown and thick, and the pulp is yellow and excellent.[5]

O. longifolius Benth. & Hook. f.

East Indies. The fruit is similar to an acorn in size and appearance. Between the stone and the rind is a soft, pulpy juice of rosewater flavor, considered very agreeable by some.[6] Its fruit is delicious to the taste.[7]

Ocimum basilicum Linn. *Labiatae.* SWEET BASIL.

Western and tropical Asia. A fragrant and aromatic plant of tropical Asia, which, as a culinary plant, has been celebrated from a very early period. McIntosh[8] says it was condemned by Chrysippus more than 200 years before Christ as an enemy to the sight and a robber of the wits. Diodorus and Hollerus entertained equally superstitious notions regarding it. Philistis, Plistonicus and others extolled its virtues and recommended it as strongly as it had been formerly condemned. Pliny says the Romans sowed the seeds of this plant with maledictions and ill words, believing the more it was cursed the better it would prosper; and when they wished for a crop, they trod it down with their feet and prayed to the gods that it might not vegetate. It seems to have been first cultivated in Britain in 1548 and is now valued for the leaves and leafy tops, which are much employed for seasoning soups, stews, sauces and various other dishes. It reached America before 1806 as it is then mentioned by McMahon[9] as a well-known plant. Sweet basil seeds, according to Miss Bird,[10] are eaten in Japan.

[1] Speke, J. H. *Journ. Disc. Source Nile* 561. 1864.

[2] Pursh, F. *Fl. Amer. Septent.* 1:177. 1814. (*N. candicans*)

[3] Mueller, F. *Sel. Pls.* 299. 1891.

[4] Browne, D. J. *Trees Amer.* 427. 1846. (*N. candicans*)

[5] Don, G. *Hist. Dichl. Pls.* 1:619. 1831. (*Mammea africana*)

[6] Firminger, T. A. C. *Gard. Ind.* 207. 1874. (*Calysaccion longifolium*)

[7] Pickering, C. *Chron. Hist. Pls.* 712. 1879. (*Calysaccion longifolium*)

[8] McIntosh, C. *Book Gard.* 2:4. 1855.

[9] McMahon, B. *Amer. Gard. Cal.* 199. 1806.

[10] Bird *Unbeat. Tracks Jap.* 1:238. 1881.

O. gratissimum Linn.

East Indies. This species is recorded as indigenous in India, the South Sea Islands and Brazil.[1] According to Loureiro,[2] it occurs in the kitchen gardens of Cochin China. It was cultivated in England in 1752 by a Mr. Miller.[3] Forskal[4] gives as the Arabic name, *hobokbok*. In French gardens, this plant is called *basilic en arbre*. Vilmorin[5] thinks, however, that the French form may be the *O. suave* Willd., but of this he is not certain.

Ocotea pretiosa Benth. & Hook. f. *Laurineae.*

A Brazilian tree which yields a bark whose properties are similar to those of cinnamon.[6]

Odina schimperi Hochst. *Anacardiaceae.*

Abyssinia. This plant is the *m'oooomboo* of the upper Nile. The fruit is scarcely edible, according to Grant.[7]

Oenanthe peucedanifolia Pollich. *Umbelliferae.* WILD PARSLEY.

Europe and adjoining Asia. The roots have occasionally been eaten.[8]

O. pimpinelloides Linn. MEADOW PARSLEY.

Mediterranean countries. Its fleshy tubercles, according to Lindley,[9] have occasionally been eaten.

O. sarmentosa Presl.

Western North America. The tubers form one of the dainty dishes of the Oregon Indians. They are black, but, when boiled like potatoes, they burst open lengthwise, showing a snowy-white, farinaceous substance, which has a sweet, cream-like taste with a slight parsley flavor.[10]

O. stolonifera Wall.

East Indies, Java and China. The plant is served as a green in Japan.[11]

Oenocarpus bacaba Mart. *Palmae.* BACABA OIL PALM.

Guiana and the Amazon. The fruit yields a colorless, sweet oil, used at Para for adulterating olive oil and excellent for cooking and for lamps. It is called bacaba.[12]

---

[1] Mueller, F. *Sel. Pls.* 143. 1876.

[2] Loureiro *Fl. Cochin.* 369. 1790.

[3] Martyn *Miller's Gard. Dict.* 1807.

[4] Forskal *Fl. Aeg.-Arab* c. xiv. 1775.

[5] Vilmorin *Les Pls. Potag.* 33. 1883.

[6] *Treas. Bot.* 2:738, 739. 1870.

[7] Speke, J. H. *Journ. Disc. Source Nile* 565. 1864.

[8] Pickering, C. *Chron. Hist. Pls.* 291. 1879

[9] Ibid.

[10] *U. S. D. A. Rpt.* 407. 1870. (*Helosciadium californicum*)

[11] Georgeson *Amer. Gard.* 653. 1891.

[12] Smith, A. *Treas. Bot.* 2:804. 1870.

O. bataua Mart. BATAVA PALM.

Brazil. This is the *patawa* of the Amazon and yields a colorless, sweet oil, used for adulterating olive oil at Para and for cooking.[1]

O. distichus Mart. BACABA WINE PALM.

Brazil. Bates[2] says this is one of the palms called bacaba. The fruit is much esteemed by the natives who manufacture a pleasant drink from it.

Oenothera biennis Linn. *Onagraceae.* EVENING PRIMROSE. GERMAN RAMPION.

Northeastern America. This plant was formerly cultivated in English gardens for its edible roots, which, when boiled, are wholesome and nutritious.[3] In Germany the roots are used as scorzonera and the young shoots in salads.[4] The roots are sweet to the taste, somewhat resembling parsnips. The roots may be used as scorzonera, but the plant is cultivated in France only as a curiosity.[5] It is said by Loudon[6] to be cultivated in Germany, and, in Carniola, the roots are eaten in salad. It first reached Europe in 1614.[7] It is given by Burr[8] for American gardens in 1863, under the name German Rampion.

Olax zeylanica Linn. *Olacineae.* MALLA.

Ceylon. It is said the leaves are used as potherbs and as salads.[9]

Olea europaea Linn. *Oleaceae.* OLIVE.

Mediterranean region. The olive has been in cultivation from the earliest periods of history. It is found wild in Syria, Greece and Africa and even in Spain but whether truly indigenous or escaped from cultivation is in doubt. The olive belongs to the fruits which were promised to the Jews in Canaan. Homer mentions green olives in the garden of Alcinous and Laertes, which were brought by Cecrops, the founder of Athens, to Greece. The cultivated tree was distinguished from the wild tree by Dioscorides. This tree was first brought to Italy, says Unger,[10] 571 B. C. and, at the time of Pliny, had been carried over the Alps to Gaul and Spain. At the time of Cato, the Romans were acquainted with only 9 kinds of olives, in the time of Pliny with 12 and at the present time with 20. Humboldt[11] says that, under the reign of Tarquin the Elder, this tree did not exist in Italy, in Spain or in Africa. Under the Consulate of Appius Claudius, the olive was still very rare in Rome, but, at the time of Pliny, the olive had already passed into France and Spain. It is said by others, however, that the olive was brought to France by the

[1] Smith, A. *Treas. Bot.* 2:804. 1870.

[2] Bates, H. W. *Nat. Amaz.* Humboldt *Libr. Sci.* 694. 1879–80.

[3] Johnson, C. P. *Useful Pls. Gt. Brit.* 104. 1862.

[4] Loudon, J. C. *Hort.* 653. 1860.

[5] Vilmorin *Les Pls. Potag.* 202. 1883.

[6] Loudon, J. C. *Hort.* 653. 1860.

[7] Linnaeus *Sp. Pl.* 492. 1763.

[8] Burr, F. *Field, Gard. Veg.* 35. 1863.

[9] Wight, R. *Illustr. Ind. Bot.* 1:101. 1840.

[10] Unger, F. *U. S. Pat. Off. Rpt.* 323. 1859.

[11] Humboldt, A. *Essai sur Geog. Pls.* 4:26. 1807.

Phocian colony which inhabited Marseilles, 680 B. C. It is now extensively cultivated in Italy, southern France, Spain, Portugal, northern Africa, western Asia and Australia, and, of late years, its culture seems to be making rapid progress in southern California.

In 1560, three plants were carried to Lima, Peru, one of these was stolen and carried to Chile and from this origin flourishing plantations became established.[1]

In 1755, the olive was introduced into South Carolina and, in 1785, it is reported as successfully grown.[2] In this year, also, the South Carolina Society imported cuttings of olives. In 1833, two varieties were introduced at Beaufort, South Carolina, and are said to have succeeded fairly well.[3] In 1869 and 1871, mention is made of the fruiting of olives at this place. In 1760, the olive was introduced into Florida by a colony of Greeks and Minorcans who founded New Smyrna, and about 1760 Anastasia Island, opposite St. Augustine, was remarkable for its fine olive trees.[4] In 1867, fine crops were gathered in gardens in St. Augustine. On Cumberland Island, Georgia, a number of trees bore abundantly for many years prior to 1835 and, in 1825 at Darien, some 200 trees were planted.[5] In 1854, olive trees were under cultivation in Louisiana, and Jefferys,[6] 1760, speaks of olive trees there yielding palatable fruit and excellent oil but he may have referred to the wild olive, *O. americana*. In 1817, an attempt by a colony to cultivate the olive in Alabama was made, a grant of land being given conditionally on success, but the enterprise was not prosecuted and fell through. In California, the olive is said to have been planted in 1700.[7]

The use of the fruit for the expression of an oil and for pickling is very extensive, and these products are largely an object of export from southern Europe. In Cephalonia,[8] according to Mrs. Brassey, the press cake is used by the peasants as a staple diet.

Olneya tesota A. Gray. *Leguminosae.* IRONWOOD. OLNEYA.

Mexico. This tree grows in the most desolate and rocky parts of Arizona and Sonora. The seeds are eaten raw or roasted by the Indians. When care is taken to parch them they equal peanuts with no perceptible difference in taste. The Mohave Indians of Arizona store them for winter use.[9]

Ombrophytum sp.? *Balanophoreae.* MOUNTAIN MAIZE.

Peru. These plants, according to Poppig, are boiled and eaten like fungi. They spring up suddenly in Peru after rain and are called mountain maize.[10]

---

[1] Markham, C. R. *Trav. Cieza de Leon.* Hakl. Soc. Ed. **33**:401. 1864.

[2] Porcher, F. P. *Res. So. Fields, Forests* 567. 1869.

[3] *U. S. Pat. Off. Rpt.* 310. 1855.

[4] *Hist. Mass. Hort. Soc.* 30. 1880.

[5] Couper *Farm. Libr.* **3**:196. 1848.

[6] Jefferys, T. *Nat. Hist. Amer.* **1**:155. 1760.

[7] *Hist. Mass Hort. Soc.* 39. 1880.

[8] Brassey *Sunshine, Storm East* **1**:179. 1880.

[9] *U. S. Dept. Agr. Rpt.* 411. 1870.

[10] Masters, M. T. *Treas. Bot.* **2**:811. 1870.

Omphalea diandra Linn. *Euphorbiaceae.* COBNUT.

West Indies. This tree is cultivated in Santo Domingo and Jamaica under the name of *noisettier*, or cobnut, from the resemblance of the flavor of the seeds to that of the European nuts. The embryo is deleterious and requires to be extracted.[1]

O. triandra Linn. COBNUT.

Tropical America. The seeds are edible after the deleterious embryo is extracted.[2] The tree is called cobnut in Jamaica. The kernels of the nuts in the raw state are delicately sweet and wholesome. When roasted they are equal, if not superior, to any chestnut. By compression, they yield a sweet and fine-flavored oil.[3]

Oncoba spinosa Forsk. *Bixineae.*

Tropical Africa and Arabia. This is a large tree called in Yemen *onkob*. The fruit is eaten by boys.[4]

Oncocarpus vitiensis A. Gray. *Anacardiaceae.*

Fiji Islands. The fleshy disk of the fruit, which is of a beautiful red when ripe, is much esteemed by the Fijians, who use it extensively bruised in water and fermented into a liquor resembling cider. The kernel, when boiled, is edible.[5]

Oncosperma filamentosum Blume. *Palmae.* NIBUNG PALM.

Malay. This is the nibung of the Malays. The heart, or cabbage, is delicately white with a very sweet, nutty flavor.[6] Adams [7] says the cabbage is certainly a most delicious vegetable and, when boiled, resembles asparagus or kale; in its raw state, it furnishes fictitious cucumbers and an excellent salad.

Oncus esculentus Lour. *Dioscoraceae.*

India. Royle [8] says this plant has large, farinaceous and edible tubers.

Onobrychis crista-galli Lam. *Leguminosae.* HEDGEHOG.

Mediterranean region. This singular plant is grown in vegetable gardens as a curiosity on account of the peculiar shape of the seed-pods. It has no utility. Its seed appears in some of our seedsmen's lists.

Ononis arvensis Linn. *Leguminosae.* REST-HARROW.

Europe. Rest-harrow, according to Gerarde,[9] furnishes a food. " The tender sprigs or crops of this shrub before the thornes come forth, are preserved in pickle, and be very pleasant sauce to be eaten with meat as sallad, as Dioscorides teacheth."

---

[1] *Treas. Bot.* 2:812. 1870.

[2] Ibid.

[3] Lunan, J. *Hort. Jam.* 1:201. 1814.

[4] Pickering, C. *Chron. Hist. Pls.* 390. 1879.

[5] Seemann, B. *Fl. Viti.* 51. 1865–73.

[6] Seemann, B. *Pop. Hist. Palms* 275. 1856.

[7] Adams, A. *Voy. Samarang* 2:426. 1848.

[8] Royle, J. F. *Illustr. Bot. Himal.* 1:379. 1839.

[9] Gerarde, J. *Herb.* 1323. 1633.

Onopordon acanthium Linn. *Compositae.* COTTON THISTLE.

Europe, north Africa, the Orient and naturalized in eastern North America. The receptacles of the flowers, says Lightfoot,[1] and the tender stalks, peeled and boiled, may be eaten in the same manner as artichokes and cardoons. Johnson[2] says an oil expressed from the seeds has been used for culinary purposes.

Opuntia camanchica Engelm. & Bigel. *Cacteae.* BASTARD FIG.

American Southwest. The fruit is much eaten by the Indians, and the leaves are roasted.[3] It has very sweet, juicy pulp.[4]

O. engelmanni Salm-Dyck. INDIAN FIG.

American Southwest. The fruit is palatable and the leaves are roasted by the Indians.[5] The large, yellowish or purple fruit is of a pleasant taste and is much relished by the inhabitants of California.[6]

O. rafinesquii Engelm. PRICKLY PEAR.

Mississippi Valley, Illinois, Missouri, Arkansas and north to Wisconsin, east to Kentucky and south to Louisiana and Texas. The fruit is one and one-half to two inches long, less than half that in diameter, naked by the disappearance of the bristles, and edible, somewhat acid or sweetish.[7] The leaves are roasted and eaten by the Indians, as is also the fruit.[8]

O. tuna Mill. INDIAN FIG. TUNA.

Southern California, Mexico, New Granada, Ecuador and the West Indies. The tuna is cultivated in the Los Angeles Valley, California, for its fruit and forms hedges 15 or 20 feet high. The Indians and Mexicans are very fond of the fruit, which serves them for food during its season.[9] The fruit of the tuna, which grew wild, says Prescott,[10] had to satisfy at times the cravings of appetite of the Spaniards under Cortez in their march upon Mexico in 1519. On the lava slopes of Mt. Etna, the fruit, according to J. Smith,[11] is collected and sold in the markets, forming an extensive article of food.

O. vulgaris Mill. BARBERRY FIG. PRICKLY PEAR.

Central America, northward to Georgia, southward to Peru and introduced into southern Europe where it has been cultivated for a considerable period. About the close of the last century, the fleet of Admiral Collingwood took a stock of the leaves of this plant, salted, among their provisions from Malta. In Sicily, this cactus flourishes on the

---

[1] Lightfoot, J. *Fl. Scot.* 1:459. 1789.

[2] Johnson, C. P. *Useful Pls. Gt. Brit.* 150. 1862.

[3] *U. S. D. A. Rpt.* 417. 1870.

[4] Engelmann and Bigelow *Pacific R. R. Rpt.* 4:40. 1856.

[5] *U. S. D. A. Rpt.* 417. 1870.

[6] Engelmann and Bigelow *Pacific R. R. Rpt.* 4:38. 1856.

[7] Engelmann and Bigelow *Pacific R. R. Rpt.* 4:41. 1856.

[8] *U. S. D. A. Rpt.* 417. 1870.

[9] Bigelow, J. N. *Pacific R. R. Rpt.* 4:16. 1856.

[10] Prescott, W. H. *Conq. Mex.* 1:424. 1843.

[11] Smith, J. *Dict. Econ. Pls.* 219. 1882.

bare lavas. The figs are very juicy, sweet, wholesome and refreshing. A variety with dark red fruit is cultivated at Catania and is much esteemed.[1] Hogg seems to think that this is the *kaktus* of Theophrastus, now called in Athens the Arabian fig, *arabosuke*,[2] but in this he is mistaken.

Orchis coriophora Linn. *Orchideae.* BUG ORCHIS.

Europe and adjoining Asia. In the Levant, its dried root is cooked and eaten [3] and is also used to furnish salep.[4]

O. longicruris Link.

Mediterranean region. This orchid furnishes a portion of the salep of commerce.[5]

O. mascula Linn. SPOTTED ORCHIS.

Europe and Asia Minor. The spotted orchis yields part of the inferior English salep. In the Peloponnesus, its dried root is cooked and eaten.[6]

O. militaris Linn.

North Asia and Europe. This orchid produces a starchy, mucilaginous substance known as salep, obtained by macerating the pulp in water.[7]

O. morio Linn. GANDERGOOSE. SALEP ORCHIS.

Europe and adjoining Asia. In the Levant, the dried root is cooked and eaten.[8] This is one of the species which furnishes salep to commerce.[9]

O. pyramidalis Linn.

Europe and north Africa. This is one of the species used to furnish salep to commerce.[10]

O. ustulata Linn.

Europe. This is one of the species which furnish salep to commerce.[11] Large quantities of salep are prepared in Macedonia and Greece, but the finest comes from Turkey. In the Himalayas and Kashmir regions, many species of bulbous-rooted orchids yield salep, which is largely used as food by the natives.

Oreodoxa oleracea Mart. *Palmae.* CABBAGE PALM.

West Indies. This is the cabbage palm of tropical America. The terminal bud, of a white color internally and of delicate flavor, serves as a vegetable.[12] Seemann [13] says

---

[1] Hooker, W. J. *Journ. Bot.* 1:121. 1834. (*Cactus opuntia*)

[2] Ibid.

[3] Pickering, C. *Chron. Hist. Pls.* 502. 1879.

[4] Flückiger and Hanbury *Pharm.* 654. 1879.

[5] Ibid.

[6] Pickering, C. *Chron. Hist. Pls.* 502. 1879.

[7] Smith, J. *Dom. Bot.* 183. 1871.

[8] Pickering, C. *Chron. Hist. Pls.* 502. 1879.

[9] Flückiger and Hanbury *Pharm.* 654. 1879.

[10] Ibid.

[11] Ibid.

[12] Masters, M. T. *Treas. Bot.* 1:88. 1870. (*Areca oleracea*)

[13] Seemann, B. *Pop. Hist. Palms* 278. 1856.

the heart is made into pickles or, when boiled, is served at table. The pith makes a sort of sago.

Origanum heracleoticum Linn. *Labiatae*. WINTER SWEET MARJORAM.

Mediterranean region. This species has been identified with the *Cunila gallinacea* of Pliny.[1] It is mentioned in the early botanies, is said to have reached England in 1640[2] and is recorded in American gardens in 1806.[3] It finds mention by Burr in 1863 but seems now to have disappeared from our seed-lists. It is frequently mentioned by early garden writers under the name winter sweet marjoram and has a variegated variety. It is an aromatic of sweet flavor and is much used for soups, broths and stuffings.

O. majorana Linn. SWEET MARJORAM.

Europe. Sweet marjoram was introduced into British gardens in 1573.[4] This is the species usually present in the herb garden. It is supposed to be the *amaracus* of Pliny,[5] who speaks of it as cultivated. It is also the *marjorana* of Albertus Magnus[6] in the thirteenth century and is mentioned as cultivated in the early botanies. Its modern culture is quite extended, and at Bombay it is considered sacred to Siva and Vishnu.[7] It is said to have reached Britain in 1573[8] and was a well-known inmate in American gardens in 1806.[9] This biennial, always treated as an annual, is highly aromatic and is much used, both in the green state and when dried, for flavoring broths, soups and stuffings.

O. onites Linn. POT MARJORAM.

Southeast Europe, Asia Minor and Syria. Pot marjoram is a perennial species from Sicily. Pliny[10] speaks of this species as called *onitin*, or *prasion*, in the first century. Its introduction into Britain is said to have taken place in 1759.[11] It was in American gardens in 1806[12] but does not appear to have been much cultivated, although recorded by Burr in 1863. Its name does not now occur in our seed-lists as it is inferior to the preceding variety.

O. vulgare Linn. ORGANY. WILD MARJORAM.

North Africa, Europe and adjoining Asia. This species has become sparingly naturalized in eastern America. Don[13] says it is used in cookery only in default of one of the other majorams. McIntosh[14] says that the leaves and tender tops are in constant demand

---

[1] Pliny lib. 20, c. 62.
[2] McIntosh, C. *Book Gard.* 2:239. 1855.
[3] McMahon, B. *Amer. Gard. Cal.* 199. 1806.
[4] McIntosh, C. *Book Gard.* 2:239. 1855.
[5] Pliny lib. 21, c. 35.
[6] Albertus Magnus *Veg.* Jessen Ed. 537. 1867.
[7] Birdwood *Veg. Prod. Bomb.* 242, 368. 1865.
[8] McIntosh, C. *Book Gard.* 2:239. 1855.
[9] McMahon, B. *Amer. Gard. Cal.* 199. 1806.
[10] Pliny lib. 20, c. 67.
[11] McIntosh, C. *Book Gard.* 2:239. 1855.
[12] McMahon, B. *Amer. Gard. Cal.* 583. 1806.
[13] Don, G. *Hist. Dichl. Pls.* 4:765. 1838.
[14] McIntosh, C. *Book Gard.* 2:238. 1855.

and that the leaves are used in many places as a substitute for tea.   Lightfoot [1] says in some parts of Sweden the peasantry put the leaves into their ale to give it an intoxicating quality and to prevent its turning sour.   It is included among garden herbs by Burr.[2]

Ornithogalum pilosum Linn. f.   *Liliaceae.*

South Africa.   The roots, according to Pallas,[3] are eaten by the Greeks of the Crimea.

O. pyrenaicum Linn.   PRUSSIAN ASPARAGUS.   STAR-OF-BETHLEHEM.

Europe and adjoining Asia.   In England, the young shoots of this plant [4] are used as asparagus.

O. umbellatum Linn.   DOVE'S DUNG.   STAR-OF-BETHLEHEM.

Northern Africa, Asia Minor and Europe.   The bulbs, says Johnson,[5] are very nutritious and form a palatable and wholesome food when boiled.   In the East they are often eaten and were probably the dove's dung mentioned in the Bible.

Orontium aquaticum Linn.   *Aroideae.*   GOLDEN CLUB.

North America.   The seeds of this species were gathered and dried by the Indians. Repeated boilings were necessary to fit them for use, the product resembling peas.[6]   The root is acrid but is rendered edible by roasting.[7]

Orthanthera viminea Wight   *Asclepiadeae.*

Northwest India.   In India, the flower-buds, raw or cooked, according to Brandis,[8] are eaten as a vegetable.

Orthosiphon rubicundus Benth.   *Labiatae.*

East Indies and Burma.   The tubers are said to be eaten in Madagascar.[9]

Oryza sativa Linn.   *Gramineae.*   RICE.

Tropical Asia.   This important grain, which supplies food for a greater number of human beings than are fed on the produce of any other known plant, is supposed to be of Asiatic origin.   Unger [10] says it is indigenous to further India and the Isle of Sunda. Barth [11] says it grows wild in central Africa, and recent travelers mention the plant as growing wild in South America.   Rice had been introduced into China 3000 years before

---

[1] Lightfoot, J.   *Fl. Scot.* 317.   1789.

[2] Burr, F.   *Field, Gard. Veg.* 427.   1863.

[3] Pallas, P. S.   *Trav. Russia* 2:449.   1803.

[4] Smith, A.   *Treas. Bot.* 2:823.   1870.

[5] Johnson, C. P.   *Useful Pls. Gt. Brit.* 272.   1862.

[6] Kalm, P.   *Trav. No. Amer.* 1:389.   1772.

[7] Porcher, F. P.   *Res. So. Fields, Forests* 623.   1869.

[8] Brandis, D.   *Forest Fl.* 335.   1874.

[9] Henfrey, A.   *Bot.* 327.   1870.   (*Ocimum sp.*)

[10] Unger, F.   *U. S. Pat. Off. Rpt.* 304.   1859.

[11] Barth, H.   *Trav. Disc. No., Cent. Afr.* 2:345.   1857.

Christ. Even in the time of Strabo, rice was cultivated in Babylon, Khuzistan and Syria. The Arabians brought it to Sicily.[1] It was found by Alexander's expedition under cultivation in Hindustan but the account of Theophrastus seems to imply that the living plant continued unknown in the Mediterranean countries. Rice was known, however, to Celsus, Pliny, Dioscorides and Galen. According to some, rice was known in Lombardy in the tenth century but Targioni-Tozzetti[2] says that in the year 1400 it was still known in Italy only as an article of import from the East. Its cultivation was introduced into Piedmont and Lombardy in the end of the fifteenth, or commencement of the sixteenth, century, either directly from India by the Portuguese or through Spain and Naples by the Spaniards. It was not cultivated in fields in Lombardy until 1522.

Rice was introduced into Virginia by Sir William Berkeley in 1647, who caused half a bushel of seed to be sown, and the yield was fifteen bushels of excellent rice.[3] This grain is stated to have been first brought into Charleston, South Carolina, by a Dutch brig from Madagascar in 1694, the captain of which left about a peck of paddy with Governor Smith, who distributed it among his friends for cultivation.[4] Another account is that Ashby sent a bag of seed rice, 100 pounds, from which in 1698 sixty tons were shipped to England.[5] The culture of rice was introduced into Louisiana by the *Company of the West* in 1718.[6] Upland, or mountain rice, was introduced into Charleston, South Carolina, from Canton, in 1772.[7] Father Baegert,[8] 1751–68, speaks of rice as flourishing in California.

The varieties of rice are almost endless. At the Madras exhibition of 1857, one exhibitor sent 190 varieties from Tanjore; another sent 65 from Travancore; 50 were received from Chingleput; 50 from Paghot; and from these 107 varieties of paddy were selected as distinct.[9] In Moon's *Catalogue of Ceylon Plants*,[10] no less than 161 varieties are enumerated as growing in Ceylon, and Carey[11] describes 40 varieties in Coromandel, all well known to native farming. The most general divisions are into upland rice, valley rice, summer rice and spring rice. The finest rice in the world is that raised in North and South Carolina. Rice in the husk is called paddy.

Oryzopsis asperifolia Michx. *Gramineae.* MOUNTAIN RICE.

North America. The grain is large and affords a fine and abundant farina, deserving the attention of agriculturists.[12]

---

[1] Unger, F. *U. S. Pat. Off. Rpt.* 304. 1859.
[2] Targioni Tozzetti *Journ. Hort. Soc. Lond.* 137. 1854.
[3] *Perf. Desc. Va.* 14. 1649. Force Coll. Tracts **2:** 1838.
[4] *U. S. Pat. Off. Rpt.* 165. 1853.
[5] Ibid.
[6] Ibid.
[7] Ibid.
[8] *Smithsonian Inst. Rpt.* 356. 1864.
[9] *Bot. Soc. Edinb.* **7:**276. 1863
[10] Ainslie, W. *Mat. Ind.* **1:**341. 1826.
[11] Roxburgh, W. *Hort. Beng.* 25. 1814.
[12] Nuttall, T. *Gen. No. Amer. Pls.* **1:**40. 1818.

O. cuspidata Benth.

Nevada, Arizona and New Mexico. This grass produces a small, black, nutritious seed, which is ground into flour and made into bread by the Zuni Indians, who, when their crops fail, become wandering hunters after these seeds.[1]

Osmanthus americana Benth. & Hook. f. *Oleaceae.* AMERICAN OLIVE. DEVIL WOOD.

Carolinas and southward. The fruit is eatable according to Pursh.[2] The fruit is of no value according to Vasey.[3]

O. fragrans Lour. FRAGRANT OLIVE.

Himalayan region, China and Japan. The scented flowers are used for flavoring teas in China and Japan.[4]

Osteomeles anthyllidifolia Lindl. *Rosaceae.*

Islands of the Pacific and China. The fruit is said to be white and sweet.[5]

Osyris arborea Wall. *Santalaceae.*

East Indies. In Kumaun, the leaves are used as a substitute for tea.[6], [7]

Owenia acidula F. Muell. *Meliaceae.*

Australia. This plant bears a dark red or crimson fruit the edible part of which is red. It is eaten raw and is very acid.[8]

O. cerasifera F. Muell. SWEET PLUM.

Australia. The pulp of the fruit when ripe is wholesome.[9]

O. venosa F. Muell. SOUR PLUM.

Australia. The ripe pulp is wholesome.[10]

Oxalis acetosella Linn. *Geraniaceae.* OXALIS. WOOD SORREL.

North temperate regions. This plant has for a long period been one of the minor vegetables in gardens although it seems to have been but rarely cultivated even in localities where the pleasant acidity of the leaves is esteemed in salads. Quintyne,[11] 1690, grew it in the Royal Gardens in France, and it is described among garden esculents by Vilmorin[12] but as one not often grown. The leaves have been used in Iceland from time

---

[1] *U. S. D. A. Rpt.* 419. 1870. (*Ericoma cuspidata*)

[2] Pursh, F. *Fl. Amer. Septent.* 1:7. 1814. (*Olea americana*)

[3] *U. S. D. A. Rpt.* 168. 1875. (*Olea americana*)

[4] Meyen, F. J. F. *Geog. Pls.* 392. 1846. (*Olea americana*)

[5] Gray, A. *U. S. Explor. Exped.* 507. 1854.

[6] Smith, A. *Treas. Bot.* 2:828. 1870.

[7] Royle, J. F. *Illustr. Bot. Himal.* 1:322. 1839.

[8] Palmer, E. *Journ. Roy. Soc. New So. Wales* 17:102. 1884.

[9] Jackson, J. R. *Treas. Bot.* 2:1324. 1876.

[10] Ibid.

[11] Quintyne *Comp. Gard.* 186. 1693.

[12] Vilmorin *Les Pls. Potag.* 397. 1883.

immemorial as a spring salad [1] and are likewise thus used by the French peasantry,[2] as well as elsewhere throughout Europe, but the references imply generally the use of the wild plant.

O. barrelieri Linn.

South America.   The acid leaves are eaten in America.[3]

O. carnosa Molina.   OCA.

Chile.   The tubercles are the oca of Peru.[4]

O. cernua Thunb.

South Africa.   The leaves are eaten.[5]

O. compressa Linn. f.

South Africa.   The acid leaves are eaten at the Cape of Good Hope.[6]

O. corniculata Linn.

Borders of temperate and tropical regions.   In India, the leaves are used as a pot-herb.[7]

O. crassicaulis Zucc.

Peru and Mexico.   This seems one of the best of the wood sorrels which yield an edible root.[8]   It has nutritious tubers and edible leaves.[9]

O. crenata Jacq.   ARRACACHA.   OCA.

Peru.   This species is cultivated in South America for its tuberous roots, which are about the size of hen's eggs, the skin being full of eyes like a potato.   Herndon [10] calls these tubers, when boiled or roasted, very agreeable to the taste.   Carruthers [11] says the plant is cultivated about Lima for its very acid leaf-stalks.   It was introduced into England in 1829 but was found to be watery and insipid.   There is a red and a yellow variety.[12]

O. deppei Lodd.

South America and Mexico.   The plant produces fleshy, edible roots of moderate size.   The roots are served boiled.   The young leaves are dressed like sorrel, put in soups or used as greens, and the flowers are excellent in salad, alone or mixed with corn salad.[13]

---

[1] Johnson, C. P.   *Useful. Pls. Gt. Brit.* 65.   1862.

[2] Noisette *Man. Jard.* 322.   1829.

[3] Baillon, H.   *Hist. Pls.* 5:32.   1878.

[4] Ibid.

[5] Unger, F.   *U. S. Pat. Off. Rpt.* 355.   1859.

[6] Baillon, H.   *Hist. Pls.* 5:32.   1878.

[7] Dutt, U. C.   *Mat. Med. Hindus* 124.   1877.

[8] Mueller, F.   *Sel. Pls.* 312.   1891.

[9] Unger, F.   *U. S. Pat. Off. Rpt.* 355.   1859.

[10] Herndon, W. L., and Gibbon, L.   *Explor. Vall. Amaz.* 1:48.   1854.

[11] Carruthers, W.   *Treas. Bot.* 2:830.   1870.

[12] *Bon Jard.* 543.   1882.

[13] Morren *Gard. Chron.* 68.   1841.

It was introduced into cultivation in England in 1827 [1] and is now also cultivated in France, the stalks and leaves being used.[2]

O. enneaphilla Cav.   SCURVY GRASS.

Falkland Islands.   The plant is eaten.[3]

O. frutescens Ruiz & Pav.

Peru.   The acid leaves are eaten in America.[4]

O. plumieri Jacq.

South America and Antilles.   Its leaves are eaten.

O. tetraphylla Cav.

Mexico.   It yields edible roots of not high quality.[5]

O. tuberosa Molina.   OCA.

Chile.   Oca is cultivated in the Andes from Chile to Mexico for its tubers, which vary from the size of peas to that of nuts and, says Unger,[6] are of no very pleasant taste.

O. violacea Linn.

North America.   This species is edible.[7]

Oxycoccus macrocarpus Pers.   *Vacciniaceae.*   CRANBERRY.

Temperate regions.   The American cranberry grows in bogs from Virginia to Wisconsin and extends to the Pacific coast.   It is mentioned by Roger Williams [8] under the name *sasemineash* and was eaten by the Indians of New England.   The fruit is boiled and eaten at the present day by the Indians of the Columbia River under the name *soolabich.*   The fruit is an article of commerce among the tribes of the Northwest.   About 1820, a few vines were cared for at Dennis, Massachusetts, but not until about 1840 can the trials at cultivation be said to have commenced, and not until 1845 was the fact established that the cranberry could be utilized as a marketable commodity.   Cranberries are now very extensively grown at Cape Cod and in New Jersey and Wisconsin.   Under favorable conditions, the vines are exceedingly productive.   In New Jersey, in 1879, a Mr. Bishop raised over 400 bushels on one acre and parts of acres have yielded at the rate of 700 to 1000 bushels per acre, but such prolificacy is exceptional.   There are several recognized varieties.

O. palustris Pers.   CRANBERRY.   MOSSBERRY.

Northern climates.   This is the cranberry of Britain which is in occasional cultivation.   The fruit is considered of superior flavor to the American cranberry but is smaller. The latter is a plant of peat bogs in the northern United States and on uplands in the

---

[1] Loudon, J. C.   *Hort.* 654.   1860.

[2] Smith, J.   *Dom. Bot.* 495.   1871.

[3] Ross *Voy. Antarct. Reg.* 2:269.   1847.

[4] Baillon, H.   *Hist. Pls.* 5:32.   1878.

[5] Unger *U. S. Pat. Off. Rpt.* 311.   1859.

[6] Ibid.

[7] Ibid.

[8] Williams, R.   *Key.* 1643.   Narragansett Hist. Coll. 1:121.   1866.

British territory.   One authority says that on the Nipigan coast of Lake Superior " the surface is flaming red with berries, more delicious than anything of the kind I have ever tasted."

Oxyria digyna Hill.   *Polygonaceae.*   MOUNTAIN SORREL.

Mountains of the north and arctic region, northern America as far as latitude 64° to 80° north.[1]   The leaves are chopped with scurvy grass or water cress and are fermented and eaten by the Alaska Indians, who are very partial to this dish.[2]

Oxystelma esculentum R. Br.   *Aclepiadeae.*

Australia.   Royle[3] says this plant is described as being edible.

Pachira aquatica Aubl.   *Malvaceae.*   MALABAR CHESTNUT.

Tropical America.   The mealy seeds of this tree, when roasted, taste like chestnuts. The young leaves and flowers are used as a vegetable.[4]   There is nothing better than this chestnut cooked with a little salt.[5]

P. grandiflora Tussac.

West Indies.   The seeds are eaten as chestnuts are.[6]

P. insignis Savign.

Mexico and Guiana.   The seeds, young leaves and flowers serve as food.[7]

Pachyrhizus angulatus Rich.   *Leguminosae.*

Tropical Asia, Central America, the East and West Indies, Mauritius and Fiji Islands. The root, a single turnip-formed tuber, when young, is eaten, both raw and boiled, by the inhabitants of India and the Mauritius.[8]   Its coarse roots furnish food to the poor in China, when boiled, or when dried, and pounded into a flour.[9]   In the Malay Archipelago, the plant produces a large, edible, tuberous root.[10]   The Fiji Islanders, who call the plant *yaka* or *wayaka*, obtain a tough fiber from the stems, with which they make fishing nets.[11]   In China and Cochin China, where it is cultivated, the tubers, which are cylindrical and about two feet long, are eaten boiled as yams are.[12]   Smith[13] says the tubers are eaten but are deleterious if not thoroughly cooked.   A kind of arrowroot is made from the root

[1] Kane, E. K.   *Arctic Explor.* 2:460.   1857.   App. XVIII.
[2] Dall, W. H.   *U. S. D. A. Rpt.* 422.   1870.
[3] Royle, J. F.   *Illustr. Bot. Himal.* 1:274.   1839.
[4] Unger, F.   *U. S. Pat. Off. Rpt.* 315.   1859.   (*Carolinea princeps*)
[5] Belanger *Trans. N. Y. Agr. Soc.* 568.   1858.   (*Carolinea princeps*)
[6] Tussac *Fl. Antill.* 4:12.   1808–1827.
[7] Unger, F.   *U. S. Pat. Off. Rpt.* 315.   1859.   (*Carolinea insignis*)
[8] Don, G.   *Hist. Dichl. Pls.* 2:361.   1832.
[9] Williams, S. W.   *U. S. Pat. Off. Rpt.* 474.   1860.   (*Dolichos bulbosus*)
[10] Pickering, C.   *Chron. Hist.* 680.   1879.
[11] Smith, A.   *Treas. Bot.* 2:834.   1870.
[12] Loudon, J. C.   *Arb. Frut. Brit.* 2:649.   1844.
[13] Smith, F. P.   *Contrib. Mat. Med. China* 88.   1871.

in some places.   The roots are eaten in Viti.   Seemann [1] says they are of a dirty white color when cooked and have a slightly starchy, insipid flavor.

P. tuberosus Spreng.   POTATO BEAN.

West Indies.   The plant has large, tuberous roots, which, as well as the seeds, serve as food.[2]   It is called *yalai* by the people of New Caledonia, and the roots are roasted and eaten.[3]

Paederia foetida Linn.   *Rubiaceae.*

East Indies, Malay and Hindustan.   This is a long, cylindrical plant, which gives off a most offensive odor when bruised.   The leaves, boiled and made into soup, are considered wholesome and suitable for the sick and convalescent, as Dutt [4] writes.

Paeonia albiflora Pall.   *Ranunculaceae.*   PAEONY.

Northern Asia.   This species is to be seen in ornamental gardens.   The roots are used as food in Mongolia, being boiled and eaten by the Tartars, who also powder the seeds to mix with their tea.

Panax fruticosum Linn.   *Araliaceae.*   PANAX.

Tropical Asia, Malay and Polynesia.   This aromatic plant is much cultivated in the Island of Ternate by the natives for food and for medicine.   The boiled leaves are eaten as greens.[5]

Pancratium maritimum Linn.   *Amaryllideae.*   SEA DAFFODIL.

Europe.   This plant is said to have properties resembling those of the squill.   The bulbs were shown among food specimens at the International Exhibition of 1862.[6]

Pandanus leram Jones.   *Pandaneae.*

Nicobar Islands.   In the Nicobar Islands, the immense fruit cones consist of several single, wedge-shaped fruits, which, when raw, are uneatable, but, boiled in water and subjected to pressure, they give out a sort of mealy mass.   This is the *melori* of the Portuguese and the *larohm* of the natives.   It is also occasionally used with the fleshy interior of the ripe fruit and forms the daily bread of the islanders.   The flavor of the mass thus prepared strongly resembles that of apple marmalade and is by no means unpalatable to Europeans.

P. odoratissimus Linn. f.   BREADFRUIT.   PANDANG.   SCREW PINE.

The terminal bud is eaten under the name of cabbage; the tender white base of the leaves is also eaten raw or boiled, during famines.[7]   Kotzebur [8] says it constitutes the chief

---

[1] Seemann, B.   *Fl. Viti.* 63.   1865–73.

[2] Unger, F.   *U. S. Pat. Off. Rpt.* 311.   1859.   (*Dolichos tuberosus*)

[3] Labillardière *Voy. Recherche Pérouse* 2:217.   1799.

[4] Dutt, U. C.   *Mat. Med. Hindus* 178.   1877.

[5] Rumphius *Herb. Ambon.* 4:78.   1741–1755.

[6] *Bot. Soc. Edinb.* 8:163.   1866.

[7] Royle, J. F.   *Illustr. Bot. Himal.* 1:408.   1839.

[8] Hooker, W. J.   *Bot. Misc.* 1:309.   1830.

food of the people of Radack. It is chewed raw for the aromatic juice and is also baked in pits.

P. pedunculatus R. Br. BREADFRUIT. SCREW PINE.

Australia and New Holland. Fraser[1] says this plant is called breadfruit and is eagerly eaten by the natives.

P. sp.? SCREW PINE.

Under the name of *kapupu*, a staple article of food is prepared in the. islands of the Gilbert group from the soft, central portion of the fruit heads of species of pandanus.[2] Adams[3] says, among the Meia-co-shimah Islands, he first had the curiosity to taste the fruit of the screw pine and found it refreshing and juicy but very insipid. When perfectly mature, he continues, they certainly look very tempting and resemble large, rich-colored pineapples. The stones, though very hard, contain a pleasant kernel.

Pangium edule Reinw. *Bixineae.*

Java. The bark is used for poisoning fish, and the nuts, when macerated in water, are rendered partially wholesome but are used only as a condiment.[4]

Panicum colonum Linn. *Gramineae.* MILLET.

Tropics. This millet grows wild in parts of India in sufficient plenty to be collected in times of scarcity to be employed as food.[5]

P. decompositum R. Br. AUSTRALIAN MILLET.

East Indies and Australia. The aborigines convert the small, millet-like grains into cakes.[6]

P. miliaceum Linn. MILLET.

Tropics. This species was cultivated in southern Europe in the time of Hippocrates and Theophrastus[7] and was known to the Romans in the time of Julius Caesar. It is the *kegchros* of Strabo, who states that it thrives excellently in Gaul and is the best protection against famine.[8] It is described by Pliny[9] as constituting the principal food of the Sarmatians, who say that the Ethiopians know of no other grain but millet and barley. It is also mentioned by Hesiod[10] and is referred to as cultivated in Italy by Columella[11] and Virgil.[12] In the embassy of Theodosius[13] to Attila, 448–9 A. D., beyond the Danube,

---

[1] Hooker, W. J. *Bot. Misc.* 1:250. 1830.
[2] *Gard. Chron.* 1878.
[3] Adams, A. *Voy. Samarang* 2:302. 1848.
[4] Smith, J. *Dom. Bot.* 403. 1871.
[5] Simmonds, P. L. *Trop. Agr.* 338. 1889.
[6] Mueller, F. *Sel. Pls.* 316. 1891. 8th Ed.
[7] Mueller, F. *Sel. Pls.* 318. 1891. 8th Ed.
[8] Unger, F. *U. S. Pat. Off. Rpt.* 305. 1859.
[9] Pickering, C. *Chron. Hist. Pls.* 79. 1879.
[10] Hooker, W. J. *Journ. Bot.* 1:214. 1834.
[11] Phillips, H. *Comp. Kitch. Gard.* 1:334. 1831.
[12] Virgil *Georgics* lib. 1, line 216.
[13] Guizot, F. P. G. *Hist. Civil.* 3:220. 1857.

millet was brought the party as provisions, and Johann Schultberger,[1] 1396–1427, speaks of millet as the only grain crop of Siberia and at Zepun on the Black Sea. In France, this millet is cultivated at the present time almost exclusively for forage; in Germany for the grain and also for fodder; in England it is unknown as an agricultural crop. It is cultivated largely in southern and western Asia, in northeastern Africa and to some extent in Italy and in Spain. It appears to be but little known as an agricultural crop in America. Jared Elliot,[2] 1747, speaks of seed being sent him under the name of East India wheat, but he says it was a millet, with small grain, the bigness of a turnip or cabbage seed and of a yellowish color. In 1822 and 1823, there are records of large crops of seed and hay grown in this country under the name of millet, but these may have been of other species than this. There are many varieties grown. Some 30 kinds are given for Ceylon. At the Madras exhibition of 1857, seven kinds were shown.

P. pilosum Sw.

South America. This grain is cultivated in India as a bread corn, under the name *bhadlee*.[3]

P. sanguinale Linn. CRAB GRASS. FINGER GRASS.

Cosmopolitan. This grain grows in abundance in Poland where it is sometimes cultivated for its seed and is in cultivation in waste ground in America, naturalized from Europe. In Europe, the small-hulled fruit furnishes a wholesome and palatable nourishment called manna grit.[4] This is the common crab grass, or finger grass, of America.

Papaver nudicaule Linn. *Papaveraceae.* ARCTIC POPPY.

This poppy was found by Kane [5] at all the stations on his two voyages to the Arctic seas and it extends probably, he says, to the furthest limit of vegetation. The leaves, and especially the seeds, which are very oleaginous, are a great resort in scorbutic affections and very agreeable to the taste. Pursh [6] gives its habitat as Labrador.

P. orientale Linn. ORIENTAL POPPY.

Asia Minor and Persia. This species was observed in the fields about Erzerum, Armenia. This is a very fine species of poppy which the Turks and Armenians call *aphion* as they do the common opium. They do not extract the opium from this kind but eat the heads as a delicacy when they are green, though very acrid and of a hot taste.[7]

P. rhoeas Linn. CORN POPPY. FIELD POPPY.

Europe, the Orient and north Africa. On the continent of Europe, this poppy is cultivated as an oil plant, the oil being esteemed next to that of the olive. The plant is in French flower gardens.[8]

---

[1] Schiltberger, J. *Trav.* 1397–1427. Hakl. Soc. Ed. 41. 1879.

[2] Elliot, Jared. *Essays Husb.* 51. 1811.

[3] *Treas. Bot.* 2:841. 1870.

[4] Unger, F. *U. S. Pat. Off. Rpt.* 306. 1859. (*Digitaria sanguinale*)

[5] Kane, E. K. *Arctic Explor.* 2:449. 1856.

[6] Pursh, F. *Fl. Amer. Septent.* 2:366. 1814.

[7] Tournefort *Voy. Levant* 2:118. 1718.

[8] Vilmorin *Fl. Pl. Ter.* 822. 1870. 3rd Ed. (*Pavot coquelicot*)

P. somniferum Linn. OPIUM POPPY.

Greece and the Orient. There are several varieties of the opium poppy, of which the two most prominent are called white and black from the color of their seeds. The opium poppy is a native of the Mediterranean region but is at present cultivated in India, Persia, Asiatic Turkey and occasionally, by way of experiment, in the United States, for the purpose of procuring opium. It is grown in northern France and the south of Germany for its seeds. This poppy is supposed to have been cultivated by the ancient Greeks and is mentioned by Homer as a garden plant. Galen speaks of the seeds as good to season bread and says the white are better than the black. The Persians sprinkle the seeds of poppies over their rice, and the seeds are used in India as a food and a sweetmeat. The seeds are also eaten, says Masters,[1] in Greece, Poland and elsewhere. In France, the seeds are made to yield by expression a bland oil, which is used as a substitute for olive oil. In Sikkim, Edgeworth[2] remarks, the seeds afford oil as well as an agreeable food, remarkably refreshing during fatigue and abstinence. Carpenter[3] says the peasants of Languedoc employ young poppies as food. The Chinese drink, smoke or chew opium to produce intoxication, and this depraved use has extended more or less to other countries.

Pappea capensis Eckl. & Zeyh. *Sapindaceae*. WILD PLUM.

South Africa. The fruit is edible. A vinous beverage and a vinegar are prepared from it, and an edible, though slightly purgative, oil is expressed from its seeds.[4] Mueller[5] says the fruit is the size of a cherry, savory and edible.

Parietaria officinalis Linn. *Urticaceae*. PELLITORY.

Southern Europe and the Orient. This plant is mentioned by Theophrastus as cooked and eaten.[6]

Parinarium campestre Aubl. *Rosaceae*.

French Guiana. The drupe is small, oval, yellow. The single seed is edible.[7]

P. excelsum Sabine. ROUGH-SKINNED OR GRAY PLUM.

Tropical Africa. The fruit is greatly esteemed by the negroes and is plentifully supplied in the markets. It is produced in the greatest abundance and is about the size and shape of an Imperatrice plum, with a coarse skin of a grayish color. The pulp is dry, farinaceous, small in quantity and of an insipid taste.[8]

P. macrophyllum Sabine. GINGERBREAD PLUM.

Tropical Africa. The fruit is oblong in form, twice the size of that of *P. excelsum* but otherwise resembling it in flavor and appearance.[9]

---

[1] Masters, M. T. *Treas. Bot.* 2:842. 1870.
[2] Hooker, W. J. *Journ. Bot.* 2:269. 1840.
[3] Carpenter, W. B. *Veg. Phys. Bot.* 203. 1844.
[4] Smith, A. *Treas. Bot.* 2:844. 1870.
[5] Mueller, F. *Sel. Pls.* 323. 1891.
[6] Pickering, C. *Chron. Hist. Pls.* 276. 1879.
[7] Don, G. *Hist. Dichl. Pls.* 2:478. 1832.
[8] Sabine, J. *Trans. Hort. Soc. Lond.* 5:451. 1824.
[9] Ibid.

P. montanum Aubl.

French Guiana.   The drupe is large, ovate, smooth and fibrous, has a thick, acrid rind, and the nut, or kernel, is sweet and edible.[1]

P. nonda F. Muell.   NONDA.

Northeast Australia.   This species bears edible, mealy, plum-like fruit.[2]

Paris polyphylla Sm.   *Liliaceae.*

Himalayan region and China.   The seeds are eaten by the Lepchas of the Himalayas. They are sweet but mawkish.[3]

Parkia africana R. Br.   *Leguminosae.*   AFRICAN LOCUST.

Tropical western Africa.   The natives of Sudan, who call the tree *dours,* roast the seeds and then bruise and allow them to ferment in water until they become putrid, when they are carefully washed, pounded into powder and made into cakes, which are excellent sauce for all kinds of food but have an unpleasant smell.   An agreeable beverage is prepared from the sweet, farinaceous pulp surrounding the seeds.   Sweetmeats are also made of it.[4]   The pods contain a yellow, farinaceous substance enveloping the seeds, of which the negroes of Sierra Leone are fond, its flavor being similar to that of the monkey-bread. This is the fruit mentioned by Park as a mimosa called by the negroes *nitta,* which furnishes a nutritive and agreeable food from its seed-pods.

P. biglandulosa Wight & Arn.

Malay.   The seeds are eaten by the Malays, who relish them as well as the mealy matter which surrounds them.   The former taste like garlic.[5]

Parmentiera edulis DC.   *Bignoniaceae.*

Mexico.   The fruit resembles a cucumber in shape, with a rough surface and is eaten. The tree is middle-sized.[6]

Paropsia edulis Thou.   *Passifloreae.*

Madagascar.   The aril of the seeds is edible.[7]

Paspalum ciliatum H. B. & K.   *Gramineae.*

Brazil.   This is a perennial and a lauded cereal grass of tropical South America.[8]

P. exile Kippist

Tropical Africa.   This is a food grass called *fundunjii* in west Africa.[9]

---

[1] Don, G.   *Hist. Dichl. Pls.* 2:478.   1832.

[2] Mueller, F.   *Sel. Pls.* 324.   1891.

[3] Hooker, J. D.   *Illustr. Himal. Pls.* Pl. 24.   1855.

[4] Smith, A.   *Treas. Bot.* 2:847.   1870.

[5] Royle, J. F.   *Illustr. Bot. Himal.* 1:183.   1839.

[6] Seemann, B.   *Treas. Bot.* 2:848.   1870.

[7] Don, G.   *Hist. Dichl. Pls.* 3:46.   1834.

[8] Mueller, F.   *Sel. Pls.* 324.   1891.

[9] Henfrey, A.   *Bot.* 399.   1870.

P. scorbiculatum Linn. KODA MILLET.

Old World tropics. This grain is grown to some extent in most parts of India. The seed is an article of diet with the Hindus, particularly with those who inhabit the hill regions and the most barren parts of the country, for it is in such districts it is chiefly cultivated, being an unprofitable crop and not sown where others more beneficial will thrive.[1] It is used only by the poorest classes, says Elliott[2] and is not reckoned very wholesome. Graham[3] says this millet is very common and cheap about Bombay but unwholesome. It is the *agrion krithon*, furnishing good bread and gruel but which, at first, killed the horses of the Greeks until by degrees they became accustomed to it, as related by Theophrastus.

Passiflora alata Ait. *Passifloreae.* PASSION FLOWERS.

Peru. A plant of climbing habit, grown in greenhouses for its flowers. The fruit is edible.

P. bournapartea Baxt.

Tropical Africa. This species is cultivated in greenhouses for its beautiful red, white and blue flowers. The fruit is edible.

P. caerulea Linn. BLUE PASSION FLOWER.

Brazil. The fruit is egg-shaped, the size of a Mogul plum and yellow when ripe.[4] It is cultivated in the gardens of Egypt.

P. coccinea Aubl.

Guiana. The aril of the fruit is edible.[5]

P. edulis Sims.

Brazil and the West Indies. The pulp of the fruit is orange-colored, the taste acid and the flavor somewhat like that of an orange.[6] The fruit in India is the size of an egg, green at first but, when ripe, is of a beautiful plum color[7] and of an agreeable and and cooling taste.[8]

P. filamentosa Cav.

South America. It has edible fruit.[9]

P. foetida Linn. LOVE-IN-A-MIST. WILD WATER LEMON.

Brazil and Jamaica. The fruit is yellow, enclosed in a netted calyx and has a pleasant smell; though all the other parts of the plant have a disagreeable odor when touched.

[1] Simmonds, P. L. *Trop. Agr.* 340. 1889.
[2] Elliott, W. *Bot. Soc. Edinb.* 7:289. 1863.
[3] Pickering, C. *Chron. Hist. Pls.* 332. 1879.
[4] Don, G. *Hist. Dichl. Pls.* 3:53. 1834.
[5] Don, G. *Hist. Dichl. Pls.* 3:50. 1834.
[6] Don, G. *Hist. Dichl. Pls.* 3:53. 1834.
[7] Firminger, T. A. C. *Gard. Ind.* 197. 1874.
[8] Smith, J. *Dict. Econ. Pls.* 197. 1882.
[9] Masters, M. T. *Treas. Bot.* 2:851. 1870.

The fruit is about the size of a Golden Pippin apple, white within, membranous and contains numerous seeds involved in an agreeable, sweet-acid pulp.[1]

P. herbertiana Bot. Reg.

Australia. According to Fraser, in New Holland the oval fruit is produced in great quantities and affords a grateful flavor.[2]

P. incarnata Linn. MAYPOPS.

Subtropical America from Virginia to Kentucky and southward. It has been cultivated by the Indians from early times. This is the *maracock* observed by Strachey[3] on the James River, " of the bigness of a green apple, and hath manie azurine or blew kernells, like as a pomegranat, a good sommer cooling fruit."

P. laurifolia Linn. WATER LEMON.

Tropical America. In Jamaica, the fruit is much esteemed, says Lunan,[4] being very delicate. It is the size of an egg and full of a very agreeable, gelatinous pulp in which the seeds are lodged. Titford[5] says the fruit is very good.

P. ligularis A. Juss.

Tropical America. The fruit is edible.[6]

P. lutea Linn.

West Indies. The plant bears edible fruit.[7]

P. macrocarpa Mast. PASSION FLOWER.

Rio Negro region of South America and cultivated in greenhouses for its large flowers. The fruits are very large, sometimes weighing as much as eight pounds. The fleshy aril attached to the seeds or the juicy pulp is the part eaten.[8]

P. maliformis Linn. CONCH APPLE. CONCH NUT. SWEET CALABASH. WATER LEMON.

West Indies. The fruit is round, smooth, about two inches in diameter, of a dingy color when ripe. It has a pale yellow, agreeable, gelatinous pulp, which is eaten with wine and sugar.[9]

P. quadrangularis Linn. GRANADILLA.

Tropical America. The fruit is of an oval shape and of various sizes from that of a goose egg to a middling-sized muskmelon; it is of a greenish-yellow color, having a spongy rind about a finger in thickness, which becomes soft as the fruit ripens, contains a succulent pulp of a water color and sweet smell, is of a very agreeable, pleasant, sweet-acid taste

---

[1] Lunan, J. *Hort. Jam.* 1:466. 1814.

[2] Hooker, W. J. *Bot. Misc.* 1:247, 248. 1830.

[3] Strachey, W. *Trav. Va.* Hakl. Soc. Ed. 6:119. 1849.

[4] Lunan, J. *Hort. Jam.* 1:39. 1814.

[5] Titford, W. J. *Hort. Bot. Amer.* 91. 1812.

[6] Masters, M. T. *Treas. Bot.* 2:851. 1870.

[7] Ibid.

[8] Ibid.

[9] Don, G. *Hist. Dichl. Pls.* 3:51. 1884.

and contains a multitude of black seeds, which are eaten with the pulp.[1] Titford [2] says it is delicious. The granadilla is cultivated in tropical America and in India and is grown in conservatories for its flowers. If fruit be wanted, the flowers must be artifically fertilized.

P. serrata Linn.

Mauritius. It has edible fruit.[3]

Paullinia cupana H. B. & K. *Sapindaceae.*

Brazil. The seeds are mingled with cassava and water and allowed to ferment, forming the favorite drink of the Orinoco Indians.[4] The pounded seeds form *guarana* bread. This bread is made by the Indians and is highly esteemed in Brazil. About 16000 pounds are exported from Santarem.[5] The bread is grated into sugar and water and forms a diet drink.[6] Its active principle is a substance called guaranine, which is identical in composition with the thein of tea.[7]

P. subrotunda Pers.

Royle [8] says this plant has an edible aril. Henfrey [9] says the seeds are eaten.

Pavetta indica Linn. *Rubiaceae.*

Asia and tropical Australia. The fruit, which is of a green color, is eaten by the natives but is oftener made into a pickle.[10]

Pectinaria articulata Haw. *Asclepiadeae.*

South Africa. Thunberg [11] says this thick plant without leaves, is eaten, after being pickled, by the Hottentots, and also by the colonists.

Pedalium murex Linn. *Pedalineae.*

Tropical eastern Asia. The leafy stems, says Drury,[12] are used in thickening buttermilk, to which they give a rich appearance. Roxburgh [13] says venders of buttermilk are in the habit of diluting their merchandise with water and then thickening the mixture with this plant, which makes the adulterated article seem rich and of the best sort. A. Smith [14] says that water becomes mucilaginous by being simply stirred with the fresh branches of this plant.

---

[1] Lunan, J. *Hort. Jam.* 1:334. 1814.

[2] Titford, W. J. *Hort. Bot. Amer.* 91. 1812.

[3] Lindley, J. *Veg. King.* 333. 1853.

[4] Moore, T. *Treas. Bot.* 2:853. 1870.

[5] Simmonds, P. L. *Trop. Agr.* 26. 1889.

[6] Herndon, W. L., and Gibbon, L. *Explor. Vall. Amaz.* 1:266. 1854. Note.

[7] Smith, A. *Treas. Bot.* 2:853. 1870.

[8] Royle, J. F. *Illustr. Bot. Himal.* 1:137. 1839.

[9] Henfrey, A. *Bot.* 234. 1870. (*P. sorbilis*)

[10] Ainslie, W. *Mat. Ind.* 2:289. 1826.

[11] Thunberg, C. P. *Trav.* 2:171. 1796. (*Stapelia articulata*)

[12] Drury, H. *Useful Pls. Ind.* 334. 1873.

[13] Wight, R. *Icon. Pls.* 4: Pl. 1615. 1850.

[14] Smith, A. *Treas. Bot.* 2:855. 1870.

Pedicularis langsdorffi Fisch. *Scrophularineae.* LOUSEWORT.

Arctic regions. Ainslie[1] says the leaves are employed as a substitute for tea by the inhabitants of the Kurile Islands.

Pelargonium acetosum Soland. *Geraniaceae.* STORK'S BILL.

Cape of Good Hope. The buds and acid leaves are eaten.[2]

P. peltatum Ait.

South Africa. At the Cape of Good Hope, the buds and acid leaves are eaten.[3]

P. triste Ait.

South Africa. Syme[4] says the tubers are eaten at the Cape of Good Hope.

P. zonale L'Hérit.

South Africa. The leaves and stalks are eaten in Yemen.[5]

Peltandra virginica Rafin. *Ariodeae.* ARROW ARUM. VIRGINIAN WAKE ROBIN.

Eastern North America. Bartram told Kalm that the Indians ate the boiled spadix and berries as a luxury. When the berries are raw they have a harsh, pungent taste, which they lose in great measure upon boiling. The Indians also eat the roots cooked but never raw, as they are then reckoned poisonous.[6]

Peltaria alliacea Jacq. *Cruciferae.* GARLIC CRESS.

Central Europe. This plant is classed as an edible by botanists.

Pemphis acidula Forst. *Lythraceae.*

Tropical Asia and islands of the Pacific. The leaves are used as a potherb along the shores.[7]

Pennisetum dasystachyum Desv. *Gramineae.*

Guiana. Barth, in *Travels in Northern Africa*, says, at Agades, the slaves were busy collecting and pounding the seeds of the *karengia*, or *uzak*, which constitutes a great part of their food. Livingstone says the seeds are collected regularly by the slaves over a large portion of central Africa and are used as food.

P. typhoideum Rich. SPIKED MILLET.

Tropics. This grass is supposed by Pickering[8] to be a native of tropical America. It is extensively cultivated about Bombay and forms a very important article of food to the natives.[9] In Africa, Livingstone[10] found it cultivated in great quantities as food for

---

[1] Ainslie, W. *Mat. Ind.* 1:128. 1826.

[2] Baillon, H. *Hist. Pls.* 5:32. 1878.

[3] Ibid.

[4] Syme, J. T. *Treas. Bot.* 1:856. 1870.

[5] Forskal *Fl. Aeg. Arab.* XCIII. 1775.

[6] Kalm, P. *Trav. No. Amer.* 1:98, 387, 388. 1772. (*Arum virginicum*)

[7] Lindley, J. *Veg. King.* 575. 1853.

[8] Pickering, C. *Chron. Hist. Pls.* 898. 1879.

[9] Ibid.

[10] Livingstone, D. *Trav. Research. So. Afr.* 350. 1858.

man. This species is cultivated in many varieties in India, where it is a native. Drury [1] says it is much cultivated in Coromandel, and that the grain is a very essential article of diet among the natives of the northern Circars. The seeds, says Unger, [2] constitute the principal article of food for the negroes in various parts of Africa. Four varieties are cultivated by the native farmers of Bengal who eat the grain and feed their cattle with the straw. [3]

Pentaclethra macrophylla Benth. *Leguminosae.*

Tropical Africa. A tree, known in Gabun as *owala* and in the Eboo country as *opachalo.* The seeds are eaten by the natives, who also extract a limpid oil from them. [4]

Pentadesma butyracea Sabine. *Guttiferae.* BUTTER TREE. TALLOW TREE.

Tropical Africa. The fruit is eaten. [5] The yellow, greasy juice, which flows from the fruit when it is cut, is mixed by the inhabitants of Sierra Leone with their food but is not used by Europeans on account of the strong, turpentine flavor. [6]

Pentatropis cynanchoides R. Br. *Asclepiadeae.*

Abyssinia, Persia and northwest India. Its follicles are eaten. [7]

Peplis portula Linn. *Lythrarieae.* WATER PURSLANE.

Europe and adjoining Asia. This plant is mentioned by Theophrastus as cultivated, by Dioscorides as esculent; it is mentioned also by Pliny, Varro and Columella. About Athens, it is eaten in salads. [8]

Pereskia aculeata Mill. *Cacteae.* BARBADOES GOOSEBERRY.

West Indies. The fruit is yellow, edible, pleasant to the taste and is used in the West Indies for preserving. [9]

P. bleo DC.

Mexico and New Granada. The leaves are eaten as a salad in Panama and are called *bleo* by the natives. [10]

Pergularia edulis Thunb. *Asclepiadeae.*

South Africa. The young leaves are eaten as a potherb in Japan. [11]

---

[1] Drury, H. *Useful Pls. Ind.* 335. 1873.

[2] Unger, F. *U. S. Pat. Off. Rpt.* 306, 307. 1859. (*Penicillaria spicata*)

[3] Roxburgh, W. *Hort. Beng.* 7. 1814.

[4] Jackson, J. R. *Treas. Bot.* 2:1327. 1876.

[5] *Treas. Bot.* 2:860. 1870.

[6] Don, G. *Hist. Dichl. Pls.* 1:619. 1831.

[7] Pickering, C. *Chron. Hist. Pls.* 390. 1879. (*Asclepias spiralis*)

[8] Pickering, C. *Chron. Hist. Pls.* 244. 1879.

[9] Smith, A. *Treas. Bot.* 2:863. 1870.

[10] Ibid.

[11] Seemann, B. *Treas. Bot.* 2:863. 1870.

Perilla arguta Benth. *Labiatae.*

China and Japan. An infusion of this plant is used, says Mueller,[1] to impart to table vegetables and other substances a deep red color. The plant is an inmate of French flower gardens.[2]

Periploca aphylla Decne. *Asclepiadeae.*

Northwest India, Afghanistan, south Persia, Arabia and Egypt. The flower-buds, says Brandis,[3] are sweet and are eaten, raw or cooked, as a vegetable.

Persea gratissima Gaertn. f. *Laurineae.* ABACATE. AHUACATE. ALLIGATOR PEAR. AVOCADO. AVOCATE. VEGETABLE MARROW.

A tree of tropical America. The avocado has been naturalized on the islands of Bourbon and Mauritius since 1758. In Brazil, it is one of the most highly-prized fruits. The fruit is like a large pear, with a green, leathery rind and a tender, juicy flesh which incloses a hard nut. The flesh, made into a sauce with citron juice and sugar, has a delightful taste. In itself, the flesh is insipid but tender and soft, tasting like artichokes. Moritz Wagner says it may be called vegetable butter as it melts upon the tongue.[4] Arruda[5] says the fruit is very pleasant and that there are in Brazil two varieties, one of which is called *cayenne*. Morelet[6] says the variety in Central America called *avocate* is a pulpy fruit with a thin, smooth, leathery skin of a green color, spotted with red, resembling much a large pear. It contains a large, oval stone, which, when the fruit ripens and is ready to eat, becomes loose and rattles in its center. The pulp is of a delicate coffee color, unctuous, without odor, resembles fresh butter and is eaten with a spoon. This fruit is rarely palatable at first to the stranger, but it finally recommends itself by its wonderfully delicate, agreeable and peculiar flavor. The second variety is called by the Indians *omtchon*. It differs from the first by the contraction of the part nearest the stem, by its sharp, conic base, by its thick, wrinkled, light green skin and by the tenacity with which the skin adheres to the pulp. A third kind is also known, called *anison*. It is not as highly esteemed as the others and has a very strong, peculiar odor. In Jamaica, says Long,[7] there are two species, the green and the red, the latter preferred, but the quality of the fruit varies; that produced in a wild state is small and often bitter. The pulp is in universal esteem and is called by some vegetable marrow and is generally eaten with sugar and lime juice or pepper and salt. It has a delicate, rich flavor. Lunan[8] says few people relish the fruit at first but it soon becomes agreeable. In an immature state, the fruit is very dangerous. It is cultivated to a limited extent in south Florida.

---

[1] Mueller, F. *Sel. Pls.* 330. 1891.

[2] Vilmorin *Fl. Pl. Ter.* 839. 1870. 3rd Ed.

[3] Brandis, D. *Forest Fl.* 330. 1876.

[4] Unger, F. *U. S. Pat. Off. Rpt.* 348. 1859.

[5] Koster, H. *Trav. Braz.* 2:363. 1817. (*Laurus persea*)

[6] Morelet *Trav. Cent. Amer.* 264, 265. 1871.

[7] Long *Hist. Jam.* 3:808. 1774.

[8] Lunan, J. *Hort. Jam.* 1:37. 1814.

Petasites japonicus F. Schmidt. *Compositae.*

Sakhalin Islands. The young, tender petioles of the leaves are said by Penhallow to be largely used by the Japanese of Yeso as a food. The native name is *fuki*. It is held in high esteem among the Ainos, although devoid of flavor. The plants are cultivated for their succulent petioles.[1]

Peteria scoparia A. Gray. *Leguminosae.*

New Mexico. This is a stout, spiny, suffruticose herb with a small, edible, tuberous rootstock.[2]

Peucedanum ambiguum Nutt. *Umbelliferae.* BISCUITROOT. BREADROOT. KONSE.

Western North America. The root is called breadroot or biscuitroot by travelers and *konse* by the Indians of Oregon and Idaho. The Canadians call it *racine blanc*. When fresh, it is like the parsnip in taste and, as the plant dies, the root becomes brittle and very white with an agreeable taste of mild celery. It is easily reduced to flour and is much used for food.[3]

P. farinosum Geyer.

Western North America. The round to oblong, white root is gathered by the Oregon Indians.

P. foeniculaceum Nutt.

Western North America. The roots are eaten by the Indians.[4]

P. geyeri S. Wats.

The tubers are an Indian food.[5]

P. graveolens Benth. & Hook. f. DILL.

Europe and Asia. This hardy, biennial plant was introduced to Britain in 1570. Masters [6] says this is supposed to be the plant which is called *arrise* in the New Testament narrative. Dill is commonly regarded as the *anethon* of Dioscorides and the *anethum* of Pliny, Palladius and others. The name dill is found in writings of the Middle Ages, and dill is spoken of as a garden plant in the early botanies. In England, it was called *dyll* by Turner,[7] 1538, which proves its presence at that date. It also occurs in the vocabulary of Alfric, Archbishop of Canterbury, in the tenth century.[8] Dill was in American gardens before 1806.[9] It seems to be spontaneous in the far West as its roots are used as food by the Snake and Shoshoni Indians, by whom it is called *yampeh*.[10] It is

---

[1] Penhallow, D. P. *Amer. Nat.* **16**:120. 1882.

[2] Havard, V. *Proc. U. S. Nat. Mus.* 501. 1885

[3] *U. S. D. A. Rpt.* 407. 1870.

[4] Brown, R. *Bot. Soc. Edinb.* **9**:380. 1868.

[5] Havard, V. *Torr. Bot. Club Bul.* **22**:110. 1895.

[6] Masters, M. T. *Treas. Bot.* **1**:66. 1870. (*Anethum graveolens*)

[7] Turner *Libellus* 1538.

[8] Flückiger and Hanbury *Pharm.* 328. 1879.

[9] McMahon, B. *Amer. Gard. Cal.* 199. 1806.

[10] *U. S. D. A. Rpt.* 405. 1870.

cultivated for its leaves and seeds.   The former are used as flavors in soups and sauces, and the seeds are added to pickled cucumbers to heighten the flavor.   In India, the seeds are much used for culinary and medicinal purposes.   The seeds are to be found in every Indian bazaar and form one of the chief ingredients in curry powder.[1]

P. nudicaule Nutt.   SYMRNIUM.

Western North America.   The Indians boil the tops in soups the same as we use celery.[2]   Beckwith [3] says the roots are used as food by the Indians of the West.

P. ostruthium Koch.   MASTERWORT.

Europe.   The foliage was formerly boiled and eaten as a potherb.[4]

P. palustre Moench.   MARSH HOG'S FENNEL.   MILK PARSLEY.

Europe.   The roots are used in Russia as a substitute for ginger.[5]

P. sativum Benth. & Hook. f.   PARSNIP.

Europe and North America.   The parsnip is a biennial, the root of which has been in use as an esculent from an early period.   The Emperor Tiberius, according to Pliny,[6] was so fond of parsnips that he had them brought annually from Germany, from the neighborhood of Gelduba on the Rhine, where they were said to be grown in great perfection.   The wild plant, according to Don,[7] is a native of Europe even to the Caucasus; in North America, on the banks of the Saskatchewan and Red River; in South America about Buenos Aires; and is naturalized in northeastern America.   The root of the wild plant is spindle-shaped, white, aromatic, mucilaginous and sweet, with a degree of acrimony. From the seeds of the wild variety in the garden of the Royal Agricultural Society at Cirencester,[8] originated the highly-appreciated garden variety known as Student.   It has been supposed that the *pastinaca* of the Romans included the carrot and the parsnip, and that the *elaphoboscon* of Pliny [9] was the parsnip.   Pliny describes the medicinal virtues of the *elaphoboscon* and says it is much esteemed as a food.   The references, however, do not prove this plant to be cultivated, nor do the references to the *pastinaca* satisfactorily indicate the parsnip.   One is willing to accept such evidence as we find that the cultivated parsnip was known to the ancient Greeks and Romans.   Among the early botanists, there is much confusion in names between the carrot and the parsnip.   The root must, however, have come into general use long before these records and perhaps its culture started in Germany, as it seems to have been unknown to Ruellius,[10] 1536, but is recorded by Fuchsius [11] in Germany, 1542, who gives a figure but calls it *gross zam mosen*.   The

---

[1] Drury, H.   *Useful Pls. of Ind.* 43.   1873.

[2] Pursh, F.   *Fl. Amer. Septent.* 1:196.   1814.

[3] Beckwith *Pacific R. R. Rpt. Survey* 2:121.   1855.

[4] Johnson, C. P.   *Useful Pls. Gt. Brit.* 126.   1862.

[5] Ibid.

[6] Booth, W. B.   *Treas. Bot.* 2:851.   1870.

[7] Don, G.   *Hist. Dichl. Pls.* 3:338.   1834.

[8] *Journ. Roy. Agr. Soc.* 15:125.   1854.

[9] Pliny lib. 22, c. 37.

[10] Ruellius *Nat. Stirp.* 1536.

[11] Fuchsius *Hist. Stirp*   1542.

parsnip is figured by Roeszlin,[1] 1550, under the name *pestnachen* and in 1552 is recorded by Tragus [2] as having a sweet root, used especially by the poor and better known in the kitchens than fat.

The following is a synonymy founded on pictures and descriptions combined, all representing our long parsnip-form of root but some indicating the hollow crown, upon which some of the modern varieties are founded, especially Camerarius in 1586:

Sisarum sativum magnum. Fuch. 751. 1542.

Pestnachen. Roeszl. 106. 1550.

Pastinaca sativa. Matth. 353. 1558; 500. 1570; 548. 1598; *Pin.* 318. 1561.

Pastinaca domestica vulgi. Lob. *Obs.* 407. 1576; *Icon.* **1**:709. 1591.

De Pastinaca. Pastenay, gerlin oder moren. Pictorius 94. 1581.

Pastinaca domestica. Cam. *Epit.* 507. 1586; Dur. C. 837. 1617

Pastinaca sativa vulgi, Matthioli. Dalechamp 719. 1587.

Pastinaca latifolia sativa. Ger. 870. 1597; Dod. 680. 1616.

Pastinaca sativa latifolia, Germanica, luteo flore. Bauh. J. **2**: pt. 2, 150, 151. 1651.

Long parsnips of the moderns

In 1683, the long parsnips are figured in England as in great use for a delicate, sweet food;[3] are spoken of by Ray,[4] 1686; Townsend,[5] 1726; Mawe,[6] 1778; and Miller,[7] 1807.

The round parsnip is called *siam* by Don,[8] 1834. Its roots are funnel-shaped, tapering very abruptly, often curving inwards. There is little known of its early history. It was noted in the *Bon Jardinier* for 1824; as also by Pirolle [9] in *Le Hort. Français;* by McIntosh,[10] Burr [11] and other more recent writers.

The parsnip was brought to America by the earliest colonists. It is mentioned at Margarita Island by Hawkins,[12] 1564; in Peru by Acosta,[13] 1604; as cultivated in Virginia in 1609 [14] and 1648;[15] in Massachusetts in 1629 [16] and as common in 1630;[17] and was among the Indian foods destroyed by Gen. Sullivan [18] in western New York in 1779.

P. triternatum Nutt.

Western North America. The roots are of the size of peanuts and are collected very

---

[1] Roeszlin *Krauterb.* 106. 1550.

[2] Tragus *Stirp.* 441. 1552.

[3] Worlidge, J. *Syst. Hort.* 175. 1683.

[4] Ray *Hist. Pl.* 410. 1686.

[5] Townsend *Seedsman* 22. 1726.

[6] Mawe and Abercrombie *Univ. Gard. Bot.* 1778. (*Pastinaca sativa*)

[7] Martyn *Miller's Gard. Dict.* 1807.

[8] Don, G. *Hist. Dichl. Pls.* **3**:339. 1834.

[9] Pirolle *L'Hort. Franc.* 1824.

[10] McIntosh, C. *Book Gard.* **2**:230. 1855.

[11] Burr, F. *Field, Gard. Veg.* 50. 1863.

[12] Hawkins *Voy.* Hakl. Soc. Ed. 27. 1878.

[13] Acosta *Nat. Mor. Hist. Ind.* 261. 1604.

[14] *True Decl. Va.* 13. 1610. Force Coll. Tracts **3**: 1844.

[15] *Perf. Desc. Va.* 4. 1649. Force Coll. Tracts **2**: No. 8. 1838.

[16] Higginson *Mass. Hist. Soc. Coll.* 1st ser. **1**:118.

[17] *New Eng. Annoy.* 1630. Anon. The first recorded poem in America.

[18] Conover, G. S. *Early Hist. Geneva* 47. 1879.

largely by the Indians. When dried, they are hard and brittle and have a mild, sweet taste. They afford a good proportion of the food of some tribes.[1] The fusiform root when roasted is one of the grateful vegetables of the Indians.[2]

Peumus boldus Molina. *Monimiaceae.* BOLDU.

Chile. The white, buttery pulp of the fruit is of an agreeable taste.[3] The aromatic fruits, about the size of haws, are eaten.

Phaseolus aconitifolius Jacq. *Leguminosae.* MOTH BEAN. TURKISH GRAM.

East Indies. This bean is cultivated in India and is called, in Hindustan, *moot.* It is a variety that does not twine and is used principally for feeding domestic animals but also serves as a food for man.[4]

P. adenanthus G. F. W. Mey.

East Indies. This bean is cultivated for its seeds. A variety with edible roots occurs,[5] and its use in India by the natives is mentioned by Graham.

P. asellus Molina.

Chile. This species was in cultivation by the natives of Chile before the conquest. The bean is spherical and pulpy.[6]

P. calcaratus Roxb. RICE BEAN.

East Indies and Malay. This bean is generally cultivated in India for its pulse. The plant is a twining one.[7]

P. caracalla Linn. CARACOL. CORKSCREW-FLOWER. SNAIL-FLOWER.

Tropics. Under the name of caracol, this species is often grown in the gardens of South America, North America, southern Europe and sometimes in India for its large, showy and sweet-scented flowers.[8] It seems doubtful if the pod or pulse is eaten.

P. derasus Schrank.

South America. The beans are used as a vegetable.[9]

P. lunatus Linn. CIVET BEAN. LIMA BEAN. SIEVA BEAN.

Tropics. The lima bean is unquestionably of American origin, and De Candolle assigns its original habitat to Brazil, where the variety *macrocarpus* Benth. has been found growing wild.[10] Seeds have been found in the mummy graves of Peru by Squier,[11] at

---

[1] Beckwith *Pacific R. R. Rpt.* 2:121. 1855.
[2] Pursh, F. *Fl. Amer. Septent.* 1:197. 1814. (*Seseli triternatum*)
[3] Molina *Hist. Chili* 1:128. 1808.
[4] Unger, F. *U. S. Pat. Off. Rpt.* 318. 1859.
[5] Mueller, F. *Sel. Pls.* 333. 1891.
[6] Molina *Hist. Chili* 1:91. 1808.
[7] Roxbury, W. *Hort. Beng.* 54. 1814.
[8] Booth, W. B. *Treas. Bot.* 2:874. 1870.
[9] Unger, F. *U. S. Pat. Off. Rpt.* 318. 1859.
[10] De Candolle, A. *Orig. Cult. Pls.* 345. 1885.
[11] Squier *Peru* 78. 1877.

Pachacamac, and by Reiss and Stubel at Ancon.[1] In southern Florida, the lima bean —
the seeds white, blotched or speckled with red — is found growing spontaneously in abandoned Indian plantations, and various forms are recorded by authors under specific names
as found in America and other countries; as *P. bipunctatus* Jacq., *P. inamoenus* Linn.,
P. puberulus H. B. & K., *P. saccharatus* Macfad.,[2] *P. derasus* Schrank (Martens), *P.
rufus* Jacq. In the mentions of beans by voyagers, this form is not discriminated from
the kidney bean, and hence we cannot offer precise statement of its occurrence from such
authorities.

The lima bean is now widely distributed. It has not been found wild in Asia nor
has it any modern Indian or Sanscrit name. Ainslie[3] says it was brought to India from
the Mauritius and that it is the *Vellore*, or *Duffin*, bean of the southern provinces. Wight
says it is much cultivated and is seldom if ever found in a wild state, and the large-podded
sort is said to have been brought by Dr. Duffin from the Mauritius.[4] This bean is not
mentioned by the early Chinese writers,[5] but Luoreiro mentions it in Cochin China in
1790. A dark red form came to Martens from Batavia and an orange-red from farther
India.[6] Martens[7] received it also from Sierra Leone; the form *bipunctatus* came from
the Cape of Good Hope to Vienna;[8] and Martens received it from Réunion under the name
pois du cap. Jaquin, 1770, fixed its appearance in Austria, but it first reached England
in 1779.[9] The form *inamoenus* was considered by Linnaeus to belong to Africa, but he
advances, as De Candolle remarks, no evidence of this habitat, and we may remark that
the slave trade may well be responsible for the transmission very quickly of South American
species of food plants of convenient characters for ship use to the African coast. *P. derasus*
Schrank, considered by Sprengel a variety of *P. inamoenus*, was found at Rio Janeiro.[10]

The lima bean is the scimitar-podded kidney bean and sugar bean of Barbados;[11]
it was mentioned in Jamaica by Lunan;[12] it may have been the " bushel bean," " very
flat, white and mottled with a purple figure," of the Carolinas in 1700–08,[13] as this description applies very closely to the lima beans now spontaneous in Florida. Two types, the
Carolina, or sieva, and the lima, were grown in American gardens in 1806. Eight varieties, some scarcely differing, are now offered for sale by our seedsmen; Vilmorin enumerates
four for France; the speckled form occurs in Brazil [14] and in Florida; a black form (*P.*

---

[1] De Candolle, A. *Orig. Cult. Pls.* 341. 1885.

[2] Ibid.

[3] Ainslie, W. *Mat. Ind.* 1:28. 1826.

[4] Wight, R. *Icon. Pls.* 3: Pl. 755. No date.

[5] Bretschneider, E. *On Study.* 1870.

[6] Martens *Gartenbohne* 96. 1869.

[7] Ibid.

[8] Martyn *Miller's Gard. Dict.* 1807.

[9] Ibid.

[10] Martens *Gartenbohne* 96. 1869.

[11] Schomburgk *Hist. Barb.* 605. 1848.

[12] Lunan, J. *Hort. Jam.* 1:434. 1814.

[13] Lawson *Hist. Car.* 130. 1860.

[14] Martens *Gartenbohne* 96. 1869.

derasus) in Brazil; the blood-red in Texas;[1] the dark red with light or orange-ruddy spots in the Bourbon Island; the black, white-streaked in Cochin China; and the large white, the small white or sieva, the red, the white sort striped and speckled with dark red and the green are found in our gardens. In central Africa, but two seeds are ever found in a pod;[2] in our most improved varieties there are five or even six. The synonymy is as follows:

> *Phaseoli magni late albi.* Lob. *Icon.* 2:60. 1591.
> B. *peregrini I. genus alterrun.* Clus. *Hist.* 2:223. 160. (Seen in 1576.) Fig.
> *Phaseolus, lato, striata, sive radiato semine.* Bauh. J. 2:267. 1651. Fig.
> P. *novi, orbis, latis, totus candidus similaci hortensis affinis.* Bauh. J. 2:268. 1651.
>   Fig. Chabr. 137. 1673. Fig.
> *Phaseolus lunatus.* Linn. *Sp.* 1016. 1763.
> P. *inamoenus.* Linn. *Sp.* 1016. 1763.
> P. *bipunctatus.* Jacq. *Hort.* I, t. 100, ex. *Mill. Dict.*
> P. *rufus.* Jacq. *Hort.* I, 13, t. 34, ex. *Mill. Dict.*
> P. *saccharatus.* Macfad. 282. 1837.
> P. *puberulus.* Kunth. *Syn.* 6:106. 1825.
> *Bushel or Sugar Bean.* A *Treat. on Gard.* (1818?).
> *Sugar Bean.* Maycock *Barb.* 293. 1830.
> *Lima Bean.* McMahon 1806.

This bean requires a warm season and hence is not grown so much in northern and central Europe as in this country. Vilmorin[3] describes three varieties and names two others. Martens,[4] however, describes six well-marked types.

TYPES OF LIMA BEANS.

1. The large, white lima is among those figured by Lobel[5] and by J. Bauhin,[6] and this places its appearance in Europe in 1591. According to Martens this is the *Phaseolus inamoenus* Linn. This type was in American gardens[7] in 1828 and probably before.

2. The Potato lima is a white bean, much thickened and rounded as compared with the first. This type seems to be fairly figured by Lobel,[8] 1591, and seems to be the *Phaseolus limensis* Macfad.,[9] justly esteemed in Jamaica.

3. The small, white lima, or sieve, saba, Carolina, Carolina sewee and West Indian, is esteemed on account of its greater hardiness over the other types. It is also well figured by Lobel, 1591, under the name *Phaseoli parvi pallico-albi ex America delati*. On account of the names and the hardiness of the plant and from the fact that it probably was cultivated by the Indians, this may be the bushel or sugar bean, which was esteemed

---

[1] Martens *Gartenbohne* 96. 1869.

[2] Schweinfurth, G. *Heart Afr.* 1:249. 1874.

[3] Vilmorin *Les Pls. Potag.* 278. 1883.

[4] Martens *Gartenbohne* 96. 1869.

[5] Lobel *Icon.* 260. 1591.

[6] Bauhin, J. *Hist. Pl.* 2:268. 1651.

[7] Fessenden *New Amer. Gard.* 36. 1828.

[8] Lobel *Icon.* 260. 1591.

[9] Macfadyen, *Jam.* 280. 837.

very delicate, appeared in various colors, as white. marbled, and green and was grown in Virginian gardens before 1818.[1] Lawson,[2] 1700-08, says: "The Bushel bean, a spontaneous growth, very flat, white, and mottled with a purple figure, was trained on poles" in the Carolinas. The sieva, if a synonym of the bushel bean, is the white form and was in American gardens before 1806. Vilmorin mentions a variety of the sieva spotted with red.

4. The speckled lima has white seeds striped and spotted with a deep, dark red. The figures of Lobel, 1591, under *Phaseoli rubri*, very well represent the cultivated variety, as also a sort said to be growing spontaneously in Florida in abandoned Indian fields.

5. The large red cannot be traced; it may be the blood-red bean Martens received from Texas, Sierra Leone and Batavia. It differs from the next but in size.

6. The small red answers well to the description given of *Phaseolus rufus* Jacq. by Martens, who put its appearance at 1770.

These six beans, with their synonyms, include all the lima beans now known, but there are a number of other types described which sooner or later will appear and will be claimed as originations. A careful reflection will convince that our varieties are all of ancient occurrence and that there have been no originations under culture within modern times. A black, white-streaked form is recorded in Cochin China by Loureiro; a white, black-streaked form is figured by Clusius in 1601; a black, as *Phaseolus derasus* Schrank, is reported in Brazil. The *P. bipunctatus* Jacq. has not as yet reached our seedsmen, although grown at Réunion under the name of *pois du cap*. Martens describes several others with a yellow band about the eye and variously colored; and one with an orange ground and black markings occurs among the beans from the Peruvian graves at Ancon at the National Museum.

P. multiflorus Willd. DUTCH CASEKNIFE BEAN. SCARLET RUNNER.

Mexico. This species has tuberous, poisonous roots.[3] It has annual, twining stems and is grown in the garden. The young pods are tender and well flavored. In Britain, the green pods alone are used; in Europe, the ripened seeds, though in Holland they are grown for both the pod and seed. In India, it is mentioned by Firminger[4] as grown. Burr[5] describes three varieties. In 1806, McMahon[6] says this bean was cultivated exclusively for ornament. In 1828, Fessenden[7] mentions it among garden beans. The culture of the Scarlet Runner is very modern. In Johnson's edition of Gerarde, 1630, it is said to have been procured by Tradescant; in Ray's time, 1686, it was grown for ornament; Miller, about 1750, was the first to bring it into repute in England as a vegetable.[8]

---

[1] Randolph *Treat. Gard.* 275. 1818.

[2] Lawson, J. *Hist. Car.* 76, 77. 1860.

[3] Balfour, J. H. *Treas. Bot.* 2:874. 1870.

[4] Firminger, T. A. C. *Gard. Ind.* 151. 1874.

[5] Burr, F. *Field, Gard. Veg.* 497, 498, 499. 1863.

[6] McMahon *Amer. Gard. Cal.* 580. 1806. (*Vicia coccinea*)

[7] Fessenden *New Amer. Gard.* 36. 1828.

[8] Martyn *Miller's Gard. Dict.* 1807. (*P. coccineus*)

P. mungo Linn. MUNG BEAN.

Tropical Asia. Elliott [1] says this is one of the most useful and largely cultivated of the Indian pulses, the green variety being more esteemed than the black. It is cultivated, according to Delile,[2] by the modern Egyptians, and Schweinfurth [3] says it is eaten by the Bongo tribe of central Africa.

P. pallar Molina.

Chile. This species was cultivated by the natives before the Conquest. The beans are half an inch long.[4]

P. retusus Benth. PRAIRIE BEAN.

Western North America and common on the prairies west of the Pecos. The seeds are about the size of peas; when still green, they make an acceptable dish [5] after thorough cooking.

P. triolobus Ait.

Asia and tropical Africa. This bean is cultivated in several varieties for its seeds, which are eaten by the poorer classes.

P. tuberosus Lour.

Cochin China. This bean has edible, tuberous roots.[6]

P. vulgaris Linn. COMMON BEAN. HARICOT. KIDNEY BEAN.

Cultivated everywhere. When the bean was first known, it was an American plant, and its culture extended over nearly the whole of the New World. It finds mention by nearly all the early voyagers and explorers, and, while the records were not kept sufficiently accurately to justify identification in all cases with varieties now known, the mass of the testimony is such that we cannot but believe that beans, as at present grown, were included. The evidence for the antiquity of the bean in America is both circumstantial and direct. The number of names given in the northern parts of America, alone, indicate an antiquity of culture: as, *sahe* or *sahu* on the St. Lawrence (Cartier); *ogaressa* by the Hurons (Sagard); *tuppuhguam-ash*, " twiners," by the northern Algonquins (Elliott); *a'teba'kwe* by the Abenaki of the Kennebec (Rasle); *mushaquissedes* by the Pequods (Stiles); *malachxil* by the Delawares (Zeisberger); and *okindgier* on the Roanoke. Moreover, in these few cases, for illustration, we find no common root. The number of varieties that were grown by the Indians is another indication of antiquity of culture, but this fact of varieties will receive illustration in quotations from early voyagers.

John Verazanno, in a letter written in July, 1524, says of the Indians of Norum-Bega: " Their ordinairie food is of pulse, whereof they have great store, differing in colour and taste from ours, of good and pleasant taste." Evidently this first visitor to

---

[1] Elliott, W. *Bot. Soc. Edinb.* **7**:292. 1863.

[2] De Candolle, A. *Geog. Bot.* **2**:962. 1855.

[3] Schweinfurth, G. *Heart Afr.* **1**:249. 1874.

[4] Molina *Hist. Chili* **1**:91. 1808.

[5] Havard, V. *Proc. U. S. Nat. Mus.* 501. 1885.

[6] Don, G. *Hist. Dichl. Pls.* **2**:349. 1832.

the New England coast had not seen kidney beans previously.[1] In 1605, Champlain, writing of the Indians of the Kennebec region, says: " With this corn they put in each hill three or four Brazilian beans (*Febues du Brésil*), which are of different colors. When they grow up they interlace with the corn, which reaches to the height of from five to six feet; and they keep the ground very free from weeds." [2] In 1614, Capt. John Smith mentions beans among the New England Indians,[3] and when the Pilgrims first landed, November 19, 1620, Miles Standish unearthed from a pit not only corn but " a bag of beans." Wood also mentions " Indian's beans " as among the foods of the Massachusetts Indians, 1629–33.[4] Lescarbot [5] says that the Indians of Maine, 1608, like those of Virginia and Florida, plant their corn in hills, " and between the kernels of corn they plant beans marked with various colors, which are very delicate: these, because they are not so high as the corn, grow very well among it." [6] The most complete enumeration of varieties is, however, given in Josselyn, before 1670: " French beans: or rather, American beans. The herbalists call them kidney-beans from their shape and effects: for they strengthen the kidneys. They are variegated much, some being bigger, a great deal, than others; some white, black, red, yellow, blue, spotted: besides your Bonivis and Calavances, and the kidney-bean that is proper to Roanoke. But these are brought into the country; the others are natural to the climate." [7] In 1535, Cartier, at the mouth of the St. Lawrence, found beans of every color, yet differing from ours.

In 1609, Hudson, exploring the river which now bears his name, found, within the limits of what is now Rensselaer County, New York, " beans of the last year's growth." [8] In 1653, Von der Donck, in his *Description of the Netherlands*, says: " Before the arrival of the Netherlanders (1614) the Indians raised beans of various kinds and colors but generally too coarse to be eaten green, or to be pickled, except the blue sort, which are abundant." [9] In 1633, DeVries " proceeded in the yacht up the (Delaware) river, to procure beans from the Indians." [10]

" Beans " were seen by Newport, 1607, in ascending the James River,[11] but Heriot, 1586, describes the *okindgier* of Virginia, " called by us beans, because in greatness and partly in shape they are like to the beans in England, saving that they are flatter, of more divers colours, and some pied. The leaf also of the stem is much different." [12] In 1700–08, Lawson [13] says: " The kidney-beans were here before the English came, being very plentiful in Indian corn-fields. The bushel-bean, a spontaneous growth, very flat, white and

[1] Hakluyt, R. *Divers Voy. Amer.* Hakl. Soc. Ed. 61. 1840.

[2] Champlain *Voy.* Prince Soc. Ed. 2:64. 1878.

[3] Smith, J. *Disc. New Eng.* 16. 1616. Force Coll. Tracts 2: No. 1. 1838.

[4] Wood, W. *New Eng. Prosp.* 75. 1865.

[5] Lescarbot *Hist. Nouv. France* 835. 1612.

[6] Gray and Trumbull *Amer. Journ. Sci. Arts* 132. Aug. 1883.

[7] Josselyn, J. *Voy.* 59. 1865.

[8] *N. Y. Hist. Soc. Coll.* 2nd ser. 1:300. 1841.

[9] Gray and Trumbull *Amer. Journ. Sci. Arts* 134. 1883.

[10] Hazard, S. *Annals Pa.* 31. 1850.

[11] Pickering, C. *Chron. Hist. Pls.* 575. 1879.

[12] Pinkerton *Coll. Voy.* 12:595. 1812.

[13] Lawson, J. *Hist. Car.* 130. 1860.

mottled with a purple figure, was trained on poles. (This is undoubtedly the lima, as it answers to the description given by a very creditible person who secured for me samples from a spontaneous plant in Florida: ' the trunk as large as a man's thigh, and the plant known for the past twenty-five years, some years yielding as much as fifty bushels of pods,' and the seeds smaller than the cultivated lima, very flat, white and mottled with purple.) Indian *rounceval* or miraculous pulse, so called from their large pods and great increase; they are very good, and so are the *bonavis, calavances, nanticokes* and abundance of other pulse, too tedious to mention, which we find the Indians possessed of when first we settled in America." *Bonavis* is perhaps Bonavista, a variety of bean sold by Thorburn, a New York seedsman, in 1828. The bonavista bean (Long) of Jamaica, is said to be *Lablab vulgaris; calavances* is the Barbados name for *Dolichos sinensis* Linn., as used by Long, a red bean; and *galavangher* pea is the Barbados name for *D. barbadensis* Mayc. In *A True Declaration of Virginia*, London, 1610, p. 12, " the two beans (planted with the corn) runne upon the stalks of the wheat, as our garden pease upon stickes."

In 1528, Narvaes found beans in great plenty in Florida and westward, and de Vaca found beans in New Mexico or Sonora in 1535. De Soto, 1539, also found beans in abundance [1] and mentions that " the granaries were full of maes and small beans," but we have no clue to the species. Beans are also mentioned in Ribault's *Voyage*, 1562, as cultivated by the Florida Indians.

The mention of beans in Mexico is frequent. The Olmecs raised beans before the time of the Toltecs; beans were a product of the Nahua tillage;[2] they are mentioned by Acosta in 1590; Alarcon speaks of their culture by the Indians of the Colorado River in 1758. The native Mexican name was *ayacotle*, according to Humboldt, and Bancroft says that they were the *etl* of the Aztecs; when boiled in the pod *exotl*.

In November, 1492, Columbus, in Cuba, found " a sort of bean "[3] or " fields planted with *faxones* and *habas* very different from those of Spain;" [4] and red and white beans were afterwards seen by him in Honduras, according to Pickering.[5] Gray and Trumbull quote Oviedo as saying that on the island and on the main many bushels are produced yearly of these and of *fesoles* of other sorts and different colors.[6]

The Indians of Peru, according to de la Vega, had three or four kinds of beans called *purutu*.[7] Squier found lima beans in the mummy covering of a woman from the huaca at Pachacamac, Peru;[8] Wittmack, who studied the beans brought from Peruvian tombs by Reiss and Strobel, identified the lima beans and also three kidney beans with *P. vulgaris purpurens* Martens, *P. vulgaris ellipticus praecox* Alefield, and *P. vulgaris ellipticus atrofuscus* Alefield.[9]

---

[1] De Soto *Disc. Conq. Fla.* 1557. Hakl. Soc. Ed. **9**:117. 1851.

[2] Bancroft, H. H. *Native Races* **2**:347. 1882.

[3] Knox, J. *Coll. Voy.* **1**:83. 1767.

[4] Gray and Trumbull *Amer. Journ. Sci. Arts* 130. 1883.

[5] Pickering, C. *Chron. Hist. Pls.* 575. 1879.

[6] Gray and Trumbull *Amer. Journ. Sci. Arts* 131. 1883.

[7] Vega, G. de la *Roy. Comment.* Hakl. Soc. Ed. **2**:358. 1871.

[8] Squier, E. G. *Peru* 78. 1877.

[9] De Candolle, A. *Orig. Cult. Pls.* 341. 1885.

In Chile, Molina says that before the country was conquered by the Spaniards, 13 or 14 kinds of the bean, varying but little from the common European bean, were cultivated by the natives. One of these has a straight stalk, the other 13 are climbers.[1]

Commentators have quite generally considered *P. vulgaris* as among the plants cultivated by the ancients, and De Candolle,[2] who has given the subject much thought, thinks the best argument is in the use of the modern names derived from the Greek *fasiolos* and the Roman *faseolus* and *phasiolus*. In 1542, Fuchsius[3] used the German word *Faselen* for the bean; in 1550, Roeszlin[4] used the same word for the pea, as did also Tragus[5] in 1552. Fuchsius gives also an alternative name, *welsch Bonen* and Roeszlin, *welsch Bonen* and *welsch Phaselen* for the bean; the same word, *welsch Bonen*, is given for the bean by Tragus, 1552, and Kyber,[6] 1553. This epithet, *welsch* or *foreign*, would seem to apply to a kind not heretofore known. Albertus Magnus,[7] who lived in the thirteenth century, used the word *faselus* as denoting a specific plant; as *"faba et faseolus et pisa et alia genera eguminis," " cicer, fava, faseolus."* He also says, *"Et sunt faseoli multorum colorum, sed quodlibet granorum habet maculam nigram in loco cotyledonis."* Now *Dolichos unguiculatus* Linn. is a plant which produces beans with a black eye (the black eye appears in many varieties of cowpea of the southern states) and is stated by Vilmorin to be grown in Italy in many varieties. Of 219 bottles of true beans, each with a distinct name, many, however, synonyms, not one has a black eye. The seeds of *Dolichos unguiculatus*, as well as 12 named varieties of cowpea all have a circle of black about the white eye, also one variety of cowpea which is all black has a white eye, and one red-speckled form does not have the black. It seems, therefore, reasonable to conclude that the *faselus* of Albertus Magnus was a Dolichos. In the list of vegetables Charlemagne ordained to be planted on his estates the word *fasiolum* occurs without explanation.[8]

Passing now to the Roman writers, Columella[9] speaks of *longa fasellus*, an epithet which well applies to the pods of the Dolichos; he gives directions for field culture, not for garden culture, and recommends planting in October. Pliny[10] says the pods are eaten with the seed, and the planting is in October and November. Palladius[11] recommends the planting of *faselus* in September and October, in a fertile and well-tilled soil, four *modii per jugerum*. Virgil's[12] epithet, *vilemque phaselum*, also indicates field culture, as to be cheap implies abundance.

Among the Greek writers, Aetius,[13] in the fourth century, says the Dolichos and

---

[1] Molina *Hist. Chili* 1:91. 1808.

[2] De Candolle, A. *Orig. Cult. Pls.* 339. 1885.

[3] Fuchsius *Hist. Stirp.* 708. 1542.

[4] Roeszlin *Kreuterb.* 149. 1550.

[5] Tragus *Stirp.* 611. 1552.

[6] Kyber *Lexicon* 404. 1553.

[7] Albertus Magnus *Veg.* Jessen Ed. 118, 167, 515. 1867.

[8] De Candolle, A. *Orig. Pls. Cult.* 340. 1885.

[9] Columella lib. 10, c. 378; lib. 2, c. 10; lib. 11, c. 2.

[10] Pliny lib. 18, c. 33.

[11] Palladius lib. 10, c. 12; lib. 11, c. 1.

[12] Virgil *Georgics* 1:227.

[13] Theophrastus *Hist. Pl.* Bodaeus Ed. 925. 1644.

the Phaseolus of the ancients were now called by all *lobos*, and by some *melax kepea*. This word *lobos* of Aetius is recognizable in the Arabic *loubia*,[1] applied to *Dolichos lubia* Forsk., a bean with low stalks, the seed ovoid, white, with a black point at the eye.

From these and other clues to be gleaned here and there from the Greek authors, one is disposed to think that the low bean of the ancients was a Dolichos, and that the word *phaselus* referred to this bean whenever used throughout the Middle Ages in speaking of a field crop.

The Roman references to Phaseolus all refer to a low-growing bean fitted for field culture and so used. There is no clear indication to be found of garden culture. Aetius seems the first among the Greeks to refer to a garden sort, for he says the *lobos* are the only kind in which the pod is eaten with the bean; and, he says, this *lobos* is called by some *melax kepea* (*Smilax hortensis*), the Dolichos and Phaseolus of his predecessors. Galen's use of the word *lobos*, or the pod plant, would hence imply garden culture in Greece in the second century.

The word *loubion* is applied by the modern Greeks to *Phaseolus vulgaris*, as is also the word *loba* in Hindustani. The word *lubia* is used by the Berbers, and in Spain the form *alubia*, for *Phaseolus vulgaris*.[2] The words *fagiuolo* in Italian, *phaseole* in French, are also used for this species. It is so easy for a name used in a specific sense to remain while the forms change, as is illustrated by the word squash in America, that we may interpret these names to refer to the common form of their time, to a Dolichos (even now in some of its varieties called a bean) in ancient times and to a Phaseolus now.

Theophrastus[3] says the *dolichos* is a climber, bears seeds and is not a desirable vegetable. The word *dolichos* seems to be used in a generic sense. There is no other mention of a climber by the ancient authors. The *dolichos* of Galen is the *faselus* of the Latins for he says that some friends of his had seen the *dolichos* (a name not then introduced in Rome) growing in fields about Caria, in Italy. We may, therefore, be reasonably certain that the pole beans which were so common in the sixteenth century were not then cultivated.

The English name, kidney beans, is derived, evidently, from the shape of the seed. Turner, 1551, uses the name first, but these beans were not generally grown in England until quite recent times. Parkinson, 1629, speaks of them as oftener on rich men's tables; and Worlidge, 1683, says that within the memory of man they were a great rarity, although now a common, delicate food. The French word *haricot*, applied to this plant, occurs in Quintyne,[4] 1693, who calls them *aricos* in one place, and *haricauts* in another. The word does not occur in *Le Jardinier Solitaire*, 1612, and Champlain,[5] 1605, uses the term *febues du Brésil*, indicating he knew no vernacular name of closer application. De Candolle[6] says the word *araco* is Italian and was originally used for *Lathyrus ochrus;* it is apparently thus used by Oribasius and Galen.

The two species of Linnaeus, *Phaseolus vulgaris* and *P. nanus*, correspond to the

---

[1] Delile, A. R.   *Mem. Pls. Cult. Egypt.* 24.   1824.

[2] De Candolle, A.   *Orig. Cult. Pls.* 341.   1885.

[3] Theophrastus *Hist. Pl.*   Bodaeus Ed. 914.   1644.

[4] Quintyne *Comp. Gard.* 142, 185.   1693.

[5] Champlain *Voy.*   Prince Soc. Ed. 64.   1878.

[6] De Candolle, A.   *Orig. Cult. Pls.* 343.   1885.

popular grouping into pole and dwarf beans. But there is this to be remarked, that Linnaeus's synonyms for *P. nanus* apply to a Dolichos and not to a Phaseolus, for the descriptions of *Phaseolus vulgaris italicus humilis s. minor, albus cum orbita nigricante* of Bauhin's [1] *History* answer well to the cowpea, as does also C. Bauhin's [2] *Smilax silique sursum rigente s. Phaseolus parvus italicus*, and do not apply to the bush bean. The figures given by Camerarius,[3] 1586, by Matthiolus,[4] 1598, and by Bauhin, 1651, are all cowpeas, although the names given are those used for the true bean, thus indicating the same confusion between the species and the names which kept pace with the introduction of new varieties of the bean from America, for Pena and Lobel,[5] 1570, say that many sorts of *fabas Pheseolosve* were received from sailors coming from the New World.

BUSH BEAN.
(*P. nanus* Linn.)

The first figure of the bush bean is by Fuchsius,[6] 1542, and his drawing resembles very closely varieties that may be found today — not the true bush, but slightly twining. In 1550, Roeszlin [7] figures a bush bean, as does Matthiolus,[8] 1558, Pinaeus,[9] 1561, and Dalechamp,[10] 1587. Matthiolus says the species is common in Italy in gardens and oftentimes in fields, the seed of various colors, as white, red, citron and spotted. Dalechamp figures the white bean. The dwarf bean is not mentioned by Dodonaeus,[11] 1566 nor in 1616. A list of varieties cultivated in Jamaica is given by Macfadyen,[12] 1837, which includes the one-colored black, yellow and red; the streaked, in which the seeds are marked with broad, linear, curved spots; the variegated, the seeds marked with rubiginose, leaden, more or less rounded spots; and the saponaceous, with the back of the seeds white, the sides and concavity marked with spots so as to resemble a common soap-ball.

Gerarde,[13] 1597, does not mention this bean in England but it is mentioned by Miller,[14] 1724, in varieties which can be identified with those grown at the present time, five in all. In 1765, Stevenson [15] names 7 varieties; in 1778, Mawe [16] names 11; in 1883, Vilmorin [17] describes 69 varieties and names others.

---

[1] Bauhin, J. *Hist. Pl.* 2:258. 1651.
[2] Bauhin, C. *Pinax* 339. 1623.
[3] Camerarius *Epit.* 212. 1586.
[4] Matthiolus *Opera* 341. 1598.
[5] Pena and Lobel *Advers.* 394. 1570.
[6] Fuchsius *Hist. Stirp.* 708. 1542.
[7] Roeszlin *Kreuterb.* 149. 1550.
[8] Matthiolus *Comment.* 237. 1558.
[9] Pinaeus *Hist. Pls.* 140. 1561.
[10] Dalechamp *Hist. Gen. Pl.* (Lugd.) 472. 1587.
[11] Dodonaeus *Frument.* 1566; *Dod. Pempt.* 1616.
[12] Macfadyen *Jam.* 1:283. 1837.
[13] Gerarde, J. *Herb.* 1038. 1597.
[14] Martyn *Miller's Gard. Dict.* 1807.
[15] Stevenson *Gard. Kal.* 66. 1765.
[16] Mawe and Abercrombie *Univ. Gard. Bot.* 1778.
[17] Vilmorin *Les Pls. Potag.* 250. 1883.

POLE BEANS.

(*P. vulgaris* Linn.)

Pole beans are figured by Tragus,[1] 1552, who speaks of them as having lately come into Germany from Italy and calls them *welsch*, or foreign and enumerates the various colors as red, purplish-white, variegated, white, black and yellowish. Dodonaeus,[2] 1566 and 1616, figures the pole bean; as does Lobel,[3] 1576 and 1591; Clusius,[4] 1601; and Castor Durante,[5] 1617. In 1597, Gerarde[6] figures four varieties in England: the white, black, red and yellow. Barnaby Googe[7] speaks of French beans, 1572, indicating by the name the source from which they came. In 1683, Worlidge[8] names two sorts as grown in English gardens, and the same varieties are given by Mortimer,[9] 1708. In France, 1829, 19 sorts are enumerated by Noisette;[10] and in 1883, Vilmorin[11] describes 38 varieties and names others.

Phillyrea latifolia Linn. *Oleaceae.*

Mediterranean region. This species is cultivated in Sicily, Italy[12] and Spain[13] for its olive-like fruit.

Phalaris canariensis Linn. *Gramineae.* CANARY GRASS.

Europe, north Africa and now naturalized in America. Canary grass is cultivated for its seeds, which are fed to canary birds. In Italy, the seeds are ground into meal and made into cakes and puddings, and, in the Canary Islands, they are used in the same manner and also made into groats for porridge.[14] The common yield is from 30 to 34 bushels of seed per acre in England, but occasionally the yield is as much as 50 bushels. The chaff is superior for horse food and the straw is very nutritious.[15] Canary grass is sparingly grown in some parts of the United States as a cultivated plant.

Phlomis tuberosa Linn. *Labiatae.*

Southern Europe, east and north Asia. Its roots are eaten cooked by the Kalmucks, who call the plant *bodmon sok*.[16]

---

[1] Tragus *Stirp.* 611. 1552.

[2] Dodonaeus *Frument.* 1566.

[3] Lobel *Obs.* 511. 1576; *Icon.* 2:60. 1591.

[4] Clusius *Hist.* 2:222. 1601.

[5] Durante, C. *Herb.* 1617.

[6] Gerarde, J. *Herb.* 1038. 1597.

[7] *Gard. Chron.* 1181. 1864.

[8] Worlidge, J. *Syst. Hort.* 197. 1683.

[9] *Gard. Chron.* 1013. 1864.

[10] Noisette *Man. Jard.* 361. 1829.

[11] Vilmorin *Les Pls. Potag.* 246. 1883.

[12] Parsons, S. B. *U. S. Pat. Off. Rpt.* 113. 1859. (*Olea latifolia*)

[13] Downing, A. J. *Fr. Fr. Trs. Amer.* 576. 1890.

[14] Johnson, C. P. *Useful Pls. Gt. Brit.* 280. 1862.

[15] Loudon, J. C. *Enc. Agr.* 832. 1866.

[16] Pickering, C. *Chron. Hist. Pls.* 793. 1879.

Phoenix acaulis Buch.-Ham. *Palmae.*

East Indies and Burma. The astringent fruits are eaten by the Lepchas, who call the tree *schap*.[1]

P. dactylifera Linn. DATE PALM.

Northern Africa and Arabia. In the East, the date tree has ever been the benefactor of mankind. The life of the wandering tribes in the desert circles around the date tree, and the Arabian poets ascribed such high importance to it that they maintain that the noble tree was not formed with other plants but from the clods which remained after the creation of Adam. The native land of the date palm seems to have been originally the region along the east side of the Persian Gulf, whence it has been distributed in the earliest periods of commerce to Arabia, Persia, Hindustan and westward over the whole of north Africa. Hartt[2] mentions a few date palms which bore fruit at Macei, Brazil, and the tree is in gardens in Florida, whence they were probably received from the United States Patent Office about 1860. In 1867, Atwood[3] says numerous, large and beautiful specimens may be seen in the gardens of St. Augustine. Redmond,[4] 1875, says the date is cultivated to a limited extent in south Florida. In the oasis of Siwah, St. John found four kinds cultivated: the *Sultani* with long, blue fruit; the *Farayah*, white ones of a kind said not to be grown in Egypt; the *Saidi*, or common date; and the *Weddee*, good only for camels and donkeys. Some yellow dates, he says, were much less elongated than others he had seen, with more flesh in comparison to the size of the stone and very luscious. The female flowers of the date are fertilized artificially. In Sind, in Arabia and elsewhere, this is done before the flower-sheaths open; a hole is made in the sheath of the female flower and a few bits of the male panicle are inserted. At Multan, India, Mr. Edgeworth[5] states that there is a date tree which bears a stoneless fruit and that in former times it was considered a royal tree, and the fruits were reserved for royal use. The fruit furnishes, fresh or dried, the staple food of large regions. The large, succulent head cut from among the mass of leaves is also eaten. The sap is sweetish and may be used as a drink or distilled into a kind of spirit.

P. farinifera Roxb.

A dwarf palm common in the country between the Ganges and Cape Comorin. Its exterior, or woody part, consists of white fibers matted together; these envelope a large quantity of farinaceous substance, which the natives use for food in times of scarcity.[6]

P. humilis Royle.

East Indies, Burma and China. The fruit, of a purple-black color, is sweet and is eaten in India.[7]

---

[1] *Treas. Bot.* 2:1340. 1876.

[2] Hartt *Geog. Braz.* 425. 1870.

[3] Atwood *U. S. D. A. Rpt.* 145. 1867.

[4] Redmond *Amer. Pom. Soc.* 55. 1875.

[5] Edgeworth *Journ. Agr. Hort. Soc. India.* Nov. 20, 1867.

[6] Seemann, B. *Pop. Hist. Palms* 314. 1856.

[7] Brandis, D. *Forest Fl.* 555. 1874.

P. pusilla Gaertn.

East Indies and south China. The shining, black berry has a sweet, mealy pulp.[1]

P. reclinata Jacq.

Tropical and south Africa. The seeds are frequently drawn into use as a substitute for coffee.[2] This species is said by Williams[3] to yield in western Africa a wine; the fruits are said to be much relished by the negro tribes.

P. sylvestris Roxb. WILD DATE.

East Indies. In India, the juice is fermented or boiled down into sugar and molasses. A large portion of the sugar made in Bengal, on the Coromandel coast and in Guzerat comes from this source.[4] The fruit is of a very inferior character.[5] The sap is drunk in India, either fresh or fermented, and is called *tari*.[6]

Phragmites communis Trin. *Gramineae.* BENNELS. REED.

Cosmopolitan. In 1751–68, Father Baegert[7] says he saw the natives of the Californian peninsula " eat the roots of the common reed, just as they were taken out of the water." Durand and Hilgard[8] state that this is the grass from which the Indians of Tejon Valley extract their sugar, and it is elsewhere stated that the gum which exudes from the stalks is collected by the Indians and gathered into balls to be eaten at pleasure. The gum is a sweet, manna-like substance.

Phrynium capitatum Willd. *Scitamineae.*

Tropical eastern Asia. Loureiro observed this plant in Annam and tropical China, its leaves wrapped around articles of food previous to boiling to impart color and grateful flavor.[9]

Phyllanthus acidissimus Muell. *Euphorbiaceae.*

Philippine Islands, Cochin China and China. The plant furnishes an edible fruit.[10]

P. distichus Muell. OTAHEITE GOOSEBERRY.

East Indies, tropical Asia and Madagascar. The fruits, in size like those of a gooseberry, are green, three or four-furrowed and somewhat acid and cooling. Firminger[11] says it is of a sour, sorrel-like flavor, unfit to be eaten raw but making a delicious stew. It is commonly used by the natives for pickling and is sold in the bazaars.

---

[1] Mueller, F.   *Sel. Pls.* 163.   1876.

[2] Ibid.

[3] Williams, B. S.   *Choice Stove, Greenhouse Pls.* 32.   1876.

[4] Brandis, D.   *Forest Fl.* 555.   1874.

[5] Firminger, T. A. C.   *Gard. Ind.* 172.   1874.

[6] *Treas. Bot.* 2:1125.   1876.

[7] *Smithsonian Inst. Rpt.* 364.   1864.

[8] *Pacific R. R. Rpt.* 5:15.   1856.

[9] Pickering, C.   *Chron. Hist. Pls.* 537.   1879.

[10] Unger, F.   *U. S. Pat. Off. Rpt.* 337.   1859.   (*Cicca racemosa*)

[11] Firminger, T. A. C.   *Gard. Ind.* 188.   1874.   (*Emblica distichus*)

P. emblica Linn. EMBLIC.

Tropical Asia. This tree is found wild and cultivated in various parts of India and the Indian Archipelago. The fruits are eaten by the natives in the Konkan and Deccan.[1] In India, a preserve of the ripe fruit made with sugar is considered a wholesome article of diet;[2] the fruit is also pickled and eaten.[3] The fruits are exceedingly acid in a raw state. Dried, this fruit forms the emblic myrobalan, used as a medicine and for dyeing and tanning.

Phyllarthron bojeranum DC. *Bignoniaceae.*

Madagascar. The fruit is edible.[4]

P. comorense DC.

In the Maritius Islands, the fruit is used for jellies.[5]

Phyllocactus biformis Labour. *Cacteae.*

Honduras. The fruit is of a shining, deep crimson color, shaped like a florence flask, and contains numerous seeds imbedded in a soft, pinkish pulp of a sweetish, subacid taste.[6]

Physalis alkekengi Linn. *Solanaceae.* STRAWBERRY TOMATO. WINTER CHERRY.

Europe and Japan. This species has long been grown for its red, smooth, round, berry-like fruits enclosed in bladder-like leaves. It was described by Dioscorides. In Arabia and even in Germany and Spain, the fruits, which have a slightly acid taste, are eaten for dessert. It was called *struchnon halikakabon* or *phusalis* by Dioscorides and is named by the modern Boeotians *keravoulia.*[7]

P. angulata Linn. GROUND CHERRY.

Tropics. The fruit is sweetish and subacid and is commonly eaten with safety if perfectly ripe.[8] The leaves are used as a vegetable in central Africa. This species is found widely dispersed over tropical regions, extending to the southern portion of the United States and to Japan. It is first described by Camararius,[9] 1588, as a plant hitherto unknown and an excellent figure is given. It was seen in a garden by C. Bauhin[10] before 1596 and is figured in the *Hortus Eystettensis,*[11] 1613. J. Bauhin[12] speaks of its presence in certain gardens in Europe. Linnaeus describes a variety with entire leaves, and both his species and variety are figured by Dillenius,[13] who obtained the variety from Holland

---

[1] Pickering, C. *Chron. Hist. Pls.* 408. 1879. (*Emblica officinalis*)

[2] Dutt, U. C. *Mat. Med. Hindus* 226. 1877.

[3] Brandis, D. *Forest Fl.* 454. 1874.

[4] Seemann, B. *Treas. Bot.* 2:880, 881. 1870.

[5] Ibid.

[6] Smith, A. *Treas. Bot.* 1:419. 1870. (*Disocactus biformis*)

[7] Hooker, W. J. *Journ. Bot.* 1:132. 1834.

[8] Nuttall, T. *Gen. No. Amer. Pls.* 1:130. 1818.

[9] Camerarius *Hort. Med.* 70. 1588. Fig. 17.

[10] Bauhin, C. *Phytopin* 297. 1596.

[11] *Hortus Eystet.* 1613 (also 1713).

[12] Bauhin, J. *Hist. Pl.* 3:609. 1651.

[13] Dillenius *Hort. Elth.* 14. 1774, f. 12, t. 12; p. 12, f. 11, t. 11.

in 1732.   When it first appeared in our vegetable gardens is not recorded.   Its synonymy seems to be as below:

> *Halicacabum sive Solanum Indicum.*   Cam. *Hort.* 70.   1588.   *cum. ic.*
> *Solanum vesicarium Indicum.*   Bauh. *Phytopin.* 297. 1596; *Pin.* 166.   1623; Ray *Hist.* 681.   1686.
> *Halicacabum seu Solanum Indicum.*   Camer. *Hortus. Eystet.*   1613.   *cum. ic.*
> *Solanum sive Halicabum Indicum.*   Bauh. J. **3**:609.   1651.   *cum. ic.*
> *Alkekengi Indicum majus.*   Tourn. *Inst.* 151.   1719.
> *Pops.*   Hughes *Barb.* 161.   1750.
> *Physalis angulata* Linn.   Gray *Syn. Fl.* **2**: pt. I, 234.

P. lanceolata Michx.   STRAWBERRY TOMATO.

Western North America.   This species was among the strawberry tomatoes grown at the New York Agricultural Experiment Station in 1886 and occurred in two varieties; the ordinary sort and another with broader leaves and more robust growth.   Its habitat is given by Gray as from Lake Winnipeg to Florida and Texas, Colorado, Utah and New Mexico.

P. obscura Michx.   GROUND CHERRY.

Eastern United States.   It produces an edible ground cherry.[1]

P. peruviana Linn.   ALKEKENGI.   BARBADOS GOOSEBERRY.   CHERRY TOMATO.   GROUND CHERRY.   WINTER CHERRY.

Tropics.   This species is sometimes grown in gardens for its fruit.   It is a hardy, annual plant, which bears a roundish fruit half an inch in diameter, yellow, semitransparent at maturity and enclosed in an inflated, membranaceous calyx.   The fruit has a juicy pulp and, when first tasted, a pleasant, strawberry-like flavor, but the after taste is not so agreeable.   This South American species seems to have become fairly well distributed through cultivation.   Birdwood[2] records it as cultivated widely in India and gives native names in the various dialects, and Speede[3] mentions it also.   In France, it is classed among garden vegetables by Vilmorin.[4]   Descourtilz gives a Carib name, *sousourouscurou.*   Drummond,[5] who introduced the plant into Australia, after ten years, reports it as completely naturalized in. his region.   This species differs but slightly from *P. pubescens.*[6]   Gray,[7] 1878, says it was introduced into cultivation several years ago but has now mainly disappeared.

P. philadelphica Lam.   PURPLE GROUND CHERRY.   PURPLE STRAWBERRY TOMATO.   PURPLE WINTER CHERRY.

North America.   The fruit is edible.[8]   Although the habitat of this species is given

---

[1] Nuttall, T.   *Gen. No. Amer. Pls.* 1:130.   1818.
[2] Birdwood *Veg. Prod. Bomb.* 173.   1865.
[3] Speede *Ind. Handb. Gard.* 233.   1842.
[4] Vilmorin *Les Pls. Potag.* 4.   1883.
[5] Hooker, W. J.   *Journ. Bot.* 2:347.   1840.
[6] Vilmorin *Les Pls. Potag.* 4.   1883.
[7] Gray, A.   *Synopt. Fl.* **2**: Pt. I. 233.   1878.
[8] Nuttall, T.   *Gen. No. Amer. Pls.* 1:130.   1818.

by Gray [1] as in fertile soil, Pennsylvania to Illinois and Texas, yet it seems to be the *miltomatl* figured by Hernandez [2] in his Mexican history, published in 1651. It is described by Burr [3] under the names given above. The *petite tomato du Mexique*, as received from Vilmorin, in 1883, can be assigned to this species, as can also a strawberry tomato grown in 1885 at the New York Agricultural Experiment Station.

P. pubescens Linn. GROUND CHERRY. HUSK TOMATO. STRAWBERRY TOMATO.

North America. This is the *camaru*.[4] It is also found wild in the United States. The fruit is edible.[5] This species has a wide range, extending from New York to Iowa, Florida and westward from Texas to the borders of California and southward to tropical America. It is described by Marcgrav [6] and Piso [7] in Brazil about the middle of the seventeenth century, and Feuille,[8] 1725, mentions it as cultivated and wild in Peru. It has been introduced into many regions. Loureiro [9] records it in Cochin China; Bojer,[10] as cultivated in the Mauritius and in all the tropical countries; and it also occurs in the descriptions of garden vegetables in France and America. It was cultivated by Miller in England in 1739 [11] and was described by Parkinson in 1640. It had not reached the kitchen garden in 1807 but had before 1863. Its synonymy seems as given below:

Camaru. Marcg. 12. 1648; Piso 223. 1658.
Halicacabum sive Alkekengi Virginense. Ray 681. 1686.
Alkekengi Virginianum, fructu luteo. Tourn. 151. 1719.
Alkekengi Virginianum, fructu luteo, vulgo Capuli. Feuille **3**:5. 1725.
Alkekengi Barbadense nanum, Alliariae folio. Dill. *Elth.* 10. f. 9. t. 9. 1774.
Physalis pubescens. Linn. *Sp.* 262. 1762.

P. virginiana Mill. STRAWBERRY TOMATO.

North America. This species has also been grown from seedsmen's strawberry tomato. It is a low, spreading plant.

P. viscosa Linn.

Eastern United States. The berry is edible.[12]

Phytelephas macrocarpa Ruiz et Pav. *Palmae.* IVORY PALM.

Tropical America. The seed at first contains a clear, insipid fluid, with which travelers allay their thirst, afterwards this liquor becomes milky and sweet; at last the fruit is almost as hard as ivory.[13] This hard albumen furnishes a vegetable ivory of commerce.

[1] Gray, A. *Synopt. Fl.* **2**: Pt. 1. 233. 1878.
[2] Hernandez *Nova Hist. Mex.* 295. 1651.
[3] Burr, F. *Field, Gard. Veg.* 593. 1863.
[4] Masters, M. T. *Treas. Bot.* **2**:882. 1870.
[5] Nuttall, T. *Gen. No. Amer. Pls.* **1**:130. 1818.
[6] Piso *Hist. Rerum Nat. Braz.* 12. 1648.
[7] Piso *De Ind.* 223. 1658.
[8] Feuillee *Obs.* **3**:5. 1725.
[9] Loureiro *Fl. Cochin.* 133. 1790.
[10] Bojer, W. *Hort. Maurit.* 237. 1837.
[11] Martyn *Miller's Gard. Dict.* 1807.
[12] Nuttall, T. *Gen. No. Amer. Pls.* **1**:130. 1818.
[13] Seemann, B. *Pop. Hist. Palms* 327. 1856.

Phyteuma spicatum Linn. *Campanulaceae.* SPIKED RAMPION.

Europe. The roots, which are thick and fleshy, were formerly eaten, either boiled or in salad, but the plant is no longer used in England, though still in favor in some parts of continental Europe.[1]

Phytocrene gigantea Wall. *Olacineae.* FOUNTAIN TREE.

Burma. A watery and drinkable sap flows from sections of the porous stem.[2]

P. palmata Wall.

Malays. A watery and drinkable sap flows from sections of the porous stem.[3]

Phytolacca acinosa Roxb. *Phytolaccaceae.* INDIAN POKE.

Himalayas and China. This plant is cultivated in Jaunsar and Kamaon, India, where its leaves are eaten boiled as a vegetable.[4,5] In 1852, it was cultivated in Germany as a spinach.[6] This species has been recommended in France as a culinary vegetable but it does not appear to have met with much success. Its leaves cooked as spinach and its young shoots as asparagus were both said to possess an excellent flavor.[7]

P. decandra Linn. GARGET. POCAN. SCOKE. VIRGINIAN POKE.

Originally from North America, this species has been distributed throughout Mexico Brazil, the Sandwich Islands and the region of the Mediterranean, even to Switzerland. It is occasionally used as a vegetable, and Barton[8] says the young shoots are brought in great abundance to the Philadelphia market as a table vegetable. In Louisiana, says Rafinesque,[9] it is called *chou-gras* and the leaves are eaten boiled in soup.

P. octandra Linn. CALALU.

Guiana and Jamaica. From this species comes a palatable, wholesome green. It is cultivated in most kitchen gardens in Jamaica.[10] In Mexico, it is called *verbachina*. In China, it is an edible plant.[11]

Picea excelsa Link. *Coniferae.* NORWAY SPRUCE.

Norway, Russia and the mountainous parts of Europe. The spray is used in making beer.[12]

P. nigra Link. BLACK SPRUCE. DOUBLE SPRUCE.

North America. Great quantities of spruce beer are made from the new shoots.[13]

---

[1] Johnson, C. P. *Useful Pls. Gt. Brit.* 162. 1862.

[2] Baillon, H. *Hist. Pls.* 5:307. 1878.

[3] Ibid.

[4] Brandis, D. *Forest Fl.* 371. 1874.

[5] Royle, J. F. *Illustr. Bot. Himal.* 1:326. 1839.

[6] Unger, F. *U. S. Pat. Off. Rpt.* 358. 1859. (*P. esculenta*)

[7] Smith, A. *Treas. Bot.* 2:895. 1870. (*Pircunia esculenta*)

[8] Barton, W. P. C. *Med. Bot.* 2:217. 1817-18.

[9] Rafinesque, C. S. *Fl. La.* 31. 1817.

[10] Titford, W. J. *Hort. Bot. Amer.* 67. 1812.

[11] Smith, F. P. *Contrib. Mat. Med. China* 171. 1871.

[12] Masters, M. T. *Treas. Bot.* 1:2. 1870. (*Abies excelsa*)

[13] Emerson, G. B. *Trees, Shrubs of Mass.* 1:99. 1875. (*Abies nigra*)

Picraena excelsa Lindl. *Simarubeae.* BITTER ASH. QUASSIA.

West Indies. This tree yields the bitter wood known as Jamaica quassia. Brewers are said to use the chips as a substitute for hops.[1]

Picridium vulgare Desf. *Compositae.* FRENCH SCORZONERA.

Europe and the Mediterranean region. This salad plant is cultivated in Italian gardens, where it is much esteemed.[2] It is also used somewhat in France [3] and was introduced into England in 1882. It is also of recent introduction into French culture.[4] In the United States, the species is noted by Burr,[5] 1863. The young leaves and the roots are eaten.[6]

Picris echioides Linn. *Compositae.* OX-TONGUE.

Europe and north Africa. Johnson [7] says this plant has been used as a potherb when in the young state.

P. hieracioides Linn.

Temperate Asia, Australia, New Zealand and Europe. The plant is used as a potherb.[8]

Pimenta officinalis Lindl. *Myrtaceae.* ALLSPICE. PIMENTO.

West Indies. The allspice tree is cultivated in the West Indies, where it is common. The allspice, or pimento, berries of commerce are of the size of a small pea and in order are supposed to resemble a combination of cinnamon, cloves and nutmeg. This tree is also cultivated now in the East Indies. The seeds are used as a condiment.[9]

Pimpinella anisum Linn. *Umbelliferae.* ANISE.

Greece and Egypt. *Anison* was known to the ancient Greeks. Dioscorides says the best came from Crete, the next best from Egypt. It is also mentioned by Theophrastus.[10] Pliny,[11] in the first century, says " *anesum*, green or dry, is desirable in all seasonings or sauces." The seeds, he says, are sprinkled in the under crust of bread and are used for flavoring wine. He quotes Pythagoras as praising it whether raw or cooked. Palladius,[12] in the beginning of the third century, gives directions for its sowing. Charlemagne,[13] in the ninth century, commanded that anise should be sown on the imperial farms in

---

[1] Masters, M. T. *Treas. Bot.* **2**:886. 1870. (*Picrasma excelsa*)

[2] *Trans. Hort. Soc. Lond.* **6**:583. 1826

[3] *Bon Jard.* 549. 1882.

[4] Noisette *Man. Jard.* **2**:422. 1860.

[5] Burr, F. *Field, Gard. Veg.* 390. 1863.

[6] Unger, F. *U. S. Pat. Off. Rpt.* 328. 1859. (*Scorzonera picroides*)

[7] Johnson, C. P. *Useful Pls. Gt. Brit.* 143. 1862. (*Helminthia echioides*)

[8] Ibid.

[9] Don. G. *Hist. Dichl. Pls.* **2**:866. 1832.

[10] Theophrastus *Hist. Pl.* Bodaeus Ed. 744. 1644.

[11] Pliny lib. 20, c. 72.

[12] Palladius lib. 3, c. 24; lib. 4, c. 9.

[13] Flückiger and Hanbury *Pharm.* 310. 1879.

Germany. Anise is mentioned also by Albertus Magnus [1] in the thirteenth century. It sems to have been grown in England as a potherb prior to 1542, as Boore,[2] in his *Dyetary of Helth*, printed in that year, says of it and fennel, " These herbes be seldom used but theyr seedes be greatly occupyde."   Ruellius [3] records anise in France in 1536 and gives the common name as Roman fennel, the name Albertus Magnus used in the thirteenth century. It is classed amóng culinary herbs by McMahon,[4] 1806.

In the seventeenth century, Quintyne records the use of the leaves in salads. The seeds now serve to flavor various liquors; in Italy, they appear in diverse pastries; in Germany they are put into bread; in England, in special bread, in rye bread and even in cheese. In Malta, localities in Spain, France, southern Italy, Germany and Russia the plant is grown on a large scale for the seed, which also enters commerce in northern India and Chile. The plant is indigenous to Asia Minor, the Greek islands and Egypt but is nowhere to be found undoubtedly growing wild. There is no indication of its having formed varieties under cultivation, except that Bauhin records one sort having rounder and smaller seeds than the common variety.

Pinanga dicksonii Blume. *Palmae.*

East Indies. This is a wild species, the nuts of which are utilized by the poorer classes as a substitute for the betel-nut.[5]

Pinus cembra Linn. *Coniferae.* RUSSIAN CEDAR. SWISS STONE PINE.

Southern Europe and northern Asia. According to Gmelin,[6] the seeds form about the sole winter food of the peasantry in Siberia. Nuttall [7] says an oil is extracted from them.

P. cembroides Zucc.

Western United States. The seeds are as large as large peas, says Newberry,[8] the flavor agreeable, and the Indians eat them whenever they can be obtained. The edible nuts are collected, says Parry,[9] by the Indians along the Mexican boundary, and Torrey says, when fresh or slightly roasted, they are very palatable.

P. contorta Dougl.

Western United States. In times of scarcity, says R. Brown,[10] the Indians will eat the liber. Along both sides of the trail in the passes of the Galton and Rocky Mountains, many of the young trees of this species are stripped of their bark for a foot or so above the ground to a height of six or seven feet. The Indians of Alaska, says Dall,[11] in the spring

---

[1] Albertus Magnus *Veg.* Jessen Ed. 476. 1867.

[2] Flückiger and Hanbury *Pharm.* 311. 1879.

[3] Ruellius *Nat. Stirp.* 701. 1536.

[4] McMahon, B. *Amer. Gard.* 199. 1806.

[5] Drury, H. *Useful Pls. Ind.* 50. 1873.

[6] Pickering, C. *Chron. Hist. Pls.* 652. 1879.

[7] Nuttall, T. *No. Amer. Sylva* 2:168. 1865.

[8] Newberry *Pacific R. R. Rpt.* 6:45. 1857. (*Abies williamsonii*)

[9] Parry *Bot. U. S. Mex. Bound. Surv.* 21. 1859.

[10] Brown, R. *Bot. Soc. Edinb.* 9:382. 1868.

[11] *U. S. D. A. Rpt.* 411. 1870.

are in the habit of stripping off the outer bark and scraping the newly formed cambium from the trunk, and this is eaten fresh or dried. When fresh it is not unpleasant but as the season advances it tastes strongly of turpentine.

P. coulteri D. Don.

California. The seeds, says Nuttall,[1] are of the size of an almond and are edible.

P. edulis Engelm. NUT PINE. PINON PINE.

Southwestern United States. The nut is sweet and edible, about the size of a hazelnut. It is used as an article of trade by the New Mexicans of the upper Rio Grande, with those below and about El Paso. The fruit has a slightly terebinthine taste but the New Mexicans are very fond of it.[2]

P. excelsa Wall. BHOTAN PINE.

Himalayan mountains. The tree is called *cheel*.[3] In Kamaon, a kind of manna, which is eaten, is collected from this tree [4] in a dry winter.

P. flexilis James.

Western United States. The large seeds are used as food by the Indians.[5]

P. gerardiana Wall. NEPAL NUT PINE.

Himalayas. The cones are plucked before they open and are heated to make the scales expand and to get the seeds out. Large quantities of the seeds are stored for winter use, and they form a staple food of the inhabitants of Kunawar. They are eaten ground and mixed with flour. It is a common saying in Kunawar, says Brandis,[6] " one tree a man's life in winter." They are oily, with a slight but not unpleasant turpentiny flavor and are called *neozar*.

P. koraiensis Sieb. & Zucc. KOREAN PINE.

Korea, Kamchatka, China and Japan. The tree produces edible nuts.[7]

P. lambertiana Dougl. GIANT PINE. SUGAR PINE.

Northwest coast of America. The resin which exudes from partially burned trees for the most part loses its terebinthine taste and smell and acquires a sweetness nearly equal to that of sugar and is sometimes used for sweetening food. It has, however, decided cathartic properties and is oftener used by the frontiersmen as a medicine than a condiment.[8] The seeds have a sweet and pleasant-tasting kernel and are eaten roasted or pounded into coarse cakes by the Indians.[9]

---

[1] Nuttall, T. *No. Amer. Sylva* 2:172. 1865.

[2] Bigelow, J. M. *Pacific R. R. Rpt.* 4:19. 1856.

[3] Pickering, C. *Chron. Hist. Pls.* 328. 1879.

[4] Brandis, D. *Forest Fl.* 512. 1874.

[5] Brewer and Watson *Bot. Cal.* 2:124. 1880.

[6] Brandis, D. *Forest Fl.* 509. 1874.

[7] Mueller, F. *Sel. Pls.* 354. 1891.

[8] Newberry *Pacific R. R. Rpt.* 6:44. 1857.

[9] Nuttall, T. *No. Amer. Sylva* 2:181. 1865.

P. longifolia Roxb. EMODI PINE.

Himalaya Mountains.   The seeds, says Brandis,[1] are eaten in India and are of some importance as food in times of scarcity.

P. monophylla Torr. & Frem. NUT PINE. STONE PINE.

Western North America.   The seeds are of an almond-like flavor and are consumed in quantity by the natives.[2]

P. parryana Engelm.

California.   The seeds are eaten by the Indians.[3]

P. pinea Linn. STONE PINE.

Southern Europe and the Levant.   This pine is said by Grigor[4] to be cultivated for its fruit about Naples.   It was known to the ancients, and with the Greeks was a tree sacred to Neptune.   The seeds are commonly called *pignons* by the French and *pinocchi* by the Italians.   They are eaten as dessert, made into sweetmeats or used in puddings and cakes.   They are very commonly used in Aleppo and in Turkey.[5]

P. sabiniana Dougl. DIGGER PINE.

California.   This is one of the nut pines of California and furnishes a most important food to the Indians, says Brewer.[6]   The seeds are as large as large beans, are very palatable, having, however, a slightly terebinthine taste.   Thousands of beings, red-skinned but human, look to this pine tree for their winter store of food.[7]

P. sylvestris Linn. SCOTCH PINE.

Northern Europe and Asia.   In Norway, the inner bark furnishes a bark-bread.[3] In Sweden, in times of scarcity, much bark is collected from the forests for food, being kiln-dried, ground into flour, mixed with a small portion of oatmeal and made into thin cakes.[9]   The inner part of the bark, says Morlot,[10] properly prepared, furnishes when boiled a very edible broth; the Laplanders are quite fond of it.   When they prepare a meal of it, they bark the tree all around up to a certain height.   The tree then dies and thus the routes of migration in Lapland are marked by a track of dead pines which is continually widening.

P. torreyana Parry.

California.   This pine bears large and edible seeds.[11]

---

[1] Brandis, D. *Forest Fl.* 508.   1874.

[2] Mueller, F.   *Sel. Pls.* 357.   1891.

[3] Newberry *Pop. Sci. Monthly* 32:36.   1888.

[4] Morton *Cyc. Agr.* 2:609.   1869.

[5] Hooker, W. J.   *Journ. Bot.* 1:205.   1834.

[6] Brewer and Watson *Bot. Cal.* 2:127.   1880.

[7] Newberry *Pacific R. R. Rpt.* 6:41.   1857.

[8] Balfour, J. H.   *Man. Bot.* 599.   1875.

[9] Johnson, C. P.   *Useful Pls. Gt. Brit.* 262.   1862.

[10] Morlot, A.   *Smithsonian Inst. Rpt.* 309.   1860.

[11] Brewer and Watson *Bot. Cal.* 2:125.   1880.

Piper amalago Linn. *Piperaceae.*

West Indies. Browne [1] says the seeds may replace pepper for seasoning.

P. betle Linn. BETLE PEPPER.

East Indies and Malay. The leaves are chewed with betel-nut by the Malays and other Indian races.

P. capense Linn. f. STAART PEPPER.

South Africa. The pepper is used by the country people in Kaffraria as a spice.[2]

P. chaba Hunter.

Indian Archipelago. The long pepper which is imported by the Dutch is the fruit-spike, collected and dried before it reaches maturity.

P. clusii C. DC.

Tropical Africa. This spice was imported as early as 1364 to Rouen and Dieppe from Liberia under the name pepper. In tropical western Africa, it is used as a condiment.[3]

P. cubeba Linn. f. CUBEB PEPPER.

Malay, Java and Penang. Pereira [4] states that as early as 1305 the product of this tree was used as a condiment in London, although now it is considered a medicine.

P. longum Linn. LONG PEPPER.

A shrub indigenous to Malabar, Ceylon, eastern Bengal, Timor and the Philippines and cultivated along the eastern and western coasts of India.[5] Its fruits consist of very small, one-sided berries or grains embedded in a pulpy matter, green when immature, and becoming red as it ripens. The fruit is gathered in the green state to form pepper, as it is then hotter than when perfectly ripe. This is the long pepper of commerce.

P. methysticum Forst. f.

Sandwich Islands and the Fiji Islands. The root of this plant is used to form an intoxicating drink under the name of *ava*, *kava* or *kawa*. The root is chewed, thrown into a bowl and water is poured on. It is then strained through cocoa-nut husks, when it is ready for use.

P. nigrum Linn. PEPPER TREE.

Indigenous to the forests of Travancore and Malabar, whence it has been introduced into Sumatra, Java, Borneo, the Malay peninsula, Siam, the Philippines and the West Indies.[6] This tree furnishes the black pepper of commerce which is the berries gathered before they are perfectly ripe and dried. The white pepper is formed from the decorticated fruits. It is frequently mentioned by Roman writers of the Augustan age and, in the fifth century, Attila demanded 3000 pounds of pepper as a part of the ransom of the city

---

[1] Lunan, J. *Hort. Jam.* 2:51. 1814.

[2] Thunberg, C. P. *Trav.* 1:170. 1795.

[3] Flückiger and Hanbury *Pharm.* 589. 1879.

[4] *U. S. Disp.* 340. 1865.

[5] Flückiger and Hanbury *Pharm.* 524. 1879.

[6] Flückiger and Hanbury *Pharm.* 576. 1879.

of Rome. An account of the growing of pepper in India is given by Mandeville, who traveled there in 1322–1356.

P. sarmentosum Roxb. LONG PEPPER.

East Indies and Malay. The fruit, according to Wight, is gathered and sold as long pepper.

P. sylvaticum Roxb. MOUNTAIN LONG PEPPER.

East Indies and Burma. The spikes, both green and ripe, are used in Bengal as long pepper.[1]

P. umbellatum Linn.

Tropics. The leaves may be boiled and eaten.[2]

Piptadenia peregrina Benth. *Leguminosae.* BLACK PARICA.

Brazil and British Guiana. The native tribes intoxicate themselves with the fumes of the burning seeds.[3]

Pipturus velutinus Wedd. *Urticaceae.*

Moluccas. This species bears a sweet but rather insipid fruit.[4]

Pisonia alba Span. *Nyctagineae.* TREE LETTUCE.

East Indies, Malay and common in the gardens about Madras. In taste, the leaves somewhat resemble lettuce, but Wight says, to his taste, it is but an indifferent substitute.[5]

Pistacia atlantica Desf. *Anacardiaceae.* MASTIC TREE.

Mediterranean region. The Moors eat the fruits and bruise them to mix with their dates.[6]

P. lentiscus Linn. MASTIC TREE.

Southern Europe, northern Africa and western Asia; introduced into the United States by the Patent Office in 1855 for trial in southern California and the Gulf States.[7] Mastic is the resin obtained from incisions in the bark of this tree and is produced principally in the Island of Scio and in Asiatic Turkey. Mastic is consumed in large quantities by the Turks for chewing to sweeten the breath and to strengthen the gums. The tree is cultivated in Italy and Portugal but is said to produce no resin in these climates. From the kernel of the fruit, an oil may be obtained, which is fine for table use.

P. mexicana H. B. & K.

Mexico. This is a small tree with edible nuts found by Bigelow near the mouth of the Pecos.[8]

---

[1] Pickering, C. *Chron. Hist. Pls.* 579. 1879.
[2] Sloane, H. *Nat. Hist. Jam.* 1:136. 1707.
[3] Hooker, W. J. *Journ. Bot.* 2:132. 1840.
[4] Wight, R. *Icon. Pls.* 2: Pl. 676. 1843. (*Morus paniculatus*)
[5] Wight, R. *Icon. Pls.* 5:Pl. 1765. 1852. (*P. morindifolia*)
[6] Loudon, J. C. *Arb. Frut. Brit.* 2:548. 1844.
[7] *U. S. Pat. Off. Rpt.* LVIII. 1855.
[8] Havard, V. *Proc. U. S. Nat. Mus.* 511. 1885.

P. terebinthus Linn. CYPRUS TURPENTINE. TEREBINTH.

Southern Europe and Mediterranean region. This is the cultivated form of *P. vera*, grown in Palestine and Syria.[1] The plant is a large and stout tree of the Mediterranean flora and furnishes Cyprus turpentine. The nuts are shaped like the filbert, long and pointed, the kernel pale, greenish, sweet and more oily than the almond. It is the *terebinthus* of Theophrastus,[2] and the *senawber* or *snowber* of the Arabs. The species was introduced into the United States for trial culture in 1859.[3]

P. vera Linn. PISTACIA NUT.

Mediterranean and the Orient. The tree is indigenous to Persia, Bactria and Syria but is cultivated in the Mediterranean regions. Seeds of the nut were distributed from the United States Patent Office in 1854.[4] The fruit is oval, about the size of an olive and contains a kernel, oily and mild to the taste.[5] The nuts are used in ices, creams, conserves and all kinds of confectionery.[6] The nut is eaten raw like almonds and is much esteemed by the Turks, Greeks and Italians. There are several varieties, of which the Aleppo is considered the best for its fruits.[7] In Kabul, pistacia trees are said by Harlan [8] to yield a crop of fruit one year, followed always by a crop of blighted fruit destitute of a kernel the next.

Pisum arvense Linn. *Leguminosae.* FIELD PEA. GREY PEA.

Eurasia. This is the pea most commonly cultivated in Egypt and it is also grown in India.[9] In China, this pea is eaten and seems to have been introduced from the country of the Vigurs, during the T'ang time.[10] This species is considered by Lindley as the original of all our cultivated peas. In Scotland and England, some 13 or more varieties of the field pea are grown. A variety allied to this species has been found in the ancient lacustrine deposits of Switzerland.[11]

P. jomardi Schrank. EGYPTIAN PEA.

Egypt. This species is edible and is perhaps cultivated.[12]

P. sativum Linn. PEA.

Europe and northern Asia. The pea in India goes back to a remote period as is shown by its Sanscrit name. The discovery of its seed in a tomb at Thebes proves it to have been an ancient Egyptian plant. It was seen in Japan by Thunberg,[13] 1776. Its

---

[1] Unger, F. *U. S. Pat. Off. Rpt.* 323. 1859.
[2] Theophrastus lib. 3, c. 14.
[3] *U. S. Pat. Off. Rpt.* 20. 1859.
[4] *U. S. Pat. Off. Rpt.* XXXII. 1854.
[5] Loudon, J. C. *Arb. Frut. Brit.* 2:546. 1844.
[6] Hooker, W. J. *Journ. Bot.* 1:109. 1834.
[7] Loudon, J. C. *Arb. Frut. Brit.* 2:546. 1844.
[8] *U. S. Pat. Off. Rpt.* 533. 1861. Note.
[9] De Candolle, A. *Geog. Bot.* 2:960. 1855.
[10] Smith, F. P. *Contrib. Mat. Med. China* 172. 1871.
[11] Heer, O. *Garden.* July 15, 1876.
[12] Unger, F. *U. S. Pat. Off. Rpt.* 317. 1859.
[13] Thunberg, C. P. *Fl. Jap.* XXXIII. 1784.

culture among the Romans is evident from its mention by Columella, Pliny and Palladius.[1] There is every reason to believe, from the paucity of description, that peas were not then in their present esteem as a vegetable and were considered inferior to other plants of the leguminous order. The first distinct mention of the garden peas is by Ruellius in 1536, who says there are two kinds of peas, one the field pea and trailing, the other a climbing pea, whose fresh pods with their peas were eaten. Green peas, however, were not a common vegetable at the close of the seventeenth century. The author of a life of Colbert, 1695, says: "It is frightful to see persons sensual enough to purchase green peas at the price of 50 crowns per litron." This kind of pompous expenditure prevailed much at the French Court, as will be seen by a letter of Madame de Maintenon, dated May 10, 1696. " This subject of peas continues to absorb all others," says she, " the anxiety to eat them, the pleasure of having eaten them and the desire to eat them again, are the three great matters which have been discussed by our princes for four days past. Some ladies, even after having supped at the Royal table and well supped too, returning to their own homes, at the risk of suffering from indigestion, will again eat peas before going to bed. It is both a fashion and a madness."[2]

In England, it is not until after the Norman Conquest and the establishment of monastic communities that we read of green peas being used. In Fosbrook's *British Monasticon*, it is stated that at Barking Nunnery the annual store of provisions consisted among other things of green peas for Lent, and, in *Archaeologia* in *Order and Government of a Nobleman's House*, they are again mentioned. In 1299, the English forces, while besieging a castle in Lothian, were compelled to feed on the peas and beans of the surrounding fields.[3] At the present time, in varieties, they are grown as far north as Hammerfest and Lapland.

Peas were early introduced to the American Continent, but, in notices of this plant, the word *peason* refers sometimes, it is probable, to beans. In 1493, *peason* are mentioned by Peter Martyr as grown at Isabela Island by Columbus; in 1535, *peason* are mentioned by Cartier as grown by the Indians of Hochelaga, now Montreal; and in 1613, peas were obtained from the French traders grown by the Indians of the Ottawa River;[5] in 1540, peas are mentioned in New Mexico by Alarcon and " small, white peas " by Coronado; in 1562, *peason* were cultivated by the Florida Indians, as related by Ribault.[6] In 1602, peas were sown by Gosnold on the Elizabeth Islands off the coast of Massachusetts, according to Smith;[7] in 1629, in Massachusetts, there was a " store of green peas," " as good as ever I eat in England," growing in the governor's garden, according to Rev. Francis Higginson.[8] In 1614, peas were mentioned by Smith[9] as grown by the New England

[1] Columella lib. 2, c. 10; lib. 11, c. 1.; Pliny lib. 18, c. 31; Palladius lib. 10, c. 6.

[2] *Gard. Chron.* 71. 1843.

[3] Glasspoole, H. G. *Rpt. Ohio State Bd. Agr.* 30:519. 1875.

[4] Cartier, J. *Third Voy.* Pinkerton Coll. 12:656. 1812.

[5] Parkman, F. *Pion. France* 379. 1894.

[6] Hakluyt, R. *Divers Voy. Amer.* Hakl. Soc. Ed. 102. 1840.

[7] Pinkerton *Coll. Voy.* 13:20. 1812.

[8] Higginson, Rev. Francis. *New Eng. Plant.* Mass. Hist. Soc. Coll. 1st Ser. 1:118. 1792.

[9] Smith, J. *Desc. New Eng.* 16. 1616. Force Coll. Tracts 2: 1838.

Indians. In 1690, Bancroft [1] says Spanish peas were grown by the Indians of Mexico, and, in 1775, Romans [2] says green peas were obtained the year round at Mobile, Alabama. In 1779, Gen. Sullivan's expedition against the Indians of western New York destroyed the growing peas of the Indians who occupied the territory near Geneva. [3]

If we trace the antiquity of the various forms which include varieties, we find the varieties noted are innumerable and occur with white and green seed, with smooth and with wrinkled seed, with seed black-spotted at the hilum, with large and small seed, as well as with plants of large and small aspects, dwarf, trailing, and tall plants, and those with edible pods.

White and Green Peas.— Lyte, in his edition of Dodonaeus, 1586, mentions the trailing pea, or what Vilmorin classifies as the half-dwarf, as having round seed, of color sometimes white, sometimes green.

Smooth Seeded.— Dodonaeus, in his *Frumentorum*, 1566, describes this form under *Pisum minus*, a tall pea, called in Germany *erweyssen;* in Brabant, *erwiten;* in France, *pois;* by the Greeks, *ochron;* the pods containing eight to ten round peas of a yellow color at first, then green. This pea was called in England, Middle Peason, in 1591. [4]

Wrinkled Seed.— The first certain mention of wrinkled seed is by Tragus in 1552, under Phaseolus. These are also recorded in Belgian and German gardens by Dodonaeus in his *Frumentorum*, 1566, under *Pisum majus*, the dry seed being angular, uneven, of a white color in some varieties and of a sordid color in others. He calls them *roomsche erwiten, groote erwiten, stock erwiten,* and the plant he says does not differ from his *Pisum minus* and indeed he uses the same figure for the two. Pena and Lobel, [5] 1570, describe the same pea as in Belgian and English gardens, under the name *Pisum angulosum hortorum quadratum Plinii*, with seed of a ferruginous and reddish color. Lobel, [6] 1591, figures the seed, using the name *Pisum quadratum*, and it seems to be the Great Peason, Garden Peason, or Branch Peason of Lyte in 1586, as he gives Dodonaeus' common names as synonyms. In 1686, Ray [7] describes this class under the name *Rouncival* and refers to Gerarde's picture of *Pisum majus*, or *Rowncivall* Pease, in 1597, as being the same. This word *Rouncival*, in white and green varieties, was used by McMahon [8] in 1806, and *Rouncivals* by Gardiner and Hepburn [9] in 1818 and Thorburn in 1828. The first good description of the seed is, however, in 1708, when Lisle [10] calls it honey-combed or pitted. Knight, a nurseryman of Bedfordshire, before 1726, [11] did much for the

[1] Bancroft, H. H. *Native Races* 1:652. 1875.

[2] Romans *Nat. Hist. Fla.* 1:115. 1775.

[3] Conover, G. S. *Early Hist. Geneva* 47. 1879.

[4] Lobel *Icon.* 2:66 and index. 1591.

[5] Pena and Lobel *Advers.* 396. 1570.

[6] Lobel *Icon.* 2:66 and index. 1591.

[7] Ray *Hist. Pl.* 892. 1686.

[8] McMahon, B. *Amer. Gard. Cal.* 582, 1806.

[9] Gardiner and Hepburn *Amer. Gard.* 59. 1818; Thorb. *Cat* 1828

[10] Lisle *Husb.* 169. 1757.

[11] Townsend *Seedsman* 2. 1726.

improvement of the pea and sent out several wrinkled varieties. Up to Knight's time the wrinkled peas do not seem to have been in general esteem. The Knight pea, the seed rough, uneven, and shrivelled, the plant tall, was in American gardens in 1821,[1] and a number of Knight's peas are under cultivation at present.

Black-eyed Peas.— These are mentioned as an old sort by Townsend [2] in 1726 and are now grown under the name of Black-eyed Marrowfat.

Dwarf Peas.— These are mentioned by Tournefort [3] in 1700 and are referred by him to 1665. There is no earlier distinct reference.

Half-Dwarfs.— These are the ordinary trailing peas as mentioned by the earlier botanies, as, for instance, the *Pisum minus* of Camerarius, 1586.

Tall Peas.— These are the forms described by the early botanies as requiring sticking, as the *Pisum majus* of Camerarius, 1596, the *Pisum* of Fuchsius, 1542, and *Phasioli* or *faselen* of Tragus, 1552.

Edible-Podded or Sugar Peas.— The pods and peas of the large, climbing pea, as also the green pods of the trailing form, are recorded as eaten by Ruellius [4] in 1536, and this manner of eating is recorded by later authors. We now have two forms, those with straight and those with contorted pods. The first of these is figured by Gerarde,[5] 1597; is described by Ray [6] in 1686 and Tournefort in 1700. The second form is mentioned by Worlidge [7] in 1683 as the Sugar pease with crooked pods, by Ray [8] as Sickle pease. In the *Jardinier Français*, 1651, Bonnefonds describes them as the Dutch pea and adds that until lately they were very rare. Roquefort says they were introduced into France by the French ambassador in Holland about 1600.[9] In 1806, McMahon includes three kinds among American esculents.

Number of Varieties.— About 1683, Meager [10] names 9 kinds in English culture; in 1765 Stevenson,[11] 34 kinds; in 1783, Bryant [12] names 14; in 1806, McMahon [13] has 22 varieties; Thorburn's Calendar, 1821, contains 11 sorts, and this seed catalog of 1828 has 24 sorts; in 1883, Vilmorin describes 149; in the report of the New York Agricultural Experiment Station for 1884, 93 varieties are described in full.

Pithecolobium bigeminum Mart. *Leguminosae.* SOAP-BARK TREE.

East Indies and Malay. The tree has long, twisted fruit, sweet to the taste but

---

[1] Cobbett, W. *Amer. Gard.* 154. 1846.

[2] Townsend *Seedsman* 2. 1726.

[3] Tournefort *Inst.* 394. 1719.

[4] Ruellius *Nat. Stirp.* 439. 1536.

[5] Gerarde, J. *Herb.* 1045. 1597.

[6] Ray *Hist. Pl.* 891. 1686.

[7] Worlidge, J. *Syst. Hort.* 197. 1683.

[8] Ray *Hist. Pl.* 891. 1686.

[9] *Gard. Chron.* 71. 1843.

[10] Meager *Eng. Gard.* 89. 1683.

[11] Stevenson *Gard. Kal.* 90. 1765.

[12] Bryant *Fl. Diet.* 305. 1783.

[13] McMahon, B. *Amer. Gard. Cal.* 582. 1806.

inducing dysentery and it, therefore, was prohibited by Alexander.[1] It is called *ta nyen* in Burma, where the natives are extravagantly fond of the seeds as a condiment to preserve fish, notwithstanding sometimes disastrous consequences.[2]

P. dulce Benth.

American tropics. The sweet pulp of the pod is wholesome.[3] The plant is extensively cultivated in India as a hedge plant. In Mexico, it is called *guamuchil*, and the fruit is boiled and eaten. In Manila, the species is grown for its fruit, which is eaten. The sweet, firm pulp in the curiously twisted pods is eaten.[4]

P. lobatum Benth.

A large tree of Burma. The seeds are eaten as a condiment.[5]

P. saman Benth. RAIN TREE. SAMAN. ZAMANG.

Tropical America. This is a Mexican tree yielding edible pods.[6]

P. unguis-cati Benth. CAT'S CLAW.

Mexico and the West Indies. The pulp about the seed is eaten by the natives.[7] In the West Indies it is eaten by the negroes.[8]

Plantago coronopus Linn. *Plantagineae.* BUCKSHORN PLANTAIN. STAR-OF-THE-EARTH.

Mediterranean countries and Middle Europe. The leaves are used in France as a salad.[9] This species is mentioned as grown in gardens by Camerarius,[10] 1586, and by many of the other botanists of the sixteenth and seventeenth centuries; it is described by Ray[11] in 1686 as cultivated in England and as not differing from the wild plant except in size and in the other accidents of culture. Townsend,[12] 1726, says the seed is now " in all the Seedsmen's Bills, tho' it is seldom in the Gardens." It is described and figured by Vilmorin[13] among French vegetables. During the three hundred years in which we find it pictured, we see no evidence of any essential changes produced by cultivation.

P. major Linn. CART-TRACK PLANT. PLANTAIN.

Europe, Asia and North America. In China, this plant was formerly eaten as a potherb.[14]

---

[1] Pickering, C. *Chron. Hist. Pls.* 331. 1879. (*Inga bigemin*)
[2] Ibid.
[3] Mueller, F. *Sel. Pls.* 27. 1891.
[4] Pickering, C. *Chron. Hist. Pls.* 650. 1879. (*Inga dulcis*)
[5] Brandis, D. *Forest Fl.* 575. 1876.
[6] Mueller, F. *Sel. Pls.* 28. 1891.
[7] Pickering, C. *Chron. Hist. Pls.* 650. 1879. (*Inga saman*)
[8] Don, G. *Hist. Dichl. Pls.* 2:391. 1832.
[9] *Bon Jard.* 478. 1882.
[10] Camerarius *Epit.* 276. 1586.
[11] Ray *Hist. Pl.* 879. 1686.
[12] Townsend *Seedsman* 18. 1726.
[13] Vilmorn *Les Pls. Potag.* 169. 1883.
[14] Smith, F. P. *Contrib. Mat. Med. of China* 172. 1871.

P. maritima Linn. SEASIDE PLANTAIN.

Shores of Europe and of the United States from New Jersey northward. Kalm[1] says the French boil its leaves in a broth on their sea voyages, or eat them as a salad. It may likewise be pickled like samphire.

Platonia insignis Mart. *Guittiferae.*

Brazil. The fruit, called *pacoury-uva* in Brazil, is said to be very sweet and delicious, whilst the seeds have the flavor of almonds.[2]

Platycrater arguta Sieb. & Zucc. *Saxifrageae.* TEA-OF-HEAVEN.

Japan. In Japan, the leaves are used as a tea substitute.[3]

Plectranthus ternatus Sims. *Labiatae.*

Comoro Islands and Madagascar. This perennial plant was carried to the Mauritius and is there cultivated as a potherb. It is called in Madagascar *omime.*[4]

Plectronia parvifolia Benth. & Hook. f. *Rubiaceae.*

Burma and Malay. The leaves of this thorny shrub are largely consumed by the natives in their curries. The pulp enclosing the seeds is eaten by the natives but, to the European taste, is not very palatable[5] In India, says Ainslie,[6] the fruit is eaten by the natives, and the leaves are also used as food, being put in curries as seasoners.

Plegerina odorata Arruda.

Brazil. This plant produces an oval or oblong drupe, very little smaller than an egg, yellow at ripening, the kernel of which is covered with a sweet, aromatic and nutritious pulp.[7]

P. rufa Arruda.

Brazil. The fruit is an irregular drupe, of which the kernel is covered with a sweet fecula, somewhat aromatic, pleasant and nutritive. It is large enough to satisfy one person. It is sold in the markets of Brazil and by some inhabitants it is now cultivated.[8]

P. umbrosissima Arruda.

Brazil. The sweet fruit is sold in the markets of Pernambuco.[9]

Plukenetia corniculata Sm. *Euphorbiaceae.*

East Indies and Malay. The leaves are said to be eaten as a vegetable.[10]

---

[1] Kalm, P. *Trav. No. Amer.* 2:345. 1772.

[2] *Treas. Bot.* 2:901. 1870.

[3] *U. S. D. A. Rpt.* 199. 1870.

[4] Pickering, C. *Chron. Hist. Pls.* 385. 1879.

[5] Wight, R. *Illustr. Ind. Bot.* 2:76. 1850. (*Canthium parviflorum*)

[6] Ainslie, W. *Mat. Ind.* 2:63. 1826. (*Webera tetrandra*)

[7] Koster, H. *Trav. Braz.* 378. 1817.

[8] Ibid.

[9] Martius *Mat. Med. Bras.* 77. 1854.

[10] Royle, J. F. *Illustr. Bot. Himal.* 1:329. 1839.

Poa abyssinica Jacq. *Gramineae.* TEFF.

A mountain plant of Abyssinia, cultivated everywhere there, at a height of from 2500 to 8000 feet where gentle heat and rain favor its development. Its seeds furnish the favorite bread of the Abyssinians in the form of thin, highly leavened and spongy cakes. Four varieties of this grain are cultivated.[1] Parkyns[2] writes that teff is considered by the Abyssinians wholesome and digestible, but so far from being satisfied of this, he is doubtful of its containing much nutritive property and as for its taste, he says, "fancy yourself chewing a piece of sour sponge and you will have a good idea of what is considered the best bread in Abyssinia."

P. flabellata Hook. f.

Fuego and the Falkland Islands. Ross[3] says the lower part of the culm in the tussock is so fleshy and juicy that when a tuft of leaves is drawn out from a tussock-bog, an inch of the base, about the thickness of a finger, affords a very sweet morsel, with flavor like nuts. Two men subsisted almost entirely upon this substance for 14 months.

Podocarpus andina Poepp. *Coniferae.* PLUM FIR.

Chile. This species forms a stately tree bearing at fruiting season clusters of edible, cherry-like fruits.[4]

P. dacrydioides A. Rich. WHITE PINE.

New Zealand. The white, sweet fruit is eaten by the natives.[5] The drupe is also eaten.

P. spicata R. Br. BLACK PINE.

New Zealand. Its young shoots are made into a beverage like spruce beer.[6] It has sweet, edible drupes.

P. totara G. Benn. MAHOGANY PINE. TOTARA PINE.

New Zealand. The fruit is eaten.[7]

Podococcus barteri Mann & H. Wendl. *Palmae.*

Western tropical Africa. The fruit is edible.

Podophyllum emodi Wall. *Berberideae.* HIMALAYAN MAY APPLE.

India. The berry is edible but the roots and leaves are poisonous.

P. peltatum Linn. MANDRAKE. MAY APPLE. RACCOON-BERRY. WILD LEMON.

Northeast America. "Certaine ground apples, a pleasant fruite" were seen by

---

[1] Unger, F. *U. S. Pat. Off. Rpt.* 306. 1859. (*Eragrostis abyssinica*)

[2] Parkyns, M. *Life Abyss.* 1:306. 1856.

[3] Ross, J. C. *Voy. Antarct. Reg.* 2:269. 1847.

[4] Mueller, F. *Sel. Pls.* 292. 1891.

[5] Ibid.

[6] Masters, M. T. *Treas. Bot.* 1:378. 1870. (*Dacrydium taxifolium*)

[7] Masters, M. T. *Treas. Bot.* 2:908. 1870.

[8] Mueller, F. *Sel. Pls.* 376. 1891. 8th Ed.

Newport on James River.   Porcher[1] says the fruit is relished by many persons.   It is extremely delicious to most persons but to many is an aperient.   In France, it is grown in the flower gardens.[2]

Polyalthia cerasoides Benth. & Hook. f.   *Anonaceae.*

East Indies.   The fruits, cherry-shaped and dark red, are eaten by the natives but are astringent.[3]   The plant has black berries, fleshy, smooth and of an acid-sweet taste.[4]

Polygala siberica Linn.   *Polygaleae.*

Temperate and tropical Asia.   The roots and tender leaves were eaten in China in the fourteenth century.[5]

P. theezans Linn.

Java and Japan.   The Japanese and Javanese use the leaves as tea.[6]

P. vulgaris Linn.   MILKWORT.

Europe and Asia Minor.   This plant is said to be used in adulterating green tea.[7]

Polygonatum japonicum C. Morr. & Decne.   *Liliaceae.*

Japan.   It is called *amatokoro* by the Japanese and the root is used.[8]

P. multiflorum All.   SOLOMON'S SEAL.

Northern regions.   The root, says Johnson,[9] macerated for some time in water, yields a substance capable of being used as food and consisting principally of starch.   The young shoots form an excellent vegetable when boiled and eaten like asparagus and are largely consumed in Turkey.   The European form of the species, mentioned by Titford,[10] is well known to the negroes in Jamaica, who eat it boiled, and the Indians in North America also feed upon the root.   Parkman[11] states that the roots of Solomon's Seal were used as food by starving Frenchmen.

P. officinale All.   SOLOMON'S SEAL.

Europe and Siberia.   The roots have been used, says Withering,[12] made into bread in times of scarcity but they require boiling or baking before use.

---

[1] Porcher, F. P.   *Res. So. Fields, Forests* 23.   1869.

[2] Vilmorin *Fl. Pl. Ter.* 899.   1870.   3rd Ed.

[3] Don, G.   *Hist. Dichl. Pls.* 1:98.   1831.

[4] Pickering, C.   *Chron. Hist. Pls.* 725.   1879.   (*Gautteria cerasoides*)

[5] Bretschneider, E.   *Bot. Sin.* 51.   1882.

[6] Baillon, H.   *Hist. Pls.* 5:84.   1878.

[7] Ibid.

[8] Pickering, C.   *Chron. Hist. Pls.* 418.   1879.

[9] Johnson, C. P.   *Useful Pls. Gt. Brit.* 270.   1862.   (*Convallaria multiflora*)

[10] Titford, W. J.   *Hort. Bot. Amer.* 56.   1811.

[11] Parkman, F.   *Pion. France* 438.   1894.

[12] Johnson, C. P.   *Useful Pls. Gt. Brit.* 270.   1862.   (*Convallaria polygonatum*)

Polygonum alpinum All. *Polygonaceae.* ALPINE KNOTWEED.

Southern Europe and northern Asia. This plant is called by the Russians *kizlez* or *kapousta*, by the Baschkirs *kamouslouk* and is eaten.[1]

P. bistorta Linn. BISTORT. SNAKEWEED.

Northern regions. The leaves " are by some boiled in the spring and eaten as greens." [2] Though very astringent and bitter to the taste in a raw state, says Johnson,[3] the root contains an abundance of starch and, after being steeped in water and roasted, becomes edible. A considerable quantity of the root thus prepared is consumed in Russia and Siberia in times of scarcity, as a substitute for bread. In the southern counties of England, the young shoots were formerly in request as an ingredient in herb puddings and as a green vegetable but they are now little used. The root, called *ma-shu* by the western Eskimos, says Seemann,[4] is an article of food with them and, after being roasted in the ashes, is not unlike a potato, though not so soft and nutritious.

P. multiflorum Thunb.

China and Japan. The roots are used as food.[5]

P. odoratum Lour.

Cochin China. This species, according to Loudon,[6] is cultivated throughout Cochin China as an excellent vegetable for eating with boiled meat and fish.

P. viviparum Linn. SERPENT GRASS.

Arctic regions and mountains south to the shore of Lake Superior. Its roots, according to Gmelin,[7] are collected by the Samoyedes and eaten. Lightfoot [8] says the people of Kamchatka and sometimes the Norwegians, when pressed with hunger, feed upon the roots. In Sweden it is called *mortog* or *swinegrass*.[9]

Polypodium fragrans. *Polypodiaceae.* POLYPODY.

East Siberia. This fern is called *serlik* by the Bouriates and is used as a substitute for tea.[10]

Polystichum munitum Kaulf. *Polypodiaceae.*

The roots of this fern, says Hooker,[11] are roasted on the embers and constitute an article of food for the Indians of the northwest.

---

[1] Pickering, C. *Chron. Hist. Pls.* 779. 1879. (*P. undulatum*)

[2] Lightfoot, J. *Fl. Scot.* 1:206. 1789.

[3] Johnson, C. P. *Useful Pls. Gt. Brit.* 218. 1862.

[4] Seemann, B. *Journ. Anthrop. Soc. Lond.* 3:CCCIII. 1865.

[5] Thunberg, C. P. *Trav.* 4:123. 1796.

[6] Loudon, J. C. *Enc. Agr.* 935.

[7] Pickering, C. *Chron. Hist. Pls.* 779. 1879.

[8] Lightfoot, J. *Fl. Scot.* 1:207. 1789.

[9] Pickering, C. *Chron. Hist. Pls.* 780. 1879.

[10] Pickering, C. *Chron. Hist. Pls.* 753. 1879.

[11] Hooker, W. J. *Fl. Bor. Amer.* 2:261. 1840. (*Aspidium munitum*)

Pometia pinnata Forst. *Sapindaceae.*

Islands of the Pacific. This species is planted around dwellings for its sweet and edible fruit.[1]

Populus alba Linn. *Salicineae.* WHITE POPLAR.

Northern regions. The inner bark of this species, of *P. nigra* Linn. and *P. tremula* Linn. is occasionally used in northern Europe and Asia as a substitute for flour in making bread.[2] The soft, new wool of the poplar, says Dall,[3] is cut fine and mixed with his tobacco by the economical Indian of Alaska.

Porcela nitidifolia Ruiz et Pav. *Anonaceae.*

Peru. The berries as well as the flowers are eaten by the inhabitants of Peru.[4]

Porphyra laciniata Agardh. *Algae.* LAVER. SLOKAM. SLOKE.

Northern regions. In England, this membranous seaweed is stewed to a pulp and brought to table served with lemon juice. It is a favorite article of food with many persons.[5]

P. vulgaris Agardh. LAVER.

Northern regions. This seaweed is cultivated in the neighborhood of Tokio, Japan. Branches of oak are placed in the shallow waters of the bay in spring time; on these the laver appears and is collected from October to the following March and is sold as food in the markets.

Portulaca lutea Soland. *Portulaceae.* YELLOW PURSLANE.

Society Islands. This plant is used as a vegetable in the Society Islands and in New Zealand.

P. oleracea Linn. PURSLANE.

A native of tropical and subtropical regions but now spread over nearly the whole world. The fact that this plant is recorded as having reached England only in 1582 would seem to indicate its origin as recent in Europe.[6] Unger[7] says it is the *andrachen* of Theophrastus and Dioscorides and is a widely-distributed plant of the Mediterranean region, occurring everywhere and readily entering the loose soil of the gardens. In the thirteenth century, Albertus Magnus[8] does not mention its culture in gardens and apparently refers to the wild form, " the stems extending over the soil." In 1536, Ruellius[9] describes the erect, green-leaved, cultivated form, as well as the wild, procumbent form, and in this he is followed by many of the succeeding botanists. Three varieties are

---

[1] Gray, A. *U. S. Explor. Exped.* 259. 1854. (*Nephelium pinnatum*)

[2] Johnson, C. P. *Useful Pls. Gt. Brit.* 252. 1862.

[3] Dall, W. H. *Alaska* 81. 1897.

[4] Don, G. *Hist. Dichl. Pls.* 1:92. 1831.

[5] Harvey, W. H. *Phycol. Brit.* 4: Pl. XCII. 1846–51. Fig.

[6] McIntosh, C. *Book Gard.* 2:171. 1855.

[7] Unger, F. *U. S. Pat. Off. Rpt.* 355. 1859.

[8] Albertus Magnus *Veg.* Jessen Ed. 548. 1867.

[9] Ruellius *Nat. Stirp.* 482. 1536.

described; the green, the golden and the large-leaved golden. The golden varieties are not mentioned by Bauhin in his *Phytopinax*, 1596, nor in his *Pinax*, 1623, but are mentioned as if well known in *Le Jardinier Solitaire*, 1612. The green variety is figured by nearly all the earlier botanists. The golden has the following synonymy:

Pourpier doré. *Le Jard. Solit.* 378. 1612; Tourn. 236. 1719; Vilm. 518. 1883.
Red or Golden. Quintyne 199. 1693.
Portulaca sativa lutea sive aurea. Ray 1039. 1688.
Golden purslane. Ray 1039. 1688; Townsend 19. 1726; Mawe. 1778; Burr 392.
1863.

In England, McIntosh[1] says the young shoots and leaves are used in summer salads and are sometimes used in French and Italian soups and in pickles. This purslane is cultivated in Yemen,[2] sold in bundles at Mocha[3] and, in Burma, is used by the natives for a potherb.[4] In 1605, Champlain[5] says the Indians on the Maine coast brought him "*purslane,* which grows in large quantities among the Indian corn, and of which they made no more account than of weeds." Cutler, 1785, says it occurs in cornfields and is eaten as a potherb and is esteemed by some as little inferior to asparagus. It was previously mentioned by Josselyn[6] prior to 1670. Purslane has never been much valued in America. In 1819, Cobbett[7] mentions it in his *American Gardener,* as "a mischievous weed that Frenchmen and pigs eat when they can get nothing else. Both use it in salad, that is to say, raw." Sir Richard Hawkins,[8] at the Island of Saint Anna, off Cape Saint Thomas, found great store "of the hearbe purslane" which was very useful to his scurvy-suffering crew. Purslane is also mentioned by Nieuhoff[9] as cultivated in Brazil in 1647.

P. quadrifida Linn.
Old World tropics. This species is much used as a potherb in India.[10]

P. retusa Engelm.
Western North America. This species is eaten by the Apache Indians.

Potentilla anserina Linn. *Rosaceae.* GOOSE GRASS. GOOSE TANSY. SILVER-WEED.
Temperate regions. In some of the Hebrides, says Lightfoot,[11] the roots have often supported the inhabitants for months together. Boiled or roasted, they taste like parsnips.

---

[1] McIntosh, C. *Book Gard.* 2:171. 1855.
[2] Pickering, C. *Chron. Hist. Pls.* 611. 1879.
[3] Ibid.
[4] Ibid.
[5] Champlain *Voy.* 1604–1610. Prince Soc. Ed. 2:75. 1878.
[6] Josselyn, J. *New Eng. Rar.* 81. 1672.
[7] Cobbett, W. *Amer. Gard.* 157. 1846.
[8] Hawkins, R. *Voy. So. Seas.* Hakl. Soc. Ed. 1:86. 1847.
[9] Churchill *Coll. Voy.* 2:132. 1732.
[10] Royle, J. F. *Illustr. Bot. Himal.* 1:221. 1839.
[11] Lightfoot, J. *Fl. Scot.* 269. 1789.

P. fruticosa Linn. SHRUBBY CINQUEFOIL.

North temperate regions. This plant is called in Siberia *kouril-skoi-tchai* or Kurile tea. The leaves are used by peasants and Tartars as a tea.[1]

P. rupestris Linn. PRAIRIE TEA. ROCK CINQUEFOIL.

Europe and northern Asia. This plant is called by the Mongols *khaltalsa* and is used as a substitute for tea, as also in Siberia where it is called *polvoi-tchai* or prairie tea.[2]

P. tormentilla Neck. TORMENTIL.

Northern Asia and Europe. Johnson[3] says by long boiling the tannin of the root is converted into gum and the roots so treated have occasionally been eaten in times of scarcity.

Poterium sanguisorba Linn. *Rosaceae.* BURNET.

North temperate regions. The young and tender leaves of burnet taste somewhat like a green cucumber and are employed in salads. It is rarely cultivated in the gardens but occurs in all our books on gardening. Three varieties are described by Burr: the Smooth-leaved, the Hairy-leaved and the Large-seeded. This latter he deems but a seminal variation and a subvariety only. The following synonymy seems clear:

I.

Pimpinella sanguisorba minor laevis. Bauh. *Phytopin.* 282. 1596.
Poterium sanguisorba, var. B. Linn. *Sp.* 1411.
Smooth-leaved. Burr 319. 1863.

II.

Sanguisorba minor. Fuch. 790. 1542.
Pimpinella and Bipinelia. Ang. Burnet *Advers.* 320. 1570; Lob: *Obs.* 412. 1576;
     ic. **1:**718. 1591.
Small or Garden Pimpernell. Lyte's *Dod.* 152. 1586.
Pimpinella minor. Lugd. 1087. 1587.
Pimpinella sanguisorba minor hirsuta. Bauh. *Phytopin.* 282. 1596.
Pimpinella vulgaris sive minor. Ray 401. 1686.
Poterium sanguisorba. Linn. *Sp.* 1411.
Hairy-leaved Burnet. Burr 319. 1863.

The garden culture of burnet is implied in Lyte's *Dodoens' Herball,*[4] 1586. Ray,[5] however, a hundred years later, does not mention its culture. In 1693, Quintyne[6] grew it in the royal vegetable garden in France, and, in 1726, Townsend[7] says it is " a good plant for Sallads." Mawe,[8] 1778, says it has long been cultivated as a salad plant; while

---

[1] Pickering, C. *Chron. Hist. Pls.* 813. 1879.
[2] Pickering, C. *Chron. Hist. Pls.* 793. 1879.
[3] Johnson, C. P. *Useful Pls. Gt. Brit.* 93. 1862.
[4] Dodoens *Herb.* 152. 1586. Lyte Ed.
[5] Ray *Hist. Pl.* 401. 1686.
[6] Quintyne *Comp. Gard.* 1693.
[7] Townsend *Seedsman* 33. 1726.
[8] Mawe and Abercrombie *Univ. Gard. Bot.* 1778.

Bryant,[1] 1783, says it is so frequently cultivated in gardens that to describe it would be unnecessary. Burnet is recorded for American gardens in 1832 and it was then doubtless, a long-grown plant. It is now grown in the Mauritius.[2]

Pourouma cecropiaefolia Mart. *Urticaceae.*

Brazil. This is a cultivated plant of the Amazon, says Bates,[3] bearing a round, juicy berry, in large bunches and resembling grapes in taste.

Pouzolzia viminea Wedd. *Urticaceae.*

East Indies. A small shrub the leaves of which are eaten in Sikkim.[4]

Prangos pabularia Lindl. *Umbelliferae.* PRANGOS.

Himalayan region. Burnes says this plant is greedily cropped by sheep and is eaten even by his fellow travelers, a statement confirmed by Kinnier.[5]

Premna integrifolia Linn. *Verbenaceae.* HEADACHE TREE.

East Indies and Malay. Ainslie [6] says the leaves are eaten by the inhabitants of the Coromandel coast.

P. latifolia Roxb.

East Indies. The leaves have a strong but not disagreeable odor and are eaten by the natives in their curries.[7]

Primula officinalis Jacq. *Primulaceae.* PRIMROSE.

Europe and Asia Minor. The leaves are eaten in salads.[8]

P. vulgaris Huds. COWSLIP. PRIMROSE.

Europe and adjoining Asia. The flowers are picked when first open and fermented with water and sugar. The liquor, when well prepared, is pleasant in flavor and very intoxicating, resembling in taste some of the sweet wines of the south of France. In many parts of England, primrose flowers are collected in large quantities for this purpose. The leaves also are wholesome and may be eaten as a salad or boiled as a green potherb.[9]

Pringlea antiscorbutica R. Br. *Cruciferae.* KERGUELEN'S LAND CABBAGE.

Antarctics. This plant was first discovered by Captain Cook and was subsequently observed by Hooker [10] on Kerguelen's Land, a cold, humid, barren, volcanic rock of the

---

[1] Bryant *Fl. Diet.* 107. 1783.

[2] Bojer, W. *Hort. Maurit.* 127. 1837.

[3] Bates, H. W. *Nat. Amaz.* Humboldt *Libr. Sci.* 1:728. 1879–80.

[4] Brandis, D. *Forest Fl.* 405. 1876.

[5] Pickering, C. *Chron. Hist. Pls.* 328. 1879.

[6] Ainslie, W. *Mat. Ind.* 2:210. 1826.

[7] Drury, H. *Useful Pls. Ind.* 354. 1873.

[8] De Candolle, A. P., and LaMarck, J. B. *Flore Franc.* 3:446. 1805.

[9] Johnson, C. P. *Useful Pls. Gt. Brit.* 212. 1862. (*P. veris*)

[10] Hooker, J. D. *Bot. Antarctic Voy.* 2:239. 1847.

southern ocean.   Its rootstocks are from three to four feet long and lie close to the ground, bearing at their extremities large heads of leaves closely resembling cabbages.[1]   Ross[2] says the root tastes like horseradish, and the young leaves or hearts resemble in flavor coarse mustard and cress.   For 130 days his crews required no fresh vegetables but this.

Prinsepia utilis Royle.   *Rosaceae.*

Himalayan region.   In India, an oil is expressed from the seeds, which is used as food and for burning.[3]

Printzia aromatica Less.   *Compositae.*

South Africa.   Henfrey[4] says the leaves are used as a tea at the Cape of Good Hope.

Prionium palmita E. Mey.   *Juncaceae.*   PALMITE RUSH.

South Africa.   The plant grows in the beds of rivers and the heart is edible.[5]

Prioria copaifera Griseb.   *Leguminosae.*

Jamaica and Panama.   The enormous seeds have edible embryos.[6]   They are sold in Panama under the name *cativa.*

Pritchardia filifera Linden.   *Palmae.*

Southwestern North America.   This species is found in rocky canons near San Felipe, Cal., attaining a height of 50 feet.   The fruit is small, black and pulpy and is used as food by the Indians.[7]

Priva laevis Juss.   *Verbenaceae.*

Chile and the Argentine Republic.   The small tubers can be used for food.[8]

Prosopis algarobilla Griseb.   *Leguminosae.*

Argentine Republic.   The seeds are sweet and nutritious.[9]

P. dulcis Kunth.   ALGAROBA.   CASHAU.

Tropical America.   The legumes of this tree, gathered a little before they are ripe, are used in South America to fatten cattle.   Later, its seeds, ground to powder, constitute the principal food of many of the inhabitants of Brazil, who call it algaroba.[10]   To this species is referred the fruit mentioned by de la Vega[11] as called *paccay* by the

[1] McIntosh, C.   *Book Gard.* 2:90.   1855.

[2] Ross, J. C.   *Voy. Antarct. Reg.* 1:87.   1847.

[3] Brandis, D.   *Forest Fl.* 196.   1876.

[4] Henfrey, A.   *Bot.* 300.   1870.

[5] Smith, A.   *Treas. Bot.* 2:928.   1870.

[6] Baillon, H.   *Hist. Pls.* 2:161.   1872.

[7] Vasey   *U. S. D. A. Rpt.* 186.   1875.   (*P. filamentosa*)

[8] Mueller, F.   *Sel. Pls.* 382.   1891.

[9] Baillon, H.   *Hist. Pls.* 2:52.   1872.

[10] Waddell *Trans. Hort. Soc. Lond.* 179.   1851.

[11] DeVega *Roy. Comment.*   Hakl. Soc. Ed. 2:362.   1871.

Indians of Peru and *guava* by the Spaniards, of which he says: " It consists of a pod about a quarta long, more or less, and two fingers in width. On opening it one finds some white stuff exactly like cotton. It is so like, that Spaniards, who did not know the fruit, have been known to scold the Indians who gave it to them to eat, thinking they were offering cotton by way of joke. They are very sweet and after being exposed to the sun, will keep very long. Within the white pulp there is a black pip, like a bean, which is not good to eat." Don [1] says the pulp contained in the pods is very sweet and is eaten in Brazil. Pickering [2] says it is called *pacai* in Peru, and that its pods are sold in the markets of Lima.

P. juliflora DC. ALGAROBA. HONEY MESQUITE. MESQUITE. SCREW BEAN.

Tropical America. Cieza de Leon [3] says the pods of this algaroba are " somewhat long and narrow and not so thick as the pods of beans. In some parts they make bread of these algarobas." Markham [4] says the tree is called *guaranga*. Don [5] says the natives of the coast of Peru and Chile eat the pulp contained in the pods. The abundant fruit is eaten by the Indians and often by the whites.[6] E. L. Greene says the mesquite-meal, which the Indians and Mexicans manufacture by drying and grinding these pods and their contents, is perhaps the most nutritious breadstuff in use among any people. The pods, from seven to nine inches long, of a buff color, are chewed by both Indians and whites as they journey, as a preventive of thirst. The pods in their fresh state are prepared and eaten by the Indians and are among the luxuries of the Apaches, Pimas, Maricopas, Tumas and other tribes of New Mexico, Utah, Nevada and southern California. A gum exudes from the tree which closely resembles gum arabic.[7]

P. pubescens Benth. SCREW BEAN OR SCREW-POD MESQUITE. TORNILLA.

Texas, Mexico and California. The pods are pounded into meal and are used as food by the Indians.[8] Whipple [9] says it forms a favorite article of food with the Indians of the Gila and Colorado rivers. Greene [10] says it has the same nutritious properties as *P. juliflora*.

P. spicigera Linn.

Persia and East Indies. The mealy, sweetish substance which surrounds the seeds is an article of food in the Punjab, Gujarat and the Deccan. The pods are collected before they are quite ripe, and the mealy pulp is eaten raw, or boiled with vegetables, salt and butter.[11]

[1] Don, G. *Hist. Dichl. Pls.* 2:400. 1832.

[2] Pickering, C. *Chron. Hist. Pls.* 663. 1879.

[3] Markham, C. R. *Trav. Cieza de Leon.* 1532–50. Hakl. Soc. Ed. 235. 1864.

[4] Pickering, C. *Chron. Hist. Pls.* 668. 1879. (*P. horrida*)

[5] Don, G. *Hist. Dichl. Pls.* 2:400. 1832.

[6] Brewer and Watson *Bot. Cal.* 1:163. 1880.

[7] *U. S. D. A. Rpt.* 410. 1870.

[8] Brewer and Watson *Bot. Cal.* 1:163. 1880.

[9] Whipple *Pacific R. R. Rpt.* 3:115. 1856.

[10] Greene, E. L. *Amer. Nat.* 30. 1881.

[11] Brandis *Forest Fl.* 171. 1874.

Protea mellifera Thunb. *Proteaceae.* HONEY-FLOWER. SUGAR-BUSH.

South Africa. In the Cape Colony, a saccharine fluid is obtained from the flowers called bush-syrup.[1]

Prunus americana Marsh. *Rosaceae.* AMERICAN PLUM. AUGUST PLUM. GOOSE PLUM. HOG
PLUM. RED PLUM. SLOE. YELLOW PLUM.

Canada to the Gulf of Mexico. This plum is cultivated for its fruit and has a number of varieties. It was, says Pickering,[2] from early times planted by the New England Indians. During the ripening of the fruit, the western Indians live sumptuously and collect quantities for drying.

P. amygdalus Stokes. ALMOND.

North Africa and the Orient. The chief distinction between the almond and the peach lies in the fruit, which, in the almond, consists of little more than a stone covered with a thick, dry, wooly skin, while the peach has in addition a rich and luscious flesh. The almond has long been known to cultivation. Those with sweet and bitter kernels were known to the Hebrews[3] and were carried by the Phoenicians to the Hesperian peninsula. The almond was sacred to Cybele, in Greece, where even at that time there were ten kinds, with sweet and with bitter nuts. Phyllis hung herself on an almond tree and was transfigured into it. Cato[4] called it *nux Graica* and Pliny[5] mentions it. Charlemagne[6] caused *amandalarios* to be planted on his estate.

Unger[7] deems the tree indigenous to western Asia and north Africa. Pickering[8] ascribes its origin to the Tauro-Caspian countries and others to Barbary, Morocco, Persia and China. Brandis[9] says it is indigenous about Lebanon, Kurdistan and in Turkestan. At the present time, it is distributed over the whole of southern Europe, the Levant, Persia, Arabia, China, Java, Madeira, the Azores and the Canary Islands. As a garden plant, it has existed in England since 1548 certainly. In the United States, certain varieties are deemed hardy in the latitude of New York.

There are many varieties and as many as seven are described by Downing[10] as recommended for culture in America. The more common classification is into sweet and bitter almonds, but De Candolle establishes five groups: the bitter almond, the sweet almond, the sweet almond with a tender shell, the sweet almond with large fruit and the peach almond.

The kernels of the sweet variety are eaten as dessert and are largely used in confectionery and in cooking; those of the bitter almond are used in the preparation of noyau

---

[1] *Treas. Bot.* 2:930. 1870.

[2] Pickering, C. *Chron. Hist. Pls.* 805. 1879.

[3] De Candolle, A. *Orig. Cult. Pls.* 221. 1885.

[4] Flückiger and Hanbury *Pharm.* 244. 1879.

[5] Ibid.

[6] Ibid.

[7] Unger, F. *U. S. Pat. Off. Rpt.* 320. 1859. (*Amygdalus communis*)

[8] Pickering, C. *Chron. Hist. Pls.* 116. 1869. (*Amygdalus communis*)

[9] Brandis, D. *Forest Fl.* 190. 1874.

[10] Downing, A. J. *Fr. Fr. Trees Amer.* 231. 1857.

and for flavoring confectionery.   Both varieties yield by pressure an odorless, fixed oil which is of an innocent nature.   The bitter almond contains a crystalizable substance called amygdalin, which, by the action of the nitrogenous emulsion present, when in contact with water, is converted into a fragrant volatile oil, the essential oil of bitter almonds and prussic acid.   The sweet almond contains the emulsion but no amygdalin, hence is not harmful as food.   When a tree is raised frcm either variety both bitter and sweet almonds are frequently found borne by the same tree.[1]

P. armeniaca Linn.   APRICOT.

Caucasus.   The native country of the apricot is usually said to be Armenia, Arabia and the higher regions of central Asia.   Harlan[2] says the species grows spontaneously in the mountains about Kabul, bearing a yellow, acid and inferior fruit.   Erman[3] mentions it as wild in Siberia; Pallas[4] saw it in the Caucasus; Grossier[5] in the mountains to the west of Pekin, China; and Regnier[6] and Sickler[7] assign it to a parallel extending between the Niger and the Atlas.   Unger[8] says that Alexander the Great brought the apricot from Armenia to Greece and Epirus, from which countries it reached Italy.   It seems not to have been known to the Greeks in the time of Theophrastus but was the *mela armeniaca* of later authors, as Dioscorides.   The apricot was referred to under the name *Armeniaca* by Columella and Pliny.   It is said to have been brought to England from Italy in 1524,[9] but others give its date of introduction 1548.[10]   Disraeli[11] says, however, the elder Tradescant in 1620, entered himself on board of a privateer armed against Morocco solely with a view of finding an opportunity of stealing apricots into Britain and it appears that he succeeded.

In the United States, there is no mention of this fruit earlier than 1720, when they were said to be growing abundantly in Virginia.[12]   In 1835, there were 17 varieties in Britain.   Downing[13] names 26 in his edition of American Fruits of 1866 and the American Pomological Society 11 in 1879.   In Ladakh, according to Moorcroft,[14] 10 varieties are cultivated, all raised from seed but one, which is propagated by budding.   In Kabul, 5 sorts are grown, according to Harlan.[15]   The apricot is cultivated throughout the entire East even to Cashmere and northern India, in China and Japan, northern Africa and

---

[1] Loudon, J. C.   *Arb. Frut. Brit.* **2**:676.   1844.

[2] Harlan   *U. S. Pat. Off. Rpt.* 529.   1861.

[3] Pumpelly, R.   *Across Amer., Asia* 399.   1871.

[4] McIntosh, C.   *Book Gard.* **2**:517.   1855.

[5] Downing, A. J.   *Fr. Fr. Trees Amer.* 235.   1857.

[6] McIntosh, C.   *Book Gard.* **2**:517.   1855.

[7] Ibid.

[8] Unger, F.   *U. S. Pat. Off. Rpt.* 340.   1859.

[9] Thompson, R.   *Treas. Bot.* **2**:932.   1870.

[10] McIntosh, C.   *Book Gard.* **2**:517.   1855.

[11] Disraeli *Curios Lit.* **2**:329.   1858.

[12] *Hist. Mass. Hort. Soc.* 21.   1880.

[13] Downing, A. J.   *Fr. Fr. Trees Amer.* 235.   1857.

[14] Darwin, C.   *Ans. Pls. Domest.* **1**:366.   1893.

[15] Harlan   *U. S. Pat. Off. Rpt.* 529.   1861.

southern Europe. About Damascus, it is cultivated extensively and a marmalade is made from the fruit for sale. In the oases of Upper Egypt, the fruit of a variety called *musch-musch* is dried in large quantities for the purpose of commerce. The fruit in general is roundish, orange or brownish-orange, with a more or less deep orange-colored flesh; the kernel in some sorts is bitter, in others as sweet as a nut.[1] Erdman describes the " wild peach " of Nerchinsk, Siberia, as a true apricot, containing a very agreeable kernel in a fleshless envelope. Harlan[2] describes a variety of Kabul as so especially lucious as to require careful manipulation in gathering, so delicate that if one should fall to the ground, the shape would be destroyed.

P. aspera Thunb.

Japan. The blue drupe is eaten.[3]

P. avium Linn. BIRD CHERRY. GEAN. MAZZARD. SWEET CHERRY. WILD CHERRY.

Europe and the Caucasus. This is the species from which sweet cherries have sprung, The wild species is small and of little value for eating. The fruits are employed in Switzerland and Germany in the distillation of a spirit known as *kirschwasser*.[4] Of the cultivated fruits of this species, more than 75 varieties are described. The fruit is well esteemed, but Hasselquist[5] says the gum may also be eaten and that a hundred men during a siege were kept alive for two months on the gum of the cherry alone. Cherry stones were among the seeds mentioned in 1629 to be sent the Massachusetts Company;[6] they were also planted at Yonkers, N. Y., about 1650,[7] as well as in Rhode Island,[8] and, in 1669. Shrigley[9] says they were cultivated in Virginia and Maryland.

P. brigantiaca Vill. ALPINE PLUM. BRIANCON PLUM. MARMOTTES. OIL PLANT.

Gallia. The fruit is borne in clusters, is round, yellow and plum-like but is scarcely eatable. In France and Piedmont, the kernels are used to procure the *huille des marmottes*, an oil considered superior to olive oil.[10]

P. buergeriana Miq.

A large tree of Japan. The fruit is small and inferior but is sometimes gathered and pickled in salt, when it is eaten as a condiment or appetizer.[11]

P. capollin Zucc.

Mexico. The cherries are of a pleasant taste.[12]

---

[1] Thompson, R. *Treas. Bot.* 2:932. 1870.

[2] Harlan *U. S. Pat. Off. Rpt.* 529. 1861.

[3] Don, G. *Hist. Dichl. Pls.* 2:513. 1832. (*Cerasus aspera*)

[4] Thompson, R. *Treas. Bot.* 1:251. 1870. (*Cerasus avium*)

[5] Johnson, C. P. *Useful Pls. Gt. Brit.* 87. 1862.

[6] *Mass. Records* 1:24.

[7] *U. S. Pat. Off. Rpt.* 293. 1853.

[8] Ibid.

[9] Shrigley *True Rel. Va., Md.* 5. 1669. Force Coll. Tracts **3**: 1844.

[10] Downing, A. J. *Fr. Fr. Trees Amer.* 242. 1857.

[11] Georgeson *Amer. Gard.* 12:78. 1891.

[12] Unger, F. *U. S. Pat. Off. Rpt.* 351. 1859. (*Cerasus capollin*)

P. cerasifera Ehrh. CHERRY PLUM.

Turkey and nearby countries. The fruit is round, about an inch in diameter, of a lively red, with little bloom. The flesh is greenish, melting, soft, very juicy, with a pleasant, lively subacid flavor.[1]

P. cerasus Linn. CHERRY. PIE CHERRY. SOUR CHERRY.

Europe and Orient. More than 50 varieties of this cherry are under cultivation. About Lake Como, Italy, a variety grows abundantly which is a sort of Morello.[2] In Asia Minor, Walsh[3] describes two delicious varieties as growing wild and cultivated in gardens. This cherry is mentioned by Theophrastus,[4] about 300 B. C., and Pliny[5] states that it was brought to Italy by Lucullus after his victory over Mithridates, and he also states that, in less than 120 years after, other lands had cherries even as far as Britain beyond the ocean. Disraeli[6] remarks that " to our shame it must be told that these cherries from the King of Pontus' city of Cerasuntis are not the cherries we are now eating; for the whole race of cherry-trees was lost in the Saxon period and was only restored by the gardener of Henry VIII who brought them from Flanders." Loudon[7] says the Romans had 8 kinds and, in England in 1640, there were 24 sorts. The Red Kentish, referred to this class, was the cherry grown by the Massachusetts colonists.

P. chamaecerasus Jacq.

Southern Europe and northern Asia. This cherry is mentioned by Pliny[8] as growing in Macedonia and the fruit is said to be dried and to yield profit to the farm. According to Jacquin,[9] this cherry grows on the Austrian Alps; according to Persoon,[10] it is cultivated.

P. chicasa Michx. CHICKASAW PLUM. INDIAN CHERRY. MOUNTAIN CHERRY.

Southeastern United States. This plum was seen by De Soto's[11] expedition at or near New Madrid, where it furnished the natives with food. The tree usually grows from 12 to 20 feet high but Marcy,[12] on the Red River of the South, found it forming small bushes from two to six feet high and bearing very large and sweet fruit varying in color from a light pink to a deep crimson. The fruit varies much and several varieties are in cultivation.

P. cocomilia Tenore. COCOMILLA PLUM.

Italy. The fruit is yellow, bitter or sour.[13]

---

[1] Downing, A. J. *Fr. Fr. Trees Amer.* 375. 1857.

[2] Thompson, R. *Treas. Bot.* 1:252. 1870. (*Cerasus*)

[3] Walsh, R. *Trans. Hort. Soc. Lond.* 6:43. 1826.

[4] Theophrastus *Hist. Pl.* 3, 13.

[5] Thompson, R. *Treas. Bot.* 1:252. 1870. (*Cerasus*)

[6] Disraeli *Curios Lit.* 2:330. 1858.

[7] Loudon, J. C. *Hort.* 553. 1860.

[8] Pickering, C. *Chron. Hist. Pls.* 398. 1879. (*Cerasus chamaecerasus*)

[9] Ibid.

[10] Ibid.

[11] Bancroft, G. *Hist. U. S.* 1:53. 1839.

[12] Marcy, R. B. *Explor. Red River* 20. 1854.

[13] Don, G. *Hist. Dichl. Pls.* 2:498. 1832.

P. dasycarpa Ehrh. BLACK APRICOT.

Orient. This apricot with dark purple, velvety fruit is cultivated in Kashmir, Afghanistan, Baluchistan and in Europe.[1]

P. divaricata Ledeb.

Turkestan. The fruits are red, yellow and black and of the size, form and taste of the Mirabelle plum. According to Capus, the natives collect and dry the fruit but do not cultivate the tree.[2]

P. domestica Linn. EUROPEAN PLUM. PLUM.

Europe and the Caucasus. The common plum came originally, says Unger,[3] from the Caucasus and is cultivated extensively in Syria, where it has passed into numerous varieties. It is now naturalized in Greece and in other regions of temperate Europe. Cultivated varieties, according to Pliny, were brought from Syria into Greece and thence into Italy. Faulken [4] says the plum was introduced from Asia into Europe during the crusades. Gough [5] says the Perdrigon plum was brought into England in the time of Henry VII. Plum stones were among the seeds mentioned in the Memorandum of Mar. 16, 1629, to be sent to the Massachusetts Company. The fruit of the plum ranges through many colors, from black to white, and is covered with a rich, glaucous bloom About 150 varieties appear in the catalogs of American nurserymen.[6] The plum is not only delicious eating, in its best varieties, but the fruit of some is largely used for prunes, and, in Hungary, an excellent brandy is distilled from the fermented juice of the fruit.

P. emarginata Walp. OREGON CHERRY.

Western North America. The fruit is eaten by the Indians.[7]

P. fasciculata A. Gray. WILD ALMOND. WILD PEACH.

Western North America. Although this fruit is almost devoid of the delicious interior of the cultivated peach, yet it has exactly the appearance and Gray says is its nearest North American relative.

P. gracilis Engelm. & Gray. PRAIRIE CHERRY.

Texas and Indian Territory. This species is cultivated by the pioneers.

P. ilicifolia Walp. EVERGREEN CHERRY. ISLAY. MOUNTAIN HOLLY. WILD CHERRY.

An evergreen of southern California. The fruit of this Prunus is yellowish-pink when ripe, with a pulpy external portion scarcely exceeding a line in thickness. Though the fruit has a pleasant taste, Parry says it would scarcely be considered worth eating in a country which was less destitute of wild fruits.

---

[1] Brandis, D. *Forest Fl.* 192. 1874.

[2] *Gard. Chron.* 22:377. 1884.

[3] Unger *U. S. Pat. Off. Rpt.* 340. 1859.

[4] *U. S. Pat. Off. Rpt.* 287. 1853.

[5] Ibid.

[6] Wood, A. *Class Book Bot.* 328. 1864.

[7] Brown, R. *Bot. Soc. Edinb.* 9:383. 1868.

P. incisa Thunb.

Japan. The fruits are eaten.[1]

P. insititia Linn. BULLACE. DAMSON.

Europe, Asia Minor and Himalayas. This plum is found wild in the Caucasus and throughout Europe. The fruit is globular, black or white, of an acid taste but not unpleasant, especially when mellowed by frost; it makes a good conserve.[2] A variety with yellow fruit is sold in the London markets under the name of the White Damson, according to Thompson.[3] From this species has come the cultivated damson plums. The damson plum, says Targioni-Tozzetti,[4] was introduced from the East since the day of Cato, who was born 232 B. C. The damson plum was brought into Europe, according to Michaud,[5] by the Duke of Anjou, in the fifth crusade, 1198–1204, from a visit to Jerusalem.

P. japonica Thunb. JAPANESE PLUM.

Japan and China. This plum is much grown in Japan for ornament and for fruit. The plum has a sweet and agreeable flavor.[6]

P. jenkinsii Hook. f.

Assam. This Prunus thrives and bears fruit at Gowhatty, India. The fruit is only eatable in tarts or preserved in brandy.[7]

P. laurocerasus Linn. *Rosaceae.* CHERRY LAUREL.

Orient. The cherry laurel is mentioned by Gerarde in 1597 as a choice garden shrub in England. The water distilled from the leaves has been used extensively for flavoring puddings and creams.[8] Sweetmeats and custards flavored with leaves of this plant have occasionally proved fatal on account of the prussic acid, yet they seem to be sometimes used.[9]

P. maritima Wangenh. BEACH PLUM.

Eastern North America. The beach plum forms a low bush or small tree on the seacoast extending from Maine to the Gulf;[10] it seldom ripens its fruit in the interior.[11] This is probably one of the plums mentioned by Edward Winslow,[12] 1621, and by Rev. Francis Higginson,[13] 1629. The fruit is from a half-inch to an inch in diameter, varies from crimson to purple and is agreeable to eat. It is preserved in considerable quantities in

---

[1] *Gard. Chron.* **25**:458. 1886. New series.

[2] Don, G. *Hist. Dichl. Pls.* **2**:498. 1832.

[3] Thompson, R. *Treas. Bot.* **2**:931. 1870.

[4] Targioni-Tozzetti *Journ. Hort. Soc. Lond.* **9**:162. 1855.

[5] Michaud *Hist. Crusades* **3**:329. 1853.

[6] Georgeson *Amer. Gard.* **12**:76. 1891.

[7] Firminger, T. A. C. *Gard. Ind.* 244. 1874. (*Cerasus jenkinsii*)

[8] Flückiger and Hanbury *Pharm.* 254. 1879.

[9] Masters, M. T. *Treas. Bot.* **1**:251. 1870. (*Cerasus laurocerasus*)

[10] Burbidge, F. W. *Cult. Pls.* 477. 1877.

[11] Downing, A. J. *Fr. Fr. Trees Amer.* 350. 1857.

[12] Young, A. *Chron. Pilgr.* 234. 1841.

[13] Higginson, Rev. Francis *New Eng. Plant.* Mass. Hist. Soc. Coll. 1st Ser. **1**:118. 1792.

Massachusetts.[1]   Downing[2] says the plum is red or purple, covered with a bloom, pleasant but somewhat astringent.

P. mume Sieb. & Zucc.   JAPANESE APRICOT.

Japan.   The fruit is hard and sour and as a rule is eaten salted or dried.   It is also made into vinegar.   This species is cultivated chiefly on account of its blossoms.[3]   In China, the blossoms are used for scenting tea.[4]

P. padus Linn.   BIRD CHERRY.   HAGBERRY.

Europe and northern Asia.   The fruit is sour, with a slight mawkish, astringent flavor but is much eaten by the Hill People of India.   In Sweden and Lapland and some parts of Russia, the bruised fruit is fermented and a spirit is distilled from it.[5]   Lightfoot[6] says the black fruit, of the size of grapes, of a nauseous taste, is eaten in Sweden and Kamchatka and is used in brandy in Scotland.   The hagberry of Scotland is said by Macgillivray[7] to be small, round, black, harsh and nauseous.   De Candolle[8] says a variety occurs with yellow fruit.

P. paniculata Thunb.

Japan.   This is the *Yung-fo* of China but cultivated there only for ornament at Canton, where it rarely fruits.   This species was introduced into England in 1819.   The cherries are said by Knight[9] to be middle-sized, reddish-amber in color, very sweet, juicy and excellent.   Smith[10] says, in China, its fruit is preserved as a sweetmeat with honey.

P. pennsylvanica Linn. f.   BIRD CHERRY.   PIN CHERRY.   WILD RED CHERRY.

Eastern North America.   Vasey[11] says the fruit is sour and unpleasant; Pursh,[12] that it is agreeable to eat; Wood,[13] that it is red and acid.

P. persica Stokes.   PEACH.

Orient.   The peach was known to Theophrastus,[14] 322 B. C., who speaks of it as a fruit of Persia, but Xenophon,[15] 401 B. C., makes no mention of the peach.   The Hebrew books are also without mention and there seems to be no Sanscrit name.[16]   The peach

---

[1] Emerson, G. B.   *Trees, Shrubs Mass.* 2:511.   1875.
[2] Downing, A. J.   *Fr. Fr. Trees Amer.* 350.   1857.
[3] Rein *Indust. Jap.* 86.   1889.
[4] Rein *Indust. Jap.* 123.   1889.
[5] Brandis, D.   *Forest Fl.* 194.   1874.
[6] Lightfoot, J.   *Fl. Scot.* 1:254.   1789.
[7] Macgillivray, W.   *Journ. Agr.* 2:506.   1831.
[8] De Candolle, A.   *Geog. Bot.* 2:1083.   1855.   (*Cerasus padus*)
[9] Knight, T. A.   *Phys. Hort. Papers* 295.   1841.
[10] Smith, F. P.   *Contrib. Mat. Med. China* 58.   1871.
[11] Vassey   *U. S. D. A. Rpt.* 161.   1875.
[12] Pursh, F.   *Fl. Amer. Septent.* 1:331.   1814.
[13] Wood, A.   *Class Book Bot.* 327.   1864.
[14] De Candolle, A.   *Geog. Bot.* 2:883.   1855.   (*Amygdalus persica*)
[15] Ibid.
[16] Ibid.

seems to have reached Europe at about the commencement of the Christian era. Dioscorides,[1] who flourished about 60 A. D., speaks of the peach, and Pliny,[2] A. D. 79, expressly states that it was imported by the Romans from Persia not long before. He also adds that this tree was brought from Egypt to the Isle of Rhodes, where it could never be made to produce fruit, and thence to Italy. He says it was not then a common fruit in Greece.[3] At this time, from two to five varieties alone were known and the nectarine was unknown.[4,5] No mention is made of the peach by Cato,[6] 201 B. C., and Columella,[7] 42 A. D., speaks of it as being cultivated in France. In China, De Candolle[8] says its culture dates to a remote antiquity and the Chinese have a multitude of superstitious ideas and legends about the properties of the different varieties, whose number is very large. He also says the peach is mentioned in the books of Confucius, fifth century before Christ, and it is represented in sculpture and on porcelain. Brandis[9] says the cultivation of the peach in China has been traced back to the tenth century, B. C.

The peach is raised with such facility from the stone that its diffusion along routes of communication must necessarily have been very rapid. If its origin is to be ascribed to China, the stones may have been carried with the caravans into Kashmir or Bokhara and Persia between the time of the Sanscrit emigration and the intercourse of the Persians with the Greeks. It is quite possible that the long delay in its diffusion was caused by the inferior quality of the peach in its first deviation over that which it possesses at present. The peach was introduced from China into Cochin China and Japan.[10] McIntosh[11] says it reached England about the middle of the sixteenth century, probably from France. Peach stones were among the seeds ordered by the Governor and Company for the Massachusetts Bay Colony in New England in 1629.[12] About 1683, Stacy,[13] writing from New Jersey, said " we have peaches by cart loads." *A Description of New Albion*,[14] 1648, records, " Peaches better than apricocks by some doe feed Hogs, one man hath ten thousand trees." Hilton[15] says of Florida, 1664, " The country abounds with Grapes, large Figs, and Peaches." William Penn,[16] in a letter dated Aug. 16, 1683, says of Philadelphia, " There are also very good peaches, and in great quantities; not an Indian plantation

[1] De Candolle, A. *Geog. Bot.* 2:881. 1855.

[2] *U. S. Pat. Off. Rpt.* 283. 1853.

[3] Ibid.

[4] Targioni-Tozzetti *Journ. Hort. Soc. Lond.* 9:167. 1855.

[5] De Candolle, A. *Geog. Bot.* 2:885. 1855. (*Amygdalus persica*)

[6] *U. S. Pat. Off. Rpt.* 283. 1853.

[7] Ibid.

[8] De Candolle, A. *Geog. Bot.* 2:883. 1855. (*Amygdalus persica*)

[9] Brandis, D. *Forest Fl.* 191. 1874.

[10] De Candolle, A. *Geog. Bot.* 2:883. 1855. (*Amygdalus persica*)

[11] McIntosh, C. *Book Gard.* 2:485. 1855. (*Amygdalus persica*)

[12] *U. S. Pat. Off. Rpt.* 284. 1853.

[13] Watson *Annals Phil.* 18. 1856.

[14] *Desc. New Albion* 31. 1648. Force Coll. Tracts 2: No. 7. 1838.

[15] Hilton *Rel. Disc. Fla.* 8. 1664. Force Coll. Tracts 4: No. 2. 1846.

[16] Watson *Annals Phil.* 63. 1856.

without them . . . not inferior to any peach you have in England, except the Newington." Beverly [1] mentions the peach as growing abundantly in Virginia in 1720. Colden [2] mentions the peach trees killed by frost in New York in 1737. At Easton, Maryland,[3] Peach Blossom Plantation was established about 1735.

So abundantly distributed had peaches become in the middle of the eighteenth century, that Bartram [4] looked upon them as an original American fruit and as growing wild in the greater par of America. Du Pratz,[5] 1758, says: " The natives had doubtless got the peach trees and fig trees from the English colony of Carolina, before the French established themselves in Louisiana. The peaches are of the kind we call Alberges, are of the size of the fist, adhere to the stone and are very juicy." In 1799, the peach trees of the Mogui Indians of New Mexico and Sonora yielded abundantly.[6] In 1649, Norwood,[7] in his *Voyage to Virginia*, found peach trees in fruit at Fayal. The peach is also abundantly distributed in South America. Darwin [8] writes that the islands near the mouth of the Parana are thickly clothed with peach and orange trees, springing from seeds carried there by the waters of the river.

The nectarine is a peach having a smooth skin. Darwin [9] gives a number of instances where peach trees have produced nectarines and even nectarines and peaches on the same tree. A still more curious case is also given where a nectarine tree produced a fruit half peach, half nectarine and subsequently perfect peaches. Nectarines usually reproduce themselves from seed and always possess their own peculiar flavor and are smooth and small. The varieties run in parallel lines with the peach. The nectarine was unknown at the commencement of the Christian era.[10] The first mention is by Cieza de Leon, who, in 1532–50, described the Caymito of Peru as " large as a nectarine." The nectarine is now found in gardens in Europe and America in numerous varieties. It is mentioned by Beverley [11] as growing abundantly in Virginia in 1720. Downing [12] describes 19 varieties and mentions others. According to Brandis, the nectarine is found in gardens in northern India, where it is called *shuftaloo* and *moondla aroo*, smooth peach, probably introduced from Kabul.

P. prostrata Labill.

Mediterranean regions and the Orient. The fruit is eaten.[13]

---

[1] *U. S. Fat. Off. Rpt.* 284. 1853.

[2] Ibid.

[3] Ibid.

[4] Kalm, P. *Trav. No. Amer.* 1:99. 1772.

[5] Du Pratz *Hist. La.* 1758, from *Agr. Mo.* 361. 1867.

[6] *Pacific R. R. Rpt.* 3:122. 1856.

[7] Norwood *Voy. Va.* 5. Force Coll. Tracts 3: 1844.

[8] Darwin, C. *Voy. H. M. S. Beagle* 120. 1884.

[9] Darwin, C. *Ans. Pls. Dom.* 1:360. 1893.

[10] Darwin, C. *Ans. Pls. Dom.* 1:363. 1893.

[11] Beverley *U. S. Pat. Off. Rpt.* 284. 1853.

[12] Downing, A. J. *Fr. Fr. Trees Amer.* 645. 1857.

[13] Brandis, D. *Forest Fl.* 194. 1874.

P. puddum Roxb.

Himalayan region. The fruit is acid and astringent, not much eaten or valued.[1] Royle[2] says it is not edible but is employed for making a well-flavored cherry brandy.

P. pumila Linn. DWARF CHERRY. SAND CHERRY.

Northern United States. The fruit is small, dark red and eatable. In the Indian Territory, every Indian goes to the plum ground in the season to collect the fruit, which is dried and preserved. From Lake Superior to Elk River on the 57th parallel, Richardson[3] found what he took to be this species with very sweet fruit.

P. rivularis Scheele. CREEK PLUM.

Texas. This is a small shrub, not uncommon on the Colorado and its tributaries, bearing excellent, red plums in August and September.[4]

P. serotina Ehrh. RUM CHERRY. WILD BLACK CHERRY.

North America. In Mexico, this cherry is called *capuli*. Burbridge[5] says the succulent fruit resembles apricots and is sold in Mexican markets under the name of *capulinos*.

P. sibirica Linn.

Siberia. The fruit is small, sour or acid, and contains a bitter kernel.[6]

P. simonii Carr. APRICOT PLUM. SIMON PLUM.

China. This plum was introduced into America from France. The fruit, though large, handsome and of firm flesh, has little merit.[7]

P. sphaerocarpa Sw.

Tropical America. From the seeds, cherry, plum and damson wine is flavored.[8]

P. spinosa Linn. BLACKTHORN. SLOE.

Europe, north Africa, the Orient and now naturalized in the United States. The fruit is like a small plum, nearly glabrous, black, covered with a bluish bloom and has a very austere taste. The fruit is eaten in some districts of northern Europe and with sugar makes a very good conserve. The leaves are used to adulterate tea.[9] The juice of the ripe fruit is said to enter largely into the manufacture of the cheaper kinds of port wine. In France, the unripe fruit is pickled, as a substitute for olives, and, in Germany and Russia, the fruit is crushed, fermented with water and a spirit is distilled from it.[10]

---

[1] Brandis, D. *Forest Fl.* 194. 1874.

[2] Royle, J. F. *Illustr. Bot. Himal.* 1:205. 1839.

[3] Richardson, J. *Arctic Explor.* 2:288. 1851. (*P. americana*)

[4] Havard, V. *Proc. U. S. Nat. Mus.* 512. 1885.

[5] Burbidge, F. W. *Cult. Pls.* 478. 1877. (*P. salicifolius*)

[6] Don, G. *Hist. Dichl. Pls.* 2:498. 1832. (*Armeniaca sibirica*)

[7] Bailey, L. H. *Cornell Bul.* 51:57. 1893.

[8] Baillon, H. *Hist. Pls.* 1:441. 1871.

[9] Johnson, C. P. *Useful Pls. Gt. Brit.* 85. 1862.

[10] Loudon, J. C. *Arb. Frut. Brit.* 2:686. 1844.

P. subcordata Benth. PACIFIC PLUM.

California. The fruit is large, pleasantly acid and excellent;[1] it is gathered in considerable quantities by both Indians and Whites.[2]

P. tomentosa Thunb.

East Asia. This species is a bush or very small tree. The fruit ripens early in the summer, is of cherry size and of good quality. The unripe fruit is also pickled or boiled in honey and is served as a delicacy.[3]

P. triflora Roxb. JAPANESE PLUM. TRIFLORA PLUM.

Burma, China and Japan. This plant is now common in the gardens of India.[4] It is cultivated in China, Japan and now in Europe and America.

P. umbellata Ell. SLOE OF THE SOUTH.

A small tree from Georgia to Florida. The fruit is pleasantly acid and is employed in preserves.[5]

P. ursina Kotschy. BEAR PLUM.

Syria. This plum bears sweet, pleasant fruit, the size of a damson and serves as food.[6]

P. virginiana Linn. CHOKE CHERRY.

A tall shrub of North America, seldom a tree, the fruit of which is very austere and astringent until perfectly ripe.[7] The fruit differs much on different plants, being sometimes very austere, sometimes very juicy and pleasant with little astringency. Wood,[8] in his *New England's Prospects*, mentions choke cherries and says they are very austere and as yet " as wilde as the Indians." Tytler [9] says the fruit is not very edible but forms a desirable addition to pemmican when dried and bruised. The fruit is now much used by the Indians of the West, and the bark is made into a tea and drunk by some of them. The purplish-black or red fruit is sweet and edible but is somewhat astringent.[10]

Psammisia bicolor Klotzsch. *Vacciniaceae.*

Of the cold zone of the Peruvian Andes. A high, evergreen bush with red berries of the size of a hazelnut.[11]

Pseudospondias microcarpa Engl. *Anacardiaceae.*

Guinea. The small, black fruit is edible.[12]

---

[1] Newberry *Pacific R. R. Rpt.* **6**:73. 1857.

[2] Brewer and Watson *Bot. Cal.* **1**:167. 1880.

[3] Georgeson *Amer. Gard.* **12**:75. 1891.

[4] Royle, J. F. *Illustr. Bot. Himal.* **1**:205. 1839.

[5] Elliott, S. *Bot. So. Car., Ga.* **1**:542. 1821.

[6] Unger, F. *U. S. Pat. Off. Rpt.* 340. 1859.

[7] Gray, A. *Man. Bot.* 149. 1868.

[8] Wood, W. *New Eng. Prosp.* 16. 1865.

[9] Tytler *Prog. Disc. No. Coast Amer.* 311. 1833.

[10] Brewer and Watson *Bot. Cal.* **1**:167. 1880. (*P. demissa*)

[11] Mueller, F. *Sel. Pls.* 498. 1891. (*Vaccinium bicolor*)

[12] Don, G. *Hist. Dichl. Pls.* **2**:79. 1832. (*Spondias zanzee*)

Psidium acutangulum DC. *Myrtaceae.*

A tree of the higher regions on the Amazon River. Its fruit is pale yellow and of apple size.[1]

P. araca Raddi. GUAVA.

West Indies and Guiana to Peru and southern Brazil. The greenish-yellow fruit is of excellent taste.[2] The berry is the size of a nutmeg.[3]

P. arboreum Vell. GUAVA.

Brazil. This guava measures about an inch and is of excellent flavor.[4]

P. cattleianum Sabine PURPLE GUAVA.

Probably a native of Brazil, though originally brought to Europe from China.[5] The fruits are large, spherical, of a fine, deep claret color, with a soft, fleshy pulp, purplish-red next the skin but white at the center and of a very agreeable, acid-sweet flavor.[6]

P. chrysophyllum F. Muell.

South Brazil. The fruit is generally not larger than a cherry.[7]

P. cinereum Mart.

Brazil. The fruit is edible.[8]

P. cuneatum Cambess.

Brazil. The fruit is greenish and of the size of a Mirabelle plum.[9]

P. grandifolium Mart.

Brazil. The fruit is the size of a walnut.[10]

P. guajava Linn. APPLE GUAVA. YELLOW GUAVA.

Tropical America. There are two varieties which are by some classed as species: *P. pomiferum* Linn., the apple-shaped, and *P. pyriforme* Griseb. or *pyriferum* Linn., the pear-shaped. This species is very largely cultivated in the vicinity of Campos, Brazil. The fruit is made into a sweetmeat and is exported in great quantities.[11] In the Quito region, says Herrera,[12] there are *guayabos* that produce fruit like apples, with many kernels, some white and some red, well tasted and wholesome. The fruit is globular, varying from the size of a plum to that of an apple and resembles an orange. The taste is rather bitter but the fruit makes an excellent preserve. The cultivation of the guava has been carried on from time immemorial, as is shown by the fruit frequently being seedless. The guava

[1] Mueller, F. *Sel. Pls.* 188. 1876. (*P. acidum*)

[2] Mueller, F. *Sel. Pls.* 391. 1891.

[3] Don, G. *Hist. Dichl. Pls.* 2:831. 1832. (*P. guineense*)

[4] Mueller, F. *Sel. Pls.* 391. 1891.

[5] Smith, A. *Treas. Bot.* 2:934. 1870.

[6] Don, G. *Hist. Dichl. Pls.* 2:832. 1891.

[7] Mueller, F. *Sel. Pls.* 391. 1891.

[8] Mueller, F. *Sel. Pls.* 392. 1891.

[9] Ibid.

[10] Don, G. *Hist. Dichl. Pls.* 2:831. 1832.

[11] Hartt *Geog. Braz.* 47. 1870.

[12] Herrera *Hist. Amer.* Stevens Trans. 5:61. 1740.

reached the East Indies through the agency of the Portuguese and Spaniards. It has but recently reached China and the Philippines, the west coast of Africa and the Island of Mauritius. Voight [1] says, in India, its fruit is of a delicious flavor. Firminger [2] states that those he has gathered have been nothing better than a hard, uneatable berry. The guava is cultivated in the West Indies, in Florida and elsewhere, and the fruits are occasionally seedless. The fruit is smooth, crowned with the calyx, not unlike in shape and size to a pomegranate, having an agreeable smell and turning yellow when ripe. The rind is about an eighth of an inch in thickness, brittle and fleshy and contains a firm pulp of white, red or yellow color in the different varieties and is of an agreeable taste. It is full of bony seeds. [3] The fruit is esteemed raw and also in preserves.

P. incanescens Mart.

Brazil. The berry is edible. [4]

P. indicum Raddi.

Brazil. The species is cultivated for its fruit. [5]

P. montanum Sw. SPICE GUAVA.

A large tree of West Indies. The fruit is eatable, green in color and soft when ripe. It has a very pleasing smell, like that of strawberries, which the pulp also resembles in taste, leaving its rich flavor on the palate for some time after eating. This fruit makes excellent marmalade. [6] The fruit is edible. [7]

P. pigmeum Arruda.

A shrub of Brazil. The fruit is about the size of a gooseberry and is greatly sought after on account of its delicious flavor which resembles that of the strawberry. It is the *marangaba* of the Brazilians. [8]

P. polycarpon Lamb.

Tropical America. The berries are yellow, the size of a cherry and of exquisite taste. [9] The fruit is yellow inside, the size of a plum and of a delicate taste. [10]

P. rufum Mart.

Brazil. The plant produces a palatable fruit. [11]

Psophocarpus tetragonolobus DC. *Leguminosae.* GOA BEAN.

This plant is grown in India for the sake of its edible seeds and also for use as a string bean. The pod is six to eight inches long, half an inch wide, with a leafy kind of

[1] Firminger, T. A. C. *Gard. Ind.* 263. 1874. (*P. pumilum*)

[2] Ibid.

[3] Lunan, J. *Hort. Jam.* 1:350. 1814.

[4] Mueller, F. *Sel. Pls.* 392. 1891.

[5] Don, G. *Hist. Dichl. Pls.* 2:833. 1832.

[6] Lunan, J. *Hort. Jam.* 1:351. 1814.

[7] Mueller, F. *Sel. Pls.* 188. 1876. (*P. cordatum*)

[8] Gardner, G. *Trav. Braz.* 146. 1846.

[9] Mueller, F. *Sel. Pls.* 393. 1891.

[10] Don, G. *Hist. Dichl. Pls.* 2:831. 1832.

[11] Mueller, F. *Sel. Pls.* 393. 1891.

fringe running along the length of its four corners. The pod is cooked whole and, says Firminger,[1] is a vegetable of little value. Wight[2] calls it a passable vegetable. In the Mauritius, the plant is called *pois carrés* and is cultivated for the seeds.[3] In Burma and the Philippines, the pods are eaten. Pickering[4] says it is a native of equatorial Africa and says " the kidney beans of the finest quality," observed by Cada Mosto[5] in Senegal in 1455, belong here.

Psoralea californica S. Wats. *Leguminosae.*

California. The tuberous roots are eaten by the Piutes.[6]

P. canescens Michx.

Southern states of North America. This plant has esculent roots.[7]

P. castorea S. Wats.

Colorado to California. The roots afford food to the Piute Indians.[8]

P. esculenta Pursh. BREAD ROOT. INDIAN TURNIP. POMME BLANCHE. PRAIRIE POTATO.

Upper Missouri and Rocky Mountain region.[9] This root is a special luxury to the Indians of Kansas and Nebraska, and the Sioux use it very extensively.[10] It is eaten roasted while fresh or carefully dried and stored for winter use.[11] The stringy, dry and tough roots are eaten by the Cree Indians of the northwest, either raw or roasted.[12]

P. glandulosa Linn. JESUIT TEA.

Chile. The roots are dried and smoked. The plant has been introduced into the Mauritius[13] where the leaves are used as a tea substitute. In Chile, it is called *culen.*[14]

P. hypogaea Nutt.

North America. The tubers are edible.[15]

P. subacaulis Torr. & Gray.

Tennessee. The plant has edible roots.[16]

---

[1] Firminger, T. A. C. *Gard. Ind.* 150. 1874.

[2] Wight, R. *Illustr. Ind. Bot.* 1:192. 1840.

[3] Pickering, C. *Chron. Hist. Pls.* 823. 1879.

[4] Ibid.

[5] Ibid.

[6] Havard, V. *Torr. Bot. Club Bul.* 22:108. 1895.

[7] Ibid.

[8] Ibid.

[9] Smith, A. *Treas. Bot.* 2:935. 1870.

[10] Fremont *Explor. Exped.* 107. 1845.

[11] Pursh, F. *Fl. Amer. Septent.* 2:475. 1814.

[12] Hooker, W. J. *Fl. Bor. Amer.* 1:137. 1840. (*P. brachiata*)

[13] Smith, A. *Treas. Bot.* 2:935. 1870.

[14] *Gard. Chron.* 242. Aug. 19, 1882. New series.

[15] Havard, V. *Torr. Bot. Club Bul.* 22:108. 1895.

[16] Ibid.

Ptelea trifoliata Linn. *Rutaceae.* HOP TREE. SHRUBBY TREFOIL.

Eastern United States. The fruit, a winged seed, is bitter and has been used as a substitute for hops.[1]

Pteris aquilina Linn. *Polypodiaceae.* BRACKEN. BRAKE.

Northern regions. The rhizomes, says Lindley, have been used as a substitute for hops and furnish a wretched bread. Pickering[2] says it is enumerated by Epicharnus as edible. Lightfoot says the people of Normandy have sometimes been compelled to subsist on bread made of brake roots. In 1683, says Lacombe, such was the destitution in some districts of France that the Abbé Grandel writes " some of the inhabitants are living upon bread made of ferns;" and in 1745 the Duke of Orleans, giving Louis XV a piece of bread made of fern, said, " Sire, this is what your subjects live upon." In Siberia, says Johnson,[3] the rhizomes are employed with about two-thirds their weight of malt for brewing a kind of beer. The brake is enumerated by Thunberg among the edible plants of Japan, and Bohmer says the young shoots are much prized by the Japanese. The fronds are gathered when still undeveloped and used in soups. The roots serve the inhabitants of Palma and Gomera for food, as Humboldt states; they grind them to powder, mix with barley meal and this composition, when boiled, is called *gofio*. In 1405, Betançon found the people of the Canaries in Ferro living on fern roots, " as for grain they had none; their bread was made of fern roots;" it was the only edible root of Palma when Europeans first visited the island. Professor Brewer says that the young, tender shoots are boiled by the California miners and eaten like asparagus, being found mucilaginous and palatable. The fronds of the brake are used as a potherb in New England. Everywhere in Vancouver Island and the neighboring country, says R. Brown, the Indians gather the roots and boil and eat them as food and they look upon them as a great luxury.

P. esculenta. TARA FERN.

The root is universally eaten by the Maoris of New Zealand. To these roots, the natives of New South Wales have resource whenever their sweet potatoes or maize crops fail. In the *Voyage of the Novara*, these roots are said to have formed the chief subsistence of the Maoris before the introduction of the potato and to have been called *raoras*.

Pterocarya caucasica C. A. Mey. *Juglandeae.*

Orient. The plant produces an edible nut.[4]

Pueraria thunbergiana Benth. *Leguminosae.*

China and Japan. The roots are fleshy and yield a starch of excellent quality. The wild plants are dug for their roots.[5] The roots contain starch, while the leaves and shoots are used as food.[6]

---

[1] Gray. A. *Man. Bot.* 110. 1868.

[2] Pickering, C. *Chron. Hist. Pls.* 97. 1879.

[3] Johnson, C. P. *Useful Pls. Gt. Brit.* 294. 1862.

[4] Unger, F. *U. S. Pat. Off. Rpt.* 321. 1859.

[5] Georgeson *Amer. Gard.* 13:387. 1892.

[6] *Science* 498. 1884.

P. tuberosa DC.

Tropical India and Burma. Brandis [1] says the large, tuberous roots are eaten.

Pulicaria odora Reichb. *Compositae.*

South Europe. In Yemen, this species is cultivated for its pleasant odor and edible leaves.[2]

Pulmonaria officinalis Linn. *Boragineae.* JERUSALEM COWSLIP. LUNGWORT.

Europe. Gerarde [3] says the leaves are used among potherbs.

Punica granatum Linn. *Lythrarieae.* POMEGRANATE.

Asia Minor,[4] Armenia, central Caucasus [5] and the Himalayas.[6] The pomegranate is of very ancient culture in Palestine, Persia, northern India and has been distributed eastward to northern China.[7] On account of the profusion of its seeds, it was with the ancients a mystical fruit, typifying procreation, increase and abundance.[8] Yet seedless fruits from Djillalabad are enumerated by Harlan [9] as among the fruits in the market at Kabul. Sir A. Barnes mentions a famous pomegranate without seeds grown in gardens near the Kabul River, and in 1860 cuttings from a seedless variety from Palestine were distributed as a much esteemed variety from the United Patent Office.[10] Burnes,[11] in his *Travels in Bokhara*, remarks on the pomegranate seeding in Mazenderan as a remarkable peculiarity. According to Athenaeus, Aphrodite first planted the pomegranate on Cyprus and in Greece. The fancy of the Greeks derived this fruit from the blood of Dionysius Zagreus. The pomegranate was known in Egypt and was cultivated even in the time of Moses. It was raised in the gardens about Carthage. Darius Hystaspes, according to Herodotus, ate of its fruit. Homer mentions the pomegranate as present in the gardens of Alcinous. The Romans brought it from Carthage to Italy, for which reason they call its fruits *mala punica*. Pliny enumerates nine different kinds and these at the present day have increased greatly. The pomegranate is now found growing wild in the southern Tyrol, southern Switzerland, as also in Spain, southern France and Greece.[12] The pomegranate was observed by Wm. Bartram,[13] about 1773, growing out of the ruins of Frederica, Georgia, and it now thrives everywhere on the Gulf coast of Florida.[14] It was mentioned as found in California by Father Baegert,[15] 1751–1768.

---

[1] Brandis, D. *Forest Fl.* 141. 1876.

[2] Pickering, C. *Chron. Hist. Pls.* 211. 1879.

[3] Gerarde, J. *Herb.* 663. 1597.

[4] De Candolle, A. *Geog. Bot.* 2:892. 1855.

[5] Ibid.

[6] Royle, J. F. *Illustr. Bot. Himal.* 1:208. 1839.

[7] Unger, F. *U. S. Pat. Off. Rpt.* 342. 1859.

[8] Hooker, W. J. *Journ. Bot.* 1:119. 1834.

[9] *U. S. Pat. Off. Rpt.* 530. 1861.

[10] *U. S. Pat. Off. Rpt.* 34. 1860.

[11] Darwin, C. *Ans. Pls. Domest.* 2:152 Note. 1893.

[12] Unger, F. *U. S. Pat. Off. Rpt.* 342. 1859.

[13] *Hist. Mass. Hort. Soc.* 27. 1880.

[14] Redmond, D. *Amer. Pom. Soc.* 57. 1875.

[15] *Smithsonian Inst. Rpt.* 356. 1864.

There are many varieties, some with sour, others with subacid, others with sweet fruit. These are generally described as about the size of the fist, with a tough, leathery rind of a beautiful, deep golden color tinged with red and are crowned with the remains of the calyx lobes.[1] The wild fruit is brought down to India from the Hill Regions for sale,[2] but the best fruit, that having sweet juice and very small seeds, comes from Kabul.[3] Burton[4] describes in Arabia 'three kinds: *Shami*, red outside, and very sweet — than which he never saw a finer fruit in the East, except at Mecca — it was almost stoneless, deliciously perfumed and as large as an infant's head; *Turki*, large, and of a white color; *Misri*, with a greenish rind and a somewhat subacid and harsh flavor.

Pyrularia edulis A. DC. *Santalaceae*.

Himalayan region. This is a large tree whose drupaceous fruit is used for food.[5] The fruit is eaten by the natives.[6]

P. pubera Michx. BUFFALO-NUT. OIL-NUT.

Pennsylvania to Georgia. The plant yields an edible fruit, according to Unger.[7]

Pyrus angustifolia Ait. *Rosaceae*. AMERICAN CRAB.

North America. This species differs little from the *P. coronaria* of which it may be a variety. Its range is not well known but it occurs in Virginia, Kansas and the western states.[8] It is good for preserves and sauces.[9]

P. arbutifolia Linn. f. CHOKEBERRY.

Northeast America. Josselyn[10] mentions its fruit as " of a delicate, aromatic taste but somewhat stiptick." The fruit is well known for its puckery quality, but occasionally a variety is found which is rather pleasant tasting and is eaten by children.

P. aria Ehrh. CHESS APPLE. WHITE BEAM TREE.

Europe and northern Asia. The berries of this species occur in the debris of the lake settlements of Switzerland.[11] Johnson[12] says the fruit is edible when mellowed by frost and that, fermented and distilled, it yields a good spirit. Dried and formed into a bread, it has been eaten in France and Sweden in time of scarcity.[13] In India, the fruit is eaten when half rotten.[14]

---

[1] Smith, A. *Treas. Bot.* 2:941. 1870.

[2] Royle, J. F. *Illustr. Bot. Himal.* 1:208. 1839.

[3] Dutt, U. C. *Mat. Med. Hindus* 166. 1877.

[4] Burton, R. F. *Pilgr. Medina, Meccah* 249. 1856.

[5] Mueller, F. *Sel. Pls.* 396. 1891.

[6] Dickie, G. D. *Treas. Bot.* 2:1080. 1870. (*Sphaerocarya edulis*)

[7] Unger, F. *U. S. Pat. Off. Rpt.* 321. 1859. (*Hamiltonia oleifera*)

[8] Vasey *Amer. Pom. Soc. Rpt.* 56. 1877.

[9] Hunt *U. S. D. A. Spec. Rpt.* 3:62. 1883.

[10] Josselyn, J. *Voy.* 59. 1865. Reprint.

[11] Pickering, C. *Chron. Hist. Pls.* 285. 1879.

[12] Johnson, C. P. *Useful Pls. Gt. Brit.* 103. 1862.

[13] Loudon, J. C. *Arb. Frut. Brit.* 2:911. 1844.

[14] Brandis, D. *Forest Fl.* 206. 1870.

P. aucuparia Ehrh. MOUNTAIN ASH. QUICKBEAM. ROWAN TREE.

Europe and northern Asia. This species is a native of Europe but is cultivated for ornament in America and, in France, is grafted on the service tree to increase the size of the berries. The round fruit is small, scarlet, very juicy, sour and bitter but, when made into a jam, is called palatable. In Wales and the Scottish Highlands, in Livonia, Sweden and Kamchatka, the berries are eaten when ripe as a fruit, and a liquor is produced from the femented berries. In various parts of the north of Europe, in times of scarcity, the dried fruit is ground into a meal and is used as a bread-food.

P. baccata Linn. SIBERIAN CRAB.

Himalayan region and northern Asia. This species is cultivated in our gardens for ornament and is highly esteemed for preserving.[1] The fruit, in India, says Brandis,[2] is small and sour but palatable, with a true apple flavor. It is much prized by the Hill People.

P. betulaefolia Bunge. BIRCH-LEAVED PEAR.

China. The flowers, leaves and fruit are edible. It was noted in China in the fourteenth century.[3]

P. communis Linn. PEAR.

Europe, northern Asia and the Himalayan region. The pear is a native of Europe and the Caucasian countries. It has been in cultivation from time immemorial. The fruit tree figured in one of the tombs at Gurna seems to belong here, and Heer[4] states that a small-fruited kind appears in the debris of the earliest lake villages of Switzerland. Unger[5] states that pears were raised in the gardens of the Phoenicians, and Thasos was celebrated in ancient times on account of the excellence of its pears. The primitive festival of the Ballachrades of the Argives with the wild pear (*achras*) had reference to this first article of food of their forefathers. The Jews were acquainted with greatly improved varieties, but the Romans first occupied themselves more closely with its cultivation and produced numerous sorts.[6] Theophrastus[7] knew 3 kinds of pears; Cato,[8] 6; Pliny,[9] 41; and Palladius,[10] 56. Targioni-Tozzetti[11] says that in Tuscany, under the Medici, in a manuscript list of the fruits served at the table of the Grand Duke Cosmo III, is an enumeration of 209 different varieties, and another manuscript of that time raises the number to 232. In Britain, in 1640, 64 kinds were cultivated,[12] and in 1842 more than 700

---

[1] Downing, A. J. *Fr. Fr. Trees Amer.* 228. 1857.

[2] Brandis, D. *Forest Fl.* 205. 1874.

[3] Bretschneider, E. *Bot. Sin.* 52. 1882.

[4] De Candolle, A. *Orig. Pls. Cult.* 231. 1885.

[5] Unger, F. *U. S. Pat. Off. Rpt.* 344. 1859.

[6] Ibid.

[7] Ibid.

[8] Ibid.

[9] Ibid.

[10] Ibid.

[11] Targioni-Tozzetti *Journ. Hort. Soc. Lond.* **9**:159. 1855.

[12] McIntosh, C. *Book Gard.* **2**:447. 1855.

sorts had been proved in the Horticultural Society's [1] gardens to be distinct.   In 1866, Field [2] gives a catalog of 850 varieties, of which 683 are of European origin.   The American Pomological Society's Catalog of 1879,[3] names 115 distinct kinds which are considered desirable for culture.   The pear is now found in Europe, Circassia, central Asia, the north of China and Japan, as well as in America but is not grown in southern India, nor in Norway.[4]   Pear seeds were mentioned in the Memorandum [5] of March 16, 1629, to be sent to the Massachusetts Company; in or about 1640, a tree was imported by Governor Prince [6] and planted at Eastman, Massachusetts, and one about the same time was planted at Yarmouth,[7] Massachusetts.   The Stuyvesant [8] pear tree was planted in New Amsterdam in 1647 and is said to have been imported from Holland.   In 1648, it is said in *A Perfect Description of Virginia* [9] that " Mr. Richard Kinsman hath had for this three or four years forty or fifty Butts of Perry made out of his orchard, pure and good."   On the banks of the Detroit River pears were planted as early as 1705 by the French settlers.[10]

P. coronaria Linn.   AMERICAN CRAB APPLE.   GARLAND CRAB.   SWEET-SCENTED CRAB.

Eastern North America.   This is, perhaps, the apple seen by Verazzano [11] in 1524 on the New England coast.   The fruit is about an inch in diameter, very acid and uneatable; it is, however, used for preserves and for making cider.[12]

P. cydonia Linn.   QUINCE.

Mediterranean and Caucasus regions.   The quince was held in high repute by the ancients and was dedicated to the Goddess of Love.   Theophrastus speaks of a kind of quince as *struthion* and Dioscorides speaks of the tree as *kudonea*.   Athenaeus says Corinth furnished the Athenians with quinces as delicious to the taste as they were beautiful to the eye.   The quince was brought to Italy from Kydron, a city of Crete, according to Pliny. Columella [13] knew it in his time, for he says " quinces not only yield pleasure but health." In 812, Charlemagne [14] enjoined its cultivation in France.   In England, it was known to Chaucer [15] in the latter part of the fourteenth century, for he speaks of it under the name of *coine*.   In 1446, baked quinces were served at a banquet in England.[16]   Quinces

---

[1] Loudon, J. C.   *Hort.* 546.   1860.

[2] Field, T. W.   *Pear Cult.* 271.   1858.

[3] *Amer. Pom. Soc. Cat.*   1879.

[4] *Treas. Bot.* 2:945.   1870.   [4]

[5] *Hist. Mass. Hort. Soc.* 11.   1880.

[6] *Hist. Mass. Hort. Soc.* 3.   1880.

[7] Ibid.

[8] *Hist. Mass. Hort. Soc.* 20.   1880.

[9] *Perf. Desc. Va.* 14.   1649.   Force Coll. Tracts 2: No. 8.   1838.

[10] *Hist. Mass. Hort. Soc.* 22.   1880.

[11] Tytler *Prog. Disc. No. Coasts Amer.* 36.   1833.

[12] Sargent *U. S. Census* 9:72.   1884.

[13] McIntosh, C.   *Book Gard.* 2:560.   1855.

[14] Flückiger and Hanbury *Pharm.* 240.   1879.

[15] Pickering, C.   *Chron. Hist. Pls.* 177.   1879.

[16] Flückiger and Hanbury *Pharm.* 240.   1879.

reached America in colonial times, for quince kernels were in the Memorandum of March 16, 1629, of seeds to be sent the Massachusetts Company.[1] They are mentioned in Virginia in 1648 [2] and again by Shrigley in 1669.[3] In 1720, they are mentioned as growing abundantly.[4] At Santa Cruz, Bartlett [5] writes: " There are two varieties of the quince here, one hard and tart like our own, the other sweet and eatable in its raw state, yet preserving the rich flavor of the former. The Mexicans gathered and ate them like apples but I found them too hard for my digestive organs." In Chile, says Molina,[6] the quinces are of large size, though, like those of Europe, they have an acid and astringent taste but, if suffered to attain perfect maturity, they are very sweet and good.

P. germanica Hook. f. MEDLAR.

Eastern Europe and the Orient. The medlar, although distributed throughout almost the whole of Europe, is not indigenous but is a native of northern Persia. It was brough, to Greece at an early period, and Theophrastus was acquainted with three varieties. At the time of Cato, it was unknown in Italy and was first brought there from Macedonia after the Macedonian war. The fact that the Romans found the medlar in Gaul proves only that it came there earlier in the way of trade.[7] Three varieties are considered worthy of cultivation in England. The skin of the fruit is brown and the flesh firm and austeret not at all fit to eat when first gathered and requiring to be kept until it begins to decay, but, when it becomes completely disorganized and its green color has entirely gone, the pulp, in its incipient state of decay has, to many tastes, an agreeable acidity. There is a seedless variety which keeps longer than the other kinds.[8]

P. glabra Boiss.

Southern Persia. This species furnishes a fruit which is eaten.[9] In Luristan it bears a substance which, according to Haussknecht, is collected by the inhabitants and is extremely like oak manna.[10]

P. intermedia Ehrh.

Europe. The fruit is red and eatable.[11]

P. japonica Thunb. JAPANESE QUINCE.

The Japanese quince is said to have been first introduced into Europe in 1815. The fruit of the variety, says Downing,[12] is dark green, very hard and has a peculiar and not unpleasant smell. In the *Michigan Pomological Society's Report*,[13] the fruit is said to be

---

[1] *Mass. Records* 1:24.

[2] *Perf. Desc. Va.* 14. 1649. Force Coll. Tracts. **2**: 1838.

[3] Shrigley *True Rel. Va., Md.* 5. 1669. Force Coll. Tracts **3**: 1844.

[4] *Hist. Mass. Hort. Soc.* 21. 1880.

[5] Bartlett, J. R. *Explor. Tex.* 1:414. 1854.

[6] Molina *Hist. Chili* 1:134. 1808.

[7] Unger, F. *U. S. Pat. Off. Rpt.* 341. 1859. (*Mespilus germanica*)

[8] Thompson, R. *Treas. Bot.* 2:739. 1870.

[9] Unger, F. *U. S. Pat. Off. Rpt.* 345. 1859.

[10] Flückiger and Hanbury *Pharm.* 373. 1879.

[11] Don, G. *Hist. Dichl. Pls.* 2:647. 1832.

[12] Downing, A. J. *Fr. Fr. Trees Amer.* 654. 1857.

[13] *Mich. Pom. Soc. Rpt.* 469. 1879. (*Cydonia japonica*)

sometimes used in jellies.   E. Y. Teas,[1] a correspondent of *Case's Botanical Index*, says he has seen specimens two by three inches in diameter, with a fine fleshy texture, abounding in a rich, aromatic juice, as tart as and very much like a lemon, readily producing a jelly of the finest quality and most delightful flavor.   When baked or stewed, the fruit becomes very fine.

P. lanata D. Don.

Himalayan region.   The fruit is edible.[2]

P. malus Linn.   APPLE.

Forests of temperate Europe and Asia.   The apple has been cultivated from remote time.   Carbonized apples have been found in the ancient lake habitations of Switzerland, at Wangen, at Robenhausen and at Concise, but these are small and resemble those which still grow wild in the Swiss forests.[3]   Apples were raised in the gardens of the Phoenicians.[4]   They are noticed by Sappho, Theocritus and Tibullus.[5]   Theophrastus[6] knew 2 kinds of apples; Cato,[7] 7; Pliny,[8] 36; Palladius,[9] 37.[10]   Varro, in the first century B. C., reports that, when he led his army through Transalpine Gaul as far as the Rhine, he passed through a country that had not the apple.   According to Targioni-Tozzetti,[11] in a manuscript list of the fruits served up in the course of the year 1670 at the table of the Grand Duke Cosmo III, of Tuscany, 56 sorts are described, 52 of which are figured by Costello.[12]   In England, 1640, Parkinson[13] enumerates 59 sorts.   In 1669, Worlidge[14] gives a list of 92, chiefly cider apples.   In 1697, Meager[15] gives a list of 83 as cultivated in the London nurseries of his day.   Yet Hartlibb,[16] 1651, mentions 200 and was of opinion that 500 varieties existed.

In 1524, Verazzano,[17] on the coast of what is supposed to be the present Massachusetts, mentions apples but we know not to what fruit he could have referred.   Apple seeds were in the Memorandum of 1629[18] of seeds to be sent the Massachusetts Company.   In 1648, Peregrin White,[19] the first European born in New England, planted apples at Marsh-

---

[1] Case *Bot. Index*.   Apr. 1880.

[2] Royle, J. F.   *Illustr. Bot. Himal.* 1:206.   1839.

[3] Lubbock *Amer. Journ. Sci. and Art* 34:181

[4] Unger *U. S. Pat. Off. Rpt.* 344.   1859.

[5] Pickering, C.   *Geog. Dist. Ans., Pls.* 39.   1863.

[6] Unger *U. S. Pat. Off. Rpt.* 344.   1859.

[7] Ibid.

[8] Ibid.

[9] Ibid.

[10] Ibid.

[11] Targoni-Tozzetti *Journ. Hort. Soc. Lond.* 9:159   1855.

[12] Ibid.

[13] McIntosh, C.   *Book Gard.* 2:412.   1855.

[14] Ibid.

[15] Ibid.

[16] Ibid.

[17] Tytler *Prog. Disc. No. Coast Amer.* 36.   1833.

[18] *Mass. Records* 1:24.

[19] *Hist. Mass. Hort. Soc.* 3.   1880.

field. In 1639, Josselyn [1] was treated with " half a score very fair pippins " from Governor's Island in Boston Harbor, though there was then " not one apple tree nor pear planted yet in no part of the country but upon that island." In 1635, at Cumberland, Rhode Island, a kind called Yellow Sweeting was originated.[2] In 1635, as Josselyn [3] states, Mr. Wolcott, a distinguished Connecticut magistrate, wrote that he had made " five hundred hogsheads of cider " out of his own orchard in one year and yet this was not more than five years after his colony was planted. In 1648, " Mr. Richard Bennett (of Virginia) had this yeere out of his orchard as many apples as he made 20 Butts of excellent cider." [4] In Downing's *Fruits*,[5] edition of 1866, some 643 varieties are noticed, and the American Pomological Society, 1879, endorses 321 varieties of the apple and 13 of crabs. In 1779, in Gen. Sullivan's Campaign, at Geneva, New York, Colonel Dearborn says under date of September 7th, " Here are considerable number of apple and other fruit trees;" the *Journal* of Capt. Nukerck says, " a great plenty of apple and peach trees;" Dr. Campfield writes, " a considerable number of apple trees 20 or 30 years old;" and Gen. Sullivan in his official report says, " a great number of fruit trees." In a pamphlet of 1798,[6] it is stated that one farmer near Geneva sold cider this year to the amount of $1200.[7] About five miles from Harrodsburg, Kentucky, in 1779, apple seeds were sown by colonists.[8]

In 1643, Henry Brewer [9] found on the coast of Chile " very good apples." In Chiloe, Darwin [10] says he never saw apples anywhere thrive so well, and " they are propagated by cuttings." Bridges [11] speaks of the houses in portions of Chile being placed in groves of apple trees. About Quito, says Hall,[12] the apples are plentiful but small and ill-flavored. In Jamaica, says Lunan,[13] no apple yet introduced thrives and the fruits are usually seedless. Among the introduced fruits of New Zealand, Wilkes,[14] 1840, mentions the apple. Thunberg does not mention them in Japan in 1776, but Hogg does in 1864; they are cultivated in the north of China and in northern India, small in some districts, remarkably fine in others.[15] In Turkestan, in 1219, Ye-iu-Tch'u-tsai, a Chinese traveler, found dense forests of apple trees.[16] The apple is generally cultivated throughout the Arab countries

[1] Josselyn, J.   *New Eng. Rar.* note. 142.   1865.

[2] Lincoln *Mass. Hort. Soc.* 14.   Sept. 20 1837.

[3] Josselyn, J.   *Voy.* 145.   1865.

[4] *Perf. Desc. Va.* 14.   1649.   Force Coll. Tracts. 2:   1838.

[5] Downing, A. J.   *Fr. Fr. Trees Amer.* 71.   1857.

[6] *Document. Hist. N. Y.* 2:1125.   1798.

[7] Conover, G. S.   *Early Hist. Geneva* 35–47.   1879

[8] *Amer. Pom. Soc. Cat.* 76.   1871.

[9] Churchill *Coll. Voy.* 1:403.   1744.

[10] Darwin, C.   *Voy. H. M. S. Beagle* 297.   1884.

[11] Hooker, W. J.   *Journ. Bot.* 1:177.   1834.

[12] Hooker, W. J.   *Journ. Bot.* 1:333.   1834.

[13] Lunan, J.   *Hort. Jam.* 1:34.   1814.

[14] Wilkes, C.   *U. S. Explor. Exped.* 2:411.   1845.

[15] Royle, J. F.   *Illustr. Bot. Himal.* 1:206.   1839.

[16] Schuyler *Turkistan* 1:394.   1876.

but is hardly edible, being prized for its odor.[1]   At Ismailia, Egypt, the apple grows but does not bear fruit.[2]   The fruit grows at Tonquin, north Africa, but is scarcely fit to be eaten.

The apple grows in Scandinavia as far as 62° north, in the Orkneys 60° north and, according to Rhind,[3] bears very fair fruit.   Apples are grown in northern Russia but the most esteemed come to St. Petersburg from the Crimea.   They are plentiful in Britain, France, Switzerland and Germany.   The fruit is said to be poor in Italy, as in Greece. In America, the apple bears fair fruit as far north as Quebec and is found in varieties in all the states even to Mexico.   In Venezuela, the fruit is noted by Humboldt to be of good quality.   In Peru, the apple is said to be uneatable.   In La Plata, the tree grows well, but the fruit is of poor quality.   A dwarf form is called the Paradise apple and another, in France, the Doucin, or St. Johns apple.   On account of rapid and low growth, these dwarfs are principally used as stocks for dwarf apples.

P. pashia Buch.-Ham.   WILD PEAR.

The hills of India.   The fruit is edible when it has become somewhat decayed.[4]   It is even then harsh and not sweet.[5]

P. prunifolia Willd.   PLUM-LEAVED APPLE.

Southern Siberia, northern China and Tartary.   This is one of the forms of the tree cultivated as the Siberian Crab.[6]

P. rivularis Dougl.   OREGON CRAB APPLE.

Alaska, Oregon, northern California and Nevada.   The fruit is about the size of a cherry and is employed by the Indians of Alaska as a part of their food supply.[7]   They are also used by the Indians of California [8] and of Oregon.[9]   The Oregon crab is called by the Chinooks *powitch*.[10]   In the early settlement of Oregon, this fruit was used largely for preserves.   Aside from the great proportion of seeds, it does not make a bad sauce.[11]

P. salicifolia Pall.   WILLOW-LEAVED PEAR.

Caucasus, Greece, Turkey, Persia and southwest Russia.   The fruit is edible, but the tree is utilized more as a superior stock for grafting.[13]

P. salvifolia DC.   SAGE-LEAVED PEAR.

This species is wild and cultivated about Aurelia in France.   The fruit is thick, long and fit for perry.[13]

---

[1] Pickering, C.   *Chron. Hist. Pls.* 181.   1879.   (*Malus sylvestris*)
[2] *Gard. Chron.* 18:458.   1882.
[3] Rhind, W.   *Hist. Veg. King.* 321.   1855.
[4] Royle, J. F.   *Illustr. Bot. Himal.* 1:206.   1839.
[5] Brandis, D.   *Forest Fl.* 204.   1874.   (*P. variolosa*)
[6] Vasey *Amer. Pom. Soc. Rpt.* 56.   1877.
[7] Vasey   *U. S. D. A. Rpt.* 162.   1875.
[8] Brewer and Watson *Bot. Cal.* 1:189.   1880.   (*Crataegus rivularis*)
[9] Hooker, W. J.   *Fl. Bor. Amer.* 1:203.   1840.
[10] Ibid.
[11] Case *Bot. Index* 38.   1881.
[12] Mueller, F.   *Sel. Pls.* 399.   1891.
[13] Loudon, J. C.   *Arb. Frut. Brit.* 2:888.   1844.

P. sieboldi Regel.

Japan. The fruit is edible after frosts.[1]

P. sinensis Lindl. CHINESE PEAR. SAND PEAR.

China. This species is known in the gardens of India as a good baking fruit.[2]

P. sinensis Poir.

China. This species furnishes a quince in China.[3]

P. sorbus Gaertn. SERVICE TREE.

North Africa and Europe. The fruit is about the size of a gooseberry and is acerb. It is used in Brittany for making a cider, which, however, has an unpleasant smell.[4] There is a pear-shaped, an apple-shaped and a berry-shaped variety.[5] In the Crimea, there is a variety with a large, red fruit the shape of a pear.[6]

P. spectabilis Ait. CHINESE FLOWERING APPLE.

China. The fruit is small, round, angular and about the size of a cherry, yellow when ripe but flavorless and fit to eat only when in a state of incipient decay at which period it takes the color and taste of the medlar.[7] There are several varieties in cultivation.[8]

P. syriaca Boiss.

Asia Minor and Syria. The mellow fruit is eaten.[9]

P. torminalis Ehrh. MAPLE SERVICE. WILD SERVICE.

Europe. The small fruits, which are greenish, with dark spots, have an extremely acid flavor but, when affected by frost, become mealy and rather agreeable to the taste. They are sometimes collected and sold in the shops in England.[10] The fruit is sold in the London markets.[11]

P. trilobata DC. THREE-LOBED-LEAVED PEAR.

Syria. This species has fruits of a pleasant flavor, tasting like pears, according to Kotschy;[12] they are frequently collected and brought to market in Damascus.[13]

Quercus aegilops Linn. *Cupuliferae.* CAMATA OR CAMATINA OAK. VALONIA OAK.

South Europe and Syria. The cups, known as valonia, are used for tanning and

---

[1] Georgeson *Amer. Gard.* **12**:12. 1891. (*P. toringo*)

[2] Royle, J. F. *Illustr. Bot. Himal.* **1**:206. 1839.

[3] Unger, F. *U. S. Pat. Off. Rpt.* 1859.

[4] Smith, J. *Dom. Bot.* 406. 1871.

[5] Loudon, J. C. *Hort.* 552. 1860.

[6] Pallas, P. S. *Trav. Russia* **2**:436. 1803.

[7] Loudon, J. C. *Arb. Frut. Brit.* **2**:909. 1844.

[8] Vasey *Amer. Pom. Soc. Rpt.* 56. 1877.

[9] Unger, F. *U. S. Pat. Off. Rpt.* 345. 1859.

[10] Johnson, C. P. *Useful Pls. Gt. Brit.* 102. 1862.

[11] Martyn *Miller's Gard. Dict.* 1807.

[12] Unger, F. *U. S. Pat. Off. Rpt.* 345. 1859.

[13] Unger, F. *U. S. Pat. Off. Rpt.* 345. 1859. (*Crataegus trilobata*)

dyeing as are the unripe acorns called camata or camatina. The ripe acorns are eaten raw or boiled.[1, 2]

Q. agrifolia Née. CALIFORNIA FIELD OAK.

The acorns are eaten by the Indians.[3]

Q. alba Linn. WHITE OAK.

Northeast America. The dried acorns are macerated in water for food by the natives on the Roanoke.[4] Acorns were dried and boiled for food by the Narragansetts.[5] Oak acorns were mixed with their pottage by the Indians of Massachusetts. Baskets full of parched acorns, hid in the ground, were discovered by the Pilgrims December 7, 1620.[6] White oak acorns were boiled for "oyl" by the natives of New England.[7] The fruit of some trees is quite pleasant to the taste, especially when roasted.

Q. cerris Linn. TURKISH OAK.

Europe and the Orient. The trees are visited in August by immense numbers of a small, white coccus insect, from the puncture of which a saccharine fluid exudes and solidifies in little grains. The wandering tribes of Kurdistan collect this saccharine secretion by dipping the branches on which it forms into hot water and evaporating to a syrupy consistence. In this state, the syrup is used for sweetening food or is mixed with flour to form a sort of cake.[8]

Q. coccifera Linn. KERMES OAK.

Mediterranean region. The acorns were used as food by the ancients.[9]

Q. cornea Lour.

China. The acorns are used for food.[10] Loudon [11] says the acorns are ground into a paste in China, which, mixed with the flour of corn, is made into cakes.

Q. cuspidata Thunb.

Japan. This species is enumerated by Thunberg [12] among the edible plants of Japan.

Q. emoryi Torr.

Western North America. This tree furnishes acorns, which are used by the Indians of the West as a food.

---

[1] Mueller, F. *Sel. Pls.* 400. 1891.

[2] Unger, F. *U. S. Pat. Off. Rpt.* 314. 1859.

[3] *U. S. D. A. Rpt.* 409. 1870.

[4] Pickering, C. *Chron. Hist. Pls.* 772. 1879.

[5] Williams, R. *Key.* 1643. Narragansett Hist. Coll. **1**:120. 1866.

[6] Young, A. *Chron. Pilgr.* 154. 1841.

[7] Josselyn, J. *New Eng. Rar.* 94. 1865. Orig. 1672.

[8] Flückiger and Hanbury *Pharm.* 372. 1879.

[9] Hooker, W. J. *Lond. Journ. Bot.* **1**:146. 1834.

[10] Mueller, F. *Sel. Pls.* 403. 1891.

[11] Loudon, J. C. *Enc. Agr.* 158. 1866.

[12] Thunberg, C. P. *Fl. Jap.* 176. 1784.

Q. garryana Dougl. WESTERN OAK.

Western North America. The acorns furnish the Indians with food and are stored by them for future use.[1]

Q. ilex Linn. BALLOTA, BELLOOT OR BELOTE OAK. HOLLY OAK.

Mediterranean region and the Orient. From varieties of this tree, says Mueller,[2] are obtained the sweet and nourishing ballota and chestnut acorns. Figuier[3] says this species is common in the south of France, and that the acorns are sweet and eatable. Brandis[4] says the acorns form an important article of food in Spain and Algeria. The acorns are eaten in Barbary, Spain and Portugal under the name of belote. In Arabia, also, they are eaten cooked, and an oil is extracted from them.[5] In Palestine, they are sold in all the bazaars.[6]

Q. lobata Née. CALIFORNIA WHITE OAK.

California. The acorns form a large proportion of the winter food of the Indians of North California.[7] The acorns, from their abundance and edible nature, form a very important part of the subsistence of the Digger Indians and are collected and stored for winter use.[8]

Q. michauxii Nutt. BASKET OAK. COW OAK.

North America. The large, sweet, edible acorns are eagerly devoured by cattle and other animals.[9]

Q. oblongifolia Torr. EVERGREEN OAK. LIVE OAK.

California and New Mexico. This species furnishes the Indians of the West with acorns for food use.[10]

Q. persica Jaub. et Spach. MANNA OAK.

Persia. The acorns are eaten in southern Europe[11] and, in southern Persia, afford material for bread. The leaves also furnish a manna.[12] In olden times, as we read in Homer and Hesiod, the acorn was the common food of the Arcadians. There is, however, much reason to suppose that chestnuts, which were named in the times of Theophrastus and Dioscorides Jupiter acorns and Sardian acorns, are often alluded to when we read of people having lived on acorns in Europe; and, in Africa, dates are signified, because they were likewise called by Herodotus and Dioscorides acorns and palm-acorns. Bar-

---

[1] *U. S. D. A. Rpt.* 409. 1870.

[2] Mueller, F. *Sel. Pls.* 194. 1876.

[3] Figuier *Veg. World* 353. 1867.

[4] Brandis, D. *Forest Fl.* 481. 1874.

[5] Masters *Treas. Bot.* 951. 1870. (*Q. ballota*)

[6] Smith, J. *Dom. Bot.* 218. 1871.

[7] Mueller, F. *Sel. Pls.* 405. 1891.

[8] Flückiger and Hanbury *Pharm.* 372. 1879.

[9] Sargent *U. S. Census* 9:141. 1884.

[10] *U. S. D. A. Rpt.* 409. 1870.

[11] Unger, F. *U. S. Pat. Off. Rpt.* 314. 1879.

[12] Flückiger and Hanbury *Pharm.* 372. 1879.

tholin[1] says that in Norway acorns are used to furnish a bread.   During a famine in France, in 1709, acorns were resorted to for sustenance.[2]   In China, the fruits of several species of oak are used as food for man, and a kind of curd is sometimes made from the ground meal.[3]   Oak bark is pounded by the Digger Indians of California [4] and used as food in times of famine.

Q. phellos Linn.   WILLOW OAK.

Eastern States of North America.   The acorns are edible.[5]

Q. prinus Linn.   CHESTNUT OAK.

Northeastern America.   The fruit is sweet and abundant.[6]

Q. robur Linn.   BLACK OAK.   TRUFFLE OAK.

Europe and western Asia.   Varieties are mentioned by Tenore [7] as bearing edible acorns.   This species yields a manna-like exudation in Kurdistan.[8]   Hanbury [9] says a saccharine substance called *diarbekei* manna, is found upon the leaves of the dwarf oaks about Smyrna, from which it is collected by the peasants, who use it instead of butter in cooking their food.   The taste is saccharine and agreeable.

Q. suber Linn.   CORK OAK.

South Europe and northern Africa.   Bosc alleges that its acorns may be eaten in cases of necessity, especially when roasted.   This species was distributed from the Patent Office in 1855.[10]

Q. undulata Torr.   ROCKY MOUNTAIN SCRUB OAK.

California.   The acorns are sweet and edible.[11]

Q. virginiana Mill.   LIVE OAK.

Eastern North America.   Eastern Indians consumed large quantities of the acorns and also obtained from them a sweet oil much used in cookery.[12]

Rajania brasiliensis Griseb.   *Dioscoreaceae.*

South Brazil.   The plant has edible roots.[13]

Randia dumetorum Lam.   *Rubiaceae.*

Old World tropics and India.   The unripe fruit is bruised, pounded and used to poison fish; when ripe it is roasted and eaten.[14]

[1] Pavy, F. W.   *Food, Diet.* 264.   1875.

[2] Ibid.

[3] Smith, F. P.   *Contrib. Mat. Med. China* 4.   1871.

[4] Brewer, Prof.   *Letter to Dr. Sturtevant.*   Oct. 20, 1879.

[5] Mueller, F.   *Sel. Pls.* 407.   1891.

[6] Emerson, G. B.   *Trees, Shrubs Mass.* 1:155.   1875.   (*Q. castanea*)

[7] Hooker, W. J.   *London Journ. Bot.* 2:182.   1840.

[8] Masters, M. T.   *Treas. Bot.* 2:951.   1870.

[9] Hanbury, D.   *Sci. Papers* 287.   1876.

[10] *U. S. Pat. Off. Rpt.* XIX.   1855.

[11] Brewer and Watson *Bot. Cal.* 2:96.   1880.

[12] Havard, V.   *Torr. Bot. Club Bul.* 22:119.   1895.

[13] Mueller, F.   *Sel. Pls.* 154.   1891.   (*Dioscorea brasiliensis*)

[14] Brandis, D.   *Forest Fl.* 273.   1876.

R. ruiziana DC.

Peru. The fruit is eaten by the Indians of Chile.[1]

R. uliginosa Poir.

East Indies and Burma. The ash-colored fruit is sold in bazaars in Oudh and Bihar and is eaten when cooked.[2]

Ranunculus bulbosus Linn. *Ranunculaceae.* BUTTERCUP.

Europe and naturalized in the United States. Lightfoot [3] says the roots when boiled become so mild as to be eatable.

R. edulis. Boiss. & Hohen. EGG-YOLK.

Asia Minor and north Persia. The small tubers, together with the young stems and leaves of the blossoms, serve as food. It is called *morchserdag* or egg-yolk, on account of the yellow color of the flowers.[4]

R. ficaria Linn. BUTTERCUP. LESSER CELANDINE. SMALL CELANDINE.

Caucasus and Europe. The young leaves, according to Linnaeus, may be eaten in the spring with other potherbs.

R. repens Linn. BUTTER DAISY. CREEPING CROWFOOT. YELLOW GOWAN.

North temperate regions. This species has less of the acrid quality which is found in most species of the genus and is said to be eaten in Europe as a potherb.

R. sceleratus Linn.

North temperate regions. After boiling, the shepherds in Wallachia eat this species.[5]

Raphanus landra Moretti. *Cruciferae.* ITALIAN RADISH. LANDRA.

Italy. The radical leaves are prepared with oil and eaten as a salad by the poor inhabitants of Insubri.[6]

R. maritimus Sm. BLACK RADISH. SPANISH RADISH.

Western Europe. The leaves and slender roots are mentioned by Dioscorides as eaten as a potherb.[7] The large, succulent roots, according to Walker,[8] are preferable to horseradish for the table.

R. raphanistrum Linn. JOINTED CHARLOCK. RUNCH. WILD MUSTARD. WILD RADISH.

A troublesome weed of Europe naturalized in northeastern America. In the outer Hebrides, its leaves are eaten as a salad. In the grain fields of England, it is so common

---

[1] Ruiz and Pavon *Fl. Peru* 2:67. 1798–1802.
[2] Brandis, D. *Forest Fl.* 273. 1876.
[3] Lightfoot, J. *Fl. Scot.* 1:292. 1789.
[4] Unger, F. *U. S. Pat. Off. Rpt.* 356. 1859.
[5] Don, G. *Hist. Dichl. Pls.* 1:33. 1831.
[6] Don, G. *Hist. Dichl. Pls.* 1:263. 1831.
[7] Pickering, C. *Chron. Hist. Pls.* 207. 1879. (*Raphanistrum maritimum*)
[8] Don, G. *Hist. Dichl. Pls.* 1:263. 1831.

that its seed is separated from the grain and sold as Durham mustard seeds.[1]   The seeds
are very pungent and form an excellent substitute for mustard.[2]

R. sativus Linn.   RADISH.

China may be considered the native land of the radish where, as in the neighboring
country of Japan, it runs into many varieties, among them an oil plant.[3]   The radish,
however, is found wild in the Mediterranean region, as in Spain, in Sardinia, more frequently in Greece and is mentioned so frequently by ancient writers that some authors
think it may be a cultivated form of *R. raphanistrum*.[4]   Radishes were extensively cultivated in Egypt in the time of the Pharaohs.   So highly did the ancient Greeks esteem the
radish, says McIntosh,[5] that, in offering their oblations to Apollo, they presented turnips
in lead and beets in silver, whereas radishes were presented in beaten gold.   The Greeks
appear to have been acquainted with three varieties, and Moschian,[6] one of their physicians,
wrote a book on the radish.   Tragus,[7] 1552, mentions radishes that weighed 40 pounds, and
Matthiolus,[8] 1544, declares having seen them weighing 100 pounds each.

This root does not appear, says Booth,[9] to have reached England until 1548.   Gerarde [10]
mentions four varieties as being grown in 1597, " eaten raw with bread " but for the most
part " used as a sauce with meates to procure appetite."   Radishes are mentioned in
Mexico by P. Martyr;[11] as abounding in Hayti by Benzoni,[12] 1565; and as cultivated in
Massachusetts by Wm. Wood,[13] 1629–33.   In 1806, McMahon [14] mentions 10 sorts in
his list of American garden esculents.   Thorburn [15] offers 9 varieties in his catalog of
1828 and 25 in 1881.   At present, radishes are usually eaten raw with salt as a salad but
are said also to be used occasionally otherwise; the leaves may be boiled as greens or eaten
as a cress; the old roots may be boiled and served as asparagus; or the seed-pods may be
used for pickles.   In China, a variety whose root is not fleshy is cultivated for the oil
which is procured from the seeds.   In Japan, the roots are in general and universal use,
being served as a vegetable and in almost every dish.   Miss Bird [16] says the *daikon* is the
abomination of Europeans.   The Lew-Chew radishes often grow, says Morrow,[17] between
two and three feet long, more than a foot in circumference and are boiled for food.   In

---

[1] Loudon, J. C.   *Enc. Agr.* 934.   1866.

[2] Johnson, C. P.   *Useful Pls. Gt. Brit.* 48.   1862.

[3] Unger, F.   *U. S. Pat. Off. Rpt.* 327.   1859

[4] *Treas. Bot.* 2:959.   1870.

[5] McIntosh, C.   *Book Gard.* 2:6.   1855.

[6] Ibid.

[7] Ibid.

[8] Ibid.

[9] Booth, W. B.   *Treas. Bot.* 2:959.   1870.

[10] Gerarde, J.   *Herb.* 184, 185.   1597.

[11] Eden *Hist. Trav.* 1577.

[12] Benzoni *Hist. New World* Smyth Trans.   1857.

[13] Wood, W.   *New Eng. Prosp.* 11.   1865.

[14] McMahon, B.   *Amer. Gard. Cal.* 582.   1806.

[15] Thorburn *Cat.* 1828.

[16] Bird *Unbeat. Tracks Jap.* 1:238.   1881.

[17] Perry *Japan* 2:16.   1852–54.

Sikh, India, the radish is cultivated principally for the vegetable formed of the young pods and for its oil.[1] In upper Egypt, a peculiar kind is cultivated, of which, says Klunzinger,[2] the leaves only are eaten, and Pickering[3] says also that the leaves are eaten in Egypt. Bayard Taylor[4] says the Arabs are very fond of radish-tops and eat them with as much relish as donkeys.

I.
ROUND, OR TURNIP, RADISH.

The round, or turnip, radish has the root swollen into a spherical form, or an oval tube rounding at the extremity to a filiform radicle. The root has several shades of color, from white to red or purple. Its savor is usually milder than that of the other sorts. This seems to be the *boeotion* of Theophrastus,[5] who described this form as the least acid, of a rotund figure and with small leaves; it is the *syriacan* of Columella[6] and of Pliny.[7] This sort does not appear to have received extensive distribution northward during the Middle Ages, as it is seldom mentioned in the earlier botanies. In 1586, Lyte[8] says they are not very common in Brabant; but they are figured in two varieties by Gerarde. Here might be put the *Raphanus vulgaris* of Tragus, 1552, which he describes as round, small and common in Germany. Bontius,[9] 1658, mentions the round radish in Java, and, in 1837, Bojer[10] describes it as grown at the Mauritius. In 1842, Speede[11] gives an Indian name, *gol moolee*, for the red and white kinds.

> *Raphanus radicula.* Pers. Baillon *Hist. Pls.* 3:222.
> *Raphanus orbiculatus.* Round radish. Ger. 184. 1597.
> *Scarlet French Turnip.* Vilm. 485. 1885.
> *Small Early White Turnip.* Vilm. 487. 1885.
> *Radicula sativa minor.* Small garden radish. Ger. 183. 1597.
> *White olive-shaped.* Vilm. 490. 1885.
> *Olive-shaped Scarlet.* Vilm. 488. 1885.

II.
LONG RADISH.

The root of this class is long, nearly cylindrical, diminishing insensibly to a point at the extremity. This is now the common garden radish. It has a variety of colors from white to red and is noteworthy for the transparency of the flesh. This radish may well be the *radicula* of Columella,[12] and the *algidense* of Pliny,[13] which he describes

---

[1] Hooker, W. J. *Journ. Bot.* 2:273.

[2] Klunzinger, C. B. *Upper Egypt* 139. 1877

[3] Pickering, C. *Geog. Distrib. Ans., Pls.* Pt. 1:59. 1863.

[4] Taylor, B. *Cent. Afr.* 105. 1859.

[5] Theophrastus lib. 7, c. 4.

[6] Columella lib. 10, c. 114; lib. 11, c. 3.

[7] Pliny lib. 19, c. 28.

[8] Dodoens *Herb.* 687. 1586. Lyte Ed.

[9] Bontius *De Ind.* 12. 1658.

[10] Bojer, W. *Hort. Maurit.* 16. 1837.

[11] Speede *Ind. Handb. Gard.* 147. 1842.

[12] Columella lib. 4, c. 8; lib. 11, c. 2.

[13] Pliny lib. 19, c. 26.

as having a long and translucent root. This type is not described in England by Lyte nor by Gerarde; it is described as in the gardens of Aleppo in 1573–75.[1] In 1658, Bontius[2] calls them, in Java, Dutch radish. In 1837, Bojer[3] names them in the Mauritius and in 1842 Speede[4] gives an Indian name, *lumbee moolee.*

> *Raphanus sativus.* Mill. Baillon *Hist. Pls.* 3:222.
> *Raphanus minor purpureus.* Lob. *Obs.* 99.   1576; *Icon.* 1:201.   1591.
> *Raphanus longus.* Cam. *Epit.* 224.   1586.
> *Raphanus purpureus minor.* Lob. Dalechamp. 636.   1587.
> *Radicula sativa minor.* Dod. 676.   1616.
> *Raphanus corynthia.* Bodaeus. 769.   1644.
> *Long Scarlet.* Vilm. 490. 1885.
> *Long White Vienna.* Vilm. 492. 1885.

III.

Long White Late Radish.

The long, white, late, large radishes cannot be recognized in the ancient writings, unless it be the reference by Pliny[5] to the size; some radishes, he says, are the size of a boy infant, and Dalechamp[6] says that such could be seen in his day in Thuringia and Erfordia. In Japan, so says Kizo Tamari,[7] a Japanese commissioner to the New Orleans Exposition of 1886, the radishes are mostly cylindrical, fusiform or club-shaped, from one-fourth of an inch to over a foot in diameter, from six inches to over a yard in length. J. Morrow[8] says that Lew Chew Radishes often grow between two and three feet long and more than twelve inches in circumference. In 1604, Acosta[9] writes that he had seen in the Indies " redish rootes as bigge as a man's arme, very tender and of good taste." These radishes are probably mentioned by Albertus Magnus[10] in the thirteenth century, who says that the *radix* are very large roots of a pyramidal figure, with a somewhat sharp savor, but not that of *raphanus;* they are planted in gardens. This type seems to have been the principal kind in northern Europe a few centuries later and is said by Lyte,[11] 1586, to be the common radish of England. In 1790, Loureiro[12] describes this type as cultivated in China and Cochin China, and this seems to be the form described by Kaempfer[13] in Japan, in 1712. The radishes figured by the early botanists enable us to connect very closely with modern varieties.

---

[1] Gronovius *Fl. Orient.* 81.   1755.
[2] Bontius *De Ind.* 12.   1658.
[3] Bojer, W.   *Hort. Maurit.* 16.   1837.
[4] Speede *Ind. Handb. Gard.* 147.   1842.
[5] Pliny lib. 19, c. 26.
[6] Dalechamp *Hist. Gen. Pl.* (Lugd.) 634.   1857.
[7] *Amer. Hort.*   Sept. 9, 1886.
[8] Perry *Japan* 2:16.   1852–54.
[9] Acosta *Nat. Mor. Hist. Ind.* 261.   1604.   Hakl. Soc. Ed. 1880.
[10] Albertus Magnus *Veg.*   Jessen Ed. 556, 645.   1867.
[11] Dodoens *Herb.* 687.   1586. Lyte Ed.
[12] Loureiro *Fl. Cochin.* 396.   1790.
[13] Kaempfer *Amoen.* 822.   1712.

a.—*Raphanus longus.*   Trag. 732.   1552.
  Raphanus.   Matth. 214.   1558; 332.   1570.
  Raphanus sive radix.   Pin. 145.   1561.
  Raphanus magnus.   Lob. *Obs.* 99.   1576; *Icon.* **1**:201.   1591.
  Raphanus alba.   Cam. *Epit.* 223.   1586.
  Raphanus sativus Matthiol.   Dalechamp 635.   1587.
  Raphanus sive radicula sativa.   Dod. 676.   1616.
  White Strasbourg.   Vilm. 494.   1885.
b.—*Raphanus II.*   Matth. 332.   1570; 349.   1598.
  Raphanus secundus Matthiol.   Dalechamp 635.   1598.
  Laon long gray Winter.   Vilm. 496.   1885.
c.—*Raphanus.*   Matth. 241.   1558; 332.   1570.
  Raphanus sive radix.   Pin. 145.   1561.
  Raphanus sativus Matthiolus.   Dalechamp 635.   1587.
  Radice.   Dur. C. 383.   1885.
  White Spanish Winter.   Vilm. 497.   1885.
d.—*Raphanus sativus.*   Garden Radish.   Ger. 183.   1597.
  Large White Russian.   Vilm. 497.   1885.

IV.

LONG BLACK RADISH.

This radish does not seem to have been mentioned by the ancients. In 1586, Lyte says: " The radish with a black root has of late years been brought into England and now beginnith to be common."

  Raphanus nigra.   Cam. *Epit.* 223.   1586.
  Raphanus sive radicula sativa nigra.   Dod. 676.   1616.
  Raffano longo.   Dur. C.   1617.   ap.
  Long-rooted Black Spanish.   Bryant 40.   1783.
  Long Black Spanish Winter.   Vilm. 496.   1885.

V.

ROUND BLACK RADISH.

This is a turnip-rooted or round form of a black radish, usually included among winter sorts.

  Raphanus pyriformis.   Ger. 184.   1597.
  Raphanus I.   Matth. 394.   1598.
  Large Purple Winter.   Vilm. 495.   1885.

There is another form of black radish figured in the early botanies, of quite a distinct appearance. It answers suggestively to the description by Vilmorin of the *Radis de Mahon* a long, red radish, exceedingly distinct, growing in part above ground and peculiar to some districts in southern France and to the Balearic Isles.

  Raphanus niger.   Lob. *Icon.* **1**:202.   1591.
  Radice selvatica.   Dur. C. 384.   1617.
  Raphanus niger.   Bod. 770.   1644.
  Radis de Mahon.   Vilm. 499.   1885.

Theophrastus mentions the Corinthian sort as having full foliage and the root, unlike other radishes, growing partly out of the earth, but the Long Normandy answers to this description as well as the Mahon.

VI.

EDIBLE-PODDED RADISH.

This radish has pods a foot or more in length and these find use as a vegetable. The species became known to Linnaeus in 1784;[1] it reached England from Java about 1816[2] and was described by Burr[3] as an American kitchen-garden plant in 1863. According to Firminger,[4] the plant has but lately come into cultivation in India and there bears pods often three feet in length. These pods make excellent pickles. It was at first called in England tree radish from Java;[5] in India, rat-tailed radish,[6] the name it now holds in the United States; by Burr,[7] 1863, Madras radish; by some, aerial radish.

Raphia hookeri G. Mann & H. Wendl. *Palmae.*

Tropical Africa. Wine or toddy is obtained in large quantities and of excellent quality from this palm.[8]

R. pedunculata Beauv.

Madagascar. This palm yields sago but of a very indifferent quality.[9]

R. vinifera Beauv. BAMBOO PALM. WINE PALM.

Tropical Africa. This species furnishes a palm wine.[10]

Raphiolepis indica Lindl. *Rosaceae.* INDIAN HAWTHORN.

China. This species produces an edible fruit.[11]

Ravenala madagascariensis J. F. Gmel. *Scitamineae.* TRAVELERS' TREE.

Madagascar. Ellis[12] says when a spear is struck into the thick, firm end of the leaf-stalk, a stream of pure, clear water gushes out. There is a kind of natural cavity, or cistern, at the base of the stalk of each of the leaves, and the water collected on the broad and ribbed surface of the leaf, flows down a groove and is stored. The seeds are edible.[13]

Ravensara aromatica J. F. Gmel. *Laurineae.* MADAGASCAR CLOVE NUTMEG. RAVENSARA.

A tree of Madagascar. The fruit, leaves and young bark, having the taste of cloves, afford one of the best spices of the island.[14] The kernel of the fruit affords the Madagascar clove nutmegs.[15]

---

[1] Martyn *Miller's Gard. Dict.* 1807.

[2] *Gard. Chron.* 779. 1866.

[3] Burr, F. *Field, Gard. Veg.* 384. 1863.

[4] Firminger, T. A. C. *Gard. Ind.* 140. 1874.

[5] *Gard. Chron.* 779. 1866.

[6] Firminger, T. A. C. *Gard. Ind.* 140. 1874.

[7] Burr, F. *Field, Gard. Veg.* 384. 1863.

[8] Williams, B. S. *Choice Stove, Greenhouse Pls.* 32. 1876

[9] Pickering, C. *Chron. Hist. Pls.* 630. 1879. (*Sagus farinifera*)

[10] Smith, A. *Treas. Bot.* 2:960. 1870.

[11] Loudon, J. C. *Arb. Frut. Brit.* 933. 1844.

[12] Ellis, W. *Three Visits Madagas.* 335. (Fig. 333.) 1859.

[13] Masters, M. T. *Treas. Bot.* 2:961. 1870.

[14] Pickering, C. *Chron. Hist. Pls.* 707. 1879. (*Agathophyllum aromaticum*)

[15] Masters, M. T. *Treas. Bot.* 1:28. 1870.

Reptonia buxifolia A. DC. *Myrsineae.*

A large shrub or small tree of India. The drupe is sessile, globose, one-third of an inch in diameter or more, glabrous, greenish, with a fleshy, sweet pericarp in a coriaceous rind. This fruit is much esteemed and during the season is sold in most bazaars. The pulp is sweet but there is not much of it.[1] The Afghans sell the fruits in their bazaars under the name of *goorgoora*.[2]

Reseda phyteuma Linn. *Resedaceae.*

Mediterranean shores and Asia Minor. Sibthorp[3] found the leaves of this plant cooked and eaten in Greece.

Reynosia latifolia Griseb. *Rhamneae.* RED IRONWOOD.

Cuba and semitropical Florida. The edible fruit ripens in April and May and is of an agreeable flavor.[4]

Rhamnus caroliniana Walt. *Rhamneae.* BUCKTHORN. INDIAN CHERRY.

Long Island, west along the Ohio to southern Illinois. The edible fruit is sweet and agreeable.[5]

R. crocea Nutt.

Western North America. The berries are collected by the Apache Indians and used as food, mixed with whatever animal substances may be at hand. The berries impart a red color to the mixture, which is absorbed into the circulation and tinges the skin.[6]

R. persica Boiss.

Persia and the Himalayan region. In Persia, the fruit is sweet and edible but emetic.[7]

R. purshiana DC. BEARBERRY..

North America. The purple berries are much esteemed among the Indians.[8]

R. staddo A. Rich.

Abyssinia. This species forms part of a kind of beer in which its bitter bark supplies the place of hops.[9]

Rhapidophyllum hystrix H. Wendl. & Drude. *Palmae.*

Georgia and Florida. The plant bears a brown, edible berry of a sweet flavor.[10]

---

[1] Brandis, D. *Forest Fl.* 287. 1874.
[2] Black, A. A. *Treas. Bot.* 2:966. 1870.
[3] Pickering, C. *Chron. Hist. Pls.* 481. 1879.
[4] Sargent *U. S. Census* 9:39. 1884.
[5] Sargent *U. S. Census* 9:40. 1884.
[6] *U. S. D. A. Rpt.* 414. 1870.
[7] Brandis, D. *Forest Fl.* 93. 1874.
[8] Don, G. *Hist. Dichl. Pls.* 2:32. 1832.
[9] Baillon, H. *Hist. Pls.* 6:72. 1880. (*R. inebrians*)
[10] Seemann, B. *Pop. Hist. Palms* 145. 1856.

Rhazya stricta Decne. *Apocynaceae.*

A shrubby plant of western Asia. Its leaves, which are very bitter, are collected and sold in the bazaars in Scinde, the natives using them in the preparation of cool drinks in hot weather.[1]

Rheedia edulis Planch. & Triana. *Guttiferae.*

Panama. The edible fruit is the size of a hazelnut.[2]

R. lateriflora Linn. WILD MAMMEE.

Tropical America. The fruit, from one to four inches long, yellow when ripe, has a pleasant, acid taste.[3]

R. madruno Planch. & Triana.

New Granada. The fruits are eaten.[4]

Rheum compactum Linn. *Polygonaceae.* PIEPLANT. RHUBARB.

Tartary and China; first known in Europe in 1758. In the *Bon Jardinier*, 1882, this is said to be the species principally grown in France as a vegetable, but Vilmorin[5] refers his varieties to *Rheum hybridum.*

R. emodi Wall. PIEPLANT. RED-VEINED PIEPLANT. RHUBARB.

Himalayas. This species was introduced into Britain about 1828. It is said by Loudon[6] to have an excellent flavor, somewhat resembling that of apples, and is excellent for a late crop, and the *Bon Jardinier*, 1882, says the petioles are longer and more esteemed than those of other species. On the contrary, Burr,[7] 1863, says the leaf-stalks, although attaining an immense size, are unfit for use on account of their purgative properties, but the plant is sometimes cultivated for its leaves, often a yard in diameter, which are useful for covering baskets containing vegetables or fruit. The wild rhubarb about Kabul is blanched for use as a vegetable and, under the name of *rewash*, is brought to the market. Gravel is piled about the sprout as it breaks from the earth, and by continuing the process, the plant is forced to grow to the height of 18 or 20 inches. Another process is to cover the plant with an earthen jar, and the sprout then curls itself spirally within the jar and becomes white, crisp and free from fiber. It is eaten in its raw state with either salt or sugar and makes a favorite preserve.[8]

R. hybridum Murr. PIEPLANT. RHUBARB.

Mongolia. This is the species to which our largest and finest varieties are usually referred. Rhubarb was first noticed in England in 1773 or 1774[9] but it did not come into

---

[1] Smith, A. *Treas. Bot.* 2:971. 1870.
[2] Black, A. A. *Treas. Bot.* 2:971. 1870.
[3] Ibid.
[4] Smith, A. *Treas. Bot.* 1:201. 1870. (*Calophyllum madruño*)
[5] Vilmorin *Les Pls. Potag.* 538. 1883. (*R. hybridum*)
[6] Loudon, J. C. *Hort.* 688. 1860.
[7] Burr, F. *Field, Gard. Veg.* 631. 1863.
[8] Harlan *U. S. Pat. Off. Rpt.* 528. 1861.
[9] Martyn *Miller's Gard. Dict.* 1807.

use as a culinary plant until about 1827. In 1829, a footstalk was noted as sixteen inches long.[1] The Victoria rhubarb of our gardens is referred to this species.

R. nobile Hook. f. & Thoms. SIKKIM RHUBARB.

Himalayas. This is a handsome ornamental plant. The stems, called *chuka* by the people of Sikkim, are pleasantly acid and much eaten.

R. palmatum Linn. PIEPLANT. RHUBARB.

Mongolia. This plant first reached Europe in 1763[2] or 1758.[3] The footstalks are much smaller than those of other kinds, hence it is not in general cultivation.[4] It is yet rare in France, although this species is superior in quality, as it is quite tender.[5]

R. rhaponticum Linn. PIEPLANT. RHUBARB.

Southern Siberia and the region of the Volga. This species, the commonest of the rhubarbs, was introduced into Europe about 1608. It was cultivated at Padua by Prosper Alpinus, and seeds from this source were planted by Parkinson in England about 1640 or before.[6] There is no reference, however, to its use as a vegetable by Alpinus,[7] 1627, nor by Ray,[8] 1686, although the latter refers to the acid stalks being more grateful than that of garden sorrel. In 1778, however, Mawe,[9] says its young stalks in spring, being cut and peeled, are used for tarts. In 1806, McMahon,[10] mentions rhubarb in American gardens and says the footstalks are very frequently used and are much esteemed for tarts and pies. In 1733, Bryant,[11] describes the footstalks as two feet long and thicker than a man's finger at the base.

" Thirty years ago," says J. Lowell [12] in the *Massachusetts Agricultural Repository*, 1822, " we were strangers to rhubarb, now in general use and constantly in our markets, and we are indebted for its introduction to an amateur in the State of Maine." T. S. Gold [13] of Connecticut writes that his father purchased a small package of pieplant seeds in 1820 and raised the first plants then known in his vicinity. The seed was sold by Thorburn [14] in 1828. The globular pouch of unopened flowers is said to form a dish of great delicacy. Stalks weighing two pounds, eleven and one-half ounces have been exhibited at the Massachusetts Horticultural Society.

R. ribes Linn. CURRANT-FRUITED RHUBARB.

Syria, Persia and Afghanistan. This plant is considered to be the *Ribes arabum* of

[1] Rhind, W. *Hist. Veg. King.* 309. 1855.
[2] Noisette *Man. Jard.* 297. 1826.
[3] *Veg. Subst.* 205. 1840.
[4] Ibid.
[5] *Bon Jard.* 706. 1882.
[6] Flückiger and Hanbury *Pharm.* 500. 1879.
[7] Alpinus *Pl. Exot.* 188. 1627.
[8] Ray *Hist. Pl.* 170. 1686.
[9] Mawe and Abercrombie *Univ. Gard. Bot.* 1778.
[10] McMahon, B. *Amer. Gard. Cal.* 205. 1806.
[11] Bryant *Fl. Diet.* 67. 1783.
[12] Lowell, J. *Mass. Agr. Reposit.* 133. 1822.
[13] Gold, T. S. Letter to Dr. Sturtevant 4–29–1880.
[14] Thorburn *Cat.* 1828.

Rauwolf, who traveled in the Orient in 1573-5, and who found it in the region of the Lebanon.[1]   Its habitat is also given as eastern Persia.   Decaisne and Naudin [2] refer to it as grown in gardens in France but not as esteemed as the *R. hybridum*, while the *Bon Jardinier*, 1882, says it is reported the best as an esculent and is greatly praised.

R. tataricum Linn. f.   TARTARIAN RHUBARB.

Tartary.   The leaf-stalks and unexpanded flower-masses are edible.[3]

R. undulatum Linn.   BUCHARIAN RHUBARB.   PIEPLANT.

Asia.   This species is said to have been introduced into Europe in 1734 from China. It yields some of the forms of garden rhubarb, especially those with red leaf-stalks.[4]   In 1810, a Mr. Myatts, Deptford, England, sent five bunches of garden rhubarb to the borough market and could sell but three.   In the United States in 1828, the seed of this variety was sold by Thorburn.[5]   Decaisne and Naudin [6] say this rhubarb is grown in gardens but is not as esteemed as is the Victoria rhubarb.

Rhizophora mucronata Lam.   *Rhizophoreae*.   MANGROVE.

Old World tropics.   The fruit is said to be edible.[7]   Masters [8] says the fermented juice is made into a kind of light wine

Rhododendron arboreum Sm.   *Ericaceae*.   TREE RHODODENDRON.

East Indies, Himalayan region and Ceylon.   In India, the flowers are made into a pleasant, subacid jelly.   They are at times intoxicating.[9]   Royle [10] says the flowers are eaten by the Hill People and are used for jelly by European visitors.

R. lapponicum Wahlenb.   LAPLAND ROSE-BAY.

Northern and arctic regions.   Richardson [11] says an infusion of the leaves and flowering tops was drunk by his party as a tea but it makes a less grateful beverage than *Ledum palustre*.

Rhodomyrtus tomentosa Wight.   *Myrtaceae*.   HILL GOOSEBERRY.   HILL GUAVE.

Tropical eastern Asia and the Malayan Archipelago.   In India, this species is found amongst the jungles of the Neilgherries.   Firminger [12] says the fruit, a pale, dirty yellow berry, is used for jellies.   In China, Pickering [13] says the fruit is eaten and preserved.

[1] Gronovius *Fl. Orient.* 49.   1755.

[2] Decaisne and Naudin *Man.* 4:190.

[3] Mueller, F.   *Sel. Pls.* 199.   1876.   (*R. rhaponticum*)

[4] Booth, W. B.   *Treas. Bot.* 2:972.   1870.

[5] Thorburn *Cat.*   1828.

[6] Decaisne and Naudin *Man.* 4:190.

[7] Brandis, D.   *Forest Fl.* 217.   1874.

[8] Masters, M. T.   *Treas. Bot.* 2:975.   1870.   (*R. mangle*)

[9] Brandis, D.   *Forest Fl.* 281.   1874.

[10] Royle, J. F.   *Illustr. Bot. Himal.* 1:259.   1839.

[11] Richardson, J.   *Arctic Explor.* 2:306.   1851.

[12] Firminger, T. A. C.   *Gard. Ind.* 264.   1874.   (*Myrtus tomentosa*)

[13] Pickering, C.   *Chron. Hist. Pls.* 745.   1879.   (*Myrtus tomentosa*)

Rhodymenia palmata Grev. *Algae.* DILLISK. DULSE.

This seaweed is the dulse of the Scotch and the dillisk of the Irish. It is much eaten in both countries, as well as in most of the northern states of Europe, by the poor along the shores and is transmitted as an article of humble luxury over most parts of the country. It is generally eaten raw, either fresh from the sea or after having been dried, but is sometimes cooked. It is exposed for sale in the markets of Irish towns and also in the Irish quarters of New York. In the Mediterranean, it forms a common ingredient in soups.[1]

Rhopalostylis sapida H. Wendl. & Drude. *Palmae.* NIKA PALM.

New Zealand. The natives eat the young inflorescence.[2]

Rhus albida Schousb. *Anacardiaceae.*

Arabia, Syria and northern Africa. The fruit is edible and is eaten as a condiment.[3]

R. aromatica Ait. FRAGRANT SUMACH.

Northern United States. According to Nuttall,[4] the drupes are acid and edible.

R. copallina Linn. DWARF SUMACH. MOUNTAIN SUMACH.

North America. Elliott[5] says the berries are possessed of an agreeable, acid taste and, infused in water, form a pleasant beverage. Pursh[6] says the leaves are used as tobacco by the Indians of the Missouri and Mississippi.

R. coriaria Linn. ELM-LEAVED SUMACH. TANNER'S SUMACH.

Mediterranean region and Persia. At Aleppo, the seeds are used as an appetizer at meals[7] as mustard is in Britain.[8] In India, Brandis[9] says the acid fruit is eaten. Pallas[10] says this is the *sumagh* or *redoul* of the Tartars and is employed by them as well as by the Turks in their meat broths, to which they impart a very agreeable acid.

R. cotinus Linn. SMOKE-PLANT.

Mediterranean region, the Orient, Himalayas and China. The leaves were used in China in the fourteenth century[11]

R. glabra Linn. SCARLET SUMACH. VINEGAR TREE.

North America. Emerson[12] says the velvety, crimson berries of this sumach are of an agreeable, acid taste and are sometimes used as a substitute for lemon juice. Kalm[13] says the boys of Philadelphia eat the berries but they are very sour.

[1] Harvey, W. H. *Phycol. Brit.* 2: Pl. CCXVIII. 1846–51.
[2] Seemann, B. *Pop. Hist. Palms* 60. 1856. (*Areca sapida*)
[3] Baillon, H. *Hist. Pls.* 5:300. 1878.
[4] Loudon, J. C. *Arb. Frut. Brit.* 2:557. 1844.
[5] Elliott, S. *Bot. So. Car., Ga.* 1:362. 1821.
[6] Pursh, F. *Fl. Amer. Septent.* 1:205. 1814.
[7] Don, G. *Hist. Dichl. Pls.* 2:71. 1832.
[8] Loudon, J. C. *Arb. Frut. Brit.* 2:554. 1844.
[9] Brandis, D. *Forest Fl.* 120. 1876.
[10] Pallas, P. S. *Trav. Russia* 2:210. 1803.
[11] Bretschneider, E. *Bot. Sin.* 52. 1882.
[12] Emerson, G. B. *Trees, Shrubs Mass.* 2:573. 1875.
[13] Kalm, P. *Trav. No. Amer.* 1:59. 1772.

R. integrifolia Benth. & Hook. f.

California.   The fresh, red berries are described by Palmer [1] as coated with an icy-looking, white substance, which is pleasantly acid and is used by the Indians to make a cooling drink.

R. parviflora Roxb.

India.   Mixed with salt, the fruit is used like tamarind in the Benar Valley and Bhawar.[2]

R. punjabensis J. L. Stew.

Himalayan region.   In India, the fruit is eaten.[3]

R. semialata Murr.   NUT-GALL TREE.

Eastern Asia.   The pulp of the fruit is acid and is eaten in Sikkim and Nepal and used medicinally.[4]

R. typhina Linn.   STAGHORN SUMACH.   VIRGINIAN SUMACH.

North America.   The leaves can be used as ordinary sumach, as Mueller [5] says.

Rhynchosia volubilis Lour.   *Leguminosae.*

China and Japan.   The seeds of the wild plant are used for food in Japan.[6, 7]

Ribes aciculare Sm.   *Saxifragaceae.*   NEEDLE-SPINED GOOSEBERRY.

Siberia.   The berries are glabrous, yellowish or purplish, sweet and of a grateful taste.[8]

R. alpinum Linn.   ALPINE CURRANT.

Europe and northern Asia.   The fruit is sweet and not very acid but is much less palatable than that of the red currant.[9]

R. ambiguum Maxim.

Japan.   The fruit is a large, orange-yellow berry nearly half an inch in diameter. The country people eat these berries.[10]

R. americanum Mill.   BLACK CURRANT.

North America.   Josselyn [11] says the black currants "are reasonably pleasant in eating." Emerson [12] says the fruit is black, watery and insipid.   In Nebraska, Thompson [13] says the fruit is large, musky but palatable.

---

[1] Brewer and Watson *Bot. Cal.* 1:111.   1880.

[2] Brandis, D.   *Forest Fl.* 119.   1874.

[3] Brandis, D.   *Forest Fl.* 120.   1874.

[4] Ibid.

[5] Mueller, F.   *Sel. Pls.* 418.   1891.

[6] Rein *Indust. Jap.* 62.   1889.

[7] Georgeson *Amer. Gard.* 14:84.   1893.

[8] Don, G.   *Hist. Dichl. Pls.* 3:178.   1834.

[9] Johnson, C. P.   *Useful Pls. Gt. Brit.* 109.   1862.

[10] Georgeson *Amer. Gard.* 12:205.   1891.

[11] Josselyn, J.   *Voy.* 59.   1865.   Reprint.

[12] Emerson, G. B.   *Trees, Shrubs Mass.* 2:478.   1875.   (*R. floridum*)

[13] Thompson, R. O.   *U. S. D. A. Rpt.* 126.   1866.   (*R. floridum*)

R. aureum Pursh. BUFFALO CURRANT. GOLDEN CURRANT. MISSOURI CURRANT.

Missouri and Columbia Rivers. This currant was brought by Lewis and Clark from the Rocky Mountains to our gardens, where it is now very common and admired for its fragrant, yellow blossoms. In Utah, this currant is extensively cultivated for its fruit, which is much like the black currant.[1] Its oval, blue berries are relished, says Downing, by some persons. Pursh[2] says the berries, red or brown, are of an exquisitely fine taste and larger than a garden currant. Both black and yellow varieties of this wild currant occur and are much used by the Indians of Colorado, Utah, Arizona, Texas, Oregon, California and Alaska

R. bracteosum Dougl. CALIFORNIAN BLACK CURRANT.

Western North America. At Sitka, the fruit is eaten.[3]

R. cynosbati Linn. DOG BRAMBLE. PRICKLY GOOSEBERRY.

Northern and western United States. The fruit is brownish-purple and eatable.

R. diacantha Pall. TWO-SPINED GOOSEBERRY.

Siberia. The berries are about the size of currants, red and of a sweetish-acid taste.[4]

R. divaricatum Dougl.

Northwest America. The berry, black, smooth, and spherical, one-third of an inch in diameter, is pleasant to the taste. The dried fruit furnishes winter food for the Indians.[5] Lindley[6] says that of all the species which came under his observation during his journeys in America, this was the finest in the flavor of its berries as well as in their size, being half an inch in diameter, sweet and juicy.

R. fragrans Pall. FRAGRANT-FLOWERED GOOSEBERRY.

Siberia and Tartary. This gooseberry bears red berries that are sweet and pleasant to the taste.

R. gracile Michx. SLENDER-BRANCHED GOOSEBERRY.

North America. Pursh[7] says the purple or blue berries of this species are of excellent taste. The berries are glabrous, purple or blue and of excellent flavor.[8] The fruit has a rich, subacid, vinous, rather perfumed flavor, which is extremely agreeable. It is rather too acid to be eaten raw but when ripe makes delicious tarts.[9]

R. griffithii Hook. f. & Thoms.

Himalayas at heights of 10,000 to 13,000 feet. The berries are somewhat austere in taste.[10]

---

[1] Case Bot. Index 10. Jan. 1881.

[2] Pursh, F. Fl. Amer. Septent. 1:164. 1814.

[3] Dall, W. H. U. S. D. A. Rpt. 187. 1868.

[4] Don, G. Hist. Dichl. Pls. 3:185. 1834.

[5] Brown, R. Bot. Soc. Edinb. 9:384. 1868.

[6] Douglas, D. Trans. Hort. Soc. Lond. 7:516. 1830. (R. irriguum)

[7] Pursh, F. Fl. Amer. Septent. 1:165. 1814.

[8] Loudon, J. C. Arb. Frut. Brit. 2:971. 1844.

[9] Lindley, J. Bot. Reg. Aug. 1834.

[10] Mueller, F. Sel. Pls. 419. 1891.

R. grossularia Linn. GOOSEBERRY.

Europe, North Africa and Himalayan region.   The gooseberry is a native of northern Europe and mountains farther south even to India.   This fruit is not alluded to by writers of the classical period.   It is mentioned by Turner,[1] 1573; and Parkinson,[2] 1629, specifies eight varieties, while now, in England, where it is a popular fruit, the varieties are enumerated by the hundreds.   In 1882, the Leveller variety with a berry weighing 818 grains was exhibited in England.[3]   On the continent of Europe, this species is little cultivated, and with us, says Downing,[4] south of Philadelphia, it succeeds but indifferently.   In the eastern states, on strong soils, when the best sorts are chosen, it thrives admirably.   On account however, of the mildew, the English varieties have now been almost entirely superceded, by those of American origin.

R. hudsonianum Richards. HUDSON BAY CURRANT.

Northern North America.   At Yukon, this species offers a fruit that is edible.[5]

R. lacustre Poir. SWAMP GOOSEBERRY.

Northern America.   In Utah, the fruit seems to be eaten; in Alaska, the fruit is poor but is used.[6]

R. magellanicum Poir.

Fuego.   This is a tall shrub with black fruit, which is said by Hooker [7] to have a very agreeable flavor.

R. menziesii Pursh.

Western North America.   The fruit is utilized by the inhabitants of southern California in making jams.[8]

R. nigrum Linn. BLACK CURRANT.

Europe and northern Asia.   The black currant is said by Pickering [9] to be a native of northeastern America, but most authors say of Europe and Siberia.   It is common wild, says Loudon,[10] in woods in Russia and Siberia.   The shrub is cultivated for its fruit, which is valued for jelly-making.   The fruit is sometimes used as dessert, and, in Scotland, the berries are eaten in puddings and tarts.   In Russia and Ireland, they are put into spirits, as cherries are in England.[11]   The leaves, when dried, have been used as a tea substitute.

R. oxyacanthoides Linn. SMOOTH WILD GOOSEBERRY.

Northern America.   This is the gooseberry probably seen by Smith in New England

---

[1] Darwin, C.   *Ans. Pls. Domest.* 1:376.   1893.

[2] Ibid.

[3] *Gard. Chron.* 466.   1882.

[4] Downing, A. J.   *Fr. Fr. Trees Amer.* 294.   1857.

[5] Dall, W. H.   *U. S. D. A. Rpt.* 187.   1868.

[6] Ibid.

[7] Gray, A.   *U. S. Explor. Exped.* 662.   1854.

[8] Palmer   *U. S. Nat. Mus.* 1:   1890.

[9] Pickering, C.   *Chron. Hist. Pls.* 871.   1879.

[10] Loudon, J. C.   *Hort.* 567.   1860.

[11] Ibid.

in 1609 and mentioned by Edward Winslow [1] among the wild fruits of Massachusetts in 1621, also by Wood,[2] 1629-33. The fruit is smooth, small, purple, sweet and pleasant flavored and is much used by the Indians of Colorado, Arizona, Oregon, California and Utah.[3] To this species may be referred the gooseberries of American origin, now so generally cultivated. Houghton's Seedling, one of the first, was disseminated in 1848 and was exhibited at the Massachusetts Horticultural Society in 1847.

R. procumbens Pall.

Siberia. The berries are very grateful to the taste and are rufescent when ripe.[4]

R. prostratum L'Herit. FETID CURRANT.

Northern America. The fruit is black, watery and insipid. It is, however, eaten in Alaska.[5]

R. rotundifolium Michx. ROUND-LEAVED GOOSEBERRY.

North America. Wood [6] says the purple fruit is delicious. Fuller [7] says it is smooth and pleasant flavored. In the *Flora of North America*,[8] the fruit is said to be about the size of the black currant, purple in color and delicious. In Illinois, it is a good deal cultivated for its fruit.[9]

R. rubrum Linn. RED CURRANT.

Northern countries, extending southward along mountain ranges. While in some regions its fruit is nauseous and unpalatable, in others it has received commendation for the purposes of a jelly. These contrasts show the currant to be a plant variable in nature. As a cultivated plant, it began to receive notice in England towards the close of the sixteenth century; it is not enumerated in Tusser's list of 1557 but is noticed by Gerarde in 1597 as appearing in the London markets, but he gives it no English name and no very particular description. In 1586, however, Lyte gives the English names as Red Gooseberryes and Bastarde Corinthes; the word *currans* appears in Lovell, 1665, and Ray, 1686, uses our word currants. "Currant plants" were mentioned in the Memorandum of March 16, 1629, of seeds and plants to be provided for the New England colonists. The spelling of the word probably did not become fixed for some time, as Evelyn in his translation of Quintyne, 1693, yet uses the word *currans*. McIntosh says the first mention of *corans*, our currant, is by Bacon, who says, "The earliest fruits are strawberries, gooseberries, corans, etc."

By the herbalists and early writers on horticulture, the first mention of the currant is by Ruellius,[10] 1536, a French author, who praises it as a border plant and its fruit as an

---

[1] Young, A. *Chron. Pilgr.* 234. 1841.

[2] Wood, W. *New Eng. Prosp.* Prince Soc. Ed. 15. 1865.

[3] *U. S. D. A. Rpt.* 414. 1870.

[4] Loudon, J. C. *Arb. Frut. Brit.* 2:981. 1844.

[5] Dall, W. H. *U. S. D. A. Rpt.* 187. 1868.

[6] Wood, A. *Class Book Bot.* 362. 1864.

[7] Fuller *Sm. Fr. Cult.* 215. 1867.

[8] Gray, A. *Fl. No. Amer.* 1:547. 1840.

[9] *Amer. Pom. Soc. Rpt.* 97. 1871.

[10] Ruellius *Nat. Stirp.* 283. 1536.

appetizer.   In 1539, Ammonius[1] says " we cherish it in our gardens," but adds nothing of further interest in this connection.   Fuchsius,[2] 1542, gives a figure which may be called a poor specimen of the Common Red and which resembles certain seedlings which are now frequently obtained.   Tragus,[3] 1552, gives a figure of the garden currant, which may well be the Common Red.   In 1558, Matthiolus[4] refers to it as common in gardens and it is also spoken of by Mizaldus[5] in 1560.   Pinaeus, 1561,[6] gives a figure which may be that of a Common Red, while Lobel,[7] 1576 and 1591, offers figures which are to be called Common Red, but which are of a far better appearance than those heretofore figured and mentions also a sweet kind.   Lyte's translation of *Dodoens*, edition of 1586, speaks of the currant in England, but translates one name as " beyond the sea " gooseberry.   This same year, 1586, Camerarius[8] figures the Common Red, as does Dalechamp[9] in 1587. The next year, Camerarius[10] gives directions for sowing the seed of the wild plant in gardens and says these seedlings quickly come to fruit.   We have hence the first clue as to how new varieties might originate, if this recommendation was generally followed. Camerarius also refers to a larger-fruited currant than common that was growing in the gardens of the Archduke of Austria.   This is the first indication of improvement in varieties, such as might well be anticipated from the practice of growing seedlings.   This *Ribes bacci rubris majoribus* may perhaps be considered as the Red Dutch variety, or at least its prototype.   In 1597, Gerarde,[11] as before stated, scarcely recognized the currant as being in general culture in England, but the next year, or 1598, brings us to what may well be called a picture of the Red Dutch variety, given in Bauhin's edition of Matthiolus, as also a mention of a white-fruited variety and another described as sweet.

In these early days the exchange of plants might be expected to be in their most condensed state, that is as seeds.   We have noted the appearance of a new variety of the currant, and now, as we examine the records of the next century, we shall find additional records of improved varieties just as if the advice of growing seedlings had been followed, and the better forms gained had been propagated by cuttings.

In 1601, Clusius[12] speaks of a sweet variety found growing wild upon the Alps and differing not at all, as his figure also shows, from the Common Red; and of a larger-fruited sort with a red flower, which may not be our species, yet he believes the variety was grown in the gardens of Brussels.   He also refers to a white-fruited sort, but what this may be is quite doubtful from the context.   In 1613, we have some fine drawings of the currant

[1] Ammonius *Med. Hort.* 310.   1539.

[2] Fuchsius *Hist. Stirp.* 662.   1542.

[3] Tragus *Stirp.* 994.   1552.

[4] Matthiolus *Comment.* 101.   1558.

[5] Mizaldus *Secret.* 105.   1560.

[6] Pinaeus *Hist. Pl.* 67.   1561.

[7] Lobel *Obs.* 615.   1576; *Icon.* 2:202.   1591.

[8] Camerarius *Epit.* 88.   1586.

[9] Dalechamp *Hist. Gen. Pl.* (Lugd.) 1:131.   1587.

[10] Camerarius *Hort. Med.* 141.   1588.

[11] Gerarde, J.   *Herb.* 1143.   1597.

[12] Clusius *Hist.* 1:119.   1601.

in the *Hortus Eystettensis*,[1] representing unmistakably highly improved forms, and these varieties may well be called the Common Red, the Red Dutch and the White Dutch. The Large Red is said to be the same as the large-fruited sort described by Clusius. Dodonaeus,[2] 1616, figures what may be called the Common Red, as common in gardens and useful for topiary work. In 1623, Bauhin[3] names the Common Red, the Sweet-fruited Red, the Red Dutch and the White Dutch (for so we interpret the types) under Latin names and synonyms and says, at Florence, he had seen fruit larger than a hazelnut. J. Bauhin,[4] in his history of plants, published in 1651 but written long before, for he died in 1613, figures what may be the Common Red and describes what may be the Red Dutch and the White Dutch. In 1654, Swertius[5] figures the Common Red and two very fine, large sorts, which we may call the Red and White Dutch type, yet somewhat larger. Jonstonus,[6] 1662, figures the Common Red and, as a compiler, makes mention of the Large Red and White. In 1665, Lovell[7] speaks of the Red and White in gardens in England. In 1677, Chabraeus[8] figures the Common Red, and Pancovius,[9] 1673, what may be the Red Dutch. Turre,[10] 1685, refers to two sorts, the Red and White, as growing among the hills of Italy, but the latter the more infrequent. In 1686, Ray[11] describes the three forms, the Common, the Large Red and the White, while in 1690, Quintyne[12] mentions the Red and White Dutch by name, and Meager[13] gives directions for growing the White.

In the eighteenth century, we have like mention by botanists of the large and small forms, both red and white, and come to the use of common names for varieties. In 1757, Blackwell's *Herbarium* represents in colors what may be the Common Red, Common White, and the Red Dutch in Germany; Salberg and Trenborg, 1763 and 1764, name the Red and White Currant for Sweden; and Langley, in his *Pomona*, 1729, speaks only of Red and White Dutch in England. Mawe's *Gardener*, 1778, under Ribes, names for varieties in England, the Common Small Red, Large Red Dutch, Long-bunched Red, Champagne Pale Red, Common Small White, Large White Dutch, Yellow Blotched-leaved, Silver-striped-leaved, Gold-striped-leaved and Gooseberry-leaved.

In 1807, *Miller's Dictionary* names the Common Red, Common White, Champagne, White Dutch and Red Dutch. In 1834, Don[14] names 13 sorts as under English cultivation. Downing describes in the various editions of his exhaustive work on fruit culture 8 varieties

---

[1] *Hortus Eystet.* 1713; an edition corresponding to that of 1613.
[2] Dodonaeus *Pempt.* 748. 1616.
[3] Bauhin, C. *Pinax.* 455. 1623.
[4] Bauhin, J. *Hist. Pl.* 11, 98. 1651.
[5] Sweertius *Floril.* t. 33. 1654.
[6] Jonstonus *Dendrograph.* 221. 1662.
[7] Lovell *Herb.* 118. 1665.
[8] Chabraeus *Sciag.* and *Icon.* 112. 1677.
[9] Pancovius *Herb.* 1673.
[10] Turre *Dryadum.* 588. 1685.
[11] Ray *Hist. Pl.* 11, 1486. 1686.
[12] Quintyne *Comp. Gard.* Evelyn Ed. 143. 1693.
[13] Meager *Eng. Gard.* 45. 1683.
[14] Don, G. *Hist. Dichl. Pls.* 111, 188. 1834.

in 1856, 25 varieties in 1866 and 23 varieties in 1885. The *Report of the American Pomological Society* for 1883 names as worthy of culture the following: Angers, Cherry, Fay's Prolific, Knight's Red, Palluau, Prince Albert, Red Dutch, Red Grape, Versailles, Victoria White Dutch and White Grape, or 12 varieties in all.

The currant fruit has not changed at all in type under culture, but has furnished variety characteristics in increased size, diminished seed and improved quality. The wild plant bears currants like those of the cultivated, but more seedy and fewer on the bunch. Removed to the garden and placed under protective influences, the plant becomes more upright and more prolific and the bunches better filled, but the berries are no larger than those that may be found in the woods. Seedlings in general present the characters of but a slightly improved wild plant. Some individuals bear bunches but little, if at all, better than those borne by selected wild plants, and it is doubtful whether, from the examination of plants, botanists could determine whether a given plant was truly wild or but an escape from cultivation. If the testimony of the herbalists be credited, red, white and sweet currants are found in nature. Hence we may believe that these natural varieties are the prototypes of those that occur in gardens, and that horticultural gain has been only in that expansion which comes from high culture, protective influence and selection propagated by cutting or division.

The currant reached Massachusetts [1] from England about 1529, and this would indicate its culture in the British Isles, yet, as before stated, the currant does not appear in Tusser's list of fruits in 1557, nor in Turner's *Libellus* 1538, is scarcely mentioned by Gerarde in 1597, and in Lyte's English translation of *Dodoens* is distinguished by the English names " Red Gooseberries, Beyond-sea Gooseberries, Bastarde Corinthes and Common ribes." Plat's *Garden of Eden*, 1653, does not mention currants, although it purports to give " an accurate description of all Flowers and Fruits now growing in England," yet Parkinson's *Paradisus*, published in 1629, mentions the red and the white sorts. The French and Dutch names of *transmarina* or *outre mer* or *over zee* in various combinations indicate that the plant was brought from beyond their boundaries, while the old French name of *ribetts*, as given by Pinaeus, 1561, Cameraius, 1586, and Castor Durante, 1617, seems derived from the Danish *ribs* and Swedish *resp* or *risp*. In general, however, the vernacular name in the various countries was founded upon the generic name of the gooseberry. De Candolle thinks the currant reached culture from the Danes or the Normans, that is from the northern countries, and in this opinion we concur. It seems, moreover, quite certain that the improved currant originated in the Low Countries, whence it received distribution where better varieties were appreciated.

The botanical names and synonyms of the currant are:

I.

Common Red.

This type differs but slightly from the wild form, the bunches being slightly larger and usually better filled, or in some cases not differing. It may be considered as the wild form improved by slight selection and high culture.

---

[1] *Mass. Records* **1**:24. 1853.

Ribes rubrum. Linn. *Sp.* 290. 2nd Ed.

Rubra grossula vel transmarina. Ruell. 283. 1536.

Ribes. Ammon. 310. 1539; Fuch. 663. *fig.* 1542; Chabr. 112. *fig.* 1677.

Ribes hortense. Trag. 995. *fig.* 1552.

Ribes officin. Matth. 101. 1558.

Grossula seu grosella rubra vel transmarina. Miz. *Secret.* 105. 1560.

Ribes vulgaria. Pin. 67. *fig.* 1561; Cam. *Epit.* 88. *fig.* 1586.

Ribes Arabum. Lob. *Obs.* 615. *fig.* 1576; *Icon.* **2**:202. 1591.

Grossulae rubrae, Ribes rubrum. Lyte. *Dod.* 792. 1586.

Grossularia rubra. **1**:131. *fig.* 1587. Dalechamp.

Ribes vulgare baccis rubris. Cam. *Hort.* 141. 1588.

Ribes rubra vulgaris. *Hort. Eyst. fig.* 1613.

Ribesium rubentis baccae. Dod. 748. *fig.* 1616.

Grossularia multiplici acino, sive non spinosa hortensis rubra, sive Bibes officinarum. Bauh. C. *Pin.* 455. 1623.

Ribes vulgaris acidus ruber. Bauh. J. 11, 97. *fig.* 1651.

Ribes rubra minor. Sweert. t. 33. *fig.* 2. 1654.

Grossularia non spinosa hortensis acino multiplici rubra vulgaris sive Ribes officinarium. Jonst. 221. *fig.* 1662.

Ribes rubra, Turre. 588. 1685. Jonst. 221. *fig.* 1662.

Ribes vulgaris fructu rubro. Ray *Hist.* 11, 1485. 1688.

II.
COMMON WHITE.

This type also occurs in our references as a wild form which has been brought under culture. Ray in his synonyms refers to the *Ribes vulgaris fructu albo,* as does Gerarde, 2nd ed., 1630, which is probably this form.

Ribes vulgaris acidur, albas baccas ferens. Bauh, J. 11, 98. 1651; Ray *Hist.* 11, 1486. 1688.

Ribes alba. Turre, 588. 1685.

III.
LARGE-FRUITED RED.

This is an improved variety and in its historical references is carried forward to the Red Dutch.

Ribes baccis rubris majorib. Cam. *Hort.* 141. 1588.

Ribes vulgaris. Matth. *Op.* 151. *fig.* 1598.

Grossularia majore fructu. Clus. *Hist.* **1**:120. 1601.

Ribes fructu rubro, majore. *Hort. Eyst. fig.* 1613; Ray *Hist.* 11. 1486. 1688.

Grossularis hortensis majore fructu rubro. Bauh. C. *Pin.* 455. 1623.

Ribes rubra major. Sweert. t. 33. *fig.* 3. 1654.

Ribes. Pancov. 341. *fig.* 1674.

Red Dutch. Quint. 143. 1693.

IV.
LARGE-FRUITED WHITE.

This is an improved form of the Common White.

Ribes . . . . *unionum instar.* Matth. *Op.* 1. 32. 152. 1598.

Ribes fructu albo. *Hort. Eyst. fig.* 1613.

Grossularia hortensis fructu margaritas simili. Bauh. C. *Pin.* 455. 1623. (excel. Clus.)

Ribes alba. Sweert. t. 33, p. 1. 1654.
Grossularia non spinosa, fructu margaritis similis. Jonst. 221. 1662.
White Dutch. Quint. 143. 1693.

V.

SWEET.

The figure of Clusius shows this fruit to be the Common Red in form of plant and berry. Sweet-fruited currants, or currants not as acid as other sorts, are known among our modern varieties, and Ray in his *Synopsis*, 1724, mentions sweet currants of the common species as in Lord Ferrer's garden at Stanton, Leicestershire, England, brought from the neighboring woods.

Ribes . . . . fructu dulci. Matth. *Op.* 152, 1. 31. 1598.
Ribes vulgaris fructu dulce. Clus. *Hist.* 5, 119, *fig.* 1601.
Grossularia vulgaris fructu dulci. Bauh. C. *Pin.* 455. 1623. (exc. Eyst.)

This review of the history of the currant shows that the types of our cultivated varieties have existed in nature and have been removed to gardens. We have no evidence that these cultivated varieties have originated by gradual improvement under cultivation. When we come to subvarieties, we conclude that these have undoubtedly originated in gardens, or at least have been disseminated from gardens. The influence of fertile soil and sunlight upon growth would be to effect a greater prolificacy and increased size of bunches; through seedlings, and the process of selection, perhaps continued through successive generations, these plants which originate larger fruit might have been preserved and propagated. In the first woodcut, that by Fuchsius in 1542, we have apparently the normal wild currant grown under protected conditions; in Castor Durante, 1585, a figure which suggests an improvement over Fuchsius; in 1588, the appearance of the prototype or the original of the Red Dutch. We may hence say that the currant received its modern improved form between 1542 and 1588, or within 46 years. This amelioration of a wild fruit within such a limited period should serve for encouragement and should emphasize the belief, warranted also by the study of other fruits and vegetables, that the seeking of wild prototypes of varieties, and intelligent growing and selecting seedlings, might give great improvement, even within the lifetime of the experimenter, in the case of other wild fruits.

To this conclusion our argument leads, yet the fact attained may be stated more concisely, that, in the currant as in the American grape, the improved variety came directly through selecting the wild variation and transferring it to the garden, or from a direct seminal variation from the seed of the common kind.

R. saxatile Pall. ROCK GOOSEBERRY.

Siberia. The berries are smooth, globose, dark purple when ripe and full of edible pulp. The acid fruit, mixed with water, forms a refreshing drink.[1]

R. setosum Lindl. BRISTLY GOOSEBERRY. MISSOURI GOOSEBERRY.

North America. The berries are black, spherical and hispid, with a subacid, pleasant flavor, a little musky.[2]

---

[1] Pickering, C. *Chron. Hist. Pls.* 582. 1879.
[2] Lindley, J. *Trans. Hort. Soc. Lond.* **7**:243. 1830.

Ricinus communis Linn. *Euphorbiaceae.* CASTOR OIL PLANT.

Tropics. In China, S. Wells Williams [1] says castor oil is used in cooking. Smith [2] says in his *Materia Medica of China* that a species or variety of Ricinus is said to have smooth fruit and to be innocuous.

Robinia flava Lour. *Leguminosae.*

North China. The taste of the root is sweetish and mucilaginous and would seem to justify, says Smith, [3] its consumption as a food in times of scarcity, as mentioned for China in the *Pen Ts'au.*

R. pseud-acacia Linn. FALSE ACACIA. LOCUST.

South Pennsylvania, southward along the mountains and naturalized in some other places. Yellow locust is commonly cultivated as an ornamental tree. The seeds, upon pressure, yield a large quantity of oil. They are quite acid but lose this quality upon boiling; they furnish a pleasant, nutritious article of food, much esteemed by the aborigines. [4]

Rollinia sieberi A. DC. *Anonaceae.* SUGAR APPLE.

Mexico. This is one of the fruit trees cultivated in the Public Gardens of Jamaica. [5] It is also cultivated in the Moluccas. The flesh of the fruit is very soft and of an unpleasant taste. [6]

R. sylvatica Warm.

Brazil. The plant is called *araticu do mato* and its fruit is good to eat. [7]

Rosa acicularis Lindl. *Rosaceae.*

Northern Asia and North America. In the Amur country, a much larger and better fruit than that of *R. canina* is afforded by this species. [8]

R. canina Linn. BRIER ROSE. DOG-BRIER.

Europe and temperate Asia. The fruits of this wild rose have a scanty, orange, acid, edible pulp and were collected in ancient times in Europe when garden fruits were few and scarce. Galen [9] mentions them as gathered by country people in his day, as they still are in Europe. Gerarde [10] remarks that " the fruit when it is ripe makes most pleasant meats and banqueting dishes, as tarts and such like." [11] Lightfoot [12] says the pulp of the

---

[1] Williams, S. W. *U. S. Pat. Off. Rpt.* 474. 1860.

[2] Smith, F. P. *Contrib. Mat. Med. China* 55. 1871.

[3] Smith, F. P. *Contrib. Mat. Med. China* 51. 1871.

[4] Millspaugh *Amer. Med. Pls.* 1: No. 50. 1. 1887.

[5] Morris *Rpt. Pub. Gard. Jam.* 35. 1880.

[6] Don, G. *Hist. Dichl. Pls.* 1:89. 1831. (*Anona mucosa*)

[7] Don, G. *Hist. Dichl. Pls.* 1:88. 1831.

[8] Flückiger and Hanbury *Pharm.* 268. 1879.

[9] Flückiger and Hanbury *Pharm.* 238. 1879.

[10] Ibid.

[11] Ibid.

[12] Lightfoot, J. *Fl. Scot.* 1:262. 1789.

fruit separated from the seeds and mixed with wine and sugar, makes a jelly much esteemed in some countries. Johnson [1] says the leaves have been used as a tea substitute.

R. centifolia Linn. CABBAGE ROSE.

In China, the blossoms are used for scenting tea.[2]

R. cinnamomea Linn. CINNAMON ROSE.

North temperate zone. The berries, or seed capsules, are eaten, says Dall,[3] by the Alaska Indians. They are sweet and juicy. The fruit is eaten by the Kamchatkians.[4]

R. fraxinellaefolia Andr. ASH-LEAVED ROSE.

Western Oregon. The haws are eaten by the Indians of the Cascade Mountains [5] and by the Nez Percés.[6] R. Brown [7] says the tender shoots in the spring are eaten by the Indians.

R. macrophylla Lindl.

Himalayan region and China. In India, Brandis [8] says the fruit is eaten.

R. nutkana Presl.

Northern Pacific coast to the Rocky Mountains. The fruit is juicy, pleasantly acidulous and is an excellent antiscorbutic for the Alaska Indians.[9]

R. rubiginosa Linn. EGLANTINE. SWEETBRIAR.

Europe and Caucasus. Berries of this species are collected and sold in Norway.[10]

R. rugosa Thunb. TURKESTAN ROSE.

Eastern Asia. This rose is called *mau*, or in Japanese *humanasi*, and the fruit is generally eaten by the Ainos.[11]

R. semperflorens Curt. MONTHLY ROSE. RED CHINA ROSE.

China. The Chinese serve the flowers of this rose dressed whole, as a ragout.[12]

R. spinosissima Linn. BURNET ROSE.

Europe and Asia Minor. The deep purple fruit of this rose, so abundant on sandy shores in Britain, is very sweet and pleasant to the taste.[13]

R. villosa Linn.

Europe and Asia. The fruit has a pleasant, acid pulp, which is sometimes served at dessert in the form of conserves or sweetmeats.

[1] Johnson, C. P. *Useful Pls. Gt. Brit.* 97. 1862.

[2] Rein *Indust. Jap.* 123. 1889.

[3] Dall, W. H. *U. S. D. A. Rpt.* 178. 1868.

[4] Pickering, C. *Chron. Hist. Pls.* 417. 1879. (*R. kamtchatica*)

[5] *U. S. D. A. Rpt.* 415. 1870.

[6] Irving, W. *Advent. Capt. Bonneville* 99. 1849.

[7] Brown, R. *Bot. Soc. Edinb.* 9:385. 1868.

[8] Brandis, D. *Forest Fl.* 203. 1874.

[9] Havard, V. *Torr. Bot. Club Bul.* 22:122. 1895.

[10] *Gard. Chron.* 823. 1857.

[11] Pickering, C. *Chron. Hist. Pls.* 417. 1879.

[12] Davis *Journ. Lond. Hort. Soc.* 9:262. 1855.

[13] Johnson, C. P. *Useful Pls. Gt. Brit.* 97. 1862.

Rosmarinus officinalis Linn. *Labiatae.* ROSEMARY.

West Mediterranean countries and grown in gardens for its use in flavoring meats and soups. This aromatic herb had many virtues ascribed to it by Pliny and is also mentioned by Dioscorides and Galen. Rosemary was also familiar to the Arab physicians of Spain in the thirteenth century and is mentioned in an Anglo-Saxon herbal of the eleventh century.[1] The first notice of its use as a condiment is by Lignamine, 1475,[2] who describes rosemary as the usual condiment with salted meats. In 1783, rosemary is described by Bryant[3] as so common in gardens as to be known to every one. It finds mention in nearly all the earlier botanies. In 1778, Mawe[4] names four varieties: Common Narrow-leaved, Broad-leaved, the Silver-striped and Gold-striped-leaved. It was in American gardens in 1806 or earlier.

Roupellia grata Wall. & Hook. *Apocynaceae.* CREAM-FRUIT.

Tropical Africa. In Sierra Leone, this plant affords a delicious fruit, according to Henfrey.[5]

Rubus arcticus Linn. *Rosaceae.* ARCTIC BRAMBLE. CRIMSON BRAMBLE.

Northern and arctic regions. This species, says Loudon,[6] has a highly flavored fruit. In Lapland, its fruit is valued and is extolled by Linnaeus. In northern Scandinavia, the fruit is delicious, having the aroma of the pineapple.[7] It affords in Labrador, says Pursh,[8] amber-colored, very delicious fruit. In Alaska, the berries are eaten.[9] The western Eskimo, according to Seemann,[10] use the berries of this species as a winter food. They are collected in autumn and frozen.

R. biflorus Buch.-Ham.

India and Himalayas up to 10,000 feet. The fruit is either red or orange.[11]

R. borbonicus Pers.

The fruit is like that of *R. caesius* Linn.[12]

R. buergeri Miq.

Japan. In Japan, this species furnishes edible fruit.[13]

R. caesius Linn. DEWBERRY OF ENGLAND.

Europe, Orient and northern Asia. The fruit is small, says Loudon,[14] with few grains but these are large, juicy, black, with a fine, glaucous bloom and are very agreeably acid.

---

[1] Flückiger and Hanbury *Pharm.* 488. 1879.

[2] Ibid.

[3] Bryant *Fl. Diet.* 141. 1783.

[4] Mawe and Abercrombie *Univ. Gard. Bot.* 1778.

[5] Henfrey, A. *Bot.* 317. 1870.

[6] Loudon, J. C. *Hort.* 569. 1860.

[7] Du Chaillu *Land Midnight Sun* 1:152. 1882.

[8] Pursh, F. *Fl. Amer. Septent.* 1:349. 1814.

[9] Dall, W. H. *U. S. D. A. Rpt.* 187. 1868.

[10] Seemann, B. *Anthrop. Journ.* 3: CCCIII. 1865. (*R. acaulis*)

[11] Mueller, F. *Sel. Pls.* 427. 1891.

[12] Don, G. *Hist. Dichl. Pls.* 2:530. N. 14. 1832.

[13] Georgeson *Amer. Gard.* 12:204. 1891.

[14] Loudon, J. C. *Arb. Frut. Brit.* 2:739. 1844.

By some it is preferred for cultivation on account of its fruit.   Johnson [1] says the berries are far superior in flavor to the ordinary bramble.

R. canadensis Linn. DEWBERRY. LOW BLACKBERRY. TRAILING BLACKBERRY.

Eastern North America. This trailing plant often furnishes a fine fruit, which is generally preferred to that of other blackberries. The fruit varies from half an inch to an inch in diameter and is very sweet and juicy, high-flavored and excellent.

R. chamaemorus Linn. BAKEAPPLE. CLOUDBERRY. MOLKA. SALMONBERRY. YELLOW-
BERRY.

Northern and arctic climates. The fruit is large, yellow or amber-colored, sweet and juicy. Geo. Lawson says it is brought abundantly to the Halifax markets.[2] This species furnishes winter food to the western Eskimos, who collect the berries in autumn and preserve them by freezing.[3] The fruit is also preserved by the Indians of Alaska.[4] The Swedes and Norwegians preserve great quantities of the fruit in the autumn to make tarts and other confections,[5] and, in Sweden, vinegar is made by fermenting the berries. The Laplanders preserve the berries by burying them in the snow.[6]

R. corchorifolius Linn. f.

Japan. The fruit is edible, according to Kinch.[7] The species furnishes an edible fruit.[8]

R. crataegifolius Bunge.

China. This species is said in *Transon's Trade Catalogue* of 1880–81 [9] to have been introduced into France from Manchuria some years ago. In July it gives a great quantity of transparent, scarlet fruits, the taste of which is sugary and agreeable.

R. cuneifolius Pursh. SAND BLACKBERRY.

Long Island to Florida. Pursh [10] says the berries are hard and dry; Elliott,[11] that they are juicy and eatable; Wood,[12] that they are black, juicy and well-flavored; Gray [13] calls them well-flavored; Fuller [14] says the fruit is of medium size, good flavor, black and ripens late.

R. deliciosus Torr. ROCKY MOUNTAIN RASPBERRY.

Western North America. The fruit is delicious, according to Torrey. In Colorado, it is a fine fruit of peculiar flavor.[15]

[1] Johnson, C. P. *Useful Pls. Gt. Brit.* 90. 1862.

[2] *Gard. Chron.* 18:716. 1882.

[3] Seemann, B. *Anthrop. Journ.* 3: CCCIII. 1865.

[4] Dall, W. H. *U. S. D. A. Rpt.* 178. 1868.

[5] Lightfoot, J. *Fl. Scot.* 1:267. 1879.

[6] Johnson, C. P. *Useful Pls. Gt. Brit.* 91. 1862.

[7] Rein *Indust. Jap.* 92. 1889.

[8] Georgeson *Amer. Gard.* 12:204. 1891.

[9] Transon *Nurs. Cat.* 23. 1880–81. Orleans, France.

[10] Pursh, F. *Fl. Amer. Septent.* 1:347. 1814.

[11] Elliott, S. *Bot. So. Car., Ga.* 1:568. 1821.

[13] Wood, A. *Class Book Bot.* 339. 1855.

[13] Gray, A. *Man. Bot.* 158. 1868.

[14] Fuller *Sm. Fr. Cult.* 169. 1867.

[15] Thompson, R. O. *U. S. D. A. Rpt.* 126. 1866.

R. fruticosus Linn. BRAMBLE. BUMBLEKITES. EUROPEAN BLACKBERRY. SCALDBERRY.

Europe, north and south Africa, middle and northern Asia.[1] The fruits in some parts of England are called bumblekites and in others scaldberries and have been eaten by children, says Loudon,[2] in every country where they grow wild since the time of Pliny. The fruit, says Johnson,[3] is wholesome and pleasant. The berries are sometimes fermented into a wine of very indifferent quality and, abroad, are sometimes used for coloring more generous liquor. The Red Muscat wine of Toulon owes its tint to the juice of blackberries. In China, the berries are gathered and eaten.[4]

R. geoides Sm.

Magellan, Falkland Islands, Fuego, Patagonia and Chiloe. This species is a raspberry-like plant, with greenish-yellow fruits resembling the cloudberry and is of a very agreeable taste.[5]

R. gunnianus Hook.

Tasmania. The fruit is red and juicy but not always well-developed.[6]

R. hawaiensis A. Gray.

Sandwich Islands. The fruit is ovoid, half an inch in length and breadth, red and edible.[7]

R. hispidus Linn. RUNNING BLACKBERRY. SWAMP BLACKBERRY.

Northern America. The fruit consists of a few large grains, red or purple, and sour.[8] The fruit is quite good tasting but is not worth picking in the presence of better varieties.

R. idaeus Linn. EUROPEAN RASPBERRY. FRAMBOISE.

Europe, Orient and northern Asia and thrives as far north as 70° in Scandinavia.[9] This species furnishes the European varieties of the cultivated raspberry and those cultivated in American gardens prior to about 1866.[10] This species is now occasionally found wild, as an escape, in Vermont and Connecticut.[11] The fruit of the wild plant is crimson or amber-colored; this is the raspberry of European gardens.[12] According to Unger,[13] this species is mentioned by Palladius as a cultivated plant. Unger says further that " there are now varieties grown with red fruit, yellow fruit and white fruit and those which bear twice in the year." [14] The fruit of this berry has been found in the debris of the lake

---

[1] Mueller, F. *Sel. Pls.* 429. 1891.
[2] Loudon, J. C. *Arb. Frut. Brit.* 2:743. 1844.
[3] Johnson, C. P. *Useful Pls. Gt. Brit.* 89. 1862.
[4] Smith, F. P. *Contrib. Mat. Med. China* 188. 1871.
[5] Mueller, F. *Sel. Pls.* 428. 1891.
[6] Mueller, F. *Sel. Pls.* 206. 1876.
[7] Gray, A. *U. S. Explor. Exped.* 505. 1854.
[8] Gray, A. *Man. Bot.* 158. 1868.
[9] Du Chaillu *Land Midnight Sun* 1:152. 1882.
[10] Downing, A. J. *Fr. Fr. Trees Amer.* 655. 1857.
[11] Wood, A. *Class Book Bot.* 340. 1864.
[12] Babington, C. C. *Brit. Rubi* 43. 1869.
[13] Unger, F. *U. S. Pat. Off. Rpt.* 347. 1859.
[14] Loudon, J. C. *Arb. Frut. Brit.* 2:737. 1844.

villages of Switzerland.[1] In 1867, Fuller[2] describes 41 varieties known to American gardens and 23 which are from native American species. As types of this class of cultivated fruit, we may mention the Antwerp, brought to this country about 1820; the Franconia, introduced from France about 1850; Brinckle's Orange, originated in Pennsylvania in 1845, and Clarke, raised from seed at New Haven, Connecticut, in 1856.

R. imperialis Cham. et Schlecht.

Brazil. The fruit is edible.[3]

R. incisus Thunb.

China and Japan. The fruit is small, bluish-black and of no great merit. Country people hold the berries in great esteem.[4]

R. jamaicensis Linn.

Tropical America. The berries are black and very agreeable. If pickled when red and unripe, they make an excellent tart.[5]

R. laciniatus Willd. CUT-LEAVED BLACKBERRY. EVERGREEN BLACKBERRY. PARSLEY-LEAVED BLACKBERRY.

This species has been sparingly cultivated in Europe for many years and in this country since 1845. It is scarcely worth growing, says Fuller,[6] except as a curiosity, but others say the fruit is large and juicy and that this plant is worthy a place in the garden.[7]

R. lasiocarpus Sm. HILL RASPBERRY. MYSORE RASPBERRY.

India. This species is cultivated in India for its fruits, which are of excellent flavor and are used in tarts, according to Firminger.[8] Brandis[9] says the fruit is very good to eat, and Royle[10] says that it is called *kul-anchoo* and affords a grateful fruit.

R. leucodermis Dougl.

Northwest America. The fruit is yellowish-red, rather large, with a white bloom and agreeable flavor[11] and is dried and preserved by the natives.[12] In Utah, the fruit surpasses the common black raspberry in flavor, size of berry and productiveness.[13] In Oregon, the berry is large, borne in great abundance, of excellent flavor but rather soft for market purposes.[14]

[1] Pickering, C. *Chron. Hist. Pls.* 134. 1879.

[2] Fuller *Sm. Fr. Cult.* 149–167. 1867.

[3] Don, G. *Hist. Dichl. Pls.* 2:537. 1832.

[4] Georgeson *Amer. Gard.* 12:204. 1891.

[5] Lunan, J. *Hort. Jam.* 1:98. 1814.

[6] Fuller *Sm. Fr. Cult.* 173. 1867.

[7] *Gard. Chron.* 18:44. 1882.

[8] Firminger, T. A. C. *Gard. Ind.* 249. 1870. (*R. albescens*)

[9] Brandis, D. *Forest Fl.* 198. 1874.

[10] Royle, J. F. *Illustr. Bot. Himal.* 1:203. 1839.

[11] Brewer and Watson *Bot. Cal.* 1:172. 1880.

[12] Brown, R. *Bot. Soc. Edinb.* 9:384. 1868.

[13] Case *Bot. Index* 10. 1881.

[14] Case *Bot. Index* 37. 1881.

R. microphyllus Linn. f.

Japan. The fruit is yellow, esculent and sapid.[1]

R. morifolius Siebold.

Japan. This species bears large black raspberries of excellent quality.

R. nessensis W. Hall.

Northern Europe. Loudon[3] says the fruit consists of a small number of dark red, or blood-colored, aggregate grains, said to be agreeably acid, with some flavor of the raspberry, whence it has been recommended by some as perhaps not unworthy of cultivation.

R. nutkanus Moç. SALMONBERRY. THIMBLEBERRY.

Alaska and Oregon. The fruit is red, large, hemispherical, sweet and pleasantly flavored.[4] The fruit is dried and eaten by the Indians. The tender shoots are also eaten. In the season, canoe loads may be seen on their way to Indian villages.[5] In Oregon, the berry is considered of excellent quality but is too small to pay for the trouble of gathering.[6]

R. occidentalis Linn. BLACKCAP. BLACK RASPBERRY. THIMBLEBERRY.

Eastern North America. Wood[7] says the fruit is of a lively, agreeable taste. It is an inferior fruit, says Emerson,[8] but has been improved by cultivation. Downing[9] says this berry is frequently cultivated in gardens, where its fruit is much larger and finer than in the uncultivated state, and its rich, acid flavor renders it, perhaps, the finest sort for kitchen use. In its wild state, says Fuller,[10] this species is most variable; he describes wild fruit in cultivation as pale or deep yellow, black, reddish-purple, light crimson or dark scarlet. He refers to this species, wild plants and seedlings, 12 varieties of blackcaps and 5 purple-canes. Downing[11] describes a white variety.

R. odoratus Linn. FLOWERING RASPBERRY.

Eastern North America. This species is found cultivated in ornamental shrubberies, but it seldom bears an edible fruit in New England. Emerson,[12] however, says the fruit is flattish, red, pleasant, though less agreeable than that of the true raspberry. Pursh[13] says, in a wild state, the fruit is yellow and of a very fine flavor and of large size. It is not considered, however, by Downing[14] or Fuller[15] as a fruit-shrub. Specimens with white and pink flowers occur about Cayuga Lake, N. Y.

---

[1] Don, G. *Hist. Dichl. Pls.* **2**:540. 1832.

[2] Georgeson *Amer. Gard.* **12**:204. 1891.

[3] Loudon, J. C. *Arb. Frut. Brit.* **2**:735. 1844. (*R. suberectus*)

[4] Brewer and Watson *Bot. Cal.* **1**:172. 1880.

[5] Brown, R. *Bot. Soc. Edinb.* **9**:384, 385. 1868.

[6] Case *Bot. Index* 37. 1881.

[7] Wood, A. *Class Book Bot.* 340. 1864.

[8] Emerson, G. B. *Trees, Shrubs Mass.* **2**:488. 1875.

[9] Downing, A. J. *Fr. Fr. Trees Amer.* 658. 1857.

[10] Fuller *Sm. Fr. Cult.* 141. 1867.

[11] Downing, A. J. *Fr. Fr. Trees Amer.* 658. 1857.

[12] Emerson, G. B. *Trees, Shrubs Mass.* **2**:487. 1875.

[13] Pursh, F. *Fl. Amer. Septent.* **1**:348. 1814.

[14] Downing, A. J. *Fr. Fr. Trees Amer.* 655. 1857.

[15] Fuller *Sm. Fr. Cult.* 114. 1867.

R. paniculatus Sm.

Himalayan region. The fruit is eaten by the natives of Viti and is made into puddings and pies by the whites.[1]

R. parvifolius Linn.   AUSTRALIAN BRAMBLE.

Malay, Australia and China. This species fruited in England in 1825. The fruit was small, of a clear and brilliant pink color, very juicy, with a subacid, extremely pleasant flavor, but the grains were few, large and pointed.[2]

R. pedatus Sm.

Western North America. The small, red berry has an excellent flavor and is eaten by the natives of Alaska.[3]

R. phoenicolasius Maxim.   WINEBERRY.

Japan. The fruit is concealed by the sepals until ripe. At first white, the berry turns bright red and is of a sweet and delicious flavor, between that of the common red and the blackcap.[4]

R. rosaefolius Sm.   MAURITIUS RASPBERRY.

Tropical Asia. In India, this shrub bears a fruit similar to the common raspberry but the berry is filled with hard seeds and is of rather a poor taste.[5] The fruit is red when ripe.[6]

R. saxatilis Linn.   ROEBUCK BERRY.   STONE BRAMBLE.

North temperate and arctic regions. The fruits, says Lightfoot,[7] are very acid alone but eaten with sugar they make an agreeable dessert. The Russians ferment the fruit with sugar and extract a potent spirit. Johnson[8] says the berries are more acid and agreeable to the taste than those of the European blackberry.

R. sellowii Cham. & Schlecht.

Argentina and Brazil. The fruit is edible.[9]

R. spectabilis Pursh.   SALMONBERRY.

Northwest America. The yellow fruits, says Loudon,[10] are of an acid and somewhat astringent taste and make excellent tarts. The young shoots, as well as the berries, are eaten by the Indians, the former being tied in bundles and steamed over the fire. There are said to be two forms in Oregon: one rather soft, yellow, somewhat insipid, subacid, about one inch in diameter when expanded; the other with red berries of a firmer texture and more acid, a shy bearer.[11]

---

[1] Seemann, B.   *Fl. Viti.* 76.   1865–73.   (*R. tiliaceus*)

[2] Lindley, J.   *Trans. Hort. Soc. Lond.* **7**:247.   1830.

[3] Coville *U. S. Nat. Herb.* **3**: No. 6. 331.   1896.

[4] Georgeson *Amer. Gard.* **12**:203.   1891.   Fig. p. 205.

[5] Firminger, T. A. C.   *Gard. Ind.* 249.   1870.

[6] Brandis, D.   *Forest Fl.* 198.   1874.

[7] Lightfoot, J.   *Fl. Scot.* **1**:265, 266.   1879.

[8] Johnson, C. P.   *Useful Pls. Gt. Brit.* 90.   1862.

[9] Don, G.   *Hist. Dichl. Pls.* **2**:537.   1832.

[10] Loudon, J. C.   *Arb. Frut. Brit.* **2**:741.   1844.

[11] Case *Bot. Index* 38.   1881.

R. strigosus Michx. RED RASPBERRY.

Northern America. In 1607, the Frenchmen of L'Escarbot's [1] expedition " amused themselves with gathering raspberries." It is among the wild fruits of Massachusetts mentioned by Edward Winslow [2] in 1621. Its fruits were greatly relished by the Indians wherever they were to be found. The fruits of the wild plants vary much in color from a dark red to a light, bright crimson. The fruits are large or small. In northern Iowa, a chance wilding, called the Elisdale, bears a very large, bright red berry, with light bloom and is very sweet and rich. Fuller,[3] in 1867, mentions six varieties as under cultivation.

R. tagallus Cham. et Schlecht.

China and Island of Luzon. The red fruit is eatable.[4]

R. thunbergii Sieb. & Zucc.

Japan. This species furnishes edible fruit.[5]

R. tokkura Siebold.

Japan. The fruit is small, red and consists of but few drupes. It is not of much value but is utilized as an article of food in Japan.[6]

R. trifidus Thunb.

Japan. The red fruit is of a grateful taste.[7]

R. triflorus Richards. DWARF RASPBERRY.

New England to Pennsylvania, Wisconsin and northward.[8] The fruit is eaten in Colorado.[9]

R. trivialis Michx. LOW-BUSH RASPBERRY.

Maryland to Florida. Elliott [10] says the berries are large, black and well-flavored.

R. ursinus Cham. & Schlecht. SALMONBERRY. WESTERN BLACKBERRY.

Northwest America. This species has been introduced into cultivation in California.[11] The berries, in Oregon, are of medium size, solid and highly flavored, ripening in July. In the season, large quantities are collected for market. The fruit varies considerably. Sometimes it is large and highly flavored, almost sweet; at other times it is large but sour or rather insipid.[12]

R. villosus Ait. BLACKBERRY. DEWBERRY.

Eastern North America. This species varies much in its fruit and several of the cultivated varieties are chance seedlings taken from the field: such as the Kittatinny,

[1] Parkman, F.   *Pion. France* 274.   1894.

[2] Young, A.   *Chron. Pilgr.* 234.   1841.

[3] Fuller *Sm. Fr. Cult.* 149.   1867.

[4] Don, G.   *Hist. Dichl. Pls.* 2:530.   1832.

[5] Georgeson *Amer. Gard.* 12:204.   1891.

[6] Ibid.

[7] Don, G.   *Hist. Dichl. Pls.* 2:539.   1832.

[8] Gray, A.   *Man. Bot.* 157.   1868.

[9] Thompson, R. O.   *U. S. D. A. Rpt.* 126.   1866.

[10] Elliott, S.   *Bot. So. Car., Ga.* 1:569.   1821.

[11] Fuller *Sm. Fr. Cult.* 116.   1867.   (*R. macropetalus*)

[12] Case *Bot. Index* 38.   1881.

found growing wild in New Jersey about 1845; New Rochelle, found in New York; New-man's Thornless, also in New York; and Wilson's Early, discovered in New Jersey about 1854. In 1867, Fuller [1] describes 18 sorts in cultivation. There is a variety cultivated abroad, says Downing,[2] with white fruits. The commencement of the cultivation of improved varieties seems to date from the appearance of the Dorchester, first exhibited at the Massachusetts Horticultural Society in 1841. The fruit is highly esteemed by the Indians of Missouri, Texas, California and Minnesota. Cabeza de Vaca,[3] 1528–35, says the Indians of the Southwest eat blackberries during four months of the year. Eight varieties, in 1879, were cataloged by the American Pomological Society [4] as worthy of cultivation.

Ruellia tuberosa Linn. *Acanthaceae.* MENOW-WEED. SNAPDRAGON.

Jamaica. Browne [5] says the plant has oblong, fleshy roots, which are frequently used among the negroes. These, when fresh, have a little pungency, which soon wears upon the palate but when dry they are quite insipid.

Rumex abyssinicus Jacq. *Polygonaceae.*

Eastern equatorial Africa. Grant [6] says the people of Fipa are said to eat its leaves.

R. acetosa Linn. SORREL. SOUR DOCK.

Europe and northern Asia. This plant was formerly cultivated in gardens for its leaves, which were used in Britain as spinach or in salads, and, in the time of Henry VIII, it was held in great repute. Sorrel is mentioned in nearly all of the earlier botanies as under culture in England; Gerarde,[7] 1597, also figures the blistered variety. It is spoken of by nearly all the later writers on garden subjects and was in common use in 1807;[8] but, in 1874, is said to have been for many years entirely discarded, the French sorrel having usurped its place.[9] The common sorrel, says McIntosh,[10] has been cultivated from time immemorial as a spinach and salad plant.[11] Johnson says it is still used to a great extent for salads in France. In Ireland, it is largely consumed by the peasantry. Sorrel seems to be particularly relished by the Hebrideans.[12] The Laplanders boil a large quantity of the leaves in water and mix the juice, when cold, in the milk of their reindeer, which they esteem an agreeable and wholesome food.[13] In Scandinavia, the plant has been used in times of scarcity to put into bread. It is mentioned as an inmate of American

[1] Fuller *Sm. Fr. Cult.* 172. 1867.

[2] Downing, A. J. *Fr. Fr. Trees Amer.* 663. 1857.

[3] Smith, B. *Rel. De Vaca* 79. 1871.

[4] *Amer. Pom. Soc. Cat.* XVIII. 1879.

[5] Lunan, J. *Hort. Jam.* 2:194. 1814.

[6] Speke, J. H. *Journ. Disc. Source Nile* 580. **1864.**

[7] Gerarde, J. *Herb.* 319. 1597.

[8] Martyn *Miller's Gard. Dict.* 1807.

[9] Booth, W. B. *Treas. Bot.* 2:998. 1870.

[10] McIntosh, C. *Book Gard.* 2:139. 1855.

[11] Johnson, C. P. *Useful Pls. Gt. Brit.* 222. 1862.

[12] *Journ. Agr.* 2:379. 1831.

[13] Lightfoot, J. *Fl. Scot.* 1:191. 1789.

gardens by McMahon,[1] 1806, and Bridgeman,[2] 1832. It is mentioned by Dall[3] among the edible and useful plants of Kotzebue Sound. In China it is eaten.[4]

R. alpinus Linn. MOUNTAIN RHUBARB.

Europe and the Caucasus. This species is sometimes grown in France but does not appear to have entered American culture. It was grown in England by Gerarde in 1597 for use in " physicke " and is described as cultivated there in *Miller's Dictionary*, 1807. It is eaten as an herb in China.[5]

R. crispus Linn. CURLED DOCK.

Europe and now naturalized in northeastern America. The leaves of this weed make a spinach highly esteemed by some.

R. hydrolapathum Huds. WILD RHUBARB.

Europe and Asia. This sorrel is eaten in China.[6]

R. hymenosepalus Torr. CANAIGRE.

Western North America. The leaves are occasionally used as a potherb.[7] In southern California, this species is extensively used as a substitute for cultivated rhubarb.[8]

R. longifolius H. B. & K.

South America. The acid leaves, immediately they appear above the ground and, indeed, throughout the summer, are eaten by the Eskimos of the West, by handfuls as an antiscorbutic.[9]

R. luxurians Linn.

South Africa. This species serves as a culinary sorrel.[10]

R. montanus Desf. FRENCH SORREL.

Europe. This species is cultivated in France and is much used as a salad. It is an important article of diet in the extreme north of Europe. The Norwegians eat the leaves with milk or mixed with meal and baked. In India, this sorrel is used in soups and for imparting a peculiarly fine flavor to omelets. This species occurs in French gardens under two types, the green-leaved and the crimped-leaved. In 1863, Burr[11] describes French sorrel among American garden esculents. In India, it is said by Firminger[12] to be an excellent ingredient of soups and imparts a peculiarly fine flavor to omelets.

---

[1] McMahon, B. *Amer. Gard. Cal.* 320. 1806.

[2] Bridgeman *Young Gard. Asst.* 107. 1857.

[3] Dall *U. S. D. A. Rpt.* 423. 1870.

[4] Smith, F. P. *Contrib. Mat. Med. China* 87. 1871.

[5] Ibid.

[6] Ibid.

[7] Saunders, W. *U. S. D. A. Rpt.* 364. 1879.

[8] *Pacific Rur. Press* 371. 1879.

[9] Seemann, B. *Journ. Anthrop. Soc.* 3: CCCIII. 1865. (*R. domesticus*)

[10] Mueller, F. *Sel. Pls.* 208. 1876.

[11] Burr, F. *Field, Gard. Veg.* 308. 1863.

[12] Firminger, T. A. C. *Gard. Ind.* 142. 1874.

R. patientia Linn. GARDEN PATIENCE. HERB PATIENCE. MONK'S RHUBARB. PATIENCE DOCK.

Southern Europe and the Orient and formerly common in gardens as a spinach plant. This plant was introduced into England in 1573. Gerarde [1] says " it is an excellent, wholesome pot-herbe." The name monk's rhubarb or *rhabarbarum monachorum* of Tragus, 1552, indicates its presence in the gardens of the monasteries. It was called *patientia* by Parkinson, 1640, and is noted by Turner,[2] 1538, as having in England the common name of patience. It was included among America esculents by McMahon,[3] 1806, and by Bridgeman,[4] 1832. Pallas [5] says the young leaves are eaten with avidity by the Greeks of the Crimea. It was known to Pliny, who calls it *Rumex sativus*.

R. sanguineus Linn. BLOODWORT. BLOODY-VEINED DOCK.

Europe and naturalized in eastern North America. This weed of waste and cultivated grounds of America is mentioned, under the name bloodwort, by Josselyn,[6] about the middle of the seventeenth century, as introduced into America. As Gerarde,[7] 1630, says, it was sown in his time for a potherb in most gardens and as Ray,[8] 1686, also says, it was planted in gardens as a vegetable, we may believe that it was in former use in colonial gardens in Massachusetts. Its use is as a spinach, and for this purpose the leaves of the wild plant are occasionally collected at the present time.

R. scutatus Linn. GARDEN SORREL.

Europe and the Orient and said to have been introduced into England in 1596. This species is mentioned in England by Gerarde [9] in 1597, but he does not indicate its general cultivation; he calls it *oxalis franca seu romana*. It is more acid than the preceding species and has displaced it largely from English culture. This species is mentioned by many of the early botanists and is under extensive culture in continental Europe.[10] It was formerly cultivated in English gardens as a spinach and is still grown extensively on the continent of Europe for this purpose.[11] The leaves are also used as a salad. Garden sorrel was mentioned among American garden products by McMahon,[12] 1806, and by Bridgeman,[13] 1832. The seed is still offered by some of our seedsmen who recommend it under the name garden sorrel.

R. vesicarius Linn. BLADDER DOCK.

South Europe, middle Asia and north Africa. This species is used as a sorrel.[14]

---

[1] Gerarde, J. *Herb.* 391. 1633 or 1636. 2nd Ed.

[2] Turner *Libellus* 1538.

[3] McMahon, B. *Amer. Gard. Cal.* 550. 1806.

[4] Bridgeman *Young Gard. Asst.* 107. 1857.

[5] Pallas, P. S. *Trav. Russia* 2:449. 1803.

[6] Josselyn, J. *New Eng. Rar.* 114. 1672.

[7] Gerarde, J. *Herb.* 390. 1633.

[8] Ray *Hist. Pl.* 174. 1686.

[9] Gerarde, J. *Herb.* 319. 1597.

[10] McIntosh, C. *Book Gard.* 2:139. 1855.

[11] McIntosh, C. *Book Gard.* 2:138. 1855.

[12] McMahon, B. *Amer. Gard. Cal.* 583. 1806.

[13] Bridgeman *Young Gard. Asst.* 1832.

[14] Mueller, F. *Sel. Pls.* 433. 1891.

Ruscus aculeatus Linn. *Liliaceae.* BOX HOLLY. BUTCHER'S BROOM. JEW'S MYRTLE.

Europe and the Orient. The tender shoots are eaten in the spring by the poor in Europe as an asparagus.[1]

Ruta graveolens Linn. *Rutaceae.* RUE. HERB-OF-GRACE.

Mediterranean countries and cultivated in gardens. Formerly the English as well as the Germans and Dutch used the green leaves of rue in their ragouts. The leaves are also used as a pickle. The Italians are said to eat the leaves in salads. It was introduced into Britain before 1562.[2] Rue is included among American garden medicinal plants by McMahon,[3] 1806, and by succeeding writers on American gardening.

Sabal adansoni Guerns. *Palmae.*

Southern United States. The soft interior of the stem is edible.[4]

S. palmetto Lodd. PALMETTO PALM.

Coast of North Carolina and southward. In Florida, the cabbage is eaten and is excellent. The drupes are said to afford nourishing food to the Indians and hunters but are not palatable to whites until they become accustomed to them. In *Plaine Description of Barmudas*,[5] 1613, it is said: " there is a tree called a Palmito tree, which hath a very sweet berry, upon which the hogs doe most feede; but our men, finding the sweetnesse of them, did willingly share with the hogs for them, they being very pleasant and wholesome, which made them carelesse almost of any bread with their meate." " The head of the Palmito tree is verie good meate either raw or sodden." " Of necessitie, I must needs mention a Palme-tree once againe, I have found it so good; take a hatchet and cut him, or an augur and bore him, and it yields a very pleasant liquor, much like unto your sweete wines."

Saccharum officinarum Linn. *Gramineae.* SUGAR CANE.

Tropics. From the elaborate investigation of Ritter,[6] it appears that this species was originally a native of Bengal and of the Indo-Chinese countries, as well as of Borneo, Java, Bali, Celebes and other islands of the Malay Archipelago. There is no evidence that it is now found anywhere in a wild state. The first historical allusion to sugar seems to be by Theophrastus (others say by Strabo),[7] who lived 321 B. C. He speaks of a sort of honey procured from canes or reeds. Varro, 68 B. C., mentions the exceeding sweetness of the Indian reed, but says the juice is derived from the root of the plant. Lucan [8] says of the Indians near the Ganges " they drink the sweet juices of the tender reed." Dioscorides says there is a sort of concreted honey which is called sugar and is found upon

[1] *Gard. Chron.* 214. 1877.

[2] McIntosh, C. *Book Gard.* 2:242. 1855.

[3] McMahon, B. *Amer. Gard. Cal.* 584. 1806.

[4] Seemann, B. *Pop. Hist. Palms* 336. 1856.

[5] *Plaine Desc. of Barmudas* 13. 1613. Force Coll. Tracts 3: No. 3. 1844.

[6] Flückiger and Hanbury *Pharm.* 650. 1879.

[7] Hooker, W. J. *Journ. Bot.* 1:217. 1834.

[8] Ibid.

canes in India and Arabia Felix and it is as hard as salt and is brittle under the teeth. Pliny adds to this description by saying it comes in fragments as large as a filbert and is used only in medicine. Paulus Aegineta quotes Archigenes as saying, " The Indian salt is like common salt in color and consistence but resembles honey in taste." Sugar is mentioned, however, in the *Institutes of Menu*,[1] and the *Sama Veda*.[2]

The Venetians[3] imported sugar cane from India by the Red Sea, prior to 1148, and it is supposed to have been introduced into the islands of Sicily, Crete, Rhodes and Cypress by the Saracens,[4] as an abundance of sugar was made in those islands previous to the discovery of the West Indies. Cane was cultivated afterwards in Spain, in Valentia, Granada and Murcia by the Moors, and sugar is still made in these provinces.[5] Other authorities believe that, in the ninth century, the Arabians obtained sugar from the sugar cane which at that time was cultivated in Susiana. Sugar was brought from Alexandria to Venice in the year 996. In 1087, 10,000 pounds of sugar are said to have been used at the wedding of the Caliph Mostadi Bemvillah. In 1420, Don Henri transported sugar cane from Sicily to Madeira, whence it was carried to the Canary Isles in 1503.[6] Thence it was introduced into Brazil in the beginning of the sixteenth century.[7] Columbus carried sugar canes from Spain to the West Indies before 1494, for at this time he says " the small quantity that we have planted has succeeded very well.[8] Sugar cane was carried to Santo Domingo about 1520.[9] In 1610, the Dutch began to make sugar in the Island of St. Thomas,[10] and, from the cane introduced in 1660, sugar was made in Jamaica in 1664.[11] Sugar cane reached Guadeloupe[12] about 1644 and Martinique[13] about 1650. It was carried to Bourbon at the formation of the colony.[14] In 1646, the Barbados began to export sugar. Plants appear to have been carried to Cuba by Velasquez about 1518 and to Mexico by Cortez[15] about 1524, and, before 1530, we find mention of sugar mills on the estates of Cortez.[16] The plant seems to have been cultivated on the banks of the Mississippi for the first time about 1751, and the first sugar mill was erected in 1758. In 1770, sugar had become one of the staple products of the colony about New Orleans. The first variety cultivated was the Creole. The Ribbon cane, originally from Java,

---

[1] Pickering, C.   *Chron. Hist. Pls.* 267.   1879.

[2] Ibid.

[3] Loudon, J. C.   *Enc. Pls.* 74.   1855.

[4] Ibid.

[5] Ibid.

[6] De Candolle, A.   *Geog. Bot.* 2:837.   1855.

[7] Ibid.

[8] Columbus *Sel. Letters 2nd Voy.* 1494.   Hakl. Soc. Ed. 78.   1847.

[9] De Candolle, A.   *Geog. Bot.* 2:837.   1855.

[10] Loudon, J. C.   *Enc. Pls.* 74.   1855.

[11] Lunan, J.   *Hort. Jam.* 2:205.   1814.

[12] De Candolle, A.   *Geog. Bot.* 2:837.   1855.

[13] Ibid.

[14] Ibid.

[15] Prescott, W. H.   *Conq. Mex.* 3:332.   1843.

[16] Ibid.

was introduced about 1820 to 1825.[1] The Otaheite cane, brought to the West Indies by Bougainville and Bligh, was introduced far later.[2]

According to Hallam,[3] Gesner, who died in 1564, was the first botanist who mentions sugar cane. Sugar cane, according to various observers, never bears seed in the West Indies, Malaga, India, Cochin China, or the Malay Archipelago,[4] but Lunan speaks of the seed in Jamaica as being oblong, pointed and ripening in the valve of the flower.

The use of sugar is well known. In South America a cane-wine called *guarapo* is in common use, prepared from the juice of the stalk allowed to run into fermentation.[5] The natives of Easter Island, who suffer great distress from want of fresh water, drink the juice.[6] In southern China, the stalks, cut into six- or ten-inch lengths, raw and boiled, are continually hawked around the streets for eating.[7] The elephant cane of Cochin China is grown for the stalks, which are chewed. The epidermis of the stalk is so brittle, that, instead of crushing in the mills, the stalks break into small fragments.[8] In central Africa, a red-stalked variety is the most frequent and the negroes make no further use of it than eating the cane,[9] and the Uganda may often be seen passing, chewing the end of a long cane that trails behind them.[10] This cane also appears in the markets of Paraguay, where it is eaten.[11] This species is, undoubtedly, says Unger,[12] a plant peculiar to China, and has been cultivated there independently and perhaps still earlier than the Indian sugar cane. This is also the sugar cane of the Malays, according to Ainslie.[13] De Candolle[14] says it was introduced into the gardens of Calcutta in 1796.

S. sara Roxb. PENREED GRASS.

East Indies, Afghanistan and India. In the southern part of the Punjab, the delicate part of the pith in the upper part of the stem is eaten by the poor.[15]

Sageretia brandrethiana Aitch. *Rhamneae.*

Orient and northwestern India. The fruit is sweet and is a great favorite with the Afghans.[16]

---

[1] Brown, J. N. *U. S. Pat. Off. Rpt.* 168. 1849.

[2] Humboldt, A. *Views Nat.* 25. 1850.

[3] Hallam *Lit. Europe* 1:241. 1856.

[4] Darwin, C. *Ans. Pls. Domest.* 2:153. 1893.

[5] Boussingault *Rur. Econ.* 194. No year.

[6] Humboldt, A. *Views Nat.* 25. 1850.

[7] Williams, S. W. *U. S. Pat. Off. Rpt.* 474. 1860.

[8] Morris *Rpt. Pub. Gard. Jam.* 21. 1880.

[9] Speke, J. H. *Journ. Disc. Source Nile* 586. 1864.

[10] Long, C. C. *Cent. Afr.* 127. 1877.

[11] Robertson, J. P. and W. P. *Letters Paraguay* 1:294. 1838.

[12] Unger, F. *U. S. Pat. Off. Rpt.* 326. 1859.

[13] Ainslie, W. *Mat. Ind.* 1:409. 1826.

[14] De Candolle, A. *Geog. Bot.* 2:836. 1855.

[15] Drury, H. *Useful Pls. Ind.* 376. 1873.

[16] Brandis, D. *Forest Fl.* 95. 1874.

S. oppositifolia Brongn.

East Indies and Malay. The sweetish fruit is eaten in India.[1]

S. theezans Brongn.

Northwestern India, Burma and China. The poor in China use the leaves as a tea.[2] The fruit is also eaten in China and the Himalayas. It is globular, the size of a small pea, dark brown when ripe,[3] and is called *tia* by the Chinese.[4]

Sagittaria chinensis Sims. *Alismaceae.* ARROW-HEAD.

China. The Chinese arrow-head is sold in the markets of China and Japan as food, the corns being full of starch.[5] It is extensively cultivated about San Francisco, California, to supply the Chinese markets, and the tubers are commonly to be found on sale.[6]

S. sagittifolia Linn. SWAMP POTATO. SWAN POTATO.

Europe, Asia and North America. The bulbs, which dig themselves into the solid earth below the mud, constitute an article of food with the Chinese, and, on that account, the plant is extensively cultivated. This species is enumerated by Thunberg[7] as among the edible plants of Japan. In eastern America, the Indians boil or roast this root which they called *katniss*.[8] It is called by the Oregon Indians *wapstoo* and constitutes an important article of diet.[9]

Salacia dulcis Benth. *Celastrineae.*

A shrub of Brazil. The fruit is the size of a crab apple, yellow, sweet, and juicy and is much eaten by the Indians on the Rio Negro, who call it *waiatuma*.[10]

S. pyriformis Steud.

Tropical Africa. This plant produces a sweet-tasted fruit the size of a Bergamot pear.[11] Wight[12] says the fruit is eatable and is said to be of a rich and sweet flavor.

S. roxburghii Wall.

East Indies. The plant bears a dull red fruit the size of a crab apple, of which the white pulp is eaten.[13]

S. scabra DC.

Guiana. The berries are edible.[14]

---

[1] Brandis, D. *Forest Fl.* 95. 1874.

[2] Don, G. *Hist. Dichl. Pls.* 2:28. 1832.

[3] Brandis, D. *Forest Fl.* 96. 1874.

[4] Smith, A. *Treas. Bot.* 2:1005. 1870.

[5] Lindley, J. *Med. Econ. Bot.* 62. 1849.

[6] Case *Bot. Index* 9. 1881.

[7] Thunberg, C. P. *Fl. Jap.* 242. 1784.

[8] Kalm, P. *Trav. No. Amer.* 1:386. 1772.

[9] Torrey, J. *Pacific R. R. Rpt.* 6:91. 1857.

[10] Black, A. A. *Treas. Bot.* 2:1007. 1870.

[11] Ibid.

[12] Wight, R. *Illustr. Ind. Bot.* 1:132. 1840.

[13] Black, A. A. *Treas. Bot.* 2:1007. 1870.

[14] Smith, A. *Treas. Bot.* 2:1007. 1870.

Salicornia brachiata Roxb. *Chenopodiaceae.*

East Indies. The shoots are pickled by the natives of India.[1]

S. fruticosa Linn

Europe and Africa. The plant is of a brackish taste but is eaten as a salad by the soldiers and some few others at the Cape of Good Hope.[2]

S. herbacea Linn. CRAB GRASS. MARSH SAMPHIRE. SALTWORT.

Seashores of the Mediterranean and north Atlantic and interior salines throughout North America and Asia. The tender shoots of this plant in England are used as a pickle and are sometimes boiled for the table.[3] This species is found about the salt springs in Syracuse, New York, and is much used for pickling.[4]

Salix alba Linn. *Salicineae.* WHITE WILLOW.

Europe, Asia and north Africa. The inner bark, though extremely bitter in the fresh state, when dried and powdered, Johnson[5] says, is used in northern countries in times of scarcity for making bread. Dall[6] says the half-digested willow-tips in the stomach of the adult deer are regarded as a delicacy by the Eskimos of the Yukon River, and the mess is eaten as a salad. The bark of a species of willow is mixed with tobacco and smoked by the Indians of Maine. In China, the leaves of this and other willows are often eaten by poor people in times of want. Willow leaves have long been used to make " sweet-tea," and about Shanghai the leaves of *S. alba* are used to adulterate tea.[7]

S. fragilis Linn. CRACK WILLOW.

Europe and Asia. In Persia, this willow yields a saccharine exudation, as stated by Haussknecht.[8]

Salvadora persica Linn. *Salvadoraceae.* MUSTARD TREE. TOOTH-BRUSH TREE.

Orient, East Indies and north Africa. The fruit is sweet and is eaten largely in the Punjab; when dried it forms an article of trade and tastes somewhat like currants. The fruit is globose, two and one-half lines in diameter, yellow when ripe, dark brown or red when dry.[9] The shoot and leaves are pungent, says Brandis,[10] and are eaten as salad and are celebrated as antidotes against poison. This shrub or small tree has been identified as the mustard tree of Scripture. The small, red, edible berries, says Ainslie,[11] have an aromatic smell and taste not unlike the garden cress. According to Stewart,[12] these berries

---

[1] Drury, H. *Useful Pls. India* 377. 1873.

[2] Thunberg, C. P. *Trav.* 1:292. 1795.

[3] Lightfoot, J. *Fl. Scot.* 1:69. 1789.

[4] Vick *Gard. Monthly* 250. 1878.

[5] Johnson, C. P. *Useful Pls. Gt. Brit.* 247. 1862.

[6] Dall, W. H. *Alaska* 148. 1897.

[7] Smith, F. P. *Contrib. Mat. Med. China* 214, 232. 1871.

[8] Flückiger and Hanbury *Pharm.* 373. 1879.

[9] Brandis, D. *Forest Fl.* 315. 1874.

[10] Brandis, D. *Forest Fl.* 316. 1874.

[11] Ainslie, W. *Mat. Ind.* 2:266. 1826.

[12] Pickering, C. *Chron. Hist. Pls.* 426. 1879.

are much eaten, and Royle [1] says the seeds, having an aromatic pungency, are substituted for mustard.

Salvia columbariae Benth. *Labiatae.* CHIA.

Southern and central California. The seeds are collected, roasted, ground by the Indians and used as a food by mixing with water and enough sugar to suit the taste. This mixture soon develops into a copious, mucilaginous mass several times the original bulk. The taste for it is soon acquired, and it is then found very palatable and nutritious.[2]

S. horminum Linn. HORMIUM CLARY.

South Europe; introduced into Britain in 1596. The leaves are used as a sage.[3] Gerarde [4] says of it, that the leaves are good to be put into pottage or broths among other potherbs. It is included in Thorburn's [5] seed catalog of 1881.

S. indica Linn.

East Indies. This species, according to Ainslie,[6] is much cultivated in India for its leaves, which are put into country beer because of their fresh and pleasant smell.

S. lanata Roxb.

Himalayan region. The stems are peeled and eaten.[7]

S. officinalis Linn. SAGE.

Mediterranean region. This plant is one of the most important occupants of the herb garden, being commonly used for seasoning and also in domestic medicine. It has been under cultivation from a remote period and is considered to be the *elelisphakos* of Theophrastus, the *elelisphakon* of Dioscorides, the *salvia* of Pliny. Its medicinal virtues are noted by Oribasius and others of the early writers on medicine. In the Middle Ages, sage found frequent mention, as by Albertus Magnus in the thirteenth century, and the plant and its uses are noticed in nearly all of the early botanies. Although but one variety is now grown in our gardens, yet formerly a number of sorts were noted, the red, green, small and variegated being named by Worlidge [8] in 1683. Sage was in American gardens in 1806 [9] and doubtless long before. Six varieties are described by Burr,[10] 1863, all of which can perhaps be included among the four mentioned in 1683 and all by Mawe in 1778.

The French make an excellent pickle of the young leaves. The Chinese value the leaves for making a tea, and at one time the Dutch carried on a profitable trade in exchanging sage for tea, pound for pound. In Zante, the apples or tumors on the sage, the effect

[1] Royle, J. F. *Illustr. Bot. Himal.* 1:319. 1839.

[2] Rothrock, J. T. *Bot. U. S. Geog. Surv.* 6:48. 1878.

[3] McIntosh, C. *Book Gard.* 2:235. 1855.

[4] Gerarde, J. *Herb.* 2nd. Ed. 773. 1633 or 1636.

[5] Thorburn *Cat.* 1881.

[6] Ainslie, W. *Mat. Ind.* 1:360. 1826.

[7] Pickering, C. *Chron. Hist. Pls.* 736. 1879.

[8] Worlidge, J. *Syst. Hort.* 218. 1683.

[9] McMahon, B. *Amer. Gard. Cal.* 583. 1806.

[10] Burr, F. *Field, Gard. Veg.* 438. 1863.

of a puncture of a species of Cynips, are made into a conserve with honey, according to Sibthorp.

S. plebeia R. Br.

Eastern Asia and Australia. The seeds are used as a mustard by the Hindus.[1]

S. sclarea Linn. CLARY.

Mediterranean region and the Orient; introduced into Britain in 1562. In Europe, the leaves are said to be put into wine to impart to it a muscatel taste. Clary was formerly much more cultivated in gardens than at present. Townsend,[2] 1726, says, " the leaves of it are used in Omlets, made with Eggs and so must be in a garden." In 1778, Mawe[3] gives three varieties; the broad-leaved, the long-leaved and the wrinkled-leaved. Clary is mentioned as cultivated in England by Ray,[4] 1686; Gerarde,[5] 1597; and it is the *Orminum* of Turner,[6] 1538. It was in American gardens preceding 1806[7] and now occurs wild in Pennsylvania, naturalized as an escape. The leaves are used for seasoning, but their use in America has been largely superceded by sage; although the seed is yet sold by some of the seedsmen, it is now but little grown.

Sambucus caerulea Rafin. *Caprifoliaceae.*

Western North America. In California, the Indians eat the berries.[8] In Utah, its clusters of fruit often weigh several pounds, and the berries are more agreeable than those of *S. canadensis.*[9]

S. canadensis Linn. CANADIAN ELDERBERRY.

North America. The unopened flower-buds form, when pickled, an excellent substitute for capers.[10] The berries are often used to make a domestic wine.

S. ebulus Linn. DANEWORT. DWARF ELDER. WALLWORT.

Europe and adjoining Asia. The plant has a nauseous smell and drastic properties.[11] Buckman[12] says the berries are used as are those of *S. nigra.*

S. mexicana Presl.

Western North America. The berries are deep purple when ripe, agreeable to the taste and almost equal to the blackberry. The plant bears flowers, green and ripe fruit on the same branches.[13]

---

[1] Pickering. C. *Chron. Hist. Pls.* 736. 1879.

[2] Townsend *Seedsman* 34. 1726.

[3] Mawe and Abercrombie *Univ. Gard. Bot.* 1778.

[4] Ray *Hist. Pl.* 543. 1686.

[5] Gerarde, J. *Herb.* 626. 1597.

[6] Turner *Libellus* (facsimile reprint). 1877.

[7] McMahon, B. *Amer. Gard. Cal.* 583. 1806.

[8] Vasey *U. S. D. A. Rpt.* 164. 1875.

[9] Case *Bot. Index* 10. 1881.

[10] Emerson, G. B. *Trees, Shrubs Mass.* 2:410. 1875.

[11] Johns, C. A. *Treas. Bot.* 2:1013. 1870.

[12] Buckman, J. *Treas. Bot.* 2:1013. 1870.

[13] Durand and Hilgard *Pacific R. R. Rpt.* 5:8. 1856.

S. nigra Linn. ELDERBERRY. EUROPEAN ELDER.

Europe and northern Asia. The elderberry is cultivated for its fruits, which are generally purplish-black, but a variety occurs of a greenish-white hue. In Europe, a wine is made from the berries and they are even marketed in London for this purpose. The berries are largely consumed in Portugal for coloring port wine. The flowers are fried in a batter and eaten. There are many superstitions which cluster about the elderberry.

S: xanthocarpa F. Muell. AUSTRALIAN EDLER.

Australia. This species furnishes one of the edible wild fruits of Australia.[1]

Sandoricum indicum Cav. *Meliaceae.* SANDAL.

Tropical Asia. In the Moluccas, Lindley[2] says the fruit is globular, the size of a small orange and somewhat three-sided. Its color is dull yellow, and it is filled with a firm, fleshy, agreeable, acid pulp, which forms a thick covering around the gelatinous substance, in which the seeds are lodged. Rumphius[3] says the fruit is chiefly used for culinary purposes. Mason[4] says the fleshy, acid pulp of the mangosteen-like fruit is highly relished by the natives.

Santalum lanceolatum R. Br. *Santalaceae.* SANDALWOOD.

Australia. The fruit is a brown or a black drupe, oblong, of a sweet taste and is the size of a small plum.[5]

Sapindus attenuatus Wall. *Sapindaceae.*

Himalayan region. The fruit is eaten by the natives of Silhet.[6]

S. esculentus A. St. Hil. PITTOMBERA.

Gardner[7] says the fruit is produced in large bunches, resembling in size the common grape. The outer covering is hard but the embryo, or kernel, is covered with a thin, transparent, sweetish-acid pulp, which alone is eaten.

S. fruticosus Roxb.

Moluccas. Unger[8] says this plant furnishes a sweetish-sour, edible fruit.

S. marginatus Willd. SOAPBERRY.

Northern North America. The Alaska Indians pound the berries and press the pulpy mass into round cakes to be used for food. It is an exceedingly repulsive food to Whites.[9]

---

[1] Unger, F.   *U. S. Pat. Off. Rpt.* 347. 1859.

[2] Lindley, J.   *Trans. Hort. Soc. Lond.* **5**:116. 1824.

[3] Ibid.

[4] Pickering, C.   *Chron. Hist. Pls.* 208. 1879.

[5] Palmer, E.   *Journ. Roy. Soc. New So. Wales* **17**:103. 1884.

[6] Royle, J. F.   *Illustr. Bot. Himal.* **1**:138. 1839.

[7] Gardner, G.   *Trav. Braz.* 176. 1849.

[8] Unger, F.   *U. S. Pat. Off. Rpt.* 344. 1859.

[9] Dall, W. H.   *U. S. D. A. Rpt.* 412. 1870.

S. senegalensis Poir. CHERRY OF SENEGAL.

Tropical Africa. The pulp of its fruit is edible but the seeds are poisonous.[1]

Sapium indicum Willd. *Euphorbiaceae.*

East Indies. The young fruit is acid and is eaten as a condiment while at the same time the fruit is one of the ingredients used for poisoning alligators.[2]

Sarcocephalus esculentus Afzel. *Rubiaceae.*

Tropical Africa. Sabine[3] says the plant bears a large, fleshy fruit of the size of a peach, with a brown and granulated surface. The core is solid and rather hard but edible, much resembling the center of a pineapple in substance. The surrounding flesh is softish, full of small seeds and, in consistence and flavor, much resembles a strawberry.

Sarcostemma brevistigma Wight & Arn. *Asclepiadeae.*

East Indies and Burma. Royle[4] says this plant yields a milky juice of an acid nature, which is taken by the natives of India to quench thirst.

S. forskalianum Schult.

Arabia. The young shoots are eaten.[5]

S. intermedium Decne.

East Indies. Wight[6] says the young, succulent branches yield a large quantity of mild, milky, acid juice, which the natives suck to allay thirst or eat as a sort of salad.

S. stipitaceum Schult.

Arabia. The young shoots are eaten.[7]

Sassafras officinale Nees & Eberm. *Laurineae.* SASSAFRAS.

Eastern United States. The dried leaves are much used as an ingredient in soups, for which they are well adapted by the abundance of mucilage they contain.[8] For this purpose, the mature, green leaves are dried and powdered, the stringy portions being separated, and are sifted and preserved for use. This preparation, mixed with soups, gives them a ropy consistence and a peculiar flavor much relished by those accustomed to it. To such soups are given the names of *gombo file* or *gombo zab.* Rafinesque[9] says it is called *gombo sassafras.* In Pennsylvania, says Kalm,[10] the flowers of sassafras are gathered and used as a tea. Sassafras tea, mixed with milk and sugar, says Masters,[11] forms the drink,

---

[1] Smith, A. *Treas. Bot.* 2:1017. 1870.

[2] Black, A. A. *Treas. Bot.* 2:1018. 1870.

[3] Sabine, J. *Trans. Hort. Soc. Lond.* 5:442. 1824. Fig.

[4] Royle, J. F. *Illustr. Bot. Himal.* 1:274. 1839.

[5] Seemann, B. *Treas. Bot.* 2:1021. 1870.

[6] Wight, R. *Illustr. Ind. Bot.* 2:167. 1850. (*S. viminale*)

[7] Seemann, B. *Treas. Bot.* 2:1021. 1870.

[8] Emerson, G. B. *Trees, Shrubs Mass.* 2:362. 1875.

[9] Rafinesque, C. S. *Fl. La.* 26. 1817. (*Laurus sassafras*)

[10] Kalm, P. *Trav. No. Amer.* 1:115. 1772. (*Laurus sassafras*)

[11] Masters, M. T. *Treas. Bot.* 2:1023. 1870.

known as saloop, which is still sold to the working classes in the early morning at the corners of the London streets. In Virginia, the young shoots are made into a kind of beer.

Satureia hortensis Linn. *Labiatae.* SUMMER SAVORY.

South Europe; supposed to have been introduced into Britain in 1562 and known to Gerarde in 1597. This species seems to be the *satureia* of Palladius [1] in the third century and of Albertus Magnus [2] in the thirteenth and is mentioned in England by Turner,[3] 1538, which would indicate its presence there at this date. Summer savory was also well known to all the earlier botanists and is mentioned as a common potherb by all the earlier writers on gardening. In 1783, Bryant [4] says that, besides being used as a potherb, it is frequently put into cakes, puddings and sausages. Summer savory was in American gardens in 1806 or earlier [5] and, as an escape from gardens, is now sparingly found. The whole plant is highly odoriferous and it is usually preferred to the other species.

S. montana Linn. WINTER SAVORY.

Caucasus and south Europe. This species was known to the earlier botanists and was probably known in ancient culture, although it is not identified with any certainty. It is mentioned in Turner's *Herbal*, 1562, and this is as far back as we have printed registers; but there can be little doubt that this, with summer savory, was much cultivated in far earlier times in England.[6] It was in American gardens in 1806.[7] The uses are the same as for the preceding species.

Saurauja napaulensis DC. *Ternstroemiaceae.*

Himalayan region. A fine tree of Nepal, called *gokul*. The natives eat the berries.[8] This is the *gogina* or *goganda* of northwest India. The palatable, viscid fruit is eaten.[9]

Sauvagesia erecta Linn. *Violarieae.*

Tropical America. The negroes and creoles of Guiana use the leaves as a spinach.[10] It is called in Guiana *adima* or *yaoba;*[11] in Peru *Yerba de St. Martin.*[12]

Saxifraga crassifolia Linn. *Saxifrageae.*

Siberia. This plant is called *badan*, and its leaves are used by the Mongols and Bouriates as a substitute for tea.[13] It is an inmate of French flower gardens.

---

[1] Palladius *Lib.* 3: c. 24.

[2] Albertus Magnus *Veg.* Jessen Ed. 569. 1867.

[3] Turner *Libellus* 1538.

[4] Bryant *Fl. Diet.* 143. 1783.

[5] McMahon, B. *Amer. Gard. Cal.* 583. 1806.

[6] Martyn *Miller's Gard. Dict.* 1807.

[7] McMahon, B. *Amer. Gard. Cal.* 583. 1806.

[8] Wallich *Pl. Asiat.* 2:40. 1830–32.

[9] Brandis, D. *Forest Fl.* 25. 1876.

[10] Don, G. *Hist. Dichl. Pls.* 1:378. 1831.

[11] Lindley, J. *Veg. King.* 343. 1846.

[12] Pickering, C. *Chron. Hist. Pls.* 673. 1879.

[13] Pickering, C. *Chron. Hist. Pls.* 793. 1879.

Scaevola koenigii Vahl. *Goodenovieae.*

Tropical regions. The leaves are eaten as potherbs. Some miraculous qualities are ascribed to its berries. The pith, which is soft and spongy, is fashioned by the Malays into artificial flowers.[1]

Scandix grandiflora Linn. *Umbelliferae.*

Eastern Europe and Asia Minor. This is an annual herb much liked as a salad for its pleasant, aromatic taste.[2]

S. pecten-veneris Linn. SCANDIX. VENUS COMB. WILD CHERVIL.

East Mediterranean countries. This is the *skanthrix*, sold, according to scandal, by the mother of Euripides. *Skanthrix* is mentioned also as a potherb by Opion, Theophrastus and Erisistratris. This, too, is the *skanthrox* of Dioscorides, eaten either raw or cooked. Scandix is enumerated by Pliny among the esculent plants of Egypt. It was observed by Honorius Bellus to be eaten in Crete.[3]

Schinus dependens Orteg. *Anacardiaceae.*

Brazil and Chile. The inhabitants prepare from the berries a kind of red wine of an agreeable flavor but very heating.[4] The fruits have a less disagreeable flavor than *S. molle.*

S. latifolius Engl.

Chile. Dr. Gillies[5] states that the Pehuenco Indians of Chile prepare by fermentation an intoxicating liquor from the fruit of this or a nearly allied species.

S. molle Linn. AUSTRALIAN PEPPER. MOLLE.

Tropical America. Acosta[6] says that the molle tree possesses rare virtues, and that the Indians make a wine from the small twigs. Garcilasso de la Vega[7] says, in Peru, they make a beverage of the berries. Molina[8] says the people of Chile prepare a red wine, very heating, from the berries. The tree was introduced into Mexico after the time of Montezuma[9] and is now found in southwestern United States.

Schizandra grandiflora Hook. f. & Thoms. *Magnoliaceae.*

Himalayan region. The fruits are pleasantly acid and are much eaten in Sikkim. The seeds are very aromatic.[10] Royle[11] says the fruit is eaten by the Hill People in the Himalayas.

---

[1] Balfour, J. H. *Man. Bot.* 523. 1875. (*S. taccada*)

[2] Mueller, F. *Sel. Pls.* 445. 1891.

[3] Pickering, C. *Chron. Hist. Pls.* 265. 1879.

[4] Molina *Hist. Chili* 1:117. 1808. (*S. huygan*)

[5] Loudon, J. C. *Arb. Frut. Brit.* 2:558. 1844. (*Duvaua latifolia*)

[6] Markham, C. R. *Trav. Cieza de Leon.* Hakl. Soc. Ed. 33:397. 1864. Note.

[7] Ibid.

[8] Molina *Hist. Chili* 117. 1808.

[9] Pickering, C. *Chron. Hist. Pls.* 853. 1879.

[10] Hooker, J. D., and Thomson, J. *Fl. Brit. Ind.* 1:44. 1855.

[11] Royle, J. F. *Illustr. Bot. Himal.* 1:62. 1839.

Schizostachyum hasskarlianum Kurz. *Gramineae.*

Java. The young shoots of this bamboo, when bursting out of the ground, are cooked as a vegetable in Java.[1]

S. serpentinum Kurz.

Java. Mueller[2] says the young shoots are used as a vegetable.

Schleichera trijuga Willd. *Sapindaceae.* GUM-LAC.

A handsome tree of India. Wight[3] says the subacid aril of the seed is eaten, and from the seeds a lamp-oil is expressed in Malabar.

Schmidelia edulis A. St. Hil. *Sapindaceae.* FRUTA DE PARAO.

Brazil. The fruits are of a sweet and agreeable taste and are sought for by the inhabitants of the places where they grow.[4]

Schotia speciosa Jacq. *Leguminosae.* CAFFIR BEAN.

Tropical and south Africa. The beans of this poisonous shrub are said by Thunberg[5] to be boiled and eaten by the Hottentots. According to Atherstone,[6] the beans are roasted and eaten in the Albany districts, where they are called *boer boom.*

Scindapsus cuscuaria Presl. *Aroideae.*

Malay. The corms are baked and eaten by the Polynesians.[7]

Scirpus articulatus Linn. *Cyperaceae.*

Africa, East Indies and Australia. This species is enumerated by Thunberg[8] among the edible plants of Japan.

S. grossus Linn. f.

East Indies and Malay. In portions of India in time of famine, the root is eagerly dug for human food. The fibers and dark cuticle being removed, the solid part of the root is dried, ground and made into bread, a little flour being sometimes mixed with it.[9]

S. lacustris Linn. BULRUSH. TULE.

Northern climates. In California, the plant is called tule and the roots are eaten by the Sierra Indians;[10] they are also eaten by the Indians of Arizona and the upper Missouri.

S. maritimus Linn. SEASIDE BULRUSH.

In India, the roots, which are large, have been ground and used as a flour in times of scarcity.[11]

---

[1] Mueller, F. *Sel. Pls.* 450. 1891.

[2] Ibid.

[3] Wight, R. *Illustr. Ind. Bot.* 1:140. 1840.

[4] Saint Hilaire, A. *Fl. Bras. Merid.* 1:294. 1825.

[5] Thunberg, C. P. *Trav.* 1:207. 1795.

[6] Black, A. A. *Treas. Bot.* 2:1035. 1870.

[7] Seemann, B. *Fl. Viti.* 287. 1865-73.

[8] Thunberg, C. P. *Fl. Jap.* XXXIII. 1784.

[9] King, Dr. *Bot. Soc. Edinb.* 10:198, 243. 1870. (*Hymenochaeta grossa*)

[10] Fremont *Explor. Exped.* 364. 1844.

[11] Royle, J. F. *Illustr. Bot. Himal.* 1:413. 1839.

Sclerocarya birroea Hochst. *Anacardiaceae.*

Eastern equatorial Africa. This plant is a forest tree called *m'choowee* on the upper Nile. The kernels of the fruit, whose unripe sarcocarp is apple-scented, are milky and are eaten like ground nuts.[1] This species affords to the natives of Abyssinia an edible kernel, while its fruits are employed in Senegal in the preparation of an alcoholic drink.[2]

S. caffra Sond.

South Africa. This species is known on the Zambezi as *mooroola*, and the seeds are eaten by the natives.[3]

Scolymus grandiflorus Desf. *Compositae.*

Egypt. The Arabs eat the stalks, both raw and boiled.[4]

S. hispanicus Linn. GOLDEN THISTLE. SPANISH OYSTER PLANT.

Mediterranean region. The root of the wild plant is collected and is used as a salsify. According to Pickering,[5] this plant is mentioned by Theophrastus, who says, " its edible root, becoming milky;" by Dioscorides, who says " the young plant, eaten as greens;" by Sibthorp, as eaten in Greece; and by Clusius who says " the root and young plant, eaten in Spain." This plant is supposed to be the *skolumus* and *leimonia* of Theophrastus, 322 B. C.; it is the *scolymus* of Pliny, A. D. 79, recorded as a food plant. The wild plant was seen in Portugal and Spain by Clusius [6] in 1576. The plant was described by Gerarde [7] in England, 1597, but he does not appear to have grown it. It was in the botanic gardens at Oxford [8] in 1658 but receives only a quoted mention from Clusius by Ray [9] in 1686. The vegetable appears not to have been in English culture in 1778,[10] nor in 1807,[11] and, in 1869, it is recorded as a new vegetable.[12] In 1597, Gerarde [13] mentions its culture in Holland, and, in 1616, Dodonaeus [14] says it was planted in Belgian gardens. In France, in 1882, it is said not to be under culture, but that its long, fleshy root is used as a kitchen vegetable in Provence and Languedoc.[15] In 1883, it is included among kitchen esculents by Vilmorin.[16] It is recorded by Burr [17] for American gardens in 1863, and its seed was offered in American seed catalogs of 1882, perhaps a few years earlier.

[1] Speke, J. H. *Journ. Disc. Source Nile* 565. 1864.

[2] Masters, M. T. *Treas. Bot.* 2:1087. 1870. (*Spondias birrea*)

[3] Jackson, J. R. *Treas. Bot.* 2:1341. 1876.

[4] Martyn *Miller's Gard. Dict.* 1807.

[5] Pickering, C. *Chron. Hist. Pls.* 187. 1879.

[6] Clusius *Hisp.* 448. 1576; *Hist.* 2:153. 1601.

[7] Gerarde, J. *Herb.* 993. 1597.

[8] Martyn *Miller's Gard. Dict.* 1807.

[9] Ray *Hist. Pl.* 257. 1686.

[10] Mawe and Abercrombie *Univ. Gard. Bot.* 1778.

[11] Martyn *Miller's Gard. Dict.* 1807.

[12] *Gard. Chron.* 584. 1869.

[13] Gerarde, J. *Herb.* 993. 1597.

[14] Dodonaeus *Pempt.* 726. 1616.

[15] *Bon Jard.* 566. 1882.

[16] Vilmorin *Les Pls. Potag.* 548. 1883

[17] Burr, F. *Field. Gard. Veg.* 94. 1863.

S. maculatus Linn. SPOTTED GOLDEN THISTLE.

Mediterranean region. This plant is thought by Unger [1] to be the *skolumos* of Dioscorides. The young leaves are eaten as a spinach. Fraas [2] says the young leaves are eaten in Greece.

Scoparia dulcis Linn. *Scrophularineae.* SWEET BROOM.

Peru and neighboring tropical America. The plant is called in Brazil *basourinha* or *vacourinha*.[3] In the Philippines, it is sometimes used as a substitute for tea and is called in Tagalo *chachachachan*.[4]

Scorpiurus sp.? *Leguminosae.* CATERPILLARS.

A strange taste causes various species of Scorpiurus to be included among garden vegetables, the caterpillar-like forms of the seed pods being used as salad-garnishing by those fond of practical jokes. As a vegetable their flavor is very indifferent. The species enumerated by Vilmorin are *Scorpiurus vermiculata* Linn., the common caterpillar; *S. muricata* Linn., the prickly caterpillar; *S. sulcata* Linn., the furrowed caterpillar; and *S. subvillosa* Linn., the hairy caterpillar. The latter species is figured by Dodonaeus, 1616, and is said even then to be sometimes grown in gardens. They are all native to southern Europe.

Scorzonera crocifolia Sibth. & Sm. *Compositae.*

Greece. The leaves, according to Heldreich,[5] are used for a favorite salad and spinach.

S. deliciosa Guss.

Sicily. This species is in most extensive cultivation in Sicily on account of its sweet roots of very grateful flavor.[6] It is considered by Mueller [7] equal, if not superior, in its culinary use to the allied salsify.

S. hispanica Linn. BLACK OYSTER PLANT. BLACK SALSIFY. VIPER'S GRASS.

Central and southern Europe. The slimy, sweetish roots have gained considerably by cultivation. The roots are long, black and tapering and are eaten, boiled or stewed, after soaking in water to extract the bitter taste. This plant was not mentioned by Matthiolus,[8] 1554, but, in 1570, was described as a new plant, called by the Spaniards *scurzonera* or *scorzonera*. In 1576, Lobel [9] says the plant was in French, Belgian and English gardens from Spanish seed. Neither Camerarius,[10] 1586, nor Dalechamp,[11] 1587, nor

---

[1] Unger, F. *U. S. Pat. Off. Rpt.* 358. 1859.

[2] Pickering, C. *Chron. Hist. Pls.* 187. 1879.

[3] Pickering, C. *Chron. Hist. Pls.* 740. 1879.

[4] Ibid.

[5] Mueller, F. *Sel. Pls.* 451. 1891.

[6] Clark, B. *Treas. Bot.* 2:1041. 1870.

[7] Mueller, F. *Sel. Pls.* 451. 1891.

[8] Matthiolus *Comment.* 558, 370. 1570; 409. 1598.

[9] Lobel *Obs.* 298. 1576.

[10] Camerarius *Epit.* 314. 1586.

[11] Dalechamp *Hist. Gen. Pl.* (Lugd.) 1206. 1587.

Bauhin,[1] 1596, nor Clusius,[2] 1601, indicates it as a cultivated plant, and Gerarde,[3] 1597, calls it a stranger in England but growing in his garden. In 1612, *Le Jardinier Solitaire* [4] calls this salsify the best root which can be grown in gardens. The use of the root as a garden vegetable is recorded in England by Meager,[5] 1683, Worlidge,[6] 1683, and by Ray,[7] 1686. Quintyne,[8] in France, 1690, calls it " one of our chiefest roots." Its cultivation does not, therefore, extend back to the sixteenth century. No varieties are recorded under culture. Black salsify was in American gardens in 1806. It was first known in Spain about the middle of the sixteenth century for its medicinal qualities as a supposed remedy for snake-bite. Black salsify was introduced into France from Spain about the beginning of the seventeenth century.

S. parviflora Jacq.

Europe, northern and western Asia. This plant is called by the Kirghis *idschelik* and is eaten as greens.[9]

S. tuberosa Pall.

Turkestan. This species yields an edible root.[10]

Scrophularia aquatica Linn. *Scrophularineae.* BISHOP'S LEAVES. BROWNWORT. WATER-BETONY.

Europe and adjoining Asia. In France, this plant is called *herbe du siège*, according to Burnett, from its roots having been eaten by the garrison of Rochelle during the siege in 1628.[11]

S. frigida Boiss.

Persia. According to Haussknecht,[12] this species yields a saccharine exudation in Persia.

Secale cereale Linn. *Gramineae.* RYE.

Orient. Rye, according to Karl Koch,[13] is found wild in the mountains of the Crimea. De Candolle [14] thinks he has discovered rye in a wild state in Australia, and a species seems to have existed in the Bronze Age of Europe, as shown by the lacustrine debris of Switzerland. Kotzebur [15] is said to have found it growing wild near Fort Ross, North America,

[1] Bauhin, C. *Phytopinax* 537. 1596.
[2] Clusius *Hist.* 2:137. 1601.
[3] Gerarde, J. *Herb.* 597. 1596.
[4] *Jard. Solit.* 210. 1612.
[5] Meager *Eng. Gard.* 61. 1683.
[6] Worlidge, J. *Syst. Hort.* 186. 1683.
[7] Ray *Hist. Pl.* 248. 1686.
[8] Quintyne *Comp. Gard.* 200. 1693. Evelyn Ed.
[9] Pickering, C. *Chron. Hist. Pls.* 587. 1879. (*S. caricifolia*)
[10] Mueller, F. *Sel. Pls.* 452. 1891.
[11] Pickering, C. *Chron. Hist. Pls.* 637. 1879.
[12] Flückiger and Hanbury *Pharm.* 373. 1879.
[13] Morton *Enc. Agr.* 2:820. 1869.
[14] De Candolle, A. *Orig. Cult. Pls.* 372. 1885.
[15] *Rpt. Ohio State Bd. Agr.* 16:164. 1861.

where it is gathered by the Indians. Syria, Armenia, Candia and south Russia have all been indicated as the native locality of rye. Pickering [1] says it is native in northeastern Europe and the adjoining portions of Asia. Rye is now found in Norway, at 67° north, but its cultivation is usually given as extending between 50° and 60° north in Europe and Asia and in America between 40° and 50° north. Fraser [2] found rye in large fields at an elevation of 11405 feet near the temple of Milun in the Himalayas. Neither the people of ancient India nor the Egyptians were acquainted with rye. The Greeks received rye from Thrace and Macedonia. [3] Pliny mentions its cultivation at the foot of the Alps [4] and thought the grain detestable and good only to appease extreme hunger. [5] Rye early reached northeastern America. In 1606, L'Escarbot sowed rye at Port Royal, Nova Scotia, [6] and, in 1610, it was growing in Champlain's garden at Quebec. [7] Rye is mentioned in New England, 1629–1633, by Wood. [8] Rye is less variable than other cultivated plants and there are but few varieties.

Sechium edule Sw. *Cucurbitaceae.* CHAYOTE.

West Indies. This species is cultivated in tropical America, the West Indies and Madeira for its fruit, which is about four inches long, three inches in diameter, of a green color outside and white within. It is used as a vegetable. [9] The roots of the old vine, on being boiled, are farinaceous and wholesome, and the seeds are very good boiled and fried in butter. It is called *chocho.* [10] In South America, it is known as *choko* and *chayote* and the fruit is used. [11] In Mexico, chayote was cultivated by the Aztecs, who called it *chayotli.* [12] In Madeira, the unripe fruit is eaten boiled and called *chocho.* In the London market, where it is sent, it is known under the name, chayote.

Sedum album Linn. *Crassulaceae.* STONECROP.

Europe, north Asia. The leaves serve as a salad. [13]

S. anacampseros Linn. EVERGREEN ORPINE.

Europe. The plant is used in soup as a vegetable. [14]

S. roseum Scop. ROSY-FLOWERED STONECROP.

Europe. In Greenland, this species is eaten. [15]

---

[1] Pickering, C. *Chron. Hist. Pls.* 513. 1879.

[2] *Enc. Brit.* **17**:630.

[3] Unger, F. *U. S. Pat. Off. Rpt.* 303. 1859.

[4] Ibid.

[5] Bostock and Riley *Nat. Hist. Pliny* **4**:52. 1856.

[6] Parkman, F. *Pion. France* 266. 1894.

[7] Parkman, F. *Pion. France* 360. 1894.

[8] Wood, W. *New Eng. Prosp.* 14. 1865.

[9] Smith, J. *Dict. Econ. Pls.* 113. 1882.

[10] Long *Hist. Jam.* **3**:802. 1774.

[11] Don, G. *Hist. Dichl. Pls.* **3**:37. 1834.

[12] Smith, A. *Treas. Bot.* **2**:1044. 1870.

[13] Loudon, J. C. *Hort.* 683. 1860.

[14] Baillon *Hist. Pls.* **3**:318. 1874.

[15] Don, G. *Hist. Dichl. Pls.* **3**:114. 1834. (*S. rhodiola*)

S. rupestre Linn. STONECROP.

Europe and adjoining Asia. The Dutch cultivated this species to mix with their salads.[1] Gerarde[2] mentions its use as a salad under the name of small summer *sengreene* and says it has a fine relish.

S. telephium Linn. ORPINE.

Europe and northern Asia. This plant is used in preparation of soups as a vegetable.[3]

Semecarpus anacardium Linn. f. *Anacardiaceae.* MARKING-NUT TREE. VARNISH TREE.

Asia and Australian tropics. The ripe fruit is collected. Fresh, it is acrid and astringent; roasted, it is said to taste somewhat like roasted apples; and when dry somewhat like dates.[4]

S. cassuvium Roxb.

Burma and Malay. The fruit has a fleshy, edible peduncle.[5]

S. forstenii Blume.

Moluccas. The fruit has a fleshy, edible peduncle.[6]

Senebiera coronopus Poir. *Cruciferae.* SWINE CRESS. WART CRESS.

Cosmopolitan. The whole herb is nauseously acrid and fetid and requires much boiling to render it eatable.[7]

S. nilotica DC.

Egypt. The cress is eaten as a salad in Egypt.[8]

Senecio cacaliaster Lam. *Compositae.*

In Thibet, this plant serves for the manufacture of *chong*, a spirituous and slightly acid liquor.[9]

S. ficoides Sch.

South Africa. The leaves are wholesome.[10]

Sesamum indicum Linn. *Pedalineae.* SESAME.

Tropics; cultivated from time immemorial in various parts of Asia and Africa. The seeds are largely consumed as food in India and tropical Africa, but their use in European countries is mainly for the expression of oil. In Sicily, the seeds are eaten scattered on bread, an ancient custom mentioned by Dioscorides.[11] In central Africa, sesame is culti-

---

[1] Phillips, H. *Comp. Kitch. Gard.* 1:268. 1831.

[2] Gerarde, J. *Herb.* 2nd Ed. 515. 1633 or 1636.

[3] Baillon, H. *Hist. Pls.* 3:318. 1874. Note.

[4] Brandis, D. *Forest Fl.* 125. 1874.

[5] Baillon, H. *Hist. Pls.* 5:305. 1878.

[6] Ibid.

[7] Don, G. *Hist. Dichl. Pls.* 1:216. 1831.

[8] Don, G. *Hist. Dichl. Pls.* 1:217. 1831.

[9] Loudon, J. C. *Enc. Agr.* 163. 1866. (*Cacalia sarracenica*)

[10] Dickie, G. D. *Treas. Bot.* 1:187. 1870. (*Cacalia ficoides*)

[11] Hooker, W. J. *Journ. Bot.* 1:135. 1834.

vated as an article of food, also for its oil.   This oil, which is largely exported from British India and Formosa, is an excellent salad oil; it is used in Japan for cooking fish.   In China, the species is extensively cultivated for the seeds to be used in confectionery.[1]   During a famine in Rajputana, the press-refuse was sold at a high price for food.   This seems to be the species, which is used by the negroes of South Carolina, who parch the seeds over the fire, boil them in broths, and use them in puddings.

Sesame was cultivated for its oil in Babylonia in the days of Herodotus and Strabo, also in Egypt in the time of Theophrastus, Dioscorides and Pliny.   Its culture in Italy is mentioned by Columella, Pliny and Palladius.   The seeds are used as a food by the Hindus, after being parched and ground into a meal which is called, in Arabic, *rehshee*. The expressed oil has a pleasant taste and is also used in cookery.   In Japan, sesame is highly esteemed,[2] but Miss Bird [3] says the use of this oil in frying is answerable for one of the most horrific smells in Japan.   In China also, the oil is used.[4]   In Greece, the seeds are made into cakes.[5]

Sesbania cavanillesii S. Wats.   *Leguminosae.*

Mexico.   The seeds are used as a substitute for coffee.[6]

S. grandiflora Poir.   VEGETABLE HUMMING-BIRD.

East Indies, Malay and Australia.   Its flower, says La Billardière,[7] is the largest of that of any of the leguminous plants, of a beautiful white, or sometimes red color, and the natives of Amboina often eat it dressed, and occasionally even raw, as a salad.   About Bombay, the plant is cultivated for its large flowers and pods, both of which are eaten by the natives.[8]   The pods are upwards of a foot long, compressed, four sided, and the tender leaves, pods and flowers are eaten as a vegetable in India.[9]   In Burma, this is a favorite vegetable with the natives,[10] and, in the Philippines, its flowers are cooked and eaten.[11]   In the West Indies the flower is not used as a food but is called, at Martinique, vegetable humming-bird.[12]

Sesuvium portulacastrum Linn.   *Ficoideae.*   SAMPHIRE.   SEASIDE PURSLANE.

Common on the sandy shores of the tropical and warm regions of the Western Hemisphere.   Sloane [13] says this plant is pickled in Jamaica and eaten as English samphire. Royle [14] says the succulent leaves are used as a potherb.

---

[1] Smith, F. P.   *Contrib. Mat. Med. China* 195.   1871.
[2] Ainslie, W.   *Mat. Med.* 2:255.   1826.
[3] Bird *Unbeat. Tracks Jap.* 1:176.   1881.
[4] Lunan, J.   *Hort. Jam.* 2:251.   1814.
[5] Ainslie, W.   *Mat. Med.* 2:255.   1826.
[6] Havard, V.   *Proc. U. S. Nat. Mus.* 500.   1885.
[7] La Billardière *Voy. Recherche Pérouse* 1:357.   1799.
[8] Pickering, C.   *Chron. Hist. Pls.* 699.   1879.
[9] Brandis, D.   *Forest Fl.* 138.   1876.
[10] Pickering, C.   *Chron. Hist. Pls.* 699.   1879.
[11] Ibid.
[12] Berlanger *Trans. N. Y. Agr. Soc.* 568.   1858.   (*Agati grandiflora*)
[13] Lunan, J.   *Hort. Jam.* 2:157.   1814.
[14] Royle, J. F.   *Illustr. Bot. Himal.* 1:223.   1839.

Setaria glauca Beauv. *Gramineae.*

Europe, temperate Asia and eastern equatorial Africa. This plant is infested with a small, round fungus, the dust of which is eaten by the natives. It was observed by Grant at 2° north and was described by Hochst.[1]

S. italica Beauv. BENGAL GRASS. ITALIAN MILLET. JAPANESE MILLET.

Tropics and subtropics. This species is frequently cultivated in Italy and other warm countries.[2] The seeds are found in the debris of the lake villages of Switzerland.[3] This millet was introduced into France in 1815, where its cultivation as a forage plant has become considerably extended.[4] In the United States, its seed was distributed through the Patent Office in 1854,[5] and its cultivation as a fodder crop has become quite extended.

This plant seems to have been known to the ancient Greeks as *elumos* and to the Romans as *panicum*.[6] It is now grown in Italy as a fodder plant and for the grain to form polenta.[7] This millet forms a valued crop in southern Europe as also in some parts of central Europe. It is not mentioned among American grasses by Flint, 1857, and is barely mentioned by Gould, 1870, except by description. It is mentioned as introduced from Europe and now spontaneous, by Gray,[8] 1868, but millet, probably this species, is mentioned prior to 1844. In India, this millet is considered by the natives as one of the most delicious of cultivated grains and is held in high estimation by the Brahmans. At Mysore, three varieties are cultivated: *bili*, on watered land; *kempa*, in palm gardens, and *mobu*, in dry fields. In more western tracts, other varieties are grown.[9]

Shepherdia argentea Nutt. *Elaeagnaceae.* BUFFALO BERRY.

Western plains of the United States. This plant is somewhat cultivated for ornament. Catlin[10] speaks of it in its native region as producing its fruit in incredible quantities, hanging in clusters to every limb and to every twig, about the size of ordinary currants and not unlike them in color and even in flavor, being exceedingly acid and almost unpalatable until they are bitten by the frosts of autumn, when they are sweetened and their flavor becomes delicious. They are dried by the Indians as winter food.

S. canadensis Nutt.

Vermont and Wisconsin northward to beyond the Arctic circle and very common on the Mackenzie. Its small, red, juicy, very bitter and slightly acid berry is useful; says Richardson,[11] for making an extempore beer, which ferments in twenty-four hours and is an agreeable beverage in hot weather. Gray[12] calls the fruit insipid.

---

[1] Pickering, C.   *Chron. Hist. Pls.* 733.   1879.   (*S. aurea*)

[2] Loudon, J. C.   *Enc. Agr.* 833.   1866.   6th Ed.

[3] Heer, O.   *Gard. Chron.* 1068.   1866.

[4] Flint, C. L.   *Grasses, Forage Pls.* 145.   1867.   (*Panicum germanicum*)

[5] *U. S. Pat. Off. Rpt.* XXII.   1854.   (*Panicum germanicum*)

[6] Unger, F.   *U. S. Pat. Off. Rpt.*   1859.

[7] Morton *Enc. Agr.* 2:550.   1869.

[8] Gray, A.   *Man. Bot.* 650.   1868.

[9] Ainslie, W.   *Mat. Med.* 1:226.   1826.   (*Panicum italicum*)

[10] Catlin, G.   *No. Amer. Indians* 1:73.   1842.

[11] Richardson, J.   *Arctic Explor.* 2:307.   1851.

[12] Gray, A.   *Man. Bot.* 425.   1868.

Sicana odorifera Naud. *Cucurbitaceae.* COROA. CURUA.

Brazil. The odor of the fruit is agreeable. The taste is sweet and at first not unpleasant but it soon nauseates. Notwithstanding this, there are some persons, says Correa de Mello,[1] but not many, who eat it.

Sicyomorpha sp. *Celastrineae.*

A genus of plants from Peru. The fruit is said to be edible and is similar in form to a cucumber.[2]

Sicyos angulata Linn. *Cucurbitaceae.* BUR CUCUMBER.

Eastern United States. In New Zealand, this plant is boiled for greens.[3] In France, it is an inmate of the flower garden.[4]

Sideroxylon australe Benth. & Hook. f. *Sapotaceae.*

Australia. The plants yield a tolerably good fruit.[5]

S. dulcificum A. DC. MIRACULOUS BERRY.

Tropical Africa. The fruit is eaten by the English residents of western Africa to counteract acidity of any article of food or drink, the sweet flavor being retained by the palate for a considerable time.[6]

S. tomentosum Roxb.

East Indies. The fruit is about the size of a crab and not unlike one, agreeing moreover with the sour, austere taste of that fruit. It is made into pickles, and the natives cook and eat it in their curries.[7]

Silaus flavescens Bernh. *Umbelliferae.* MEADOW SAXIFRAGE. PEPPER SAXIFRAGE.

Middle Europe. This species is mentioned by Pliny. It is cooked as an acid potherb.[8]

Silene cucubalus Wibel. *Caryophylleae.* BLADDER CAMPION.

Europe, north Africa, Himalayan region and naturalized in America. Johnson[9] says the young shoots resemble green peas in taste and make a very good vegetable for the table when boiled. In 1685, the crops in Minorca having been nearly destroyed by locusts, this plant afforded support to many of the inhabitants. Pickering[10] says it is used throughout the Levant, the leaves being cooked and eaten.

---

[1] De Mello *Bot. Soc. Edinb.* **10**:348. 1870.

[2] Masters, M. T. *Treas. Bot.* **2**:1342. 1876.

[3] Pickering, C. *Chron. Hist. Pls.* 989. 1879.

[4] Vilmorin *Fl. Pl. Ter.* 1067. 1870. 3rd Ed.

[5] Mueller, F. *Sel. Pls.* 17. 1891. (*Achras australis*)

[6] Smith, A. *Treas. Bot.* **2**:1057. 1870.

[7] Wight, R. *Icon. Pls.* **4**:Pl. 1218. 1850. (*Sapota elengoides*)

[8] Pickering, C. *Chron. Hist. Pls.* 507. 1879. (*Cnidium silaus*)

[9] Johnson, C. P. *Useful Pls. Gt. Brit.* 54. 1862. (*S. inflata*)

[10] Pickering, C. *Chron. Hist. Pls.* 289. 1879. (*S. inflata*)

Siler trilobum Crantz. *Umbelliferae.*

Orient, middle and south Europe. The stems are edible and the fruit serves as a condiment.[1] This plant is called on the lower Volga *gladich*. This is the *baltracan* described by Barbaro as having the smell of rather musty oranges, its stem single, hollow, thicker than one's finger and more than a " braccio " high; leaf like rape; seed like fennel but larger, pungent, but pleasant to taste and when in season, if broken as far as the soft part, can be eaten without salt. The water in which the leaves are boiled is drunk as wine and is very refreshing.[2]

Silphium laeve Hook. *Compositae.* ROSIN-WEED.

North America. The tuberous roots are eaten by the Indians along the Columbia River.[3]

Silybum marianum Gaertn. *Compositae.* HOLY THISTLE. MILK THISTLE.

Europe. This plant was formerly cultivated in gardens in England but has now fallen into disuse. The young leaves were once used in spring salads or boiled as a substitute for spinach. The young stalks, peeled and soaked in water to extract the bitterness, were cooked and eaten much in the manner of sea kale. The roots, when two years old, were used much in the way of salsify, which they resemble, and the receptacle of the flowers was cooked and eaten as an artichoke.[4] Bryant,[5] in his *Flora Dietica*, says the young shoots in the spring surpass the finest cabbage when boiled as a vegetable. Johnson[6] says the roots were sometimes baked in pies. Lightfoot[7] says, in Scotland, the tender leaves are by some boiled and eaten as garden stuff.

Simmondsia californica Nutt. *Euphorbiaceae.*

Southern California. The ripe fruit is the size of a hazelnut and has a thin, smooth, three-valved husk, which, separating spontaneously, discloses a brown, triangular kernel. This fruit, though edible, can hardly be termed palatable. Its taste is somewhat intermediate between that of the filbert and acorn. It is employed by the Indians as an article of diet and is called by them *jajoba*.[8]

Sison amomum Linn. *Umbelliferae.* HONEWORT. STONE PARSLEY.

Europe and Asia Minor. Lindley[9] says the seeds are pungent and aromatic but have a nauseous smell when fresh. Mueller[10] says they can be used for a condiment.

---

[1] Mueller, F. *Sel. Pls.* 251. 1891. (*Laserpitium aquilegifolium*)
[2] Pickering, C. *Chron. Hist. Pls.* 815. 1879. (*Laserpitium trilobum*)
[3] Black, A. A. *Treas. Bot.* 2:1059. 1870.
[4] McIntosh, C. *Book Gard.* 2:134. 1855. (*Carduus marianus*)
[5] Bryant *Fl. Diet.* 60. 1783.
[6] Johnson, C. P. *Useful Pls. Gt. Brit.* 149. 1862. (*Carduus marianus*)
[7] Lightfoot, J. *Fl. Scot.* 1:454. 1789. (*Carduus marianus*)
[8] Parry *Bot. U. S. Mex. Bound. Surv.* 2:17. 1859.
[9] Pickering, C. *Chron. Hist. Pls.* 320. 1879.
[10] Mueller, F. *Sel. Pls.* 458. 1891.

Sisymbrium alliaria Scop.   *Cruciferae.*   GARLICWORT.   SAUCE-ALONE.

This plant, of Europe and adjoining Asia, is the sauce-alone of Gerarde,[1] who says " divers eat the stamped leaves hereof with salt fish, for a sauce, as they do those of ransons." It is the garlicwort of Turner [2] and is eaten with meat, having a strong odor of garlic. According to Neill,[3] when gathered as it approaches the flowering state, if boiled separately and then eaten with boiled mutton, it forms a desirable potherb. In Wales, it is often fried with bacon or herrings and is sometimes eaten as a salad. The Germans call it *sasskraut* and use it much as a salad in the spring. In England, it is used with lettuce.

S. canescens Nutt.   TANSY MUSTARD.

North and South America. The seeds are collected by the Indians of California.[4]

S. officinale Scop.   BANK CRESS.   CRAMBLING ROCKET.   HEDGE MUSTARD.

Europe and north Africa. This European herb, now naturalized in the United States, is used as greens or spinach in many parts of Britain. Don [5] says the plant smells strongly of garlic and was formerly used in Europe by country people in sauces and salads. Bridgeman, 1832, in his work on American gardening says it is used as an early potherb and has a warm and acrid flavor. Johnson [6] says it is occasionally cultivated as a pot-herb but is not very palatable.

Sium decumbens Thunb.   *Umbelliferae.*   JELLICO.

Japan. The leaves are eaten in Cochin China.[7]

S. helenianum Hook. f.   JELLICO.

St. Helena Islands. This species is called jellico at St. Helena, where the green stems are sold in the markets for eating raw.[8]

S. latifolium Linn.   WATER PARSNIP.

North America and Europe. The leaves are cooked and eaten in Italy.[9]

S. sisarum Linn.   SKIRRET.

Eastern Asia. This plant is a hardy perennial, usually grown as an annual, a native of China; introduced into Britain before 1548. It is mentioned by Gerarde.[10] The Emperor Tiberius is said to have demanded this sweet and somewhat aromatic root as a tribute from the Germans living on the Rhine. In America, it was seen by Romans [11] at Mobile, Alabama, in 1775. In 1806, it is mentioned among garden products by

[1] Gerarde, J.   *Herb.* 650.   1597.

[2] Pickering, C.   *Chron. Hist. Pls.* 634.   1879.   (*Erysimum alliaria*)

[3] Johnson, C. P.   *Useful Pls. Gt. Brit.* 35.   1862.   (*Erysimum alliaria*)

[4] Brewer and Watson *Bot. Cal.* 40.   1880.

[5] Don, G.   *Hist. Dichl. Pls.* 1:209.   1831.   (*Alliaria officinalis*)

[6] Johnson, C. P.   *Useful Pls. Gt. Brit.* 35.   1862.

[7] Loureiro *Fl. Cochin.* 179.   1790.

[8] *Treas. Bot.* 2:1308.   1876.

[9] Pickering, C.   *Chron. Hist. Pls.* 172.   1879.

[10] Gerarde, J.   *Herb.* 201.   1597.

[11] Romans *Nat. Hist. Fla.* 1:115.   1775.

McMahon.[1] The root is composed of fleshy tubers about the size of the little finger and, formerly more than now, was esteemed when boiled as among the sweetest, whitest and most pleasant of roots. McIntosh[2] says skirret is much used in French cookery. Skirret seed appears for sale in American catalogs.

This plant seems to have been unknown to the ancients; certainly no mention can be found of an umbellifer with grouped and divergent roots, the peculiarity of skirret alone among European cultivated plants of this order. In the sixteenth century, the name *siser* was applied to the carrot as well as to skirret: as, by Camerarius,[3] who describes *siser*, the *sisaron* of the Greeks, as a skirret; and *siser alterum*, Italian *carota bianca*, German *gierlin*, Spanish *chirivia*, French *chervy* or *girolle* or *carotte blanche*, as a carrot; other illustrations of this period and earlier might be given. Fuchsius,[4] 1542, figures skirret, as does also Ruellius,[5] 1550, Tragus,[6] 1552, and many others after this time. Skirret was well known in Europe as a plant of culture at this period. It perhaps came, says De Candolle,[7] from Siberia to Russia and thence into Germany. Skirret is not named by Turner,[8] 1538, but is in 1551.[9] In 1570, the *Adversaria* gives the English name as scyrret.

Sloanea dentata Linn. *Tiliaceae.*

Brazil and Guiana. The species yields an edible fruit.[10]

Smilacina racemosa Desf. *Liliaceae.* FALSE SPIKENARD. TREACLE-BERRY.

Siberia and northeast North America. The berries are pale red, speckled with purple and are aromatic.[11] Wood[12] mentions this among edible wild fruits. Josselyn[13] says it is called " treacle-berries, having the perfect taste of treacle when they are ripe — and will keep good for a long while. Certainly a very wholesome berry and medicinal."

Smilax china Linn. *Liliaceae.* CHINA-ROOT.

China, Cochin China and Japan. The rootstocks are eaten by the Chinese on account of the abundance of the starch.[14]

S. glyciphylla Sm. SARSAPARILLA. SWEET TEA PLANT.

Australia. The leaves are used as tea.[15]

---

[1] McMahon, B. *Amer. Gard. Cal.* 583. 1806.

[2] McIntosh, C. *Book Gard.* 2:229. 1855.

[3] Camerarius *Epit.* 226, 227. 1586,

[4] Fuchsius *Hist. Stirp.* 752. 1542.

[5] Dioscorides Ruellius Ed. 239. 1550.

[6] Tragus *Stirp.* 911. 1552.

[7] De Candolle, A. *Orig. Pls. Cult.* 39. 1885.

[8] Turner *Libellus*. 1538.

[9] Bauhin, C. *Pinax* 155. 1623.

[10] Unger, F. *U. S. Pat. Off. Rpt.* 315. 1859.

[11] Gray, A. *Man. Bot.* 530. 1868.

[12] Wood, W. *New Eng. Prosp.* 15. 1865.

[13] Josselyn, J. *New Eng. Rar.* 87, note. 1865. Orig. 1672.

[14] Lindley, J. *Med. Econ. Bot.* 64. 1849.

[15] Masters, M. T. *Treas. Bot.* 2:1066. 1870.

S. laurifolia Linn.

Southeastern United States. The young shoots are eaten as asparagus in the southern states.[1] The roots were used by the Indians to obtain a fecula for food.[2]

S. pseudo-china Linn.

New Jersey to Kentucky and southward. The Indians of Carolina boiled and ate the root.[3] The Seminoles of Florida obtained their red meal from the root.[4] The young shoots are used as an asparagus in the southern states and the roots were used by the Confederate soldiers in the manufacture of an extemporaneous beer.[5]

S. rotundifolia Linn. GREEN BRIAR.

Pennsylvania to Kentucky and southward. Griffith[6] says the fecula obtained from the root was employed by the Indians as a meal.

S. tamnoides Linn.

New Jersey, Virginia and southward. The fecula of the root is used as a meal by the Indians.[7]

Smyrnium olusatrum Linn. *Umbelliferae.* ALEXANDERS. HORSE PARSLEY.

Europe and the adjoining portion of Asia; formerly much cultivated. Alexanders was mentioned by Dioscorides,[8] and, in the time of Gerarde,[9] the root was sent to the table raw as a salad herb. In the United States, it is mentioned by McMahon,[10] 1806, as used for culinary purposes as cardoon and blanched in like manner, but it does not appear in his general list of kitchen-garden esculents. The young shoots and leaf-stalks are the part eaten; they have, when raw, a rather agreeable taste, not very unlike that of celery, though more pungent; they are likewise used to flavor soups and stews and are still so employed in England by the country people. The stalks are blanched in the manner of celery.[11] This vegetable was formerly much esteemed in Italy.

The name alexanders is said to be a corruption of Olusatrum, but Ray[12] says it is called so either because it came from the Egyptian city of that name or it was so believed. The Italian name *macerone* is believed by Ray to have been corruptly derived from Macedonia but a more probable origin is from *maceria*, the Italian for wall, as Columella[13] says, "*Pastinato loco semine debet conseri maxime juxta maceriam.*"

In this umbellifer, as De Candolle remarks, we can follow the plant from the begin-

[1] Porcher, F. P. *Res. So. Fields, Forests* 616. 1869

[2] Griffith, W. *Med. Bot.* 660. 1847.

[3] Porcher, F. P. *Res. So. Fields, Forests* 617. 1869.

[4] Ibid.

[5] Porcher, F. P. *Res. So. Fields, Forests* 616. 1869.

[6] Griffith, W. *Med. Bot.* 660. 1847.

[7] Ibid.

[8] Gerarde, J. *Herb.* 1019. 1636.

[9] Ibid.

[10] McMahon, B. *Amer. Gard. Cal.* 198. 1806.

[11] Johnson, C. P. *Useful Pls. Gt. Brit.* 124. 1862.

[12] Ray *Hist. Pl.* 437. 1686.

[13] Columella lib. II, c. 3.

ning to the end of its culture. Theophrastus, who flourished about 322 B. C., speaks of alexanders as an officinal plant, under the name of *hipposelinon*. Dioscorides, who lived in the first century after Christ, speaks of the edible properties of the roots and leaves, while Columella and Pliny, authors of the same century, speak of its cultivation. Galen, in the second century, classes it among edibles, and Apicius, in the third century, gives a recipe for its preparation for the table. Charlemagne, who died A. D. 814, included this vegetable among those ordered to be planted on his estates. Ruellius's edition of *Dioscorides*, 1529, does not speak of its culture, nor does Leonicenus, 1529; but Fuchsius, 1542, says it is planted in gardens. Tragus, 1552, received seed from a friend, so it was apparently not generally grown in his part of Germany at this date. Matthiolus, in his *Commentaries*, 1558, refers to its edible qualities. Pena and Lobel, 1570, say in England it occurs abundantly in gardens and that the cultivated form is far better than the wild plant. Camerarius, 1586, says, " *in hortis seritur.*" Gerarde, 1597, does not speak of its culture but says, " groweth in most places of England," but in his edition of 1630 says, " The root hereof is also in our age served to the table raw for a sallade herbe." Dodonaeus, 1616, refers to its culture in the gardens of Belgium, and Bodaeus à Stapel, in his edition of *Theophrastus*, 1644, says it is much approved in salads and is cultivated as a vegetable. *Le Jardinier Solitaire*, 1612, mentions the culture of celery, but not that of alexanders, in French gardens. Quintyne, in the English edition of his *Complete Gard'ner*, 1704, says " it is one of the furnitures of our winter-sallads, which must be whitened like our wild Endive or Succory." In 1726, Townsend, in his *Complete Seedsman*, refers to the manner of use, but adds, " 'tis but in few gardens." Mawe's *Gardener*, 1778, refers to this vegetable, but it is apparently in minor use at this time; yet Varlo, in his *Husbandry*, 1785, gives directions for continuous sowing of the seed in order to secure a more continuous supply. McMahon, in his *American Gardeners' Kalendar*, 1806, includes this vegetable in his descriptions but not in his general list of kitchen garden esculents; it is likewise enumerated by later American writers and is included by Burr, 1863, among garden vegetables, a survival of mention apparently not indicating use; and Vilmorin, in his *Les Plantes Potagères*, 1883, gives a heading and a few lines to *maceron*. Its seed is not now advertised in our catalogs.

S. perfoliatum Linn. ALEXANDERS.

Southern Europe. This form of alexanders is thought by some to be superior to *S. olusatrum*.[1] This species is perhaps confounded with *S. olusatrum* in some of the references already given. Loudon says it was formerly cultivated, and McIntosh says it is thought by many superior to *S. olusatrum*, a remark which Burr[2] includes in his description. Although the species is separated by a number of the older botanists, yet Ruellius, 1529, is the only one who refers to its edible qualities. This plant, which De Candolle says has been under common culture for fifteen centuries, has shown no change of type during that time. The figures, which occur in so many of the herbals, all show the same type of plant, irrespective of the source from which the illustration may have been taken, unless perhaps the root is drawn rather more enlarged in some cases than in others.

[1] McIntosh, C. *Book Gard.* 2:129. 1855.
[2] Burr, F. *Field, Gard. Veg.* 315. 1863.

Solanum aethiopicum Linn. *Solanaceae.* GOLDEN APPLE. LOVE APPLE.

Asia and tropical Africa; cultivated there and elsewhere for its edible berries, which are large, red, globular and uneven. The fruits are eaten in China, Japan and in Egypt.

S. anguivi Lam. MADAGASCAR POTATO.

Madagascar. The small, red, glabrous berries are eaten.[1]

S. aviculare Forst. f. KANGAROO APPLE.

New Zealand, Australia and Tasmania. The fruit is eaten by the islanders of the Pacific.[2] The greenish-yellow berry, the size of a plum, is edible but acerb unless fully ripe.[3] The berries lose their unpleasant acidity only after they have dropped in full maturity from the branches, and then their taste resembles, in some degree, *Physalis peruviana*, to which they are also similar in size.[4] The native tribes eagerly collect the fruit as an article of food.

S. cari Molina.

Chile. This is a distinct species of potato which has been long cultivated in Chile but is still unknown not only in Europe but also in Quito and Mexico

S. commersonii Dun.

Valparaiso to Buenos Aires. The species resembles the common potato.[5]

S. elaeagnifolium Cav.

Tropical America. The Mexicans use the fruit for curdling milk and, according to Dr. Gregg, call it *trompillo*.[6]

S. fendleri A. Gray.

This species is found growing in great abundance in northern New Mexico. The tuber is one of the chief articles of winter diet with the Navajo Indians. These tubers are quite small, one-half to three-quarters of an inch in diameter, of a good taste and are somewhat like a boiled chestnut. This species has been suggested as the original of the cultivated potato, but the history of the cultivated potato is against this theory.[7]

S. gilo Raddi.

Brazil. The plant is much cultivated for its large, spherical, orange-colored berries, which are eatable.[8]

S. maccai Dun.

Guiana. The red, globose berry is edible.[9]

[1] Don, G. *Hist. Dichl. Pls.* 4:437. 1838.

[2] Unger, F. *U. S. Pat. Off. Rpt.* 337. 1859.

[3] Masters, M. T. *Treas. Bot.* 2:1071. 1870. (*S. laciniatum*)

[4] Hooker, W. J. *Journ. Bot.* 8:338. 1856.

[5] De Candolle, A. *Geog. Bot.* 814. 1855.

[6] Torrey, J. *Bot. U. S. Mex. Bound. Surv.* 2:152. 1859.

[7] *U. S. D. A. Rpt.* 409. 1870.

[8] Mueller, F. *Sel. Pls.* 460. 1891.

[9] Don, G. *Hist. Dichl. Pls.* 4:431. 1838.

S. maglia Schlecht.

Chile. This is a wild potato of Chile called *maglia* by the natives. The tubers are very small and of a slightly bitter taste.[1]

S. melongena Linn. EGGPLANT. JEW'S APPLE. MAD APPLE.

Old World tropics. The eggplant seems not to have been known in Europe in the time of the ancients. The Arab physician, Ebn Baithar, who wrote in the thirteenth century, speaks of it and cites Rhases, who lived in the ninth century.[2] Albertus Magnus,[3] who lived in Europe in the thirteenth century, mentions it. Ibn-al-awam, a Moorish Spaniard of the twelfth century, describes four species, and six are noted in the Nabathaean agriculture.[4] According to Jessen,[5] Avicenna, who flourished about A. D. 595, knew it, and called it *badingan*. Bretschneider [6] says the eggplant can be identified in the *Ts'i min yao shu*, a Chinese work on agriculture of the fifth century, and is described in later writings of 1590, 1640, and 1742. Acosta [7] mentions, as among the vegetables carried from Spain to America, the " *berengenas*, or apples of Love;" and Piso,[8] 1658, figures the eggplant among Brazilian plants, under the name of *belingela*.

The eggplants first known in Europe appear to belong to the class we now grow for ornament, the fruit resembling an egg. They were of various colors. Fuchsius, 1542, mentions the purple and the yellow; Tragus, 1552, who says they have recently reached Germany from Naples, names the same colors; Lyte's *Dodoens*, 1586, names two kinds, one purple and the other pale or whitish. In 1587, Dalechamp figures three kinds, the one long, another obscurely pear-shaped and the third rounded; he mentions the colors purple, yellow and ash-colored; Gerarde, 1597, says white, yellow or brown; Dodonaeus, 1616, mentions the oblong and round, white and purple; Marcgravius, 1648, describes a round and yellow fruit; J. Bauhin, 1651, names various sorts, the long, the deep and the round, yellow, purple and whitish. Bontius, 1658, describes the wild plant of Java as oblong and round, or spherical, the color yellow; the cultivated sorts purple or white. Rauwolf particularly describes these plants at Aleppo, 1574, as ash-colored, yellow and purple.

At present, the purple eggplant is almost the only color grown in our kitchen gardens but there are many sorts grown in other regions. The purple and the white ornamental are mentioned for American gardens in 1806; as also in England, 1807; in France, 1824. In the Mauritius, Bojer [9] names three varieties of purple and white colors. In India, Carey [10] says, there are several varieties in constant cultivation by the natives, such as

[1] De Candolle, A. *Geog. Bot.* 2:812. 1855.

[2] De Candolle, A. *Orig. Pls. Cult.* 287. 1885.

[3] Albertus Magnus *Veg.* Jessen Ed. 204. 1867.

[4] Ibn-al-awam *Livre d'Agr.* 2: pt. 1, pp. 236–239. 1866.

[5] Albertus Magnus *Veg.* Jessen Ed. 204. 1867.

[6] Bretschneider, E. *Bot. Sin.* 59. 1882.

[7] Acosta *Nat. Mor. Hist. Ind.* 1:265. 1880. Hakl. Soc. Ed.

[8] Piso *De Ind.* 210. 1658.

[9] Bojer, W. *Hort. Maurit.* 240. 1837.

[10] Roxburgh, W. *Hort. Beng.* 16. 1814.

green, white, purple, yellow.   Firminger [1] describes purple-, black- and white-fruited forms; and Speede [2] names the purple and white in six varieties.   In Cochin China, Loureiro describes five sorts: purple, white, and variegated.

There are two sorts of plants to be recognized: (a) The one with the stems, leaves and calyxes unarmed, or nearly so. (b) The other with the stems, leaves and calyxes more or less aculeate.   The first sort is figured by Fuchsius, 1542, and by succeeding authors up to the present date.   The second sort is first noticed by Camerarius, 1588, and has continued to the present time.

The varieties now grown in American gardens can be divided very readily into four types, the oval, round, long and the oblong or pear-shaped.   The following synonymy can be established:

I.

THE OVAL.

This, at present, includes but ornamental sorts, and present forms show a marked improvement in evenness and regularity over the older forms.

Calyx not spiny.—

Mala insana.   Fuch. 513.   1542; Roeszl. 117.   1550; Tragus 894.   1552; Pineaus
        514.   1561; Ger. 274.   1597; Sweert. t. 20, p. 1.   1612; Dod. 458.   1616.
Melongena sive mala insana vel melanzana.   Lob. *Obs.* 138.   1576; *Icon.* i, 268.   1591.
Melongena, seu mala insana.   Cam. *Epit.* 820.   1586.
Melongena.   Matth. *Opera.* 760.   1598.
Melanzane.   Dur. C. 279.   1617.
Solanum pomiferum fructu rotundo.   Bauh. J. **3**:618.   1651.
Melongena arabum.   Chabr. 524.   1673.
Aubergine blanche.   Vilm. 27.   1883.

Calyx spiny.—

Melanzana fructu pallido.   Hort. Eyst.   1713; *Aut. Ord.* **1**:3; also ib.; 1613.
White Egg-Plant.   N. Y. Sta.   1886.

II.

THE ROUND.

Calyx not spiny.—

Belingela.   Marcg. 24.   1648; Piso. 210.   1658.
Aubergine ronde de Chine.   Decaisne and Naudin. *Man.* **4**:288.
Black Pekin.   Ferry.   1883; Hovey.   1866.

Calyx spiny.—

Black Pekin.   Greg.   1886; Thorb.   1886.

III.

THE LONG.

This type varies much in size and proportion, if the Chinese variety described by Kizo Tamari [3] as recently introduced into Japan belongs to this class.   He says it is about one inch in diameter by one foot and a half long.   This form may be either straight or curved.

---

[1] Firminger, T. A. C.   *Gard. Ind.* 155.   1874.

[2] Speede *Ind. Handb. Gard.* 177.   1842.

[3] *Amer. Hort.* 10.   1886.

Calyx not spiny.—

    Melantzana arabum melongena. Dalechamp **2**: app. 23. 1587.

    Solanum pomiferum fructu incurvo. Bauh. J. **3**:619. 1651; Chabr. 524. 1673;
        Pluk. *Phyt.* t. 226, p. 2. 1691.

    Aubergine violette longue. Decaisne and Naudin. *Man.* **4**:287.

Calyx spiny.—

    Aubergine violette longue. Vilm. 24. 1883.

IV.

THE OBLONG OR PEAR-SHAPED.

This form is a swollen fruit with an elongation towards the summit, in some of its varieties shaped like the powder-horn gourd.

Calyx not spiny.—

    Melantzana nigra. Dalechamp. **2**: app. 23. 1587.

    Aubergine violette nain tres hative. Vilm. 26. 1883.

    Early Round Violet. Damman. 1884.

Calyx spiny.—

    Solanum pomiferum magnus fructu, etc. Pluk. *Phyt.* t. 226, p. 3. 1691.

    Melongena. Tourn. t. 65. 1719.

    American Large Purple. Burr. 609. 1863.

We may note that the Arabic words *melongena* and *bedengaim* were applied by Rauwolf to the long-fruited form, the calyx not spiny, while the word *betleschaim* or *melanzana batleschaim* was applied to the spiny-calyx form of the pear-shaped, if Gronovius's [1] synonymy is to be trusted.

Every type in the varieties under cultivation can with certainty be referred to one of the four forms above named. The oval type is figured in 1542, as we have shown; the round type in 1648, in Brazil; the long type, by Dalechamp, in 1587; and the pear-shaped type also in 1587. All the colors now noted, and more, receive notice by the ancient writers. As we have confined our synonymy to those authors who have given figures and have omitted those who but described, however certainly the descriptions would apply, we can claim accuracy as to our facts.

We, hence, have no evidence that types have originated through cultivation in recent years and we have strong evidence that types have continued unchanged through long-continued cultivation under diverse climates. It is but as we examine variation within types that we see the influences of cultivation. The oval-fruited is described by Dodonaeus, 1616, as of the form and size of an egg, but he says that in Egypt, where the plant is wild, it attains double or three times the size which it has in France and Germany. Ray, 1686, compares the size of the long-fruited to that of an egg, or of a cucumber, a comparison that would answer for to-day, as cucumber-size covers a wide range; but, he adds, that the curved form is like a long gourd. The figures of the pear-shaped in 1719 indicate a fruit which compares well with the usual sizes grown at the present time. It is in regularity of form and in the large size of selected strains that we see the influence arising from careful selection and protected growth. What other influence has climate exercised? We do not know.

---

[1] Gronovius *Fl. Orient.* 25, 26. 1755.

This sketch illustrates the point already made in studies of the dandelion, celery and other vegetables — that types of varieties have great fixity, are not produced through human selection and cultivation, and, we wish we could add in this case, originated from wild prototypes; but, unfortunately, there are no records of the variation observed in feral or spontaneous plants.

S. montanum Linn.

Peru.   The Peruvian Indians are stated to use the roots in soups.[1]

S. muricatum Ait.   PEPINO.

Chile and Peru.   This is a shrubby species with egg-shaped, edible berries, which are white, with purple spots, and attain a length of six inches.[2]

S. nigrum Linn.   BLACK NIGHTSHADE.   COMMON NIGHTSHADE.

Cosmopolitan.   This plant, says Vilmorin, is not as yet used in France as a vegetable, but, in warm countries, the leaves are sometimes eaten as spinach.[3]   It is mentioned by Galen[4] among aliments in the second century but was not cultivated in Germany in Fuchsius'[5] time, 1542, although it retained its name, *Solanum hortense*, perhaps from its former cultivation.   It is a plant of wide distribution, occurring in the northern hemisphere from Sweden and the northeast of America from Hudson Bay, even to the equatorial regions; as, for example, at Timor, the Galapagos, the Antilles, Abyssinia, the Mascarene Isles, Mauritius, Van Diemen's Land and Chile.[6]   It is found as a potherb in the markets of Mauritius[7] and is used as a spinach in central Africa.[8]   In China, the young shoots are eaten, as also its black berries,[9] and, in the Mississippi Valley, the little black berries are made into pies and other pastry.[10]

S. quitoënse Lam.

Peru.   The berries resemble in size, color and taste small oranges and are of a peculiar fragrance.[11]   The Peruvians eat this fruit.[12]

S. repandum Forst. f.

Pacific Isles.   In Viti, the fruit is eaten by the natives, either in soups or with yams.[13]

S. sessiliflorum Dun.

Brazil.   The berries are eaten in Para, where they are called *cubios*,[14] and the leaves are also eaten in Brazil.[15]

---

[1] Masters, M. T.   *Treas. Bot.* **2**:1235.   1870.

[2] Mueller, F.   *Sel. Pls.* 462.   1891.

[3] Vilmorin *Veg. Gard.* 355.   1885.

[4] Galen *Aliment.* lib. 2. Bruns. Ed. 153.   1547.

[5] Fuchsius *Hist. Stirp.* 69.   1542.

[6] De Candolle, A.   *Geog. Bot.* **2**:573.   1855.

[7] Seemann, B.   *Gard. Chron.* 622.   1861.

[8] Speke, J. H.   *Journ. Disc. Source Nile* 576.   1864.

[9] Smith, F. P.   *Contrib. Mat. Med. China* 201.   1871.

[10] Bessey *Bot.* 502.   1880.

[11] Mueller, F.   *Sel. Pls.* 462.   1891.

[12] Masters, M. T.   *Treas. Bot.* **2**:1070.   1870.

[13] Seemann, B.   *Gard. Chron.* 697.   1861.

[14] Don, G.   *Hist. Dichl. Pls.* **4**:436.   1838.

[15] Masters, M. T.   *Treas. Bot.* **2**:1070.   1870.

S. topiro Humb. & Bonpl. TURKEY BERRY.

Banks of the Orinoco. The berry is edible.[1]

S. torvum Sw.

Cosmopolitan tropics. West Indies to Peru. This species is shrubby with yellow, spherical berries of good size which seem wholesome.[2]

S. trilobatum Linn.

Tropical Asia. The leaves are eaten by the Hindus.[3]

S. tuberosum Linn. POTATO.

Western South America. A native of southern Chile, becoming an object of cultivation in northern Chile and Peru in the time of the Incas.[4] Mueller[5] says the potato is found wild also in Argentina. Darwin[6] states that the wild potato now grows on the islands of the Chonos Archipelago in great abundance, on the sandy, shelly soil near the sea beach. The tubers were generally small, but he found one of oval shape two inches in diameter, resembling in every respect and having the same smell as English potatoes. When boiled, these potatoes shrunk much and were watery and insipid, without any bitter taste. They grow as far south as latitude 50 and are called *aquinas* by the wild Indians of that part. Frezier,[7] 1732, speaks of the potatoes of the Chile Indians as called by them *papas* and as being quite insipid in taste.

According to Humboldt,[8] the potato was cultivated at the time of the discovery of America in all the temperate regions of Chile to New Granada but not in Mexico. The earliest mention of the potato, if it be not the sweet potato, is that of Peter Martyr, who, referring to the time of Columbus' voyages, says that the Indians of Darien " dygge also out of the grounds certayne rootes growing of themselves, which they call *betatas*, muche lyke unto the navie rootes of Millane, or the great puffes or mushroomes of the earth. Howsoever they be dressed, eyther fryed or sodde, they geve place to no suche kynde of meate in pleasant tendernes. The skinne is somewhat tougher than eyther the navies or mushromes, and of earthy colour, but the inner meate thereof is very white: These are nourished in gardens. . . . They are also eaten rawe and have the taste of rawe chestnuts but are somewhat sweeter." In 1519, Pigafetta Vicentia, the chronicler of the voyage of Magellan. says, on the coast of Brazil, 20° south, the natives brought the Spaniards baskets of potatoes, or " batates," a root resembling " turnips, and tasted like chestnuts," but these may have been the sweet potato.

In 1553, Peter Cieca[9] says the inhabitants of Peru and vicinity had a tuberous root which they eat and call *papas*. Cieza de Leon,[10] who traveled between 1532 and 1550,

[1] Don, G. *Hist. Dichl. Pls.* 4:410. 1838.

[2] Mueller, F. *Sel. Pls.* 462. 1891.

[3] Ainslie, W. *Mat. Ind.* 2:427. 1826.

[4] Pickering, C. *Chron. Hist. Pls.* 660. 1879.

[5] Mueller, F. *Sel. Pls.* 462. 1891.

[6] Darwin, C. *Voy. H. M. S. Beagle* 285. 1845.

[7] Frezier *Rel. Voy.* 61. 1732.

[8] De Candolle, A. *Geog. Bot.* 2:810. 1855.

[9] McAdam, R. S. *Journ. Agr.* 5:323. 1835.

[10] Markham, C. R. *Trav. Cieza de Leon.* Hakl. Soc. Ed. 33:360. 1864.

says the country of the Collao has for the principal food of its inhabitants potatoes, which are like the earth-nut. They dry these potatoes in the sun and keep them from one harvest to another. After they are dried, they call them *chunus*, and they are highly esteemed and valued among them. *Chunus*, or frozen potatoes, are still the ordinary food in the Collao. Garcilasso de la Vega [1] also speaks of the *papas* of the Collao, round and moist, and inclined to rot soon. Prescott [2] says the potato formed the great staple of the more elevated plains of Peru, under the Incas. Acosta,[3] who wrote about 1590, says they call " papas these rootes (which) are like to ground nuttes, they are small roots which cast out many leaves. They gather this *papas*, and dry it well in the sunne, then beating it they make that which they call *chuno* which keepes many daies, and serves for bread . . . they likewise eat of these *papas* boyled or roasted." Zarata,[4] 1555, speaks of the potato being cultivated by the Peruvians and called papas. In 1565, Hawkins [5] found potatoes at Santa Fe de Bogata and carried some thence.

In the West Indies, we find no mention of the potato until some time after the discovery of the islands. In 1564, Hawkins [6] says the potatoes at Margarita Island, just, off the coast of Venezuela, are " the most delicate rootes that may be eaten, and doe far exceede parssnips or carets." In 1595, Captain Preston [7] and Sommers, on their way to Virginia, stopped at Dominica Islands, and the Indians brought to them " plantans and potatos." In 1633, White [8] found this root in great abundance in Barbados.

It is quite possible that Hawkins [9] carried the potato to North America in 1565 when he relieved the famine among the French on the banks of the river May, now St. Johns, Florida, and sailed northward towards Virginia, where, in 1584, Hariot [10] describes under the name of *openawk* what is supposed to be the potato: " The roots of this plant grow in damp soils, many hanging together as if fixed on ropes. They are good food, either boiled or roasted." Round potatoes, says Jefferson,[11] " were found in Virginia when first visited by the English; but it is not said whether of spontaneous growth, or by cultivation only." In 1597, Gerarde [12] says, " it groweth naturally in America, where it was first discovered, as reports Clusius, since which time I have received roots thereof from Virginia, otherwise called Norembega;" his description applies to the potato. The potato is mentioned under cultivation in Virginia in 1609,[13] in 1648 [14] and in 1649 as better than

[1] Vega *Roy. Comment.* Hakl. Soc. Ed. 2:17. 1871.

[2] Prescott, W. H. *Conq. Peru* 1:141. 1860.

[3] Acosta *Sierras Peru* 259. 1601.

[4] Zarate *Hist. Conq. Peru.* 1555.

[5] Hawkins *Second Voy.* 1564. Hakl. Soc. Ed. 27. 1878.

[6] Ibid.

[7] Preston and Sommers *Voy.* Hakl. Voy. 10:215. 1904.

[8] White *Rel. Md.* 14, 15. 1664. Force Coll. Tracts 4: No. 2. 1846.

[9] Hawkins *Second Voy.* 1588. Hakl. Soc. Ed. 66. 1878.

[10] Hariot *Narrative Va.* 1588. Quaritch Reprint. 26. 1893.

[11] Jefferson *Notes Va.* Trenton 54. 1803.

[12] Gerarde, J. *Herb.* 781. 1597.

[13] *True Decl. Va.* 13. 1610. Force Coll. Tracts 3: No. 1. 1844.

[14] *Perf. Desc. Va.* 4. 1649. Force Coll. Tracts 2: No. 8. 1838.

those grown in England, " excellently delicious and strongly nourishing." [1] Potatoes are said to have been introduced into New England by a colony of Presbyterian Irish, who settled in Londonderry, New Hampshire, in 1719, but cultivation did not become general for many years; potatoes appeared in Salem, Massachusetts, about 1762, as a field crop. In 1830, Col. Morris, then in his ninetieth year, informed Watson [2] that the potatoes used in his early life were very inferior to those of the present; they were called Spanish potatoes and were very sharp and pungent in the throat and smell, but a better sort was received from Liverpool.

Tench Frances, of Philadelphia, first imported an improved stock, which, by frequent cultivation, he much improved. About 1817, says Goodrich, [3] the potato bore seed to the amount, perhaps, of a gill to the hill; from 1842 to 1847, in the annual cultivation of two and a half acres, he recollects having found but two branches, and his experience, he says, has not been exceptional. In 1806, McMahon [4] mentions but one kind; and in 1832, Bridgeman [5] says there are many varieties. In 1848, nearly 100 kinds were exhibited at the Massachusetts Horticultural Society; in 1876, at the Centennial Exhibition, 500 named varieties were shown. The potato now extends over North America to Labrador and Fort Simpson, 65° north, where Richardson [6] says they yield well.

Sir J. Banks [7] considers that the potato was first brought into Europe from the mountainous parts of South America in the neighborhood in Quito in the early part of the sixteenth century. Yet the Spanish name of *battatas* corresponds to the " betatas " of Peter Martyr and would indicate that these tubers came from the coast region of South America; yet, strangely enough, they are now called *batatas Inglezas* according to McIntosh. [8] Bowles, in his introduction to the *Natural History of Spain*, is quoted by M. Drouyn de Thuys as saying that the potato was first transported from Spain into Galicia and thence to Italy where it was so common in the sixteenth century as to be fed to animals; but the first date we find is from Nuttall, [9] who says that, according to Bauhin, the potato was introduced into Europe from the mountainous parts of Peru in the year 1590, and this strangely enough — too strange to be true — is after the potato was known elsewhere. In Bauhin's *Phytopinax*, 1596, appears, according to Hallam, [10] the first accurate description of the potato, which he says was already cultivated in Italy. In Italy, it received the name of the truffle, *taratoufle*, which reminds one of the description of P. Martyr. Sismondi, [11] whose work on agriculture was published in 1801, says the potato, little known in Lombardy, was introduced by himself into the hills of Tuscany, where it was then known only to the

[1] Williams, E. *Virginia* 48. 1650. Force Coll. Tracts 3: No. 11. 1844.

[2] Watson, J. F. *Annals Phil.* 2:487. 1845.

[3] Goodrich *Trans. N. Y. Agr. Soc.* 447. 1847.

[4] McMahon, B. *Amer. Gard. Cal.* 582. 1806.

[5] Bridgeman, J. *Young Gard. Asst.* 85. 1857.

[6] Richardson, J. *Arctic Explor.* 1:165. 1851.

[7] Loudon, J. C. *Enc. Agr.* 845. 1866.

[8] McIntosh, C. *Book Gard.* 2:223. 1855.

[9] Nuttall, T. *Gen. No. Amer. Pls.* 1:128. 1818.

[10] Hallam, H. *Lit. Europe* 1:243. 1856.

[11] Loudon, J. C. *Enc. Agr.* 53. 1866.

gardeners of Florence and Leghorn. Glasspoole[1] says its cultivation in Tuscany began in 1767. In 1588, Clusius,[2] at Vienna, received a present of two of the tubers from Flanders and gives a plate of the plant in his book published in 1601.[3] In 1600, Olivier de Serres speaks of the potato as recently brought to France from Switzerland. It was not, however, until the middle of the eighteenth century that, under the urging of Parmentier,[4] it became an object of general culture. The potato was introduced into Sweden in 1720, where, notwithstanding the exertions of Linnaeus,[5] it did not come into general cultivation until aided by royal edict in 1764. It has now reached the North Cape, where it is grown in gardens.[6] The potato has been grown on a large scale in Saxony only since 1717; in Prussia, since 1738;[7] in Germany since 1710.[8]

It is said by Glasspoole,[9] that Hawkins, in 1565, brought the potato into Ireland, but Lindley says it was first introduced by Raleigh on his Irish estate. As the return of Raleigh's ships and the acquisition of these estates took place in 1585, this is probably the date of the introduction. Dr. Campbell,[10] however, in his *Political Survey*, says the potato was not introduced into Ireland until 1610. In 1597, Gerarde[11] had the potato growing in his garden in England. Woolridge,[12] who wrote in 1687, says: "I do not hear that it has been yet essayed whether they may not be propagated in great quantities for the use of swine and other cattle." Lisle,[13] in his *Husbandry*, 1694–1722, does not mention potatoes. Mortimer,[14] in his *Gardeners' Kalendar* for 1708, says, "The root is very near the nature of the Jerusalem artichoke, although not so good and wholesome, but it may prove good to swine." Bradley,[15] about 1719, says, "They are of less note than horse-radish, radish, scorzoners, beets and skirret; but, as they are not without their admirers, I will not pass them by in silence." Miller,[16] 1754, says they are "despised by rich and deemed only proper food for the meaner sort of persons." The potato was introduced into Lancashire in 1728, where its cultivation soon became general and whence it gradually spread over other counties of England. In Scotland, the potato was first cultivated in 1739, in the county of Sterling, and was not known in the Highlands until 1743.[17] Booth[18] says it was introduced in 1725 and came into field culture about 1760.

---

[1] Glasspoole, H. G. *Ohio State Bd. Agr. Rpt.* 29:420. 1874.

[2] *Journ. Agr.* 1:679. 1829.

[3] Ibid.

[4] Glasspoole, H. G. *Ohio State Bd. Agr. Rpt.* 29:420. 1874.

[5] Ibid.

[6] Stephens, G. *Journ. Agr.* 6:93. 1836.

[7] Boussingault, J. B. *Rur. Econ.* 154. 1865.

[8] Ibid.

[9] Glasspoole, H. G. *Ohio State Bd. Agr. Rpt.* 29:414. 1874.

[10] Ibid.

[11] *Journ. Agr.* 1:679. 1829.

[12] Glasspoole, H. G. *Ohio State Bd. Agr. Rpt.* 29:414. 1874.

[13] Glasspoole, H. G. *Ohio State Bd. Agr. Rpt.* 29:422. 1874.

[14] Ibid.

[15] Ibid.

[16] *Journ. Agr.* 1:679. 1829.

[17] *Journ. Agr.* 5:327. 1835.

[18] Booth, W. B. *Treas. Bot.* 2:1071. 1870.

The potato is mentioned as among the edible products of Japan by Thunberg,[1] 1776, and its cultivation, says Humboldt,[2] has become common. In New Zealand, where it had become common by 1840, the first tubers were left by Captain Cook 1770.[3] In China, at the present time, the potato is grown chiefly for consumption by foreigners and has not found favor with the natives.[4] It is now also grown in the Island of Java, in the Buton, in Bengal and from the extremity of Africa to Labrador, Iceland and Lapland, says Humboldt[5] in 1811.

The tenor of the whole history of the potato seems such as to imply that at first its tuber was of such poor quality as not to obtain general liking, that it was only as the quality was improved that its acceptance became assured and that it is to the effort of growers that it has secured at the present time a quality that forces universal approval.

The varieties of the potato are now innumerable and, while of several distinct types of form and color, are all supposed to have been derived from a common wild progenitor. It is interesting to observe, therefore, that varieties were under culture in South America even before the discovery. In a vocabulary of a now extinct tribe, the Chibcha, who once occupied the region about the present Bogota, ten different varieties are identified, one of which, " black inside," has not as yet appeared in modern culture.[6] At the present time, Vilmorin[7] makes an extremely artificial classification as follows: (1) The round, yellow varieties. (2) The long, yellow varieties. (3) The variegated, long, yellow varieties. (4) The round, red varieties. (5) The flat, pink, or red varieties. (6) The smooth, long, red varieties. (7) The notched, long, red varieties. (8) The violet-colored and variegated varieties. The yellow and red varieties are mentioned by Bauhin,[8] 1596, as the tawny and the purple. In 1726, Townsend[9] mentions the white and the red in England, as does Bryant[10] in 1783. In 1785, Varlo[11] describes eight sorts: " the White Round, the Red Round, the Large Irish White Smooth, the Large Round Red, the Culgee, the Early-wife, the White Kidney, the Bull's-eye Red." In further description he says " the Jerusalem is long and full of eyes, the Culgee is red on one side, the Early-wife does not blossom and is of a light red, and the Toadback is nearly akin to the large Irish, the skin almost black, and rough like a russetting; the Kidney is oblong, white with a yellowish cast." In 1828, Fessenden says there are many varieties, and, in 1832, Bridgeman says the varieties are very numerous. In 1848, nearly 100 sorts were exhibited at the Massachusetts Horticultural Society in Boston. Decaisne and Naudin give the number of varieties in France in 1815 as 60, in 1855 as 493, in 1862 as 528.

---

[1] Thunberg, C. P. *Fl. Jap.* XLII. 1784.

[2] Humboldt, A. *Polit. Essay New Spain* 2:352. 1811.

[3] Wilkes, C. *U. S. Explor. Exped.* 2:412. 1845.

[4] Williams, S. *U. S. Pat. Off. Rpt.* 474. 1860.

[5] Humboldt, A. *Polit. Essay New Spain* 2:352. 1811.

[6] *Gard. Chron.* 26:720. 1886.

[7] Vilmorin *Veg. Gard.* 443. 1885.

[8] Bauhin, C. *Phytopinax* 301. 1596.

[9] Townsend *Seedsman* 23. 1726.

[10] Bryant, C. *Fl. Diet.* 15. 1783.

[11] Varlo *Husbandry* 2:97. 1785.

A number of wild varieties of the potato have been grown at the New York Agricultural Experiment Station, including the *Solanum maglia*. One sort, which has not as yet been identified with its specific name, corresponds to the notched class of Vilmorin. The *maglia* corresponds to the round and oblong-flattened forms; the *jamesii* to the round form. The colors of these wild potatoes are said by some growers to include the white, the red, and the variegated. In their habits of growth, the *maglia* forms its tubers deep under the ground, the *jamesii* very much scattered and extending a long distance from the plant.

The synonymy of our types can include those described by Vilmorin, as follows:

I.— Round yellow. Vilm. 1885.
    Round as a ball. Ger. 781. 1597; 927. 1633.
    Solanum tuberosum. Blackw. *Herb*. pl. 523. b. 1773.
    White round. Varlo *Husb*. 2:97. 1785.
II.— Long yellow. Vilm. 1885.
    Ovall or egge fashion. Ger. 781. 1597; 927. 1633.
    Oblonga. Bauh. *Prod*. 90. 1671; Matth. 757. cum ic. 1598.
    Papas peruanorum. Clus. *Rar*. 2:79. cum ic. 1601.
III.— Variegated long yellow. Vilm. 1885.
IV.— Round red. Vilm. 1885.
    Pugni magnitudine. Matth. 757. 1598.
    Red round. Varlo *Husb*. 2:97. 1785.
V.— Flat pink or red. Vilm. 1885.
VI.— Smooth long red. Vilm. 1885.
    ? Solanum tuberosum. Blackw. *Herb*. pl. 523. b. 1773.
VII.— Notched long red. Vilm. 1885.
    ? Membri virilis forma. Bauh. *Prod*. 90. 1671.
VIII.— Violet colored and variegated.
    ? Atrorubens. Bauh. *Phytopin*. 301. 1596.
    Toadback. Varlo. *Husb*. 2:97. 1785.
    Solanum tuberosum tuberibus nigricantibus. Blackw. *Herb*. 7. 586.

The figures which seem to be referable to the *maglia* species are:

Batata virginiana sive virginianorum pappus. Ger. 781. 1597.
Solanum tuberosum esculentum. Matth. *Op*. 758. 1598; Bauh. *Prod*. 89. 1671.
Arachidna theophrasti forte, Papas peruanorum. Clus. *Rar*. 2:79. 1601.
Papas americanus. Sweertius *Florelig*. 7. 28. fig. 4. 1612.

The potatoes which are now grown in the United States were derived from several sources; from England of late years; from Bogota [1] in 1847; and from Chile [2] in 1850.

S. uporo Dun.

Islands of the Pacific. In Viti, the fruit is prepared by the natives into a sauce which is used at their cannibal feasts. The white settlers occasionally use the fruit to prepare a sauce like the tomato and use the leaves as a potherb.[3] It is used as a vegetable in the Society Islands and New Zealand.[4]

---

[1] Couper *Farm. Lib*. 382. 1847.
[2] *Trans. N. Y. Agr. Soc*. 726. 1850; 367. 1851.
[3] Seemann, B. *Fl. Viti*. 176. 1865–1873.
[4] Unger, F. *U. S. Pat. Off. Rpt*. 357. 1859. (*S. viride*)

S. xanthocarpum Schrad. & Wendl. YELLOW-BERRIED NIGHTSHADE.

Old World tropics. This species is cultivated for its fruit in the Circars. The fruits are much esteemed by the natives, who eat them in their curries.[1]

Solidago odora Ait. *Compositae.* SWEET GOLDEN-ROD.

Eastern North America. Pursh[2] says the dried flowers make a pleasant and wholesome tea substitute. In the *American Naturalist,*[3] 1879, it is said this plant is used as a tea in Pennsylvania.

Sonchus oleraceus Linn. *Compositae.* SOW THISTLE.

Europe, Asia and naturalized in the United States. This thistle is mentioned as an esculent by Dioscorides. Pliny records that the hospitable Hecate regaled Theseus before his encounter with the bull of Marathon with a dish of sow thistles. In Germany, the young leaves are put into salads, and this common weed is exceedingly wholesome.[4] Hooker[5] says it is eaten by the natives of New Zealand.

S. tenerrimus Linn.

Mediterranean region. This thistle is eaten in Italy as a salad.[6]

Sonneratia acida Linn. f. *Lythrarieae.*

Malay and shores of the East Indies. The fruit is eaten by the natives.[7] A. Smith[8] says the acid, slightly bitter fruits are eaten as a condiment by the Malays.

Sophora secundiflora Lag. *Leguminosae.*

Mexico. This is the *frijolillo* of Texas, according to Bellanger. The Indians near San Antonio formerly used it for an intoxicant.[9]

Sorghum vulgare Pers. *Gramineae.* BROOM CORN. DURRA. EGYPTIAN CORN. KAFFIR
       CORN. NEGRO CORN. PAMPAS RICE. RICE CORN. SORGHUM. TENNESSEE RICE.

Tropics and subtropics. This species is supposed to be a native of Africa, perhaps of Abyssinia, and has been cultivated in China from a remote period. Doolittle[10] says the Chinese make a coarse kind of bread from the flour of the seeds of sorghum, eaten principally by the poorer classes. The best kind of Chinese whiskey, often called Chinese wine, is distilled from the seeds. This Chinese form was imported into France from the north of China about 1851 and, through the agency of the Patent Office, it was obtained from France in 1854 and distributed in the United States. Of the French importation

---

[1] Drury, H. *Useful Pls. Ind.* 397. 1873.

[2] Porcher, F. P. *Res. So. Fields, Forests* 458. 1869.

[3] *Amer. Nat.* 345. 1879.

[4] Johnson, C. P. *Useful Pls. Gt. Brit.* 142, 143. 1862.

[5] Hooker, J. D. *Bot. Antarctic Voy.* 2:324. 1847.

[6] Johns, C. A. *Treas. Bot.* 2:1072. 1870.

[7] Pickering, C. *Chron. Hist. Pls.* 727. 1879.

[8] Smith, A. *Treas. Bot.* 2:1073. 1870.

[9] Havard, V. *Torr. Bot. Club Bul.* 23:39. 1896.

[10] Doolittle, J. *Social Life Chinese* 25. 1868. Note.

from Shanghai, it is interesting to note that but one seed of all that was received, germinated. The Zulu Kaffirs cultivated the African variety, called *imphee*, about their huts for the purpose of chewing and sucking the stalks, and Mr. Wray [1] recognized 15 varieties, which he introduced to this country in 1857. He found this species in 1851 and engaged in the distribution of the seed in Europe and Asia before bringing it to America. There are some mentions of this plant, however, far earlier. In 1786, a Signor Pietro Arduino [2] is said to have attempted its introduction into Italy from Kaffirland but did not succeed, and Wilkinson in his *Ancient Egyptians* states that the plant grows about Assuan in Nubia, in the oases, and is called by the Arabs *dokhn*. One writer attempts, indeed, to identify this plant with the variety mentioned by Pliny, *S. nigrum*, and described by the earlier herbalists. Barth [3] speaks of its being extensively grown in Africa, and Livingstone [4] says the stalks are chewed as sugar cane and the people are fat thereon. Pallas says it is cultivated by the Tartars of the Crimea.

Sorghum is now cultivated throughout India, tropical Asia, Africa, southern Europe, the West Indies and America. Next to rice, says Carey,[5] this may be said to be the most extensively cultivated of all the culmiferous tribe and forms a very considerable part of the diet of the natives of the countries where it is grown. There are many varieties. Pliny [6] speaks of the black-seeded millet brought to Italy from the East Indies, and Fuchsius, 1542, describes the *shorgi;* Tragus, 1552, gives it the name *Panicum Dioscorides et Plinii;* Gesner, 1591, calls it *sorghum;* Matthiolus, 1595, *milium indicum;* Lobel, 1576, describes this species as *sorgo melica Italorum;* Dodonaeus, 1583, as *melica sorghum;* and Lonicer, 1589, and Gerarde, 1597, describe several varieties. Durra, or Guinea corn, was introduced into Jamaica and thence into our southern states in the last century and was reported as growing in Georgia in 1838. In the West Indies, negro corn is largely consumed by the colored population when made into bread. In the United States, a variety is largely grown for the making of brooms under the name of broom corn. In western Kansas, varieties are grown for the seed in regions which are too arid for the certain growing of maize under the names Egyptian corn, rice corn, pampas rice, Tennessee rice and durra. In 1805, a specimen of Egyptian corn was exhibited to the Massachusetts Society for Promoting Agriculture as grown in New Hampshire.[7] In Egypt, six varieties are enumerated as cultivated for the seed used as food. In Algeria, two kinds are grown, the red and the white seeded. The *dari*, from Jaffa, is considered the best in the Mediterranean region and is exported. In Italy, the seeds, apparently of the black variety, are used for bread. At the Madras exhibition of 1857, 56 varieties were shown, and Elliott [8] says he has seen it in all parts of India, Arabia, Abyssinia, Egypt, Asia Minor, Turkey and Italy. Sorghum is also found in Natal, where it is called Kaffir corn.

[1] Stewart, F. L. *Sorghum Prod.* 20. 1867.

[2] Olcott, H. S. *Sorghum* 23. 1857.

[3] *U. S. Disp.* 1602. 1865.

[4] Waller, H. *Last Journ. Livingstone* 51. 1875. (*S. saccharatum*)

[5] Roxburgh, W. *Hort. Beng.* 7. 1814.

[6] Pliny lib. 18, c. 10.

[7] *Commentators to the Mass. Soc.* 26. 1806.

[8] Elliott, W. *Bot. Soc. of Edinb.* 7:282. 1863.

Thunberg[1] enumerates sorghum among the edible plants of Japan. In Europe, says Unger,[2] sorghum is raised to advantage in Hungary, Dalmatia, Italy and Portugal. In the United States, sorghum will probably not be grown as a food grain except in the arid regions.

Sorindeia madagascariensis DC. *Anacardiaceae.*

Africa and Madagascar. On the upper Nile, the fruit is eaten. The bunches are two feet long with 200 plums each, the size of a sparrow egg, taste like a mango, are yellow and hang curiously from the main trunk and boughs like parasites. The fruits grow also from among the leaves.[3]

Sparaxis bulbifera Ker-Gawl. *Irideae.* HARLEQUIN FLOWER.

South Africa. The bulbous tubers are edible.[4]

Specularia speculum A. DC. *Campanulaceae.* VENUS'S LOOKING-GLASS.

Europe and Mediterranean region. Henfrey[5] says this plant has been used in salads. It is grown in the flower garden in France.[6]

Spergula arvensis Linn. *Caryophylleae.* CORN SPURRY. TOADFLAX.

Europe; naturalized in North America. In Finland and Scandinavia, says Johnson,[7] in time of scarcity bread has sometimes been made of the seeds.

Sphaerococcus cartilaginens Good. & Wood. *Algae.*

Balfour[8] says this seaweed is used in China as a substitute for edible birds-nests. It is to be found in Chinese markets and differs but little from Irish moss and is used as a substitute for the more expensive birds-nest.

Sphagnum obtusifolium Ehrh. *Sphagnales.* BOG MOSS. SPHAGNUM.

Temperate climates. Sphagnum, says Lindley,[9] is a wretched food in barbarous countries.

Spilanthes acmella Murr. *Compositae.* ALPHABET-PLANT. PARA CRESS.

Cosmopolitan tropics and subtropics. This plant is used as a salad plant in Brazil.[10] It is the *Cresson du Brésil* of the French and is cultivated as a seasoning plant.[11] In South America, it is the cress of Para and is cultivated as a salad and potherb in tropical countries.[12]

---

[1] Thunberg, C. P. *Fl. Jap.* XXXIII. 1784.

[2] Unger, F. *U. S. Pat. Off. Rpt.* 306. 1859.

[3] Speke, J. H. *Journ. Disc. Source Nile* 565. 1864.

[4] Seemann, B. *Treas. Bot.* 2:1076. 1870.

[5] Henfrey, A. *Bot.* 303. 1870.

[6] Vilmorin *Fl. Pl. Ter.* 220. 1870. 3rd Ed. (*Campanula speculum*)

[7] Johnson, C. P. *Useful Pls. Gt. Brit.* 53. 1862.

[8] Balfour, J. H. *Man. Bot.* 520. 1844.

[9] Lindley, J. *Med. Econ. Bot.* 23. 1849.

[10] Unger, F. *U. S. Pat. Off. Rpt.* 356. 1859. (*S. oleracea*)

[11] *Bon Jard.* 567. 1882. (*S. fusca*)

[12] Black, A. A. *Treas. Bot.* 2:1083. 1870. (*S. oleracea*)

It is eaten as a salad in the Mascarenhas, in the East Indies, South America [1] and in Japan, where it is called *hoko so*.

Spinacia oleracea Linn.   *Chenopodiaceae*.   SPINACH.

Cultivated everywhere. Spinach appears to have been introduced into Europe through Spain by the Mauro-Spaniards.[2] According to Beckman, the first notice of its use as an edible in Europe occurs in 1351 in a list of vegetables used by monks on fast days, but, in the Nabataean agriculture in Spain, in the twelfth century,[3] Ibn-al-Awam speaks of it as a prince of vegetables. Albertus Magnus,[4] who lived in Germany and died in the year 1280, knew the prickly-seeded form, and the *Ortus Sanitatis* of 1511 figures spinach and gives a Greek name *aspenach*. It was also well known to Agricola in 1539.[5] In England, the name *spynoches* occurs in a cook book of 1390, compiled under the name of *The Forme of Cury* for the use of the court of King Richard the Second; in 1538, spinach is spoken of by Turner [6] in his *Libellus* as well known in England and, in 1536 by Ruellius, as if well known in France. These dates are interesting, as De Candolle calls it new to Europe in the sixteenth century and other authors date its first mention in England as not preceding 1568. The smooth-seeded spinach is described by Tragus in 1552. According to Sprengel, spinach is noticed by Crescentius in the thirteenth century and is badly figured in the *Ortus Sanitatis*, edition of 1491. According to Bretschneider, spinach is noticed in a Chinese work on husbandry of the seventh or eighth century.[7] There is no early notice of its introduction into America, but, in 1806, three varieties were known to our gardens.[8]

Two races are now known in American gardens; one with prickly seed, and the other with smooth seed. These have been described as follows:

I.

PRICKLY-SEEDED SPINACH.

Spinacia spinosa Moench.

Spinachia. Alb. Mag. 13th Cent.   Jessen Ed. 563; Fuchsius. 666. cum ic. 1542; Dod. 619. cum ic. 1616.
Binetach, Spinat, Spinacia. Roeszl. cum ic. 1550.
Olus hispanicus. Trag. 325. cum ic. 1552.
Spinacia. Matth. 342. cum ic. 1570; Lob. *Obs*. 129. 1576. cum ic. 1591; ic. **1**:257. 1591; Dalechamp 544 cum ic. 1587; Ger. 260. cum ic. 1597.
Spanachum. Cam. *Epit*. 245. cum ic. 1586.
Lapathum hortense alterum, sue spinacia semine spinoso. Bauh. *Phytopin*.
Spinachia mas. Bauh. J. **2**:964. cum ic. 1651.

---

[1] Unger, F.   *U. S. Pat. Off. Rpt.* 356. 1859.
[2] Targioni-Tozzetti *Trans. Hort. Soc. Lond.* **9**:148. 1855.
[3] Heuze, G.   *Pls. Aliment.* I, IV. 1873.
[4] Albertus Magnus *Veg.* Jessen Ed. 563. 1867.
[5] Ammonius *Med. Herb.* 323. 1539.
[6] Turner *Libellus* 1538.
[7] Bretschneider, E.   *On Study* 16. 1870.
[8] *N. Y. (Geneva) Agr. Sta. Rpt.* **6**:226. 1887.

Spinacia oleraceae. Linn. var. A. Linn. *Sp.* 2d ed. 1456.
Epinard d'Angleterre. Vilm. 203. 1883.
Large Prickly or Winter Spinage. Vilm. 533. 1885.

II.

SMOOTH-SEEDED SPINACH.

Spinacia inermis Moench.

Spinachia nobilis. Trag. 324. 1552.
Lapathum hortense alterum spinacia, semine non spinoso. Bauh. *Phytopin.* 184. 1596.
Spinacia II. Ger. 260. 1597.
Spinachia foemina. Bauh. J. 2:964. 1651.
Spinachia semine non pungente, folio majore rotundiore. Ray 162. 1686; Chabr.
   303. cum ic. 1677.
Spinacia glabra. Mill. *Dict.* 1733.
Spinacia oleracea. Linn. var. B. Linn. *Sp.* 1456. 1762.
Epinards à graine ronde. Vilm. 204. 1883.
Round-seeded Spinage. Vilm. 534. 1885.

Spinach was in American gardens in 1806.[1] But one variety of the prickly-seeded is described by Vilmorin[2] and five of the smooth-seeded form.

Spiraea filipendula Linn. *Rosaceae.* DROPWORT. MEADOW SWEET.
   Europe and northern Asia; common in gardens in the United States. Linnaeus[3] says the roots have been eaten by men instead of bread.

Spondias lutea Linn. *Anacardiaceae.* BRAZILIAN PLUM. JEW PLUM. OTAHEITE APPLE.
   Cosmopolitan tropics. At Tahiti, says Ellis,[4] the *vi*, or Brazilian plum, is an abundant and excellent fruit of an oval or oblong shape and bright yellow color. In form and taste, it somewhat resembles a Magnum Bonum plum but is larger and, instead of a stone, has a hard and spiked core containing a number of seeds. Firminger[5] says its appearance is very inviting, as is also its exquisite fragrance, resembling that of the quince; to the taste, however, it is very acid, with a flavor like that of an exceedingly bad mango. This is the Jew plum of Mauritius.[6] Lunan[7] says the fruit is purple, yellow, or variegated; pulp sweet, slightly acidulated, yellow, thin, having a singular but not unpleasant taste and a sweet smell. It varies somewhat in form. The seed scarcely ever ripens, but the tree is readily increased by cuttings, and if a branch laden with young fruit be set in the ground it will grow and the fruit will come to maturity. Masters[8] says the flower-buds are used as a sweetmeat with sugar.

---

[1] McMahon, B. *Amer. Gard. Cal.* 583. 1806.
[2] Vilmorin *Les Pls. Potag.* 202. 1883.
[3] Lightfoot, J. *Fl. Scot.* 1:259. 1789.
[4] Ellis, W. *Polyn. Research.* 1:61. 1833.
[5] Firminger, T. A. C. *Gard. Ind.* 234. 1874. (*S. dulcis*)
[6] Morris *Rpt. Pub. Gard. Jam.* 35. 1880.
[7] Lunan, J. *Hort. Jam.* 1:185. 1814. (*S. mombin*)
[8] Masters, M. T. *Treas. Bot.* 2:1086. 1870. (*S. mombin*)

S. mangifera Willd.   HOG PLUM.

Tropical Asia.   The fruit, when largest, is of the size of a goose egg, of a rich olive-green, mottled with yellow and black, with but a trifling degree of scent and none of the quince-like odor of the other species.   The inner part nearest the rind is rather acid; that being removed, the part nearest the stem is sweet and eatable, but withal it is not an agreeable fruit.[1]   Brandis[2] says the ripe fruit has an astringent acid and turpentine taste but is eaten and pickled.

S. purpurea Linn.   HOG PLUM.   SPANISH PLUM.

Tropical America; cultivated in the northern regions of the tropical parts of Brazil.[3] This fruit has very recently been introduced at Jacksonville, Florida, under the name of Spanish plum.   Lunan[4] says the fruits are yellow with sometimes a slight mixture of redness, sweet smelling, covered with a thin skin, the size of a pigeon's egg, having within a little sweetish, acidulous pulp and a very large nut; eaten by some.   The natives, says Unger,[5] eat the sweetish, acid flesh, prepare a sauce and manufacture a drink from it.

S. tuberosa Arruda.

Brazil.   The fruit is about twice the size of a large gooseberry, of an oblong shape and of a yellowish color when ripe; beneath its coriaceous skin there is a juicy pulp of a pleasant, sweetish-acid taste.   The fruit is fit to eat only when it is so ripe as to fall to the ground, when a large quantity may be eaten without inconvenience.[6]

Stachys affinis Fresen.   *Labiatae.*   CHINESE ARTICHOKE.   KNOT ROOT.

Egypt and Arabia.   This plant was introduced into cultivation by Vilmorin-Andrieux et Cie. in 1886.[7]   The roots are thick and fleshy and are useful for pickles and may be used fried.   According to Bretschneider,[8] the roots were eaten as a vegetable in China in the fourteenth and sixteenth centuries and are described as a cultivated vegetable by Chinese writings of 1640 and 1742.   The species is a cultivated vegetable in Japan and is called *choro-gi*, and is esteemed.

S. heraclea All.

Southern Europe.   Archer says the leaves and stems, shown at the International Exhibition of 1862 as a tea substitute, are used by the modern Greeks and are believed to be the *sideritis* of the ancients.

S. palustris Linn.   ALL-HEAL.   WOUNDWORT.

Northern climates.   Lightfoot[9] says the roots have been eaten in times of necessity, either boiled or dried and made into bread.   Henfrey[10] says the fleshy, subterranean

---

[1] Firminger, T. A. C.   *Gard. Ind.* 235.   1874.

[2] Brandis, D.   *Forest Fl.* 128.   1874.

[3] Unger, F.   *U. S. Pat. Off. Rpt.* 349.   1859.

[4] Lunan, J.   *Hort. Jam.* 2:186.   1814.

[5] Unger, F.   *U. S. Pat. Off. Rpt.* 349.   1859.

[6] Gardner, G.   *Trav. Braz.* 176.   1849.

[7] Vilmorin-Andrieux et Cie.   *Seed Cat.*   1886.

[8] Bretschneider, E.   *Bot. Sin.* 53, 59, 83, 85.   1882.

[9] Lightfoot, J.   *Fl. Scot.* 1:313.   1789.

[10] Henfrey, A.   *Bot.* 327.   1870.

rhizomes are sometimes collected as a table vegetable. Loudon says these, when grown on rich moist soil, are white, crisp and agreeable to the taste. Johnson[1] says the young shoots, though of agreeable taste, are of disagreeable smell but may be eaten as asparagus.

Stachytarpheta indica Vahl. *Verbenaceae.*

Austria. The leaves are sold as Brazilian tea, which Lindley[2] says is a rather poor article.

Staphylea pinnata Linn. *Sapindaceae.* EUROPEAN BLADDER NUT.

Europe; cultivated in shrubberies. Haller[3] says the kernels of the fruit taste like those of pistachios and are eaten in Germany by children.

S. trifolia Linn. AMERICAN BLADDER NUT.

Eastern North America. The seeds contain a sweet oil; they are sometimes eaten like pistachios.[4]

Stauntonia hexaphylla Decne. *Berberideae.*

Japan. The Japanese eat its roundish, watery berries and use their juice as a remedy for opthalmia.[5]

Stellaria media Cyrill. *Caryophylleae.* CHICKWEED. STARWORT. STITCHWORT.

Temperate regions. This plant is found in every garden as a weed. It forms when boiled, says Johnson,[6] an excellent green vegetable, much resembling spinach in flavor and is very wholesome.

Stemona tuberosa Lour. *Roxburghiaceae.*

Tropical Asia. The thick, tuberous roots, after a previous preparation with lime-water, are candied with sugar in India and are taken with tea but are said to be insipid.[7]

Sterculia alata Roxb. *Sterculiaceae.* BUDDHA'S COCOANUT.

East Indies. The winged seeds of its large fruit are eaten.[8]

S. balanghas Linn.

Tropical eastern Asia. The seeds, when roasted, are nearly as palatable as chestnuts. Rumphius[9] says the seeds are considered esculent by the inhabitants of Amboina, who roast them. Unger[10] says the nuts are eaten by the natives of the South Sea Islands generally.

---

[1] Johnson, C. P. *Useful Pls. Gt. Brit.* 207. 1862.

[2] Lindley, J. *Med. Econ. Bot.* 222. 1849. (*S. jamaicensis*)

[3] Loudon, J. C. *Arb. Frut. Brit.* 1:494. 1854.

[4] Baillon, H. *Hist. Pls.* 5:388. 1878.

[5] Smith, A. *Treas. Bot.* 2:1093. 1870.

[6] Johnson, C. P. *Useful Pls. Gt. Brit.* 53. 1862.

[7] *Treas. Bot.* 2:994. 1870. (*Roxburghia*)

[8] Pickering, C. *Chron. Hist. Pls.* 112. 1879.

[9] Don, G. *Hist. Dichl. Pls.* 1:515. 1831.

[10] Unger, F. *U. S. Pat. Off. Rpt.* 323. 1859.

S. carthaginensis Cav.

Tropical America. The seeds are called *chica* by the Brazilians and *panama* by the Panamanians and are commonly eaten by the inhabitants as nuts.[1]

S. chicha A. St. Hil. CHICA.

Brazil. The inhabitants of Goyaz eat the almonds, which are of an agreeable taste.

S. diversifolia G. Don. BOTTLE TREE.

A tree of tropical Australia. The seeds are eaten and the taproots are used, when young, as an article of food by the natives.[2]

S. foetida Linn.

Old World tropics. Rheede[3] says its fruit is edible. Graham[4] says, at Bombay, the seeds are roasted and eaten like chestnuts. Mason[5] says, in Burma, its seeds are eaten like filberts. Blanco[6] says its seeds are eaten in the Philippines.

S. guttata Roxb.

Tropical India. The seeds are eaten by the natives of Bombay.

S. rupestris Benth. BOTTLE TREE.

Northeastern Australia. The trunk of this tree bulges out in the form of a barrel. The stem abounds in a mucilaginous or resinous substance resembling gum tragacanth, which is wholesome and nutritious and is said to be used as an article of food by the aborigines in cases of extreme need.[7]

S. scaphigera Wall.

Burma and Malay. The seeds when macerated in water swell into a large, gelatinous mass. This jelly is valued by the Siamese and Chinese, who sweeten it and use it as a delicacy.

S. tomentosa Guill. & Perr.

Equatorial Africa. The seeds are eaten in famines.[8]

S. urens Roxb.

East Indies. The seeds are roasted and eaten by Gonds and Kurkurs in Central India, according to Brandis.[9] The plant yields a gum like gum tragacanth, and the seeds, according to Drury,[10] are roasted and eaten and also made into a kind of coffee.

Stereospermum zylocarpum Benth. & Hook. f. *Bignoniaceae.*

East Indies. Its tender pods are eaten.[11]

---

[1] Smith, A. *Treas. Bot.* 2:1097. 1870.

[2] Black, A. A. *Treas. Bot.* 1:162. 1870. (*Brachychiton populneum*)

[3] Rheede *Hort. Malabar.* 4:75 t. 36. 1750.

[4] Pickering, C. *Chron. Hist. Pls.* 332. 1879.

[5] Ibid.

[6] Ibid.

[7] Black, A. A. *Treas. Bot.* 1:389. 1870. (*Delabechea rupestris*)

[8] Pickering, C. *Chron. Hist. Pls.* 269. 1879.

[9] Brandis, D. *Forest Fl.* 34. 1874.

[10] Pickering, C. *Chron. Hist. Pls.* 333. 1879.

[11] Pickering, C. *Chron. Hist. Pls.* 739. 1879. (*Bignonia xylocarpa*)

Sticta pulmonaria (Linn.) Schaer. *Lichenes.* LUNG LICHEN. LUNGWORT.

Northern climates. This lichen, found growing on the ground in woods, is used as a substitute for Iceland moss.[1]

Stilbocarpa polaris A. Gray. *Araliaceae.*

New Zealand. This is an herbaceous plant with long roots, which are saccharine and have served ship-wrecked people for a lengthened period as sustenance.[2]

Strelitzia reginae Ait. *Scitamineae.* BIRD OF PARADISE FLOWER.

South Africa. The seeds are gathered and eaten by the Kaffirs.[3]

Strychnos innocua Delile. *Loganiaceae.*

Nubia. The pulp of the fruit is eaten by the natives of Egypt and Senegal.[4]

S. nux-vomica Linn. NUX-VOMICA TREE. STRYCHNINE.

Tropical India and Burma. Mason[5] says in Burma the pulp of the fruit is a favorite repast with children.

S. potatorum Linn. f. CLEARING NUT. WATER-FILTER NUT.

East Indies. The fruit, when very young, is made into a preserve and eaten.[6] The pulp of the fruit is edible[7] and the ripe seeds are dried and sold in the bazaars to clear muddy water.[8]

S. pseudo-quina A. St. Hil. COPALCHI.

Brazil. The pulpy portion of the fruit is eaten by the natives.[9]

S. spinosa Lam.

Madagascar. The fruit, according to Flacourt,[10] is as large as a quince, with a gourd-like shell full of large, flat seeds; the juice and watery pulp are agreeable when ripe. The pulp of the fruit is commonly eaten by the natives wherever it grows; it is somewhat acid and is said to be delicious.[11]

S. tieute Lesch.

Java. The bark of its root yields one of the most dangerous poisons known, called *tshettik* or *tjettik* or *upas radja*.[12] The pulp of the fruit is said to be edible.[13]

---

[1] Smith, J. *Dict. Econ. Pls.* 253. 1882.
[2] Mueller, F. *Sel. Pls.* 468. 1891.
[3] Masters, M. T. *Treas. Bot.* 2:1103. 1870.
[4] Masters, M. T. *Treas. Bot.* 2:1106. 1870.
[5] Pickering, C. *Chron. Hist. Pls.* 638. 1879.
[6] Ainslie, W. *Mat. Ind.* 2:420. 1826.
[7] Brandis, D. *Forest Fl.* 317. 1874.
[8] Drury, H. *Useful Pls. Ind.* 408. 1873.
[9] Royle, J. F. *Illustr. Bot. Himal.* 1:272. 1839.
[10] Pickering, C. *Chron. Hist. Pls.* 707. 1879.
[11] Black, A. A. *Treas. Bot.* 1:168. 1870. (*Brehmia spinosa*)
[12] Pickering, C. *Chron. Hist. Pls.* 445. 1879.
[13] Masters, M. T. *Treas. Bot.* 2:1106. 1870.

Styrax benzoin Dryand. *Styraceae.* BENZOIN. STORAX.

Malay. This plant furnishes gum benzoin, used for flavoring by chocolate manufacturers. That from Siam is preferred.

Suaeda maritima Dum. *Chenopodiaceae.* SEA-BLITE.

Temperate regions. Roxburgh[1] says the leaves are eaten by the natives of India and considered very wholesome. Graham[2] says the leaves are eaten about Bombay.

Symphoricarpos racemosus Michx. *Caprifoliaceae.* SNOWBERRY.

North America. The fruit is eaten by the Indians of Oregon and Washington.[3]

Symphytum officinale Linn. *Boragineae.* BONESET. COMFREY.

Europe and adjoining Asia. The leaves, when young, form a good green-vegetable and are not infrequently eaten by country people. They are sometimes used to flavor cakes and other culinary preparations.[4] The blanched stalks form an agreeable asparagus.[5]

Symplocos alstonia L'Hérit. *Styraceae.*

New Granada. According to Gardner,[6] the leaves are employed as a tea substitute,[7] and an infusion of one of the species is used likewise in Brazil.

Tabernaemontana utilis Arn. *Apocynaceae.* COW TREE. HYA-HYA.

Guiana. From an incision in the bark is obtained a good flow of thick, white, creamy sap of a rich, nutty flavor, but Brown[8] says a little of it goes a long way. Brandis[9] calls it a thick, sweet, nutritious milk.

Tacca dubia Schult. f. *Taccaceae.* TACCA.

Malayan Archipelago. It is used as tacca.[10]

T. palmata Blume. TACCA.

Java. This is one of the taccas of the Malayan Archipelago which furnishes a food-fecula.[11]

T. pinnatifida Forst. PIA. SALEP. TACCA.

Asia and African tropics and islands of Pacific. The tubers of the tacca furnish a mealy nutriment to the inhabitants of the Society Islands and the Moluccas, where the plant is found both wild and in a state of cultivation. In the latter case, the tuberous

---

[1] Drury, H. *Useful Pls. Ind.* 377. 1873.

[2] Pickering, C. *Chron. Hist. Pls.* 519. 1879. (*Salsola indica*)

[3] *U. S. D. A. Rpt.* 415. 1870.

[4] Johnson, C. P. *Useful Pls. Gt. Brit.* 182. 1862.

[5] Loudon, J. C. *Hort.* 673. 1860.

[6] Smith, A. *Treas. Bot.* 2:1115. 1870.

[7] Don, G. *Hist. Dichl. Pls.* 4:1. 1838.

[8] Brown, C. B. *Camp Life Brit. Guiana* 46. 1877.

[9] Brandis, D. *Forest Fl.* 322. 1874.

[10] Royle, J. F. *Illustr. Bot. Himal.* 1:377. 1839.

[11] Rumphius *Herb. Ambon.* 5:330, t. 115. 1750.

root loses some of its original acridity and bitterness.[1]   The roots are rasped and macerated for four or five days in water and a fecula is separated in the same manner that sago is and, like it, is employed as an article of food by the inhabitants of the Malayan Islands and the Moluccas.[2]   In Otaheite, they make cakes of the meal of the tubers.   The tubers form an article of diet in China and Cochin China [3] and in Travancore, where they are much eaten, the natives mix agreeable acids with them to subdue their natural pungency.[4] From the tubers, the main supply of the Fiji arrowroot is prepared,[5] and an arrowroot is also made from this plant in the East Indian province of Arracan.

Tacsonia mollissima H. B. & K.   *Passifloreae.*

New Granada.   In India, says Firminger,[6] this plant bears a great abundance of a pale green fruit of the size of a goose egg and of a rather agreeable flavor.

T. mixta Juss.

Tropical America.   The fruit is edible.[7]

T. tripartita Juss.

Ecuador.   It bears edible fruit.[8]

Tagetes lucida Cav.   *Compositae.*   SWEET MACE.

Mexico.   This plant, says Loudon,[9] is much used in Nottinghamshire, England, as an ingredient of soups instead of tarragon.   In France, it is grown in the flower garden.[10]

Talauma plumierii DC.   *Magnoliaceae.*

West Indies.   The flowers are used by the distillers of Martinique to sweeten liquors.[11]

Talinum patens Willd.   *Portulaceae.*

Tropical America.   In Brazil, St. Hilaire [12] says the leaves are cooked as are those of purslane.

Talisia olivaeformis Radlk.   *Sapindaceae.*

New Granada.   The fruit is the size and shape of an olive, jet black and of a pleasant taste.[13]

---

[1] Unger, F.   *U. S. Pat. Off. Rpt.* 308.   1859.

[2] Royle, J. F.   *Illustr. Bot. Himal.* 1:377.   1839.

[3] Ibid.

[4] Ibid.

[5] Mueller, F.   *Sel. Pls.* 473.   1891.

[6] Firminger, T. A. C.   *Gard. Ind.* 198.   1874.

[7] Carruthers *Treas. Bot.* 2:1119.   1870.

[8] Ibid.

[9] Loudon, J. C.   *Hort.* 685.   1860.

[10] Vilmorin *Fl. Pl. Ter.* 1123.   1870.   3rd Ed.

[11] Don, G.   *Hist. Dichl. Pls.* 1:85.   1831.

[12] St. Hilaire, A.   *Fl. Bras. Merid.* 2:193.   1829.

[13] Don, G.   *Hist. Dichl. Pls.* 1:672.   1831.

Tamarindus indica Linn. *Leguminosae.* TAMARIND.

Asia and tropical Africa. The tamarind furnishes a fruit in southern Asia and middle Africa, which is used for food and is manufactured into cooling drinks. This large tree is planted before the houses in Senegal, Egypt, Arabia and India. The acid pulp in India is used in the preparation of a beer.[1] The seeds or stones in India in times of famine are boiled or fried and then eaten [2] as they are also in Ceylon.[3] Tamarinds form an important ingredient in Indian cookery, especially in curries, and in western India are used in preserving or pickling fish. In Timor, Cunningham [4] saw the fruit exposed in large quantities for sale in the markets, the husk having been taken off and the fruit then dried in the sun.

The West Indian form of *T. indica* is cultivated for its fruit in the West Indies, the pulp of which is mixed and boiled with sugar and forms an important article of commerce. In Curacao, the natives eat the pulp raw. In Martinique, they eat even the unripe fruit.[5] Fresh tamarinds are occasionally brought to this country. They have an agreeable, sour taste, without any mixture of sweetness. As we usually find them, in the preserved state, they form a dark colored, adhesive mass, consisting of syrup mixed with the pulp, membrane, strings and seeds of the pod. They are of a sweet, acidulous taste. On account of their laxative and refrigerant effect, convalescents often find the pulp a pleasant addition to their diet The tree is very abundant in Jamaica and is grown in the government collection of fruits at Washington.

Tamarix art'culata Vahl. *Tamariscineae.*

Arabia, Persia and East Indies. Tamarisk manna is produced on the twigs by the puncture of an insect in parts of the Punjab and in Sind. This manna is chiefly collected during the hot weather and is used medicinally or to adulterate sugar.[6] This plant is said by Prosper Alpinus [7] to be the *atle* of the Egyptians, written *atl* by Forskal [8] and *atleh* by Delile.[9]

T. gallica Linn. MANNA PLANT.

Europe, Asia and Africa. This species descends in Senegal to the neighborhood of the equator. It is called in Egypt and Fezzan *attil* and *tarfe* by the Arabs, whence the name *taray* of the Spaniards, and *tarajol* of the Canarians.[10] It supplies a manna in the southern Punjab.[11] Burckhardt [12] states that this manna is used by the Bedouin Arabs near Mt. Sinai with their food. Arnold [13] says, in Persia, the ground beneath the bushes

---

[1] Unger, F. *U. S. Pat. Off. Rpt.* 337. 1859.

[2] Ainslie, W. *Mat. Ind.* 1:427. 1826.

[3] Masters, M. T. *Treas. Bot.* 2:1121. 1870.

[4] Hooker, W. J. *Journ. Bot.* 4:252. 1842.

[5] Don, G. *Hist. Dichl. Pls.* 2:438. 1832. (*T. occidentalis*)

[6] Brandis, D. *Forest Fl.* 23. 1874.

[7] Hooker, W. J. *Journ. Bot.* 3:428. 1841.

[8] Ibid.

[9] Ibid.

[10] Hooker, W. J. *Journ. Bot.* 3:429. 1841.

[11] Brandis, D. *Forest Fl.* 21. 1874.

[12] *U. S. Disp.* 532. 1865. Note.

[13] Arnold, A. *Through Persia Caravan* 227. 1877.

is swept clean and a cotton cloth spread under the branches. The trees are then shaken, the manna collected and made into cakes with sugar or honey and flour. Sweet almonds are sometimes added to the sweetmeat before it is baked.

Tamus communis Linn. *Dioscoreaceae.* BLACK BRYONY. MANDRAKE.

Europe, Persia and north Africa. Dioscorides says the young shoots were eaten, and the young shoots are now cooked and eaten in Cyprus.[1] Gerarde[2] says " they are served at men's tables also in our age in Tuscania; others report the like also to be done in Andalusia." The young suckers, in which the acrid principle is not much developed, are eaten as asparagus, as Lindley[3] says, after careful boiling and changing the water. In France, black bryony is grown in the flower gardens.[4]

Tanacetum vulgare Linn. *Compositae.* TANSY.

A strong-scented plant of Europe and Asia; now naturalized in the United States. Tansy is still included in the herb garden as a condimental and medicinal herb, yet it is very little grown, the wild plant usually sufficing for all purposes. Tansy very readily becomes an escape, thriving in out-of-the-way places without culture. It was formerly in greater esteem than at present. In 1633, Gerarde[5] says: " In the spring-time are made with the leaves hereof newly sprung up, and with egs, cakes, or tansies, which be pleasant in taste, and good for the stomacke." In 1778, Mawe[6] says: " This herb, for its economical uses in the kitchen and medicine, merits culture in every garden," and names for varieties the plain-leaved, the curled-leaved, the variegated-leaved and the scentless. Both the common and the curled are figured by Dodonaeus,[7] 1616, and are mentioned in other botanies of this period. It was in American gardens before 1806.

Tanaecium lilacinum Seem. *Bignoniaceae.*

Panama. Dr. Seemann[8] says the edible berry is called in Guiana *emosse-berry*.

Taraxacum officinale Wigg. *Compositae.* DANDELION.

Temperate regions, north and south. The dandelion is highly spoken of as a spring green by various authors and has been used as a food plant in many regions but it has only recently come under cultivation. When a swarm of locusts destroyed vegetation in the Island of Minorca, the inhabitants subsisted on this plant, and, in Gottingen, the dried root has been used as a substitute for coffee. In 1749, Kalm[9] speaks of the French in New York preparing and eating the roots as a common salad but not usually employing the leaves. The plant is now eaten raw or cooked by the Digger Indians of Colorado

[1] Pickering, C. *Chron. Hist. Pls.* 162. 1879.

[2] Gerarde, J. *Herb.* 872. 1633 or 1636.

[3] Lindley, J. *Med. Econ. Bot.* 62. 1849.

[4] Vilmorin *Fl. Pl. Ter.* 1125. 1870. 3rd Ed.

[5] Gerarde, J. *Herb.* 651. 1633.

[6] Mawe and Abercrombie *Univ. Gard. Bot.* 1778.

[7] Dodonaeus *Pempt.* 36. 1616.

[8] Hooker, W. J. *Journ. Bot.* 9:142. 1857.

[9] Kalm, P. *Trav. No. Amer.* 2:190. 1772. (*Leontodon taraxacom*)

and the Apaches of Arizona. In 1828, Fessenden[1] says the wild plant is used by our people but is never cultivated. In 1853, McIntosh,[2] an English author, had never heard of dandelions being cultivated. They are now extensively cultivated in France, and, in 1879, five varieties appeared in the French catalogs.

Dandelions are blanched for use as a winter salad. They are now very largely grown by our market gardeners, and Thorburn,[3] in 1881, offers seed of two sorts. In 1871, four varieties were exhibited at the Massachusetts Horticultural Society under the names of the French Large-leaved, French Thick-leaved, Red-seeded and the American Improved. Fearing Burr, who exhibited them, makes no mention of dandelions in his *Garden Vegetables*, 1866. The common name is a corruption of *dent de lion*, a word which is found in the Welsh *Dant y Llew* of the thirteenth century. Its vernacular names in various languages have usually reference to the peculiar indentation of the leaves, or to some other resemblance or character of the plant. By commentators, the dandelion has been identified with the *aphake* of Theophrastus, *a* in composition signifying absence of and *phake*, lentils, or the name, perhaps, signifying that the plant can be used as a green before lentils appear in the spring. The dandelion may be the *ambubeia* of Pliny and the name may suggest the scattering of the seed, *ambulo* meaning the going backward and forward, but some commentators assign this name to the wild endive or chicory; the *hedypnois* of Pliny is but doubtfully identified with our dandelion and appears to be derived from two Greek words signifying sweet breath and may refer to the sweet smell of the flowers.

Bauhin, in his *Pinax*, 1623, enumerates two varieties of dandelion: one, the *Dens Leonis latiore filio*, carried back in his synonymy to Brunselsius, 1539; the other, *Dens Leonis angustiore folio*, carried back in like manner to Caesalpinus, 1583. The first kind, he says, has a large and a medium variety, the leaves sometimes pointed, sometimes obtuse. In the *Flore Naturelle et Economique*, Paris, 1803, the same varieties, apparently, are mentioned, one with narrow leaves and the other with large and rounded leaves. In Martyn's *Miller's Dictionary*, 1807, the leaves of the dandelion are said to vary from pinnatifid or deeply runcinate in a very dry situation to nearly entire in a very moist one, generally smooth but sometimes a little rough; and *Leontodon palustris* is described as scarcely more than a variety, varying much in its leaves, which have few notches or are almost entire, the plant smoother, neater, more levigated and more glaucous than the common dandelion.

In Geneva, New York, on the grounds of the New York Agricultural Experiment Station, a large number of variations are to be commonly noted, both in the habit and appearance of the plant and irrespective of difference of soil or exposure, as varieties may readily be separated whose roots are intertwined. Some plants grow with quite erect leaves, others with their leaves closely appressed to the soil; some have broad, others narrow leaves; some have runcinate leaves, others leaves much cut and almost fringed and yet others the leaves nearly entire; some have almost sessile leaves; some have smooth leaves, others roughened leaves; some have thin, others thick leaves; some grow

[1] Fessenden *New Amer. Gard.* 98. 1828. (*Leontodon taraxacom*)
[2] McIntosh, C. *Book Gard.* 2:166. 1855.
[3] Thorburn *Cat.* 1881.

to a larger size, others are always dwarfer; some have an open manner of growth, others a close manner.

The use of the wild plant as a vegetable seems to have been common from remote times, but its culture is modern. In 1836, a Mr. Corey, Brookline, Massachusetts, grew dandelions for the Boston market from seed obtained from the largest of the wild plants.[1] In 1863, dandelions are described among garden esculents by Burr,[2] but the context does not indicate any especial varieties. In 1874, perhaps earlier, the seed appears for sale in seed catalogs,[3] and the various seed catalogs of 1885 offer six names, one of which is the "common." In England, dandelion culture is not mentioned in Mawe's *Gardener*, 1778, nor in Martyn's *Miller's Dictionary*, 1807; the first notice is in the *Gardeners' Chronicle*,[4] where an instance of cultivation is noted, the herbage forming "a beautiful and delicate blanched salad." In 1880, its culture had not become common, as this year its cultivation in France, and not in England, is noted.[5] In France, Noisette [6] gives cultural directions and says the wild plant furnishes a spring potherb. The dandelion is not, however, mentioned in *L'Horticulteur Française*,[7] nor in *Nouveau Dictionnaire du Jardinage*, 1826. Vilmorin [8] mentions its culture in France as dating from 1868, and the firm of Vilmorin-Andrieux et Cie., 1885, offers four sorts of seed, one, the Improved Moss, as new. In Vilmorin's *Les Plantes Potagères*,[9] 1883, two forms are figured: *Pissenlit améliore à coeur plein* and *Pissenlit améliore très hatif*. The first of these is named in *Album de Cliches*, *Pissenlit améliore frise*, and a fourth name or third form is figured, the *Pissenlit mousse*.

The type of the *Pissenlit mousse* can be readily found among the wild plants on the grounds of the New York Agricultural Experiment Station, very closely resembling Vilmorin's figure in every respect when growing on rich soil, except that the leaf divisions are scarcely as much crowded.

The type of the *Pissenlit améliore à coeur plein* is perhaps to be recognized in Anton Pinaeus' figure, 1561, and is certainly to be found growing wild at the New York Agricultural Experiment Station.

The *Pissenlit améliore très hatif* is figured in 1616; the resemblance between the two figures, the one by Dodonaeus and the other by Vilmorin, is very close. It is also to be found growing wild on the New York Station grounds.

Taxus baccata Linn. *Coniferae.* YEW.

North temperate Europe and Asia. The berries, says Johns,[10] are of a mawkish, disagreeable taste but are eaten with impunity by children. The nut contains a kernel

[1] *Mass. Hort. Soc. Trans.* 128. 1884.

[2] Burr, F. *Field, Gard. Veg.* 345. 1863.

[3] Briggs Bros. *Cat.* 1874.

[4] *Gard. Chron.* 340. 1846.

[5] Jenkins *Journ. Roy. Agr. Soc.* 16:94.

[6] Noisette *Man. Jard.* 356. 1829.

[7] Pirolle *L'Hort. Franc.* 1824.

[8] *Bon Jard.* 485. 1882.

[9] Vilmorin *Veg. Gard.* 229. 1885.

[10] Johns, C. A. *Treas. Bot.* 2:1126. 1870.

which has an agreeable flavor like that of the stone-pine. Brandis[1] says the berries are sweet and harmless and are eaten by the natives of the northwest Himalayas.

Telfairia occidentalis Hook. f. *Cucurbitaceae.*

Tropical Africa. The plant is cultivated for its seeds, which the natives boil and eat.[2]

T. pedata Hook.

Tropical Africa. The plant is a climber, the stems of which often attain the length of a hundred feet. The fruit attains a weight of 60 pounds and contains at times as many as 500 seeds. These seeds, when boiled, are eatable and a large quantity of oil can be expressed from them.[3]

Terminalia arjuna Wight & Arn. *Combretaceae.*

East Indies. In India, a decoction of the bark with milk is given as a nourishment. It is considered tonic, astringent and cooling.[4]

T. bellerica Roxb.

Tropical India and Burma. The kernels of the fruit are eaten.[5]

T. catappa Linn. INDIAN ALMOND.

Tropical eastern Asia. This plant is cultivated in gardens in India and in south Florida.[6] The kernel of the drupe has the taste and virtues of the almond, though, says Ainslie,[7] perhaps the flavor is more that of the English filbert. The drupe is nearly three inches long, egg-shaped, grooved, and contains but one kernel, which is considered a nourishing food for weak people and from which a pleasant, edible oil is prepared. Firminger[8] says, beyond comparison, this is the most delicious fruit of any kind the country affords.

T. citrina Roxb. CITRON MYROBALAN. HARANUT.

East Indies. This plant is ranked amongst the fruits of India. It is about the size of a French plum and is often made into a pickle.

T. glabrata Forst. f.

Friendly and Society Islands. The kernels of the fruit are eaten and have the flavor of almonds.[9]

T. latifolia Sw.

Jamaica. The kernels are eaten and have the flavor of almonds.[10]

---

[1] Brandis, D. *Forest Fl.* 541. 1874.

[2] Smith, A. *Treas. Bot.* 2:1130. 1876.

[3] Mueller, F. *Sel. Pls.* 477. 1891.

[4] Dutt, U. C. *Mat. Med. Hindus* 163. 1877.

[5] Royle, J. F. *Illustr. Bot. Himal.* 1:210. 1839.

[6] Nuttall, T. *No. Amer. Sylva* 1:126. 1865.

[7] Ainslie, W. *Mat. Ind.* 2:230. 1826.

[8] Firminger, T. A. C. *Gard. Ind.* 279. 1874.

[9] Don, G. *Hist. Dichl. Pls.* 2:658. 1832.

[10] Ainslie, W. *Mat. Ind.* 2:231. 1826.

T. litoralis Seem.

Fiji Islands.   The seeds are sometimes eaten by children in Viti.[1]

T. mauritiana Lam.   FALSE BENZOIN.

Mauritius and Bourbon.   The kernels of the fruit are eaten.[2]

T. pamea DC.

Guiana.   The tree is cultivated on the Isle of France and elsewhere.   The almond-like kernels are good to eat and are served on the better tables of the country.[3]

T. platyphylla F. Muell.

Australia.   The fruit is oblong, pointed, blue when ripe, and is eaten raw.[4]

Testudinaria elephantipes Salisb.   *Dioscoreaceae.*   ELEPHANT'S FOOT.   HOTTENTOT BREAD.

South Africa.   This plant bears a bulb entirely above ground, which grows to an enormous size, frequently three feet in height and diameter.   It is closely studded with angular, ligneous protuberances, which give it some resemblance to the shell of a tortoise. The inside is a fleshy substance, which may be compared to a turnip, both in substance and color.   The taste is thought to resemble that of the yam of the East Indies.

Tetracera alnifolia Willd.   *Dilleniaceae.*   WATER TREE.

Tropical Africa.   The climbing stems of this tree yield a good supply of clear water when cut across.[5]

Tetragonia expansa Murr.   *Ficoideae.*   NEW ZEALAND SPINACH.

New Zealand and Australia.   This plant was first found by Sir Joseph Banks, in 1770, at Queen Charlotte Sound, New Zealand, and its merits were discovered by the sailors of Captain Cook's expedition around the world.   It reached Kew Gardens in 1772.[6] This spinach also occurs in Australia, both on the coast and in the desert interior, in New Caledonia, China, Japan and Chile.[7]   Don[8] says three varieties are found in Chile: one with smooth leaves, one with leaves hoary beneath and a third small and glabrous.   The plant was cultivated as a spinach plant in England in 1821 or earlier.[9]   It was in use in France in 1824 or earlier.[10]   In the United States, its seed was distributed among members of the New York Horticultural Society in 1827 and in 1828 it appeared in seed catalogs.[11]   St. Hilaire[12] records its use as a spinach in south Brazil, and Bojer[13] records it

---

[1] Seemann, B.   *Fl. Viti.* 94.   1865–1873.

[2] Unger, F.   *U. S. Pat. Off. Rpt.* 323.   1859.

[3] Aublet *Hist. Pls. Guiane* 2:949.   1775.

[4] Palmer, E.   *Journ. Roy. Soc. New So. Wales* 17:104.   1884.

[5] Smith, A.   *Treas. Bot.* 2:1134.   1870.   (*T. potatoria*)

[6] Don, G.   *Hist. Dichl. Pls.* 3:152.   1834.

[7] Mueller, F.   *Sel. Pls.* 237.   1876.

[8] Don, G.   *Hist. Dichl. Pls.* 3:152.   1834.

[9] Ibid.

[10] Pirolle *L'Hort. Franc.* 256.   1824–25.

[11] Thorburn *Cat.* 88.   1828.

[12] Saint Hilaire, A.   *Fl. Bras. Merid.* 1824.

[13] Bojer, W.   *Hort. Maurit.* 155.   1837.

in the Mauritius. The plant is used as a spinach in Tongatabu but not in New Zealand.[1]

T. implexicoma Hook. f. AUSTRALIAN SPINACH. ICE PLANT.

Extra-tropic Australia, New Zealand and Chatham Island. As a spinach plant, this species is as valuable as *T. expansa.*[2]

Tetramicra bicolor Rolfe. *Orchideae.*

Brazil. The fragrant fruit of this orchid has the odor of the Tonquin bean. It is sweeter than vanilla and is less penetrating.[3]

Teucrium scorodonia Linn. *Labiatae.* WOOD GERMANDER. WOOD SAGE.

Europe. This is an extremely bitter plant with the smell and taste of hops and is said to be substituted for hops in ale in the Island of Jersey.[4]

Thapsia moniza Masf. *Umbelliferae.* CARROT TREE.

Canary Islands. This plant can be gathered, says Black,[5] only by expert cragsmen let down the cliffs by ropes. The roots are eaten raw or boiled, when raw tasting like earth-nuts, and stringy and insipid when boiled. It is called the carrot tree, says Mueller,[6] but the root is inferior to a carrot.

Thelygonum cynocrambe Linn. *Urticaceae.* DOG'S CABBAGE.

Orient, East Indies and Mediterranean countries. This plant, says Syme,[7] is sub-acid and slightly purgative but is sometimes used as a potherb.

Theobroma bicolor Humb. & Bonpl. *Sterculiaceae.* CACAO.

New Granada. This species replaces the cacao in part in the West Indies and South America and the seeds are brought into commerce.[8]

T. cacao Linn. CACAO. COCOA.

Tropical America. This is the best-known species of the genus and the bulk of the cacao, or cocoa, of commerce is produced by it.[9] It is largely cultivated in Guayaquil, Venezuela, Trinidad, Grenada, Jamaica and elsewhere in tropical America. Cacao is also grown as an introduced plant in the Mauritius and Bourbon. The fruit is an oblong-ovate capsule or berry, six or eight inches in length, with a thick, coriaceous and somewhat ligneous rind, enclosing a whitish pulp in which numerous seeds are embedded. These are ovate, somewhat compressed, about the size of an almond and consist of an interior thin shell and a brown, oily kernel. Separated from the matter in which they are enveloped,

---

[1] Unger, F.   *U. S. Pat. Off. Rpt.* 356. 1859.

[2] Mueller, F.   *Sel. Pls.* 478. 1891.

[3] Moore, T.   *Treas. Bot.* 2:675. 1870.   (*Leptotes bicolor*)

[4] Smith, A.   *Treas. Bot.* 2:1137. 1870.

[5] Black, A. A.   *Treas. Bot.* 2:750. 1870.   (*Moniza edulis*)

[6] Mueller, F.   *Sel. Pls.* 478. 1891.   (*T. edulis*)

[7] Syme, J. T.   *Treas. Bot.* 2:1142. 1870.

[8] Unger, F.   *U. S. Pat. Off. Rpt.* 321. 1859.

[9] Smith, A.   *Treas. Bot.* 2:1143. 1870.

they constitute the cacao of commerce. Chocolate and cocoa are variously prepared from the nuts.

When Cortez was entertained at the court of the Aztec Emperor, Montezuma, he was treated to a sweet preparation of the cocoa, called *chocollatl*, flavored with vanilla, and other aromatic spices. Cacao was carried to Spain from Mexico, and the Spaniards kept the cacao secret for many years, selling it very profitably as chocolate to the wealthy and luxurious classes of Europe. Chocolate reached France, however, only in 1661 and did not reach Britain until a few years later. It is now more largely consumed in Spain than elsewhere in Europe. The European consumption of chocolate is estimated at quite 40,000,000 pounds. In the United States, the imports in 1880 were 7,411,045 pounds. Cacao was cultivated by the nations of Central America before the arrival of Europeans. The Nahua nations used the nibs, or grains, as circulating medium instead of money.[1] Stephens[2] states that the nuts are still used in Yucatan as currency, as of old, by the Indians. After maize, says Landa,[3] cacao was perhaps the crop to which the most attention was paid. It was called *cacaguat* in Nicaragua and several species which grew wild were also much used. In the month of Muan, the cacao planters even held a festival in honor of their patron deities Ekohuah, Chac and Hobnil.[4] Humboldt[5] states that he met with no tribe on the Orinoco that prepared a beverage with the seeds of the cacao, but the savages sucked the pulp of the pod and threw away the seeds. Hartt[6] says the cacao tree is quite extensively cultivated at Bahia but is not often cultivated south of the Amazon. In Jamaica, Lunan[7] rates the average produce of cacao per acre at 1000 pounds, allowing for bad years. It is called in Mexican *cacautl*.

T. guyanensis Voigt.

Guiana. This species furnishes a portion of the cacao of the West Indies and South America.[8]

T. speciosa Willd.

Brazil. In the West Indies, this species replaces cacao and its seeds enter into commerce.[9]

Theophrasta jussieui Lindl. *Myrsineae*.

South America and Santo Domingo. The fruit is succulent, and bread is made from the seeds.[10]

Thladiantha dubia Naud. *Cucurbitaceae*.

China. The fruit is oblong, very succulent and is eaten by the natives of the Himalayas.[11]

---

[1] Bancroft, H. H. *Native Races* 2:381. 1882.

[2] Stephens, J. L. *Trav. Yucatan* 2:196. 1841.

[3] Bancroft, H. H. *Native Races* 2:718. 1882.

[4] Bancroft, H. H. *Native Races* 2:692. 1882.

[5] Humboldt, A. *Trav.* 2:58. 1889.

[6] Hartt, C. F. *Geog. Braz.* 244. 1870.

[7] Lunan, J. *Hort. Jam.* 1:187. 1814.

[8] Unger, F. *U. S. Pat. Off. Rpt.* 321. 1859.

[9] Ibid.

[10] Masters, M. T. *Treas. Bot.* 2:1144. 1870.

[11] Moore, T. *Treas. Bot.* 2:1145. 1870.

Thlaspi arvense Linn. *Cruciferae.* PENNY CRESS.

Europe and northern Asia. This plant is classed as an edible cress by Loudon. It is a cultivated vegetable.[1]

Thrinax argentea Lodd. *Palmae.* BROOM PALM. SILVER THATCH.

A palm of the West Indies and Panama. The undeveloped leaves, or cabbage, form an excellent vegetable.[2]

Thuya gigantea Nutt. *Coniferae.*

Western North America. Nuttall[3] says the cambium is used as food by the Indians of Oregon.

T. occidentalis Linn. AMERICAN ARBOR VITAE. WHITE CEDAR.

North America and Siberia. Thoreau,[4] *In the Maine Woods*, says, "This night we had a dish of arbor-vitae, or cedar tea, which the lumberman sometimes uses when other herbs fail." He did not find it very palatable.

Thymus capitatus Hoffmgg. & Link. *Labiatae.* HEADED SAVORY.

The Levant; introduced into Britain in 1596. This plant is used as savory for seasoning.[5] This species is omitted from our most modern books on gardening, although recorded in American gardens as late as 1863.[6] It is mentioned as under culture in many of the early works on botany and gardening.

T. serpyllum Linn. LEMON THYME. WILD THYME.

Europe and sparingly naturalized in some localities in northeastern America. In 1726, Townsend[7] speaks of it in English gardens but not as a potherb. It is placed among American potherbs by McMahon,[8] 1806. At the present time, lemon thyme is occasionally used for seasoning in England. In Iceland, it is used to give an agreeable flavor to sour milk. The odor of the leaves is quite agreeable, and they are thought to be a desirable seasoning for veal. Don[9] says the flavor of the leaves is milder and more grateful than those of *T. vulgaris*.

T. vulgaris Linn. THYME.

Southern countries of Europe but long cultivated in more northern countries. In English culture, thyme is recorded about 1548[10] and is mentioned by Gerarde, 1597, and succeeding authors. It succeeds as an annual even in Iceland[11] and is recorded as grown in the tropical gardens of the Mauritius.[12] Three varieties are known: the narrow-leaved,

---

[1] Bretschneider, E. *Bot. Sin.* 53. 1882.

[2] Smith, A. *Treas. Bot.* 2:1147. 1870.

[3] Nuttall, T. *No. Amer. Sylva* 2:163. 1865.

[4] Thoreau *Me. Woods* 72. 1877.

[5] McIntosh, C. *Book Gard.* 2:238.. 1855 (*Satureja capitata*)

[6] Burr, F. *Field, Gard. Veg.* 442. 1863. (*Saturjea capitata*)

[7] Townsend *Seedsman* 35. 1726.

[8] McMahon, B. *Amer. Gard. Cal.* 583. 1806.

[9] Don, G. *Hist. Dichl. Pls.* 4:768. 1838.

[10] Booth, W. B. *Treas. Bot.* 2:1149. 1870.

[11] Flückiger and Hanbury *Pharm.* 487. 1879.

[12] Bojer, W. *Hort. Maurit.* 248. 1837.

Thymus vulgaris, tenuiore folio of Bauhin,[1] 1596; the broad-leaved, *Thymus vulgaris, latiore folio* of Bahuin,[2] 1596; and the variegated, *Thymus variegato folio* of Tournefort[3] and also mentioned by Bauhin,[4] 1623. Thyme was known in American gardens in 1806[5] or earlier. The broad-leaved kind is the one now principally grown in the herb garden for use in seasonings.

Tigridia pavonia Ker-Gawl. *Irideae.* TIGER FLOWER.

Mexico. Its farinaceous root was eaten by the ancient Mexicans.[6]

Tilia. *Tiliaceae.* BASSWOOD. LIME. LINDEN. WHITEWOOD.

Several species of Tilia are extensively grown as shade trees in Europe, where they are indigenous, and all may often be found introduced in the northeastern states of America. The flowers and leaves are sometimes used as a tea substitute and sugar has been made from the sap.[7] During the last century, Missa,[8] a French chemist, found that the fruit of the lime, ground up with some of the flowers in a mortar, furnished a substance much resembling chocolate in flavor. Some attempts were made in Prussia to introduce the manufacture of this lime-chocolate but were abandoned on account of the great liability of the paste to decompose. Lime-chocolate contains much nutritious matter and has an agreeable flavor.

Tinguarra sicula Benth. & Hook. f. *Umbelliferae.*

Countries about the Mediterranean Sea. The root is edible and celery-like.[9]

Tococa guianensis Aubl. *Melastomaceae.*

Brazil. The fruit is edible.[10]

Toddalia aculeata Pers. *Rutaceae.* LOPEZ ROOT.

Tropical India. The ripe berries, says Roxburgh,[11] are fully as pungent as black pepper and with nearly the same kind of pungency. They are pickled by the natives and are most excellent.

Torreya nucifera Sieb. & Zucc. *Coniferae.* KAYA.

Japan. The nuts are carefully gathered by the Japanese and the kernels are eaten.[12] An oil used for culinary purposes is expressed from them. In China, the

---

[1] Bauhin, C. *Phytopinax* 414. 1596.

[2] Ibid.

[3] Tournefort *Inst.* 196. 1719.

[4] Bauhin, C. *Pinax* 219. 1623.

[5] McMahon, B. *Amer. Gard. Cal.* 583. 1806.

[6] Pickering, C. *Chron. Hist. Pls.* 650. 1879.

[7] Browne, D. J. *Trees Amer.* 45. 1846.

[8] Johnson, C. P. *Useful Pls. Gt. Brit.* 61. 1862.

[9] Mueller, F. *Sel. Pls.* 482. 1891.

[10] Masters, M. T. *Treas. Bot.* 2:1154. 1870.

[11] Roxburgh, W. *Fl. Ind.* 1:617. 1820.

[12] Alcock, R. *Capital Tycoon* 2:485. 1863.

seeds are eaten like hazelnuts and, although reputed somewhat laxative, are considered wholesome.[1]

Trachycarpus fortunei H. Wendl.   *Palmae.*

China. The clusters of young flower-buds are eaten in China in much the same way as bamboo sprouts.[2]

T. martianus H. Wendl.

Himalayan region. The fruit is eaten, though the pulp is scanty and almost taste-less.[3]

Tragopogon crocifolius Linn.   *Compositae.*

Mediterranean countries. This species is enumerated by Pliny [4] among the esculent plants of Egypt, and Sprengel [5] says the root is edible.

T. porrifolius Linn.   OYSTER PLANT.   SALSIFY.   VEGETABLE OYSTER.

Mediterranean countries. The roots are long, white and fleshy, tapering like the parsnip but never attaining the same diameter. The roots are used, boiled or fried, and the flavor is mild and sweetish and reminds one of the oyster, whence its name oyster plant. McIntosh [6] says that, when dressed as asparagus, there is some resemblance in taste and that the flower-stalks, if cut in the spring of the second year before they become hard, and dressed like asparagus, make an excellent dish. The roots, says Burr,[7] thinly sliced, are sometimes used as a salad.

In the thirteenth century, Albertus Magnus [8] describes a wild plant, *Oculus porce* or *flos campi*, which commentators identify with the salsify, as having a delectable root, which is eaten, but he makes no mention of cultivation. Salsify is described, but apparently not under kitchen-garden culture, by Matthiolus in 1570 and 1598 [9] but it is not mentioned by him in 1558, when he refers to the yellow-flowered species; there is no mention of salsify culture by Camerarius 1586, but, in 1587, Dalechamp [10] says it is planted in gardens. In 1597, Gerarde [11] describes it but apparently as an inmate of the flower garden. In 1612, *Le Jardinier Solitaire* speaks of salsify as under kitchen-garden culture in France; and Dodonaeus,[12] 1616, J. Bauhin,[13] 1651, and Ray,[14] 1686, refer to it as apparently cultivated. After this period its culture seems to have been quite general as it is

---

[1] Hanbury, D. *Sci. Papers* 234. 1876.
[2] Smith, F. P. *Contrib. Mat. Med. China* 111. 1871.
[3] Brandis, D. *Forest Fl.* 547. 1874.
[4] Pickering, C. *Chron. Hist. Pls.* 361. 1879.
[5] Ibid.
[6] McIntosh, C. *Book Gard.* 2:228. 1855.
[7] Burr, F. *Field, Gard. Veg.* 52. 1863.
[8] Albertus Magnus *Veg.* Jessen Ed. 546. 1867.
[9] Matthiolus *Comment.* 379. 1570.
[10] Dalechamp *Hist. Gen. Pl.* (Lugd.) 1079. **1587.**
[11] Gerarde, J. *Herb.* 596. 1597.
[12] Dodonaeus *Pempt.* 256. 1616.
[13] Bauhin, J. *Hist. Pl.* 2:1059.
[14] Ray *Hist. Pl.* 252. 1686.

referred to in the works on gardening beginning with Quintyne, 1693.   McMahon,[1] 1806, includes salsify among American garden esculents, and, in 1822, John Lowell[2] says, " though it has been in our gardens for ten years, it has never been extensively cultivated for the market."

T. pratensis Linn.   GOAT'S BEARD.

Northwest India, Europe and the adjoining portions of Asia.   In 1640, this species was cultivated in gardens in England, as mentioned by Parkinson.   Evelyn, in his *Acetaria*, mentions its cultivation, but this vegetable has now given way to salsify.[3]   Lightfoot[4] mentions the use of the roots, boiled, and of the spring shoots as greens.[5]

Trapa bispinosa Roxb.   *Onagrarieae.*   SINHARA NUT.

Old World tropics.   This species grows abundantly in the lakes about Cashmere and at Wurler lake and is said to yield annually ten million pounds of nuts.   These are scooped up from the bottom of the lake in small nets and constitute almost the only food of at least 30,000 persons for five months in the year.   When extracted from the shell, they are eaten raw, boiled, roasted, fried, or dressed in various ways after being reduced to flour.[6]   They are also eaten in Lahore.

T. cochinchinensis Lour.

Cochin China.   The seeds are eaten as are those of the ling.[7]

T. incisa Sieb. & Zucc.

Japan.   This species is grown in Yezo and is largely used by the Ainus and to some extent by the Japanese for food.[8]

T. natans Linn.   JESUIT NUT.   LING.   SALIGOT.   TRAPA NUT.   WATER CALTROPS.   WATER CHESTNUT.

Europe and eastern Asia.   The Thraceans, according to Pliny, baked bread from the flour of the seeds, and the seeds are thus used even now in some parts of southern Europe and, at Venice, are sold under the name of Jesuit nuts.[9]   Grant[10] found trapa nuts on the Victoria Nyanza in Africa, and the Waganda use the four-pronged nuts for food.   It is enumerated by Thunberg among the edible plants of Japan.   Introduced into America, trapa is said to have become naturalized in the waters of the Concord River, Massachusetts.   This water plant is extensively cultivated in China and furnishes, in its strangely-shaped fruits, a staple article of nutriment.   It has run into several varieties.[11]

[1] McMahon, B.   *Amer. Gard. Cal.* 582.   1806.

[2] Lowell, J.   *Mass. Agr. Reposit.* 135.   1822.

[3] Glasspoole, H. G.   *Rpt. Ohio St. Bd. Agr.* **30**:541.   1875.

[4] Lightfoot, J.   *Fl. Scot.* **1**:427.   1789.

[5] Pickering, C.   *Chron. Hist. Pls.* 844.   1879.

[6] *U. S. Pat. Off. Rpt.* XXX.   1855.

[7] Unger, F.   *U. S. Pat. Off. Rpt.* 325.   1859.

[8] Penhallow, D. P.   *Amer. Nat.* **16**:120.   1882.

[9] Don, G.   *Hist. Dichl. Pls.* **2**:700.   1832.

[10] Speke, J. H.   *Journ. Disc. Source Nile* 569.   1864.

[11] Unger, F.   *U. S. Pat. Off. Rpt.* 325.   1859.

Williams [1] says its cultivation is in running water and the nuts are collected in autumn by people in punts or tubs, who look for the ripe ones as they pull themselves through the vines over the surface of the patch.   The dried nuts are often ground into a sort of arrow-root flour.   The taste of the fresh boiled nuts is like that of new cheese.

Treculia africana Decne.   *Urticaceae*.   BREADFRUIT TREE.

A tropical African tree called *okwa*.   The nuts contain an edible embryo and are collected by the negroes and ground into meal.[2]

Trianthema portulacastrum Linn.   *Ficoideae*.

Tropical Asia.   Royle [3] says this plant is used as a potherb in India.   Wight [4] says the leaves are sometimes employed as a potherb.   Ainslie [5] says it is eaten by the natives; Stewart,[6] that it is a common weed eaten in the Punjab in times of dearth but is apt to produce diarrhea and paralysis.

Tribulus terrestris Linn.   *Zygophylleae*.   LAND CALTROPS.

The unexpanded capsules, reduced to powder and formed into cakes, served as food during a famine in Rajputana, India.[7]

Trichosanthes anguina Linn.   *Cucurbitaceae*.   CLUB GOURD.   SERPENT CUCUMBER.   SNAKE
             GOURD.   VIPER'S GOURD.

India.   The fruit of this plant is a large, greenish-white, club-shaped gourd of the length of a man's arm and about four inches thick.   The fruit is eaten sliced and dressed in the manner of French beans.[8]   The gourd is commonly cultivated about Bombay [9] and is in very general demand for vegetable curries in Burma.[10]   The seed appears in some of the Prussian seed catalogs under the name of *melonengurkin*.   In Central America, it is called serpent cucumber or viper's gourd from the remarkable, snake-like appearance of its fruits, which are frequently six or more feet long, at first striped with different shades of green but ultimately a bright, orange color.[11]

T. cucumerina Linn.

Tropical India.   Its seed appears for sale in the Erfurt seed catalogs.   The unripe fruit is very bitter but is eaten by the natives of India in their curries.[12]

---

[1] Williams, S. W.   *U. S. Pat. Off. Rpt.* 471.   1860.

[2] Moore, J.   *Treas. Bot.* 2:1322.   1876.

[3] Royle, J. F.   *Illustr. Bot. Himal.* 1:221.   1839.

[4] Wight, R.   *Illustr. Ind. Bot.* 2:43.   1850.

[5] Ainslie, W.   *Mat. Ind.* 2:370.   1826.   (*T. monogyna*)

[6] Drury, H.   *Useful Pls. Ind.* 431.   1873.

[7] King, G.   *Bot. Soc. Edinb.* 10:198.   1870.   (*T. lanuginosus*)

[8] Firminger, T. A. C.   *Gard. Ind.* 129.   1874.

[9] Pickering, C.   *Chron. Hist. Pls.* 723.   1879.

[10] Ibid.

[11] Smith, A.   *Treas. Bot.* 2:1168.   1870.   (*T. colubrina*)

[12] Drury *Useful Pls. Ind.* 441.   1858.

T. dioica Roxb.

Tropical India. Firminger[1] says this plant produces a small, oblong, green gourd about four inches long and two broad; boiled, it affords rather an insipid dish, yet it is found very acceptable from the season in which it occurs. Dutt[2] says it is extensively cultivated in Bengal, and that the unripe fruit is much used by the natives as a vegetable and is the most palatable one of the country. The tender tops are also used as a potherb.

Trifolium fucatum Lindl. *Leguminosae.*

Western North America. Professor W. H. Brewer[3] writes that this clover is eaten by the Digger Indians of California.

T. involucratum Ortega. TREFOIL.

Western North America. This clover is eaten by the Digger tribes.[4]

T. pratense Linn. RED CLOVER.

Europe and temperate Asia. Clover is among the most generally cultivated fodder plants, but its use as a human food plant is unknown to Europeans. Some of the clovers are eaten cooked or raw by the Digger Indians of California and by the Apaches of Arizona. The former tribe cooks it by placing layers of clover, well moistened, between hot stones; it is consumed in large rations. The Apaches boil clover, young grass, dandelions and pigweed together. Where clover is found growing wild, the Indians practice a sort of semicultivation by irrigating it and harvesting.[5] Clover was introduced into America from Europe at an early period as Bartram[6] saw it before the American Revolution. In 1797, Samuel Deane[7] speaks of it as a plant highly valued in New England. In Ireland, says Lightfoot,[8] when food is scarce, the powdered flowers are mixed with bread and eaten. As an agricultural plant, clover first secured attention in England in 1635.

T. repens Linn. WHITE CLOVER.

Everywhere common in Europe and America. Johnson[9] says the flowers and pods in time of famine in Ireland and Scotland have been ground into powder and used as a food.

Trigonella caerulea Ser. *Leguminosae.*

Eastern Europe and Caucasian region. In Switzerland, this plant is called *kraut curd-herb* and is used to give odor and flavor to schabzieger, or sapsago, cheese. The dried flowers are reduced to powder and worked into a paste with the curd.[10]

---

[1] Firminger, T. A. C. *Gard. Ind.* 130. 1874.

[2] Dutt, U. C. *Mat. Med. Hindus* 169. 1877.

[3] Letter of Oct. 20, 1879, to Dr. E. L. Sturtevant.

[4] Pickering, C. *Chron. Hist. Pls.* 582. 1879.

[5] *U. S. D. A. Rpt.* 423. 1870.

[6] De Candolle, A. *Geog. Bot.* 2:748. 1855.

[7] Gould *Trans. N. Y. Agr. Soc.* 32:17. 1872-6.

[8] Lightfoot, J. *Fl. Scot.* 1:406. 1879.

[9] Johnson, C. P. *Useful Pls. Gt. Brit.* 74. 1862.

[10] Smith, A. *Treas. Bot.* 1:732. 1870. (*Melilotus caerulea*)

T. corniculata Linn.

South Europe and Asia Minor. In Bengal, this plant serves as a vegetable food.[1]

T. foenum-graecum Linn. FENUGREEK. HELBEH.

Europe and the Orient. Fenugreek is cultivated in Morocco, in the south of France near Montpelier, in Alsace, in a few places in Switzerland, in some provinces of the German and Austrian Empires, as Thuringia and Moravia, and on a large scale in Egypt, where it is known as helbeh.[2] In Egypt, fenugreek is eaten crude and its sprouting seeds are often mixed in a ragout with honey.[3] *Helbeh* conserve, says Pickering,[4] was once an article of export, even to Britain, and to the present day is employed by Arabs along the east African coast for child-stealing. At Rosetta, the seeds are used as a coffee. Fenugreek is a favorite article of diet with the Parsees of India, says Pickering,[5] It is extensively cultivated in India, says Dutt,[6] the seeds to be used as a condiment and the aromatic leaves as a potherb. In 1859,[7] seeds of helbeh were introduced into the United States through the Patent Office from Palestine, and they are now offered in our seed catalogs.

T. radiata Boiss.

Asia Minor and Persia. In China the curved legumes were formerly eaten.[8]

T. suavissima Lindl.

Australia. This species is mentioned by Mueller as a food plant of Australia.[9]

Trilisa odoratissima Cass. *Compositae.* CAROLINA VANILLA. DEER'S TONGUE.

Virginia and southward. The leaves exhale the odor of vanilla when bruised, and, in Florida, the plant has become in some degree an article of commerce, being used by tobacconists for flavoring smoking tobacco.[10]

Triosteum perfoliatum Linn. *Caprifoliaceae.* FEVER ROOT. WILD COFFEE.

Eastern North America. Barton[11] reports that Muhlenburg told him that the dried and toasted berries were considered by some of the Germans of Pennsylvania an excellent substitute for coffee.

Triphasia aurantiola Lour. *Rutaceae.* LIME BERRY.

A shrub of tropical Asia. Loureiro[12] says the berry is red, ovate, half the size of a coffee bean, covered with a thin pellicle and contains a sweet, clammy, inodorous, edible

[1] Unger, F. *U. S. Pat. Off. Rpt.* 359. 1859. (*T. esculenta*)
[2] Flückiger and Hanbury *Pharm.* 151. 1879.
[3] Pickering, C. *Chron. Hist. Pls.* 174. 1879.
[4] Ibid.
[5] Pickering, C. *Chron. Hist. Pls.* 37. 1879.
[6] Dutt, U. C. *Mat. Med. Hindus* 144. 1877.
[7] *U. S. Pat. Off. Rpt.* 20. 1859.
[8] Smith, F. P. *Contrib. Mat. Med. China* 145. 1871.
[9] Unger, F. *U. S. Pat. Off. Rpt.* 357. 1859.
[10] *U. S. D. A. Rpt.* 170. 1871.
[11] Barton, W. P. C. *Med. Bot.* 1:63. 1817.
[12] Loureiro *Fl. Cochin.* 152. 1790.

pulp. The berry, like an orange in miniature, says Mason, is often found in Chinese preserves. Firminger[1] says, in India, the fruit is of the size of a large currant. It has a stone surrounded by a small quantity of pulp, juicy and of an agreeable, aniseed-like flavor. The plant is cultivated in the East and West Indies. The fruits, says A. Smith,[2] are about as large as hazelnuts and have a red skin. When ripe they have an agreeable taste but, if gathered green, they have a strong flavor of turpentine and the pulp is very sticky. They are sometimes preserved whole in syrup and are occasionally sent to England.

Tripsacum dactyloides Linn. *Gramineae.* BUFFALO GRASS.

Central and North America. Mueller[3] says the seeds are available for food.

Triticum bicorne Forsk. *Gramineae.* SPELT.

Egypt and Syria. The name spelt is given generally to all wheats in which the grain adheres to the chaff. Spelt is little cultivated except in the warmer districts of south-eastern Europe and the African and Asiatic shores of the Mediterranean. This appears to be botanically the same species as the *T. bicorne* of Forskahl's *Egyptian Flora*.

T. dicoccum Schrank. EMMER. GERMAN WHEAT. TWO-GRAINED WHEAT.

Europe; of ancient cultivation and, according to Unger,[4] the *zeia dipokpos* of Dioscorides. Emmer is grown in southern Europe more than in central Europe.

T. monococcum Linn. KUSSEMETH. LESSER SPELT. ONE-GRAINED WHEAT.

Greece and Asia Minor. This is the kussemeth of the Scriptures From it the Syrians and Arabians make their bread. Its cultivation has not extended to India, Egypt or Greece.[5] In its wild state, says Bentham[6] this species has been described under the name of *Crithodium aegilopoides*. The produce of lesser spelt is too small to be of any importance except in very poor soils.

T. polonicum Linn. POLISH WHEAT.

Polish wheat is cultivated in the warmer regions of Europe.[7]

T. spelta Linn. SPELT.

Some think this to be the grain called *olura* or *zeia* or *zea* by the ancient Greeks.[8] Spelt is at present cultivated to a small extent in Europe. It was seen by Alexander the Great[9] as a cultivated plant in his campaign in Pontus. Its origin in Mesopotamia and Hamadam, in Persia, is doubtful; especially as its cultivation in these countries cannot be carried back to any very remote antiquity.

[1] Firminger, T. A. C. *Gard. Ind.* 217. 1874.

[2] Smith, A. *Treas. Bot.* 2:1173. 1870. (*T. trifoliata*)

[3] Mueller, F. *Sel. Pls.* 489. 1891.

[4] Unger, F. *U. S. Pat. Off. Rpt.* 304. 1859. (*T. amyleum*)

[5] Ibid.

[6] Morton *Cyc. Agr.* 2:1005. 1869.

[7] Unger, F. *U. S. Pat. Off. Rpt.* 304. 1859.

[8] De Candolle, A. *Geog. Bot.* 2:933. 1855.

[9] De Candolle, A. *Geog. Bot.* 2:934. 1855.

This is the species which includes all the true wheats, excepting the spelts. It is said to have been found wild in various parts of Asia where it is not likely to have escaped from cultivation.[1] According to Grecian fable, it was originally native on the plains of Enna and in Sicily, but it is much more probable that it is a native of the plains about the Caspian.

Isis was supposed to have introduced wheat into Egypt; Demeter, into Greece; and the Emperor Chin-nong, into China about 3000 B. C.[2] Standing crops of bearded wheat are figured in Egypt under the Fourth Dynasty, about 2440 B. C., at Gizeh, but nowhere on these nor on subsequent monuments with the minute accuracy required for distinguishing species.[3] In Greece, Theophrastus [4] mentioned eight varieties and among the carbonized seeds exhumed by Dr. Schliemann [5] in Greece is a very hard, fine-grained, sharp wheat, very flat on the furrowed side, which is said to differ from any wheat hitherto known. In Europe, wheat was cultivated before the period of written history as samples have been removed from the debris of the lacustrine habitations in Switzerland which do not differ in size and form from our varieties.[6] Wheat is mentioned by Diodorus as growing wild in Sicily, and ears of bearded wheat appear on most of the ancient Sicilian coins. On two Leontine brass coins are figures of Ceres in addition to the usual ears of corn.[7]

In France, wheat was the most valued cereal in the eighth century as shown by the maximum price fixed by an edict of Charlemagne wherein oats were to be sold at one denier, barley at two deniers, rye at three deniers and wheat at four deniers a bushel.[8] It is probable, says C. W. Johnson,[9] that wheat was not cultivated by the early Britons for the climate, owing to the immense preponderance of woods and undrained soil, was so severe and wet that, in winter, they could attempt no agricultural employments, and even when Bede [10] wrote, early in the eighth century, the Anglo-Saxons sowed their wheat in spring. Wheat remained an article of comparative luxury until nearly the seventeenth century. That the cultivation of wheat in England was unimportant in the reign of Elizabeth, is attested by Tussar.[11] Yet wheat was cultivated by the Romans and is mentioned by Columella,[12] Pliny,[13] Cicero,[14] Caesar [15] and many others.

In India, wheat seems not to be native but introduced, if we can trust to the Sanscrit name, which, translated, is food of the Barbarians, but this may mean that the center

[1] De Candolle, A. *Geog. Bot.* **2**:931, 932. 1855.

[2] Unger, F. *U. S. Pat. Off. Rpt.* 303. 1859.

[3] Pickering, C. *Chron. Hist. Pls.* 59. 1879. (*T. turgidum*)

[4] Hooker, W. J. *Journ. Bot.* **1**:216. 1834.

[5] Schliemann, Dr. *Amer. Antiq.* 66. 1880.

[6] Lubbock *Amer. Journ. Sci. Art.* **34**:181. 1862.

[7] Hooker, W. J. *Journ. Bot.* **1**:216. 1834.

[8] Guizot, M. *Hist. Civil.* **3**:25. 1857.

[9] Johnson, C. W. *Journ. Agr.* **11**:482. 1841.

[10] Ibid.

[11] Ibid.

[12] Andrews *Latin Lexicon* 1570. 1861.

[13] Ibid.

[14] Ibid.

[15] Ibid.

and south of India, too hot for wheat-growing, received their grain from the Hill Tribes of the north, where the climate suited it.[1] In the *Bhavaprakasa*, two types are mentioned, the large-grained and small-grained, or beardless. The first variety is said to come from the west, the second to be indigenous to middle India.[2] About 1330, in the wonders described by Friar Jordanus,[3] it is said, " wheaten bread is there not eaten by the natives, although wheat they have in plenty." In China, according to Stanislas Julien,[4] wheat was cultivated in the year 2822 B. C.

The first wheat raised in the New World was sown by Spaniards on the Island of Isabela. The foundation of the wheat harvests of Mexico is said to have been three or four grains, carefully preserved by a negro slave of Cortez in 1530, which were found in some rice brought from Spain for the use of the troops.[5] In Quito, says Humboldt,[6] the first wheat was raised by a Franciscan monk in front of his convent. The first wheat introduced into Peru was by a Spanish woman who took great pains to disseminate it among the colonists, says Prescott,[7] but no dates are given. Garcilasso de la Vega [8] affirms that, up to 1547, no wheaten bread had been sold at Cusco, Peru. In 1542, John Alphonse,[9] chief pilot to Roberval, in speaking of the region about the present Montreal, says, " I have told in one ear of corn 120 grains, like the corn of France and you need not to sow your wheat until March and it will be ripe in the midst of August." The first wheat grown in New England was that sown by Gosnold,[10] on the Elizabeth Islands, off the coast of Massachusetts, " which sprang up eight or nine inches in fourteen days." In 1604, on the Island of St. Croix, near Calais, Maine, the French had some wheat sown, which flourished freely,[11] and, in 1606, wheat was sown by L'Escarbot near the port of Port Royal, Annapolis Basin, Nova Scotia. In 1610, wheat was among the plants in Champlain's garden at Quebec.[12] In Virginia, the first wheat appears to have been sown in 1611;[13] in 1626, samples of wheat grown in the Dutch colony of New Netherlands were taken to Holland for exhibit.[14] In 1629, wheat was ordered by the Plymouth Colony, from England, for seed.[15] In 1718, wheat was introduced into the Valley of the Mississippi by the Western Company.[16] In California, wheat is spoken of by Father Baegert,[17] as

[1] Pictet *Anthrop. Rev. and Journ.* 1:241. 1863.

[2] Dutt, U. C. *Mat. Med. Hindus* 269. 1877.

[3] Jordanus, Fr. *Wonders East.* Hakl. Soc. Ed. 12. 1863.

[4] De Candolle, A. *Geog. Bot.* 2:931. 1855.

[5] Humboldt, A. *Views Nat.* 130. 1850.

[6] Ibid.

[7] Prescott, W. H. *Conq. Peru* 1:142. 1860. Note.

[8] Walton *Journ. Agr.* 2nd Ser. 1:615. 1845.

[9] Pinkerton *Coll. Voy.* 12:674. 1812.

[10] Hubbard, W. *New Eng.* Mass. Hist. Soc. Coll. 5:11. 1818. 2nd Ser.

[11] Champlain *Voy.* Prince Soc. Ed. 2:34. 1878.

[12] Parkman, F. *Pion. France* 360. 1894.

[13] Flint, C. L. *U. S. D. A. Rpt.* 280. 1872.

[14] Ibid.

[15] Ibid.

[16] *U. S. D. A. Rpt.* 127. 1853.

[17] Baegert, F. *Smithsonian Inst. Rpt.* 356. 1863.

flourishing, 1751–1768; and it was cultivated by the Pimas Indians of the Gila River in 1799.[1]

The northern limit to the growing of wheat is 57° north in Britain, 64° in Norway, 60° in Russia and lower in Siberia.[2] In North America, wheat is raised with profit at Fort Liard, 60° north. The fine harvests of Egypt and of Algiers, says Humboldt, as well as those of the valleys of Aragua and Cuba, prove that the augmentation of heat is not prejudicial to the harvests of wheat, unless it be attended with an excess of drought or moisture. In the moist region on the slopes of the mountains of Mexico and Xalapa, the luxuriance of the vegetation is such that wheat does not form ears.[3]

The varieties of wheat are almost endless, and their characteristics vary widely under the influence of cultivation and climate. There are 180 distinct sorts in the museum of Cornell University;[4] Darwin says Dalbret cultivated during 30 years from 150 to 160 kinds; Colonel Le Conteur[5] possessed upwards of 150; and Philippar,[6] 322 varieties. The summer and winter kinds were classed by Linnaeus as distinct species but it has been proved that the one can be converted into the other by cultivation. Godron[7] describes five species of wheat and De Candolle[8] four. Reports come from little-known regions of distinct kinds; in Japan there is said to be a variety which cannot be forced to grow higher than 20 or 24 inches, though the length of the heads may increase. In general, wheat is the most esteemed of the cereal productions but, so far does habit govern, that in Abyssinia, according to Parkyns,[9] the flour of teff, or *dagussa*, scarcely palatable to Europeans, is preferred by the natives to that of any other grain.

Tropaeolum edule Paxt. *Geraniaceae.* NASTURTIUM.

Chile. Mr. Bridges, writing in the *Journal of Botany*, 1842, says the roots are eaten in times of scarcity in Peru.[10]

T. majus Linn. INDIAN CRESS. TALL NASTURTIUM.

Peru. The plant is grown more for ornament than for food purposes, but the flowers and young leaves are frequently used to mix in salads, and the seeds, gathered while young and green, are used for pickling and as an excellent substitute for capers.[11] " The seeds of this rare and faire plant came first from the Indies into Spaine and those hot regions, and from thence into France and Flanders, from whence I have received seeds that hath borne with me both flowers and seeds," says Gerarde, 1597.[12] We cannot agree with those

---

[1] Whipple and Turner *Pacif. R. R. Rpt.* **3**:123. 1856.

[2] *Enc. Brit.* **17**:630.

[3] Humboldt, A. *Trav.* **1**:498. 1889.

[4] Gould *Agr. Conn.* 25. 1872.

[5] Darwin, C. *Ans. Pls. Domest.* **1**:332. 1893.

[6] Ibid.

[7] Godron *Journ. Roy. Agr. Soc.* **19**:104. 1858.

[8] De Candolle, A. *Geog. Bot.* **2**:930. 1855.

[9] Parkyns *Life Abyss.* **1**:306. 1856.

[10] *Gard. Chron.* 301. 1842.

[11] McIntosh, C. *Book Gard.* **2**:170. 1855.

[12] Gerarde, J. *Herb.* 196. 1597; 251. 1633.

authors who consider this the dwarf form, as the figure given comes nearer to the tall, as it was figured by J. Bauhin,[1] in his works printed in 1651, with the name *scandens*, 33 years before its introduction by Linnaeus. Ray,[2] 1686, speaks of its use as a vegetable, and this use is also spoken of by Townsend,[3] 1726. In American gardens, this nasturtium was noticed by McMahon,[4] 1806, and by all the early garden writers as being the predominant kind in culture. The synonymy is as follows:

Nasturtium Indicum. Cam. *Icon.* t. 31. 1588.
Nasturtium Indicum. Indian cresses. Ger. 196. 1597.
Nasturtium indicum folio peltato scandens. Bauh, J. **2**:75. 1651.
Cardamindum ampliore folio and *majore flore.* Feuille, *Peru.* **3**: t. 8. 1725.

T. minus Linn. DWARF NASTURTIUM.

Peru. The Dwarf nasturtium was first brought into Europe from Peru, where it is a native. It reached England in 1596 and is described by Gerarde[5] as coming from the Indies into Spain and thence into France and Flanders, whence he received seeds. The plant, like the tall nasturtium, is grown principally as an ornament, but the flowers and leaves and green fruit may be used in salads or for pickling. This species seems to have been first known in Europe about 1574; was described by Monardes;[6] is figured by Lobel,[7] 1576; and is generally spoken of about this period as a new and rare plant. It was in the vegetable garden in England in 1726,[8] probably before, and is mentioned in American gardens in 1806.[9]

T. pentaphyllum Lam. FIVE-LEAVED NASTURTIUM.

Brazil and Chile. This species furnishes an edible cress.[10] It bears a three-lobed, sweet, fleshy, edible berry, black, juicy and not unlike in appearance and flavor to the Zante, or currant, grape.[11]

T. sessilifolium Poepp. & Endl.

Chile. Philippi says this is one of the most eligible of the species of this genus for its tubers, which can be eaten even in a raw state.[12]

T. tuberosum Ruiz & Pav. PERUVIAN NASTURTIUM.

Bolivia and Peru; long cultivated on the Peruvian Andes for its tuberous roots.[13] The tubers are called *ysano*, are yellow and red and about the size of small pears. They

---

[1] Bauhin, J. *Hist. Pl.* **2**:75. 1651.
[2] Ray *Hist. Pl.* 487. 1686.
[3] Townsend *Seedsman* 40. 1726.
[4] McMahon, B. *Amer. Gard. Cal.* 318. 1806.
[5] Gerarde, J. *Herb.* 251. 1633 or 1636; 195. 1597.
[6] *Hortus Eystet.* ord. 13, fol. 1. 1713.
[7] Lobel *Obs.* 338. 1576.
[8] Townsend *Seedsman* 40. 1726.
[9] McMahon, B. *Amer. Gard. Cal.* 318. 1806.
[10] Unger, F. *U. S. Pat. Off. Rpt.* 356. 1859.
[11] Moore, T. *Treas. Bot.* **1**:280. 1870. (*Chymocarpus pentaphyllum*)
[12] Mueller, F. *Sel. Pls.* 493. 1891.
[13] Pickering, C. *Chron. Hist. Pls.* 678. 1879.

are cooked and then frozen before being eaten; the women of La Paz are very fond of this frozen dish.[1]

Trophis americana Linn.   *Urticaceae.*   RAMOON TREE.

West Indies.   The berries, which are about the size of large grapes, have a very pleasant flavor.[2]

Tsuga canadensis Carr.   *Coniferae.*   HEMLOCK.

North America.   The Indians of Maine prepare a tea from the leaves of hemlock and this tea is relished as a drink.   The spray is also used in New England and elsewhere to a limited extent in the domestic manufacture of spruce beer.   According to McKenzie,[3] the aborigines of the West employ the inner bark as a food; it is taken off early in the spring and made into cakes, which are eaten with salmon oil and are considered dainties. Langsdorff [4] speaks of the Thlinkets at Sitka eating cakes made of bark of spruce fir, mixed with roots, berries and train oil.

Typha angustifolia Linn.   *Typhaceae.*   SMALL BULRUSH.

Europe and North America.   The young shoots are edible and resemble asparagus.[5]

T. elephantina Roxb.   ELEPHANT'S GRASS.

Mediterranean region and East Indies.   A kind of bread, called *boor* or *booree*, is made in Scinde from the pollen.[6]

T. latifolia Linn.   BULRUSH.   CAT TAIL.   COSSACK ASPARAGUS.   REED MACE.

Europe and North America.   In Virginia, the poorer settlers ate the root of the bulbrush and were very fond of it; it has a sweetish taste.[7]   Haller [8] says the roots are eaten in salads.   Long [9] says the seeds are esculent, roasted; Lindley, that it is sometimes used as food under the name of Cossack asparagus.   This plant, says Clarke,[10] flourishes luxuriantly in the shallows of the Don.   He found the people devouring it raw; " with a degree of avidity as though it had been a religious observance.   It was to be seen in all the streets and in every house, bound into faggots."   " They peel off the outer rind and find near the root a tender, white part of the stem, which, for about the length of 18 inches, affords a crisp, cooling, and very pleasant article of food."

T. laxmanni Lepech.   SCENTED FLAG.

Europe and northern Asia.   The rhizomes furnish a meal which is made into cakes. They are used also as a vegetable.[11]

---

[1] *Journ. Hort. Soc. Lond.* **9**:59.   1855.

[2] Lunan, J.   *Hort. Jam.* **2**:140.   1814.

[3] Nuttall, T.   *No. Amer. Sylva* **2**:163.   1865.   (*Thuja gigantea*)

[4] Langsdorff *Voy.* **2**:131.   1813–14.

[5] Drury, H.   *Useful Pls. Ind.* 435.   1869.

[6] *Treas. Bot.* **2**:1269.   1870.

[7] Forster, J. R.   *Fl. Amer. Septent.* 41.   1771.

[8] Lunan, J.   *Hort. Jam.* **1**:169.   1814.

[9] Ibid.

[10] Clarke *Trav. Russia* **1**:175.

[11] Smith, F. P.   *Contrib. Mat. Med. China* 223.   1871.

Ullucus tuberosus Caldas. *Chenopodiaceae.* MELLOCO. ULLUCO.

Andes of Bolivia, Peru and New Granada. The ulluco, or melloco, is a juicy plant with a creeping stem, the sprouts of which swell at the tips into tubers from the size of a hazelnut to that of a pigeon's egg, like the sweet potato.[1] In Peru, it is called *oca quina* and Herndon[2] says is more glutinous than the oca and not as pleasant to the taste. The plant is extensively cultivated and, from the tubers by alternately freezing and steeping, a starchy substance is obtained, which is called by the Indians *chuna* and is relished. When the failure of the potato crop was dreaded in England, this plant was one of the substitutes proposed, but the tubers were not considered sufficiently agreeable to the British palate. Ulluco was introduced into France in 1848, but trial showed its unfitness for that climate.[3]

Ulmus campestris Linn. *Urticaceae.* ENGLISH ELM.

Europe and the Orient. The English elm was early introduced into Boston and is now grown here and there as a shade tree. In Norway, the inhabitants kiln-dry the bark and in time of scarcity grind it into a meal to be mixed with flour for bread. The fruit, in a green state, according to Browne,[4] is sometimes eaten as a salad. Some years ago, in England, says Johnson,[5] an immense quantity of dried elm leaves were used for adulterating tea and for manufacturing a substance intended to be used as a substitute for it. In Russia, the leaves of a variety are used as tea.[6] In times of great scarcity, the ground bark, the leaves and the membranous fruit are all eaten as food in China.[7]

U. fulva Michx. RED ELM. SLIPPERY ELM.

New England to Wisconsin and Kentucky. Flour prepared from the bark by drying and grinding, mixed with milk, like arrowroot, is said by Emerson[8] to be a wholesome and nutritious food for infants and invalids.

Umbellularia californica Nutt. *Laurineae.* BALM OF HEAVEN. CAJEPUT TREE. CALI-
FORNIAN OLIVE. MOUNTAIN LAUREL. SASSAFRAS LAUREL. SPICE BUSH.

Northwestern America. The foliage, when bruised, gives out a camphor-like scent. Hunters often, according to Douglas,[9] make use of a decoction of the leaves, which stimulates the system and produces a glow of warmth. The Spanish-Americans use the leaves as a condiment.[10]

Uncaria gambier Roxb. *Rubiaceae.* GAMBIR.

Malacca, Sumatra, Cochin China and other parts of eastern Asia; largely cultivated in the Islands of Bintang, Singapore and Prince of Wales. Gambir is prepared by boiling

---

[1] Unger, F. *U. S. Pat. Off. Rpt.* 311. 1859.

[2] Herndon, W. L., and Gibbon, L. *Explor. Vall. Amaz.* 1:48. 1854.

[3] *Bon Jard.* 649. 1882.

[4] Browne, D. J. *Trees Amer.* 497. 1846.

[5] Johnson, C. P. *Useful Pls. Gt. Brit.* 236. 1862.

[6] Browne, D. J. *Trees Amer.* 497. 1846.

[7] Smith, F. P. *Contrib. Mat. Med. China* 92. 1871.

[8] Emerson, G. B. *Trees, Shrubs Mass.* 2:335. 1875.

[9] Hooker, W. J. *Fl. Bor. Amer.* 2:137. 1840. (*Tetranthera californica*)

[10] Smith, A. *Treas. Bot.* 2:821. 1870. (*Oreodaphne californica*)

the leaves and evaporating the decoction until it acquires the consistence of clay.   This gambir is used for tanning leather, also by dyers and curers, forming an article of export. Among the Malays, the chief use is as a masticatory, in combination with the areca-nut and the betel-leaf.[1]

Unona concolor Willd.   *Anonaceae.*

Guiana.   This plant has an acrid and aromatic fruit, used as a pepper by the negroes in Guiana.[2]

U. discolor Vahl.

Tropical Asia.   The fruit is used in the same way as is that of the species above.[3]

U. discreta Linn. f.

Guiana.   The purple, aromatic, berries are of a very good taste.[4]

U. dumetorum Dun.

Cochin China.   The pulp of the fruit is sparing but is of a grateful taste.[5]

U. undulata Dun.

Tropical Africa.   The plant has an aromatic fruit, which is used as a condiment at Wari in Guinea.[6]

Urceola elastica Roxb.   *Apocynaceae.*   RUBBER TREE.

Indian Archipelago.   This plant is a gigantic climber which yields Borneo rubber.[7] Its fruit, the size of an orange, contains numerous, kidney-shaped seeds nestling in a copious, tawny-colored pulp, which is much relished both by natives and European residents and is said to taste like well-rotted medlars.[8]

Urginea sp.?   *Liliaceae.*

Equatorial Africa.   A species which has nauseous and bitter roots and white flowers and furnishes a vegetable to the natives.   Grant [9] writes, " the men of the Moon roast its leaves and stalks and cook them as a spinach."

Urtica dioica Linn.   *Urticaceae.*   NETTLE.

North temperate regions; naturalized in America from Europe.   The nettle, according to Sir Walter Scott,[10] was at one time cultivated in Scotland as a potherb.   Nettle tops, in the spring, says Lightfoot,[11] are often boiled and eaten by the common people of Scotland

---

[1] Smith, A.   *Treas. Bot.* 2:779.   1870.   (*Nauclea gambir*)

[2] Don, G.   *Hist. Dichl. Pls.* 1:95.   1831.   (*U. aromatica*)

[3] Smith, A.   *Treas. Bot.* 1:564.   1870.   (*Habzelia aromatica*)

[4] Don, G.   *Hist. Dichl. Pls.* 1:95.   1831.

[5] Ibid.

[6] Ibid.

[7] Brandis, D.   *Forest Fl.* 320.   1874.

[8] Smith, A.   *Treas. Bot.* 2:1193.   1870.

[9] Speke, J. H.   *Journ. Disc. Source Nile* 584.   1864.

[10] Masters, M. T.   *Treas. Bot.* 2:1196.   1870.

[11] Lightfoot, J.   *Fl. Scot.* 2:579.   1789.

as greens, and the young leaves are often boiled in soup in the outer Hebrides and form a very palatable article of food, it is said.[1] The tender tops are much more commonly eaten in Germany, Belgium and other parts of Europe than in England[2] and are also used in northern Persia.[3]

Uvaria burahol Blume *Anonaceae.*
Java. Baillon[4] says the fruit is eaten in tropical Asia.

U. cordata Schum. & Thonn.
Tropical Africa. The plant bears edible fruits.[5]

U. dulcis Dun.
Burma, Malay and tropical Asia. The perfumed fruit is eaten. In the Public Gardens of Jamaica, this species is grown as a fruit tree.[6]

U. zeylanica Linn.
East Indies. The fruit is eatable, of a vinous taste, resembling that of an apricot.[7]

Uvularia perfoliata Linn. *Liliaceae.* BELWORT.
Eastern North America. Griffith[8] says the roots are edible when cooked, and the young shoots are a very good substitute for asparagus.

U. sessilifolia Linn. BELWORT.
Eastern North America. This pretty herb is mentioned as yielding a good substitute for asparagus.[9]

Vaccinium caespitosum Michx. *Vacciniaceae.* DWARF BILBERRY.
Alpine regions of northeastern United States. A small bush, says Mueller,[10] with bluish, edible berries.

V. canadense Kalm. SOUR-TOP OR VELVET-LEAF BLUEBERRY.
Canada and Maine to Wisconsin and the Rocky Mountains. The berry is blue and sweet.[11]

V. corymbosum Linn. HIGH BLUEBERRY. SWAMP BLUEBERRY.
Northeastern United States and southward. The berries are often large, black, with a bluish bloom and of a sprightly, acidulous taste. This blueberry has been recommended by horticulturists for cultivation and in some of its varieties is very deserving.

---

[1] *Journ. Agr.* 2:378. 1831.

[2] Masters, M. T. *Treas. Bot.* 2:1196. 1870.

[3] Unger, F. *U. S. Pat. Off. Rpt.* 356. 1859.

[4] Baillon, H. *Hist. Pls.* 1:272. 1871.

[5] Masters, M. T. *Treas. Bot.* 2:1198. 1870.

[6] Morris *Rpt. Pub. Gard. Jam.* 35. 1880.

[7] Don, G. *Hist. Dichl. Pls.* 1:92. 1831.

[8] Griffith, W. *Med. Bot.* 641. 1847.

[9] Mueller, F. *Sel. Pls.* 498. 1891.

[10] Mueller, F. *Sel. Pls.* 499. 1891.

[11] Wood, A. *Class Book Bot.* 482. 1864.

V. erythrocarpum Michx.

Pennsylvania to Georgia on high mountains. The transparent, scarlet berries are of excellent taste.

V. leschenaultii Wight.

Neilgherries. The berries, about the size of red currants, are agreeably acid and make excellent tarts.[1]   Mueller[2] says of Ceylon also, a tree, flowering and fruiting throughout the year.

V. leucanthum Schlecht.

Mexico. The black fruit is edible.[3]

V. maderense Link. MADERIA WHORTLEBERRY.

Madeira. The berries are black, juicy, eatable and gratefully acid.[4]

V. meridionale Sw. JAMAICA BILBERRY.

Jamaica. The berries are sapid, red, acid, astringent, bitter and, like bilberries, they make good jelly.[5]   This species is grown in the Public Gardens of Jamaica.[6]

V. mortinia Benth. MORTINIA.

Ecuador and the mountains of Columbia. The berries come to the Quito market under the name of mortinia.[7]

V. myrtillus Linn. BILBERRY. BLAEBERRY. WHINBERRY. WHORTLEBERRY.

North temperate and arctic regions. The Highlanders of Scotland frequently eat the berries in milk and sometimes make them into tarts and jellies.[8]   In the Orkneys, the blaeberry grows in abundance, the fruit of large size; wine of fine flavor has been made from it.   Johnson[9] says the berries are slightly acid and sweetish but do not possess much flavor in the raw state, though liked by some persons.   They are sold in the English markets. This is a favorite food of the Rocky Mountain Indians.[10]

V. ovalifolium Sm.

Northern North America. The berries are gathered before quite ripe, are pressed into a cake, then dried and laid by. When used, a quantity is put into a vessel of cold water and stirred rapidly with the hand until it assumes a form not unlike soapsuds. It is pleasant to the taste, with a slightly bitter flavor.[11]

---

[1] Wight, R.   *Icon. Pls.* 4:Pl. 1188.   1850.

[2] Mueller, F.   *Sel. Pls.* 499.   1891.

[3] Don, G.   *Hist. Dichl. Pls.* 3:855.   1834.

[4] Don, G.   *Hist. Dichl. Pls.* 3:854.   1834.

[5] Titford, W. J.   *Hort. Bot. Amer.* 60.   1812.

[6] Morris *Rpt. Pub. Gard. Jam.* 35.   1880.

[7] Mueller, F.   *Sel. Pls.* 500.   1891.

[8] Lightfoot, J.   *Fl. Scot.* 1:201.   1789.

[9] Johnson, C. P.   *Useful Pls. Gt. Brit.* 163.   **1862.**

[10] *U. S. D. A. Rpt.* 415.   1870.

[11] Brown, R.   *Bot. Soc. Edinb.* 9:384.   1868.

V. parvifolium Sm. RED HUCKLEBERRY.

Northwest coast of North America. The berries are red and make excellent tarts.[1] The berries are of good size and flavor.[2]

V. pensylvanicum Lam. EARLY BLUEBERRY. LOW SWEET BLUEBERRY.

Northern America, producing many varieties. The berries says Pursh,[3] are large, bluish-black, extremely sweet and agreeable to eat. Gray[4] says the berries are large and sweet and the earliest blueberry in the market. Emerson[5] says the berries are blue, very sweet, rather soft for marketing, but are particularly suited to be preserved by drying. Kalm[6] says the Indians formerly plucked huckleberries in abundance every year, dried them in the sun, and preserved them for eating. In 1615, Champlain[7] found the Indians near Lake Huron gathering blueberries for their winter store. Roger Williams[8] says of the New England Indians that they "gathered *attitaash*, worthleberries, of which there are divers sorts: sweet, like currants, some opening, some of a binding nature. *Sautaash* are these currants dried and so preserved all the year, which they beat to powder and mingle with their parched meal and make a delicate dish which they call *sautauthig*, which is as sweet to them as plum or spice cake to the English." The Indians of the Northwest coast are very fond of this fruit and smoke-dry it in large quantities for winter use.[9]

V. praestans Lamb. KAMCHATKA BILBERRY.

Kamchatka. This is a minute plant but with large, delicious fruits.[10]

V. salicinum Cham. & Schlecht.

Alaska. The berries are collected and dried by the natives.[11]

V. stamineum Linn. DEERBERRY. SQUAW HUCKLEBERRY.

Northern United States. Elliott[12] says the berries are eaten. The Indians of Wisconsin and Michigan make extensive use of the fruit.[13] Emerson[14] says the fruit is scarcely eatable.

V. uliginosum Linn. BOG BILBERRY. MOORBERRY.

Northern climates. Don[15] says the berries are large, juicy, black, covered with a mealy bloom, eatable, but neither grateful nor wholesome. The berries, says Johnson,[16]

[1] Don, G. *Hist. Dichl. Pls.* 3:854. 1834.

[2] Case *Bot. Index* 38. 1881.

[3] Pursh, F. *Fl. Amer. Septent.* 1:288. 1814.

[4] Gray, A. *Man. Bot.* 291. 1868.

[5] Emerson, G. B. *Trees, Shrubs Mass.* 2:456, 457. 1875.

[6] Kalm, P. *Trav. No. Amer.* 2:390. 1772.

[7] Parkman, F. *Pion. France* 394. 1894.

[8] Williams, R. *Key.* Narragansett Club Ed. 1:122. 1643.

[9] *U. S. D. A. Rpt.* 415. 1870.

[10] Mueller, F. *Sel. Pls.* 502. 1891.

[11] Pickering, C. *Chron. Hist. Pls.* 581. 1879.

[12] Elliott, S. *Bot. So. Car., Ga.* 1:496. 1821.

[13] *U. S. D. A. Rpt.* 415. 1870.

[14] Emerson, G. B. *Trees, Shrubs Mass.* 2:454. 1875.

[15] Don, G. *Hist. Dichl. Pls.* 3:853. 1834.

[16] Johnson, C. P. *Useful Pls. Gt. Brit.* 163. 1875.

are eaten occasionally but in any "large quantity cause giddiness and headache." In Siberia, the berries are fermented, distilled and furnish a strong alcoholic spirit. It is said that the berries are used in France to color wine. Richardson [1] says, beyond the Arctic circle this species is, in good seasons, plentiful to an extraordinary degree and is of a finer quality than in more southern localities.

V. vacillans Soland. LOW BLUEBERRY.

From Massachusetts and Vermont to Pennsylvania. This vaccinium has a small bush, with rather late-ripening berries.

V. vitis-idaea Linn. COWBERRY. CRANBERRY. FOXBERRY.

Northern and arctic regions. This is the *wi-sa-gu-mina* of the Crees and the cranberry most plentiful and most used throughout Rupert's Land. This berry, says Richardson, [2] is excellent for every purpose to which a cranberry can be applied. Thoreau, [3] in the Maine woods, made his desserts on these berries stewed and sweetened, but Gray [4] says they are barely edible in America. The fruit is not much eaten in Britain but is greatly valued in Sweden. The berries are tasteless and but little acid when gathered but, after exposure to frost, they become very sour. They are often sold in the London market as cranberries. In Siberia, they are kept in water in winter, where they acquire their proper acidity and are eaten in spring. [5]

Valeriana cornucopiae Linn. *Valerianeae.* AFRICAN VALERIAN.

African valerian is a recent introduction into gardens and furnishes in its leaves a salad of excellent quality. The plant is native to the Mediterranean region in grain fields and in waste places. C. Bauhin, [6] 1596, speaks of it as if of recent introduction to botanical gardens in his time; and Clusius, [7] 1601, J. Bauhin, [8] 1651, and Ray, [9] 1686, all describe it. This valerian is not spoken of as under cultivation in *Miller's Dictionary*, 1807, nor does Don in his *Gardener's Dictionary*, 1834, speak of any use, although he is usually very ready with such information. In 1841, the *Bon Jardinier*, in France, refers to it as being a good salad plant. As neither Noisette, [10] 1830, nor Petit, [11] 1826, nor Pirolle, [12] 1824, mentions it, we may assume that it had not entered the vegetable garden at these dates. In 1863, Burr [13] describes African valerian among American garden vegetables, as does Vilmorin [14]

---

[1] Richardson, J. *Arctic Explor.* 2:300. 1851.

[2] Richardson, J. *Arctic Explor.* 2:301. 1851.

[3] Thoreau *Me. Woods* 30. 1877.

[4] Gray, A. *Man. Bot.* 290. 1868.

[5] Johnson, C. P. *Useful Pls. Gt. Brit.* 164. 1862.

[6] Bauhin, C. *Phytopinax* 293. 1596; *Pinax* 164. 1623; *Prod.* 87. 1671.

[7] Clusius *Hist.* 2:54. 1601.

[8] Bauhin, J. *Hist. Pl.* 3:Pt. 2, 212. 1651.

[9] Ray *Hist. Pl.* 394. 1686.

[10] Noisette *Man. Jard.* 1830.

[11] Petit *Dict. Jard.* 1826.

[12] Pirolle *L'Hort. Franc.* 1824–25.

[13] Burr, F. *Field, Gard. Veg.* 401. 1863.

[14] Vilmorin *Les Pls. Potag.* 562. 1883. (*Fedia cornucopiae*)

in France in 1883, and it is described in England in 1885. No varieties are described, although a purple and a white-flowered form are mentioned by Bauhin as occurring in the wild plant. The one sort now described has pink- or rose-colored flowers.

V. edulis Nutt. TOBACCO ROOT. VALERIAN.

Ohio to Wisconsin and westward. This is the principal edible root among the Indians who inhabit the upper waters of the streams on the western side of the Rocky Mountains. It has a very strong and remarkably peculiar taste and an odor most offensive.[1] The root is large, of a very bright yellow color, is full of nutriment and, to some, the taste is agreeable. The Indians of the Northwest collect the roots in the spring and, after baking, use them as food. From a bitter and somewhat pernicious substance, it is converted by baking into a soft, pulpy mass of sweet taste which is not unwholesome.[2]

Valerianella coronata DC. *Valerianaceae.*

Europe and the Orient. In France, this species furnishes a salad.[3]

V. eriocarpa Desv. ITALIAN CORN SALAD.

Europe and north Africa. This plant is much used in Europe as a substitute for lettuce in the spring and also, when grown in rich soil and of a considerable size, for spinach.[4] This species occurs in gardens in two varieties. It has a lighter green, somewhat longer leaf than the ordinary corn salad, slightly hairy and a little dentate on the borders towards the base.[5] It has the same uses. It is described for American gardens in 1863.[6] Under its common name *greese mâche*, it is noticed in France in 1829 and also as *mâche d'Italie* in 1824.[7]

V. olitoria Pollich. CORN SALAD. LAMB'S LETTUCE.

This annual plant has been found spontaneous in all temperate Europe as far as 60° north; in southern Europe to the Canary Isles, Madeira and the Azores; in north Africa, Asia Minor and in the region of the Caucasus.[8] This species seems quite variable in nature, and, as long ago as 1623, Bauhin [9] records its variability in size, saying it occurs with narrow, broad and entire leaves. Corn salad is described by Lobel,[10] 1576; Dalechamp,[11] 1587; as also by Camerarius [12] 1588; but with all, as occurring in fields and without mention of culture, although its value as a salad is recognized. In 1597, Gerarde [13] says it has

[1] Fremont, J. C. *Explor. Exped.* 135, 160. 1845.

[2] Hooker, W. J. *Fl. Bor. Amer.* 1:291. 1840. (*Patrinia ceratophylla*)

[3] *Bon Jard.* 522. 1882.

[4] McIntosh, C. *Book Gard.* 2:172. 1855.

[5] Vilmorin *Les Pls. Potag.* 325. 1883.

[6] Burr, F. *Field, Gard. Veg.* 340. 1863.

[7] Noisette *Man. Jard.* 1829.

[8] De Candolle, A. *Orig. Cult. Pls.* 92. 1885.

[9] Bauhin, C. *Pinax* 19:165. 1623.

[10] Lobel *Obs.* 413. 1576. Fig. p. 412.

[11] Dalechamp *Hist. Gen. Pl.* (Lugd.) 554, 1127, fig. 1587.

[12] Camerarius *Hort. Med.* 175. 1588.

[13] Gerarde, J. *Herb.* 243. 1597.

grown in use among the French and Dutch strangers in England, and " hath beene sowen in gardens as a sallad herbe." He figures two varieties. J. Bauhin [1] describes two sorts and gives Tabernaemontanus as a witness that it was found in gardens as well as in fields and vineyards. Ray,[2] 1686, quotes J. Bauhin only; Chabraeus,[3] 1677, describes it as grown in gardens as a salad herb; Worlidge,[4] 1683, Maeger,[5] 1683, Quintyne,[6] 1693 and 1704, Townsend,[7] 1726, Stevenson,[8] 1765, Mawe,[9] 1778, Bryant,[10] 1783, all refer to its culture in England. In France, according to Heuze,[11] the species is spoken of as cultivated by Olivier de Serres and is referred to as if a well-known cultivated salad in *Le Jardinier Solitaire*, 1612. Corn salad was in American gardens previous to 1806.[12] Vilmorin [13] describes four varieties, which are distinct. All these have blunt leaves. The variety quite frequently distributed in American gardens is that which is figured by the herbalists as having pointed leaves; as, for instance:

> *Phu minimum alterum.* Lob. 412. 1576; Dalechamp 1127. 1587.
> *Polypremnum.* Dalechamp 554. 1587.
> *Lactuca agnina.* Ger. 242. 1597.

The round-leaved form, the *mâche ronde* of Vilmorin, has its type figured by Dodonaeus in his *Pemptades*, 1616, under the name *album olus*.

Vangueria madagascariensis J. F. Gmel. *Rubiaceae.* TAMARIND OF THE INDIES.

Tropical Africa. The fruit is eaten under the name of *voa-vanga*.[14] It is the size of an apple and is eaten both raw and roasted but is far from palatable.[15] In Bengal, the fruit is eaten by the natives.[16] At Martinique, it is called tamarind of the Indies; the flavor of its pulp and its color recall the medlar of Europe.[17]

V. spinosa Roxb.

Tropical Asia. The berry is the size of a cherry, succulent and edible.[18]

---

[1] Bauhin, J. *Hist. Pl.* 3:324. 1651.

[2] Ray *Hist. Pl.* 392. 1686.

[3] Chabraeus *Sciag. and Icon.* 437. 1677.

[4] Worlidge, J. *Syst. Hort.* 214. 1683.

[5] Meager *Eng. Gard.* 61. 1683.

[6] Quintyne *Comp. Gard.* 144. 1693; 205. 1704.

[7] Townsend *Seedsman* 16. 1726.

[8] Stevenson *Gard. Kal.* 34. 1765.

[9] Mawe and Abercrombie *Univ. Gard. Bot.* 1778. (*V. locusta*)

[10] Bryant *Fl. Diet.* 116. 1783.

[11] Heuze, G. *Pls. Aliment.* I, V. 1873.

[12] McMahon, B. *Amer. Gard. Cal.* 455. 1806. (*V. locusta*)

[13] Vilmorin *Veg. Gard.* 202. 1885.

[14] Masters, M. T. *Treas. Bot.* 2:1203. 1870.

[15] Pickering, C. *Chron. Hist. Pls.* 700. 1879. (*V. edulis*)

[16] Wight, R. *Illustr. Ind. Bot.* 2:76. 1850. (*V. edulis*)

[17] Belanger *Trans. N. Y. Agr. Soc.* 18:567, 568. 1858. (*V. edulis*)

[18] Don, G. *Hist. Dichl. Pls.* 3:550. 1834.

Vanilla aromatica Sw. *Orchideae.* VANILLA.

Tropical America. This species is said to be cultivated in the isles of France and Bourbon. The pods constitute one of the vanillas of commerce.[1]

V. guianensis Splitg.

Tropical America. This species is described as yielding an aromatic fruit.

V. planifolia Andr. VANILLA.

West Indies and Mexico. The best vanilla is the produce of this species but several other South American species are also used. The product is employed very extensively for flavoring.

Vateria indica Linn. *Dipterocarpeae.* DAMMAR.

East Indies. This species is a tree of Ceylon from whose seeds the natives make a kind of bread.[2]

Veitchia joannis H. Wendl. *Palmae.*

Fiji Islands. The kernel has a slightly astringent taste but is eaten readily by the natives of Viti, especially the youngsters.[3]

Veltheimia. *Liliaceae.*

Eastern equatorial Africa. This plant grows in the swamps of the Nile, and its flowers are utilized as a spinach.[4]

Veratrum viride Ait. *Liliaceae.* INDIAN POKE. WHITE HELLEBORE.

North America. Josselyn [5] probably referred to this plant when mentioning a small, round-leafed tobacco as utilized by the New England Indians.

Veronica anagallis Linn. *Scrophularineae.* WATER SPEEDWELL.

Northern climates. The plant is considered to be antiscorbutic.[6]

V. beccabunga Linn. BROOKLIME. WATER PIMPERNEL.

Northern climates. Lightfoot [7] says of brooklime, " it is esteemed an anti-scorbutic and is eaten by some in the spring as a sallet, but it is more bitter and not so agreeable to the palate as watercresses." Loudon [8] says it is used in Britain as a salad.

V. officinalis Linn. FLUELLEN. SPEEDWELL.

Northern climates. The leaves of this species were recommended by Hoffman [9] as a tea substitute, but Withering [10] says it is more astringent and less grateful than tea.

---

[1] *U. S. Disp.* 849. 1865.

[2] Hooker, W. J. *Journ. Bot.* 2:239. 1840.

[3] Seemann, B. *Fl. Viti.* 272. 1865–73.

[4] Speke, J. H. *Journ. Disc. Source Nile* 584. 1864.

[5] Josselyn, J. *New Eng. Rar.* 103. 1865. 1672 original date.

[6] Masters, M. T. *Treas. Bot.* 2:1211. 1870.

[7] Lightfoot, J. *Fl. Scot.* 1:73. 1789.

[8] Loudon, J. C. *Hort.* 683. 1860.

[9] Johnson, C. P. *Useful Pls. Gt. Brit.* 193. 1862.

[10] Sinclair, G. *Hort. Gram. Woburn.* 330. 1869·

Viburnum cotinifolium D. Don. *Caprifoliaceae.* VIBURNUM.

Himalayan regions.   The ripe fruit is sweetish and is eaten in India.[1]

V. foetens Decne.

Himalayan regions.   In India, the sweetish fruit is eaten.[2]

V. lentago Linn. NANNYBERRY. SHEEPBERRY. SWEET VIBURNUM. WILD RAISIN.

Northeastern America to Georgia.   The berries are said by Wood[3] to be well-flavored, black, and sweetish.

V. nudum Linn. NAKED VIBURNUM. WITHE-ROD.

Newfoundland to Georgia.   The fruit is apple-shaped, compressed, about a quarter of an inch long, of a deep blue color, of a sweetish taste and may be eaten.[4]

V. opulus Linn. CRANBERRY TREE. GUELDER ROSE. PIMBINA. SNOWBALL TREE. WHITTEN TREE.

Middle and northern Europe and northern America.   The fruit is a poor substitute for cranberries, hence the name cranberry tree.[5]   The fruit, when ripe, is of a pleasant, acid taste and is sometimes substituted for cranberries.[6]   Thoreau[7] stewed them with sugar and says the lumbermen of Maine cook them with molasses; he afterwards saw them in a garden in Bangor.   In Norway and Sweden, the berries are eaten with honey and flour, and a spirit is distilled from them.[8]   A miserable food for savage nations, says Lindley.[9]   On the Winnipeg river, the fruit is of an orange color, fleshy and agreeable to the taste.   This plant is the *nipi minan* of the Crees.   Probably this is the fruit brought from the North and called by the Narragansett Indians *wuchipoquameneash*, described by Roger Williams[10] as " a kind of sharp fruit like a barberry in taste."

V. prunifolium Linn. BLACK HAW.

New York to Georgia.   The blackish berries are sweet and eatable.[11, 12]

V. stellulatum Wall.

Himalayan regions.   The small, acid fruit is eaten in the mountains of India.[13, 14]

Vicia cracca Linn. *Leguminosae.* TUFTED VETCH.

Asia, Europe and northern America.   This vetch has been occasionally cultivated, as affording provender of good quality, but it does not ripen a sufficient quantity of seed

---

[1] Brandis, D.   *Forest Fl.* 258.   1874.

[2] Brandis, D.   *Forest Fl.* 259.   1874.

[3] Wood, A.   *Class Book Bot.* 398.   1864.

[4] Emerson, G. B.   *Trees, Shrubs Mass.* 2:411.   1875.

[5] Gray, A.   *Man. Bot.* 207.   1868.

[6] Emerson, G. B.   *Trees, Shrubs Mass.* 2:416.   1875.

[7] Thoreau *Me. Woods* 173.   1877.

[8] Masters, M. T.   *Treas. Bot.* 2:1213.   1870.

[9] Lindley, J.   *Veg. King.* 767.   1846.

[10] Pickering, C.   *Chron. Hist. Pls.* 806.   1879.

[11] Wood, A.   *Class Book Bot.* 398.   1864.

[12] Rafinesque, C. S.   *Fl. La.* 77.   1817.

[13] Brandis, D.   *Forest Fl.* 258.   1874.

[14] Royle, J. F.   *Illustr. Bot. Himal.* 1:236.   1839.

to make it easy to grow it as an annual green crop. Johnson [1] says the seeds may be used as food.

V. ervilia Willd.

North Africa and Europe. This vetch, according to Loudon,[2] is cultivated in some places as a lentil. This vetch is cultivated by the French.

V. faba Linn. BROAD BEAN. ENGLISH BEAN. EUROPEAN BEAN. HORSE BEAN. WINDSOR BEAN.

Europe and Asia. The European bean appears to be among the most ancient of our cultivated esculents. A variety has been found in the lacustrine deposits of Switzerland ascribed to the Bronze Age. It was cultivated by the ancient Greeks and Romans, by the Hebrews and by the ancient Egyptians, although it is not among the seeds found in the catacombs, perhaps, De Candolle [3] remarks, because it was reported unworthy for the nourishment of priests, or certain priests, or from motives of superstition. Herodotus [4] states that the priests in Egypt held beans in such aversion that none were sown throughout the land; if by chance a single plant anywhere sprang up, they turned away their eyes from it as from an impure thing. Wilkinson [5] remarks that this statement applied, apparently, only to the priests for the people were allowed to eat these beans.

Pythagorus is said to have eaten beans very frequently, but his disciples seem to have forbidden their eating, and it is related that their aversion was carried to such an extent that a party of Pythagoreans allowed themselves to be slaughtered by the soldiers of Dionysius rather than to escape by passing through a field of these vegetables.[6] Porphyrus says, " take the flowers of the bean when they begin to grow black, put them in a vessel and bury it in the ground; at the end of ninety days, when it is opened, the head of a child will be found in the bottom." [7] Diogenes Laertius says, " beans are the substance which contains the largest portion of that animated matter of which our souls are particles." [8] One of the noble families of Rome, the Fabii, derived their name from this plant, and the Romans had a solemn feast called Fabaria, at which they offered beans in honor of Carna, the wife of Janus. At one time, the Romans believed the souls of such as had died resided in beans and Clemens Alexandrinus, and even Cicero, entertained equally extravagant notions of them. The Flamen Dialis were not permitted to mention the name, and Lucian represents a philosopher in Hades as saying that to eat beans and to eat one's father's head were equal crimes.[9] A temple dedicated to the God of Beans, Kyanites, stood upon the sacred road to Elensis, and the

---

[1] Johnson, C. P. *Useful Pls. Gt. Brit.* 81. 1862.

[2] Loudon, J. C. *Enc. Agr.* 843. 1866.

[3] De Candolle, A. *Geog. Bot.* 2:956. 1855. (*Faba vulgaris*)

[4] Barthelemy, J. J. *Voy. Anacharsis Greece* 6:2. 1825.

[5] Wilkinson, J. G. *Anc. Egypt.* 1:323. 1854.

[6] Barthelemy, J. J. *Voy. Anacharsis Greece* 6:2, 3, 4. 1825.

[7] Barthelemy, J. J. *Voy. Anacharsis Greece* 5:466. 1825.

[8] Ibid.

[9] McIntosh, C. *Book Gard.* 2:62. 1855. (*Faba vulgaris*)

Kyampsia or bean feast, which the Athenians celebrated in honor of Apollo, was characterized by the use of beans. What the Greeks called the Egyptian bean was the seed of *Nelumbium speciosum*.[1]

The Emperor Chin-nong [2] is said to have introduced the bean into China in the year 2822 B. C. The period of its introduction into Britain is unknown but Gerarde,[3] 1597, appears to have known only two varieties. At Teneriffe, at the discovery, the people are said to have had beans and peas or vetches, all of which they call *hacichei*.[4] In 1667, Father Carli [5] speaks of "kidney beans and common beans" in Congo. In 1776, they were seen by Thunberg [6] in Japan. The first introduction into the North American colonies was by Captain Gosnold, 1602, who planted them on the Elizabeth Islands near the coast of Massachusetts, where they flourished well. They were also cultivated in Newfoundland as early as 1622, in New Netherlands in 1644, and in Virginia prior to 1648.[7] Beans are mentioned as cultivated in New England prior to 1671 by Josselyn.[8] In McMahon's [9] work of 1806, fourteen kinds are enumerated. In 1828, Thorburn [10] gives, in his seed list, six kinds and in 1881 but four. European beans are seldom cultivated in America now, their place being taken by the kidney beans.

The vague indications of the supposed habitat of the bean in Persia or on the shores of the Caspian, says Targioni-Tozzetti,[11] have not been confirmed by modern researches. "May it not," says he, "have originated from *Vicia narbonensis*, a species not uncommon in the Mediterranean region from Spain to the Caucasus and very much resembling the bean in every respect except in the thinness of the pod and the smallness of the seeds?"

Linnaeus forms this bean into two botanical varieties, as does also Moench, who names the one *hortensis*, or the garden bean, the other *equina*, or the horse bean. These are both figured or mentioned by the early botanists; the *hortensis*, or garden bean, by Fuchsius, 1542, and Tragus, 1552. The *equina* is described by Pena and Lobel in their *Adversaria*, 1570, and by Lyte in his *Dodoens*, 1586, as well as by Dodonaeus, 1566. R. Thompson,[12] 1850, describes ten varieties, giving synonyms and these include all known to him. Let us follow up his synonymy, in order to see whether varieties of modern origination appear. This synonymy is founded upon identity of names in most instances and applies to the garden bean only, yet collateral evidence would seem to indicate a substantial correctness:

---

[1] De Candolle, A. *Geog. Bot.* 2:956. 1855.

[2] Ibid.

[3] Gerarde, J. *Herb.* 1038. 1597.

[4] *Gen. Coll. Voy. Portugese* 183. 1789.

[5] Churchill *Coll. Voy.* 1:500. 1744.

[6] Thunberg, C. P. *Fl. Jap.* 284. 1784.

[7] *Perj. Desc. Va.* 4. 1649. Force Coll. Tracts 2: No. 8. 1838.

[8] Josselyn, J. *New Eng. Rar.* 143. 1865.

[9] McMahon, B. *Amer. Gard. Cal.* 580. 1806.

[10] Thorburn *Cat.* 1828 and 1881.

[11] Targioni-Tozzetti *Journ. Hort. Soc. Lond.* 138. 1855.

[12] Thompson, R. *Gard. Chron.* 84. 1850.

1. *Early mazagan.* Thompson. 1850. Brought from a settlement of the Portuguese on the coast of Africa, just without the Straits of Gibralter. *Mill. Dict.* 1807.

   Early mazagan. Mawe 1778; Bryant 1783; McMahon 1806; Thorb. *Cat.* 1828; Thorb. *Cat.* 1884.

   Fève naine hâtive. Noisette 1829; Vilm. 1882.

2. *Marshall's Early Dwarf Prolific.* Thompson. 1850.

3. *Long-pod.* Thompson. 1850.

   Long-pod. McMahon 1806.

   Early long-pod. Mawe 1778; Bridgeman 1832; Loudon 1860.

   Early Portugal or Lisbon. Mawe 1778; *Mill. Dict.* 1807.

   Early Lisbon. McMahon 1806; Bridgeman 1832.

   Turkey long-pod. Mawe 1778; McMahon 1806; Bridgeman 1832.

   Tall long-pod. Mawe 1778.

   Sandwich. J. W. Gent. 1683; Townsend 1726; Stevenson 1765; Mawe 1778; Bryant 1738; Bridgeman 1832.

   Sword long-pod. Thorb. *Cat.* 1828; Fessenden 1828; Bridgeman 1832; Thorb. *Cat.* 1884.

   Hang-down long-pod. Vilm. 1883.

   Fève à longue cosses. Noisette 1829; Vilm. 1883.

4. *Green long-pod.* Thompson. 1850.

   Green Genoa. McMahon 1806; Bridgeman 1832.

   Green Nonpareil. McMahon 1806; Thorb. *Gard. Kal.* 1821; Fessenden 1828; Bridgeman 1832; Thorb. *Cat.* 1884.

5. *Dutch long-pod.* Thompson. 1850; Loudon 1860.

6. *Windsor.* Thompson. 1850.

   Broad Windsor. *Mill. Dict.* 1807; Fessenden 1828; Loudon 1860; Thorb. 1884.

   Kentish Windsor. Bridgeman 1832.

   Taylor's Windsor. Bridgeman 1832.

   Mumford. Mawe 1778; Bryant 1783; McMahon 1806; Bridgeman 1832.

   Small Spanish. Mawe 1778; Bryant 1783.

   Windsor. Stevenson 1765; Mawe 1778; Bryant 1783.

   Large Windsor. Van der Donck 1653; in present New York.

7. *Green Windsor.* Thompson. 1850.

   Toker. Stevenson 1765; Mawe 1778; Bryant 1783; Bridgeman 1832.

   Fève de Windsor verte. Vilm. 1883.

8. *Green China.* Thompson. 1850.

9. *Dwarf crimson-seeded.* Thompson. 1850.

   Fève très naine rouge. Vilm. 1883.

10. *Dwarf fan.* Thompson. 1850.

    Dwarf fan or *cluster.* Mawe 1778.

    Dwarf cluster. McMahon 1806; Bridgeman 1832.

    Fève naine hâtive à châssis. Vilm. 1883.

11. *Red-blossomed.* Mawe 1778; McMahon 1806; Bridgeman 1832; Thompson 1850.

12. *White-blossomed.* Mawe 1778; McMahon 1806; Bridgeman 1832; Thompson 1850.

The only two other varieties advertised lately are Beck's Dwarf Green Gem and Seville Long-pod. There is certainly no indication here that types have appeared in modern culture. The crowd of new names which appear during a decade gradually becomes reduced to a synonymy, and we find at last that the variation gained has been within types only.

V. gemella Crantz. SMOOTH TARE.

Europe and the Orient; a weed of Britain, which is said to be cultivated in some places. It is now naturalized in the United States near the coast.

V. gigantea Hook.

California to Sitka. The seeds are eaten by the Indians.[1] Gray remarks that the seeds are eatable, when young, like green peas.

V. hirsuta S. F. Gray. HAIRY TARE.

Europe, northern Africa and Asia. This species is said by Loudon [2] to be cultivated in some places as a lentil. This plant is naturalized in the United States from Massachusetts to Virginia.[3]

V. monanthos Desf.

Mediterranean region. This is a lens cultivated by the French.[4]

V. narbonensis Linn. NARBONNE VETCH.

Orient and Mediterranean region. This species is supposed by Targioni-Tozzetti [5] to be the original of the English bean. The seeds are of excellent quality.[6]

V. pallida Turcz. WOOD VETCH.

Himalayan regions. This vetch has been cultivated chiefly in cold, northern regions, being remarkably hardy. It is found wild even within the arctic regions.[7]

V. pisiformis Linn.

Europe. This is the *lentille du Canada* of the French and, according to Loudon,[8] is cultivated in some places as a lentil.

V. sativa Linn. TARE. WHITE VETCH.

Europe, North Africa and the Orient. In 1686, according to Ray,[9] this tare was grown throughout Europe for feeding animals. There are a number of varieties, the most prominent of which are the spring and winter tares. The seed of the white vetch is eaten in some countries. The seeds are said by Johnson [10] to be neither very palatable nor nutritious. In many cantons of France, the seeds are, however, eaten in soup and enter into the composition of flours used for breadmaking.[11]

V. sepium Linn. BUSH VETCH.

Northern Asia, Himalayan regions and Europe. The seeds may be used as food.[12]

---

[1] Brown, R. *Bot. Soc. Edinb.* 9:382. 1868.

[2] Loudon, J. C. *Enc. Agr.* 843. 1866. (*Ervum hirsutum*)

[3] Gray, A. *Man. Bot.* 139. 1868.

[4] Vilmorin *Les Pls. Potag.* 320. 1883. (*Ervum monanthos*)

[5] Targioni-Tozzetti *Journ. Hort. Soc. Lond.* 9:138. 1855.

[6] Mueller, F. *Sel. Pls.* 505. 1891. 8th Ed.

[7] Morton *Cyc. Agr.* 2:1071. 1869. (*V. sylvatica*)

[8] Loudon, J. C. *Enc. Agr.* 843. 1866.

[9] Loudon, J. C. *Enc. Agr.* 841. 1866.

[10] Johnson, C. P. *Useful Pls. Gt. Brit.* 80. 1862.

[11] *Bon Jard.* 621. 1882.

[12] Johnson, C. P. *Useful Pls. Gt. Brit.* 81. 1862.

V. villosa Roth. LARGE RUSSIAN VETCH.

Russia. This species has been cultivated of late years with much success in several parts of northern and central Europe.

Victoria regia Lindl. *Nymphaeceae.* WATER LILY. WATER MAIZE.

Guiana. The Spaniards collect the seeds and eat them roasted.[1]

Vigna catjang Walp. *Leguminosae.* COWPEA. JERUSALEM PEA. MARBLE PEA.

East Indies. This plant is cultivated in Portugal and Italy.[2] In India, varieties with white, brown and black seeds are cultivated.[3] In Martinique, the seeds are highly esteemed as an article of food. In the southern states, this species has many permanent varieties, as Red Cowpea, Black-eyed pea and so on. So conspicuous is this species that in some localities it is made to carry the name of all others, all being referred to as the cowpea.[4] This plant is extensively cultivated in India for its pods, which are often two feet in length, contain a number of pea-like seeds, called by the Hindus *chowlee*, and form a considerable article of food. In China, the green pods are used as a vegetable.[5]

V. glabra Savi. CHINESE DOLICHOS. CLAY PEA.

A native of tropical Africa; cultivated at Karagwe on the upper Nile, where it is called *koondii*. The seeds are eaten.[6] This plant is commonly cultivated about Bombay for its pods and pulse.[7] There are several varieties of this bean in India, white, red, dun, green, black; they vary also greatly in size but are distinguished by their form, which differs from all the other kinds in the beans being truncated at either end.[8] Firminger[9] speaks of it, however, as a bean of indifferent quality. In China, the pods are eaten as a string bean. In Egypt, it furnishes a vegetable food.[10] In the Barbados, this species furnishes the *calavances*, or red beans, of Long[11] and is also called Chinese dolichos and clay pea.[12] The pulse is called by the Hindus *chowlu*, by the Chinese *tow-cok*.

V. lanceolata Benth. VIGNA.

Tropical and subtropical Australia. According to Mueller,[13] the plant is available for culinary purposes.

Villaresia congonha Miers. *Olacineae.*

Brazil. The leaves, dried and pulverized, are used as tea in Brazil.

[1] Masters, M. T. *Treas. Bot.* 2:1215. 1870.

[2] Unger, F. *U. S. Pat. Off. Rpt.* 318. 1859. (*Dolichos catjang*)

[3] Roxburgh, W. *Hort. Beng.* 55. 1814.

[4] Stille, J. P. *West. Farm. Almanac.* 1881.

[5] Smith, J. *Dom. Bot.* 418. 1871.

[6] Pickering, C. *Chron. Hist. Pls.* 730. 1879. (*V. luteola*)

[7] Pickering, C. *Chron. Hist. Pls.* 286. 1879.

[8] Elliott, W. *Bot. Soc. Edinb.* 7:293. 1863. (*Dolichos sinensis*)

[9] Firminger, T. A. C. *Gard. Ind.* 149. 1874. (*Dolichos sinensis*)

[10] Unger, F. *U. S. Pat. Off. Rpt.* 318. 1859. (*Dolichos glycinoides*)

[11] Long, E. *Hist. Jam.* 786. 1774.

[12] Schomburgkh, R. H. *Hist. Barb.* 606. 1848. (*Dolichos sinensis*)

[13] Mueller, F. *Sel. Pls.* 507. 1891.

Viola odorata Linn. *Violarieae.* VIOLET.

Europe, Africa and northern Asia. This violet is esteemed by the Egyptians and Turks for use in sorbet, which they make of violet sugar dissolved in water.

V. palmata Linn. VIOLET. WILD OKRA.

Eastern North America. The plant is mucilaginous and is employed by negroes in the southern United States for making soup and is called wild okra.[1]

Vitex cienkowskii Kotschy & Peyr. *Verbenaceae.*

Tropical Africa. The sweet, olive-shaped fruit, says Schweinfurth,[2] is relished exceedingly by the natives of central Africa.

V. doniana Sweet.

Tropical Africa. The fruit is eatable, says Sabine,[3] but is inferior to both the sugar and yellow plums of that country.

Vitis acetosa F. Muell. *Ampelideae.* AUSTRALIAN GRAPE.

Australia. The stems are herbaceous rather than shrubby, erect. The whole plant is pervaded with acidity and proves valuable in cases of scurvy. The berries are edible.[4]

V. acida Chapm.

South America and West Indies. The whole plant has an acid taste.[5]

V. adnata Wall.

Asia and Australian tropics. The acid leaves are eaten.[6]

V. aestivalis Michx. BUNCH GRAPE. PIGEON GRAPE. SUMMER GRAPE.

Eastern America. The berries are pleasant and the flowers fragrant. This grape is referred to by Wood[7] in his *New England's Prospects* as the "smaller kinde of grape which groweth in the Islands, which is sooner ripe and more delectable." As it occurs wild, it presents many varieties in its fruit and has produced, according to William Saunders,[8] the cultivated forms known as Lenoir, Herbemont, Devereaux, Alvey, Cynthiana and Norton's Virginia; according to Ravenel, Clinton and Delaware. This species was introduced into England in 1656.[9]

V. africana Spreng.

Tropical Africa. The berries are black and eatable.[10]

---

[1] Porcher, F. P. *Res. So. Fields, Forests* 80. 1869.

[2] Schweinfurth, G. *Heart Afr.* 1:221. 1874.

[3] Sabine, J. *Trans. Hort. Soc. Lond.* 5:455. 1824. (*V. umbrosa*)

[4] Mueller, F. *Sel. Pls.* 508. 1891.

[5] Don, G. *Hist. Dichl. Pls.* 1:691. 1831. (*Cissus acida*)

[6] Unger, F. *U. S. Pat. Off. Rpt.* 359. 1859. (*Cissus latifolia*)

[7] Wood, W. *New Eng. Prosp.* 20. 1865.

[8] Saunders, W. *Amer. Pom. Soc.* 70. 1879.

[9] Loudon, J. C. *Arb. Frut. Brit.* 1:479. 1854.

[10] Don, G. *Hist. Dichl. Pls.* 1:694. 1831. (*Ampelopsis botria*)

V. antarctica Benth.

East Australia. This species is an evergreen, bearing small and edible berries.[1]

V arborea Linn.

Orient and North America. The fruit is said to become agreeable when perfectly matured, but Nuttall [2] says, to his taste, it is always nauseous.

V. arizonica Engelm. CANYON GRAPE.

Arizona and Utah. The fruit is small, borne in small clusters and is said to be quite luscious.[3]

V. auriculata Wall.

Himalayan region, Burma and Java. The berries are large and juicy.[4]

V. berlanderi Planch.

Texas and northern Mexico. This vine bears a very large cluster of rich, though remarkably small, fruit.[5] The quality is fine for wine.[6]

V. bicolor Le Conte. BLUE GRAPE. SUMMER GRAPE.

New Hampshire to North Carolina and westward. The berries are small and generally sweet and agreeable.[7]

V. caesia Sabine.

Tropical Africa. The berries are round and black, with an austere, acid taste not very agreeable to Europeans; the grapes are eaten chiefly by the negroes, who are very fond of them.[8]

V. californica Benth.

Southwestern United States. The quantity of the fruit that an Indian will consume at one time is scarcely credible. The ancient Pueblo Indians were in the habit of cultivating this grape as is evident from the peculiar distribution of the plant near reined settlements. In Arizona, near Fort Whipple, they are found arranged in rows and the vines are very old.[9] The berry is small and round and much resembles the ordinary frost grape of New England but it is larger, more juicy and richer in flavor.

V. candicans Engelm.

Southwestern United States. The berries are large, black or dark purple; skin thin, beneath which is a cuticle containing a red and very acid juice. The true pulp is edible. This species bears fruit unfit for eating owing to the biting pungency of its skin and the tough pulp [10] but may have promise as a wine grape.

---

[1] Mueller, F. *Sel. Pls.* 509. 1891. (*V. baudiniana*)

[2] Nuttall, T. *Gen. No. Amer. Pls.* 1:144. 1818.

[3] Brewer and Watson *Bo'. Cal.* 1:105. 1880.

[4] Mueller, F. *Sel. Pls.* 348. 1880.

[5] Munson *Gard. Forest* 475. 1890.

[6] Munson *Amer. Gard.* 12:659. 1891.

[7] *U. S. Pat. Off. Rpt.* 230. 1857.

[8] Sabine, J. *Trans. Hort. Soc. Lond.* 5:447. 1824.

[9] *U. S. D. A. Rpt.* 415. 1870.

[10] Munson *Gard. Forest* 475. 1890.

V. capensis Burm.

South Africa. The berry is said to be excellent but with a different flavor from our grapes. It is brought to the table at the Cape of Good Hope.[1]

V. caribaea DC.   CARIBEAN GRAPE.

West Indies and moist thickets in Florida and along the shores of the Gulf of Mexico as far as southern Texas. This grape was found in Arkansas by Nuttall.[2] Its grapes are small, sour and generally unpalatable, yet sometimes it has fruit agreeably acid. Its vines are said to be so full of sap as to be used in the West Indies to allay thirst.[3] Sloane [4] says, in Jamaica, it is red or deep purple and the size of a currant and agreeably acid, as well as astringent. Loudon [5] says it was introduced into England in 1800.

V. cordifolia Michx.   CHICKEN GRAPE. FROST GRAPE. WINTER GRAPE.

Eastern United States. The fruit hangs in short clusters, is dark purple, almost black when ripe, with a dark blue bloom, about the size of a large pea. It is very acid, says Emerson,[6] but pleasant, with a rich, spicy taste and without any acerbity remaining after eating. Natural varieties of this grape have been transferred to gardens in Massachusetts and the berries of these plants are described as of " a juicy, agreeable, wine taste," " oval, sweet and spicy," " round and sweet," " sweet and agreeable." This species has been strongly recommended for wine-making. Some of the varieties have red, others black fruits.

V. elongata Wall.

East Indies. The berries are large and juicy.[7]

V. geniculata Miq.

Java. The fruit is eaten.[8]

V. heterophylla Thunb.

China and Japan. The leaves are used for food.[9]

V. hypoglauca F. Muell.

East Australia. This species is an evergreen climber of enormous length. The black berries attain the size of small cherries.[10]

V. imperialis Miq.

Sumatra and Borneo. Its berries are large and juicy.[11]

---

[1] Lindley, J.   *Trans. Hort. Soc. Lond.* **5**:92.   1824.   (*Cissus capensis*)

[2] Buckley *U. S. Pat. Off. Rpt.* 483.   1861.

[3] Ibid.

[4] Loudon, J. C.   *Arb. Frut. Brit.* **1**:481.   1854.

[5] Ibid.

[6] Emerson, G. B.   *Trees, Shrubs Mass.* **2**:534.   1875.

[7] Mueller, F.   *Sel. Pls.* 510.   1891.

[8] Don, G.   *Hist. Dichl. Pls.* **1**:693.   1831.   (*Cissus elongata*)

[9] Bretschneider, E.   *Bot. Sin.* 51.   1882.

[10] Mueller, F.   *Sel. Pls.* 510.   1891.

[11] Ibid.

V. indica Linn.

East Indies and India. The small berries are edible.[1]

V. labrusca Linn. FOX GRAPE. SKUNK GRAPE.

Eastern United States. This is probably the grape seen by the Northmen at Vinland, when the two Scotch slaves sent out to explore brought back a bunch of grapes in 1006. This grape was mentioned by Edward Winslow[2] in Massachusetts, 1621, as " white and red and very sweet and strong also." Master Graves[3] says " vines doe grow here plentifully laden with the biggest grapes that ever I saw; some I have seen four inches about." The fox grape is often mentioned by the colonists. In 1769, the French settlers on the Illinois River made upwards of one hundred hogsheads of strong wine from the wild grape. The fruit varies much in size, color and taste, and some of the natural varieties are very fair fruit and may be found even now around many New England homesteads, although they all have more or less of the strong, musky flavor, which in some varieties is disagreeably intense. Emerson[4] says he has gathered grapes in the woods decidedly superior to the Isabella.

This species has given origin to many cultivated varieties, such as Isabella, Concord, Moore's Early and Hartford Prolific. Emerson[5] says also, the Catawba, Blands Grape, Schuylkill, Elsinberg and others; Ravenal includes Diana and Rebecca. The Isabella and Catawba were introduced to notice in 1816, the Concord about 1854. Diana was exhibited in 1843, and Moore's Early for the first time in 1872. At the present time, 1879, 46 varieties of American grapes are approved by the American Pomological Society, and many others are before the public on probation. Oh account of the immunity of the grape vines derived from this species from the phylloxera, large numbers of vines have been exported to France for use in vineyards as stocks for grafting. At present, this species promises to be as prolific of valuable varieties as is the *V. vinifera* of Europe and Asia.

V. latifolia Roxb.

East Indies. The acid leaves are eaten.[6]

V. linsecomii Buckl. PINE-WOOD GRAPE. POST-OAK GRAPE. TURKEY GRAPE.

Texas. The grapes are from one-half to three-quarters of an inch in diameter, of a deep purple, tender, pleasant and free from musky flavor. It is cultivated in a few gardens in Texas.[7]

V. monticola Buckl. MOUNTAIN GRAPE.

Texas; occasionally cultivated in gardens. The berries are large, white or amber-colored; skin thin; pulp tender, juicy and sweet.[8]

---

[1] Mueller, F. *Sel. Pls.* 510. 1891.

[2] Young, A. *Chron. Pilgr.* 234. 1841.

[3] *Mass. Hist. Soc. Coll.* 1st Ser. 1:124. 1806. Reprint of 1792.

[4] Emerson, G. B. *Trees, Shrubs Mass.* 2:532. 1875.

[5] Emerson, G. B. *Trees, Shrubs Mass.* 2:531. 1875.

[6] Unger, F. *U. S. Pat. Off. Rpt.* 1859.

[7] Buckley *U. S. Pat. Off. Rpt.* 485. 1861.

[8] Ibid.

V. mutabilis Miq.

Java.   The berries are large and edible.[1]

V. opaca F. Muell.

East Australia.   The vine produces as many as eight to ten large tubers.   Though insipid, these are eagerly sought by the natives for food.[2]

V. pallida Wight & Arn.

Asia and African tropics.   The berries are large, edible and particularly sweet.[3]

V. quadrangularis Wall.

Arabia to India and central Africa.   The berries are eaten in India, and the young shoots and leaves are used by the natives as a potherb.[4][5]

V. riparia Michx.   FROST GRAPE.   RIVERBANK GRAPE.

Eastern North America.   The berries are usually small, blackish or amber-colored and very acid.   This species has given origin to the Clinton, Taylor, Elvira and other grapes now under cultivation.

V. rotundifolia Michx.   MUSCADINE.   BULLACE.   SOUTHERN FOX GRAPE.   SCUPPERNONG.

Southeastern United States.   This species bears its berries in loose clusters, scarcely exceeding five or six berries, changing from reddish-brown to black in ripening, with a thick skin and large pulp.   In a cultivated form, it occurs in several white and black varieties. In the southern states, it is highly relished and is used for domestic winemaking.

V. rubifolia Wall.

Himalayan regions.   The berries are esculent.[6]

V. rupestris Scheele.   BUSH GRAPE.   MOUNTAIN GRAPE.   ROCK GRAPE.   SAND GRAPE.   SUGAR GRAPE.

Southwestern America.   This species is the mountain grape of Texas.   The stems are upright and but two or three feet high.   The bunches are small and the berries are of the size of peas, black and very sweet and grateful to the taste.

V. schimperiana Hochst.

Abyssinia.   Barter compares the edible berries to clusters of Frontignac grapes.[7]

V. sicyoides Miq.

Tropical America.   The black berries are eaten.[8]

V. thrysiflora Miq.

Sumatra.   The berries are large and edible.[9]

---

[1] Mueller, F.   *Sel. Pls.* 510.   1891.

[2] *Gard. Chron.* 365.   1866.

[3] Mueller, F.   *Sel. Pls.* 255, 256.   1876.

[4] Wight, R.   *Illustr. Ind. Bot.* 1:151.   1840.   (*Cissus quadrangularis*)

[5] Ainslie, W.   *Mat. Ind.* 2:303.   1826.

[6] Don, G.   *Hist. Dichl. Pls.* 1:711.   1831.

[7] Mueller, F.   *Sel. Pls.* 513.   1891.

[8] Don, G.   *Hist. Dichl. Pls.* 1:691.   1831.   (*Cissus ovata*)

[9] Mueller, F.   *Sel. Pls.* 510.   1891.

V. trifolia Linn.

Asia and Australian tropics. The leaves are acid and edible.[1]

V. uvifera Baker.

Tropical Africa. The berries are black, pulpy, of an austere, acid taste but are eaten by the natives.[2]

V. vinifera Linn. EUROPEAN GRAPE. WINE GRAPE.

The European grape is found wild on the coast of the Caspian, in Armenia and in Karamania. From Asia, it passed into Greece and thence into Sicily. The Phocians carried it to the south of France; the Romans planted it on the banks of the Rhine. This grape is of the most ancient culture. Full details of wine-making and vineyards are figured under the Fourth (2440 B. C.), Seventeenth (1680 B. C.) and Eighteenth (1525 B. C.) Dynasties in Egypt, and vineyards and wine are mentioned in the Scriptural history of Noah. Its introduction into all parts of the world has but multiplied its peculiarities. Virgil [3] says " we neither can recount how numerous the species, nor what are their names, nor imports it to comprise their number; which whoever would know the same may seek to learn how numerous are the sands of the Libyan sea tossed by the zephyr; as to know how many waves of the Ionian sea come to the shores, when Eurus, more violent, falls upon the ships." In the time of Chaptal,[4] about 1825, there were 1400 varieties enumerated in the Luxembourg catalog obtained from France alone; the Geneva catalog numbered 600; Presl [5] describes 44 varieties as cultivated in Sicily; Redding [6] notices 12 kinds near Shiraz, Persia; and Burnes [7] 10 kinds at Cabul. The Pinceau variety of France was known as long ago as 1394.[8]

Some believe that the vine was introduced into England by the Romans, while, according to others, it was first brought by the Phoenicians, who also have the credit of having transplanted it from Palestine to the islands of the Mediterranean. The earliest English chronicles make mention of vineyards, and vine culture is said to have continued until the Reformation; but the English climate is not suitable and the grape is grown only under glass except in a few favored locations. The vine was brought to the New World by Columbus, and, in 1494 at Hayti, " cuttings from European vines already began to form their clusters." [9] In 1741, there were some thousands of vines from Portugal thriving at Augusta, Georgia,[10] and there are accounts of this vine in New Albion in 1647.[11] There are accounts of wine-making from grapes of unknown species in Virginia in 1630, 1647,

---

[1] Unger, F. *U. S. Pat. Off. Rpt.* 359. 1859. (*Cissus crenata*)

[2] Don, G. *Hist. Dichl. Pls.* 1:690. 1831.

[3] Virgil *Georgics* lib. 2, verse 103–108.

[4] *U. S. Pat. Off. Rpt.* 540. 1859.

[5] Hooker, W. J. *Journ. Bot.* 1:106. 1834.

[6] *U. S. Pat. Off. Rpt.* 367. 1860.

[7] *U. S. Pat. Off. Rpt.* 368. 1860.

[8] Daubeny, C. *Trees, Shrubs Anc.* 71. 1865.

[9] Irving, W. *Columbus* 1:380. 1848.

[10] *Desc. Ga.* 4. 1741. Force Coll. Tracts **2**: 1838.

[11] *Desc. New Albion* 8. 1648. Force Coll. Tracts **2**: 1838.

1651; in Massachusetts, in 1634; in Pennsylvania, in 1683 and 1685; and in Indiana in 1804.   In Chile and in California, its culture seems successful.   In California, its introduction was due to the Missions which were mainly established from 1769 to 1820. Except in California, here and there a single vine in exceptional localities may succeed.

The currant, or Zante, grape is the variety which furnishes the dried currants of commerce, the individual grapes being no larger than peas, entirely free from seeds and of an agreeable flavor.   This vine was introduced into the United States in 1855 and is now grown in California, where, however, it troubles the cultivator by occasionally producing seeds.   At present, our supply of currant grapes comes from the Ionian Islands chiefly but they are also grown in France.   Unlike other grape vines, this, in Zante, will not succeed upon the hills but flourishes in low lands, retentive of moisture, incapable of drainage and flooded for two months of the year.

Voandzeia subterranea Thou.   *Leguminosae.*   GROUNDNUT.

African tropics; extensively cultivated from Bambarra and the coast of Guinea to Natal, its esculent pods and seeds forming a common article of food.   In 1682, Father Merolla describes this species in the Congo under the name of *incumbe*, growing under ground.   He says, " it is like a musquet-ball and very wholesome and well tasted." Montiero[1] says it is sparingly cultivated at Cambambe and the surrounding district. The plant is commonly found now in Brazil and in Surinam.

Voyria rosea Aubl.   *Gentianeae.*

Guiana.   The tuberous roots are baked and eaten in Guiana like potatoes.   They are of a reddish color externally and white within.[2]

Washingtonia filifera H. Wendl.   *Palmae.*

This palm is found in rocky canyons near San Felipe, California, attaining a height of 50 feet.   The fruit is small, black, pulpy and is used as food by the Indians.

Weinmannia racemosa Linn. f.   *Saxifrageae.*

New Zealand.   This tree resembles the beech in leaf and general appearance and bears a fruit the color and size of a Damson plum.   The fruit is sweet and pleasant.[3]

Willughbeia edulis Roxb.   *Apocynaceae.*

Himalayas, Burma, India and Malay.   The fruit is of a dark orange color, the size of a large lemon, and is filled with a soft, yellowish pulp, in which are immersed a few seeds the size of a horse bean.   It is thought good by the natives.[4]

Wistaria chinensis DC.   *Leguminosae.*   WISTARIA.

China.   The flowers are used for food.[5]

---

[1] Montiero, J. J.   *Angola, River Congo* 2:111.   1875.

[2] Masters, M. T.   *Treas. Bot.* 2:1225.   1870.

[3] *Gard. Chron.* 703.   1841.   (*Leiospermum racemosum*)

[4] Roxburgh, W.   *Pls. Corom.* 3:77.   1819.

[5] Bretschneider, E.   *Bot. Sin.* 52.   1882.

Xanthium strumarium Linn. *Compositae.* BUR WEED.

Cosmopolitan. In China, the leaves and shoots are eaten as a vegetable.[1]

Xanthoceras sorbifolia Bunge. *Sapindaceae.*

China. The flowers, leaves and fruit are used for food.[2]

Xanthorrhoea arborea R. Br. *Juncaceae.* GRASS GUM TREE.

An Australian tree. The tender, white center of the leaves is used as a vegetable.[3]

X. hastilis R. Br. GRASS TREE.

Southern Australia. The tender, inner leaves are esculent and far from disagreeable, having a milky taste with a slight, balsamic flavor.[4]

Xanthosoma sagittifolium Schott. *Aroideae.*

Tropical America. This plant is generally planted in Jamaica for the use of the table. Lunan[5] says, in wholesomeness and delicacy, it is superior to spinach and vies with any European vegetable whatever. The roots are said to be edible. Starch is obtained from the rootstocks.[6]

Ximenia americana Linn. *Olacineae.* HOG PLUM. SEASIDE PLUM.

Cosmopolitan tropics. The fruits resemble yellow plums, are edible and of an agreeable taste.[7] They have an acid-sweet, aromatic taste, with some degree of austerity.[8] The plant bears round, orange-colored fruits, of which the natives of the Fiji and other islands of the Pacific Ocean are very fond, though they are rather tart. Before they are ripe they possess a powerful odor of essential oil of almonds.[9] In the Circars, its yellow fruit, which is about the size of a pigeon's egg, is eaten by the natives.[10]

Xylopia aethiopica A. Rich. *Anonaceae.* ETHIOPIAN PEPPER. GUINEA PEPPER. NEGRO PEPPER.

Tropical Africa. A tall shrub whose fruit, consisting of a number of smooth, pod-like carpels about the thickness of a quill and two inches long, is dried and used instead of pepper. The seeds have an aromatic, pungent taste and were formerly sold in English shops under the name of Ethiopian pepper, Guinea pepper and Negro pepper.[11]

---

[1] Smith, F. P. *Contrib. Mat. Med. China* 233. 1871.
[2] Bretschneider, E. *Bot. Sin.* 52. 1882.
[3] Smith, A. *Treas. Bot.* 2:1239. 1870.
[4] Pickering, C. *Chron. Hist. Pls.* 564. 1879.
[5] Lunan, J. *Hort. Jam.* 1:415. 1814.
[6] Masters, M. T. *Treas. Bot.* 2:1239. 1870.
[7] Vasey, G. *U. S. D. A. Rpt.* 156. 1875.
[8] Smith, A. *Treas. Bot.* 2:1241. 1870.
[9] Ibid. (*X. elliptica*)
[10] Pickering, C. *Chron. Hist. Pls.* 856. 1879. (*X. spinosa*)
[11] Don, G. *Hist. Dichl. Pls.* 1:95. 1831. (*Unona aethiopica*)

X. frutescens Aubl.

Tropical America. The seeds have an acrid, aromatic taste and are used by the negroes in Guiana instead of pepper.[1]

X. glabra Linn.   BITTERWOOD.

Jamaica. The wood, bark and berries have an agreeable, bitter taste, not unlike that of the orange seed. Freshly gathered from the tree, the berries are agreeable to the palate and grateful to the stomach.[2]

X. sericea A. St. Hil.

Brazil. Arruda[3] says the capsules have the taste and pungency of black pepper and are used by many as a spice in cooking and by some are preferred even to pepper. The fruit, says St. Hilaire,[4] has the odor and taste of pepper but is not as strong. It can be employed as a spice.

X. undulata Beauv.

Tropical Africa. It also furnishes a similar spice.[5]

Xysmalobium heudelotianum Decne. *Asclepiadeae*

Tropical Africa. The plant has a watery, turnip-shaped root, called *yakhop* by the negroes, by whom it is eaten.[6]

Yucca acaulis H. B. & K. *Liliaceae*. MAGUEY.

Venezuela. The sweet and fermented juice of this plant yields a spirit by distillation; the young leaves are eaten.[7]

Y. baccata Torr.   SPANISH BAYONET.

Southwestern North America and Mexico. The fruit is the size of a large fig with a sweet, edible pulp.[8] The Indians of Arizona, New Mexico and Utah are very fond of the fruit and dry it for winter use. The young flower-buds, when about to expand, are also roasted but to Whites are insipid food. Bartlett[9] saw in an Apache camp a pot of the flowers boiling for food.

Y. filamentosa Linn.   ADAM'S NEEDLE.   NEEDLE PALM.

Southwestern North America. This yucca bears large, fleshy fruits which are edible; they are called *datile*.[10] The fruit, the size of a peach, is used as an article of food.

---

[1] Don, G. *Hist. Dichl. Pls.* 1:96. 1831.

[2] Loudon, J. C. *Enc. Pls.* 481. 1855.

[3] Koster, H. *Trav. Braz.* 2:362. 1817. (*Unona carminativa*)

[4] Saint Hilaire, A. *Fl. Bras. Merid.* 1:33. 1825.

[5] Smith, A. *Treas. Bot.* 1:564. 1870. (*Habzelia undulata*)

[6] Smith, A. *Treas. Bot.* 2:1243. 1870.

[7] Humboldt, A. *Trav.* 1:484. 1889.

[8] Torrey, J. *Bot. U. S. Mex. Bound. Surv.* 2:221. 1859.

[9] Bartlett, J. R. *Explor. Texas* 2:492. 1854.

[10] Torrey, J. *Bot. U. S. Mex. Bound. Surv.* 2:221. 1859. (*Y. puberula*)

Y. glauca Nutt.

America. The plant bears an edible fruit often three inches long and one-half inch across.[1]

Y. treculeana Carr.

Mexico and western Texas. The fruit is said to resemble a pawpaw and to be edible.

Zalacca affinis Griff. *Palmae.*

Malay. This palm is found in Malacca and is called by the natives *salak batool*. The fruit is edible.[2]

Z. conferta Griff.

Malay and Sumatra. The fruit is large, deep brown and hangs sometimes quite down in the mud in deeply clustered branches, almost hidden by the half-decayed bracts. The pulp surrounding the seeds is intensively acid and is much used by the Malays as a condiment.

Z. edulis Blume.

Burma and Malay. The fruit is much sought after by the Burmese on account of the fleshy and juicy covering of the seeds, which has a pleasantly acid and refreshing taste.[3] The fruit is eaten.[4] It is about the size of a walnut and is covered with scales like those of a lizard; below the scales are two or three sweet, yellow kernels, which the Malays eat. A preserve is also made of the fruit.[5]

Zamia chigua Seem. *Cycadaceae.*

New Granada. The seeds are boiled and reduced to a mash which is served with milk and sugar. Bread is also made from them.[6]

Z. furfuracea Ait. SAGO CYCAD.

Mexico. This plant yields a sago which is much used in Jamaica.[7]

Z. integrifolia Ait. SAGO CYCAD.

West Indies and Florida. This cycad furnishes the Seminole Indians with their white meal.[8] An arrowroot has been prepared from it at St. Augustine. It is now cultivated to a limited extent.[9]

Z. pumila Linn.

West Indies. The plant furnishes a kind of arrowroot.[10]

---

[1] Case *Bot. Index* 92. 1880.

[2] Griffith, W. *Palms Brit. East Ind.* 12. 1850.

[3] Wallich *Pl. Asiat.* 3:15. Pls. 222, 223, 224. 1830–32.

[4] Griffith, W. *Palms Brit. East Ind.* 15. 1850. (*Z. macrostachya*)

[5] Cook, Capt. *Gard. Chron.* 584. 1875.

[6] Seemann, B. *Bot. Voy. Herald* 1:257. 1853.

[7] Smith, J. *Dict. Econ. Pls.* 362. 1882.

[8] Porcher, F. P. *Res. So. Fields, Forests* 617. 1869.

[9] Havard, V. *Torr. Bot. Club Bul.* 22:107. 1895.

[10] Balfour, J. H. *Man. Bot.* 601. 1875.

Z. tenuis Willd.

Bahama Islands. The plant yields from its trunk a pure starch, used as a fine arrow-root in the Bahamas.

Zanthoxylum alatum Roxb. *Rutaceae.*

Himalayas and China. This is a small tree, the fruits of which are used in China as well as in India as a condiment.[1] Its aromatic capsules are used as a condiment in India.[2]

Z. budrunga Wall.

Himalayas and Burma. The capsules are used for their warm, spicy, pepper-like pungency.[3]

Z. piperitum DC.

China and Japan. The bark, leaves and fruits are used as a spice.[4]

Z. rhetsa DC.

East Indies. The unripe capsules are like small berries and are gratefully aromatic, tasting like the peel of a fresh orange.[5] The seeds are used as a condiment in Malabar.[6] On the Coromandel Mountains, its aromatic bark is put in food as a condiment, and its seeds are used as a pepper substitute.[7]

Zea mays Linn. *Gramineae.* CORN. MAIZE.

Tropical America. The earliest record of maize is in the *Popol Vuh*, the sacred book of the Quicke Indians of western Guatemala, whose records extend back to the eighth century. In the *Popol Vuh* the legend runs: " In Paxil, or Cayala (land of divided and stagnant waters) as it is called, were the ears of yellow maize and of white. These are the names of the barbarians who went to seek food the Fox, the Jackal, the Paroquet and the Crow — four barbarians who made known to them the ears of the white maize and of the yellow, who came to Paxil and guided them thither. There it was they obtained at last the food that was to enter into the flesh of man, of man created and formed; this it was that was his blood, that became the blood of man — this maize that entered into him by the provision of him who creates, of him who gives being. And they rejoiced that they had at last arrived in this most excellent land, so full of good things, where the white and yellow maize did abound, also the cacao, where were sapotes and many fruits and honey; all was overflowing with the best of food in this country of Paxil, or Cayala. There was food of every kind; there were large and small plants, to which the barbarians had guided them. Then they began to grind the yellow and white maize and of them did Xmucane make nine drinks, which nourishment was the beginning of

---

[1] Hanbury, D. *Sci. Papers* 230. 1876.
[2] Royle, J. F. *Illustr. Bot. Himal.* 1:157. 1839.
[3] Ibid.
[4] Don, G. *Hist. Dichl. Pls.* 1:802. 1831.
[5] Wight, R. *Illustr. Ind. Bot.* 1:168. 1840.
[6] Pickering, C. *Chron. Hist. Pls.* 522. 1870.
[7] Ibid.

strength, giving unto man flesh and stature. Such were the deeds of the begetter and giver of being, Tepeuh, Gucumatz. Thereupon they began to speak of creating our first mother and our first father. Only yellow maize and white maize entered into their flesh and these alone formed the legs and arms of man; and these were our first fathers, the four men who were formed, into whose flesh this food entered."

This Paxil, or Cayala, is suggested by Bancroft to have been the region of the Usumacinta River, in what is now the Mexican province of Tabasco. In a Nahua record, written in Aztec with Spanish letters by an anonymous native author, referring to the Pre-Toltec period, it is said: " At that time Azcatl, the ant, going to Tonacatepetl, mount of our subsistence, for maize, was met by Quetzalcoatl, who said ' where hast thou been to obtain that thing? Tell me.' At first the ant would not tell but the Plumed Serpent insisted and repeated, ' whither shall I go? ' They went there together, Quetzalcoatl meta-morphosing himself into a black ant. Tlattlauhqui Azcati, the yellow ant, accompanied Quetzalocoatl respectfully, as they went to seek maize and brought it to Tamoanchan. Then the gods began to eat and put some of the maize in our mouths that we might become strong."

Another tradition of the Pre-Toltec period is also given by Bancroft[1] in which an old man and old woman pulled out the broken teeth of precious stones from the jaw of Vucub Cakix, in which he took great pride, and substituted grains of maize. In the golden age of Mexico, during the reign of Quetzalocoatl, tradition says, maize was abundant, and a head of it was as much as a man could carry clasped in his arms. During the reign of Nopaltzin, King of the Chichimecs, which Humboldt[2] ascribes to 1250 A. D., the culture of maize and the art of making bread, long neglected and in danger of being lost, was revived by a Toltec named Xinhtlato. In Mexico, Centeotl was goddess of maize and had various appellations, such as Tonacajohua, " she who sustains us," Tzinteotl, "original goddess," and during her festival a sort of porridge made of maize, called mazamorra, was given to the youths, who walked through the maize fields, carrying stalks of maize and other herbs called mecoatl with which they afterwards strewed the image of the god of cereals that every one had in his house.

At harvest time in Quegolani, the priests of the maize god, ceremonially visited the corn fields, sought the fairest and best-filled ear, which, after worshipping, they wrapped in cloth and at next seedtime, with processions and solemn rites, buried, wrapped in a deer skin, in a hole lined with stems in the midst of the fields. When another harvest came, if it were a fruitful one, the earth was dug up and the decayed remains dis-tributed in small parcels to the happy populace as talismans against all kinds of evil. The Mexican god Tlaloc is represented with a stalk of maize in the one hand and in the other an instrument with which he is digging the ground. This sanguinary deity seems to have required the sacrifice of a boy in April, whose dead body was put in the granaries or the fields. In the great temple at Mexico, there was a chapel dedicated to the god Cinteutl, called Cinteupan, the god of maize and of bread. In 1880, Charnay[3] found

---

[1] Bancroft, H. H. *Native Races* 5:173. 1886.

[2] Pickering, C. *Chron. Hist. Pls.* 741. 1879.

[3] Charnay *No. Amer. Rev.* 306. 1880.

a statue in Mexico upon whose base, among other things, are sculptured representations of ears of corn.

Maize was seen first by Europeans on the mainland, in 1498, on the shore of the Gulf of Paria, where the natives brought to the ships maize and a beverage made therefrom.[1]   In 1503, Diego Bartholemew [2] " saw above six leagues of ground full of maize and cultivated."   As for liquor, he says, " they have plenty of a very palatable kind of beer made of maez."   Vasco Nunez,[3] 1513, speaks of maize at Darien.   In 1520, the Spaniards in their battle with the Tepeacans were embarrassed by the tall maize that covered part of the plain. Cortez [4] also found corn in Honduras in plantations and everywhere throughout Yucatan, where it had previously been seen by Columbus [5] in 1502.   In this region, Morelet,[6] more than three centuries later found the plains covered with maize often seven to eight metres in height.   Among the varieties cultivated in Mexico, Humboldt [7] mentions one in which the ear ripens in two months after planting; Oviedo [8] mentions one in Nicaragua which is reaped in between 30 and 40 days from planting.

The first corn seen by Europeans was by Columbus, in November, 1492, in Cuba, " a kind of grain called *maiz*, of which was made a very well-tasted flour."[9]   Peter Martyr,[10] in his *First Decade*, said by Robertson to have been written in 1493, says, " the *panicum* of this country is longer by a spanne, somewhat sharpe towards the ende and as bygge as a man's arme in ye brawne: the grains whereof are set in a marvellous manner and are in forme somewhat lyke a Pease.   Whyle they be soure and unripe, they are whyte but when they are ripe, they be very blacke, and when they be broken, they be whiter then snowe: this kynde of grayne they call *maizim*."   In his *Third Decade* he adds, " bearing also more than a thousand graynes."   Acosta,[11] strangely enough, says that this grain occurred on the mainland but that he did " not find that in old time, on the islands of Barloventa, as Cuba, S. Dominique, Jamaigue, and S. Jean, that they used *mayo*." Gomara,[12] however, asserts that the islanders were acquainted with maize and Oviedo describes maize without any intimation of its being a plant that was not natural to Hispaniola.   In 1564, Hawkins [13] found maize at Margarita Island " in bigness of a pease, the eare whereof is much like to a teasell but a span in length, having thereon a number of grains."

[1] Irving, W. *Columbus* 2:116. 1849.

[2] Harshberger, J. W. *Maize* 137. 1893.

[3] Andagoya, P. de. *Narrative*. Hakl. Soc. Ed. 29. 1865.

[4] Prescott, W. H. *Conq. Mex.* 3:284. 1843.

[5] Irving, W. *Columbus* 2:335. 1849.

[6] Morelet *Trav. Cent. Amer.* 326. 1871.

[7] Humboldt, A. *Polit. Essay New Spain* 2:313. 1811.

[8] Ibid.

[9] Knox *Coll. Voy.* 1:83. 1767.

[10] Eden *Hist. Trav.* 10. 1577.

[11] Acosta *Nat. Mor. Hist. Ind.* 254. 1604. Hakl. Soc. Ed. 1880.

[12] Pickering, C. *Geog. Dist. Ans. Pls.* Pt. 1:135. 1863.

[13] Hawkins *Second Voyage*. Hakl. Soc. Ed. 57:27. 1877.

In South America, in 1498, maize was brought to Columbus [1] off the coast of Venezuela. In 1541, Benzoni [2] speaks of the wine of maize, made in the region of the Gulf of Paria. Hans Stade,[3] about 1550, during his captivity in eastern Brazil, speaks of maize under the names *abaty, abatij, abashi, ubatim,* and *milhe de Guine.* In 1520, Magellan found maize at Rio Janeiro, and, in 1647, Nienhoff [4] says it was called *maiz* by the Indians. In 1596, Masham [5] says that in Guiana there " is great store of Guiny-wheat (whereof they make passing good drinke) which after it is once sowed, if you cut off the eare, in the same stalke groweth another." Dobrizhoffer,[6] 1749–67, speaks of several kinds grown in Paraguay: the best known, the *abati hata,* composed of very hard grains; the *abati moroti,* which consists of very soft and white ones; the *abati miri,* which ripens in one month and has very small, dwarfish grains; and *bisingallo,* the most famous of all, the grains of which are angular and pointed. On the western coast, maize was found by Cavendish [7] in 1587 at the Isle of Mocha and on the coast of Chile. In 1649, Alonzo de Ovalle [8] says the ordinary diet of the people of Chile is boiled maize. Molina,[9] 1787, says eight or nine varieties are cultivated, one called *curagua* having smaller grains than the other varieties. This seems to have been a pop corn, as under *Zea curagua,* the Valparaiso corn, Loudon [10] says a distinct variety, to which a sort of religious reputation is attached, on account of the grains which, when roasted, split regularly in the form of a cross.

In Peru, Squier [11] found in an ancient burial place ears of maize, thick, short and variegated, and a very good carving in a variegated talc of an ear of maize three inches long and of just proportions, besides one jar filled with maize. Tschudi [12] describes two kinds which were taken from tombs, apparently dating back to the dynasty of the Incas. Darwin [13] found on the coast, at 85 feet elevation, embedded amidst shells, a head of Indian corn, apparently identical with those taken from the old Peruvian tombs. Garcilasso de la Vega [14] says there are two kinds of *sara,* the Inca name for maize, the one hard and called *muruchu,* the other tender and called *capia.* De la Vega [15] says the Peruvians made a beverage from the stalks before they were ripe.

So much was this grain esteemed that the palace gardens of the Incas were decorated with maize in gold and silver, with all the grains, stalks, spikes, leaves, and, in one instance, in " the gardens of gold and silver " there was an entire corn field of some size, representing

[1] Irving, W. *Columbus* 2:116. 1849.

[2] Benzoni *Hist. New World.* Hakl. Soc. Ed. 21:9. 1857.

[3] *Captiv. Hans Stade.* Hakl. Soc. Ed. 51:49. 1874.

[4] Churchill *Coll. Voy.* 2:135. 1732.

[5] Masham *Raleigh's Third Voy. Guiana.* Hakl. Voy. 11:14. 1904.

[6] Dobrizhoffer *Acct. Abipone* 1:425. 1749–67.

[7] *Lives, Voy. Drake, Cavendish* 132. 1854.

[8] Churchill *Coll. Voy.* 3:73. 1732.

[9] Molina *Hist. Chili* 1:90. 1808.

[10] Loudon, J. C. *Enc. Agr.* 829. 1866.

[11] Squier, E. G. *Peru* 91. 1877.

[12] Darwin, C. *Ans. Pls. Domest.* 1:338. 1893.

[13] Darwin, C. *Voy. H. M. S. Beagle* 370. 1884.

[14] Vega *Roy. Comment.* Hakl. Soc. Ed. 2:355. 1871.

[15] Vega *Roy. Comment.* Hakl. Soc. Ed. 2:357. 1871.

the maize in its natural shape. De la Vega [1] notices the curious workmanship with which the golden ear was half-disclosed amidst the broad leaves of silver and the light tassel of the same material that floated gracefully from its top. At Titiaca, the sacred temple was surrounded with broad fields of maize, which imbibed a portion of its sanctity, and the yearly produce was distributed among the different public magazines, in small quantities to each, as something that would sanctify the remainder of the store.[2] Acosta [3] says they take a certain portion of the most fruitful of the maize that grows on their farms, " the which they put in a certain grenier which they do call Pirua, with certain ceremonies, watching them nights: they put this Mays in the richest garment they have, and being thus wrapped and dressed, they worship this Pirua and hold it in great veneration, saying it is the mother of the Mays of their inheritance, and that by this means the mays augments and is preserved." Rivers and Tschudi say, " the corn-stalks with many ears or with double ears were considered as sacred things but not as Deities: they were called by the Indians Hirantazara, or Aryherazara, because they danced with the dance Arihuay, when the corn was suspended by branches of willow; in the same way did they worship the ears, the grains of which were of various colors, or were arranged in rows, united in the shape of a cone."

In 1532-50, Cieza de Leon [4] found maize abundant in fields, requiring four months for its growth. Gibbon,[5] 1851, describes the corn at Tarma as being small-grained and of four colors: red, white, yellow and blue. Herndon [6] says, on the Montana, three crops are made in a year. On the Island of Titraca, says Squier,[7] the stalks of the maize are scarcely three feet high, and the ears, not longer than one's finger, are closely covered with compact, vitreous grains. On the coast of Peru, says de la Vega,[8] the sowing is done by the ancient Peruvians, " by making holes with thick stakes, into which they put the heads of fish together with two or three grains of maize." This seems to be the same method now in vogue among the Indians in some parts of Mexico and as described in part by Bancroft,[9] for the ancient Aztecs.

The first mention of corn in the present territory of the United States and Canada, seems to have been in the Icelandic Sagas. At Hop, supposed by Prof. Rafn [10] to be in the vicinity of Taunton River, Massachusetts, Karlsefne, in 1006, " found there upon the land self sown fields of wheat, there where the ground was low but vines there where it rose somewhat."[11] Karlsefne [12] is said to have sent out two Scotch people to explore and

[1] Vega *Roy. Comment.* Hakl. Soc. Ed. 1:283. 1869.

[2] Vega *Roy. Comment.* Hakl. Soc. Ed. 1:288. 1869.

[3] Acosta *Nat. Mor. Hist. Ind.* 403. 1604. Hakl. Soc. Ed. 1880.

[4] Markham, C. R. *Trav. Cieza de Leon.* Hakl. Soc. Ed. 33:55. 1864

[5] Herndon, W. L.. and Gibbon, L. *Explor. Vall. Amaz.* 2:1. 1854.

[6] Herndon, W. L., and Gibbon, L. *Explor. Vall. Amaz.* 1:86. 1854.

[7] Squier, E. G. *Peru* 341. 1877.

[8] Vega *Roy. Comment.* Hakl. Soc. Ed. 2:13. 1871.

[9] Bancroft, H. H. *Native Races* 1:625. 1875.

[10] Rafn *Voy. Northmen Amer.* Prince Soc. Ed. 116. 1877.

[11] Karlsefne *Voy. Northmen Amer.* Prince Soc. Ed. 51. 1877.

[12] Ibid.

when they returned they brought back " a bunch of grapes and a new sowen ear of wheat." Again, in 1002, Thorwald,[1] on an island far to the westward of Vinland, " met with a wooden Kornhjalmr " (corn shed?), but saw no other signs of inhabitants, nor of wild beasts.

The first mention in more modern time is in Florida and westward, where it was found by Narvaez in 1528.[2] During De Soto's invasion, 1540, *maes* was found everywhere along his route, from Florida, Alabama, to the upper part of Mississippi, probably on the western bank of the Yazoo, in fields or stored in granaries. Ribault,[3] 1562, says the Florida Indians sow their fields with *Mahiz*. When Cartier visited Hochelaga, now Montreal, in 1535, that town was situated in the midst of extensive corn fields, the grain " even as the millet of Brazil, as great and somewhat bigger than small peason." The Indians called the grain *carracony* and stored it in granaries situated on the top of their habitations. In 1613, Champlain[4] mentions corn growing in fields " feebly scratched with hoes of wood or bone " at Lake Coulonge, on the Ottawa River. In 1540, Colonado,[5] in marching from Mexico to Quivira — supposed by Bancroft[6] to be within the present territory of Kansas — found corn everywhere in abundance, wherever arable soil, apparently, could be found. He mentions that the Zuni Indians practiced irrigation. Alarcon,[7] in 1540, found the Indians of the Colorado River growing abundance of corn as did Espijo in 1583.

The Navajo Indians have this tradition: " All the wise men being one day assembled, a turkey hen came flying from the direction of the morning star and shook from her feather an ear of blue corn into the midst of the company."[8] At the present time, blue, yellow, white, red and even black corn is cultivated in New Mexico, the blue being predominant and most esteemed.[9] In Virginia, in 1585, Sir Richard Grenville[10] is recorded as having destroyed the standing corn of the natives. Heriot[11] 1586, mentions a kind of grain called *mayze* in the West Indies. Corn is mentioned by Strachey[12] under the name of *poketawes*. In *A True Declaration of Virginia*,[13] 1610, the corn is said to grow to a height of twelve or fourteen feet, " yielding some four, five, or six eares, on every stalke and in every eare some five hundred, some seaven hundred cornes." Corn cultivated after the Indian method was grown in 1608, the first successful attempt by Englishmen on record.[14]

[1] Pickering, C. *Chron. Hist. Pls.* 616. 1879.
[2] Smith, B. *Rel. De Vaca* 47. 1871.
[3] *Divers Voy. Amer.* Hakl. Soc. Ed. 7:102. 1840.
[4] Parkman, F. *Pion. France* 374. 1894. 25th Ed.
[5] *Pacific R. R. Rpt.* 3:110. 1856.
[6] Bancroft, H. H. *Native Races* 1:538. 1875.
[7] Whipple and Turner *Pacific R. R. Rpt.* 3:112. 1856.
[8] Bancroft, H. H. *Native Races* 3:83. 1882.
[9] Massie *U. S. Pat. Off. Rpt.* 346. 1852–53.
[10] Bancroft, G. *Hist. U. S.* 1:96. 1839.
[11] Hariot, T. *Narrative Va.* 1588. Quaritch reprint 21. 1893.
[12] Strachey, W. *Trav. Va.* Hakl. Soc. Ed. 6:116. 1849.
[13] *True Decl. Va.* 12. 1610. Force Coll. Tracts 3: No. 1. 1844.
[14] *U. S. Pat. Off. Rpt.* 98. 1853.

In New England, corn was mentioned in 1605 by Champlain,[1] who saw it in cultivation by the Indians at the mouth of the Kennebec. At Cape Cod, a little later, he saw fields of corn and also fields lying fallow. He mentions the method used for storing to be n pits dug in sand on the slopes of the hills, into which the large grass sacks of corn are stored and then buried. In 1620, Miles Standish,[2] exploring for the Pilgrims, found the fields in stubble for it was November and finally under the heap of sand " newly done: we might see how they paddled it with their hands," " a fine, great, new basket, full of very faire corn, of this year, with some six and thirty goodly ears of corn, some yellow and some red and others mixt with blue."[3] In 1629, Higginson [4] says, " There is not such greate and plentiful eares of corne, I suppose, any where else to be found but in this country: because, also, of varietie of colours — as red, blew, and yellow, etc.: and of one corne there springeth four or five hundred." Josselyn [5] says, " Indian wheat, of which there is three sorts,— yellow, red and blew. The blew is commonly ripe before the other, a month."

In August, 1636, when the English made their attack on the Indians at Block Island, " two hundred acres of corn were under cultivation and the maize, already partly harvested, was piled in heaps to be stored away for winter use."[6] The Indians have a tradition, says Roger Williams,[7] that " the crow brought them at first an Indian Grain of Corn in one Eare, and an Indian, or French, Beane is another, from the great God *Kautantouwits'* field in the Southwest, from whence they hold came all their corne and beanes." Indian corn was found as a common food when Europeans first landed at New York in 1609, extensive fields being cultivated and the grain preserved.[8] In 1653, when Le Moine [9] navigated Lake Ontario and landed among the Senecas, they gave him " bread made from Indian corn, of a kind to be roasted at the fire." In 1687, in an invasion into the country of the Senecas by Marquis de Nouville, the quantity of corn destroyed was esti- mated at 1,200,000 bushels. In 1696, the French army under Frontenac [10] invaded the country of the Onondagas and spent three days in destroying the growing crops in the fields which extended a league and a half from the fort.

In 1633, De Vries [11] obtained from the Indians on the Delaware River Indian corn and peas. In 1696, the Rev. John Campanius,[12] in his Delaware and Swedish translation of the Catechism, accommodates the Lord's Prayer to the circumstances of the Indians: thus, instead of " give us our daily bread," he has it, " a plentiful supply of venison and

---

[1] Champlain *Voy.* 1604–10. Prince Soc. Ed. 2:64, 121. 1878.

[2] Young, A. *Chron. Pilgr.* 130, 132. 1841.

[3] Mourt *Rel.* Mass. Hist. Soc. Ser. 1. 8:210. 1802.

[4] Higginson, Rev. Francis. *New Eng. Plant.* 1629. Mass. Hist. Coll. 1:118. 1792.

[5] Josselyn, J. *New Eng. Rar.* 83. 1638–63.

[6] Harshberger, J. W. *Maize* 131. 1893.

[7] Williams, R. *Key.* 1643. Narragansett Club Ed. 1:144. 1866.

[8] Delafield *Trans. N. Y. Agr. Soc.* 10:386. 1850.

[9] Delafield *Trans. N. Y. Agr. Soc.* 10:387. 1850.

[10] Frontenac *Doc. Hist. N. Y.* 1:213. 1850.

[11] Hazard, S. *Annals Pa.* 31, 32. 1850.

[12] Hazard, S. *Annals Pa.* 101. 1850.

corn." The Indians on the Delaware were very fond of hasty pudding, which they called *sappaun*, and Campanius [1] relates that the sachems and other Indians were feasted upon it in 1654. In 1680, Hennepin [2] found corn everywhere in his journey from Niagara to the Mississippi River. Marquette,[3] 1673, Allouez,[4] 1676, and Membre,[5] 1679, all mention the cultivation of corn by the Illinois Indians. The Mandan Indians, according to Catlin,[6] cultivate a variety whose ears are not longer than a man's thumb. The Tuscarora corn is thought to be the variety cultivated by the North Carolina Indians upon the settlement of their country and was introduced into the State of New York in 1712, when the Tuscarora Indians migrated thither. The corn raised by the Yakima Indians of Washington is an eight-rowed variety, small and attenuated, the ears not over five inches long.

We thus see that the culture of corn was general in the New World at the time of the discovery; that it reigned from Brazil to Canada, from Chile to California; that it was grown extensively in fields; and that it had produced many varieties — always an indication of antiquity of culture. It furnished food in its grain, and, from its stalks, sugar to the Peruvians, honey to the Mexicans and a kind of wine or beer to all the natives of the tropics.

In Europe, maize is said by Benzoni,[7] who wrote in 1572, to have been brought with Columbus on his return from America to Spain, along with parrots and other new Indian articles. Descourlitz,[8] 1829, asserts that maize was introduced by the Spaniards from Peru. There is a statement that it came to the northern provinces of Spain, across the Isthmus of Panama, brought by Basques who accompanied Pizarro to Peru. But Oviedo [9] states in his work, printed in 1525, says Boussingault,[10] that he had seen corn growing in Andalusia and the neighborhood of Madrid, and the Spaniards under Pizarro landed at Tumbez, for the conquest, only in 1532. Yet it could not have been generally known in Spain, for Hernandez,[11] who returned to Europe from Mexico in 1571 or 1593 (the authorities differ), in a long chapter on maize, expresses indignation that the Spaniards had not yet introduced into their country so useful a plant. The Haitian name of *mahiz* and the Peruvian name of *sara*, both used in Spain, without indicating a date, perhaps indicate its introduction from both countries. Gerarde,[12] 1597, writes that maize was brought to Spain out of America and the islands adjoining, as out of Florida and Virginia, but the old herbalist need not be expected to be very accurate in his histories.

In Germany, corn is mentioned by Bock,[13] or Tragus as he is often called, who is one

[1] Hazard, S. *Annals Pa.* 152. 1850.

[2] Hennepin *Voy.* Reprint Amer. Antiq. Soc. 1:66. 1820.

[3] Flagg, W. C. *Agr. Ill.* 13:301.

[4] Ibid.

[5] Ibid.

[6] Catlin, G. *No. Amer. Indians* 1:121. 1842.

[7] Benzoni *Hist. New World.* 1572. Hakl. Soc. Ed. 23. 1857.

[8] Descourlitz, M. E. *Fl. Antill.* 8:57. 1829.

[9] Brewer *U. S. Census* 3:94. 1880.

[10] Boussingault, J. B. *Rur. Econ.* 179. 1865.

[11] De Candolle, A. *Geog. Bot.* 2:946. 1855.

[12] Gerade, J. *Herb.* 77. 1597.

[13] Bonafous *Hist. Nat. Mais* 11. 1836.

of the earliest writers on German plants and published in 1539. But Bonafous,[1] 1532, asserts the plant came from Arabia. In Kyber's *Botany*, 1552, an edition of Tragus, corn is called *Turkish Korn*, but in those days everything foreign was likely to be called " Turkish;"[2] but he also calls it *welschkorn* and says (page 650) that everything strange and hitherto unknown receives this name. Fuchsius,[3] 1542, also declares that corn came from Asia to Greece, thence to Germany. We may, therefore, assert with considerable certainty that maize became known in Germany early in the sixteenth century.

Ruellius,[4] a native of France, 1536, asserts that maize came from Arabia and calls it *Turcicum frumentum*. This seems to indicate that he knew the grain in France. The variety of names used for this grain in various parts of France, such as: " wheat of Turkey," " wheat of Rome," " wheat of Barbary," " wheat of Guiana " and " wheat of Spain," indicate that in the course of cultivation the seed had been received from diverse sources.

It was not until after the year 1610, says Targioni-Tozzetti,[5] that maize found its way through Spain and Sicily. Cardan,[6] 1553, and Matthiolus, 1570, both Italians, mentioned the plant in their writings, but the former does not affirm that it was known in Italy, nor does the latter in his edition of 1645, and, indeed, says that it should be called " Indian wheat " and not " Turkish wheat," because it came from the West Indies and not from Asia nor from Turkey. In 1685, George de Turre [7] says that the maize, or Turkish wheat, was imported into Italy " since a few years." Ramusio,[8] who died in 1557, is quoted by Pickering [9] as stating that the plant was first seen in Italy in his time.

In Asia, we have record of the early introduction of corn to Java by the Portuguese in 1496, according to Rumphius.[10] In 1521, maize was found by Magellan [11] at the island of Limasava. In 1665, white and red varieties are mentioned by Nieuhoff at Batavia. Adams,[12] 1484, says of Borneo, that the magnificent maize springs up often in large and vivid patches. Corn reached China in 1516, according to Malte-Brun.[13] Bretschneider [14] says Li-shi-chen was the first Chinese author who mentioned corn, the date being the close of the sixteenth century. He states that maize came to China from central Asia. Corn is enumerated by Thunberg,[15] 1775, as among the edible plants of Japan. At Lew Chew,

---

[1] Bonafous *Hist. Nat. Mais* 11. 1836.

[2] Brewer *U. S. Census* **3**:94. 1880.

[3] Flint *Trans. N. Y. Agr. Soc.* 292. 1849.

[4] Ibid.

[5] Targioni-Tozzetti *Trans. Hort. Soc. Lond.* **9**:137. 1855.

[6] *Trans. Ill. Agr. Soc.* 472. 1856–57.

[7] Turre, G. *Dryadum* 478. 1685.

[8] Pickering, C. *Geog. Dist. Ans. Pls.* Pt. **1**:135. 1863.

[9] Ibid.

[10] De Candolle, A. *Geog. Bot.* **2**:950. 1855.

[11] *Lives, Voy. Drake, Cavendish* 33. 1854.

[12] Adams, A. *Voy. Samarang* **2**:424. 1848.

[13] De Candolle, A. *Geog. Bot.* **2**:950. 1855.

[14] Bretschneider, E. *Bot. Sin.* 59. 1882.

[15] Thunberg, C. P. *Fl. Jap.* 37. 1784.

no maize was found or was believed to exist at the time of the visit of the Perry expedition,[1] although it is mentioned as being there by Hall,[2] 1818, and by Belcher,[3] 1848. Roxburgh[4] says corn is cultivated in different parts of India in gardens but nowhere on a large scale. Firminger[5] says corn has now become thoroughly naturalized in all parts of India but seems to be much degenerated as compared with that raised from seed annually brought from America. Dutt[6] says corn has no Sanscrit name but is largely cultivated in Bihar and upper India. Ebn Barthon,[7] an Arab physician of the thirteenth century, who traveled extensively in Asia, makes no mention of any plant which appears to be maize.[8] Friar Odorri,[9] who traveled in 1316–1330 to China, makes no mention of maize, nor does Monticorvino,[10] 1292–1338. Batuta,[11] who traveled from 1325 to 1355, mentions in China almost every cultivated product but not maize. Varthema,[12] who in 1503–8 visited Egypt, Arabia, Persia, India and Ethiopia, mentions many fruits and vegetables but makes no reference to maize. Forskal,[13] in 1774, found maize cultivated in the mountains of Yemen but the mention of corn as coming from Arabia is made by Bock, 1532, Ruellius, 1536 and Fuchsius, 1542, as has been mentioned before.

Barbot[14] in his *Description of the Coast of Guinea* says the Portuguese first enriched these African countries with the Indian wheat, or maize, bringing the seed from the Island of St. Thomas in the bight of Guinea, to the Gold Coast. He says there are two sorts, the red and the white. In the early part of the sixteenth century, a Portuguese writing, translated into Italian and inserted in Ramusio's collections (Ramusio died in 1557, and the publication of his collection began in 1550), states that at St. Jago, Cape de Verde Islands, " they sow a grain called *Zaburso*, the same that grows in the West Indies under the name of maize. This grain is as common on the coast of Africa as in these islands and is the chief sustenance of both these countries. They gather their crop in forty days." About 1550, Hans Stade[15] uses the words *zaburso* and *milho de Guine*, and, in 1586, Heriot[16] speaks of " Guinea wheat," a striking commentary on the extent of its distribution in that portion of Africa. In 1593, Hawkins[17] found at the Canary Islands

[1] Perry *Japan* 2:33. 1852–54.
[2] Ibid.
[3] Ibid.
[4] Roxburgh, W. *Fl. Ind.* 3:568. 1832.
[5] Firminger, T. A. C. *Gard. Ind.* 3:111. 1874.
[6] Dutt, U. C. *Mat. Med. Hindus* 270. 1877.
[7] De Candolle, A. *Geog. Bot.* 2:948. 1855.
[8] Ibid.
[9] *Cathay, Way Thither.* Hakl. Soc. Ed. 1866.
[10] Ibid.
[11] Ibid.
[12] Jones, J. W. *Trav. Varthema.* Hakl. Soc. Ed. 1863.
[13] Forskal, P. *Fl. Aeg. Arab.* LXXV. 1775.
[14] Churchill *Coll. Voy.* 5:196. 1746.
[15] *Captiv. Hans Stade.* Hakl. Soc. Ed. 49. 1874.
[16] Pinkerton *Coll. Voy.* 12:595. 1812.
[17] Hawkins, R. *Voy. So. Seas.* Hakl. Soc. Ed. 1:48. 1847.

"mayes, which wee call Guynnewheate." Maize is mentioned in the Congo by Father Angelo [1] in 1667 and by Father Merolla [2] in 1682. In Barbot's *Description of the Coasts of East Africa and Malabar* in the beginning of the sixteenth century, there is ample mention of almost every kind of vegetable which might be looked for in this region but not of maize, except in a misprint (page 14, Hakluyt Society Edition) for yams. Prosper Alpinus,[3] who wrote of the agriculture of Egypt in 1592, makes no mention of maize. In 1775, Forskal [4] found corn little cultivated and it then had not a name distinct from Sorgho.[5] Delile's account of the Egyptian name and tradition indicates that the plant was received from the North by way of Syria and Turkey. Barth [6] mentions finding maize in northern Africa and Parkyns,[7] in Abyssinia.

In Polynesia, corn does not seem to be much grown. In 1595, Mendana [8] "sowed maize before the Indians" in the Marquesas group. In 1792, "a little tolerably good maize" was found by Vancouver [9] at Tahiti. In the Fiji Islands, corn is grown by the white settlers but not as yet (1865) by the natives. There is but one kind, a small, yellow-grained one, and it is called *sila ni papalagi*, foreign sila, by the natives. At Tongatabu, in 1840, a little corn was growing.[10]

At the French exposition of 1852, specimens of maize were exhibited from Algeria, Canada, Australia, Portugal, Hungary and Syria. At the London Exhibition of 1862, 200 varieties, collected by Professor Brignoli of the Modena Royal Botanical Gardens, were shown.[11] In 1880, the writer hastily collected from northern America and exhibited before the Massachusetts Board of Agriculture, 307 varieties. Although these are but a tithe of the various kinds that could be gathered together from the various regions of the globe, yet they all belong to one botanical species, *Zea mays* Linn., although Steudel [12] in his synopsis of plants catalogs six others, namely: *Zea hirta* Bonaf., the hairy maize, from California; *Z. rostrata* Bonaf., of Peru; *Z. macrosperma* Klotz., of Peru; *Z. curagua* Molina, of Chile; *Z. cryptosperma* Bonaf., of Buenos Aires; *Z. erythrolepis* Bonaf., or red-husked corn. In popular language, we have hard corns and soft corns; flints, dents, pop corns and sweets; yellow, red, white, black and variegated and many other colors and shades. The rows vary in varieties from 8 to 32 and in individual specimens from 4 to 48; the length of ear, in varieties from 2 inches to 12, in specimens from 1 inch to 16. Some ears are cylindrical, others tapering, others forming a cone, and some small pop corns are globular egg-shaped. The variation in the form of kernel is also as marked,

---

[1] Churchill *Coll. Voy.* 1:491. 1744.

[2] Churchill *Coll. Voy.* 1:563. 1744.

[3] Churchill *Coll. Voy.* 5:196. 1746.

[4] Pickering, C. *Geog. Dist. Ans. Pls.* Pt. 1:135. 1863.

[5] Ibid.

[6] Barth, H. *Trav. No. Cent. Afr.* 276. 1857.

[7] Parkyns, M. *Life Abyss.* 1:306. 1856.

[8] Dalrymple *Coll. Voy.* 1:70. 1770.

[9] Vancouver, G. *No. Pacific Voy.* 1:339. 1801.

[10] Seemann, B. *Fl. Viti.* 327. 1865–73.

[11] Wilkes, C. *U. S. Explor. Exped.* 3:32. 1845.

[12] Simmonds, P. L. *Trop. Agr.* 306. 1889.

from large to small, wrinkled and smooth, dented, rounded, flat, pointed and tipped with a spine. There is no genus of plant more variable unless it be Brassica.

The history of the appearance of sweet corn in gardens shows it to be quite modern. In the *New England Farmer*, Aug. 3, 1822,[1] it is said, " a writer in the Plymouth paper asserts that sweet corn was not known in New England until a gentleman of that place, who was in Gen. Sullivan's expedition against the Indians in 1779, brought a few ears to Plymouth, which he found among the Indians on the border of the Susquehannah." A writer the following September [2] adds that this sweet corn was brought by Lieut. Richard Bagnal from Gen. Sullivan's expedition against the Six Nations in 1779 and was called *papoon corn*. " That was the first of the species ever seen here and has since that time been more and more diffused; and, I believe within a few years only, has been generally and extensively cultivated for culinary purposes. The species has undergone some change since it was first introduced — then the core was a bright crimson, and after being boiled and the corn taken off, if the corn was laid in contact with any linen, it communicated an indelible stain. This inconvenience has disappeared. This species, also, like what is distinguished by the appellation of southern, or flat, corn, by repeated plantings here, assimilates it to our local corn."

Sweet corn is not referred to by Jefferson in his *Notes on Virginia*, 1781; nor by McMahon, 1806; nor by Gardiner and Hepburn, 1818; nor by Thorburn, 1817; nor by Randolph, 1818; nor by Fessenden, 1828. In 1801, Bordley [3] mentions the "'sweet corn, having a white, shrivelled grain when ripe " as yielding richer juice in the stalks than common corn. In 1832, " sweet or sugar " corn is mentioned among garden vegetables by Bridgeman.[4] In 1851, Buist [5] mentions two varieties. In 1853, Bement [6] says of the " Early Sweet corn, the variety introduced by Cape Bagnoll [7] of Plymouth, that one kind has a white cob, the other a red cob." In 1854, Schenck [8] mentions the Extra Early, the Eight-rowed Sweet, and Stowells Sugar, which has been brought into notice within a few months. In 1858, Klippart [9] mentions in addition the Mammoth Sugar and says the yellow, blue and red sugars are all mere sports from the New England and are not desirable. In 1866, Burr describes 12 varieties. The seed catalog of Thorburn,[10] 1828, offers one variety, the Sugar, or Sweet; in 1881, 16 varieties.

Zephyranthes atamasco Herb. App. *Amaryllideae.* ATAMASCO LILY.

Southern states of North America. The bulbous roots were eaten by the Creek Indians in times of scarcity.[11] In France, this species is cultivated in the flower gardens.

---

[1] *New Eng. Farm.* Aug. 3, 1822.

[2] *New Eng. Farm.* Sept. 1822.

[3] *New Eng. Farm.* June 14, 1823.

[4] Bridgeman *Gard. Asst.* 1832.

[5] Buist, R. *Family Kitch. Gard.* 61. 1851.

[6] Bement *Trans. N. Y. Agr. Soc.* 13:336. 1853.

[7] Ibid.

[8] Schenck, P. A. *Gard. Text Book* 185. 1851.

[9] Klippart *Rpt. State Bd. Agr. Ohio* 13:518. 1858.

[10] Thorburn *Cat.* 1828.

[11] Pickering, C. *Chron. Hist. Pls.* 776. 1879.

Zilla myagroides Forsk. *Cruciferae.*

Egypt and Arabia. The leaves are boiled and eaten by the Arabs.[1]

Zingiber mioga Rosc. *Scitamineae.* WILD GINGER.

Japan. This is a kind of wild ginger of Japan where the root is said to be utilized.

Z. officinale Rosc. GINGER.

Tropics. The rhizomes of this species furnish the well-known ginger. The plant is largely cultivated both in the East and West Indies, as well as in Africa and China. It is supposed that there are two varieties, one producing darker-colored rhizomes than the other, this difference in color being independent of the mode of preparation. The young rhizomes, preserved in syrup, are imported for the delicious conserve known as preserved ginger — that imported from the West Indies being preferred to the Chinese kind.[2]

Z. zerumbet Rosc. WILD GINGER.

Tropical Asia and the Malayan Archipelago. The leaves and shoots are used as greens in Bengal.

Zizania aquatica Linn. *Gramineae.* INDIAN RICE. WILD RICE.

North America and eastern Asia. Wild rice is found on the swampy borders of streams and in shallow water, common in the United States, especially northwestward. Gould[3] has found it nine feet tall at the foot of Lake Champlain and in places on the Hudson and Delaware Rivers, where the tibe ebbs and flows, over twelve feet high. The seeds have furnished food from early times to the Indians and the plant has been considered worthy of cultivation. In 1791, seeds from Canada were sent to England and attempts were made at its culture.[4] Father Hennepin,[5] in 1680, in his voyage on the upper Mississippi, ate the grain and pronounced it better and more wholesome than rice. In 1784, Jonathan Carver[6] speaks of wild rice as being the most valuable of all the spontaneous productions of the Northwest. Jefferys,[7] 1760, says the people of Louisiana gather the seeds and make them into a bread. Flint[8] says, but for this grain the Canadian traders and hunters could hardly exist. Pinkerton[9] says, " this plant seems to be designed by nature to become the bread corn of the north." Almost every observer who has mentioned it has used terms of praise. Gould[10] says the plant seems especially adapted for the soiling of cattle and that its use increases the yield and the richness of milk. In Louisiana, its use is recommended for hay, and in Savannah, Georgia, says Elliott,[11] under

---

[1] Don, G. *Hist. Dichl. Pls.* 1:255. 1831.

[2] Masters, M. T. *Treas. Bot.* 2:1250. 1870.

[3] Gould, J. *Trans. N. Y. Agr. Soc.* 224. 1869.

[4] Banks, Sir J. *Trans. Hort. Soc. Lond.* 1:22. 1815.

[5] *Amer. Antiq. Soc. (Arch. Amer.)* 1:89. 1820.

[6] Carver, J. *Trav. No. Amer.* 210. 1784.

[7] Jefferys, T. *Nat. Hist. Amer.* 1:157. 1760.

[8] Flint, T. *West. States* 1:84. 1828.

[9] Gould, J. *Trans. N. Y. Agr. Soc.* 225. 1869.

[10] Ibid.

[11] Elliott, S. *Bot. So. Car., Ga.* 2:586. 1821.

the name of wild oats, it is used almost exclusively during the summer as green fodder for cows and horses. The one objection to its culture seems to come from the seed dropping so readily when ripe. The northern Indians, of the lakes and rivers between the Mississippi and Lake Superior, gather the seed by pushing the canoe amongst the stems and shaking the heads over the boat. An acre of wild rice is supposed to be equal to an acre of wheat in the nutriment afforded. The seeds are black, smooth, narrow, cylindrical, about half an inch long, white and farinaceous when cooked and are very palatable.

This is the *kaw-sun* of China and is found in the lakes of Anam, Manchuria, China and Japan. From Dr. Hance,[1] we know that the solid base of the stem forms a very choice vegetable largely used in China, where it is cultivated.

Zizyphus agrestis Roem. & Schult. *Rhamneae.*

China and Cochin China. The globose, red drupe is eatable.[2]

Z. joazeiro Mart.

Brazil. This plant is recommended as yielding fruit in arid regions.[3]

Z. jujuba Lam. CHINESE DATE. JUJUBE.

East Indies and Malay; cultivated generally in the East Indies. More than 1200 years ago this plant was introduced into China by way of Persia [4] and now yields an excellent dessert fruit for the Chinese, who recognize many varieties, differing in shape, color and size of the fruits. Those of one variety are called Chinese date. In India, the fruit is more or less globose in the wild and common sorts and is ovoid or oblong in the cultivated and improved plant. The pulp is mealy, sweetish, with a pleasant taste, and, in South India, an oil is extracted from the kernel.[5] Wallich [6] describes a variety which produces a fruit of a long form, about the size of an egg, and which is of excellent quality. A variety with a small, sour berry is a great favorite with the Burmese.[7] In Abyssinia, its fruits are made into a substance like dry cheese.[8] In Mauritius, six varieties are described, of these four are pleasant tasting and two not good.[9]

Z. lotus Lam. AFRICAN DATE PALM. JEW THORN. LOTUS.

Mediterranean region. The roundish, purplish fruit has the appearance of olives and a sweet taste resembling figs or dates.[10] According to Theophrastus, the *lotos* was so common in Zerbi, the island of the Lotophagi, that a Roman army on its way to Carthage was nourished several days on its fruit. Homer also mentions this attractive fruit, from which Ulysses succeeded, only by violence, in turning away his companions. It

[1] Hance, Dr. *Gard. Chron.* 633. 1872.

[2] Don, G. *Hist. Dichl. Pls.* 2:27. 1832.

[3] Mueller, F. *Sel. Pls.* 527. 1891.

[4] Pickering, C. *Chron. Hist. Pls.* 222. 1879.

[5] Brandis, D. *Forest Fl.* 88. 1874.

[6] Ainslie, W. *Mat. Med. Ind.* 2:95. 1826.

[7] Pickering, C. *Chron. Hist. Pls.* 222. 1879.

[8] Grant *Treas. Bot.* 2:1308. 1876.

[9] Hooker, W. J. *Journ. Bot.* 1:320. 1834.

[10] Unger, F. *U. S. Pat. Off. Rpt.* 343. 1859.

forms an important article of food in Tunis and Barbary and is also cultivated in southern Europe at the present time.

Z. lycioides A. Gray.

Texas and the neighboring Mexican states. The plant bears round, black, edible but rather astringent berries, about the size of a rifle ball, which are called *gerambuyo prieto* and *cornudo de cuervo*.[1]

Z. mucronata Willd.

Tropical Africa, Cape of Good Hope and Senegal. The red fruit is eaten[2] and is used in Africa for making into a bread and also for the preparation of a pleasant beverage.[3]

Z. napeca Willd.

East Indies. The fruit is the size of a pea, smooth, shining, black. The taste is acid and astringent, but it is eaten by the natives.[4]

Z. obtusifolia A. Gray.

Texas. The large, round, black berries are eaten by Mexicans although nearly tasteless.[5]

Z. oxyphylla Edgew.

Himalayan region. The very acid fruit is eaten.[6]

Z. reticulata DC.

South America. The fruit is eatable.[7]

Z. rotundifolia Lam.

Persia and East Indies. The fruit is eaten and during famines has supported thousands. The taste is sweet and acidulous.[8]

Z. rugosa Lam.

East Indies and Burma. The fruit is eaten but has a peculiar, mawkish flavor.[9] The fruit is yellow and the size of a small cherry.[10]

Z. sativa Gaertn. JUJUBE.

Mediterranean and temperate Asia. The jujube is indigenous in Syria, in the Himalayas, in Greece and is cultivated on both shores of the Mediterranean. It has been naturalized in Italy since the time of Augustus when it was brought from Syria, where it is said to have been brought from India by the way of Palmyra. It is now cultivated in Spain, France and Italy as far north as Genoa.[11] The fruit is scarlet, about an inch

---

[1] Torrey, J. *U. S. Pat. Off. Rpt.* 240. 1857.
[2] Don, G. *Hist. Dichl. Pls.* 2:24. 1832.
[3] Smith, A. *Treas. Bot.* 2:1251. 1870. (*Z. baclei*)
[4] Don, G. *Hist. Dichl. Pls.* 2:25. 1832.
[5] Havard, V. *Proc. U. S. Nat. Mus.* 508. 1885.
[6] Brandis, D. *Forest Fl.* 86. 1874.
[7] Don, G. *Hist. Dichl. Pls.* 2:25. 1832.
[8] Brandis, D. *Forest Fl.* 89. 1874. (*Z. nummularia*)
[9] Brandis, D. *Forest Fl.* 90. 1874.
[10] Don, G. *Hist. Dichl. Pls.* 2:26. 1832. (*Z. xylocarpa*)
[11] Loudon, J. C. *Arb. Frut. Brit.* 2:525. 1844. (*Z. vulgaris*)

long, and has an edible pulp. Brandis[1] says that, while the fruit of the Mediterranean variety is sweet, that of the Indian variety is acid but well flavored. This shrub was introduced into South Carolina in 1837, and the seed was distributed from the Patent Office in 1855.[2]

Z. spina-christi Willd. CHRIST'S THORN. NUBK TREE.

North Africa and the Orient. The fruit is oblong, about the size of a sloe and has a pleasant, subacid taste. It is used as food by the inhabitants of Egypt and Arabia.[3]

Z. xylopyrus Willd.

East Indies. The fruits are not eaten by men but the kernels are.[4]

Zostera marina Linn. *Naiadaceae.* EEL GRASS. GRASS-WRACK. SEA GRASS.

Europe. In the outer Hebrides, the root of this plant, which after storms is cast upon the shores in great abundance, is chewed for the saccharine juice which it contains.[5] The plant is much used as a manure.

Zygophyllum coccineum Linn. *Zygophylleae.*

North Africa and Arabia. The aromatic seeds are employed by the Arabs in the place of pepper.[6]

Z. fabago Linn. BEAN CAPER.

Spain, north Africa and western Asia. The flowers are used as a caper substitute.[7]

---

[1] Brandis, D. *Forest Fl.* 85. 1874. (*Z. vulgaris*)

[2] *U. S. Pat. Off. Rpt.* 311. 1855.

[3] Loudon, J. C. *Arb. Frut. Brit.* 2:526. 1844.

[4] Brandis, D. *Forest Fl.* 90. 1874.

[5] *Journ. Agr.* 2:379. 1831.

[6] Masters, M. T. *Treas. Bot.* 2:1254. 1870.

[7] Balfour, J. H. *Man. Bot.* 466. 1875.

AUTHORS AND TITLES QUOTED IN STURTEVANT'S NOTES ON EDIBLE PLANTS

Adams, A. *Voy. Samarang.*
Adams, Arthur: The Zoology of the Voyage of H. M. S. Samarang. London, 1850.

Aegineta, P. *Pharm. Simp.*
Aegineta, Paulus: Pharmaca simplicia, Othone Brunfelsio interprete. Idem De ratione victus Gulielmo Copo Basiliensi interprete. In Paulum Aeginetam de simplicibus iuxta ac de ratione victus, index tum utilis, tum necessarius. Argentorati, Sept. 1531.

Agassiz *Journ. Braz.*
Agassiz, Professor and Mrs. Louis: A Journey in Brazil. Boston, 1868.

Agr. Gaz.
Agricultural Gazette of New South Wales. Sydney, 1890. Issued by direction of the minister for mines and agriculture. (Monthly.)

Ainslie, W. *Mat. Ind.*
Ainslie, Whitelaw, M.D.: Materia Indica; or, Some Account of Those Articles Which are Employed by the Hindoos, and other Eastern Nations, in their Medicine, Arts, and Agriculture. London, 1826. 2 vols.

Albertus Magnus *Veg.* Jessen Ed.
Albertus Magnus: Ex ordine praedicatorum de vegetabilibus libri vii, historiae naturalis pars xviii. Editionem criticam ab Ernesto Meyero coeptam absolvit Carolus Jessen. Berolini, 1867.

Alcock, R. *Capital Tycoon.*
Alcock, Sir Rutherford: The Capital of the Tycoon: A Narrative of a Three Years' Residence in Japan. London, 1863. 2 vols.

Alexander, J. E. *Exped. Disc. Afr.*
Alexander, Sir James Edward: An Expedition of Discovery into the Interior of Africa, through the hitherto undescribed Countries of the Great Namaquas, Boschmans, and Hill Damaras. Performed Under the Auspices of Her Majesty's Government, and The Royal Geographical Society; and Conducted by Sir James Edward Alexander. London, 1838. 2 vols.

Alpinus *Pl. Aegypt.*
Alpinus, Prosperus: De plantis Aegypti liber......Accessit etiam liber de balsamo aliàs editus. Venetiis, 1592.

—— *Pl. Exot.*
Alpinus, Prosperus: De plantis exoticis libri duo......Opus completum, editum studio ac opera Alpini Alpini. Venetiis, 1627.

Amer. Agr.
American Agriculturist. Weekly published by the Orange Judd Co. New York, Springfield, Mass. and Chicago, 1842.

Amer. Antiq. Soc.
> Archeologia Americana.   Transactions and Collections of the American Antiquarian
> Society.   Worcester, Mass., 1820–1885.   Vol. 1–7.

Amer. Gard.
> American Gardening.   A Weekly Illustrated Journal of Horticulture.   New York,
> 1892–1904.   Before its union with Popular Gardening in 1892, the publication
> was known as The American Garden.

Amer. Journ. Pharm.
> American Journal of Pharmacy.   Philadelphia, 1835.

Amer. Journ. Sci. Art.
> American Journal of Science and Arts.   Four Series.   New York and New Haven,
> 1818–1905.

Amer. Nat.
> American Naturalist.   Monthly.   Boston, Mass., 1868.

Amer. Pom. Soc. Rpt.
> American Pomological Society Reports.   Issued usually biennially from 1850 to date.
> First published as the Proceedings of the National Convention of Fruit Growers
> in 1848.

Ammonius *Med. Herb.* 1539.

Andagoya, Pascual de: *Narrative.*   See Hakluyt.

Anderson, C. J. *Lake Ngami.*
> Anderson, Charles John: Lake Ngami; or, Explorations and Discoveries during Four
> Years' Wanderings in the Wilds of Southwestern Africa.   New York, 1856.

Andrews, H. C. *Bot. Reposit.*
> Andrews, Henry C.:   The Botanist's Repository for New and Rare Plants containing
> coloured Figures of Such Plants, as Have Not Hitherto Appeared in Any Similar
> Publication.   To Each Description is added A Short History of the Plant.
> London, 1797–(1812).   10 vols.

Andrews, E. A. *Latin Lexicon.*
> Andrews, Ethan Allen: A Copious and Critical Latin-English Lexicon founded on
> the Larger Latin-German Lexicon of Dr. William Freund: with Additions and
> Corrections.   New York, 1861.

Angelo, Father.   See Churchill Collection.

Anghiera, Peter Martyr de: The Decades of the New World, or West India: written in
> the Latin tongue, and translated into Englysche by Rycharde Eden.   London,
> 1555.

Anthrop. Journ.
> Journal of the Anthropological Society of London, Eng.   Containing in 1865, vol. 3,
> an article by Berthold Seemann.

Antiq. Culin.
> Antiquitates Culinariae; or Curious tracts relating to the culinary affairs of the old
> English.   With a preliminary discourse, notes and illustrations, by the Reverend
> Richard Warner.   London, 1791.

Apicius *Opson.*
> Apicius, Coelius: De Opsoniis.   1709.

Archer, T. C.   *Profit. Pls.*
  Archer, Thomas Croxen: Profitable Plants: A Description of the Principal Articles of Vegetable Origin used for Food, Clothing, Tanning, Dyeing, Building, Medicine, Perfumery, etc. London, 1865.

Arnold, A.   *Through Persia Caravan.*
  Arnold, Arthur: Through Persia by Caravan. New York, 1877.

Aublet *Hist. Pls. Guiane.*
  Aublet, J. B. C. F.: Histoire des plantes de la Guiane Françoise. Londres, 1775. 4 vols.

Babington, C. C.   *Brit. Rubi.*
  Babington, Charles Cardale: The British Rubi; An attempt to discriminate the species of Rubus known to inhabit the British Isles. London, 1869.

Baillon, H.   *Hist. Pls.*
  Baillon, Henry Ernst: The Natural History of Plants. Translated by Marcus M. Hartog, Trinity College, Cambridge. London, Vol. 1, 1871; 2, 1872; 3, 1874; 4, 1875; 5, 1878; 6, 1880; 7, 1881; 8, 1888.

Balfour, J. H.   *Man. Bot.*
  Balfour, John Hutton: A Manual of Botany, being an Introduction to the Study of the Structure, Physiology, and Classification of Plants. Fifth Ed. Edinburgh, 1875.

Balfour, J. H.   See Treasury of Botany.

Bancroft, G.   *Hist. U. S.*
  Bancroft, George: History of the United States from the Discovery of the American Continent. Fifth Ed. Boston, 1838–75. 11 vols.

Bancroft, H. H.   *Native Races.*
  Bancroft, Hubert Howe: The Native Races of the Pacific States of North America. Vol. 1. Wild Tribes. New York, 1875. Vol. II. Civilized Nations. San Francisco, 1882. Vol. III. Myths and Languages. San Francisco, 1882. Vol. IV. Antiquities. San Francisco, 1886. Vol. V. Primitive History. San Francisco, 1886.

Barbot *Desc. Coasts E. Afr.*
  A Description of the Coasts of East Africa. See Churchill Collection.

Barbot *Desc. Coasts Guinea.*
  A Description of the Coasts of Guinea. See Churchill Collection.

Barrow, J.   *Voy. Disc. Arctic Reg.*
  Barrow, Sir John: Voyages of Discovery and Research within The Arctic Regions, from the year 1818 to the present time. London, 1846.

Barthelemy, J. J.   *Voy. Anacharsis Grèce.*
  Voyage d'Anacharsis En Grèce Vers Le Milieu Du Quatrième Siècle. Paris, 1822.

Barth, H.   *Trav. Disc. No., Cent. Afr.*
  Barth, Henry: Travels and Discoveries in North and Central Africa. Being A Journal of an Expedition Undertaken Under the Auspices of H. B. M.'S Government in the Years 1849–1855. New York, 1857. 3 vols.

Bartlett, J. R.   *Explor. Texas.*

Bartlett, John Russel: Personal Narrative of Explorations and Incidents in Texas, New Mexico, California, Sonora, and Chihuahua. Connected with the United States and Mexican Boundary Commission, during the Years 1850, '52, and '53. New York, 1854.

Barton, W. P. C.   *Med. Bot.*

Barton, William P. C., M. D.: Vegetable Materia Medica of the United States; or Medical Botany: containing a Botanical, General, and Medical History, of Medicinal Plants Indigenous to the United States. Philadelphia, Vol. 1, 1817; vol. 2, 1818.

Barton and Castle *Brit. Fl. Med.*

Barton, B. H. and Castle, T.: British Flora Medica: A history of the medicinal plants of Great Britain. London, 1837. 2 vols. Second Ed. by J. R. Jackson. 1877.

Bartram, W.   *Trav. No., So. Car.*

Bartram, William: Travels through North and South Carolina, Georgia, East and West Florida, the Cherokee Country, Containing An Account of the Soil and Natural Productions of those regions. Philadelphia, 1791. Reprinted London, 1792.

Bates, H. W.   *Nat. Amaz.*

Bates, Henry Walter: The Naturalist on the River Amazons. A Record of Adventures, Habits of Animals, Sketches of Brazilian and Indian Life, and Aspects of Nature under the Equator, during Eleven years of Travel. In the Humboldt Library of Popular Science Literature. This pamphlet is No. 12. New York, 1879–80.

Bauhin, C.   *Phytopinax.*

Bauhin, Caspar: ΦΥΤΟΠΙΝΑΞ seu enumeratio plantarum ab Herbariis nostro seculo descriptarum, cum earum differentiis. Basileae. (no date; 1596 fide Pritzel)

—— *Pinax.*

Bauhin, Caspar: ΠΙΝΑΞ Theatri Botanici. Basileae. Helvet., 1623. Bound with Bauhinus, C., Πρόδρομος Theatri Botanici. 1620.

—— *Prodromus.*

Bauhin, Caspar: ΠΡΟΔΡΟΜΟΣ Theatri Botanici in quo plantae supra sexcentae ab ipso primum descriptae cum plurimis figuris proponuntur. Editio altera emendatior. Basiliae, 1671. Bound with Bauhinus, C., Πίναξ Theatri Botanici. (Imp. Jo. Reg.), 1671.

Bauhin, J.   *Hist. Pl.*

Bauhin, Johann, *and* Cherler, Johann Heinrich: Historia plantarum universalis, nova, et absolutissima cum consensu et dissensu circa eas. . . . Quam recensuit & auxit Dominicus Chabraeus. Ebroduni, vol. 1, 1650; 2, 3, 1651. 3 vols.

Bennett, G.   *Gath. Nat. Austral.*

Bennett, George, M. D.: Gatherings of a Naturalist in Australasia Being Observations principally on the Animal and Vegetable Productions of New South Wales, New Zealand and some of the Austral Islands. London, 1860.

Benzoni, G.   *Hist. New World.* See Hakluyt.

Berkley, M. J. See Treasury of Botany.

Berlanger in Transactions New York Agricultural Society. Albany, 1858.

Bessey, C. E. *Bot.*
> Bessey, Charles Edwin: Botany for High Schools and Colleges. New York, 1880. (American science series.)

Beverley *Hist. Va.*
> Beverley, Robert: History of Virginia, by a native and inhabitant of the place. London, 1705.

Bigelow, J. *Med. Bot.*
> Bigelow, Jacob, M. D.: American Medical Botany, being a Collection of the Native Medicinal Plants of the United States, Containing their Botanical History and Chemical Analysis, and Properties and Uses in Medicine, Diet and the Arts, with Coloured Engravings. Vol. 1, 1817; 2, 1818; 3, 1820. Boston, Mass.

Bigelow, J. M. See Pacific Railroad Reports.

Bird, I. L. *Unbeat. Tracks Jap.*
> Bird, Isabella L.: Unbeaten Tracks in Japan, An Account of Travels on Horseback in the Interior including Visits to the Aborigines of Yezo and the Shrines of Nikko and Ise. With Map and Illustrations. New York, 1881. 2 vols.

Birdwood *Veg. Prod. Bomb.*
> Birdwood, G. C. M.: Catalogue of the Vegetable productions of the Presidency of Bombay . . . Second Ed. Bombay, 1865.

Black, A. A. See Treasury of Botany.

Bojer, W. *Hort. Maurit.*
> Bojer, Wenzel: Hortus mauritianus, ou énumération des plantes . . . à île Maurice. Maurice, 1837.

Bonafous, M. *Hist. Nat. Mais.*
> Bonafous, Matthieu, Directeur du Jardin Royal D'Agriculture de Turin: Histoire Naturelle, Agricole et Economique du Mais. Paris, 1836.

Bontius, Jacobus. See Piso, Gulielmus De Ind.

Booth, W. B. See Treasury of Botany.

Bostock and Riley *Nat. Hist. Pliny.*
> Bostock, John, M. D., and Riley, H. T., Esq.: The Natural History of Pliny. London, 1855. 6 vols.

Boussingault, J. B. *Rur. Econ.*
> Rural Economy In its relations with Chemistry, Physics and Meteorology or Chemistry applied to Science. Translated from French by George Law, Agriculturist. New York, 1865.

Brandis, D. *Forest Fl.*
> Brandis, Dietrich: The Forest Flora of North-West and Central India: A Handbook of the Indigenous Trees and Shrubs of those Countries. Commenced by the Late J. Lindsay Stewart. Continued and Completed by Dietrich Brandis. Prepared at the Herbarium of the Royal Gardens, Kew. London, 1874.

Brassey *Sunshine, Storm East.*
> Brassey, Mrs.: Sunshine and Storm in the East, or Cruises to Cyprus and Constantinople. Leipzig, 1880. 2 vols.

Bretschneider, E. *Bot. Sin.*

Bretschneider, Emil, M. D.: Botanicon Sinicum. Notes on Chinese Botany from Native and Western Sources. London, 1882.

—— *On Study.*

Bretschneider, Emil, M. D.: On the Study and Value of Chinese Botanical Works, with Notes on the History of Plants and Geographical Botany From Chinese Sources. Foochow, Preface dated December 17, 1870.

Brewer and Watson *Bot. Cal.*

Botany of California. Vol. 1, Polypetalae, By W. H. Brewer and Sereno Watson. Gamopetalae, By Asa Gray. Vol. 2, By Sereno Watson. Cambridge, Mass., 1876–1880. Second (Revised) Ed.

Bridgeman, T. *Young Gard. Asst.*

Bridgeman, Thomas: Young Gardener's Assistant. Practical Directions For the Cultivation of Culinary Vegetables and Flowers, Fruit Trees, Grape Vines, etc. New York, 1857.

Britten, J. See Treasury of Botany.

Brown, C. B. *Camp Life Brit. Guiana.*

Brown, C. Barrington: Canoe and Camp Life in British Guiana. With Map and Illustrations. London, 1876.

Brown, R. See Edinborough Botanical Society Transactions.

Browne, D. J. *Trees Amer.*

Browne, Daniel Jay: The Trees of America; Native and Foreign, Pictorially and Botanically Delineated, and Scientifically and Popularly Described. New York, 1846.

Bryant, C. *Fl. Diet.*

Bryant, Charles: Flora diaetetica; or, History of esculent plants, both domestic and foreign. London, 1783.

Buckman, J. See Treasury of Botany.

Buist, R. *Fam. Kitch. Gard.*

Buist, Robert: The Family Kitchen Gardener; containing Plain and Accurate Descriptions of all the Different Species and Varieties of Culinary Vegetables. New York, 1851.

Burbidge, F. W. *Cult. Pls.*

Burbidge, Frederick William: Cultivated Plants; Their Propagation and Improvement. Edinburgh and London, 1877.

Burr, F. *Field, Gard. Veg.*

Burr, Fearing, Jr.: The Field and Garden Vegetables of America; containing Full Descriptions of Nearly Eleven Hundred Species and Varieties; with Directions for propagation, Culture and Use. Boston, 1863.

Burton, R. F. *Explor. Braz.*

Burton, Captain Richard F.: Explorations of the Highlands of the Brazil; with a full account of the Gold and Diamond Mines; also, Canoeing down 1500 miles of the Great River São Francisco, from Sabara to the Sea. London, 1869. 2 vols.

—— *Lake Reg. Cent. Afr.*

Burton, Captain Richard F.: The Lake Regions of Central Africa. A Picture of Explorations. New York, 1860.

Burton, R. F. *Pilgr. Medina, Meccah.*
Burton, Richard F.: Personal Narrative of a Pilgrimage to El-Medinah and Meccah. With Introduction by Bayard Taylor. New York, 1856.

Cal. State Bd. Hort. Rpt.
California State Board of Horticulture Reports. Sacramento, 1884.

Camerarius *Epit.*
Camerarius, Joachimus: De plantis epitome utilissima, Petri Andreae Matthioli. . . . Accessit, praeter indicem quam exactissimum, . . . auctore Francisco Calceolario. Francofurti ad Moenum, 1586.

—— *Hort. Med.*
Camerarius, Joachimus: Hortus medicus et philosophicus: in quo plurimarum stirpium breves descriptiones. Francofurti ad Moenum, 1588.

Cardanus *Rerum var.*
Cardanus, Hieronymus: De rerum varietate. Basiliae, 1581.

Captivity of Hans Stade. See Hakluyt.

Carpenter, W. B. *Veg. Phys. Bot.*
Carpenter, William Benjamin: Vegetable Physiology and Botany. London, 1844. Forming vol. 1 of the Popular Cyclopedia. Reprinted Philadelphia, 1850.

Carruthers, W. See Treasury of Botany.

Cartier, J. *Bref. Récit.*
Cartier, Jacques: Brief récit, et succinte narration, de la nauigation faicte es ysles de Canada. 1545. Reimpr. Tross. Paris, 1863.

Cartier, Jacques. *Third Voyage.* See Pinkerton Collection.

Carver, J. *Trav. No. Amer.*
Carver, Jonathan: Travels through the interior parts of North America in the years 1766, 1767, and 1768. London, 1778.

Case *Bot. Index.*
Botanical Index. An illustrated quarterly botanical magazine. Published by L. B. Case. Richmond, Ind., 1877–1881.

Cathay and the Way Thither. See Hakluyt.

Catlin, G. *No. Amer. Indians.*
Catlin, George: Letters and Notes on the Manners, Customs and Condition of the North American Indians. Written during eight years' travel amongst the wildest tribes of Indians in North America, 1832–39. New York, 1842. 2 vols.

Cato *Script. Rei Rust.* See Scriptores rei rusticae.

Chabraeus *Sciag. and Icon.*
Chabraeus, Dominicus: Omnium stirpium sciagraphia et icones, quibus plantarum et radicum tum in hortis cultarum, tum in urbium fossis . . . spontè provenientium. Genevae, 1677.

Champlain *Voyage.* See Prince Society Ed.

Church, A. H. *Food.*
Church, Arthur Herbert: Food; Some Account of the Sources, Constituents, and Uses. London, 1887.

Churchill *Coll. Voy.*

> A collection of Voyages and Travels, some Now first Printed from Original Manuscripts, others Now first Published in English. With a General Preface, giving an Account of the Progress of Navigation, from its first Beginning. Illustrated with a great Number of useful Maps and Cuts, Curiously Engraven. Printed by Assignment from Messrs. Churchill. London, 1732. 6 vols. 3rd 1744.

—— Angelo.

> A Curious and Exact Account of a Voyage to Congo In the Years 1666 and 1667 By the R. R. F. F. Michael Angelo of Gatino and Dennis de Carli of Pacenza, Capuchius and Apostolick Missioners into the said Kingdom of Congo. In Vol. 1.

—— Baumgarten.

> The Travels of Martin Baumgarten A Nobleman of Germany through Egypt, Arabia, Palestine and Syria. In Three Books. In Vol. 1.

—— Brewer.

> A Voyage To the Kingdom of Chili in America, Performed by Mr. Henry Brewer, and Mr. Elias Herckeman, In the Years 1642 and 1643 With a description of The Isle of Formosa and Japan. Translated from the High Dutch Original, Printed at Frankford upon the Maine, 1649. In Vol. 1.

—— Merolla.

> A Voyage to Congo, And Several Other Countries chiefly in Southern Africk. By Father Jerom Merolla da Sorrento, a Capuchin and Apostolick Missioner in the year 1682. Made English from the Italian. In Vol. 1.

Clusius *Hist.*

> Clusius, Carolus: Rariorum plantarum historia. Antverpiae, 1601.

Cobbett, W. *Amer. Gard.*

> Cobbett, William: The American Gardener; or, A Treatise On the situation, soil, fencing and laying-out of gardens; on the making and managing of hot-beds and green-houses; and on the propagation and cultivation of the several sorts of vegetables, herbs, fruits and flowers. New York, 1846.

Columna *Minus cognit. stirp. pars altera.*

> Columna, Fabius: Minus cognitarum stirpium pars altera. Romae, 1616.

Commelin, J. Horti med. amstelod . . . Amst. 1697–1701. 2 vols.

Conover, G. S. *Early Hist. Geneva.*

> Conover, George S.: Early History of Geneva (formerly called Kanadesaga). From the Geneva Courier, March 1879. Geneva, N. Y.

Couper *Farm. Libr.*

> Farmer's Library and Monthly Journal of Agriculture. New York, 1846–48.

Dalechamp, J. *Hist. Gen. Pls.* (Lugd.)

> Dalechamp, Jacques: Historia generalis plantarum, in libros xviii per certas classes artificiose digesta. Lugdini, Vol. 1, 1587; vol. 2, 1586

Dall, W. H. *Alaska.*

> Dall, William H.: Alaska and Its Resources. Boston, 1897.

Dalyrmple *Coll. Voy.*

> Dalyrmple, Alexander: Collection of Voyages in the South Pacific Ocean. London, 1770–71.

Darlington, W. *Weeds, Useful Pls.*
> Darlington, William: American Weeds and Useful Plants. New York, 1863.

Darwin, C. *Ans. Pls. Domest.*
> Darwin, Charles: The Variation of Animals and Plants Under Domestication. Second Ed., Revised. London, 1893. 2 vols.

———— *Voy. H. M. S. Beagle.*
> Darwin, Charles: Journal of Researches into the Natural History and Geology of the Countries Visited During the Voyage of H. M. S. Beagle Round the World, under the Command of Capt. Fitz Roy, R. N. New York, 1884.

Daubeny, C. *Trees, Shrubs Anc.*
> Daubeny, Charles Giles Bridle: Essay on the Trees and Shrubs of the Ancients: Being the Substance of Four Lectures Delivered before The University of Oxford. Oxford and London, 1865.

Decaisne and Naudin *Man. Jard.*
> Decaisne, Joseph and Naudin, Charles: Manuel de l'Amateur des Jardins; Traité Général d'Horticulture. Paris, (1862–66).

De Candolle, A. *Geog. Bot.*
> De Candolle, Alphonse: Géographie Botanique Raisonnée ou Exposition des Faits Principaux et des Lois Concernant la Distribution Géographique des Plantes de l'Époque Actuelle. Deux Tomes. Paris, 1855.

———— *Orig. Cult. Pls.*
> De Candolle, Alphonse: Origin of Cultivated Plants. New York, 1885.

De Candolle, Alphonse P. See London Horticultural Society Transactions.

De Candolle, A. P. *Veg. Organ.*
> De Candolle, Augustin Pyramus: Organographie végétale. Paris, 1827. English translation, Vegetable Organography, by B. Kingdon. London, 1839–40. Second Ed. New York, 1840. 2 vols.

De Candolle, A. & C. *Monog.*
> Monographiae Phaneroganum. Prodromi nunc continuatio, nunc revisio. Vol. 3 containing among others Cucurbitaceae by Alfred Cogniaux. Paris, 1881.

De Candolle and LaMarck *Flore Franc.*
> De Candolle, A. P. and LaMarck, J. B.: Flore française. Paris, 1805. 4 vols. Third Ed. Paris, 1815. 5 vols.

Delile, A. R. *Mem. Pls. Cult. Egypt.*
> Delile, Alire Raffeneau: Flore d'Égypte. Second Ed. Paris, 1824. First Ed. appeared in Mémoires botaniques.

De Morga *Philippine Islands.*   See Hakluyt.

Descourtilz, M. E. *Fl. Antill.*
> Descourtilz, Michel Étienne: Flore pittoresque et médicale des Antilles. Paris, 1827–33. 8 vols.

Description of Georgia.   See Force Collection.

Description of New Albion.   See Force Collection.

De Soto *Discovery and Conquest of Florida.*   See Hakluyt.

Dewey, C. *Rpt. Herb. Flow. Pls. Mass.*

Dewey, Chester: Report on the Herbaceous Flowering Plants of Massachusetts, Arranged According to the Natural Orders of Lindley, and Illustrated Chiefly by Popular Descriptions of their Character, Properties, and Uses. Cambridge, Mass., 1840.

Dickie, G. D. See Treasury of Botany.

Dillenius *Hort. Elth.*

Dillenius, Johannes Jacobus: Horti Elthamensis plantarum rariorum icones et nomina . . . Additis denominationibus Linnaeanis. Lugduni Batavorum, 1774. 2 vols. in one.

Dioscorides (Amatus Lusitanus Ed.)

In Dioscoridis Anazarbei de medica materia libros quinque enarrationes eruditissimae Doctoris Amati Lusitani. Argentorati, 1554.

———— (Ruellius Ed.)

P. Dioscoridae pharmacorum simplicium, reique medicae libri viii. Io. Ruellio interprete. Argentorati, 1529.

———— (Vergelius Ed.)

Pedacii Dioscoridae Anazarbei simplicium medicamentorum . . . Interprete Marcello Vergilio Secretario Florentino. Basiliae, 1532.

Disraeli, I. *Curios. Lit.*

Disraeli, Isaac: Curiosities of Literature. With a View of the Life and writings of the Author by his son. Boston, 1858. 4 vols.

Dobrizhoffer *Acct. Abipones.*

Dobrizhoffer, Martin: An account of the Abipones, an equestrian people of Paraguay. Translated from the Latin. London, 1822. 3 vols.

Dodge. See U. S. Dept. of Agriculture.

Dodonaeus *Frument.*

Dodonaeus, Rembertus (Dodoens): Frumentorum, leguminum, palustrium et aquatilium herbarum, ac eorum, quae eo pertinent, historia . . . Antverpiae, 1566.

———— *Pempt.*

Dodonaeus, Rembertus (Dodoens): Stirpium historiae pemptades sex, sive libri xxx. Antverpiae, 1583.

Dodoens *Herb.* Lyte Ed.

Dodoens, Rembert: A nieuve herball, or historie of plantes: wherein is contayned the whole discourse and perfect description of all sortes of herbes and plantes: their divers & sundry kindes: Translated out of French into English by Henry Lyte Esquyer. London, 1578.

Don, G. *Hist. Dichl. Pls.*

Don, George: History of Dichladymeous Plants. London, 1831–38. 4 vols. Founded on Miller's Garden Dictionary but never completed.

Doolittle, J. *Social Life Chinese.*

Doolittle, Rev. Justus: Social Life of the Chinese. A Daguerreotype of daily Life in China. Edited and Revised by the Rev. Paxton Hood. London, 1868.

Downing, A. J. *Fr. Fr. Trees Amer.*
Downing, Andrew J.: The Fruits and Fruit Trees of America: or the culture, propagation and management, in the garden and orchard, of fruit trees generally with Descriptions of All The Finest Varieties of Fruit,— First Revision by Charles Downing. New York, 1857. Second Revision by Charles Downing. New York, 1869.

Drury, H. *Useful Pls. Ind.*
Drury, Major Heber: The Useful Plants of India Alphabetically Arranged With Botanical Descriptions, Vernacular Synonyms, and Notices of Their Economical Value in Commerce, Medicine and the Arts. Madras, 1858.

Du Chaillu, P. B. *Land Midnight Sun.*
Du Chaillu, Paul B.: The Land of the Midnight Sun; Summer and Winter Journeys through Sweden, Norway, Lapland and Northern Finland. New York, 1882. 2 vols.

Dunal, M. F. *Synop. Solan.*
Solanorum . . . synopsis. Monspelii, 1816.

Durante, C. *Herb.*
Durante, Castor: Herbario novo. Venetia, 1617.

Dutt, U. C. *Mat. Med. Hindus.*
Dutt, Udoy Chand: The Materia Medica of the Hindus, Compiled from Sanskrit Medical Works. With a Glossary of Indian Plants, By George King. Calcutta, 1877.

Dyer, W. T. See Treasury of Botany.

Eden *Hist. Trav.*
Eden, Rycharde: History of Travel. London, 1577.

Edinb. Bot. Soc. Trans.
Transactions of the Botanical Society. Edinburgh, Scotland: Printed For the Botanical Society. Vol. VI, 1860; VII, 1863; VIII, 1866; IX, 1868; X, 1870.

Eliot, J. *Essays Husb.*
Eliot, Jared: Essays on Field Husbandry. 1811. (Massachusetts agricultural repository and journal.)

Elliott, S. *Bot. So. Car., Ga.*
Elliott, Stephen: A Sketch of the Botany of South-Carolina and Georgia. Charleston, S. C., Vol. 1, 1821; vol. 2, 1824.

Ellis, W. *Polyn. Research.*
Ellis, William: Polynesian Researches, during a Residence of Nearly Eight Years in the Society and Sandwich Islands. New York, 1833. 4 vols.

Ellis, W. *Three Visits Madagas.*
Ellis, Rev. William: Three Visits to Madagascar During the Years 1853–1854–1856. Including a Journey To The Capital; With Notices of the Natural History of The Country and Of The Present Civilization of the People. New York, 1859.

Emerson, G. B. *Trees, Shrubs Mass.*
Emerson, George B.: A Report on the Trees and Shrubs Growing Naturally In The Forests of Massachusetts. Second Ed. Boston, 1875.

Enc. Brit.

> The Encyclopaedia Brittanica or Dictionary of Arts, Sciences, and General Literature. Eighth Ed. With Extensive Improvements and Additions; and Numerous Engravings. Vol. 17 Boston, 1859. (Containing quotation by Fraser on buckwheat.) Vol. 21 1860. (Containing article on tea by several authors.) 22 vols. 22nd (1860) being index.

Englemann *Bot. Works.*

> Englemann, George: Botanical Works. Cambridge, Mass., 1887.

Fendler, A., and Gray, A.: Plantae fendlerianae. Boston, 1849.

Fessenden *New Amer. Gard.*

> Fessenden, Thomas Green: New American Gardener; containing practical directions on the culture of fruits and vegetables. Boston, 1828.

Feuillée *Peru.*

> Feuillée, Louis: Descriptions of medicinal plants which are in particular use in the South American countries of Peru and Chile. Paris, 1725.

———— *Obs.*

> Feuillée, Louis: Journal des observations physiques, mathématiques et botaniques. Paris, vols. 1 and 2, 1714; vol. 3, 1725. Contains many botanical plates and descriptions, especially in vol. 3.

Field, T. W. *Pear Cult.*

> Field, Thomas W.: Pear Culture: A manual For the Propagation, Planting, Cultivation and Management of The Pear Tree. New York, 1859.

Figuier, L. *Veg. World.*

> Figuier, Louis: The Vegetable World; Being a History of Plants, With their Botanical Descriptions and Peculiar Properties. London, 1867.

Firminger, T. A. C. *Gard. Ind.*

> Firminger, Thomas A. C.: A Manual of Gardening for Bengal and Upper India. Third Ed. Calcutta and London, 1874.

Fletcher, J. C. and Kidder, D. P. *Braz.*

> Fletcher, Rev. James C. and Kidder, Rev. D. P.: Brazil and The Brazilians portrayed in Historical and Descriptive Sketches. Boston, 1879.

Flint, C. L. *Grasses, Forage Pls.*

> Flint, Charles Louis: Grasses and Forage Plants. A Practical Treatise comprising Their Natural History; comparative Nutritive Value, etc. Boston, 1867.

Flint, T. *West. States.*

> Flint, Timothy: A Condensed Geography and History of the Western States, or The Mississippi Valley. Cincinnati, 1828. 2 vols.

Flückiger, F. A.: *Science Record.* 1874.

Flückiger and Hanbury *Pharm.*

> Flückiger, Frederich A. and Hanbury, Daniel: Pharmacographia; A History Of The Principal Drugs Of Vegetable Origin Met With in Great Britain and British India. London, 1874. Second Ed. 1879.

Force Coll. Tracts.

> Tracts and Other Papers, Relating Principally to the Origin, Settlement, and Progress of the Colonies in North America, From the Discovery of the Country to the Year 1776. Collected by Peter Force. Washington: Printed by Peter Force. Vol. 2, 1838; vol. 3, 1844.

Force Coll. Tracts *Desc. Ga.*

A Description of Georgia, by a gentleman who has resided there upwards of seven Years, and was one of the first settlers. London, 1741. 8 pages. 2: No. 12. 1838.

—— Hilton, W. *Rel. Disc. Fla.*

A Relation of a Discovery lately made on the Coast of Florida By William Hilton Commander, and a Commissioner with Capt. Anthony Long, and Peter Fabian, in the Ship Adventure. 1664. 27 pages. 4: No. 2. 1846.

—— *Perf. Desc. Va.*

A Perfect Description of Virginia: being, a full and true Relation of the present State of the plantation — also, A Narration of the Countrey, within a few days journey of Virginia, West and by South where people come to trade: being related to the Gouvernour, Sir William Berckley,— London, 1649. 20 pages. 2: No. 8. 1838.

—— *Plaine Desc. Barmudas.*

A Plaine Description of the Barmudas, now called Sommer Ilands. With the manner of their discoverie Anno 1609, by the shipwrack and admirable deliverance of Sir Thomas Gates, and Sir George Sommers, wherein are truly set forth the commodities and profits of that Rich, Pleasant, and Healthfull Countrie. 1613. 24 pages. 2: No. 3. 1838.

—— Plantagent *Desc. New Albion.*

A Description of the Province of New Albion, and a Direction for Adventurers with small stock to get two for one, and good land freely:— and a former Description reprinted of the healthiest, pleasantest, and richest Plantation of New Albion in North Virginia, proved by thirteen witnesses. 1648. 36 pages. 2: No. 7. 1838.

—— Shrigley *True Rel. Va., Md.*

A True Relation of Virginia and Mary-land; with the Commodities therein, which in part the Author saw; the rest he had from knowing and credible persons, by Nathaniel Shrigley. London, 1669. 8 pages. 3: No. 7. 1844.

—— Smith, J. *Desc. New Eng.*

A Description of New England: or the Observations and Discoveries of Captain John Smith in the North of America, in the Year of our Lord 1614:— London, 1616. 48 pages. 2: No. 1. 1838.

—— *True Decl. Va.*

A True Declaration of the estate of the Colonie in Virginia, with a confutation of such scandalous reports as have tended to the disgrace of so worthy an enterprise. Published by advice and direction of the Councill of Virginia. London, 1610. 28 pages. 3: No. 1. 1844.

—— White, A. *Rel. Md.*

A Relation of the Colony of the Lord Bacon of Baltimore, in Md. near Virginia; a Narrative of the Voyage to Maryland, by Father Andrew White; and sundry reports from Fathers Andrew White, John Altham, John Brock, and other Jesuit Fathers of the Company, to Superior General at Rome. 48 pages. no date. 4: No. 3. 1846

Forme of Cury. See Antiquitates Culinariae.

Forskal, P. *Fl. Aeg. Arab.*

Forskal, Petrus: Flora Aegyptiaco-Arabica sive Descriptiones Plantarum, quas per Aegyptum Inferiorem et Arabiam Felicem Detexit, Illustravit. Post Mortem Auctoris Edidit Carsten Niebuhr. Hauniae, 1775.

Forster, J. R. *Obs.*
    Forster, John Reinold: Observations made during a Voyage Round the World, on Physical Geography, Natural History, and Ethic Philosophy. London, 1778.

—— *Fl. Amer. Septent.*
    Forster, John Reinold: Florae Americae septentrionalis. London, 1771.

Fortune, R. *Resid. Chinese.*
    Fortune, Robert: A Residence Among the Chinese: Inland, on the Coast, and At Sea. Being a Narrative of Scenes and Adventures During a Third Visit to China, from 1853 to 1856. Including notices of many natural productions and works of art, the culture of silk, &c. With Suggestions on the Present War. London, 1857.

—— *Wand. China.*
    Fortune, Robert: Wanderings in China. London, 1847.

Franklin, J. *Narr. Journ. Polar Sea.*
    Franklin, Capt. John: Narrative of a Journey To the Shores of The Polar Sea, in the Years 1819–22. With an Appendix on Various Subjects Relating to Science and Natural History. London, 1823.

Fraser, J. B. *Mesopotamia.*
    Fraser, J. Baillie: Mesopotamia and Assyria, from the Earliest Ages to the Present Time; with Illustrations of their natural History. Edinburgh, 1842.

Fremont, J. C. *Explor. Exped.*
    Fremont, John Charles: Report of the exploring expedition to the Rocky mountains, Oregon and California. Washington, 1845.

Frezier *Rel. Voy.*
    Frezier, Amadée François: Relation du voyage de la Mer de Sud aux côtes du Chily et du Pérou, fait pendant les années 1712, 1713, & 1714......Paris, 1732.

Fuchsius *Hist. Stirp.*
    Fuchsius, Leonhartus: De historia stirpium commentarii insignes. Basileae, 1542.

Fuller, A. S. *Sm. Fr. Cult.*
    Fuller, Andrew Samuel: The Small Fruit Culturist. New York, 1867.

Galen *De Aliment.*
    Galenus, Claudius: De alimentorum facultatibus libri tres. Lugdini, 1547.

Gallesio, G. Traité du Citrus. Paris, 1811.

Gard. and For.
    Garden and Forest: A Journal of Horticulture, Landscape Art and Forestry. Conducted by Charles S. Sargent. Illustrated. Vol. I–X. New York, 1888–1897.

Gard. Chron.
    The Gardener's Chronicle; A weekly illustrated journal of horticulture. London, 1841.

Gardiner and Hepburn *Amer. Gard.*
    American Gardener. New Ed. Georgetown, D. C., 1818.

Gardner, G. *Trav. Braz.*
    Gardner, George: Travels in the Interior of Brazil, the Northern Provinces, and the Gold and Diamond Districts. London, 1846.

Gasparin *Cours Agr.*
Cours d'Agriculture. Troisième Édition. Tome Quatrième. Paris. No date.

General Collections of the Voyages of the Portugese. 1789.

Geoffrey *Materia Medica.* 1841.

Gerarde, J. *Herb.*
The Herball or generall historie of plantes. Gathered by John Gerarde of London, Master in Chirurgerie. First Ed. London, 1597. Enlarged and amended by Thomas Johnson. 1636. Also a 1633 Ed.

Gibbon, L. *Valley of the Amazon.* See Herndon and Gibbon.

Glasspoole, H. G. *Rpt. Ohio State Bd. Agr.*
Twenty Ninth Annual Report of the Ohio State Board of Agriculture For the Year 1874. Article by Glasspoole, on the history of our common cultivated vegetables, 412–450.

Gmelin, J. G. *Fl. Sibir.*
Gmelin, Joannes Georgius: Flora Sibirica sive historia plantarum Sibiriae. Petropoli, vol. 1, 1747; vol. 2, 1749; vol. 3, 1768; vol. 4, 1769. Vols. 3 and 4 edited by Samuel Gottlieb Gmelin.

Gordon, G. and Glendinning, R. *Pinetum.*
The Pinetum: being a Synopsis of All the Coniferous Plants at present known, with Descriptions, History and Synonyms, and a comprehensive systematic index. Second Ed. London, 1875. First Ed. London, 1858. Supplement 1862. Second Ed. Index by H. G. Bohn, 1875.

Grandsagne *Hist. Nat. Pline.*
de Grandsagne, Ajasson: Histoire naturelle de Pline. Traduction nouvelle. Paris, 1829–1833. 20 vols.

Gray, A. *Bot. U. S. Explor. Exped.*
Gray, Asa: United States Exploring Expedition During the Years 1838, 1839, 1840, 1841, 1842 Under the Command of Charles Wilkes, U. S. N. Vol. XV Botany Phanerogamia by Asa Gray, M.D. Part 1. Philadelphia, 1854.

—— *Flora of North America.* See Torrey and Gray.

—— *Man. Bot.*
Gray, Asa: Manual of the Botany of the Northern United States. Boston and Cambridge, 1848. Many editions and extensions.

—— and Trumbull in Amer. Journ. Sci. and Arts. See American Journal of Science and Arts.

—— *Synopt. Fl. No. Amer.*
Gray, Asa: Synoptical Flora of North America; The Gamopetalae. Being a Second Ed. of Vol. 1 Part 2 and Vol. 2 Part 1, collected. Published By The Smithsonian Institution, Washington. New York, 1886.

Gregorius: De Siliquastris in genere; See Clusius, Carolus. Curae Posteriores....pages 105–108.

Griffith, W. *Med. Bot.*
Griffith, William: Medical Botany. 1847.

Griffith, W.   *Palms Brit. Ind.*

Griffith, William: Palms of British East India. Arranged by John McLelland. Calcutta, 1850.

Grisebach, A. H. R.   *Fl. Brit. W. Ind.*

Grisebach, August Heinrich Rudolph: Flora of the British West Indian Islands. London, 1864.

Gronovius *Fl. Orient.*

Gronovius, Johan. Fredericus: Flora Orientalis sive recensio plantarum, quas botanicorum coryphaeus Leonhardus Rauwolffus......annis 1573, 74, 75......observit, & collegit......Lugduni Batavorum, 1755.

———— *Fl. Virg.*

Gronovius, Johan. Fredericus: Flora Virginica exhibens plantas, quas nobilissimus vir D. D. Johannes Claytonus......in Virginia crescentes observavit, collegit and obtulit......Lugduni Batavorum, 1762.

Guizot, F. P. G.   *Hist. Civil.*

The History of Civilization from the Fall of the Roman Empire to the French Revolution. Translated by William Hazlitt. New York, 1856.   3 vols.

Hakluyt Society Publications. Vols. 1–79. London, 1847–89.

———— Acosta, J.   *Nat. Mor. Hist. Ind.*

The Natural and Moral History of the Indies, by Father Joseph de Acosta.   Reprinted from the English Translated Edition of Edward Grimston, 1604, and edited by Clements R. Markham. London, 1880.

———— Andagoya, P.   *Narrative.*

Narrative of The Proceeding of Pedrarias Davila Written by The Adelantado Pascual De Andagoya. Translated by Clements R. Markham. London, 1865.

———— Benzoni   *Hist. New World.*

History of the New World By Girolamo Benzoni of Milan Shewing His Travels in America, From A. D. 1541 to 1556: Translated and Edited by Rear Admiral W. H. Smyth. London, 1857.

———— *Captiv. Hans Stade.*

The Captivity of Hans Stade of Hesse, in A. D. 1547–1555, Among the wild Tribes of Eastern Brazil. Translated by Albert Tootal, Esq., of Rio de Janiero, and annotated by Richard F. Burton. London, 1874.

———— *Cathay, Way Thither.*

Cathay and the Way Thither; being a collection of Medieval Notices of China, Translated and Edited By Colonel Henry Yule, C. B. with a Preliminary Essay. London, 1866.

———— Columbus *Sel. Letters.*

Select Letters of Christopher Columbus With Other original Documents, Relating to His Four Voyages to The New World. Translated and Edited by R. H. Major, Esq. Of The British Museum. London, 1847.

———— De Morga *Philip. Islands.*

The Philippine Islands Mulaccas, Siam, Cambodia, Japan & China, At the Close of The Sixteenth Century By Antonia de Morga Translated from the Spanish by Henry E. J. Stanley. London, 1868.

Hakluyt Society Publications. De Soto *Disc. Conq. Fla.*

    The Discovery and Conquest of Terra Florida, by Don Ferdinando de Soto, and six
    hundred Spaniards his followers. Written by a gentleman of Elvas, employed
    in all the action, and translated out of Portuguese, By Sir Richard Hakluyt.
    Reprinted from the edition of 1611. Edited, With Notes and an Introduction,
    and a translation of a Narrative of the Expedition by Luis Hernandez de Biedma,
    factor to the same, By William B. Rye, of the British Museum. London, 1851.

—— Hakluyt, R. *Divers Voy. Amer.*

    Divers Voyages Touching The Discovery of America And the Island Adjacent Collected
    and Published By Sir Richard Hakluyt Edited by John Winter Jones Of British
    Museum. London, 1850.

—— Hawkins, R. *Voy. So. Seas.*

    The Observations of Sir Richard Hawkins, Knt. in his Voyage into The South Sea
    in the Year 1593. Reprinted from the Edition of 1622. Edited by C. R. Drink-
    water Bethune, Captain R. N. London, 1847.

—— Jones, J. W. *Trav. Varthema.*

    The Travels of Ludovico di Varthema in Egypt, Syria, Arabia Deserta and Arabia
    Felix, in Persia, India and Ethiopia, A. D. 1503 to 1508. Translated From the
    Original Italian Edition of 1510, with a preface, by John Winter Jones, Esq.
    and Edited, with notes and an introduction, By George Percy Badger. London,
    1863.

—— Jordanus *Wonders East.*

    Mirabilla Descripta. The Wonders of the East, By Friar Jordanus, of the order
    of Preachers and Bishop of Columbum in India the Greater, (circa 1330). Trans-
    lated from the Latin Original, as published at Paris in 1839, in the Recueil de
    Voyages et de Memories, of the Society of Geography, with the addition of a
    commentary, By Colonel Henry Yule, C. B. London, 1863.

—— Markham, C. R. *Trav. Cieza de Leon.*

    The Travels of Pedro de Cieza de Leon, A. D. 1532–50, contained in the First Part
    of His Chronicle of Peru. Translated and Edited, with notes and an introduction
    By Clements R. Markham. London, 1864.

—— Raleigh, R. *Disc. Guiana.*

    The Discovery of the Large, rich, and Beautiful Empire of Guiana with a relation of
    The Great and Golden City of Manoa Performed in the year 1595, by Sir W.
    Raleigh, Knt. Reprinted from the Edition of 1596, with some Unpublished
    Documents Relative to that country. Edited, with copious explanatory notes
    and a biographical memoir, by Sir Robert H. Schomburgk, Ph. D. London,
    1848.

—— Schiltberger, J. *Bondage, Trav.*

    The Bondage and Travels of Johann Schiltberger In Europe, Asia and Africa 1396–
    1427. Translated by Commander J. Buchan Telfer, R. N. London, 1879.

—— Strachey, W. *Trav. Va.*

    The Historie of Travaile into Virginia Britannia; expressing the Cosmographie and
    Commodities of the Country, together with the manners and customes of the
    people. William Strachey, Gent., The First Secretary of the Colony. Edited
    by R. H. Major. London, 1849.

Hakluyt Society Publications.   Vega, G. de la *Roy. Comment.*
> Royal Commentaries of The Yncas by the Ynca Garcillaso de la Vega.   Translated and Edited, With Notes and an Introduction, By Clements R. Markman.   2 vols. London, 1869–1871.

Hakluyt Voyages.
> The Principal Navigations Voyages Traffiques & Discoveries Of the English Nation Made by Sea or Over-land to the Remote and Farthest Distant Quarters Of the Earth at any time within the Compasse of these 1600 yeeres.   By Richard Hakluyt.   Glasgow: 1904.

—— Masham, Thomas   *Raleghs Third Voyage.*
> The 3 Voyage set forth by Sir Walter Ralegh to Guiana with a pinnesse called The Wat, begun in the yere 1596, written by M. Thomas Masham a gentleman of the company.   Hakluyt 11: 14.   1904.

—— May, Henry   *Voyage.*
> A briefe note of a voyage to the East Indies, begun the 10 of April 1591, wherein were three tall ships, the Penelope of Captain Raimond, Admirall, ...:......... ....Written by Henry May, who in his returne homeward by the West Indies suffered shipwracke upon the Isle of Bermuda.   Hakluyt 10:   1904.

—— Nicols, Thomas.
> A Description of the fortunate Ilands, otherwise called the Ilands of Canaria, with their strange fruits and commodities, composed by Thomas Nicols Englishman, who remained there the space of seven years together.   Hakluyt 6:   1904.

—— Preston and Sommers   *Voyage.*
> The victorious voyage of Captaine Anias Preston now knight, and Captaine George Sommers to the West India, begun in March 1595.   Wherein the yle of Puerto Santo, the yle of Coche neare Margarita, the fort and towne of Coro, the stately city of S. Iago de Leon were taken sacked and burned and the town of Cumana ransomed and Jamaica entered.   Written by Robert Diare one of the company.

Hallam, H.   *Lit. Europe.*
> Hallam, Henry: Introduction to the Literature of Europe In the Fifteenth, Sixteenth and Seventeenth Centuries.   New York, 1856.   2 vols.

Hanbury, D.   *Sci. Papers.*
> Hanbury, Daniel: Science Papers, chiefly Pharmacological and Botanical.   Edited, with memoir, by Joseph Ince.   London, 1876.

Hariot, T.   *Narrative Va.* Quaritch Reprint.
> Hariot, Thomas: Narrative Of The First English Plantation of Virginia.   First printed at London in 1588 now reproduced after De Bry's illustrated ed. printed at Frankfort in 1590.   The illustrations having been designed in Virginia in 1585.   By John White.   London, 1893.

Harshberger, J. W.   *Maize.*
> Contributions from the Botanical Laboratory of the University of Pennsylvania. Philadelphia, 1893.   Maize — A   Botanical and Economic Study.   John W. Harshberger.   1: No. 2.   1893.

Hartt, C. F. *Geog. Braz.*
Hartt, Charles Fred: Geology and Physical Geography of Brazil. Scientific Results of A Journey in Brazil. By Louis Agassiz and his traveling companions; The Thayer Expedition. Boston, 1870.

Harvey, W. H. *Man. Brit. Algae.*
Harvey, William Henry: Manual of The British Algae containing Generic and Specific Descriptions of all The British Species of Sea-Weeds, Confervae, Both Marine and Fresh-Water. London, 1841.

——— *Phycol. Brit.*
Harvey, William Henry: Phycologia Brittanica or A History of British Sea-Weeds, Containing Coloured Figures, Generic and Specific Characters, Synonymes, and Descriptions of All the Species of Algae Inhabiting the Shores of The British Islands. London, 1846–1851.

Havard, V. See Torrey Botanical Club Bulletins and United States National Museum.

Hawkins, R. *Voy. So. Seas.*
Hawkins, Sir Richard: Voyage into the South Seas. 1593. See Hakluyt.

Hazard, S. *Annals Pa.*
Hazard, Samuel: Annals of Pennsylvania, from the Discovery of the Delaware. 1609–1682. Philadelphia, 1850.

Henfrey, A. *Bot.*
Henfrey, Arthur: An Elementary Course of Botany, Structural, Physiological and Systematic. Second Ed. Revised, and in part Re-written By Maxwell T. Masters, M.D. London, 1870.

Hennepin *Voy.*
Hennepin, Father Louis: *Voyage.* See Amer. Antiq. Soc. 1820.

Hernandez *Nova Hist. Mex.*
Hernandez, Father: Nova Plantarum, Animalium et Mineralium Mexicanorum Historia. Romae, 1651.

Herndon, W. L. and Gibbon, L. *Explor. Vall. Amaz.*
Herndon, William Lewis and Gibbon, Lardner: Exploration of the Valley of the Amazon, Made under direction of The Navy Department. Vol. 1 By Lieut. Herndon. Vol. 2 By Lieut. Gibbon. Washington, 1854.

Herrera *Hist. Amer.*
Herrera, Antonio de: General history of the vast continent and islands of America, commonly called the West-Indies, from the first discovery thereof. Translation by John Stevens. London, 1725. 6 vols.

Heuze, G. *Pls. Aliment.*
Heuze, Gustave: Les plantes alimentaires. Paris, 1873.

Higginson, Rev. Francis *New England's Plantation.* 1630. See Massachusetts Historical Society Collections.

Hippocrates *Opera* Cornarius Ed.
Hippocratis coi medicorum omnium longe principis, opera quae apud nos extant omnia. Per Ianum Cornarium......conscripta. Parisiis, 1546.

Hilton *Relation of Florida.* See Force Collection.

Hist. Gen. Pl. See Dalechamps.

Hist. Mass. Hort. Soc.
> History of the Massachusetts Horticultural Society. 1829–1878. Edited by Robert Manning. Boston, 1880.

Hobday, E.   *Cottage Gard.*
> Cottage Gardening; or, Flowers, fruits, and vegetables for small gardens. London, 1878.

Hodge, H. C.   *Arizona.*
> Hodge, Hiram C.: Arizona As It Is; or, The Coming Country. Compiled from Notes of Travel During the Years 1874, 1875, and 1876. New York, Boston, Cambridge, 1877.

Hooker, J. D.   *Bot. Antarctic Voy.*
> Hooker, Joseph Dalton, M. D.: Botany of The Antarctic Voyage of H. M. Discovery Ships Erebus and Terror in the Years 1839–1843, Under the Command of Captain Sir James Clark Ross. London, Vol. 1, 1844; vol. 2, 1847.

——— *Fl. Brit. Ind.*
> Hooker, Joseph Dalton: Flora of British India. London, 1872. Assisted by several other botanists.

——— *Himal. Journ.*
> Hooker, Joseph Dalton, M.D.: Himalayan Journals or Notes of a Naturalist in Bengal, The Sikkim and Nepal Himalayas The Khasia Mountains &c. With Maps and Illustrations. London, 1854. 2 vols.

——— *Illustr. Himal. Pls.*
> Hooker, Joseph Dalton, M.D.: Illustrations of Himalayan plants. London, 1855.

——— **and Ball** *Marocco, Gt. Atlas.*
> Hooker, Joseph Dalton and Ball, John: Journal of A Tour in Marocco and The Great Atlas. With an Appendix including A Sketch of the Geology of Marocco, by George Maw. London, 1878.

Hooker, W. J.   *Bot. Misc.*
> Hooker, Sir William Jackson: Botanical Miscellany containing Figures and Descriptions of Such Plants As Recomment Themselves By Their Novelty, Rarity or History or by The Uses to Which they are applied in The Arts, In Medicine and In Domestic Oeconomy; Together with Occasional Botanical Notices and Information. 3 vols. London: Vol. 1, 1830; vol. 2, 1831; vol. 3, 1833.

——— *Fl. Bor. Amer.*
> Hooker, Sir William Jackson: Flora Boreali-Americana; or, the Botany of the Northern Parts of British America: Compiled principally from The Plants collected by Dr. Richardson and Mr. Drummond on the late northern expeditions, under command of Captain Sir John Franklin, R. N. to which are added those of Mr. Douglas, from north-west America, and of other naturalists. London, 1840. 2 vols.

——— *Journ. Bot.*
> Hooker, Sir William Jackson: The Journal of Botany, Being a second series of the Botanical Miscellany; containing Figures and Descriptions of Such Plants as Recommend Themselves by Their Novelty, Rarity, or History, Or by the Uses to which they are applied In the Arts, in Medicine, and in Domestic Oeconomy. 4 vols. London, Vol. 1, 1834; vol. 2, 1840; vol. 3, 1841; vol. 4, 1842.

Hooker, W. J. *Journ. Bot.*
   Hooker, Sir William Jackson: Journal of Botany and Kew Garden Miscellany. London,˙ 1849–57.   9 vols.

—— *Lond. Journ. Bot.*
   Hooker, Sir William Jackson: London Journal of Botany.   London, 1842–48.   5 vols.

Hortus Eystet.
   Hortus eystettensis.   Probable author is Besler.   1613.

Horto, G. ab. *Aromatum.*
   Horto, Garcia ab: Aromatum, et simplicium aliquot medicamentorum apud Indos nascentium historia . . . Nunc vero primum Latina facta & in Epitomen contracta à Carolo Clusio Atrebate.

Hough, F. B. *Elem. For.*
   Hough, Franklin B.: The Elements of Forestry Designed to Afford Information Concerning the Planting and Care of Forest Trees For Ornament or Profit and Giving Suggestion upon The Creation and Care of Woodlands.   Cincinnati, 1882.

Hughes, G. *Nat. Hist. Barb.*
   Hughes, Rev. Griffith: The Natural History of Barbadoes.   In ten books.   London, 1750.

Humboldt, A. *Polit. Essay New Spain.*
   Humboldt, Alexander de: Political Essay on the Kingdom of New Spain.   Translated from the Original French, By John Black.   New York, 1811.   2 vols.

—— *Trav.*
   Humboldt, Alexander de: Personal Narrative of Travels to the Equinoctial Regions of America, during the years 1799–1804.   By Alexander Von Humboldt and Aime Bonpland.   Written in French by Alexander Von Humboldt: Translated and Edited by Thomasina Ross.   London, 1889.   3 vols.

—— *Views Nat.*
   Humboldt, Alexander de: Views of Nature: or Contemplations on The Sublime Phenomena of Creation; with Scientific Illustrations.   Translated from the German By E. C. Otte, and Henry G. Bohn.   London, 1850.

Humboldt, F. A. von and Bonpland, A.:   La géographie des plantes.   Paris, 1805.

Hutchinson *Hist. Mass.*
   History of the Colony of Massachusetts-Bay, with a Collection of original papers relative to the history of the colony.   By Gov. Thomas Hutchinson.   Third Ed. Salem, Mass. and London, 1795–1828.   3 vols.

Ibn-al-Awam. *Livre d'Agr.*
   Le livre de l'agriculture.   Traduit de l'Arabe par J. J. Clement-Mullet.   Paris. Vol. 1, 1864; vol. 2, part 1, 1866; vol. 2, part 2, 1867.   2 vols. in one.   From the twelfth century, A.D.

Illinois Agricultural Society, Transactions of.   Springfield, Ill.   1855–71.

Illinois Horticultural Society, Transactions of.   Chicago, Ill.   1861–1913.

Irving, W. *Astoria.*
   Irving, Washington: Astoria or, Anecdotes of an Enterprise beyond the Rocky Mountains.   Author's Revised Ed.   New York, 1849.

Irving, W. *Advent. Capt. Bonneville.*

Irving, Washington: The Adventures of Captain Bonneville, U. S. A., in the Rocky Mountains and the Far West. Digested from his Journal and Illustrated from Various other Sources. Author's Revised Ed. New York, 1849.

—— *Columbus.*

Irving, Washington: The Life and Voyages of Christopher Columbus; to which are added those of His Companions. Author's Revised Ed. New York, Vol. 1, 1848; vol. 2, 3, 1847. 3 vols.

Jackson, J. R. See Treasury of Botany.

Jard. Solit.

Jardinier solitaire, ou dialogues entre un curieux & un jardinier solitaire. Contenant la méthode de faire & de cultiver un jardin fruitier & potager......Quatrième Ed. Paris, 1612.

Jefferson, T. *Notes Va.*

Jefferson, Thomas: Notes on the State of Virginia — with a map of Virginia, Maryland, Delaware and Pennsylvania. Philadelphia, 1801.

Jefferys, T. *Nat. Hist. Amer.*

Jefferys, Thomas: The Natural and Civil History of the French Dominions in North and South America Giving a particular account of the Climate, Soil, Minerals, Animals, Vegetables, Manufactures, Trade, Commerce and Language. London, Part 1, 1760; Part 2, 1761.

Johns, C. A. See Treasury of Botany.

Jonstonus *Dendrograph.*

Jonstonus, Johannes: Dendrographias sive historiae naturalis de arboribus et fructibus......Francofurti ad Moenum, 1662.

Johnson, C. P. *Useful Pls. Gt. Brit.*

Johnson, C. Pierpont: The Useful Plants of Great Britain: A Treatise Upon the Principal Native Vegetables Capable of Application as Food, Medicine, or in the Arts and Manufactures. London, 1862.

Jones, J. W. *Travels of Varthema.* See Hakluyt.

Jordanus, Father *Wonders of the East.* See Hakluyt.

Josselyn, J. *New Eng. Rar.*

Josselyn, John: New-England's Rarities Discovered in Birds, Beasts, Fishes, Serpents and Plants of That Country With an Introduction and Notes by Edward Tuckerman, M. A. Boston, 1865. Originally published in London, 1672.

—— *Voy.*

Josselyn, John: An Account of Two Voyages to New England Made during Years 1638, 1663. Boston, 1865. Originally published in London, 1674

Journ. Agr.

Journal of Agriculture. London, 1829. The Journal of Agriculture. New Series. Edinburgh, London, 1845.

Journ. Hort. Soc. Lond.

The Journal of the Horticultural Society of London. London, 1855. Vol. 9 contains Article XIII by Dr. Antonio Targioni-Tozzetti.

Kaempfer, E. *Amoen.*

Kaempferus, Engelbertus: Amoenitatum exoticarum politico-physico-medicarum fasciculi v, ...Lemgoviae, 1712.

Kalm, P. *Trav. No. Amer.*

Kalm, Peter: Travels into North America, Containing Its Natural History, and A Circumstantial Account of its Plantations and Agriculture in general. Translated into English By John Reinhold Forster. Second Ed. London, 1772. 2 vols.

Kane, E. K. *Arctic Explor.*

Kane, Elisha Kent, M.D., U. S. N.: Arctic Explorations: The Second Grinnell Expedition in Search of Sir John Franklin, 1853, '54, '55. Philadelphia, 1857. 2 vols.

Kansas Bd. Agr. Rpt.

Kansas State Board of Agriculture Report. Topeka, Kan. 1872–96.

Karlsefne. See Voyages of Northmen. Prince Society Collection.

Kenrick, W. *New Amer. Orch.*

Kenrick, William: The New American Orchardist, or An Account of the Most Valuable Varieties of Fruit, of all climates, Adapted to Cultivation in The United States, With their history, modes of culture, management, uses . . . Second Ed. Enlarged and Improved. Boston, 1835.

King, Dr. See Edinborough Botanical Society Transactions.

Klunzinger, C. B. *Upper Egypt.*

Bilder aus Oberaegypten, der Wuste und dem Rothen Meere. Stuttgart, 1877.

Knight, T. A. *Phys. Hort. Papers.*

Knight, Thomas Andrew: A Selection from the Physiological and Horticultural Papers — (Edited by Bentham, G. and Dr. Lindley). London, 1841.

Knox, J. *Coll. Voy.*

A New Collection of Voyages, Discoveries and Travels: containing Whatever is worthy of Notice, in Europe, Asia, Africa and America: In respect to The Situation and Extent of Empires, Kingdoms, and Provinces; their Climates, Soil, Produce, &c. London, 1767. 7 vols.

Koster, H. *Trav. Braz.*

Koster, Henry: Travels in Brazil. Second Ed. London, 1817. 2 vols.

Kunth, C. S. Synopsis plantarum. Paris, 1822–25. 4 vols.

Kyber *Lexicon.*

Kyberus, Davidus: Lexicon rei herbariae trilingue. Argentinae, 1553.

La Billardière *Voy. Recherche Pérouse.*

La Billardière, J. J. H. de: Voyage à la recherche de la Pérouse. Paris, 1799. 2 vols. Copies exist with the imprint " Londres, 1800."

Lahontan, L. *New Voy. Amer.*

Lahontan, Louis Armand de Lom d'Arce, Baron de: New Voyages to North America Containing an account of the Several Nations of that Vast Continent, etc. etc. 1666–1735. Vol. 2 has title: New voyages to North America. Giving a full account of the customs, commerce, religion, and strange opinions of the savages of that country. London, 1835. 2 vols.

Lambert, A. B. *Desc. Genus Pinus.*

Lambert, Aylmer Bourke: A Description of the Genus Pinus with Directions Relative to The Cultivation and Remarks on the Uses of the Several Species of the Family of Coniferae. London, 1832. 2 vols.

Langsdorff *Voyage.* 1813-14.

Lankester, E. *Veg. Food.*
Lankester, Edwin: Vegetable Substances used for the Food of Man. London, 1846.
Second Ed. Library of Entertaining Knowledge Nos. 29 and 30.

Laurembergius *Apparat. Plant.*
Laurembergius, Petrus: Apparatus plantarius primus: tributus in duos libros.
I. De plantis bulbosis. II. De plantis tuberosis. Francofurti ad Moenum, 1632.

——— *Hort.*
Laurembergius, Petrus: Horticultura, libris ii. comprehensa; * * * Francofurti
ad Moenum, 1632.

Lawson, J. *Hist. Car.*
Lawson, John: The History of Carolina Containing Exact Description and Natural
History of That Country. London, 1714. Reprinted. Raleigh, 1860.

Lawson, P. *Prize Essays Highland Soc.*
Prize Essays and Transactions of the Highland Society of Scotland. Second Ed.
Edinburgh, Vol. 1, 1812.

Le Maire and Schoutin *Voyage.* 1615. See Dalyrmple Collection.

Leon, Cieza de. *Travels.* See Markham under Hakluyt.

Lescarbot *Hist. Nouv. France.*
Lescarbot, Marc: Histoire de la nouvelle France. 1612. In Collection (A) of
Voyages and Travels. 1745. Vol. 2.

Lightfoot, J. *Fl. Scot.*
Lightfoot, John: Flora Scotica or a Systematic Arrangement in the Linnaean Method
of the Native Plants of Scotland and the Hebrides. Second Ed. To which is
now prefixed the Life of the Author, by T. Pennant. London, 1789. 2 vols.

Lindley, J. *Med. Econ. Bot.*
Lindley, John: Medical and Oeconomical Botany. London, 1849.

——— *Veg. King.*
Lindley, John: The Vegetable Kingdom; or, The Structure, Classification, and Uses
of Plants, Illustrated upon the Natural System. London, 1846. Third Ed.
1853.

——— **and Moore, T.** *Treas. Bot.*
The Treasury of Botany: A Popular Dictionary of The Vegetable Kingdom; with
which is incorporated A Glossary of Botanical Terms. Edited by John Lindley
and Thomas Moore. Assisted by Numerous Contributors. New Ed. London,
1870. 2 vols. Same. Revised Ed. with supplement. 1876.
List of Contributors to The Treasury of Botany.

Professor Balfour — (J. H. B.)	Mr. R. Heward — (R. H.)
Rev. M. J. Berkeley — (M. J. B.)	Rev. C. A. Johns — (C. A. J.)
Mr. A. A. Black — (A. A. B.)	Dr. Masters — (M. T. M.)
Mr. W. B. Booth — (W. B. B.)	Dr. Moore — (D. M.)
Professor Buckman — (J. B.)	Dr. Seemann — (B. S.)
Mr. W. Caruthers — (W. C.)	Mr. A. Smith — (A. S.)
Mr. B. Clarke — (B. C.)	Mr. J. T. Syme — (J. T. S.)
Professor Dickie — (G. D.)	Mr. R. Thompson — (R. T.)
Mr. W. B. Hemsley — (W. B. H.)	Mr. W. Thompson — (W. T.)

Lindley, J. and Paxton, J. *Flow. Gard.*

Flower Garden. London, 1851–53. 3 vols. Second Ed. 1880. Re-issue, by A. Murray, Nos. 1–7 (1873–74), discontinued after page 112. Second Ed. by T. Baines is entirely recast and must not be confounded with original ed.

Linnaeus *Sp. Pl.*

Linnaeus, C.: Species plantarum. 1753. Second Ed. 1762–63. 2 vols.

Lisle *Husb.*

Lisle, Edward: Observations in Husbandry. London, 1757. Edited by Thomas Lisle.

Lives and Voyages of Drake, Cavendish et al. 1854.

Livingstone, D. *Trav. Research. So. Afr.*

Livingstone, David: Missionary Travels and Researches in South Africa; Including a Sketch of Sixteen Years' Residence in the Interior of Africa, And a Journey from the Cape of Good Hope to Loanda on the West Coast; Thence across the Continent, Down the River Zambesi, to the Eastern Ocean. New York, 1858.

—— **and C.** *Exped. Zambesi.*

Livingstone, David and Charles: Narrative of an Expedition To The Zambesi and its Tributaries and of the Discovery of the Lakes Shirwa and Nyassa. 1858–1864. New York, 1866.

Livingstone, J. in Trans. Hort. Soc. Lond.

Lobel *Icon.*

Lobel, Matthias: Icones Stirpium, sev plantarum tam exoticarum quam indigenarum, in gratiam rei herbariae . . . Antwerp, 1591. 2 vols. in one.

—— *Pl. Stirp. Hist.*

Lobel, Matthias: Plantarum sev stirpium historia. Antwerp, 1576.

—— *Stirp. Illustr.*

Lobel, Matthias: Stirpium illustrationes. Plurimas elaborantes inauditas plantas subreptitiis Joh: Parkinsoni rhapsodiis sparsim gravatae. London, 1655.

London Hort. Soc. Trans.

Transactions of the London Horticultural Society. London, England, 1812–1848.

London Hort. Soc. Journ.

Journal of the London Horticultural Society. London, England, 1846.

Long, C. C. *Cent. Afr.*

Long, Col. C. Chaillé: Central Africa; Naked Truths Of a Naked People. An Account of Expeditions to the Lake Victoria Nyanza and The Makraka Niam-Niam West of The Bahr-El-Abiad (White Nile). New York, 1877.

Long, E. *Hist. Jam.*

Long, Edward: The History of Jamaica or A General Survey of the Antient and Modern State of That Island. London, 1774. 3 vols.

Loudon, J. C. *Arb. Frut. Brit.*

Arboretum and Fruticetum Britannicum; or The Trees and Shrubs of Great Britain Native and Foreign, Hardy and Half Hardy. Second Ed. London, 1854. 8 vols.

—— *Enc. Agr.*

Encyclopedia of Agriculture. Sixth Ed. Illustrated. London, 1866.

Loudon, J. C.   *Enc. Pls.*

Loudon's Encyclopaedia of Plants: Comprising the Specific Character, Description, Culture, History, Application in the Arts, and every other Desirable Particular Respecting all the Plants Indigenous to, Cultivated in, or Introduced into Britain. New Ed. Corrected to the Present Time. Edited by Mrs. Loudon; Assisted by George Don; and David Wooster. London, 1855.

———— *Hort.*

The Horticulturist; or An Attempt to teach the Science and Practice of The Culture and Management of The Kitchen, Fruit, and Forcing Garden to Those who have had no previous knowledge or practice in these departments of gardening. New Ed. London, 1860.

Loureiro *Fl. Cochin.*

Loureiro, J.: Flora cochinensis . . . Ulyssipone, 1790. 2 vols. Also Berlin, 1793.

Lovell, R.   *Herb.*

Lovell, Robert: Sive, Enchiridion botanicum, or, a compleat herball, containing the summe of ancient and moderne authors, both galenical and chymical, toughing trees, shrubs, plants, fruits, flowers, etc. Oxford, 1665.

Lunan, J.   *Hort. Jam.*

Lunan, John: Hortus Jamaicensis, or a Botanical Description, (According to the Linnean System) and an Account of the Virtues, &c. of its Indigenous Plants Hitherto Known, As Also of the Most Useful Exotics. Compiled from the Best Authorities, and Alphabetically Arranged. Jamaica, 1814. 2 vols.

Macer Floridus *Herb. Virt.*

De herbarum virtutibus Aemilii . . . Cum carmine de herba quadam exotica, cuius nomen mulier est rixosa, eodem D. Georgio Pictorio Villingano autore.— Basileae, 1581.

———— *Vir. Herb.*   Sillig Ed.

De viribus herbarum una cum Walafridi Strabonis . . . Accedit anonymi carmen Graecum de herbis, quod e codice Vindobonensi auxit et cum Godofredi Hermanni suisque emendationibus edidit Iulius Sillig. Lipsiae, 1832.

Macfadyen *Jam.*

Macfadyen, James: The flora of Jamaica; a description of the plants of that island, arranged according to the natural orders. London, 1837.

Madden, E.   *Obs. Himal. Coniferae.*

Observations on Himalayan Coniferae. Calcutta, 1850.

Me. Farm.

Maine Farmer. (Weekly) Augusta, Me. 1833.

Marcgravius   See Piso *Hist. Rerum Nat. Bras.*

Marcy, R. B.   *Explor. Red River.*

Marcy, Randolph B.: Exploration of the Red River of Louisiana, in the year 1852. Washington, 1854.

Markham, C. R.   *Travels of Cieza de Leon.*   See Hakluyt.

Martens *Gartenbohnen.*

Martens, Georg von: Die Gartenbohnen; ihre verbreitung, cultur, und benützung. Second Ed. Ravensburg, 1869.

Martius *Mat. Med. Bras.*
   Martius, Karl Friedrich Philipp von: Materia Medica Brasiliensis. 1854.

Martyn *Fl. Rust.*
   Martyn, Thomas: Flora Rustica. London, 1792–94. 4 vols.

Martyn See Miller *Gard. Dict.*

Martyr, Peter. See Anghiera, Peter Martyr de.

Masham *Ralegh's Third Voyage to Guiana.* See Hakluyt.

Massachusetts Agricultural Repository and Journal. Boston, Mass. 1793–1832.

Mass. Hist. Soc. Coll.
   Massachusetts Historical Society Collections. Vols. I–X, Boston, 1792–1809. (Vol.
      I reprinted in 1806 and 1859; vol. V in 1816 and 1835).
   Second series I–X, Boston, 1814–23 (reprinted 1838–43).
   Third series I–X, Boston, 1825–49 (vol. 1 reprinted, 1846).
   Fourth series I–X, Boston, 1852–71.
   Higginson, Rev. Francis: *New England's Plantation.* London, 1630.
   First series, Vol. I, 1792.
   Hubbard, William: *History of Indian Wars in New England.*
   Second series, Vol. V.
   Gookin, Daniel: Historical Collections of the Indians in New England, 1792.

Mass. Hort. Soc. Trans.
   Massachusetts Horticultural Society Transactions. Boston, Mass., 1837.

Mass. Records.
   Massachusetts Records: Records of the Governor and Company of Massachusetts
      Bay in New England. Edited by Nathaniel Shurtleff, M. D. 1853–54.

Masters, Dr. M. T. See Treasury of Botany.

Matthiolus *Comment.*
   Matthiolus, Petrus Andrea: Commentarii secundo aucti, in libros sex Pedacii
      Dioscoridis . . . Venetiis, 1558.

—— *Comment.*
   Matthiolus, Petrus Andrea: Commentarii in sex libros Pedacii Dioscoridis Anazarbei
      de medica materia . . . Venetiis, 1570.

—— *Opera.*
   Matthiolus, Petrus Andrea: Opera quae extant omnia: Hoc est, commentarii in
      vi libros Pedacii Dioscorides . . . Basiliae, 1598.

Mawe and Abercrombie *Univ. Gard. Bot.*
   Mawe, Thomas and Abercrombie, John: The Universal Gardener and Botanist; or,
      A General Dictionary of Gardening and Botany. Exhibiting in Botanical
      Arrangement, according to the Linnaean System, Every Tree, Shrub, and Her-
      baceous Plant, that merit Culture, either for Use, Ornament, or Curiosity, in
      Every Department of Gardening, Together with Practical Directions for Perform-
      ing the various Mechanical Operations of Gardening in General. London, 1778.

May, Captain H. *Voyage.* See Hakluyt.

McIntosh, C. *Book Gard.*
   M'Intosh, Charles: The Book of the Garden. Practical Gardening Edinburgh,
      London, 1855. 2 vols.

McMahon, B.   *Amer. Gard. Cal.*
> M'Mahon, Bernard: The American Gardener's Calendar; adapted To the Climates and Seasons of the United States.   Philadelphia, 1806.

Meager   *Eng. Gard.*
> Meager, L.   The English Gardener; or a sure guide to young planters and gardeners. In three parts.   London, 1683.

Merolla, Father   *Voyage to Congo.*   See Churchill Collection.   1682.

Meyen   *Geog. Pls.*
> Meyen, F. J. F.: Outlines of the Geography of Plants; The Native Country, the Culture and the Use of the Principal Cultivated Plants on Which the Prosperity of Nations is Based.   Translated by Margaret Johnston.   London, 1846.

Michaud   *Hist. Crusades.*
> Michaud, Joseph Francois: History of the Crusades.   London, 1852.   Translated by W. Robson.

Michaux, F. A.   *No. Amer. Sylva.*
> Michaux, F. Andrew: The North American Sylva; or, A Description of the Forest Trees of the United States, Canada, and Nova Scotia.   To which is added A Description of the most Useful of the European Forest Trees.   Illustrated by 156 Colored Engravings.   Translated from the French.   Philadelphia, 1865. 3 vols.

Miers, J.   *Illustr. So. Amer. Pls.*
> Miers, John: Illustrations of South American Plants.   London, 1846–57.   2 vols.

Miller, J.   *Bot. officinale.*
> Botanicum officinale; or A compendious herbal.   London, 1722.

Miller   *Gard. Dict.*
> Miller, Phillip: Gardener's and Botanist's Dictionary.   Containing The Best and Newest Methods of Cultivating and Improving the Kitchen, Fruit, Flower Garden and Nursery . . .   To which is now added A complete Enumeration and Description of all Plants Hitherto known, with their Generic and Specific Characters By Thomas Martyn.   1807.   2 vols.

Millspaugh, C. F.   *Amer. Med. Pls.*
> Millspaugh, Charles F., M. D.:   American medicinal plants; an illustrated and descriptive guide to American plants used as homoeopathic remedies.   The Work is Illustrated from Drawings of Each Plant in Situ, by the Author. Philadelphia, 1884.   2 vols.

Mizaldus   *Secret.*
> Mizaldus, Antonius: Secretorum agri Enchiridion primum, hortorum curam . . . Lutetiae, 1560.

Molina   *Hist. Chili.*
> Molina, Abbe Don J. Ignatius: The Geographical Natural and Civil History of Chili.   Illustrated by a half-sheet Map of the Country.   Translated from the Original Italian By an American Gentleman.   1808.   2 vols.

Monteiro, J. J.   *Angola, River Congo.*
> Monteiro, Joachim John: Angola and The River Congo.   With Map and Illustrations.   London, 1875.   2 vols.

Moon, A. *Indig. Exot. Pls. Ceylon.*
Indigenous and exotic plants growing in Ceylon . . . Colombo, 1824.

Moore, T. See Treasury of Botany.

Morelet *Trav. Cent. Amer.*
Travels in Central America. 1871.

Morignolli *Cathay and The Way Thither.* See Hakluyt.

Morison, R. *Hort. Reg. Bles.*
Morison, Robertus: Hortus Regius Blesensis auctus, . . . Praeludiorum
botanicorum pars prior. Londini, 1669.

Morris Report of the Public Gardens of Jamaica. 1880.

Mortimer *Whole Art Husb.*
Mortimer, John: Whole Art of Husbandry; or, The Way of managing and improving
of land. London, 1708.

Morton *Cyc. Agr.*
Morton, John Chalmers: Cyclopedia of Agriculture. Glasgow, Edinburgh and
London, 1869.

Mourt *Relation.* See Massachusetts Historical Society Collection.

Mueller, F. *Sel. Pls.*
Mueller, Baron Ferdinand von: Select Extra-Tropical Plants, Readily Eligible for
Industrial Culture or Naturalization, With Indications of Their Native Countries
and Some of Their Uses. Eighth Ed. Melbourne, 1891. Indian Ed. Calcutta,
1880.

Nature: A Weekly Illustrated Journal of Science. Vol. XXIX. Nov. 1883 to April
1884. London and New York, 1884.

New England Annoyances. Poem 1630. The first published in America. Anonymous
author.

New England Farmer. Brattleboro, Vt., 1822.

New Description of Virginia. See Force Collection.

Newes from the Barmudas. 1613. See Force Collection.

New York Agricultural Experiment Station Reports. Geneva, N. Y., 1883.

New York Farmer. Port Jervis, N. Y., 1881.

N. Y. Hist. Soc. Coll.
Collections of the New York Historical Society. Second Series Vol. 1 New. Printed
for the Society. 1841. Containing Article No. VII " Extracts From The
New World or A Description of the West Indies " By John de Laet, Director of
the Dutch West India Co.

Newberry, J. S. See Pacific Railroad Report.

Newberry *Pop. Sci. Month.*
Newberry, J. S. in Popular Science Monthly. 1887.

Nicols, Thomas *Voyage.* See Hakluyt.

Nieuhoff's Voyages. See Churchill Collection.

Noisette *Man. Jard.*
> Noisette, Louis: Manuel du Jardinier. Paris, 1829.

Nordhoff, C. *No. Cal., Sandwich Is.*
> Nordhoff, Charles: Northern California, Oregon, and the Sandwich Islands. London, 1874.

Nuttall, T. *Gen. No. Amer. Pl.*
> Nuttall, Thomas: Genera of North American Plants, and a catalogue of the species, to the year 1817. Philadelphia, 1818. 2 vols.

—— *No. Amer. Sylva.*
> Nuttall, Thomas: The North American Sylva; or, a Description of the Forest Trees of the United States, Canada, and Nova Scotia, not described in the work of F. Andrew Michaux, and containing all the Forest Trees discovered in the Rocky Mountains, the Territory of Oregon, down to the shores of the Pacific, and into the confines of California, as well as in various parts of the United States. Philadelphia, 1865. 3 vols. in 2.

Olcott, H. S. *Sorghum.*
> Olcott, Henry S.: Sorgho and Imphee, The Chinese and African Sugar Canes. A Treatise upon their Origin, Varieties and Culture. New York, 1857.

Oliver, D. *Fl. Trop. Afr.*
> Oliver, Daniel: Flora of Tropical Africa. Assisted by other Botanists. London, 1868. 3 vols.

Ovalle *Voyages.* See Churchill Collection.

Pacific R. R. Rpt.
> Pacific Railroad Reports. Report of Explorations and Surveys to ascertain the most practicable and economical route for a railroad from the Mississippi River to the Pacific Ocean. Washington, 1855–61. 12 vols.
>> Containing botanical contributions by A. Gray, J. M. Bigelow, G. Engelmann, J. Torrey, J. S. Newberry, et al.

Pacific Rural Press. (Weekly) San Francisco, 1870.

Paillieux, A.: *Le Soja.* Paris, 1881.

Palladius Contributor to Vol. III of Scriptores rei rusticae veteres Latini e recensione Jo. Matth. Gesneri cum ejusdem praef. et lexico rustico.— Biponti, 1787–88. 4 vols.

Pallas, P. S. *Trav. Russia.*
> Pallas, Peter Simon: Travels through the Southern Provinces of the Russian Empire, in the years 1793 and 1794. Translated from the German of P. S. Pallas, Counsellor of State to His Imperial Majesty of all the Russias, Knight, &c. London, 1802–03. 2 vols.

Palmer, E. *Journ. Roy. Soc. New So. Wales.*
> Journal and Proceedings of the Royal Society of New South Wales, for 1883. Incorporated 1881. Vol. XVII. Edited by A. Liversidge. Sydney, 1884.
> Article III.— On plants used by the Natives of North Queensland, Flinders, and Mitchell Rivers, for food, medicine, &c. By Edward Palmer.

Pancovius, T. *Herb.*
> Pancovius, Thomas: Thomae Pancovii . . . herbarium, oder kräuter-und gewächs-buch darinn so wol einheimische als auszländische kräuter. Cölln, 1673.

Parkinson, J. *Par. Terr.*
> Parkinson, John: Paradisi in Sole Paradisus Terrestris. Reprinted from the ed. of 1629. London, 1904.

Parkman, F. *Pion. France.*
> Parkman, Francis: Pioneers of France in the New World. Revised, with additions. Boston, 1894.

Parkyns, M. *Life Abyss.*
> Parkyns, Mansfield: Life in Abyssinia, Being Notes Collected During Three Years Residence and Travel In That Country. New York, 1856. 2 vols. in one.

Parry *Bot. U. S. Mex. Bound. Surv.*
> Parry, Charles Christopher: Botany of the U. S. and Mexican Boundary Survey. Washington, 1854.

Pavy, F. W. *Food Diet.*
> A Treatise on Food and Dietetics, Physiologically and Therapeutically Considered. Second Ed. London, 1875.

Pena and Lobel *Advers.*
> Pena, Petrus and Lobel, Mathia de: Stirpium adversaria nova. Londini, 1570.

Penhallow, D. P. See American Naturalist.

Perry, M. C. *Japan.*
> Perry, Matthew Calbraith: Narrative of the Expedition of an American squadron to the China Seas and Japan, performed in the years 1852, 53 and 54. Compiled from the original notes and journals of Comm. Perry. By F. L. Hawkes, D. D. New York, 1856.

Perfect Description of Virginia. See Force Collection.

Peschel, O. *Races Man.*
> Peschel, Oscar: The Races of Man and Their Geographical Distribution. From the German. New York, 1876.

Petit *Dict. Jard.*
> Dictionaire du Jardin. 1826.

Pharm. Journ., Trans.
> Pharmaceutical Journal and Transactions of the Pharmaceutical Society. London, Vol. 1, 1841.

Phillips, H. *Comp. Kitch. Gard.*
> Phillips, Henry: The Companion for the Kitchen Garden. History of Cultivated Vegetables; Comprising Their Botanical, Medicinal, Edible, and Chemical Qualities; Natural History. New Ed. London, 1831. 2 vols.

—— *Comp. Orch.*
> Phillips, Henry: The Companion For the Orchard. An Historical and Botanical Account of Fruits Known in Great Britain. New Ed. London, 1831.

Pickering, C. *Chron. Hist. Pls.*
> Pickering, Charles, M. D.: Chronological History of Plants: Man's Record of his own existence illustrated through their names, uses, and companionship. Boston, 1879.

—— *Geog. Dist. Ans., Pls.*
> Pickering, Charles, M. D.: The geographical distribution of animals and plants. Boston, 1863–76.

Pickering, C. *Races Man.*

    Pickering, Charles, M. D.: The Races of Man; and Their Geographical Distribution. New Ed. To which is prefixed, An Analytical Synopsis of the Natural History of Man. By John Charles Hall, M. D. London, 1888. First Ed. Boston, 1863.

Pictet. See Anthropological Revue and Journal.

Pinaeus *Hist. Pl.*

    Pinaeus, Anton.: Historia plantarum. Earum imagines, nomenclaturae, qualitates, & natale solum.— Lugduni, 1561.

Pinkerton, J. *Coll. Voy.*

    Pinkerton, John: General Collection of the Best and Most Interesting Voyages and Travels In All Parts of the World, Many of Which are for the First Translated into English Digested on a new plan. Several Vols. London, 1812.

Pirolle *L'Hort. Franc.*

    L'Hortciulteur francaise. 1824.

Piso *De Ind.*

    Piso, Gulielmus: De Indiae utriusque re naturali et medica libri quatuordecim.— Amstelodami, 1658.

———— *Hist. Rerum Nat. Bras.*

    Piso, Gulielmus: De medicina Brasiliensi libri quatuor . . . et Georgi Marcgravi de Liebstad, historiae rerum naturalium Brasiliae, libri octo . . . Lugdini Batavorum, et Amstelodami, 1648.

Plaine Description of the Barmudas. See Force Collection.

Plantagent. See Force Collection.

Pliny. See Bostock *Hist. Nat. Pliny.*

Pluc'netius *Almag. Bot.*

    Pluc'netius, Leonardus: Almagesti botanici mantissa plantarum novissimè detectarum ultrà millenarium numerum complectens. Londini, 1700.

Pomet *Hist. Drugs.*

    Pomet, Pierre: A complete history of drugs. Written in French by Monsieur Pomet. Done into English from the originals. The fourth ed., carefully corrected, with large additions.— London, 1748.

Porcher, F. P. *Res. So. Fields, Forest.*

    Porcher, Francis Peyre, M. D.: Resources of the Southern Fields and Forests, Medical, Economical and Agricultural; being also a Medical Botany of the Southern States; with practical information on the useful properties of the trees, plants, and shrubs. New Ed.— Revised and largely Augmented. Charleston, 1869.

Prescott, W. H. *Conq. Peru.*

    Prescott, William H.: History of the Conquest of Peru, with a preliminary view of the Civilization of the Incas. Philadelphia, 1860. 2 vols.

———— *Conq. Mex.*

    Prescott, William H.: History of the Conquest of Mexico with a preliminary view of the Ancient Mexican Civilization, and the Life of the Conqueror, Hernando Cortes. New York, 1843. 3 vols.

Prestoe, H. *Trinidad Bot. Gard. Rpt.*

    Trinidad Botanical Garden, Rpt. of. Port of Spain, Trinidad, 1880.

Preston and Sommers *Voyage.* See Hakluyt.

Prince *Coll. Voy.*

Voyage of Samuel de Champlain Translated from the French By Charles Pomeroy Otis. With Historical Illustrations and a Memoir By the Rev. Edmund F. Slafter. Five Illustrations. Vol. 1 (1567–1635) 1880. Vol. 2 (1604–1610) Heliotype Copies of twenty local maps. 1878. Vol. 3 (1611–1618) Heliotype Copies of ten maps and illustrations. 1882. Boston, 1880.

——

Voyages of the Northmen to America Including Extracts From Icelandic Sagas Relating to Western Voyages By Northmen in the Tenth and Eleventh Centuries In an English Translation by North Ludlow Beamish; With a Synopsis of the Historical Evidence and Opinion of Professor Rafn as to the Places Visited By The Scandanavians On The Coast of America. Edited with an Introduction By the Rev. Edmund F. Slafter. Boston, 1877.

Pumpelly, R. *Across Amer., Asia.*

Pumpelly, Raphael: Across America and Asia; Notes of a Five Years Journey Around the World And of Residence In Arizona, Japan and China. Fifth Ed. Revised. New York, 1871.

Pursh, F. *Fl. Amer. Septent.*

Pursh, Frederick: Flora Americae Septentrionalis; or A Systematic Arrangement and Description of The Plants of North America. Containing, Besides what have been Described by Preceding Authors, Many new and rare Species, Collected During Twelve Years Travels and Residence in That Country. London, 1814. 2 vols.

Quintyne, J. *Comp. Gard.*

Quintinye, Joannes de la: The Complete Gard'ner. . . . now compendiously abridg'd, and made of more use, with very considerable improvements. By George London, and Henry Wise. The fourth ed. corrected.— London, 1704.

—— *Comp. Gard.* Evelyn Ed.

Quintinye, Joannes de la: The Compleat Gard'ner; or, directions for cultivating and right ordering of fruit-gardens and kitchen-gardens. In six books. To which is added his treatise of orange-trees, with the raising of melons. Made English by John Evelyn.— London, 1693.

Rafinesque, C. S. *Fl. La.*

Rafinesque, Constantine Samuel: Flora Ludoviciana; or A Flora of the State of Louisiana. Translated, revised and improved From the French of C. C. Robin. New York, 1817.

Rafn. See Prince Collection Voyages.

Raleigh *Discovery of Guiana.* See Hakluyt.

Randolph, J. *Treat. Gard.*

Randolph, John: Treatise on Gardening. (In Gardiner and Hepburn. The American Gardener.) 1818.

Ramusio. See General Collections of the Voyages of the Portugese. 1789.

Ray, J. *Hist. Pl.*

Raius, Joannes: Historia plantarum.— Londini, vol. I, 1686; vol. II, 1688; vol. III, 1704. 3 vols.

Ray, J. *Synop. methodica.*
Raius, Joannes: Synopsis methodica stirpium Britannicarum: tum indigenis, tum in agris cultis locis suis dispositis. Third ed. Londini, 1724.

―――― *Trav. through Low-Countries.*
Ray, John: Travels through the Low-Countries, Germany, Italy and France, with curious observations, natural, topographical, moral, physiological, &c. Also, a catalogue of plants, found spontaneously growing in those parts, and their virtues. Second ed.— London, vol. I, 1738. Vol. II, A collection of curious travels and voyages. 2 vols. in one.

Regnier *Econ. Publ. Celt.*
De l'Économie Publique des Celtes. 1818.

Rein *Indust. Jap.*
Rein, Johann Justice: Industry of Japan. London, 1889. Translated from the German.

Rheede *Hort. Malabar.*
Rheede tot Draakenstein, H. A.: Hortus indicus malabaricus . . . Amst. 1678– 1703. 12 vols.

Rhind, W. *Hist. Veg. King.*
Rhind, William: A History of The Vegetable Kingdom; embracing The Physiology of Plants, with Their Uses to Man and The Lower Animals, and their application in the Arts, Manufactures, and Domestic Economy. Glasgow, Edinburgh & London, 1855.

Ribault *Voyage.* See Hakluyt.

Richardson, J. *Arctic Explor.*
Richardson, Sir John: Arctic Searching Expedition; A Journal of a Boat-Voyage Through Ruperts Land and the Arctic Sea In Search of The Discovery Ships under the Command of Sir John Franklin. With an appendix of The Physical Geography of North America. London, 1851. 2 vols.

Rigil See Gardeners Chronicle.

Robertson, J. P. and W. P. *Letters Paraguay.*
Letters on Paraguay Comprising An Account of a Four Years Residence in That Republic Under The Government of The Dictator Francia. London, 1838. 2 vols.

Robinson, W. *Hist. Amer.*
Robinson, William, D. D.: The History of the Discovery and Settlement of America. 1856.

―――― *Parks, Gard. Paris.*
Robinson, William: The Parks and Gardens of Paris, considered in Relation to the wants of other cities and of Public and Private Gardens. Illustrated. London, 1878.

Roezlin, E. *Kreuterb.*
Roeszlin, Eucharius: Kreuterbuch, von natürlichem Nutz, und gründtlichem Gebrauch der Kreutter, Bäum, Gesteud, etc. Franckfurt am Meyn, 1550.

Romans *Nat. Hist. Fla.*
Romans, Bernard: A Concise Natural History of East and West Florida. New York, 1775.

Ross, J. C. *Voy. Antarct. Reg.*
Ross, Captain Sir James Clark: A Voyage of Discovery and Research in the Southern and Antarctic Regions, during the years 1839–43. London, 1847. 2 vols.

Rothrock, J. T. *U. S. Geog. Surv. Bot.*
Engineer Department, U. S. Army. Report upon United States Geographical Surveys West of the one hundredth meridian. Published by Authority of the Honorable Secretary of War. In Seven Vols. accompanied by one topographical and one geological atlas. Vol. VI.— Botany. Washington, 1878.

Roxburgh, W. *Fl. Ind.*
Roxburgh, William: Flora Indica, or, Descriptions of Indian Plants. Serampore, 1820–24. 2 vols.

———— *Hort. Beng.*
Roxburgh, William: Hortus bengalensis, or a Catalogue of the Plants growing in the H. E. I. C.'s Botanic Garden at Calcutta. Serampore, 1814. With an introduction by W. Carey.

———— *Pls. Corom. Coast.*
Roxburgh, William: Plants of the Coast of Coromandel Selected From Drawings and Descriptions Presented to The Hon. Court of Directors of the East India Company. Published under the Direction of Sir Joseph Banks. London, vol. 1, 1795; vol. 2, 1798; vol. 3, 1819.

Roy. Agr. Soc. Journ.
Royal Agricultural Society of England, Journal of. London, 1840–1914.

Royle, J. F. *Illustr. Bot. Himal.*
Royle, J. Forbes, M. D.: Illustrations of the Botany and Other Branches Of The Natural History Of The Himalayan Mountains and of the Flora of Cashmere. London, 1839. 2 vols.

Ruellius *Nat. Stirp.*
Ruellius, Joannes: De natura stirpium libri tres. Parisiis, 1536.

Ruiz and Pavon *Fl. Peru.*
Ruiz, Lopez H. and Pavon, J.: Flora peruviana et chilensis. (Matriti). 1798–1802. 4 vols.

Rumphius *Herb. Ambon.*
Rumphius, Georg. Everhard: Herbarium Amboinense, . . . edidit . . . Joh. Burmannus.— Amstelaedami, Hagae Comitis, Ultrajecti, 1741–1750. 6 vols.

Rur. N. Y.
Rural New Yorker. A Journal for the Suburban and Country Home. Illustrated. Rochester and New York, 1850.

Sabine, J. See London Hort. Soc. Trans.

Sachs *Bot.*
Sachs, Julius: Text Book of Botany, Morphological and Physiological. Edited by Sydney H. Vines. Second Ed. Oxford, 1882.

Saint Hilaire, A. *Fl. Bras. Merid.*
Saint-Hilaire, Auguste de: Flora Brasiliae Meridionalis Auctore. Accedunt Tabulae Dilineatae a Turpinio Aerique Incisae. Tomus Primus. Parisiis, 1825. Tomus Secundus, 1829.

Scaliger *Aristotle.*
> Scaliger, Julius Caesar: In libros de plantis Aristoteli inscriptos, commentarii. Lugduni, 1566.

Schenck, P. A. *Gard. Text Book.*
> Schenck, Peter Adam: The Gardener's Text-Book: containing Practical Directions upon the Formation and Management of The Kitchen Garden; and for The culture and Domestic Use of its Vegetables, Fruits, and Medicinal Herbs. New York, 1851.

Schiltberger, J. *Bondage, Trav.* See Hakluyt.

Schomburgk, R. H. *Hist. Barb.*
> Schomburgk, Sir Robert H.: The History of Barbadoes; comprising A Geographical and Statistical Description of the Island. London, 1848.

——— Discovery of Guiana. See Raleigh under Hakluyt.

Schuyler, E. *Turkistan.*
> Schuyler, Eugene: Notes of A Journey in Russian Turkistan, Kohokand, Bukhara, and Kuldja. New York, 1876. 2 vols.

Schweinfurth, G. *Heart Afr.*
> Schweinfurth, Dr. Georg: The Heart of Africa; Three Years Travels and Adventures In The Unexplored Regions of Central Africa from 1868 to 1871. Translated by Ellen E. Frewer. New York, 1874. 2 vols.

Script. Rei Rust.
> Scriptores rei rusticae veteres Latini e recensione Jo. Matth. Gesneri cum ejusdem praef. et lexico rustico. Biponti, 1787-8. 4 vols.

Seemann, B. See Anthropological Journal.

——— *Bot. Voy. Herald.*
> Seemann, Berthold: Botany of the Voyage of H. M. S. Herald. London, 1852-57.

——— *Fl. Viti.*
> Seemann, Berthold: Flora Vitiensis: A Description of the Plants of the Viti or Fiji Islands with An Account of Their History, Uses, and Properties. With One Hundred Plates By Walter Fitch. London, 1865-73.

——— *Journ. Bot.*
> Seemann, Berthold: Journal of Botany. London, 1863-71. 9 vols.

——— *Pop. Hist. Palms.*
> Seemann, Berthold: Popular History of the Palms and their allies, containing A Familiar Account of Their Structure, Geographical and Geological Distribution, History, Properties, and Uses, And a Complete List of all the Species Introduced into our Gardens. London, 1856.

Shrigley. See Force Collection.

Sibthorp, J. *Fl. Graecae.*
> Sibthorp, Johannes, M.D.: Florae Graecae Prodromus: sive Plantarum omnium enumeratio, quas in Provinciis aut Insulis Graeciae invenit. Londini, Vol. 1, 1806; vol. 2, 1813.

Simmonds, P. L. *Trop. Agr.*
> Simmonds, Peter Lund: Tropical Agriculture: A Treatise on the Culture, Preparation, Commerce and Consumption Of The Principal Products Of The Vegetable Kingdom. New Ed. London and New York, 1889.

Simpson, G. *Journ. Round World.*
Simpson, Sir George: Narrative of a Journey Round the World During the Years 1841 and 1842. London, 1847. 2 vols.

Sinclair, G. *Hort. Gram. Woburn.*
Sinclair, George: Hortus gramineus woburnensis......Lond. 1816. Fifth Ed. 1869. The first edition was illustrated with actual specimens, the subsequent ones by figures.

Sloane, H. *Cat.*
Sloane, Hans: Catalogus plant . . . in Jamaica. London, 1696.

——— *Nat. Hist. Jam.*
Sloane, Hans, M.D.: A Voyage To the Islands Madera, Barbadoes, Nieves, St. Christophers, and Jamaica; with the Natural History Of the last of those Islands. London, 1707–25. 2 vols.

Smith, A. See Treasury of Botany.

Smith, B. *Rel. De Vaca.*
Smith, Buckingham: Relation of Alvar Nunez Cabeza De Vaca. Translated from the Spanish. New York, 1871.

Smith, F. P. *Contrib. Mat. Med. China.*
Smith, Frederick Porter: Contributions toward the Materia Medica and Natural History of China. For the use of Medical Missionaries and Native Medical Students. Shanghai and London, 1871.

Smith, J. Description of New England. See Force Collection.

Smith, J. *Dict. Econ. Pls.*
Smith, John: A Dictionary of Popular Names of the Plants which furnish the Natural and Acquired Wants of Man, in all matters of Domestic and General Economy, Their History, Products and Uses. London, 1882.

——— *Dom. Bot.*
Smith, John: Domestic Botany. London, 1871.

Smithsonian Inst. Rpt.
Smithsonian Institution Reports. Washington, D. C., 1846.

Soyer, A. *Pantroph.*
The Pantropheon or History of Food From Earliest Ages of the World. London, 1853.

Sparks, J. *Essays on Husbandry.* 1747, 1811.

Speede, G. T. F. *Ind. Handb. Gard.*
Speede, G. T. Frederic: The Indian Handbook of Gardening or Guide to the Management of the Kitchen, Fruit, and Flower Garden in India To Which are Added A Hindostanee Vocabulary of Horticultural Terms, and a List of Plants. Second Ed. Calcutta, 1842.

Speke, J. H. *Journ. Disc. Source Nile.*
Speke, Capt. John Hanning: Journal of The Discovery of The Source of the Nile. New York, 1864.

Sprengel, K. *Hist.*
Sprengel, Kurt: Historia rei herbariae. Amst. 1807–8. 2 vols. (Second Ed.) Geschichte der Botanik. Altenburg, 1817–8. 2 vols.

Spry *Cruise Challenger.*
> Spry, William James Joseph: Cruise of H. M. S. Challenger.   New York, 1887.

Squier, E. G.   *Peru.*
> Squier, E. George: Peru; Incidents of Travel and Exploration In The Land of the Incas.   New York, 1877.

Squier, M. F.   *Trav. Cent. Amer.*
> Squier, Mrs. M. F.:   Travels in Central America Including Accounts of Some Regions Unexplored since the Conquest From The French Of The Chevalier Arthur Morelet.   Introduction and Notes By E. Geo. Squier.   New York, 1871.

Stansbury, H.   *Rpt. Great Salt Lake.*
> Stansbury, Capt. Howard: Exploration and Survey of the Valley of the Great Salt Lake of Utah, including A Reconnoissance of a new route through the Rocky Mountains.   Washington, 1853.

Stephens, J. L.   *Trav. Yucatan.*
> Stephens, John L.:   Incidents of Travel in Central America, Chiapas and Yucatan.   1841.   2 vols.

Stevenson, D.   *Gard. Kal.*
> Stevenson, Davis: The new and complete gardener's kalendar.   Sixth ed. Dublin, 1765.   The first ed. under another title, was published in 1746.

Steudel, E. G.   *Synop. Pl.*
> Steudel, Ernst Gottlieb: Synopsis Plantarum Glumacearum.   Stuttgartiae, 1855.

Stewart, F. L.   *Sorghum, Prod.*
> Sorghum and its Products.   An Account of Recent Investigations concerning the Value of Sorghum in Sugar Production, together with a description of A new method of making sugar and Refined Sugar from this Plant.   Philadelphia, 1867.

Stille, A.   *Therap. Mat. Med.*
> Stille, Alfred, M. D.:   Therapeutics and Materia Medica.   A Systematic Treatise on the Action and Uses of Medicinal Agents, including their Description and History.   Fourth Ed.   Philadelphia, 1874.   2 vols.

Sweet, R.   *Brit. Flow. Gard.*
> Sweet, Robert: British Flower Garden.   First series, 3 vols.   London, 1823–29. Second series, 4 vols. 1831–38.

Sweertius, E.   *Floril.*
> Sweertius, Emanuel: Florilegium.   Amsterdam, 1612.   Part Second, Amsterdam, 1654.

Switzer, S.   *Raising Veg.*
> Switzer, Stephen: A compendious method for the raising of the Italian brocoli, Spanish cardoon, celeriac, finochi and other foreign kitchen vegetables.   London, 1729.

Syme, J. T.   See Treasury of Botany.

Targioni-Tozzetti   See Journal of Horticultural Society of London.

Taylor, B.   *Cent. Afr.*
> Taylor, Bayard: A Journey to Central Africa or Life and Landscapes From Egypt To the Negro Kingdom Of The White Nile.   Tenth Ed.   New York, 1859.

Taylor B. *Siam.*
Taylor, Bayard: Siam, the Land of the White Elephant as it was and is. New York, 1892.

Tennent, J. E. *Ceylon.*
Tennent, Sir James Emerson: Ceylon: An Account of the Island Physical, Historical, and Topographical with Notices of its Natural History, Antiquities and Productions. Third Ed. London, 1859.

Theophrastus *Hist. Pl.* Bodaeus Ed.
De historia plantarum libri decem, Graece & Latinè. . . . . . .illustravit Joannes Bodaeus a Stapel. Amsterdam, 1644.

Thorburn *Cat.*
Thorburn (American Seed House) Catalogs. New York.

Thoreau *Me. Woods.*
Thoreau, Henry David: Maine Woods. Ninth Ed. New York, 1877.

Thunberg, C. P. *Fl. Jap.*
Thunberg, Caroli Petri: Flora Japonica sistens Plantas Insularum Japonicarum secundum Systema sexvale emendatum redactas ad XX Classes, Ordines, Genera et Species. Lipsiae, 1784.

———— *Travs.*
Thunberg, Charles Peter, M.D.: Travels in Europe, Africa, and Asia, made Between the Years 1770 and 1779. Third Ed. London, vol. 1, 1795; vol. 2, 3, 4, 1796. 4 vols.

Tillus *Cat. Hort. Pisa.*
Tillus, Michael Angelus: Catalogus plantarum Horti Pisani.— Florentiae, 1723.

Tinburg *Hort. Culin.* 1764.

Titford, W. J. *Hort. Bot. Amer.*
Titford, William Jowit, M.D.: Sketches towards a Hortus Botanicus Americanus; or, Coloured Plates of New and Valuable Plants of the West Indies and North and South America. Also of Several Others, Natives of Africa and the East Indies: Arranged after the Linnaean System. London, 1812.

Torrey Bot. Club Bul.
Torrey Botanical Society Bulletins. New York, 1870. Containing V. Havard's article on foods used by American Indians.

Torrey, J. *Bot. U. S. Mex. Bound. Surv.*
Torrey, John: Report on the United States and Mexican Boundary Survey. Washington, 1859.

———— **and Gray, A.** *Fl. No. Amer.*
Torrey, John, M.D. and Gray, Asa, M.D.: A Flora of North America containing Abridged Descriptions of all Known Indigenous and Naturalized Plants Growing North of Mexico. New York, 1840.

Tournefort *Inst.*
Tournefort, Josephus Pitton: Institutiones rei herbariae. Editio tertia, appendicibus aucta ab Antonio de Jussieu.— Parisiis, Vols. I-III, 1719. 3 vols. in two.

———— *Voy. Levant.*
Tournefort, J. Pitton: Rélation d'un Voyage Du Levant Fait Par Ordre du Roi, Enrichie de Déscriptions & de Figures. Tomes Deux. Amsterdam, 1718.

Townsend *Seedsman.*

> Townsend, Benj.: The Complete Seedsman, shewing the best and easiest method for raising and cultivating every sort of seed belonging to a kitchen and flower-garden. To which is added, a catalogue of the seeds, plants, etc. London, 1726.

Tragus *Stirp.*

> Tragus, Hieronymus: De stirpium, maxime earum, quae in Germania nostra nascuntur . . . libri tres......Argentinae, 1552. 2 vols.

Treasury of Botany. See Lindley, J. and Moore, T.

Trinidad, Report of Royal Botanical Garden of. Port of Spain, 1881.

True Declaration of Virginia. See Force Collection.

Turner *Libellus.*

> Turner, William: Libellus de re herbaria novus, * * * originally published in 1538, reprinted in facsimile, with notes, modern names, and a life of the author, by Benjamin Daydon Jackson. Privately printed. London, 1877.

Turre, G. *Dryadum.*

> Turre, Georgius a: Dryadum, Amadryadum Chloridisque triumphus, ubi plantarum uniuersa natura spectatur, affectiones expenduntur, facultates explicantur. Patavii, 1685.

Tussac *Fl. Antill.*

> Tussac, F. R. Flora Antillarum. Paris, 1808-27. 4 vols.

Tytler *Prog. Disc. No. Coast Amer.*

> Tytler, Patrick F.: Progress of Discovery on the More Northern Coasts of America. New York, 1833.

Unger, F. See U. S. Patent Office Reports.

U. S. D. A. Pom. Bul.

> U. S. Department of Agriculture. Division of Pomology. Bulletin No. 1. Report on The Condition of Tropical and Semi-tropical Fruits in the United States in 1887. Washington, 1888.

U. S. D. A. Rpt.

> Reports of the U. S. Dept. of Agriculture. Washington, D. C., 1862-1894.

U. S. Nat. Mus.

> United States National Museum. See Smithsonian institution.

U. S. Pat. Off. Rpt.

> Reports of the Agricultural Section of the United States Patent Office. Washington, D. C., 1837-1861.

Vancouver, G. *Voy. No. Pacific.*

> Vancouver, Capt. George: A Voyage of Discovery to the North Pacific Ocean, and Round the World; In which the Coast of North-west America has been carefully examined and accurately surveyed. Dedicated by Permission, to His Majesty. A new ed. with corrections. London, 1801. 6 vols.

Vega, Garcillaso de la. *Roy. Comment.* See Hakluyt.

Venegas *Hist. Cal.*

> Venegas, Miguel: A Natural and Civil History of California; translated from the Spanish. London, 1759. 2 vols.

Vick, J. *Cat.*
    Vick, James: Catalogues of Seed House. Rochester, N. Y.

―――― *Gard. Month.*
    Vick, James: Garden Monthly. A periodical devoted to the improvement of home and commercial gardens. Dansville, N. Y., 1878.

Vilmorin *Fl. Pl. Ter.*
    Vilmorin-Andrieux et Cie: Les Fleurs de Pleine Terre comprenant La Description et la Culture des Fleurs Annuelles Vivaces et Bulbeuses de Pleine Terre. Troisième Édition. Illustrée de près de 1300 gravures. Paris, 1870.

―――― *Les. Pls. Potag.*
    Vilmorin-Andrieux et Cie: Les Plantes Potagères Description et Culture des Principaux Légumes des climats tempérés. Paris, 1883.

―――― *Veg. Gard.*
    Vilmorin-Andrieux et Cie: The Vegetable Garden. Illustrations, Descriptions, and Culture of The Garden Vegetables of Cold and Temperate Climates. English Ed. Published under the Direction of W. Robinson, Editor of " The Garden." London, 1885.

Vilmorin-Andrieux et Cie: *Seed Cat.*
    Catalogues of Seed House. Paris, France.

Voy. Northmen Amer.
    Voyage of Northmen to America. See Prince Society Ed.

Voyage to Virginia. See Force Collection.

Wafer *Voy. Isthmus Amer.*
    Wafer, Lionel: Voyage and Description of the Isthmus of America. London, 1699.

Wallace, A. R. *Malay Arch.*
    Wallace, Alfred Russel: The Malay Archipelago; The Land of The Orang-Utan, and The Bird Of Paradise; A Narrative of Travel With Studies of Man and Nature. New York, 1869.

―――― *Trav. Amaz.*
    Wallace, Alfred Russel: A Narrative of Travels on the Amazon and Rio Negro, with an account of the Native Tribes, and Observations on the climate, geology, and Natural History of the Amazon Valley. London, 1853.

―――― *Trop. Nat.*
    Wallace, Alfred Russel: Natural Selection and Tropical Nature Essays on Descriptive and Theoretical Biology. New Ed. with Corrections and Additions. London and New York, 1895.

Waller, H. *Last Journ. Livingstone.*
    Waller, Horace: The Last Journals of David Livingstone, in Central Africa. From 1865 to his death. Continued by a narrative of His last moments and sufferings, obtained from His faithful servants Chuma and Susi. New York, 1875.

Wallich, N. *Pls. Asiat.*
    Wallich, Nathaniel: Plantae asiaticae rariores . . . London, 1830–32. 3 vols.

Walsh, R. See London Horticultural Society Transactions.

Warner, R. See Antiquitates Culinariae.

Watson, J. F. *Annals Phil.*
Annals of Philadelphia. Philadelphia, 1856.

Wesley *Nat. Hist. Book Cir.*
Natural History Book Circular No. 71. 1886.

Wheeler *Bot., Gard. Dict.*
Wheeler, James: Botanists' and Gardeners' New Dictionary, containing names, classes, &c., according to the system of Linnaeus. London, 1763.

White *Rel. Voy. Md.*
Relation of a Voyage to Maryland. See Force Collection.

Wight, R. *Icon. Pls.*
Wight, Robert, M.D.: Icones Plantarum Indiae Orientalis or Figures of Indian Plants. Madras, Vol. 1, 1840; 2, 1843; 3, no date given; 4, 1850; 5, 1852; 6, 1853.

———— *Illustr. Ind. Bot.*
Wight, Robert, M.D.: Illustrations of Indian Botany or Figures Illustrative of Each of the Natural Orders of Indian Plants Described in the Author's Prodromus Florae Peninsulae Indiae Orientalis: With observations on their botanical relations, economical uses, medicinal properties. Madras, Vol. 1, 1840; vol. 2, 1850.

Wilkes, C. *U. S. Explor. Exped.*
Wilkes, Charles, U. S. N.: Narrative of United States Exploring Expedition during the years 1838, 1839, 1840, 1841, 1842. In Five Volumes and An Atlas. Philadelphia, 1845.

Wilkinson, J. G. *Anc. Egypt.*
Wilkinson, Sir J. Gardner: A Popular Account of The Ancient Egyptians. Revised and Abridged from His Larger Work. New York, 1854. 2 vols.

Williams, B. S. *Choice Stove, Greenhouse Pls.*
Williams, Benjamin Samuel: Choice Stove and Greenhouse Ornamental-Leaved Plants. Second Ed. Comprising Descriptions of More Than Nine Hundred Species and Varieties. London, 1876.

Williams, E. *Virginia.* See Force Collection.

Williams, R. *Key.*
Williams, Roger: A Key into the Language of America or An Help to the Language of the Natives. London, 1643. Reprinted in Publications of the Narragansett Club. First Series. Vol. 1. Providence, R. I., 1866.

Williams, S. W. *Mid. King.*
Williams, S. Wells: The Middle Kingdom: A Survey of the Geography, Government, Education, Social Life, Arts, Religion, &c. Of The Chinese Empire and Its Inhabitants. New York, 1848. 2 vols.

Williams, S. W. See United States Patent Office Reports.

Wood, A. *Class Book Bot.*
Wood, Alphonso: Class-Book of Botany: Being Outlines of the Structure, Physiology, and Classification of Plants; with A Flora of the United States and Canada. New York and Troy, 1864.

Wood, W. *New Eng. Prosp.*
The Publications of the Prince Society, Established May 25th 1858. Wood's New-England Prospect. Boston, 1865.

Woods, J. *Ill. Country.*

Woods, John: Two Years' Residence in the settlement on the English Prairie, in the Illinois Country, United States. With an account of its Animal and Vegetable Productions, Agriculture, &c. London, 1822.

Worlidge, J. *Syst. Hort.*

Worlidge, John: Systema horti-culturae: or, the art of gardening. In three books. The second ed. with large additions. By J. W. Gent. London, 1683.

Young, A. *Chron. Pilgr.*

Young, Alexander: Chronicles of The Pilgrim Fathers of The Colony of Plymouth From 1602 to 1625. Now First Collected From Original Records and Contemporaneous Printed Documents. Boston, 1841.

Zanonius *Stirp. Hist.*

Zanonius, Jacobus: Rariorum stirpium historia ex parte olim edita. Latine reddidit, supplevitque Cajetanus Montius. Bononiae, 1742.

Zarate *Hist. Conq. Peru.*

Zarate, Augustin de: Histoire de la Découverte et de la Conquête du Perou. Paris, 1774. 2 vols. Translated from Spanish print of 1555.

INDEX TO SYNONYMS

INDEX TO COMMON NAMES

Chickweed, 557; sea, 64
Chicory, 167
Chicot, 296
Chillies, 136
China tree, 358
China-root, 537
Chinquapin, 153; water, 382
Chive, 39
Chocolate, Indian, 289
Chokeberry, 472
Chrysanthemum, corn, 163
Chufa, 230
Chupa-chupa, 356
Ciboul, 36
Cicely, sweet, 379
Cider tree, 258
Cigar-box wood, 154
Cinnamon, 168; American, 381; wild, 131
Cinnamon vine, 240
Cinquefoil, rock, 452; shrubby, 452
Citron, 173, 176
Citron myrobalan, 566
Cive, 39
Clary, 521
Clearing nut, 559
Cleavers, 285
Clotbur, 62
Cloudberry, 506
Clove, 259; wild, 258
Clover, bur, 357; red, 575; sweet, 359; white, 575
Clove-root, 290
Cobnut, 193, 194, 394
Coca, 257
Cocklebur, 28
Coco de Mer, 339
Cocoanut, 182; Buddha's, 557; double, 339
Cocum, 285
Coffee, 183; Liberian, 184; Swedish, 74; wild, 260, 576
Coffee-tree, Kentucky, 296
Cokernut, little, 318
Colanut, 184
Cole, red, 180
Coleus, 185
Colewort, 195
Colic-root, 30
Collards, 100
Colocynth, 169
Columbine, wild, 59
Comfrey, 560
Conch nut, 410
Convolvulus, water, 314
Cool-tankard, 97
Copalchi, 559
Coquito habraso, 23
Coral tree, 257
Coral-bead plant, 17
Corazon, 52
Corchorus, 189
Coriander, 191; Roman, 388
Cork tree, 24

Corkscrew-flower, 418
Cork-wood, 52
Corn, 608; broom, 551; Egyptian, 551; Kaffir, 551; negro, 551; rice, 551
Corn salad, 589; Italian, 589
Cornus, 192
Coroa, 534
Corossol, 51, 52
Costmary, 163
Cotton, 293
Cotton tree, 97
Cow parsnip, 301, 302; American, 301; downy, 301; yellow, 301
Cow plant, 296
Cow tree, 365, 560
Cowa, 285
Cowa-mangosteen, 285
Cowberry, 588
Cowhage, 371
Cowitch, 371
Cowpea, 597
Cowslip, 127, 453; Jerusalem, 471
Cow-tree, 121
Crab, American, 472; garland, 474; Siberian, 473; sweet-scented, 474
Crab's eye, 330
Crakeberry, 253
Cranberry, 402, 588; Australian, 338
Cranberry tree, 592
Cranberry-myrtle, 380
Crataegus, 197
Cream of tartar tree, 24
Cream-fruit, 505
Creamnut, 89
Creashak, 63
Creeping crowfoot, 483
Creosote plant, 326
Cress, 332; American, 82; bank, 536; Belle Isle, 82; bitter, 82, 140; early winter, 82; garlic, 412; hairy, 141; hoary, 331; Indian, 381, 580; lamb's, 141; land, 82; March, 381; meadow, 141; New Zealand, 332; para, 553; penny, 570; swine, 531; wart, 531; water, 380, 381; winter, 82
Crookneck, Canada, 211; winter, 211
Crowberry, 253
Crow-corn, 30
Cuckold, 62
Cuckoo flower, 141
Cuckoo flowers, round-leaved, 141
Cuckoo pint, 70
Cucumber, 208; bur, 201, 534; globe, 207; Indian, 357; serpent, 574; snake, 207; wild, 201
Cucumber tree, 79
Cumin, 223; black, 388
Currant, alpine, 494; Australian, 266, 334; black, 494, 496; Buffalo, 495; Californian black, 495; fetid, 497; golden, 495; Hudson bay, 496; Indian, 179; Missouri, 495; mountain, 65; red, 497; wild, 163
Currant tree, 99
Curry-leaf tree, 372

A CATALOGUE OF SELECTED DOVER BOOKS
IN ALL FIELDS OF INTEREST

A CATALOGUE OF SELECTED DOVER BOOKS
IN ALL FIELDS OF INTEREST

AMERICA'S OLD MASTERS, James T. Flexner. Four men emerged unexpectedly from provincial 18th century America to leadership in European art: Benjamin West, J. S. Copley, C. R. Peale, Gilbert Stuart. Brilliant coverage of lives and contributions. Revised, 1967 edition. 69 plates. 365pp. of text.

21806-6 Paperbound $3.00

FIRST FLOWERS OF OUR WILDERNESS: AMERICAN PAINTING, THE COLONIAL PERIOD, James T. Flexner. Painters, and regional painting traditions from earliest Colonial times up to the emergence of Copley, West and Peale Sr., Foster, Gustavus Hesselius, Feke, John Smibert and many anonymous painters in the primitive manner. Engaging presentation, with 162 illustrations. xxii + 368pp.

22180-6 Paperbound $3.50

THE LIGHT OF DISTANT SKIES: AMERICAN PAINTING, 1760-1835, James T. Flexner. The great generation of early American painters goes to Europe to learn and to teach: West, Copley, Gilbert Stuart and others. Allston, Trumbull, Morse; also contemporary American painters—primitives, derivatives, academics—who remained in America. 102 illustrations. xiii + 306pp. 22179-2 Paperbound $3.00

A HISTORY OF THE RISE AND PROGRESS OF THE ARTS OF DESIGN IN THE UNITED STATES, William Dunlap. Much the richest mine of information on early American painters, sculptors, architects, engravers, miniaturists, etc. The only source of information for scores of artists, the major primary source for many others. Unabridged reprint of rare original 1834 edition, with new introduction by James T. Flexner, and 394 new illustrations. Edited by Rita Weiss. 6⅝ x 9⅝.

21695-0, 21696-9, 21697-7 Three volumes, Paperbound $13.50

EPOCHS OF CHINESE AND JAPANESE ART, Ernest F. Fenollosa. From primitive Chinese art to the 20th century, thorough history, explanation of every important art period and form, including Japanese woodcuts; main stress on China and Japan, but Tibet, Korea also included. Still unexcelled for its detailed, rich coverage of cultural background, aesthetic elements, diffusion studies, particularly of the historical period. 2nd, 1913 edition. 242 illustrations. lii + 439pp. of text.

20364-6, 20365-4 Two volumes, Paperbound $6.00

THE GENTLE ART OF MAKING ENEMIES, James A. M. Whistler. Greatest wit of his day deflates Oscar Wilde, Ruskin, Swinburne; strikes back at inane critics, exhibitions, art journalism; aesthetics of impressionist revolution in most striking form. Highly readable classic by great painter. Reproduction of edition designed by Whistler. Introduction by Alfred Werner. xxxvi + 334pp.

21875-9 Paperbound $2.50

AMERICAN FOOD AND GAME FISHES, David S. Jordan and Barton W. Evermann. Definitive source of information, detailed and accurate enough to enable the sportsman and nature lover to identify conclusively some 1,000 species and sub-species of North American fish, sought for food or sport. Coverage of range, physiology, habits, life history, food value. Best methods of capture, interest to the angler, advice on bait, fly-fishing, etc. 338 drawings and photographs. l + 574pp. 6⅝ x 9⅜.

22383-1 Paperbound $4.50

THE FROG BOOK, Mary C. Dickerson. Complete with extensive finding keys, over 300 photographs, and an introduction to the general biology of frogs and toads, this is the classic non-technical study of Northeastern and Central species. 58 species; 290 photographs and 16 color plates. xvii + 253pp.

21973-9 Paperbound $4.00

THE MOTH BOOK: A GUIDE TO THE MOTHS OF NORTH AMERICA, William J. Holland. Classical study, eagerly sought after and used for the past 60 years. Clear identification manual to more than 2,000 different moths, largest manual in existence. General information about moths, capturing, mounting, classifying, etc., followed by species by species descriptions. 263 illustrations plus 48 color plates show almost every species, full size. 1968 edition, preface, nomenclature changes by A. E. Brower. xxiv + 479pp. of text. 6½ x 9¼.

21948-8 Paperbound $5.00

THE SEA-BEACH AT EBB-TIDE, Augusta Foote Arnold. Interested amateur can identify hundreds of marine plants and animals on coasts of North America; marine algae; seaweeds; squids; hermit crabs; horse shoe crabs; shrimps; corals; sea anemones; etc. Species descriptions cover: structure; food; reproductive cycle; size; shape; color; habitat; etc. Over 600 drawings. 85 plates. xii + 490pp.

21949-6 Paperbound $3.50

COMMON BIRD SONGS, Donald J. Borror. 33⅓ 12-inch record presents songs of 60 important birds of the eastern United States. A thorough, serious record which provides several examples for each bird, showing different types of song, individual variations, etc. Inestimable identification aid for birdwatcher. 32-page booklet gives text about birds and songs, with illustration for each bird.

21829-5 Record, book, album. Monaural. $2.75

FADS AND FALLACIES IN THE NAME OF SCIENCE, Martin Gardner. Fair, witty appraisal of cranks and quacks of science: Atlantis, Lemuria, hollow earth, flat earth, Velikovsky, orgone energy, Dianetics, flying saucers, Bridey Murphy, food fads, medical fads, perpetual motion, etc. Formerly "In the Name of Science." x + 363pp.

20394-8 Paperbound $2.00

HOAXES, Curtis D. MacDougall. Exhaustive, unbelievably rich account of great hoaxes: Locke's moon hoax, Shakespearean forgeries, sea serpents, Loch Ness monster, Cardiff giant, John Wilkes Booth's mummy, Disumbrationist school of art, dozens more; also journalism, psychology of hoaxing. 54 illustrations. xi + 338pp.

20465-0 Paperbound $2.75

JOHANN SEBASTIAN BACH, Philipp Spitta. One of the great classics of musicology, this definitive analysis of Bach's music (and life) has never been surpassed. Lucid, nontechnical analyses of hundreds of pieces (30 pages devoted to St. Matthew Passion, 26 to B Minor Mass). Also includes major analysis of 18th-century music. 450 musical examples. 40-page musical supplement. Total of xx + 1799pp.

(EUK) 22278-0, 22279-9 Two volumes, Clothbound $15.00

MOZART AND HIS PIANO CONCERTOS, Cuthbert Girdlestone. The only full-length study of an important area of Mozart's creativity. Provides detailed analyses of all 23 concertos, traces inspirational sources. 417 musical examples. Second edition. 509pp. (USO) 21271-8 Paperbound $3.50

THE PERFECT WAGNERITE: A COMMENTARY ON THE NIBLUNG'S RING, George Bernard Shaw. Brilliant and still relevant criticism in remarkable essays on Wagner's Ring cycle, Shaw's ideas on political and social ideology behind the plots, role of Leitmotifs, vocal requisites, etc. Prefaces. xxi + 136pp.

21707-8 Paperbound $1.50

DON GIOVANNI, W. A. Mozart. Complete libretto, modern English translation; biographies of composer and librettist; accounts of early performances and critical reaction. Lavishly illustrated. All the material you need to understand and appreciate this great work. Dover Opera Guide and Libretto Series; translated and introduced by Ellen Bleiler. 92 illustrations. 209pp.

21134-7 Paperbound $1.50

HIGH FIDELITY SYSTEMS: A LAYMAN'S GUIDE, Roy F. Allison. All the basic information you need for setting up your own audio system: high fidelity and stereo record players, tape records, F.M. Connections, adjusting tone arm, cartridge, checking needle alignment, positioning speakers, phasing speakers, adjusting hums, trouble-shooting, maintenance, and similar topics. Enlarged 1965 edition. More than 50 charts, diagrams, photos. iv + 91pp. 21514-8 Paperbound $1.25

REPRODUCTION OF SOUND, Edgar Villchur. Thorough coverage for laymen of high fidelity systems, reproducing systems in general, needles, amplifiers, preamps, loudspeakers, feedback, explaining physical background. "A rare talent for making technicalities vividly comprehensible," R. Darrell, *High Fidelity*. 69 figures. iv + 92pp. 21515-6 Paperbound $1.00

HEAR ME TALKIN' TO YA: THE STORY OF JAZZ AS TOLD BY THE MEN WHO MADE IT, Nat Shapiro and Nat Hentoff. Louis Armstrong, Fats Waller, Jo Jones, Clarence Williams, Billy Holiday, Duke Ellington, Jelly Roll Morton and dozens of other jazz greats tell how it was in Chicago's South Side, New Orleans, depression Harlem and the modern West Coast as jazz was born and grew. xvi + 429pp.

21726-4 Paperbound $2.50

FABLES OF AESOP, translated by Sir Roger L'Estrange. A reproduction of the very rare 1931 Paris edition; a selection of the most interesting fables, together with 50 imaginative drawings by Alexander Calder. v + 128pp. 6½x9¼.

21780-9 Paperbound $1.25

PLANETS, STARS AND GALAXIES: DESCRIPTIVE ASTRONOMY FOR BEGINNERS, A. E. Fanning. Comprehensive introductory survey of astronomy: the sun, solar system, stars, galaxies, universe, cosmology; up-to-date, including quasars, radio stars, etc. Preface by Prof. Donald Menzel. 24pp. of photographs. 189pp. 5¼ x 8¼.
21680-2 Paperbound $1.50

TEACH YOURSELF CALCULUS, P. Abbott. With a good background in algebra and trig, you can teach yourself calculus with this book. Simple, straightforward introduction to functions of all kinds, integration, differentiation, series, etc. "Students who are beginning to study calculus method will derive great help from this book." Faraday House Journal. 308pp. 20683-1 Clothbound $2.00

TEACH YOURSELF TRIGONOMETRY, P. Abbott. Geometrical foundations, indices and logarithms, ratios, angles, circular measure, etc. are presented in this sound, easy-to-use text. Excellent for the beginner or as a brush up, this text carries the student through the solution of triangles. 204pp. 20682-3 Clothbound $2.00

TEACH YOURSELF ANATOMY, David LeVay. Accurate, inclusive, profusely illustrated account of structure, skeleton, abdomen, muscles, nervous system, glands, brain, reproductive organs, evolution. "Quite the best and most readable account,' *Medical Officer.* 12 color plates. 164 figures. 311pp. 4¾ x 7.
21651-9 Clothbound $2.50

TEACH YOURSELF PHYSIOLOGY, David LeVay. Anatomical, biochemical bases; digestive, nervous, endocrine systems; metabolism; respiration; muscle; excretion; temperature control; reproduction. "Good elementary exposition," *The Lancet.* 6 color plates. 44 illustrations. 208pp. 4¼ x 7. 21658-6 Clothbound $2.50

THE FRIENDLY STARS, Martha Evans Martin. Classic has taught naked-eye observation of stars, planets to hundreds of thousands, still not surpassed for charm, lucidity, adequacy. Completely updated by Professor Donald H. Menzel, Harvard Observatory. 25 illustrations. 16 x 30 chart. x + 147pp. 21099-5 Paperbound $1.25

MUSIC OF THE SPHERES: THE MATERIAL UNIVERSE FROM ATOM TO QUASAR, SIMPLY EXPLAINED, Guy Murchie. Extremely broad, brilliantly written popular account begins with the solar system and reaches to dividing line between matter and nonmatter; latest understandings presented with exceptional clarity. Volume One: Planets, stars, galaxies, cosmology, geology, celestial mechanics, latest astronomical discoveries; Volume Two: Matter, atoms, waves, radiation, relativity, chemical action, heat, nuclear energy, quantum theory, music, light, color, probability, antimatter, antigravity, and similar topics. 319 figures. 1967 (second) edition. Total of xx + 644pp. 21809-0, 21810-4 Two volumes, Paperbound $5.00

OLD-TIME SCHOOLS AND SCHOOL BOOKS, Clifton Johnson. Illustrations and rhymes from early primers, abundant quotations from early textbooks, many anecdotes of school life enliven this study of elementary schools from Puritans to middle 19th century. Introduction by Carl Withers. 234 illustrations. xxxiii + 381pp.
21031-6 Paperbound $2.50

THE PHILOSOPHY OF THE UPANISHADS, Paul Deussen. Clear, detailed statement of upanishadic system of thought, generally considered among best available. History of these works, full exposition of system emergent from them, parallel concepts in the West. Translated by A. S. Geden. xiv + 429pp.

21616-0 Paperbound $3.00

LANGUAGE, TRUTH AND LOGIC, Alfred J. Ayer. Famous, remarkably clear introduction to the Vienna and Cambridge schools of Logical Positivism; function of philosophy, elimination of metaphysical thought, nature of analysis, similar topics. "Wish I had written it myself," Bertrand Russell. 2nd, 1946 edition. 160pp.

20010-8 Paperbound $1.35

THE GUIDE FOR THE PERPLEXED, Moses Maimonides. Great classic of medieval Judaism, major attempt to reconcile revealed religion (Pentateuch, commentaries) and Aristotelian philosophy. Enormously important in all Western thought. Unabridged Friedländer translation. 50-page introduction. lix + 414pp.

(USO) 20351-4 Paperbound $2.50

OCCULT AND SUPERNATURAL PHENOMENA, D. H. Rawcliffe. Full, serious study of the most persistent delusions of mankind: crystal gazing, mediumistic trance, stigmata, lycanthropy, fire walking, dowsing, telepathy, ghosts, ESP, etc., and their relation to common forms of abnormal psychology. Formerly *Illusions and Delusions of the Supernatural and the Occult.* iii + 551pp.   20503-7 Paperbound $3.50

THE EGYPTIAN BOOK OF THE DEAD: THE PAPYRUS OF ANI, E. A. Wallis Budge. Full hieroglyphic text, interlinear transliteration of sounds, word for word translation, then smooth, connected translation; Theban recension. Basic work in Ancient Egyptian civilization; now even more significant than ever for historical importance, dilation of consciousness, etc. clvi + 377pp. 6½ x 9¼.

21866-X Paperbound $3.95

PSYCHOLOGY OF MUSIC, Carl E. Seashore. Basic, thorough survey of everything known about psychology of music up to 1940's; essential reading for psychologists, musicologists. Physical acoustics; auditory apparatus; relationship of physical sound to perceived sound; role of the mind in sorting, altering, suppressing, creating sound sensations; musical learning, testing for ability, absolute pitch, other topics. Records of Caruso, Menuhin analyzed. 88 figures. xix + 408pp.

21851-1 Paperbound $2.75

THE I CHING (THE BOOK OF CHANGES), translated by James Legge. Complete translated text plus appendices by Confucius, of perhaps the most penetrating divination book ever compiled. Indispensable to all study of early Oriental civilizations. 3 plates. xxiii + 448pp.   21062-6 Paperbound $3.00

THE UPANISHADS, translated by Max Müller. Twelve classical upanishads: Chandogya, Kena, Aitareya, Kaushitaki, Isa, Katha, Mundaka, Taittiriyaka, Brhadaranyaka, Svetasvatara, Prasna, Maitriyana. 160-page introduction, analysis by Prof. Müller. Total of 826pp.   20398-0, 20399-9 Two volumes, Paperbound $5.00

MATHEMATICAL PUZZLES FOR BEGINNERS AND ENTHUSIASTS, Geoffrey Mott-Smith. 189 puzzles from easy to difficult—involving arithmetic, logic, algebra, properties of digits, probability, etc.—for enjoyment and mental stimulus. Explanation of mathematical principles behind the puzzles. 135 illustrations. viii + 248pp.

20198-8 Paperbound $1.25

PAPER FOLDING FOR BEGINNERS, William D. Murray and Francis J. Rigney. Easiest book on the market, clearest instructions on making interesting, beautiful origami. Sail boats, cups, roosters, frogs that move legs, bonbon boxes, standing birds, etc. 40 projects; more than 275 diagrams and photographs. 94pp.

20713-7 Paperbound $1.00

TRICKS AND GAMES ON THE POOL TABLE, Fred Herrmann. 79 tricks and games— some solitaires, some for two or more players, some competitive games—to entertain you between formal games. Mystifying shots and throws, unusual caroms, tricks involving such props as cork, coins, a hat, etc. Formerly *Fun on the Pool Table.* 77 figures. 95pp.

21814-7 Paperbound $1.00

HAND SHADOWS TO BE THROWN UPON THE WALL: A SERIES OF NOVEL AND AMUSING FIGURES FORMED BY THE HAND, Henry Bursill. Delightful picturebook from great-grandfather's day shows how to make 18 different hand shadows: a bird that flies, duck that quacks, dog that wags his tail, camel, goose, deer, boy, turtle, etc. Only book of its sort. vi + 33pp. 6½ x 9¼.   21779-5 Paperbound $1.00

WHITTLING AND WOODCARVING, E. J. Tangerman. 18th printing of best book on market. "If you can cut a potato you can carve" toys and puzzles, chains, chessmen, caricatures, masks, frames, woodcut blocks, surface patterns, much more. Information on tools, woods, techniques. Also goes into serious wood sculpture from Middle Ages to present, East and West. 464 photos, figures. x + 293pp.

20965-2 Paperbound $2.00

HISTORY OF PHILOSOPHY, Julián Marias. Possibly the clearest, most easily followed, best planned, most useful one-volume history of philosophy on the market; neither skimpy nor overfull. Full details on system of every major philosopher and dozens of less important thinkers from pre-Socratics up to Existentialism and later. Strong on many European figures usually omitted. Has gone through dozens of editions in Europe. 1966 edition, translated by Stanley Appelbaum and Clarence Strowbridge. xviii + 505pp.

21739-6 Paperbound $3.00

YOGA: A SCIENTIFIC EVALUATION, Kovoor T. Behanan. Scientific but non-technical study of physiological results of yoga exercises; done under auspices of Yale U. Relations to Indian thought, to psychoanalysis, etc. 16 photos. xxiii + 270pp.

20505-3 Paperbound $2.50

Prices subject to change without notice.
Available at your book dealer or write for free catalogue to Dept. GI, Dover Publications, Inc., 180 Varick St., N. Y., N. Y. 10014. Dover publishes more than 150 books each year on science, elementary and advanced mathematics, biology, music, art, literary history, social sciences and other areas.